PHILIP'S

COMPLETE ROAD ATLAS Britain and Ireland

II Key to map symbols
III Motorway service areas
VI The Speed Limit: 80mph or 70mph? Or even 60mph?
VIII Route planning maps
XVIII Road map of Ireland
XX Distances and journey times

1 Key to road map pages
2 Road maps of Britain

161 Urban approach maps
161 Bristol *approaches*
162 Birmingham *approaches*
164 Cardiff *approaches*
165 Edinburgh *approaches*
166 Glasgow *approaches*
167 Leeds *approaches*
168 London *approaches*
172 Liverpool *approaches*
173 Manchester *approaches*
174 Newcastle *approaches*

175 Town plans
175 Aberdeen, Bath, Blackpool
176 Birmingham, Bournemouth, Bradford
177 Brighton, Bristol, Cambridge
178 Canterbury, Cardiff, Cheltenham, Chester
179 Colchester, Coventry, Derby, Dundee
180 Durham, Edinburgh, Exeter
181 Glasgow, Gloucester, Hanley (Stoke-on-Trent)
182 Harrogate, Hull, Ipswich, Leicester
183 Leeds, Liverpool
184 London
186 Lincoln, Luton, Manchester
187 Maidstone, Middlesbrough, Milton Keynes, Newcastle upon Tyne
188 Newport, Northampton, Norwich, Nottingham
189 Oxford, Peterborough, Plymouth, Portsmouth
190 Reading, Salisbury, Scarborough, Southampton
191 Sheffield, Southend-on-Sea, Stoke
192 Stratford-upon-Avon, Sunderland, Swansea, Swindon
193 Taunton, Telford, Windsor, Winchester
194 Wolverhampton, Worcester, Wrexham, York

195 Index to town plans
205 Index to road maps of Britain
Inside back cover: **County and unitary authority boundaries**

www.philips-maps.co.uk

First published in 2009 by Philip's
a division of Octopus Publishing Group Ltd
www.octopusbooks.co.uk
Endeavour House, 189 Shaftesbury Avenue
London WC2H 8JY
An Hachette UK Company
www.hachette.co.uk

Fourth edition 2012
First impression 2012

ISBN 978-1-84907-214-4 (spiral)
ISBN 978-1-84907-215-1 (hardback)

Cartography by Philip's

Data for the speed cameras provided by **PocketGPSWorld.com Ltd**.

Information for National Parks, Areas of Outstanding Natural Beauty, National Trails and Country Parks in Wales supplied by the Countryside Council for Wales.

Information for National Parks, Areas of Outstanding Natural Beauty, National Trails and Country Parks in England supplied by Natural England. Data for Regional Parks, Long Distance Footpaths and Country Parks in Scotland provided by Scottish Natural Heritage.

Gaelic name forms used in the Western Isles provided by Comhairle nan Eilean.

Data for the National Nature Reserves in England provided by Natural England. Data for the National Nature Reserves in Wales provided by Countryside Council for Wales. Darparwyd data'n ymwneud â Gwarchodfeydd Natur Cenedlaethol Cymru gan Gyngor Cefn Gwlad Cymru.

Information on the location of National Nature Reserves in Scotland was provided by Scottish Natural Heritage.

Data for National Scenic Areas in Scotland provided by the Scottish Executive Office. Crown copyright material is reproduced with the permission of the Controller of HMSO and the Queen's Printer for Scotland. Licence number C02W0003960.

Photographic acknowledgements: page VI Mark Sykes / Alamy; page VII, bottom, George Clerk / iStockphoto.com.

Printed in China

*Independent research survey, from research carried out by Outlook Research Limited, 2005/06.
**Estimated sales of all Philip's UK road atlases since launch.

Road map symbols

M6
4 5
S S

- **Motorway, toll motorway**
- **Motorway junction** – full, restricted access
- **Motorway service area** – full, restricted access
- **Motorway under construction**

A453
S
4 5

- **Primary route** – dual, single carriageway
- **Service area, roundabout, multi-level junction**
- **Numbered junction** – full, restricted access
- **Primary route under construction**
- **Narrow primary route**

Derby

- **Primary destination**

A34

- **A road** – dual, single carriageway
- **A road under construction, narrow A road**

B2135

- **B road** – dual, single carriageway
- **B road under construction, narrow B road**
- **Minor road** – over 4 metres, under 4 metres wide
- **Minor road with restricted access**

2

- **Distance in miles**
- **Scenic route**

40 40

- **Speed camera** – single, multiple

TOLL

- **Toll, steep gradient** – arrow points downhill
- **Tunnel**
- **National trail** – England and Wales
- **Long distance footpath** – Scotland
- **Railway with station**
- **Level crossing, tunnel**
- **Preserved railway with station**
- **National boundary**
- **County / unitary authority boundary**
- **Car ferry, catamaran**
- **Passenger ferry, catamaran**
- **Hovercraft**

CALAIS 1:30

- **Ferry destination, journey time** – hrs : mins

Ferry

- **Car ferry** – river crossing
- **Principal airport, other airport**
- **National park**
- **Area of Outstanding Natural Beauty** – England and Wales **National Scenic Area** – Scotland
- **forest park / regional park / national forest**
- **Woodland**
- **Beach**
- **Linear antiquity**
- **Roman road**

1066

- **Hillfort, battlefield** – with date

795

- **Viewpoint, nature reserve, spot height** – in metres
- **Golf course, youth hostel, sporting venue**
- **Camp site, caravan site, camping and caravan site**

P&R

- **Shopping village, park and ride**

29

- **Adjoining page number** – road maps

Road map scale 1: 200 000 or 3·15 miles to 1 inch

0 1 2 3 4 5 6 miles

0 1 2 3 4 5 6 7 8 9 10 km

Approach map symbols

M6

- **Motorway**
- **Toll motorway**

6 5

- **Motorway junction** – full, restricted access

S

- **Service area**
- **Under construction**

A6

- **Primary route** – dual, single carriageway

S

- **Service area**
- **Multi-level junction**
- **roundabout**
- **Under construction**

A195

- **A road** – dual, single carriageway

B1288

- **B road** – dual, single carriageway
- **Minor road** – dual, single carriageway
- **Ring road**

3

- **Distance in miles**
- **Congestion charge area**

COSELEY

- **Railway with station**

LOXDALE

- **Tramway with station**

M

- **Underground or metro station**

Town plan symbols

- **Motorway**
- **Primary route** – dual, single carriageway
- **A road** – dual, single carriageway
- **B road** – dual, single carriageway
- **Minor through road**
- **One-way street**
- **Pedestrian roads**
- **Shopping streets**
- **Railway with station**

City Hall

- **Tramway with station**
- **Bus or railway station building**
- **Shopping precinct or retail park**
- **Park**
- **Building of public interest**
- **Theatre, cinema**

P

- **Parking, shopmobility**

Bank

- **Underground station**

West St

- **Metro station**

H

- **Hospital, Police station**

PO

- **Post office**

Tourist information

- **Abbey, cathedral or priory**
- **Ancient monument**
- **Aquarium**
- **Art gallery**
- **Bird collection or aviary**
- **Castle**
- **Church**
- **Country park**
  - England and Wales
  - Scotland
- **Farm park**
- **Garden**
- **Historic ship**
- **House**
- **House and garden**
- **Motor racing circuit**
- **Museum**
- **Picnic area**
- **Preserved railway**
- **Race course**
- **Roman antiquity**
- **Safari park**
- **Theme park**
- **Tourist information centre**
  - open all year
  - open seasonally
- **Zoo**
- **Other place of interest**

Relief

Feet	metres
3000	914
2600	792
2200	671
1800	549
1400	427
1000	305
0	0

Speed Cameras

Fixed camera locations are shown using the 40 symbol.

In congested areas the 40 symbol is used to show that there are two or more cameras on the road indicated.

Due to the restrictions of scale the camera locations are only approximate and cannot indicate the operating direction of the camera. Mobile camera sites, and cameras located on roads not included on the mapping are not shown. Where two or more cameras are shown on the same road, drivers are warned that this may indicate that a SPEC system is in operation. These cameras use the time taken to drive between the two camera positions to calculate the speed of the vehicle.

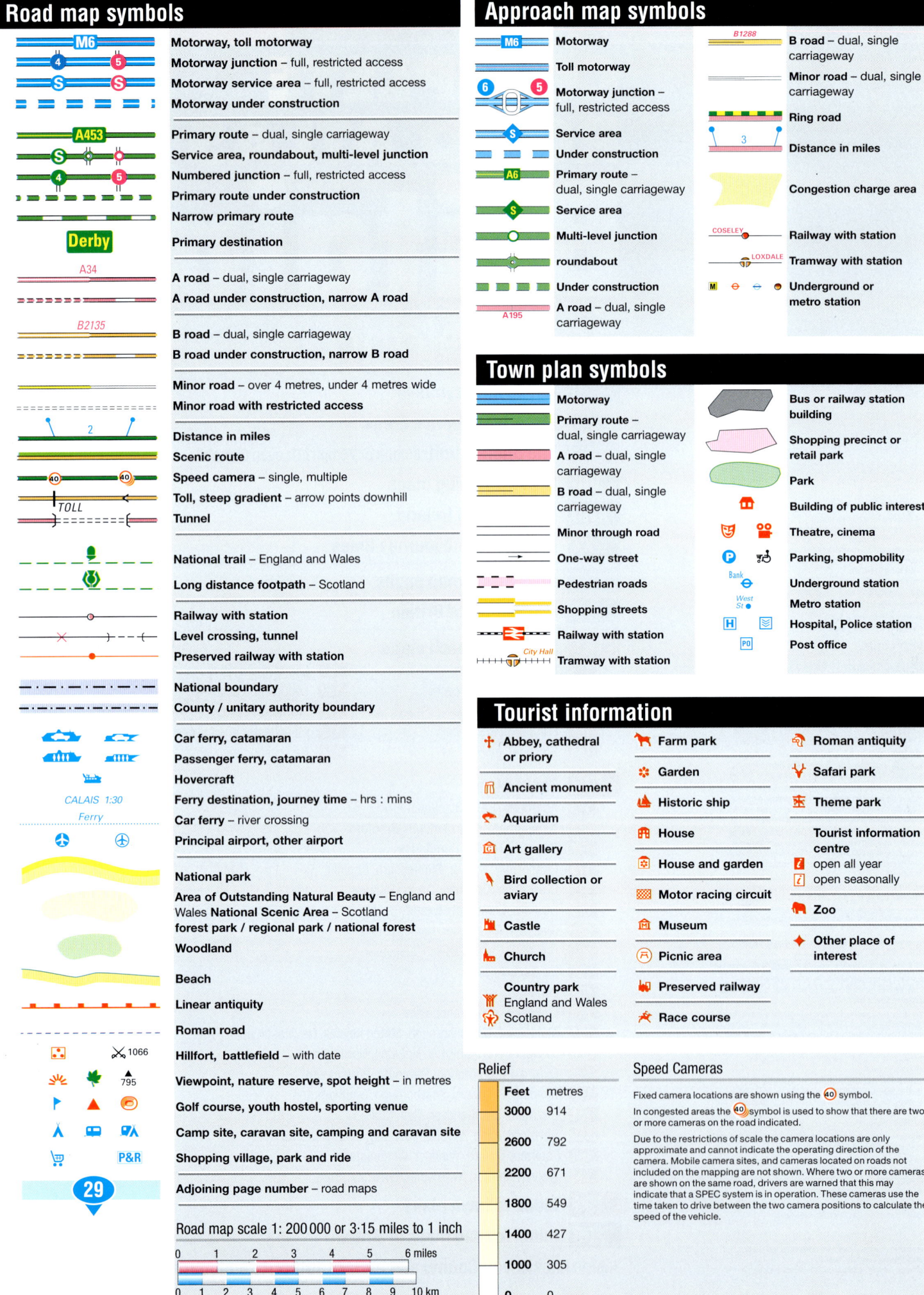

Motorway service areas

England

A1(M) Baldock — Extra MSA

A1(M) J10 • Northbound and southbound 54 F3 TL23443661

M&S Simply Food • WH Smith • KFC • Le Petit Four • McDonald's • Pizza Hut Express • Starbucks *Shell*

Days Inn 2hrs

A1(M), Junction 10, Baldock, Hertfordshire SG7 5TR

www.extraservices.co.uk

McDonald's open 24 hrs

A1(M) Peterborough Extra MSA

A1(M) J17 • Northbound and southbound 65 E8 TL13939395

M&S Simply Food • McColls • Namco • KFC • Le Petit Four • McDonald's • Pizza Hut Express *Shell, LPG* *Days Inn* 2 hrs

Great North Road, Haddon, Peterborough PE7 8UQ

www.extraservices.co.uk

Shop in forecourt is open 24 hrs

A1(M) Blyth — Moto

A1(M) Junction 34 • Northbound and southbound 89 F7 SK62568827

Costa • Burger King • EDC • WH Smith • Coffee Nation *Esso* *Travelodge* Hill Top Roundabout, Blyth S81 8HG 01909 591841

A1(M) Wetherby — Moto

A1(M): J46 • Northbound and southbound 95 D7 SE41525025

M&S Simply Food • Upper Crust • WH Smith • Burger King • Costa Coffee • EDC *BP* *Days Inn* 2 hrs Kirk Deighton, North Yorkshire LS22 5GT 01937 545080 www.moto-way.co.uk

Forecourt outlets open 24 hrs

A1(M) Durham — RoadChef

A1(M) J61 • Northbound and southbound 111 F6 NZ30843718

WH Smith • The Burger Company • Costa Coffee • Restbite *Total* *Premier Inn* 2 hrs

Tursdale Road, Bowburn, County Durham DH6 5NP 0191 377 9222 www.roadchef.com

Fast food outlet and shop in forecourt open 24 hrs

A1(M) Washington — Moto

A1(M) just north of J64 • Northbound and southbound 111 D5 NZ28375506

WH Smith • Burger King • Coffee Nation • Costa Coffee • EDC *BP* *Travelodge* 2 hrs

Portobello, Birtley, County Durham DH3 2SJ 0191 410 3436 www.moto-way.co.uk

WH Smith and outlets on forecourt open 24 hrs

M1 London Gateway Welcome Break

M1 between J2 and J4 • Northbound and southbound 41 E5 TQ20269369

WH Smith • Burger King • Eat In • Starbucks *Shell* *Days Inn* 2 hrs M1 J2/4, Mill Hill, London NW7 3HB 0208 906 0611 lgw.enquiry@welcomebreak.co.uk

www.welcomebreak.co.uk

WH Smith open 24 hrs

M1 Toddington — Moto

M1, 1 mile south of J12 • Northbound and southbound 40 B3 TL03092878

M&S Simply Food • WH Smith • Burger King • Coffee Nation • Costa Coffee • EDC • Krispy Kreme Doughnuts *BP, LPG available*

Travelodge 2 hrs

Toddington, Bedfordshire LU5 6HR 01525 878400

www.moto-way.co.uk

Outlets on forecourts open 24 hrs

M1 Newport Pagnell Welcome Break

M1, north of J14 • Northbound and southbound 53 E6 SP85834351

WH Smith • Eat In • KFC • Starbucks *Shell* *Days Inn* 2 hrs

M1 Motorway, J14/15, Newport Pagnell, Buckinghamshire MK16 8DS 01908 217722

newport.enquiry@welcomebreak.co.uk

www.welcomebreak.co.uk

WH Smith and shop in forecourt open 24 hrs

M1 Northampton — RoadChef

M1 J15A • Northbound and southbound 52 D5 SP72285732

Fonebitz • WH Smith • The Burger Company • Costa Coffee • Hot Food Co (southbound) • Restbite (northbound) • Wild Bean Cafe *BP* 2 hrs

M1 Junction 15A, Northampton, Northamptonshire NN4 9QY 01604 831888

www.roadchef.co.uk

WH Smith and shop in forecourt open 24 hrs

M1 Watford Gap — RoadChef

M1 between J16 and J17 • Northbound and southbound 52 C4 SP59956802

Fonebitz • WH Smith • Costa Coffee • Hot Food Co • Wimpy (northbound); The Burger Company • Costa Coffee • Restbite (southbound) *BP* *Premier Inn (southbound)*

2 hrs M1 Motorway, Northamptonshire NN6 7UZ

01327 879001

www.roadchef.co.uk

M1 Leicester Forest East Welcome Break

M1 between J21 and J21A • Northbound and southbound 64 D2 SK53860267

Waitrose • WH Smith • Burger King • Eat In • KFC • Starbucks *BP, LPG available (northbound)* *Days Inn* 2 hrs

Leicester Forest East, M1, Leicester, Leicestershire LE3 3GB 0116 238 6801 lfe.enquiry@welcomebreak.co.uk

www.welcomebreak.co.uk

Eat In and WH Smith are open 24 hrs

Symbols

- Accommodation
- Baby change
- Barber shop
- Bureau de change
- Cash machine
- Footbridge
- Fuel
- Meeting room
- Free parking
- Showers
- Toilets
- Disabled toilets
- RADAR key scheme
- Truckstop
- Truck wash
- Free WiFi
- Work space
- Address
- Telephone number
- e-mail address
- website
- Details of shops and catering outlets that are normally open 24 hours are listed at the end of each entry. Other listed outlets may not be open 24 hours.

M1 Leicester — Moto

M1 just off J22 • Northbound and southbound 64 C1 SK47651111

Costa • Burger King] • Coffee Nation *BP, LPG available*

Littleshaw Lane, Markfield LE67 9PP 01530 244777

www.moto-way.co.uk

M1 Donington Park — Moto

M1 J23A • Northbound and southbound 64 B1 SK46712513

Fone Bitz • M&S Simply Food • WH Smith • Burger King • Coffee Nation • Costa Coffee • EDC *BP, LPG available* *Travelodge*

2 hrs Castle Donington, Derby, East Midlands DE74 2TN

01509 672220

www.moto-way.co.uk

Shop in forecourt and WH Smith open 24 hrs

M1 Trowell — Moto

M1 between J25 and J26 • Northbound and southbound 76 E4 SK49354073

M&S Simply Food • WH Smith • Burger King • Coffee Nation • Costa Coffee • EDC *BP* *Travelodge*

2 hrs Ilkeston, Trowell, Nottinghamshire NG9 3PL

01159 320291

www.moto-way.co.uk

WH Smith and forecourt outlets are open 24 hrs

M1 Tibshelf — RoadChef

M1, 2 miles north of J28 • Northbound and southbound 76 C4 SK44856031

Fone Bitz • WH Smith • The Burger Company • Costa Coffee • Restbite *Shell* *Premier Inn (northbound only)* 2 hrs

Newton Wood Lane, Newton, Alfreton DE55 5TZ 01773 760607 www.roadchef.co.uk

WH Smith and forecourt shop open 24 hrs

M1 Woodall — Welcome Break

M1, 2.5 miles north of J30 • Northbound and southbound 89 F5 SK47928006

WH Smith • Burger King • Eat In • KFC • Starbucks *Shell, LPG available (southbound)* *Days Inn* 2 hrs

M1 Motorway, Sheffield, South Yorkshire S26 7XR

0114 248 7992 woodall.enquiry@welcomebreak.co.uk

www.welcomebreak.co.uk

Eat In, WH Smith and outlets on forecourt open 24 hrs

M1 Woolley Edge — Moto

M1, just north of J38 • Northbound and southbound 88 C4 SE29841400

M&S Simply Food • WH Smith • Burger King • Coffee Nation • Costa Coffee • EDC *Esso* *Travelodge*

2 hrs West Bretton, Wakefield, West Yorkshire WF4 4LQ 01924 830371

www.moto-way.co.uk

WH Smith and outlets on forecourt are open 24 hrs

M2 Medway — Moto

M2 between J4 and J5 • Eastbound and westbound 30 C2 TQ81756344

WH Smith • Burger King • Coffee Nation • Costa Coffee *BP, LPG available (eastbound)*

Travelodge 2 hrs

M2, Rainham, Gillingham, Kent ME8 8PQ 01634 236900 www.moto-way.co.uk WH Smith and shop in forecourt are open 24 hrs

M3 Fleet — Welcome Break

M3 between J4A/J5 • Eastbound and westbound 27 D5 SU79885583

Waitrose • WH Smith • Burger King • Eat In • KFC • Starbucks *Shell (southbound, LPG available); BP (northbound)* *Days Inn* 2 hrs

Fleet, Hampshire GU51 1AA

01252 788 500 fleet.enquiry@welcomebreak.co.uk

www.welcomebreak.co.uk

Eat In and WH Smith open 24 hrs

M3 Winchester — Moto

M3, 4 miles north of J9 • Northbound and southbound 26 F3 SU52303550

WH Smith • Burger King • Coffee Nation • Costa Coffee • EDC *Shell, LPG available* *Premier Inn*

2 hrs Shroner Wood, Winchester, Hampshire SO21 1PP

01962 791140

www.moto-way.co.uk

Outlets on forecourt open 24 hrs

M4 Heston — Moto

M4 1 mile east of J3 • Eastbound and westbound 28 B2 TQ11777778

WH Smith • Burger King • Coffee Nation • Costa Coffee • EDC • Krispy Kreme Doughnuts *BP, LPG (westbound)* *Travelodge*

2 hrs Phoenix Way, Heston, Hounslow, London TW5 9NB 0208 590 2101 www.moto-way.co.uk Coffee Nation and WH Smith are open 24 hrs

M4 Reading – eastbound Moto

M4 Junctions 11-12 • Eastbound
26 C4 SU67177012
M&S • Costa • Burger King • EDC • WH Smith • Krispy Kreme • Coffee Nation BP Travelodge 2 hrs Burghfield, Reading RG30 3UQ 01189 566966 www.moto-way.co.uk WH Smith and outlets in the forecourt are open 24 hrs

M4 Reading – westbound Moto

M4 Junctions 11-12 • Westbound
26 C4 SU67046985
M&S • Costa • Burger King • EDC • WH Smith • Upper Crust • Krispy Kreme • Coffee Nation BP Travelodge 2 hrs Burghfield, Reading RG30 3UQ 01189 566966 www.moto-way.co.uk WH Smith and outlets in the forecourt are open 24 hrs

M4 Chieveley Moto

M4 J13 • Eastbound and westbound 26 B2 SU48157268
M&S Simply Food • WH Smith • Burger King • Coffee Nation • Costa Coffee • EDC BP, LPG available Travelodge 2 hrs Oxford Road, Hermitage, Thatcham, Berkshire, RG18 9XX 01635 248024 www.moto-way.co.uk WH Smith open 24 hrs

M4 Membury Welcome Break

M4, 4 miles west of J14 • Eastbound and westbound
25 B8 SU30847601
Waitrose • WH Smith • Burger King • Eat In • KFC • Starbucks BP LPG available (eastbound) Days Inn 2 hrs Woodlands Road, Membury, near Lambourn, Berkshire RG17 7TZ 01488 674360 membury.enquiry@welcomebreak.co.uk www.welcomebreak.co.uk Eat In, WH Smith and forecourt shop open 24 hrs

M4 Leigh Delamere Moto

M4 just west of J17 • Eastbound and westbound
24 B3 ST89077899
Fonebitz • M&S Simply Food • WH Smith • Burger King • Coffee Nation • Costa Coffee • EDC BP, LPG available Travelodge 2 hrs Chippenham, Wiltshire SN14 6LB 01666 837691 (eastbound); 01666 842015 (westbound) www.moto.co.uk WH Smith and shop and coffee shops in the forecourt are open 24 hrs

M5 Frankley Moto

M5 J3 • Northbound and southbound 62 F3 SO98938120
M&S Simply Food • WH Smith • Burger King • Coffee Nation • Costa Coffee • EDC Esso Travelodge (southbound only) 2 hrs Illey Lane, Birmingham, West Midlands B32 4AR 0121 550 3131 www.moto-way.co.uk Coffee Nation and WH Smith open 24 hrs

M5 Strensham – southbound RoadChef

M5 southbound, just before J8 • Southbound only
50 F4 SO9041393
Cotton Traders • Fonebitz • WH Smith • Costa Coffee • Hot Food Company • McDonalds • Soho Coffee Company BP 2 hrs M5 Motorway, Lower Strensham, Worcestershire WR8 9LJ 01684 290577 www.roadchef.co.uk The outlets on the forecourt are open 24 hrs

M5 Strensham – northbound RoadChef

M5, 1 mile north of J8 • Northbound only
50 E3 SO89344072
Cotton Traders • Fonebitz • Subway • WH Smith • Costa Coffee • Pizza Hut Express • Restbite • Wimpy Texaco, LPG available Premier Inn 2 hrs M5 Motorway, Lower Strensham, Worcestershire WR8 9LJ 01684 293004 www.roadchef.co.uk The outlets on the forecourt are open 24 hrs

M5 Michaelwood Welcome Break

M5, just north of J14 • Northbound and southbound
36 E4 ST7409541
WH Smith • Burger King • Eat In • KFC • Starbucks BP Days Inn 2 hrs Lower Wick, Dursley, Gloucestershire GL11 6DD 01454 260631 michaelwood.enquiry@welcomebreak.co.uk www.welcomebreak.co.uk WH Smith and shop in forecourt open 24 hrs

M5 Gordano Welcome Break

M5 J19 • Northbound and southbound 23 B7 ST50977563
Waitrose • WH Smith • Burger King • Eat In • KFC • Starbucks Shell Days Inn 2 hrs Portbury, Bristol BS20 7XG 01275 373624 gordano.enquiry@welcomebreak.co.uk www.welcomebreak.co.uk WH Smith open 24 hrs

M5 Sedgemoor Southbound RoadChef

M5, 7 miles south of J21
23 D5 ST35815259
WH Smith • The Burger Company • Costa Coffee • Restbite Total Days Inn 2 hrs M5 Southbound Rooksbridge, Axbridge, Somerset BS24 0JL 01934 750888

www.roadchef.co.uk Shop on forecourt is open 24 hrs

M5 Sedgemoor Northbound Welcome Break

M5, 3 miles north of J22
23 D5 ST35815259
WH Smith • Burger King • Coffee Primo • Eat in Shell Days Inn 2 hrs M5 Motorway Northbound, Bridgwater, Somerset BS24 0JL 01934 750730 sedgemoor.enquiry@welcomebreak.co.uk www.welcomebreak.co.uk WH Smith and shop on forecourt are open 24 hrs

M5 Bridgwater Moto

M5, J24 • Northbound and southbound 22 F5 ST30403441
WH Smith • Burger King • Coffee Nation • Costa Coffee • EDC BP Travelodge 2 hrs Huntsworth Business Park, Bridgwater, Somerset TA6 6TS 01278 456800 www.moto-way.co.uk WH Smith and shop in forecourt are open 24 hrs

M5 Taunton Deane RoadChef

M5 between J25 and J26 • Northbound and southbound
11 B7 ST19592035
Fonebitz (southbound only) • WH Smith • The Burger Company • Costa Coffee • Restbite Shell Premier Inn (southbound only) 2 hrs Trull, Taunton, Somerset TA3 7PF 01823 271111 www.roadchef.co.uk Outlets on forecourt are open 24 hrs

A38 / M5 Tiverton Moto

M5 Junction 27. • Northbound and southbound
11 C5 ST04901386
Costa • Burger King Travelodge 2 hrs. No HGVs Tiverton EX16 7HD 01884 829423

M5 Cullompton Extra MSA

M5, J28 • Northbound and southbound 10 D5 ST02660798
WH Smith • Le Petit Four • McDonald's Shell 2 hrs Old Station Yard, Station Road, Cullompton, Devon EX15 1NS 01522 523737 http://extraservices.co.uk WH Smith and shop in forecourt open 24 hrs

M5 Exeter Moto

M5 J30 • Northbound and southbound 10 E4 SX96779180
M&S Simply Food • WH Smith • Burger King • Coffee Nation • Costa Coffee • EDS • Harry Ramsden BP Travelodge 2 hrs Sandygate, Exeter, Devon EX2 7HF 01392 436266 www.moto-way.co.uk WH Smith open 24 hrs

M6 Corley Welcome Break

M6, 2.5 miles west of J3 • Eastbound and westbound
63 F7 SP30898604
Waitrose • WH Smith • Burger King • Eat In • KFC • Starbucks Shell Days Inn 2 hrs Highfield Lane, Corley, Staffordshire CV7 8NR 01676 540111 corleyenquiry@welcomebreak.co.uk www.welcomebreak.co.uk WH Smith open 24 hrs

M6 Norton Canes Road Chef

M6 Toll between JT6 and JT7 • Eastbound and westbound
62 D4 SK02290745
WH Smith • The Burger Company • Costa Coffee • Restbite BP Premier Inn 2 hrs Norton Canes, Cannock, Staffordshire WS11 9UX 01543 272540 www.roadchef.co.uk WH Smith and shop in forecourt open 24 hrs

M6 Hilton Park Moto

M6 J10A and J11 • Northbound and southbound
62 D3 SJ96200500
M&S Simply Food • Fone Bitz • WH Smith • Burger King • Coffee Nation • Costa Coffee • EDC BP Travelodge 2 hrs Essington, Wolverhampton, Staffordshire WV11 2AT 01922 412237 www.moto-way.co.uk Coffee shops in forecourt and WH Smith are open 24 hrs

M6 Stafford – northbound Moto

M6, 3 miles north of J14 • Northbound only
75 F5 SJ88613186
Fonebitz • M&S Simply Food • WH Smith • Burger King • Coffee Nation • EDC BP, LPG available Travelodge 2 hrs Stone, Staffordshire ST15 0EU 01785 811188 www.moto-way.co.uk The outlets on the forecourt are open 24 hrs

M6 Stafford – southbound RoadChef

M6, 7.5 miles south of J15 • Southbound only
75 F5 SJ89243065
Fonebitz • WH Smith • The Burger Company • Costa Coffee • Restbite Esso Premier Inn 2 hrs M6 Southbound, Stone, Staffordshire ST15 0EU 01785 826300 www.roadchef.co.uk

M6 Keele Welcome Break

M6, 6 miles north of J15 • Northbound and southbound
74 E5 SJ80624406
WH Smith • Burger King • Eat In • KFC • Starbucks Shell, LPG available (southbound) 2 hrs Three Mile Lane, Keele, Newcastle under Lyme, Staffordshire ST5 5HG 01782 634230 keele.enquiry@welcomebreak.co.uk www.welcomebreak.co.uk Eat In and WH Smith are open 24 hrs

M6 Sandbach RoadChef

M6, just south of J17 • Northbound and southbound
74 C4 SK02290745
WH Smith • The Burger Company • Costa Coffee • Restbite Esso 2 hrs M6 Northbound, Sandbach, Cheshire CW11 2FZ 01270 767134 www.roadchef.co.uk The outlets in the forecourt are open 24 hrs

M6 Knutsford Moto

M6, between J18 and J19 • Northbound and southbound
74 B4 SJ73267826
M&S Simply Food • WH Smith • Burger King • Coffee Nation • Costa Coffee • EDC • Krispy Kreme Doughnuts BP, LPG available Travelodge 2 hrs Northwich Road, Knutsford, Cheshire WA16 0TL 01565 634167 www.moto-way.co.uk Shop in forecourt open 24 hrs

M6 Charnock Richard Welcome Break

M6, 2.5 miles north of J27 • Northbound and southbound
86 C3 SD54411521
WH Smith • Burger King • Coffee Primo • Eat In (northbound only) • KFC Shell (southbound, LPG available); Texaco (northbound) Days Inn 2 hrs Mill Lane, Chorley, Lancashire PR7 5LR 01257 791746 www.welcomebreak.co.uk Eat In and WH Smith open 24 hrs

M6 Lancaster (Forton) Moto

M6 south of J33 • Northbound and southbound
92 D5 SD50145198
Fone Bitz • M&S Simply Food • WH Smith • Burger King • Coffee Nation • Costa Coffee • EDC BP, LPG available Travelodge 2 hrs White Carr Lane, Bay Horse, Lancaster, Lancashire LA2 9DU 01524 791775 www.moto-way.co.uk WH Smith and shop in forecourt are open 24 hrs

M6 Burton-in-Kendal Moto

M6 between J35 and J36 • Northbound only
92 B5 SD52207617
WH Smith • Burger King • Coffee Nation Costa Coffee • EDC BP Travelodge 2 hrs Burton West, Carnforth, Lancashire LA6 1JF 01524 781234 www.moto-way.co.uk

M6 Killington Lake RoadChef

M6 just south of J37 • Southbound only
99 E7 SD58779111
WH Smith • The Burger Company • Costa Coffee • Restbite BP, LPG available Premier Inn 2 hrs M6 Southbound, near Kendal, Cumbria LA8 0NW 08701 977 145 www.roadchef.co.uk WH Smith and shop in forecourt open 24 hrs

M6 Tebay – northbound Westmorland

M6, just north of J38 • Northbound only
99 D8 NY60510626
Farm shop • butchers counter • Cafe • cake shop Total, LPG available Westmorland Hotel Yes M6, Old Tebay, Cumbria CA10 3ZA 01539 624511 www.westmorland.com Main site and shop on forecourt open 24 hrs

M6 Tebay – southbound Westmorland

M6, 4.5 miles south of J39 • Southbound only
99 D8 NY60790650
Butcher's counter • Cafe • coffee shop Total Yes M6, Old Tebay, Cumbria CA10 3SB 01539 624511 www.westmorland.com Made to Go snack bar and forecourt shop open 24 hrs

M6 Southwaite Moto

M6 Junctions 41-42 • Northbound and southbound
108 E4 NY44164523
M&S • Costa • Burger King • EDC • WH Smith • Coffee Nation BP Travelodge 2 hrs Broadfield Road, Carlisle CA4 0NT 01697 473476 www.moto-way.co.uk WH Smith and outlets on the forecourts are open 24 hours

M11 Birchanger Green Welcome Break

M11 at J8/J8a • Northbound and southbound 41 B8 TL51202149
Waitrose • WH Smith • Burger King • Eat In • KFC • Starbucks Shell, LPG available Days Inn 2 hrs Old Dunmow Road, Bishop's Stortford, Hertfordshire CM23 5QZ 01279 653388 www.welcomebreak.co.uk WH Smith open 24 hrs

M18 Doncaster North Moto

M18 J5, at the western end of the M180 • Northbound and southbound 89 C7 SE66791104
WH Smith • Burger King • Coffee Nation • Costa Coffee • EDC BP, LPG available Travelodge 2 hrs Hatfield, Doncaster, South Yorkshire DN8 5GS 02920 891141 www.moto-way.co.uk WH Smith open 24 hrs

M20 Maidstone RoadChef

M20 J8 30 D2 TQ82455523
WH Smith • The Burger Company • Costa Coffee • Restbite Esso Premier Inn 2 hrs M20 J8, Hollingbourne, Maidstone, Kent ME17 1SS 01622 739647 www.roadchef.co.uk WH Smith and shop in forecourt are open 24 hrs

M20 Stop24 (Folkestone) Stop 24

M20 J11 19 B8 TR13283729

Julian Graves • WH Smith • Breakfast Break • Burger King • Eat • KFC • Starbucks • Shell, LPG available

2 hrs Junction 11 M20, Stanford Intersection, Stanford, Kent CT21 4BL 01303 760273 info@stop24.co.uk www.stop24.co.uk Outlets on forecourt are open 24 hrs

M23 Pease Pottage Moto

M23 J11 • Northbound and southbound 28 F3 TQ26183310

M&S Simply Food • WH Smith • Burger King • Coffee Nation • Costa Coffee • EDC • Krispy Kreme Doughnuts • BP, LPG available

2 hrs Brighton Road, Pease Pottage, Crawley, West Sussex RH11 9AE 01293 562852 www.moto-way.co.uk WH Smith and outlets in forecourt open 24 hrs

M25 Clacket Lane RoadChef

M25 between J5 and J6 • Eastbound and westbound 28 D5 TQ42335457

Fone Bitz • WH Smith • Costa Coffee (westbound only) • Restbite • Wimpy • Total • Premier Inn (westbound only) 2hrs M25 Westbound, Westerham, Kent TN16 2ER 01959 565577 www.roadchef.com Restbite open 24 hrs

M25 Cobham Extra MSA

M25 J9-10 (due to open July 2012) • Clockwise and anti-clockwise 28 D2 TQ11345768

Days Inn • Eat In • KFC • McDonalds • Shell • Starbucks • WH Smith • Shell • Days Inn customerservices@extraservices.co.uk http://extraservices.co.uk

M25 South Mimms Welcome Break

M25 J23 and A1(M) J1 • Clockwise and anti-clockwise 41 D5 TL23000023

Waitrose • WH Smith • Burger King • Eat In • KFC • Starbucks • BP • Days Inn 2 hrs Bignells Corner, Potters Bar, Hertfordshire EN6 3QQ 01707 621001 mimms.enquiry@welcomebreak.co.uk www.welcomebreak.co.uk Eat In, WH Smith and the outlets on the forecourt are open 24 hrs

M25 Thurrock Moto

M25, signposted from J30/J31 • Clockwise and anti-clockwise 29 B6 TQ57837947

M&S Simply Food • WH Smith • Burger King • Coffee Nation • Costa Coffee • EDC • Krispy Kreme Doughnuts • Esso • Travelodge 2 hrs Arterial Road, West Thurrock, Grays, Essex RM16 3BG 01708 865487 www.moto-way.co.uk WH Smith and shop on forecourt open 24 hrs

M27 Rownhams RoadChef

M27, between J3 and J4 • Eastbound and westbound 14 C4 SU38791769

WH Smith • Costa Coffee • Restbite (both sides); Wimpy (southbound only) • Esso • Premier Inn 2 hrs M27 Southbound, Southampton, Hampshire SO16 8AP 02380 734480 www.roadchef.co.uk The outlets in the forecourts are open 24 hrs

M40 Beaconsfield Extra MSA

M40 J2 • Eastbound and westbound 40 F2 SU95098897

M&S Simply Food • WH Smith • KFC • Le Petit Four • McDonald's • Presto • Starbucks • Shell, LPG available • Etap Hotel 2 hrs A355 Windsor Drive, Beaconsfield, Buckinghamshire HP9 2SE www.extraservices.co.uk McDonald's open 24 hrs

M40 Oxford Welcome Break

M40 J8A • Northbound and southbound 39 D6 SP62440479

Waitrose • WH Smith • Burger King • Eat In • KFC • Starbucks • BP • Days Inn 2 hrs M40 Junction 8A, Waterstock, Oxfordshire OX33 1JN 01865 877000 oxford.enquiry@welcomebreak.co.uk www.welcomebreak.co.uk WH Smith and shop in forecourt open 24 hrs

M40 Cherwell Valley Moto

M40 J10 • Northbound and southbound 39 B5 SP55162822

M&S Simply Food • WH Smith • Burger King • Coffee Nation • Costa Coffee • EDC • Esso • Travelodge 2 hrs Northampton Road, Ardley, Bicester, Oxfordshire OX27 7RD 01869 346060 www.moto-way.co.uk Coffee Nation and WH Smith open 24 hrs

M40 Warwick South Welcome Break

M40 between J12 and J13 • Southbound 51 D8 SP34075801

WH Smith • Burger King • Eat In • KFC • Starbucks • BP, LPG available • Days Inn 2 hrs Banbury Road, Ashorne, Warwick CV35 0AA 01926 651681 warwicksouth.enquiry@welcomebreak.co.uk www.welcomebreak.co.uk Eat In, WH Smith and forecourt outlets open 24 hrs

M40 Warwick North Welcome Break

M40 between J12 and J13 • Northbound 51 D8 SP33885770

Waitrose • Coffee Primo • Eat In • Burger King • KFC • WH Smith • Shell • Days Inn 2 hrs Banbury Road, Ashorne, Warwick CV35 0AA 01926 650681 warwick.rdm@welcomebreak.co.uk www.welcomebreak.co.uk

M42 Hopwood Park Welcome Break

M42 Junction 2 • Eastbound and westbound 50 B5 SP03637389

Waitrose • Coffee Primo Lounge • EatIn Restaurant • Burger King • KFC • WH Smith • Shell 2 hrs Redditch Road, Alvechurch B48 7AU 0121 4474000 hopwood.training@welcomebreak.co.uk www.welcomebreak.co.uk

M42 Tamworth Moto

M42, just north of J10 • Northbound and southbound 63 D6 SK24440112

M&S Simply Food • WH Smith • Burger King • Coffee Nation • Costa Coffee • EDC • Esso • Travelodge 2 hrs Green Lane, Tamworth, Staffordshire B77 5PS 01827 260120 www.moto-way.co.uk WH Smith and outlets on forecourt are open 24 hrs

M48 Severn View Moto

M48 J1 • Eastbound and westbound 36 F2 ST57118959

WH Smith • Burger King • Coffee Nation • Costa Coffee • BP • Travelodge 2 hrs Aust, South Gloucestershire BS35 4BH 01454 623851 www.moto-way.co.uk Forecourt outlets open 24 hrs

M54 Telford Welcome Break

M54 J4 • Eastbound and westbound 61 D7 SJ73050890

WH Smith • Burger King • Eat In • Starbucks • Shell • Days Inn 2 hrs Priorslee Road, Shifnal, Telford, Shropshire TF11 8TG 01952 238400 telford.gm@welcomebreak.co.uk www.welcomebreak.co.uk WH Smith and shop on forecourt open 24 hrs

M56 Chester RoadChef

M56 J14 • Eastbound and westbound 73 B8 SJ46537491

WH Smith • Costa Coffee • Restbite • The Burger Company • Shell • Premier Inn 2 hrs Elton, Chester, Cheshire CH2 4QZ 01928 728500 www.roadchef.com Costa Coffee and Restbite open 24 hrs

M61 Rivington Euro Garages

M61 between J6 and J7 • Northbound and southbound 86 C4 SD62111168

Burger King • Spar • Starbucks • Subway • BP • Rivington Lodge (southbound) 2 hrs M61, Horwich, Bolton, Lancashire BL6 5UZ 01254 56070 enquiries@eurogarages.com www.eurogarages.com/rivington-services Spar shop and forecourt open 24hrs

M62 Burtonwood Welcome Break

M62 J8 • Eastbound and westbound 86 E3 SJ57749129

WH Smith • KFC • Starbucks • Shell 2 hrs M62 Great Sankey, Warrington, Cheshire WA5 3AX 01925 651656 burtonwood.enquiry@welcomebreak.co.uk www.welcomebreak.co.uk WH Smith open 24 hrs

M62 Birch Moto

M62 1.5 miles east of J18 • Eastbound and westbound 87 D6 SD84700797

Coffee Nation • M&S Simply Food • WH Smith • Burger King • Costa Coffee • Fresh Express • the Eat and Drink Co • BP • Travelodge 2 hrs Heywood, Lancashire OL10 2HQ 0161 643 0911 www.moto-way.co.uk WH Smith is open 24 hrs

M62 Hartshead Moor Welcome Break

M62, between J25 and J26 • Eastbound and westbound 88 B2 SE16892413

WH Smith • Burger King • Eat In • KFC • Starbucks • Shell • Days Inn Bradford 2 hrs Clifton, Brighouse, West Yorkshire HD6 4JX 01274 876584 hartshead.enquiry@welcomebreak.co.uk www.welcomebreak.co.uk Eat In is open 24 hrs

M62 Ferrybridge Moto

M62 Junction 33. Also A1(M) J40 (northbound) or J41 (southbound) • Northbound and southbound 89 B5 SE48512262

M&S Simply Food • WH Smith • Burger King • Coffee Nation • Costa Coffee • EDC • Esso • Travelodge 2 hrs Ferrybridge, Knottingly, West Yorkshire WF11 0AF 01977 672767 www.moto-way.co.uk Coffee Nation and WH Smith open 24 hrs

M65 Darwen Extra MSA

M65 J4. • Eastbound and westbound 86 B4 SD68592414

Somerfield Essentials • Le Petit Four • McDonald's • Shell, LPG • Travelodge 2 hrs Darwen Motorway Services Area, Darwen, Lancashire BB3 0AT www.extraservices.co.uk Shop in forecourt is open 24 hrs

Scotland

M9 Stirling Moto

M9 J9 • Northbound and southbound 127 F7 NS80438870

WH Smith • Burger King • Coffee Nation • Costa Coffee • EDC • BP • Travelodge 2 hrs Pirnhall, Stirling FK7 8EU 01786 813614 www.moto-way.co.uk WH Smith is open 24 hrs

M74 Bothwell RoadChef

M74, south of J4 • southbound only 119 D7 NS70855980

WH Smith • Costa • Restbite • BP, LPG available 2hrs M74 Southbound, Bothwell, Lanarkshire G71 8BG 01698 854123 www.roadchef.com Shop in forecourt is open 24 hrs

M74 Hamilton RoadChef

M74, 1 mile north of J6 • northbound only 119 D7 NS72572672

WH Smith • Costa Coffee • Restbite • BP • Premier Inn 2hrs M74 Northbound, Hamilton, South Lanarkshire ML3 6JW 01698 282176 www.welcomebreak.co.uk Shop in forecourt is open 24hrs

M74 Happendon Cairn Lodge

M74 between J11 and J12 on B7078 • Northbound and southbound 119 F8 NS85243364

Yes • Coffee shop • restaurant • Shell 2hrs Cairn Lodge, Douglas, Lanark, South Lanarkshire ML11 0RJ 01555 851880 Shop in forecourt open 24 hrs

A74(M) Abington Welcome Break

A74(M) J13 • Northbound and southbound 114 B2 NS93222505

WH Smith • Burger King • Eat In • Starbucks • Shell, LPG available • Days Inn 2 hrs Abington, Biggar, South Lanarkshire ML12 6RG 01864 502637 abington.enquiry@welcomebreak.co.uk www.welcomebreak.co.uk Eat In open 24 hrs. Tourist information office

A74(M) Annandale Water Road Chef

A74(M) J16 • Northbound and southbound 114 E4 NY10389261

WH Smith • Costa Coffee • Restbite • The Burger Company • Wild Bean Cafe • BP • Premier Inn 2hrs Johnstone Bridge, near Lockerbie, Dumfries and Galloway DG11 1HD 01576 470870 www.roadchef.com Restbite and forecourt shop are open 24 hrs

A74(M) Gretna Green Welcome Break

A74(M), just north of J22 • Northbound and southbound 108 C3 NY30746872

WH Smith • Burger King • Eat In • KFC • Starbucks • BP, LPG available • Days Inn 2 hrs M74A Trunk Road, Gretna Green, Dumfries and Galloway DG16 5HQ 01461 337567 gretna.enquiry@welcomebreak.co.uk www.welcomebreak.co.uk Eat In and WH Smith open 24 hrs

M80 Old Inns

M80 • Eastbound and Westbound 119 B7 NS77187671

Shell Select • Old inns Cafe • Silk Cottage Cantonese buffet restaurant and takeaway • Shell Castlecary Road, Cumbernauld G68 0BJ 0843 259 0190 (filling station) http://www.shell.co.uk • http://www.oldinnscafe.com

M90 Kinross Moto

M90 J6 • Northbound and southbound 128 D3 NO10800282

WH Smith • Burger King • Coffee Nation • Costa Coffee • EDC • Esso • Travelodge 2 hrs M90, Kinross, Perth and Kinross KY13 7NQ 01577 863123 www.moto-way.co.uk WH Smith and shop in forecourt open 24 hrs

Wales

M4 Magor First

M4 J23A • Eastbound and westbound 35 F8 ST42068796

Yes • Burger King • cafe • Esso • Travelodge 2 hours M4 Magor, Caldicot, Monmouthshire NP26 3YL 01633 881887 info@firstmotorway.co.uk www.firstmotorway.co.uk Cafe open 24 hrs

M4 Cardiff Gate Welcome Break

M4 J30 • Eastbound and westbound 35 F6 ST21658283

Waitrose • WH Smith • Burger King • Starbucks • Total, LPG available 2 hrs Cardiff Gate Business Park, Cardiff, South Glamorgan CF23 8RA 01758 822102 www.welcomebreak.co.uk Shop in forecourt open 24 hrs

M4 Cardiff West Moto

M4, off J33 • Eastbound and westbound 22 B2 ST09417967

Moto Shop • WH Smith • Burger King • Coffee Nation • Costa Coffee • EDC • Esso • Travelodge 2 hrs Pontyclun, Mid Glamorgan CF72 8SA 02920 891141 www.moto-way.co.uk WH Smith is open 24 hrs

M4 Sarn Park Welcome Break

M4 J36 • Eastbound and westbound 34 F3 SS90688290

WH Smith • Burger King • Eat In • Shell • Days Inn 2 hrs M4 Motorway, Junction 36, Sarn Park, Bridgend CF32 9RW 01656 655332 sarn.enquiry@welcomebreak.co.uk www.welcomebreak.co.uk WH Smith and shop in forecourt are open 24 hrs

M4 Swansea Moto

M4 at J47 • Eastbound and westbound 33 E7 SS62159969

WH Smith • Burger King • Coffee Nation • Costa Coffee • BP • Travelodge 2 hrs Penllergaer, Swansea, West Glamorgan SA4 1GT 01792 896222 www.moto-way.co.uk The outlets on the forecourt are open 24 hrs

M4 Pont Abraham RoadChef

M4 J49 • Eastbound and westbound 33 D6 SN57470743

WH Smith • Costa Coffee • JJ Beanos • Restbite • Texaco 2 hours Llanedi, Pontarddulais, Swansea SA4 0FU 01792 884663 www.roadchef.co.uk Forecourt outlets open 24 hrs

The Speed Limit: 80mph or 70mph? Or even 60mph?

By Stephen Mesquita, Philip's *On the Road* Correspondent

It was one of those moments, described in phrasebooks as 'At the Car Hire Desk'. A moment to make the heart sink and the spirit to travel wither. It was at Frankfurt airport. 'I'm very sorry, sir, we don't have the Compact you ordered.' Visions of scooters and mopeds appeared before my eyes.

'But we do have a Mercedes blah blah blah, which we can offer you in its place at no extra charge' (sorry Mercedes fans, the specification escapes me).

So there I was, on the autobahn, with over 100 miles to drive to my appointment. An autobahn with no speed limit and a Mercedes blah blah blah which also seemed to have no speed limit. It was a pleasant autumn's afternoon. The traffic was relatively light.

We have reached the stage in this tale where I need to break the flow to state my credentials. I am not a boy racer. I never have been a boy racer (except for an incident in my long lost youth which I may decide to relate later). Speed comes a very poor second to safety when I am driving. I'm normally very happy to pootle along the motorway at 70mph, if not a bit slower.

But here I was with an opportunity to conduct an experiment – purely for the sake of research, you understand. How fast could I go in this speed machine at whose wheel I now found myself? Looking in my mirror at the outside lane I could see another Merc way back on the autobahn. Within a few seconds it passed me in a blur. Now was my chance. I put the pedal to the metal, manoeuvred into the outside lane and held on tight.

To try to answer this question, I left my house at 4.40am on a damp February morning

From a quick calculation, 240kph is 150mph. That was the stage at which I decided that my driving skills probably weren't up to going any faster. The worrying thing was that, even at 240kph, there were still cars appearing with alarming speed in my rear view mirror, impatient to overtake.

Where is all this leading?

When, last year, the government floated the idea of raising the speed limit on motorways to 80mph, my mind went back to my experience outside Frankfurt. But it also went back even further. To my first driving experience, in the mid 1970s, on the freeways of the Mid West. It was just after the oil crisis and the speed limit, even on the freeway, was 55mph. My job entailed a lot of driving in a car with automatic everything – a car that more or less drove itself.

The freeways were, for the most part, empty and the journeys were long. 55mph seemed mind-numbingly slow. The radio played the same hits over and over. Combating boredom was nearly impossible.

So which was it to be? The German experience, the status quo or the US experience of the mid-70s?

To try to answer this question, I left my house at 4.40am on a damp February morning. The first challenge was to find a stretch of road where I could conduct my experiment. Out here, in deepest East Anglia, there are no three-lane motorways. There are also, in some area, forests of speed cameras. I needed to drive on an east-west axis to neutralise the effect of a north wind. And I needed to be out at a time of day when lorries were least likely to be overtaking each other in the outside lane and when all good law enforcement officers were tucked up in bed.

This was the plan – to drive 30 miles at 80mph and 30 miles at 60mph and a bit in between at regulation 70mph. I chose the A14, A11 and M11 from Bury St Edmunds and back. It's dual carriageway all the

way. It's comparatively speed camera free on the outward leg (at least I hope so) and, although it's busy, it's not too busy at 5.30am when I started the 80mph stretch.

The advantage of driving faster is that you get there faster. So you save time. The advantage of driving slower is that you use less petrol, so you save money. I am not qualified to talk about road safety, although the Road Safety Pressure Groups all argue that faster is more dangerous. I am also not qualified to comment on the environmental issues, although it follows that less petrol means less pollution.

I would not normally bore you with spreadsheets – but, on this occasion, it seems to be the simplest way to express the argument.

If you're a professional driver clocking up 25,000 miles a year, it totals out at nearly £1,000 more

The important thing is to understand – as all motorists surely do – that the faster you drive, the more petrol you consume. In my trusty 10-year old VW Passat Estate 1.9 TDi (I do remember the specification of my own car), I would normally expect to do about 45 miles per gallon on a long journey.

At 80mph, over 30 miles, the petrol consumption was 36.6mpg; at 70mph over 20 miles (10 miles into the wind and 10 miles with the wind behind) the average was 42.9mpg; and, at 60mph, the consumption was 47.3mpg.

Now for the maths. At the time of going to press, diesel costs £1.40 per gallon. So my 30 miles at 80mph cost me £5.21 and my 30 miles at 60mph cost me £4.03. It may not sound much – but multiply it up over a year and it turns into a sum of money that you notice. In fact, if you're a professional driver clocking up 25,000 miles a year, it totals out at nearly £1,000 more.

So here is my Ready Reckoner (table 1)

Based on my experience, if I drove at 60mph on long journeys, it could save me 23% on my fuel costs compared with driving at 80mph and 9% compared with driving at 70mph. You'll notice that the differential is greater between 70 and 80 than between 60 and 70mph.

But time is also money. Is it possible that the savings in petrol would be wiped out by the cost of the additional journey time? Back to the spreadsheet (table 2):

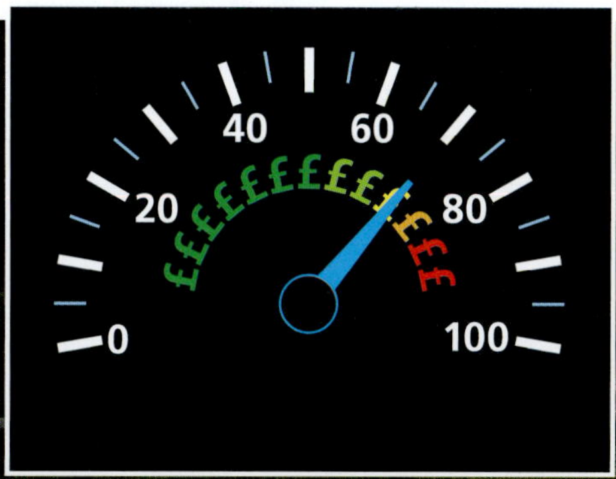

So you'll see that, although it's 23% cheaper to drive at 60mph compared with 80, it takes 32% longer. The 104 hours lost by the professional driver would cost considerably more than the £983 gained in the petrol saving.

'Hours lost' is a concept that is not always easy to quantify. How many of those hours would otherwise be downtime, so not really lost? If this is what the bean counters call a Cost Benefit Analysis, it doesn't really give us a conclusive answer.

Quite a few other drivers – and not just lorries – were also keeping to 60

Back to the A14. Here are some considerations which you can't deduce from the spreadsheets. First, I didn't actually drive at 80mph. The needle of my speedometer was at, or over, 80mph for most of the journey. But when I came to check my average speed, I had actually driven the 30 miles at 77mph. Thanks to those nice people at VW, my speedometer was set to register 3–4mph faster than I was actually driving. Anyone who uses sat nav can see this as they drive. Their speedometer registers a higher speed than the sat nav tells them they are actually driving.

But I was happy not to be averaging 80. If it had been a fine day on an empty motorway, I would probably have been very comfortable doing 80. But on a dual carriageway, with overtaking lorries which threw up spray, and in the dark, 77mph was fast enough. Actually, it was probably too fast.

And then I had a surprise when I was driving at 60mph on the return leg. Quite a few other drivers – and not just lorries – were also keeping to 60. In these tough times, many drivers have already worked out for themselves the economies of driving more slowly – without a law being needed to stop those who want or need to drive faster. The law does not force you to drive at 70.

It may make for a dull conclusion to this otherwise sparkling article (spreadsheets and all) – but my vote is to keep the speed limit at 70mph. If we were really trying to be green in this country, we would reduce it – but that's currently left to you as an individual. My dawn sortie has convinced me that raising the speed limit to 80mph on our crowded motorways does not have my vote. Sorry all you budding Jensons and Lewis's out there.

So, after breaking the law to bring you this research, I'll be going back to driving at 70mph – or, now I've done the sums, maybe a little bit slower.

Oh yes – that incident from my long lost past. I nearly forgot. Well, I didn't always keep to the 55mph speed limit during my stint on the road in the USA. In fact, on an empty freeway between Chicago and Minneapolis, I got stopped. Despite my poor impression of Bertie Wooster pleading ignorance as a foreigner, a request for $115 arrived from a court in Wisconsin. I remember thinking as I wrote the cheque, that in 1975 $115 was quite a lot of money.

1

	80	70	60	70	60	70	60
	36.6mpg	**42.9mpg**	**47.3mpg**	**Amount saved***			**% Saved***
5,000 miles	£869	£742	£673	£127.68	£196.69	17%	23%
10,000 miles	£1,739	£1,484	£1,346	£255.37	£393.38	17%	23%
15,000 miles	£2,608	£2,225	£2,018	£383.05	£590.06	17%	23%
20,000 miles	£3,478	£2,967	£2,691	£510.74	£786.75	17%	23%
25,000 miles	£4,347	£3,709	£3,364	£638.42	£983.44	17%	23%

Price per litre – diesel: £1.40
Price per gallon – diesel: £6.36

*compared to 80mph

2

	Time taken (hours)			**Additional time taken** (hours)			**% Additional time taken** at 60mph compared to:	
	80	70	60	80	70	60	80	70
5,000 miles	62.50	71.43	83.33	0	8.93	20.83	32%	13%
10,000 miles	125.00	142.86	166.67	0	17.86	41.67	32%	13%
15,000 miles	187.50	214.29	250.00	0	26.79	62.50	32%	13%
20,000 miles	250.00	285.71	333.33	0	35.71	83.33	32%	13%
25,000 miles	312.50	357.14	416.67	0	44.64	104.17	32%	13%

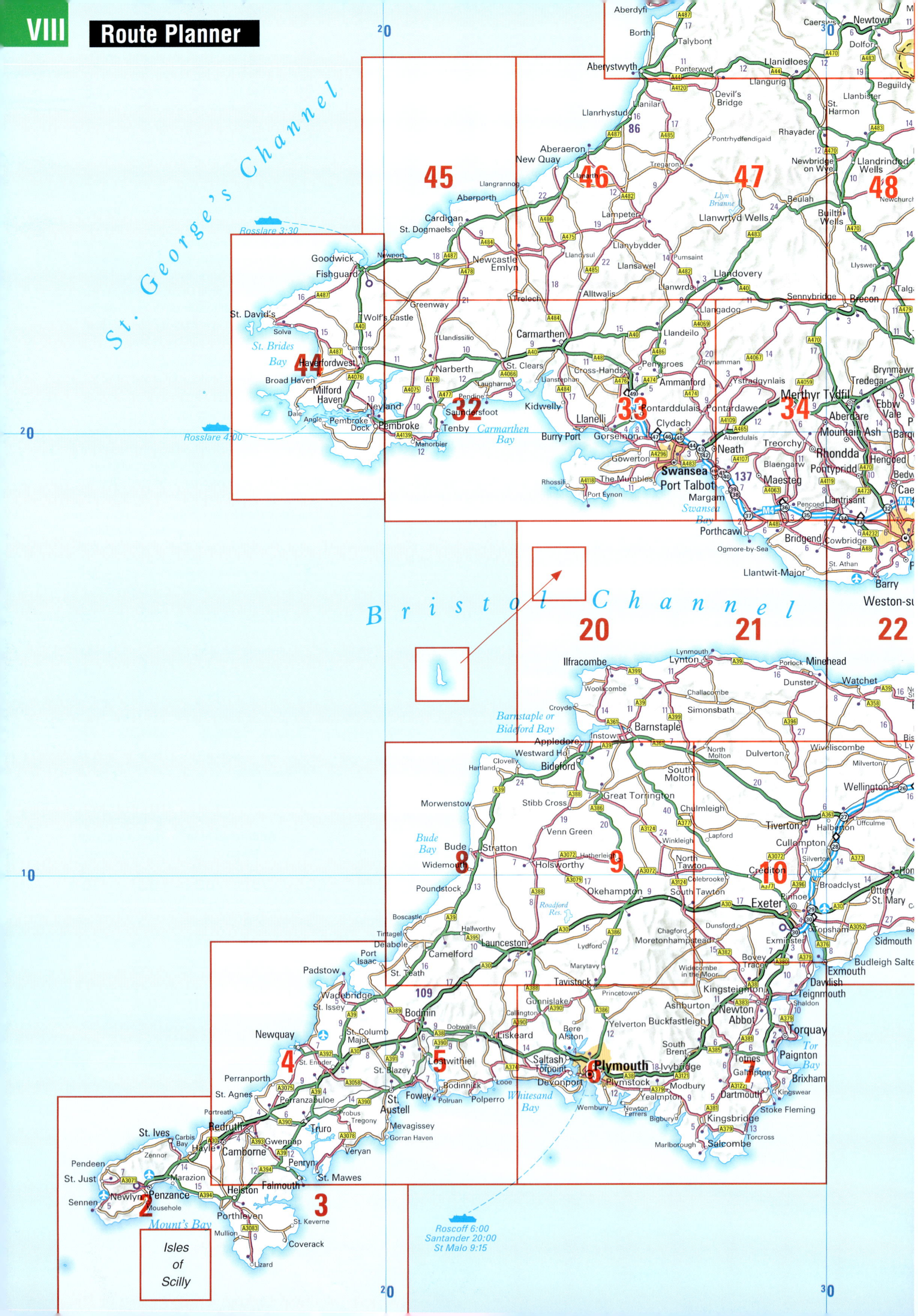
St. George's Channel
Bristol Channel
Rosslare 3:30
Rosslare 4:00
Roscoff 6:00
Santander 20:00
St Malo 9:15
Isles of Scilly
20
30
10
2
3
4
5
6
7
8
9
10
20
21
22
32
33
34
44
45
46
47
48
86
109
137
Aberdyfi
Borth
Talybont
Aberystwyth
Ponterwyd
Llanidloes
Llangurig
Devil's Bridge
Caersws
Newtown
Dolfor
Beguildy
Llanbister
St. Harmon
Rhayader
Llanrhystud
Llanilar
Pontrhydfendigaid
Aberaeron
New Quay
Llanarth
Tregaron
Newbridge on Wye
Llandrindod Wells
Newchurch
Llangrannog
Aberporth
Llyn Brianne
Beulah
Builth Wells
Cardigan
St. Dogmaels
Lampeter
Llanwrtyd Wells
Llanybydder
Llandysul
Newcastle Emlyn
Pumsaint
Llansawel
Llyswen
Goodwick
Fishguard
Newport
Llandovery
Llanwrda
Alltwalis
Trelech
Greenway
Sennybridge
Brecon
Talgarth
St. David's
Solva
Wolf's Castle
St. Brides Bay
Camrose
Haverfordwest
Broad Haven
Milford Haven
Dale
Angle
Pembroke Dock
Neyland
Pembroke
Llandissilio
Narberth
Carmarthen
St. Clears
Laugharne
Pendine
Saundersfoot
Tenby
Manorbier
Carmarthen Bay
Kidwelly
Llansteffan
Llangadog
Llandeilo
Cross-Hands
Penygroes
Ammanford
Brynamman
Ystradgynlais
Merthyr Tydfil
Tredegar
Brynmawr
Ebbw Vale
Aberdare
Mountain Ash
Bargoed
Pontarddulais
Pontardawe
Llanelli
Burry Port
Gorseinon
Clydach
Swansea
Neath
Aberdulais
Treorchy
Rhondda
Hengoed
Pontypridd
Blaengarw
Maesteg
Gowerton
Rhossili
The Mumbles
Port Eynon
Port Talbot
Margam
Swansea Bay
Porthcawl
Bridgend
Pencoed
Llantrisant
Cowbridge
Ogmore-by-Sea
Llantwit-Major
St. Athan
Barry
Weston-super
Caerphilly
Ilfracombe
Lynmouth
Lynton
Porlock
Minehead
Watchet
Dunster
Woolacombe
Challacombe
Simonsbath
Croyde
Barnstaple or Bideford Bay
Barnstaple
Instow
Appledore
Westward Ho!
Bideford
Clovelly
Hartland
North Molton
South Molton
Dulverton
Wiveliscombe
Milverton
Wellington
Great Torrington
Stibb Cross
Morwenstow
Chulmleigh
Lapford
Tiverton
Halberton
Uffculme
Venn Green
Winkleigh
Bude Bay
Bude
Stratton
Widemouth
Hatherleigh
Holsworthy
North Tawton
Cullompton
Silverton
Crediton
Colebrooke
Broadclyst
Poundstock
Okehampton
South Tawton
Pinhoe
Exeter
Ottery St. Mary
Boscastle
Roadford Res.
Tintagel
Delabole
Hallworthy
Launceston
Lydford
Chagford
Moretonhampstead
Dunsford
Topsham
Exminster
Sidmouth
Port Isaac
Camelford
Marytavy
Bovey Tracey
Budleigh Salterton
Exmouth
Padstow
St. Teath
Tavistock
Widecombe in the Moor
Dawlish
Teignmouth
Shaldon
Wadebridge
St. Issey
Princetown
Kingsteignton
Gunnislake
Callington
Bodmin
Ashburton
Newton Abbot
Newquay
Dobwalls
Bere Alston
Yelverton
Buckfastleigh
Torquay
St. Columb Major
Liskeard
South Brent
Tor Bay
Paignton
St. Enoder
St. Blazey
Lostwithiel
Saltash
Torpoint
Plymouth
Ivybridge
Plympstock
Totnes
Galmpton
Brixham
Perranporth
Bodinnick
Looe
Devonport
Modbury
Dartmouth
Kingswear
St. Agnes
Perranzabuloe
Fowey
Polruan
Polperro
Whitsand Bay
Wembury
Yealmpton
Stoke Fleming
Portreath
St. Austell
Probus
Tregony
Newton Ferrers
Bigbury
Kingsbridge
Redruth
Truro
Mevagissey
Gorran Haven
Torcross
St. Ives
Carbis Bay
Hayle
Camborne
Gwennap
Veryan
Marlborough
Salcombe
Zennor
Penryn
Pendeen
St. Just
Marazion
Falmouth
St. Mawes
Sennen
Newlyn
Penzance
Helston
Mousehole
Porthleven
St. Keverne
Mount's Bay
Mullion
Coverack
Lizard

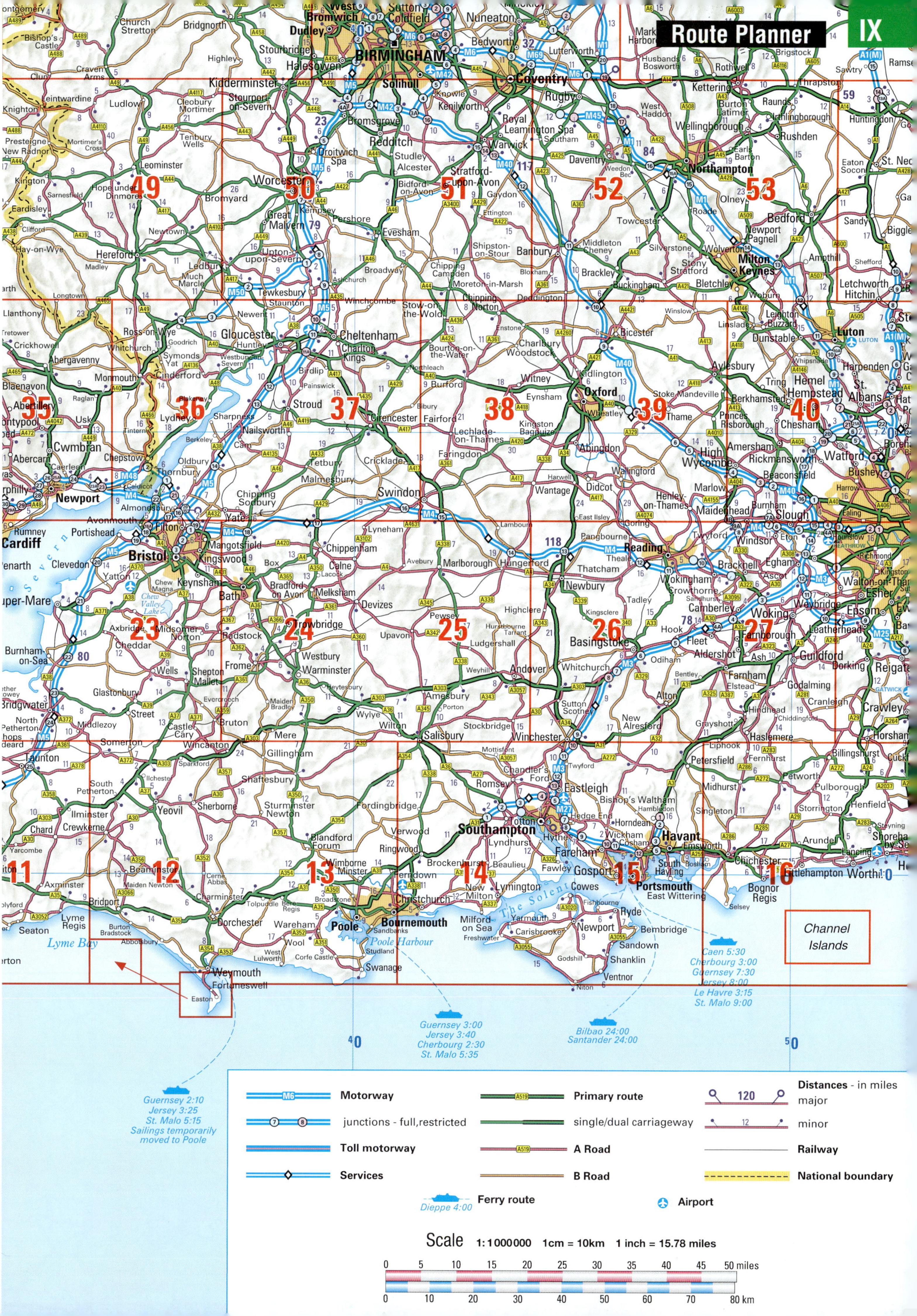
Channel Islands
Caen 5:30
Cherbourg 3:00
Guernsey 7:30
Jersey 8:00
Le Havre 3:15
St. Malo 9:00
Guernsey 3:00
Jersey 3:40
Cherbourg 2:30
St. Malo 5:35
Bilbao 24:00
Santander 24:00
Guernsey 2:10
Jersey 3:25
St. Malo 5:15
Sailings temporarily moved to Poole
Motorway
junctions - full,restricted
Toll motorway
Services
Primary route
single/dual carriageway
A Road
B Road
Distances - in miles
major
minor
Railway
National boundary
Ferry route
Dieppe 4:00
Airport
Scale 1:1 000 000 1cm = 10km 1 inch = 15.78 miles
0 5 10 15 20 25 30 35 40 45 50 miles
0 10 20 30 40 50 60 70 80 km

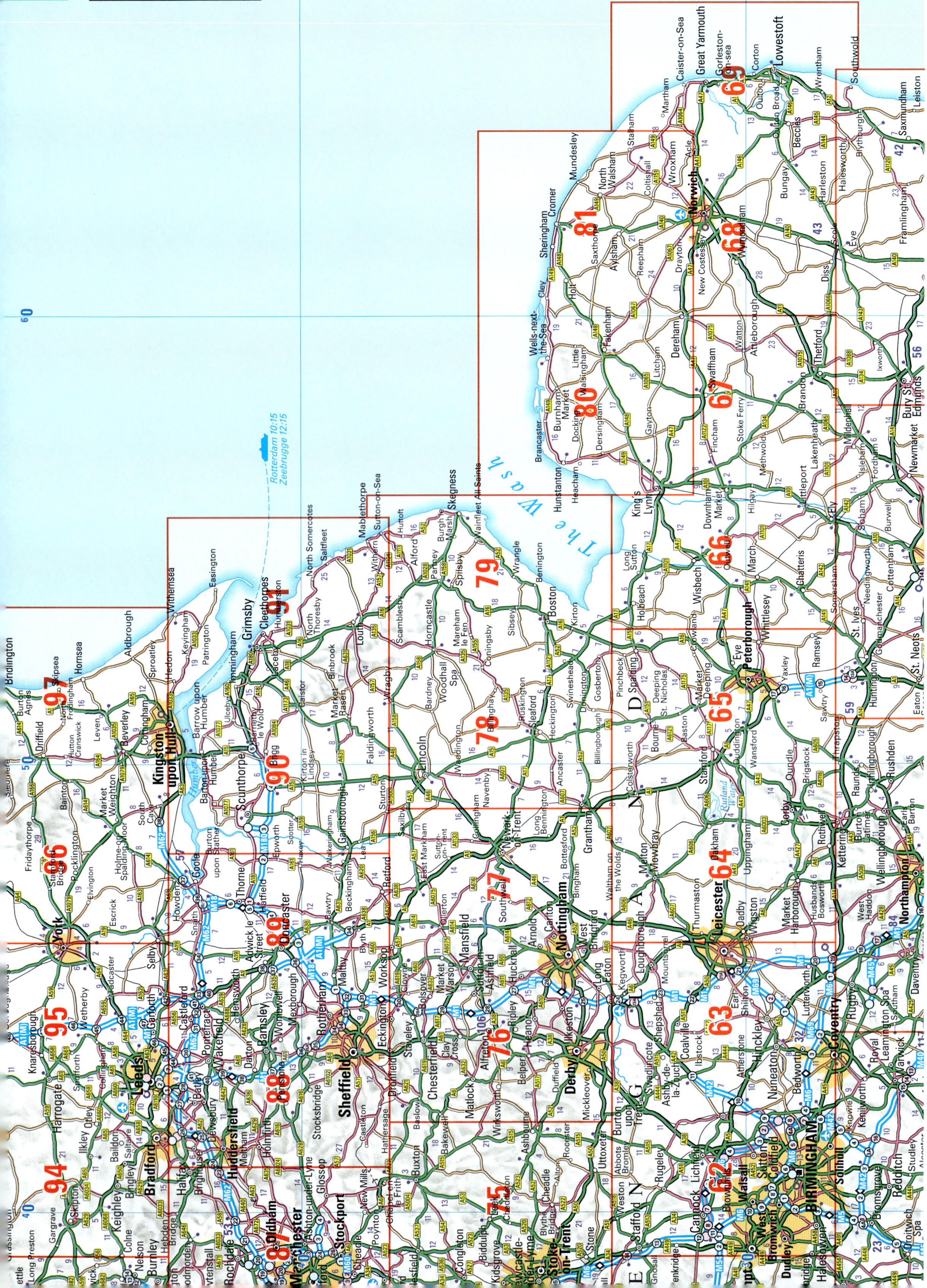
The Wash
Rotterdam 10:15
Zeebrugge 12:15
York
Leeds
Bradford
Sheffield
Nottingham
Leicester
Derby
Coventry
Lincoln
Norwich
Peterborough
Northampton
BIRMINGHAM
Kingston upon Hull
Doncaster
Grimsby
Boston
Great Yarmouth
Lowestoft
Stoke-on-Trent
Huddersfield
Oldham
Manchester

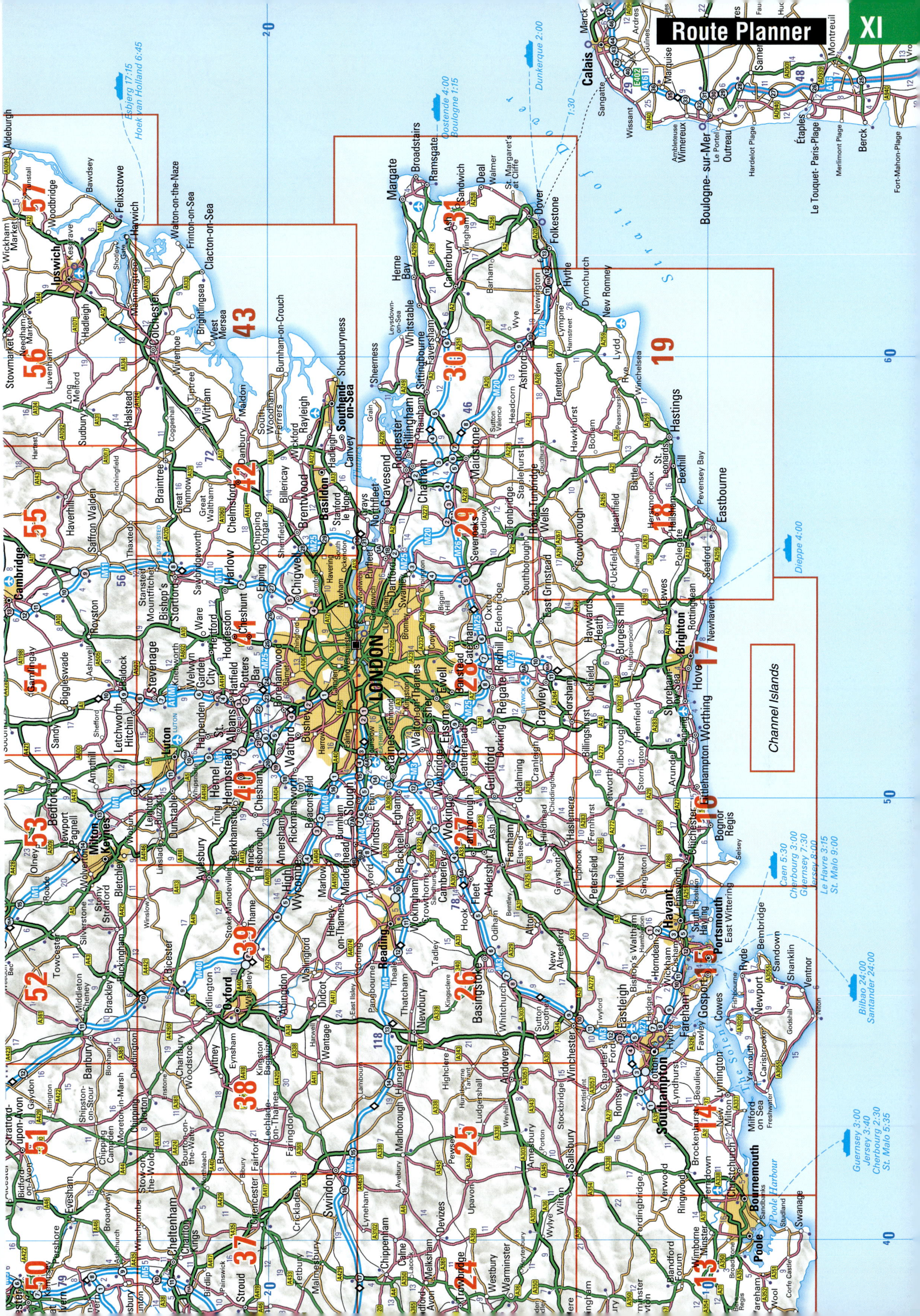
LONDON
Channel Islands
Calais
Boulogne-sur-Mer
Dunkerque 2:00
Dover
Folkestone
Brighton
Southampton
Portsmouth
Bournemouth
Oxford
Reading
Cambridge
Ipswich
Colchester
Southend-on-Sea
Maidstone
Canterbury
Hastings
Eastbourne
Luton
Milton Keynes
Swindon
Salisbury
Winchester
Guildford
Chelmsford
Harwich
Felixstowe
Dieppe 4:00

104
105
106
107
108
109
98
99
84
92
93
85
86
82
83
72
73
74
70
71
58
59
60
61
IRISH SEA
Isle of Man
Cardigan Bay
Solway Firth
Luce Bay
Wigtown Bay
Morecambe Bay
Liverpool Bay
Holyhead Bay
Conwy Bay
Caernarfon Bay
Tremadog Bay
Bardsey Sd.
Anglesey
WALES
Belfast 2:55
Dublin 2:55
3:15
2:30
Belfast 8:00
Dublin 7:30
Dublin 1:49
Dun Laoghaire 2:00
Stewart
Kirkcowan
Glenluce
Lochans
Portpatrick
Sandhead
Port William
Port Logan
Drummore
Whauphill
Garlieston
Whithorn
Isle of Whithorn
Wigtown
Creetown
Gatehouse of Fleet
Laurieston
Castle Douglas
Dalbeattie
New Abbey
Kirkcudbright
Dundrennan
Borgue
Caulkerbush
Kirkbean
Ruthwell
Annan
Gretna
Carlisle
Brampton
Smithfield
Gilsland
Greenhead
Haltwhistle
Lambley
Alston
Wetheral
Croglin
High Hesket
Dalston
Thursby
Wigton
Kirkbride
Newton Arlosh
Silloth
Abbey Town
Beckfoot
Aspatria
Maryport
Flimby
Workington
Bothel
Caldbeck
Lazonby
Langwathby
Cockermouth
Greystoke
Penrith
Temple Sowerby
Appleby-in-Westmorland
Distington
Whitehaven
Thornthwaite
Keswick
Threlkeld
Hackthorpe
Derwent Water
Buttermere
Ullswater
Patterdale
Frizington
St. Bees
Egremont
Borrowdale
Grasmere
Shap
Haweswater
Hoff
Kirkby Stephen
Orton
Tebay
Gosforth
Wast Water
Ambleside
Seascale
Windermere
Grayrigg
Coniston
Torver
Bowness-on-Windermere
Kendal
Ravenglass
Broughton-in-Furness
Coniston Water
Newby Bridge
Sedbergh
Garsdale Head
Bootle
Oxenholme
Grizebeck
Millom
Milnthorpe
Arnside
Kirkby Lonsdale
Askam-in-Furness
Ulverston
Dalton-in-Furness
Grange-over-Sands
Burton
Carnforth
Ingleton
Barrow-in-Furness
Vickerstown
Rampside
High Bentham
Caton
Morecambe
Heysham
Lancaster
Galgate
Slaidburn
Fleetwood
Garstang
Cleveleys
Clitheroe
Poulton-le-Fylde
Longridge
Blackpool
Kirkham
Preston
Blackburn
Padiham
Lytham St. Anne's
Leyland
Darwen
Southport
Chorley
Horwich
Ormskirk
Bury
Formby
Skelmersdale
Wigan
Bolton
Worsley
Maghull
Crosby
Kirkby
Leigh
Bootle
St Helens
Wallasey
Liverpool
Hoylake
Birkenhead
Bebington
Widnes
Warrington
Speke
Runcorn
Heswall
Prestatyn
Rhyl
Rhuddlan
Ellesmere Port
Helsby
Northwich
Holywell
Connah's Quay
Flint
Kelsall
Queensferry
Chester
Winsford
Middlewich
Mold
Buckley
Sandbach
Hope
Rossett
Crewe
Wrexham
Nantwich
Holt
Malpas
Audlem
Madeley
Overton
Whitchurch
Market Drayton
Chirk
Ellesmere
Prees
Wem
Whittington
Oswestry
Hodnet
Baschurch
Shawbury
Newport
Llanymynech
Crudgington
Shrewsbury
Wellington
Oakengates
Welshpool
Westbury
Telford
Minsterley
Cressage
Ironbridge
Wolverhampton
Berriew
Chirbury
Much Wenlock
Montgomery
Church Stretton
Bridgnorth
Bishop's Castle
Newtown
Highley
Clun
Craven Arms
Kidderminster
Leintwardine
Ludlow
Cleobury Mortimer
Stourport-on-Severn
Ramsey
Andreas
Kirk Michael
Peel
Laxey
Foxdale
Douglas
Ballasalla
Port Erin
Port St. Mary
Castletown
Cemaes
Amlwch
Moelfre
Llanerchymedd
Benllech
Holyhead
Pentraeth
Valley
Llangefni
Menai Bridge
Beaumaris
Llanfairfechan
Conwy
Llandudno
Colwyn Bay
Abergele
St. Asaph
Trefnant
Denbigh
Rhosneigr
Bangor
Bethesda
Aberffraw
Y Felinheli
Dolgarrog
Llansannan
Newborough
Caernarfon
Llanberis
Capel Curig
Llanrwst
Betws-y-Coed
Ruthin
Waunfawr
Dolwyddelan
Penygroes
Cerrigydrudion
Rhosllanerchrugog
Llanaelhaearn
Beddgelert
Blaenau Ffestiniog
Ffestiniog
Corwen
Llangollen
Nefyn
Porthmadog
Penrhyndeudraeth
Bala
Llandrillo
Tudweiliog
Pwllheli
Criccieth
Trawsfynydd
L. Bala
Llanbedrog
Harlech
Aberdaron
Rhiw
Abersoch
Llanbedr
Llanuwchllyn
L. Vyrnwy
Penybontfawr
Dolgellau
Barmouth
Llanwddyn
Llanfyllin
Llwyngwril
Foel
Guilsfield
Tal-y-llyn
Corris
Mallwyd
Aberg'ynolwyn
Bryncrug
Llanfair Caereinion
Llanbrynmair
Tywyn
Machynlleth
Carno
Aberdyfi
Caersws
Borth
Talybont
Dolfor
Llanidloes
Aberystwyth
Ponterwyd
Llangurig
Devil's Bridge
Llanbister
Beguildy
Llanilar
Portavogie
Ballywalter
Donaghadee

Newcastle-Upon-Tyne
Tynemouth
South Shields
Gateshead
Sunderland
Hexham
Consett
Durham
Hartlepool
Redcar
Middlesbrough
Stockton-on-Tees
Darlington
Whitby
Robin Hood's Bay
Scarborough
Northallerton
Thirsk
Ripon
Harrogate
Knaresborough
York
Bridlington
Bridlington Bay
Flamborough
Filey
Beverley
Kingston upon Hull
Humber
Withernsea
Grimsby
Cleethorpes
Scunthorpe
Rotterdam 10:15
Zeebrugge 12:15
Leeds
Bradford
Halifax
Huddersfield
Wakefield
Castleford
Pontefract
Selby
Goole
Doncaster
Barnsley
Rotherham
Sheffield
Manchester
Oldham
Stockport
Chesterfield
Mansfield
Lincoln
Skegness
The Wash
Boston
Nottingham
Derby
Stoke-on-Trent
Newcastle-under-Lyme
Grantham
Newark-on-Trent
Hunstanton
King's Lynn
Leicester
Peterborough
Wisbech
Stamford
Melton Mowbray
Loughborough
Coalville
Nuneaton
Hinckley
Coventry
BIRMINGHAM
Walsall
West Bromwich
Dudley
Solihull
Lichfield
Stafford
Tamworth
Rugby
Kettering
Corby
Market Harborough
Rutland Water
Spalding
E N G L A N D
110 111 100 101 102 103 94 95 96 97 87 88 89 90 91 75 76 77 78 79 80 62 63 64 65 66 67

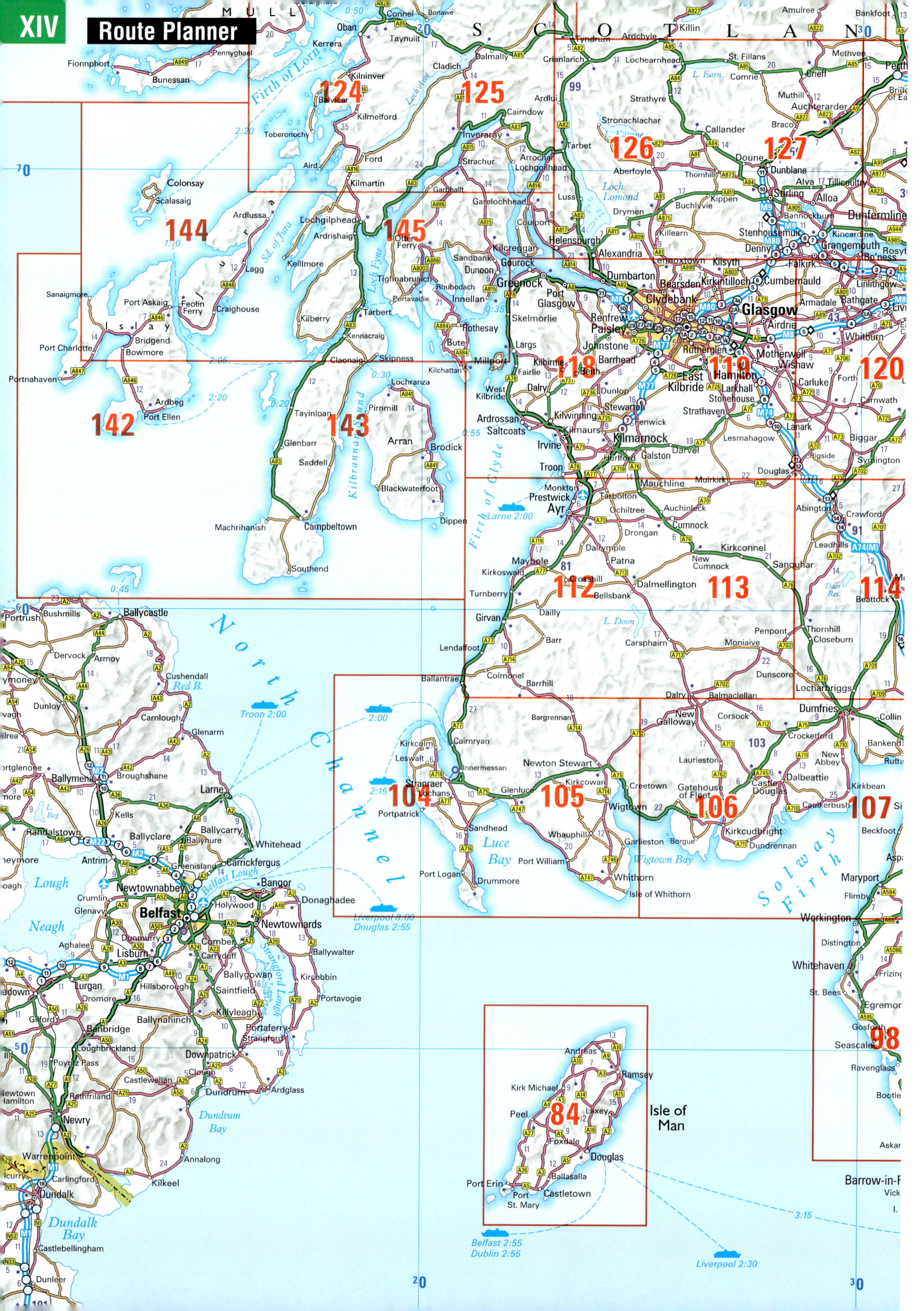
S C O T L A N D
MULL
Oban
Firth of Lorn
Colonsay
Islay
Port Ellen
Campbeltown
Arran
Brodick
Firth of Clyde
Glasgow
Clydebank
Paisley
Greenock
Dumbarton
Stirling
Falkirk
Perth
Dunfermline
Cumbernauld
Airdrie
Motherwell
Hamilton
East Kilbride
Kilmarnock
Irvine
Ayr
Prestwick
Troon
Girvan
Stranraer
Newton Stewart
Wigtown Bay
Luce Bay
Dumfries
Solway Firth
Kirkcudbright
Workington
Whitehaven
North Channel
Larne
Ballymena
Antrim
Belfast
Bangor
Newtownards
Lisburn
Lough Neagh
Newry
Downpatrick
Dundalk
Dundalk Bay
Isle of Man
Douglas
Ramsey
Peel
Castletown
Liverpool 2:30
Liverpool 8:00
Douglas 2:55
Belfast 2:55
Dublin 2:55
Troon 2:00
Larne 2:00
124
125
126
127
142
143
144
145
118
119
120
112
113
114
104
105
106
107
103
98
84

NORTH SEA
Firth of Forth
Firth of Tay
Morecambe Bay
Dundee
Carnoustie
Monifieth
Invergowrie
Tayport
Newport-on-Tay
Leuchars
Newburgh
Cupar
St. Andrews
Auchtermuchty
Ladybank
Ceres
Crail
Anstruther
St. Monance
Falkland
Leslie
Kinross
Markinch
Glenrothes
Leven
Elie
Buckhaven
I. of May
Lochgelly
Kirkcaldy
Cowdenbeath
Burntisland
Inverkeithing
North Berwick
Gullane
Dunbar
Queensferry
Edinburgh
Prestonpans
Musselburgh
Tranent
Haddington
East Linton
Cockburnspath
Dalkeith
Gifford
Loanhead
Bonnyrigg
St. Abb's
Coldingham
Eyemouth
Grantshouse
Ayton
Chirnside
Penicuik
Gorebridge
Preston
Duns
Berwick-upon-Tweed
Leadburn
Westruther
Fountainhall
Lauder
Greenlaw
Swinton
Scremerston
Blyth Bridge
Stow
Leitholm
Peebles
Gordon
Coldstream
Lowick
Innerleithen
Earlston
Galashiels
Flodden
Broughton
Kelso
Belford
Bamburgh
Melrose
Maxwellheugh
Seahouses
Selkirk
Doddington
Beadnell
Yarrow
Ancrum
Town Yetholm
Wooler
Chatton
North Charlton
Morebattle
Jedburgh
Embleton
Wooperton
Denholm
Longhoughton
Roberton
Hawick
Alnwick
Lesbury
Ramseycleuch
Alnmouth
Alwinton
Warkworth
Teviothead
Catcleugh
Rothbury
Amble
Longframlington
Eskdalemuir
Rochester
Widdrington
Kielder
Kielder Res.
Otterburn
Longhorsley
Boreland
West Woodburn
Ashington
Pegswood
Newbiggin-by-the-Sea
Hartburn
Langholm
Newcastleton
Morpeth
Kirkwhelpington
Bedlington
Lockerbie
Bellingham
Whalton
Blyth
Cramlington
Eaglesfield
Belsay
Wark
Colwell
Whitley Bay
Canonbie
Ponteland
Longbenton
Ecclefechan
Kirkpatrick Fleming
Humshaugh
Newcastle-Upon-Tyne
Tynemouth
Longtown
Haydon Bridge
South Shields
Amsterdam 15:30
Annan
Gretna
Smithfield
Gilsland
Blaydon
Jarrow
Brampton
Greenhead
Haltwhistle
Hexham
Corbridge
Gateshead
Sunderland
Kirkbride
Lambley
Catton
Prudhoe
Whickham
Carlisle
Wetheral
Allendale Town
Stanley
Washington
Newton Arlosh
Thursby
Dalston
Consett
Chester-le-Street
Houghton-le-Spring
Abbey Town
Wigton
High Hesket
Croglin
Alston
Lanchester
Hetton-le-Hole
Seaham
Durham
Peterlee
Wearhead
Stanhope
Bothel
Caldbeck
Lazonby
Willington
Hartlepool
Spennymoor
Trimdon
Langwathby
Greystoke
Penrith
Bishop Auckland
Ferryhill
Sedgefield
Cockermouth
Temple Sowerby
Middleton-in-Teesdale
Redcar
Marske-by-the-Sea
Billingham
Newton Aycliffe
Saltburn-by-the-Sea
Threlkeld
Keswick
Appleby-in-Westmorland
Staindrop
Stockton-on-Tees
Middlesbrough
Hackthorpe
Cotherstone
Thornaby-on-Tees
Loftus
Staithes
Derwent Water
Buttermere
Ullswater
Patterdale
Hoff
Barnard Castle
Darlington
Guisborough
Shap
Brough
Yarm
Whitby
Borrowdale
Kirkby Stephen
Bowes
Grasmere
Haweswater
Orton
Sleights
Ambleside
Stokesley
Wast Water
Tebay
Richmond
Scotch Corner
Robin Hood's Bay
Windermere
Keld
Reeth
Grayrigg
Coniston
Catterick
Torver
Bowness-on-Windermere
Kendal
Northallerton
Garsdale Head
Muker
Broughton-in-Furness
Coniston Water
Sedbergh
Hawes
Leyburn
Burniston
Newby Bridge
Kirkbymoorside
Scalby
Scarborough
Oxenholme
Aysgarth
Bedale
Grizebeck
Thornton-le-Dale
Millom
Milnthorpe
Kirkby Lonsdale
Masham
Thirsk
Helmsley
Pickering
Snainton
Filey
Arnside
Ulverston
Sowerby
Grange-over-Sands
Burton
Hovingham
Dalton-in-Furness
Carnforth
Ingleton
Horton in Ribblesdale
Kettlewell
Kirkby Malzeard
Ripon
Stillington
Norton
Rampside
High Bentham
Pateley Bridge
Boroughbridge
Sledmere
Rudston
Morecambe
Caton
Settle
Grassington
Heysham
Lancaster
Long Preston
Knaresborough
Fridaythorpe
Burton Agnes
Driffield
Galgate
Gargrave
Harrogate
York
Stamford Bridge
Slaidburn
Skipton
Spofforth
Bainton
Hutton Cranswick
North Frodingham
Fleetwood
Barnoldswick
Ilkley
Otley
Wetherby
Pocklington
Elvington
Cleveleys
Garstang
Clitheroe
Keighley
Baildon
Collingham
Tadcaster
Escrick
Market Weighton
Leven
128
129
121
122
123
115
116
117
108
109
110
111
99
100
101
102
103
92
93
94
95
96
97

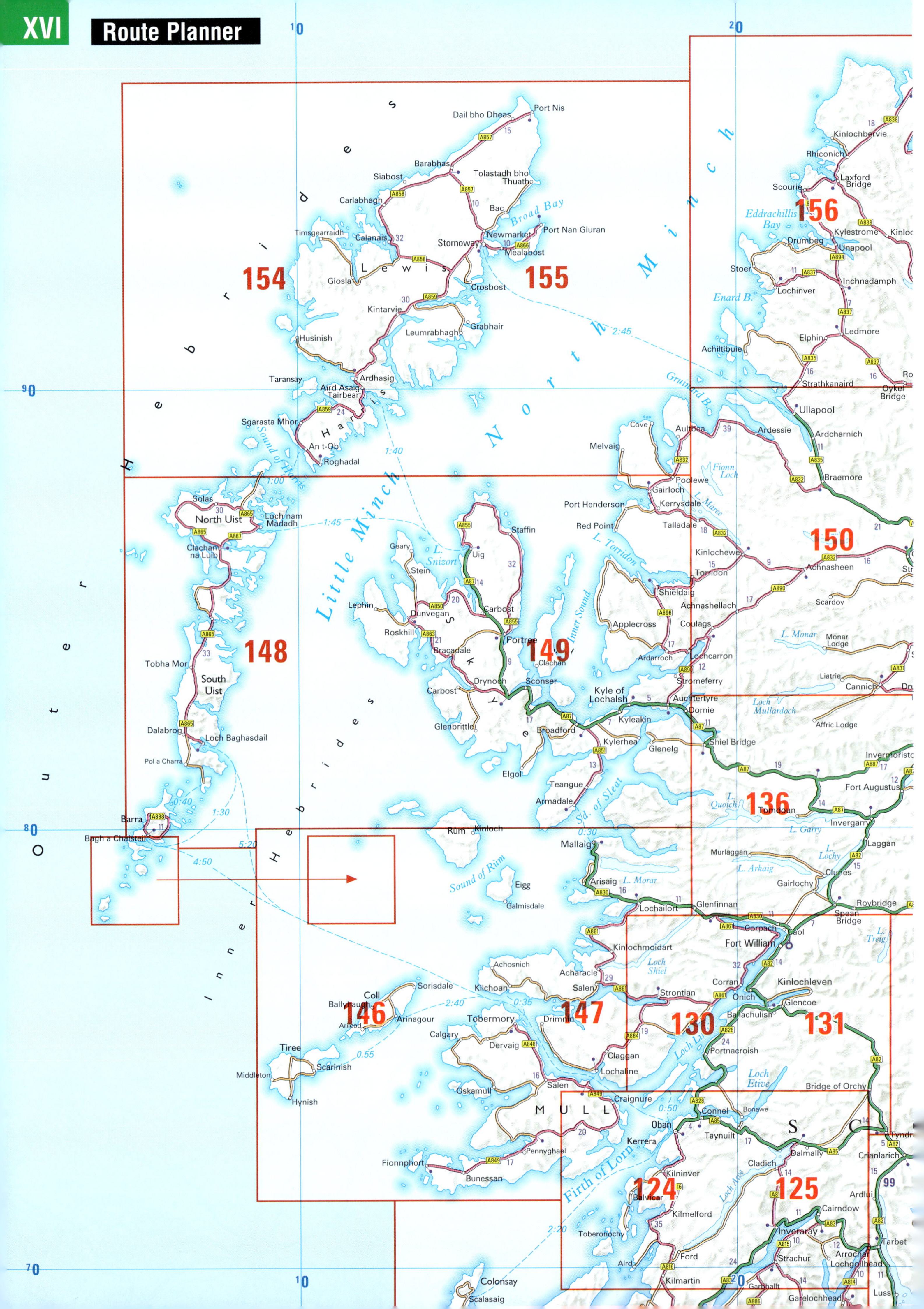
154
155
156
148
149
150
136
146
147
130
131
124
125
North Minch
Little Minch
Outer Hebrides
Inner Hebrides
Lewis
Harris
Skye
MULL
Stornoway
Port Nis
Tarbert
Portree
Kyle of Lochalsh
Ullapool
Mallaig
Fort William
Oban
Tobermory
Barra
North Uist
South Uist
Coll
Tiree
Rum
Eigg
Colonsay

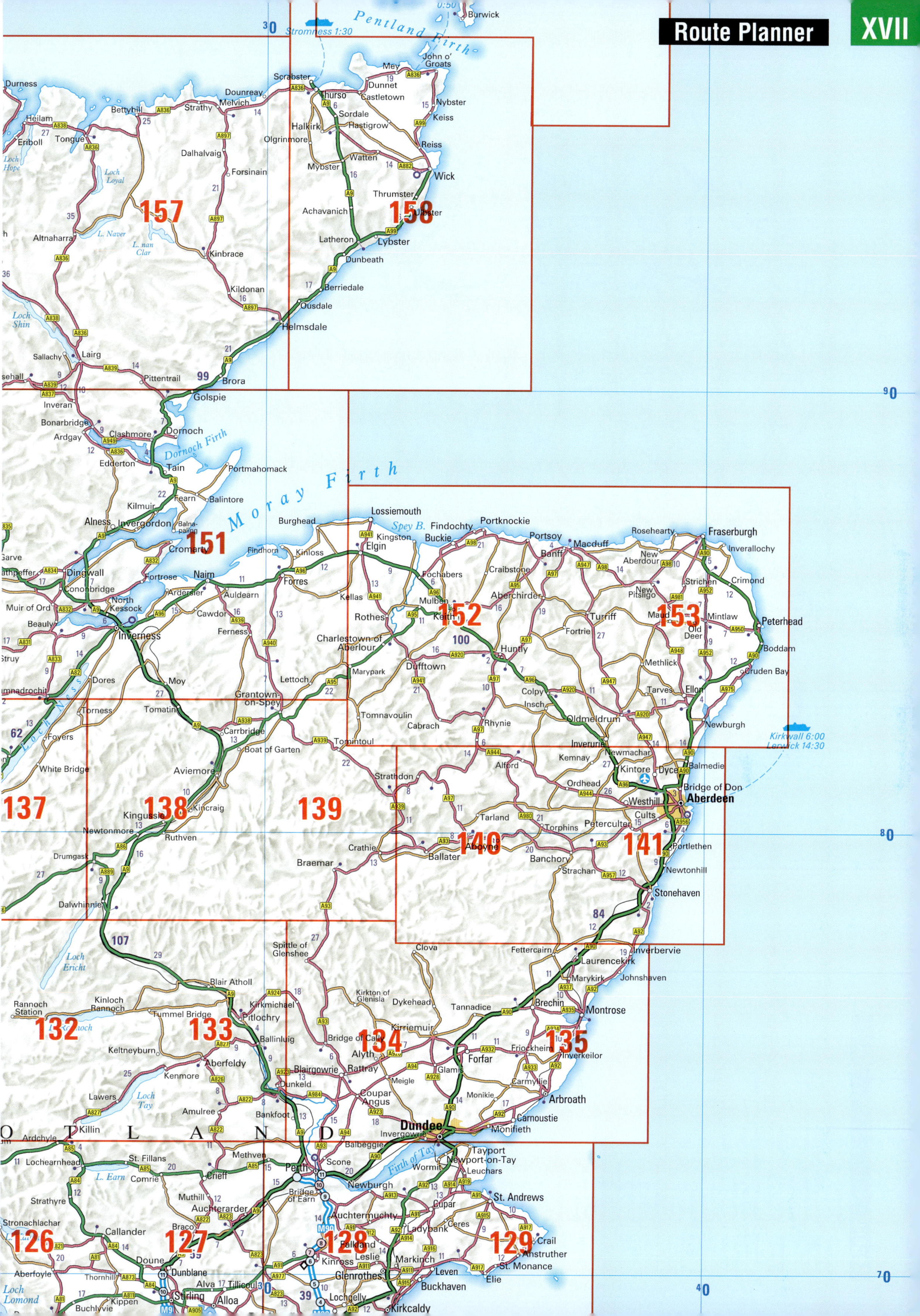
Pentland Firth
Stromness 1:30
Burwick
John o' Groats
Mey
Dunnet
Castletown
Scrabster
Thurso
Durness
Dounreay
Melvich
Strathy
Bettyhill
Heilam
Eriboll
Tongue
Loch Hope
Loch Loyal
Halkirk
Sordale
Hastigrow
Olgrinmore
Nybster
Keiss
Reiss
Watten
Mybster
Wick
Dalhalvaig
Forsinain
Thrumster
Ulbster
Achavanich
Latheron
Lybster
Dunbeath
Altnaharra
L. Naver
L. nan Clar
Kinbrace
Kildonan
Berriedale
Ousdale
Helmsdale
Loch Shin
Lairg
Sallachy
Pittentrail
Brora
Golspie
Inveran
Bonarbridge
Ardgay
Clashmore
Dornoch
Dornoch Firth
Edderton
Tain
Portmahomack
Fearn
Balintore
Moray Firth
Kilmuir
Alness
Invergordon
Balnapaling
Cromarty
Burghead
Lossiemouth
Spey B.
Findochty
Portknockie
Portsoy
Macduff
Rosehearty
Fraserburgh
Inverallochy
Kingston
Buckie
Elgin
Banff
New Aberdour
Findhorn
Kinloss
Forres
Nairn
Dingwall
Conon Bridge
Fortrose
Ardersier
Auldearn
Cawdor
Muir of Ord
North Kessock
Beauly
Inverness
Struy
Ferness
Kellas
Rothes
Fochabers
Mulben
Keith
Craibstone
Aberchirder
Turriff
Fortrie
New Pitsligo
Strichen
Crimond
Maud
Mintlaw
Old Deer
Peterhead
Boddam
Charlestown of Aberlour
Huntly
Dufftown
Marypark
Methlick
Cruden Bay
Tarves
Ellon
Dores
Moy
Lettoch
Grantown-on-Spey
Colpy
Insch
Oldmeldrum
Newburgh
Kirkwall 6:00
Lerwick 14:30
Foyers
Torness
Tomatin
Carrbridge
Boat of Garten
Tomnavoulin
Cabrach
Rhynie
Tomintoul
Inverurie
Kemnay
Newmachar
Alford
Kintore
Dyce
Balmedie
Bridge of Don
Aberdeen
White Bridge
Aviemore
Strathdon
Ordhead
Westhill
Cults
Kingussie
Kincraig
Newtonmore
Ruthven
Tarland
Torphins
Peterculter
Portlethen
Crathie
Ballater
Aboyne
Banchory
Braemar
Strachan
Newtonhill
Stonehaven
Drumgask
Dalwhinnie
Loch Ericht
Spittle of Glenshee
Clova
Fettercairn
Inverbervie
Laurencekirk
Marykirk
Johnshaven
Blair Atholl
Kirkton of Glenisla
Dykehead
Tannadice
Brechin
Montrose
Rannoch Station
Kinloch Rannoch
Tummel Bridge
Kirkmichael
Pitlochry
Kirriemuir
Ballinluig
Bridge of Cally
Alyth
Friockheim
Inverkeilor
Keltneyburn
Aberfeldy
Kenmore
Blairgowrie
Rattray
Glamis
Forfar
Dunkeld
Meigle
Carmyllie
Lawers
Loch Tay
Coupar Angus
Monikie
Arbroath
Amulree
Bankfoot
Carnoustie
Killin
Dundee
Invergowrie
Monifieth
Ardchyle
Balbeggie
Tayport
Newport-on-Tay
Lochearnhead
St. Fillans
Methven
Scone
Wormit
Leuchars
L. Earn
Comrie
Crieff
Perth
Firth of Tay
Newburgh
Bridge of Earn
St. Andrews
Strathyre
Muthill
Auchterarder
Cupar
Auchtermuchty
Stronachlachar
Callander
Braco
Ladybank
Ceres
Crail
Anstruther
St. Monance
Falkland
Leslie
Markinch
Kinross
Doune
Dunblane
Glenrothes
Leven
Elie
Aberfoyle
Thornhill
Alva
Tillicoultry
Buckhaven
Loch Lomond
Kippen
Stirling
Alloa
Lochgelly
Buchlyvie
Kirkcaldy
SCOTLAND
157
158
151
152
153
137
138
139
140
141
132
133
134
135
126
127
128
129

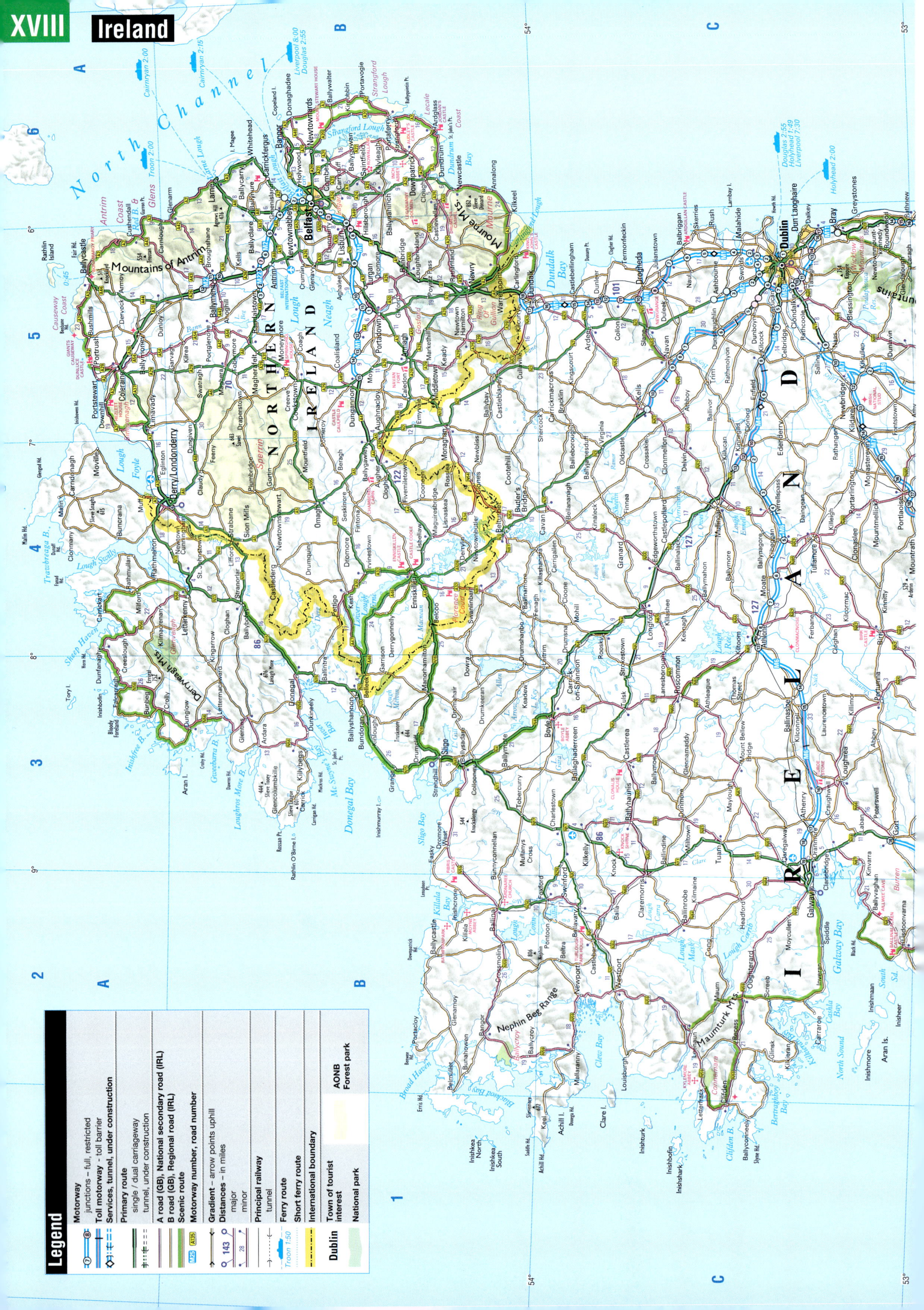
Legend
Motorway
junctions – full, restricted
Toll motorway – toll barrier
Services, tunnel, under construction
Primary route
single / dual carriageway
tunnel, under construction
A road (GB), National secondary road (IRL)
B road (GB), Regional road (IRL)
Scenic route
Motorway number, road number
Gradient – arrow points uphill
Distances – in miles
major
minor
Principal railway
tunnel
Ferry route
Short ferry route
International boundary
Dublin
Town of tourist interest
AONB
Forest park
National park
NORTHERN IRELAND
IRELAND
North Channel
Belfast
Dublin
Derry/Londonderry
Galway
Sligo
Mountains of Antrim
Mourne Mts
Donegal Bay
Galway Bay
Nephin Beg Range
Derryveagh Mts
Maumturk Mts

Index to Ireland

A

Abbey	C3
Abbeydorney	D2
Abbeyfeale	D2
Abbeyleix	D4
Adare	D3
Adrigole	E2
Aghalee	B5
Ahoghill	B5
Allihies	E1
Anascaul	D1
Annalong	B6
Annestown	D4
Antrim	B5
Ardagh	D2
Ardara	B3
Ardee	C5
Ardfert	D2
Ardglass	B6
Ardgroom	E2
Ardkearagh	E1
Arklow	D5
Armagh	B5
Armoy	A5
Arthurstown	D5
Ashbourne	C5
Askeaton	D3
Athboy	C5
Athea	D2
Athenry	C3
Athleague	C3
Athlone	C4
Athy	D5
Augher	B4
Aughnacloy	B5
Aughrim	D5

B

Bailieborough	C5
Balbriggan	C5
Balla	C2
Ballaghaderreen	C3
Ballina	B2
Ballinalack	C4
Ballinamore	B4
Ballinascarty	E3
Ballinasloe	C3
Ballindine	C3
Ballingarry, *Limerick*	D3
Ballingarry, *Tipperary*	D4
Ballingeary	E2
Ballinhassig	E3
Ballinrobe	C2
Ballinskellings	E1
Ballinspittle	E3
Ballintra	B3
Ballivor	C5
Ballon	D5
Ballybay	B5
Ballybofey	B4
Ballybunion	D2
Ballycanew	D5
Ballycarry	B6
Ballycastle, *Antrim*	A5
Ballycastle, *Mayo*	B2
Ballyclare	B6
Ballyconneely	C1
Ballycotton	E3
Ballycroy	B2
Ballydehob	E2
Ballyferriter	D1
Ballygawley	B4
Ballygowan	B6
Ballyhaunis	C3
Ballyheige	D2
Ballyjamesduff	C4
Ballylanders	D3
Ballylynan	D4
Ballymahon	C4
Ballymena	B5
Ballymoe	C3
Ballymoney	A5
Ballymore	C4
Ballymote	B3
Ballynacorra	E3
Ballynagore	C4
Ballynahinch	B6
Ballynure	B6
Ballyragget	D4
Ballysadare	B3
Ballyshannon	B3
Ballyvaghan	C2
Ballyvourney	E2
Ballywalter	B6
Baltimore	E2
Baltinglass	D5
Banbridge	B5
Bandon	E3
Bangor, *Down*	B6
Bangor, *Mayo*	B2
Banteer	D3
Bantry	E2
Beaufort	D2
Belcoo	B4
Belfast	B6
Belgooly	E3
Bellananagh	C4
Bellavary	C2
Belleek	B3
Belmullet	B2
Beltra	C2
Belturbet	B4
Beragh	B4
Birr	C4
Blackwater	D5
Blarney	E3
Blessington	C5
Borris	D5
Borris-in-Ossory	D4
Borrisokane	D3
Borrisoleigh	D4
Boyle	C3
Bracklin	C5
Bray	C5
Broadford	D3
Broughshane	B5
Bruff	D3
Bunahowen	B2
Bunbeg	A3
Bunclody	D5
Buncrana	A4
Bundoran	B3
Bunmahon	D4
Bunnyconnellan	B2
Bunratty	D3
Bushmills	A5
Butler's Bridge	B4
Buttevant	D3

C

Caher	D4
Caherciveen	E1
Caherdaniel	E1
Caledon	B5
Callan	D4
Camp	D2
Cappamore	D3
Cappoquin	D4
Carlingford	B5
Carlow	D5
Carndonagh	A4
Carnew	D5
Carnlough	B6
Carraroe	C2
Carrick	B3
Carrick-on-Shannon	C3
Carrick-on-Suir	D4
Carrickart	A4
Carrickfergus	B6
Carrickmacross	C5
Carrigallen	C4
Carryduff	B6
Cashel	D4
Castlebar	C2
Castlebellingham	C5
Castleblaney	B5
Castlebridge	D5
Castlecomer	D4
Castlederg	B4
Castledermot	D5
Castleisland	D2
Castlemaine	D2
Castlemartyr	E3
Castlepollard	C4
Castlerea	C3
Castletown Bearhaven	E2
Castletownroche	D3
Castlewellan	B6
Cavan	C4
Celbridge	C5
Charlestown	C3
Charleville	D3
Clarecastle	D3
Claregalway	C3
Claremorris	C2
Clarinbridge	C3
Clashmore	D4
Claudy	B4
Clifden	C1
Clogh	D4
Cloghan, *Donegal*	B4
Cloghan, *Offaly*	C4
Clogheen	D4
Clogher	B4
Cloghjordan	D3
Clonakilty	E3
Clonaslee	C4
Clondalkin	C5
Clones	B4
Clonmany	A4
Clonmel	D4
Clonmellon	C4
Clonord	C4
Clonroche	D5
Cloone	C4
Clough	B6
Cloyne	E3
Coachford	E3
Coagh	B5
Coalisland	B5
Cóbh	E3
Coleraine	A5
Collon	C5
Collooney	B3
Comber	B6
Cong	C2
Conna	D3
Connaugh	D3
Cookstown	B5
Coolgreany	D5
Cooneen	B4
Cootehill	B4
Cork	E3
Craughwell	C3
Creeslough	A4
Creeve	B5
Crolly	A3
Crookhaven	E2
Crookstown	E3
Croom	D3
Crossakiel	C4
Crosshaven	E3
Crossmolina	B2
Crumlin	B5
Crusheen	D3
Cullaville	B5
Cushendall	A5

D

Daingean	C4
Darragh	D2
Delvin	C4
Derry/Londonderry	B4
Derrygonnelly	B4
Derrylin	B4
Dervock	A5
Dingle	D1
Donaghadee	B6
Donegal	B3
Doonbeg	D2
Downhill	A5
Downpatrick	B6
Dowra	B3
Draperstown	B5
Drimoleague	E2
Drogheda	C5
Dromahair	B3
Dromcolliher	D3
Dromore, *Down*	B5
Dromore, *Tyrone*	B4
Dromore West	B3
Drumcliff	B3
Drumkeeran	B3
Drumquin	B4
Drumshanbo	B3
Drumsna	C4
Dublin	C5
Duleek	C5
Dun Laoghaire	C5
Dunboyne	C5
Dundalk	B5
Dundrum	B6
Dunfanaghy	A4
Dungannon	B5
Dungarvan	D4
Dungiven	B5
Dunglow	B3
Dungourney	E3
Dunkineely	B3
Dunlavin	C5
Dunleer	C5
Dunloy	A5
Dunmanway	E2
Dunmore	C3
Dunmore East	D5
Dunmurry	B5
Dunshaughlin	C5
Durrow	D4
Durrus	E2

E

Easky	B3
Edenderry	C4
Edgeworthstown	C4
Eglinton	A4
Emyvale	B5
Enfield	C5
Ennis	D3
Enniscorthy	D5
Enniskean	E3
Enniskillen	B4
Ennistimon	D2

F

Falcarragh	A3
Farranfore	D2
Feeny	B4
Fenagh	B4
Fenit	D2
Ferbane	C4
Fermoy	D3
Ferns	D5
Fethard, *Tipperar y*	D4
Fethard, *Wexford*	D5
Finnea	C4
Fintona	B4
Fivemiletown	B4
Fontstown	C5
Foxford	C2
Foynes	D2
Freshford	D4

G

Galway	C2
Garrison	B3
Garvagh	B5
Gilford	B5
Glenamoy	B2
Glenarm	B6
Glenavy	B5
Glenbeigh	D2
Glencolumbkille	B3
Glendalough	C5
Glenealy	D5
Glengarriff	E2
Glennamaddy	C3
Glenties	B3
Glin	D2
Glinsk	C2
Gorey	D5
Gort	C3
Gortin	B4
Gowran	D4
Graiguenamanagh	D5
Granard	C4
Grange	B3
Greenisland	B6
Greystones	C5

H

Hacketstown	D5
Headford	C2
Herbertstown	D3
Hillsborough	B5
Holycross	D4
Holywood	B6
Hospital	D3

I

Inagh	D2
Inishannon	E3
Inishcrone	B2
Inveran	C2
Irvinestown	B4

J

Johnstown	D4
Julianstown	C5

K

Kanturk	D3
Keadew	B3
Keady	B5
Keel	C1
Keenagh	C4
Kells, *Antrim*	B5
Kells, *Meath*	C5
Kenmare	E2
Kesh	B4
Kilbaha	D2
Kilbeggan	C4
Kilcock	C5
Kilconnell	C3
Kilcormac	C4
Kilcullen	C5
Kilcurry	B5
Kildare	C5
Kildorrery	D3
Kilgarvan	E2
Kilkee	D2
Kilkeel	B6
Kilkelly	C3
Kilkenny	D4
Kilkieran	C2
Kilkinlea	D2
Kill	D4
Killadysert	D2
Killala	B2
Killaloe	D3
Killarney	D2
Killashandra	B4
Killashee	C4
Killeigh	C4
Killenaule	D4
Killimor	C3
Killinaboy	D2
Killinick	D5
Killorglin	D2
Killucan	C4
Killybegs	B3
Killyleagh	B6
Kilmacrenan	A4
Kilmacthomas	D4
Kilmaine	C2
Kilmallock	D3
Kilmeadan	D4
Kilmeedy	D3
Kilmore Quay	D5
Kilnaleck	C4
Kilrea	B5
Kilrush	D2
Kiltoom	C3
Kingarrow	B3
Kingscourt	C5
Kinlough	B3
Kinnegad	C4
Kinnitty	C4
Kinsale	E3
Kinvarra	C3
Kircubbin	B6
Knock	C3
Knocktopher	D4

L

Laban	C3
Lanesborough	C4
Laragh	C5
Larne	B6
Lauragh	E2
Laurencetown	C3
Leap	E2
Leenaun	C2
Leighlinbridge	D5
Leitrim	C3
Letterfrack	C2
Letterkenny	B4
Lettermacaward	B3
Lifford	B4
Limavady	A5
Limerick	D3
Lisbellaw	B4
Lisburn	B5
Liscannor	D2
Lisdoonvarna	C2
Lismore	D4
Lisnaskea	B4
Lissycasey	D2
Listowel	D2
Littleton	D4
Longford	C4
Loughbrickland	B5
Loughrea	C3
Louisburgh	C2
Lucan	C5
Lurgan	B5

M

Macroom	E3
Maghera	B5
Magherafelt	B5
Maguiresbridge	B4
Malahide	C5
Malin	A4
Mallaranny	C2
Mallow	D3
Manorhamilton	B3
Markethill	B5
Maum	C2
Maylough	C3
Middletown	B5
Midleton	E3
Milford	A4
Millstreet, *Cork*	D2
Millstreet, *Waterford*	D4
Milltown, *Galway*	C3
Milltown, *Kerry*	D1
Milltown Malbay	D2
Mitchelstown	D3
Moate	C4
Mohill	C4
Monaghan	B5
Monasterevin	C4
Moneygall	D4
Moneymore	B5
Mount Bellew Bridge	C3
Mountfield	B4
Mountmellick	C4
Mountrath	D4
Moville	A4
Moy	B5
Moycullen	C2
Muckross	D2
Muff	A4
Muine Bheag	D5
Mullanys Cross	B3
Mullinavat	D4
Mullingar	C4

N

Naas	C5
Naul	C5
Navan	C5
Nenagh	D3
New Ross	D5
Newbliss	B4
Newbridge	C5
Newcastle	B6
Newcastle West	D2
Newinn	D4
Newmarket	D3
Newmarket-on-Fergus	D3
Newport, *Mayo*	C2
Newport, *Tipperar y*	D3
Newry	B5
Newtown Cunningham	B4
Newtown Hamilton	B5
Newtown Sands	D2
Newtownabbey	B6
Newtownards	B6
Newtownbutler	B4
Newtown-mountkennedy	C5
Newtownshandrum	D3
Newtownstewart	B4
Ninemilehouse	D4

O

Oilgate	D5
Oldcastle	C4
Omagh	B4
Oranmore	C3
Oughterard	C2

P

Pallas Green	D3
Parknasilla	E2
Passage East	D5
Passage West	E3
Patrickswell	D3
Paulstown	D4
Peterswell	C3
Pettigo	B4
Plumbridge	B4
Pomeroy	B5
Pontoon	C2
Portacloy	B2
Portadown	B5
Portaferry	B6
Portarlington	C4
Portavogie	B6
Portglenone	B5
Portlaoise	C4
Portmagne	E1
Portroe	D3
Portrush	A5
Portstewart	A5
Portumna	C3
Poyntz Pass	B5

R

Randalstown	B5
Rathangan	C5
Rathcoole	C5
Rathcormack	D3
Rathdrum	D5
Rathfriland	B5
Rathkeale	D3
Rathmelton	A4
Rathmolyon	C5
Rathmore	D2
Rathmullan	A4
Rathnew	D5
Rathvilly	D5
Ratoath	C5
Recess	C2
Ringaskiddy	E3
Roosky	C4
Roscommon	C3
Roscrea	D4
Rosmult	D4
Rosslare	D5
Rosslare Harbour	D5
Rosslea	B4
Roundwood	C5
Rush	C5

S

Saint Johnstown	B4
Saintfield	B6
Sallins	C5
Scarriff	D3
Screeb	C2
Seskinore	B4
Shanagolden	D2
Shercock	C5
Shillelagh	D5
Silvermines	D3
Sion Mills	B4
Skerries	C5
Skibbereen	E2
Slane	C5
Sligo	B3
Sneem	E2
Spiddle	C2
Strabane	B4
Stradbally	D1
Strandhill	B3
Strangford	B6
Stranorlar	B4
Strokestown	C3
Swanlinbar	B4
Swatragh	B5
Swinford	C3
Swords	C5

T

Tallaght	C5
Tallow	D4
Tarbert	D2
Templederry	D3
Templemore	D4
Termonfeckin	C5
Thomas Street	C3
Thomastown	D4
Thurles	D4
Timoleague	E3
Timolin	D5
Tipperary	D3
Tobercurry	B3
Tobermore	B5
Toomyvara	D3
Toormore	E2
Tralee	D2
Tramore	D4
Trim	C5
Tuam	C3
Tulla	D3
Tullamore	C4
Tullow	D5
Tulsk	C3
Tyrrellspass	C4

U

Urlingford	D4

V

Virginia	C4

W

Warrenpoint	B5
Waterford	D4
Watergrasshill	D3
Waterville	E1
Wellingtonbridge	D5
Westport	C2
Wexford	D5
Whitegate	E3
Whitehead	B6
Wicklow	D5

Y

Youghal	E4

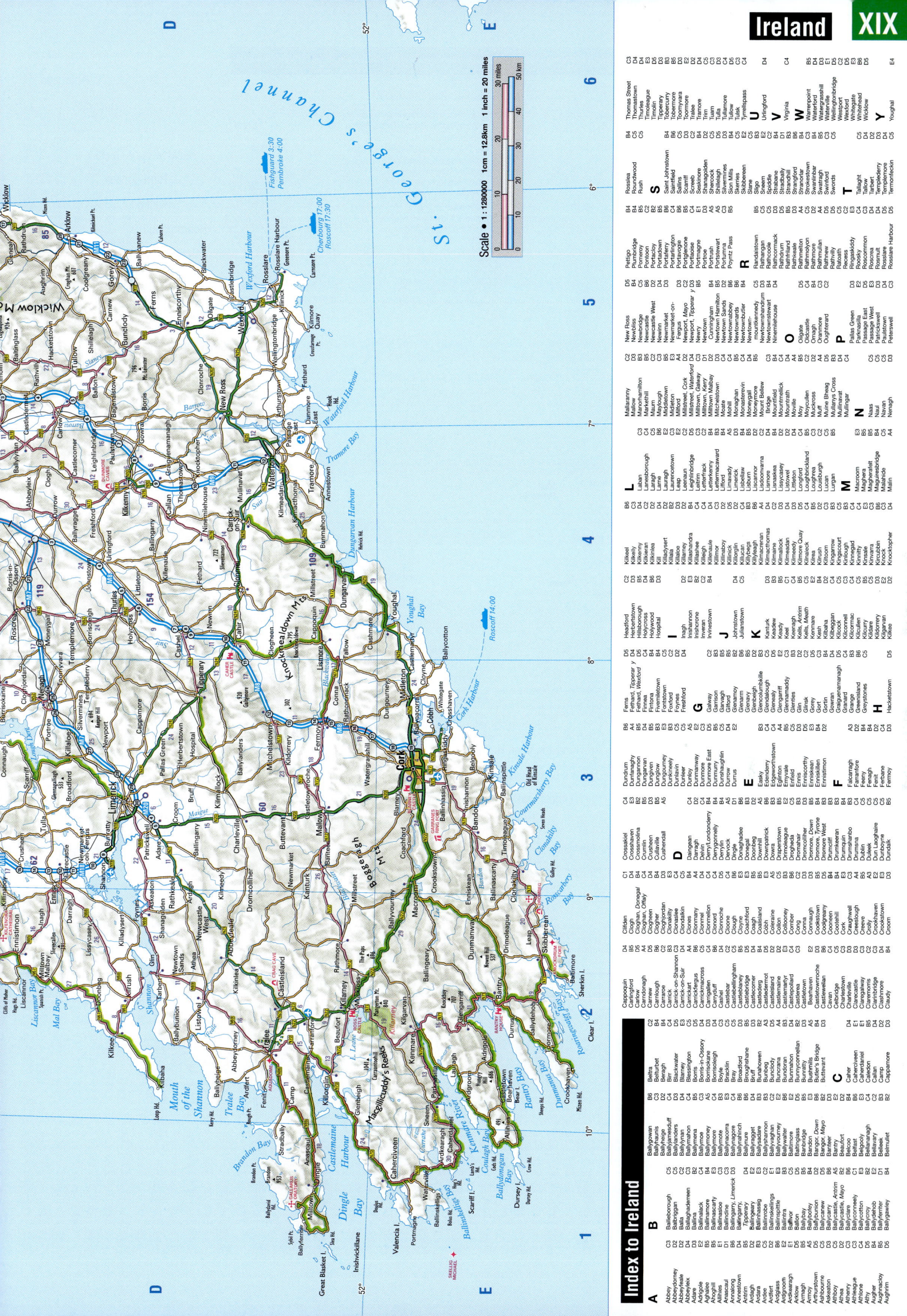

Distance table

How to use this table

Distances are shown in miles and kilometres with estimated journey times in hours and minutes.

For example: the distance between Dover and Fishguard is 331 miles or 533 kilometres with an estimated journey time of 6 hours, 20 minutes.

Estimated driving times are based on an average speed of 60mph on Motorways and 40mph on other roads. Drivers should allow extra time when driving at peak periods or through areas likely to be congested.

	Dover	Dundee	Edinburgh	Exeter	Fishguard
Dundee	523 / 842 / 9:10				
Edinburgh	462 / 744 / 8:10	56 / 90 / 1:30			
Exeter	248 / 399 / 4:40	518 / 834 / 9:10	450 / 724 / 8:00		
Fishguard	331 / 533 / 6:20	460 / 740 / 8:30	399 / 642 / 7:30	230 / 370 / 4:30	
Fort William	596 / 959 / 11:00	127 / 204 / 3:10	144 / 232 / 3:30	560 / 901 / 10:20	486 / 782 / 9:30

(Each cell: miles / kilometres / journey time)

	London	Aberdeen	Aberystwyth	Ayr	Berwick-upon-Tweed	Birmingham	Blackpool	Bournemouth	Braemar	Brighton	Bristol	Cambridge	Cardiff	Carlisle	Doncaster	Dover	Dundee	Edinburgh	Exeter	Fishguard	Fort William	Glasgow	Gloucester	Great Yarmouth	Harwich	Holyhead	Inverness	John o' Groats	Kingston upon Hull	Kyle of Lochalsh	Land's End	Leeds	Leicester	Lincoln	Liverpool	Manchester	Newcastle upon Tyne	Norwich	Nottingham	Oban	Oxford	Plymouth	Portsmouth	Sheffield	Shrewsbury	Southampton	Stranraer	Swansea
Aberdeen	517 / 832 / 11:20
Aberystwyth	211 / 340 / 4:40	445 / 716 / 8:40
Ayr	394 / 634 / 7:20	183 / 295 / 4:20	317 / 510 / 6:10
Berwick-upon-Tweed	352 / 567 / 7:30	182 / 293 / 4:40	311 / 501 / 6:20	134 / 216 / 3:00
Birmingham	117 / 188 / 2:50	420 / 676 / 8:30	114 / 183 / 2:50	289 / 465 / 5:30	274 / 441 / 5:30
Blackpool	226 / 364 / 4:30	308 / 496 / 6:20	153 / 246 / 3:20	180 / 290 / 3:30	181 / 291 / 3:50	123 / 198 / 2:40
Bournemouth	107 / 172 / 2:40	564 / 908 / 10:20	207 / 333 / 4:30	436 / 702 / 8:00	412 / 663 / 7:50	147 / 237 / 3:10	270 / 435 / 5:00
Braemar	482 / 776 / 10:30	59 / 95 / 1:30	405 / 652 / 7:50	143 / 230 / 3:00	148 / 238 / 3:20	385 / 620 / 7:10	281 / 452 / 5:20	524 / 843 / 9:30
Brighton	52 / 84 / 1:50	573 / 922 / 10:30	253 / 407 / 5:10	446 / 718 / 8:00	409 / 658 / 7:40	163 / 262 / 3:20	286 / 460 / 5:20	92 / 148 / 2:10	534 / 859 / 9:40
Bristol	122 / 196 / 2:50	493 / 793 / 9:10	125 / 201 / 3:00	370 / 595 / 6:40	362 / 583 / 6:50	81 / 130 / 2:00	204 / 328 / 3:50	82 / 132 / 2:30	477 / 768 / 8:40	147 / 237 / 4:10
Cambridge	54 / 87 / 1:30	471 / 758 / 10:00	214 / 344 / 4:20	357 / 575 / 6:20	306 / 493 / 5:40	100 / 161 / 2:10	208 / 335 / 3:50	154 / 248 / 3:00	438 / 705 / 7:50	116 / 187 / 2:20	169 / 272 / 3:10
Cardiff	157 / 253 / 3:20	505 / 813 / 9:20	105 / 169 / 2:40	382 / 615 / 7:00	368 / 592 / 7:00	103 / 166 / 2:20	209 / 336 / 4:00	117 / 188 / 3:00	483 / 778 / 8:40	182 / 293 / 3:40	45 / 72 / 1:20	190 / 306 / 3:30
Carlisle	301 / 484 / 5:40	221 / 356 / 4:30	224 / 360 / 4:30	93 / 150 / 2:00	87 / 140 / 2:10	196 / 315 / 3:50	87 / 140 / 1:50	343 / 552 / 6:20	196 / 316 / 3:50	370 / 596 / 6:40	277 / 446 / 5:00	264 / 425 / 4:40	289 / 465 / 5:20
Doncaster	171 / 275 / 3:30	344 / 554 / 6:50	176 / 283 / 3:40	235 / 378 / 4:20	184 / 296 / 3:50	94 / 151 / 2:00	94 / 151 / 1:50	235 / 378 / 4:20	310 / 499 / 5:40	236 / 380 / 4:30	175 / 282 / 3:20	116 / 187 / 2:10	209 / 336 / 4:00	142 / 229 / 3:00
Dover	71 / 114 / 2:00	588 / 947 / 10:40	297 / 478 / 5:50	478 / 769 / 8:30	424 / 683 / 7:50	194 / 312 / 3:50	312 / 502 / 5:40	174 / 280 / 4:30	553 / 890 / 9:50	82 / 132 / 2:20	202 / 325 / 3:50	125 / 201 / 2:30	238 / 383 / 4:30	389 / 626 / 7:00	242 / 390 / 4:30
Dundee	448 / 721 / 8:40	67 / 108 / 1:50	376 / 605 / 7:10	117 / 188 / 2:30	113 / 182 / 2:40	349 / 562 / 6:20	239 / 385 / 4:30	495 / 797 / 8:50	52 / 84 / 1:20	517 / 832 / 9:10	430 / 692 / 7:40	406 / 654 / 7:10	441 / 710 / 8:00	152 / 245 / 3:00	275 / 443 / 5:00	523 / 842 / 9:10
Edinburgh	390 / 628 / 7:20	125 / 201 / 3:10	320 / 515 / 6:20	73 / 117 / 1:50	57 / 92 / 1:40	292 / 470 / 5:30	183 / 295 / 3:30	439 / 707 / 8:00	91 / 146 / 2:10	456 / 734 / 8:20	373 / 600 / 6:50	345 / 555 / 6:10	385 / 620 / 7:00	96 / 154 / 2:00	219 / 352 / 4:00	462 / 744 / 8:10	56 / 90 / 1:30
Exeter	181 / 291 / 3:40	569 / 916 / 10:20	201 / 323 / 4:10	446 / 718 / 7:50	428 / 689 / 7:50	157 / 253 / 3:10	282 / 454 / 5:10	82 / 132 / 2:20	550 / 885 / 9:40	184 / 296 / 5:00	76 / 122 / 1:40	249 / 401 / 4:30	121 / 195 / 2:30	353 / 568 / 6:20	251 / 404 / 4:30	248 / 399 / 4:40	518 / 834 / 9:10	450 / 724 / 8:00
Fishguard	260 / 418 / 5:20	504 / 811 / 10:10	56 / 90 / 1:30	373 / 600 / 7:00	371 / 597 / 7:20	170 / 274 / 3:40	209 / 336 / 4:10	222 / 357 / 4:40	493 / 794 / 9:10	291 / 468 / 5:40	154 / 248 / 3:20	270 / 435 / 5:10	112 / 180 / 2:40	297 / 478 / 5:40	247 / 398 / 4:50	331 / 533 / 6:20	460 / 740 / 8:30	399 / 642 / 7:30	230 / 370 / 4:30
Fort William	510 / 821 / 9:50	149 / 240 / 3:50	430 / 692 / 8:40	133 / 214 / 3:20	190 / 306 / 4:40	392 / 631 / 7:40	296 / 476 / 6:00	539 / 867 / 10:10	125 / 201 / 3:10	575 / 926 / 10:50	486 / 782 / 9:10	479 / 771 / 9:00	485 / 781 / 9:10	206 / 332 / 4:30	357 / 575 / 7:00	596 / 959 / 11:00	127 / 204 / 3:10	144 / 232 / 3:30	560 / 901 / 10:20	486 / 782 / 9:30
Glasgow	397 / 639 / 7:30	145 / 233 / 3:30	320 / 515 / 6:20	33 / 53 / 1:10	101 / 163 / 2:40	292 / 470 / 5:30	183 / 295 / 3:40	439 / 707 / 8:00	110 / 177 / 2:30	468 / 753 / 8:30	373 / 600 / 6:50	372 / 599 / 6:40	385 / 620 / 7:00	96 / 154 / 2:10	249 / 401 / 4:40	488 / 786 / 8:40	83 / 134 / 2:00	44 / 71 / 1:20	449 / 723 / 8:00	376 / 605 / 7:10	101 / 163 / 2:50
Gloucester	109 / 175 / 2:30	468 / 753 / 8:30	102 / 164 / 2:30	330 / 531 / 5:50	318 / 512 / 6:00	56 / 90 / 1:20	174 / 280 / 3:10	99 / 159 / 2:40	443 / 713 / 8:00	159 / 256 / 3:10	35 / 56 / 1:00	123 / 198 / 2:20	56 / 90 / 1:20	247 / 398 / 4:20	150 / 241 / 2:50	191 / 307 / 3:30	410 / 660 / 7:10	349 / 562 / 6:10	111 / 179 / 2:10	153 / 246 / 3:10	454 / 731 / 8:30	346 / 557 / 6:10
Great Yarmouth	128 / 206 / 3:40	517 / 832 / 10:50	294 / 473 / 6:20	402 / 647 / 7:40	345 / 555 / 7:00	180 / 290 / 4:10	252 / 406 / 5:10	240 / 386 / 5:00	477 / 768 / 9:10	180 / 290 / 4:10	275 / 443 / 5:40	82 / 132 / 2:10	284 / 457 / 5:50	320 / 515 / 6:20	167 / 269 / 3:40	185 / 298 / 4:00	484 / 779 / 9:00	386 / 621 / 7:30	335 / 539 / 6:30	366 / 589 / 7:20	527 / 848 / 10:20	419 / 674 / 8:00	225 / 362 / 4:40
Harwich	76 / 122 / 2:20	535 / 861 / 11:20	281 / 452 / 5:50	425 / 684 / 8:00	372 / 599 / 7:20	167 / 269 / 3:40	275 / 443 / 5:20	187 / 301 / 4:00	504 / 811 / 9:20	128 / 206 / 3:00	217 / 349 / 4:30	67 / 108 / 1:50	246 / 396 / 5:00	336 / 541 / 6:20	194 / 312 / 4:00	125 / 201 / 2:50	469 / 755 / 8:40	413 / 665 / 7:40	279 / 449 / 5:20	337 / 542 / 6:40	543 / 874 / 10:30	432 / 695 / 8:10	196 / 316 / 4:00	82 / 132 / 2:10
Holyhead	269 / 433 / 5:40	439 / 707 / 8:40	111 / 179 / 2:50	305 / 491 / 6:10	311 / 501 / 6:30	148 / 238 / 3:30	141 / 227 / 3:20	288 / 463 / 5:50	426 / 686 / 8:20	334 / 538 / 6:40	206 / 332 / 4:30	270 / 435 / 5:20	216 / 348 / 5:40	231 / 372 / 4:50	181 / 291 / 3:50	360 / 580 / 7:00	394 / 634 / 7:30	333 / 536 / 6:40	282 / 454 / 5:40	167 / 269 / 4:00	438 / 705 / 8:50	330 / 531 / 6:40	191 / 307 / 4:00	334 / 538 / 7:00	349 / 562 / 7:10
Inverness	550 / 885 / 10:40	105 / 169 / 2:50	486 / 782 / 9:40	199 / 320 / 4:30	215 / 346 / 5:10	458 / 737 / 9:00	348 / 560 / 7:00	597 / 961 / 11:20	75 / 121 / 2:00	617 / 993 / 11:30	539 / 867 / 10:10	505 / 813 / 9:30	549 / 884 / 10:20	262 / 422 / 5:30	383 / 617 / 7:30	622 / 1001 / 11:30	132 / 212 / 3:20	158 / 254 / 3:50	618 / 995 / 11:30	542 / 872 / 10:30	66 / 106 / 1:40	166 / 267 / 4:00	504 / 811 / 9:30	553 / 890 / 11:00	569 / 916 / 11:00	474 / 763 / 9:40
John o' Groats	663 / 1067 / 13:30	232 / 373 / 5:50	601 / 967 / 12:40	328 / 528 / 7:40	342 / 550 / 8:10	574 / 924 / 11:50	478 / 769 / 10:00	724 / 1165 / 14:20	202 / 325 / 5:00	741 / 1193 / 14:40	668 / 1075 / 13:20	630 / 1014 / 12:30	680 / 1094 / 13:30	391 / 629 / 8:40	507 / 816 / 10:30	746 / 1201 / 14:40	259 / 417 / 6:30	285 / 459 / 7:00	744 / 1197 / 14:30	671 / 1080 / 13:40	195 / 314 / 5:00	295 / 475 / 7:10	628 / 1011 / 12:30	677 / 1090 / 14:00	693 / 1116 / 14:00	603 / 970 / 12:40	129 / 208 / 3:20
Kingston upon Hull	184 / 296 / 3:50	364 / 586 / 7:20	223 / 359 / 4:40	251 / 404 / 4:40	185 / 298 / 3:50	134 / 216 / 2:50	127 / 204 / 2:30	264 / 425 / 5:00	327 / 526 / 6:10	245 / 394 / 4:40	233 / 375 / 4:20	139 / 224 / 3:10	244 / 393 / 4:40	158 / 254 / 3:00	47 / 76 / 1:10	256 / 412 / 4:50	295 / 475 / 5:30	234 / 377 / 4:30	309 / 497 / 5:40	280 / 451 / 5:30	369 / 594 / 7:20	254 / 409 / 4:50	169 / 272 / 3:10	207 / 333 / 5:20	196 / 316 / 4:10	231 / 372 / 4:50	394 / 634 / 7:50	518 / 834 / 10:50
Kyle of Lochalsh	586 / 943 / 11:40	189 / 304 / 4:50	499 / 803 / 10:20	212 / 341 / 5:10	263 / 423 / 6:20	471 / 758 / 9:40	372 / 599 / 7:50	618 / 995 / 12:10	159 / 256 / 4:00	651 / 1048 / 12:40	552 / 888 / 10:50	555 / 893 / 10:50	564 / 908 / 11:10	275 / 443 / 6:10	432 / 695 / 8:40	671 / 1080 / 12:50	186 / 299 / 4:40	216 / 348 / 5:20	628 / 1011 / 12:00	567 / 913 / 11:20	79 / 127 / 2:00	179 / 288 / 4:40	528 / 850 / 10:20	602 / 969 / 12:10	611 / 983 / 12:10	514 / 827 / 10:40	84 / 135 / 2:10	189 / 304 / 4:40	445 / 716 / 9:00
Land's End	297 / 478 / 6:30	692 / 1114 / 13:10	313 / 504 / 6:50	570 / 917 / 10:50	552 / 888 / 10:40	281 / 452 / 6:00	405 / 652 / 8:00	205 / 330 / 5:20	665 / 1070 / 12:30	308 / 496 / 7:50	200 / 322 / 4:40	374 / 602 / 7:20	245 / 394 / 5:20	477 / 768 / 9:10	374 / 602 / 7:20	381 / 613 / 7:40	642 / 1033 / 12:00	574 / 924 / 10:50	123 / 198 / 3:20	353 / 568 / 7:20	686 / 1104 / 13:20	573 / 922 / 10:50	235 / 378 / 5:00	446 / 718 / 9:10	390 / 628 / 8:00	405 / 652 / 8:30	741 / 1193 / 14:20	868 / 1397 / 17:20	421 / 678 / 8:20	763 / 1228 / 15:10
Leeds	189 / 304 / 3:50	327 / 526 / 6:50	169 / 272 / 3:40	212 / 341 / 4:00	156 / 251 / 3:20	113 / 182 / 2:30	72 / 116 / 1:40	255 / 410 / 4:50	293 / 472 / 5:30	260 / 419 / 5:00	194 / 312 / 3:50	145 / 233 / 2:50	232 / 373 / 4:20	119 / 192 / 2:30	29 / 47 / 0:50	260 / 418 / 4:50	258 / 415 / 4:50	202 / 325 / 4:00	270 / 435 / 5:00	237 / 381 / 4:40	329 / 530 / 6:40	215 / 346 / 4:10	174 / 280 / 3:20	196 / 315 / 4:20	223 / 359 / 4:30	176 / 283 / 4:00	360 / 579 / 7:10	487 / 784 / 10:20	55 / 89 / 1:30	394 / 634 / 8:20	405 / 652 / 8:00
Leicester	97 / 156 / 2:20	414 / 666 / 7:40	153 / 246 / 3:20	299 / 481 / 5:20	252 / 406 / 5:00	39 / 63 / 1:10	140 / 225 / 2:40	158 / 254 / 3:10	389 / 626 / 7:00	166 / 267 / 3:20	120 / 193 / 2:30	68 / 109 / 1:20	154 / 248 / 3:00	206 / 332 / 3:50	74 / 119 / 1:30	185 / 298 / 3:30	349 / 562 / 6:20	296 / 476 / 5:20	196 / 315 / 3:40	209 / 336 / 4:10	422 / 679 / 8:00	314 / 505 / 5:40	85 / 137 / 1:40	140 / 225 / 3:20	147 / 237 / 3:10	190 / 306 / 4:00	461 / 742 / 8:50	588 / 947 / 11:50	102 / 164 / 2:10	500 / 805 / 9:50	320 / 515 / 6:30	95 / 153 / 2:00
Lincoln	131 / 211 / 3:10	383 / 616 / 7:20	199 / 320 / 4:20	274 / 441 / 5:10	224 / 360 / 4:40	90 / 145 / 2:10	128 / 206 / 2:40	209 / 336 / 4:10	357 / 575 / 6:40	197 / 317 / 4:00	183 / 295 / 3:40	85 / 137 / 2:20	208 / 335 / 4:10	191 / 307 / 3:40	39 / 63 / 1:10	202 / 325 / 4:00	314 / 505 / 5:50	258 / 415 / 5:00	247 / 398 / 4:40	272 / 438 / 5:30	399 / 642 / 7:50	291 / 468 / 5:30	159 / 256 / 3:10	128 / 206 / 3:20	155 / 249 / 3:30	216 / 348 / 4:40	427 / 687 / 8:30	554 / 892 / 11:30	44 / 71 / 1:20	476 / 766 / 9:40	371 / 597 / 7:30	68 / 109 / 1:50	51 / 82 / 1:20
Liverpool	202 / 325 / 4:10	341 / 549 / 6:40	104 / 167 / 2:40	213 / 343 / 4:10	219 / 352 / 4:30	93 / 150 / 2:10	49 / 79 / 1:20	234 / 377 / 4:30	318 / 512 / 6:00	272 / 438 / 5:10	161 / 259 / 3:10	194 / 312 / 3:40	169 / 272 / 3:20	120 / 193 / 2:30	86 / 138 / 1:50	299 / 481 / 5:30	286 / 460 / 5:20	216 / 348 / 4:10	237 / 381 / 4:30	160 / 257 / 3:30	329 / 530 / 6:40	216 / 348 / 4:10	140 / 225 / 2:40	240 / 386 / 5:00	265 / 427 / 5:20	102 / 164 / 2:40	382 / 615 / 7:40	511 / 822 / 10:40	130 / 209 / 2:40	407 / 655 / 8:30	361 / 581 / 7:20	75 / 121 / 1:50	130 / 209 / 2:40	129 / 208 / 2:50
Manchester	185 / 298 / 3:50	340 / 547 / 6:30	129 / 208 / 3:00	212 / 341 / 4:00	196 / 315 / 4:00	80 / 129 / 2:00	48 / 77 / 1:20	227 / 365 / 4:20	318 / 512 / 6:00	257 / 414 / 4:50	161 / 259 / 3:10	165 / 266 / 3:10	183 / 295 / 3:40	119 / 192 / 2:30	61 / 98 / 1:30	276 / 444 / 5:10	285 / 459 / 5:20	215 / 346 / 4:10	236 / 380 / 4:20	197 / 317 / 4:00	329 / 530 / 6:40	215 / 346 / 4:10	126 / 203 / 2:30	212 / 341 / 4:30	228 / 367 / 4:40	124 / 200 / 3:00	373 / 600 / 7:30	500 / 805 / 10:30	95 / 153 / 2:10	406 / 654 / 8:30	361 / 581 / 7:20	40 / 64 / 1:10	92 / 148 / 2:00	84 / 135 / 2:00	35 / 56 / 1:10
Newcastle upon Tyne	286 / 460 / 5:40	235 / 378 / 4:50	257 / 414 / 5:20	149 / 240 / 3:00	64 / 103 / 1:50	207 / 333 / 4:10	129 / 208 / 2:40	347 / 558 / 6:30	201 / 323 / 4:00	352 / 567 / 6:30	299 / 481 / 5:30	241 / 388 / 4:20	325 / 523 / 6:00	57 / 92 / 1:50	114 / 183 / 2:20	358 / 576 / 6:30	166 / 267 / 3:20	110 / 177 / 2:20	364 / 586 / 6:30	329 / 529 / 6:20	253 / 407 / 5:20	148 / 238 / 3:10	266 / 428 / 4:50	281 / 452 / 5:40	308 / 496 / 6:00	272 / 438 / 5:40	268 / 431 / 5:40	395 / 636 / 8:50	132 / 212 / 2:50	318 / 512 / 7:00	498 / 802 / 9:40	92 / 148 / 2:10	187 / 301 / 3:40	159 / 256 / 3:20	168 / 270 / 3:20	132 / 212 / 2:50
Norwich	114 / 183 / 3:30	496 / 798 / 9:40	276 / 444 / 6:00	382 / 615 / 7:20	328 / 528 / 6:40	166 / 267 / 3:50	232 / 373 / 4:50	214 / 344 / 4:40	457 / 735 / 8:40	175 / 282 / 4:00	252 / 406 / 5:10	62 / 100 / 1:50	262 / 422 / 5:20	289 / 465 / 5:40	147 / 237 / 3:20	174 / 280 / 3:50	422 / 679 / 8:00	366 / 589 / 7:00	308 / 496 / 6:00	343 / 552 / 7:00	504 / 811 / 10:00	385 / 620 / 9:00	204 / 328 / 4:10	20 / 32 / 0:40	73 / 117 / 2:00	311 / 501 / 6:40	529 / 852 / 10:30	654 / 1053 / 13:30	149 / 240 / 4:00	582 / 937 / 11:50	421 / 678 / 8:40	176 / 283 / 3:50	119 / 192 / 3:20	105 / 169 / 2:50	220 / 354 / 4:40	185 / 298 / 4:30	264 / 425 / 5:20
Nottingham	122 / 196 / 2:40	393 / 633 / 7:30	164 / 264 / 3:40	274 / 441 / 5:10	221 / 356 / 4:30	50 / 80 / 1:20	111 / 179 / 2:20	183 / 295 / 3:40	353 / 568 / 6:30	193 / 311 / 3:50	145 / 233 / 3:00	83 / 134 / 1:40	172 / 277 / 3:20	194 / 312 / 3:40	43 / 69 / 1:10	205 / 330 / 3:50	328 / 528 / 6:00	262 / 422 / 4:50	221 / 356 / 4:10	220 / 354 / 4:30	401 / 646 / 7:50	293 / 472 / 5:30	110 / 177 / 2:10	153 / 246 / 3:30	150 / 241 / 3:20	185 / 298 / 4:00	430 / 692 / 8:20	557 / 896 / 11:30	90 / 145 / 2:00	479 / 771 / 9:40	345 / 555 / 7:00	70 / 113 / 1:40	25 / 40 / 0:50	35 / 56 / 1:10	98 / 158 / 2:10	73 / 118 / 1:40	157 / 253 / 3:10	130 / 209 / 3:40
Oban	499 / 803 / 9:30	178 / 286 / 4:20	412 / 663 / 8:10	94 / 151 / 2:20	180 / 290 / 4:20	384 / 618 / 7:30	285 / 459 / 5:40	530 / 853 / 9:50	141 / 227 / 3:30	565 / 910 / 10:30	465 / 748 / 8:40	468 / 753 / 8:40	477 / 768 / 9:00	188 / 303 / 4:00	346 / 557 / 6:40	585 / 942 / 10:40	117 / 188 / 2:50	123 / 198 / 3:00	549 / 884 / 10:00	481 / 774 / 9:10	49 / 79 / 1:20	92 / 148 / 2:30	441 / 710 / 8:10	515 / 829 / 10:00	524 / 843 / 10:00	427 / 687 / 8:30	117 / 188 / 3:00	244 / 393 / 6:10	346 / 557 / 6:40	128 / 206 / 3:10	665 / 1070 / 12:50	307 / 494 / 6:00	419 / 674 / 7:50	387 / 623 / 7:30	308 / 496 / 6:10	307 / 494 / 6:00	233 / 375 / 4:50	492 / 792 / 9:40	390 / 628 / 7:30
Oxford	57 / 92 / 1:40	483 / 777 / 8:50	154 / 248 / 3:20	353 / 568 / 6:20	324 / 521 / 6:10	64 / 103 / 1:30	187 / 301 / 3:30	90 / 145 / 2:00	465 / 749 / 8:20	108 / 174 / 2:20	74 / 119 / 1:40	83 / 134 / 1:40	108 / 174 / 2:20	260 / 418 / 4:40	145 / 233 / 2:40	141 / 227 / 2:50	433 / 697 / 7:40	372 / 599 / 6:40	156 / 251 / 3:00	205 / 330 / 4:10	472 / 760 / 9:00	356 / 573 / 6:30	52 / 84 / 1:30	200 / 322 / 4:20	145 / 233 / 3:10	238 / 383 / 4:50	532 / 856 / 10:00	656 / 1056 / 13:00	192 / 309 / 3:40	550 / 885 / 10:40	274 / 441 / 5:40	168 / 270 / 3:10	73 / 117 / 1:30	137 / 221 / 2:50	172 / 277 / 3:20	144 / 232 / 2:50	260 / 418 / 4:50	145 / 233 / 3:50	109 / 175 / 2:10	462 / 744 / 8:30
Plymouth	218 / 351 / 4:40	615 / 990 / 11:20	237 / 382 / 5:10	492 / 792 / 9:00	474 / 763 / 9:00	203 / 327 / 4:20	328 / 528 / 6:10	128 / 206 / 3:30	587 / 945 / 10:40	224 / 361 / 6:00	122 / 196 / 2:50	293 / 472 / 5:30	167 / 269 / 3:40	399 / 642 / 7:20	297 / 478 / 5:40	300 / 483 / 5:50	552 / 888 / 10:00	496 / 798 / 9:00	46 / 74 / 1:30	264 / 425 / 5:30	595 / 958 / 11:20	495 / 797 / 9:10	157 / 253 / 3:20	365 / 588 / 7:20	309 / 497 / 6:10	328 / 528 / 6:40	664 / 1069 / 12:30	790 / 1271 / 15:40	355 / 571 / 6:40	674 / 1085 / 13:10	89 / 143 / 2:20	316 / 509 / 6:00	242 / 389 / 4:40	293 / 472 / 5:50	283 / 455 / 5:30	283 / 455 / 5:30	410 / 660 / 7:40	343 / 552 / 7:00	267 / 430 / 5:10	587 / 945 / 11:00	199 / 320 / 4:00
Portsmouth	70 / 113 / 2:00	560 / 901 / 10:10	222 / 357 / 4:40	430 / 692 / 7:40	401 / 645 / 7:30	141 / 227 / 3:00	264 / 425 / 4:50	52 / 84 / 1:30	547 / 881 / 9:50	48 / 77 / 1:40	97 / 156 / 2:10	144 / 232 / 2:50	142 / 229 / 3:00	348 / 560 / 6:10	234 / 377 / 4:20	130 / 209 / 2:50	514 / 827 / 9:00	453 / 729 / 8:10	135 / 217 / 2:40	251 / 404 / 5:00	555 / 893 / 10:20	448 / 721 / 8:10	119 / 192 / 3:00	221 / 356 / 4:40	166 / 267 / 3:40	311 / 501 / 6:10	613 / 987 / 11:30	737 / 1186 / 14:30	269 / 433 / 5:00	633 / 1019 / 12:10	259 / 417 / 5:40	257 / 414 / 4:50	162 / 261 / 3:10	201 / 323 / 4:00	254 / 409 / 4:50	236 / 380 / 4:30	337 / 542 / 6:10	207 / 333 / 4:20	191 / 307 / 3:40	545 / 877 / 10:00	77 / 124 / 1:40	176 / 283 / 4:50
Sheffield	159 / 256 / 3:20	360 / 579 / 6:50	159 / 256 / 3:30	245 / 394 / 4:30	190 / 306 / 4:00	76 / 122 / 1:50	86 / 138 / 1:50	216 / 348 / 4:10	320 / 515 / 6:00	226 / 364 / 4:20	161 / 259 / 3:10	120 / 193 / 2:20	194 / 312 / 3:40	152 / 245 / 3:00	18 / 29 / 0:40	245 / 394 / 4:30	291 / 468 / 5:20	235 / 378 / 4:20	237 / 381 / 4:20	215 / 346 / 4:20	348 / 560 / 6:50	248 / 399 / 4:40	126 / 203 / 2:20	166 / 267 / 3:40	187 / 301 / 3:50	168 / 270 / 3:40	393 / 632 / 7:40	520 / 837 / 10:50	65 / 105 / 1:30	427 / 687 / 8:40	361 / 581 / 7:10	33 / 53 / 1:00	62 / 100 / 1:20	46 / 74 / 1:20	72 / 116 / 1:40	38 / 61 / 1:00	125 / 201 / 2:40	146 / 235 / 3:20	37 / 60 / 1:00	339 / 546 / 6:30	135 / 217 / 2:40	283 / 455 / 5:30	230 / 370 / 4:20
Shrewsbury	160 / 258 / 3:20	399 / 642 / 7:30	77 / 124 / 2:10	269 / 433 / 5:00	265 / 426 / 5:10	45 / 72 / 1:20	98 / 158 / 2:00	185 / 298 / 3:40	371 / 597 / 6:50	226 / 364 / 4:20	103 / 166 / 2:50	159 / 256 / 3:00	111 / 179 / 2:20	176 / 283 / 3:20	109 / 175 / 2:10	251 / 404 / 4:30	330 / 531 / 6:00	274 / 441 / 5:00	179 / 288 / 3:20	145 / 233 / 3:10	382 / 615 / 7:20	272 / 438 / 5:00	77 / 124 / 1:30	225 / 362 / 4:40	240 / 386 / 4:40	113 / 182 / 2:50	438 / 705 / 8:20	567 / 912 / 11:30	169 / 272 / 3:10	451 / 726 / 9:00	303 / 488 / 6:10	109 / 175 / 2:20	84 / 135 / 1:40	133 / 214 / 2:50	58 / 93 / 1:50	69 / 111 / 1:40	201 / 323 / 3:50	205 / 330 / 4:20	93 / 150 / 2:00	364 / 586 / 7:00	106 / 171 / 2:10	225 / 362 / 4:40	207 / 333 / 3:50	82 / 132 / 2:10
Southampton	77 / 124 / 2:00	547 / 880 / 10:00	201 / 323 / 4:10	417 / 671 / 7:30	388 / 624 / 7:10	128 / 206 / 2:40	251 / 404 / 4:40	31 / 50 / 1:00	532 / 856 / 9:30	61 / 98 / 1:50	76 / 122 / 2:20	148 / 238 / 2:50	121 / 195 / 2:30	324 / 521 / 5:50	209 / 336 / 3:50	143 / 230 / 2:50	500 / 805 / 8:50	438 / 705 / 7:50	105 / 169 / 3:00	233 / 375 / 4:40	541 / 871 / 10:00	433 / 697 / 7:40	105 / 169 / 2:40	220 / 354 / 4:40	164 / 264 / 3:30	293 / 472 / 5:50	598 / 963 / 11:10	723 / 1164 / 14:10	256 / 412 / 4:40	618 / 995 / 12:00	228 / 367 / 5:00	232 / 373 / 4:20	137 / 220 / 2:40	204 / 328 / 4:00	239 / 385 / 4:30	221 / 356 / 4:10	324 / 521 / 5:50	206 / 332 / 4:20	176 / 283 / 3:20	530 / 853 / 9:40	64 / 103 / 1:30	151 / 243 / 4:10	21 / 34 / 0:50	199 / 320 / 3:40	185 / 298 / 4:10
Stranraer	402 / 647 / 7:50	228 / 367 / 5:10	325 / 523 / 6:50	51 / 82 / 1:20	170 / 274 / 4:10	297 / 478 / 6:00	188 / 303 / 4:00	444 / 715 / 8:30	194 / 312 / 4:20	475 / 765 / 9:00	378 / 608 / 7:20	379 / 610 / 7:10	390 / 628 / 7:30	101 / 163 / 2:40	257 / 414 / 5:10	496 / 798 / 9:10	167 / 269 / 3:40	124 / 200 / 3:00	454 / 731 / 8:30	392 / 631 / 7:50	195 / 314 / 4:50	84 / 135 / 2:30	343 / 552 / 6:30	426 / 686 / 8:40	410 / 660 / 8:10	338 / 544 / 7:00	262 / 422 / 6:00	379 / 610 / 9:00	259 / 417 / 5:20	263 / 423 / 6:30	585 / 942 / 11:30	220 / 354 / 4:40	330 / 531 / 6:20	298 / 480 / 6:00	221 / 356 / 4:40	220 / 354 / 4:40	158 / 254 / 3:40	403 / 649 / 8:10	290 / 467 / 5:50	148 / 238 / 3:40	379 / 610 / 7:10	500 / 805 / 9:40	461 / 742 / 8:40	263 / 423 / 5:20	277 / 446 / 5:30	445 / 716 / 8:20
Swansea	194 / 312 / 4:00	507 / 816 / 9:20	73 / 117 / 2:00	379 / 610 / 6:50	383 / 616 / 7:10	119 / 192 / 2:30	216 / 348 / 4:00	167 / 269 / 3:20	505 / 813 / 9:00	222 / 357 / 4:20	85 / 137 / 1:50	227 / 365 / 4:10	41 / 66 / 1:10	309 / 497 / 5:30	232 / 373 / 4:10	274 / 441 / 5:00	473 / 761 / 8:20	412 / 663 / 7:20	161 / 259 / 3:00	67 / 108 / 1:50	496 / 798 / 9:20	409 / 658 / 7:20	89 / 143 / 1:50	329 / 530 / 6:30	267 / 430 / 5:10	184 / 296 / 4:50	572 / 921 / 10:40	696 / 1120 / 13:40	264 / 425 / 4:50	594 / 956 / 11:30	285 / 459 / 6:00	248 / 399 / 4:40	177 / 285 / 3:20	233 / 375 / 4:30	195 / 314 / 3:40	187 / 301 / 3:30	347 / 559 / 6:20	301 / 485 / 6:00	192 / 309 / 3:40	506 / 815 / 9:20	141 / 227 / 2:40	206 / 332 / 4:10	182 / 293 / 3:30	217 / 349 / 4:00	118 / 190 / 2:20	161 / 259 / 3:00	417 / 671 / 7:50
York	207 / 333 / 4:10	319 / 513 / 6:10	195 / 314 / 4:10	214 / 344 / 4:00	148 / 238 / 3:10	130 / 209 / 2:40	96 / 154 / 2:00	269 / 433 / 5:00	285 / 459 / 5:20	275 / 443 / 5:10	222 / 357 / 4:10	165 / 266 / 3:10	244 / 393 / 4:40	121 / 195 / 2:30	34 / 55 / 1:00	282 / 454 / 5:10	250 / 402 / 4:40	194 / 312 / 3:40	287 / 462 / 5:10	261 / 420 / 5:10	330 / 531 / 6:30	217 / 349 / 4:10	189 / 304 / 3:30	201 / 323 / 4:20	228 / 367 / 4:40	204 / 328 / 4:20	352 / 566 / 7:00	479 / 771 / 10:10	37 / 60 / 1:10	407 / 655 / 8:20	411 / 661 / 8:00	24 / 39 / 0:50	108 / 174 / 2:10	75 / 121 / 1:50	99 / 159 / 2:10	64 / 103 / 1:30	84 / 135 / 2:20	181 / 291 / 4:20	77 / 124 / 1:40	309 / 497 / 6:00	181 / 291 / 3:20	333 / 536 / 6:20	278 / 448 / 5:10	52 / 84 / 1:20	133 / 214 / 2:40	258 / 415 / 5:10	222 / 357 / 4:40	272 / 438 / 5:10

Supporting

THINK!

Travel safe – Don't drive tired

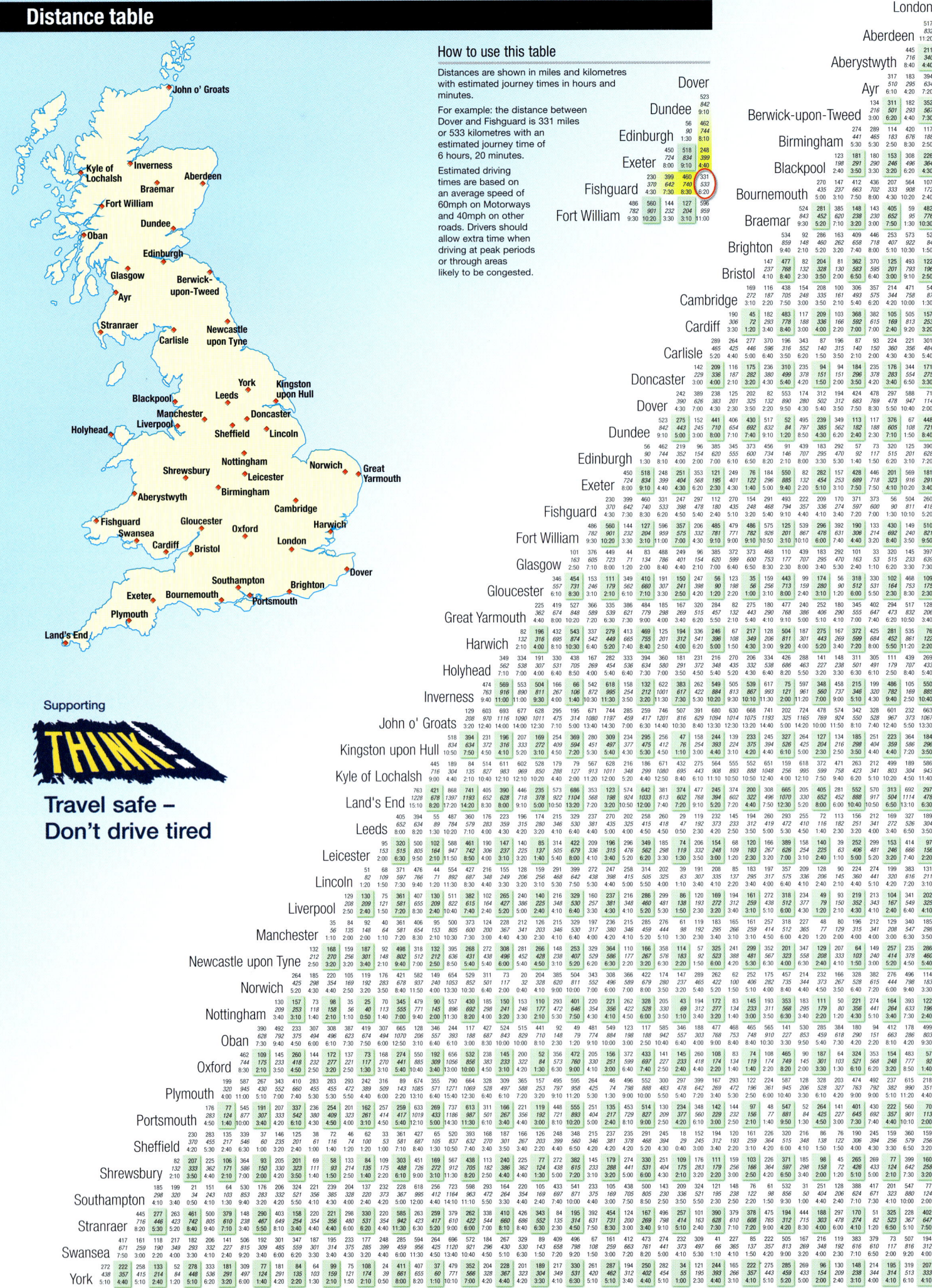

Key to 3-mile map pages

Shetland Islands 160
Lerwick
Fair Isle
Orkney Islands
Kirkwall 159
Thurso
Wick 158
Lewis
Stornoway
154 155
Harris
Scourie
156 157
A9
Ullapool
Dornoch
A835
150 151
Inverness
Elgin
Fraserburgh
152 153
A96 A90
North Uist
Skye
148 149
South Uist
Kyle of Lochalsh
A87 A82 A95
136 137 138 139
Aberdeen
140 141
A830 A86
Mallaig
Fort William
A9 A90
Coll
Tiree
146 147 130 131 132 133 134 135
Mull
Dundee
A828
Oban
124 125
A85
126 127
Perth
St Andrews
M90 A92
128 129
Colonsay
A83
M9
144 145
Jura
A82
Stirling
Glasgow
Edinburgh
122 123
M8
Islay
118 119 120 121
Berwick-upon-Tweed
142 143
M74 A702
Arran
Campbeltown
Ayr
A76
Hawick
A68 A1
Alnwick
112 113 114 115
A74(M) A7
116 117
A77
Stranraer
A75
Dumfries
Newcastle upon Tyne
104 105 106 107
110 111
Carlisle
A69
Sunderland
108 109
Durham
A19
Whitehaven
A66
Middlesbrough
A591 M6
A1(M)
98 99 100 101 102 103
Isle of Man
84
Kendal
A595 A1
A19 A171
Scarborough
Douglas
Barrow in Furness
Lancaster
A59
Harrogate
York
A64 A165
92 93 94 95 96 97
Blackpool
Bradford
Leeds
M62 A63
Hull
Preston
86 87
Grimsby
M180
85
Manchester
M62
88 89 90 91
Doncaster
82 83
Liverpool
M53 M62
Holyhead
A55
Anglesey
Sheffield
Lincoln
A16
Llandudno
Chester
A49
Macclesfield
M1
Mansfield
A46
Skegness
Bangor
72 73 74 75 76 77 78 79
M6 A6
A487
Hanley
A17
80 81
Wrexham
A5 A483
Stoke
A50
Derby
Nottingham
Boston
Cromer
70 71
Dolgellau
Shrewsbury
A458
Stafford
Leicester
A16
A17 A148
King's Lynn
A47
Great Yarmouth
60 61 62 63 64 65 66 67
Norwich
M54
A47 A47
58 59
Telford
Birmingham
M69
Peterborough
68 69
Newtown
Wolverhampton
Coventry
A43 A1(M)
A10
A11 A12
Aberystwyth
A44
A49
Worcester
Stratford-upon-Avon
M1
Kettering
Newmarket
Bury St Edmunds
45 46 47 48 49
Northampton
A14
Cambridge
A14
A487
Builth Wells
A470
A44
50 51 52 53 54 55 56 57
Ipswich
A483
Hereford
M50 M5
Banbury
A43
Milton Keynes
M11 A12
Felixstowe
Fishguard
A40
Merthyr Tydfil
A49
Gloucester
Cheltenham
M40
Luton
A1(M)
Chelmsford
Colchester
44
32 33 34 35 36 37 38 39 40 41 42 43
A470
A40
M1
M25
Pembroke
Llanelli
M4
Swansea
Newport
Swindon
Oxford
A34 M40
London
Southend-on-Sea
Cardiff
Bristol
Bath
M4
Reading
30 31
Newbury
Windsor
28 29
M2
Canterbury
20 21 22 23 24 25 26 27
M3
Croydon
Lundy
Ilfracombe
M5 A37
A36
A3
Maidstone
Dover
Winchester
Bideford
A361
Taunton
Salisbury
M27
Southampton
A23
Ashford
A386
A303
A259
Lewes
8 9 10 11 12 13 14 15 16 17 18 19
A39 A30
Exeter
Dorchester
Poole
Portsmouth
A27
Chichester
Brighton
A35
Bournemouth
Weymouth
Isle of Wight
Newquay
Plymouth
A38
Torquay
4 5 6 7
Penzance
A30
Truro
2 3
Isles of Scilly
Alderney
Channel Islands
Guernsey
Jersey

CORNWALL
SW
Godrevy Island
Godrevy Pt.
Navax Pt.
TEHIDY
Clodgy Pt.
The Island
St Ives Bay
TATE ST IVES
BARBARA HEPWORTH MUSEUM
St Ives
SOUTH WEST COAST PATH
The Carracks
Gwithian
Kehelland
A30
A3047
Gurnard's Head
Zennor
247
Towednack
Halsetown
Carbis Bay
Phillack
Connor Downs
Roseworthy
TREVITHICK COTTAGE
WAYSIDE FOLK MUSEUM
Porthmeor
Lelant
Copperhouse
Barripper
Carnhell Green
Cripplesease
PARADISE PARK
Hayle
B3306
252
Morvah
Bojewyan
Nancledra
Canon's Town
Praze-an-Beeble
Fraddam
B3280
Crowan
CHYSAUSTER ANCIENT VILLAGE
GEEVOR TIN MINE MUSEUM
Pendeen
Higher Boscaswell
Trewellard
Newmill
St Erth
Leedstown
Drym
Botallack
Carnyorth
PENZANCE HELIPORT
Ludgvan
Crowlas
Townshend
Cape Cornwall
B3318
A3071
TRENGWAINTON
Madron
Gulval
Relubbus
Nancegollan
Godolphin Cross
St Just
Newbridge
Heamoor
PENZANCE
Chyandour
A394
St Hilary
GODOLPHIN HOUSE
Trescowe
The Bisons
BALLOWALL BARROW
LAND'S END
Bosavern
Marazion
Goldsithney
Crowntown
Kelynack
224
Sancreed
Res.
Penzance
ST MICHAEL'S MOUNT
Perranuthnoe
Germoe
Ashton
Sithney
CARN EUNY ANCIENT VILLAGE
Tredavoe
Breage
LAND'S END
Lower Drift
Newlyn
NEWLYN ART GALLERY
SOUTH WEST COAST PATH
Praa Sands
B3302
Brane
Whitesand Bay
Catchall
Paul
Cudden Pt.
Rinsey
Crows-an-wra
B3283
Kerris
Mousehole
Sennen Cove
A30
St Buryan
Trewavas Hd.
B3304
Longships
Sennen
Trewoofe
St Clement's Island
Porthleven
The Loe
LAND'S END
B3315
SOUTH WEST COAST PATH
MOUNT'S BAY
Polgigga
Lamorna
Porthleven Sands
TREGIFFIAN BURIAL CHAMBER
Porthcurno
Boskenna
Lamorna Cove
ISLES OF SCILLY 2:40 (Mar-Nov)
Treen
St Levan
MINACK OPEN AIR THEATRE
Gwennap Hd.
Runnel Stone
Isles of Scilly
White Island
St Helens
KING CHARLES CASTLE
St Martin's
Bryher
41
47
CROMWELL'S CASTLE
New Grimsby
Higher Town
Tresco
Bryher
TRESCO ABBEY GARDENS
Crow Sound
Eastern Isles
Samson
BANT'S CARN
The Road
51
INNISIDGEN CAIRNS
North West Passage
Newford
Maypole
LONGSTONE HERITAGE CEN
A3110
St Mary's
Hugh Town
ST MARY'S
Old Town
GARRISON WALLS
Broad Sound
Smith Sound
St Mary's Sound
PENZANCE 2:40 (Mar-Nov)
Annet
St Agnes
Gugh
St Agnes
1
2
3
4
5
A
B
C
D
E
F
0 1 2 3 4 5 6 miles
0 1 2 3 4 5 6 7 8 9 10 km

5
6
7
8
9
A
B
C
D
E
F
SW
C O R N W A L L
Penhale Pt.
Holywell
HOLYWELL BAY FUN PARK
Carines
Ligger or Perran Bay
Penhale Sands
Cubert
Rejerrah
Mount
Rose
PERRAN ROUND
SOUTH WEST COAST PATH
Perranporth
PERRANPORTH
Goonhavern
Bolingey
Perranzabuloe
Trevellas
St Agnes Hd.
St Agnes
Mithian
Callestick
CORNISH CYDER FARM
Goonbell
Porthtowan
Mount Hawke
Three Burrows
Blackwater
Portreath
Mawla
Scorrier
TOLGUS MILL
CORNISH GOLD
Illogan
CORNISH MINES & ENGINES
Roscroggan
Pool
Tuckingmill
Carnkie
CAMBORNE
Camborne
SHIRE HORSE FARM
Troon
Redruth
St Day
Carharrack
GWENNAP PIT
Lanner
Four Lanes
Penhalvaen
Stithians
Stithians Res.
Penmarth
Burras
Carnkie
Releath
Porkellis
POLDARK MINE
Wendron
Seworgan
HELSTON RAILWAY
Trewennack
Helston
Gweek
NATIONAL SEAL SANCTUARY
FLAMBARDS EXPERIENCE
Mawgan
Garras
HALLIGGYE FOGOU
TRELOWARREN
Newtown
Berepper
Gunwalloe
Cury
Cross Lanes
Mullion
Mullion Cove
Mullion Island
Penhale
THE LIZARD
Goonhilly Downs
Trelan
Predannack Wollas
Vellan Hd.
St Ruan
Grade
Ruan Minor
Cadgwith
SOUTH WEST COAST PATH
Kynance Cove
Lizard
LIZARD
LIZARD POINT
Hot Pt.
Kuggar
Gwenter
COVERACK
Coverack
Chynhalls Pt.
Black Hd.
Lowland Pt.
Traboe
St Keverne
The Manacles
Manacle Pt.
Porthoustock
Porthallow
Tregidden
St Martin
Manaccan
Helford
Helford River
Nare Pt.
St Anthony-in-Meneage
Helford Passage
TREBAH
GLENDURGAN
Porth Navas
Mawnan
Mawnan Smith
Rosemullion Hd.
Constantine
Treverva
Penjerrick
Falmouth Bay
Budock Water
Rame
Longdowns
Mabe Burnthouse
ART GALLERY
Falmouth
NATIONAL MARITIME
PENDENNIS CASTLE
Pendennis Pt.
Penryn
Flushing
Mylor Bridge
Burnthouse
Ponsanooth
Perranarworthal
Devoran
Penpol
Gwennap
Carnon Downs
Bissoe
Twelve Heads
Chacewater
Baldhu
Threemilestone
ROYAL CORNWALL MUS
Truro
Kea
Playing Place
Feock
Old Kea
Malpas
Kenwyn
CATHEDRAL
Merther
St Clement
Shortlanesend
Allet
Marazanvose
Zelah
St Allen
Trispen
St Erme
Ladock
Tresillian
Carrick Roads
Fal
Trelissick
TRELISSICK
St Michael Penkevil
Lamorran
Ruan Lanihorne
Philleigh
Treworga
Treworlas
Trewithian
St Just in Roseland
Gerrans
Portscatho
Greeb Pt.
St Mawes
Bohortha
Zone Pt.
Gerrans Bay
Nare Hd.
Carne
Veryan
Portloe
SOUTH WEST COAST PATH
Veryan Bay
Portholland
Tregony
Tresawle
Probus
Grampound
TREWITHEN
Creed
Grampound Road
St Ewe
THE LOST GARDENS OF HELIGAN
Polmassick
Kestle
Trevarrick
St Michael Caerhays
Gorran Churchtown
Gorran Haven
Boswinger
BOSWINGER
Penare
Dodman Pt.
Chapel Pt.
Portmellon
Mevagissey
WORLD OF MODEL RAILWAYS
Mevagissey Bay
Pentewan
Black Hd.
Trenarren
Hewas Water
TORTOISE GARDEN
Sticker
Polgooth
Porthpean
Charlestown
SHIPWRECK HERITAGE
ST AUSTELL BREWERY
Holmbush
St Austell
St Mewan
Trewoon
Coombe
St Stephen
New Mills
High Street
Foxhole
Nanpean
WHEAL MARTYN CHINA CLAY HERITAGE CENTRE
Carthew
CHINA CLAY
Trethurgy
EDEN PROJECT
Carclaze
Tregrehan Mills
Penwithick
Stenalees
St Blazey
Bugle
Hensbarrow Downs
Whitemoor
St Dennis
Indian Queens
Trezaise
Treviscoe
Trethosa
Retew
Brighton
Summercourt
Fraddon
Penhale
St Enoder
St Columb Road
Kestle Mill
DAIRY LAND FARM WORLD
TRERICE
Gummow's Shop
St Newlyn East
LAPPA VALLEY STEAM RAILWAY
Newlyn Downs
Mitchell
Carland Cross
Trelassick
A30
A39
A390
A394
A3075
A3076
A3058
A3078
A3083
A3047
A393
B3285
B3284
B3277
B3298
B3301
B3280
B3297
B3293
B3294
B3296
B3289
B3275
B3279
B3287
B3273
B3274
P&R

CORNWALL
Tintagel Hd.
TINTAGEL
Start Pt.
SOUTH WEST COAST PATH
Port Isaac Bay
Port Isaac
Port Quin
Port Quin Bay
Port Gaverne
Pentire Pt.
New Polzeath
Padstow Bay
Polzeath
LONG CROSS
Trelights
Pendoggett
Gulland Rock
Trebetherick
St Endellion
Trelill
Gunver Hd.
St Minver
TREVOSE HEAD
Crugmeer
Pityme
Trewethern
St Kew
St Kew Highway
Chapel Amble
Trevone
PRIDEAUX PLACE
Rock
Constantine Bay
NATIONAL LOBSTER HATCHERY
Padstow
St Merryn
Camel
TREYARNON
Treyarnon
Shop
Trevanson
Bodieve
St Mabyn
Wadebridge
Porthcothan
Little Petherick
Whitecross
St Breock
Egloshayle
PENCARROW HOUSE
Penrose
St Issey
St Ervan
Rumford
Tredinnick
Burlawn
Park Hd.
St Jidgey
Washaway
CREALY GREAT ADVENTURE PARK
ST BREOCK DOWNS MONOLITH
St Eval
Trenance
Nanstallon
Berryl's Pt.
Trevarrian
CORNISH BIRDS OF PREY CENTRE
St Mawgan
Rosenannon
Ruthernbridge
St Lawrence
Withiel
Talskiddy
WATERGATE BAY
Tregurrian
NEWQUAY
St Wenn
St Columb Major
Tregonetha
Lanivet
Towan Hd.
Newquay Bay
Porth
St Columb Minor
Fistral Bay
Pentire
CASTLE AN DINAS
Belowda
Victoria
Trebudannon
Kelsey Hd.
West Pentire
BLUE REEF AQUARIUM
NEWQUAY ZOO
Colan
SPRINGFIELDS FUN PARK & PONY CENTRE
Ruthvoes
Lockengate
Newquay
Quintrell Downs
Mountjoy
Tregoss
Crantock
Lane
GOSS MOOR
Trevarren
Roche
Bilberry
HOLYWELL BAY FUN PARK
Kestle Mill
St Columb Road
Indian Queens
Trezaise
Penhale Pt.
Carines
Fraddon
Bugle
Holywell
DAIRY LAND FARM WORLD
Penhale
St Dennis
Hensbarrow
Ligger or Perran Bay
Cubert
TRERICE
St Enoder
Whitemoor
Downs
Stenalees
Penhale Sands
St Newlyn East
Gummow's Shop
Retew
CHINA CLAY
Penwithick
Rejerrah
Treviscoe
Nanpean
Carthew
Mount
LAPPA VALLEY STEAM RAILWAY
Summercourt
Trethurgy
Rose
PERRAN ROUND
Trethosa
Foxhole
Perranporth
Newlyn Downs
Mitchell
Brighton
WHEAL MARTYN CHINA CLAY HERITAGE CENTRE
EDEN PROJECT
PERRANPORTH
Goonhavern
High Street
Carclaze
Bolingey
Carland Cross
St Austell
Boscoppa
Perranzabuloe
Trelassick
St Stephen
Holmbush
St Agnes Hd.
Zelah
Trewoon
Trevellas
SW
New Mills
Coombe
St Mewan
Charlestown
St Agnes
Mithian
St Allen
Polgooth
ST AUSTELL BREWERY
Callestick
St Erme
Ladock
Grampound Road
Sticker
Porthpean
Goonbell
CORNISH CYDER FARM
Marazanvose
Trispen
Hewas Water
TORTOISE GARDEN
Allet
Trenarren
Porthtowan
Mount Hawke
Probus
Grampound
Black Hd.
Shortlanesend
TREWITHEN
Pentewan
Three Burrows
Creed
THE LOST GARDENS OF HELIGAN
Mevagissey Bay
Blackwater
Tresillian
St Ewe
P&R
Truro
Kenwyn
Tresawle
Polmassick
Kestle
Portreath
Mawla
CATHEDRAL
Merther
WORLD OF MODEL RAILWAYS
TOLGUS MILL
CORNISH GOLD
Scorrier
Threemilestone
Tregony
Mevagissey
PORTREATH
Illogan
Chacewater
ROYAL CORNWALL MUS.
Portmellon
CORNISH MINES & ENGINES
St Day
Baldhu
St Clement
Chapel Pt.
Twelve Heads
Kea
Ruan Lanihorne
Trevarrick
Gorran Churchtown
Redruth
Malpas
St Michael Caerhays
Pool
Tuckingmill
Cambrea
Carharrack
Bissoe
Playing Place
St Michael Penkevil
Lamorran
Gorran Haven
Carnkie
GWENNAP PIT
Gwennap
Carnon Downs
Old Kea
Treworga
Portholland
Boswinger
BOSWINGER
CAMBORNE
Lanner
Perranarworthal
Penpol
Trelissick
Philleigh
Penare
SHIRE HORSE FARM
Four Lanes
Devoran
Feock
TRELISSICK
Veryan
Portloe
Veryan Bay
Dodman Pt.
Troon
Ponsanooth
Treworlas
Carne
Penhalvaen
Gerrans Bay
Stithians
Burnthouse
Trewithian
Nare Hd.
Stithians Res.
Mylor Bridge
St Just in Roseland
Penmarth
Carrick Roads
Gerrans
Portscatho
Crowan
Burras
Carnkie
Penryn
Flushing
Greeb Pt.
Falmouth
St Mawes
Relea
NATIONAL MARITIME
Bohortha
Nancegollan
GALLERY
PENDENNIS CASTLE
Wendron
Seworgan
Treverva
Pendennis Pt.
Zone Pt.
Crowntown
0 1 2 3 4 5 6 miles
0 1 2 3 4 5 6 7 8 9 10 km

5
6
7
8
9
4
A
B
C
D
E
F
Boscastle
Tintagel
Treknow
Trewarmett
Trebarwith
Treligga
Delabole
Camelford
Valley Truckle
Helstone
St Teath
Treveighan
Michaelstow
St Tudy
St Breward
Row
Wenfordbridge
Blisland
Bradford
Davidstow
Trewassa
Tremail
Davidstow Moor
Crowdy Res.
High Moor
BROWN WILLY
GARROW TOR
THE ARTHURIAN CENTRE
CORNWALL AT WAR
MUSEUM OF SMUGGLING
Hallworthy
Treneglos
Tremaine
Tresmeer
Tregeare
Cold Northcott
St Clether
Laneast
Trewen
Polyphant
Altarnun
Trewint
Codda
Bolventor
BODMIN MOOR
Dozmary Pool
Colliford Lake
Temple
Maidenwell
Millpool
Helland
Camel
Bodmin Forest
Bodmin
BODMIN
Cardinham
Warleggan
Mount
St Neot
Ley
CARNGLAZE SLATE CAVERNS
Commonmoor
GOLITHA FALLS
KING DONIERT'S CIRCLE
St Cleer
Tremar
TRETHEVY QUOIT
Darite
CARADON HILL
Minions
Siblyback Lake
THE HURLERS STONE CIRCLES
Upton Cross
Henwood
KILMAR TOR
North Hill
Trebartha
Congdon's Shop
Lewannick
Piper's Pool
TRETHORNE LEISURE FARM
HIDDEN VALLEY DISCOVERY PARK
Tregadillett
Launceston
LAUNCESTON STEAM RAILWAY
CASTLE
Egloskerry
North Petherwin
Yeolmbridge
Langore
St Stephen's
Dutson
Werrington
Bridgetown
Broadwoodwidger
Cross Green
Stowford
DINGLE'S FAIRGROUND HERITAGE CENTRE
Thrushelton
Lewdown
Portgate
Liftondown
Lifton
Tinhay
Daw's House
South Petherwin
Lawhitton
Kelly
Bradstone
Chillaton
Milton Abbot
Dunterton
Lezant
Trekenner
Rezare
Trebullett
Treburley
Coad's Green
Bathpool
Rilla Mill
Bray Shop
Linkinhorne
South Hill
Stoke Climsland
Sydenham Damerel
Horsebridge
Luckett
Latchley
Downgate
Chilsworthy
Gunnislake
Gulworthy
Kelly Bray
KIT HILL
St Ann's Chapel
Drakewalls
Albaston
Golberdon
Haye
Callington
DUPATH WELL HOUSE
Harrowbarrow
COTEHELE
Calstock
St Dominick
TAMAR VALLEY
Bere Alston
Weir Quay
Pensilva
Trevigro
Gang
St Ive
Newbridge
Merrymeet
Pengover Green
Quethiock
St Mellion
Pillaton
Liskeard
Dobwalls
Doublebois
East Taphouse
West Taphouse
St Pinnock
Fowey
LANHYDROCK HOUSE
BODMIN AND WENFORD RAILWAY
TOWN MUSEUM
Trebyan
Sweetshouse
Redmoor
RESTORMEL CASTLE
Braddock
Cornwall
Herodsfoot
St Keyne
MAGNIFICENT MUSIC MACHINES
Menheniot
Blunts
Tideford Cross
Landrake
Hatt
Botusfleming
Cargreen
Landulph
SALTASH SERVICES
Tamerton Foliot
Lostwithiel
Lanlivery
Luxulyan
Couch's Mill
Milltown
Bocaddon
Lerryn
Trewidland
Duloe
Widegates
Trerule Foot
Hessenford
Tideford
Trematon
Saltash
St Erney
St Stephens
St Germans
Polbathic
MARY NEWMAN'S COTTAGE
St Budeaux
ANTONY HOUSE
Sheviock
Crafthole
Antony
Torpoint
Devonport
Penpillick
St Blazey
GOLANT
Golant
Tywardreath
Par
St Veep
Penpoll
Lanreath
Muchlarnick
Pelynt
Sandplace
Morval
St Martin
MONKEY SANCTUARY
Seaton
Downderry
Portwrinkle
Looe
East Looe
West Looe
OLD GUILDHALL
Looe Bay
St George's or Looe I.
Lanteglos Highway
Trenewan
Porthallow
Polperro
HERITAGE MUSEUM
Talland Bay
Lansallos
Bodinnick
Fowey
Polruan
Polkerris
Menabilly
SHIPWRECK & HERITAGE CENTRE
ST CATHERINE'S CASTLE
SOUTH WEST COAST PATH
Pencarrow Hd.
ST. AUSTELL BAY
Gribbin Hd.
Whitsand Bay
Freathy
St John
Cremyll
Millbrook
Kingsand
Cawsand
Rame
Rame Hd.
Penlee Pt.
SX
ROSCOFF 6:00 (Feb-Nov)
SANTANDER 20:00 (Mar-Nov)
ST MALO 9:15 (Nov-Mar)
A30
A395
A388
A39
A38
A390
A387
A374
A3082
B3266
B3262
B3263
B3314
B3267
B3254
B3257
B3362
B3268
B3269
B3359
B3252
B3251
B3253
B3247
B3249
B3271

6
Broadwoodwidger
Cross Green
Thrushelton
Stowford
Lewdown
Lewtrenchard
Bridestowe
Bridestowe and Sourton Common
BLACK-A-TOR COPSE
HIGH WILLHAYS
621
Gidleigh
Murchington
Sandypark
Easton
Teign
Chagford
DINGLE'S FAIRGROUND HERITAGE CENTRE
Portgate
Shortacombe
OKEMENT HILL
Teigncombe
Dutson
Liftondown
Lifton
Tinhay
LAUNCESTON STEAM RAILWAY
Lydford
LYDFORD
HANGINGSTONE HILL
Frenchbeer
DARTMOOR
Coryton
LYDFORD GORGE
Lettaford
THE MINIATURE PONY CENTRE
North Bovey
Lawhitton
Kelly
North Brentor
Black Down
Willsworthy
CUT HILL
SITTAFORD TOR
GRIMSPOUND
A388
Bradstone
Chillaton
DARTMOOR
HAMELDOWN TOR
Dunterton
Milton Abbot
Horndon
POSTBRIDGE INFORMATION CENTRE
Postbridge
Mary Tavy
ROUGH TOR
HOUND TOR
Trekenner
Rezare
Cudliptown
NATIONAL
FOREST
Bellever
Bonehill
Sydenham Damerel
Lamerton
Wilminstone
Peter Tavy
GT. MIS TOR
WISTMAN'S WOOD
BELLEVER (Dartmoor)
Widecombe in the Moor
Stoke Climsland
Horsebridge
Merrivale
PREHISTORIC SETTLEMENT
Two Bridges
B3387
Luckett
Latchley
Tavistock
Rundlestone
RIPPON TOR
Ponsworthy
Downgate
HIGH MOORLAND VISITOR CENTRE
Princetown
W. Dart
Hexworthy
Dartmeet
Chilsworthy
Gulworthy
Whitchurch
Sampford Spiney
Buckland in the Moor
Gunnislake
Grenofen
Poundsgate
Kelly Bray
KIT HILL
St Ann's Chapel
TOLL
PARK
Drakewalls
Higher Walreddon
Whiteworks
RIVER DART ADVENTURES
Callington
Albaston
Horrabridge
Walkhampton
Harrowbarrow
DUPATH WELL HOUSE
COTEHELE
Calstock
Buckland Monachorum
THE GARDEN HOUSE
PAPERWEIGHT CENTRE
Dousland
Burrator Res.
RYDER'S HILL
Holne
Newbridge
St Dominick
TAMAR
Crapstone
Yelverton
Sheepstor
D
e
v
BUCKFAST ABBEY
Buckfast
Bere Alston
BUCKLAND ABBEY
Meavy
Buckfastleigh
St Mellion
VALLEY
Milton Combe
UPPER PLYM VALLEY
Weir Quay
Clearbrook
Lopwell
SX
Dean
Pillaton
Plym
Shaugh Prior
SHELL TOP
Ugborough Moor
Dean Prior
PENNYWELL FARM & WILDLIFE CENTRE
A388
Cargreen
Bere Ferrers
Didworthy
Hatt
Landulph
A386
Bickleigh
DENDLES WOOD
Botusfleming
Tamerton Foliot
Roborough
Wotter
Lee Moor
Rattery
Landrake
SALTASH SERVICES
CROWNHILL FORT
P&R
Plym Forest
South Brent
Tideford
Trematon
A38
Saltash
Crownhill
Drakeland Corner
Lutton
Cornwood
Harford
UGBOROUGH BEACON
Cheston
St Erney
St Stephens
Plymouth
DARTMOOR ZOOLOGICAL PARK
Lincombe
St Germans
MARY NEWMAN'S COTTAGE
St Budeaux
Eggbuckland
PLYM VALLEY RAILWAY
Sparkwell
Bittaford
Avonwick
ANTONY HOUSE
MERCHANT'S HOUSE
P&R
Plympton
Lee Mill
Ivybridge
North Huish
Diptford
Sheviock
Torpoint
Devonport
Plymouth
SALTRAM
A38
Ugborough
Crafthole
Antony
Westlake
Curtisknowle
Portwrinkle
St John
Cremyll
ROYAL CITADEL
Plymstock
Elburton
Ermington
Brownston
SOUTH WEST COAST PATH
MOUNT EDGCUMBE
Drake's I.
Hooe
Brixton
Yealmpton
Modbury
Freathy
Millbrook
MOUNT EDGCUMBE
The Sound
Staddiscombe
Whitsand Bay
Kingsand
Bovisand Bay
Down Thomas
Holbeton
Cawsand
Luson
Rame
Knighton
Battisborough Cross
Loddiswell
Woodleigh
Penlee Pt.
Heybrook Bay
Wembury
Newton Ferrers
Aveton Gifford
Rame Hd.
Wembury Bay
Noss Mayo
Mothecombe
St Ann's Chapel
Great Mew Stone
Worswell
Kingston
Bigbury
SORLEY TUNNEL ADVENTURE WORLDS
Stoke Pt.
SOUTH WEST COAST PATH
Ringmore
Churchstow
E
Bigbury on Sea
Burgh I.
West Alvington
BIGBURY BAY
Bantham
Buckland
Kingsbridge
5
ROSCOFF 6:00 (Feb-Nov)
SANTANDER 20:00 (Mar-Nov)
ST MALO 9:15 (Nov-Mar)
Thurlestone
South Milton
Woolston
Galmpton
4
Hope
Malborough
SOUTH
Bolt Tail
Bolberry
Salcombe
East Portlemouth
Soar
SALCOMBE
OVERBECKS MUSEUM AND GARDEN
Bolt Hd.
F
0 1 2 3 4 5 6 miles
0 1 2 3 4 5 6 7 8 9 10 km
25
3
4
5

Dunsford
Shillingford St George
Topsham
Clyst St George
Salterton
Newton Poppleford
Sidmouth
Moretonhampstead
Doccombe
Bridford
Bridfordmills
Doddiscombsleigh
Exminster
Kennford
Ebford
Exton
Woodbury
Colaton Raleigh
Yettington
Bicton Park
Otterton
Otterton Mill
Ladram Bay
Christow
Higher Ashton
Lower Ashton
Kenn
Powderham
Powderham Castle
River Exe
Lympstone
A La Ronde
East Budleigh
South West Coast Path
Withycombe Raleigh
Knowle
Budleigh Salterton
Danger Pt.
Canonteign Falls
Trusham
Exeter
Kenton
Starcross
Littleham
Lustleigh
Manaton
Water
Bovey
Hennock
Cockwood
Exmouth
World of Country Life
Fairlynch Arts Centre and Museum
Dawlish Warren
Exmouth Model Railway
Straight Pt.
Ashcombe
Bovey Tracey
Chudleigh
Chudleigh Knighton
East Dartmoor Woods & Heaths
Haytor Information Centre
Craft Centre
Ugbrooke House
Brimley
Haytor Vale
Ilsington
Heathfield
Ideford
Luton
Little Haldon
Dawlish
Liverton
Stover
Trago Mills
Coldeast
Preston
Holcombe
Teigngrace
Bishopsteignton
Sigford
Kingsteignton
Teignmouth
Teign
Shaldon
Shaldon Wildlife Trust
Bickington
Highweek
Newton Abbot
Combeinteignhead
Netherton
Stokeinteignhead
Ashburton
West Ogwell
Bradley
Wolborough
Plant World
East Ogwell
Decoy
Prickly Ball Hedgehog Hospital
Babbacombe Bay
Woodland
Denbury
Abbotskerswell
Coffinswell
Kingskerswell
Maidencombe
Forder Grn.
Torbryan
Ipplepen
North Whilborough
Barton
Watcombe
Landscove
Broadhempston
Buckfast Butterflies & Dartmoor Otter Sanctuary
Shiphay
Model Village
Babbacombe
SX
SY
Compton
Compton Castle
Torre
Torre Abbey
Torquay
Kent's Cavern Prehistoric Caves
Staverton
Cockington
Wellswood
Hope's Nose
Dartington
Littlehempston
Marldon
Living Coasts
Dartington Cider Press Centre
Dartington Hall
Oldway Mansion
Shinner's Bridge
Berry Pomeroy Castle
Hollicombe
South Devon Railway
Bladgon
Torbay
Cott
Totnes
Berry Pomeroy
Kirkham
Paignton
Tigley
Collaton St Mary
Dartmouth Steam Railway
Torbay
Belsford
Zoo
Tor Bay
Harberton
Dart
Goodrington
Golden Hind
Ashprington
Stoke Gabriel
Brixham
Berry Head
Harbertonford
Churston Ferrers
Galmpton
Tuckenhay
Cornworthy
Crabadon
Berry Head
St Mary's Bay
Washbourne
Dittisham
River Dart
Sharkham Pt.
Halwell
Allaleigh
Capton
Hillhead
Moreleigh
Woodlands Leisure Park
Dartmouth
Newcomen Engine House
Kingswear
Scabbacombe Hd.
Woodford
Blackawton
Ferry
Warfleet
Coleton Fishacre
Millcombe
Bayards Cove Fort
Dartmouth Castle
Bowden
Mew Stone
East Allington
Stoke Fleming
Strete
Blackpool
Goveton
South West Coast Path
Harleston
Slapton
Sherford
Frittiscombe
Slapton Sands
Slapton Ley
Start Bay
Frogmore
Stokenham
Charleston
Chillington
Torcross
Kernborough
Beeson
South Pool
Beesands
Kellaton
Hallsands
South Allington
Start Point
East Prawle
Lannacombe Bay
Prawle Pt.
Devon
A
B
C
D
E
F
5
6
7
8
9

HARTLAND POINT
NORTH
BIDEFORD
Titchberry
Windbury Pt.
HARTLAND ABBEY
Stoke
Hartland Quay
Hartland
CLOVELLY VILLAGE
Clovelly
Higher Clovelly
SOUTH WEST COAST PATH
DOCTON MILL
Philham
Milford
Eddistone
ELMSCOTT
Elmscott
Tosberry
Buck's Cross
THE MILKY WAY ADVENTURE PARK
Woolfardisworthy
South Hole
Hartland Forest
Alminstone Cross
Knaps Longpeak
Welcombe
Meddon
Ashmansworthy
Woolley
Gooseham
Eastcott
Youlstone
Morwenstow
Dinworthy
Higher Sharpnose Pt.
Shop
A39
Woodford
Bradworthy
Lower Sharpnose Pt.
Bradworthy Cross
Kilkhampton
Alfardisworthy
Coombe
Sutcombe
Stibb
Soldon Cross
BUDE
Poughill
DUNSDON
Flexbury
Hersham
Bude Haven
Stratton
Grimscott
Chilsworthy
Bude
Launcells
A3072
Pancrasweek
BAY
Holsworthy
Upton
Tamar
Derril
Derriton
Marhamchurch
Bridgerule
Widemouth Bay
Pyworthy
Chasty
Widemouth Sand
Budd's Titson
Leworthy
Millook
Coppathorne
Dizzard Pt.
Poundstock
Treskinnick Cross
Tregole
Whitstone
SOUTH WEST COAST PATH
St Gennys
Trewint
Week St Mary
North Tamerton
PENHALLAM
Cambeak
Crackington Haven
Rosecare
Jacobstow
Tetcott
Lana
CORNWALL
SS
SX
Wainhouse Corner
Luffincott
Fire Beacon Pt.
Tresparrett Posts
B3263
South Wheatley
West Curry
Beeny
A39
Maxworthy
BOSCASTLE
Tresparrett
Marshgate
Bennacott
Northcott
Canworthy Water
Boyton
Boscastle
Otterham
Brazacott
Trevalga
Lesnewth
TAMAR OTTER & WILDLIFE CENTRE
Warbstow
Langdon
CASTLE
Trelash
Tintagel Hd.
OLD POST OFFICE
TINTAGEL
Bossiney
Tremaine
Ottery
North Petherwin
Bridgetown
Tintagel
B3266
Hallworthy
Treneglos
Werrington
Treknow
308
Davidstow
Yeolmbridge
Trewarmett
B3262
Tresmeer
B3263
Trewassa
Tremail
Egloskerry
Langore
THE ARTHURIAN CENTRE
Start Pt.
Trebarwith
CORNWALL AT WAR
Davidstow Moor
Tregeare
St Stephen's
Dutson
Cold Northcott
A395
HIDDEN VALLEY DISCOVERY PARK
Treligga
B3314
Piper's Pool
Launceston
CASTLE
SOUTH WEST COAST PATH
Delabole
St Clether
Laneast
Tregadillett
A30
Camelford
Trewen
Daw's House
Port Isaac Bay
Crowdy Res.
TRETHORNE LEISURE FARM
A388
Valley Truckle
B3314
B3267
Helstone
Polyphant
South Petherwin
Port Isaac
Port Quin Bay
Port Quin
Port Gaverne
St Teath
400 ROUGH TOR
High Moor
Altarnun
Lewannick
Inny
LONG CROSS
B3267
Trelights
Pendoggett
Treveighan
420 BROWN WILLY
Trewint
B3257
Lezant
Polzeath
Michaelstow
369
A30
Codda
Congdon's Shop
Trekenner
331 GARROW TOR
BODMIN MOOR
Trebullett
St Breward
MUSEUM OF SMUGGLING
Trebartha
Treburley
Row
Bolventor
North Hill
Coad's Green
Chapel Amble
St Kew
Rock
Bradford
B3254
B3257
0 1 2 3 4 5 6 miles
0 1 2 3 4 5 6 7 8 9 10 km

Barnstaple
Bideford
Great Torrington
Okehampton
South Molton
Appledore
Westward Ho!
Northam
Instow
Fremington
Bickington
Newport
Bishops Tawton
Landkey
Swimbridge
Westacott
Goodleigh
Chivenor
Braunton Burrows
Pilton
Yelland
Bickleton
Tawstock
Horwood
Eastleigh
Westleigh
Orchard Hill
Abbotsham
Buck's Mills
Horns Cross
Fairy Cross
Ford
Woodtown
Littleham
Handy Cross
Landcross
East-the-Water
Goldworthy
Parkham
Parkham Ash
Buckland Brewer
Monkleigh
Weare Giffard
Frithelstock
Frithelstock Stone
Taddiport
Little Torrington
Tythecott
West Putford
East Putford
Bulkworthy
Abbots Bickington
Newton St Petrock
Langtree
Stibb Cross
Peters Marland
Woollaton
Winswell
Venn Green
Milton Damerel
Holsworthy Beacon
Thornbury
Shebbear
Buckland Filleigh
Woodacott
Bradford
Black Torrington
Sheepwash
Cookbury
Holemoor
Highampton
Brandis Corner
Whimble
Hollacombe
Chilla
Graddon Moor
Halwill Junction
Halwill
Clawton
Beaworthy
Northlew
Patchacott
Ashbury
Quoditch
Broadbury
Ashwater
Henford
Chapmans Well
Virginstow
East Panson
St Giles on the Hth.
Gridley Corner
Germansweek
Eworthy
Boasley Cross
Grinacombe Moor
Roadford Res.
Bratton Clovelly
Broadwoodwidger
Cross Green
Thrushelton
Stowford
Lewdown
Liftondown
Lifton
Tinhay
Portgate
Lewtrenchard
Coryton
Lydford
Lawhitton
Kelly
Bradstone
Chillaton
North Brentor
Black Down
Willsworthy
Milton Abbot
Dunterton
Rezare
Sydenham Damerel
Lamerton
Mary Tavy
Horndon
Cudliptown
Peter Tavy
Wilminstone
Merrivale
Newton Tracey
Ensis
Hiscott
Chapelton
Fishleigh Barton
Woodtown
Alverdiscott
Yarnscombe
Atherington
Langridge Ford
Sherwood Green
High Bullen
St Giles in the Wood
Kingscott
Roborough
Beaford
Riddlecombe
Merton
Huish
Dolton
Dowland
Petrockstow
Meeth
Iddesleigh
Monkokehampton
Hatherleigh
Jacobstowe
Inwardleigh
Oak Cross
Folly Gate
Sourton
Meldon
Okehampton Camp
Okehampton Common
Bridestowe
Bridestowe and Sourton Common
Shortacombe
Thorndon Cross
Newland
Herner
Cobbaton
East Stowford
Chittlehampton
Umberleigh
Warkleigh
Satterleigh
Clapworthy
High Bickington
Chittlehamholt
Burrington
Ashreigney
Hollocombe
Winkleigh
Broadwood Kelly
Bondleigh
Honeychurch
Exbourne
Sampford Courtenay
North Tawton
Taw Green
Sticklepath
Belstone
South Tawton
South Zeal
Whiddon Down
Spreyton
Itton
Throwleigh
Wonson
Gidleigh
Murchington
Chagford
Teigncombe
Frenchbeer
Drewsteignton
Sandypark
Easton
Lettaford
North Bovey
Manaton
Postbridge
Bellever
Widecombe in the Moor
Bonehill
Haytor Vale
Gunn
Brayford
High Bray
North Heasley
Heasley Mill
South Radworthy
Charles
West Buckland
East Buckland
Filleigh
North Molton
Bish Mill
Bishops Nympton
Alswear
George Nympton
Romansleigh
King's Nympton
Cadbury Barton
Elstone
Chulmleigh
Week
West Worlington
Cheldon
Chawleigh
Ashley
Wembworthy
Filleigh
Eastington
Lapford
Coldridge
Brushford
Nymet Rowland
West Leigh
East Leigh
Zeal Monachorum
Down St Mary
Bow
Nymet Tracey
Colebrooke
Hillerton
Ettisleigh
Cheriton Bishop
Crockernwell
BAY
DEVON
Devon
DARTMOOR NATIONAL PARK
DARTMOOR FOREST
SS
SX
LUNDY 2:00 (Mar-Oct)
NORTH DEVON MARITIME MUSEUM
NORTHAM BURROWS
TAPELEY PARK GDNS
THE BIG SHEEP
BURTON ART GALL & MUS
ATLANTIC VILLAGE
DARTINGTON CRYSTAL
R.H.S. GARDEN ROSEMOOR
GNOME RESERVE & GARDEN
WINSFORD WALLED GARDEN
MUSEUM OF NORTH DEVON
NORTH DEVON FARM PARK
COBBATON COMBAT COLL
QUINCE HONEY FARM
DARTMOOR RAILWAY
FINCH FOUNDRY
OKEHAMPTON (Dartmoor)
CASTLE
BRACKEN TOR
SOURTON CROSS SERVICES
BLACK-A-TOR COPSE
YES TOR 619
HIGH WILLHAYS 621
OKEMENT HILL 566
HANGINGSTONE HILL 604
COSDON HILL 550
CUT HILL 604
SITTAFORD TOR 537
DINGLE'S FAIRGROUND HERITAGE CENTRE
LYDFORD
LYDFORD GORGE
CASTLE DROGO
THE MINIATURE PONY CENTRE
GRIMSPOUND
HAMELDOWN TOR 529
POSTBRIDGE INFORMATION CENTRE
ROUGH TOR 546
WISTMAN'S WOOD
GT. MIS TOR 539
PREHISTORIC SETTLEMENT
LLEVER (Dartmoor)
HOUND TOR
Two Bridges
A39
A377
A386
A388
A361
A3124
A3072
A3079
A30
A382
B3233
B3232
B3227
B3226
B3217
B3220
B3096
B3042
B3215
B3206
B3212
B3362
B3387
P&R
Taw
Torridge
Mole
Yeo
Lew
Carey
Thrushel
Tamar
Teign
E. Dart
5
6
7
8
9
10
20
A
B
C
D
E
F
G

Brayford
High Bray
Radworthy
North Heasley
South Radworthy
Heasley Mill
Charles
West Buckland
East Buckland
Winsford
Exton
Liscombe
Bridgetown
TARR STEPS
Hawkridge
Withiel Florey
Brompton Regis
Clatworthy Res.
Wimbleball Lake
Molland Common
Twitchen
Danes Brook
Anstey Common
West Anstey
East Anstey
Molland
North Molton
A361
Filleigh
Dulverton
Battleton
Barle
Bury
Skilgate
Huish Champflower
HADDON HILL
HEYDON HILL
Chipstable
Upton
QUINCE HONEY FARM
East Stowford
South Molton
Chittlehampton
Yeo Mill
Nightcott
Brushford
Morebath
Oldways End
Exebridge
Petton
Shillingford
Clayhanger
Bish Mill
Newtown
Bishops Nympton
Clapworthy
George Nympton
Alswear
Ash Mill
Knowstone
Roachill
Oakfordbridge
Bampton
Satterleigh
Mariansleigh
Rose Ash
Oakford
Huntsham
Chittlehamholt
Romansleigh
Meshaw
STOODLEIGH BEACON
Stoodleigh
Cove
Hockworthy
King's Nympton
Creacombe
Rackenford
EXE VALLEY
Cadbury Barton
Week
Queen Dart
Little Dart
Loxbeare
Washfield
Chevithorne
East Mere
Whitnage
Elstone
Lutworthy
Templeton Bridge
Bolham
KNIGHTSHAYES COURT
Uplowman
Chulmleigh
West Worlington
East Worlington
Witheridge
Templeton
Calverleigh
Chettiscombe
Sampford Peverell
Cheldon
Drayford
Nomansland
TIVERTON CASTLE
Cowleymoor
Halberton
GRAND WESTERN CANAL
Chawleigh
Thelbridge Barton
Washford Pyne
SS
Cruwys Morchard
Withleigh
Cotteylands
Tiverton
Ashley
Pennymoor
Ash Thomas
Black Dog
Way Village
Willand
Filleigh
Dalch
Puddington
Well Town
Wembworthy
Eastington
DIGGERLAND
CULLOMPTON SERVICES
Brushford
Coldridge
Nymet Rowland
Lapford
Morchard Bishop
Woolfardisworthy
Poughill
Upham
Cadeleigh
Butterleigh
BICKLEIGH MILL
Cullompton
Kennerleigh
Stockleigh English
BICKLEIGH CASTLE
Bickleigh
DEVON RAILWAY CENTRE
Oldborough
A377
West Leigh
Taw
Cheriton Fitzpaine
Colebrook
East Leigh
Ash Bullayne
East Village
Cadbury
FURSDON HOUSE
Bradninch
Mutterton
Westcott
Zeal Monachorum
Down St Mary
Newbuildings
Stockleigh Pomeroy
Exe
Silverton
Culm
Copplestone
Sandford
Upton Hellions
Up Exe
Hele
Langford
Clyst Hydon
North Tawton
Bow
Knowle
Thorverton
Ellerhayes
THE COLLEGIATE CHURCH OF THE HOLY CROSS
Shobrooke
Efford
Shute
Nether Exe
Clyst St Lawrence
Nymet Tracey
Coleford
KILLERTON HOUSE
Colebrooke
Crediton
Rewe
Budlake
Westwood
Itton
Sweetham
Brampford Speke
Hillerton
Yeoford
Uton
Hookway
M5
Broadclyst
Venny Tedburn
Newton St Cyres
Stoke Canon
Upton Pyne
Whimple
Spreyton
Poltimore
Dog Village
Jack in the Green
SX
Cowley
Hittisleigh
Tedburn St Mary
Pinhoe
Rockbeare
South Tawton
South Zeal
Whiddon Down
Whitestone
Exwick
Whipton
Clyst Honiton
EXETER INTERNATIONAL
A30
Cheriton Bishop
EXETER
CATHEDRAL
Heavitree
Sowton
EXETER SERVICES
Marsh Green
Crockernwell
Aylesbeare
Longdown
Wheatley
St Thomas
Clyst St Mary
Farringdon
Drewsteignton
CASTLE DROGO
Ide
Countess Wear
CREALY ADVENTURE PARK
Throwleigh
Sandypark
Alphington
EXETER
Woodbury Salterton
Wonson
Easton
Teign
Dunsford
Shillingford St George
Clyst St George
Gidleigh
Murchington
Ebford
Woodbury
Topsham
MUS
A376
Chagford
Bridfordmills
Kenn
Exminster
Exton
Teigncombe
Doccombe
Bridford
Kennford
Doddiscombsleigh
River Exe
BLACK HILL
Frenchbeer
Moretonhampstead
Christow
Higher Ashton
Powderham
Lympstone
Lower Ashton
A LA RONDE
THE MINIATURE PONY CENTRE
North Bovey
POWDERHAM CASTLE
Kenton
Withycombe Raleigh
Lettaford
CANONTEIGN FALLS
A38
Starcross
Littleham
Manaton
Lustleigh
Trusham
A380
Exmouth
GRIMSPOUND
HAMELDOWN TOR
Water
Hennock
Cockwood
DAWLISH WARREN
EXMOUTH MODEL RAILWAY
Straight Pt.
Postbridge
Bovey
EAST DARTMOOR HEATHS
Bovey Tracey
Chudleigh
Ashcombe
Chudleigh Knighton
UGBROOKE HOUSE
Dawlish Warren
BELLEVER
CRAFT CENTRE
Brimley
Ideford
Luton
HAYTOR INFORMATION CENTRE
Ilsington
Heathfield
Little Haldon
Dawlish
Dart
0 1 2 3 4 5 6 miles
0 1 2 3 4 5 6 7 8 9 10 km

Taunton
Wellington
Wiveliscombe
VALE OF TAUNTON DEANE
BLACKDOWN HILLS
BLACKDOWN HILLS
Ilminster
Chard
Crewkerne
South Petherton
Honiton
Axminster
Ottery St Mary
Sidmouth
Sidford
Seaton
Beer
Beer Hd.
Lyme Regis
Charmouth
Budleigh Salterton
Danger Pt.
Ladram Bay
Seaton Bay
Charlton Bay
LYME BAY
EAST DEVON
West Sedge Moor
Culm Valley
Isle
Parrett
Tone
Axe
Yarty
Otter
Tale
Char
ST
SY
A
B
C
D
E
F
G
5
6
7
8
9
M5
A30
A35
A303
A358
A38
A375
A3052
22
12
Langport
Curry Rivel
North Curry
Hatch Beauchamp
Ilton
Donyatt
Dowlish Wake
Cricket St Thomas
Winsham
Forde Abbey and Gardens
Thorncombe
Hawkchurch
Membury
Stockland
Dunkeswell
Upottery
Hemyock
Culmstock
Uffculme
Churchinford
Buckland St Mary
Broadhembury
Payhembury
Feniton
Gittisham
Colyton
Colyford
Axmouth
Uplyme
Musbury
Shute
Kilmington
Branscombe
Salcombe Regis
Otterton
East Budleigh
Knowle
Newton Poppleford
Whitchurch Canonicorum
Chideock
Seatown
Symondsbury
Bishops Lydeard
Staplegrove
Bathpool
Creech St Michael
Ruishton
Henlade
Thornfalcon
Stoke St Mary
Orchard Portman
Pitminster
Corfe
Blagdon Hill
Staple Fitzpaine
Bickenhall
Ashill
Broadway
Horton
Whitestaunton
Yarcombe
Wambrook
Tatworth
South Chard
Tytherleigh
Chardstock
Wilmington
Offwell
Northleigh
Southleigh
Farway
Whitford
Combpyne
Rousdon
Wootton Fitzpaine
Marshwood
Bettiscombe
Pilsdon
Burstock
Broadwindsor
Drimpton
Clapton
Seaborough
Misterton
Hinton St George
Merriott
Chillington
Cudworth
Chaffcombe
Wadeford
Combe St Nicholas
Kingstone
Seavington St Michael
Seavington St Mary
Lopen
Dinnington
Puckington
Stocklinch
Barrington
Shepton Beauchamp
Kingsbury Episcopi
East Lambrook
Hambridge
Fivehead
Isle Abbotts
Isle Brewers
Curry Mallet
Beercrocombe
Drayton
Huish Episcopi
Burrowbridge
Lyng
Athelney
Stathe
Durston
North Newton
Hedging
Thurloxton
Kingston St Mary
Cheddon Fitzpaine
Monkton Heathfield
West Monkton
Nailsbourne
Fulford
Pickney
Cothelstone
Cushuish
Broomfield
Norton Fitzwarren
Hillcommon
Oake
Hillfarance
Bradford-on-Tone
Nynehead
Runnington
Rockwell Green
West Buckland
Trull
Staplehay
Angersleigh
Wrangway
Ford Street
Sampford Arundel
Holcombe Rogus
Westleigh
Burlescombe
Nicholashayne
Appledore
Ashbrittle
Thorne St Margaret
Holywell Lake
Langford Budville
Milverton
Bathealton
Kittisford
Appley
Waterrow
Halse
Fitzhead
Combe Florey
Lydeard St Lawrence
Tolland
Brompton Ralph
Clatworthy
Maundown
Kentisbeare
Blackborough
Sheldon
Kerswell
Dulford
Norman's Green
Plymtree
Talaton
Fenny Bridges
Alfington
Fairmile
Tipton St John
Venn Ottery
Harpford
Bowd
Colaton Raleigh
Hawkerland
Yettington
Wiggaton
West Hill
Combe Raleigh
Awliscombe
Buckerell
Colestocks
Church Green
Harcombe
Weston
Vicarage
Cotleigh
Monkton
Wick
Luppitt
Rawridge
Beacon
Smeatharpe
Bolham Water
Clayhidon
Rosemary Lane
Churchstanton
Bishopswood
Marsh
Howley
Newcott
Furley
Millhayes
Heathstock
Dalwood
Alston
Churchill
Smallridge
Holditch
Birdsmoorgate
Marshalsea
Weycroft
Craddock
Smithincott
Ashill
Abbey
Sidbury
Cotmaton
SOUTH WEST COAST PATH
SEATON TRAMWAY
DINOSAURLAND
AQUARIUM
WORLD OF COUNTRY LIFE
FAIRLYNCH ARTS CENTRE AND MUSEUM
BICTON PARK
OTTERTON MILL
ESCOT PARK
BURROW FARM
SHUTE BARTON
BLACKBURY CAMP
BEER QUARRY CAVES
MARINE HOUSE
AXMOUTH TO LYME REGIS UNDERCLIFFS
CHARMOUTH HERITAGE COAST CENTRE
HORNSBURY MILL
PERRYS CIDER
BARRINGTON COURT
E. LAMBROOK MANOR
THE CRAFT AND DESIGN CENTRE
COLDHARBOUR MILL
COTHAY
SHEPPY'S CIDER
TAUNTON DEANE SERVICES
SOMERSET CRICKET MUS
HESTERCOMBE GARDENS
FYNE COURT
WILLOWS & WETLANDS VISITOR CENTRE
LANGPORT & R PARRETT VISITOR CENTRE
BRIDGWATER & TAUNTON CANAL MAUNSEL LOCKS
STEMBRIDGE TOWER
BARRINGTON HILL
STAPLE HILL
HACKPEN HILL
BLACK DOWN

King's Sedge Moor
Somerset Levels
Middlezoy
Othery
Pathe
Moorland
High Ham
Henley
Dundon
Compton Dundon
Butleigh
Barton St David
Baltonsborough
Southwood
Brue
West Lydford
East Lydford
Hornblotton Green
Sutton
Alford
Lovington
Ansford
Castle Cary
Pitcombe
Cole
Redlynch
Hardway
Stoney Stoke
Alfred's Tower
Shepton Montague
Charlton Musgrove
Leigh Common
Stemp
Tower Mill
Littleton
Kingweston
Keinton Mandeville
Lydford-on-Fosse
Galhampton
Hadspen Garden
Wincanton
Bratton Seymour
Bayford
Burrowbridge
Athelney
Stathe
Aller
Low Ham
Pitney
Somerton
Charlton Adam
Charlton Mackerell
Babcary
North Barrow
Haynes Motor Mus
Yarlington
Stoke St Gregory
West Sedge Moor
Langport
Huish Episcopi
Curry Rivel
Langport & R Parrett Visitor Centre
WS & Wetlands Visitor Centre
Drayton
Muchelney
Long Sutton
Lytes Cary Manor
Kingsdon
Cary Fitzpaine
South Barrow
Sparkford
North Cadbury
Holton
Maperton
Lattiford
North Cheriton
South Cheriton
South Cadbury
Compton Pauncefoot
Blackford
Fivehead
Isle
Yeo
Long Load
Podimore
Northover
Ilchester
Fleet Air Arm Mus
Yeovilton
Limington
West Camel
Queen Camel
Bridgehampton
Chilton Cantelo
Marston Magna
Sutton Montis
Corton Denham
Charlton Horethorne
Horsington
Abbas Combe
Templecombe
Isle Brewers
Isle Abbotts
Hambridge
Kingsbury Episcopi
Stapleton
Ash
Coat
Ashington
Rimpton
Sandford Orcas Manor House
Sandford Orcas
Adber
Stowell
Yenston
Henstridge Ash
Henstridge Marsh
Henstridge
Milborne Wick
Milborne Port
Stalbridge
Westport
East Lambrook
Martock
Treasurer's Ho
Tintinhull
Tintinhull Garden
Chilthorne Domer
Yeovil Marsh
Mudford
Trent
Poyntington
Oborne
West Lambrook
E. Lambrook Manor
Puckington
Barrington
Barrington Court
South Petherton
Hurst
Bower Hinton
Stoke sub Hamdon
Montacute House
Ilton
Stocklinch
Shepton Beauchamp
Stoke-sub-Hamdon Priory
Montacute
Preston Plucknett
Yeovil
Nether Compton
Over Compton
Sherborne Old Castle
Goathill
Purse Caundle
Sherborne
Sherborne Castle
Stalbridge Weston
Ashwell
Ilminster
Seavington St Michael
Norton sub Hamdon
Ham Hill
Odcombe
Brympton
Bradford Abbas
North Wootton
Haydon
Stourton Caundle
Bishop's Caundle
Donyatt
Perrys Cider
Seavington St Mary
Over Stratton
Lopen
Chiselborough
West Coker
North Coker
Barwick
Yeovil
Alweston
Folke
Lydlinch
Kingstone
Dinnington
West Chinnock
East Chinnock
Hardington Moor
East Coker
Stoford
Thornford
Lillington
Longburton
Holwell
Dowlish Wake
Hinton St George
Merriott
Hardington Mandeville
Ryme Intrinseca
Beer Hackett
Woodbridge
Cricket Malherbie
Chillington
Haselbury Plucknett
Res
Closworth
Yetminster
Crouch Hill
King's Stag
Hornsbury Mill
Cudworth
Pendomer
Chaffcombe
Cricket St Thomas
Crewkerne
North Perrott
Hardington Marsh
Holnest
Glanvilles Wootton
Hewish
Misterton
Halstock
Melbury Osmond
Leigh
Chetnole
Hermitage
Middlemarsh
Pulham
Hazelbury Bryan
Lydden
Whatley
Winsham
Wayford
Clapton
South Perrott
West Chelborough
Melbury Sampford
Melbury Bubb
Westfields
Seaborough
Mosterton
Chedington
Corscombe
Evershot
Hilfield
Lyon's Gate
Dunfish
Mappowder
Chard
Forde Abbey and Gardens
Drimpton
Buckland Newton
Minterne House & Gardens
Minterne Magna
Thorncombe
Burstock
Broadwindsor
Rampisham
Holywell
Frome St Quintin
Batcombe
Up Cerne
Alton Pancras
Holditch
The Craft and Design Centre
Beaminster
Plush
Birdsmoorgate
Hawkchurch
Wraxall
Up Sydling
Cerne Abbas
Cerne Abbas Giant
Stoke Abbott
Marshalsea
Bettiscombe
Netherbury
Mapperton
Hooke
Cattistock
Sydling St Nicholas
Piddletrenthide
Marshwood
Pilsdon
Melplash
Toller Porcorum
Chilfrome
Maiden Newton
Nether Cerne
White Lackington
Piddlehinton
North Poorton
Hog Cliff
Godmanstone
Wootton Fitzpaine
Whitchurch Canonicorum
Broad Oak
Salwayash
West Milton
Powerstock
Toller Fratrum
Forston
Ryall
Dottery
Nettlecombe
Wynford Eagle
Charlton Down
Char
Morcombelake
Bradpole
Eggardon
Loders
Uploders
West Compton
Frampton
Grimstone
Charmouth
Charmouth Heritage Coast Centre
Symondsbury
Bridport
Askerswell
Muckleford
Stratton
Charminster
Hardy's Cottage Garden
Lyme Regis
Aquarium
Dinosaurland
Chideock
Eype
Walditch
Bothenhampton
Kingston Russell
Compton Valence
Bradford Peverell
Dorchester
Stinsford
Seatown
South West Coast Path
West Bay
Shipton Gorge
Chilcombe
Litton Cheney
Long Bredy
Winterbourne Abbas
The Tutankhamun Exhibition
Nine Stones
Military Museum
The Dinosaur Museum
Kingston Maurward
West Stafford
Burton Bradstock
Poor Lot Barrows
Winterbourne Steepleton
Martinstown
Maiden Castle
Whitcombe
Swyre
Puncknowle
Littlebredy
Valley of Stones
Black Down
Hardy Monument
Winterborne Monkton
Winterborne Herringston
West Knighton
West Bexington
Kingston Russell Stone Circle
Portesham
Broadmayne
Abbotsbury
Abbotsbury Children's Farm
Sub Tropical Gardens
St Catherine's Chapel
Swannery
Rodden
Upwey
Bincombe
White Horse
Poxwell
Broadwey
Littlemoor
Preston
Upton
Langton Herring
Nottington
Overcombe
Osmington
Radipole
Jordan Hill Roman Temple
Osmington Mills
Bennetts Water Gardens
Chickerell
Sea Life
Melcombe Regis
Chesil Beach
Westham
Weymouth
Charlestown
Nothe Fort
Brewer's Quay and Timewalk
Rodwell
Wyke Regis
Portland Harbour
Weymouth Bay
Guernsey 2:10
Jersey 3:25
St. Malo 5:15
Sailings temporarily moved to Poole
Weymouth & Portland National Sailing Academy
Portland Castle
Fortuneswell
West Bay
Grove
Easton
Portland
Weston
Museum
Southwell
Bill of Portland
Dorset
Blackmoor Vale
SY
ST
0 1 2 3 4 5 6 miles
0 1 2 3 4 5 6 7 8 9 10 km

Stourton
Zeals
Penselwood
Bourton
Mere
Queen Oak
West Knoyle
The Green
Berwick St Leonard
Hindon
Fonthill Bishop
Fonthill Gifford
East Knoyle
Chilmark
Ridge
Teffont Magna
Teffont Evias
Chicksgrove
Dinton
Baverstock
Barford St Martin
Burcombe
Ditchampton
Wilton
Quidhampton
Bemerton
Stratford sub Castle
Old Sarum
New Sarum
Netherhampton
West Harnham
East Harnham
Salisbury
Coombe Bissett
Odstock
Nunton
Homington
Huntingford
Milton on Stour
Cucklington
Gillingham
Elm Hill
Ham Common
Wyke
Sedgehill
Newtown
Hatch
Tisbury
Sutton Mandeville
Fovant
Compton Chamberlayne
Swallowcliffe
Ansty
Semley
Motcombe
Buckhorn Weston
Kington Magna
West Stour
Knap Corner
East Stour
Shaftesbury
Ivy Cross
Donhead St Andrew
Donhead St Mary
Milkwell
West End
Berwick St John
Ludwell
Charlton
Cann
Cann Common
Win Green
Alvediston
Ebbesbourne Wake
Fifield Bavant
Broad Chalke
Bishopstone
Stoke Farthing
Croucheston
Stratford Tony
Mount Sorrel
Bowerchalke
Woodminton
Martin Drove End
Rockbourne Down
Wick Down
Fifehead Magdalen
Stour Provost
Stour Row
Guy's Marsh
Todber
Pillwell
Marnhull
Melbury Abbas
Melbury Down
Margaret Marsh
Bedchester
East Orchard
West Orchard
Compton Abbas
Ashmore
Tollard Royal
Fontmell Magna
Manston
Sutton Waldron
Hinton St Mary
Sturminster Newton
Fiddleford
Hammoon
Iwerne Courtney or Shroton
Iwerne Minster
Child Okeford
Newton
Broad Oak
Fifehead Neville
Okeford Fitzpaine
Shillingstone
Woodcutts
Deanland
Sixpenny Handley
Woodyates
Pentridge
Martin
Tidpit
Whitsbury
Upper Street
Rockbourne
Outwick
Burgate
Sandleheath
Fordingbridge
Dean
Farnham
Stubhampton
Chettle
Tarrant Gunville
Tarrant Hinton
Cashmoor
Gussage St Michael
Monkton Up Wimborne
Wimborne St Giles
Cranborne
Cripplestyle
Edmondsham
Alderholt
Bickton
Charing Cross
Gussage All Saints
Long Crichel
Moor Crichel
Knowlton
Verwood
Woodlands
Ibsley
Ringwood Forest
Blashford
Ringwood
Kingston
Stourpaine
Pimperne
Tarrant Launceston
Tarrant Monkton
Manswood
Durweston
Ibberton
Turnworth
Woolland
Bryanston
Blandford Forum
Blandford St Mary
Tarrant Rawston
Tarrant Rushton
Witchampton
Chalbury
Chalbury Common
Horton
Hinton Martell
Gaunt's Common
Mannington
Three Legged Cross
Ashley
Ashley Heath
St Ives
St Leonards
Stoke Wake
Higher Ansty
Winterborne Houghton
Winterborne Stickland
Winterborne Clenston
Charlton Marshall
Thorncombe
Tarrant Keyneston
Tarrant Crawford
Stanbridge
Holt
Broom Hill
West Moors
Hilton
Melcombe Bingham
Whatcombe
Milton Abbas
Spetisbury
Shapwick
Clapgate
Colehill
Canford Bottom
Stapehill
Hillbutts
Trickett's Cross
Ferndown
Pamphill
Wimborne Minster
Charlton Down
Winterborne Whitechurch
Sturminster Marshall
Cheselbourne
Dewlish
Almer
Winterborne Kingston
Winterborne Zelston
Hampreston
Longham
West Parley
Parley Cross
Oakley
Canford Magna
Merley
Corfe Mullen
East End
Bearwood
Bear Cross
Kinson
Ensbury
Holdenhurst
Jumpers Green
Milborne St Andrew
Anderson
Morden
East Morden
Hill View
Broadstone
Canford Heath
Bournemouth
Moordown
Puddletown
Athelhampton
Tolpuddle
Burleston
Affpuddle
Bere Regis
Turners Puddle
Bloxworth
Lytchett Matravers
Slepe
Lytchett Minster
Waterloo
Newtown
Talbot Village
Winton
Tincleton
Briantspuddle
Lane End
Wareham Forest
Holton Heath
Upton
Hamworthy
Poole
Branksome
Westbourne
Pokesdown
Boscombe
Southbourne
Wick
Woodsford
Parkstone
Lilliput
Branksome Park
Canford Cliffs
Moreton
Bovington Camp
Trigon Hill
Sandford
Northport
Poole Harbour
Brownsea I.
Crossways
Wareham
Arne
Sandbanks
POOLE BAY
Stokeford
Wool
East Burton
Warmwell
Owermoigne
East Stoke
Stoborough
Ridge
West Holme
Stoborough Green
Middlebere Heath
Wytch Heath
Studland
Newton Heath
East Knighton
Winfrith Newburgh
Coombe Keynes
Grange Heath
Holworth
Chaldon Herring or East Chaldon
Norden Heath
East Creech
Corfe Castle
Church Knowle
Studland
The Foreland
Chaldon Down
West Lulworth
East Lulworth
Purbeck Hills
Steeple
Nine Barrow Down
Ulwell
New Swanage
Swanage Bay
Swanage
Ringstead Bay
Durdle Door
Lulworth Cove
Worbarrow Bay
Tyneham
Kimmeridge
Kimmeridge Bay
Kingston
Harman's Cross
Langton Matravers
Acton
Worth Matravers
Peveril Pt.
Durlston Head
Tilly Whim Caves
CRANBORNE CHASE AND WEST WILTSHIRE DOWNS
DORSET
ISLE OF PURBECK
VALE OF WARDOUR
SU
SZ
GUERNSEY 3:00
JERSEY 3:40
ST. MALO 5:35
CHERBOURG 2:30
(Apr-Oct)
(May-Sept)

Salisbury
Wilton
Newton
Lower Woodford
Winterbourne Earls
Firsdown
East Winterslow
Middle Winterslow
The Common
Broughton
Little Somborne
Up Somborne
West Winterslow
Pitton
Houghton
Quidhampton
Stratford sub Castle
Old Sarum
Laverstock
Ditchampton
Barford St Martin
Burcombe
Netherhampton
Bemerton
West Harnham
East Harnham
Milford
Britford
Alderbury
Farley
West Tytherley
Horsebridge
King's Somborne
Ashley
Sparsholt
Farley Mount
East Tytherley
Brook
Coombe Bissett
Stratford Tony
Odstock
Homington
Nunton
Whaddon
Bodenham
West Grimstead
East Grimstead
West Dean
East Dean
Lockerley
Pepperbox Hill
Butt's Green
Mottisfont
Mottisfont Abbey
Michelmersh
Standon
Braishfield
Hursley
Bishopstone
Stoke Farthing
Croucheston
Ebble
Charlton-All-Saints
Whiteparish
Carter's Clay
Kent's Oak
Timsbury
Pucknall
Hillier Gardens
Newtown
Awbridge
Abbotswood
Ampfield
Newton
Upper Ratley
Cupernham
Romsey
Romsey Abbey
Whitenap
Chandler's Ford
Rockbourne Down
Wick Down
Wick
Downton
Morgan's Vale
Redlynch
Newhouse
Langley Wood
Sherfield English
Landford Manor
Plaitford
East Wellow
West Wellow
North Baddesley
Chilworth
Martin Drove End
Woodfalls
Lover
Martin
Martin Down
Tidpit
Whitsbury
Breamore House & Museum
Upper Street
North Charford
Hale
Hamptworth Lodge
Landford
Canada
Broadlands
Toothill
Ridge
Lee
Pentridge
Pentridge Hill
Rockbourne
Breamore
Nomansland
Outwick
Roman Villa
Burgate
Damerham
Woodgreen
Wigley
Ower
Paultons Park
Rownhams Services
Rownhams
Nursling
Upton
Bassett
Swaythling
Sandleheath
Ashford
Alderholt Mill
Fordingbridge
Godshill
Bramshaw
Newbridge
Brook Hill
Brook
Calmore
Testwood
Coxford
Southampton
Cranborne
Alderholt
Blissford
Fritham
Cadnam
Copythorne
Winsor
Totton
Wimpson
Portswood
Shirley
Manor Garden
Cripplestyle
Edmondsham Ho
Edmondsham
Charing Cross
Bickton
Stuckton
Hyde
Hungerford
North Gorley
South Gorley
Furzey Gdns
Stoney Cross
Broomy Lodge
Minstead
Newtown
Bartley
Netley Marsh
Woodlands
Ashurst
Eling
Eling Tide Mill
Millbrook
City Art Gall
Bitterne
Northam
Itchen
Woolston
Maritime Mus
Heavy Horse Centre
Verwood
Woodlands
Ibsley
Mockbeggar
Linwood
Moyles Court
Rockford
Hampshire
New Forest National Park
Emery Down
Lyndhurst
New Forest Centre
Longdown Farm
Pooksgreen
New Forest Wildlife Park
Marchwood
Netley Abbey
Ringwood Forest
Blashford
Linford
Reptiliary
Bank
Clayhill
Dibden
Hythe
Dibden Purlieu
Buttsash
Three Legged Cross
Moors Valley
Mannington
Holt Heath
Ashley
Ashley Heath
Ringwood
Picket Post
Burley Lodge
Denny Lodge
Beaulieu Heath
Hardley
Holbury
West Moors
St Ives
St Leonards Services
Mortown
Raptor and Reptile Centre
Burley Street
Burley
Bisterne Close
New Park
Balmerlawn
Broom Hill
St Leonards
Avon Heath
Matchams
Kingston
Kingston Great Common
Brockenhurst
Palace Ho
Beaulieu
Abbey
National Motor Mus
Hill Top
Blackfield
Langley
Ferndown
Trickett's Cross
Stapehill
Hatchet Gate
East Boldre
Setley
Beaulieu Heath
Bucklers Hard
Maritime Museum
Exbury
Lepe
Knoll Gdns
West Parley
Longham
Parley Cross
Bournemouth Airport
Avon
Ripley
Thorney Hill
Bransgore
Wootton
Sway
Battramsley
Bull Hill
Boldre
Pilley
Spinners
Norleywood
East End
Portmore
Hampshire
Needs Ore Pt.
Hurn
Adventure Wonderland
Ensbury
Kinson
Bear Cross
Sopley
Neacroft
Winkton
Jumpers Green
Burton
Bashley
Beckley
Godwinscroft
Hinton
New Milton
Sammy Miller's Motorcycle Mus
Golden Hill
Hordle
Ashley
Mount Pleasant
Buckland
Lymington
Pennington
Walhampton
South
Waterford
Woodside
Bournemouth
Holdenhurst
Moordown
Newtown
Talbot Village
Branksome
Westbourne
Lilliput
Branksome Park
Canford Cliffs
Compton Acres
Boscombe
Pokesdown
Red House Mus
Christchurch
Priory Church
Wick
Southbourne
Purewell
Somerford
Highcliffe
Highcliffe Castle
Walkford
Old Milton
Barton on Sea
Everton
Downton
Lymore
Braxton
Lower Pennington
Keyhaven & Pennington Marshes
Keyhaven
Hurst Castle
Milford on Sea
Mudeford
Christchurch Bay
Hengistbury Head
Bournemouth
Oceanarium
Art Gall and Mus
Poole Bay
Sandbanks
Studland Beach and Nature Reserve
Studland Bay
The Foreland
South West Coast Path
Swanage Bay
Peveril
SU
SZ
Guernsey 3:00
Jersey 3:40
St. Malo 5:35
Cherbourg 2:30
(Apr-Oct)
(May-Sept)
Sconce Pt.
Fort Victoria
Island Planetarium
Yarmouth
Norton
Colwell Bay
Totland
Totland Bay
Norton Green
Pound Green
Freshwater
Chessell Pottery Barns
Freshwater Bay
Afton
Alum Bay
The Needles
The Needles Park
The Needles Old Battery
Freshwater Bay
Hulverstone
Brook
The Undercliff
Mottistone
Moortown
Brighstone
Limerstone
Yafford
Thorncross
Brighstone Bay
Brighstone Forest
Shalcombe
Calbourne
Calbourne Water Mill
Newbridge
Wellow
Ningwood
Thorley
Thorley Street
Shalfleet
Cranmore
Newtown
Newtown Harbour
Porchfield
Hamstead
Old Town Hall
Newtown Bay
Thorness Bay
Isle of Wight
The Solent
Atherfield Pt.
0 1 2 3 4 5 6 miles
0 1 2 3 4 5 6 7 8 9 10 km

Winchester
Kings Worthy
Martyr Worthy
Itchen Abbas
Itchen Stoke
New Alresford
Alresford
Gundleton
Bishop's Sutton
North Street
Four Marks
Kitwood
Ropley
Ropley Dean
Monkwood
Newton Valence
Selborne
Blackmoor
Whitehill
Conford
Liphook
Greatham
Longmoor Camp
East Tisted
Colemore
Littleton
Headbourne Worthy
Weeke
Winnall
Easton
Avington
Ovington
Tichborne
Cheriton
West Tisted
Hawkley
Liss Forest
West Liss
East Liss
Liss
Rake
Milland
Hill Brow
Langley
Stanmore
Oliver's Battery
Chilcomb
ST CATHERINE'S HILL
INTECH SCIENCE CENTRE & PLANETARIUM
MID-HANTS RAILWAY
GILBERT WHITE'S HOUSE & THE OATES MUSEUM
New Cheriton
Hinton Ampner
Bramdean
Privett
High Cross
Stoner Hill
Steep Marsh
Froxfield Green
Steep
Sheet
Petersfield
Borden
Rogate
Chithurst
Iping
ASHFORD HANGERS
Compton
Longwood Warren
Beauworth
Kilmeston
Brockwood
Twyford
Shawford
Otterbourne
Morestead
Lane End
Owslebury
Baybridge
Colden Common
MARWELL ZOOLOGICAL PARK
SOUTH DOWNS NATIONAL PARK
SOUTH DOWNS WAY
BEACON HILL
West Meon
Warnford
OLD WINCHESTER HILL
East End
East Meon
Langrish
Ramsdean
Stroud
Weston
ST PETER'S CHURCH
THE BEAR MUS
Rother
Dumpford
Nyewood
Trotton
Minsted
Upham
Exton
Coombe
BUTSER HILL
Nursted
Buriton
East Harting
South Harting
Elsted
Didling
Fisher's Pond
EASTLEIGH
Bishopstoke
Lower Upham
Ashton
Dean
Corhampton
Meonstoke
Brockbridge
Droxford
War Down
QUEEN ELIZABETH
Treyford
LINCH DOWN
Fair Oak
Wintershill
Newtown
Hoe
SOUTHAMPTON
Horton Heath
Durley
PALACE
Bishop's Waltham
Swanmore
Soberton
Chidden
Clanfield
Chalton
UPPARK
North Marden
ITCHEN VALLEY
SU
Hambledon
Compton
Up Marden
West Marden
East Marden
Long Common
Waltham Chase
Shirrell Heath
Catherington
Blendworth
Horndean
Finchdean
Forestside
KINGLEY VALE
West Dean
WEST DEAN GARDENS
West End
Curdridge
Shedfield
Soberton Heath
Hoe Gate
Anthill Common
Lovedean
Rowlands Castle
Stoughton
Hedge End
Botley
Newtown
Denmead
Cowplain
Thornhill
Sholing
Hamble
MANOR FARM
Burridge
Curbridge
WHITELEY VILLAGE
Wickham
Hundred Acres
North Boarhunt
FOREST OF BERE
Waterlooville
STAUNTON
STANSTED PARK
Walderton
BOW HILL
Old Netley
Lowford
Bursledon
Lower Swanwick
Swanwick
SOUTHWICK BREWHOUSE
Southwick
Leigh Park
Woodend
West Stoke
Mid Lavant
Hound
HOLLY HILL WOODLAND PARK
Park Gate
Funtley
Boarhunt
FORT NELSON
Ports Down
Purbrook
Stockheath
Westbourne
Funtington
East Ashling
Woodmancote
Summersdale
ROYAL VICTORIA
Hamble-le-Rice
Locks Heath
ABBEY
Wallington
Bedhampton
HAVANT
Warblington
West Ashling
SOUTHAMPTON WATER
Warsash
Newtown
ST ANDREWS
Titchfield
Fareham
Portchester
Wymering
Cosham
Drayton
Hermitage
Hambrook
Nutbourne
Emsworth
Southbourne
Chichester
Fawley
Ashlett
CALSHOT CASTLE
CALSHOT ACTIVITY CENTRE
Calshot
TITCHFIELD HAVEN
Peel Common
Stubbington
Fleetlands
Bridgemary
PORTCHESTER CASTLE
Portsmouth
Portsmouth Harbour
Hilsea
Langstone
FARLINGTON MARSHES
Northney
Thorney
CHICHESTER HARBOUR
Chidham
Broadbridge
Bosham
BOSHAM WALK
Fishbourne
FISHBOURNE PALACE
Apuldram
Donnington
Hunston
Hill Head
Lee-on-the-Solent
FORT BROCKHURST
Brockhurst
Hardway
North End
Langstone Harbour
Stoke
North Hayling
West Thorney
West Itchenor
1642 LIVING HISTORY VILLAGE
EXPLOSION
GUNWHARF QUAYS
HMS VICTORY
MARY ROSE
DICKENS BIRTHPLACE
Portsea
PORTSMOUTH
Fleet
HAYLING ISLAND
Chichester Harbour
Shipton Green
SUSSEX FALCONRY
Birdham
Street End
LEPE
GOSPORT
SUBMARINE
CATHEDRAL
Fratton
Milton
Eastney
FORT
West Town
ROYAL MARINES MUSEUM
South Hayling
Eastoke
EAST HAYLING LIGHT RAILWAY
West Wittering
Acre Street
Somerley
Highleigh
EARNLEY BUTTERFLIES AND GARDENS
Earnley
East Wittering
Bracklesham
Stone Pt.
Stokes Bay
Alverstoke
BLUE REEF AQUARIUM
Southsea
SOUTHSEA CASTLE
Gilkicker Pt.
SOLENT
SPITHEAD
Cowes
MARITIME MUSEUM
East Cowes
Osborne Bay
OSBORNE HOUSE
Gurnard Bay
Gurnard
Rew Street
Northwood
Whippingham
Norton
Selsey
SELSEY BILL
Isle of Wight
Parkhurst
Parkhurst Forest
Medina
Fishbourne
Wootton Bridge
Binstead
RYDE
TOLL
Nettlestone Pt.
SEAVIEW WILDLIFE ENCOUNTER
Seaview
Elmfield
Nettlestone
BRICKFIELDS
Wootton Common
Havenstreet
BUTTERFLY WORLD
Staplers
ISLE OF WIGHT STEAM RAILWAY
WALTZING WATERS
St Helens
Gunville
Hunny Hill
NEWPORT
Carisbrooke
ROBIN HILL ADVENTURE PARK
Bembridge
Foreland
Lane End
WINDMILL
Clatterford
ROMAN VILLA
Shide
Downend
Brading
Steyne Cross
CARISBROOKE CASTLE
Bowcombe
ARRETON MANOR
Arreton
Alverstone
MORTON MANOR
Hillway
Whitecliff Bay
Blackwater
Merstone
DINOSAUR ISLE
Yaverland
Culver Cliff
ISLE OF WIGHT ZOO
Gatcombe
Rookley
Horringford
Newchurch
Sandown
Chillerton
AMAZON WORLD
Winford
Branstone
Lake
Shorwell
NATURAL HISTORY CENTRE
Apse Heath
SZ
Sandown Bay
Godshill
Sandford
Kingston
MODEL VILLAGE
Whiteley Bank
Shanklin
SHANKLIN CHINE
Little Atherfield
APPULDURCOMBE HOUSE
Roud
Chale Green
Wroxall
Luccombe Village
Luccombe Chine
Pyle
Stenbury Down
Dunnose
Chale Bay
Chale
HERITAGE MUSEUM
Bonchurch
Blackgang Chine
ST CATHERINE'S ORATORY
Whitwell
Ventnor
Blackgang
Niton
BOTANIC GARDEN & VISITOR CENTRE
St Lawrence
The Undercliff
BLACKGANG CHINE
CAEN 5:30
LE HAVRE 3:15
ST. MALO 9:00
BILBAO 24:00
SANTANDER 24:00 (Mar-Nov)
CAEN 3:45 (April-Sept)
CHERBOURG 3:00 (April-Nov)
GUERNSEY 7:30
JERSEY 8:00
0:23
0:55
0:10
0:40
0:22
M27
M3
M275
A3(M)
A3
A27
A31
A32
A272
A334
A3054
A3020
A3021
A3055
A3056
B3047
B3035
B3037
B3354
B3385
B3330
B3395
B2146
B2177
B2149
B2148
B2145
B2179
B2070
26
16
5
6
7
8
9
A
B
C
D
E
F
G

SOUTH DOWNS NATIONAL PARK
West Sussex
SU
SZ
Haslemere
Liphook
Petersfield
Midhurst
Petworth
Billingshurst
Pulborough
Storrington
Arundel
Chichester
Bognor Regis
Littlehampton
Rustington
Angmering
Ferring
Middleton-on-Sea
East Wittering
Selsey
SELSEY BILL
Bosham
Southbourne
CHICHESTER HARBOUR
Emsworth
Liss
Rogate
Fernhurst
Northchapel
Kirdford
Wisborough Green
Fittleworth
Amberley
Washington
Findon
Goring-by-Sea
West Worthing
Singleton
West Dean
Charlton
Goodwood
Halnaker
Boxgrove
Fontwell
Slindon
Walberton
Barnham
Yapton
Felpham
Pagham
Sidlesham
Earnley
West Wittering
Bracklesham
Church Norton
Norton
Alderney
3½ miles to 1 inch
Braye
St Anne
Quesnard Pt.
Longis Bay
Clonque Bay
Telegraph Bay
Brehou
ALDERNEY
Guernsey
3½ miles to 1 inch
GUERNSEY
St Peter Port
St Sampson
L'Islet
Le Villocq
Mont Saint
Carmel
Fort George
Mouilpied
La Planque
Le Planel
Pointe de la Moye
Icart Pt.
St Martin's Pt.
Herm
Jethou
Lihou I.
Rocquaine Bay
Pleinmont Pt.
Cobo Bay
Vazon Bay
Grand Havre
L'Ancresse Bay
Le Plomb
La Fontenelle
Belle Greve Bay
Moulin Huet Bay
POOLE 3:00 (Apr-Oct)
WEYMOUTH 2:30
PORTSMOUTH 7:30
SARK 0:45
ST. HELIER 2:00
ST. HELIER 1:00
ST. MALO 3:00
DIELETTE 1:00
CARTERET 1:30
ALDERNEY 1:00
DIELETTE 0:45
ST. PETER PORT 1:00
0 1 2 3 4 5 6 miles
0 1 2 3 4 5 6 7 8 9 10 km

Horsham
St Leonard's Forest
Roffey
Colgate
Pease Pottage
Tilgate Forest Row
Balcombe
Handcross
Nymans Garden
Staplefield
Slaugham
Mannings Heath
Monk's Gate
Ashfold Crossways
Southwater
Nuthurst
Copsale
Lower Beeding
Leonardslee Lakes & Gardens
Warninglid
Crabtree
Maplehurst
Cowfold
West Grinstead
Cuckfield
Ansty
Bolney
Slough Green
Brook Street
Borde Hill Garden
Whitemans Green
Lindfield
HAYWARDS HEATH
Scayne's Hill
Balcombe Lane
Selsfield Common
West Hoathly
Priest House
Wakehurst Place
Sharpthorne
Highbrook
Ardingly
Horsted Keynes
Chelwood Gate
Chelwood Common
Danehill
Coleman's Hatch
Wych Cross
Ashdown Forest
Nutley
Duddleswell
Crowborough
Poundfield
Jarvis Brook
Fairwarp
High Hurstwood
Butcher's Cross
Cackle Street
Sheffield Green
Sheffield Park
Splayne's Green
Fletching
Bluebell Railway
Maresfield
Pound Green
Buxted
Ringles Cross
Uckfield
Framfield
Blackboys
Newick
Grisling Common
North Chailey
Chailey
Wivelsfield Green
Wivelsfield
BURGESS HILL
Hickstead
Kent Street
Wineham
Twineham
Sayers Common
Partridge Green
Dial Post
West End
Henfield
Blackstone
Albourne
Washbrooks Farm Centre
Woodmancote
Hurstpierpoint
Hurst Wickham
Hassocks
Keymer
Ditchling
Ditchling Museum
Ditchling Common
Plumpton Green
Plumpton
South Street
East Chiltington
Chiltington
Streat
Westmeston
Spithurst
Isfield
Lavender Line Steam Railway
Barcombe Cross
Barcombe
Cooksbridge
Offham
Mt. Harry
Hamsey
Little Horsted
Ridgewood
Rose Hill
Halland
East Hoathly
Shortgate
Broyle Side
Laughton
Whitesmith
Chiddingly
Golden Cross
Ringmer
Glyndebourne
Mark Cross
Lower Dicker
Ripe
Chalvington
Arlington
Selmeston
Ashurst
Steyning
Bramber
Upper Beeding
St Mary's House
Botolphs
Coombes
Small Dole
Fulking
Edburton
Poynings
Saddlescombe
Truleigh Hill
Devil's Dyke
Clayton
Pyecombe
Ditchling Beacon
Stanmer Park
Stanmer
Patcham
Coldean
Falmer
Kingston near Lewes
Lewes
South Malling
Cliffe Hill
Anne of Cleves Ho
Wallands Park
Glynde
Glynde Place
Lewes Downs (Mount Caburn)
Beddingham
Firle Place
West Firle
Charleston Farmhouse
Alciston
Firle Beacon
Berwick
Drusillas Park
Wilmington
The Long Man of Wilmington
Alfriston
Clergy House
Lullington Heath
Litlington
Charleston Manor
Westdean
Seven Sisters
Friston
Birling Gap
Brighton and Hove
Mile Oak
Westdene
Withdean
Portslade
West Blatchington
Preston Manor
Preston
Moulsecoomb
Bevendean
Woodingdean
Castle Hill
Iford
Rodmell
Monks Ho
Southease
Tarring Neville
South Heighton
Denton
Norton
Bishopstone
Paradise Park
Newhaven
Newhaven Fort
Seaford
East Blatchington
Piddinghoe
Telscombe
Saltdean
Telscombe Cliffs
Peacehaven
Ovingdean
Rottingdean
Kemp Town
Brighton Marina
Volk's Electric Railway
Royal Pavilion
Brighton Sea Life
HOVE
BRIGHTON
Portslade-by-Sea
Southwick
Kingston by Sea
SHOREHAM-BY-SEA
Shoreham
Lancing
South Lancing
North Lancing
Sompting
Broadwater
East Worthing
Worthing
Marlipins Museum
Dieppe 4:00
SOUTH DOWNS
South Downs Way
TQ
TV
Jersey
3½ miles to 1 inch
Plémont Pt.
Grosnez Pt.
Sorel Pt.
Ronez Pt.
St John's Bay
Belle Hougue Pt.
North Coast Visitor Centre
St John's
Bouley Bay
Tour de Rozel
Rozel
St Mary's
Trinity
La Coupe Pt.
JERSEY
St Ouens
Carrefour Selous
Durrell Wildlife Conservation Trust (Zoo)
Kempt Tower Visitor Centre
St Ouen's Bay
St Peter's
St Martin's
St Catherine's Bay
La Hougue Bie
Mont Orgueil Castle
Five Oaks
Gorey
Red Houses
Corbière Pt.
St Brelade
St Aubin
St Helier
Jersey Museum
Grouville
Royal Bay of Grouville
St Brelades Bay
St Aubin's Bay
St Clements
Elizabeth Castle
Fort Regent Leisure Centre
Noirmont Pt.
Le Nez Pt.
St Clements Bay
La Rocque Pt.
Carteret 1:00
St. Peter Port 1:10 (Apr-Oct)
Sark 1:00 (Apr-Oct)
St. Peter Port 1:00
Weymouth 3:40
Poole 3:00 (Apr-Oct)
St. Peter Port 2:00
Portsmouth 8:00
St. Malo 1:15
Granville 1:00
St. Peter Port 1:00
Carteret 2:00
(Apr-Oct)

ROYAL TUNBRIDGE WELLS
Southborough
Pembury
Crowborough
Mayfield
Wadhurst
Hawkhurst
Cranbrook
Staplehurst
Headcorn
Uckfield
Heathfield
Hailsham
Polegate
Willingdon
Eastbourne
Seaford
Newhaven
Battle
Hastings
St Leonards
BEXHILL
Hollington
Robertsbridge
Burwash
Etchingham
Bodiam
Pevensey
Pevensey Bay
Pevensey Levels
Hurst Green
Ticehurst
Frant
Rotherfield
Buxted
Maresfield
Nutley
Hartfield
Groombridge
Forest Row
Herstmonceux
Ninfield
Sedlescombe
Westfield
Baldslow
Ore
Alfriston
East Dean
Friston
Birling Gap
BEACHY HEAD
ASHDOWN FOREST
Bedgebury Forest
Bewl Water
H I G H   W E A L D
E a s t   S u s s e x
TQ
TV
A21
A22
A26
A27
A259
A265
A267
A271
A272
DIEPPE 4:00
0 1 2 3 4 5 6 miles
0 1 2 3 4 5 6 7 8 9 10 km

Ashford
Willesborough
Sevington
Kingsnorth
Great Chart
Godinton House
Hinxhill
Willesborough Lees
Mersham
Brabourne
Brabourne Lees
Lymbridge Green
Stowting
Smeeth
Sellindge
Lees
Postling
Stanford
Etchinghill
Lyminge
Rhodes Minnis
Ottinge
Elham
Swingfield Minnis
Densole
Hawkinge
Paddlesworth
Kent Battle of Britain Museum
Butterfly Centre
Drellingore
West Hougham
Capel le Ferne
Channel Tunnel
Beachborough
Newington
Folkestone
Cheriton
Elham Valley Rly Mus
Pedlinge
Saltwood
Sandgate
Rotunda
Cliff Lift
Hythe
Palmarsh
Brockhill
Lympne
Port Lympne Wild Animal Park and Gardens
Court-at-Street
Newingreen
Aldington
Clap Hill
Aldington Frith
Bonnington
Bilsington
Cheeseman's Green
Bromley Green
Ham Street Woods
Orlestone
Ruckinge
Hamstreet
Military Canal
Royal
E. Stour
West Hythe
Burmarsh
Newchurch
Romney, Hythe and Dymchurch Railway
Dymchurch
Martello Tower
Romney Marsh
St Mary in the Marsh
Romney Warren
St Mary's Bay
Ivychurch
TR
Littlestone on Sea
Romney Sands
New Romney
Old Romney
Greatstone on Sea
Lydd (London Ashford)
Lydd on Sea
Lydd
Denge Marsh
Lydd International Raceway
Dungeness
Denge Beach
Dungeness Power Station & Information Centre
The Old Lighthouse
DUNGENESS
Brookland
Brenzett
Aeronautical Museum
Snargate
Snave
Walland Marsh
Warehorne
Kenardington
Appledore Heath
Appledore
Horne's Place Chapel
Stone
South of England Rare Breeds Cen
Shirkoak
Henghurst
Woodchurch
Shadoxhurst
Stubbs Cross
Bethersden
Tandon
High Halden
Biddenden
Biddenden Vineyard
Standen
Smarden
Smarden Bell
Headcorn
Haffenden Quarter
Wissenden
Maltman's Hill
St Michael's
Kent & East Sussex Railway
Tenterden
Colonel Stephens Railway Museum
Leigh Green
Parkgate
Brook Street
Reading Street
Small Hythe
Smallhythe Place
Rolvenden Layne
Isle of Oxney
Peening Quarter
Wittersham
Ham Green
The Stocks
Rother
Rother Levels
Farm World
Four Oaks
Beckley
Peasmarsh
Iden
Houghton Green
Rye Foreign
Playden
East Guldeford
Rye
Rye Heritage Centre
Tillingham
Udimore
Rye Harbour
Camber Castle
Camber
Rye Bay
Brede
Winchelsea
Winchelsea Court Hall Museum
Winchelsea Beach
Icklesham
Pett
Guestling Green
Cliff End
Fairlight
Fairlight Cove
Hastings
Water World
ENGLISH CHANNEL
M20
A20
A28
A259
A2070
A262
A261
A268
B2067
B2080
B2082
B2089
B2075
B2068
North Downs Way
Stop 24 Services
Folkestone

1
2
3
4
5
A
B
C
D
E
F
North West Point
North East Point
LUNDY MARINE NATURE RESERVE
LUNDY
142
ILFRACOMBE 2:00
BIDEFORD 2:00
(Mar-Oct)
South West Point
Surf Point
SS
NORTH DEVON
LUNDY 2:00
(Mar-Oct)
OLD CORN MILL
Rillage Pt.
Combe Martin Bay
Trentishoe
Ilfracombe
ILFRACOMBE MUSEUM
Hele
WATERMOUTH CASTLE
Girt Down
349
Heale
Bull Pt.
Rockham Bay
Lee
206
Berrynarbor
Combe Martin
Whitestone
Slade
Sterridge
WILDLIFE & DINOSAUR PARK
Morte Point
Mortehoe
A361
B3230
A399
269
A3123
Woolacombe
Trimstone
Berry Down Cross
Kentisbury
MORTE BAY
B3343
Cheglinch
Berry Down
B3229
210
Dean
Patchole
Kentisbury Ford
Woolacombe Sand
Bittadon
SOUTH WEST COAST PATH
West Down
East Down
Pickwell
North Buckland
Baggy Pt.
Putsborough
Churchill
Arlington
ARLINGTON COURT
Georgeham
Nethercott
Croyde Bay
Halsinger
Milltown
Croyde
Darracott
Muddiford
Loxhore
158
Lobb
B3231
Knowle
A39
Marwood
Guineaford
Shirwell
Bratton Fleming
Saunton
Pippacott
Kingsheanton
198
Braunton
MARWOOD HILL GARDENS
BROOMHILL
Shirwell Cross
Yeo
Stoke Rivers
ELLIOT GALLERY
Heanton Punchardon
Prixford
Saunton Sands
Wrafton
Ashford
Burridge
TOLL
Braunton Burrows
A361
Chivenor
Barnstaple
Goodleigh
Taw
Pilton
Gunn
LUNDY 2:00
(Mar-Oct)
MUSEUM OF BARNSTAPLE & NORTH DEVON
Fremington
Westacott
Yelland
B3233
Bickington
P&R
Bickleton
A39
Newport
Landkey
Bishops Tawton
NORTH DEVON MARITIME MUSEUM
NORTHAM BURROWS
BIDEFORD BAY
Instow
Swimbridge Newland
NORTH DEVON FARM PARK
Appledore
Swimbridge
Westward Ho!
Torridge
A386
TAPELEY PARK GDNS
Northam
Westleigh
Orchard Hill
Eastleigh
Horwood
Newton Tracey
A377
East Stowford
THE BIG SHEEP
Bideford
Cobbaton
Herner
Abbotsham
BURTON ART GALL & MUS
Ensis
COBBATON COMBAT COLL
Hiscott
Chapelton
Woodtown
Handy
East-the-Water
Chittlehampton
Titchberry
CLOVELLY VILLAGE
0 1 2 3 4 5 6 miles
0 1 2 3 4 5 6 7 8 9 10 km
9

Pyle
(Y Pîl)
Kenfig
Kenfig Hill
North Cornelly
South Cornelly
Kenfig Burrows
KENFIG POOL AND DUNES
Cefn Cribbwr
Cefn Cross
Aberkenfig
Tondu
Sarn
SARN PARK SERVICES
Bryncethin
Pencoed
Llanilid
Coity
COITY CASTLE
Bridgend
(Pen-y-bont ar Ogwr)
Laleston
Coychurch
Treoes
Corntown
Ewenny
St Mary Hill
Llangan
Llansannor
Craig Penllyn
Penllyn
Vale of Glamorgan (Bro Morgannwg)
Ystradowen
Maendy
Aberthin
Welsh St Donats
Cowbridge
(Y Bont-Faen)
Llanblethian
St Hilary
Llandough
Llysworney
Llandow
Pentre Meyrick
Colwinston
Penuchadre
Wick
Broughton
Llanmihangel
St Mary Church
OLD BEAUPRE CASTLE
Sigingstone
Flemingston
Llanmaes
Eglwys-Brewis
Llanbethery
Llantwit Major
(Llanilltud Fawr)
Boverton
St Athan
East Aberthaw
Rhoose
(Y Rhws)
Monknash
Marcross
St Donat's
Nash Pt.
Trwyn yr As
Breaksea Pt.
Trwyn Breaksea
Porthcawl
ROYAL PORTHCAWL
Nottage
Newton
Hutchwns
Tythegston
Merthyr Mawr
OGMORE CASTLE
MERTHYR MAWR WARREN
CONEY BEACH
Ogmore
Ogmore-by-Sea
St Brides Major
Southerndown
GLENMORGAN HERITAGE COAST CENTRE
Tusker Rock
MÔR HAFREN
BRISTOL CHANNEL
SS
Foreland Pt.
Highveer Pt.
Woody Bay
Lynmouth Bay
Lynmouth
Lynton
CLIFF RAILWAY
Countisbury
WATERSMEET HOUSE
Martinhoe
Barbrook
East Ilkerton
Cheriton
Furzehill
Shallowford
Brendon
Malmsmead
Oare
CULBONE HILL
Brendon Common
Hurlstone Pt.
Porlock Bay
Porlock Weir
Bossington
EXMOOR FALCONRY
SOUTH WEST COAST PATH
SELWORTHY BEACON
Allerford
Selworthy
Porlock
West Luccombe
Luccombe
HAWKCOMBE WOODS
Holnicote Estate
DUNKERY BEACON
THE DUNKERY & HORNER WOOD
Minehead
WEST SOMERSET RAILWAY
BUTLINS
Alcombe
Woodcombe
Periton
Marsh Street
Dunster
DUNSTER CASTLE
DUNKERY VINEYARD
Wootton Courtenay
Cowbridge
Timberscombe
Carhampton
Blue Anchor Bay
Blue Anchor
Old Cleeve
Withycombe
Bilbrook
CLEEVE ABBEY
Rodhuish
BRENDON FOREST
CROYDON HILL
EXMOOR FOREST
EXMOOR NATIONAL PARK
LYNTON AND BARNSTAPLE RLY
Martinhoe Cross
Parracombe
Blackmoor Gate
Challacombe Common
Challacombe
Pinkworthy Pond
PINKERY
Exe Plain
EXMOOR ZOO
Shoulsbarrow Common
Knightacott
Leworthy
Simonsbath
Edgcott
Exford
Luckwell Bridge
Cutcombe
Wheddon Cross
LYPE HILL
Luxborough
Roadwater
Kingsbridge
Treborough
BRENDON HILLS
Benton
Lydcott
HORSEN HILL
Withypool Common
Withypool
WINSFORD HILL
Winsford
Exton
Brayford
High Bray
North Radworthy
North Heasley
Heasley Mill
South Radworthy
Charles
West Buckland
East Buckland
Liscombe
TARR STEPS
Hawkridge
Bridgetown
Withiel Florey
Brompton Regis
Clatworthy Res.
Wimbleball Lake
Molland Common
Twitchen
Dane's Brook
Anstey Common
Molland
West Anstey
East Anstey
Dulverton
Battleton
Nightcott
Yeo Mill
Filleigh
QUINCE HONEY FARM
South Molton
HADDON HILL
Bury
Skilgate
Upton
Huish Champflower
Chipstable
Waterrow

Pencoed
Llantrisant
Talbot Green
Pontyclun
Cardiff
(Caerdydd)
CARDIFF
(CAERDYDD)
Whitchurch
Llanishen
Rumney
Lisvane
Castleton
Marshfield
St Brides Wentlooge
Peterstone Wentlooge
Newton
Llandaff
Canton
Cathays
Roath
Ely
Caerau
St Fagans
Radyr
Tongwynlais
Taff's Well
Creigiau
Pentyrch
Peterston super-Ely
St Brides super Ely
St George's
Michaelston-super-Ely
Butetown
Grangetown
Leckwith
Michaelston-le-Pit
Wenvoe
Llandough
Cogan
PENARTH
Dinas Powys
St Andrews Major
Cadoxton
Sully
Lower Penarth
Lavernock Pt.
Trwyn Larnog
Sully Island
Ynys Sili
Flat Holm
Steep Holm
BARRY
(Y BARRI)
Barry Island
Colcot
Merthyr Dyfan
Porthkerry
Rhoose
(Y Rhws)
East Aberthaw
Gileston
Breaksea Pt.
Trwyn Breaksea
Vale of Glamorgan
(Bro Morgannwg)
Cowbridge
(Y Bont-Faen)
Llanblethian
Llantwit Major
(Llanilltud Fawr)
Boverton
St Athan
Llanbethery
Penmark
Llancarfan
Moulton
Flemingston
Walterston
Bonvilston
St Nicholas
Wallston
St Lythans
St Hilary
Llantrithyd
Welsh St Donats
Pendoylan
Ystradowen
Aberthin
Maendy
Penllyn
Llansannor
Llangan
Craig Penllyn
St Mary Hill
Llandow
Llysworney
Meyric
Pentre
Sigingstone
Llanmaes
Eglwys-Brewis
St Mary Church
Llanmihangel
Llanharan
Llanharry
Brynsadler
Brynna
Bryncae
Dolau
Llanilid
Cross Inn
Groes-faen
Capel Llanilltern
Talygarn
Efail Isaf
Thornhill
Llanedeyrn
Cyncoed
Heath
Birchgrove
Rhiwbina
ABER HAFREN
MOUTH OF THE SEVERN
MÔR HAFREN
BRISTOL CHANNEL
ST
BRIDGWATER BAY
Sand Pt.
Sand Bay
Kewstoke
Milton
Weston-super-Mare
Weston Bay
Brean Down
Uphill
Hutton
Bleadon
Brean
BERROW FLATS
Lympsham
Eastertown
Gore Sands
Berrow
Brent Knoll
East Brent
Burnham-on-Sea
Edithmead
Highbridge
Watchfield
STERT FLATS
Stolford
Steart
Huntspill
Bason Bridge
East Huntspill
Stretcholt
Pawlett
Woolavington
Puriton
Dunball
Bawdrip
Combwich
Otterhampton
Stockland Bristol
Stogursey
Shurton
Burton
Lilstock
Kilton
Stringston
Kilve
Holford
Nether Stowey
Fiddington
Rodway
Cannington
Chilton Trinity
Charlynch
Wembdon
Bridgwater
Chedzoy
Spaxton
Four Forks
Durleigh
Enmore
Goathurst
North Petherton
Huntworth
Lower Aisholt
Courtway
Broomfield
Cothelstone
Northmoor Green or Moorland
North Newton
Thurloxton
Hedging
Lyng
West Lyng
Durston
Creech Heathfield
Creech
North End
Meare Green
Knapp
Kingston St Mary
West Monkton
Monkton Heathfield
Cheddon Fitzpaine
Bathpool
Staplegrove
Nailsbourne
Pickney
Fulford
Cushuish
Bishops Lydeard
East Combe
Combe Florey
Ash Priors
Tarr
Tolland
Lydeard St Lawrence
Willett
West Bagborough
Flaxpool
Crowcombe
QUANTOCK FOREST
QUANTOCK HILLS
Over Stowey
Somerset
Bicknoller
Sampford Brett
Williton
Staple
West Quantoxhead
East Quantoxhead
Watchet
Washford
Old Cleeve
Blue Anchor
Blue Anchor Bay
Carhampton
Dunster
Minehead
Alcombe
Woodcombe
Marsh Street
Timberscombe
Withycombe
Bilbrook
Rodhuish
Roadwater
Yard
Vellow
Stogumber
Monksilver
Lower Vexford
Elworthy
Luxborough
Kingsbridge
Treborough
BRENDON HILLS
BRENDON FOREST
LYPE HILL
Withiel Florey
Clatworthy Res.
Clatworthy
Brompton Regis
Brompton Ralph
Wimbleball Lake
Upton
Champflower
Langley Marsh
Wiveliscombe
Fitzhead
Halse
VALE OF TAUNTON DEANE
Preston Bowyer
Milverton
Hillcommon
Heathfield
Norton
Waterrow
Bury
0 1 2 3 4 5 6 miles
0 1 2 3 4 5 6 7 8 9 10 km

Avonmouth
Portishead
Portbury
Clevedon
North Somerset
Nailsea
Yatton
Congresbury
Wrington
Bristol
BRISTOL
FILTON
Patchway
MANGOTSFIELD
Kingswood
Hanham
KEYNSHAM
Bath
Bath and N.E. Somerset
Chew Valley Lake
Blagdon Lake
Cheddar
Axbridge
Wedmore
Wells
Shepton Mallet
Glastonbury
Street
Somerton
Radstock
Midsomer Norton
Paulton
Peasedown St John
Chipping Sodbury
Evercreech
Bruton
Castle Cary
Wincanton
Langport
Mendip Hills
Polden Hills
King's Sedge Moor
Battery Pt.
Redcliff Bay
Chilcompton
Chewton Mendip
Pensford
Timsbury
Frome
Westhay
Meare
Butleigh
Charlton Mackerell
Kingsdon
Keinton Mandeville
Babcary
Sparkford
North Cadbury
Middlezoy
Othery
High Ham
Burrowbridge
Stoke St Gregory
Curry Rivel
Huish Episcopi

MANGOTSFIELD
Kingswood
Hanham
KEYNSHAM
Yate
Chipping Sodbury
Bath
Corsham
Chippenham
Calne
Melksham
Devizes
Bradford-on-Avon
Trowbridge
Westbury
Frome
Warminster
Radstock
Midsomer Norton
Paulton
Peasedown St John
Holt
Mere
Bruton
Castle Cary
Gillingham
Evercreech
Wilt
SALIS
PLA
CRANBORNE CHASE
VALE OF WAR
COTSWOLD
Summer Down
West Lavington Down
Littleton Down
Keysley Down
Great Ridge
Bruton Forest
Kennet & Avon Canal
Avon
M4
A4
A36
A46
A350
A361
A303
A420
A3102
LEIGH DELAMERE SERVICES
WARMINSTER SERVICES
CASTLE COMBE
DYRHAM PARK
SHELDON MANOR
LACKHAM
BOWOOD HOUSE
LACOCK ABBEY
FOX-TALBOT MUS
CORSHAM COURT
GREAT CHALFIELD MANOR
THE COURTS
AMERICAN MUS
ROMAN BATHS
PRIOR PARK
NO 1 ROYAL CRESCENT
AVON VALLEY RAILWAY
GRENVILLE'S MON
BRATTON CAMP & WHITE HORSE
WESTWOOD MANOR
TITHE BARN
BARTON FARM
PETO
BROKERSWOOD
NUNNEY CASTLE
LONGLEAT
WARMINSTER DEWEY MUSEUM
EAST SOMERSET RAILWAY
RADSTOCK MUSEUM
PRISTON MILL
LONG BARROW
STOURHEAD
STOURTON HOUSE
ALFRED'S TOWER
BUSH FARM BISON CENTRE
HADSPEN GARDEN
WINCANTON
OLD WARDOUR CASTLE
FARMER GILES FARMSTEAD
BROADLEAS GARDENS
WYLYE DOWN
PRESCOMBE DOWN
PARSONAGE DOWN
0 1 2 3 4 5 6 miles
0 1 2 3 4 5 6 7 8 9 10 km

Swindon
Royal Wootton Bassett
The Marsh
North Wroughton
Wroughton
Coate
Coate Water
Wanborough
Hinton Parva
Idstone
Bishopstone
Liddington
Ashdown House
Kingston Warren
Lambourn Downs
Bassett
Upper Lambourn
Lambourn
Fawley
South Fawley
Farnborough
Lilley
Brightwalton
Catmore
Elcombe
Chiseldon
Badbury
Broadtown Lane
Broad Town
Bushton
Clyffe Pypard
Broad Hinton
Uffcott
Barbury Castle
Upper Upham
Baydon
Eastbury
East Garston
Chaddleworth
Leckhampstead Thicket
Leckhampstead
Clevancy
Winterbourne Bassett
Marlborough Downs
Hackpen Hill
Woodsend
Aldbourne
Membury Services
Woodlands St Mary
Great Shefford
Shefford Woodlands
Weston
Welford
Berwick Bassett
Southend
Ogbourne St George
Ogbourne St Andrew
Preston
Whittonditch
Winterbourne Monkton
Windmill Hill
Yatesbury
Rockley
The Ridgeway
Fyfield Down
Ogbourne Maizey
Ramsbury
Hungerford Newtown
Wickham
Winterbourne
Westbrook
Boxford
Snelsmore Common
Avebury Manor
Avebury
Stone Circle
W Kennett Avenue
Silbury Hill
Mildenhall
Axford
Kennet
Chilton Foliat
Hungerford
Halfway
Stockcross
Bagnor
Donnington
Beckhampton
West Kennett
Fyfield
Marlborough
Manton
Lockeridge
West Overton
East Kennett
Long Barrow
The Sanctuary
Savernake Forest
Cadley
Froxfield
Avington
Kintbury
Enborne
Newbury
Speen
Tan Hill
Milk Hill
Pewsey Downs
Clench Common
Chisbury
Chisbury Chapel
Little Bedwyn
Laylands Green
Hamstead Marshall
Bagshot
Inkpen
Upper Green
Horton
Allington
Stanton St Bernard
West Stowell
Huish
Oare
Wootton Rivers
Durley
Great Bedwyn
Shalbourne
Ham
West Woodhay
Ball Hill
North End
Woolton Hill
Broad Laying
All Cannings
Alton Priors
Honey Street
New Mill
Crofton
Crofton Beam Engines
Stibb Green
Eastcourt
Burbage
Wilton
Wilton Windmill
Walbury Hill
Combe
East Woodhay
East End
Rivar
Buttermere
Highclere
Wilcot
Woodborough
Bottlesford
Pewsey
Easton Royal
Milton Lilbourne
West Grafton
East Grafton
Marten
Beechingstoke
Patney
Wedhampton
Chirton
Marden
Henge
Southcott
Manningford Bruce
Wexcombe
Oxenwood
Linkenholt
Faccombe
Highclere Castle
North Newnton
Wilsford
Hilcott
Manningford Bohune
Pewsey Down
Tidcombe
Fosbury
Vernham Street
Netherton
Ashmansworth
Charlton
Rushall
Upavon
Brunton
Aughton
Collingbourne Kingston
Haydown Hill
Vernham Dean
Crux Easton
Woodcott
Upton
Upper Chute
Chute Standen
Lower Everleigh
Everleigh
Sunton
Cadley
Collingbourne Ducis
Ibthorpe
Dunley
Binley
Hurstbourne Tarrant
West Chisenbury
East Chisenbury
Compton
Lower Chute
Collingbourne Forest
Tangley
Black Heath
Compton Down
Enford
Fifield
Coombe
Haxton Down
Ludgershall
Wildhern
Doles Wood
Stoke
St Mary Bourne
West Down
Enford Down
Fittleton
Netheravon
Dovecote
Tidworth
North Tidworth
South Tidworth
Hatherden
Clanville
Enham Alamein
Little London
Smannell
Whitchurch
Orcheston Down
Figheldean
Ablington
Appleshaw
Penton Mewsey
Weyhill
Picket Piece
Finkley Down Farm Park
Hurstbourne Priors
Knighton Down
Kimpton
Fyfield
Thruxton
The Hawk Conservancy Trust
Weyhill Services
Charlton
Andover
Andover Down
Orcheston
Milston
Shipton Bellinger
Elston
Shrewton
Larkhill
Durrington
Bulford Camp
Beacon Hill
Quarley
Amport
Monxton
Abbotts Ann
Anna Valley
Upper Clatford
Harewood Forest
Middleton
Longparish
Forton
Tidbury Ring
Stonehenge
Woodhenge
Countess
Bulford
Cholderton Rare Breeds
Cholderton
Grateley
Goodworth Clatford
Wherwell
Bullington
Barton Stacey
Newton Stacey
Winterbourne Stoke
West Amesbury
Amesbury
Avon
Palestine
Berwick St James
Wilsford
Newton Tony
Chilbolton
Sutton Scotney Services
Lake
Great Durnford
Boscombe
Allington
Fullerton
Museum of Army Flying
Stapleford
Upper Woodford
Bourne
Over Wallop
Middle Wallop
Nether Wallop
Longstock
Leckford
Little Wishford
Middle Woodford
Idmiston
Porton
Gomeldon
Great Wishford
Stoford
South Newton
Lower Woodford
Winterbourne Dauntsey
Winterbourne Gunner
Lopcombe Corner
Stockbridge
Crawley
Worthy Down
Grovely Wood
Chilhampton
Winterbourne Earls
East Winterslow
Firsdown
Little Somborne
Up Somborne
Littleton
Barford St Martin
Ditchampton
Stratford sub Castle
Old Sarum
New Sarum
Middle Winterslow
The Common
Whiteshoot Hill
Broughton
Houghton
All Saints Church
Flowerdown Barrows
Wilton
Quidhampton
Laverstock
West Winterslow
Pitton
King's Somborne
Ashley
Sparsholt
Burcombe
Wilton House
Bemerton
Salisbury
Horsebridge
Farley Mount
Weeke
Netherhampton
West Harnham
East Harnham
Milford
Mompesson House
Farley
West Tytherley
East Tytherley
Brook
Salisbury Racecourse
Coombe Bissett
Britford
Alderbury
East Grimstead
West Dean
Lockerley
Mottisfont Abbey
Stanmore
Stratford Tony
Odstock
Whaddon
West Grimstead
East Dean
Butt's Green
Mottisfont
Michelmersh
Standon
Ebble
Bishopstone
Homington
Nunton
Bodenham
Pepperbox Hill
Braishfield
Oliver's Battery
SU
Swindon
North
Wessex
Downs
Vale of Pewsey
Shire
Bury
Wiltshire
M4
A4
A34
A36
A303
A338
A346
A345
A342
A354
A360
A361
A419
A3026
A3057
A3093
A343
A30
A272
B4192
B4000
B4001
B4005
B3087
B3086
B3083
B3084
B3048
B3400
B3420
B3049
37
38
26
14
15
16

Berkshire
West
Hampshire
Reading
Newbury
Basingstoke
Andover
Winchester
Hungerford
Thatcham
Tilehurst
Caversham
Whitley
Goring
Streatley
Moulsford
South Stoke
Checkendon
Stoke Row
Highmoor Cross
Satwell
Shepherd's Green
Rotherfield Greys
Rotherfield Peppard
Sonning Common
Kidmore End
Cane End
Binfield Heath
Dunsden Green
Tokers Green
Emmer Green
Mapledurham
Whitchurch Hill
Whitchurch
Pangbourne
Purley
Tidmarsh
Sulham
Calcot Row
Theale
Englefield
Tutts Clump
North Street
Bradfield
Southend
Chapel Row
Beenham
Woolhampton
Midgham
Aldermaston Wharf
Aldermaston
Padworth
Ufton Nervet
Sheffield Bottom
Sulhamstead
Burghfield
Burghfield Hill
Burghfield Common
Grazeley
Shinfield
Threemile Cross
Arborfield
Spencers Wood
Farley Hill
Swallowfield
Wokefield Park
Mortimer
Stratfield Mortimer
Mortimer West End
Beech Hill
Riseley
Stratfield Saye
Silchester
Tadley
Pamber Heath
Pamber Green
Pamber End
Little London
Baughurst
Heath End
Ashford Hill
Headley
Plastow Green
Kingsclere
Wolverton
Wolverton Common
West Heath
Ramsdell
Charter Alley
Monk Sherborne
Sherborne St John
Bramley
Sherfield on Loddon
Hartley Wespall
Turgis Green
Stratfield Turgis
Hazeley
Mattingley
Hound Green
Heckfield
Bramshill
Lyde Green
West Green
Church End
Rotherwick
Newnham
Hook
Chineham
Popley
Daneshill
Old Basing
North Warnborough
Greywell
Odiham
Up Nately
Hatch
Mapledurwell
Oakridge
South View
Winklebury
Worting
South Ham
Buckskin
Kempshott
Oakley
Deane
East Oakley
Brighton Hill
Cliddesden
Tunworth
Upton Grey
Long Sutton
South Warnborough
Winslade
Herriard
Weston Patrick
Farleigh Wallop
Ellisfield
Broadmere
Southrope
Dummer
Nutley
Axford
Preston Candover
Bradley
Lower Wield
Upper Wield
Lasham
Shalden
Golden Pot
Holybourne
Bentworth
Beech
Alton
Wilsom
Chawton
West Worldham
Holt End
Wivelrod
Medstead
Hattingley
South Town
Lower Farringdon
Upper Farringdon
Four Marks
Selborne
Newton Valence
Kitwood
East Tisted
Monkwood
Ropley
Ropley Dean
Colemore
Hawkley
Bighton
Soldridge
North Street
Gundleton
Bishop's Sutton
New Alresford
Old Alresford
Itchen Stoke
Itchen Abbas
Martyr Worthy
Kings Worthy
Headbourne Worthy
Easton
Avington
Ovington
Tichborne
Cheriton
New Cheriton
Bramdean
Hinton Ampner
Kilmeston
Brockwood
Beauworth
Longwood Warren
Chilcomb
Privett
High Cross
Stoner Hill
Brown Candover
Northington
Micheldever
Micheldever Wood
Micheldever Forest
East Stratton
West Stratton
Stoke Charity
Woodmancott
Popham
North Waltham
Steventon
Overton
Ashe
Laverstoke
Whitchurch
Quidhampton
Newfound
Upper Wootton
Wootton St Lawrence
Ibworth
Hannington
North Oakley
Sydmonton
Ecchinswell
Burghclere
Old Burghclere
Highclere
Whitway
Crux Easton
Ashmansworth
Faccombe
Linkenholt
Netherton
Woodcott
Dunley
Litchfield
Binley
Hurstbourne Tarrant
Ibthorpe
Upton
Doles Wood
Stoke
St Mary Bourne
Cole Henley
Little London
Smannell
Enham Alamein
Picket Piece
Charlton
Hurstbourne Priors
Tufton
Andover Down
Middleton
Longparish
Forton
Harewood Forest
Upper Clatford
Anna Valley
Goodworth Clatford
Wherwell
Newton Stacey
Bullington
Barton Stacey
Chilbolton
Fullerton
Wonston
Sutton Scotney
South Wonston
Longstock
Leckford
Crawley
Worthy Down
Little Somborne
Up Somborne
Littleton
Sparsholt
Ashley
King's Somborne
Weeke
Winnall
Stockbridge
Brook
Michelmersh
Braishfield
Bullington
Wash Common
Newtown
Greenham
Crookham
Brimpton
Wasing
Speen
Shaw
Donnington
Stockcross
Bagnor
Boxford
Westbrook
Winterbourne
Chieveley
Curridge
Hermitage
Oare
Little Hungerford
Longlane
Frilsham
Stanford Dingley
Bucklebury
Upper Bucklebury
Cold Ash
Clay Hill
Yattendon
Hampstead Norreys
Ashampstead
Quicks Green
Upper Basildon
Lower Basildon
Aldworth
Compton
East Ilsley
West Ilsley
Farnborough
Catmore
Lilley
Stanmore
Beedon
Peasemore
World's End
Downend
Leckhampstead
Leckhampstead Thicket
Chaddleworth
Brightwalton
Fawley
South Fawley
East Garston
Great Shefford
Shefford Woodlands
Woodlands St Mary
Weston
Welford
Wickham
Hungerford Newtown
Halfway
Avington
Kintbury
Enborne
Hamstead Marshall
Inkpen
Upper Green
West Woodhay
Ball Hill
North End
Woolton Hill
Broad Laying
East Woodhay
East End
Buttermere
Combe
Walbury Hill
Highclere Castle
Donnington Castle
Snelsmore Common
Basildon Park
Beale Park
Mapledurham
The Living Rainforest
Streatley on Thames
St Bartholomew's
Mus. of English Rural Life
Roman Town
Stratfield Saye House
Wellington
The Vyne
Milestones
Sandham Memorial Chapel
Tidbury Ring
Finkley Down Farm Park
Northington Grange
Curtis Museum
Jane Austen's Ho
Mid-Hants Railway
Gilbert White's House & The Oates Museum
Ashford Hangers
All Saints Church
Flowerdown Barrows
Farley Mount
Intech Science Centre & Planetarium
St Catherine's Hill
Chieveley Services
Reading Services
Tothill Services
Micheldever Services
Sutton Scotney Services
Winchester Services
Kennet
Lambourn
Pang
Ashford Hill
M4
M3
A34
A33
A303
A339
A31
A4
A30
A343
A32
0 1 2 3 4 5 6 miles
0 1 2 3 4 5 6 7 8 9 10 km

Windsor
Maidenhead
Slough
SLOUGH
WINDSOR
Uxbridge
Hayes
Southall
Brentford
Isleworth
HOUNSLOW
HEATHROW AIRPORT
Feltham
Staines-upon-Thames
EGHAM
Ashford
Teddington
Sunbury-on-Thames
Walton-on-Thames
Esher
Henley-on-Thames
Twyford
Woodley
Earley
Binfield
WOKINGHAM
Bracknell
Bracknell Forest
Crowthorne
Sandhurst
CAMBERLEY
Yateley
Fleet
Frimley
FARNBOROUGH
ALDERSHOT
Farnham
Ascot
Sunninghill
Virginia Water
CHERTSEY
Addlestone
WEYBRIDGE
Byfleet
Cobham
Chobham
Bagshot
WOKING
Guildford
Shalford
Godalming
Milford
Haslemere
Hindhead
Grayshott
Bordon
Liphook
Cranleigh
Fetcham
Great Bookham
East Horsley
SURREY
Hog's Back
Chobham Ridges
Hurt Wood
Cole Park
Billingshurst

Uxbridge
Willesden
Camden
Islington
East Ham
Barking
Ealing
Acton
Paddington
City
Hayes
Southall
Kensington
Westminster
Southwark
Bermondsey
Blackwall Tunnel
Woolwich Ferry
Woolwich
Chiswick
Hammersmith
Chelsea
LAMBETH
Deptford
Greenwich
Brentford
Kew Br.
Fulham
Battersea
Heston
Heathrow Airport
Hounslow
Isleworth
Richmond
Wandsworth
Camberwell
Lewisham
Greater London
Feltham
Twickenham
Catford
Staines upon-Thames
Ashford
Teddington
Wimbledon
Mitcham
Streatham
Penge
Bromley
Chislehurst
Sunbury-on-Thames
Kingston upon Thames
Morden
Beckenham
Chertsey
Walton-on-Thames
Surbiton
New Malden
Croydon
Weybridge
Esher
Cheam
Sutton
Wallington
Byfleet
Ewell
Purley
Cobham
Oxshott
Epsom
Banstead
Coulsdon
Whyteleafe
Warlingham
Biggin Hill
Ashtead
Leatherhead
Burgh Heath
Chipstead
Tadworth
Kingswood
Caterham
Woldingham
Westerham
Limpsfield
Oxted
Merstham
Redhill
Dorking
Reigate
Surrey
Westcott
Salfords
Edenbridge
Horley
Lingfield
Gatwick Airport
Cranleigh
East Grinstead
Three Bridges
Crawley
Horsham
Balcombe
M25
M23
M3
M4
A3
A23
A22
A24
A25
A264
40
41
27
17
0 1 2 3 4 5 6 miles
0 1 2 3 4 5 6 7 8 9 10 km

Dagenham
Hornchurch
South Hornchurch
Rainham
Creekmouth
Thamesmead
Wennington
Aveley
Thurrock
South Ockendon
North Ockendon
North Stifford
Baker Street
Orsett
Horndon on the Hill
Stanford-le-Hope
Fobbing
Corringham
Coryton
CANVEY ISLAND
Leigh Beck
Thames Haven
London Gateway under construction
THAMES ESTUARY
Linford
Chadwell St Mary
West Tilbury
East Tilbury
Tilbury
Grays
Little Thurrock
South Stifford
West Thurrock
Purfleet
Dartford Crossing
THURROCK SERVICES
Belvedere
Erith
Plumstead
Abbey Wood
Welling
Bexleyheath
Crayford
Slade Green
DARTFORD
Stone
Greenhithe
Swanscombe
SWANSCOMBE SKULL SITE
NORTHFLEET
MILTON CHANTRY
GRAVESEND
Chalk
Bexley
Sidcup
Foots Cray
North Cray
Coldblow
Wilmington
Darenth
Bean
Betsham
Perry Street
SECRET COLD WAR BUNKER
Singlewell
Shorne
Higham
Lower Higham
Church Street
Cliffe
Cliffe Woods
Cooling
Halstow Marshes
St Mary's Marshes
St Mary Hoo
High Halstow
Allhallows
Lower Stoke
Isle of Grain
Stoke
North Street
Medway
Chattenden
Hoo St.Werburgh
Upnor
Frindsbury
Strood
ROCHESTER
CHATHAM
Gillingham
Brompton
Grange
Ham Green
Upchurch
Rainham
Hextable
Swanley Village
Sutton at Hone
South Darenth
Horton Kirby
Swanley
St Paul's Cray
St Mary Cray
Crockenhill
Orpington
Farningham
EYNSFORD CASTLE
Eynsford
LULLINGSTONE ROMAN VILLA
Maplescombe
West Kingsdown
Fawkham Green
Ash
New Ash Green
Hartley
Longfield
Southfleet
Istead Rise
New Barn
Meopham Station
Meopham
Sole Street
Cobham
Hook Green
Luddesdown
Cuxton
North Halling
Upper Halling
Halling
Wouldham
Blue Bell Hill
Walderslade
Wayfield
Luton
Hempstead
Wigmore
Moor Street
Newington
Hartlip
Bredhurst
Stockbury
Chelsfield
Green St Green
Pratt's Bottom
Badger's Mount
Halstead
Shoreham
Knockholt
Knockholt Pound
Otford
Kemsing
Heaverham
Wrotham
Fairseat
Stansted
Culverstone Green
Vigo Village
Trottiscliffe
Birling
Snodland
Ryarsh
New Hythe
Burham
Eccles
Aylesford
Boxley
Detling
Thurnham
Bicknor
Hucking
Broad Street
Chevening
Dunton Green
Chipstead
Riverhead
Sevenoaks
Seal
Borough Green
Platt
Wrotham Heath
Addington
West Malling
Offham
Leybourne
Ditton
East Malling
British Legion Village
Sandling
Maidstone
Bearsted
Roseacre
Hollingbourne
Ightham
Stone Street
Ivy Hatch
IGHTHAM MOTE
Crouch
Claygate Cross
Plaxtol
Dunk's Green
Mereworth
Kent Street
King's Hill
Teston
East Barming
Tovil
Shepway
Otham
Leeds
LEEDS CASTLE
Broomfield
Brasted
Sundridge
Brasted Chart
Cross Keys
Whitley Row
Ide Hill
Toy's Hill
Sevenoaks Weald
Underriver
Shipbourne
Old Soar Manor
West Peckham
Wateringbury
Nettlestead
Nettlestead Green
West Farleigh
East Farleigh
Loose
Boughton Monchelsea
Langley
Langley Heath
Kingswood
Coxheath
Oakhurst
Coldharbour
Pittswood
Hadlow
Yalding
Hunton
Linton
Chart Corner
Sutton Valence
Ulcombe
Pootings
Four Elms
Hildenborough
Hilden Park
Higham Wood
Golden Green
East Peckham
Hale Street
Beltring
Laddingford
Benover
Chainhurst
Rabbit's Cross
How Green
Bough Beech
Chiddingstone Causeway
Leigh
Brook Street
TONBRIDGE
Five Oak Green
Barnes Street
Whetsted
Queen Street
Collier Street
Cross-at-Hand
Milebush
Southernden
Hever
Chiddingstone
Penshurst
Bidborough
Tudeley
Paddock Wood
Claygate
Marden
Hawkenbury
Headcorn
Staplehurst
Markbeech
Chiddingstone Hoath
Speldhurst
Southborough
High Brooms
Matfield
Pembury
Castle Hill
Brenchley
Petteridge
Horsmonden
Marden Beech
Marden Thorn
Sinkhurst Green
Frittenden
Knox Bridge
Winchet Hill
Curtisden Green
Cowden
Blackham
Fordcombe
Rusthall
ROYAL TUNBRIDGE WELLS
Hazel Street
Cranbrook Common
Three Chimneys
Ashurst
Langton Green
Hawkenbury
Lamberhurst Quarter
Lamberhurst
Bells Yew Green
Goudhurst
Iden Green
Wilsley Pound
Sissinghurst
Groombridge
Hartfield
Withyham
Eridge Green
Frant
Hook Green
Kilndown
Hartley
Cranbrook
East End
Upper Hartfield
Lye Green
Cousley Wood
Wood's Green
Bewl Water
Bedgebury Forest
Parkgate
Coleman's Hatch
Friar's Gate
Boarshead
Mark Cross
Durgates
Wadhurst
Three Leg Cross
Gill's Green
Benenden
Crowborough
Poundfield
Town Row
Riseden
Best Beech Hill
Shover's Green
Wallcrouch
Union Street
Flimwell
High Street
Hawkhurst
Iden Green
Four Throws
Dingleden
Rolvenden
ASHDOWN FOREST
Jarvis Brook
Rotherfield
Tidebrook
Ticehurst
Horns Corner
The Moor
Sandhurst
Duddleswell
Coggins Mill
Stonegate
Swiftsden
Hurst Green
Sandhurst Cross
Newenden
Cackle Street
Fairwarp
High Hurstwood
Butcher's Cross
Mayfield
Witherenden Hill
Etchingham
Bodiam
HIGH WEALD
KENT DOWNS
Kent

CANVEY ISLAND
Coryton
Thames Haven
Leigh Beck
Shoeburyness
Cambridge Town
THAMES ESTUARY
42
43
Halstow Marshes
St Mary's Marshes
Allhallows-on-Sea
Allhallows
St Mary Hoo
Lower Stoke
Isle of Grain
Grain
Cliffe
Cooling
High Halstow
Stoke
North Street
Cliffe Woods
Medway
Chattenden
Hoo St.Werburgh
Upnor
Frindsbury
Brompton
ROCHESTER
Gillingham
CHATHAM
Luton
Wayfield
Walderslade
Grange
Rainham
Ham Green
Lower Halstow
Upchurch
Iwade
Breach
Moor Street
Wigmore
Hempstead
Newington
Bobbing
Hartlip
Sheerness
West Minster
Halfway Houses
Minster
Queenborough
Rushenden
Eastchurch
Warden Pt.
Warden
Leysdown-on-Sea
Chetney Marshes
ISLE OF SHEPPEY
Isle of Harty
Shell Ness
The Swale
WHITSTABLE
Tankerton
Swalecliffe
Seasalter
Chestfield
South Street
Kemsley
Milton Regis
SITTINGBOURNE
Conyer
Uplees
Borden
Bapchild
Oad Street
Barrow Green
Teynham
Oare
Graveney
Faversham
Goodnestone
Yorkletts
Dargate
Hernhill
Honey Hill
Tyler Hill
Blean
Hales Place
Rough Common
Harbledown
Thanington
Chartham
Chartham Hatch
Bredhurst
Stockbury
South Green
Bredgar
Tunstall
Highsted
Rodmersham
Lynsted
Ospringe
Preston
Boughton Street
Dunkirk
Swanton Street
Bicknor
Hucking
Thurnham
Detling
Boxley
Sandling
Maidstone
Broad Street
Roseacre
Bearsted
Hollingbourne
Eyhorne Street
Wormshill
Frinsted
Milstead
Newnham
Doddington
Eastling
Sheldwich
Wichling
North Street
Selling
Throwley
Badlesmere
Shottenden
Old Wives Lees
Chilham
Shalmsford Street
Street End
Garlinge Green
Petham
Tovil
East Farleigh
Shepway
Otham
Leeds
Broomfield
Harrietsham
West Street
Warren Street
Stalisfield Green
Leaveland
Molash
Loose
Boughton Monchelsea
Langley
Langley Heath
Kingswood
Lenham
Sandway
Lenham Heath
Charing
Challock
Godmersham
Sole Street
Crundale
Waltham
Linton
Chart Corner
Chart Sutton
Sutton Valence
Ulcombe
Grafty Green
Boughton Malherbe
Charing Heath
Westwell Leacon
Westwell
Boughton Aluph
Bilting
Boughton Lees
Wye
Hassell Street
Bodsham
Stelling Minnis
Elmsted
Egerton
Egerton Forstal
Little Chart
Ram Lane
Goat Lees
Kennington
Brook
Hastingleigh
Cross-at-Hand
Milebush
Marden
Hawkenbury
Headcorn
Southernden
Pluckley
Pluckley Thorne
Hothfield
Hinxhill
Lymbridge Green
Marden Beech
Marden Thorn
Staplehurst
Sinkhurst Green
Smarden Bell
Smarden
Maltman's Hill
Great Chart
Ashford
Willesborough
Willesborough Lees
Brabourne
Winchet Hill
Curtisden Green
Knox Bridge
Frittenden
Lashenden
Haffenden Quarter
Wissenden
Sevington
Brabourne Lees
Stowting
Standen
Bethersden
Stubbs Cross
Kingsnorth
Mersham
Smeeth
Postling
Collier's Green
Cranbrook Common
Three Chimneys
Biddenden
Tanden
Shadoxhurst
Cheeseman's Green
Sellindge
Sellindge Lees
Beach
Stanford
Wilsley Pound
Sissinghurst
High Halden
Bromley Green
Aldington Frith
Clap Hill
Aldington
Newingreen
Cranbrook
East End
St Michael's
Henghurst
Shirkoak
Bonnington
Court-at-Street
Lympne
Pedlinge
Hartley
Woodchurch
Orlestone
Bilsington
Parkgate
Tenterden
Ruckinge
West Hythe
Gill's Green
Benenden
Leigh Green
Brook Street
Kenardington
Hamstreet
Warehorne
Royal Military Canal
Palmarsh
Iden Green
Dingleden
Rolvenden
Burmarsh
Newchurch
High Street
Hawkhurst
Four Throws
Small Hythe
Reading Street
Appledore Heath
Snave
The Moor
Rolvenden Layne
ISLE OF OXNEY
Appledore
ROMNEY MARSH
Dymchurch
St Mary in the Marsh
Peening Quarter
Stone
Snargate
Brenzett
Ivychurch
St Mary's Bay
Hurst Green
Wittersham
Ham Green
The Stocks
Bodiam
Brookland
M2
M20
A2
A20
A28
A249
A299
A229
A274
A252
A251
A262
A2070
A259
A268
TQ
KENT
NORTH DOWNS
0 1 2 3 4 5 6 miles
0 1 2 3 4 5 6 7 8 9 10 km

5
6
7
8
9
A
B
C
D
E
F
G
TR
TURNER CONTEMPORARY
THE SHELL GROTTO
Margate
Cliftonville
Foreness Pt.
Kingsgate
NORTH FORELAND
LIGHTHOUSE
Westgate on Sea
MARGATE
Northdown
St Peter's
BROADSTAIRS
BLEAK HOUSE
DICKENS HOUSE MUSEUM
RECULVER
RECULVER TOWERS AND ROMAN FORT
Minnis Bay
HERNE BAY
Reculver
Birchington
Hillborough
QUEX HOUSE
Isle of Thanet
SPITFIRE AND HURRICANE MEM
Northwood
Dumpton
Newington
Ramsgate
MARITIME MUSEUM
Beltinge
A299
A28
Acol
Greenhill
Broomfield
St Nicholas at Wade
Herne
Boyden Gate
Sarre
WINDMILL
A253
KENT INTERNATIONAL
Manston
Way
Cliffsend
Pegwell
Hoath
Chislet
Monkton
Minster
Calcott
Upstreet
Stour
West Stourmouth
PEGWELL BAY
SANDWICH & PEGWELL BAY
OOSTENDE 4:00
BOULOGNE 1:15
Hersden
ST. AUGUSTINE'S CROSS
Pegwell Bay
Broadoak
Grove
STODMARSH
East Stourmouth
A256
Westmarsh
Sturry
Westbere
Preston
Ware
RICHBOROUGH CASTLE
Fordwich
Stodmarsh
Elmstone
Hoaden
AMPHITHEATRE
Great Stonar
P&R
Canterbury
Wickhambreux
WINGHAM BIRD PARK
A257
Sandwich Bay
Ickham
Sandwich
Littlebourne
Wingham
Guilton
Ash
ROYAL ST. GEORGE'S
ST. AUGUSTINE'S ABBEY
CANTERBURY
HOWLETTS WILD ANIMAL PARK
Marshborough
TOLL
Stone Cross
Bramling
Staple
Woodnesborough
Bekesbourne
Worth
A2050
A2
Nackington
Patrixbourne
Goodnestone
Gore
Ham
A258
Bridge
Adisham
GOODNESTONE PARK
Eastry
Finglesham
Lower Hardres
Knowlton
Chillenden
Bishopsbourne
Aylesham
Betteshanger
Sholden
MARITIME AND LOCAL HISTORY MUSEUM
DEAL
THE DOWNS
NORTH DOWNS WAY
Nonington
Easole Street
Northbourne
DEAL CASTLE
Upper Hardres Court
Kingston
B2046
Snowdown
Tilmanstone
Great Mongeham
Walmer
Barham
Womenswold
Elvington
WALMER CASTLE AND GARDENS
Derringstone
Barfrestone
Ripple
Bossingham
EAST KENT RLY
East Studdal
Sutton
Woolage Green
Eythorne
ELHAM VALLEY VINEYARD
Coxhill
Shepherdswell
West Langdon
Ringwould
Kingsdown
Denton
Martin
LYDDEN
A256
East Langdon
Wingmore
Wootton
Coldred
Martin Mill
Lyminge Forest
A260
Selsted
Lydden
Whitfield
Guston
St Margaret's at Cliffe
ST JOHN'S COMMANDERY
LYDDEN TEMPLE EWELL
Ewell Minnis
Temple Ewell
West Cliffe
THE BAY MUSEUM
Rhodes Minnis
Elham
Swingfield Street
St Margaret's Bay
BUTTERFLY CENTRE
CRABBLE CORN MILL
THE PINES GARDEN
SOUTH FORELAND
Swingfield Minnis
Buckland
Ottinge
ROMAN PAINTED HOUSE
WHITE CLIFFS
Densole
Drellingore
Alkham
Maxton
CASTLE & HELLFIRE CORNER
CALAIS 1:30
DUNKERQUE 2:00
KENT BATTLE OF BRITAIN MUSEUM
Lyminge
Paddlesworth
Hawkinge
West Hougham
Farthingloe
DOVER
Etchinghill
B2011
A20
Aycliff
DE BRADELEI WHARF
CHANNEL TUNNEL
Capel le Ferne
SAMPHIRE HOE
borough
Newington
EAST CLIFF & WARREN
East Wear Bay
ELHAM VALLEY RLY MUS
Cheriton
Folkestone
Saltwood
ROTUNDA
Sandgate
CLIFF LIFT
Hythe
19
CHANNEL
TUNNEL

MYNYDD PRESELI
Pontfaen
Crymych
Tegryn
Cwmorgan
Tanglwst
Pentre-galar
Hermon
Llanfyrnach
Hen-feddau fawr
Bryn-Iwan
Cwmduad
New Inn
Rosebush
Mynachlog-ddu
Dinas
Trelech
Puncheston
Castlebythe
Tufton
Henry's Moat
Glandwr
Hebron
Blaen-waun
Cynwyl Elfed
Blaen-y-coed
Pen-y-bont
Maenclochog
Llangolman
Glandy Cross
Pant-y-Caws
Llanglydwen
Cefn-y-pant
WELSH CHOCOLATE FARM
Cwmbach
Llanwinio
Woodstock
Wallis
New Moat
Efailwen
Cwmfelin Mynach
Talog
Bwlchnewydd
LLYS-Y-FRAN RESERVOIR
Llys-y-frân
Llanycefn
Maesgwynne
Cross-hands
Llanboidy
Ty-hen
Abernant
Newchurch
Walton East
Pen-ffordd
Login
Gellywen
Llandissilio
Dyffryn
Hiraeth
SN
Tre-vaughan
Clarbeston
Clarbeston Road
Bletherston
Henllan Amgoed
Meidrim
Merthyr
Carmarthen
(Caerfyrddin)
Llanfallteg
Clunderwen
Llangynin
Sarnau
Gelli
Cwmfelin Boeth
Bancyfelin
Llanllwch
CORS GOCH, LLANLLWCH
LLAWHADEN CASTLE
Wiston
Bethesda
Pwll-trap
Llawhaden
Robeston Wathen
Llanddewi Velfrey
Whitland
Trevaughan
Backe
St Clears
(Sanclêr)
Llangynog
Llangain
The Rhos
Narberth
(Arberth)
Crinow
Lampeter Velfrey
Llwyn-y-brain
Llanddowror
Afon Tâf
Blackpool
WILSON MUSEUM
PICTON CASTLE & GARDENS
BLUE LAGOON
HERONS BROOK
Morfa Bach
Afon Tywi
Minwear
Cross Hands
Cold Blow
Princes Gate
Taverspite
Halfpenny Furze
Llanybri
OAKWOOD
Landshipping
Templeton
Red Roses
Landawke
DYLAN THOMAS BOATHOUSE
Llansteffan
Landshipping Quay
Martletwy
Ludchurch
Longstone
Llanteg
Llansadurnen
Laugharne
CASTLE
Ferryside
Black Tar
Yerbeston
FOLLY FARM
Reynalton
Thomas Chapel
Marros
Brook
Broadway
Broadlay
Port Lion
Houghton
Loveston
Stepaside
COLBY WOODLAND GARDEN
MUSEUM OF SPEED
Pendine
East Marsh
Llansaint
Cresswell Quay
Jeffreyston
Begelly
Kilgetty
Amroth
Pendine Sands
Traeth Pentywynn
Lawrenny
West Williamston
Cresselly
Broadmoor
Carew Newton
PEMBROKESHIRE COAST
ARFORDIR PENFRO
Saundersfoot
East Williamston
Redberth
Cosheston
CAREW CASTLE
Carew
Broadfield
Pembrey Forest
Milton
Sageston
New Hedges
Pembroke
(Penfro)
Carew Cheriton
TENBY DINOSAUR PARK
TUDOR MERCHANT'S HOUSE
CARMARTHEN
LAMPHEY BISHOP'S PALACE
MANOR HOUSE WILDLIFE PARK
Lamphey
St Florence
Gumfreston
Tenby
(Dinbych-y-Pysgod)
PEMBREY
Hodgeston
Jameston
Penally
BAY
Freshwater East
Lydstep
Giltar Pt.
Caldey Sound
BAE CAERFYRDDIN
Cheriton or Stackpole Elidor
MANORBIER CASTLE
Manorbier
MANORBIER
Caldey Island
Ynys Bŷr
Trewent Pt.
Trwyn Trewent
Old Castle Hd.
Chapel Pt.
Trwyn Capel
STACKPOLE
Stackpole Hd.
Pen Stackpole
SS
Burry Holms
Rhossili Bay
Bae Rhossili
Worms Head
Penrhyn-Gŵyr
0 1 2 3 4 5 6 miles
0 1 2 3 4 5 6 7 8 9 10 km

Carmarthenshire
(Sir Gaerfyrddin)
Swansea
(Abertawe)
Brechfa Forest
Llandovery
Llandeilo
Llanelli
Swansea
(Abertawe)
Neath
(Castell-Nedd)
Port Talbot
Ammanford
(Rhydaman)
Pontarddulais
Gorseinon
Clydach
Pontardawe
Ystradgynlais
Ystalyfera
Kidwelly
(Cydweli)
Burry Port
(Porth Tywyn)
The Mumbles
(Y Mwmbwls)
Carmarthen
Brynamman
Black Mountain
Y Mynydd Du
Vale of Tywi
Dyffryn Tywi
Swansea Valley
Cwm Abertawe
Swansea Bay
Bae Abertawe
Gower
Port Eynon Pt.
Trwyn Port Eynon
Mumbles Hd.
Trwyn yr Mwmbwls
Pwlldu Hd.
Pen Pwlldu
Oxwich Bay
Bae Oxwich
Port Eynon Bay
Bae Port Eynon
Whiteford Pt.
Trwyn Whiteford
Llanrhidian Sands
Traeth Llanrhidian
Mynydd y Gwair
Mynydd March-Hywel
SN
SS
A40
A48
A483
A4138
A484
M4
46
47
34
5
6
7
8

Llandovery
Halfway
Nant Bran
Pont-faen
Pwllgloyw
Sarnau
Garthbrengy
Felinfach
Talachddu
Llandefaelog Fach
Llanddew
Pentre-bach
Myrtle Hill
Llanwrda
Cilgwyn
Myddfai
Llywel
Pentre'r-felin
Trallong
Aberyscir
Brecon
(Aberhonddu)
Llanywern
Llechfaen
Usk Reservoir
Trecastle
Sennybridge
(Pont Senni)
Defynnog
Penpont
Llanspyddid
Llanfaes
BRECON GAER ROMAN FORT
CATHEDRAL
SOUTH WALES BORDERERS
BRECKNOCK MUSEUM
Llanhamlach
Llangadog
Cwmwysg
Pont ar Hydfer
Talsarn
Twynllanan
Llanddeusant
LLANDDEUSANT
Glas Fynydd Forest
Crai
Felin-Crai
Heol Senni
Mynydd Illtyd
MOUNTAIN CENTRE
Tai'r-Bull
Libanus
Llanfrynach
Pencelli
Dyffryn Ceidrych
Pont-ar-llechau
Capel Gwynfe
TRICHRUG
Neuadd
Pont Aber
SN
802 FAN BRYCHEINIOG
Cray Res.
LLWYN Y CELYN
CRAIG CERRIG GLEISIAD A FAN FRYNYCH
Glyn Tarell
A470
886 PEN Y FAN
BRECON BEACONS
769
DANYWENALLT
Talybont Res.
BLACK MOUNTAIN
Y MYNYDD DU
BRECON BEACONS
FFOREST FAWR
FOEL FRAITH 604
575 FAN GIHIRYCH
734 FAN FAWR
Beacons Res.
Neuadd Reservoirs
Ystradfellte Res.
Abercynafon
THE NATIONAL SHOWCAVES FOR WALES
DAN-YR-OGOF
Glyntawe
CRAIG-Y-NOS
Craig-y-nos
Penwyllt
OGOF FFYNNON DDU
Cantref Res.
Nant-ddu
Pen-y-cae
Brynamman
Rhosaman
Cwmllynfell
Ystradowen
Gwaun-Leision
Tairgwaith
Gwaun-Gurwen
Abercraf
Caehopkin
CEFN-YR-ERW
Coelbren
Upper Cwm-twrch
Cwmgiedd
Lower Cwm-twrch
Cwmgors
Gurnos
Ystradgynlais
Penrhos
Ystradfellte
Llwyn-on Res.
GARWNANT VISITOR CENTRE
Pontsticill Reservoir
BRECON MOUNTAIN RAILWAY
Pontsticill
Vaynor
460
Ystalyfera
Onllwyn
Dyffryn Cellwen
Seven Sisters
Nant-y-cafn
Pontneddfechan
Glyn-neath
(Glynedd)
Morfa Glas
Penderyn
Pontbren Llwyd
Cefn-coed-y-cymmer
Dowlais
A4060
CASTLE MUS. & ART GALL.
Gellideg
Pen-yr-Heolgerrig
Merthyr Tydfil
(Merthyr Tudful)
YNYSFACH ENGINE HOUSE HERITAGE CEN.
Godre'r-graig
Climaen-gwyn
Ynys-meudwy
Rhyd-y-fro
Pontardawe
GLANTAWE RIVERSIDE PARK
Trebanos
Alltwen
Cilybebyll
Gellinudd
Rhôs
SWANSEA VALLEY
CWM ABERTAWE
Mynydd March-Hywel
Crynant
418
CEFN COED COLLIERY MUS.
Rheola Forest
VALE OF NEATH
CWM NEDD
SARN HELEN
Rhigos
Cwm-hwnt
Blaengwrach
Cwmgwrach
A465
Hirwaun
Tre-Gibbon
Penywaun
Trecynon
Llwydcoed
Cwmdare
ABERDARE
(ABERDÂR)
DARE VALLEY
Aber-nant
Pentrebach
Abercanaid
Troedyrhiw
Cwmbach
491
Aberaman
Resolven
383 RESOLVEN MTN.
Melincourt
Neath
Rhondda
Clydach
Glais
Cilfrew
Aberdulais
FALLS
Clyne
Blaenrhondda
Bedlinog
Cwmfelin
Aberfan
Bryn-coch
Heol-las
Rhydding
Birchgrove
Neath Abbey
Skewen
Tonna
Cadoxton-Juxta-Neath
NEATH MUSEUM
Port Talbot
(Castell-Nedd
Port Talbot)
Tynewydd
Glyncorrwg
Treherbert
Cwmaman
MOUNTAIN ASH
(ABERPENNAR)
Penrhiwceiber
Merthyr Vale
A470
Treharris
Neath
(Castell-Nedd)
Cimla
Pentre-dwr
Llansamlet
Blaen-gwynfi
Aber-gwynfi
Cwm-parc
Maerdy
Treorchy
(Treorci)
Pentre
Ferndale
St Gwynno Forest
Cynon Taff
Duffryn
Cymer
Croeserw
VISITOR CENTRE
Briton Ferry
GNOLL
SOUTH WALES MINERS MUSEUM
RHONDDA
Ystrad
Ton-Pentre
Gelli
Tylorstown
Ynysboeth
Abercynon
Pontrhydyfen
Caerau
Spelter
FOEL Y DYFFRYN 366
568 WERFA
Nant-y-moel
535 CRAIG Y GEIFR
Clydach Vale
Llwynypia
Pont-y-gwaith
Wattstown
Ynysybwl
Baglan
Pwll-y-glaw
Brynbryddan
AFAN FOREST PARK
Dyffryn
Blaengarw
CLYDACH VALE
327
Trealaw
Ynyshir
MYNYDD DINAS 528
Cwmafan
Bryn
Nantyffyllon
Wyndham
Price Town
Tonypandy
Penygraig
Porth
RHONDDA HERITAGE PARK
Glyncoch
Cilfy
Aberavon
Port Talbot
MAESTEG
Pontycymer
Trebanog
PONTYPRIDD
Rhydyfelin
Glyntaff
Goytre
Garth
Cwmfelin
Pont Rhyd-y-cyff
Ogmore Vale
Ogmore Forest
Evanstown
Gilfach Goch
(Rhondda
Cynon Taf)
Bryn Golau
Tonyrefail
Pen-y-coedcae
Treforest
Taibach
Llangynwyd
344 MYNYDD MARGAM
Bridgend
(Pen-y-bont ar Ogwr)
Lewistown
Pant-yr-awel
Hendreforgan
Glynogwr
Margam
SWANSEA BAY
BAE ABERTAWE
Groes
319 MOEL TON-MAWR
Bettws
Llangeinor
Blackmill
Castellau
Hawthorn
Upper Church Village
Llantwit Fardre
Church Village
MARGAM
MARGAM ABBEY AND STONES MUSEUM
Coytrahen
BRYNGARW
Brynmenyn
Bryncethin
303 MYNYDD MAENDY
Coedely
Beddau
SS
BEDFORD PARK
Kenfig Hill
Cefn Cross
Aberkenfig
Tondu
Sarn
BRIDGEND
Heol-y-Cyw
Brynna
Llanharan
MODEL HOUSE CENTRE
Llantrisant
Talbot Green
Efail Isaf
Kenfig
Mawdlam
North Cornelly
Pyle
(Y Pîl)
Cefn Cribbwr
SARN PARK SERVICES
Pen-y-fai
Pendre
Coity
COITY CASTLE
Pencoed
P&R
Brynceae
Dolau
Llanilid
Cross Inn
Pontyclun
Creigiau
KENFIG POOL AND DUNES
Kenfig Burrows
South Cornelly
M4
NEWCASTLE
Bridgend
(Pen-y-bont ar Ogwr)
Llanharry
Brynsadler
Miskin
Groes-faen
Capel Llanilltern
Laleston
Coychurch
Talygarn
LLANERCH VINEYARD
ROYAL PORTHCAWL
Tythegston
Merthyr Mawr
Treoes
St Mary Hill
Craig Penllyn
Ystradowen
St Brides super Ely
Newton
Clevis
OGMORE CASTLE
MERTHYR MAWR WARREN
Ogmore
Ewenny
Corntown
Llangan
Llansannor
Maendy
Peterston super-Ely
Porthcawl
CONEY
Pentre
Penllyn
Aberthin
Welsh St Donats
Pendoylan
St George's
CRYMLYN BOG AND PANT-Y-SAIS
0 1 2 3 4 5 6 miles
0 1 2 3 4 5 6 7 8 9 10 km

BLACK MOUNTAINS
Y MYNYDDOEDD DUON
Monmouthshire
(Sir Fynwy)
Torfaen
(Tor-faen)
Caerphilly
(Caerffili)
Newport
(Casnewydd)
Cardiff
(Caerdydd)
SO
ST
Abergavenny
(Y Fenni)
Monmouth
(Trefynwy)
Cwmbran
(Cwmbrân)
Usk
(Brynbuga)
PONTYPOOL
(PONT-Y-PWL)
Blaenavon
EBBW VALE
(GLYN EBWY)
Tredegar
Rhymney
(Rhymni)
New Tredegar
(Tredegar Newydd)
Bargoed
(Bargod)
Blackwood
(Coed Duon)
Abertillery
(Abertyleri)
Llanhilleth
(Llanhiledd)
Abersychan
Brynmawr
Blaina
Nantyglo
Crumlin
(Crymlyn)
Oakdale
Risca
(Rhisga)
Crosskeys
Abercarn
Pontnewydd
Griffithstown
Hengoed
Gelligaer
CAERPHILLY
(CAERFFILI)
Caerleon
(Caerllion)
Chepstow
Caldicot
Magor
Rogiet
Portishead
Battery Pt.
Redcliff Bay
Avonmouth
Whitchurch
Rumney
Llandaff
Crickhowell
Talgarth
Tretower
Grosmont
Skenfrith
Raglan
Llanfihangel-Crucorney
Pandy
Llangorse Lake
Mynydd Llangatwg
Mynydd Llangynidr
Llangattock
Gilwern
Govilon
Machen
Bedwas
Rogerstone
Bassaleg
Marshfield
Castleton
Peterstone Wentlooge
St Brides Wentlooge
Goldcliff
Whitson
Nash
Redwick
Undy
St Mellons
Lisvane
Llanishen
Rhiwbina
Tongwynlais
Taff's Well
Nelson
Ystrad-mynach
Pengam
Newbridge
Llanvaches
Penhow
Langstone
Llanwern
Bishton
Wilcrick
Shirenewton
Earlswood
Devauden
Itton Common
Trellech
Llanishen
Mitcheltroy Common
Dingestow
Wonastow
Llantilio Crossenny
Llanvetherine
Llanvapley
Llanarth
Bryngwyn
Kingcoed
Gwehelog
Llansoy
Gwernesney
Llangwm
Llanbadoc
Llantrisant
Llangybi
Tredunnock
Llandegveth
Coed-y-paen
Glascoed
Little Mill
Monkswood
Llancayo
Goytre
Penperlleni
Llanover
Llanellen
Llanfoist
Mardy
Llanddewi Rhydderch
Coed Morgan
Llangattock nigh Usk
Newcastle
Llangattock-Vibon-Avel
Rockfield
Dixton
Welsh Newton
St Maughans
Llanrothal
Garway
Kentchurch
Pontrilas
Ewyas Harold
Abbey Dore
Kilpeck
Much Dewchurch
Wormelow Tump
Llanwarne
Orcop
Walterstone
Llangua
Rowlestone
Clodock
Longtown
Oldcastle
Llanthony
Cwmyoy
Stanton
Llanbedr
Bwlch
Cwmdu
Llangynidr
Llangasty Talyllyn
Cathedine
Llangors
Llansantffraed
Talybont-on-Usk
Aber Village
Princetown
Trefil
Beaufort
Garnlydan
Sirhowy
Dukestown
Georgetown
Pontlottyn
Fochriw
Abertysswg
Tirphil
Deri
Markham
Argoed
Hollybush
Cwm
Waunlwyd
Cwmtillery
East Bank
Varteg
Cwmavon
Garndiffaith
Talywain
Trevethin
New Inn
Lowlands
Upper Cwmbran
Croesyceiliog
Llanfrechfa
Ponthir
Llantarnam
Oakfield
Henllys
Castell-y-bwch
Malpas
Bettws
Christchurch
Maindee
Duffryn
Pentre-poeth
Rhiwderin
Lower Machen
Pontywaun
Ynysddu
Cwmfelinfach
Wattsville
Maesycwmmer
Pontllanfraith
Fleur-de-lis
Senghenydd
Abertridwr
Llanbradach
Penyrheol
Trecenydd
Nantgarw
Rudry
Thornhill
Llanedeyrn
Cyncoed
Llanrumney
Heath
Birchgrove
Cathays
Roath
Canton
Ely
St Fagans
Michaelston-y-Fedw
Coedkernew
Blacktown
Newton
A40
A465
A4042
A449
A48
A48(M)
M4
M48
A466
A472
A470
A469
A479
B4521
B4233
B4347
B4598
SECOND SEVERN CROSSING
TOLL
CARDIFF

Monmouthshire
(Sir Fynwy)
South
Gloucestershire
Monmouth
(Trefynwy)
Ross-on-Wye
Chepstow
(Cas-gwent)
FOREST
OF
DEAN
Cinderford
Coleford
Lydney
Newent
Dursley
Wotton-under-Edge
Thornbury
Yate
Chipping Sodbury
Caldicot
Patchway
FILTON
MANGOTSFIELD
River Severn
The Noose
Frampton on Severn
Berkeley
Raglan
Skenfrith
Tintern Parva
St Briavels
Whitchurch
Goodrich
Much Marcle
Kilcot
Severn Beach
Redcliff Bay
Caldicot Level
Tidenham Chase
Chepstow Pk. Wood
M4
M5
M48
M49
M50
A40
A48
A449
A466
A4137
A38
A403
A46
SO
ST
0 1 2 3 4 5 6 miles
0 1 2 3 4 5 6 7 8 9 10 km

Tewkesbury
Bishop's Cleeve
Winchcombe
Cheltenham
Charlton Kings
Gloucester
Churchdown
Hucclecote
Stroud
Stonehouse
Chalford
Cirencester
Nailsworth
Tetbury
Malmesbury
South Cerney
Cricklade
Fairford
Lechlade-on-Thames
Highworth
Swindon
Stratton St Margaret
Royal Wootton Bassett
Purton
Northleach
Bourton-on-the-Water
Stow-on-the-Wold
Andoversford
Painswick
Minchinhampton
Bibury
Lydiard Millicent
COTSWOLDS
SP
SU
A40
A417
A419
A429
A433
A436
A38
A46
A350
A424
A361
A346
M4
M5
50
51
38
24
25

Batsford
Bourton on the Hill
Moreton-in-Marsh
Lemington
Great Wolford
Whichford
Hook Norton
Hook Norton Brewery Visitor Centre
Wigginton
South Newington
Barford St John
Barford St Michael
Clifton
Deddington
Hempton
Sezincote
Wellington Aviation Museum
Barton on the Heath
Long Compton
Little Compton
Great Rollright
Swerford
Worton
Cutsdean
Ford
Condicote
Longborough
Donnington
Evenlode
Chastleton
Chastleton House
Rollright Stones
Salford
Over Norton
Little Tew
Great Tew
Over Worton
Duns Tew
North Aston
Temple Guiting
Cotswold Farm Park
Upper Swell
Lower Swell
Broadwell
Stow-on-the-Wold
Adlestrop
Daylesford
Oddington
Cornwell
Chipping Norton
Heythrop
Sandford St Martin
Ledwell
Middle Barton
Somerton
Middle Aston
Upper Heyford
Kineton
Maugersbury
Westcott Barton
Church Enstone
Steeple Aston
Lidstone
Gagingwell
Enstone
Steeple Barton
Lower Heyford
Rousham House
Naunton
Upper Slaughter
Lower Slaughter
Wyck Rissington
Icomb
Kingham
Churchill
Bledington
Sarsden
Cleveley
Kiddington
Over Kiddington
Glympton
Taston
Spelsbury
Chadlington
Bruern Abbey
Lyneham
Westcote
Notgrove
Cold Aston
Bourton-on-the-Water
The Old Mill
Model Village
Birdland Park & Gardens
Clapton-on-the-Hill
Little Rissington
Upper Rissington
Idbury
Fifield
Milton under Wychwood
Shipton-under-Wychwood
Ascott-under-Wychwood
Chilson
Charlbury
Wootton
Tackley
Stonesfield
Wychwood Forest
Fawler
Bunkers Hill
Shipton on Cherwell
Turkdean
Hazleton
Great Rissington
Farmington
Cotswold Motoring Collection
Northleach
Sherborne
Windrush
Great Barrington
Taynton
Fordwells
Finstock
North Leigh Roman Villa
Combe
Woodstock
Blenheim Palace
Thrupp
London Oxford
Leafield
Ramsden
Whiteoak Green
East End
North Leigh
Long Hanborough
Bladon
Begbroke
Kidlington
Eastington
Lodge Park
Little Barrington
Burford
Fulbrook
Swinbrook
Asthall Leigh
Hailey
New Yatt
Freeland
Church Hanborough
Yarnton
Fossebridge
Coln St Dennis
Asthall
Minster Lovell
Minster Lovell Hall and Dovecote
Crawley
Witney
Barnard Gate
Cassington
Oxford Services
Coln Rogers
Winson
Aldsworth
Westwell
Signet
Charterville Allotments
Cogges
South Leigh
Eynsham
Wolvercote
Holwell
Bradwell Grove
Shilton
Cotswold Wildlife Park
Curbridge
Cogges Manor Farm Mus
High Cogges
Swinford
Wytham
Ablington
Arlington
Bibury
Arlington Row
Coln St Aldwyn's
Eastleach Turville
Eastleach Martin
Carterton
Brize Norton
Ducklington
Hardwick
Farmoor
Farmoor Reservoir
Sutton
Stanton Harcourt
Botley
North Hinksey
Ashmolean Mus
Quenington
Hatherop
Filkins
Fyfield
Broughton Poggs
Kencot
Alvescot
Black Bourton
Lew
Yelford
Brighthampton
West End
Cumnor
Chawley
Conduit House
Southrop
Broadwell
Aston
Cote
Standlake
Eaton
Northmoor
Bessels Leigh
Wootton
Boars Hill
Langford
Little Faringdon
Clanfield
Bampton
Weald
Shifford
The Thames Path
Appleton
Lamborough Hill
Foxcombe Hill
Sunningwell
Poulton
Milton End
Fairford
Horcott
Meysey Hampton
Grafton
Radcot
Chimney
Duxford
Thames or Isis
Lechlade-on-Thames
Kelmscott
Kelmscott Manor
Eaton Hastings
Carswell Marsh
Chimney Meadows
Hinton Waldrist
Longworth
Netherton
Fyfield
Tubney
Cothill
Whelford
Inglesham
Buckland
Southmoor
Kingston Bagpuize
Kingston Bagpuize House
Frilford
Shippon
Marston Meysey
Dunfield
Kempsford
Down Ampney
Latton
Buscot
Buscot Park
Littleworth
Pusey
Garford
Marcham
Caldecott
Castle Eaton
Hannington Wick
Upper Inglesham
Badbury Hill
Faringdon
Hatford
Charney Bassett
The Thames Path
Coleshill
Great Barn
Great Coxwell
Shellingford
Little Coxwell
Stanford in the Vale
Lyford
West Hanney
East Hanney
Cricklade
Hannington
Highworth
Fernham
Vale of White Horse
Goosey
Denchworth
Drayton
Milton
Steventon
Swindon and Cricklade Railway
Broad Blunsdon
Stanton Fitzwarren
Sevenhampton
Longcot
Baulking
Watchfield
Uffington
Grove
Milton Hill
Rowstock
Harwell
Blunsdon St Andrew
Stanton Park
Shrivenham
South Marston
West Challow
East Challow
West Hendred
East Hendred
Ardington
Ardington House
Lockinge
Haydon Wick
Penhill
Upper Stratton
Stratton St Margaret
Purton
Kingston Lisle
Sparsholt
Childrey
Wantage
Woolstone
Compton Beauchamp
Uffington Castle
Bourton
Gorse Hill
Pinehurst
Lydiard Millicent
Rodbourne Cheney
Rodbourne
Steam
Walcot
Swindon
Letcombe Regis
West Ginge
East Ginge
Whitehorse Hill
Wayland's Smithy
The Ridgeway
Chilton
Ashbury
Idstone
Kingston Warren
Letcombe Bassett
Hinton Parva
Bishopstone
Wanborough
Coate
Coate Water
West Ilsley
Ashdown Park
Lambourn Downs
Farnborough
East Ilsley
North Wroughton
Wroughton
Liddington
Badbury
Upper Lambourn
Fawley
Catmore
Broadtown Lane
Elcombe
Chiseldon
South Fawley
Brightwalton
Lilley
Stanmore
Lambourn
Baydon
Leckhampstead
Leckhampstead Thicket
Beedon
Peasemore
Chaddleworth
Eastbury
East Garston
World's End
Woodsend
Aldbourne
Membury Services
Woodlands
Leckhampstead
SP
SU
Oxfordshire
0 1 2 3 4 5 6 miles
0 1 2 3 4 5 6 7 8 9 10 km

Buckingham
Bletchley
Croughton
Aynho
Mixbury
Water Stratford
Radclive
Finmere
Tingewick
Gawcott
Thornborough
Nash
Tattenhoe
Far Bletchley
Souldern
Cottisford
Newton Purcell
Barton Hartshorn
Padbury
Singleborough
Great Horwood
Little Horwood
Whaddon Chase
Newton Longville
Fritwell
Baynard's Green
Hardwick
Hethe
Preston Bissett
Chetwode
Adstock
Addington
Drayton Parslow
Stoke Hammond
Fewcott
Stoke Lyne
Fringford
Hillesden
Winslow
Winslow Hall
Mursley
Swanbourne
North End
Soulbury
Ardley
Cherwell Valley Services
Bucknell
Stratton Audley
Twyford
Steeple Claydon
Middle Claydon
Claydon House
East Claydon
Granborough
Hoggeston
Stewkley
South End
Linslade
Caversfield
Poundon
Charndon
Calvert
Botolph Claydon
Dunton
Burcott
Caulcott
Middleton Stoney
Woodfield
Highfield
Bicester
Launton
Marsh Gibbon
North Marston
Creslow
Cublington
Wing
Ascott
Buckingham
Edgcott
Grendon Underwood
Oving
Whitchurch
Aston Abbotts
Chesterton
Bicester Village
Quainton Windmill
Quainton
Pitchcott
Kirtlington
Ambrosden
Blackthorn
Buckinghamshire Railway Centre
Hardwick
Mentmore
Wingrave
Weston-on-the-Green
Wendlebury
Lower Arncott
Kingswood
Westcott
Waddesdon
Weedon
Rowsham
Bletchingdon
Merton
Ludgershall
Wotton Underwood
Cheddington
Charlton on Otmoor
Upper Arncott
Piddington
Waddesdon Manor
Akeman Street
Bierton
Long Marston
Puttenham
Hampton Poyle
Murcott
Boarstall Tower
Boarstall
Brill Windmill
Brill
Dorton
Ashendon
Upper Winchendon
Aylesbury
Wilstone
Oddington
Islip
Noke
Horton-cum-Studley
Upper Pollicott
Nether Winchendon House
Lower Winchendon
Stone
Southcourt
Buckland
Little London
Chilton
Cuddington
Dinton
Weston Turville
Aston Clinton
Woodeaton
Beckley
Oakley
Chearsley
Westlington
Stoke Mandeville
Halton
Elsfield
Easington
Bishopstone
Summertown
Stanton St John
Forest Hill
Worminghall
Long Crendon
Townsend
Haddenham
Ford
Kimble Wick
North Lee
Terrick
Nash Lee
Butler's Cross
Wendover
Marston
Headington
The Oxford Story
University
Botanic Garden
Barton
Holton
Ickford
Waterperry
Waterperry Gardens
Shabbington
Aston Sandford
Little Kimble
Ellesborough
St Leonard's
Oxford
Wheatley
Shotover
Waterstock
Thame
Kingsey
Owlswick
Meadle
Great Kimble
Dunsmore
The Lee
Cowley
Horspath
Oxford Services
Rycote Chapel
Tiddington
Moreton
Towersey
Ilmer
Longwick
Askett
New Hinksey
Iffley
Cuddesdon
Great Milton
Monks Risborough
Little Hampden
Ballinger Common
South Hinksey
Littlemore
Denton
Emmington
Pitch Green
Henton
Manor House
Bledlow
Princes Risborough
Kennington
Sandford on Thames
Garsington
Great Haseley
Tetsworth
Sydenham
Saunderton
Great Hampden
Prestwood
Great Missenden
Toot Baldon
Little Milton
Little Haseley
Chinnor
Chinnor & Princes Risborough Railway
Loosley Row
Oakley
Marsh Baldon
St Katherine's
Postcombe
Crowell
Lacey Green
Speen
Kingshill
Radley
Nuneham Courtenay
Chiselhampton
Stoke Talmage
Adwell
Kingston Blount
Aston Rowant
Radnage
Bledlow Ridge
Walters Ash
Upper North Dean
Great Kingshill
Stadhampton
South Weston
Lewknor
The City
Bradenham
Cryers Hill
Widmer End
Abingdon
Drayton St Leonard
Easington
Chalgrove
Stokenchurch
Naphill
Hughenden Valley
Clifton Hampden
Berinsfield
Newington
Pyrton
Shirburn
Beacon's Bottom
West Wycombe
West Wycombe Caves
Downley
Hughenden Manor
Hazlemere
Culham
Burcot
Brightwell Baldwin
Dorchester
Dorchester Abbey
Pendon Mus
Long Wittenham
Berrick Salome
Cuxham
Watlington
Christmas Common
Ibstone
West Wycombe Park
High Wycombe
Tylers Green
Sutton Courtenay
Appleford
Little Wittenham
Warborough
Roke
Britwell Salome
The Ridgeway
Northend
Cadmore End
Bolter End
Booker
Wycombe Marsh
Loudwater
Shillingford
Benson
Ewelme
Greenfield
Turville Heath
Turville
Fingest
Lane End
Wycombe Air Park
Didcot Railway Centre
Brightwell-cum-Sotwell
Preston Crowmarsh
Cookley Green
Pishill
Skirmett
Frieth
Flackwell Heath
Didcot
East Hagbourne
Wallingford
Crowmarsh Gifford
Russell's Water
Park Corner
Stonor
Marlow Bottom
Little Marlow
Wooburn Green
North Moreton
Cholsey and Wallingford Railway
West Hagbourne
South Moreton
Nuffield
Rockwell End
Lower Woodend
Bovingdon Green
Well End
Upton
Aston Upthorpe
Cholsey
North Stoke
Nettlebed
Fawley
Hambleden
Marlow
Bourne End
Cores End
Blewbury
Aston Tirrold
Ipsden
Middle Assendon
Greenlands
Lower Assendon
Mill End
Bisham
Cookham
Stanley
Cookham Dean
Cookham Rise
Maharajah's Well
Highmoor Cross
Medmenham
Moulsford
South Stoke
Checkendon
Stoke Row
Satwell
Greys Court
Remenham
Aston
Remenham Hill
The Thames Path
Hurley
Windsor
Park Corner
Furze Platt
Woodcote
Shepherd's Green
Rotherfield Greys
Henley-on-Thames
River & Rowing Museum
Burchett's Green
Pinkneys Grn.
Maidenhead
Streatley
Goring
Cray's Pond
Rotherfield Peppard
Harpsden
Warren Row
Compton
Goring Heath
Sonning Common
Bray
Streatley on Thames
St Bartholomew's
Aldworth
Lower Basildon
Beale Park
Whitchurch Hill
Cane End
Kidmore End
Lower Shiplake
Shiplake
Wargrave
Littlewick Green
Cox Grn.
Bray Wick
Basildon Park
Binfield Hth.
Hare Hatch
White Waltham
Woodlands Park
Holyport
Hampstead Norreys
The Living Rainforest
Ashampstead
Pangbourne
Whitchurch
Mapledurham
Tokers Green
Dunsden Green
Sonning Eye
Twyford
Waltham St Lawrence
Stud Grn
Touchen End
Quicks Green
Upper Basildon
Purley
Emmer Green
Charvil
Play Hatch
Paley Street
Maidenhead
Buckinghamshire
Oxford
Chiltern
SP
SU

Central Bedfordshire
Luton
Hertfordshire
Windsor and Maidenhead
Slough
Bletchley
Woburn
Leighton Buzzard
Dunstable
Houghton Regis
Luton
HITCHIN
Aylesbury
Tring
Berkhamsted
Hemel Hempstead
St Albans
HARPENDEN
Wendover
Princes Risborough
Chesham
Amersham
Great Missenden
High Wycombe
Beaconsfield
Marlow
Maidenhead
Watford
RICKMANSWORTH
BOREHAMWOOD
Bushey
Radlett
London Colney
Abbots Langley
Kings Langley
Chalfont St Giles
Chalfont St Peter
Gerrards Cross
Uxbridge
Ruislip
Northwood
HARROW
Wembley
EALING
Southall
Hayes
Yiewsley
West Drayton
HEATHROW
WINDSOR
SLOUGH
Eton
Datchet
Burnham
Isleworth
Brentford
Stanmore
Edgware
Chiltern Hills
Stokenchurch
Loudwater
Flackwell Heath
Bourne End
Cookham
Farnham Royal
Stoke Poges
Iver
Denham
Langley
Colnbrook
Markyate
Redbourn
Wheathampstead
Kimpton
Chorleywood
Croxley Green
Oxhey
Elstree
Pinner
Eastcote
Greenford
Sudbury
Perivale
Hanwell
Heston
Cranford
Harlington
Sipson
0 1 2 3 4 5 6 miles
0 1 2 3 4 5 6 7 8 9 10 km

LETCHWORTH
Baldock
Stevenage
Buntingford
Stansted Mountfitchet
STANSTED AIRPORT
BISHOP'S STORTFORD
Hertford
Ware
Sawbridgeworth
WELWYN GARDEN CITY
Harlow
HODDESDON
Hatfield
Broxbourne
CHESHUNT
WALTHAM ABBEY
Epping
Chipping Ongar
POTTERS BAR
ENFIELD
BARNET
Loughton
Chigwell
BRENTWOOD
Romford
Hornchurch
Upminster
Dagenham
Barking
Ilford
Walthamstow
Tottenham
Edmonton
Chingford
Woodford
Finchley
Hendon
Hampstead
Willesden
Camden
Islington
Hackney
Stoke Newington
Leyton
Stratford
East Ham
Woolwich
Greenwich
Deptford
LAMBETH
Westminster
City
Hammersmith
Fulham
Chelsea
Battersea
Camberwell
Erith
Purfleet
Aveley
Grays
Dartford Crossing
M25
M11
A1(M)
A10
A414
A120
54
55
42
28
29
TL
TQ

Newport
Howlett End
Little Sampford
Howe Street
Morris Green
Hedingham
Little Maplestead
Debden
Wicken Bonhunt
Rickling
Widdington
Mole Hall Wildlife Park
Priors Hall Barn
Debden Cross
Thaxted
Little Bardfield
Finchingfield
Wethersfield
Halstead
Quendon
Hamperden End
Cutlers Green
Great Bardfield
Blackmore End
Gosfield
Colne Engaine
Wakes Colne
Ugley
Henham
Monk Street
Shalford
Church End
Beazley End
Earls Colne
Ugley Green
Elsenham
Broxted
Duton Hill
Lindsell
Shalford Green
Jasper's Green
Bocking Churchstreet
High Garrett
Greenstead Green
Stansted Mountfitchet
Molehill Green
Brick End
Great Easton
Bran End
Bardfield Saling
Great Saling
Panfield
Stisted
Great Tey
Stansted Airport
Little Easton
Stebbing
Stebbing Green
Bocking
Braintree
Pattiswick
Broad Green
Bishop's Stortford
Bambers Green
Churchend
Great Dunmow
Little Dunmow
Bannister Green
Rayne
Bradwell
Coggeshall
Takeley
Takeley Street
Smith's Green
Hope End Green
Barnston
Felsted
Great Notley
Black Notley
Tye Green
Cressing
Coggeshall Hamlet
Feering
Gore Pit
Hatfield Forest
Gt. Hallingbury
Bacon End
Bishop's Green
Hounslow Green
North End
Hartford End
Willows Grn.
Young's End
Silver End
Kelvedon
Messing
Great Canfield
High Roding
White Notley
Faulkbourne
Inworth
Lit. Hallingbury
Ford End
Little Leighs
Great Leighs
Rivenhall End
Tiptree
Hatfield Broad Oak
Aythorpe Roding
High Easter
Howe Street
Pleshey
Fuller Street
Fairstead
Terling
Flack's Green
Chipping Hill
Witham
Great Braxted
Hatfield Heath
Sheering
White Roding
Leaden Roding
Good Easter
Great Waltham
Little Waltham
Great Totham
Wickham Bishops
Matching
Matching Tye
Abbess Roding
Margaret Roding
Chignall Smealy
Mashbury
Chignall St James
Hatfield Peverel
Little Totham
Great Totham
Matching Green
Beauchamp Roding
Broomfield
Nounsley
Boreham
Langford
Broad Street Green
High Laver
Little Laver
Foster Street
Shellow Bowells
Boyton Cross
Parsonage Green
Springfield
Chelmer Village
Little Baddow
Heybridge
Magdalen Laver
Roxwell
Writtle
Chelmsford
Woodham Walter
Maldon
Heybridge Basin
Hastingwood
Fyfield
Willingale
Great Oxney Green
Moreton
Cooksmill Green
Widford
Great Baddow
Danbury
Russell Green
Northey I.
Bovinger
Bobbingworth
Norton Mandeville
Sandon
Woodham Mortimer
North Weald Bassett
Shelley
Norton Heath
Loves Green
Galleywood
Howe Green
Rudley Green
Toot Hill
Greensted
High Ongar
Chipping Ongar
Nine Ashes
Cock Clarks
Bicknacre
Mundon
Blackmore
Mill Green
Margaretting
Purleigh
Stanford Rivers
Stondon Massey
Fryerning
West Hanningfield
East Hanningfield
Cold Norton
Latchingdon
Little End
Ingatestone
Stapleford Tawney
Kelvedon Hatch
Doddinghurst
Swallows Cross
Stock
Woodham Ferrers
Stow Maries
Heybridge
Reservoir
Navestock Heath
Mountnessing
Coalhill
Rettendon
South Woodham Ferrers
North Fambridge
Navestock Side
South Hanningfield
Downham
Stapleford Abbotts
Pilgrims Hatch
Hutton
Ramsden Heath
Rettendon Place
South Fambridge
Shenfield
Billericay
Runwell
Hullbridge
Canewdon
South Weald
Brentwood
Ramsden Bellhouse
Wickford
Battlesbridge
Rawreth
Ashingdon
Havering-atte-Bower
South Green
Shotgate
Hockley
Hawkwell
Great Stambridge
Harold Hill
Ingrave
Little Burstead
Crays Hill
Stroud Green
Rayleigh
Herongate
Great Burstead
Dunton Wayletts
Nevendon
North Benfleet
Rochford
Harold Wood
Great Warley
Little Warley
Basildon
Bowers Gifford
Thundersley
Eastwood
Gidea Park
Romford
Cranham
Laindon
Pitsea
Daws Heath
Hadleigh
Prittlewell
Hornchurch
West Horndon
Langdon Hills
Vange
Hope's Grn.
Southend-on-Sea
Rush Green
Upminster
South Benfleet
Leigh on Sea
Elm Park
Bulphan
Westcliff-on-Sea
Dagenham
Hacton
Corbets Tey
North Ockendon
Horndon on the Hill
Fobbing
Canvey
Canvey Island
South Hornchurch
Corringham
Leigh Beck
Thurrock
Rainham
South Ockendon
Baker Street
Orsett
Stanford-le-Hope
Coryton
Wennington
Aveley
North Stifford
Mucking
Thames Haven
London Gateway under construction
Thames Estuary
Chadwell St Mary
Linford
Halstow Marshes
St Mary's Marshes
Allhallows-on-Sea
West Tilbury
Belvedere
East Tilbury
Cliffe
Cooling
St Mary Hoo
Allhallows
Lower Stoke
Grain
Isle of Grain
Tilbury
Slade Green
High Halstow
0 1 2 3 4 5 6 miles
0 1 2 3 4 5 6 7 8 9 10 km

Bures
Nayland
Stratford St Mary
Boxted
Dedham
Brantham
Cattawade
Upper Street
Harkstead
Holbrook Bay
Shop Corner
Shotley Gate
HARWICH
Stour
Mount Bures
Little Horkesley
Boxted Heath
Boxted Cross
Langham
Dedham Heath
Lawford
Mistley
Manningtree
Bradfield
Wrabness
Parkeston
Upper Dovercourt
Dovercourt
Wormingford
Great Horkesley
MISTLEY TOWERS
STOUR VALLEY
SIR ALFRED MUNNINGS ART MUSEUM
BRIDGE COTTAGE
HARWICH REDOUBT FORT
ESBJERG 17:15
HOEK VAN HOLLAND 6:45
EAST ANGLIAN RAILWAY MUSEUM
WESTON HOMES COMMUNITY STAD
Horkesley Heath
Ardleigh
Bradfield Heath
Little Oakley
Fordham
West Bergholt
Mile End
Little Bromley
Horsley Cross
Horsleycross Street
Wix
Great Oakley
Colne
Eight Ash Green
Parson's Heath
Fox Street
Crockleford Heath
Great Bromley
Stone's Green
Fordstreet
Aldham
HIGHWOODS
Little Bentley
Tendring Green
Colchester
Elmstead Market
ST BOTOLPH'S PRIORY
Beaumont
Marks Tey
Lexden
Stanway
Beacon End
Hare Green
Balls Green
Horsey Island
The Naze
EARTH WORKS
Abbey Field
Wivenhoe Cross
Tendring
Thorpe Green
HAMFORD WATER
Copford Green
Shrub End
Old Heath
Frating Green
Great Bentley
Thorpe-le-Soken
Kirby-le-Soken
MARITIME MUSEUM
Maypole Green
BOURNE MILL
Wivenhoe
BETH CHATTO GDNS
Weeley
Weeley Heath
COLCHESTER ZOO
Blackheath
Rowhedge
Aingers Green
Walton-on-the-Naze
Easthorpe
Heckfordbridge
Layer de la Haye
Alresford
Kirby Cross
Frinton-on-Sea
Hardy's Green
Fingringhoe
Row Heath
Smythe's Green
Birch
Birch Green
Malting Green
Thorrington
Little Clacton
CLACTON VILLAGE
Great Holland
Abberton
Abberton Reservoir
Langenhoe
St Osyth Heath
HOLLAND HAVEN
Layer Marney
Layer Breton
LAYER MARNEY TOWER
River Colne
Brightlingsea
Peldon
ST OSYTH PRIORY
St Osyth
Great Clacton
Holland-on-Sea
Clacton-on-Sea
Oxley Green
Paternoster Heath
Great Wigborough
Mersea Island
East Mersea
CUDMORE GROVE
Point Clear
Salcott
COPT HALL MARSHES
Blue Row
COLNE ESTUARY
Jaywick
Tolleshunt D'Arcy
BLACKWATER ESTUARY
West Mersea
MERSEA ISLAND MUSEUM
Colne Pt.
Tolleshunt Major
Tollesbury
The Nass
Virley Channel
Goldhanger
Sales Pt.
ST PETERS ON THE WALL
Bradwell Waterside
Blackwater
Osea I.
Bradwell on Sea
Ramsey Island
St Lawrence
Tillingham
DENGIE
TM
Steeple
Asheldham
Dengie
Mayland
Southminster
Ray Sand
Althorne
Stoneyhills
MANGAPPS RAILWAY MUS
Montsale
Deal Hall
Ostend
Creeksea
Burnham-on-Crouch
MUS
Foulness Sand
Foulness Pt.
Crouch
TR
Paglesham Churchend
WALLASEA WETLANDS
Courtsend
Paglesham Eastend
Churchend
Ballards Gore
Potton Island
FOULNESS ISLAND
MAPLIN SANDS
Barling
Little Wakering
Havengore Island
Great Wakering
Bournes Green
North Shoebury
Shoeburyness
Thorpe Bay
Cambridge Town
Shoeburyness
A12
A120
A133
A134
A137
A13
B1508
B1029
B1035
B1352
B1414
B1033
B1027
B1028
B1022
B1026
B1025
B1023
B1032
B1021
B1018
B1010
B1016
B1017
A
B
C
D
E
F
G
5
6
7
8
60
62
23
20
18
56
57
30

Pembrokeshire
(Sir Benfro)
PEMBROKESHIRE COAST
ARFORDIR PENFRO
ST. BRIDES
BAY
BAE SAIN FFRAID
SM
SR
ROSSLARE 3:30
ROSSLARE 4:00
Strumble Head
Pen Caer
Tresinwen
PWLL DERI
213
Llanwnda
Goodwick
(Wdig)
191
Lower Town
Fishguard Bay
Bae Abergwaun
Fishguard
(Abergwaun)
Dinas Head
Brynhenllan
Dinas Cross
A487
45
Trefasser
Penbwchdy
Dyffryn
Manorowen
St Nicholas
PEMBROKESHIRE COAST PATH
LLWYBR ARFORDIR PENFRO
TREGWYNT WOOLLEN MILL
A40
Scleddau
Llanychaer
Pontfaen
B4313
Ynysduellyn
Abercastle
Granston
Trecwn
Penclegyr
Porthgain
Trefin
Mathry
Newbridge
CORSYDD LLANGLOFFAN
Abereiddy
Llanrhian
16
Penparc
Castlemorris
Croes-goch
B4330
B4331
14
Little Newcastle
Puncheston
ST. DAVID'S HEAD
PENMAEN DEWI
Tretio
Treffynnon
164
Treddiog
Letterston
Castlebythe
Tufton
181
Treleddyd-fawr
Carnhedryn
Treglemais
Llanreithan
Welsh Hook
St Dogwells
Whitesand Bay
Porth-mawr
ST DAVID'S
Rhodiad
BISHOP'S PALACE
B4583
Caerfarchell
Llandeloy
Pont-yr-hafod
Wolf's Castle
B4329
Ambleston
Woodstock
A487
Rhosson
Whitchurch
Middle Mill
Trefgarn Owen
Hayscastle
Rinaston
Wallis
CATHEDRAL
St David's
(Tyddewi)
Nine Wells
Solva
Brimaston
LLYS-Y-FRAN RESERVOIR
Ramsey Island
Ynys Dewi
RAMSEY ISLAND
Ramsey Sound
Hayscastle Cross
Mountain Water
Treffgarne
Triffleton
Spittal
178
DUDWELL MT.
Leweston
Penycwm
SCOLTON MANOR
Walton East
Newgale
W. Cleddau
E. Cleddau
Wolfsdale
Roch Gate
Roch
Camrose
Rudbaxton
Clarbeston Road
Keeston
Simpson Cross
PEMBROKE MOTOR MUSEUM
15
Nolton Haven
Nolton
Tangiers
Leechpool
Pelcomb Cross
Crundale
Wiston
Lambston
Slade
Haverfordwest
(Hwlffordd)
Druidston
Pelcomb Bridge
Portfield Gate
CASTLE MUSEUM AND ART GALLERY
The Rhos
Uzmaston
BROAD HAVEN
Haroldston West
B4341
Dreenhill
Merlin's Bridge
Broad Haven
Millin Cross
PICTON CASTLE & GARDENS
B4327
Broadway
Little Haven
Walton West
Pope Hill
Boulston
Minwear
Talbenny
North Johnston
Freystrop
Landshipping
12
Walwyn's Castle
Hook
Martletwy
Tower Point
Trwyn Twr
St Bride's
82
Landshipping Quay
NATIONAL NATURE RESERVE
79
Wooltack Point
Trwyn Wooltack
Johnston
Tiers Cross
Llangwm
Black Tar
Skomer Island
Ynys Skomer
SKOMER ISLAND
Marloes
Hasguard
Robeston Cross
A4076
Rosemarket
MARLOES SANDS
Broad Sound
Thornton
Hill Mountain
Port Lion
Steynton
A477
Houghton
Sandy Haven
Herbrandston
Lawrenny
St Ishmael's
Milford Haven
(Aberdaugleddau)
Gateholm Island
Ynys Gateholm
B4325
Honeyborough
Burton
West Williamston
Dale
Hakin
Waterston
Llanstadwell
Neyland
MILFORD HAVEN
ABERDAUGLEDDYF
UPTON CASTLE GARDENS
Skokholm Island
Ynys Skokholm
Pembroke Dock
(Doc Penfro)
TOLL
Cosheston
CAREW CASTLE
71
Angle
Angle Bay
Bae Angle
PEMBROKE DOCK SUNDERLAND TRUST
Pwllcrochan
32
Milton
Pennar
B4322
St Ann's Hd.
Pentir St. Ann
Rhoscrowther
Pembroke
(Penfro)
Monkton
LAMPHEY BISHOP'S PALACE
Sheep Island
Ynys y Defaid
B4320
Hundleton
Lamphey
Freshwater West
Maiden Wells
B4584
Hodgeston
B4319
St Twynnells
Castlemartin
Freshwater East
Warren
Chenton or Stackpole Elidor
Trewent Pt.
Trwyn Trewent
Merrion
Linney Hd.
Pentir Linney
St Petrox
Stackpole
ELEGUG STACKS
STACKPOLE
Bosherston
The Wash
Stackpole Hd.
Pen Stackpole
St Govan's Hd.
Pen St Gofan
A
B
C
D
E
F
G
1
2
3
4
5
17
18
20
24
19
0 1 2 3 4 5 6 miles
0 1 2 3 4 5 6 7 8 9 10 km

CARDIGAN BAY
BAE CEREDIGION
SN
PEMBROKESHIRE COAST
ARFORDIR PENFRO
PEMBROKESHIRE COAST PATH
LLWYBR ARFORDIR PENFRO
Cwmtudu
Cwmtydu
Ynys-Lochtyn
Llangrannog
Blaencelyn
Pontgarreg
Penbryn
Penmorfa
Brynhoffnant
Sarnau
Tresaith
Aberporth
Parcllyn
Felinwynt
Mwnt
Cardigan I.
Ynys Aberteifi
Cemaes Head
Pen Cemaes
Gwbert
Y Ferwig
Blaenannerch
Aberporth West Wales Airport
Tremain
Tan-y-groes
Glynarthen
Blaenporth
Penparc
Poppit Sands
Cippyn
Cardigan
(Aberteifi)
Castle
St Dogmaels
Abbey
Bridgend
Llangoedmor
Pantgwyn
Ponthirwaun
Bryngwyn
Capel Tygwydd
Beulah
Bettws Ifan
Hawen
Rhydlewis
Brongest
Troed-yr-aur
Moylgrove
Monington
Croft
Pen-y-bryn
Coedmor
Cilgerran Castle
Llechryd
Llandygwydd
Cilgerran
Afon Teifi
Bridell
Glanrhyd
Llantood
Carreg-wen
Cwm-cou
Llandyfriog
Aber-banc
Pontgareg
Rhos-hill
Coracle Centre & Flour Mill
Abercych
Cenarth
Newcastle Emlyn
(Castell Newydd Emlyn)
Pentrecagal
Aber-Arad
National Wool Museum
Felindre
Cwmhiraeth
Newport Bay
Bae Trefdraeth
Dinas Head
Berry Hill
Nevern
Felindre Farchog
Pengelli Forest
Castell Henllys Fort
Newchapel
Clynfyw
Boncath
Cilwendeg
Penrherber
Cheese Farm
Fishguard Bay
Bae Abergwaun
Brynhenllan
Parrog
Newport
(Trefdraeth)
Dinas Cross
Lower Town
Carningli
Ty Canol
Eglwyswrw
Dyfed Shires & Leisure Farm
Bro Meigan Gardens
Llanfair-Nant-Gwyn
Blaenffos
Afon Nevern
Crosswell
Bwlchygroes
Cwmcych
Capel Iwan
Fishguard
(Abergwaun)
Llanychaer
Cilgwyn
Brynberian
Pontyglasier
Eglwyswen
Penygroes
Star
Clydey
Cwmorgan
Tanglwst
Moelfre
Pontfaen
Trecwn
Crymych
Tegryn
Mynydd Preseli
Foel Cwmcerwyn
Hermon
Bryn-Iwan
Pentre-galar
Llanfyrnach
Hen-feddau fawr
Little Newcastle
Puncheston
Castlebythe
New Inn
Rosebush
Mynachlog-ddu
Dinas
Trelech
Glandwr
Afon Taf
Hebron
Blaenwaun
Welsh Chocolate Farm
Llanwinio
Pen-y-bont
Glandy Cross
Pant-y-Caws
Llanglydwen
Cefn-y-pant
Cwmbach
Talog
Ambleston
Woodstock
New Moat
A487
A484
A478
B4548
B4546
B4582
B4570
B4332
B4333
B4334
B4321
B4571
B4313
B4329
B4299
0 1 2 3 4 5 6 miles
0 1 2 3 4 5 6 7 8 9 10 km

1
2
3
4
5
A
B
C
D
E
F
58
45
32
33
SN
ARTS CENTRE
NATIONAL LIBRARY
CLIFF RAILWAY
Aberystwyth
P&R
CASTLE
Clarach
Bow Street
Plas Gogerddan
Penrhyn-coch
Comins Coch
Capel Dewi
Llanbadarn Fawr
A44
Trefechan
Penparcau
Southgate
Glanrafon
Rhydyfelin
Moriah
Capel Seion
Llanfarian
Gors
Chancery
New Cross
Blaenplwyf
Llanilar
Pentre-llyn
A487
A485
B4575
Rhos-y-garth
B4576
Llanddeiniol
Llangwyryfon
Llanrhystud
Lledrod
Trefenter
Rhyd-Rosser
Llansantffraed
FANTASY FARM PARK
LLYN EIDDWEN
361
Bronnant
Rhydfudr
MYNYDD BACH
Llanon
Bontnewydd
Nebo
Cere
(Sir
Blaenpennal
Aberarth
Cross Inn
Bethania
Tyncelyn
Aberaeron
B4577
Pennant
188
Penuwch
Monachty
B4337
Crynfryn
B4578
New Quay (Ceinewydd)
LLANERCHAERON
Cilcennin
Llangeitho
Ffos-y-ffin
Cei-bach
Newbridge
Bwlch-Llan
Llwyncelyn
B4342
Capel Betws Lleucu
Maen-y-groes
Gilfachrheda
Oakford
Ciliau Aeron
Afon Aeron
Cwmtudu Cwmtydu
A486
Cross Inn
A482
Trefilan
Llundain-fach
Commins Capel Betws
Nanternis
Llanarth
B4339
Ystrad Aeron
Tal-sarn
Gartheli
Caerwedros
Dihewyd
Abermeurig
Llwyn-y-groes
Ynys-Lochtyn
169
A487
Felinfach
252
Blaencelyn
Llwyndafydd
Synod Inn
Mydroilyn
Felindre
Olmarch
Llangrannog
Temple Bar
Pontgarreg
Caledrhydiau
Ffynnon-oer
Llangybi
Plwmp
B4334
B4321
Penbryn
Pentregat
Llanfair Clydogau
Tresaith
Penmorfa
Brynhoffnant
B4338
Cribyn
Silian
Betws Bledrws
Aberporth
Sarnau
Gorsgoch
ABERPORTH WEST WALES AIRPORT
Talgarreg
259
Maestir
Olwen
Tan-y-groes
Capel Cynon
RHOS LLAWR CWRT
Bwlch-y-fadfa
324
Cellan
Lampeter (Llanbedr Pont Steffan)
Blaenporth
Glynarthen
314
Castell-Howell
Aber
Cwrt-newydd
Pentrefelin
B4333
Bettws Ifan
Rhydlewis
Ffostrasol
B4459
Llanwnnen
A475
Cwmann
Pantgwyn
Beulah
Hawen
Maesymeillion
Pont-siân
Cwmsychpant
Pentre-bach
Ram
185
Ponthirwaun
Penrhiw-pâl
Coed-y-bryn
Llanwenog
Dre-fach
Alltyblaca
Llanycrwys
Bryngwyn
Brongest
Troedyraur
Tregroes
Rhydowen
A485
Pencarreg
Parc-y-rhôs
Llandygwydd
Capel Tygwydd
Maesllyn
Croes-lan
Brynteg
Llanybydder
Ffaldybrenin
B4571
Prengwyn
415
Horeb
258
Capel Dewi
Rhuddlan
Glan-Duar
Ty Mawr
Mynydd Pencarreg
Harford
Cwm-cou
Llandyfriog
Aber-banc
B4476
ROCK MILL WOOLLEN MILL
Maesycrugiau
Penrhiw-llan
TEIFI VALLEY RAILWAY
Llandysul
Cenarth
Newcastle Emlyn (Castell Newydd Emlyn)
Pentrecagal
Henllan
Aber-Giâr
Esgairdawe
Llanfihangel-ar-arth
Aber-Arad
NATIONAL WOOL MUSEUM
Llangeler
B4336
Llanllwni
408
Penrherber
Drefach
Pentre-cwrt
Rhydcymerau
CHEESE FARM
Felindre
Bancyffordd
Cwmhiraeth
Drefelin
Saron
Llidiad Nenog
Capel Iwan
Cwmpengraig
New Inn
Llansawel
Cwmcych
Pencader
335
MOELFRE
Rhôs
Gwyddgrug
Cwmorgan
Carmarthenshire
(Sir Gaerfyrddin)
Tanglwst
Dolgran
Gwernogle
Abergorlech
Edwinsford
TALLEY ABBEY
MYNYDD RHOS-WEN
Afon Cothi
A484
314
329
CYNROS
Talley
B4299
Bryn-Iwan
247
Alltwalis
Brechfa Forest
Nant-y-ffin
Pen-y-garn
Cwm-byr
Hermon
Cwmduad
B4310
Halfway
Hen-feddau fawr
Trelech
Cwmdu
Llanpumsaint
192
Llanllawddog
Brechfa
Soar
Pontarsais
Horeb
Llanfynydd
Capel Isaac
B4301
B4310
Pant-glas
Salem
Afon Duad
Rhydargaeau
Llanwinio
Talog
0 1 2 3 4 5 6 miles
0 1 2 3 4 5 6 7 8 9 10 km

Hafren Forest
Llanidloes
Pen-bont Rhydybeddau
Dyffryn Castell
LLYWERNOG SILVER LEAD MINE
Pant Mawr
Glynbrochan
Cwmbelan
Capel Bangor
Dollwen
Goginan
Llanifyny
Llangurig
Cwmbrwyno
A44
GLYNDWR'S WAY
VALE OF RHEIDOL RAILWAY
Afon Rheidol
RHEIDOL HYDRO ELECTRIC STATION
Ystumtuen
Aberffrwd
Ysbytycynfyn
COED RHEIDOL
David's Well
A4120
Pisgah
Llanfihangel-y-Creuddyn
Mynydd Bach
Trisant
Devil's Bridge
B4343
610 PEN Y GARN
Blaenycwm
Nantgwyn
B4518
Pant-y-dwr
493 RED LION HI
Cnwch-coch
A470
Bwlch-y-sarnau
B4340
Abermagwr
Crosswood
New Row
B4574
HAFOD ESTATE
Cwmystwyth
Pont-rhyd-y-groes
571 GEIFAS
498
St Harmon
Llanafan
Wenallt
Mynydd Bach
371
Ysbyty Ystwyth
Wye (Gwy)
505 MOEL HYWEL
Craig-goch Res.
Tynygraig
Tanyrhydiau
572 TRAWSALLT
CLAERWEN
Rhayader (Rhaeadr Gwy)
WELSH ROYAL CRYSTAL
Gaufron
Ystradmeurig
Ffair-Rhos
Penygarreg Res.
Llansantffraed Cwmdeuddwr
Swydd-ffynnon
Pontrhydfendigaid
STRATA FLORIDA ABBEY
Elan Village
Garreg-ddu Res.
THE GIGRIN RED KITE FEEDING CENTRE
Nantmel
Glan Teifi
CORS CARON
530 DIBYN DU
Claerwen Reservoir
Nant-glas
Gwystre
Ceredigion
Ty'n-yr-eithin
Afon Claerwen
Caban-coch Res.
Llanwrthwl
Argoed
Llandrindod Wells (Llandrindod)
Llanyre
A470
A4081
249
Tywi Forest
Powys
WELSH GOLD CENTRE
Tregaron
B4343
537 DRUM-DDU
Newbridge on Wye
B4358
NATIONAL C COLLECT
Ithon
508 Y DRUM
645 DRYGARN FAWR
532 BRYN CRWN
Disserth
Howe
Cross
DOLGOCH
484 ESGAIR CERRIG
SN
Llanafan-fawr
A483
Llanddewi-Brefi
Pentre-rhew
TYNCORNEL
500
NANT IRFON
CORS Y LLYN
B4358
Pentre-llwyn-llwyd
Cwmbach
Builth Road
Soar-y-Mynydd
Llyn Brianne Res.
Troed-rhiwdalar
463
484 BRYN BRAWD
Abergwesyn
Llanelwe
456
Beulah
Cilmery
Oaklands
Llanfechan
A483
Builth Wells (Llanfair-ym-Muallt)
487
Mynydd Trawsnant
Cwm Irfon
Garth
Tyn-y-graig
ALLT RHYD Y GROES
CAMBRIAN WOOLLEN MILL
Llanwrtyd
441
Llanddewi'r Cwm
Irfon
Maesmynis
440
Ystradffin
Llanwrtyd Wells (Llanwrtud)
Llangammarch Wells
Alltma
B4519
459
Ffarmers
Afon Cothi
Mynydd Mallaen
Nant-y-Bai
Cefn-gorwydd
474 DRUM-DDU
Epynt
B4520
Cwrt-y-cadno
Rhandirmwyn
Pentre Dolau-Honddu
48
Gwenddwr
Mynydd Epynt
Crychan Forest
Llandre
434 ESGAIR FERCHON
463 BRYN DU
Pumsaint
DOLAUCOTHI GOLD MINES
Caeo Forest
Cynghordy
Tirabad
433
Upper Chapel
Cilycwm
Caio
341
Llanfair-ar-y-bryn
Llaneglwys
Porthyrhyd
Divlyn
456
Crugybar
Siloh
Blaendyryn
Merthyr Cynog
Honddu
Lower Chapel
B4302
A482
Pentre-ty-gwyn
Babel
423
Llandovery (Llanymddyfri)
A483
Mynydd Bwlch-y-groes
442
Llandeilo'r Fan
Llanfihangel Nant Bran
Pont-faen
Garthbre
Pwllgloyw
Cwmdwr
Halfway
Pentre-bach
Sarnau
B4520
Wauncluda
Llansadwrn
Llanwrda
A40
A4069
Myrtle Hill
Nant Bran
Llandefaelog Fach
Llanddew
Felindre
Pentre'r-felin
Battle
Llywel
Trallong
CATHEDRAL
Cilgwyn
33
Myddfai
440
Usk
Aberyscir
BRECON GAER ROMAN FORT
Brecon (Aberhonddu)
34
Ashfield
Usk Reservoir
Trecastle
Sennybridge (Pont Senni)
Wysg
Llanfaes
Hermon
Llangadog
Cwmwysg
Penpont
Llanspyddid
Pont ar Hydfer
Defynnog
Mynydd Illtyd
Manordeilo
Felindre
400
BRECKNOCK MUSEUM
Tai'r-Bull
Cwmifor
A4067
MOUNTAIN CENTRE
Talsarn
Llanfrynach
58
59
48
A
B
C
D
E
F
G
5
6
7
8
9

Rhayader
(Rhaeadr Gwy)
Llansantffraed Cwmdeuddwr
WELSH ROYAL CRYSTAL
THE GIGRIN FARM RED KITE FEEDING CENTRE
Gaufron
Nantmel
Nant-glas
Llanwrthwl
Argoed
St Harmon
Pant-y-dwr
Nantgwyn
Tylwch
New Chapel
MOEL HYWEL
Bwlch-y-sarnau
Abbey-cwm-hir
David's Well
RED LION HILL
GLYNDWR'S WAY
Llanbadarn Fynydd
Rhydmoelddu
Llanbister
Llandewi Ystradenny
CILFAESTY HILL
Felindre
Beguildy
Black Mountain
BEACON HILL
Dutlas
BLACK MT
Bettws-y-crwyn
Quabbs
Anchor
Hall of the Forest
Newcastle
Whitcott Keysett
Bicton
Lower Down
Clun
CLUN MILL
CASTLE
Clunton
Llwyn
Churchbank
Hobarris
Upper Treverward
Llanfair Waterdine
Purlogue
OFFA'S DYKE PATH
New Invention
Chapel Lawn
Skyborry Green
Knucklas
Stowe
Knighton
(Tref-y-Clawdd)
Milebrook
Crug
Llangunllo
Bleddfa
Monaughty
Pilleth
Rhos-y-meirch
Whitton
Norton
Dolley Green
Cascob
Maes-Treylow
Discoed
Stapleton
Presteigne
(Llanandras)
JUDGES LODGING
Lugg
Combe
Rodd
Beggar's Bush
Kinnerton
Evenjobb
Nash
Stansbatch
Knill
Titley
Dolau
Llanfihangel Rhydithon
RADNOR FOREST
Crossgates
Fron
Gwystre
Penybont
Llandegley
Llandrindod Wells
(Llandrindod)
RADNORSHIRE MUSEUM
Ridgebourne
NATIONAL CYCLE COLLECTION
Llanyre
Ithon
DRUM-DDU
Newbridge-on-Wye
Disserth
Howey
Crossway
New Radnor
Old Radnor
Yardro
Walton
STANNER ROCKS
Flintsham
Dolyhir
Burlingjobb
OFFA'S DYKE PATH
Llanfihangel-nant-Melan
Frank's Bridge
GWAUNCESTE HILL
SO
Hergest Ridge
HERGEST CROFT GDNS
Kington
Headbrook
Upper Hergest
Lower Hergest
Lyonshall
Holme Marsh
OAKLANDS SMALL BREEDS FARM
Kingswood
Gladestry
Hopley's Green
Huntington
Hengoed
Wootton
Llanafan-fawr
CORS Y LLYN
Pentre-llwyn-llwyd
Troed-rhiwdalar
Cwmbach
Builth Road
Llansantffraed-in-Elvel
Hundred House
Glascwm
Colva
Cregrina
Llanelwedd
Cilmery
Oaklands
Llanfaredd
Builth Wells
(Llanfair-ym-Muallt)
Llanfechan
Garth
Irfon
Tyn-y-graig
Maesmynis
Llanddewi'r Cwm
Aberedw
Alltmawr
Llanbadarn-y-Garreg
Rhulen
RED HILL
Bryngwyn
Newchurch
Michaelchurch on Arrow
Lower Welson
Almeley
Upcott
Kinnersley
Eardisley
Brilley
Dol-y-cannau
RHOS GOCH
Rhos-goch
Rhydspence
TOLL
Millhalf
Willersley
Ailey
Whitney-on-Wye
Winforton
Letton
Wye
Clifford
Priory Wood
Merbach
Bredwardine
GARDENS & GALLERY
Llangammarch Wells
DRUM-DDU
Llandeilo Graban
Llanbedr
Painscastle
Bronydd
Hardwicke
The Bage
Brobury
Pentre Dolau-Honddu
Gwenddwr
Erwood
Crickadarn
THE BEGWNS
Clyro
Hay-on-Wye
(Y Gelli Gandryll)
ARTHUR'S STONE
Cusop
Dorstone
BRYN DU
Upper Chapel
Llanstephan
Rhydness
Llowes
Llanigon
Snodhill
Peterchurch
Hinton
Boughrood
Cwmbach
Glasbury
Pipton
Tregoyd
Llanrosser
Llaneglwys
Llyswen
Three Cocks
Velindre
Blaendyryn
Merthyr Cynog
Lower Chapel
Honddu
Llandefalle
Bronllys
BRONLLYS
Lynfi
HAY BLUFF
Craswall
Urishay Common
Upper Maes-coed
Llanfihangel Nant Bran
Pont-faen
Pwllgloyw
Sarnau
Garthbrengy
Talachddu
Llanfilo
Talgarth
Llanelieu
THE TUMPA
Michaelchurch Escley
Middle Maes-coed
Newton
Nant Bran
Llandefaelog Fach
Llanddew
Felinfach
Tredustan
Trefecca
HOWELL HOUSE
Tredomen
Llandefaelog-tre'r-graig
TREFEINON OPEN FARM
Pengenffordd
BLACK MOUNTAINS
Afon Honddu
Llanveynoe
Lower Maes-coed
Battle
Llanfrynach
BRECON GAER ROMAN FORT
CATHEDRAL
Aberyscir
Usk (Wysg)
Brecon
(Aberhonddu)
Llanywern
BRECON
Llanfihangel Tal-y-llyn
Llechfaen
Talyllyn
Llannamlach
Llangors
Llangorse Lake
Llangasty Talyllyn
Mynydd Troed
Y MYNYDDOEDD DUON
Longtown
Llanthony
PRIORY
Clodock
OFFA'S DYKE PATH
LLWYBR CLAWDD OFFA
HATTERRALL
Bull
MOUNTAIN CENTRE
miles
km

Hopesay
Kempton
Little Brampton
Aston on Clun
Sibdon Carwood
Newington
Halford
Dinchope
Craven Arms
Stokesay
STOKESAY CASTLE
Seifton
Norton
Vernolds Common
Culmington
Great Sutton
Peaton
Hayton's Bent
St Margaret
Stoke St Milborough
Cleedownton
Aston Botterell
Loughton
Wheathill
Chorley
Stottesdon
RAYS FARM COUNTRY MATTERS
Purslow
Clunbury
Broome
Twitchen
Brandhill
THE WERNLAS COLLECTION
Onibury
Hopton Cangeford
Silvington
Farlow
Kinlet
Hopton Castle
Hoptonheath
Abcott
Clungunford
Shelderton
Wootton
Stanton Lacy
Bromfield
LUDLOW
Middleton
Bitterley
Cleeton St Mary
Catherton
Buttonoak
Bedstone
Marlow
Henley
Foxwood
Doddington
Neen Savage
Hopton Wafers
WYRE FOREST
Wyre Forest
Bucknell
Todding
Kinton
Leintwardine
Ludlow
Snitton
Farden
Knowbury
Cleehill
Hints
Knowle
Coreley
Cleobury Mortimer
Lem Hill
Far Forest
Fingerpost
Pound Bank
Callow Hill
Bliss Gate
Buckton
Downton on the Rock
Ludford
P&R
Hope Bagot
Milson
Bayton
Brampton Bryan
Teme
Walford
Burrington
Aston
Overton
Caynham
Whitton
Nash
Neen Sollars
Mamble
Clows Top
Rock
Stour
Adforton
Ashford Carbonell
Ashford Bowdler
Greete
Frith Common
Letton
Elton
Leinthall Starkes
Richards Castle
Middleton
Boraston
Wigmore
Birtley
BURFORD HOUSE & MEADOW GALLERY
Lindridge
Pensax
Ongar Street
Lower Lye
Leinthall Earls
Woofferton
Little Hereford
Newnham Bridge
Eardiston
Abberley
Yatton
Brimfield
Comberton
Gosford
Burford
Tenbury Wells
Lower Rochford
Stockton on Teme
Lingen
Limebrook
CROFT CASTLE
Orleton
Upper Rochford
Hanley William
Orleton
Stanford on Teme
Stanford Bridge
Great Witley
Aymestrey
Bircher
Middleton on the Hill
St Michaels
Callows Grave
Hanley Child
Broad Heath
Sapey Common
Kinsham
Byton
Mortimer's Cross
Yarpole
Lucton
WATER MILL AND BATTLE CENTRE
Ashton
Eye
BERRINGTON HALL
The Hundred
Leysters Pole
Kyre Magna
Stoke Bliss
Upper Sapey
Shelsley Walsh
Shelsley Beauchamp
Combe Moor
Luston
Lugg Green
Ledicot
Shobdon
Kingsland
Eyton
Kimbolton
Bank Street
Sweet Green
Clifton upon Teme
Staunton on Arrow
Cobnash
The Broad
Stockton
Whyle
Grafton
High Lane
Harpley
Shirl Heath
Cholstrey
LEOMINSTER
Leominster
Pudleston
Collington
Thornbury
Hatfield
Martley
Tedstone Wafer
Arrow
Eardisland
BURTON COURT
Lawton
Monkland
Barons Cross
Steen's Bridge
Edvin Loach
Edwyn Ralph
Tedstone Delamere
Horsham
Berrow Green
Pembridge
Marston
Ivington Green
Ivington
Humber
Docklow
Grendon Green
Bredenbury
Bromyard Downs
HERITAGE CENTRE
BROCKHAMPTON ESTATE
Whitbourne
Bearwood
DUNKERTONS CIDER
Luntley
Brierley
Stoke Prior
Risbury
Marston Stannett
Knightwick
Broadwas
Sollers Dilwyn
Dilwyn
Haven
Broxwood
Aulden
Marlbrook
Newton
Upper Hill
Hope under Dinmore
Hegdon Hill
Pencombe
Bromyard
Linley Green
Alfrick
Woonton
Birley
Knapton Green
Bowley
HAMPTON COURT
SO
Stanford Bishop
Alfrick Pound
Sarnesfield
Weobley
Weobley Marsh
Bush Bank
QUEENSWOOD
Bodenham
SHORTWOOD FAMILY FARM
Little Cowarne
Munderfield Row
Acton Beauchamp
Suckley
Leigh Sinton
King's Pyon
Westhope
Bodenham Moor
Maund Bryan
Ullingswick
Munderfield Stocks
Acton Green
Longley Green
Storridge
Ledgemoor
Canon Pyon
Urdimarsh
The Vauld
Felton
Moreton Jeffries
Stoke Lacy
Evesbatch
Stony Cross
Calver Hill
Wormsley
Wellington
Walker's Green
Burley Gate
Much Cowarne
Bishops Frome
Fromes Hill
Stifford's Bridge
Cradley
Norton Canon
Yarsop
Marden
Preston Wynne
Ridgeway Cross
Westfield
Moorhampton
Tillington Common
Sutton St Nicholas
Ocle Pychard
Lower Egleton
Castle Frome
West Malvern
Staunton on Wye
Yazor
Mansel Lacy
Tillington
Moreton on Lugg
Newtown
Norbridge
Mathon
Mansell Gamage
Brinsop
Burghill
Pipe and Lyde
KENCHESTER WATER GARDENS
Westhide
Stanley Hill
Ham Green
Monnington on Wye
Credenhill
Withington
Stretton Grandison
Canon Frome
Upper Wyche
Byford
Bishopstone
Kenchester
Stretton Sugwas
Shelwick
Shucknall
Bosbury
Colwall Stone
Preston on Wye
Bridge Sollers
Canon Bridge
THE WEIR
Swainshill
King's Acre
Holmer
Hagley
Weston Beggard
Yarkhill
Tarrington
Coddington
Colwall Green
Moccas
Ploughfield
Lulham
Breinton Common
Upper Breinton
HEREFORD
Lugwardine
Bartestree
Munsley
Staplow
Little Malvern
Blakemere
THE FLITS
Tyberton
CIDER MUSEUM
Tupsley
Dormington
Trumpet
Wellington Heath
Madley
Eaton Bishop
Breinton
Ruckhall
Hereford
Priors Frome
Alder's End
Bradlow
Shenmore
Cublington
Lower Bullingham
ROTHERWAS
Hampton Bishop
Checkley
Woolhope Cockshoot
Pixley
Aylton
Ledbury
Hollybush
Vowchurch
Brampton
Clehonger
Grafton
Mordiford
Putley
Eastnor
EASTNOR
Turnastone
Kingstone
Dinedor
Wye
Little Marcle
Golden Valley
Allensmore
Portway
Twyford Common
Holme Lacy
Woolhope
Preston
Thruxton
Winnal
Callow
Fownhope
Rushall
Donnington
Brown's End
Cockyard
Dewsall Court
Aconbury
HELLEN'S MANOR
St Margaret's
Kerry's Gate
Bolstone
Sollers Hope
Bromsberrow Hth.
Bacton
Didley
Kivernoll
King's Thorn
Little Dewchurch
Brockhampton
Much Marcle
Broom's Green
Little Birch
Falcon
COURT GARDENS
Lyne Down
Ryton
Wormbridge
ABBEY DORE COURT
St Devereux
Much Dewchurch
Much Birch
Carey
Ballingham
Crossway
Dymock
ST MARY'S CHURCH
Redmarley D'Abitot
Abbey Dore
Howton
Kilpeck
KILPECK CASTLE (REMS) & CHURCH
Wormelow Tump
Penalt
Fawley Chapel
How Caple
Kempley
Poolhill
Ewyas Harold
Orcop Hill
Hoarwithy
Llandinabo
Red Rail
King's Caple
Foy
Hole-in-the-Wall
Brand Green
Pontrilas
Llanwarne
Sellack
Upton Bishop
Rowlestone
Monmouth Cap
Pagwy Llydiart
Harewood End
Upper Grove Common
Brampton Abbotts
Phocle Green
Upleadon
Llangua
Kentchurch
Orcop
Pencoyd
Garway Hill
Michaelchurch
ROSS SPUR SERVICES
Gorsley
Newent
GROSMONT
Leadon
Teme
Lugg
Frome
Rea
Lodon
M50
A49
A44
A456
A443
A4112
A4103
A417
A438
A465
A466
A449
A4110
A4113
A4117
A480
B4368
B4367
B4385
B4364
B4363
B4199
B4201
B4202
B4204
B4203
B4197
B4214
B4220
B4218
B4216
B4224
B4399
B4348
B4349
B4352
B4347
B4362
B4361
B4360
B4529
B4457
B4230
B4530
B4215
B4221
B4024
B4208
60
61
50
35
36

Worcestershire
Stourbridge
HALESOWEN
Kidderminster
Bromsgrove
Redditch
Droitwich Spa
Worcester
Evesham
Pershore
Great Malvern
Malvern Link
Upton upon Severn
Tewkesbury
Ledbury
Bromyard
Bewdley
Stourport on Severn
Catshill
Aston Fields
Bishop's Cleeve
Newent
Kinver
Wyre Forest
Abberley Hill
Malvern Hills
Vale
Potter's Cross
Alveley
Highley
Chorley
Stottesdon
Romsley
Kingsford
Whittington
Pedmore
Hasbury
Harborne
Bartley Green
Selly Oak
Bournville
Woodgate
Illey
Frankley
Longbridge
Rubery
Northfield
Hopwood
Cofton Hackett
Lickey
Marlbrook
Barnt Green
Alvechurch
Rowney Green
Tutnall
Tardebigge
Finstall
Charford
Sidemoor
Blackwell
Lickey End
Hagley
West Hagley
Clent
Romsley
Belbroughton
Bell End
Wildmoor
Fairfield
Drayton
Bluntington
Chaddesley Corbett
Bournheath
Dodford
Rushock
Broome
Holy Cross
Blakedown
Churchill
Harvington
Mustow Green
Stone
Shenstone
Cookley
Wolverley
Franche
Caunsall
Blakeshall
Shatterford
Upper Arley
Kinlet
Trimpley
Low Habberley
Pound Green
Buttonoak
Blakebrook
Wribbenhall
Far Forest
Lem Hill
Fingerpost
Pound Bank
Ribbesford
Callow Hill
Bliss Gate
Cleobury Mortimer
Neen Savage
Hopton Wafers
Catherton
Oreton
Milson
Bayton
Neen Sollars
Mamble
Clows Top
Rock
Frith Common
Lindridge
Eardiston
Newnham Bridge
Rochford
Pensax
Stockton on Teme
Abberley
Dunley
Astley
Areley Kings
Astley Cross
Wilden
Upper Mitton
Hartlebury
Waresley
Elmley Lovett
Crossway Green
Lincomb
Cutnall Green
Elmbridge
Dunhampton
Doverdale
Hampton Lovett
Upton Warren
Wychbold
Stoke Prior
Woodgate
Webheath
Headless Cross
Bentley
Crabbs Cross
Hanbury
Ham Green
Hunt End
Woolmere Green
Astwood Bank
Feckenham
Bradley Green
Hadzor
Salwarpe
Witton
Ombersley
Holt Fleet
Holt
Holt Heath
Uphampton
Sytchampton
Oldfield
Shrawley
Noutard's Green
Great Witley
Little Witley
Stanford Bridge
Stanford on Teme
Hanley William
Hanley Child
Broad Heath
Stoke Bliss
Sapey Common
Upper Sapey
Shelsley Walsh
Shelsley Beauchamp
Clifton upon Teme
Sweet Green
High Lane
Harpley
Martley
Wichenford
Sinton Green
Grimley
Hawford
Fernhill Heath
Martin Hussingtree
Oddingley
Sale Green
Himbleton
Stock Wood
Stock Green
Holberrow Green
Moseley
Shoulton
Hallow
Lower Broadheath
Claines
Hindlip
Tibberton
Huddington
Dormston
Inkberrow
Tedstone Wafer
Tedstone Delamere
Edvin Loach
Edwyn Ralph
Horsham
Berrow Green
Whitbourne
Broad Green
Upper Broadheath
Warndon
Crowle
Grafton Flyford
Kington
Abbots Morton
Knightwick
Lulsley
Broadwas
Bromyard Downs
Linley Green
Alfrick
Brockamin
Leigh
Rushwick
St John's
Red Hill
Bredicot
Churchill
Broughton Hackett
Upton Snodsbury
North Piddle
Flyford Flavell
Abberton
Rous Lench
Ab Lench
Church Lench
Atch Lench
Spetchley
Whittington
Cherry Orchard
White Ladies Aston
Naunton Beauchamp
Bishampton
Egdon
Stanford Bishop
Munderfield Row
Acton Beauchamp
Alfrick Pound
Bransford
Suckley
Leigh Sinton
Bowling Green
Powick
Pole Elm
Norton
Littleworth
Stoulton
Peopleton
Pinvin
Throckmorton
Harvington Cross
Acton Green
Longley Green
Storridge
Stanbrook
Callow End
Kempsey
Hatfield
Drake's Broughton
Norton
Lenchwick
Evesbatch
Bishops Frome
Fromes Hill
Ridgeway Cross
Stony Cross
Cradley
Stifford's Bridge
Westfield
Newland
Madresfield
Kerswell Grn.
Pirton
Wadborough
Wyre Piddle
Lower Moor
Fladbury
Charlton
Cropthorne
Castle Frome
Norbridge
Mathon
West Malvern
Ham Green
Upper Wyche
Lower Wyche
Guarlford
Rhydd
Clifton
High Green
Besford
Defford
Severn Stoke
Kinnersley
Dunstall Common
Stanley Hill
Canon Frome
Colwall Stone
Colwall Green
Malvern Wells
Hanley Swan
Hanley Castle
Earl's Croome
Holly Grn.
Baughton
Eckington
Birlingham
Little Comberton
Great Comberton
Bricklehampton
Netherton
Hampton
Bengeworth
Fairfield
Coddington
Staplow
Munsley
Trumpet
Wellington Heath
Bradlow
Welland
Little Malvern
Newbridge Green
Naunton
Upper Strensham
Lower Strensham
Bredon's Norton
Bredon Hill
Elmley Castle
Kersoe
Ashton under Hill
Hinton on the Green
Sedgeberrow
Aston Somerville
Wormington
Pixley
Aylton
Putley
Little Marcle
Eastnor
Hollybush
Castlemorton
Birts Street
Rye Street
Camer's Green
Queenhill
Ripple
Twyning
Twyning Green
Puckrup
Shuthonger
Bredon
Kemerton
Overbury
Conderton
Kinsham
Beckford
Dumbleton
Great Washbourne
Alderton
Longdon
Sledge Green
Brown's End
Bushley
Northway
Ashchurch
Aston Cross
Teddington
Toddington
Preston
Donnington
Rushall
Much Marcle
Bromsberrow Hth.
Broom's Green
Ryton
Redmarley D'Abitot
Playley Green
Pendock
Long Green
Forthampton
Eldersfield
Walton Cardiff
Fiddington
Oxenton
Alstone
Dixton
Gretton
Greet
Hailes
Lyne Down
Dymock
Kempley
Fishpool
Pooll
Staunton
Corse Lawn
Chaceley
Deerhurst
Tredington
Stoke Orchard
Gotherington
Winchcombe
Corse
Tirley
Apperley
Hasfield
Ashleworth
Coombe Hill
Hardwicke
Elmstone Hardwicke
Woodmancote
Cleeve Hill
Leigh
Hartpury
Gorsley
Crow Hill
Southam
Swindon
Newtown
Lye
Woodgate Valley
Bartley Res.
Frankley Services
Hopwood Park Services
Strensham Services (Northbound Only)
Strensham Services (Southbound Only)
Severn Valley Railway
Wyre Forest
Rays Farm Country Matters
Bodenham Arboretum & Earth Centre
Clent Hills
Waseley Hills
Lickey Hills
West Midland
Cottage Garden
Harvington Hall
Blackstone Meadows
Worcestershire County Museum
Whitlenge Gdns
Chaddesley Woods
Avoncroft Mus of Historic Buildings
Webbs of Wychbold
Fosters Green Meadows
Hanbury Hall
Witley Court
Elgar's Birthplace
Tudor House
Guildhall
Brockhampton Estate
Heritage Centre
Worcester Woods
Leigh Court Barn
Royal Worcester Porcelain
Croome Park
Three Counties Showground
Bredon Barn
Conderton Pottery
Silk Centre
Evesham Country Park
Hellens Manor
St Mary's Church
Odda's Chapel
Eastnor
Winchcombe Pottery
Langley Hill
Sudeley Castle & Gardens
Belas Knap Long Barrow
Railway Mus
Abbey
Avon
Severn
Teme
Isbourne
Frome
Rea
Stour
SO
M5
M50
A456
A458
A491
A448
A441
A38
A449
A451
A443
A44
A4133
A422
A4440
A4103
A4104
A417
A46
A435
A438
A4172
B4211
B4084
B4082
B4090
B4092
B4204
B4197
B4196
B4199
B4202
B4203
B4214
B4220
B4209
B4208
B4218
B4232
B4424
B4024
B4221
B4215
B4213
B4079
B4077
B4078
B4632
B4080
B4636
B4363
B4201
B4188
B4551
B4184
49
61
62
36
37
0 1 2 3 4 5 6 miles
0 1 2 3 4 5 6 7 8 9 10 km

Warwick
Coventry
Solihull
Kenilworth
Royal Leamington Spa
Warwick
Stratford-upon-Avon
Banbury
Shipston-on-Stour
Moreton-in-Marsh
Stow-on-the-Wold
Chipping Norton
Broadway
Alcester
Henley-in-Arden
Studley
Southam
Cubbington
Shirley
Dorridge
Edgbaston
Sheldon
Butler's End
Meriden
Hampton in Arden
Eastcote
Knowle
Barston
Balsall Common
Berkswell
Eastern Green
Allesley
Keresley
Longford
Walsgrave on Sowe
Wyken
Binley
Binley Woods
Brandon
Wolston
Brinklow
Bretford
Willenhall
Pinley
Earlsdon
Stivichall
Tollbar End
Baginton
Ryton-on-Dunsmore
Stretton-on-Dunsmore
Princethorpe
Bourton on Dunsmore
Frankton
Draycote
Marton
Birdingbury
Eathorpe
Wappenbury
Weston under Wetherley
Hunningham
Lillington
Stoneleigh
Bubbenhall
Stareton
Ashow
Crackley
Burton Green
Tile Hill
Whoberley
Honiley
Beausale
Wroxall
Chadwick End
Baddesley Clinton
Kingswood
Lapworth
Rowington
Shrewley
Haseley
Hatton
Budbrooke
Leek Wootton
Old Milverton
Milverton
Offchurch
Radford Semele
Whitnash
Bascote
Long Itchington
Stockton
Ufton
Harbury
Chesterton
Ladbroke
Bishop's Itchington
Knightcote
Gaydon
Lighthorne
Moreton Morrell
Ashorne
Wellesbourne
Charlecote
Hampton Lucy
Newbold Pacey
Barford
Sherbourne
Wasperton
Norton Lindsey
Claverdon
Langley
Wootton Wawen
Snitterfield
Bearley
Aston Cantlow
Wilmcote
Bishopton
Shottery
Tiddington
Alveston
Loxley
Clifford Chambers
Atherstone on Stour
Preston on Stour
Alderminster
Ettington
Kineton
Combrook
Walton
Butlers Marston
Pillerton Hersey
Pillerton Priors
Oxhill
Radway
Warmington
Ratley
Edge Hill
Shotteswell
Hornton
Horley
Hanwell
Wroxton
Drayton
Balscote
Shenington
Alkerton
Epwell
Shutford
North Newington
Broughton
Tadmarton
Swalcliffe
Sibford Gower
Sibford Ferris
Bloxham
Milcombe
Hook Norton
Wigginton
South Newington
Barford St John
Barford St Michael
Hempton
Great Rollright
Swerford
Little Tew
Great Tew
Nether Worton
Over Worton
Heythrop
Enstone
Salford
Over Norton
Little Compton
Long Compton
Barton on the Heath
Great Wolford
Little Wolford
Todenham
Cherington
Stourton
Whichford
Ascott
Burmington
Willington
Barcheston
Tidmington
Upper Brailes
Lower Brailes
Sutton under Brailes
Winderton
Halford
Idlicote
Tredington
Honington
Whatcote
Lower Tysoe
Upper Tysoe
Middle Tysoe
Newbold on Stour
Armscote
Blackwell
Ilmington
Darlingscott
Admington
Upper Quinton
Lower Quinton
Wimpstone
Long Marston
Dorsington
Mickleton
Hidcote Boyce
Ebrington
Aston Subedge
Weston-Sub-Edge
Saintbury
Willersey
Charingworth
Chipping Campden
Broad Campden
Paxford
Blockley
Draycott
Aston Magna
Batsford
Bourton on the Hill
Sezincote
Longborough
Condicote
Donnington
Broadwell
Evenlode
Chastleton
Adlestrop
Cornwell
Daylesford
Oddington
Upper Swell
Lower Swell
Temple Guiting
Kineton
Ford
Cutsdean
Farmcote
Didbrook
Stanway
Snowshill
Stanton
Laverton
Buckland
Childswickham
Wickhamford
Badsey
Bretforton
Honeybourne
Aldington
Offenham
South Littleton
Middle Littleton
North Littleton
Cleeve Prior
Harvington
Marlcliff
Bidford-on-Avon
Barton
Salford Priors
Abbots Salford
Iron Cross
Dunnington
Broom
Wixford
Exhall
Ardens Grafton
Temple Grafton
Binton
Welford-on-Avon
Luddington
Weethley Gate
Arrow
Oversley Green
Haselor
Walcote
Billesley
Great Alne
Kinwarton
Coughton
King's Coughton
New End
Cookhill
Sambourne
Mappleborough Green
Morton Bagot
Oldberrow
Ullenhall
Ipsley
Gorcott Hill
Holt End
Beoley
Tanworth-in-Arden
Wood End
Branson's Cross
Portway
Earlswood
Hockley Heath
Lowsonford
Kemps Green
Preston Bagot
Yarningale Common
Wolverton
Heath End
Hampton on the Hill
Longbridge
Bishop's Tachbrook
Fenny Compton
Burton Dassett
Northend
Avon Dassett
Farnborough
Mollington
Cropredy
Claydon
Temple Herdewyke
Chadshunt
Wormleighton
Priors Hardwick
Marston Doles
Napton on the Hill
Chapel Green
Leamington Hastings
Hollywood
Drakes Cross
Whitlock's End
Monkspath
Bentley Heath
Temple Balsall
Fen End
Balsall
Catchems Corner
Meer End
Olton
Hall Green
Elmdon
Elmdon Heath
Bickenhill
Four Oaks
Copt Heath
Sparkhill
Moseley
Springfield
King's Heath
Cotteridge
King's Norton
Wythall
Hawkes End
Coundon
Spon End
Foleshill
Little Heath
Ansty
Shilton
Barnacle
Stretton under Fosse
Easenhall
King's Newnham
Church Lawford
Stretton-on-Fosse
Grand Union Canal
Oxford Canal
Stratford Canal
Avon
Stour
Itchen
M6
M40
M42
A45
A46
A429
A44
A3400
EVESHAM
SP

Coventry
Rugby
Daventry
Southam
Banbury
Brackley
Towcester
Buckingham
Middleton Cheney
N o r t h a
SP
M6
M1
M45
M40
A45
A5
A14
A43
A422
A423
A425
A426
A428
A361
A4500
Barnacle
Shilton
Withybrook
Ansty
Monks Kirby
Pailton
Cross in Hand
Cotesbach
Misterton
Walcote
North Kilworth
Husbands Bosworth
Sibbertoft
Great Oxendon
South Kilworth
Welford
Naseby Field
Clipston
Kelmarsh
Sulby Reservoir
Stanford Res.
Naseby Res.
Churchover
Gibbet Hill
Shawell
Swinford
Stanford on Avon
Stanford Hall
Easenhall
Brinklow
Harborough Magna
Newbold on Avon
Newton
Catthorpe
Lilbourne
Clay Coton
Cold Ashby
Naseby
Haselbech
Maidwell
Thornby
Binley Woods
Binley
Bretford
King's Newnham
Church Lawford
Long Lawford
Clifton upon Dunsmore
Yelvertoft
Brandon
Wolston
Ryton-on-Dunsmore
Ryton Organic Gardens
Bilton
Hillmorton
Winwick
Guilsborough
Cottesbrooke
Cottesbrooke Hall and Gdns
Baginton
Bubbenhall
Stretton-on-Dunsmore
Bourton on Dunsmore
Dunchurch
Kilsby
Crick
West Haddon
Coton
Coton Manor
Hollowell
Creaton
Ravensthorpe
Teeton
Brixworth
Spratton
Princethorpe
Thurlaston
Draycote Water
Barby
Weston under Wetherley
Wappenbury
Frankton
Draycote
Kites Hardwick
Ashby St Ledgers
Watford
Watford Gap Services
East Haddon
Holdenby
Holdenby House and Falconry Centre
Cubbington
Hunningham
Eathorpe
Marton
Birdingbury
Leamington Hastings
Woolscott
Willoughby
Long Buckby
Chapel Brampton
Church Brampton
N'Hampton & Lamport Railway
Grandborough
Sawbridge
Braunston
Welton
Great Brington
Althorp
Offchurch
Long Itchington
Bascote
Broadwell
Stockton
Nethercote
Daventry Res.
Norton
Whilton
Little Brington
Harlestone
Flecknoe
Lower Shuckburgh
Brockhall
Nobottle
New Duston
Queen's Park
Ufton
Napton on the Hill
Staverton
Daventry Mus
Dodford
Harpole
Dallington
Duston
Flore
Harbury
Chapel Green
Upper Catesby
Badby
Newnham
Upper Weedon
Weedon Bec
Upper Heyford
Nether Heyford
Kislingbury
Upton
Far Cotton
Chesterton Windmill
Chesterton
Ladbroke
Hellidon
Nene
Northamptonshire Ironstone Rly Trust
Warwick Services
Marston Doles
Priors Marston
Everdon
Church Stowe
Upper Stowe
Old Dairy Farm Country Shopping & Craft Centre
Bugbrooke
Rothersthorpe
Northampton Services
Hunsbury Hill
Cross Green
Bishop's Itchington
Priors Hardwick
Charwelton
Preston Capes
Farthingstone
Litchborough
Gayton
Milton Malsor
Lighthorne Heritage Motor Centre
Knightcote
Oxford Canal
Grand Union Canal
Gaydon
Wormleighton
Upper Boddington
Byfield
Maidford
Grimscote
Pattishall
Eastcote
Astcote
Cold Higham
Tiffield
Blisworth
Northend
Burton Dassett Hills
Fenny Compton
Boddington Reservoir
Hinton
Woodford Halse
Temple Herdewyke
Burton Dassett
Lower Boddington
Granary Museum of Bygones
Eydon
Canons Ashby House
Canons Ashby
Adstone
Blakesley
Duncote
Caldecote
Kineton
Little Kineton
Claydon
Aston le Walls
Moreton Pinkney
Woodend
Greens Norton
Shutlanger
Stoke Bruerne
The Canal Museum
Avon Dassett
Farnborough
Farnborough Hall
Chipping Warden
Cherwell
Catanger Llama Trekking
Woodend Green
Bradden
Towcester Racecourse
Stoke Park Pavilions
Radway
Warmington
Ratley
Edge Hill
Mollington
Wardington
Culworth
Weston
Weedon Lois
Slapton
Alderton
Cropredy
Upper Wardington
Sulgrave
Sulgrave Manor
Abthorpe
Pury End
Paulerspury
Shotteswell
Upton House
Great Bourton
Williamscott
Thorpe Mandeville
Wappenham
Middle Tysoe
Hornton
Horley
Helmdon
Silverstone
Whittlebury
Alkerton
Hanwell
Chacombe
Marston St Lawrence
Syresham
Silverstone Circuit
Whittlewood Forest
Shenington
Wroxton
Drayton
Grimsbury
Thenford
Greatworth
Crowfield
Radstone
Lillingstone Dayrell
Lillingstone Lovell
Balscote
Neithrop
Overthorpe
Warkworth
Halse
Biddlesden
Whitfield
Epwell
Shutford
North Newington
Farthinghoe
Wicken
Swalcliffe Barn
Broughton Castle
Easington
Sibford Gower
Tadmarton
Broughton
Upper Astrop
Newbottle
Turweston
Dadford
Stowe School and Gardens
Akeley
Leckhampstead
Swalcliffe
Bodicote
Sor Brook
Astrop
Hinton-in-the-Hedges
Shalstone
Buffler's Holt
Chackmore
Sibford Ferris
Bloxham
West Adderbury
East Adderbury
King's Sutton
Charlton
Westbury
Maids Moreton
Milcombe
Milton
Evenley
Great Ouse
Water Stratford
Radclive
Mixbury
Finmere
Thornborough
Hook Norton
Norton Visitors Centre
Barford St John
Barford St Michael
Croughton
Wigginton
South Newington
Clifton
Aynho
Tingewick
Gawcott
Swerford
Hempton
Deddington
Souldern
Cottisford
Barton Hartshorn
Newton Purcell
Padbury
Adstock
Nether Worton
Great Tew
Over Worton
North Aston
Fritwell
Baynard's Green
Hardwick
Preston Bissett
Addington
Hethe
Fringford
Hillesden
Somerton
Fewcott
Stoke Lyne
Cherwell Valley Services
Middle Aston
Ardley
Upper Heyford
Stratton Audley
Twyford
Steeple Claydon
East Claydon
Middle Claydon
Westcott Barton
Steeple Aston
Bucknell
0 1 2 3 4 5 6 miles
0 1 2 3 4 5 6 7 8 9 10 km

Kettering
Wellingborough
Northampton
Bedford
Milton Keynes
Newport Pagnell
Olney
Rushden
Higham Ferrers
Irthlingborough
Burton Latimer
Raunds
Thrapston
Rothwell
Desborough
Kempston
Bletchley
Wolverton
Stony Stratford
Leighton Buzzard
Winslow
Ampthill
Flitwick
Clophill
Shefford
Barton-le-Clay
Cranfield
Bedford
Milton Keynes
Central Bedfordshire
SP
TL
YARDLEY CHASE
Salcey Forest
Grafham Water
Pitsford Reservoir
Sywell Reservoir
M1
A6
A14
A45
A421
A428
A509
A5
A4146
A508
A43
64
65
54
39
40

Cambridge
TL
Luddington in the Brook
Thurning
Sawtry
Great Gidding
Little Gidding
Steeple Gidding
Hamerton Zoo Park
Wigsthorpe
Clopton
Winwick
Hamerton
Upton
Alconbury Weston
Old Weston
Buckworth
Alconbury
Barham
Woolley
Leighton Bromswold
Brington
Molesworth
Bythorn
Catworth
Spaldwick
Stow Longa
Easton
Covington
Tilbrook
Ellington
Brampton
Huntingdon
Hinchingbrooke
Godmanchester
Church End
Wood Walton
Great Raveley
Little Raveley
Upwood
Upwood Meadows
Monks Wood
Wennington
Abbots Ripton
Little Stukeley
Great Stukeley
Broughton
King's Ripton
Bury
Wistow
Warboys
Old Hurst
Woodhurst
Sapley
Hartford
Wyton
Houghton
Houghton Mill
Cromwell Mus
Hemingford Abbots
Hemingford Grey
St Ives
Tick Fen
Chapel Head
Ferry Hill
Pidley Fen
Horseley Fen
Langwood Fen
Mepal
Chatteris Fen
Sutton
Fenton
Pidley
Somersham
Colne
Bluntisham
Earith
Hill Row Doles
Aldreth
Needingworth
Holywell
Over
Great Ouse
Willingham
Smithey
The Busway Guided Bus
Fenstanton
Swavesey
Fen Drayton
Boxworth End
Conington
Cambridge Services
Boxworth
Longstanton
Rampton
Cottenham
Westwick
Oakington
Lolworth
Bar Hill
Dry Drayton
Histon
Impington
Girton
Madingley
Grafham Water
Grafham
Buckden Towers
Buckden
Kimbolton
Lower Dean
Upper Dean
Swineshead
Stonely
West Perry
East Perry
Dillington
Staughton Green
Staughton Highway
Great Staughton
Little Staughton
Southoe
Offord Cluny
Offord Darcy
Diddington
Great Paxton
Little Paxton
Papworth St Agnes
Graveley
Toseland
Hilton
Papworth Everard
Elsworth
Knapwell
Wood Green Animal Shelter
Galley Hill
Yelling
Keysoe
Keysoe Row
Brook End
Pertenhall
Bolnhurst
Thurleigh
Rootham's Green
Colmworth
Bushmead Priory
Hail Weston
Duloe
Staploe
St Neots
Eaton Socon
Eynesbury
Croxton
Eltisley
Cambourne
Caxton
Highfields
Hardwick
Coton
Caldecote
Toft
Comberton
Barton
Bourn
Newnham
Grantchester
Botanic Garden
Kingston
Great Gransden
Little Gransden
Abbotsley
Waresley
Longstowe
Little Barford
Wyboston
Chawston
Colesden
Duck's Cross
Wilden
Ravensden
Renhold
Salph End
Roxton
Green End
Great Barford
Blunham
Tempsford
Gamlingay
Hatley St George
East Hatley
Great Eversden
Little Eversden
Harlton
Haslingfield
Hauxton
Harston
Rupert Brooke Museum
Wimpole Hall and Home Farm
Arrington
Croydon
Orwell
New Wimpole
Barrington
Shepreth Wildlife Park
Shepreth
Foxton
Newton
Thriplow
Fowlmere
Bedford
Bedford Museum
Goldington
Priory
Fenlake
Kempston
Elstow Moot Hall
Elstow
Cardington
Harrowden
Shortstown
Cople
Moggerhanger
Moggerhanger Park
Willington
Everton
Girtford
Sandy
Beeston
Potton
Cockayne Hatley
Wrestlingworth
Tadlow
Cam or Rhee
Wendy
Meldreth
Whaddon
Chiswick End
Kneesworth
Melbourn
Bassingbourn
Hatch
Thorncote Green
Northill
Ickwell Green
Upper Caldecote
Sutton
Eyeworth
Biggleswade
Dunton
Guilden Morden
Abington Pigotts
Litlington
Steeple Morden
Royston & District Mus
Royston
Heydon
Great Chishill
Chrishall
Little Chishill
Cotton End
Littleworth
Wilstead
Haynes
Haynes Church End
Houghton Conquest
Houghton House
Shuttleworth Collection
The Swiss Garden
Bird of Prey Centre
Old Warden
Southill
Broom
Stanford
Langford
Edworth
Hinxworth
Ashwell
Caldecote
Newnham
Barley
Therfield
Kelshall
Reed
Ampthill
Maulden
Clophill
Beadlow
Shefford
Clifton
Hoo Hill Maze
Campton
Henlow
Astwick
Church End
Stotfold
Baldock Services
Bygrave
Slip End
Meppershall
Upper Gravenhurst
De Grey Mausoleum
Flitton
Flitwick
Silsoe
Wrest Park House
Greenfield
Pulloxhill
Higham Gobion
Westoning
Upper Stondon
Shillington
Stondon Transport Mus
Lower Stondon
Arlesey
Radwell
Norton
Baldock
Wallington
Roe Green
Mill End
Sandon
Buckland
Barkway
Nuthampstead
Langley Upper Green
Langley Lower Green
Anstey
Meesden
Chipping
Wyddial
Hare Street
Brent Pelham
Apsley End
Holwell
Pirton
Letchworth
Barton-le-Clay
Hexton
Pegsdon
Knocking Hoe
Hitchin
Ickleford
Willian
Walsworth
Great Wymondley
Little Wymondley
Graveley
Clothall
Weston
Rushden
Throcking
Cromer Windmill
Cromer
Cottered
Hall's Green
Aspenden
Buntingford
Westmill
Great Hormead
Furneaux Pelham
Hay Street
Gravesend
Ardeley
Walkern
Wood End
Ippollytts
Sharpenhoe
Sundon Hills
Streatley
Barton Hills
Galley Hill
Sundon
miles
km

Downham
Chettisham
West Fen
Prickwillow
Shippea Hill Sta.
Lakenheath
Wangford Warren
Thetford Warren
HIGH LODGE FOREST CENTRE
Witcham
Coveney
Witchy Hill
OLIVER CROMWELL'S HOUSE
Ely
Queen Adelaide
Kenny Hill
Lakenheath Warren
Elveden
THETFORD HEATH
EAST OF ENGLAND TANK MUSEUM
Wentworth
Witchford
Middle Fen
Stuntney
Great Fen
Mildenhall Fen
Eriswell
Holywell Row
Little Thetford
Broad Hill
Beck Row
North Hill
Haddenham
Wilburton
Stretham
Barway
Soham Cotes
WINDMILL
Isleham Fen
Thistley Green
West Row
PRIORY CHURCH
Isleham
Mildenhall
The King's Forest
Soham
Soham Mere
Worlington
Barton Mills
Icklingham
DOWN FIELD WINDMILL
Freckenham
CAVENHAM HEATH
Tuddenham
WEST STOW
West Stow
Ingham
Fen
Chittering
Wicken
WICKEN CORN WINDMILL
WICKEN FEN
Upware
New River
Fordham
Chippenham
Red Lodge
Herringswell
Lackford
Culford
Flempton
Cavenham
CHIPPENHAM FEN
River Bank
Adventurers' Fen
Landwade
Snailwell
Kennett
Hengrave
HENGRAVE HALL
Fornham All Saints
FARMLAND MUS & DENNY ABBEY
Burwell
Reach
Exning
Kentford
Risby
Higham
Waterbeach
Landbeach
LODE MILL
Commercial End
Lode
Swaffham Prior
Newmarket Heath
Newmarket
Moulton
PACKHORSE BRIDGE
Gazeley
Little Saxham
Westley
Barrow
Great Saxham
CATHEDRAL AND ABBEY RUINS
Bury St Edmunds
Milton
Horningsea
Stow cum Quy
ANGLESEY ABBEY
Swaffham Bulbeck
NEWMARKET
NATIONAL STUD
NATIONAL HORSERACING MUSEUM
Cheveley
Ashley
Dalham
Denham
Horringer
ICKWORTH HOUSE
Kings Hedges
Fen Ditton
Bottisham
Dunstall Green
Hargrave
Chevington
MUS OF TECHNOLOGY
CAMBRIDGE
Teversham
Saxton Street
Ousden
Hawstead
Whepstead
FITZWILLIAM MUS
Romsey Town
Little Wilbraham
Stetchworth
Woodditton
Upend
Lidgate
Depden Green
REDE HALL
Cambridge
Great Wilbraham
Dullingham
Ditton Green
Kirtling
Chedburgh
Depden
Rede
Fulbourn
Cherry Hinton
Six Mile Bottom
Westley Waterless
Burrough Green
Kirtling Green
Thorns
Wickhambrook
Clopton Green
Brockley Green
Trumpington
WANDLEBURY
Brinkley
Weston Colville
Great Bradley
Cowlinge
Wickham Street
Denston
Hawkedon
Great Shelford
Stapleford
TL
Weston Green
Carlton
Little Bradley
Stradishall
Stansfield
Hartest
Little Shelford
Granta
Babraham
West Wratting
Balsham
Little Thurlow
Boxted
Shimpling
FOURWENTWAYS SERVICES
Little Abington
Great Thurlow
Barnardiston
Hundon
Stanstead
Sawston
Great Abington
Hildersham
West Wickham
Great Wratting
Poslingford
Glemsford
Whittlesford
DUXFORD CHAPEL
Pampisford
Streetly End
Horseheath
Withersfield
Little Wratting
Kedington
Chilton Street
Clare
Cavendish
SUE RYDER FOUNDATION MUS
High Street
Duxford
LINTON ZOO
Linton
Bartlow
Haverhill
Boyton End
Pentlow
Long Melford
IMPERIAL WAR MUSEUM DUXFORD
Hinxton
Hadstock
Shudy Camps
Castle Camps
Sturmer
Stoke by Clare
CLARE CASTLE
CLARE ANCIENT HOUSE
Foxearth
Ickleton
Stump Cross
Great Chesterford
Wixoe
Baythorne End
Belchamp St Paul
Borley
Little Chesterford
Ashdon
Helions Bumpstead
Birdbrook
Ashen
Ovington
Belchamp Otten
Ballingdon
Bulmer
Strethall
Little Walden
Church End
Steeple Bumpstead
Ridgewell
Tilbury Juxta Clare
Belchamp Walter
Elmdon
Littlebury
Saffron Walden
SAFFRON WALDEN
Little Yeldham
Bulmer Tye
Sewards End
Stambourne
Gestingthorpe
Henny
Littlebury Green
Bridge Green
AUDLEY END HOUSE & GDNS
Radwinter
Hempstead
Stambourne Green
Toppesfield
Great Yeldham
Great Henny
Wenden Ambo
Wimbish
Audley End
COLNE VALLEY RAILWAY
HEDINGHAM CASTLE
Wickham St Paul
Duddenhoe End
Tye Green
Great Sampford
Cornish Hall End
Gainsford End
Highstreet Green
Castle Hedingham
Twinstead Green
Arkesden
Wimbish Green
Little Sampford
Great Maplestead
Alphamstone
Newport
Howlett End
Howe Street
Morris Green
Sible Hedingham
Little Maplestead
Clavering
Wicken Bonhunt
Debden
Finchingfield
Pebmarsh
Rickling
PRIORS HALL BARN
Widdington
Debden Cross
MOLE HALL WILDLIFE PARK
Thaxted
Little Bardfield
Wethersfield
Blackmore End
Halstead
Starlings Green
Hamperden End
Cutlers Green
Berden
Quendon
Great Bardfield
Gosfield
Colne
Stocking Pelham
ST MARY'S CHURCH
Henham
GLENDALE FORGE
Monk Street
Shalford
Church End
Beazley End
Earls Colne
Ugley
Ugley Green
Duton Hill
Lindsell
Shalford Green
Greenstead Green
Manuden
HOUSE ON THE HILL TOY MUS
Elsenham
Broxted
Great Easton
Bardfield Saling
Jasper's Green
Bocking Churchstreet
High Garrett
East End
Farnham Green
Molehill
Brick
Great Ouse
Lark
Kennett
Cam
Pant
Stort
Granta
A10
A11
A14
A142
A505
A1065
A134
A131
M11
A1101
A1123
A1303
A1304
A1307
A143
A1092
A1017
A1124
A1134
A1301
A1309
B1382
B1104
B1102
B1085
B1103
B1506
B1063
B1061
B1052
B1054
B1053
B1051
B1057
B1383
B1039
B1038
B1184
B1112
B1106
B1066
B1064
B1058
B1065
B1421
B1049
66
67
56
41
42
55

Thetford
Thetford Warren
Wangford Warren
Lakenheath Warren
Brettenham
Shadwell
Rushford
Gasthorpe
Garboldisham
North Lopham
South Lopham
Fersfield
Shelfanger
Mill Green
Burston
Walcot Green
Bressingham
Roydon
Diss
Ancient House Mus
Thetford Heath
Elveden
East of England Tank Museum
Barnham
Euston
Euston Hall
Knettishall
Knettishall Heath
Coney Weston
Hopton
Market Weston
Blo' Norton
Thelnetham Windmill
Thelnetham
Redgrave
Bressingham Steam Museum and Gardens
Magpie Green
Palgrave
Stuston
Wortham
Hinderclay
Thrandeston
Fakenham Magna
Barningham
Sapiston
Honington
Hepworth
Botesdale
Rickinghall
Burgate
Mellis
Langton Green
Yaxley
Eye
The King's Forest
Icklingham
Cavenham Heath
Tuddenham
Bardwell
Ixworth Thorpe
Troston
Stanton
Upthorpe
Wattisfield
Allwood Green
Thornham Parva
Walsham le Willows
Cranmer Green
Gislingham
Thornham Magna
Braiseworth
West Stow
Lackford
Culford
Ingham
Ampton
Great Livermere
Ixworth
Abbey (rem)
Langham
Four Ashes
Crownland
Wickham Street
Stoke Ash
Cavenham
Flempton
Timworth Green
Conyers Green
Stowlangtoft
Badwell Ash
Long Thurlow
Westhorpe
Finningham
Wickham Skeith
Thorndon
Hengrave
Hengrave Hall
Fornham All Saints
Fornham St Martin
Pakenham
Hunston
Great Ashfield
Wyverstone
Wyverstone Street
Bacton
Cotton
Thwaite
Brockford Street
Wetheringsett
Mid Suffolk Light Rly Mus
Great Barton
Stanton Street
Earl's Green
Ford's Green
Thurston
Norton
Bacton Green
Mendlesham
Blacksmith's Green
Bury St Edmunds
Westley
Little Saxham
Great Saxham
Barrow
Higham
Cathedral and Abbey Ruins
Tostock
Elmswell
Haughley Green
Ward Green
Canham's Green
Gipping
Mendlesham Green
Wetherup Street
Blackthorpe
Beyton
Rougham
Hessett
Woolpit
Woolpit Bygones Museum
Wetherden
Haughley Park
Haughley
Saxham Street
Middlewood Green
Mickfield
Horringer
Ickworth House
Denham
Rushbrooke
Sicklesmere
Rougham Green
Drinkstone
Drinkstone Green
Bradfield St George
Harleston
Thorney Green
Stowupland
Forward Green
Little Stonham
Hargrave
Chevington
Little Whelnetham
Hawstead
Great Welnetham
Whepstead
Bradfield St Clare
Rattlesden
Buxhall
Fen Street
Poystreet Green
Museum of East Anglian Life
Stowmarket
Earl Stonham
Stonham Aspal
Creeting Bottoms
Crowfield
Depden Green
Rede Hall
Chedburgh
Depden
Bradfield Combust
Bradfield Woods
Felsham
Gedding
Great Finborough
Combs Ford
Combs
Creeting St Mary
Beacon Hill Services
Thorns
Rede
Hoggard's Green
Cross Green
Hightown Green
High Street Green
Moats Tye
Wickhambrook
Clopton Green
Wickham Street
Lawshall
Cockfield
Great Green
Thorpe Green
Little Finborough
Battisford
Needham Market
Coddenham
Brockley Green
Denston
Hawkedon
Stansfield
Stradishall
Thorpe Morieux
Brettenham
Battisford Tye
Charles Tye
Ringshall
Needham Lake
Barking
Barking Tye
Baylham
Hartest
Shimpling Street
Shimpling
Boxted
Alpheton
Cross Green
Hitcham
Wattisham Airfield Museum
Wattisham
Ringshall Stocks
Great Bricett
Willisham Tye
Great Blakenham
Barham
Claydon
Preston St Mary
Kettlebaston
Stanstead
Lavenham
Guildhall
Bildeston
Nedging Tye
Offton
Little Blakenham
Akenham
Hundon
Poslingford
Glemsford
Kentwell Hall
Bridge Street
Monks Eleigh
Chelsworth
Naughton
Somersham
Brent Eleigh
Semer
Ash Street
Elmsett
Flowton
Whitton
Chilton Street
Cavendish
Sue Ryder Foundation Mus
High Street
Long Melford
Melford Hall
Milden
Whatfield
Bramford
Westbourne
Clare
Clare Castle
Clare Ancient House
Pentlow
Foxearth
Acton
Little Waldingfield
Great Waldingfield
Lindsey
St James's Chapel
Aldham
Sproughton
Ipswich
Borley
Mill Green
Kersey
Wolves Wood RSPB Reserve
Burstall
Hintlesham
Chantry
Ashen
Ovington
Belchamp Otten
Sudbury
Edwardstone
Hadleigh
Chattisham
Copdock
Ridgewell
Tilbury Juxta Clare
Belchamp Walter
Ballingdon
Bulmer
Great Cornard
Gainsborough's Ho
Newton
Groton
Boxford
Layham
Coles Green
Mace Green
Belstead
Little Yeldham
Bulmer Tye
Middleton
Little Cornard
Stone Street
Calais Street
Whitestreet Green
Raydon
Great Wenham
Capel St Mary
Great Yeldham
Gestingthorpe
Henny Street
Assington
Polstead
Shelley
Holton St Mary
Tattingstone
Colne Valley Railway
Hedingham Castle
Audley End
Great Henny
Twinstead
Leavenheath
Harrow Street
Stoke-by-Nayland
Bentley
The Heath
Alton Water Res
Castle Hedingham
Wickham St Paul
Great Maplestead
Twinstead Green
Lamarsh
Honey Tye
Dedham Vale
Thorington Street
Higham
Stratford St Mary
East Bergholt
East Bergholt Place
Flatford
Sible Hedingham
Little Maplestead
Alphamstone
Bures Green
Bures
Nayland
Boxted
Dedham
Bridge Cottage
Brantham
Stour Valley
Upper Street
Cattawade
Pebmarsh
Little Horkesley
Boxted Heath
Boxted Cross
Langham
Sir Alfred Munnings Art Museum
Dedham Heath
Lawford
Mistley Towers
Mistley
Manningtree
Bradfield
Mount Bures
Wormingford
Great Horkesley
Halstead
Colne Engaine
Blackmore End
Gosfield
Wakes Colne
East Anglian Railway Museum
Weston Homes Community Stad
Horkesley Heath
Ardleigh
Bradfield Heath
Beazley End
Chappel
Fordham
West Bergholt
Mile End
Fox Street
Little Bromley
Horsleycross Street
Horsley Cross
Eight Ash Green
Person's Heath
Crockleford Heath
Great Bromley
Highwoods
Colchester
St Botolph's
Tendring Green
Little Bentley
Bocking Churchstreet
Fordstreet
Colne
Stour
Little Ouse
Gipping
Brett
Dove
TL
0 1 2 3 4 5 6 miles
0 1 2 3 4 5 6 7 8 9 10 km

Harleston
Redenhall
Wortwell
Mendham
Garlic Street
Rushall
Shimpling
Dickleburgh
Needham
St Margaret South Elmham
SOUTH ELMHAM HALL
All Saints South Elmham
Ilketshall St Lawrence
Redisham
Shadingfield
Stone Street
Cox Common
Brampton
Stoven
Wrentham
Benacre
Covehithe
Frostenden
South Cove
Clay Common
Thelveton
100TH BOMB GROUP MEMORIAL MUS
Withersdale Street
St James South Elmham
Rumburgh
Spexhall
Westhall
Cove Bottom
Metfield
Thorpe Abbotts
Scole
Brockdish
BILLINGFORD WINDMILL
Oakley
Hoxne
Syleham
Fressingfield
WINGFIELD OLD COLLEGE
Wingfield
Little Whittingham Green
Linstead Parva
Wissett
Chediston
Halesworth
Holton
Blyford
Wangford
Reydon Smear
Reydon
Southwold
SOUTHWOLD MUSEUM
HEN REEDBED NATURE RESERVE
Brome Street
Cross Street
Heckfield Green
Battlesea Green
Chippenhall Green
Silverley's Green
Cratfield
Cookley
Wenhaston
Blackheath
Blythburgh
Walberswick
Blyth
Denham
Stradbroke
Pixey Green
Swan Green
Huntingfield
Walpole
Thorington
Bramfield
Ashfield Green
Banyard's Green
Cranley
Denham Street
Horham
Wootten Green
Wilby
Russel's Green
Laxfield
Heveningham
Sibton Green
SUFFOLK COAST
Dunwich
Dunwich Forest
DUNWICH UNDERWATER EXPLORATION EXHIBITION
Redlingfield
Athelington
Foals Green
Brundish Street
Crown Corner
Ubbeston Green
High Street
Hemp Green
Darsham
Occold
Fingal Street
Stanway Green
Brundish
Owl's Green
Sibton
Peasenhall
Yoxford
Middleton Moor
Westleton
WESTLETON HEATH
MINSMERE RSPB NATURE RESERVE
Rishangles
Bedingfield
Southolt
Worlingworth
Tannington
Badingham
Rotten End
Middleton
Alde
Bedfield
Maypole Green
Dennington
Bruisyard
North Green
Theberton
Eastbridge
Kenton
Saxtead
Monk Soham
SAXTEAD GREEN POST MILL
Brabling Green
Cransford
Curlew Green
Kelsale
Rendham
Carlton
LEISTON ABBEY
Debenham
Saxtead Green
Framlingham
Sweffling
Saxmundham
Leiston
Sizewell
Ashfield
Earl Soham
Great Glemham
Knodishall
Winston
Deben
Lampardbrook
Cole's Green
Benhall Street
Sternfield
Aldringham
Winston Green
Peats Corner
Brandeston
Parham
Stratford St Andrew
Benhall Green
Coldfair Green
Friston
Thorpeness
Pettaugh
Framsden
Cretingham
Kettleburgh
Hacheston
Farnham
Gromford
HELMINGHAM HALL GARDENS
Helmingham
Monewden
Easton
EASTON FARM PARK
Marlesford
Little Glemham
SNAPE MALTINGS
Snape
NORTH WARREN RSPB NATURE RESERVE
Aldeburgh
Letheringham
AKENFIELD
Charsfield
Lower Hacheston
BLAXHALL
Blaxhall
Iken
Gosbeck
Otley
Clopton Corner
Wickham Market
Campsey Ash
High Street
Aldeburgh Bay
Ashbocking
Dallinghoo
Debach
Pettistree
Tunstall
Tunstall Forest
Rendlesham
Sudbourne
Hemingstone
Swilland
Clopton
Bredfield
TM
Chillesford
Ufford
Witnesham
Grundisburgh
Burgh
Eyke
Butley
Henley
Hasketon
Melton
Bromeswell
Rendlesham Forest
ORFORD CASTLE
Orford
Orford Ness
Tuddenham St Martin
Culpho
Boot Street
Great Bealings
Woodbridge
SUTTON HOO
Butley High Corner
ORFORDNESS-HAVERGATE
Westerfield
Playford
Maidensgrave
Capel St Andrew
Rushmere St Andrew
Little Bealings
Martlesham
Boyton
CHRISTCHURCH MANSION
P&R
Waldringfield Heath
Sutton
Stores Corner
Ipswich
Kesgrave
Martlesham Heath
Waldringfield
Shottisham
Duck Corner
Hollesley Bay
MARTLESHAM HEATH CONTROL TOWER
Hollesley
Rose Hill
Stoke
Maidenhall
Warren Heath
Brightwell
Newbourne
Shingle Street
Gainsborough
Bucklesham
Hemley
Alderton
Bawdsey
Wherstead
ORWELL
Nacton
Kirton
Freston
Woolverstone
Levington
Falkenham
Pin Mill
Orwell
Thorpe Common
Trimley St Martin
Chelmondiston
Trimley Lower Street
Felixstowe Ferry
Holbrook
Trimley St Mary
Old Felixstowe
Stutton
Lower Holbrook
Erwarton
Shotley
TRIMLEY MARSHES NATURE RESERVE
Walton
Harkstead
Shotley Gate
Shop Corner
FELIXSTOWE
Holbrook Bay
Stour
HARWICH
CHARLES MANNING'S AMUSEMENT PARK
ESBJERG 17:15
HOEK VAN HOLLAND 6:45
Parkeston
HARWICH REDOUBT FORT
Wrabness
Ramsey
Upper Dovercourt
Dovercourt
Little Oakley
Wix
Great Oakley
Stone's Green
A140
A143
A144
A145
A12
A1095
A1120
A1094
A1152
A1214
A1156
A14
A120
A154
B1116
B1123
B1117
B1118
B1124
B1126
B1127
B1387
B1125
B1122
B1121
B1119
B1120
B1069
B1353
B1077
B1079
B1078
B1084
B1438
B1083
B1080
B1456
B1352
B1414
68
69
43
A
B
C
D
E
F
G
5
6
7
8
9

Gwynedd
SNOWDONIA NATIONAL PARK
PARC CENEDLAETHOL ERYRI
TREMADOG BAY
BAE TREMADOG
BARMOUTH BAY
BAE BERMO
Aberdovey Bar
Bae Aberdyfi
SH
SN
Morfa Harlech
Harlech
Glyn-cywarch
Eisingrug
623 MOEL YSGYFARNOGOD
Bronaber
Mynydd Bach
MOEL LLYFRANT
Mynydd Bryn-llech
Buarthmeini
Llanfair
LLANFAIR SLATE CAVERNS
Llandanwg
Pen-sarn
Pen-y-bont
Pentre Gwynfryn
RHINOG
720 RHINOG FAWR
SARN HELEN
Bed-y-coedwr
RHAEADR MAWDDACH
Pont Aber-Geirw
Cwm-hesgen
Llanbedr
COED Y BRENIN VISITOR CENTRE
Coed y Brenin Forest
Capel Hermon
734 RHOBELL FAWR
Pont Fronwydd
Afon Wnion
Morfa Dyffryn
MORFA DYFFRYN
754 Y LLETHR
DIFFWYS 750
Coed Ystumgwern
Llanenddwyn
Dyffryn Ardudwy
Cors-y-Gedol
Llanddwywe
COED GANLLWYD
Ganllwyd
Llanfachreth
ALLT Y BENGLOG
A494
Rhydymain
Blaen-y-cwm
Tal-y-bont
71
Llanelltyd
CYMER ABBEY
Bont Newydd
Pen-y-bryn
Plas-canol
Bontddu
TOLL
PENMAENPOOL CENTRE
Brithdir
Caerdeon
Llanaber
Cutiau
Penmaenpool
Abergwynant
Dolgellau
Y Gribin
A470
A496
A493
B4573
B4416
Afon Mawddach
Barmouth (Abermaw)
RNLI LIFEBOAT MUSEUM
KINGS
Rhydwen
Afon Cerist
670 WAUN-OER
The Bar
Arthog
Ynysgyfflog
FAIRBOURNE STEAM RAILWAY
Fairbourne
893 CADAIR IDRIS
Mynydd Ceiswyn
Mynydd Dolgoed
MEIRION MILL
Friog
CADER IDRIS
Minffordd
Dyfi Forest
Llwyngwril
Tal-y-llyn
Corris Uchaf
A487
Aberllefenni
Aberangell
Afon Dysynni
Llanfihangel-y-pennant
KING ARTHUR'S LABYRINTH & CRAFT CENTRE
CASTELL Y BERE
Corris
CORRIS RAILWAY AND MUSEUM
Cwm-Llinau
Llangelynin
Abergynolwyn
Esgairgeiliog
Dol-fôr
B4405
Rhoslefain
Llanegryn
Cemmaes
Llanfendigaid
Peniarth
Plas Llwyngwern
CENTRE FOR ALTERNATIVE TECHNOLOGY
309
Pantperthog
Tonfanau
633 TARRENHENDRE
B4404
Llanwrin
Cemmaes Road
Bryncrug
Pandy
VALLEY DYFI
Commins Coch
Pen-y-bont
A489
Abercegir
Rhyd-yr-onen
TALYLLYN RAILWAY
SENEDD-DY-OWAIN GLYNDWR
Machynlleth
Darowen
Tywyn
Pennal
Penegoes
FELIN CREWI WATER MILL
Tal-y-wern
Cwrt
DOVEY DYFFRYN
Forge
Caethle
Derwenlas
Melinbyrhedyn
Glaspwll
Pant-glâs
468 MOELFRE
279
Aberhosan
Aberdovey
Glandyfi
Dovey Dyfi
YNYS HIR RESERVE
Eglwys Fach
DYFI FURNACE
DYFI
Glaslyn
Fochno
Ynyslas
B4353
582
Llancynfelyn
Tre'r-ddôl
BORTH
Tre-Taliesin
521 MOEL-Y-LLYN
Borth
Source of R. Severn Blaen Hafren
Upper Borth
Tal-y-bont
Dôl-y-Bont
Nant-y-Moch Reservoir
PLYNLIMON PUMLUMON FAWR
752
741
Source of R. Wye Blaen Gwy
Llandre
Pen-y-garn
Bont-goch
B4572
ARTS CENTRE
Bow Street
Salem
506
NATIONAL LIBRARY
Clarach
Penrhyn-coch
CLIFF RAILWAY
148
Plas Gogerddan
Pen-bont Rhydybeddau
Aberystwyth
A4159
Comins Coch
Capel Dewi
LLYWERNOG SILVER LEAD MINE
Dyffryn Castell
P&R
Trefechan
Llanbadarn Fawr
Dollwen
Goginan
CASTLE
A44
Capel Bangor
Ponterwyd
564
Penparcau
Glanrafon
Cwmbrwyno
Southgate
VALE OF RHEIDOL RAILWAY
Afon Rheidol
RHEIDOL HYDRO ELECTRIC STAT.
46
47
Rhydyfelin
Moriah
Capel Seion
Ystumtuen
Ysbytycynfyn
Aberffrwd
Gors
A4120
Pisgah
COED RHEIDOL
Llanfarian
Llanfihangel-y-Creuddyn
Mynydd Bach
New Cross
Devil's Bridge
610 PEN Y GARN
Blaenplwyf
A485
Trisant
Blaenycwm
0 1 2 3 4 5 6 miles
0 1 2 3 4 5 6 7 8 9 10 km

Parc
Dolhendre
Llangower
Llyn Tegid or Bala
BALA LAKE RAILWAY
Llanuwchllyn
Pont-Rhyd-sarn
Cwm Cynllwyd
Talardd
Ty-nant
626 FOEL Y GEIFR
666
884
907 ARAN FAWDDWY
Aber-Hirnant
Aberhirnant Forest
Pont Cwm Pydew
Blaen-y-Cwm
827 MOEL SYCH
PISTYLL RHAEADR
Tan-y-pistyll
Tyn-y-fedwen
Llanarmon Dyffryn Ceiriog
Tyn-y-ffridd
Tregeiriog
Llechrydau
Rhiwlas
Cefn Canol
Llangadwaladr
Tai-bach
Moelfre
Llansilin
Pant-g
Llawnt
Rhydycroe
OFFA'S DYKE PATH
LLWYBR CLAWDD OFFA
Tyn-y-coed
Trefonen
Treflach
Pencraig
Llangynog
Pennant Melangell
607
Cefn Coch
Llanrhaeadr-ym-Mochnant
B4580
B4396
Llangedwyn
Pen-y-bont
Porth-y-waen
Penybontfawr
Penygarnedd
Hirnant
Afon Tanat
Rhos-y-brithdir
389
B4391
Llanyblodwel
Y BERWYN
Alltforgan
Lake Vyrnwy
B4393
Ty-uchaf
Aber-Rhiwlech
Pont y Pennant
540
Blaen-y-cwm
Abernaint
Bwlchyddar
Llanfechain
Llansantffraid-ym-Mechain
Llanymynech
Llanfyllin
Cywarch
513
Llanymawddwy
Hen Gerrig
Llanwddyn
Abertridwr
Tycrwyn
A490
A495
Bryn Sion
Aber Cowarch
TIR RHIWIOG 545
Moel y Llyn
Ddôl-Cownwy
Dyfnant Forest
Mynydd y Gadfa
Llanfihangel-yn-Ngwynfa
Bwlch-y-cibau
Waen Fach
Deuddwr
Sarnau
Arddleen
Main
SJ
Trefnanney
Geuffordd
Dinas-Mawddwy
Minllyn
Cwm-Cewydd
Mallwyd
A458
Wern
Pont-Llogel
Afon Vyrnwy (Afon Efyrnwy)
Dolanog
330
Meifod
Pentrebeirdd
Wern
Pontrobert
Glascoed
Maesgwyn-Isaf
Groes-lwyd
Guilsfield
Pool Quay
B4392
B4382
Foel
Llangadfan
Ffridd Goch
523
Pen Coed
GLYNDŴR'S WAY
Llanerfyl
Four Crosses
Heniarth
Cyfronydd
Cloddiau
Welshpool (Y Trallwng)
Buttin
WELSHPOOL & LLANFAIR LIGHT RAILWAY
POWYSLAND
POWIS CASTLE
Hope
Mynydd y Cemaes
Clegyrnant
Dolwen
Sychtyn
Neinthirion
Melin-y-grug
Melin-y-ddôl
Llanfair Caereinion
B4385
Castle Caereinion
Leighton
Pentre-Celyn
Pandy
Cwmderwen
Mynydd Waun Fawr
Bryn-penarth
364
Waun
Llanbrynmair
Powys
Tafolwern
Dolfach
440
Llanllugan
B4389
B4390
Manafon
Pant-y-ffridd
Llwynderw
MID-WALES
Fron
B4388
A483
Kingswood
Stockton
Llan
Bont-Dolgadfan
A470
Talerddig
Rhyd
Llanwyddelan
Adfa
New Mills
Berriew
Forden
B4518
Pennant
Carno
458
Tregynon
Brooks
Garthmyl
Fron
Montgomery (Trefaldwyn)
B4386
Dylife
Clatter
Bwlch-y-ffridd
Bettws Cedewain
DOLFORWYN CASTLE
Green Lane
Abermule
Llandyssil
398
Llanwnog
265
Llanllwchaiarn
Llanmerewig
Pentreheyling
Staylittle
GLYNDŴR'S WAY
Llawr-y-glyn
Gleiniant
B4569
Caersws
A489
Milford
Newtown (Y Drenewydd)
Hodley
Glanmule
Sarn
City
Trefeglwys
Kerry
B4368
Llyn Clywedog
482 FAN HILL
Van
Oakley Park
307
Little London
Llandinam
Mochdre
Dolfor
Mainstone
497
Clun Forest
Hafren Forest
Tan Hinon
Old Hall
Glan-y-nant
Llanidloes
Severn (Hafren)
Pentre
SO
Anchor
Hall of the Forest
528 CILFAESTY HILL
448 BLACK MT.
Newcastle
Glynbrochan
Newchapel
Pant Mawr
Cwmbelan
B4355
Felindre
Bettws-y-crwyn
Quabbs
Llanifyny
A44
Llangurig
Tylwch
584
Llaithddu
Beguildy
Black Mountain
GLYNDŴR'S WAY
David's Well
Llanbadarn Fynydd
Dutlas
Llanfair Waterdine
Nantgwyn
493 RED LION HILL
Rhydmoelddu
547 BEACON HILL
Pant-y-dwr
72
60
47
48
A B C D E F G

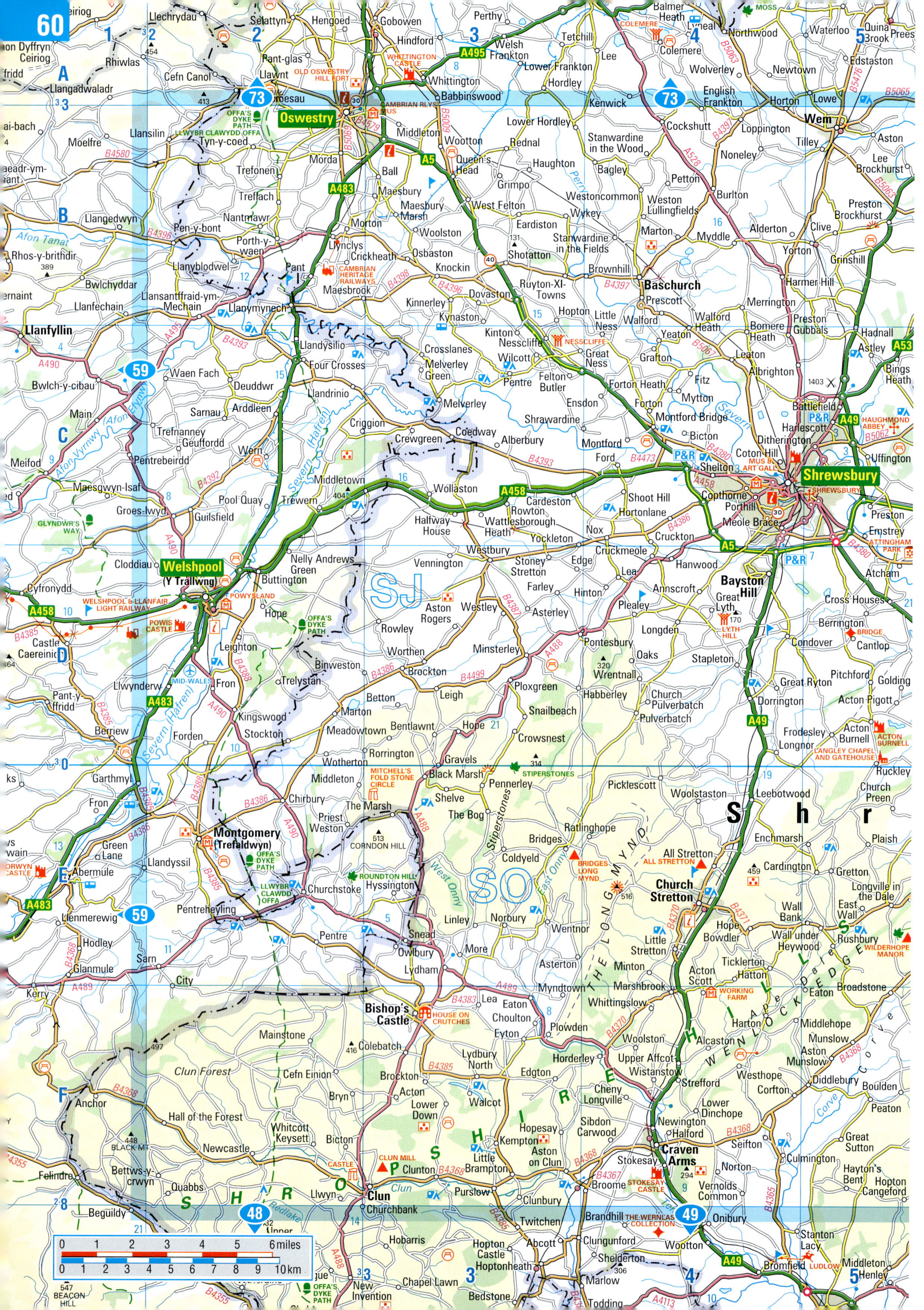
Llechrydau
Selattyn
Hengoed
Gobowen
Perthy
Welsh Frankton
Tetchill
Lee
Balmer Heath
Lyneal
Northwood
Waterloo
Quina Brook
Prees
Rhiwlas
Pant-glas
WHITTINGTON CASTLE
Lower Frankton
Hordley
Colemere
Wolverley
Newtown
Edstaston
Llangadwaladr
Cefn Canol
Llawnt
OLD OSWESTRY HILL FORT
Whittington
Babbinswood
Kenwick
English Frankton
Horton
Lowe
Wem
Oswestry
CAMBRIAN RLYS MUS
OFFA'S DYKE PATH
LLWYBR CLAWDD OFFA
Llansilin
Moelfre
Tyn-y-coed
Middleton
Wootton
Lower Hordley
Rednal
Cockshutt
Loppington
Tilley
Aston
Morda
Queen's Head
Haughton
Stanwardine in the Wood
Noneley
Lee Brockhurst
Trefonen
Ball
Grimpo
Bagley
Petton
Maesbury
Westoncommon
Weston Lullingfields
Burlton
Preston Brockhurst
Treflach
Maesbury Marsh
West Felton
Wykey
Llangedwyn
Nantmawr
Eardiston
Alderton
Clive
Afon Tanat
Pen-y-bont
Morton
Woolston
Stanwardine in the Fields
Marton
Myddle
Yorton
Porth-y-waen
Llynclys
Crickheath
Osbaston
Shotatton
Rhos-y-brithdir
Llanyblodwel
Pant
CAMBRIAN HERITAGE RAILWAYS
Knockin
Brownhill
Grinshill
Bwlchyddar
Maesbrook
Dovaston
Ruyton-XI-Towns
Baschurch
Harmer Hill
Llansantffraid-ym-Mechain
Kinnerley
Prescott
Merrington
Llanfechain
Llanymynech
Kynaston
Hopton
Little Ness
Walford
Walford Heath
Preston Gubbals
Llanfyllin
Llandysilio
Kinton
Nesscliffe
NESSCLIFFE
Yeaton
Bomere Heath
Hadnall
Crosslanes
Great Ness
Leaton
Astley
Four Crosses
Melverley Green
Wilcott
Grafton
Albrighton
Bings Heath
Bwlch-y-cibau
Waen Fach
Deuddwr
Pentre
Felton Butler
Forton Heath
Fitz
Landrinio
Forton
Mytton
Battlefield
Main
Sarnau
Arddleen
Melverley
Ensdon
Montford Bridge
Harlescott
HAUGHMOND ABBEY
Afon Efyrnwy
Trefnanney
Criggion
Shrawardine
Bicton
Ditherington
Geuffordd
Crewgreen
Coedway
Alberbury
Montford
Coton Hill
Uffington
Meifod
Wern
Ford
Shelton
MUS & ART GALL
Shrewsbury
Pentrebeirdd
Middletown
Wollaston
Cardeston
Copthorne
Porthill
SHREWSBURY
Maesgwyn-Isaf
Pool Quay
Trewern
Rowton
Shoot Hill
Groes-lwyd
Guilsfield
Halfway House
Wattlesborough Heath
Hortonlane
Meole Brace
Preston
GLYNDWR'S WAY
Yockleton
Nox
Cruckton
Emstrey
ATTINGHAM PARK
Cloddiau
Welshpool (Y Trallwng)
Nelly Andrews Green
Westbury
Stoney Stretton
Edge
Cruckmeole
Hanwood
Atcham
Vennington
Buttington
Lea
Bayston Hill
Cyfronydd
POWYSLAND
Farley
Hinton
Annscroft
Great Lyth
Cross Houses
WELSHPOOL & LLANFAIR LIGHT RAILWAY
Hope
Aston Rogers
Westley
Asterley
Pleal ey
POWIS CASTLE
LYTH HILL
Berrington
Castle Caereinion
Rowley
Pontesbury
Longden
BRIDGE
Cantlop
Leighton
Worthen
Minsterley
Condover
Oaks
Stapleton
Binweston
Brockton
Wrentnall
Pitchford
Golding
Llwynderw
Fron
Trelystan
Leigh
Ploxgreen
Habberley
Church Pulverbatch
Great Ryton
Acton Pigott
MID-WALES
Betton
Pulverbatch
Dorrington
Pant-y-ffridd
Kingswood
Marton
Snailbeach
Berriew
Forden
Stockton
Meadowtown
Bentlawnt
Hope
Crowsnest
Frodesley
Acton Burnell
ACTON BURNELL
Longnor
LANGLEY CHAPEL AND GATEHOUSE
Rorrington
Gravels
Wotherton
Garthmyl
Middleton
MITCHELL'S FOLD STONE CIRCLE
Black Marsh
STIPERSTONES
Pennerley
Picklescott
Woolstaston
Leebotwood
Ruckley
Church Preen
Fron
Chirbury
Shelve
The Marsh
Priest Weston
The Bog
Ratlinghope
Enchmarsh
Plaish
Green Lane
Montgomery (Trefaldwyn)
CORNDON HILL
Stiperstones
Bridges
All Stretton
ALL STRETTON
Cardington
Gretton
Llandyssil
Coldyeld
BRIDGES LONG MYND
Longville in the Dale
Abermule
ROUNDTON HILL
Churchstoke
Hyssington
Church Stretton
Wall Bank
East Wall
Pentreheyling
West Onny
East Onny
Hope Bowdler
Wall under Heywood
Rushbury
WILDERHOPE MANOR
Llenmerewig
Linley
Norbury
Wentnor
Little Stretton
Hodley
Pentre
Snead
Ticklerton
More
Glanmule
Sarn
Owlbury
Asterton
Minton
Acton Scott
Hatton
City
Lydham
Myndtown
Marshbrook
Broadstone
Kerry
Lea
Eaton
WORKING FARM
Bishop's Castle
HOUSE ON CRUTCHES
Whittingslow
Choulton
Plowden
Harton
Middlehope
Mainstone
Eyton
Woolston
Alcaston
Munslow
Colebatch
Lydbury North
Horderley
Upper Affcot
Aston Munslow
Clun Forest
Cefn Einion
Brockton
Edgton
Wistanstow
Westhope
Diddlebury
Boulden
Corfton
Acton
Cheny Longville
Strefford
Peaton
Anchor
Bryn
Lower Down
Walcot
Sibdon Carwood
Lower Dinchope
Hall of the Forest
Whitcott Keysett
Newington
Hopesay
Halford
Great Sutton
Kempton
Seifton
BLACK MT
Newcastle
Bicton
Aston on Clun
Stokesay
Craven Arms
Culmington
CLUN MILL
Little Brampton
Norton
Hayton's Bent
Felindre
Bettws-y-crwyn
CASTLE
Clunton
Broome
STOKESAY CASTLE
Vernolds Common
Hopton Cangeford
Quabbs
Llwyn
Clun
Purslow
Clunbury
Beguildy
Churchbank
Redlake
Twitchen
Brandhill
THE WERNLAS COLLECTION
Onibury
Hobarris
Abcott
Clungunford
Stanton Lacy
Hopton Castle
Shelderton
Wootton
Hoptonheath
Bromfield
LUDLOW
Middleton
Henley
Chapel Lawn
Marlow
New Invention
Bedstone
Todding
BEACON HILL
Shropshire
SJ
SO
THE LONG MYND
WENLOCK EDGE
APE DALE
Severn
Afon Hafren
Corve
A5
A49
A53
A458
A483
A488
A489
A495
A490
A528
A4113
B4393
B4386
B4368
B4385
B4396
B4397
B4398
B4380
B4370
B4371
B4365
B4367
B4383
B4387
B4388
B4392
B4499
B4580
B4579
B4473
B4355
B5062
B5063
B5065
B5067
B5069
B5009
B5476
B4380
0 1 2 3 4 5 6 miles
0 1 2 3 4 5 6 7 8 9 10 km
73
59
48
49

Telford and Wrekin
Shropshire
Sandford
Longford
Market Drayton
Hales
Fairoak
Wetwood
Croxtonbank
Croxton
Millmeece
Slindon
Yarnfield
Walton
Stone
Little Stoke
Milwich
Prees
Lowe
Heath
Darliston
Fauls
Bletchley
Ternhill
The Four Alls
Sutton
Woodseaves
Chipnall
Sugnall
Norton Bridge
Aston-By-Stone
Burston
Sandon
Prees Green
Lostford
Wollerton
Cheswardine
Bishop's Offley
Pershall
Eccleshall
Chebsey
Yarlet
Hawkstone Park
Wollerton Old Hall
Stoke Heath
Soudley
Izaak Walton's Cottage Museum
Whitgreave
Weston
Marchamley
Hodnet
Wistanswick
Mill Green
Goldstone Hall
Lockleywood
Adbaston
Wootton
Ellenhall
Great Bridgeford
Marston
Salt
Wixhill
Hodnet Hall
Stoke on Tern
Hinstock
Knighton
High Offley
Moston
Hopton
High Hatton
Child's Ercall
Ollerton
Ellerton
Shebdon
Woodseaves
Seighford
Holmcroft
Stafford
Stanton upon Hine Heath
Radmoor
Sambrook
Weston Jones
Norbury
Lawnhead
Knightley Dale
Ranton
Coton Clanford
Doxey
Moreton Corbet
Eaton on Tern
Howle
Pickstock
Derrington
Forebridge
Moreton Corbet
Ellerdine Heath
Puleston
Sutton
Long Compton
Ancient High House
Edgebolton
Great Bolas
Gnosall
Whitecross
Moss Pit
Weeping Cross
Shawbury
Muckleton
Cold Hatton
Meese
Tibberton
Edgmond Marsh
Forton
Aqualate Mere
Haughton
Walton
Cherrington
Edgmond
Coton
Gnosall Heath
Allimore Green
Coppenhall
Acton Trussell
Great Wytheford
Rowton
Waters Upton
Newport
Outwoods
Apeton
Bradley
Dunston
Walton
Crudgington
Adeney
Longford
Church Aston
Chetwynd Aston
Moreton
Church Eaton
Bednall
Poynton Green
High Ercall
Kynnersley
Brockton
High Onn
Levedale
Roden
Haughton
Slapeford
Preston upon the Weald Moors
Eyton upon the Weald Moors
Lilleshall
Lilleshall Abbey
Orslow
Longridge
Mitton
Longdon on Tern
Hoo Farm Animal Kingdom
Great Chatwell
Penkridge
Rodington
Muxton
Heath Hill
Whiston
Congreve
Bratton
Donnington
Brineton
Marston
Upton Magna
Withington
Admaston
Trench
Donnington Wood
Lilyhurst
Sheriffhales
Weston Heath
Blymhill
Lapley
Hunting
Wrockwardine
Hadley
Granville
Mottey Meadows
Wheaton Aston
Stretton
Walcot
Wellington
Ketley
Ketley Bank
Oakengates
Gailey
Charlton
Arleston
Priorslee
Crackleybank
Telford Services
Weston under Lizard
Weston Park
Belvide Res.
Horsebrook
Hatherton
Norton
Uppington
Aston
The Rock
Lawley
Bishop's Wood
Kiddemore Green
Wroxeter Roman City
Rushton
Telford
Haughton
Shifnal
Tong Norton
Brewood
Boscobel House & The Royal Oak
Wroxeter
Donnington
Eaton Constantine
The Wrekin
Horsehay
Dawley
Telford Wonderland
The Wyke
Tong
White Ladies Priory
Hillington Hall
Standeford
Coven
Shareshill
Longwood
Little Wenlock
Telford Steam Railway
Stirchley
Raf Museum
Hilton Park Services
Dryton
Leighton
Little Dawley
Halesfield
Kemberton
Albrighton
Codsall Wood
Featherstone
Buildwas
Rosehill Ho
Coalbrookdale
Worfe
Buildwas Abbey
Mus of Iron
Mus of the Gorge
Madeley
Blists Hill
David Austin Roses
Cound
Cressage
Sheinton
Ironbridge
Tollhouse Mus
Coalport
Brockton
Grindle
Ryton
Oaken
Codsall
Fordhouses
Moseley Old Hall
Essington
Benthall Hall
Benthall
Wyke
Jackfield Tile Mus
Boningale
Oxley
Bushbury
Homer
Broseley
Sutton Maddock
Beckbury
Harley
Much Wenlock
Norton
Burnhill Green
Wergs
Tettenhall
Wolverhampton
Wednesfield
Kenley
Willey
Stockton
Badger
Pattingham
Wightwick Manor
Bantock House
Stretton Westwood
Stableford
Ackleton
Perton
Willenhall
Hughley
Rudge
Trescott
Moseley
Presthope
Callaughton
Astley Abbotts
Chesterton
Bradmore
Blakenhall
Bilston
Acton Round
Nordley
Shipley
Lower Penn
Penn
Ettingshall
Bourton
Haughton
Worfield
Seisdon
Easthope
Cross Lane Head
Hilton
Hopstone
Trysull
Sedgley
Aston Eyre
Morville Hall
Morville
Cliff Railway
Tasley
Roughton
Claverley
Wombourne
Bagger
Tipton
Brockton
Monkhopton
Morville Heath
Stanmore
Heathton
Blakeley
Weston
Bridgnorth
Farmcote
Himley Hall
Himley
Wrens Nest
Upper Gornal
Gornalwood
Dudley Zoo & Castle
Wilderhope Manor
Shipton
Netchwood
Lower Netchwood
Upton Cressett
Oldbury
Watermill
Danesford
Wolverhampton Halfpenny Green
Halfpenny Green
Swindon
Stanton Long
Chetton
Eardington
Quatford
Highgate Common
Bobbington
Wall Heath
Dudley
Middleton Priors
Holdgate
Ditton Priors
Glazeley
Dudmaston
Quatt
Six Ashes
Kingswinford
Bromley
Netherton
Broadfield House Glass Mus
Four Ashes
Tuckhill
Brierley Hill
Tugford
Neenton
Abdon
Middleton Scriven
Chelmarsh
Chelmarsh Res.
Enville
Old Hill
Upper Heath
Brown Clee Hill
Cleobury North
Sidbury
Borle Brook
Sutton
Hampton Loade
Hampton
Wordsley
Amblecote
Red House Glass Cone
Cradley Heath
Quarry Bank
Clee St Margaret
Burwarton
Billingsley
Woodhill
Birdsgreen
Stourton
Wollescote
Aston Botterell
Potter's Cross
Stourbridge
Lye
Halesowen
Chorley
Highley
Alveley
Severn Valley
Kinver
Whittington
Hasbury
Stoke St Milborough
Loughton
Wheathill
Stottesdon
Rays Farm Country Matters
Romsley
Kingsford
Pedmore
Cleedownton
Farlow
Shatterford
Bodenham Arboretum & Earth Centre
Blakeshall
Caunsall
Hagley
Oreton
Kinlet
Upper Arley
Cookley
West Hagley
Clent
Silvington
Catherton
Pound Green
Trimpley
Wolverley
Churchill
Broome
Cleeton St Mary
Buttonoak
Low Habberley
Franche
Blakedown
Holy Cross
Bitterley
Foxwood
Doddington
Neen Savage
Wafers
Wyre Forest
Wyre
Severn Valley Railway
Blakebrook
Kidderminster
Bell End
Belbroughton
Snitton
Farden
Cleobury
Far Forest
Bewdley
West Midland Safari Park
Stone
Drayton
Wildmoor
Hopton Wafers
Sow
Severn
Tern
Roden
Worfe
Rea Brook
Shropshire Union Canal
Stour
Dale
Corve
A49
A53
A41
A442
A518
A5223
A5
A458
A454
A449
A51
A34
A456
A491
A4117
A4169
A464
A4375
A4176
A4555
A4363
A4201
B5026
B5027
B5013
B5066
B5405
B5062
B5063
B5061
B4380
B4378
B4368
B4364
B4376
B4373
B4176
B4394
B4379
B4555
B4363
B4199
B4190
B4188
B4551
M6
M54
T8
S
SJ
SO
74
62
49
50
A
B
C
D
E
F
G
5
6
7
8
9
61
Stafford Services
Telford Services
Hilton Park Services
P&R
1643
180
540
533
321
231
204
298
137
139
150
407

Stone
Uttoxeter
Eccleshall
Stafford
Weston
Abbots Bromley
Newport
Penkridge
Rugeley
Hednesford
Cannock
Lichfield
Burntwood
Brownhills
Shifnal
Albrighton
Brewood
Codsall
Wolverhampton
Tettenhall
Wednesfield
Willenhall
Bilston
Darlaston
Walsall
Aldridge
SUTTON COLDFIELD
Wednesbury
Sedgley
Coseley
Tipton
West Bromwich
Wombourne
Dudley
Oldbury
Rowley Regis
SMETHWICK
BIRMINGHAM
Kingswinford
Brierley Hill
Stourbridge
HALESOWEN
Kinver
Solihull
Shirley
Longbridge
Bewdley
S t a f f o r d
W e s t M i d l a n d s
CANNOCK CHASE
SJ
SO
M6
M54
M5
A5
A34
A38
A449
A41
0 1 2 3 4 5 6 miles
0 1 2 3 4 5 6 7 8 9 10 km

Burton upon Trent
Swadlincote
Ashby-de-la-Zouch
Coalville
Loughborough
Shepshed
Melbourne
Castle Donington
Kegworth
Long Eaton
Tamworth
Atherstone
Nuneaton
Hinckley
Bedworth
Coventry
Coleshill
Measham
Ibstock
Whitwick
Lutterworth
Earl Shilton
Anstey
Burbage
Tutbury
Repton
Willington
Chellaston
Normanton
Barton-under-Needwood
NATIONAL FOREST
FOREST
SK
SP
M1
M42
M6
M69
A5
A42
A444
A38
A50
A453
A511
A6
A47
A46
76
64
52
51

Long Eaton
Clifton
Ruddington
Keyworth
Plumtree
Normanton-on-the-Wolds
Owthorpe
Colston Bassett
Langar
Barkestone-le-Vale
Belvoir
Plungar
Stathern
Harston
Knipton
Thrumpton
Sawley
Bradmore
Kinoulton
Cavendish Bridge
Ratcliffe on Soar
Lockington
Castle Donington
Kegworth
Kingston on Soar
West Leake
East Leake
Costock
Bunny
New Kingston
Wysall
Widmerpool
Stanton-on-the-Wolds
Hickling
Hose
Eaton
Branston
Croxton Kerrial
Eastwell
Upper Broughton
Long Clawson
Goadby Marwood
Waltham on the Wolds
Willoughby-on-the-Wolds
Nether Broughton
Wycomb
Chadwell
Stonesby
Sutton Bonington
Rempstone
Diseworth
Long Whatton
Normanton on Soar
Wymeswold
Old Dalby
Wartnaby
Ab Kettleby
Holwell
Scalford
Hathern
Hoton
Grimston
Saxelbye
Coston
Garthorpe
Freeby
Belton
Stanford on Soar
Cotes
Burton on the Wolds
Six Hills
Melton Mowbray
Thorpe Arnold
Saxby
Shepshed
Thorpe Acre
Loughborough
Walton on the Wolds
Ragdale
Shoby
Asfordby
Asfordby Hill
Wyfordby
Brentingby
Burton Lazars
Stapleford
Shelthorpe
Woodthorpe
Barrow upon Soar
Seagrave
Hoby
Frisby on the Wreake
Kirby Bellars
Nanpantan
Quorndon
Thrussington
Rotherby
Whitwick
Charnwood Forest
Woodhouse
Mountsorrel
Sileby
Ratcliffe on the Wreake
Great Dalby
Little Dalby
Whissendine
Greenhill
Woodhouse Eaves
Cossington
Rearsby
East Goscote
Gaddesby
Ashby Folville
Thorpe Satchville
Bardon
Copt Oak
Swithland
Rothley
Queniborough
Pickwell
Cold Overton
Leicestershire
Cropston
Syston
Barsby
Twyford
Burrough on the Hill
Somerby
Langham
Markfield
Stanton under Bardon
Thurcaston
Birstall
Barkby
South Croxton
Barleythorpe
Field Head
Newtown Linford
Anstey
Thurmaston
Beeby
Marefield
Owston
Knossington
Thornton
Groby
Lowesby
Hungarton
Cold Newton
Keyham
Ratby
Glenfield
Leicester
Scraptoft
New Humberstone
Halstead
Tilton on the Hill
Braunston-in-Rutland
Brooke
Botcheston
Newtown Unthank
Kirby Muxloe
Bushby
Thurnby
Desford
Leicester Forest East
Braunstone Town
City
Evington
Stoughton
Houghton on the Hill
Billesdon
Skeffington
Loddington
Ridlington
Belton in Rutland
Peckleton
Stoneygate
Knighton
Oadby
Gaulby
Tugby
East Norton
Kirkby Mallory
Aylestone
King's Norton
Rolleston
Allexton
Wardley
Stapleton
Thurlaston
Enderby
Glen Parva
Little Stretton
Illston on the Hill
Noseley
Goadby
Earl Shilton
Barwell
Narborough
Blaby
Wigston
Great Glen
Carlton Curlieu
Elmesthorpe
Huncote
Littlethorpe
Whetstone
South Wigston
Newton Harcourt
Burton Overy
Horninghold
Hallaton
Stockerston
Shangton
Croft
Countesthorpe
Stoney Stanton
Cosby
Kilby
Kibworth Harcourt
Stonton Wyville
Glooston
Cranoe
Blaston
Eyebrook Reservoir
Sutton in the Elms
Slawston
Sapcote
Primethorpe
Fleckney
Kibworth Beauchamp
Tur Langton
Church Langton
Great Easton
Medbourne
Peatling Magna
Arnesby
Smeeton Westerby
Welham
Burbage
Aston Flamville
Broughton Astley
Willoughby Waterleys
Saddington
East Langton
Thorpe Langton
Drayton
Bringhurst
Sharnford
Dunton Bassett
Ashby Magna
Shearsby
Bruntingthorpe
Weston by Welland
Sutton Bassett
Ashley
Cottingham
Middleton
Frolesworth
Leire
Foxton
Gumley
Great Bowden
East Carlton
Claybrooke Magna
Claybrooke Parva
Ashby Parva
Peatling Parva
Mowsley
Laughton
Market Harborough
Stoke Albany
Wilbarston
Copston Magna
Wibtoft
Ullesthorpe
Gilmorton
Walton
Dingley
Brampton Ash
Lubenham
Little Bowden
Kimcote
Theddingworth
Marston Trussell
East Farndon
Braybrooke
Pipewell
Bitteswell
Lutterworth
Willey
Misterton
Husbands Bosworth
Withybrook
Cross in Hand
Walcote
North Kilworth
Sibbertoft
Great Oxendon
Desborough
Rushton
Monks Kirby
Cotesbach
South Kilworth
Sulby Reservoir
Clipston
Arthingworth
Harrington
Rothwell
Pailton
Churchover
Gibbet Hill
Welford
Stretton under Fosse
Shawell
Swinford
Stanford on Avon
Naseby Field
Kelmarsh
Orton
Easenhall
Harborough Magna
Naseby Reservoir
Loddington
Thorpe Malsor
King's Newnham
Naseby
Haselbech
Maidwell
Draughton
Great Cransley
Coton
Cold Ashby
Thornby
Mawsley
Broughton
Lawford
Clifton upon Dunsmore
Yelvertoft
New Bilton
SK
SP
A453
A606
A6006
A60
A6
A512
A46
A607
A47
A50
A563
A5460
A426
A5199
A427
A6
A4304
A4303
A5
A508
A14
A43
A428
M1
M69
M6
63
77
52
53
0 1 2 3 4 5 6 miles
0 1 2 3 4 5 6 7 8 9 10 km

Denton
Harlaxton
HARLAXTON MANOR
Little Ponton
Stroxton
Great Ponton
78
Hungerton
Wyville
Stoke Rochford
Easton
Bassingthorpe
Saltby
Skillington
WOOLSTHORPE MANOR
Woolsthorpe
Colsterworth
Twyford
GRANTHAM SOUTH SERVICES
Sproxton
Buckminster
Stainby
Sewstern
Gunby
North Witham
South Witham
Wymondham
CRIBBS MEADOW
Edmondthorpe
Thistleton
Market Overton
Teigh
Barrow
Stretton
RUTLAND RAILWAY MUS
Greetham
Ashwell
Cottesmore
Exton
Rutland
BARNSDALE GARDENS
Burley
FALCONRY CENTRE
Oakham
Whitwell
Empingham
Upper Hambleton
Egleton
RUTLAND WATER
Normanton
Manton
Edith Weston
Lyndon
North Luffenham
Ketton
Preston
Wing
Pilton
South Luffenham
Ayston
Glaston
Morcott
Barrowden
Tixover
Uppingham
Bisbrooke
Seaton
Stoke Dry
Lyddington
BEDE HOUSE
Harringworth
Wakerley
Laxton
Thorpe by Water
Gretton
Caldecott
KIRBY HALL
Rockingham
ROCKINGHAM CASTLE
Deene
DEENE PARK
Deenethorpe
Little Weldon
Great Weldon
Corby
Stanion
Little Oakley
Great Oakley
Brigstock
HILL FARM HERBS
FERMYN WOODS
LYVEDEN NEW BIELD
Newton
Geddington
ELEANOR CROSS
Sudborough
BOUGHTON HOUSE
Warkton
Grafton Underwood
Weekley
Kettering
Barton Seagrave
Cranford St Andrew
Cranford St John
Twywell
Woodford
Denford
Ropsley
Sapperton
Old Somerby
Humby
Pickworth
Hanby
Folkingham
Boothby Pagnell
Lenton
Ingoldsby
Keisby
Laughton
Aslackby
Birthorpe
Billingborough
Pointon
Millthorpe
Dowsby
Graby
Rippingale
Bitchfield
Irnham
Hawthorpe
Kirkby Underwood
Bulby
Dunsby
Burton-le-Coggles
Corby Glen
Stainfield
Haconby
Birkholme
Elsthorpe
Hanthorpe
Morton
Swayfield
Swinstead
Grimsthorpe
GRIMSTHORPE CASTLE
Cawthorpe
Dyke
Edenham
Scottlethorpe
Bourne
Creeton
Castle Bytham
Little Bytham
Lound
Witham on the Hill
Northorpe
Thurlby
Toft
THURLBY
Clipsham
Careby
Manthorpe
Obthorpe
Wilsthorpe
Thetford
Pickworth
Carlby
Essendine
Braceborough
Baston
Greatford
Langtoft
Tolethorpe Hall
TOLETHORPE HALL RUTLAND OPEN AIR THEATRE
Ryhall
Little Casterton
Belmesthorpe
Barholm
Towngate
Market Deeping
Frognall
Deeping St James
Tickencote
Great Casterton
Tallington
West Deeping
Deeping Gate
Northfields
Uffington
Stamford
Tinwell
BURGHLEY
Maxey
Northborough
Etton
Peakirk
Easton on the Hill
Pilsgate
Barnack
Bainton
Ufford
Helpston
Glinton
BARNACK HILLS AND HOLES
Southorpe
Collyweston
COLLYWESTON GREAT WOOD
Wittering
Thornhaugh
SACREWELL FARM & COUNTRY CENTRE
Upton
CASTOR HANGLANDS
Marholm
Werrington
Walton
Gunthorpe
Peterborough
Duddington
BEDFORD PURLIEUS
Wansford
Stibbington
Sutton
Ailsworth
Castor
NENE VALLEY RAILWAY
FERRY MEADOWS
LONGTHORPE TOWER
Longthorpe
Dogsthorpe
Newark
Eye
Fengate
FLAG FEN BRONZE AGE EXCAVATIONS
Old Fletton
Orton Longueville
Stanground
Whittlesey
King's Cliffe
Yarwell
Sibson
SIBSON
Water Newton
Alwalton
Orton Waterville
Chesterton
CROWN LAKES
Farcet
Blatherwycke
Apethorpe
Nassington
Woodnewton
Bulwick
SOUTHWICK HALL
Southwick
Fotheringhay
CASTLE SITE
ELTON HALL
Elton
Haddon
PETERBOROUGH SERVICES
Yaxley
Eaglethorpe
Warmington
Tansor
Morborne
Norman Cross
Farcet Fen
Whittlesey Mere
Glapthorn
Cotterstock
Folksworth
Upper Benefield
Lower Benefield
Oundle
Ashton
BARNWELL
Polebrook
Caldecote
Stilton
Denton
Lutton
Holme
HOLME FEN
Stoke Doyle
Barnwell St Andrew
Glatton
Conington
Pilton
Hemington
Barnwell All Saints
Luddington in the Brook
Wadenhoe
Achurch
Thurning
Great Gidding
Little Gidding
Steeple Gidding
HAMERTON ZOO PARK
Sawtry
Ramsey Heights
WOODWALTON FEN
Church End
UPWOOD MEADOWS
Wood Walton
Great Raveley
MONKS WOOD
Aldwincle
Wigsthorpe
Thorpe Waterville
Lowick
Clopton
Winwick
Coppingford
Hamerton
Titchmarsh
Islip
Thrapston
53
54
Old Weston
Upton
Alconbury Weston
Alconbury
Buckworth
Brington
Bythorn
Molesworth
Wennington
Abbots Ripton
Little Stukeley
Gosberton
Gosberton Clough
Westhorpe
Risegate
Surfleet
Crossgate
Northgate
Pinchbeck
Pinchbeck Bars
Pinchbeck West
Spalding
Pode Hole
Little London
Clay Lake
Twenty
TF
Tonque End
Deeping Fen
Deeping St Nicholas
Hop Pole
Crowland
CROWLAND
Newborough
Bedford Level (North)
Eye Green
King's Delph
Stone Bridge Corner
66
TL
Peterborough
Rockingham Forest
Welland
Nene
Witham
Chater
Harper's Brook
Ise
King Street

Donington South Ing
Quadring
Gosberton
Gosberton Clough
Westhorpe
Risegate
Surfleet
Surfleet Seas End
Fosdyke
Holbeach St Marks
Holbeach St Matthew
HOLBEACH MARSH
Gedney Marsh
Gedney Drove End
Lynn Channel
THE WASH
Crossgate
Northgate
Pinchbeck
Pinchbeck Bars
Pinchbeck West
Spalding
Pode Hole
Little London
Clay Lake
Twenty
BAYTREE OWL CENTRE
SPRINGFIELDS
SPRINGFIELDS SHOW GARDENS
Weston
Moulton
Whaplode
MOULTON MILL
Low Fulney
AYSCOUGHFEE HALL
Weston Hills
Austendike
Moulton Seas End
Halesgate
Saracen's Head
Holbeach Bank
Holbeach Clough
Holbeach Hurn
Holbeach
Fleet Hargate
Gedney Dyke
Gedney
Fleet
Gedney Broadgate
Lutton
Chapelgate
Little London
BUTTERFLY & WILDLIFE PARK
Long Sutton
Guy's Head
Terrington
Sutton Bridge
Sutton Crosses
Orange Row
Walpole Cross Keys
Whaplode St Catherine
MUS OF ENTERTAINMENT
Moulton Chapel
Cowbit
Tongue End
Deeping Fen
Deeping St Nicholas
Brotherhouse Bar
Moulton Eaugate
Holbeach St Johns
Sutton St James
Tydd St Mary
Tydd Gote
Four Gotes
Tydd St Giles
Walpole St Andrew
Walpole Marsh
Walpole St Peter
Hay Green
TF
Tydd St Giles Fen
Newton
Ingleborough
St John's Highway
Hop Pole
Whaplode Drove
Holbeach Drove
Shepeau Stow
Sutton St Edmund
Fitton End
West Walton
West Walton Highway
Walpole Highway
St John
Terrington
Marshland
St John's Fen End
Market Deeping
Frognall
Deeping St James
Crowland
CROWLAND ABBEY
Dowsdale
Gedney Hill
Throckenholt
Gorefield
Leverington
Church End
PECKOVER HOUSE
Walsoken
FENLAND & WEST NORFOLK AVIATION MUSEUM
Wisbech
WISBECH & FENLAND MUS
New Walsoken
Marshland St James
North Fen
Northborough
Nene Terrace
Morris Fen
Parson Drove
Murrow
Wisbech St Mary
Tholomas Drove
Emneth
Elm
Emneth Hungate
Peakirk
Newborough
Glinton
Rogue's Alley
Holly End
Bedford Level (North)
Eye Green
Thorney
Thorney Toll
Guyhirn Gull
Guyhirn
Waldersey
Friday Bridge
WELLE MANOR HALL
Outwell
Stow
Werrington
Gunthorpe
Eye
Ring's End
Coldham
Laddus Fens
Upwell
Walton
Dogsthorpe
Newark
Stone Bridge Corner
Chainbridge
Three Holes
Peterborough
CATH
LONGTHORPE TOWER
Longthorpe
FERRY MEADOWS
Fengate
FLAG FEN BRONZE AGE EXCAVATIONS
North Side
Eldernell
West Fen
Westry
Norwoodside
Euximoor Fen
Euximoor Drove
South District
Upwell
RAILWORLD
Orton Longueville
Old Fletton
Stanground
Whittlesey
Inham's End
Coates
Eastrea
Turves
March
Binnimoor Fen
Christchurch
Lakesend
Orton Waterville
CROWN LAKES
Farcet
King's Delph
Twenty Foot River
TL
Town End
Upwell Fen
Tipsend
PETERBOROUGH SERVICES
Yaxley
Farcet Fen
Whittlesey Mere
Pondersbridge
BEDFORD LEVEL (MIDDLE)
White Fen
Flood's Ferry
Ranson Moor
Wimblington
Welney
Gold Hill
Norman Cross
Cambridge
Nene
Benwick
Doddington
ISLE
Manea
Stilton
HOLME FEN
Middle Moor
Ramsey Mereside
Wimblington Fen
Sixteen Foot Drain
Purls Bridge
Fodder Fen
Denton
Holme
Ramsey St Mary's
Ramsey Forty Foot
Forty Foot Drain
Vermuden's Drain
Chatteris
OF
Horseway
Welches Dam
New Bedford River
Pymoor
WILDLIFE TRUST WELNEY
Glatton
Conington
Ramsey Heights
Ramsey Hollow
Ramsey
RAMSEY RURAL MUSEUM
WOODWALTON FEN
Langwood Fen
Little Downham
Sawtry
Bury
Tick Fen
Ferry Hill
Church End
UPWOOD MEADOWS
Upwood
Chapel Head
ELY
Horseley Fen
Wardy Hill
Chettisham
West Fen
Little Gidding
Wood Walton
Great Raveley
Wistow
Pidley Fen
Mepal
Coveney
Coppingford
MONKS WOOD
Little Raveley
Warboys
Fenton
Chatteris Fen
Sutton
Witcham
OLIVER CROMWELL'S HOUSE
Ely
CATHEDRAL AND MUS
Upton
Wennington
Pidley
Wentworth
Witchford
Somersham
Hill Row Doles
North Hill
Haddenham
Little Thetford
Alconbury
Little Stukeley
Ripton
Old Hurst
Woodhurst
Colne
0 1 2 3 4 5 6 miles
0 1 2 3 4 5 6 7 8 9 10 km
A17
A16
A151
A1101
A47
A141
A142
A1139
A15
A605
A1122
A1(M)
A10
A1175
A1123
B1397
B1357
B1359
B1180
B1356
B1168
B1165
B1390
B1166
B1167
B1169
B1187
B1040
B1443
B1101
B1099
B1098
B1093
B1096
B1043
B1090
B1050
B1381
B1411
B1094
B1525
B660
A1421
79
65
54
55

Snettisham
SNETTISHAM PARK
SNETTISHAM NATURE RESERVE
Shepherd's Port
Ingoldisthorpe
Shernborne
Dersingham
DERSINGHAM BOG
SANDRINGHAM
Sandringham
Wolferton
West Newton
Flitcham
Great Bircham
BIRCHAM MILL
PEDDARS WAY
Newton
Bircham Tofts
Bagthorpe
Barmer
Syderstone
Blenheim Park
Wicken Green Village
Sculthorpe
West Barsham
East Barsham
Fakenham
FAKENHAM
Little Ryburgh
Great Ryburgh
Anmer
HOUGHTON HALL
New Houghton
West Rudham
East Rudham
Tattersett
Coxford
Shereford
Dunton
Tatterford
Hempton
Toftrees
Helhoughton
Colkirk
Oxwick
West Raynham
East Raynham
Hamrow
South Raynham
Horningtoft
Whissonsett
Brisley
Harpley
Little Massingham
Great Massingham
Hillington
PEDDARS WAY & NORFOLK COAST PATH
Congham
CONGHAM HALL HERB GARDEN
Grimston
Pott Row
Roydon
ROYDON COMMON
Castle Rising
CASTLE RISING
North Wootton
South Wootton
Ongar Hill
Marsh
King's Lynn
MARITIME EXHIBITION
GUILDHALL
Gaywood
Clenchwarton
Terrington St Clement
West Lynn
Fairstead
Hardwick
Tilney High End
Tilney All Saints
Massingham Heath
Weasenham St Peter
Weasenham All Saints
Wellingham
EXTREME ADVENTURE
Tittleshall
Stanfield
East Bilney
Gayton
Ashwicken
Leziate
Gayton Thorpe
Fair Green
Tower End
Middleton
East Winch
West Winch
North Runcton
Saddle Bow
Wiggenhall St Germans
Wiggenhall St Mary the Virgin
Tilney St Lawrence
Wiggenhall St Mary Magdalen
Tottenhill Row
Tottenhill
Watlington
Setchey
Blackborough End
West Bilney
Pentney
East Walton
Narborough
West Acre
Castle Acre
CASTLE ACRE PRIORY
South Acre
Newton
West Lexham
East Lexham
Litcham
Mileham
Bittering
NORFOLK RURAL LIFE MUSEUM
Beeston
Great Dunham
Little Dunham
Drury Square
Crane's Corner
Longham
Sparrow Green
Great Fransham
Little Fransham
Wendling
Norfolk
Wormegay
Great Palgrave
Sporle
HALE GDNS & ARBORETUM
Daffy Green
Marham
Shouldham
Runcton Holme
Marshland Fen
South Runcton
Shouldham Thorpe
Beachamwell Warren
Swaffham
PEDDARS WAY & NORFOLK COAST PATH
Necton
West End
Bradenham
North Pickenham
Holme Hale
Stowbridge
Stow Bardolph
West Head
Wimbotsham
Fincham
Barton Bendish
Beachamwell
Shingham
Cockley Cley
ICENI VILLAGE AND MUSEUMS
South Pickenham
Ashill
Crowshill
Downham Market
Broomhill
Stradsett
Crimplesham
Bardolph Fen
Barroway Drove
Bexwell
Eastmoor
GOODERSTONE WATER GARDENS
Gooderstone
Saham Hills
Saham Toney
Ovington
Carbrooke
Nordelph
Denver
Wereham
Boughton
Oxborough
OXBURGH HALL, GARDEN & ESTATE
Great Cressingham
Caudlesprings
West Dereham
Fordham
Hilborough
Watton
Griston
Wretton
Stoke Ferry
Whittington
Foulden
Bodney
Little Cressingham
Merton
Northacre
Fen
Old Bedford River
Hilgay
Wissey
Northwold
The Arms
Caston
Ten Mile Bank
Brookville
Thompson
Stow
Hilgay Fen
Southery
Methwold Hythe
Methwold
Cranwich
Ickburgh
LYNFORD ARBORETUM AND LAKES
Mundford
Methwold Fens
Southery Fens
Queen's Ground
THETFORD
West Tofts
Great Hockham
Apes Hall
Brandon Creek
Feltwell
BRECKLAND
Wretham
Brandon Bank
Feltwell Fens
Hockwold cum Wilton
Weeting
WEETING CASTLE
GRIMES GRAVES
FOREST
PEDDARS WAY & NORFOLK COAST PATH
Mare Fen
Burnt Fen
Littleport
Hockwold Fens
WEETING HEATH
Little Ouse
Brandon
Santon Downham
Croxton
Bridgham
BEDFORD LEVEL (SOUTH)
BRANDON PARK
HIGH LODGE FOREST CENTRE
THETFORD WARREN LODGE
PARK
Brettenham
Shadwell
Shippea Hill Sta.
Thetford
Thetford Warren
ANCIENT HOUSE MUS
Prickwillow
Great Ouse
Lakenheath
Wangford Warren
Rushford
Queen Adelaide
Kenny Hill
Lakenheath Warren
Knettishall
KNETTISHALL HEATH
Middle Fen
Stuntney
Great Fen
Mildenhall Fen
Eriswell
Elveden
EAST OF ENGLAND TANK MUSEUM
Barnham
Euston
EUSTON HALL
Coney Weston
Broad Hill
Holywell Row
Beck Row
Fakenham Magna
Barningham
WINDMILL
Isleham Fen
Thistley Green
West Row
TF
TL

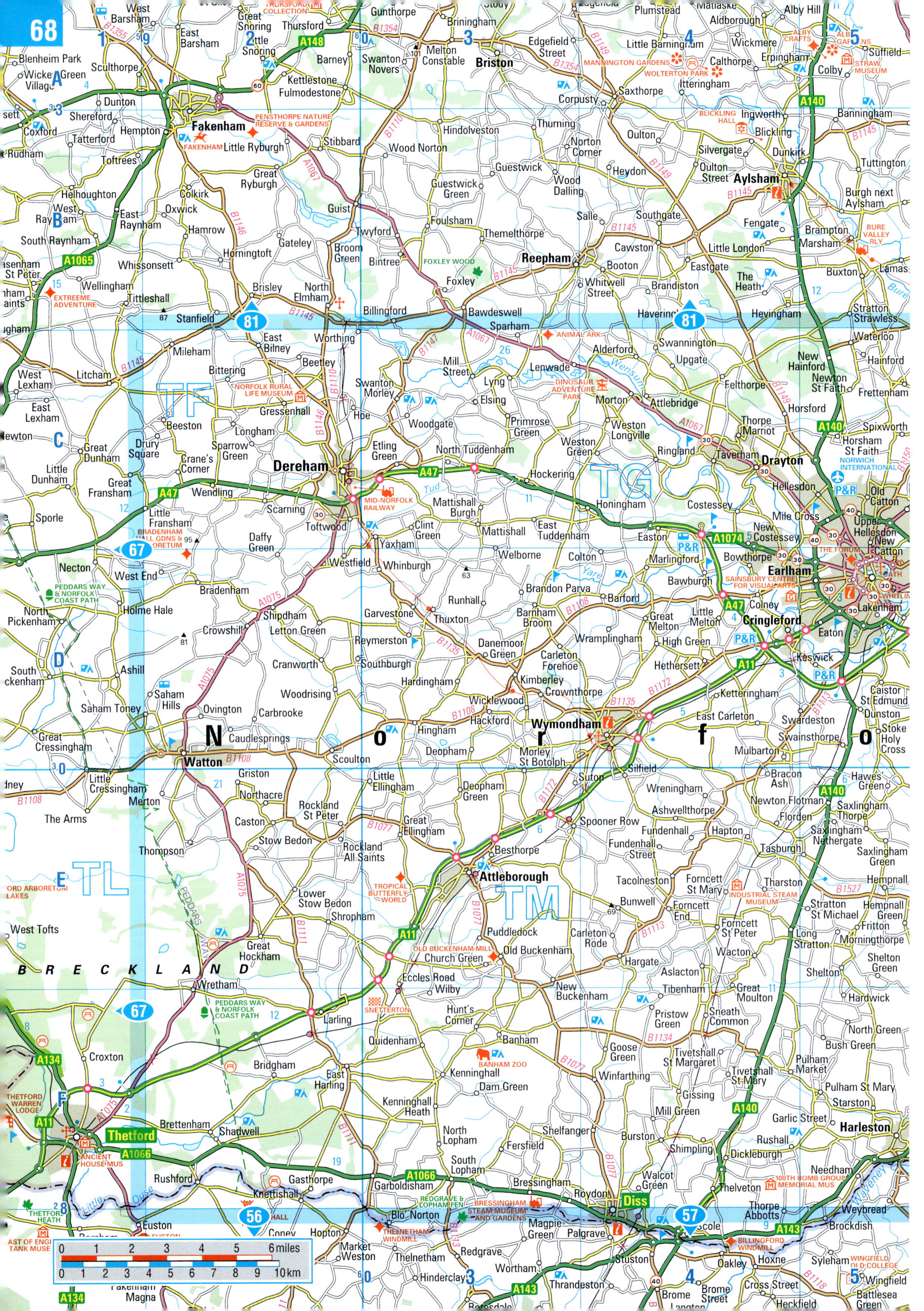
West Barsham
East Barsham
Great Snoring
Little Snoring
Thursford
Gunthorpe
Briningham
Edgefield
Edgefield Street
Plumstead
Matlaske
Aldborough
Alby Hill
Little Barningham
Wickmere
Erpingham
Colby
Suffield
Blenheim Park
Wicken Green Village
Sculthorpe
Barney
Swanton Novers
Melton Constable
Briston
Kettlestone
Fulmodestone
Mannington Gardens
Wolterton Park
Calthorpe
Itteringham
Saxthorpe
Corpusty
Dunton
Shereford
Hempton
Fakenham
Pensthorpe Nature Reserve & Gardens
Little Ryburgh
Stibbard
Hindolveston
Thurning
Norton Corner
Oulton
Blickling Hall
Ingworth
Blickling
Banningham
Coxford
Tatterford
Toftrees
Rudham
Great Ryburgh
Wood Norton
Guestwick
Guestwick Green
Wood Dalling
Heydon
Silvergate
Oulton Street
Aylsham
Dunkirk
Tuttington
Burgh next Aylsham
Helhoughton
West Raynham
East Raynham
Oxwick
Colkirk
Hamrow
Guist
Twyford
Foulsham
Themelthorpe
Salle
Southgate
Fengate
Brampton
Marsham
Bure Valley Rly
South Raynham
Whissonsett
Horningtoft
Gateley
Broom Green
Bintree
Foxley Wood
Foxley
Reepham
Booton
Cawston
Little London
Eastgate
Buxton
Lamas
Wellingham
Tittleshall
Extreme Adventure
Brisley
North Elmham
Whitwell Street
Brandiston
The Heath
Stanfield
Billingford
Bawdeswell
Sparham
Haveringland
Hevingham
Stratton Strawless
Mileham
East Bilney
Worthing
Animal Ark
Alderford
Swannington
Upgate
Waterloo
Beetley
Bittering
Mill Street
Lyng
Lenwade
Dinosaur Adventure Park
New Hainford
Hainford
Newton St Faith
Frettenham
West Lexham
Litcham
Norfolk Rural Life Museum
Gressenhall
Swanton Morley
Elsing
Morton
Attlebridge
Felthorpe
Horsford
East Lexham
Beeston
Hoe
Woodgate
Primrose Green
Weston Longville
Thorpe Marriot
Spixworth
Newton
Great Dunham
Drury Square
Longham
Sparrow Green
Crane's Corner
Etling Green
North Tuddenham
Weston Green
Ringland
Taverham
Drayton
Horsham St Faith
Norwich International
Little Dunham
Great Fransham
Dereham
Hockering
Hellesdon
Old Catton
Wendling
Scarning
Mid-Norfolk Railway
Mattishall Burgh
Honingham
Costessey
Mile Cross
Upper Hellesdon
Sporle
Little Fransham
Bradenham Hall Gdns & Arboretum
Toftwood
Clint Green
Mattishall
East Tuddenham
Easton
New Costessey
Catton
Yaxham
Daffy Green
Welborne
Colton
Marlingford
Bowthorpe
The Forum
Earlham
Necton
West End
Westfield
Whinburgh
Bawburgh
Sainsbury Centre for Visual Arts
Peddars Way & Norfolk Coast Path
Bradenham
Brandon Parva
Barford
Runhall
North Pickenham
Holme Hale
Shipdham
Garvestone
Thuxton
Barnham Broom
Great Melton
Little Melton
Colney
Cringleford
Lakenham
Eaton
Crowshill
Letton Green
Reymerston
Danemoor Green
Wramplingham
High Green
South Pickenham
Ashill
Cranworth
Southburgh
Carleton Forehoe
Hethersett
Keswick
Saham Hills
Saham Toney
Woodrising
Hardingham
Kimberley
Crownthorpe
Ketteringham
Caistor St Edmund
Ovington
Carbrooke
Wicklewood
Hackford
Wymondham
East Carleton
Swardeston
Dunston
Stoke Holy Cross
Great Cressingham
Caudlesprings
Hingham
Deopham
Morley St Botolph
Swainsthorpe
Mulbarton
Watton
Scoulton
Silfield
Bracon Ash
Hawes' Green
Little Cressingham
Griston
Little Ellingham
Deopham Green
Suton
Wreningham
Newton Flotman
Saxlingham Thorpe
Merton
Northacre
Rockland St Peter
Ashwellthorpe
Flordon
The Arms
Caston
Great Ellingham
Spooner Row
Fundenhall
Hapton
Saxlingham Nethergate
Thompson
Stow Bedon
Rockland All Saints
Besthorpe
Fundenhall Street
Tasburgh
Saxlingham Green
Attleborough
Tacolneston
Forncett St Mary
Tharston
Hempnall
Lower Stow Bedon
Tropical Butterfly World
Bunwell
Industrial Steam Museum
Stratton St Michael
Hempnall Green
Shropham
Forncett End
West Tofts
Puddledock
Carleton Rode
Forncett St Peter
Long Stratton
Fritton
Morningthorpe
Great Hockham
Old Buckenham Mill
Old Buckenham
Church Green
Wacton
Shelton Green
BRECKLAND
Hargate
Aslacton
Shelton
Eccles Road
Wilby
New Buckenham
Tibenham
Great Moulton
Wretham
Peddars Way & Norfolk Coast Path
Snetterton
Hunt's Corner
Pristow Green
Sneath Common
Hardwick
Larling
North Green
Quidenham
Banham
Goose Green
Tivetshall St Margaret
Bush Green
Croxton
Bridgham
Banham Zoo
Tivetshall St Mary
Pulham Market
East Harling
Kenninghall
Winfarthing
Thetford Warren Lodge
Dam Green
Gissing
Pulham St Mary
Kenninghall Heath
Starston
Brettenham
Shadwell
Mill Green
Garlic Street
Thetford
North Lopham
Shelfanger
Burston
Harleston
Ancient House Mus
Fersfield
Rushall
Shimpling
Dickleburgh
Rushford
South Lopham
Gasthorpe
Garboldisham
Bressingham
Walcot Green
Needham
100th Bomb Group Memorial Mus
Knettishall
Roydon
Diss
Thelveton
Redgrave & Lopham Fen
Bressingham Steam Museum and Gardens
Thorpe Abbotts
Thetford Heath
Blo' Norton
Euston
Magpie Green
Palgrave
Scole
Weybread
Brockdish
Thelnetham Windmill
Billingford Windmill
Coney
Hopton
Market Weston
Thelnetham
Redgrave
Stuston
Oakley
Hoxne
Syleham
Wingfield Old College
Hinderclay
Wortham
Thrandeston
Brome
Brome Street
Cross Street
Wingfield
Battlesea Green
Heckfield
Fakenham Magna
Norfolk
TF
TG
TL
TM
0
1
2
3
4
5
6 miles
0
1
2
3
4
5
6
7
8
9
10 km

5
6
7
8
9
A
B
C
D
E
F
G
NORFOLK
COAST
THE
BROADS
TG
TM
NORWICH
Great Yarmouth
Gorleston-on-Sea
Lowestoft
Beccles
Bungay
Halesworth
Southwold
Caister-on-Sea
North Walsham
Coltishall
Hoveton
Wroxham
Acle
Brundall
Loddon
Hemsby
Belton
Kessingland
Sprowston
Thorpe St Andrew
Knapton
Bacton
Keswick
Walcott
Bradfield
Antingham
Swafield
Broomholm
Edingthorpe
Edingthorpe Green
Witton Bridge
Ridlington
Spa Common
Crostwight
Happisburgh
Whimpwell Green
Eccles on Sea
Happisburgh Common
Felmingham
EAST RUSTON OLD VICARAGE GARDEN
Lessingham
Hempstead
Honing
East Ruston
Ingham Corner
Sea Palling
Westwick
Bengate
Worstead
Ingham
WAXHAM GREAT BARN
Waxham
Skeyton
Swanton Abbott
Sloley
Dilham
Smallburgh
Stalham
Stalham Green
Hickling
MUSEUM OF THE BROADS
Sutton
Hickling Green
Scottow
Pennygate
Barton Turf
Hickling Heath
Horsey
Little Hautbois
Tunstead
Sco Ruston
ANT BROADS AND MARSHES
Wood Street
Neatishead
Catfield
Hickling Broad
HORSEY WINDMILL
WINTERTON DUNES
WROXHAM BARNS
Ashmanhaugh
Barton Broad
RA BOAT TRIP
HICKLING BROAD
MARTHAM BROAD
East Somerton
Irstead
Sharp Street
Potter Heigham
West Somerton
Winterton-on-Sea
Horstead
Threehammer Common
Belaugh
Thurne
Martham
Lower Street
Ludham
Bastwick
HILLSIDE ANIMAL SANCTUARY
Upper Street
Horning
LUDHAM MARSHES
Repps
Newport
Wroxham Broad
Upper Street
BURE MARSHES
Thurne
Rollesby
Crostwick
Woodbastwick
Ormesby St Michael
Scratby
California
Ranworth
Clippesby
Salhouse
Filby Broad
Rackheath
FAIRHAVEN WOODLAND & WATER GARDEN
Ormesby St Margaret
P&R
Panxworth
Billockby
Burgh St Margaret
Filby
CAISTER ROMAN TOWN
New Rackheath
South Walsham
Mautby
Little Plumstead
Upton
THE CANDLEMAKER WORKSHOP
Thrigby
West Caister
THRIGBY HALL WILDLIFE GARDENS
Runham
Hemblington
Blofield Heath
North Burlingham
Stokesby
West End
YARMOUTH
Thorpe End
Great Plumstead
Bure
GREAT YARMOUTH GREAT DENES
Blofield
Lingwood
Damgate
Beighton
Tunstall
Runham
Postwick
Strumpshaw
Moulton St Mary
Halvergate Marshes
SEA LIFE GREAT YARMOUTH
Surlingham
South Burlingham
Breydon Water
Cobholm Island
Trowse Newton
Kirby Bedon
Buckenham
Halvergate
ELIZABETHAN HOUSE, MARITIME
NELSON/TOLHOUSE MUSEUMS
EXHIBITION GALLERIES
Hassingham
Freethorpe
Burgh Castle
Southtown
Arminghall
Bramerton
MID YARE
Southwood
Wickhampton
AMAZONIA-WORLD OF REPTILES
BERNEY ARMS WINDMILL
PLEASURE BEACH
Framingham Pigot
Rockland St Mary
Cantley
Limpenhoe
Bradwell
Claxton
Yare
PETTITTS ANIMAL ADVENTURE PARK
Framingham Earl
Hellington
Ashby St Mary
Poringland
Yelverton
Langley Street
Reedham
REDWINGS HORSE SANCTUARY
Bergh Apton
Hardley Street
Ferry
Howe
Thurton
ST OLAVES PRIORY
Fritton
Hopton on Sea
Shotesham
Brooke
Chedgrave
Lower Thurlton
The Dell
Lound
Stubb's Green
Sisland
Chet
Thurlton
SOMERLEYTON HALL
Seething
Mundham
Hales
Thorpe
Blundeston
Kirstead Green
Stubbs Green
Raveningham
Herringfleet
Corton
Somerleyton
PLEASUREWOOD HILLS LEISURE PARK
HALES HALL BARN & GARDENS
RAVENINGHAM GARDENS
Haddiscoe
Maypole Green
Thwaite St Mary
Toft Monks
Oulton
LOWESTOFT AND EAST SUFFOLK MARITIME MUSEUM
Road Green
Woodton
Kirby Cane
Stockton
Normanstone
Hedenham
Wheatacre
Burgh St Peter
HERITAGE/VISITOR CENTRE
Topcroft
Cobbler's Green
Ellingham
Kirby Row
Aldeby
Oulton Broad
Topcroft Street
LOWESTOFT MUSEUM
Ditchingham
Broome
Geldeston
Gillingham
Waveney
CARLTON MARSHES NATURE RESERVE
Kirkley
Shipmeadow
Barnby
Pakefield
Great Green
Earsham
Mettingham
Worlingham
Carlton Colville
Denton
Barsham
North Cove
Mutford
Ringsfield
Gisleham
NORFOLK AND SUFFOLK AVIATION MUSEUM
Ilketshall St Andrew
Ringsfield Corner
Hulver Street
Rushmere
Alburgh
Flixton
Kessingland Beach
Ilketshall St Margaret
Ellough
Henstead
Homersfield
AFRICA ALIVE
Benacre
St Cross South Elmham
St Michael South Elmham
Ilketshall St Lawrence
Redisham
Sotterley
Wortwell
Redenhall
Shadingfield
Mendham
St Margaret South Elmham
All Saints South Elmham
Stone Street
West End
BENACRE
SOUTH ELMHAM HALL
Cox Common
Wrentham
Brampton
Stoven
Clay Common
Covehithe
Withersdale Street
St James South Elmham
Rumburgh
Mill Common
Frostenden
Spexhall
South Cove
Metfield
Uggeshall
Cove Bottom
Westhall
Broadway
Wangford
Linstead Parva
Chediston
Reydon Smear
Fressingfield
Reydon
Little Whittingham Green
Holton
Blyford
HEN REEDBED NATURE RESERVE
SOUTHWOLD MUSEUM
Chippenhall Green
Silverley's Green
Cratfield
Cookley
Wenhaston
Blyth
A47
A146
A143
A12
A1117
A149
A1151
A1062
A1064
A144
A145
A1095
B1354
B1150
B1159
B1152
B1140
B1332
B1136
B1074
B1062
B1127
B1437
B1375
B1123
B1124
B1126
B1116
81
57

1
2
3
4
5
A
B
C
D
E
F
Malltraeth Bay
Bae Malltraeth
Newborough Forest
Llanddwyn I.
Ynys Llanddwyn
The Bar
Abermenai Pt.
Trwyn Abermenai
SEIONT II MARITIME MUSEUM
CASTLE & REGIMENTAL MUS.
CAERNARFON BAY
BAE CAERNARFON
CAERNARFON AIR MUSEUM
Morfa Dinlle
Dinas Dinlle
Llandwrog
GLYNLLIFON
Pontllyfni
Aberdesach
82
WELSH LIFE
Clynnog-fawr
Tainlon
Capel Uchaf
Gyrn-goch
Bryn-yr-eryr
SH
509 BWLCH MAWR
522 GYRN DDU
Trefor
564 YR EIFL
Llanaelhaearn
Pen-sarn
LLEYN
B4417
Llithfaen
Carreg Ddu
Porth Dinllaen
Pistyll
Nefyn
Llwyndyrys
Pencaenewydd
Llangybi
Morfa Nefyn
LLEYN HISTORICAL MARITIME MUSEUM
Fron
Llanarmon
Edern
Tan-y-graig
Rhos-fawr
B4354
Y Ffôr
Chwilog
Porth Ysgadan
Glanrhyd
PENARTH FAWR MEDIEVAL HOUSE
Rhos-y-llan
CORS GEIRCH
Boduan
A497
Llannor
A499
Abererch
Tudweiliog
BODVEL HALL ADVENTURE PARK
HAVEN
Dinas
PENRHYN LLYN
Efailnewydd
Rhyd-y-clafdy
Denio
Pwllheli
Porth Golmon
Garnfadryn
B4415
Carreg yr Imbill
Bryn-mawr
Llaniestyn
Penrhos
South Beach
Pen-y-graig
Llangwnnadl
Rhedyn
Penrhyn Mawr
Sarn Meyllteyrn
B4413
Ty-hen
Pen-y-groeslon
Botwnnog
Nanhoron
Llanbedrog
Methlem
Bryncroes
Mynytho
Trwyn Llanbedrog
Rhydlios
Llandegwning
304 MYNYDD RHIW
PLAS-YN-RHIW
St Tudwal's Road
Angorfa St Tudwal
Rhoshirwaun
Capel Carmel
Lawrdref Bellaf
Llangian
Rhiw
Abersoch
191
Porth Neigwl or Hell's Mouth
Llanengan
St Tudwal's Island East
Ynys St Tudwal Dwyrain
Uwchmynydd
Aberdaron
Llanfaelrhys
Sarn Bach
Bwlchtocyn
Marchroes
St Tudwal's Island West
Ynys St Tudwal Gorllewin
Bodermid
Bardsey Sound
Swnt Enlli
Pen-y-cil
Cilan Uchaf
Trwyn Cilan
167
YNYS ENLLI
Bardsey Island
Ynys Enlli
0 1 2 3 4 5 6 miles
0 1 2 3 4 5 6 7 8 9 10 km

Caernarfon
Porthmadog
Betws-y-Coed
Dolgellau
Llanrwst
Blaenau Ffestiniog
Llan Ffestiniog
Penrhyndeudraeth
Criccieth
Harlech
Barmouth (Abermaw)
Llanberis
Beddgelert
Trawsfynydd
Llanbedr
Fairbourne
Tremadog
Maentwrog
Llanelltyd
Corris
SH
Gwynedd
SNOWDONIA NATIONAL PARK
TREMADOG BAY
BAE TREMADOG
BARMOUTH BAY
BAE BERMO
Morfa Harlech
Morfa Dyffryn
Traeth Bach
Afon Mawddach
Llyn Trawsfynydd
Llyn Padarn
Llyn Peris
Llyn Cwellyn
Llyn Celyn
Llyn Conwy
Llyn Dinas
Llyn Gwynant
Gwydyr Forest
Coed y Brenin Forest
Dyfi Forest
Beddgelert Forest
Pass of Llanberis
Pass of Aberglaslyn
Migneint
1085 SNOWDON YR WYDDFA
1064 CARNEDD LLYWELYN
999 GLYDER FAWR
893 CADAIR IDRIS
872 CARNEDD MOEL SIABOD
854 ARENIG FAWR
754 Y LLETHR
720 RHINOG FAWR
A5
A470
A487
A496
A498
A4086
A4085
A494
A493
A4212
B4391
B4418
B4410
B4411
B4407
B4406
B4573
B4405
B4416
B5113
TOLL
72
82
83
58
59
5
6
7
8
9
A
B
C
D
E
F
G

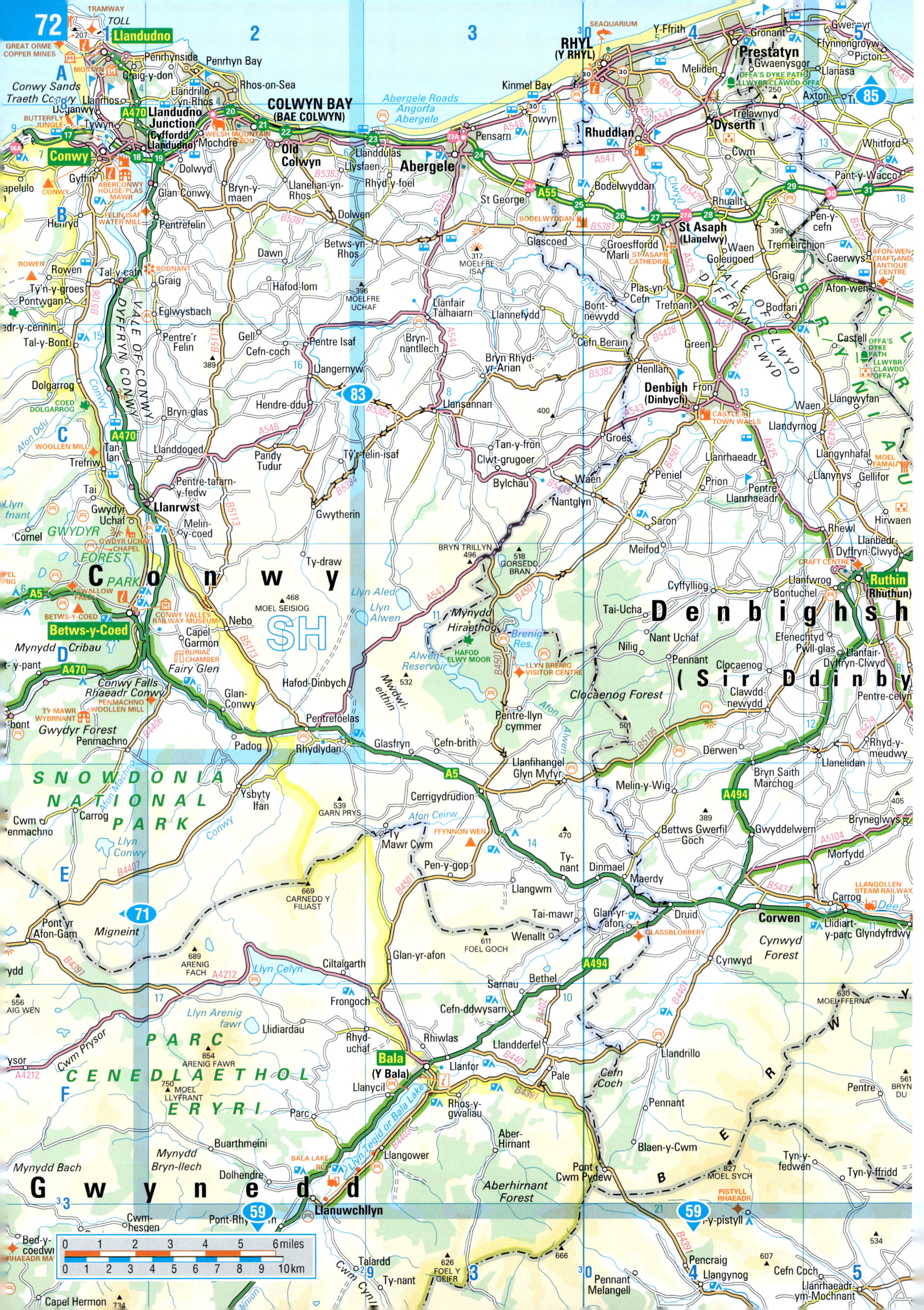

Llandudno
Great Orme Copper Mines
Tramway
Toll
Penrhynside
Penrhyn Bay
Craig-y-don
Rhos-on-Sea
Conwy Sands
Traeth Conwy
Llandrillo-yn-Rhos
Deganwy
Llandudno Junction (Cyffordd Llandudno)
Colwyn Bay (Bae Colwyn)
Welsh Mountain Zoo
Mochdre
Old Colwyn
Butterfly Jungle
Tywyn
Conwy
Gyffin
Aberconwy House/Plas Mawr
Dolwyd
Glan Conwy
Bryn-y-maen
Llanelian-yn-Rhos
Llanddulas
Llysfaen
Rhyd-y-foel
Abergele Roads
Angorfa Abergele
Abergele
Pensarn
Towyn
Kinmel Bay
Rhyl (Y Rhyl)
Seaquarium
Y-Ffrith
Gronant
Gwespyr
Prestatyn
Gwaenysgor
Ffynnongroyw
Picton
Meliden
Llanasa
Offa's Dyke Path Llwybr Clawdd Offa
Axton
Trelawnyd
Dyserth
Rhuddlan
Whitford
Cwm
Pant-y-Wacco
St George
Bodelwyddan
Bodelwyddan Castle
Rhuallt
St Asaph (Llanelwy)
St Asaph Cathedral
Pen-y-cefn
Tremeirchion
Caerwys
Afon-Wen Craft and Antique Centre
Glascoed
Groesffordd Marli
Waen
Goleugoed
Henryd
Felin Isaf Water Mill
Pentrefelin
Dolwen
Dawn
Betws-yn-Rhos
Moelfre Isaf
Moelfre Uchaf
Bodnant
Rowen
Tal-y-cafn
Graig
Ty'n-y-groes
Pontwgan
Hafod-lom
Eglwysbach
Llanfair Talhaiarn
Llannefydd
Bont-newydd
Plas-yn-Cefn
Trefnant
Bodfari
Afon-wen
Vale of Conwy
Dyffryn Conwy
Vale of Clwyd
Dyffryn Clwyd
Tal-y-Bont
Pentre'r Felin
Gell
Cefn-coch
Pentre Isaf
Bryn-nantllech
Cefn Berain
Green
Castell
Offa's Dyke Path Llwybr Clawdd Offa
Llangernyw
Bryn Rhyd-yr-Arian
Henllan
Denbigh (Dinbych)
Fron
Castle & Town Walls
Dolgarrog
Coed Dolgarrog
Hendre-ddu
Llansannan
Llangwyfan
Bryn-glas
Waen
Llandyrnog
Woollen Mill
Afon Ddu
Tan-lan
Trefriw
Llanddoged
Pandy Tudur
Ty'n-felin-isaf
Tan-y-fron
Clwt-grugoer
Groes
Llanrhaeadr
Llangynhafal
Moel Famau
Llanrwst
Pentre-tafarn-y-fedw
Bylchau
Waen
Nantglyn
Peniel
Prion
Pentre Llanrhaeadr
Llanynys
Gellifor
Tai
Gwydyr Uchaf
Gwydyr Uchaf Chapel
Melin-y-coed
Gwytherin
Saron
Rhewl
Hirwaen
Llanbedr-Dyffryn-Clwyd
Cornel
Gwydyr Forest
Bryn Trillyn
Gorsedd Bran
Meifod
Craft Centre
Forest Park
Ty-draw
Llanfwrog
Ruthin (Rhuthun)
Conwy
Cyffylliog
Bontuchel
Swallow Falls
Betws-y-Coed
Conwy Valley Railway Museum
Moel Seisiog
Llyn Aled
Llyn Alwen
Mynydd Hiraethog
Tai-Ucha
Denbighshire (Sir Ddinbych)
Nebo
Capel Garmon
Burial Chamber
Brenig Res.
Hafod Elwy Moor
Nant Uchaf
Efenechtyd
Pwll-glas
Llanfair-Dyffryn-Clwyd
Mynydd Cribau
Fairy Glen
Alwen Reservoir
Llyn Brenig Visitor Centre
Nilig
Pennant
Clocaenog
Conwy Falls
Rhaeadr Conwy
Penmachno Woollen Mill
Ty Mawr Wybrnant
Glan-Conwy
Hafod-Dinbych
Mwdwl-eithin
Clocaenog Forest
Clawdd-newydd
Pentre-celyn
Gwydyr Forest
Penmachno
Pentrefoelas
Pentre-llyn cymmer
Afon Alwen
Padog
Rhydlydan
Glasfryn
Cefn-brith
Llanfihangel Glyn Myfyr
Derwen
Rhyd-y-meudwy
Llanelidan
Snowdonia National Park
Afon Machno
Ysbyty Ifan
Garn Prys
Cerrigydrudion
Melin-y-Wig
Bryn Saith Marchog
Cwm Penmachno
Carrog
Afon Ceirw
Ffynnon Wen
Ty Mawr Cwm
Bettws Gwerfil Goch
Gwyddelwern
Bryneglwys
Llyn Conwy
Pen-y-gop
Ty-nant
Dinmael
Maerdy
Morfydd
Llangwm
Carnedd y Filiast
Tai-mawr
Glan-yr-afon
Druid
Corwen
Carrog
Llangollen Steam Railway
Pont yr Afon-Gam
Migneint
Wenallt
Foel Goch
Glassblobbery
Llidiart-y-parc
Glyndyfrdwy
Cynwyd Forest
Cynwyd
Arenig Fach
Llyn Celyn
Ciltalgarth
Glan-yr-afon
Bethel
Sarnau
Aig Wen
Frongoch
Cefn-ddwysarn
Moel Fferna
Llyn Arenig fawr
Lllidiardau
Rhyd-uchaf
Rhiwlas
Llandderfel
Llandrillo
Cwm Prysor
Parc Cenedlaethol Eryri
Arenig Fawr
Bala (Y Bala)
Llanfor
Pale
Cefn Coch
Llanycil
Moel Llyfnant
Parc
Rhos-y-gwaliau
Pennant
Pentre
Bryn Du
Llyn Tegid or Bala Lake
Aber-Hirnant
Blaen-y-Cwm
Berwyn
Buarthmeini
Llangower
Bala Lake Rly
Mynydd Bryn-llech
Mynydd Bach
Dolhendre
Aberhirnant Forest
Pont Cwm Pydew
Moel Sych
Tyn-y-fedwen
Tyn-y-ffridd
Gwynedd
Llanuwchllyn
Pistyll Rhaeadr
Cwm-hesgen
Pont-Rhyd-y-pistyll
Bed-y-coedwr
Talardd
Foel y Geifr
Pennant Melangell
Pencraig
Llangynog
Cefn Coch
Llanrhaeadr-ym-Mochnant
Ty-nant
Capel Hermon
Cwm Cynllwyd
SH
0 1 2 3 4 5 6 miles
0 1 2 3 4 5 6 7 8 9 10 km

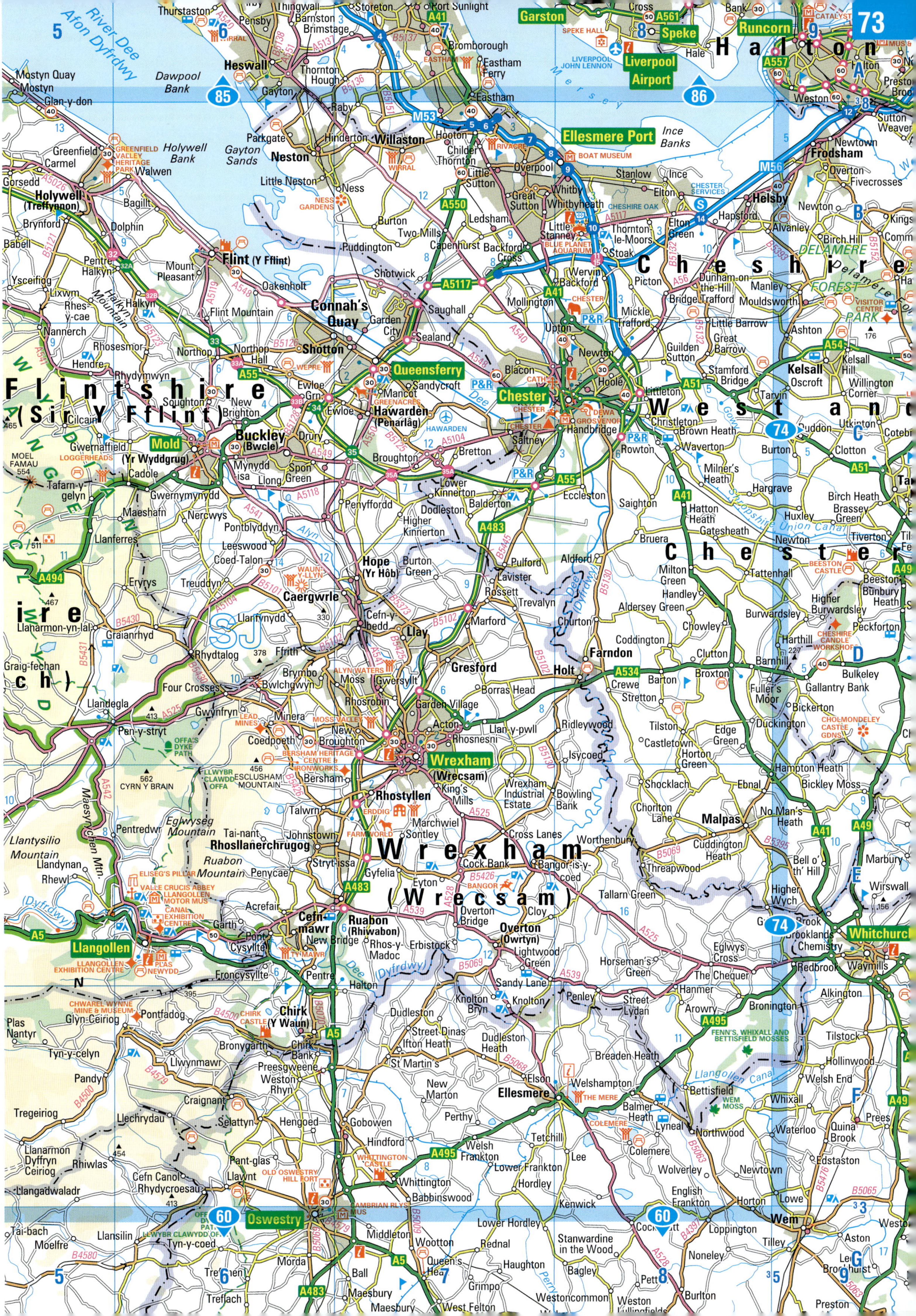
River Dee
Afon Dyfrdwy
Dawpool Bank
Holywell Bank
Gayton Sands
Mersey
Ince Banks
Halton
Runcorn
Garston
Speke
Liverpool Airport
Ellesmere Port
Frodsham
Helsby
Cheshire
Delamere Forest
Heswall
Neston
Mostyn
Holywell (Treffynnon)
Flint (Y Fflint)
Connah's Quay
Shotton
Queensferry
Chester
Hawarden (Penarlâg)
Saltney
Flintshire (Sir y Fflint)
Mold
(Yr Wyddgrug)
Buckley (Bwcle)
Hope (Yr Hôb)
Caergwrle
Llay
Gresford
Holt
Farndon
West and Chester
Tarvin
Kelsall
Tattenhall
Malpas
Wrexham (Wrecsam)
Rhostyllen
Ruabon (Rhiwabon)
Cefn-mawr
Llangollen
Chirk (Y Waun)
Overton (Owrtyn)
Ellesmere
Whitchurch
Wem
Oswestry
SJ

Halton
Runcorn
Weston
Hale
Ince Banks
Frodsham
Helsby
Newtown
Overton
Fivecrosses
Preston on the Hill
Dutton
Sutton Weaver
Aston
Daresbury
Hatton
Keckwick
Norton
Lower Stretton
Stretton
Higher Whitley
Lower Whitley
Arley
Arley Hall
High Legh
Sworton Heath
Thorn
Hoo Green
Mere
Bucklow Hill
Rostherne Mere
Ashley
Tatton House
New Mills
Thorns Green
Morley Green
Styal
WILMSLOW
Davenport Green
Knutsford
Over Knutsford
Mobberley
Knolls Green
Alderley Edge
Ollerton
Marthall
Nether Alderley
Over Peover
Chelford
Monks Heath
Peover Heath
Capesthorne Hall
Withington Green
Siddington
Jodrell Bank Visitor Centre
Blackden Heath
Goostrey
Twemlow Green
Lower Withington
Cranage
Holmes Chapel
Gleadsmoss
Swettenham
Sandlow Green
Newsbank
Brereton Green
Brereton Heath
Hulme Walfield
West Heath
Arclid
Astbury
Brownlow
Brookhouse Green
Brownlow Heath
Fourlanes End
Little Moreton Hall
Hassall Green
Scholar Green
Thurlwood
Rode Heath
Mount Pleasant
Church Lawton
Alsager
Kidsgrove
Radway Green
Talke
Red Street
Audley
Chesterton
Alsagers Bank
Bradwell
Halmer End
Knutton
Silverdale
Madeley Heath
Keele
Newcastle-under-Lyme
Clayton
Keele Services
Madeley Park
Whitmore
Hanchurch
Baldwin's Gate
Stableford
Beech
Maer
Chapel Chorlton
Cranberry
Podmore
Standon
Cotes
Chatcull
Millmeece
Wetwood
Croxtonbank
Croxton
Slindon
Sugnall
Sturbridge
Bishop's Offley
Pershall
Eccleshall
Adbaston
Knighton
High Offley
Wootton
Shebdon
Woodseaves
Ellenhall
Great Budworth
Comberbach
Gib Hill
Bate Heath
Holehouses
Cheshire County Showground
Pickmere
Tabley
Knutsford Services
Higher Wincham
Plumley
Smithy Green
Anderton Boat Lift
Marbury
Barnton
Anderton
Wincham
Marston
Lostock Gralam
Lostock Green
Lower Peover
Swan Green
Peover Hall
Northwich
Weaverham
Rudheath
Broken Cross
Hartford
Salt Mus
Lach Dennis
Davenham
Moulton
Whitegate
Bostock Green
Puddinglake
Byley
Foxwist Green
Whitegate Way
Wharton Green
Wharton
WINSFORD
Salterswall
Little Budworth
Over
Church Hill
School Green
Middlewich
Sproston Green
Occlestone Green
Moston Green
Bradwall Green
Elworth
Sandbach Crosses
Sandbach
Sandbach Services
Warmingham
Wheelock
Wheelock Heath
Hassall
Winterley
Haslington
Bradfield Green
Coppenhall Moss
Maw Green
Barrows Green
Crewe
Wistaston
Wistaston Green
Wells Green
Gresty Green
Willaston
Weston
Shavington
Barthomley
Englesea-brook
Hough
Gorstyhill
Balterley
Betley
Wrinehill
Wybunbury
Walgherton
Hatherton
Hunsterson
Blakenhall
Checkley
Madeley
Onneley
Hankelow
Audlem
Buerton
Kinsey Heath
Coxbank
Woore
Ireland's Cross
Pipe Gate
Aston
Knighton
Willoughbridge
The Dorothy Clive Garden
Bearstone
Blackbrook
Adderley
Norton in Hales
Mucklestone
Ashley Heath
Ashley
Loggerheads
Hookgate
Almington
Hales
Betton
Market Drayton
Longford
Moreton Say
Sutton
Rosehill
The Four Alls
Woodseaves
Chipnall
Cheswardine
Soudley
Tern Hill
Stoke Heath
Wistanswick
Mill Green
Lockleywood
Goldstone Hall
Hinstock
Stoke on Tern
Hodnet
Hodnet Hall
Marchamley
Hawkstone Park
Wollerton
Wollerton Old Hall
Hopton
High Ollerton
Child's Ercall
Ellerton
Kingsley
Crowton
Acton Bridge
Little Leigh
Dones Green
Commonside
Birch Hill
Alvanley
Manley
Mouldsworth
Delamere Forest
Norley
Hatchmere
Cuddington
Sandiway
Visitor Centre
Farmer for a Day
Ashton
Little Barrow
Great Barrow
Guilden Sutton
Stamford Bridge
Kelsall
Kelsall Hill
Oscroft
Willington Corner
Delamere
Oakmere
Little Budworth
Duddon
Utkinton
Cotebrook
Shire Horse Centre
Oulton Park
Rushton
Eaton
Tarporley
Clotton
Burton
Rhuddall Heath
Four Lane Ends
Tilstone Fearnall
Birch Heath
Brassey Green
Huxley
Hargrave
Wettenhall
Church Minshull
Cholmondeston
Alpraham
Calveley
Bunbury
Bunbury Heath
Beeston
Beeston Castle
Water Mill
Tiverton
Spurstow
Wardle
Aston juxta Mondrum
Barbridge
Haughton Moss
Worleston
Wistaston
Woolstanwood
Radmore Green
Burford
Burland
Faddiley
Acton
Nantwich
St Mary's
Stapeley Water Gardens
Butt Green
Stapeley
Ravensmoor
Larden Green
Chorley
Bickerton
Cholmondeley Castle Gdns
Gallantry Bank
Bulkeley
Peckforton
Higher Burwardsley
Burwardsley
Cheshire Candle Workshops
Harthill
Brown Knowl
Barnhill
Broxton
Fuller's Moor
Duckington
Hampton Heath
Bickley Moss
Ebnal
Malpas
No Man's Heath
Cuddington Heath
Threapwood
Bell o' th' Hill
Higher Wych
Wrenbury
Sound
Sound Heath
Broomhall
Aston
Newhall
Norbury
Marbury
Marley Green
Wirswall
Grindley Brook
Brooklands
Chemistry
Whitchurch
Redbrook
Waymills
Broughall
Burleydam
Lightwood Green
Wilkesley
Ash Magna
Alkington
Bronington
Ightfield
Newstreet Lane
Calverhall
Prees Heath
Tilstock
Hollinwood
Welsh End
Prees Higher Heath
Whixall
Prees
Quina Brook
Waterloo
Sandford
Darliston
Fauls
Bletchley
Prees Lower Heath
Prees Green
Edstaston
Newtown
Lowe
Horton
Wem
Loppington
Burlton
Preston
Petton
Cockshutt
English Frankton
Wolverley
Lyneal
Northwood
Bettisfield
Fenn's, Whixall and Bettisfield Mosses
Wem Moss
Hanmer
Arowry
Eglwys Cross
The Chequer
Shocklach
Chorlton Lane
Castletown
Tilston
Horton Green
Edge Green
Clutton
Barton
Chowley
Handley
Milton Green
Tattenhall
Gatesheath
Hatton Heath
Milner's Heath
Waverton
Christleton
Littleton
Bruera
Elton
Elton Green
Hapsford
Dunham-on-the-Hill
Bridge Trafford
Picton
Chester Services
Gowy
Shropshire Union Canal
Llangollen Canal
Weaver
Dane
Cheshire
West and Chester
Staffs

0 1 2 3 4 5 6 miles
0 1 2 3 4 5 6 7 8 9 10 km

PEAK DISTRICT NATIONAL PARK
SK
Cheshire East
Stafford
Macclesfield
Congleton
Buxton
Leek
Stoke-on-Trent
Ashbourne
Uttoxeter
Stone
Bakewell
Whaley Bridge
Chapel-en-le-Frith
Tideswell
Hathersage
Bollington
Prestbury
Biddulph
Cheadle
Tunstall
Burslem
Hanley
Fenton
Longton
Tutbury
Weston
Youlgrave
Ashford in the Water
Hartington
Alton
Rocester
Sudbury
Poynton
Hurdsfield
Burbage
Cheddleton
Baddeley Green
Endon
Kingsley
Waterhouses
Ilam
Thorpe
Mayfield
Clifton
Doveridge
Hatton
Great Cubley
Tissington
Longnor
Flash
Wincle
Rushton Spencer
Upper Hulme
Warslow
Alstonefield
Grindon
Calton
Blore
Okeover
Norbury
Denstone
Croxden
Hollington
Checkley
Fole
Bramshall
Gratwich
Kingstone
Marchington
Hanbury
Rolleston-on-Dove
Stretton
Anslow
Newborough
Draycott in the Clay
Scropton
Foston
Church Broughton
Sutton on the Hill
Dalbury
Longford
Alkmonton
Hollington Grove
Thurvaston
Rodsley
Yeaveley
Shirley
Osmaston
Wyaston
Snelston
Ellastone
Stanton
Wootton
Ramshorn
Oakamoor
Kingsley Holt
Froghall
Ipstones
Consall
Cellarhead
Werrington
Bucknall
Milton
Bagnall
Stanley
Brown Edge
Norton-in-the-Moors
Meir Heath
Barlaston
Trentham
Hanford
Oulton
Moddershall
Hilderstone
Milwich
Sandon
Salt
Hixon
Drointon
Stowe-by-Chartley
Gayton
Fradswell
Coton
Weaver Hills
Blackbrook
Bottom House
Onecote
Butterton
Wetton
Grindonmoor Gate
Hope
Milldale
Dove Dale
Parwich
Alsop en le Dale
Biggin
Heathcote
Newhaven
Pikehall
Aldwark
Elton
Winster
Birchover
Darley Bridge
Rowsley
Haddon Hall
Over Haddon
Monyash
Flagg
Sheldon
Taddington
Chelmorton
Earl Sterndale
Crowdicote
Pilsbury
Parsley Hay
Middleton
Sheen
Brund
Hulme End
Fawfieldhead
Newtown
Hollinsclough
Glutton Bridge
Axe Edge
Brand Side
Harpur Hill
King Sterndale
Cowdale
Fairfield
Peak Dale
Dove Holes
Combs
Tunstead
Wormhill
Millers Dale
Litton
Wardlow
Cressbrook
Great Longstone
Little Longstone
Hassop
Pilsley
Edensor
Calver
Stoney Middleton
Eyam
Foolow
Grindleford
Great Hucklow
Bretton
Abney
Bradwell
Castleton
Hope
Peak Forest
Sparrowpit
Whitehough
Chinley
Buxworth
Furness Vale
New Mills
Kettleshume
Rainow
Langley
Sutton Lane Ends
Wildboarclough
Danebridge
Bosley
Timbersbrook
Mow Cop
Kidsgrove
Knypersley
Horton
Rudyard
Meerbrook
Tittesworth Res.
Rudyard Res.
Hollingworth
M6
A50
A52
A53
A515
A6
A523
A54
A34
A520
A521
A522
A518
A51
A511
A623
A619
A537
A5004
75
76
62
87
88

Derby
Derby City
Nott
Chesterfield
Matlock
Ashbourne
Mansfield
Bakewell
Belper
Ripley
Alfreton
Heanor
Ilkeston
Eastwood
Hucknall
Kirkby in Ashfield
Sutton in Ashfield
Mansfield Woodhouse
Bolsover
Staveley
Eckington
Dronfield
Clowne
Shirebrook
Long Eaton
Beeston
Stapleford
Castle Donington
Melbourne
Repton
Willington
Hathersage
Baslow
Wirksworth
Cromford
Duffield
Allestree
Mickleover
Spondon
Chaddesden
Normanton
Alvaston
Chellaston
Littleover
Kilburn
Codnor
Somercotes
Pinxton
Tibshelf
Clay Cross
North Wingfield
Brimington
Whitwell
Creswell
Darley Bridge
Youlgrave
Rowsley
Ashford in the Water
Kimberley
Sandiacre
Kegworth
Ockbrook
Borrowash
Breaston
Draycott
Sawley
Castleton
Bradwell
Hope
Bamford
Tideswell
Eyam
Stoney Middleton
Calver
Grindleford
Holmesfield
Old Whittington
Staveley
Killamarsh
Barlborough
Renishaw
Wingerworth
Ashover
Tansley
Crich
Bullbridge
Ambergate
Holbrook
Horsley
Smalley
Morley
Breadsall
Little Eaton
Kedleston
Quarndon
Brailsford
Kirk Langley
Etwall
Burnaston
Findern
Stenson
Hilton
Sudbury
Doveridge
Clifton
Mayfield
Osmaston
Shirley
Hulland Ward
Carsington
Brassington
Tissington
Parwich
Hartington
Elton
Winster
Birchover
Stanton in Peak
Alport
Over Haddon
Sheldon
Monyash
Flagg
Taddington
Great Longstone
Pilsley
Edensor
Beeley
Two Dales
Wensley
Bonsall
Brightgate
Grangemill
Ible
Aldwark
Longcliffe
Ballidon
Bradbourne
Fenny Bentley
Thorpe
Mapleton
Kniveton
Atlow
Biggin
Hognaston
Kirk Ireton
Idridgehay
Shottle
Turnditch
Windley
Hazelwood
Milford
Holbrook
Coxbench
Denby
Loscoe
Aldercar
Langley Mill
Awsworth
Cossall
Trowell
Stanton-by-Dale
Dale Abbey
West Hallam
Stanley
Mapperley
Shipley
Marlpool
Derbyshire
Derby
Notts
Derwent
Wye
Dove Dale
Carsington Res.
East Moor
M1
A6
A38
A52
A50
A61
A619
A617
A610
A609
A615
A632
A516
A515
A5111
A6005
A514
A453
A623
A625
A621
A6020
A5012
A517
A6007
A616
A60
A611
A608
A6096
A6102
A57
29
29A
28
27
26
25
24
24A
30
88
89
75
63
0 1 2 3 4 5 6 miles
0 1 2 3 4 5 6 7 8 9 10 km

Woodsetts
Wigthorpe
Gateford
Shireoaks
Rhodesia
Darfoulds
Kilton
Manton
Worksop
Scofton
Ranby
West Retford
Babworth
Ordsall
RETFORD
BASSETLAW MUSEUM
Sutton
Hayton
Clarborough
North Leverton with Habblesthorpe
Welham
NORTH LEVERTON WINDMILL
Littleborough
Coates
South Leverton
Grove
Cottam
Treswell
SUNDOWN ADVENTURELAND
Rampton
Eaton
Headon
Woodbeck
Stokeham
Church Laneham
Gamston
Upton
Laneham
Askham
East Drayton
Elkesley
West Drayton
Markham Moor
MARKHAM MOOR SERVICES
Darlton
Ragnall
Dunham
Laughterton
Newton on Trent
Milton
West Markham
East Markham
Tuxford
WALKS OF LIFE
Fledborough
North Clifton
South Clifton
High Marnham
Low Marnham
Normanton on Trent
Weston
Grassthorpe
Sutton on Trent
Girton
Egmanton
Laxton
Moorhouse
Ompton
Kneesall
Ossington
Norwell Woodhouse
Norwell
Carlton on Trent
THE VINA COOKE MUS OF DOLLS & BYGONE CHILDHOOD
Cromwell
Collingham
Holme
Bathley
North Muskham
South Muskham
Langford
Little Carlton
Kelham
Winthorpe
NEWARK AIR MUSEUM
Coddington
Newark-on-Trent
Balderton
Hawton
Farndon
Rolleston
Averham
Staythorpe
Upton
Southwell
SOUTHWELL MINSTER
THE WORKHOUSE
Easthorpe
Halloughton
Park Hill
Morton
Fiskerton
Thurgarton
Bleasby
East Stoke
Thorpe
Elston
Syerston
Cotham
Flintham
Sibthorpe
Shelton
Hoveringham
Kneeton
Caythorpe
Lowdham
Epperstone
Gonalston
Lambley
Bulcote
Gunthorpe
East Bridgford
Burton Joyce
Gedling
Carlton
Porchester
Mapperley Park
ARNOLD
Bestwood Village
BESTWOOD
TUMBLE TOWN
Woodborough
Calverton
Oxton
Ravenshead
Blidworth
Rainworth
Haywood Oaks
White Post
Farnsfield
Edingley
Halam
Kirklington
Normanton
Maplebeck
Caunton
Knapthorpe
Winkburn
Hockerton
Eakring
Kersall
Bilsthorpe
Bilsthorpe Moor
WONDERLAND PLEASURE PARK
WHITE POST FARM CENTRE
Clipstone
Old Clipstone
Forest Town
Edwinstowe
Ollerton
Boughton
New Ollerton
Wellow
BETH SHALOM HOLOCAUST CENTRE
SHERWOOD FOREST
Lidgett
VISITORS CENTRE
RUFFORD
SHERWOOD PINES FOREST PARK
Market Warsop
Meden Vale
Church Warsop
Budby
Cuckney
Norton
Carburton
Perlethorpe
HAMLYN LODGE COTTAGE INDUSTRY
Hardwick Village
CLUMBER PARK
CRESWELL CRAGS MUSEUM
Great Lake
Bothamsall
Haughton
Bevercotes
Walesby
Kirton
LONGDALE RURAL CRAFT CENTRE
PAPPLEWICK PUMPING STATION
BURNTSTUMP
Nottingham
P&R
THE TALES OF ROBIN HOOD
GREENS MILL & SCIENCE CEN
Colwick
Radcliffe on Trent
Saxondale
Holme Pierrepont
HOLME PIERREPONT
Stoke Bardolph
Shelford
Newton
Bingham
Car Colston
Scarrington
Screveton
Hawksworth
Thoroton
Flawborough
Staunton in the Vale
Kilvington
Alverton
Orston
Aslockton
Whatton
Normanton
Bottesford
Easthorpe
Elton
Upper Saxondale
Harlequin
Cropwell Butler
Tithby
Granby
Sutton
Barnstone
Cropwell Bishop
Langar
NATURESCAPE WILD FLOWER FARM
VALE OF BELVOIR
Muston
MUSTON MEADOWS
Redmile
Barkestone-le-Vale
Plungar
Belvoir
BELVOIR CASTLE
Stenwith
Woolsthorpe by Belvoir
Denton
Harston
Knipton
Stathern
Harby
Colston Bassett
Kinoulton
Owthorpe
Cotgrave
Normanton-on-the-Wolds
Tollerton
Plumtree
Keyworth
Stanton-on-the-Wolds
Bassingfield
NOTTINGHAM
WEST BRIDGFORD
TRENT BRIDGE CRICKET GRD
Edwalton
Wilford
Lenton
Clifton
Ruddington
FRAMEWORK KNITTERS MUS
RUSHCLIFFE
GREAT CENTRAL RLY (NOTT'M)
Bradmore
Bunny
East Leake
Costock
Wysall
Widmerpool
Willoughby-on-the-Wolds
Hickling
Upper Broughton
Long Clawson
Hose
Eastwell
Goadby Marwood
Eaton
Branston
Croxton Kerrial
Waltham on the Wolds
Saltby
Skillington
Stoke Rochford
Wyville
Hungerton
Great Ponton
Stroxton
Little Ponton
Harlaxton
HARLAXTON MANOR
Old Somerby
Grantham
GRANTHAM MUS
Cold Harbour
Earlsfield
Barrowby
Sedgebrook
Allington
Great Gonerby
Manthorpe
GRANTHAM NORTH SERVICES
BOUNDARY MILLS
Syston
Barkston
Belton
BELTON HOUSE
Honington
Marston
MARSTON
Hougham
Westborough
Foston
Long Bennington
Dry Doddington
Claypole
Stubton
Brandon
Hough-on-the-Hill
Gelston
Caythorpe
Frieston
Carlton Scroop
West Willoughby
Normanton
Fenton
Barnby in the Willows
Beckingham
Stragglethorpe
Brant Broughton
Leadenham
Fulbeck
MANOR STABLES CRAFT WORKSHOPS
Stapleford
Carlton le Moorland
Norton Disney
Brough
Bassingham
Thurlby
Swinderby
Morton
Haddington
Aubourn
South Scarle
Besthorpe
North Scarle
Eagle
Eagle Barnsdale
Eagle Moor
Thorpe on the Hill
North Hykeham
South Hykeham
Whisby
Bracebridge
Boultham
New Boultham
Birchwood
Doddington
DODDINGTON HALL
HARTSHOLME
LINCOLNSHIRE ROAD TRANSPORT MUSEUM
Wigsley
Spalford
Harby
Thorney
Broadholme
Skellingthorpe
Saxilby
Odder
Burton
MUSEUM OF LINCOLNSHIRE LIFE
Kettlethorpe
Fenton
Torksey
Brampton
Sturton by Stow
Ingleby
Bransby
Broxholme
North Carlton
South Carlton
Scampton
Aisthorpe
Thorpe in the Fallows
Cammeringham
Stow
Normanby by Stow
Willingham by Stow
Gate Burton
Marton
Knaith
Sturton le Steeple
Wheatley
Mattersey
in Lindrick
TOLL
Trent
Maun
Poulter
Witham
Brant
Till
SK
Nottinghamshire
A1
A57
A614
A60
A617
A616
A6075
A638
A620
A6097
A612
A46
A52
A606
A17
A156
A1500
A607
A1133
B6045
B6079
B6420
B6034
B6035
B6030
B6020
B6386
B6011
B684
B1241
B1190
B1174
B1176
B6403
89
90
78
64

Willingham by Stow
Normanby by Stow
Ingham
Spridlington
Cold Hanworth
Friesthorpe
Bleasby
Lissington
East Torrington
West Torrington
South Willingham
Biscathorpe
Donington on Bain
Stow
Cammeringham
Hackthorn
Snarford
Wickenby
Holton cum Beckering
Benniworth
Thorpe in the Fallows
Brattleby
Welton Hill
East Barkwith
Market Stainton
Sturton by Stow
Aisthorpe
DAMBUSTERS INN & HERITAGE CENTRE
Welton
Snelland
West Barkwith
Brampton
Scampton
Dunholme
Fulnetby
Rand
RAND FARM PARK
Sotby
Torksey
Bransby
Stainton by Langworth
Wragby
Panton
Ranby
Broxholme
North Carlton
Scothern
Bullington
Hatton
Fenton
Ingleby
South Carlton
Sudbrooke
Langworth
WOODSIDE FALCONRY AND CONSERVATION CENTRE
Langton by Wragby
Great Sturton
Kettlethorpe
Saxilby
Odder
Riseholme
Nettleham
Apley
Kingthorpe
Newton on Trent
Burton
Reepham
Hemingby
MUSEUM OF LINCOLNSHIRE LIFE
Bunker's Hill
North Greetwell
Cherry Willingham
Low Barlings
Minting
Baumber
Broadholme
Ermine
ELLIS MILL
St Giles
Fiskerton
Stainfield
Thorney
CATH
Gautby
Wispington
Skellingthorpe
Clifton
Lincoln
Washingborough
Young Wood
Edlington
Harby
DODDINGTON HALL
New Boultham
Wigsley
Doddington
Birchwood
Boultham
Canwick
Heighington
Branston Booths
Bardney
Bucknall
Thimbleby
Langton
Spalford
HARTSHOLME
Bracebridge
Horsington
Thornton
Eagle Moor
LINCOLNSHIRE ROAD TRANSPORT MUSEUM
Bracebridge Heath
Branston
Potterhanworth Booths
BARDNEY LIMEWOODS
Old Woodhall
North Scarle
Eagle
Whisby
WHISBY NATURAL WORLD
Southrey
Martin
Bracebridge Low Fields
Potterhanworth
Stixwould
Reeds Beck
Dalderby
Eagle Barnsdale
North Hykeham
Thorpe on the Hill
Roughton Moor
Roughton
South Hykeham
Waddington
Wasps Nest
Nocton
Sots Hole
COTTAGE MUSEUM
Haltham
South Scarle
Morton
Swinderby
Haddington
Dunston
Woodhall Spa
Kirkstead
Kirkby on Bain
Aubourn
Harmston
Metheringham
Toft Hill
Collingham
Thurlby
Coleby
Martin Dales
Blankney
Martin
Bassingham
Boothby Graffoe
METHERINGHAM AIRFIELD VISITOR CENTRE
TIMBERLAND ART & DESIGN
Tattershall Thorpe
Coningsby
Norton Disney
Navenby
Scopwick
Timberland
TATTERSHALL COLLEGE
Tattershall
BATTLE OF BRITAIN MEMORIAL FLIGHT
Brough
Stapleford
Carlton le Moorland
SK
TF
Kirkby Green
Thorpe Tilney
Walcott
Tattershall Bridge
COLLEGIATE CHURCH OF THE HOLY TRINITY
Wellingore
Rowston
Hawthorn Hill
NEWARK AIR MUSEUM
Ashby de la Launde
BILLINGHAY COTTAGE
Dogdyke
Digby
Billinghay
Scrub Hill
New York
Coddington
Welbourn
Bloxholm
Chapel Hill
Beckingham
Brant Broughton
NORTH INGS FARM MUSEUM
Dorrington
North Kyme
Haven Bank
Wildmore
Stragglethorpe
Leadenham
Barnby in the Willows
Ruskington
Anwick
Fenton
Fulbeck
Cranwell
MANOR STABLES CRAFT WORKSHOPS
Claypole
BUBBLE CAR MUSEUM
South Kyme
Holland Fen
Stubton
Caythorpe
Leasingham
South Kyme Fen
Brandon
Evedon
Ewerby Thorpe
Dry Doddington
Frieston
North Rauceby
CRANWELL AVIATION HERITAGE CENTRE
Holdingham
COGGLESFORD WATERMILL
Ewerby
Amber Hill
Hough-on-the-Hill
Normanton
Kirkby la Thorpe
Howell
Long Bennington
Gelston
South Rauceby
Sleaford
Asgarby
HOLLAND FEN
Carlton Scroop
Sudbrook
Quarrington
East Heckington
Hougham
West Willoughby
Ancaster
Heckington
Swineshead Bridge
Westborough
MARSTON HALL
THE PEAROOM CENTRE
Marston
Honington
Silk Willoughby
Burton Pedwardine
Great Hale
HECKINGTON WINDMILL
Foston
Wilsford
Little Hale
North End
Barkston
Northbeck
BOUNDARY MILLS
GRANTHAM NORTH SERVICES
Syston
Kelby
Culverthorpe
Swarby
Helpringham
Swineshead
Allington
Belton
Scredington
Great Gonerby
BELTON HOUSE
Heydour
Aswarby
Oasby
Drayton
Sedgebrook
Manthorpe
Aisby
Aunsby
Osbournby
Spanby
Bicker
Welby
Londonthorpe
Dembleby
Swaton
Grantham
Haceby
Newton
Threekingham
Northorpe
Barrowby
Earlsfield
GRANTHAM MUS
Cold Harbour
Braceby
Bridge End
Donington
Walcot
Horbling
Church End
Ropsley
Sapperton
Pickworth
Stow
Billingborough
Donington South Ing
Woolsthorpe by Belvoir
Old Somerby
Folkingham
Birthorpe
Quadring
Denton
HARLAXTON MANOR
Humby
Hanby
Gosberton
Harlaxton
Little Ponton
Boothby Pagnell
Laughton
Pointon
Westhorpe
Stroxton
Lenton
Aslackby
Millthorpe
Gosberton Clough
Great Ponton
Dowsby
Hungerton
Ingoldsby
Graby
Risegate
Croxton Kerrial
Keisby
Bitchfield
Hawthorpe
Kirkby Underwood
Rippingale
Irnham
Bulby
Dunsby
Northgate
Gossgate
Saltby
Skillington
WOOLSTHORPE MANOR
Pinchbeck
Pinchbeck Bars
ERMINE STREET
Witham
Brant
Till
L i n c
A1500 A15 A46 A57 A158 A156 A1434 A607 A17 A153 A52 A1 A157
B1398 B1241 B1190 B1188 B1178 B1202 B1191 B1189 B1192 B1399 B1225 B1429 B1209 B6403 B1174 B1176 B1177 B1394 B1395 B1181 B1397 B1356
90 91 77 65
0 1 2 3 4 5 6 miles
0 1 2 3 4 5 6 7 8 9 10 km

Raithby
Withcall
Little Cawthorpe
South Reston
Gayton le Marsh
Trusthorpe
Tathwell
North Reston
Strubby
Sutton on Sea
Haugham
Muckton
Tothill
Withern
Maltby le Marsh
Thorpe
Stenigot
CADWELL PARK
Authorpe
Beesby
Sandilands
Cawkwell
Maidenwell
Burwell
Woodthorpe
Goulceby
WOODY'S TOP
Hannah
Scamblesby
Farforth
Ruckland
Belleau
CLAYTHORPE WATER MILL AND WILDFOWL GARDENS
Saleby
Markby
White Pit
Swaby
Aby
Oxcombe
Asserby
Ketsby
South Thoresby
ALFORD WINDMILL
ALFORD MANOR HOUSE
Bilsby
Huttoft
Belchford
South Ormsby
Rigsby
Alford
Haugh
Calceby
Anderby
ON YOUR MARQUES
Tetford
Farlesthorpe
Mumby
Authorpe Row
Fulletby
Driby
Brinkhill
Well
Salmonby
Cumberworth
Somersby
Ulceby
Chapel St Leonards
Helsey
Bonthorpe
Hogsthorpe
West Ashby
Sutterby
Bag Enderby
Harrington
Claxby
Willoughby
Ashby Puerorum
High Toynton
Langton
Sloothby
Greetham
Aswardby
Skendleby
HARDY'S ANIMAL FARM
Horncastle
Hagworthingham
Sausthorpe
Ingoldmells
Scrafield
SNIPE DALES
Partney
Welton le Marsh
Addlethorpe
FANTASY ISLAND CHILDREN'S PLAYDROME & THE MILLENNIUM ROLLERCOASTER
Mareham on the Hill
Hameringham
Lusby
Mavis Enderby
Raithby
Scremby
Candlesby
Orby
Orby Marsh
FUNCOAST WORLD
Scrivelsby
Asgarby
Spilsby
Ashby by Partney
GUNBY HALL
Burgh le Marsh
Winthorpe
Seathorne
Old Bolingbroke
Hundleby
NORTHCOTE HEAVY HORSE CENTRE
Hareby
Bratoft
Great Steeping
NATURELAND SEAL SANCTUARY
Wood Enderby
Moorby
BOLINGBROKE
Halton Holegate
Toynton All Saints
Irby in the Marsh
BURGH LE MARSH WINDMILL
CHURCH FARM MUS
Skegness
OSLINC OSTRICH FARM
Miningsby
West Keal
East Keal
THE LIFEBOAT STATION
East Kirkby
Toynton St Peter
Firsby
Little Steeping
Toynton Fen Side
Mareham le Fen
LINCOLNSHIRE AVIATION HERITAGE CENTRE
Keal Cotes
Thorpe Culvert
Thorpe St Peter
Croft
Revesby
Seacroft
Croft Marsh
Revesby Bridge
Thorpe Fendykes
Wainfleet All Saints
Stickford
New Bolingbroke
Wainfleet Bank
MAGDALEN MUSEUM
Fen Side
GIBRALTAR POINT
Tumby Woodside
Midville
New Leake
Wainfleet Tofts
Wainfleet St Mary
Stickney
Eastville
Friskney Eaudike
Medlam
Wainfleet Sand
East Fen
Sandy Bank
Friskney
Carrington
Bunker's Hill
Lade Bank
West Fen
Wrangle Bank
Friskney Tofts
Hundle Houses
Northlands
Leake Commonside
SIBSEY TRADER MILL
Sibsey
Wrangle Lowgate
Friskney Flats
Frithville
Old Leake
Gipsey Bridge
Wrangle
Fishtoft Drove
Hurn's End
Langrick
Anton's Gowt
Hill Dyke
Boston Long Hedges
Leverton Outgate
Frith Bank
Leverton Highgate
Leverton
Brothertoft
Cowbridge
Benington
Leverton Lucasgate
BOSTON DEEPS
LYNN DEEPS
Boston West
Boston
Haltoft End
Butterwick
GUILDHALL
Freiston
TF
Chain Bridge
Skirbeck
Skirbeck Quarter
Kirton Holme
Wyberton
Fishtoft
THE WASH
Frampton West End
Fenhouses
Scrane End
Hunstanton
SEA LIFE SANCTUARY
Kirton End
Frampton
Kirton
Sandholme
Asperton
Skeldyke
Heacham
Wigtoft
Seadyke
Sutterton
Bucklegate
Algarkirk
Fosdyke
Lynn Channel
SNETTISHAM NATURE RESERVE
Holbeach St Matthew
Holbeach St Marks
Dawsmere
Surfleet Seas End
HOLBEACH MARSH
Gedney Marsh
Gedney Drove End
Surfleet
DERSINGHAM
Moulton Seas End
Saracen's Head
Holbeach Hurn
THE WASH
Wolferton
Holbeach Bank
Halesgate
Holbeach Clough
Gedney Dyke
Lutton
Guy's
BAYTREE OWL CENTRE
A
B
C
D
E
F
G
5
6
7
8
9
91
66
80
A157
A153
A1104
A16
A1028
A158
A1111
A52
B1449
A1104
B1373
B1196
B1195
B1183
A155
A1121
B1184
B1192
B1397
B1391
A17
B1357
B1359

80
NATURELAND SEAL SANCTUARY
THE LIFEBOAT STATION
Skegness
Seacroft
Croft Marsh
GIBRALTAR POINT
Wainfleet Sand
TF
NORFOLK COAST
BRANCASTER ROADS
LYNN DEEPS
79
SCOLT HEAD ISLAND
Holkham Bay
Brancaster Bay
HOLME DUNES
HOLKHAM
PEDDARS WAY & NORFOLK COAST PATH
WELLS-NEXT-THE-SEA
Wells-next-the-Sea
HOLME BIRD OBSERVATORY
Holme next the Sea
Titchwell
Brancaster Staithe
Burnham Deepdale
Brancaster
Burnham Norton
Burnham Overy Staithe
Holkham
Old Hunstanton
Thornham
Burnham Westgate
Burnham Overy Town
HOLKHAM HALL
Warham
Hunstanton
Burnham Market
Burnham Thorpe
WELLS AND WALSINGHAM LIGHT RAILWAY
Ringstead
SEA LIFE SANCTUARY
HUNSTANTON
New Holkham
Wighton
CREAKE ABBEY
Copy's Green
Summerfield
North Creake
Great Walsingham
Heacham
NORFOLK LAVENDER
PEDDARS WAY & NORFOLK COAST PATH
Docking
SOUTH CREAKE MAIZE MAZE
Little Walsingham
SHIREHALL MUS
Sedgeford
Stanhoe
South Creake
Waterden
North Barsham
Houghton St Giles
Fring
Birchan Newton
Snettisham
West Barsham
Great Snoring
SNETTISHAM PARK
Great Bircham
Barmer
East Barsham
SNETTISHAM NATURE RESERVE
Shepherd's Port
Ingoldisthorpe
Syderstone
Blenheim Park
Shernborne
Bircham Tofts
BIRCHAM MILL
Bagthorpe
Wicken Green Village
Sculthorpe
Dersingham
PEDDARS WAY
67
DERSINGHAM BOG
Anmer
HOUGHTON HALL
Tattersett
Dunton
Shereford
Fakenham
West Rudham
Coxford
Hempton
Sandringham
SANDRINGHAM
Tatterford
FAKENHAM
Wolferton
East Rudham
Toftrees
West Newton
New Houghton
A148
Flitcham
Helhoughton
Colkirk
Harpley
Hillington
PEDDARS WAY & NORFOLK COAST PATH
West Raynham
Oxwick
Castle Rising
Little Massingham
East Raynham
Terrington Marsh
North Wootton
Ongar Hill
CASTLE RISING
Congham
Hamrow
Great Massingham
South Raynham
Roydon
Weasenham St Peter
A1065
Horningtoft
South Wootton
CONGHAM HALL HERB GARDEN
Whissonsett
King's Lynn
ROYDON COMMON
Grimston
Wellingham
MARITIME EXHIBITION
Weasenham All Saints
Clenchwarton
Gaywood
Pott Row
Massingham Heath
Tittleshall
EXTREEME ADVENTURE
Terrington St Clement
GUILDHALL
West Lynn
Fairstead
Gayton
Stanfield
Rougham
Hardwick
Leziate
Ashwicken
Mileham
Tilney All Saints
Gayton Thorpe
West Lexham
Litcham
Bittering
Tilney High End
Fair Green
Tower End
East Lexham
Middleton
East Walton
Castle Acre
Beeston
Saddle Bow
West Winch
North Runcton
East Winch
West Acre
CASTLE ACRE PRIORY
Newton
Longham
Terrington St John
Wiggenhall St Germans
West Bilney
Pentney
South Acre
Great Dunham
Drury Square
Sparrow Green
Tilney St Lawrence
Setchey
Blackborough End
Crane's Corner
Wiggenhall St Mary the Virgin
Tottenhill Row
Narborough
Little Dunham
Great Fransham
Wendling
Wiggenhall St Mary Magdalen
Watlington
Wormegay
Great Palgrave
Sporle
Little Fransham
Tottenhill
BRADENHAM HALL GDNS & ARBORETUM
Runcton Holme
Shouldham
Marham
Necton
Swaffham
West End
PEDDARS WAY & NORFOLK COAST PATH
Bradenham
Beachamwell Warren
North Pickenham
Holme Hale
Stow Bardolph
Fincham
Barton Bendish
Crowshill
West Head
Wimbotsham
Beachamwell
0 1 2 3 4 5 6 miles
0 1 2 3 4 5 6 7 8 9 10 km

TG
NORFOLK
COAST
Blakeney Point
BLAKENEY
Cley next the Sea
CLEY MILL
GUILDHALL
PEDDARS WAY AND NORFOLK COAST PATH
Morston
Stiffkey
Cockthorpe
Blakeney
Wiveton
Newgate
Salthouse
Kelling
Weybourne
MUCKLEBURGH COLLECTION
NORTH NORFOLK RAILWAY (THE POPPY LINE)
Sheringham
SHERINGHAM PARK
SHERINGHAM
Upper Sheringham
Beeston Regis
PRIORY MAZE & GARDENS
NORFOLK SHIRE HORSE CENTRE
West Runton
East Runton
CROMER MUSEUM
Cromer
Overstrand
Langham
Glandford
Westgate
Binham
Saxlingham
Letheringsett
Holt
High Kelling
Bodham
East Beckham
Aylmerton
Felbrigg
FELBRIGG HALL
Crossdale Street
Northrepps
Sidestrand
Trimingham
WAYSIDE CROSS
THE TEXTILE CENTRE
Field Dalling
Lower Green
PICTURECRAFT GALLERY
LETHERINGSETT WATERMILL
HOLT
West Beckham
Gresham
BACONSTHORPE CASTLE
Baconsthorpe
Sustead
Roughton
Frogshall
Southrepps
Gimingham
Mundesley
STOW WINDMILL
Bale
Sharrington
Hempstead
Hindringham
Thornage
Brinton
Hunworth
Bessingham
Hanworth
Thorpe Market
Lower Street
Trunch
Paston
Knapton
Bacton
Thursford
THURSFORD COLLECTION
Gunthorpe
Stody
Briningham
Edgefield
Plumstead
Matlaske
Aldborough
Thurgarton
Alby Hill
Antingham
Bradfield
Swafield
Edingthorpe
Broomholm
Keswick
Little Snoring
Barney
Swanton Novers
Melton Constable
Briston
Edgefield Street
Little Barningham
Wickmere
ALBY CRAFTS
ALBY GARDENS
Suffield
STRAW MUSEUM
Colby
Erpingham
Calthorpe
MANNINGTON GARDENS
WOLTERTON PARK
Itteringham
Kettlestone
Fulmodestone
Saxthorpe
Corpusty
North Walsham
Spa Common
Edingthorpe Green
Witton Bridge
Ridlington
Crostwight
PENSTHORPE NATURE RESERVE & GARDENS
Hindolveston
Thurning
BLICKLING HALL
Ingworth
Blickling
Banningham
Felmingham
Happisburgh
EAST RUSTON OLD VICARAGE GARDEN
Little Ryburgh
Stibbard
Wood Norton
Norton Corner
Oulton
Silvergate
Dunkirk
Tuttington
Westwick
Honing
East Ruston
Great Ryburgh
Guestwick
Heydon
Oulton Street
Aylsham
Burgh next Aylsham
Skeyton
Bengate
Worstead
Guestwick Green
Wood Dalling
Swanton Abbott
Sloley
Guist
Foulsham
Salle
Southgate
Fengate
Marsham
Brampton
Dilham
East Ruston
Smallburgh
Twyford
Themelthorpe
Cawston
Little London
BURE VALLEY RAILWAY
Scottow
Gateley
Broom Green
Bintree
FOXLEY WOOD
Reepham
Booton
Eastgate
Lamas
Pennygate
Barton Turf
Foxley
Whitwell Street
Brandiston
The Heath
Buxton
Little Hautbois
Tunstead
Brisley
North Elmham
Billingford
Bawdeswell
Haveringland
Hevingham
Stratton Strawless
Sco Ruston
WROXHAM BARNS
Neatishead
ANT BROADS AND MARSHES
Ashmanhaugh
East Bilney
Worthing
Sparham
ANIMAL ARK
Swannington
Coltishall
Three Hammer Common
Beetley
Mill Street
Lenwade
Alderford
Upgate
Waterloo
New Hainford
Hainford
Belaugh
Hoveton
Lower Street
NORFOLK RURAL LIFE MUSEUM
Swanton Morley
Lyng
DINOSAUR ADVENTURE PARK
Wensum
Felthorpe
Frettenham
Wroxham
Upper Street
Horning
Gressenhall
Hoe
Elsing
Morton
Attlebridge
HILLSIDE ANIMAL SANCTUARY
Horsford
Newton St Faith
Wroxham Broad
BURE MARSHES
Woodgate
Primrose Green
Weston Longville
Thorpe Marriott
Crostwick
Woodbastwick
Etling Green
North Tuddenham
Weston Green
Ringland
Taverham
Drayton
Horsham St Faith
NORWICH INTERNATIONAL
Spixworth
Rackheath
Salhouse
Dereham
Hockering
Hellesdon
Old Catton
New Rackheath
Panxworth
MID-NORFOLK RAILWAY
Scarning
Toftwood
Mattishall Burgh
Honingham
Costessey
Mile Cross
Sprowston
Thorpe End
Little Plumstead
Hemblington
Clint Green
Mattishall
East Tuddenham
Upper Hellesdon
Easton
New Costessey
Blofield Heath
Dafty Green
Yaxham
Colton
THE FORUM
New Catton
Thorpe St Andrew
Great Plumstead
Westfield
Whinburgh
Welborne
Marlingford
Bowthorpe
Earlham
CATHEDRAL
NORWICH
Blofield
Brundall
Yare
Bawburgh
SAINSBURY CENTRE FOR VISUAL ARTS
WHITLINGHAM
Brandon Parva
Runhall
Barford
Colney
Lakenham
Postwick
Shipdham
Garvestone
Thuxton
Barnham Broom
Great Melton
Little Melton
Cringleford
Trowse Newton
Kirby Bedon
Surlingham
Strumpshaw
Letton Green
Reymerston
Danemoor Green
Carleton
Wramplingham
High Green
Eaton
Keswick
Bramerton

The Skerries
Ynysoedd y Moelrhoniaid
Carmel Head
Pen Carmel
Wilfa Head
Pen Wilfa
Cemaes Bay
Bae Cemaes
Cemlyn Bay
Bae Cemlyn
WYLFA POWER STATION AND OBSERVATION TOWER
Llanbadrig
Porthllechog
Bull Bay
Porth Llechog
Amlwch Port
Point Lynas
Trwyn Eilian
Cemaes
Tregele
Amlwch
Llaneilian
Llanfairynghornwy
Llanfechell
Rhosbeirio
Bodewryd
Pengorffwysfa
Penysarn
Nebo
Dulas
Isle of Anglesey
(Sir Ynys Môn)
Church Bay
Porth Swtan
Rhydwyn
Llanrhyddlad
Llanfflewyn
Rhosgoch
Carreglefn
Rhosybol
Tyn-y-pwll
Dulas Bay
Bae Dulas
DUBLIN 1:49
DUN LAOGHAIRE 2:00
(Mar-Sept)
DUBLIN 3:15
HOLYHEAD BAY
BAE CAERGYBI
Llanfaethlu
Llanbabo
Alaw Res.
Gwredog
City Dulas
Brynrefail
Moelfre
Ty-mawr
LLYNON WINDMILL
Llanddeusant
Llandyfrydog
Mynydd Bodafon
Llanallgo
Marianglas
North Stack
BREAKWATER
HOLYHEAD MOUNTAIN 220
Llanfwrog
Elim
Llanerchymedd
Hebron
Maenaddwyn
Llaingoch
Holyhead
(Caergybi)
Llanfachraeth
Llantrisant
Carmel
Bachau
Brynteg
Tynygongl
Benllech
South Stack
ELLINS TOWER RSPB RESERVE
Goferydd
Kingsland
PENRHOS FEILW STANDING STONES
Penrhosfeilw
ANGLESEY
Newlands Park
Pen-llyn
Llanynghenedl
Llechcynfarwy
Capel Coch
CORS ERDDREINIOG
CORS GOCH
Llanbedrgoch
Red Wharf Bay
Tan-y-graig
Penrhyn Mawr
Valley
Bodedern
Trefor
Tregaian
Llangwyllog
Llanddyfnan
Pentraeth
Trearddur
Glan-traeth
Four Mile Bridge
Caergeiliog
Bryngwran
Llynfaes
Glan Gors
Rhosmeirch
THE STONE SCIENCE
CORS BODEILIO
Talwrn
Pen-y-garnedd
Holy Island
Ynys Gybi
Llanfihangel yn Nhowyn
Gwalchmai
Bodffordd
ORIEL YNYS MON
Heneglwys
Rhoscefnhir
Rhoscolyn
Llanfairyneubwll
Capel-gwyn
Ddrydwy
Llangefni
Ceint
Penmynydd
SH
Cymyran Bay
Bae Cymyran
Rhosneigr
Llanfaelog
Bryn Du
Pencarnisiog
Cerrigceinwen
Llangristiolus
HENBLAS COUNTRY PARK
Soar
Capel Mawr
Pentre Berw
Gaerwen
JAMES PRINGLE WEAVERS
PILI PALAS
(Porthaethwy)
Llanfairpwll-gwyngyll
Bethel
Trefdraeth
Afon Cefni
Llanddaniel Fab
Llangwyfan-isaf
Aberffraw
Llangadwaladr
Hermon
Malltraeth
PLAS NEWYDD
Capel-y-graig
Llangaffo
PLAS COCH GARDEN ZOO
Bodorgan
Brynsiencyn
Dwyran
SEA ZOO
Y Felinheli
GREENWOOD CENTRE
Seion
Llanddeiniolen
NEWBOROUGH WARREN AND YNYS LLANDDWYN
Newborough
Pen-lon
MODEL VILLAGE
BIRD WORLD
FOEL FARM PARK
MENAI STRAIT AFON MENAI
Bethel
Saron
Malltraeth Bay
Bae Malltraeth
Newborough Forest
SEIONT II MARITIME MUSEUM
CASTLE & REGIMENTAL MUS
Waterloo Port
Llanrug
BRYN BRAS CASTLE
Pont-rug
SEGONTIUM FORT
Cwm-y-glo
Llanddwyn I.
Ynys Llanddwyn
Caernarfon
Caeathro
The Bar
Abermenai Pt.
Trwyn Abermenai
WELSH HIGHLAND RAILWAY
Ceunant
INIGO JONES TUDOR SLATEWORKS
Llanfaglan
Croesywaun
Groeslon
Bontnewydd
Waunfawr
CAERNARFON AIR MUSEUM
Saron
Glan-rhyd
Morfa Dinlle
Rhostryfan
Llanwnda
Rhosgadfan
CAERNARFON BAY
BAE CAERNARFON
Dinas Dinlle
Ffrwd
Penyffridd
Betws-Garmon
Llandwrog
Groeslon
Fron
GLYNLLIFON
Carmel
Cilgwyn
Nantlle
Penygroes
Pontllyfni
Talysarn
Tan-yr-allt
Aberdesach
Llanllyfni
Nebo
WELSH LIFE
Tainlon
Clynnog-fawr
734
Capel Uchaf
Nasareth
Gyrn-goch
Bryn-yr-eryr
Pant-glas
509 BWLCH MAWR
522 GYRN DDU
Trefor
Uwchmynydd
Clynnog
Dafarn Faig
Afon Dwyfor
Llanfihangel
70
71
0 1 2 3 4 5 6 miles
0 1 2 3 4 5 6 7 8 9 10km

Great Ormes Head
Pen-y-Gogarth
TRAMWAY
TOLL
GREAT ORME
GREAT ORME COPPER MINES
Llandudno
Puffin Island
Ynys Seiriol
CONWY BAY
BAE CONWY
Conwy Sands
Traeth Conwy
Penrhynside
Penrhyn Bay
Rhos-on-Sea
COLWYN BAY
(BAE COLWYN)
Abergele Roads
Angorfa Abergele
Craig-y-don
Llandrillo-yn-Rhos
Llanrhos
Deganwy
Tywyn
MOSTYN
BUTTERFLY JUNGLE
Llandudno Junction
(Cyffordd Llandudno)
WELSH MOUNTAIN ZOO
Mochdre
Old Colwyn
Llanddulas
Abergele
Pensarn
Dwygyfylchi
Conwy
Penmaenmawr
Gyffin
CONWY
ABERCONWY HOUSE/PLAS MAWR
Penmaenan
Capelulo
Dolwyd
Glan-Conwy
Bryn-y-maen
Llanelian-yn-Rhos
Llysfaen
Rhyd-y-foel
Dolwen
St George
Mariandyrys
Glan-yr-afon
Caim
Penmon
Llanddona
Llangoed
Llanfaes
Llansadwrn
GAOL AND COURTHOUSE
Beaumaris
Llandegfan
Lavan Sands
Traeth Lafan
Menai Bridge
Garth
Hirael
TEGFRYN
PENRHYN
BANGOR
Bangor
Llandegai
Coed Mawr
Glan Adda
Minffordd
Tal-y-bont
Llanfairfechan
Nant-y-pandy
SH
Henryd
FELIN ISAF WATER MILL
Pentrefelin
Dawn
Betws-yn-Rhos
MOELFRE ISAF
Abergwyngregyn
Crymlyn
TAL-Y-FAN
ROWEN
Rowen
Tal-y-cafn
BODNANT
Graig
Hafod-lom
MOELFRE UCHAF
Llanfair Talhaiarn
COED ABER
Aber Falls
Rhaeadr Aber
Ty'n-y-groes
Pontwgan
COED GORSWEN
Eglwysbach
Llanbedr-y-cennin
Tal-y-Bont
Pentre'r Felin
Gell
Cefn-coch
Pentre Isaf
Bryn-nantllech
COCHWILLAN OLD HALL
Llanllechid
BANGOR SERVICES
Glasinfryn
Rachub
Tregarth
SNOWDONIA
NATIONAL
PARK
FOEL FRAS
Bethesda
Gerlan
Braichmelyn
Afon Dulyn
Llyn Eigiau
Dolgarrog
COED DOLGARROG
VALE OF CONWY
DYFFRYN CONWY
Llangernyw
Hendre-ddu
Llansannan
Pentir
Sling
Rhiwlas
Penisarwaun
Deiniolen
Clwt-y-bont
Ty'n-y-maes
Marchlyn Mawr Res.
CARNEDD LLYWELYN
CARNEDD DAFYDD
Afon Ddu
WOOLLEN MILL
Trefriw
Tan-lan
Bryn-glas
Llanddoged
Pandy Tudur
Tŷ'r-felin-isaf
Brynrefail
Llyn Padarn
Dinorwic
POWER OF WALES
LLANBERIS LAKE RAILWAY
PADARN
Llanberis
SLATE MUS
Llyn Cowlyd
Llyn Crafnant
Pentre-tafarn-y-fedw
Llanrwst
Gwytherin
Pont Pen-y-benglog
Llyn Ogwen
Pont Rhyd-goch
IDWAL COTTAGE
CWM GLAS CRAFNANT
Cornel
GWYDYR
Gwydyr Uchaf
GWYDYR UCHAF CHAPEL
Tai
Melin-y-coed
Ty-draw
BRYN TRILLYN
LLANBERIS
DOLBADARN
Llyn Peris
Nant Peris
CWM IDWAL
Pass of Llanberis
GLYDER FAWR
PARC
Capel Curig
CAPEL CURIG
FOREST PARK
SWALLOW FALLS
Conwy
MOEL SEISIOG
Llyn Aled
Llyn Alwen
Mynydd Hiraethog
PEN-Y-PASS
Pen-y-Gwryd Hotel
Pont Cyfyng
BETWS-Y-COED
Betws-y-Coed
CONWY VALLEY RAILWAY MUSEUM
Capel Garmon
BURIAL CHAMBER
Nebo
SNOWDON RANGER
SNOWDON SUMMIT VISITOR CENTRE (HAFOD ERYRI)
SNOWDON MOUNTAIN RAILWAY
CENEDLAETHOL
Mynydd Cribau
CARNEDD MOEL SIABOD
Pont-y-pant
Fairy Glen
Alwen Reservoir
HAFOD ELWY MOOR
SNOWDON YR WYDDFA
Llyn Llydaw
Rhyd-Ddu
YR WYDDFA
Conwy Falls
Rhaeadr Conwy
PENMACHNO WOOLLEN MILL
Glan-Conwy
Hafod-Dinbych
Mwdwl-eithin
Dolwyddelan
DOLWYDDELAN
TY MAWR WYBRNANT
Gwydyr Forest
Penmachno
Pentrefoelas
Ffridd-Uchaf
Llyn Gwynant
ERYRI
Garnedd
Pentre-bont
Bethania
BRYN GWYNANT
Padog
Rhydlydan
Glasfryn
Cefn-brith
Beddgelert Forest
Nantgwynant
Llyn Dinas
SYGUN COPPER MINE
MOEL PENAMNEN
Ysbyty Ifan
GARN PRYS
Cerrigydrudion
MOEL HEBOG
Pass of Aberglaslyn
Beddgelert
WELSH HIGHLAND RLY
Nantmor
Rhiwbryfdir
LLECHWEDD SLATE CAVERNS
Blaenau Ffestiniog
Bethania
Tanygrisiau
Cwm Penmachno
Carrog
Afon Machno
Llyn Conwy
Tŷ Mawr
Cwm
Pen-y-garnedd
Afon Ce
BRYNNON WEN
A55
A470
A5
A4086
A498
A4244
A545
A548
A543
A544
B5106
B5113
B5383
B5381
B5382
B5384
B5109
B4409
B4406
B4407
B4501
71
72

NX
SC
Isle of Man
POINT OF AYRE
The Ayres
Rue Pt.
The Lhen
Glentruan
Cranstal
Dhowin
Bride
Andreas
MANX CROSSES
JURBY SOUTH
Jurby Head
Jurby East
Sandygate
Jurby West
Ballasalla
Regaby
The Cronk
St Judes
Dhoor
RAMSEY BAY
Ramsey
CURRAGHS WILDLIFE PARK
GROVE MUSEUM
Sulby
MANX ELECTRIC RAILWAY
Port e Vullen
Orrisdale
Ballaugh
T.T.Course
Churchtown
Glen Auldyn
Maughold
Maughold Head
MANX CROSSES
Rhencullen
Ravensdale
Dreemskerry
Kirk Michael
565 NORTH BARRULE
Ballajora
CELTIC CRAFT CENTRE
Corrany
Ballaleigh
Res.
SNAEFELL 621
Cornaa
Glen Mona
Barregarrow
Druidale
Dhoon
MURRAYS MOTORCYCLE MUSEUM
Agneash
Bulgham Bay
MANX TRANSPORT MUSEUM
Knocksharry
544
SNAEFELL MOUNTAIN RAILWAY
LAXEY WHEEL AND MINES
Laxey
Cronk-y-Voddy
Ballaquine
St Patrick's I.
PEEL
487 COLDEN
LAXEY WOOLLEN MILLS
Old Laxey
Peel
Laxey Head
HOUSE OF MANANNAN
BALLALHEANNAGH GARDENS
Fairy Cottage
Contrary Head
TYNWALD CRAFT CENTRE
Laxey Bay
KIPPER MUSEUM
TYNWALD HILL
Creg-ny-Baa
Ballacannel
Patrick
St John's
Greeba
Baldwin
Baldrine
Glenmaye
333
Clay Head
Lower Foxdale
Crosby
Dalby Pt.
MANX CROSSES
Glen Vine
Strang
HEYSHAM 3:15
Onchan
Dalby
Tromode
GROUDLE GLEN RAILWAY
Niarbyl
Foxdale
Union Mills
Eairy
ONCHAN PLEASURE PARK
Braaid
Spring Valley
HEYSHAM 2:00 (TT race period only)
Douglas
Niarbyl Bay
483 SOUTH BARRULE
Cooil
Douglas Bay
222
Close Clark
Douglas Head
Ellenbrook
Ballaveare
CAMERA OBSCURA
St Mark's
Ballamodha
Newtown
LIVERPOOL 2:30 (March-Nov)
Little Ness
Lingague
Ronague
ISLE OF MAN STEAM RAILWAY
Fleshwick Bay
Grenaby
LIVERPOOL 4:15 (Winter only)
Surby
Ballabeg
RUSHEN ABBEY
Santon Head
Bradda Head
Bradda
Colby
Ballasalla
Port Greenaugh
Port Erin
BILLOWN
ISLE OF MAN
RAILWAY MUS
Four Roads
The Howe
Castletown
Derbyhaven
Cregneash
CASTLE RUSHEN
NAUTICAL MUS
St Michael's I.
SCARLETT VISITOR CENTRE
OLD HOUSE OF KEYS
Port St Mary
CREGNEASH VILLAGE FOLK MUSEUM
128
Scarlett Point
Spanish Head
Dreswick Pt.
Calf of Man
Chicken Rock
BELFAST 2:55 (April-Sept)
DUBLIN 2:55 (June-Sept)
0 1 2 3 4 5 6 miles
0 1 2 3 4 5 6 7 8 9 10 km

IRISH SEA
LIVERPOOL BAY
SD
SJ
Southport
Lytham St Anne's
Kirkham
Freckleton
Fairhaven
Salters Bank
Banks Sands
Great Bank
Horse Bank
Ribble
RIBBLE MARSHES
Hesketh Bank
Becconsall
Tarleton
Banks
Crossens
Marshside
Churchtown
Mere Brow
Holmeswood
Blowick
Birkdale
Hillside
Ainsdale
Ainsdale-on-Sea
Woodvale
Scarisbrick
Burscough
ORMSKIRK
Halsall
Formby
Freshfield
Formby Pt.
Little Altcar
Great Altcar
Hightown
Ince Blundell
Lydiate
Maghull
Little Crosby
Thornton
Great Crosby
LITHERLAND
Kirkby
Knowsley
Waterloo
Seaforth
Bootle
Merseyside
LIVERPOOL
Huyton
Roby
Wallasey
New Brighton
Liscard
Egremont
Seacombe
Moreton
Leasowe
Meols
HOYLAKE
West Kirby
Hilbre I.
West Hoyle Bank
Birkenhead
BEBINGTON
Heswall
Neston
Parkgate
Willaston
Garston
Speke
Liverpool Airport
Ellesmere Port
Eastham
Bromborough
Port Sunlight
Welsh Channel
Point of Ayr
Talacre
Gronant
Prestatyn
Mostyn
Holywell
River Dee
Afon Dyfrdwy
Dawpool Bank
Holywell Bank
Gayton Sands
Mockbeggar Wharf
Crosby Channel
BELFAST 8:00
DOUGLAS 4:15 (Winter only) DUBLIN 7:30
DOUGLAS 2:30 (March-Nov)
Mersey
Ince Banks
0 1 2 3 4 5 6 miles
0 1 2 3 4 5 6 7 8 9 10 km

Preston
Fulwood
Ribbleton
Kirkham
Wrea Green
Freckleton
Lytham
Ansdell
Warton
Banks Sands
Hesketh Bank
Longton
Leyland
Lancashire
Chorley
Eccleston
Mawdesley
Rufford
Burscough
Ormskirk
Skelmersdale
Wigan
Standish
Coppull
Adlington
Horwich
Blackrod
Westhoughton
Bolton
Blackburn
Darwen
Blackburn with Darwen
Hindley
Atherton
Tyldesley
Leigh
Ashton-in-Makerfield
Golborne
Haydock
Newton-le-Willows
St Helens
Rainford
Billinge
Kirkby
Maghull
Knowsley
Prescot
Huyton
Roby
Liverpool
Merseyside
Bootle
Speke
Garston
Liverpool Airport
Widnes
Runcorn
Halton
Frodsham
Helsby
Warrington
Lymm
Irlam
Partington
Cadishead
Birchwood
Culcheth
Samlesbury
Bamber Bridge
Walton-le-Dale
Penwortham
Hutton
Tarleton
Banks
Crossens
Churchtown
Formby
Halsall
Scarisbrick
Aughton
Lydiate
Melling
Knowsley Safari Park
Wrightington
Parbold
Orrell
Up Holland
Shevington
Aspull
Platt Bridge
Abram
Lowton
Glazebury
Chat Moss
Great Sankey
Penketh
Stockton Heath
Appleton Thorn
Daresbury
Preston Brook
Sutton Weaver
Aston
Dutton
Comberbach
Great Budworth
Anglezarke Moor
Rivington
Turton Moor
Edgworth
Great Harwood
Rishton
Clayton-le-Moors
Church
85
86
92
93
73
74
M6
M55
M58
M57
M62
M61
M65
M56
M60
A59
A565
A570
A580
A5209
0 1 2 3 4 5 6 miles
0 1 2 3 4 5 6 7 8 9 10 km

Padiham
Burnley
Accrington
Haslingden
Rawtenstall
Bacup
Ramsbottom
Todmorden
Hebden Bridge
Mytholmroyd
Queensbury
Illingworth
Halifax
Sowerby Bridge
Brighouse
Elland
Huddersfield
Slaithwaite
Marsden
Meltham
Holmfirth
Littleborough
Rochdale
Milnrow
Heywood
Bury
Whitworth
Wardle
Royton
Shaw
Middleton
Chadderton
Oldham
Radcliffe
Whitefield
Prestwich
Swinton
Pendlebury
Eccles
Salford
MANCHESTER
Ashton-under-Lyne
Stalybridge
Dukinfield
Mossley
Droylsden
Failsworth
Denton
Hyde
Glossop
Hadfield
Trafford Park
Urmston
Stretford
Sale
Altrincham
Gatley
Cheadle
Stockport
Bredbury
Romiley
Marple
Hazel Grove
Bramhall
Poynton
Manchester Airport
Wilmslow
Knutsford
Alderley Edge
Prestbury
Bollington
New Mills
Whaley Bridge
Chapel-en-le-Frith
Tideswell
Hayfield
Heptonstall Moor
Forest of Rossendale
Saddleworth Moor
Hope Forest
SE
SK
Greater Manchester
M60
M62
M66
M67
M56
M602
A6
A56
A58
A627(M)
A628
A646
A629
A6018
93
94
88
74
75

Bradford
LEEDS
PUDSEY
GARFORTH
Kippax
Queensbury
Halifax
Brighouse
Cleckheaton
BATLEY
MORLEY
Birstall
Middleton
Rothwell
CASTLEFORD
Sowerby Bridge
Elland
Heckmondwike
Dewsbury
OSSETT
Horbury
Wakefield
Normanton
Pontefract
Featherstone
Mirfield
Huddersfield
Slaithwaite
Marsden
Meltham
Honley
HOLMFIRTH
Skelmanthorpe
Clayton West
Denby Dale
Darton
Royston
Hemsworth
South Kirkby
Cudworth
Barnsley
Penistone
Dodworth
Darfield
Wombwell
Worsbrough
Hoyland
Wath upon Dearne
Stocksbridge
Chapeltown
Rawmarsh
Ecclesfield
Sheffield
Handsworth
GLOSSOP
Charlestown
Hathersage
Chapel-en-le-Frith
Dronfield
ECKINGTON
West Yorkshire
South Yorkshire
PEAK DISTRICT NATIONAL PARK
HOPE FOREST
HIGH PEAK
0 1 2 3 4 5 6 miles
0 1 2 3 4 5 6 7 8 9 10 km

Sherburn in Elmet
Barlby
Selby
Selby Abbey
Osgodby
Menthorpe
Breighton
Spaldington
Little Fenton
Newthorpe
Thorpe Willoughby
Lund
Cliffe
South Duffield
Wressle
Brind
North Howden
Portington
Hive
South Milford
Monk Fryston
Hambleton
Brayton
East Common
Hemingbrough
Newsholme
Howden
Cavil
Eastrington
Sandholme
Gilberdyke
Ledsham
Lumby
Barlow
Barmby on the Marsh
Staddlethorpe
Hillam
Gateforth
Burn
Long Drax
Asselby
Knedlington
Kilpin Pike
Balkholme
Fairburn
Burton Salmon
Brotherton
Birkin
West Haddlesey
Chapel Haddlesey
Drax
Boothferry
Kilpin
New Fryston
Camblesforth
Laxton
Temple Hirst
Hirst Courtney
Newland
Airmyn
Hook
Skelton
Blacktoft
Ferrybridge
Sutton
Beal
Kellington
Carlton
Saltmarshe
Yokefleet
Knottingley
Kellingley
Eggborough
Hensall
Snaith
Rawcliffe
Goole
Ousefleet
Whitgift
Reedness
Swinefleet
Rawcliffe Bridge
Old Goole
Little Reedness
Cridling Stubbs
High Eggborough
Gowdall
East Cowick
West Cowick
Whitley
Great Heck
Pollington
Southfield Reservoir
Dutch River
Adlingfleet
Chequerfield
Darrington
East Hardwick
Womersley
Balne
Aire and Calder Navigation
Goole Fields
Fockerby
Garthorpe
Burton Stather
Wentbridge
Little Smeaton
Walden Stubbs
Goole Moors
Luddington
Low Ackworth
Sykehouse
Pincheon Green
Thorpe Audlin
Kirk Smeaton
Fenwick
Moorends
Humberhead Peatlands
Thorne Waste or Moors
Amcotts
Badsworth
Norton
Campsall
Moss
Fosterhouses
Fishlake
Crowle
Upton
Wrangbrook
Instoneville
Askern
Far Bank
Thorne
North Elmsall
Sutton
Haywood
Braithwaite
Doncaster North Services
Canal Side
Wike Well End
Stainforth & Keadby Canal
Windsor
Moorthorpe
South Elmsall
Skelbrooke
Burghwallis
Owston
Kirk Bramwith
Thorpe in Balne
Stainforth
Hatfield
Hatfield Chase
Ealand
Keadby
Gunness
Hampole
Carcroft
Skellow
Adwick le Street
Barnby Dun
Dunscroft
Burringham
Althorpe
Hooton Pagnell
Kirk Sandall
Almholme
Hatfield Woodhouse
Derrythorpe
Clayton
Brodsworth
Toll Bar
Woodlands
Dunsville
West End
Sandtoft
Woodhouse
The Trolleybus Museum at Sandtoft
Grey Green
Belton
Westgate
Beltoft
Arksey
Edenthorpe
Hatfield Moors
Church Town
East Butterwick
West Butterwick
Thurnscoe
Thurnscoe East
Bentley
Armthorpe
Isle of Axholme
Hickleton
Marr
Scawsby
Cusworth
Wheatley
Intake
Nutwell
Epworth
Old Rectory
Goldthorpe
Melton Wood
Doncaster
Wroot
Epworth Turbary
Bolton upon Dearne
Barnburgh
Newton
Cusworth Hall Museum
Cantley
Branton
Low Burnham
Kelfield
Susworth
Scotter
Harlington
Sprotbrough
Hyde Park
Bessacarr
Auckley
Adwick upon Dearne
High Melton
Balby
Cadeby
Lakeside Village
Aeroventure
Lidget
Blaxton
Upperthorpe
Owston Ferry
Mexborough
Warmsworth
Haxey
East Lound
Laughton Forest
Denaby Main
Old Denaby
New Edlington
Loversall
Rossington
Finningley
Westwoodside
East Ferry
Conisbrough
Conisbrough/Ivanhoe
Craiselound
Wildsworth
Robin Hood Airport Doncaster Sheffield
Kilnhurst
Old Edlington
New Rossington
Hooton Roberts
Clifton
St Leger Horse Park
Idle
Laughton
Thrybergh
Ravenfield
Wadworth
Blyton
Misson
Misterton
West Stockwith
East Stockwith
Micklebring
Austerfield
Newington
Walkerith
Dalton
Braithwell
Stainton
Spital Hill
Bawtry
Walkeringham
Morton
Gainsborough
Bramley
Hellaby
Maltby
Tickhill
Harworth
Gringley on the Hill
Gainsborough Old Hall
Wickersley
Bircotes
Everton
Hooton Levitt
Scaftworth
Scrooby
Cuckoo Hill
Beckingham
Carr
Styrrup
Wiseton
Thurcroft
Roche Abbey
Stone
Serlby
Mattersey Thorpe
Mattersey
Oldcotes
Blyth Services
Ranskill
Brampton en le Morthen
Firbeck
Clayworth
Saundby
Ulley
Laughton en le Morthen
Langold
Torworth
Bole
Aughton
Laughton Common
Letwell
Blyth
Lound
North Wheatley
Lea
Knaith Park
Aston
Dinnington
Gildingwells
Wetlands Animal Park
South Wheatley
Sturton le Steeple
Knaith
Barnby Moor
Carlton in Lindrick
Sutton
Hayton
North Anston
Swallownest
Todwick
Woodsetts
Clarborough
North Leverton with Habblesthorpe
Gate Burton
Kiveton Park
South Anston
Wigthorpe
Bassetlaw Museum
Welham
Littleborough
Marton
Wales
North Leverton Windmill
Thorpe Salvin
Gateford
Scofton
West Retford
Coates
Norwood
Harthill
Netherthorpe
Shireoaks
Ranby
Babworth
Retford
South Leverton
Killamarsh
Woodall Services
Kilton
Ordsall
Grove
Cottam
Bramp
Spinkhill
Darfoulds
Eaton
Treswell
Sundown Adventureland
Rampton
Torksey
Manton
Barlborough
Worksop
Woodbeck
Church Laneham
Fenton
Whitwell
Hodthorpe
Headon
Upton
Stokeham
Mastin Moor
Clowne
Clumber Park
Gamston
Laneham
Laughterton

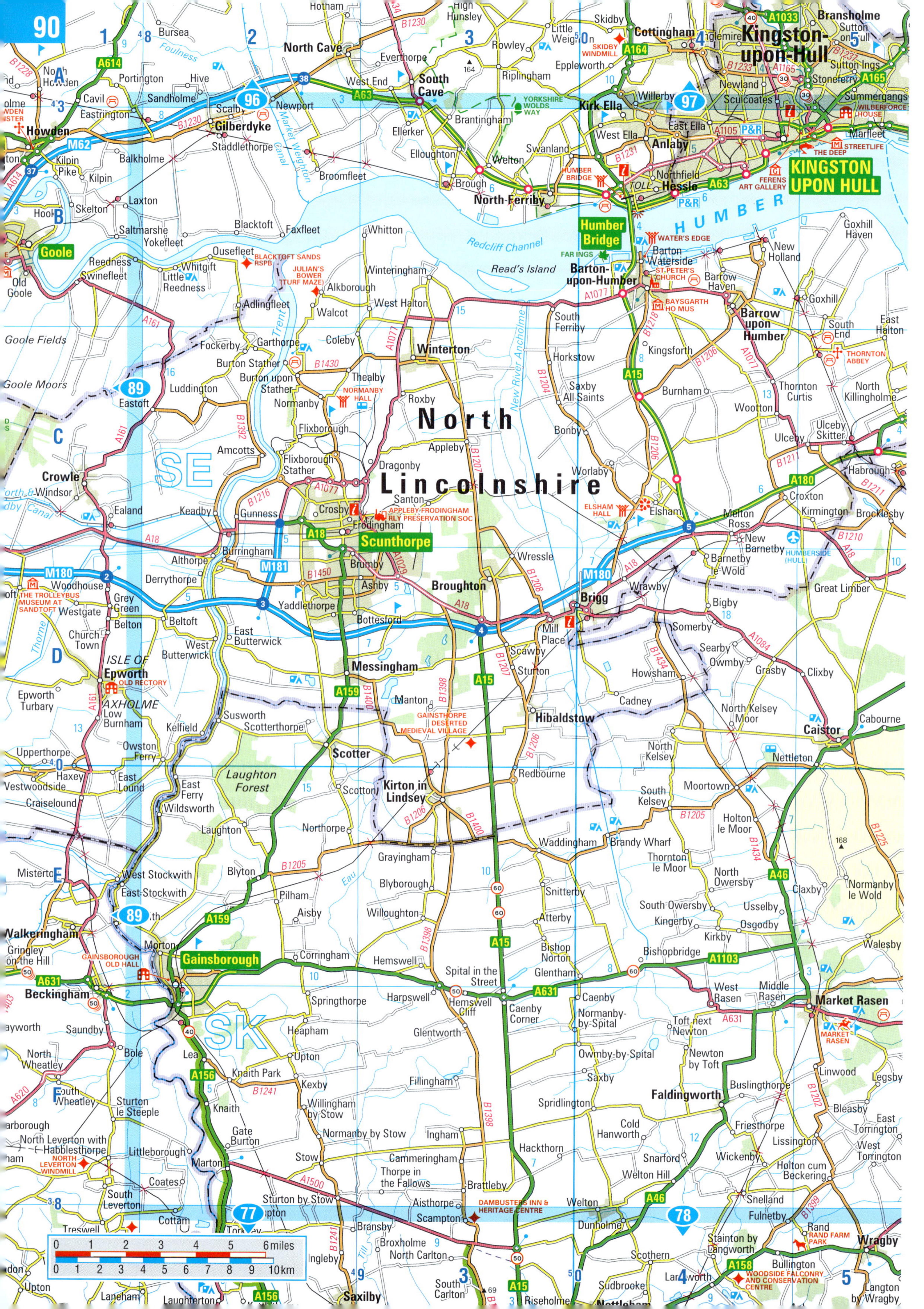
Kingston-upon-Hull
KINGSTON UPON HULL
HUMBER
Humber Bridge
North Lincolnshire
Scunthorpe
Goole
Gainsborough
Howden
Cottingham
Hessle
Anlaby
Kirk Ella
Willerby
North Ferriby
Brough
South Cave
North Cave
Newport
Gilberdyke
Barton-upon-Humber
Barrow upon Humber
New Holland
Winterton
Brigg
Broughton
Messingham
Scotter
Kirton in Lindsey
Hibaldstow
Caistor
Market Rasen
Crowle
Epworth
ISLE OF AXHOLME
Haxey
Beckingham
Walkeringham
Laughton Forest
Faldingworth
Wragby
Saxilby
Scampton
Welton
Dunholme
Spital in the Street
Hemswell
Blyton
Stow
Marton
Misterton
North Leverton with Habblesthorpe
Sturton le Steeple
Elsham
Melton Ross
Kirmington
Habrough
Ulceby
Goxhill
Thornton Curtis
Barnetby le Wold
Bigby
Grasby
Nettleton
North Kelsey
South Kelsey
Waddingham
Redbourne
Normanby le Wold
Walesby
Middle Rasen
West Rasen
Bishopbridge
Glentham
Caenby Corner
Burton upon Stather
Normanby
Flixborough
Alkborough
Whitton
Winteringham
West Halton
Amcotts
Gunness
Frodingham
Bottesford
Yaddlethorpe
Ashby
Belton
Westgate
Althorpe
Keadby
Ealand
Owston Ferry
East Ferry
Wildsworth
Morton
Lea
Knaith
Gate Burton
Willingham by Stow
Normanby by Stow
Ingham
Fillingham
Glentworth
Harpswell
Upton
Kexby
Springthorpe
Corringham
Heapham
Pilham
Aisby
Blyborough
Grayingham
Willoughton
Snitterby
Atterby
Bishop Norton
Owmby-by-Spital
Normanby-by-Spital
Saxby
Spridlington
Hackthorn
Cold Hanworth
Snarford
Friesthorpe
Wickenby
Lissington
Holton cum Beckering
Snelland
Fulnetby
Rand
Bullington
Langworth
Sudbrooke
Scothern
Riseholme
North Carlton
South Carlton
Broxholme
Bransby
Sturton by Stow
Cammeringham
Thorpe in the Fallows
Brattleby
Aisthorpe
Coates
South Leverton
Cottam
Treswell
Laneham
Littleborough
Bole
Saundby
North Wheatley
South Wheatley
Gringley on the Hill
M62
M180
M181
A15
A18
A63
A159
A161
A631
A46
A1077
A1103
A156
A614
SE
SK
0 1 2 3 4 5 6 miles
0 1 2 3 4 5 6 7 8 9 10 km

5
6
7
8
9
A
B
C
D
E
F
G
TA
TF
Thirtleby
Sproatley
Humbleton
Fitling
Hilston
Ganstead
Bilton
Lelley
Owstwick
Tunstall
Elstronwick
Preston
Burton
Pidsea
97
Roos
North End
West End
Waxholme
Salt End
A1033
Hedon
Owthorne
Withernsea
Haven Side
Rimswell
Burstwick
B1362
Halsham
East End
Paull
Thorngumbald
Camerton
FORT PAULL
Ryehill
Keyingham
Hollym
Ottringham
Little Humber
Winestead
Holmpton
Thorney Crofts
Patrington
Out Newton
Cherry Cob Sands
Welwick
Weeton
B1445
Easington
Sunk Island
Skeffling
Kilnsea
A160
South Killingholme
Immingham
MUSEUM
SPURN
Stallingborough
A180
Pyewipe
ROTTERDAM 10:15
ZEEBRUGGE 12:15
SPURN HEAD
Grimsby
Healing
West Marsh
Keelby
Great Coates
CLEETHORPES
MOUTH OF THE HUMBER
FISHING HERITAGE CENTRE
Old Clee
Riby Cross Roads
Aylesby
Freshney
A46
CLEETHORPES COAST LIGHT RAILWAY
Riby
Laceby
Nunsthorpe
PLEASURE ISLAND THEME PARK
Bradley
Scartho
A1098
CLEETHORPES
B1219
Humberston
North East
A1173
A16
Irby upon Humber
Waltham
New Waltham
A18
Barnoldby le Beck
WALTHAM WINDMILL
Holton le Clay
Swallow
Lincolnshire
A1031
Tetney Lock
A46
Brigsley
Beelsby
B1203
Ashby cum Fenby
North Cotes
Cuxwold
Hatcliffe
Waithe
Tetney
East Ravendale
Rothwell
Grainsby
Marshchapel
Donna Nook
B1201
Croxby
Eskham
North Thoresby
Wragholme
Grainthorpe
Thoresway
Thorganby
Wold Newton
North Somercotes
Fulstow
Swinhope
DONNA NOOK
A16
LINCOLNSHIRE WOLDS RLY
Skidbrooke North End
Brookenby
Ludborough
Covenham St Bartholomew
Conisholme
Saltfleet
South Somercotes
Covenham St Mary
Stainton le Vale
Binbrook
Utterby
Skidbrooke
Yarburgh
B1203
North Ormsby
Saltfleetby St Clements
ALVINGHAM MILL
Kirmond le Mire
Fotherby
Alvingham
Little Grimsby
SALTFLEETBY THEDDLETHORPE
North Cockerington
Tealby
North Elkington
Great Tows
Kelstern
Saltfleetby All Saints
Theddlethorpe St Helen
RUSHMOOR
A631
North Willingham
South Elkington
South Cockerington
Saltfleetby St Peter
Ludford
Keddington
Grimoldby
B1200
Welton le Wold
Louth
Theddlethorpe All Saints
Sixhills
Burgh on Bain
Stewton
Manby
SEAL SANCTUARY & NATURE CENTRE
ST JAMES
Grimblethorpe
Little Carlton
Meers Bridge
Gayton le Wold
Hallington
Great Carlton
Mablethorpe
Hainton
A157
Biscathorpe
Legbourne
Raithby
Trusthorpe
South Willingham
Donington on Bain
Little Cawthorpe
South Reston
Gayton le Marsh
Withcall
A153
A157
North Reston
A1104
Strubby
Tathwell
Sutton on Sea
Benniworth
Withern
Thorpe
Haugham
Muckton
Tothill
Maltby le Marsh
East Barkwith
CADWELL PARK
Authorpe
B1373
Sandilands
Market Stainton
Stenigot
Beesby
West Barkwith
B1225
Cawkwell
Woodthorpe
Maidenwell
A16
Burwell
78
79
Sotby
Goulceby
WOODY'S TOP
Hannah
Panton
Ranby
Belleau
Saleby
Scamblesby
Ruckland
CLAYTHORPE WATER AND WILDFOWL GARDENS
Markby
Farforth
White Pit
Swaby
Aby
Hatton
Oxcombe
ALFORD WINDMILL
A1111
Asserby
A52
Great Sturton
Ketsby
South Thoresby
ALFORD MANOR HOUSE
Bilsby
Huttoft
Belchford
Rigsby
Alford
B1449

Millom
MILLOM FOLK MUSEUM
Haverigg
Whicham
Green
The Hill
Kirkby-in-Furness
Beck Side
Soutergate
Broughton-Beck
Penny Bridge
Greenodd
Gawthwaite
Bridge
Arrad Foot
Mansriggs
Backbarrow
Haverthwaite
Ayside
High Newton
Low Newton
Witherslack
Town End
Mill Side
Field Broughton
Heversham
Milnthorpe
Leasgill
Crooklands
Farleton
Meathop
Lindale
Storth
Beetham
HERON CORN MILL
Holme
CLAWTHWAITE FELL
Clawthorpe
Burton-in-Kendal
Yealand Redmayne
Yealand Conyers
LEIGHTON HALL
Priest Hutton
Borwick
Capernwray
LAKELAND WILDLIFE OASIS
Arnside
ARNSIDE KNOT
GAIT BARROWS
ARNSIDE AND SILVERDALE
Silverdale
Warton
Warton Sands
OLD RECTORY
Millhead
Carnforth
Over Kellet
Nether Kellet
Bolton-le-Sands
Bolton Town End
Hest Bank
Slyne
Aughton
Caton Green
Halton
Caton
BURTON-IN-KENDAL (Northbound Only)
DUDDON SANDS
Askam in Furness
Ireleth
Lindal in Furness
SOUTH LAKES WILD ANIMAL PARK
SANDSCALE HAWS
Ulverston
LAUREL & HARDY MUS
Pennington
Swarthmoor
Great Urswick
Little Urswick
Bardsea
CONISHEAD PRIORY & MANJUSHRI KADAMPA MEDITATION CENTRE
Cartmel Sands
ROUDSEA WOOD AND MOSSES
CARTMEL
CARTMEL PRIORY
Cartmel
HOLKER HALL
Holker
Allithwaite
Grange-over-Sands
Cark
Flookburgh
Kents Bank
Ravenstown
LAKELAND RIDING CENTRE
Humphrey Head Pt.
Dalton-in-Furness
DALTON CASTLE
Stainton with Adgarley
Scales
Baycliff
NORTH WALNEY
BARROW (WALNEY ISLAND)
Hawcoat
BOW BRIDGE
Ormsgill
Newton
GLEASTON WATERMILL
Newbarns
FURNESS ABBEY
Dendron
Gleaston
Aldingham
Barrow-in-Furness
North Scale
Yarlside
Newbiggin
CUSTOM HO
THE DOCK MUSEUM
Vickerstown
Barrow Island
Leece
Roosebeck
Biggar
Rampside
Roa Island
Foulney Island
South End
Piel Island
Isle of Walney
South End Point
South Channel
MORECAMBE BAY
Morecambe
Bare
Torrisholme
Sandylands
Skerton
White Lund
MARITIME MUS
Heysham
Lancaster
PRIORY CHURCH
CITY MUS
ASHTON MEMORIAL
LEISURE PARK
Aldcliffe
Heaton
Scotforth
Quernmore
Middleton
Overton
DOUGLAS 3:15
DOUGLAS 2:00 (TT race period only)
Sunderland Pt.
Shoulder of Lune
Lune
Glasson
Conder Green
Galgate
Thurnham
Smith Green
Ortner
Dolphinholme
LANCASTER (FORTON) SERV
Cockerham Sands
Cockerham
Braides
Forton
Street
Hollins Lane
Dam Side
Stake Pool
Winmarleigh
Scorton
Pilling Lane
Pilling
Knott End-on-Sea
Preesall
Fleetwood
Rossall Point
FREEPORT FLEETWOOD
Wyre
SD
Eagland Hill
Cabus
Oakenclough
Garstang
THE FIG TREE FAIRTRADE VISITOR CENTRE
Calder Vale
Nateby
Bowgreave
Calder
Stalmine
Staynall
MARSH MILL-IN-WYRE
WYRE ESTUARY
Cleveleys
Trunnah
Hambleton
Churchtown
Catterall
Moss Edge
Out Rawcliffe
Ratten Row
Anchorsholme
Norbreck
Thornton
Little Eccleston
TOLL
St Michael's on Wyre
Claughton
Bispham
Skippool
Little Singleton
Bilsborrow
Inglewhite
Carleton
Great Eccleston
Elswick
Myerscough
Blackpool
Warbreck
North Shore
Poulton-le-Fylde
Singleton
Crossmoor
Inskip
Cuddy Hill
Queenstown
Thistleton
Roseacre
Barton
Normoss
Layton
Esprick
Staining
Catforth
Blackpool
BLACKPOOL TOWER
SEA LIFE CENTRE
LOUIS TUSSAUD'S WAXWORKS
ZOO PARK
Great Marton
Corner Row
Wharles
Woodplumpton
Broughton
Lancashire
Weeton
Great Plumpton
Little Plumpton
Wesham
Treales
Lower Bartle
Higher Bartle
Sharoe Green
Hawes Side
Mereside
South Shore
BLACKPOOL PLEASURE BEACH
Common Edge
Kirkham
Dowbridge
Lancaster Canal
Cottam
Ingol
Fulwood
Cadley
Squires Gate
Westby
Wrea Green
Lea Town
BLACKPOOL INTERNATIONAL
Moss Side
Newton
Scales
Clifton
Preston
Higher Ballam
TOY AND TEDDY BEAR MUSEUM
ROYAL LYTHAM & ST ANNES
LYTHAM HALL
Freckleton
P&R
RIBBLE STEAM RAILWAY
St Annes
Ansdell
Lytham
Warton
Bottom of Hutton
Higher Penwortham
Lytham St Anne's
Fairhaven
Salters Bank
Ribble
Hutton
Longton
Middleforth Green
Lostock
M6
M55
A590
A595
A5087
A683
A6
A585
A583
A584
A587
A588
A586
A59
A582
98
99
85
86
0 1 2 3 4 5 6 miles
0 1 2 3 4 5 6 7 8 9 10 km

YORKSHIRE DALES NATIONAL PARK
FOREST OF BOWLAND
SD
LANGSTROTHDALE CHASE
THE FOREST OF PENDLE
THE FOREST OF TRAWDEN
RIBBLESDALE
99
100
94
86
87
Old Town
Mansergh
Barbon
Lupton
Kearstwick
Casterton
Kirkby Lonsdale
Hutton Roof
Leck
Cowan Bridge
Nether Burrow
Whittington
Newton
Ireby
Masongill
Westhouse
Ingleton
Burton in Lonsdale
Cantsfield
Tunstall
Arkholme
Melling
Wrayton
Docker Park Farm
Gressingham
Hornby
Tatham
Wennington
Low Bentham
High Bentham
Bentham Pottery
Wray
Farleton
Claughton
Caton Moor
Crossgill
Salter
Goodber Common
Lowgill
Tatham Fells
Haylot Fell
Mewith Head
Keasden
Burn Moor
Catlow Fell
Wenning
Newby
Clapham
Austwick
Feizor
Lawkland
Eldroth
Yorkshire Dales Falconry and Conservation Centre
Ingleborough Common
Ingleborough
Ingleborough Show Cave
Gaping Gill
White Scar Caves
Simon Fell
Scales Moor
Chapel-le-Dale
Crag Hill
Leck Fell
Whernside
Deepdale
Blea Moor
Ribblehead
Gayle Moor
Cam Fell
Cam Beck
High Birkwith
Horton Moor
New Houses
Horton in Ribblesdale
Pen-y-ghent
Helwith Bridge
Wharfe
Little Stainforth
Stainforth
Stackhouse
Watershed Mill Visitor Centre
Langcliffe
Giggleswick
Giggleswick School Chapel
Settle
Wham
Mearbeck
Rathmell
Horses Health Farm
Long Preston
Wigglesworth
Hellifield
Tosside
Gisburn Forest
Stocks Reservoir
Grunsagill
Knotts
Halton West
Nappa
Paythorne
Newsholme
Horton
Forest Becks
Slaidburn
Newton
Lane Ends
Easington Fell
Holden
Bolton-by-Bowland
Sawley
Grindleton
West Bradford
Chatburn
Downham
Rimington
Twiston
Waddington
Clitheroe
Clitheroe Castle Museum
Low Moor
Worston
Pendle Hill
Barley
Pendleton
Newchurch
Pendle Heritage Centre
Barrowford
Sabden
Wiswell
Whalley
Whalley Abbey
Billington
Simonstone
Padiham
Read
Altham
Great Harwood
Clayton-le-Moors
Rishton
Huncoat
Church
Accrington
Oswaldtwistle
Baxenden
Dunnockshaw
Love Clough
Goodshaw
Goodshaw Chapel
Forest of Rossendale
Water
Clow Bridge
Lane Ends
Hapton
Habergham
Rose Grove
Burnley
Worsthorne
Hurstwood
Mereclough
Towneley Hall Art Gallery & Museum & Historic House
Weavers Triangle
Brunshaw
Gawthorpe Hall
Trapp Forge
Higham
Fence
Brierfield
Nelson
Little Marsden
Colne
British in India Mus
Trawden
Winewall
Wycoller
Laneshaw Bridge
Foulridge
Colne Edge
Roughlee
Blacko
Kelbrook
Salterforth
Barnoldswick
Coates
Earby
Thornton-in-Craven
Lane End
Bracewell
Gisburn
West Marton
East Marton
Broughton
Gargrave
Bank Newton
Coniston Cold
Eshton
Flasby
Bell Busk
Otterburn
Airton
Calton
Winterburn
Hetton
Kirkby Malham
Hanlith
Malham
Malham Cove
Malham Tarn
The Settle Loop
New House Farm, Malham
Bordley
Kilnsey
Kirkby Fell
Fountains Fell
Darnbrook Fell
Arncliffe
Hawkswick
Kettlewell
Litton
Littondale
Scoska Wood
Halton Gill
Foxup
Hubberholme
Yockenthwaite
Buckden
Cray
Oughtershaw
Middle Tongue
Cragdale Moor
Pennine Way
Ward's Stone
Mallowdale Fell
White Hill
Croasdale Fell
Tarnbrook Fell
Tarnbrook
Lee Fell
Lee
Abbeystead
Marshaw
Trough of Bowland
Whins Brow
Hawthornthwaite Fell
Fell Top
Sykes
Hareden
Dunsop Bridge
Sykes Fell
Bleasdale Moors
Fair Snape Fell
Bleasdale
Whitewell
Cow Ark
Leagram Gardens
Chipping
Beacon Fell
Whitechapel
Hesketh Lane
Bashall Eaves
Walker Fold
Hodder
Longridge Fell
Knowle Green
New Row
Longridge
Great Mitton
Barrow
Hurst Green
Old Langho
Langho
Goosnargh
St Saviour's Church
Little Town
Ribchester
Mus of Childhood
Roman Museum
Ribble
Grimsargh
Haighton Green
Copster Green
Balderstone
Salesbury
Osbaldeston
Wilpshire
Mellor Brook
Mellor
Samlesbury Hall
Samlesbury
Brockholes Nature Res
Ribbleton
Samlesbury Bottoms
Hoghton Tower
Blackburn
Pleckgate
Brownhill
Feniscowles
Pleasington
Riley Green
Hoghton
Coup Green
Gregson Lane
Bamber Bridge
Walton-le-Dale
Higher Walton
Lower Darwen
Ewood
Shadsworth
Guide
Cornholme
Charlestown
Lydgate
Portsmouth
Blackshaw Head
Widdop Res.
Walshaw Dean Res.
Heptonstall Moor
Boulsworth Hill
Thieveley Pike
Holme Chapel
Haggate
Harle Syke
Burnley Lane
Walk Mill
Milnshaw
Scaitcliffe
West End
Lothersdale
Elslack
Cowling
Carleton
A65
A683
A687
A682
A59
A56
A6068
A646
A671
A666
A6
M6
M65
A679
A680
A678
B6480
B6478
B6479
B6255
B6243
B6245
B6246
B6230
B6254
B6231
B6232
B6251
B6383
B6238
B6268
B5269
B6160

YORKSHIRE DALES NATIONAL PARK
NIDDERDALE
North
SD
SE
Oughtershaw
Cragdale Moor
643 MIDDLE TONGUE
Kidstones
Walden Head
100
101
Carlton Moor
Walden
Gammersgill
West Scrafton
Horsehouse
Coverdale
Braidley
Woodale
Hindlethwaite Moor
Colsterdale Moor
Colsterdale
Ellingstring
High Ellington
Low Ellington
Fearby
Healey
Masham
UREDALE GLASS
THEAKSTON BREWERY VISITOR CENTRE
Swinton
Leighton
Warthermarske
Ilton
Leighton Res.
Roundhill Res.
Masham Moor
544 GREAT HAW
605 LITTLE WHERNSIDE
Scar House Res.
Angram Res.
Yockenthwaite
Hubberholme
Cray
702 BUCKDEN PIKE
Buckden
Foxup
Halton Gill
610
Starbotton
Litton
Littondale
SCOSKA WOOD
KETTLEWELL
Kettlewell
Arncliffe
Hawkswick
Darnbrook Fell
662 FOUNTAINS FELL
PENNINE WAY
704 GREAT WHERNSIDE
Riggs Moor
Middlesmoor
Stean
Lofthouse
Stean Moor
Ramsgill
406 HAMBLETON HILL
Bouthwaite
Dallowgill Moor
Dallow
Carlesmoor
Swetton
Greygarth
Laverton
Grewelthorpe
Kirkby Malzeard
Low Grantley
Grantley
Gouthwaite Res.
Conistone Moor
Kilnsey
KILNSEY PARK
Conistone
Malham Tarn
93
MALHAM TARN
THE SETTLE LOOP
MALHAM COVE
547 KIRKBY FELL
MALHAM
Malham
Bordley
NEW HOUSE FARM, MALHAM
Threshfield
Grassington
UPPER WHARFEDALE MUSEUM
Linton
Hebden Moor
Grimwith Res.
Greenhow Hill
Pateley Bridge
NIDDERDALE MUSEUM
Wath
Heathfield Moor
Pateley Moor
Eavestone
Risplith
Sawley
Bewerley
Glasshouses
Wilsill
BRIMHAM ROCKS
Low Laithe
New York
Dacre Banks
Summer Bridge
Hebden
STUMP CROSS CAVERNS
PARCEVALL HALL GARDENS
Pockstones Moor
Skyreholme
Thorpe
Burnsall
Hanlith
Kirkby Malham
Threapland
Cracoe
Rylstone
506 Upper Barden Res.
Appletreewick
Drebley
449 Barden Fell
Thruscross Res.
West End
Padside
Darley Head
Darley
Thornthwaite
Birstwith
Kettlesing Bottom
Airton
Calton
Winterburn
Hetton
Otterburn
Hellifield
Bell Busk
Flasby
Eshton
Lower Barden Res.
Barden Scale
BOLTON ABBEY ESTATE
Bolton Abbey
Halton East
Eastby
Embsay
EMBSAY & BOLTON ABBEY STEAM RLY
BUFFERS
Hill End
Hazlewood
Pace Gate
409
Blubberhouses
Fewston Res.
Fewston
Kettlesing Head
Timble
Swinsty Res.
Bland Hill
Jack Hill
Coniston Cold
Bank Newton
Gargrave
Thorlby
SKIPTON
Skipton
Halton West
Nappa
219
Newsholme
Horton
Broughton
East Marton
West Marton
Elslack
Carleton
Draughton
Bolton Bridge
Beamsley
Langbar
Addingham
Middleton
Denton
Lindley Wood Res.
Lindley Green
Braythorn
Farnley
Stainburn
Askwith
Clifton
Weston
Newall
Otley
Leathley
Pool
CHEVIN FOREST PARK
Bracewell
Lane End
Thornton-in-Craven
388
Cononley
Low Bradley
Cringles
ILKLEY
Ilkley Moor
402
Burley in Wharfedale
Menston
East Carlton
Guiseley
Yeadon
Rawdon
Barnoldswick
Coates
Earby
EARBY
Salterforth
Kelbrook
Lothersdale
Glusburn
Farnhill
Kildwick
Silsden
Eastburn
Steeton
Sutton-in-Craven
CLIFFE CASTLE
Utley
Riddlesden
EAST RIDDLESDEN HALL
East Morton
Micklethwaite
Hawksworth
Crossflatts
Eldwick
BRACKEN HALL COUNTRYSIDE CENTRE
Baildon
Esholt
Lane Ends
Cowling
New Road Side
Keighley
Braithwaite
Knowle Park
Laycock
Goose Eye
Exley Head
Oakworth
Thwaites
Thwaites Brow
VINTAGE RAILWAY CARRIAGE MUS
BINGLEY
1853 GALLERY
Saltaire
SHIPLEY
Idle
Apperley Bridge
Horsforth
Calverley
Rodley
Foulridge
Colne Edge
Blacko
Roughlee
Laneshaw Bridge
Winewall
Trawden
Wycoller
WYCOLLER
443 KEIGHLEY MOOR
Ingrow
COLNE
BRITISH IN INDIA MUS
NELSON
Little Marsden
Brierfield
THE FOREST OF TRAWDEN
Dockroyd
Lees
BRONTE PARSONAGE MUS
HAWORTH
Haworth
Cullingworth
Harden
Cottingley
Wilsden
Moorhead
Eccleshill
Stanbury
Marsh
PENISTONE HILL
Oxenhope
KEIGHLEY AND WORTH VALLEY RAILWAY
517 BOULSWORTH HILL
PENNINE WAY
Haworth Moor
Lingbob
CARTWRIGHT HALL ART GALLERY
Frizinghall
Heaton
Manningham
Bradford
BRADFORD IND MUS
Undercliffe
Thornbury
Farsley
Bramley
Stanningley
Burnley
Harle Syke
Haggate
Walshaw Dean Res.
Wadsworth Moor
Denholme
Well Heads
Allerton
Thornton
Denholme Clough
Lidget Green
Little Horton
Great Horton
Clayton
Laisterdyke
Bowling
Holme Wood
PUDSEY
Swinnow Moor
Tong
New Farnley
Worsthorne
Hurstwood
Mereclough
Walk Mill
WEAVERS TRIANGLE
TOWNELEY HALL ART GALLERY, MUSEUM & HISTORIC HOUSE
Widdop Res.
Heptonstall Moor
451
Warley Moor Res.
Dean Head Res.
Causeway Foot
Mountain
Queensbury
NAT MEDIA MUSEUM
West Bowling
BOLLING HALL
Bierley
Wibsey
Butterhill
88
Illingworth
Ambler Thorn
Shelf
Low Moor
Oakenshaw
Birkenshaw
Drighlington
Gildersome
Adwalton
Holme Chapel
Colden
Pecket Well
87
Chiserley
Wainstalls
Hebden Bridge
Mount Tabor
Ovenden
Booth
Midgley
Wheatley
Luddenden
Mytholmroyd
WALKLEY CLOGS
BANKFIELD MUSEUM
Northowram
SHIBDEN HALL
Stone Chair
Wyke
Halifax
OAKWELL HALL
RED HOUSE
Birstall
Gomersal
BAGSHAW MUS
Portsmouth
Lydgate
Water
A59
A65
A682
A629
A56
A6068
A6034
A650
A658
A6120
A647
A644
A6036
A58
A646
M606
B6160
B6265
B6451
B6165
B6382
0 1 2 3 4 5 6 miles
0 1 2 3 4 5 6 7 8 9 10 km

Yorkshire
City of York
SE
Thirsk
Sowerby
Carlton Miniott
Sutton-under-Whitestonecliffe
Helmsley
Rye Dale
Duncombe Park
Oldstead
Kilburn
High Kilburn
Wass
Ampleforth
Byland Abbey
Coxwold
Oswaldkirk
Gilling East
Hovingham
Yearsley
Brandsby
Husthwaite
Oulston
Thormanby
Easingwold
Crayke
Stillington
Farlington
Sheriff Hutton
Sutton-on-the-Forest
Sutton Park
Huby
Tollerton
Alne
Flawith
Tholthorpe
Raskelf
Helperby
Brafferton
Cundall
Fawdington
Crakehill
Dalton
Sessay
Hutton Sessay
Birdforth
Little Sessay
Topcliffe
Asenby
Rainton
Dishforth
Baldersby
Skipton-on-Swale
Catton
Melmerby
Nunwick
Hutton Conyers
Ripon
Ripon Cathedral
Sharow
Copt Hewick
Bishopton
Littlethorpe
Bridge Hewick
Marton-le-Moor
Norton-le-Clay
Kirby Hill
Boroughbridge
Aldborough
Aldborough Roman Town
Langthorpe
Roecliffe
Minskip
Bishop Monkton
Markington
Studley Roger
Studley Royal Water Garden
Fountains Abbey
Aldfield
Skelton-on-Ure
Newby Hall
Wormald Green
Burton Leonard
South Stainley
Copgrove
Staveley
Ferrensby
Arkendale
Farnham
Brearton
Knaresborough
Knaresborough Castle & Courthouse Museum
Mother Shipton's Cave
Scotton
Scriven
Coneythorpe
Flaxby
Allerton Mauleverer
Allerton Park
Whixley
Green Hammerton
Kirk Hammerton
Upper Dunsforth
Lower Dunsforth
Myton-on-Swale
Great Ouseburn
Little Ouseburn
Aldwark
Youlton
Linton-on-Ouse
Thorpe Underwood
Newton on Ouse
Beningbrough
Beningbrough Hall
Nun Monkton
Moor Monkton
Shipton
Skelton
Wigginton
Haxby
Strensall
Towthorpe
Earswick
Huntington
New Earswick
Nether Poppleton
Upper Poppleton
Overton
Rawcliffe
Clifton
York
York Minster
Jorvik Viking Centre
National Railway Museum
Heworth
Osbaldwick
Murton
Holgate
Acomb
Knapton
Rufforth
Hessay
Marston Moor
Long Marston
Tockwith
Cattal
Hunsingore
Cowthorpe
Bickerton
Wetherby Services
Hopperton
Goldsborough
Harrogate
Starbeck
Forest Lane Head
Woodlands
Plumpton Rocks
Little Ribston
North Deighton
Kirk Deighton
Follifoot
Spofforth
Spofforth Castle
Spacey Houses
Pannal
Oatlands
Harlow Hill
Beckwithshaw
Rossett Green
Brackenthwaite
North Rigton
Kirkby Overflow
Sicklinghall
Huby
Weeton
Netherby
Dunkeswick
Castley
Wetherby
Linton
Collingham
Chapel Hill
Harewood
Harewood House
East Keswick
Boston Spa
Thorp Arch
Walton
Wighill
Healaugh
Bilton in Ainsty
Hutton Wandesley
Angram
Askham Bryan
Askham Richard
Bilbrough
Catterton
Copmanthorpe
York West Services
Acaster Malbis
Bishopthorpe
Naburn
Deighton
Escrick
Fulford
Heslington
Crockey Hill
Colton
Appleton Roebuck
Acaster Selby
Bolton Percy
Kirkby Wharfe
Ulleskelf
Newton Kyme
Tadcaster
Clifford
Bramham
Bramham Park
Stutton
Towton
Church Fenton
Little Fenton
Biggin
Ryther
Cawood
Kelfield
Stillingfleet
Riccall
Skipwith
Wistow
Barlby
Osgodby
Selby
Selby Abbey
Thorpe Willoughby
Brayton
Hambleton
Monk Fryston
Hillam
Birkin
Burton Salmon
Brotherton
Fairburn
Sherburn in Elmet
Saxton
Barkston
Steeton Hall Gateway
South Milford
Lumby
Ledsham
Ledston
Ledston Luck
Kippax
Great Preston
Allerton Bywater
Mickletown
Methley
Castleford
Garforth
Micklefield
Newthorpe
Lotherton Hall
Aberford
Barwick-in-Elmet
Potterton
Scholes
Thorner
Scarcroft
Bardsey
East Rigton
Wike
Eccup
Alwoodley
Moor Allerton
Shadwell
Roundhay
Seacroft
Whitkirk
Manston
Halton
Colton
Temple Newsam House
Swillington
Rothwell
Oulton
Woodlesford
Middleton
Morley
Beeston
Hunslet
Leeds
Holbeck
Armley
Farnley
Wortley
Headingley
Chapel Allerton
Potternewton
Harehills
Burley
Kirkstall
Meanwood
Adel
Holt Park
Bramhope
Arthington
Weardley
Tingley
East Ardsley
Churwell
Bruntcliffe
Lofthouse
Robin Hood
Carr Gate
Haigh
Cold Kirby
Scawton
Harome
Sproxton
Nunnington
Cawton
Coulton
Scackleton
Stearsby
Dalby
Skewsby
Whenby
West Lilling
Bagby
Balk
Great Thirkleby
Little Thirkleby
Carlton Husthwaite
Pickhill
Holme
Sinderby
Sandhutton
Ainderby Quernhow
Kirklington
Nosterfield
Carthorpe
Well
West Tanfield
Thornborough
Sutton Howgrave
Middleton Quernham
Wath
North Stainley
Mickley
Sutton Grange
Azerley
Galphay
Winksley
Ure Bank
Bishop Thornton
Shaw Mills
Bedlam
Burnt Yates
Ripley
Ripley Castle
Clint
Nidd
Hampsthwaite
Killinghall
New Park
South Kilvington
Cross Lanes
A1(M)
A19
A59
A64
A168
A170
A61
A1237
M1
M62
M621

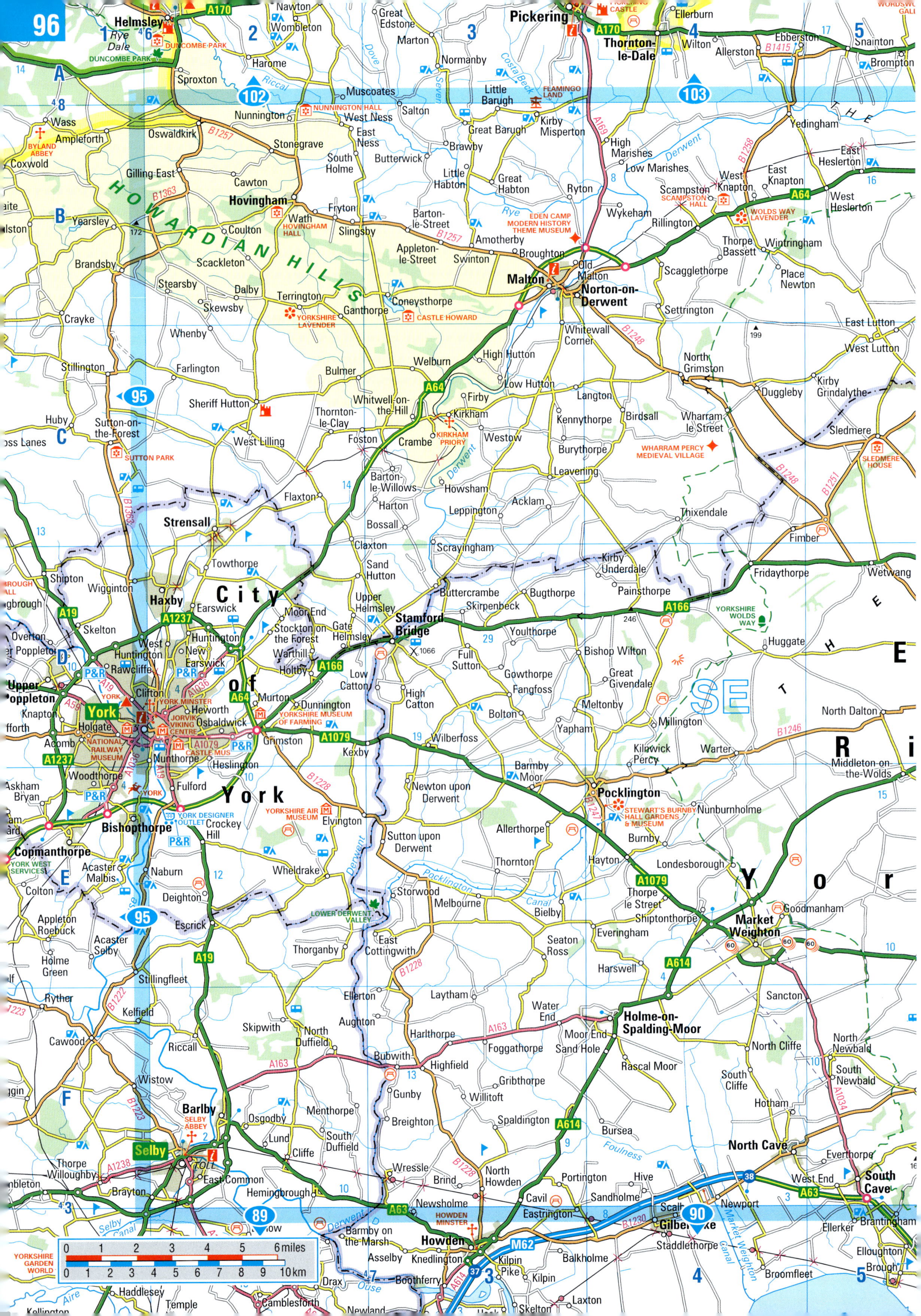

Helmsley
Rye Dale
DUNCOMBE PARK
A170
Nawton
Wombleton
Great Edstone
Marton
Pickering
Thornton-le-Dale
Ellerburn
Wilton
Allerston
Ebberston
Snainton
Brompton
Harome
Sproxton
Normanby
Riccall
102
103
Muscoates
Little Barugh
FLAMINGO LAND
Nunnington
NUNNINGTON HALL
West Ness
Salton
Great Barugh
Kirby Misperton
Wass
Ampleforth
BYLAND ABBEY
Oswaldkirk
B1257
Stonegrave
East Ness
Brawby
High Marishes
Low Marishes
Yedingham
East Heslerton
Coxwold
Gilling East
Cawton
South Holme
Butterwick
Little Habton
Great Habton
Ryton
Scampston
SCAMPSTON HALL
West Knapton
East Knapton
West Heslerton
HOWARDIAN HILLS
Hovingham
Wath
HOVINGHAM HALL
Fryton
Slingsby
Barton-le-Street
EDEN CAMP MODERN HISTORY THEME MUSEUM
Wykeham
Rillington
WOLDS WAY LAVENDER
A64
Yearsley
Coulton
Amotherby
Thorpe Bassett
Wintringham
Brandsby
Scackleton
Appleton-le-Street
Swinton
Broughton
Old Malton
Malton
Norton-on-Derwent
Scagglethorpe
Place Newton
Stearsby
Dalby
Terrington
Coneysthorpe
Skewsby
YORKSHIRE LAVENDER
Ganthorpe
CASTLE HOWARD
Settrington
Crayke
Whenby
Whitewall Corner
B1248
East Lutton
West Lutton
High Hutton
Stillington
Farlington
Bulmer
Welburn
North Grimston
Low Hutton
95
Sheriff Hutton
Whitwell-on-the-Hill
Firby
Langton
Duggleby
Kirby Grindalythe
Huby
Sutton-on-the-Forest
Thornton-le-Clay
Kirkham
Kennythorpe
Birdsall
Wharram le Street
Sledmere
SUTTON PARK
West Lilling
Foston
Crambe
KIRKHAM PRIORY
Westow
Burythorpe
WHARRAM PERCY MEDIEVAL VILLAGE
SLEDMERE HOUSE
Flaxton
Barton-le-Willows
Howsham
Leavening
Harton
Leppington
Acklam
Thixendale
Strensall
Bossall
Claxton
Scrayingham
Fimber
Towthorpe
Sand Hutton
Kirby Underdale
Fridaythorpe
Shipton
Wigginton
Buttercrambe
Bugthorpe
Painsthorpe
Wetwang
Haxby
City
Upper Helmsley
Skirpenbeck
Earswick
Moor End
A19
A1237
Stamford Bridge
A166
YORKSHIRE WOLDS WAY
Skelton
Huntington
Stockton on the Forest
Gate Helmsley
Youlthorpe
Huggate
Overton
West Huntington
New Earswick
Warthill
Full Sutton
Bishop Wilton
Upper Poppleton
Rawcliffe
Holtby
Low Catton
Gowthorpe
Great Givendale
Knapton
Clifton
of
Murton
Fangfoss
York
YORK MINSTER
Heworth
Dunnington
High Catton
Meltonby
Millington
North Dalton
Holgate
JORVIK VIKING CENTRE
Osbaldwick
YORKSHIRE MUSEUM OF FARMING
Bolton
Yapham
Acomb
NATIONAL RAILWAY MUSEUM
A1079
Grimston
Wilberfoss
Kilnwick Percy
Warter
B1246
CASTLE MUS
Kexby
Middleton-on-the-Wolds
Nunthorpe
Heslington
Barmby Moor
Woodthorpe
Askham Bryan
Fulford
Newton upon Derwent
Pocklington
York
B1228
YORKSHIRE AIR MUSEUM
Elvington
STEWART'S BURNBY HALL GARDENS & MUSEUM
Nunburnholme
Bishopthorpe
YORK DESIGNER OUTLET
Crockey Hill
Sutton upon Derwent
Allerthorpe
Burnby
Copmanthorpe
Naburn
Wheldrake
Thornton
Hayton
Londesborough
YORK WEST SERVICES
Acaster Malbis
Deighton
Storwood
Melbourne
Pocklington Canal
Thorpe le Street
Colton
LOWER DERWENT VALLEY
Bielby
Goodmanham
Appleton Roebuck
Escrick
Everingham
Shiptonthorpe
Market Weighton
Acaster Selby
East Cottingwith
Seaton Ross
A614
Holme Green
Thorganby
Harswell
Stillingfleet
Ryther
Kelfield
Ellerton
Laytham
Sancton
Aughton
Water End
Holme-on-Spalding-Moor
Cawood
Skipwith
North Duffield
Harlthorpe
A163
Moor End
Sand Hole
Foggathorpe
North Cliffe
North Newbald
Riccall
Bubwith
Highfield
Rascal Moor
South Newbald
South Cliffe
Wistow
Gunby
Gribthorpe
Willitoft
Hotham
Barlby
SELBY ABBEY
Osgodby
Menthorpe
Breighton
Spaldington
Bursea
Lund
South Duffield
North Cave
Selby
Cliffe
Foulness
Everthorpe
Thorpe Willoughby
A1238
East Common
Wressle
North Howden
Portington
Hive
South Cave
Brayton
Hemingbrough
Brind
Sandholme
West End
A63
Newsholme
Cavil
Newport
Eastrington
Scalby
Gilberdyke
89
90
Selby Canal
HOWDEN MINSTER
Barmby on the Marsh
Howden
M62
Balkholme
Staddlethorpe
Ellerker
Brantingham
Asselby
Knedlington
Kilpin Pike
Kilpin
Broomfleet
Elloughton
Brough
YORKSHIRE GARDEN WORLD
Drax
Boothferry
Ouse
Aire
Haddlesey
Temple
Camblesforth
Laxton
Skelton
Newland
Kellington
Market Weighton Canal
0 1 2 3 4 5 6 miles
0 1 2 3 4 5 6 7 8 9 10 km

Seamer
Irton
Eastfield
Yons Nab
CLEVELAND WAY
Cayton
Lebberston
Gristhorpe
Filey Brigg
Filey
Flixton
Folkton
Willerby
Staxton
Muston
Filey Bay
Primrose Valley
Hunmanby Moor
Reighton Sands
Reighton Gap
Ganton
YORKSHIRE WOLDS WAY
Sherburn
Potter Brompton
Hunmanby
Fordon
Reighton
Speeton
Wold Newton
Foxholes
Burton Fleming
Buckton
Bempton
Butterwick
Grindale
Flamborough
FLAMBOROUGH HEAD
Weaverthorpe
Helperthorpe
Octon
Thwing
SEWERBY HALL AND GARDENS
Sewerby
BONDVILLE MODEL VILLAGE
Octon Cross Roads
Boynton
PRIORY
BAYLE MUSEUM
Rudston
Bridlington
Langtoft
Bessingby
West Hill
OLD PENNY MEMORIES
Carnaby
Hilderthorpe
Cottam
Haisthorpe
BURTON AGNES HALL
Thornholme
Kilham
BURTON AGNES MANOR HOUSE
PARK ROSE BIRD OF PREY CENTRE
BRIDLINGTON BAY
Burton Agnes
Ruston Parva
Harpham
Fraisthorpe
Garton-on-the-Wolds
Lowthorpe
Nafferton
Gransmoor
Barmston
Elmswell
Little Driffield
Driffield
Great Kelk
Lissett
Gembling
Ulrome
Kelleythorpe
Foston on the Wolds
Driffield Canal
Wansford
Tibthorpe
Kirkburn
Southburn
Skerne
SKIPSEA CASTLE
TA
Skipsea
Church End
Brigham
Beeford
Skipsea Brough
Hutton
North Frodingham
Bainton
Hutton Cranswick
Rotsea
Dunnington
Watton
Hempholme
Bewholme
Atwick
Kilnwick
North Cliff
Lund
Beswick
Watton Beck
Burshill
Hornsea
Hornsea Mere
Holme on the Wolds
Lockington
Baswick Steer
Brandesburton
Seaton
HORNSEA MUSEUM
Thorpe
FREEPORT HORNSEA
Hornsea Bridge
South Dalton
Scorborough
Aike
Leven Canal
Leven
Sigglesthorne
Rolston
Arram
Catwick
Goxhill
Etton
Leconfield
Eske
Little Hatfield
Mappleton
Gardham
Cherry Burton
Routh
Rise
Great Hatfield
Great Cowden
Tickton
Long Riston
Arnold
Withernwick
Molescroft
BEVERLEY
Beverley
New Ellerby
Bishop Burton
Weel
Meaux
Skirlaugh
Marton
Aldbrough
BEVERLEY FRIARY
MINSTER
Woodmansey
West Newton
East Newton
Walkington
Wawne
Old Ellerby
BURTON CONSTABLE HALL
Flinton
Bentley
Thearne
Swine
Coniston
Garton
Grimston
Dunswell
High Hunsley
Skidby
Bransholme
Thirtleby
Sproatley
Humbleton
Fitling
Hilston
Little Weighton
Kingston-upon-Hull
Sutton on Hull
Ganstead
Rowley
SKIDBY WINDMILL
Inglemire
Lelley
Cottingham
Sutton Ings
Bilton
Owstwick
Tunstall
Eppleworth
Riplingham
Elstronwick
Stoneferry
Newland
Preston
Burton Pidsea
North End
YORKSHIRE WOLDS WAY
Kirk Ella
Willerby
Sculcoates
Summergangs
WILBERFORCE HOUSE
Roos
West End
Waxholme
Owthorne
West Ella
Anlaby
Marfleet
Salt End
Hedon
Rimswell
Swanland
Welton
STREETLIFE
THE DEEP
Haven Side
Burstwick
Halsham
Withernsea
HUMBER BRIDGE
Northfield
Hessle
FERENS ART GALLERY
KINGSTON UPON HULL
Paull
Camerton
East End
North Ferriby
Thorngumbald
FORT PAULL
Ryehill
Keyingham

1
2
3
4
A
B
C
D
E
F
NX
NY
SC
SD
LAKE DISTRICT NATIONAL PARK
CUMBRIAN MOUNTAINS
Flimby
Broughton Moor
Standingstone
Dovenby
Bridekirk
Bewaldeth
Orthwaite
Siddick
Camerton
Great Broughton
Little Broughton
Papcastle
WORDSWORTH HO
Cockermouth
CASTLEGATE HO
Embleton
Bassenthwaite
Seaton
Great Clifton
Brigham
Derwent
Wythop Mill
WYTHOP MILL
COCKERMOUTH
BASSENTHWAITE LAKE
Bassenthwaite Lake
SKIDDAW FOREST
SKIDDAW HOUSE
931 SKIDDAW
MIREHOUSE
GREAT CALVA
North Side
Workington
Stainburn
HELENA THOMPSON MUS
Bridgefoot
Greysouthen
Little Clifton
Eaglesfield
Deanscales
Westfield
Mossbay
Winscales
SANDYBECK MEADOW
Thornthwaite Forest
Thornthwaite
THORNTHWAITE GALLERIES
Whinlatter Pass
Millbeck
Applethwaite
CUMBERLAND PENCIL MUSEUM
Braithwaite
Harrington
High Harrington
Dean
Branthwaite
Low Lorton
High Lorton
Mosser
Pardshaw
Lorton Vale
Distington
Ullock
Mockerkin
Thackthwaite
HERITAGE/VISITOR CENTRE
WHINLATTER FOREST PARK
GRISEDALE PIKE
Portinscale
Keswick
Lowca
Pica
Moresby
Parton
Asby
Loweswater
Lamplugh
BRACKENTHWAITE FELL
Stair
DERWENT WATER
Bransty
Moresby Parks
Arlecdon
Loweswater Fell
Little Town
DERWENTWATER
THE RUM STORY
WALK MILL
Rowrah
HIGH LEYS
Kirkland
Croasdale
Crummock Water
Rannerdale
Derwent Fells
Grange
HIGH SEAT
Whitehaven
HAIG COLLIERY MINING MUSEUM
Hensingham
Frizington
GREAT BORNE
Buttermere
BUTTERMERE
Buttermere Fell
Watendlath
Saltom Bay
Mirehouse
Cleator Moor
Ennerdale Bridge
Ennerdale Forest
HIGH STILE
Rosthwaite
ST BEES HEAD
Sandwith
Moor Row
Wath Brow
ENNERDALE
BORROWDALE
Borrowdale
Rottington
Cleator
LONGLANDS LAKE
Ennerdale Water
Ennerdale Fell
Liza
BLACK SAIL
HONISTER HAUSE
Seatoller
Stonethwaite
St Bees
PILLAR
Seathwaite
ULLSCARF
Egremont
Wilton
GREAT GABLE
HIGH WHITE STONES
Coulderton
Thornhill
SEATALLAN
Wasdale Head
Middletown
Haile
Calder
Bleng
Nethertown
Beckermet
COPELAND FOREST
SCAFELL PIKE
BOW FELL
Langdale Pikes
Stickle Tarn
Braystones
Calder Bridge
Wast Water
High Sellafield
SELLAFIELD VISITORS CENTRE
Calder Hall
Wellington
WASTWATER
Burnmoor Tarn
Nether Wasdale
The Screes
Gosforth
Santon Bridge
HARDKNOTT FORT
Hard Knott Pass
Wrynose Pass
Brathay
Seascale
Eskdale Green
Beckfoot
Boot
ESKDALE
Eskdale
Cockley Beck
FURNESS FELLS
Holmrook
Irt
HARTER FELL
Seathwaite Tarn
CONISTON COPPERMINES
CONISTON HOLLY HOW
Drigg
Mite
Esk
Birker Fell
THE OLD MAN OF CONISTON
Saltcoats
RAVENGLASS AND ESKDALE RAILWAY & MUS
BATHHOUSE
Ravenglass
MUNCASTER CASTLE & WORLD OWL CENTRE
Devoke Water
Woodend
Hall Dunnerdale
Seathwaite
Ulpha Fell
Broad Oak
Newbiggin
Lane End
WHITFELL
Ulpha
Hoses
CAW
Torver
Stub Place
Corney
Corney Fell
Broughton Mills
Duddon
Hycemoor
Selker Bay
Bootle
Duddon Bridge
Lower Hawthwaite
High Nibthwaite
Water Yeat
Blawith
Broughton in Furness
Lowick Bridge
Black Combe
Hallthwaites
DUDDON MOSSES
Foxfield
Grizebeck
Lowick Green
Gawthwaite
Whitbeck
The Green
The Hill
Kirkby-in-Furness
Beck Side
Broughton Beck
Silecroft
Whicham
Soutergate
Kirksanton
Millom
MILLOM FOLK MUSEUM
Mansriggs
LAUREL & HARDY MUS
Haverigg
Ulverston
Pennington
DUDDON SANDS
Askam in Furness
Ireleth
Lindal in Furness
Swarthmoor
SOUTH LAKES
A596
A595
A66
A5086
B5292
B5291
A591
B5289
B5294
B5295
B5345
B5344
A593
A5084
A5092
B5281
A5093
107
92
0 1 2 3 4 5 6 miles
0 1 2 3 4 5 6 7 8 9 10 km

Penrith
Windermere
Kendal
Kirkby Lonsdale
Appleby-in-Westmorland
Sedbergh
Ambleside
Bowness-on-Windermere
Coniston
Staveley
Milnthorpe
Grange-over-Sands
Arnside
Shap
Tebay
Orton
Pooley Bridge
Glenridding
Patterdale
Grasmere
Rydal
Hawkshead
Near Sawrey
Far Sawrey
Troutbeck
Kentmere
Sadgill
Bampton
Askham
Eamont Bridge
Clifton
Temple Sowerby
Kirkby Thore
Crackenthorpe
Brampton
Long Marton
Dufton
Morland
Great Strickland
Little Strickland
Newby
King's Meaburn
Maulds Meaburn
Crosby Ravensworth
Great Asby
Raisbeck
Gaisgill
Kelleth
Grayrigg
Lambrigg Fell
Burneside
Natland
Oxenholme
Sedgwick
Levens
Crooklands
Endmoor
Heversham
Beetham
Holme
Burton-in-Kendal
Lupton
Barbon
Casterton
Dent
Gawthrop
Middleton
Killington
Millthrop
Cautley
Lowgill
Beck Foot
Crosthwaite
Winster
Cartmel
Cartmel Fell
Newby Bridge
Lakeside
Haverthwaite
Backbarrow
Ulverston
Satterthwaite
Grizedale
Force Mills
Rusland
Finsthwaite
Torver
Bowmanstead
Threlkeld
Scales
Mungrisdale
Troutbeck
Penruddock
Greystoke
Stainton
Dacre
Sockbridge
Tirril
Matterdale End
Dockray
Thirlmere
Wythburn
Helvellyn
Skiddaw
Ullswater
Haweswater Reservoir
Brothers Water
Kirkstone Pass
Windermere
Esthwaite Water
Coniston Water
Rydal Water
Grizedale Forest Park
Shap Fells
Ralfland Forest
Howgill Fells
Langdale Fell
Ravenstonedale Common
Martindale Common
Bampton Common
Long Sleddale
Borrowdale
L A K E   D I S T R I C T   N A T I O N A L   P A R K
C u m b r i a
F U R N E S S   F E L L S
NY
SD
M6
A6
A66
A591
A590
A592
A684
A685
A65
Brougham Castle
Mayburgh Henge
Dalemain
Lowther
Shap Abbey
Acorn Bank
Castlerigg Stone Circle
Aira Force
Holker Hall
Levens Hall
Sizergh
Brantwood
Hill Top
Dove Cottage and Wordsworth Museum
Rydal Mount
Townend
Holehird Gardens
Brockhole
The World of Beatrix Potter
Lakeside and Haverthwaite Railway
Aquarium of the Lakes
Killington Services
Tebay Services
Burton-in-Kendal Services
108
109
100
92
93

Ousby
Skirwith
Kirkland
893 CROSS FELL
MILBURN FOREST
Tees
Trout Beck
MOOR HOUSE-UPPER TEESDALE
639 VIEWING HILL
Harwood Beck
Harwood
Langdon Common
696 CHAPELFELL TOP
Westernhope Moor
675
Newbiggin Common
Bollihope Common
Middleton Common
A
Blencarn
Crowdundle Beck
109
Culgaith
Milburn
772
Dufton Fell
Cow Green Reservoir
767
Widdybank Fell
CAULDRON SNOUT
Langdon Beck
LANGDON BECK
Forest
Ettersgill
110
HIGH FORCE
BOWLEES VISITOR CENTRE
Newbiggin
565
ACORN BANK
Temple Sowerby
Lowmoor Row
Knock
PENNINE WAY
Maize Beck
Cronkley Fell
TEESDALE
Holwick
Middleton-in-Teesdale
B
Cliburn
Kirkby Thore
DUFTON
Dufton
Long Marton
Brampton
Murton Fell
673
NORTH
Mickle Fell
776
LUNE FOREST
Lune Moor
Bowbank
Thringarth
Mickleton
Eggleston
EGGLESTON HALL
Morland
Bolton
King's Meaburn
Crackenthorpe
Murton
Grassholme Reservoir
Grassholme
Romaldkirk
Hunderthwaite
Newby
Colby
Appleby-in-Westmorland
Hilton
Warcop Fell
Lune
Selset Reservoir
Hury
DOW CRAG 549
Hunderthwaite Moor
PENNINES
Hury Reservoir
Burrells
Eden
B6542
A66
Hoff
EDEN VALLEY RAILWAY
Great Ormside
Reagill
Stainmore Common
Balder
Balderhead Reservoir
BALDERSDALE
Clove Lodge
Cotherstone Moor
99
B6260
Maulds Meaburn
Sandford
Warcop
Hillbeck
North Stainmore
Deep Dale
Deepdale Beck
C
Crosby Ravensworth
Drybeck
BROUGH CASTLE
Brough
South Stainmore
Bowes
PENNINE WAY
Oddendale
Great Asby
Bleatarn
Great Musgrave
Little Musgrave
Brough Sowerby
Kaber
Barras
Moudy Mea
A66
Gilmonby
Soulby
A685
Winton
Heggerscales
Bowes Moor
STAINMORE FOREST
Sleightholme
GREAT ASBY SCAR
Crosby Ravensworth Fell
Crosby Garrett
Hartley
Belah
Scargill Moor
Orton
412
Little Asby
KIRKBY STEPHEN
Kirkby Stephen
Winton Fell
Sleightholme Moor
B6261
M6
Raisbeck
Smardale
Waitby
Nateby
NY
510 CLEASBY HILL
D
SMARDALE GILL
662
Lune
Gaisgill
Kelleth
Newbiggin-on-Lune
Ash Fell
B6270
Arkengarthdale Moor
Tebay
A685
Bowderdale
Coldbeck
A683
385
Stonesdale Moor
Whaw
Weasdale
Ravenstonedale
Ravenseat
ROGAN'S SEAT 671
583 GREAT PINSEAT
Birkdale
Common
West Stonesdale
Keld
Melbecks Moor
Outhgill
709
Langdale Fell
Ravenstonedale Common
B6270
494
587
Angram
Kearton
Mallerstang
708
Common
Angram Common
Thwaite
Muker
Gunnerside
Feetham
Howgill Fell
716
GREAT SHUNNER FELL
Satron
Low Row
Lowgill
676 THE CALF
BUTTERTUBS PASS
Crackpot
Beck Foot
A683
Brant Fell
Abbotside Common
YORKSHIRE
E
PENNINE WAY
Abbotside Common
Cautley
SD
Cotterdale
Askrigg Common
M6
Baugh Fell
North Yo
99
Sedbergh
FARFIELD MILL ARTS & HERITAGE CENTRE
Garsdale Head
High Shaw
Askrigg
Newbiggin
KILLINGTON SERVICES (Southbound Only)
A684
Hardrow
Sedbusk
LOW MILL OUTDOOR CENTRE
Millthrop
676
Mossdale Moor
Appersett
DALES COUNTRYSIDE MUSEUM
Bainbridge
Woodhall
Garsdale
WENSLEYDALE POTTERY
Hawes
Worton
Killington
Garsdale
HAWES
Gayle
Burtersett
WENSLEYDALE
Cubeck
Thornton Rust
Dee
556 RISE HILL
Widdale Fell
DALES
Countersett
WENSLEYDALE CREAMERY
Semer Water
Gawthrop
Cowgill
672
Wether Fell
614
Carpley Green
BISHOPDALE VALLEY
Middleton
Dent
Dentdale
Stone House
Wold Fell
B6255
Dodd Fell
Marsett
Stalling Busk
Newbiggin
F
609 CALF TOP
Deepdale
668
Bishopdale Beck
B6160
Old Town
682 CRAG HILL
PENNINE WAY
Cragdale Moor
Barbon
Whernside
Gayle Moor
Mansergh
736
Blea Moor
NATIONAL
Oughtershaw
643 MIDDLE TONGUE
Kidstones
Kearstwick
Casterton
Cam Fell
Walden Head
Kirkby Lonsdale
93
627
Ribblehead
LANGSTROTHDALE CHASE
94
Yockenthwaite
Cray
702 BUCKDEN PIKE
Hubberholme
0 1 2 3 4 5 6 miles
0 1 2 3 4 5 6 7 8 9 10 km
Dale
INGLEBOROUGH
B6479
Cam Beck
High Birkwith
Foxup
Halton Gill
Buckden
Cowan Bridge
Ireby
636
610
PARK

Pikeston Fell
487 AWLAW PIKE
Fir Tree
Hamsterley Forest
Bedburn
Redford
Hamsterley
TOLL
110
Witton-le-Wear
Hunwick
Newfield
Byers Green
Spennymoor
Ferryhill
Trimdon
Middlestone Moor
Kirk Merrington
Ferryhill Station
RISLINGTON
Fishburn
High Grange
Binchester Blocks
BINCHESTER FORT
Westerton
AUCKLAND CASTLE
Middlestone
Mainsforth
Bishop Middleham
Butterwick
Witton Park
Toronto
Escomb
ESCOMB CHURCH
Coundon
Leasingthorne
111
Chilton Lane
Chilton
HARDWICK HALL
Sedgefield
Low Etherley
High Etherley
Bishop Auckland
Rushyford
Toft Hill
ST HELEN'S
Coundon Grange
Eldon
Old Eldon
Bradbury
SEDGEFIELD
Woodland
Morley
St Helen Auckland
Shildon
Middridge
NEWTON AYCLIFFE
Mordon
Wynyard Village
Woodland Fell
Howle
Butterknowle
West Auckland
LOCOMOTION N R M SHILDON
Thorpe Larches
Copley
High Lands
Evenwood
Bildershaw
Foxton
Cockfield
Evenwood Gate
Royal Oak
Redworth
Aycliffe
Stillington
Burnt Houses
Bolam
Elstob
Wackerfield
Heighington
Whitton
Carlton
RABY CASTLE
Hilton
Redmarshall
Kinninvie
Houghton-le-Side
Great Stainton
Bishopton
Ingleton
Walworth Gate
Brafferton
Little Stainton
Staindrop
Killerby
Coatham Mundeville
Cotherstone
Langton
Denton
Skerne
Stainton
Headlam
Summerhouse
Walworth
Beaumont Hill
Barmpton
Cleatlam
Little Newsham
102
Hart
BARNARD CASTLE
THE BOWES MUSEUM
Lartington
Gainford
High Coniscliffe
Harrowgate Hill
Great Burdon
Sadberge
Elton
Startforth
Barnard Castle
Winston
Darlington
Longnewton
HEAD OF STEAM
Westwick
Whorlton
Piercebridge
Haughton-le-Skerne
Urlay Nook
Boldron
EGGLESTONE ABBEY
ROKEBY PARK
Ovington
ROMAN BRIDGE
Low Coniscliffe
Darlington
DURHAM TEES VALLEY
Egglescliffe
BOWES CASTLE
Greta Bridge
Caldwell
Manfield
Cleasby
Middleton St George
Eppleby
Forcett
Hutton Magna
Brignall
Carlton
Stapleton
Blackwell
Middleton One Row
Aislaby
STANWICK IRON AGE FORTIFICATIONS
Lane Head
Stanwick-St-John
Aldbrough St John
Low Dinsdale
Scargill
West Layton
Neasham
Low Worsall
Barningham
Newsham
East Layton
Newton Morrell
Croft-on-Tees
Hurworth Place
High
The Stang Forest
Melsonby
Barton
Eryholme
Girsby
Dalton
Dalton-on-Tees
Ravensworth
BARTON PARK SERVICES
Sockburn
Pictor
Gayles
CROFT
Kirby Hill
Hartforth
Whashton
Middleton Tyas
Hornby
Appleton Wiske
NZ
Gilling West
SCOTCH CORNER SERVICES
Great Smeaton
Scotch Corner
522
Moulton
North Cowton
West Rounton
Atley Hill
Wiske
Langthwaite
Washfold
Arkle Town
Hurst
Richmond
Skeeby
Uckerby
East Cowton
Birkby
Welbury
Arkengarthdale
Deighton
Skelton
EASBY ABBEY
Scorton
Marske
RICHMOND CASTLE
Easby
Healaugh
SWALEDALE MUSEUM
Hudswell
Reeth
Fremington
Colburn
Brompton-on-Swale
CATTERICK
Bolton-on-Swale
Whitwell
Streetlam
Lovesome Hill
East Harlsey
Grinton
Marrick
Downholme
Hipswell
Catterick Bridge
Danby Wiske
SWALE DALE
GRINTON LODGE
Walkerville
Catterick
Brompton
Catterick Garrison
Winton
Stainton
Hipswell Moor
Scotton
Tunstall
Great Langton
Kirby Sigston
SE
Stainton Moor
East Appleton
Kirkby Fleetham
411
Yafforth
Bolton Moor
Redmire Moor
Barden
East Hauxwell
Hornby
Great Fencote
Bullamoor
Hackforth
Thrintoft
Ainderby Steeple
Northallerton
Romanby
Garriston
Little Fencote
Scruton
Yorkshire
Castle Bolton
Bellerby
Hunton
Arrathorne
Langthorne
Morton-on-Swale
BOLTON CASTLE
SWINESIDE CERAMICS
Constable Burton
Warlaby
Preston-under-Scar
Patrick Brompton
Little Crakehall
CRAKEHALL WATER MILL
Redmire
Leyburn
Great Crakehall
Leeming
North Otterington
Thornton-le-Beans
Carperby
Ure
Wensley
THE WENSLEYDALE RAILWAY
Finghall
Newton-le-Willows
Leeming Bar
Sowber Gate
Swale
AYSGARTH FALLS
Swinithwaite
Harmby
Spennithorne
Gatenby
Aiskew
Bedale
Newby Wiske
Aysgarth
WHITE ROSE CANDLES
Middleham
Cowling
Londonderry
South Otterington
Thoralby
West Witton
546 PENHILL
Thornton Steward
Burrill
Exelby
Thornton-le-Street
West Burton
Agglethorpe
MIDDLEHAM CASTLE
JERVAULX ABBEY
Firby
Maunby
Coverham
Thirn
Theakston
Melmerby
East Witton
Thornton Watlass
THORP PERROW ARBORETUM
Burneston
Kirby Wiske
Newsham
Carlton
Caldbergh
SION HILL HALL & BIRDS OF PREY CENTRE
Snape
Carthorpe
Ellingstring
Carlton Moor
Walden
Gammersgill
Coverdale
West Scrafton
High Ellington
Low Ellington
AERIAL EXTREME
Pickhill
South Kilvington
Holme
Sandhutton
Horsehouse
Colsterdale
URE DALE GLASS
Low Burton
Well
Sinderby
Kirklington
Ainderby Quernhow
Colsterdale Moor
Fearby
Healey
Braidley
Hindlethwaite Moor
THEAKSTON BREWERY VISITOR CENTRE
Masham
Binsoe
Nosterfield
Howe
Carlton Miniott
Woodale
544 GREAT HAW
94
Leighton
Swinton
Warthermarske
Thornborough
95
Sutton Howgrave
Skipton-on-Swale
Baldersby
Masham Moor
Leighton Res.
West Tanfield
MARMION TOWER
Middleton Quernham
Catton
605 LITTLE WHERNSIDE
Scar House Res.
Ilton
LIGHTWATER VILLAGE
Roundhill Res.
Mickley
North Stainley
Wath
NORTON CONYERS
Melmerby
Baldersby St James
Topcliffe
Angram Res.
Grewelthorpe
LIGHTWATER VALLEY
Asenby
A68
A688
A689
A167
A1(M)
A6072
A66
A67
A66(M)
A1
A6108
A684
A61
A168
A177
B6282
B6279
B6275
B6274
B6278
B6277
B6444
B6280
B6271
B6268
B6267
B6270
B6286
B6287
B6288
B1263
B1264
B1265
B1276
A6136

Hartlepool
Seaton Carew
Tees Bay
REDCAR
Saltburn-by-the-Sea
Marske-by-the-Sea
Stockton-on-Tees
BILLINGHAM
Middlesbrough
Redcar and Cleveland
Guisborough
Darlington
Sedgefield
Yarm
Eaglescliffe
Thornaby-on-Tees
Stokesley
Great Ayton
Nunthorpe
Skelton
Brotton
Northallerton
Thirsk
Helmsley
Kirkbymoorside
Osmotherley
Brompton
Sowerby
CLEVELAND HILLS
HAMBLETON HILLS
North York Moors
NORTH YORK MOORS NATIONAL PARK
NZ
SE
101
111
95
96
0 1 2 3 4 5 6 miles
0 1 2 3 4 5 6 7 8 9 10 km

5
6
7
8
A
B
C
D
E
F
G
NZ
OV
SE
TA
CHRIS BIRKBECK INTERNATIONAL RALLY SCHOOL
Skinningrove
Carlin How
Loftus
Boulby
Staithes
Easington
Port Mulgrave
Runswick Bay
Hinderwell
Runswick Bay
Kettleness
Goldsborough
Liverton
Roxby
Newton Mulgrave
Ellerby
Scaling
Scaling Dam Res.
Mickleby
East Barnby
West Barnby
Lythe
Sandsend
Sandsend Wyke
THE DRACULA EXPERIENCE
SUTCLIFFE GALLERY
Whitby
Saltwick Bay
WHITBY ABBEY
CAPTAIN COOK MEMORIAL MUSEUM
East Row
Dunsley
Newholm
Ugthorpe
Danby Low Moor
Lealholm Moor
THE MOORS CENTRE
Danby
Ainthorpe
Stonegate
Houlsyke
Lealholm
Ruswarp
Stainsacre
Aislaby
Briggswath
Sleights
Sneaton
Ugglebarnby
High Hawsker
Sneatonthorpe
Ness Pt.
CLEVELAND WAY
Raw
Robin Hood's Bay
OLD COASTGUARD STATION
BOGGLE HOLE
Fylingthorpe
Robin Hood's Bay
Low Garth
Street
Glaisdale
MUSEUM OF VICTORIAN SCIENCE
Egton
Egton Bridge
Grosmont
GROSMONT GALLERY
Esk Valley
Littlebeck
Glaisdale Moor
Egton High Moor
Beck Hole
Goathland
Old Peak
Ravenscar
Flask Inn
Fylingdales Moor
Rosedale Moor
WHEELDALE MOOR ROMAN ROAD
Staintondale
STAINTONDALE SHIRE HORSE FARM
Y O R K   M O O R S
Harwood Dale Forest
Wheeldale Moor
Goathland Moor
Saltergate
Thorgill
Rosedale Abbey
Harwood Dale
Cloughton Newlands
Cloughton Wyke
Cloughton
PICKERING MOOR
Pickering Forest
P A R K
Langdale Forest
Broxa Forest
Cropton
Hartoft End
Stape
Cropton Forest
Spaunton Moor
Burniston
Cromer Pt.
MOORLAND EXPERIENCE
TOLL
Broxa
Silpho
Suffield
SCARBOROUGH SEA LIFE CENTRE
Scalby Ness Rocks
KINDERLAND
Lastingham
Levisham
LOCKTON
Langdale End
Hackness
Scalby
North Bay
Newton-on-Rawcliffe
Lockton
Staindale Forest
Hutton-le-Hole
Spaunton
Wrench Green
Everley
Barrowcliff
Newby
SCARBOROUGH CASTLE
ROTUNDA MUSEUM
Appleton-le-Moors
NORTH RIDING FOREST PARK
Wykeham Forest
Scarborough
Low Dalby
Falsgrave
South Bay
NORTH YORKSHIRE MOORS RAILWAY
FORGE VALLEY WOODLANDS
Keldholme
Sinnington
Wrelton
Aislaby
ST PETER AND ST PAUL CHURCH
DALBY FOREST VISITOR CENTRE
Dalby Forest
East Ayton
THE HONEY FARM
Cayton Bay
Kirkby Mills
Middleton
West Ayton
Osgodby
Great Edstone
PICKERING CASTLE
Ellerburn
Sawdon
WORDSWORTH GALLERY
Hutton Buscel
Irton
Eastfield
Yons Nab
Pickering
Ruston
Seamer
Marton
Thornton-le-Dale
Wilton
Allerston
Ebberston
Snainton
Wykeham
Cayton
Normanby
Brompton
Lebberston
Gristhorpe
Little Barugh
FLAMINGO LAND
Flixton
Folkton
Salton
Kirby Misperton
Yedingham
THE CARRS
Staxton
Muston
Great Barugh
High Marishes
East Heslerton
Sherburn
Ganton
YORKSHIRE WOLDS WAY
Brawby
Butterwick
Low Marishes
Little Habton
Great Habton
Ryton
Scampston
SCAMPSTON HALL
West Knapton
East Knapton
West Heslerton
Potter Brompton
Hunmanby
Fordon
Derwent
Esk
A171
A174
A169
A170
A165
A64
A1039
B1266
B1366
B1410
B1416
B1447
B1415
B1258
B1261
96
97
P&R

Bennane Hd.
112
Colmonell
Knockdolian
265
B734
Ballantrae Bay
Heronsford
Glen Tig
B7044
Ballantrae
Balkissock
Downan Pt.
Auchencrosh
439
BENERAIRD
A77
LARNE 1:00
(Mar-Oct)
LARNE 2:00
BELFAST 2:15
Mark
Glen App
Milleur Pt.
Corsewall Pt.
257
Barnhills
Portencalzie
North Cairn
South Cairn
Corsewall
B738
Loch Connell
Kirkcolm
Cairnryan
Penwhirn Res.
Dounan Bay
Mains of Airies
Ervie
Braid Fell
Low Salchrie
The Wig
B798
LOCH RYAN
Knocknain
Leswalt
Slouchnawen Bay
Craigencross
Innermessan
NW
B7043
A718
A751
Black Loch
CASTLE KENNEDY GARDENS
Glenstockadale
Stranraer
Aird
White Loch
Castle Kennedy
Broadsea Bay
T H E R H I
CASTLE OF ST JOHN VISITOR CENTRE
Knockglass
WIGTOWN DISTRICT MUSEUM
Soulseat Loch
A75
Mark
Lochans
182
Black Hd.
B7077
Dunskey Ho.
A77
Torrs Wa
LITTLE WHEELS
Portpatrick
Awhirk
B7084
Luce Sa
Stoneykirk
A716
Port of Spittal Bay
B7042
Cairngarroch
Sandhead
KIRKMADRINE STONES
Sandhead Bay
Cairngarroch Bay
Money Hd.
Clachanmore
Hole Stone Bay
ARDWELL GDNS
Ardwell
Ardwell Mains
Chapel Rossan Bay
Ardwell Pt.
Logan Mains
LOGAN BOTANIC GARDEN
Balgowan Pt.
Mull of Logan
LOGAN FISH POND MARINE LIFE CENTRE
Port Nessock or Port Logan Bay
Port Logan
Cairnywellan Hd.
B7065
A716
Clanyard Bay
Low Clanyard
Kirkmaiden
Laggantalluch Hd.
Drummore
164
Damnaglaur
B7041
Crammag Hd.
Cairngaan
Port Kemin
0 1 2 3 4 5 6 miles
0 1 2 3 4 5 6 7 8 9 10 km

Poundland
Pinwherry
Bellamore
335 PINDONNAN
Ballochmorrie
Black Clauchrie
Water of Tig
Dusk
Barrhill
Laggan
Eldrick
A714
112
Arecleoch Forest
Chirmorrie
B7027
Drumlamford Loch
Dornal
Loch Dornal
Loch Ochiltree
Loch Maberry
Miltonise
287
Craig Airie Fell
Loch Derry
Polbae
LAGGANGAIRN STANDING STONES
Knowe
Cross Water of Luce
Artfield Fell
244
G A L L O W A Y
F O R E S T
P A R K
Cree
Loch Moan
Water of Minnoch
Palgowan
Glentrool
Forest
Glen Trool Lodge
Trool
BRUCE'S STONE
1307
Glen
Loch Trool
Glentrool Village
GLENTROOL VISITOR CENTRE
Bargrennan
Clachaneasy
Kirroughtree Forest
Loch Middle
716 LAMACHAN HILL
Loch Dee
843 MERRICK
692 MULLWHARCHAR
Loch Enoch
Loch Neldricken
Loch Valley
SILVER FLOWE
RHINNS OF KELLS
814 CORSERINE
Loch Harrow
Loch Dungeon
Forrest Lodge
746
Clatteringshaws Forest
Clatteringshaws Loch
Dumfries and Galloway
353
WILD GOAT PARK
106
A712
Loch Grannoch
Penkiln Burn
Palnure Burn
711 CAINSMORE OF FLEET
CAIRNSMORE OF FLEET
Penninghame Forest
Carseriggan
A714
B7027
Challoch
Minnigaff
MINNIGAFF
Creebridge
Newton Stewart
NX
Black Loch
Loch Heron
Loch Ronald
213
Benfield
Palnure
Clints of Dromore
New Luce
SOUTHERN UPLAND WAY
Auchmantle
Drumphail
205
Tarf Water
Shennanton
A75
B735
B733
Kirkcowan
123
Baltersan
Cree
Causeway End
Whitecairn
Carscreugh
Craighlaw Mains
Water of Luce
GLENWHAN GARDENS
GLENLUCE ABBEY
Dunragit
CASTLE OF PARK
Glenluce
Dernaglar Loch
Knock Moss
High Mindork
Spittal
Carsegowan
GEM ROCK MUSEUM
Creetown
Glen
Torhousemuir
Bladnoch
TORHOUSE STONE CIRCLE
Wigtown Sands
Wigtown
SCOTLAND'S BOOK TOWN
131
B7052
B733
B7005
A747
Whitefield Loch
Milton
Stairhaven
Castle Loch
Fell Loch
T H E
M A C H A R S
Culmazie
Bladnoch
VISITOR CENTRE
Carsluith
CARSLUITH CASTLE
456 CAIRNHARROW
CAIRNHOLY CAIRNS
Auchenmalg
Mochrum Loch
B7005
Braehead
Kirkinner
Baldoon Sands
Ravenshall Pt.
Ringdoo Pt.
Fleet Bay
Auchenmalg Bay
Culshabbin
Alticry
197
Loch Head
Barrachan
B7052
B7085
A746
Whauphill
B7004
CHAPEL FINIAN
Elrig
MOTE OF DRUCHTAG
B7085
75
Sorbie
B7052
Garlieston
Eggerness Pt.
Mochrum
Airyhassen
Milton Pt.
Drumtroddan
Drummoddie
DRUMTRODDAN STONES
GALLOWAY HOUSE GARDENS
B7063
Port William
B7085
Monreith Mains
B7021
Moor of Ravenstone
A746
B7004
Cults
CRUGGLETON CHURCH AND CASTLE
L U C E   B A Y
BARSALLOCH FORT
Barsalloch Pt.
Monreith
Bishopton
Whithorn
Port Allen
MONREITH ANIMAL WORLD, SHORE CENTRE AND MUSEUM
PRIORY AND MUSEUM
WHITHORN TRUST DISCOVERY CENTRE
Monreith Bay
A747
Portyerrock Bay
Glasserton
A746
Cairn Hd.
146 FELL OF CARLETON
B7004
ST NINIAN'S CHAPEL
ST NINIAN'S CAVE
Isle of Whithorn
Port Castle Bay
Cutcloy
BURROW HEAD
Cailliness Pt.
MULL OF GALLOWAY
5
6
7
8
9
A
B
C
D
E
F

Dungeon
Loch Valley
Silver Flowe
746
Drumbuie
Earlstoun Loch
Millquarter
St John's Town of Dalry
Bogue
A702
Corriedoo Forest
417
Loch Urr
Sundaywell
Milton
373
Garroch
Glenlee
113
Blackcraig
Knocklearn
Clatteringshaws Forest
Clatteringshaws Loch
Loch Dee
381
New Galloway
A762
A712
B7075
Balmaclellan
Gibbshill
Glenkiln
398
Glen
Blowplain Open Farm
317
Ironmacannie
Craig
Corsock
An Hill
Clatteringshaws Forest Wildlife Centre
Raiders Road Forest Drive
Dumfries and Galloway
Merkland
Urr Water
Brooklands
353
Bennan Forest
Dee
Loch Ken
A713
Cairn Edward Hill
Drumrash
Crocketford or Ninemile Bar
Auchenreoch Loch
Wild Goat Park
Loch Grannoch
470
Fell of Fleet
Mossdale
Parton
B794
Kirkpatrick Durham
Milton
Stroan Loch
Springholm
A712
Palnure Burn
Cainsmore of Fleet
711
Cairnsmore of Fleet
Loch Skerrow
Woodhall Loch
Old Bridge of Urr
Crossmichael
105
Craig
Fleet Forest
Lochenbreck Loch
Townhead of Greenlaw
Clarebrand
Haugh of Urr
B795
Mote of Urr
Clints of Dromore
Laurieston
Palnure
Laurieston Forest
343
Loch Glentoo
Threave Castle
A711
Old Buittle Tower
182
Barhill
Big Water of Fleet
Cree
Loch Whinyeon
Loch Mannoch
A762
Loch Bargatton
Kelton Mains Open Farm
Castle Douglas
A745
Carlingwark Loch
Dalbeattie
Glengap
Threave Gardens
Bridge of Dee
Rhonehouse or Kelton Hill
366 Bengray
Forest
Glengap
Gem Rock Museum
B736
B727
Creetown
A75
Gelston
B796
Glen
Fleet
Ringford
A711
Dee
Palnackie
Wigtown Sands
Anworth
Mill on the Fleet
Gatehouse of Fleet
Valleyfield
Airieland
Barnbarroch
456
Cairnharrow
Cardoness Castle
Wigtown
Scotland's Book Town
Carsluith
Carsluith Castle
Valley
Girthon
Twynholm
Galloway Hydro Visitor Centre
Tongland
391
Bengairn
Orchardton Tower
Kippford or Scaur
Mote of Mark
Rough Island
Cairnholy Cairns
Broughton House and Garden
East Stewartry Coast
Baldoon Sands
Ravenshall Pt.
Fleet Bay
Barharrow
A755
Whinnieliggate
Sandgreen
Stewartry Museum
Kirkcudbright
Auchencairn
Hestan
Ringdoo Pt.
89
Islands of Fleet
Knockbrex
St Mary's Island
Mutehill
Kirkcarswell
Balcary Pt.
B7004
Kirkandrews
Borgue
135
Dundrennan
Rascarrel
Rascarrel Bay
Sorbie
B7052
Garlieston
Wigtown Bay
Orroland
Eggerness Pt.
Borness
Townhead
Dundrennan Abbey
Galloway House Gardens
B7063
Kirkcudbright Bay
Ross
Netherlaw
Balmae
Port Mary
Borness Pt.
108
Abbey Hd.
Cults
Cruggleton Church and Castle
Little Ross
Whithorn
Port Allen
Portyerrock Bay
Cairn Hd.
St Ninian's Chapel
Isle of Whithorn
Cutcloy
NX
0 1 2 3 4 5 6 miles
0 1 2 3 4 5 6 7 8 9 10 km

Dumfries
Lochmaben
Lockerbie
Locharbriggs
Annan
Maryport
Workington
Cockermouth
Silloth
Aspatria
Allonby
Wigton
Kirkbride
Newton Arlosh
Eastriggs
Bowness-on-Solway
Port Carlisle
Glasson
Drumburgh
Anthorn
Cardurnock
Bowness Common
Whitrigg
Skinburness
Calvo
Seaville
Causewayhead
Greenrow
Blitterlees
Kingside Hill
Abbey Town
Highlaws
Beckfoot
Pelutho
Newtown
Mawbray
Holme St Cuthbert
Edderside
New Cowper
Westnewton
Bromfield
Langrigg
Blencogo
Dundraw
Kelsick
Lessonhall
Waverbridge
Waverton
Waterside
Watchhill
Hayton
Prospect
Oughterside
Allerby
Crosscanonby
Crosby
Crosby-Villa
Bullgill
Gilcrux
Parsonby
Plumbland
Threapland
Blennerhasset
Mealsgate
Boltongate
Torpenhow
Bothel
Ireby
High Ireby
Uldale
Sunderland
Blindcrake
Bewaldeth
Bassenthwaite
Dearham
Tallentire
Bridekirk
Dovenby
Flimby
Broughton Moor
Standingstone
Great Broughton
Little Broughton
Papcastle
Embleton
Wythop Mill
Brigham
Camerton
Seaton
Siddick
Great Clifton
Little Clifton
Bridgefoot
Greysouthen
Eaglesfield
Deanscales
Dean
Low Lorton
Stainburn
Westfield
Mossbay
Harrington
Winscales
Thornthwaite Forest
Thornthwaite
Wedholme Flow
South Solway Mosses
Dubmill Pt.
Allonby Bay
Maryport Maritime Museum
Wordsworth Ho
Helena Thompson Mus
Sandybeck Meadow
Castlegate Ho
Binsey
Mirehouse
Skiddaw
Bassenthwaite Lake
Derwent
Ellen
Waver
Wampool
Over Water
Solway Coast
Solway Firth
Nith Estuary
Blackshaw Bank
Mersehead Sands
Southerness Pt.
Castlehill Pt.
Southerness
Carsethorn
Kirkbean
Arbigland Gardens
John Paul Jones Cottage Museum
Preston mill
Mainsriddle
Caulkerbush
Drumstinchall
Sandyhills
Colvend
Rockcliffe
Portling
Criffell
Drumburn
Overton
Loch Kindar
New Abbey
Sweetheart Abbey
New Abbey Corn Mill
National Mus of Costume
Kirkconnell
Glencaple
Kirkconnell Flow
Mabie Forest
Mabie
Lochaber Loch
Loch Arthur
Beeswing
Kirkgunzeon
Drumcoltran Tower
Long Fell
Islesteps
Kingholm Quay
Kelton
Lochrutton Loch
Lochfoot
Brae
Cargenbridge
Shawhead
Maxwelltown
Dumfries Museum & Camera Obscura
Burns House
Robert Burns Centre
Old Bridge House Mus
Lincluden College
Lincluden
Terregles Banks
Newbridge
Irongray
Drumpark
Holywood
Newtonairds
Galiaberry
Duncow
Amisfield
Kirkton
Tinwald
Heathhall
The Grove
Greystone
Dumfries and Galloway Aviation Mus
Torthorwald
Collin
Greenlea
Racks
Cleughbrae
Mouswald
Lochar Moss
Lochar Water
Bankend
Shearington
Blackshaw
Caerlaverock Castle
Caerlaverock
Eastpark
Bowhouse
Wildfowl and Wetland Centre
Ruthwell
Ruthwell Cross
Duncan Savings Bank Museum
Clarencefield
Cummertrees
Powfoot
Welldale
Shawhill
Dornock
Carrutherstown
Dalton
Hoddom Mains
Hoddomcross
Brydekirk
Charlesfield
Creca
Kirtlebridge
Ecclefechan
Thomas Carlyle's Birthplace
Eaglesfield
Middlebie
Waterbeck
Burnswark
Burnswark Hillfort
Bankshill
Castlemilk
Kettleholm
Middleshaw
Birkshaw Forest
Hightae
Heck
Castle Loch
Lochmaben Castle
Rammerscales House
Marjoriebanks
Applegarthtown
A74(M)
A75
A76
A701
A709
A710
A711
A595
A596
A66
A591
A594
B725
B724
B7020
B6357
B5302
B5300
B5301
B5307
B5299
B793
114
108
98
NX
NY

Lockerbie
Paddockhole
Langholm
MALCOLM MONUMENT
Tinnisburn Forest
Kershopefoot
Kershope Forest
Bankshill
Kirtleton
Caulside
115
Burnswark
BURNSWARK HILLFORT
GILNOCKIE TOWER
Claygate
Baileyhead
Waterbeck
Rowanburn
Crossings
Blackpool Gate
Evertown
Canonbie
Catlowdy
Middlebie
KIRKCONNEL CHURCHYARD
BIRRENS FORT
Springkell
Milltown
Woodhouselees
Riddings
Roughsike
Roadhead
Ecclefechan
THOMAS CARLYLE'S BIRTHPLACE
Eaglesfield
Haggbeck
Moat
Hoddomcross
Chapelknowe
SCOTS DYKE
Kirtlebridge
MERKLAND CROSS
Hoddom Mains
Netherby
Easton
Stapleton
Kirkpatrick-Fleming
Brydekirk
Creca
Newton
Hollee
GRETNA GREEN SERVICES
OLD BLACKSMITHS SHOP CENTRE
Charlesfield
107
Longtown
Boltonfellend
Kirkcambeck
Springfield
Gretna Green
Annan
Gretna
Rigg
Kirklinton
Hethersgill
Powfoot
Welldale
Shawhill
Dornock
Eastriggs
GRETNA GATEWAY
Browhouses
Sandysike
Westlinton
Smithfield
Walton
VALLUM
NY
Scaleby Hill
Scaleby
Newtown
Bowness-on-Solway
Port Carlisle
Todhills
TODHILLS SERVICES
Blackford
Laversdale
Irthington
Brampton
Rockcliffe
Eden
Glasson
COURSE OF HADRIAN'S WALL
Harker
CARLISLE
Bowness Common
Drumburgh
HADRIAN'S WALL PATH
Burgh by Sands
Beaumont
Cargo
Kingstown
Houghton
Linstock
Low Crosby
Newby East
Cardurnock
Anthorn
Easton
Boustead Hill
Grinsdale
Edentown
DRUMBURGH MOSS
Whitrigg
Kirkandrews upon Eden
Hayton
Warwick on Eden
Fingland
FINGLANDRIGG WOODS
Thurstonfield
Stanwix
Carlisle
Kirkbride
Kirkbampton
Moorhouse
CARLISLE
TULLIE HOUSE MUS & GALL
Warwick Bridge
How
Castle Carrock
Newton Arlosh
Oughterby
Little Bampton
Little Orton
CATH
Scotby
Heads Nook
Faugh
Botcherby
Great Orton
Morton
Newby West
Wetheral
Great Corby
WETHERAL PRIORY GATEHOUSE
Calvo
Seaville
Wedholme Flow
Aikton
Harraby
Upperby
Wiggonby
Cummersdale
Cumwhinton
Cumwhitton
Kingside Hill
SOUTH SOLWAY MOSSES
Baldwinholme
Carleton
CARLISLE
Brisco
Durdar
Abbey Town
Kelsick
Oulton
Lessonhall
Dalston
Cotehill
Hornsby
Cumrew
Dundraw
Waverbridge
Thursby
Buckabank
Wreay
Holmwrangle
Blencogo
Wigton
West Curthwaite
East Curthwaite
Bromfield
Waverton
Gaitsgill
Aiketgate
Ainstable
Langrigg
Waterside
Brackenthwaite
Low Hesket
Armathwaite
Red Dial
Rosley
Raughton Head
Stockdalewath
SOUTHWAITE SERVICES
Westnewton
Westward
Welton
Southwaite
High Hesket
Ruckcroft
Bolton Low Houses
HIGH HEAD SCULPTURE VALLEY
Old Town
Watchhill
Fletchertown
Ivegill
Aspatria
Brocklebank
Sebergham
Low Braithwaite
Staffield
Mealsgate
Blennerhasset
Boltongate
Cumbria
Inglewood Forest
Thomas Close
Calthwaite
Lazonby
Sandale
Sowerby Row
Threapland
Torpenhow
Caldbeck
Hesket Newmarket
Lazonby Fell
Townhead
Plumbland
Whitrigg
Ireby
Hutton End
Bothel
Fell Side
Branthwaite
Millhouse
New Rent
HUTTON-IN-THE-FOREST
Plumpton
Brockleymoor
Uldale
High Ireby
Low Row
Lamonby
Unthank
Skelton
Unthank End
Plumpton Head
BINSEY
Sunderland
High Row
Ellonby
Blindcrake
Over Water
HIGH PIKE
Bewaldeth
Hutton Roof
Orthwaite
KNOTT
Mosedale
Johnby
Little Blencow
Catterlen
Derwent
Bassenthwaite
Great Blencow
Laithes
Fair Hill
Embleton
GREAT CALVA
Greystoke
Newton Reigny
Penrith
SKIDDAW FOREST
Mungrisdale
BASSENTHWAITE LAKE
Wythop Mill
WYTHOP MILL
98
SKIDDAW HOUSE
Berrier
99
Newbiggin
Carleton
Motherby
BLENCATHRA
Eamont Bridge
Penruddock
SADDLEBACK OR BLENCATHRA
Stainton
Scales
Troutbeck
TARN MOSS
DALEMAIN
RHEGED
Sockbridge
Clifton
Hutton
Dacre
Tirril
Thornthwaite
Applethwaite
Threlkeld
CUMBERLAND
0 1 2 3 4 5 6 miles
0 1 2 3 4 5 6 7 8 9 10 km

NORTHUMBERLAND NATIONAL PARK
NY
Bellingham
Haltwhistle
Haydon Bridge
Hexham
Alston
Middleton-in-Teesdale
Greenhead
Gilsland
Bewcastle
Spadeadam Forest
Kielder Mires
Wark Forest
Hadrian's Wall Path
Course of Hadrian's Wall
Housesteads Roman Fort
Chesterholm Museum (Vindolanda)
Birdoswald Roman Fort
Roman Army Museum
Chesters Roman Fort
Brunton Turret
Pennine Way
A69
A686
A689
B6277
B6295
Allendale Town
Allenheads
Nenthead
Nenthead Mines Heritage Centre
North of England Lead Mining Museum
South Tynedale Railway
Gossipgate Gallery
Garrigill
Alston Moor
Geltsdale Middle
King's Forest of Geltsdale
Gilderdale Forest
Milburn Forest
Moor House-Upper Teesdale
Cow Green Reservoir
Cauldron Snout
High Force
Bowlees Visitor Centre
Langdon Beck
Weardale
St John's Chapel
Westgate
Cowshill
Wearhead
Burnhope Reservoir
Rookhope
Rookhope Nurseries
Blanchland
Hunstanworth
Slaley Forest
Whitfield
Ninebanks
Langley
Catton
Sinderhope
Allendale Common
Hexhamshire Common
Melmerby
Melmerby Fell
Cross Fell
Kirkland
Culgaith
Milburn
Dufton Fell
Cronkley Fell
Acorn Bank
Brougham Castle
Mayburgh Henge
Wetheriggs Country Pottery
Cliburn Moss
Temple Sowerby
Newbiggin
Knock
N O R T H P E N N I N E S
116
110
99
100

Ridsdale
Redesmouth
Sweethope Loughs
Great Bavington
Thockrington
Kirkharle
Capheaton
Wansbeck
Bolam Lake
Meldon
Bolam
Molesden
Whalton
Tranwell
Clifton
Choppington
Bedlington
Nedderton
Shilvington
Saltwick
Harnham
Belsay
Belsay Hall
Little Bavington
Kirkheaton
Ogle
Kirkley Hall
Stannington
Plessey Woods
Birtley
Wark
Colt Crag Reservoir
Hallington Reservoir
Hallington
Black Heddon
West Newham
Milbourne
Higham Dykes
Berwick Hill
Northumberland Cheese Farm
Great Swinburne
Colwell
Ingoe
Par End
Gunnerton
Ryal
Brenkley
Seaton Burn
Dinnington
Simonburn
Barrasford
Fenwick
Heugh
Ponteland
Brunswick Village
Northumberland
Haughton Castle
Chollerton
Humshaugh
Chollerford
Bingfield
Matfen
Stamfordham
Dalton
Prestwick
Hazlerigg
Darras Hall
High Callerton
Newcastle International
Woolsington
Course of Hadrian's Wall
Hadrian's Wall Path
Walwick
Low Brunton
Brunton Turret
Chesters Roman Fort
Great Whittington
Ouston
Eachwick
Medburn
Black Callerton
Kenton Bankfoot
Gosforth
Wall
Hill Head
Halton
Harlow Hill
Newbrough
Fourstones
Hadrian's Wall Path
North Walbottle
Westerhope
Kenton
Aydon Castle
Aydon
Warden
Acomb
Sandhoe
Tyne Green
Newton Hall
Horsley
Heddon-on-the-Wall
Throckley
Walbottle
Newcastle upon Tyne
George Stephenson's Birthplace
Wylam Railway Mus
Tyne Riverside
Newburn
Low Gate
Haydon Bridge
Moothall
Abbey
Corbridge
Newton
Wylam
Clara Vale
Ovingham
West Wylam
Ryton
Scotswood
Newcastle Discovery
Hexham
Border History Mus
Dilston
Dilston Physic Gdn
Ovington
Crawcrook
Blaydon
Metroland
Dunston
Cherryburn
Prudhoe
Branch End
Mickley Square
Greenside
Winlaton
Whickham Thorns Centre
Riding Mill
Broomhaugh
Stocksfield
High Mickley
Coalburns
Barlow
Whickham
Painshawfield
Leadgate
High Spen
Derwent Walk
Sunniside
Street Gate
Chowdene
Broomley
New Ridley
Hedley on the Hill
Highfield
Chopwell
Rowlands Gill
Gibside
Byermoor
Marley Hill
Lamesley
Dye House
Dalton
Slaley
Healey
Highland Cattle Centre
Whittonstall
Blackhall Mill
Derwentcote Steel Furnace
Angel of the North
Whitley Chapel
Hamsterley
St Andrew's Church
Burnopfield
Leazes
Kibblesworth
Allendale Town
Slaley Forest
Kiln Pit Hill
Newlands
Ebchester
Hobson
Tanfield Railway
High Westwood
Medomsley
Tanfield
Beamish
Urpeth
Hexhamshire Common
Broadwall House
Derwent Res.
Shotleyfield
Dipton
Tantobie
Tanfield Lea
Stanley
Catchgate
West Pelton
Perkinsville
Sinderhope
Allendale Common
Blanchland Moor
Carterway Heads
Bridgehill
Shotley Bridge
Leadgate
The Middles
Grange Villa
Pow Hill
Consett
Annfield Plain
Craghead
Chester-le-Street
Blanchland
Edmundbyers
Templetown
Iveston
Waldridge
Spartylea
Muggleswick
Allensford
Knitsley
Delves
Maiden Law
Edmondsley
Hunstanworth
Nookton Fell
Castleside
Burnhope
Muggleswick Common
Horsleyhope
Lanchester
Broom House Farm
Sacriston
Dirt Pot
Allenheads
NY
NZ
Bolt's Law
Waskerley
East Butsfield
Witton Gilbert
Diggerland
Langley Park
North
Rookhope
Rookhope Nurseries
Stanhope Common
Cornsay
Hall Hill Farm
Cornsay Colliery
Satley
Quebec
Esh
Bearpark
Lanehead
Middlehope Moor
Collier Law
Tunstall Res.
Ushaw Moor
Broompark
Esh Winning
Waterhouses
High Stoop
New Brancepeth
Cowshill
Wearhead
Crawleyside
Wolsingham Park Moor
Durham Dales Centre
Stanhope
Weardale
Westgate
Eastgate
Tow Law
East Hedleyhope
Brandon
Ireshopeburn
St John's Chapel
Daddry Shield
Weardale Railway
Frosterley
Wolsingham
Durham
Sunniside
Brancepeth
Billy Row
Thornley
Ireshope Moor
Pennines
Hill End
Wear
Crook
Helmington Row
Oakenshaw
Willington
Page Bank
Fir Tree
Byers Green
Westernhope Moor
Bollihope Common
Howden-le-Wear
Hunwick
Newfield
Middlestone Moor
Langdon Common
Chapelfell Top
Pikeston Fell
High Grange
Binchester Fort
Binchester Blocks
Westerton
Witton-le-Wear
Langdon Beck
Newbiggin Common
Middleton Common
Pawlaw Pike
Bedburn
Witton Park
Toronto
Auckland Castle
Coundon
Forest
Ettersgill
Redford
Hamsterley
Escomb Church
Escomb
Tees
High Force
Bowlees Visitor Centre
Hamsterley Forest
Low Etherley
High Etherley
Bishop Auckland
Cronkley Fell
Toft Hill
St Helen's
Eldon
Coundon Grange
Middleton-in-Teesdale
Woodland Fell
Woodland
Howle
Morley
Butterknowle
West Auckland
St Helen Auckland
Shildon
0 1 2 3 4 5 6 miles
0 1 2 3 4 5 6 7 8 9 10 km
A68
A69
A696
A1
A19
A167
A692
A693
A694
A695
A691
A689
A688
A6079
B6318
B6342
B6320
B6319
B6305
B6306
B6307
B6309
B6321
B6278
B6296
B6301
B6297
B6299
B6282
116
117
109
100
101

6
7
8
9
A
B
C
D
E
F
G
117
101
102
NZ
BLYTH
West Sleekburn
Cambois
East Sleekburn
Bedlington Station
Cowpen
Bebside
Newsham
East Hartford
New Delaval
Shankhouse
Nelson Village
New Hartley
Seaton
Seaton Sluice
SEATON DELAVAL HALL
Hartley
East Cramlington
Seaton Delaval
ST MARY'S LIGHTHOUSE
St Mary's or Bait I.
Holywell
Seghill
Annitsford
Burradon
Backworth
Earsdon
WHITLEY BAY
AMSTERDAM 15:30
Camperdown
Killingworth
Monkseaton
Shiremoor
Cullercoats
BLUE REEF AQUARIUM
TYNEMOUTH CASTLE & PRIORY
Marden
Longbenton
STEPHENSON RAILWAY MUSEUM
Tynemouth
ARBEIA ROMAN FORT AND MUSEUM
THE RISING SUN
North Shields
Willington
Jesmond
WALLSEND
ROYAL QUAYS
South Shields
SOUTH SHIELDS MUSEUM
Heaton
Tyne Tunnel
Jarrow
BEDE'S WORLD
ST PAUL'S MONASTERY
Westoe
THE LEAS AND MARSDEN ROCK
Marsden Bay
Byker
NEWCASTLE
SEGEDUNUM FORT
Harton
Marsden
CASTLE KEEP
Walker
Hebburn
SOUTER LIGHTHOUSE
Gateshead
INTERNATIONAL STADIUM
Hedworth
Whiteleas
Cleadon
Whitburn Colliery
Boldon Colliery
Pelaw
Whitburn
Felling
Carr Hill
Boldon
FULWELL WINDMILL
Fulwell
Roker
Low Fell
Downhill
Hylton Castle
Southwick
Monkwearmouth
Wrekenton
NATIONAL GLASS CENTRE
ST PETER'S CHURCH
SUNDERLAND MINSTER
STATION MUS
Usworth
Castletown
Springwell
Blackfell
South Hylton
Pallion
Birtley
WASHINGTON
High Barnes
Sunderland
WASHINGTON SERVICES
Lambton
Pennywell
Hendon
THE WILDFOWL & WETLANDS TRUST
PENSHAW MON
Ouston
New Silksworth
Barley Mow
Fatfield
Penshaw
Rickleton
East Herrington
Tunstall
Ryhope
Shiney Row
New Herrington
Doxford Park
RYHOPE ENGINES MUS
Bournmoor
Newbottle
Burdon
Seaton
Northlea
Chester Moor
Fence Houses
HOUGHTON-LE-SPRING
SEAHAM
Great Lumley
Colliery Row
West Lea
Plawsworth
East Rainton
Dalton-le-Dale
West Rainton
Hetton-le-Hole
Cold Hesledon
Kimblesworth
FINCHALE PRIORY
Leamside
Murton
Hawthorn
DALTON PARK
Pity Me
Low Moorsley
Easington Lane
South Hetton
Beacon Pt.
Framwellgate Moor
Pittington
Easington Colliery
Carrville
DURHAM LIGHT INFANTRY MUS
Littletown
Easington
Sherburn
Sherburn Hill
Haswell
Haswell Plough
Shotton Colliery
DURHAM CITY
DURHAM CATH
Horden
DURHAM UNIV ORIENTAL MUS
Ludworth
Shincliffe
Shadforth
PETERLEE
Thornley
Old Cassop
Shotton
CASTLE EDEN DENE
Blackhall Colliery
Wheatley Hill
Blackhall Rocks
Castle Eden
Sunderland Bridge
Bowburn
Old Quarrington
CASSOP VALE
High Hesleden
Hesleden
DURHAM SERVICES
Wingate
Deaf Hill
DURHAM COAST
Hett
Quarrington Hill
Croxdale
Station Town
Hart Station
Tudhoe
Kelloe
Trimdon Colliery
Hutton Henry
Coxhoe
Trimdon Grange
Sheraton
Hart
Spennymoor
Cornforth
Trimdon
ST HILDA'S PARISH CHURCH
HARTLEPOOL'S MARITIME EXPERIENCE
High Throston
Hartlepool Bay
Ferryhill
THRISLINGTON
Ferryhill Station
Fishburn
Elwick
West Park
SUMMERHILL
Hartlepool
Kirk Merrington
Mainsforth
Bishop Middleham
Dalton Piercy
Rift House
Seaton Carew
Middlestone
Chilton Lane
Butterwick
Leasingthorne
Chilton
HARDWICK HALL
Rushyford
Sedgefield
Tees Bay
Bradbury
SEDGEFIELD
Greatham
Middridge
NEWTON AYCLIFFE
Mordon
Wynyard Village
Graythorp
Newton Bewley
Salt Scar
Thorpe Larches
WYNYARD
COWPEN
A189
A192
A193
A1061
A190
A191
A1058
A19
A187
A185
A194
A1300
A184
A194(M)
A1018
A183
A1231
A1290
A693
A690
A182
A167
A1(M)
A1086
A179
A177
A181
A689
A178
B1404
B1285
B1283
B1280
B1432
B1287
B1278
B1281
B1276
B1277
Hartlepool

Troon
North Bay
South Bay
Lady Isle
LARNE 2:00 (March-Oct)
Barassie
Muirhead
Loans
Symington
Bogend
Craigie
Crossroads
Hansel Village
Millburn
Auchmillan
Mossgiel
Mauchline
Monkton
Tarbolton
BACHELOR'S CLUB
BURN'S HOUSE MUSEUM
GLASGOW PRESTWICK
Prestwick
Failford
AYR GORGE WOODLANDS
Woodfield
St Quivox
Mossblown
Haugh
Newton on Ayr
Wallacetown
Annbank
Stair
Crosshill
Whitletts
Trabboch
Ochiltree
Ayr
Belston
Seafield
Masonhill
Coylton
Coalhall
Belmont
ROBERT BURNS BIRTHPLACE MUS
MACLAURIN GALLERY & ROZELLE HOUSE
Hillhead
Drongan
Heads of Ayr
HEADS OF AYR FARM PARK
Doonfoot
Laigh Glengall
Joppa
Alloway
BURNS NATIONAL HERITAGE PARK
TAM O'SHANTER EXPERIENCE
Barbieston
Martnaham Loch
Fisherton
Sinclairston
Hayhill
Littlemill
Dunure
Rankinston
Culroy
Hollybush
Minishant
Dalrymple
ELECTRIC BRAE
Water of Coyle
Culzean Bay
Polnessan
KILMEIN HILL
NS
CULZEAN CASTLE
Whitefaulds
Maybole
COLLEGIATE CHURCH
Patna
Burnfoot
Waterside
Maidenhead Bay
Kirkmichael
Aitkenhead
Loch Spallander Reservoir
DOON VALLEY HERITAGE MUSEUM
BENBEOCH
SCOTTISH INDUSTRIAL RAILWAY CENTRE
Maidens
Kirkoswald
CROSSRAGUEL ABBEY
Crosshill
Burnton
TURNBERRY
Turnberry Bay
SOUTER JOHNNIE'S COTTAGE
Turnberry
Brest Rocks
BLAIRQUHAN
Dalmellington
CATHCARTSON VISITOR CENTRE
Bogton Loch
Straiton
Bellsbank
Ruglen
Townhead
South
Wallacetown
Dipple
Burnhead
Dailly
BIG HILL OF GLENMOUNT
BARGANY GARDENS
Old Dailly
Ayrshire
Penkill
Girvan
Houdston
Linfern Loch
Tairlaw Forest
Loch Finlas
Glendoune
Penwhapple Res.
Loch Bradan
LOCH DOON
LOCH DOON CASTLE
Lamloch
MULL OF MILJOAN
Dalwyne
Craigmalloch
Woodland Bay
South Balloch
Tormitchell
CARRICK
Pinminnoch
Barr
Changue Forest
CARRICK FOREST
Loch Riecawr
Kennedy's Pass
Auchensoul
GREY HILL
Pinmore
Loch Macaterick
Merkland
Currarie
Straid
Lendalfoot
CRAIGENREOCH
MEAUL
Pinmore Mains
Gala Lane
CARLETON CASTLE
Poundland
PINDONNAN
NX
CORSERINE
Pinwherry
GALLOWAY
MULLWHARCHAR
Loch Harrow
Colmonell
Bellamore
Knocdolian
Loch Moan
MERRICK
Loch Enoch
Ballochmorrie
Black Clauchrie
Water of Minnoch
Palgowan
Loch Neldricken
RHINNS OF KELLS
Heronsford
Glen Tig
Water of Tig
FOREST
SILVER FLOWE
Loch Valley
Barrhill
Laggan
Eldrick
Glentrool
Forest
Balkissock
BRUCE'S STONE
Glen Trool Lodge
Trool
Clatteringshaws
Arecleoch Forest
Loch Trool
Glentrool Village
GLENTROOL VISITOR CENTRE
PARK
Loch Dee
Drumlamford Loch
Dornal
Bargrennan
LAMACHAN HILL
Loch Dornal
miles
km

East Ayrshire
Dumfries and Galloway
NS
NX
Glengavel Reservoir
Avon
434 WEDDER HILL
466 MIDDLEFIELD LAW
522 NUTBERRY HILL
River Wethan
Braehead
Happendon
HAPPENDON (CAIRN LODGE) SERVICES
Uddington
406
Douglas West
Douglas Water
Roberton Law
Robertc
M74
119
Glenbuck
465 HARESHAW HILL
Netherwood
Glespin
Smallburn
Muirkirk
Kames
SORN CASTLE
Catrine
Sorn
Airds Moss
392 AUCHENSAUGH HILL
Middle Muir
Glentaggart
Crawfordjohn
593 CAIRN TABLE
Cronberry
Back Rogerton
Auchinleck
Lugar
Glenmuir
497 WARDLAW HILL
Glenmuirshaw
Holmhead
Logan
KEIR HARDIE STATUE
Cumnock
BAIRD INSTITUTE MUS.
Netherthird
Craigens
Dalblair
Glenmuir Water
Duneaton Water
DRAKE LAW 483
478 MOUNT STUART
LOWTHER HILLS
494 RAKE LAW
553 WELLGRAIN DOD
114
Skares
DOON VALLEY RARE BREEDS CENTRE
Fingland
509 KIRKLAND HILL
Kirkland
Crawick Water
Elvan Water
Leadhills
LEADHILLS & WANLOCKHEAD RLY
MUSEUM OF LEAD MINING
WANLOCKHEAD BEAM ENGINE
Wanlockhead
LOTUS LODGE
Pathhead
Mansfield
Nith
Connel Park
Bankglen
New Cumnock
Kirkconnel
A76
485 CONRIG HILL
732 GREEN LOWTHER
Kelloholm
Crawick
Sanquhar
Mennock Pass
725 LOWTHER HILL
Burnside
Dalleagles
THE KNIPE 575
Afton Water
TOLBOOTH MUSEUM
SANQUHAR POST OFFICE
Kello Water
Mennock
SOUTHERN UPLAND WAY
Potrail Water
569 ENOCH HILL
700 BLACKCRAIG HILL
Euchan Water
449 CAIRN HILL
Afton Reservoir
478
Durisdeermill
DURISDEER PARISH CH
Durisdeer
BALLENCLE
Enterkinfoot
554 CAIRNKINNA HILL
Scar Water
Enoch
Carsphairn Forest
Holestane
443
MORTON CASTLE
DRUMLANRIG CASTLE
800
797 CAIRNSMORE OF CARSPHAIRN
Corlae
580 BENBRACK
Benbuie
Auchenbrack
Shinnel Water
Carronbridge
Auchenbainzie
Gatelawbridge
Brockloch
Burnhead
Penpont
Thornhill
Water of Ken
372
Tynron
Dalwhat Water
Garryhorn
Carsphairn
CAIRN AVEL
Bardennoch
SOUTHERN UPLAND WAY
Keir Mill
Closeburn
Dundeugh Forest
Knowehead
Kendoon Loch
Craigdarroch
Moniaive
JAMES PATERSON MUSEUM
Kirkland
357
Park
Castlemaddy
Glencrosh
MAXWELTON HOUSE
THE GLENKENS
Dundeugh
Kendoon
KENDOON
Glenhoul
Black Water
385 WETHER HILL
Castlefairn
Straith
Dalmacallan Forest
Wallaceton
Glenmidge
Auldgirth
Forrest Lodge
Carsfad Loch
Holmhead
Lochinvar
Lochurr
432 BOGRIE HILL
Loch Dungeon
417
Loch Urr
Dunscore
Sundaywell
Milton
Cairn Water
Earlstoun Loch
Millquarter
Drumbuie
St John's Town of Dalry
Bogue
Corriedoo Forest
373
240
Garroch
Glenlee
Blackcraig
Newtonairds
Drumpark
Holywoo
Knocklearn
106
Irongray
Glenkiln Res.
New Galloway
Balmaclellan
Gibbshill
381
BLOWPLAIN OPEN FARM
Glenkiln
398 Glen
Terregles Banks
317
Ironmacannie
Corsock
Shawhead
CLATTERINGSHAWS FOREST WILDLIFE CENTRE
A70
A76
A713
A702
A712
A762
B729
B7000
B743
B705
B7036
B741
B740
B797
B7040
B7078
A
B
C
D
E
F
G
5
6
7
8
9

Happendon
Uddington
Douglas
Douglas Water
ST BRIDES
M74
Roberton Law
Roberton
Wiston
Newton
DUNGAVEL HILL
120
Lamington
Coulter
A702
Clyde
Cowgill Upper Reservoir
Culter Water
CULTER FELL
748
Culter Waterhead Reservoir
Drumelzier
Holms Water
BLAKEHOPE HEAD
543
PYKESTONE HILL
737
Langhaugh
Manor Water
Stanhope
637
817
DOLLAR LAW
696
BLACK LAW
Crookhaugh
Hearthstane
510
GLENWHAPPEN RIG
688
Tweedsmuir
Tweed
A701
840
BROAD LAW
Meggethead
Megget Reservoir
Talla Reservoir
Talla Linnfoots
Glenbreck
392
AUCHENSAUGH HILL
Middle Muir
B7078
Glentaggart
Crawfordjohn
ABINGTON SERVICES
Abington
569
TEWSGILL HILL
Camps Water
Camps Reservoir
DRAKE LAW
483
Kirkton
Crawford
550
B740
Wanlock Water
LOWTHER HILLS
494
RAKE LAW
WELLGRAIN DOD
553
B797
B7040
Elvanfoot
113
Elvan Water
Leadhills
LEADHILLS & WANLOCKHEAD RLY
MUSEUM OF LEAD MINING
WANLOCKHEAD BEAM ENGINE
Wanlockhead
LOTUS LODGE
732
GREEN LOWTHER
725
LOWTHER HILL
Mennock Pass
A702
Watermeetings
March
Nether Howecleuch
546
CLYDE LAW
553
CRAIGMAID
690
Fruid Reservoir
LOCHCRAIG HEAD
800
Loch Skeen
Source of River Tweed
GREY MARE'S TAIL WATERFALLS
882
WHITE COOMB
Birkhill
677
808
HART FELL
Blackhope Burn
753
SADDLE YOKE
DEVIL'S BEEF TUB
Ericstane
Granton
Howslack
Roundstonefoot
Capplegill
BLACK
B719
A74(M)
SOUTHERN UPLAND WAY
B797
Mennock
SOUTHERN UPLAND WAY
Potrail Water
Daer Reservoir
449
CAIRN HILL
A76
NS
NT
Coatsgate
Moffat
MUSEUM
Moffat Water
A708
678
CAPEL FELL
692
ETTRICK PEN
688
LOCH FELL
Garpel Water
407
Easter Earshaig
Beattock
Kinnelhead
691
BALLENCLEUCH LAW
Durisdeermill
DURISDEER PARISH CHURCH
Durisdeer
Enterkinfoot
Enoch
668
GANA HILL
Dumcrieff
Annan
Wamphray Water
Eskdale
484
Laverhay
Holestane
443
MORTON CASTLE
512
QUEENSBERRY
DRUMLANRIG CASTLE
Carronbridge
Locherben
399
A701
Black Esk Reservoir
Auchenbainzie
Scar Water
Burnhead
Penpont
Gatelawbridge
Thornhill
NX
NY
Lochwood
Newton
Kinnel Water
B7020
B7076
Waterhead
Sandyford
B723
Loch Ettrick
113
Keir Mill
Closeburn
353
Forest of Ae
St Ann's
16
Johnstonebridge
ANNANDALE WATER SERVICES
Chapelhill
Dinwoodie Mains
Boreland
Dryfe Water
357
A702
Park
Blackacre
MAXWELTON HOUSE
B729
A76
Courance
Ae Village
Water of Ae
Dumfries and
Nethermill
Sibbaldbie
Straith
Wallaceton
Dalmacallan Forest
Glenmidge
Nith
Auldgirth
Parkgate
Templand
Corrie Common
Dalswinton
Shieldhill
Millhousebridge
Dunscore
Auchencairn
A701
Applegarthtown
A74(M)
Sundaywell
Milton
Duncow
B723
Cairn Water
Gallaberry
Amisfield
Lochmaben
Marjoriebanks
17
Water of Milk
Lockerbie
240
B729
Kirkton
Tinwald
LOCHMABEN CASTLE
Castle Loch
A709
Bankshill
B7068
Newtonairds
Holywood
Locharbriggs
Heathhall
DUMFRIES AND GALLOWAY AVIATION MUS
Heck
107
18
Drumpark
Glenkiln
Irongray
LINCLUDEN COLLEGE
The Grove
Dumfries
Torthorwald
Hightae
Birkshaw Forest
Castlemilk
287
Burnswark
BURNSWARK HILLFORT
OLD BRIDGE HOUSE MUS
Greystone
RAMMERSCALES HOUSE
249
Kettleholm
Middleshaw
398
Glen
Shawhead
Maxwelltown
Collin
A75
Middlebie
B7076
0 1 2 3 4 5 6 miles
0 1 2 3 4 5 6 7 8 9 10 km

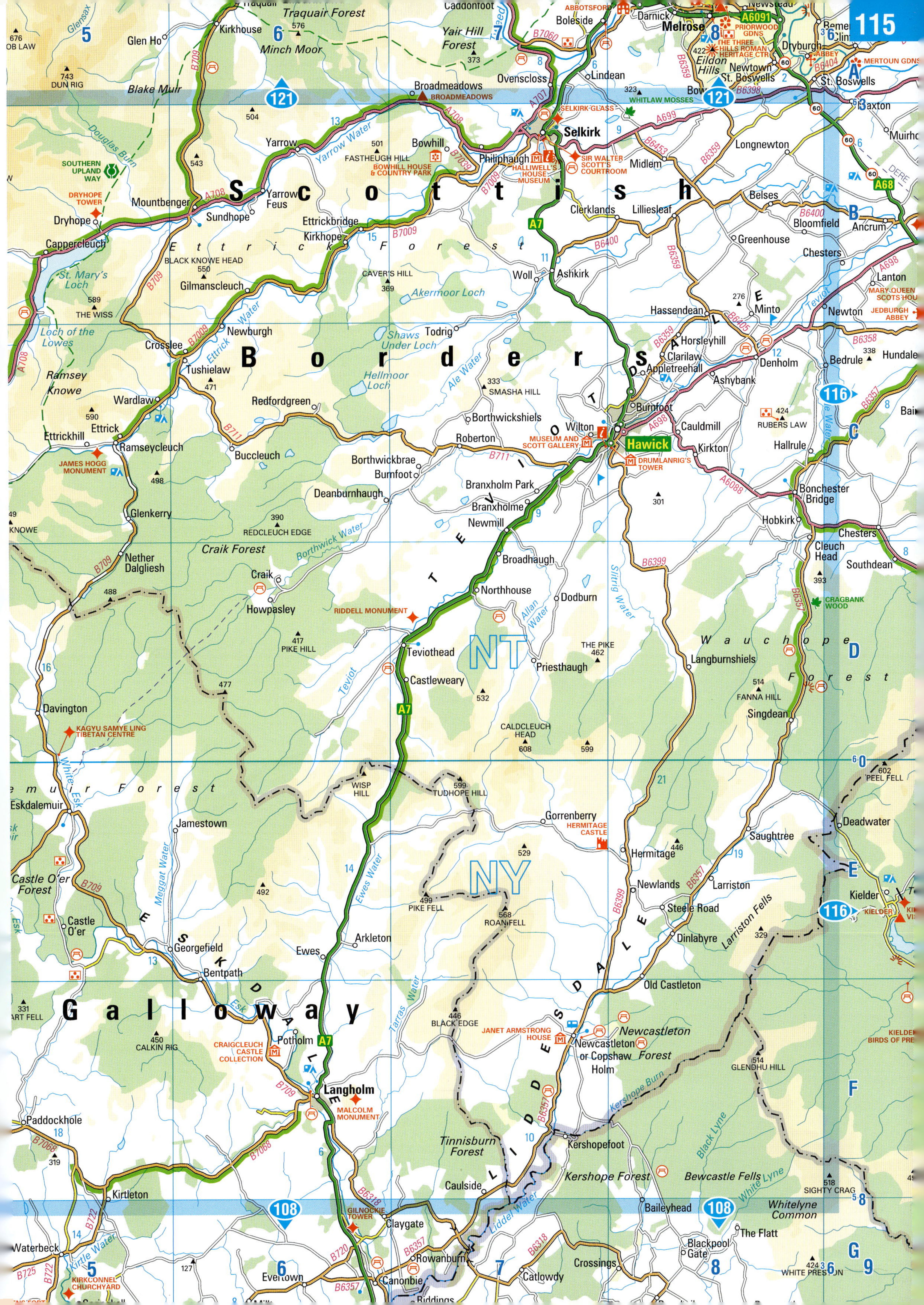
Traquair Forest
Caddonfoot
Kirkhouse
Glen Ho
Minch Moor
Yair Hill Forest
Boleside
Darnick
Melrose
Newstead
Bemersyde
Dryburgh
Eildon Hills
Newtown St. Boswells
St. Boswells
Ovenscloss
Lindean
Broadmeadows
Blake Muir
Dun Rig
Douglas Burn
Yarrow Water
Yarrow
Fastheugh Hill
Bowhill
Bowhill House & Country Park
Philiphaugh
Halliwell's House Museum
Sir Walter Scott's Courtroom
Selkirk
Selkirk Glass
Whitlaw Mosses
Midlem
Longnewton
Maxton
Muirhouselaw
Southern Upland Way
Dryhope Tower
Dryhope
Mountbenger
Yarrow Feus
Sundhope
Ettrickbridge
Kirkhope
Cappercleuch
St. Mary's Loch
Black Knowe Head
Gilmanscleuch
The Wiss
Loch of the Lowes
Caver's Hill
Akermoor Loch
Clerklands
Lilliesleaf
Belses
Bloomfield
Ancrum
Greenhouse
Chesters
Lanton
Mary Queen of Scots House
Jedburgh Abbey
Newton
Woll
Ashkirk
Hassendean
Minto
Horsleyhill
Clarilaw
Appletreehall
Denholm
Bedrule
Hundalee
Ashybank
Crosslee
Newburgh
Tushielaw
Todrig
Shaws Under Loch
Hellmoor Loch
Ale Water
Smasha Hill
Ramsey Knowe
Wardlaw
Redfordgreen
Borthwickshiels
Burnfoot
Cauldmill
Rubers Law
Hallrule
Ettrickhill
Ettrick
Ramseycleuch
James Hogg Monument
Buccleuch
Roberton
Wilton
Museum and Scott Gallery
Hawick
Drumlanrig's Tower
Kirkton
Borthwickbrae
Burnfoot
Deanburnhaugh
Branxholm Park
Branxholme
Newmill
Bonchester Bridge
Hobkirk
Glenkerry
Knowe
Redcleuch Edge
Borthwick Water
Chesters
Cleuch Head
Southdean
Craik Forest
Nether Dalgliesh
Craik
Broadhaugh
Slitrig Water
Howpasley
Northhouse
Dodburn
Cragbank Wood
Riddell Monument
Allan Water
Pike Hill
Teviothead
The Pike
Priesthaugh
Wauchope Forest
Langburnshiels
Castleweary
Fanna Hill
Singdean
Davington
Kagyu Samye Ling Tibetan Centre
Caldcleuch Head
Peel Fell
Eskdalemuir Forest
Eskdalemuir
White Esk
Wisp Hill
Tudhope Hill
Gorrenberry
Hermitage Castle
Hermitage
Deadwater
Saughtree
Jamestown
Meggat Water
Ewes Water
Newlands
Larriston
Kielder
Castle O'er Forest
Castle O'er
Pike Fell
Roan Fell
Steele Road
Dinlabyre
Larriston Fells
Georgefield
Arkleton
Ewes
Bentpath
Eskdale
Old Castleton
Liddesdale
Teviotdale
Scottish Borders
Dumfries and Galloway
Art Fell
Tarras Water
Black Edge
Janet Armstrong House
Newcastleton or Copshaw Holm
Newcastleton Forest
Kielder Birds of Prey
Calkin Rig
Craigcleuch Scottish Explorers Museum
Potholm
Glendhu Hill
Langholm
Malcolm Monument
Kershope Burn
Paddockhole
Tinnisburn Forest
Black Lyne
Kershopefoot
Kershope Forest
Bewcastle Fells
White Lyne
Kirtleton
Caulside
Sighty Crag
Baileyhead
Whitelyne Common
Gilnockie Tower
Claygate
Liddel Water
The Flatt
Waterbeck
Kirtle Water
Blackpool Gate
Rowanburn
Crossings
Kirkconnel Churchyard
Evertown
Canonbie
Catlowdy
White Preston
Riddings
121
116
108
NT
NY

Kelso
Dryburgh
Eildon Hills
Newtown St. Boswells
St. Boswells
Bowden
Maxton
Roxburgh
Heiton
Windywalls
Lempitlaw
Hoselaw
Blakelaw
Mindrum
Pawston
Kilham
Downham
Howtel
Westnewton
Kirknewton
Midlem
Longnewton
Muirhouselaw
Kalemouth
Frogden
Town Yetholm
Kirk Yetholm
Hethpool
Lilliesleaf
Belses
Nisbet
Eckford
Crookhouse
Linton
Bloomfield
Ancrum
Crailing
Morebattle
Greenhouse
Chesters
Bonjedward
Cessford
Cliftoncote
Lanton
Crailinghall
Whitton
Hassendean
Minto
Newton
Jedburgh
Howden
Hownam Mains
Mowhaugh
Sourhope
Horsleyhill
Clarilaw
Appletreehall
Denholm
Bedrule
Hundalee
Oxnam
Hownam
Craik Moor
Ashybank
Chatto
Swinside Hall
Burnfoot
Mossburnford
Bairnkine
Hawick
Kirkton
Cauldmill
Hallrule
Falla
Mervinslaw
Camptown
Bonchester Bridge
Hobkirk
Chesters
Cleuch Head
Southdean
Nether Hindhope
Blindburn
Barrowburn
Leithope Forest
Shillmoor
Alwinton
Linshiels
Wauchope Forest
Langburnshiels
Singdean
Catcleugh
Byrness
Catcleugh Reservoir
Featherwood
Redesdale Forest
Kielderhead Moor
Sills
Redesdale Camp
Rochester
Horsley
Deadwater
Saughtree
Hermitage
Newlands
Larriston
Steele Road
Dinlabyre
Kielder
Wainhope Moor
Emblehope Moor
Blackburn Common
Blakehope Fell
Elishaw
Otterburn
Otterburn Camp
Old Castleton
Newcastleton Forest
KIELDER FOREST PARK
KIELDER WATER
Shipley Shiels
Troughend Common
Gatehouse
Hareshaw Head
West Woodburn
East Woodburn
Falstone
Greenhaugh
The Eals
Lanehead
Charlton
Hesleyside
Bellingham
Ridsdale
Bower
Redesmouth
Bewcastle Fells
Hopehouse
Baileyhead
Whitelyne Common
Paddaburn
Wark Forest
Birtley
Stonehaugh
Whygate
THE CHEVIOT HILLS
THE CHEVIOT
NORTHUMBERLAND NATIONAL PARK
Kidland Forest
NT
NY
A68
A698
A6088
A699
B6357
122
115
109
0 1 2 3 4 5 6 miles
0 1 2 3 4 5 6 7 8 9 10 km

NORTHUMBERLAND COAST
Belford
North Hazelrigg
Easington
Waren Mill
Glororum
Burton
Seahouses
North Sunderland
Beadnell
Beadnell Bay
Benthall
High Newton-by-the-Sea
Low Newton-by-the-Sea
Embleton Bay
Embleton
Dunstan Steads
Castle Point
DUNSTANBURGH CASTLE
Craster
Dunstan
Howick
Howick Haven
Longhoughton
Boulmer
Boulmer Haven
Alnmouth
Alnmouth Bay
Lesbury
Hawkhill
Denwick
Alnwick
ALNWICK ABBEY
HULNE PRIORY
Shipley
Rennington
Littlemill
Littlehoughton
Rock
South Charlton
West Ditchburn
North Charlton
Brownyside
Christon Bank
Brunton
Preston
PRESTON TOWER
Ellingham
Chathill
Fleetham
Newham
Newham Hall
Newstead
Rosebrough
Warenford
Lucker
Adderstone
Bellshill
Warenton
Mousen
Bradford
Spindlestone
Elford
Swinhoe
Fenton
Nesbit
Milfield
Doddington
South Hazelrigg
West Horton
East Horton
Lanton
Coupland
Newtown
Wetwood Hall
Akeld
Humbleton
Wooler
Earle
Middleton Hall
North Middleton
South Middleton
COLD LAW
Langleeford
Harthope Burn
Haugh Head
Chatton
Greendikes
Chillingham
CHILLINGHAM CASTLE
WILD CATTLE OF CHILLINGHAM
Hepburn
Lilburn Tower
East Lilburn
Old Bewick
Ilderton
Roseden
Roddam
Wooperton
New Bewick
Eglingham
Harehope
Beanley
Brandon
Powburn
INGRAM NATIONAL PARK CENTRE
Ingram
Greensidehill
DUNMOOR HILL
Branton
Glanton
Glanton Pike
Titlington
Shawdon Hall
Bolton
Abberwick
Broome Park
Lemmington Hall
Whittingham
Thrunton
Thrunton Wood
EDLINGHAM CASTLE
Edlingham
Great Ryle
Prendwick
Alnham
Little Ryle
Yetlington
Callaly
Scrainwood
Biddlestone
Netherton
Lorbottle Hall
Lorbottle
Burradon
High Trewhitt
Harbottle
Sharperton
Coquet
LADY'S WELL
Holystone
Flotterton
Caistron
Hepple
Warton
Snitter
Cartington
Thropton
Newtown
Rothbury
CRAGSIDE HOUSE
Whitton
NATIONAL PARK VISITOR CENTRE
Great Tosson
SHIRLAW PIKE
Shilbottle
Low Buston
High Buston
Birling
Warkworth
Eastfield Hall
Newton-on-the-Moor
Hazon
Swarland Estate
Swarland
Brainshaugh
Guyzance
Gloster Hill
Amble
Coquet I.
Hauxley
North Togston
Togston
Radcliffe
Acklington
Broomhill
South Broomhill
Red Row
DRUIDGE BAY
Druidge Bay
Felton
West Thirston
East Thirston
Longframlington
LONGFRAMLINGTON GARDENS
BRINKBURN PRIORY
Weldon
Low Hesleyhurst
Eshott
Helm
West Chevington
Widdrington
Stobswood
Widdrington Station
The Scars
Cresswell
Ellington
Lynemouth
Linton
Ulgham
THE SANCTUARY WILDLIFE CENTRE
Tritlington
Fenrother
Causey Park Bridge
Longhorsley
Wingates
Forestburn Gate
TOSSON HILL
ROTHBURY FOREST
Harwood Forest
Fontburn Res.
Fallowlees Burn
Elsdon
Raylees
Nunnykirk
Ewesley
Rothley Shield East
Netherwitton
Stanton
Hebron
Longhirst
Pegswood
Ashington
COLLIERY MUSEUM
Woodhorn
Beacon Pt.
QUEEN ELIZABETH II
Newbiggin-by-the-Sea
Hirst
North Seaton
WANSBECK
Bothal
NORTHUMBRIA CRAFT CENTRE
Morpeth
Mitford
Stakeford
Guide Post
Scotland Gate
Choppington
Hepscott
West Sleekburn
Cambois
East Sleekburn
Bedlington Station
Bedlington
Cowpen
BLYTH
Bebside
Newsham
New Delaval
Clifton
Tranwell
Nedderton
BEDLINGTON
PLESSEY WOODS
East Hartford
Shankhouse
Cramlington
Southfield
East Cramlington
Nelson Village
New Hartley
Seaton Delaval
Stannington
NORTHUMBERLAND CHEESE FARM
Saltwick
Berwick Hill
KIRKLEY HALL
Ogle
Higham Dykes
West Newham
Milbourne
Shilvington
Whalton
Molesden
Meldon
Throphill
Pigdon
Longwitton
Hartburn
High Angerton
Middleton
Wansbeck
BOLAM LAKE
Bolam
Harnham
Belsay
BELSAY HALL
Black Heddon
Scots' Gap
Cambo
Rothley
HERTERTON HOUSE GARDEN
Hart Burn
Font
Knowesgate
X-TREME ADVENTURE
Kirkwhelpington
WALLINGTON
Kirkharle
Capheaton
Sweethope Loughs
Great Bavington
Thockrington
Little Bavington
Kirkheaton
Hallington
Hallington Reservoir
Colt Crag Reservoir
A1
A697
A1068
A189
A192
A196
A193
A696
A1061
B1340
B1342
B6349
B6348
B1341
B1339
B6347
B6346
B6341
B6344
B6342
B6343
B6524
B1337
B6345
B1329
B1331
B1505
B6525
DEVIL'S CAUSEWAY
123
110
NT
NU
NY
NZ
Northumberland
UMBERLAND
L PARK
Shill Moor
HAT LAW
A
B
C
D
E
F
G

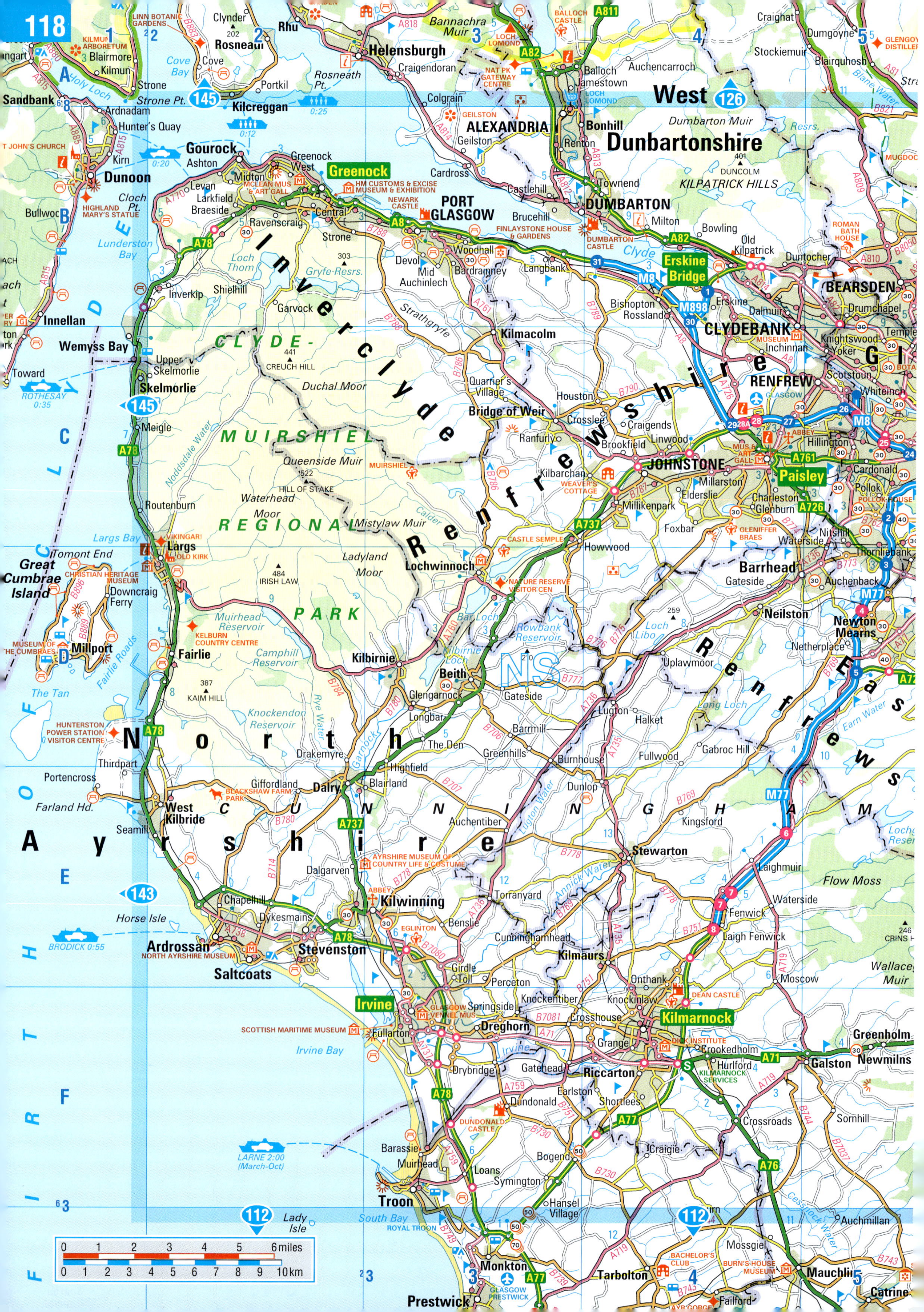
West Dunbartonshire
Dunbartonshire
Inverclyde
Renfrewshire
East Renfrewshire
North Ayrshire
CLYDE-MUIRSHIEL REGIONAL PARK
CUNNINGHAME
FIRTH OF CLYDE
Helensburgh
Rhu
Clynder
Rosneath
Kilcreggan
Cove
Portkil
Strone Pt.
Holy Loch
Sandbank
Ardnadam
Hunter's Quay
Kilmun
Blairmore
Strone
Kirn
Dunoon
Bullwood
Innellan
Toward
Gourock
Ashton
Greenock
Port Glasgow
Craigendoran
Cardross
Alexandria
Balloch
Jamestown
Bonhill
Renton
Dumbarton
Milton
Bowling
Old Kilpatrick
Duntocher
Bearsden
Clydebank
Erskine
Erskine Bridge
Bishopton
Renfrew
Paisley
Johnstone
Linwood
Kilbarchan
Howwood
Lochwinnoch
Kilmacolm
Bridge of Weir
Houston
Crosslee
Brookfield
Elderslie
Barrhead
Neilston
Newton Mearns
Uplawmoor
Kilbirnie
Beith
Glengarnock
Dalry
Kilwinning
Stevenston
Ardrossan
Saltcoats
West Kilbride
Seamill
Fairlie
Largs
Skelmorlie
Wemyss Bay
Inverkip
Millport
Great Cumbrae Island
Irvine
Dreghorn
Kilmarnock
Kilmaurs
Stewarton
Dunlop
Fenwick
Galston
Newmilns
Hurlford
Riccarton
Dundonald
Troon
Symington
Monkton
Prestwick
Tarbolton
Mauchline
Catrine
Irvine Bay
South Bay
Horse Isle
Lady Isle
Farland Hd.
Portencross
ROTHESAY 0:35
BRODICK 0:55
LARNE 2:00 (March-Oct)
M8
M77
M898
A78
A737
A77
A71
A76
A82
0 1 2 3 4 5 6 miles
0 1 2 3 4 5 6 7 8 9 10 km

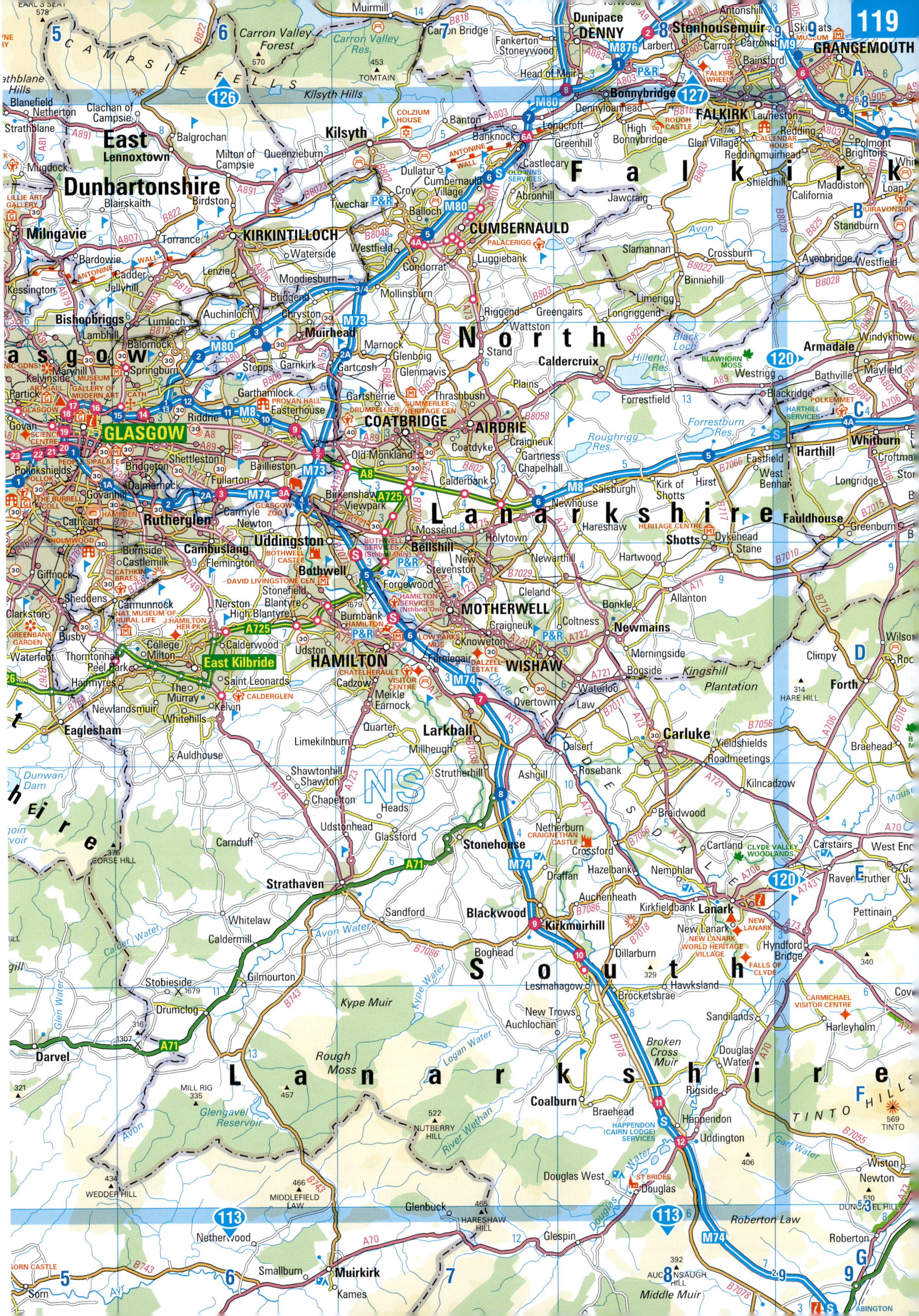
126
127
120
113
East Dunbartonshire
Falkirk
North Lanarkshire
South Lanarkshire
GLASGOW
East Kilbride
Campsie Fells
Carron Valley Forest
Carron Valley Res.
Kilsyth Hills
DENNY
Stenhousemuir
GRANGEMOUTH
Bonnybridge
FALKIRK
Kilsyth
Milngavie
KIRKINTILLOCH
CUMBERNAULD
Bishopbriggs
Muirhead
Stepps
COATBRIDGE
AIRDRIE
Caldercruix
Armadale
Harthill
Whitburn
Fauldhouse
Shotts
Rutherglen
Cambuslang
Uddingston
Bellshill
Bothwell
MOTHERWELL
Newmains
HAMILTON
WISHAW
Larkhall
Carluke
Kingshill Plantation
Forth
Strathaven
Stonehouse
Blackwood
Kirkmuirhill
Lanark
Lesmahagow
Coalburn
Douglas
Douglas West
Darvel
Eaglesham
Kype Muir
Rough Moss
Glengavel Reservoir
Tinto Hills
Muirkirk
Glenbuck
Middle Muir
Roberton Law
M80
M73
M8
M74
M876
M9
A71
A725
A8

Stenhousemuir
Larbert
Carron
Carronshore
Skinflats
GRANGEMOUTH
Bainsford
FALKIRK
Laurieston
Redding
Glen Village
Polmont
Brightons
Reddingmuirhead
Shieldhill
Maddiston
California
Bo'ness
Grangepans
Carriden
Muirhouses
Blackness
Mannerston
Grougfoot
Linlithgow
Linlithgow Bridge
Whitecross
Philpstoun
Old Philpstoun
Bridgend
Threemiletown
Charlestown
Limekilns
Rosyth
Inverkeithing
St. Margaret's Hope
Inverkeithing Bay
Forth Road Bridge
North Queensferry
Queensferry
Dalmeny
Newton
Dalgety Bay
Inchcolm
Inchmickery
Cramond I.
Drum Sands
Cramond
Cramond Bridge
Granton
Davidson's Mains
Barnton
Drylaw
Murrayfield
Corstorphine
Gorgie
Morningside
Craiglockhart
Braid
Colinton
Fairmilehead
Juniper Green
Currie
Hermiston
Sighthill
Ratho Station
Ratho
Bonnington
Ingliston
Gogar
Kirkliston
Turnhouse
Winchburgh
Broxburn
Uphall
Uphall Station
Ecclesmachan
Newbridge
Burnside
Dechmont
Wester Dechmont
Pumpherston
Wilkieston
Deans
LIVINGSTON
Mid Calder
East Calder
Oakbank
Livingston Village
Bellsquarry
Seafield
Kirknewton
Burnwynd
Balerno
Malleny Mills
Bathgate
Boghall
Whiteside
Armadale
Windyknowe
Mayfield
Bathville
Westrigg
Blackridge
Blackburn
Whitburn
East Whitburn
Croftmalloch
Harthill
Eastfield
West Benhar
Longridge
Stoneyburn
Bents
Addiewell
Loganlea
West Calder
Polbeth
Fauldhouse
Greenburn
Breich
Shotts
Dykehead
Stane
Kirk of Shotts
Hirst
Allanton
Avonbridge
Westfield
Torphichen
Standburn
Crossburn
Binniehill
Limerigg
Forrestburn Res.
Black Loch
Hillend Res.
Falkirk
West Lothian
Lothian
Edinburgh
Mid
PENTLAND HILLS REGIONAL PARK
PENTLAND HILLS
Harlaw Reservoir
Threipmuir Reservoir
Glencorse Res.
Harperrig Reservoir
Woodhouselee
Easter Howgate
Milton Bridge
Penicuik
Silverburn
Kirkhill
Howgate
Nine Mile Burn
Carlops
Leadburn
Baddinsgill Reservoir
Cobbinshaw Reservoir
Crosswood Reservoir
Woodmuir Plantation
Woolfords Cottages
Tarbrax
Wilsontown
Rootpark
Auchengray
Forth
Climpy
Kingshill Plantation
Carluke
Yieldshields
Roadmeetings
Kilncadzow
Braehead
Braidwood
Cartland
Carstairs
Carstairs Junction
West End
Carnwath
Kaimend
Newbigging
Walston
Dunsyre
Dolphinton
Melbourne
Elsrickle
West Linton
West Water Reservoir
Cowdenburn
Whim Farm
Waterheads
Halmyre Mains
Damside
Romannobridge
Mountain Cross
Eddleston
Blyth Bridge
Drochil
Kirkurd
Candy Mill
Nemphlar
Lanark
New Lanark
Kirkfieldbank
Ravenstruther
Pettinain
Libberton
Hyndford Bridge
Hawksland
Sandilands
Covington
Whitecastle
Shieldhill
Quothquan
Biggar
Skirling
Thankerton
Harleyholm
Douglas Water
Wolfclyde
Causewayend
Symington
Coulter
Rachan Mill
Broughton
Drumelzier
Dreva Forest
UPPER TWEEDDALE
Stobo
Kirkton Manor
Hallyne
Castlehill
Bellspool
TINTO HILLS
Tinto
Happendon
Uddington
Wiston
Newton
Lamington
Broken Cross Muir
Roberton Law
Stanhope
Crookhaugh
Hearthstane
Langhaugh
Cowgill Upper Reservoir
Culter Waterhead Reservoir
Culter Fell
Dollar Law
Black Law
Stob Law
Pykestone Hill
Blakehope Head
Broughton Heights
Black Meldon
White Meldon
White Craig
Bleak Law
Mendick Hill
Byrehope Mount
West Cairn Hill
East Cairn Hill
Scald Law
Black Mount
Hare Hill
Dungavel Hill
Glenwhappen Rig
NS
NT
M8
M9
A702
A70
A71
A72
A73
A701
A721
A743
119
120
127
128
114
0 1 2 3 4 5 6 miles
0 1 2 3 4 5 6 7 8 9 10 km

FIRTH OF FORTH
Inchkeith
Black Rocks
HMY BRITANNIA
Newhaven
Leith
EDINBURGH
Gullane Bay
Gullane
Dirleton
West Fenton
Fenton Barns
Kingston
Whitekirk
Aberlady Bay
Aberlady
Craigielaw
MYRETON MOTOR MUSEUM
Drem
Tyninghame
Tyne Mouth
Belhaven
West Barns
Gosford Bay
GOSFORD HOUSE
Spittal
Ballencrieff
Athelstaneford
THE CHESTERS FORT
MUSEUM OF FLIGHT
East Fortune
Preston
East Linton
PRESTON MILL & PHANTASSIE DOOCOT
Cockenzie and Port Seton
SETON COLLEGIATE CHURCH
Longniddry
Huntington
Elvington
HOPETOUN MON
JANE WELSH CARLYLE MUSEUM
HAILES CASTLE
Traprain
Pitcox
Stenton
Luggate Burn
Biel Water
Prestonpans
MUSSELBURGH INDUSTRIAL HERITAGE MUSEUM
Fisherrow Sands
Musselburgh
Portobello
Joppa
PALACE OF HOLYROOD HOUSE
Duddingston
NAT MUS OF SCOTLAND
NEWHAILES
INVERESK LODGE GDNS
Inveresk
Wallyford
Tranent
Gladsmuir
Haddington
ST MARY'S COLLEGIATE CH
Halls
Papple
Macmerry
Penston
Samuelston
Garvald
East Lothian
Craigmillar
Newcraighall
CRAIGMILLAR CASTLE
ROYAL OBSERVATORY
EDINBURGH SERVICES
Elphinstone
New Winton
New Town
Bolton
Dunbar Common
Danderhall
Whitecraig
Ormiston
Carfrae
Liberton
Gilmerton
Millerhill
Crossgatehall
Pencaitland
Kaimes
DALKEITH PARK
Dalkeith
Cousland
GLENKINCHIE DISTILLERY
East Saltoun
West Saltoun
Gifford
Danskine
Straiton
BUTTERFLY FARM
Eskbank
Peastonbank
Loanhead
Newbattle
Easthouses
Mayfield
Gilchriston
Quarryford
Longyester
Long Newton
Bilston
Polton
Bonnyrigg and Lasswade
Peaston
Pathhead
Roslin
MINING MUSEUM
VOGRIE
Newtongrange
Newlandrig
ROSSLYN CHAPEL
ROSLIN GLEN
Rosewell
Auchendinny
Crichton
Humbie
Fala Dam
Stobshiel
Blegbie
Whiteadder Reservoir
LAMMER LAW
Hopes Reservoir
MEIKLE SAYS LAW
LAMMERMUIR HILLS
ARNISTON HOUSE
Arniston
CRICHTON CASTLE
Carrington
Gorebridge
North Middleton
Tynehead
Fala
Lothian
Temple
Middleton
Fala Moor
HUNT LAW
Dye Water
Rosebery Reservoir
Falahill
Gilston
Soonhope Burn
Watch Water Reservoir
Hillhouse
HOG'S LAW
Kirktonhill
TORFICHEN HILL
Carcant
Heriot
Gala Water
Oxton
Addinston
Gladhouse Reservoir
MOORFOOT HILLS
NT
Wedderlie
COLLIE LAW
Leader Water
Westruther
Blythe
Thornydykes
Fountainhall
Torquhan
THIRLSTANE CASTLE
Lauder
Whiteburn
Thirlstane
Hounslow
Dewar
BLACKHOPE SCAR
Eden Water
Killochyett
Boon
Scottish Borders
WHITEHOPE LAW
Lugate Water
Stow
Legerwood
GREEN KNOWE TOWER
Nether Blainslie
Glentress Forest
TWEED
Leithen Water
WINDLESTRAW LAW
Bow
SOUTHERN UPLAND WAY
West Morriston
Fans
Peebles
BLACK LAW
Colquhar
GREAT LAW
Caitha Bowland
TWEEDDALE MUS & GALL
Glentress
Kings Muir
VALLEY
Langshaw
KAILZIE GARDENS
Kirkburn
ROBERT SMALL'S PRINTING WORKS
Blackhaugh
Buckholm
Earlston
MELLERSTAIN HOUSE
Cardrona
ST RONAN'S WELL INTERPRETATIVE CENTRE
Walkerburn
Galashiels
Cardrona Forest
Innerleithen
PETER ANDERSON WOOLLEN MILL
EILDON AND LEADERFOOT
Redpath
Brotherstone
TRAQUAIR HOUSE
FOREST
Clovenfords
OLD GALA HOUSE
Gattonside
ABBEY
MELROSE
Newstead
Traquair
Elibank and Traquair Forest
Caddonfoot
ABBOTSFORD
SMAILHOLM TOWER
PARK
Boleside
Darnick
Melrose
PRIORWOOD GDNS
Bemersyde
Clintmains
Kirkhouse
Yair Hill Forest
THE THREE HILLS ROMAN HERITAGE CTR
Glen Ho
Minch Moor
Eildon Hills
Dryburgh
ABBEY
MERTOUN GDNS
Newtown St. Boswells
St. Boswells
Lindean
Ovenscloss
Bowden
Blake Muir
Broadmeadows
BROADMEADOWS
WHITLAW MOSSES
Maxton
Rutherford
SELKIRK GLASS
Yarrow
Yarrow Water
Bowhill
Selkirk
Longnewton
Muirhouselaw
SOUTHERN UPLAND WAY
FASTHEUGH HILL
BOWHILL HOUSE & COUNTRY PARK
Philiphaugh
HALLIWELL'S HOUSE MUSEUM
SIR WALTER SCOTT'S COURTROOM
Midlem
DRYHOPE TOWER
Mountbenger
Yarrow Feus
Belses

1
2
3
4
5
A
B
C
D
E
F
Scoughall
Kingston
Whitekirk
St. Baldred's Cradle
Tyne Mouth
129
JOHN MUIR BIRTHPLACE
Dunbar
JOHN MUIR
Belhaven
West Barns
East Fortune
Tyninghame
Preston
East Linton
PRESTON MILL & PHANTASSIE DOOCOT
Biel Water
HAILES CASTLE
Traprain
Pitcox
Spott
Broxburn
Barns Ness
East Barns
Skateraw
Meikle Pinkerton
Luggate Burn
Stenton
Halls
Dry Burn
Innerwick
Thorntonloch
Papple
Garvald
COCKLAW HILL 319
DUNGLASS COLLEGIATE CHURCH
Reed Pt.
Cove
Cockburnspath
Siccar Pt.
Wheat Stack
FAST CASTLE
ST ABB'S HEAD
St. Abb's Head
KITTIWAKE GALLERY
Oldhamstocks
Dunbar Common
BRANSLY HILL
Carfrae
Lumsdaine
Coldingham Moor
Northfield
St Abbs
Coldingham
St. Abb's Haven
COLDINGHAM PRIORY
Danskine
121
Quarryford
Longyester
Ecclaw
HEART LAW
SOUTHERN UPLAND WAY
Grantshouse
Huxton
Ale Water
Eyemouth
Bothwell Water
Spartleton Edge
Monynut Water
Nether Monynut
Houndwood
Eye Water
Cairncross
LAMMERMUIR HILLS
Whiteadder Reservoir
Hopes Reservoir
MEIKLE SAYS LAW
CRANSHAWS HILL
Whiteadder Water
Cranshaws
Abbey St. Bathans
Reston
AYTON CASTLE
Ayton
Auchencrow
Ellemford
EDINSHALL BROCH
Prenderguest
HUNT LAW
LAMMERMUIR
Lintlaw
Preston
Chirnside
Dye Water
Longformacus
Watch Water Reservoir
NT
Chirnsidebridge
Edrom
Foulden
Clappers
FOULDEN TITHE BARN
Whiteadder Water
HOG'S LAW
DIRRINGTON GREAT LAW
JIM CLARK ROOM
Buxley
MANDERSTON
Allanton
Hutton
Paxton
Scottish Borders
Clockmill
Duns
Cheeklaw
CRUMSTANE FARM PARK
Blackadder West
PAXTON HOUSE
UNION SUSPENSION BRIDGE
Wedderlie
Choicelee
Gavinton
Sinclair's Hill
Whitsome
Fishwick
Loanend
Westruther
Polwarth
Blythe
Thornydykes
Halliburton
Sisterpath
Fogo
Fogorig
Bogend
Horndean
Horncliffe
Thornton Park
Whiteburn
Thirlestane
Houndslow
Swinton
SWINTON KIRK
Ladykirk
NORHAM CASTLE
Norham
MERSE
Swintonmill
Simprim
Shoreswood
Boon
Eden Water
Greenlaw
Blackadder Water
Grindon
Legerwood
Huntlywood
GREEN KNOWE TOWER
Gordon
Middlethird
Easter Howlaws
Lambden
Leitholm
Orange Lane
Felkington
Shellacres
West Morriston
Hume
HUME CASTLE
Falsidehill
Eccles
Lennel
Castle Heaton
Duddo
Fans
Coldstream
THE HIRSEL
HIRSEL
Cornhill-on-Tweed
HEATHERSLAW LIGHT RAILWAY
Etal
Earlston
MELLERSTAIN HOUSE
Stichill
Birgham
Carham
Wark
East Learmouth
West Learmouth
Crookham
Branxton
Ford
Nenthorn
Ednam
Tweed
Hadden
EILDON AND LEADERFOOT
Redpath
Smailholm
Brotherstone
Kerchesters
Pressen
Flodden
Newstead
SMAILHOLM TOWER
KELSO ABBEY
FLOORS CASTLE
Kelso
Sprouston
Hoselfield
Downham
Howtel
Melrose
PRIORWOOD GDNS
THE THREE HILLS ROMAN HERITAGE CTR
Eildon Hills
Bemersyde
Clintmains
Dryburgh
DRYBURGH ABBEY
MERTOUN GDNS
Manorhill
Trows
ROXBURGH CASTLE
Maxwellheugh
Windywalls
Lempitlaw
Mindrum
Milfield
Pawston
Kilham
Glen
Newtown St. Boswells
St. Boswells
Bowden
Rutherford
Roxburgh
Hoselaw
Blakelaw
Lanton
Coupland
Maxton
116
Heiton
Shotton
Westnewton
Kirknewton
KIRK YETHOLM
Frogden
Town Yetholm
Kirk Yetholm
Hethpool
Kalemouth
TEVIOT WATER GARDENS
Kale Water
Crookhouse
Linton
Belses
Nisbet
Eckford
College Burn
0 1 2 3 4 5 6 miles
0 1 2 3 4 5 6 7 8 9 10 km

5
6
7
8
9
A
B
C
D
E
F
G
NU
NORTHUMBERLAND COAST
EYEMOUTH MUSEUM
Burnmouth
Lamberton Beach
Lamberton
1333
Highfields
Berwick-upon-Tweed
BARRACKS MUSEUM & RAMPARTS
East Ord
Tweedmouth
Spittal
Tweed
Prior Park
Redshin Cove
A698
A1167
B6461
108
Murton
Thornton
Scremerston
DEVIL'S CAUSEWAY
West Allerdean
Shoresdean
Cheswick
Goswick
Ancroft
B6354
B6525
North Low
Haggerston
Berrington
South Low
Beal
A1
82
12
Bowsden
Causeway
Holy Island Sands
Holy Island
LINDISFARNE
Emmanuel Hd.
Holy Island (Lindisfarne)
LINDISFARNE CASTLE
Castle Pt.
HERITAGE CENTRE
LINDISFARNE PRIORY
Guile Pt.
Fenham
HUT SMITHY WOOD WORKSHOP
Barmoor Castle
Barmoor Lane End
B6353
West Kyloe
Fenwick
Lowick
East Kyloe
Kyloe Hills
HERSLAW MILL
LADY WATERFORD HALL
ST CUTHBERT'S WAY
Buckton
Elwick
Ross
Budle Bay
Farne Islands
Staple Sound
FARNE ISLANDS
Inner Sound
BAMBURGH CASTLE
Bamburgh
157
Holburn
Detchant
Middleton
Budle
Kimmerston
Hetton Steads
211
North Hazelrigg
Belford
Easington
B1342
Waren Mill
B1340
Fenton Town
Nesbit
Spindlestone
Glororum
Burton
Doddington
South Hazelrigg
B6349
Mousen
Bradford
B1341
Seahouses
200
West Horton
Newtown
East Horton
Bellshill
Elford
North Sunderland
Akeld
1402
Weetwood Hall
10
Warenton
Adderstone
Lucker
Newham Hall
A697
B6525
117
B6348
Beadnell
Warenford
Humbleton
Chatton
Greendikes
Newham
Swinhoe
Benthall
Wooler
WOOLER
166
Fleetham
B1340
Beadnell Bay
Newstead
Earle
Haugh Head
Chillingham
Rosebrough
Chathill
High Newton-by-the-Sea
Middleton Hall
CHILLINGHAM CASTLE
WILD CATTLE OF CHILLINGHAM
Ellingham
Newtown
Preston
15

SOUND OF MULL
Claggan
Larachbeg
KINLOCHALINE CASTLE
ARDTORNISH GARDENS
Achranich
Loch Aline
Loch Teàrnait
Rannoch
BEINN A' CHAISIL
437
Glensanda
Loch nan Clach
Shuna I.
Portnacroish
Appin House
Appin
Port Appin
Port Ramsay
Clachan
LYNN OF LORN
Eriska
North Shian
South Shian
SCOTTISH SEA LIFE SANCTUARY
Fiunary
Savary
Lochaline
GLAIS BHEINN 479
AN SLEAGHACH 513
Eignaig
Lismore
Aros Mains
Rubha Mor
Salen
Fishnish Bay
ARDTORNISH CASTLE
Ardtornish Pt.
Garbh Shlios
Camas Gorm
Achnacroish
Pennygown
Killbeg
Corrynachenchy
Inninmore Bay
147
130
Garmony
Scallastle Bay
Rubha an Ridire
Bernera I.
Achinduin
Kilcheran
Baravullin
Ferlochan
Kiel Crofts
Benderloch
Ledaig
Achnaba
ISLAND OF MULL
Knock
Loch Bà
Glen Cannel
Scallastle
Java
Craignure Bay
Craignure
Eilean Dubh
Ardmucknish Bay
766 DUN DA GHAOITHE
Duart Bay
Duart Pt.
DUART CASTLE
Eilean Musdile
0:50
Eilean Mor
DUNSTAFFNAGE CASTLE
North Connel
Connel
Black Crofts
FALLS OF LORA
A828
761 BEINN TALAIDH
Lochdon
0:45
Dunbeg
704 CORRA-BHEINN
CASTLEBAY 4:50
COLL 2:40
TIREE 3:35
Ganavan
Dunollie
OBAN LODGE
MCCAIG'S TOWER
OBAN DISTILLERY
Black Lochs
Glen More
Lussa
A849
Loch Don
Grass Pt.
Strathcoil
Coladoir
Altnacraig
Oban
Kerrera
Balliemore
Glenamachrie
Loch Airdeglais
248
Loch Spelve
BEN BUIE 717
698 CREACH BEINN
Ardmore
Loch Fuaron
Croggan
Rubha nan Sailthean
Bach I.
Loch Nell
Glen
Kinlochspelve
Gallanach
Lochbuie
Barrachandroman
Kilbride
Kilmore
Barran
Rubha Seanach
Sound of Kerrera
503 BEINN NA CROISE
Loch Uisg
Am Buth
Loch Feochan
Glen Feochan
GLENFEOCHAN HOUSE GARDENS
Kilbride
FIRTH OF LORN
Carsaig
Loch Buie
405 DRUIM FADA
Laggan Deer Forest
Kilninver
A816
B844
Barochreal
Glen Euchar
368 A'CHRUACH
Musdale
Bragleenmore
Carsaig Bay
Rubha Dubh
LORD LOVAT'S CAVE
NM
Insh I.
CLACHAN BRIDGE
Loch Scamadale
515 BEINN CHAPULL
Frank Lockwood's Island
Sound of Insh
Clachan-Seil
Seil
Clachan
AN CALA GARDENS
438 CARN DEARG
Easdale
EASDALE ISLAND FOLK MUSEUM
Balvicar
Braes of Lorn
Blaran
267 CRUACH RAREY
Loch Tralaig
Lochavich
Drissaig
Dubh-fheith
B8003
Seil Sound
Cuan
Ferry
Torsa
Melfort
Kilmun
Cullipool
94
Kilchoan
Ardanstur
Kilmelford
Loch Avich
Garbh Eileach
Garvellachs
Luing
Loch Melfort
Glenmore
Lagalochan
SCARBA, Eilean Dubh Mor
LUNGA AND THE GARVELLACHS
Sound of Luing
Achafolla
ARDUAINE GARDEN
Arduaine
Kames
365
491 CARN DUCHARA
Eileach an Naoimh
Garraron
Inverliever Forest
Kilmaha
COLONSAY 2:20
Toberonochy
Shuna Sound
Lunga
Shuna
Craobh Haven
Barravullin
Lunga
Barbreck
Liever
350 CRUACH AN EACHLAICH
Arichamish
CRUACH SCARBA 449
Shuna Pt.
Kintraw
Torran
B840
Scarba
Rubha Aird Luing
Ardfern
144
Ford
Finchairn
FINCHAIRN CASTLE
Ederline
B8002
227 CREAG MHOR
Gulf of Corryvreckan
Loch Craignish
Eilean Righ
CARNASSARIE CASTLE
458 CRUACH FHIONN
Aird
Loch Gaineamhach
Rèisa an t-Sruith
319
Kinuachdrachd
Kilmartin
GLEBE CAIRN
KILMARTIN HOUSE TRUST
Craignish Pt.
Island Macaskin
296 CRUACH NA SEILCHEIG
Glengarrisdale Bay
Kinuachdrachd Harbour
Slockavullin
KILMARTIN SCULPTURED STONES
RI CRUIN CAIRN
Glen Airigh
Poltalloch
NR
Glendebadel Bay
Loch Crinan
231 DUN DUBH
144
145
365 BEN GARRISDALE
Crinan
B8025
CUP AND RING MARKS
Loch Glashan
Kilmahumaig
B841
MOINE MHOR
DUNADD FORT
Kilmichael Glassary
Moine Mhór
Bellanoch
Bridgend
CAIRNBAAN CUP & RING MARKS
A83
Lussa
467
Lealt
265
ROCK MARKINGS
Lochgair
Asknish
0 1 2 3 4 5 6 miles
0 1 2 3 4 5 6 7 8 9 10 km
A B C D E F
1 2 3 4 5

Argyll
and
Bute
ARGYLL FOREST PARK
NN
NS
Stockdale
Elleric
Glen Creran
Fasnacloich
Invercreran
Glasdrum
GLASDRUM WOOD
Druimavuic
Creagan
South Creagan
Barcaldine
Barcaldine Forest
Gleann Salach
ARDCHATTAN PRIORY GARDENS
ARDCHATTAN PRIORY
Achnacloich
ACHNACLOICH GARDEN
Bonawe
BONAWE IRON FURNACE
INVERAWE FISHERIES AND SMOKERIES EXHIBITION
Brochroy
Taynuilt
Ichrachan
Bridge of Awe
Pass of Brander
BARGUILLEAN GARDENS
GLEN NANT
Glen Nant
Loch Nant
Kilchrenan
Annat
North Port
Sior Loch
South Port
Portsonachan
Cladich
Inverinan
Ballimeanoch
Allt Beochlich
Dalavich
Blarghour
ARDCHONNELL CASTLE
Portinnisherrich
Eredine
Durran
Eredine Forest
Loch Leacann
Auchindrain
AUCHINDRAIN OPEN AIR MUSEUM
Furnace
Crarae
CRARAE GLEN GARDENS
Minard
Tullochgorm
Lachlan Bay
Garbhallt
LACHLAN CASTLE
Newton
Strathlachlan Forest
Lephinmore
Lephinchapel
Dunans
Caol Ghleann
Loch Etive
Glen Ure
Gualachulain
Inverchanan
Glenceitlein
Glen Liver
Glen Noe
Glen Kinglass
Cruachan Reservoir
Falls of Cruachan
CRUACHAN DAM VISITOR CENTRE
Loch Tromlee
ARDANAISEIG GARDENS
Ardanaiseig
Innis Chonain
INISHAIL CHAPEL
Inishail
KILCHURN CASTLE
Lochawe
Dalmally
MCINTYRE MONUMENT
Teatle Water
Stronmilchan
Strath of Orchy
Inverlochy
Achnafalnich
Glen Strae
Allt Mhoille
Allt Fearna
Cladich
Lochan Shira
Loch Stron Mor
Brannie Burn
Glen Shira
Kilblaan Burn
Dubh Loch
Tullich
Glen Aray
Clachan
Drishaig
ARDKINGLAS WOODLAND GARDEN
Cairndow
Glen Kinglas
INVERARAY CASTLE
BELL TOWER
INVERARAY JAIL
Inveraray
Newtown
MARITIME MUSEUM
Ardno
St Catherine's
Hell's Glen
Rest and Be Thankful
Dalchenna
Douglas Water
Creggans
Clachan
Strachur
Strachur Bay
Glen Sluain
Invernoaden
Glenbranter
Glenbranter Forest
Loch Eck
Whistlefield
Bernice
Monevechadan
Drimsynie
Lochgoilhead
Corrow
Blairlomond
Loch Goil
Ardgoil Forest
Carrick Castle
CARRICK CASTLE
Garelochhead
Glen Croe
Ardgartan
Ardgartan Forest
Loch Long
Glenmallan
Portincaple
Whistlefield
Succoth
Tarbet
Arrochar
Stuckgowan
Ardmay
Glen Douglas
Inverbeg
INVERBEG GALLERY
Edentaggart
Glen Luss
Aldochlay
NAT PARK CENTRE
THISTLE BAGPIPE WORKS
Inveruglas
Inversnaid Hotel
WEST HIGHLAND WAY
ROB ROY'S CAVE
Craig Rostan
Loch Sloy
Ardlui
Inverarnan
Falls of Falloch
Glen Falloch
Ben Glas Burn
Dubh Eas
Eas a'Ghaill
Allt Fionn Ghlinne
Inverherive
Cononish
Tyndrum
Clifton
Arrivain
Glen Lochy
Glen Orchy
Arichastlich
Bridge of Orchy
Inveroran Hotel
Loch Dochard
Forest Lodge
Black Mount
BLACK MOUNT
Loch Tulla
Achallader
Allt Chonoghlais
Allt Coire a'Chaolain
Allt Dochard
Allt Hallater
Allt Easach
Abhainn Sheilach
Glenfyne Lodge
Glen Fyne
Allt na Lairige
BEN LUI
1130 BEN LUI
978 BEINN DUBHCHRAIG
739 MEALL NAN TIGHEARN
733 TROISGEACH
948 BEINN BHUIDHE
550 BEINN GHLAS
645 MAOL BREAC
941 BEN VORLICH
1011 BEINN IME
901 BEINN AN LOCHAIN
565 CRUACH NAN CAPULL
847 BEN DONICH
CNOC COINNICH
703 BEINN LOCHAIN
779 BEINN BHEULA
519 THE SADDLE
618 BEINN BHEAG
659 CREACHAN MOR
734 DOUNE HILL
702 BEINN EICH
713 BEINN CHAORACH
593 BEINN RUISG
589 CRUACH MHOR
514 AN SUIDHE
482 BEINN DEARG
515 BEINN GHLAS
897
1126 BEN CRUACHAN
989 BEINN EUNAICH
796 BEINN MHIC-MHONAIDH
840 BEINN UDLAIDH
901 BEINN ODHAR
1076 BEINN DORAIN
1004 BEINN AN DOTHAIDH
957 BEINN NAN AIGHENAN
1078 BEN STARAV
1044 STOB COIR'AN ALBANNAICH
1090 STOB GHABHAR
1099 CLACH LEATHAD
883 STOB DUBH
959 BEINN FHIONNLAIDH
937 BEINN SGULAIRD
839 BEINN TRILLEACHAN
810 CREACH BHEINN
715 BEINN MHEADHONACH
A82
A85
A83
A815
A819
A886
A814
A817
B8077
B8074
B845
B840
B828
B839
B8000
130
131
126
145

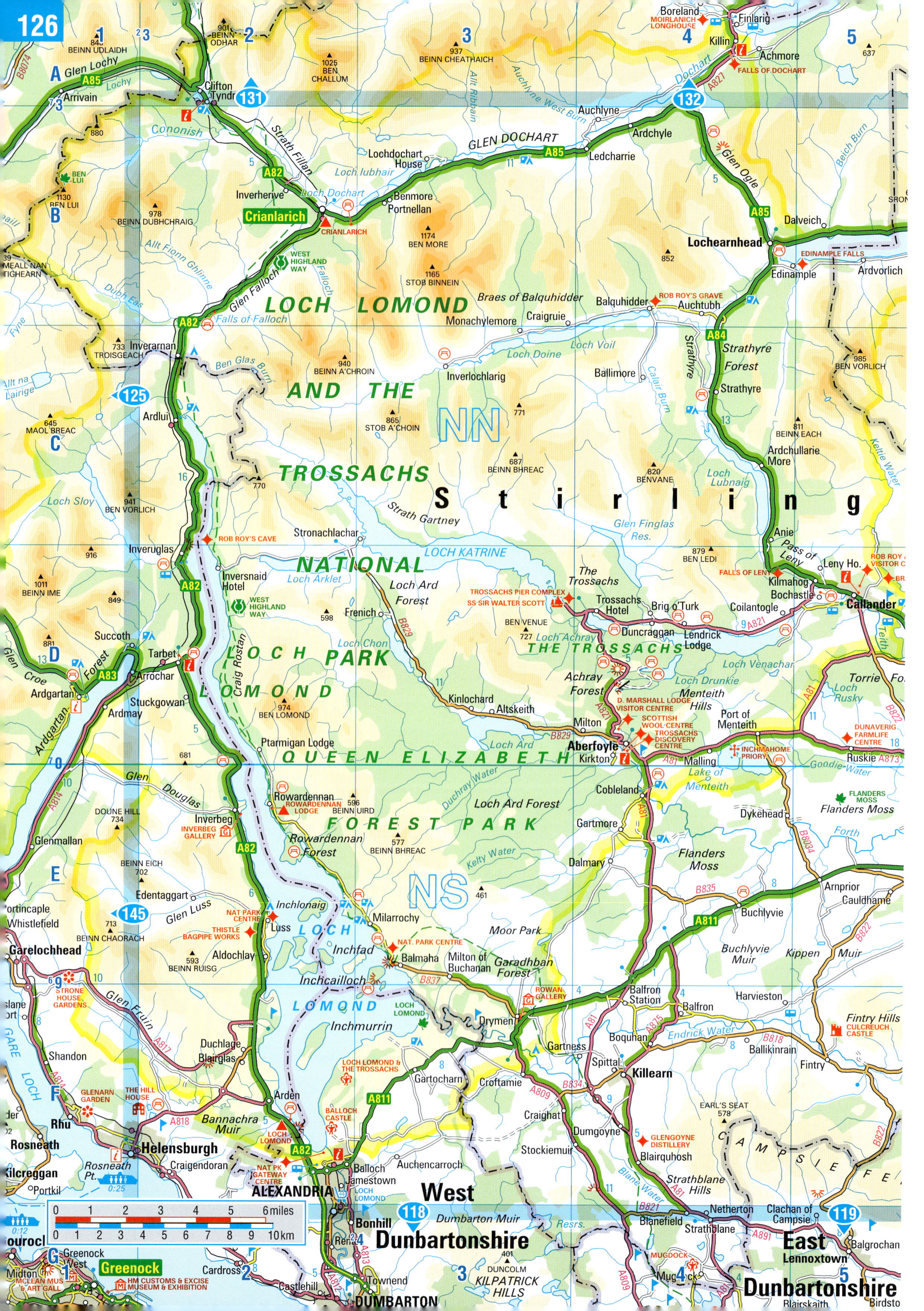
Glen Lochy
A85
Arrivain
BEINN UDLAIDH
BEINN ODHAR
Clifton
Tyndrum
131
BEN CHALLUM
BEINN CHEATHAICH
Allt Ribhain
Auchlyne West Burn
Boreland
MOIRLANICH LONGHOUSE
Finlarig
Killin
Achmore
FALLS OF DOCHART
Dochart
A827
132
Auchlyne
Ardchyle
Glen Ogle
Cononish
Strath Fillan
A82
Lochdochart House
GLEN DOCHART
A85
Ledcharrie
Beich Burn
Loch Iubhair
BEN LUI
Inverherive
Loch Dochart
Benmore
Portnellan
Crianlarich
CRIANLARICH
BEINN DUBHCHRAIG
BEN MORE
A85
Dalveich
Lochearnhead
EDINAMPLE FALLS
Edinample
Ardvorlich
MEALL NAN TIGHEARN
Allt Fionn Ghlinne
WEST HIGHLAND WAY
Falloch
STOB BINNEIN
Glen Falloch
Dubh Eas
LOCH LOMOND
Braes of Balquhidder
Balquhidder
ROB ROY'S GRAVE
Auchtubh
A82
Falls of Falloch
Monachylemore
Craigruie
A84
Strathyre Forest
Strathyre
Fyne
TROISGEACH
Inverarnan
Ben Glas Burn
Loch Voil
Loch Doine
Ballimore
BEN VORLICH
Allt na Lairige
BEINN A'CHROIN
Inverlochlarig
Calair Burn
125
AND THE
NN
Ardlui
MAOL BREAC
STOB A'CHOIN
BEINN EACH
C
Ardchullarie More
Keltie Water
TROSSACHS
BEINN BHREAC
BENVANE
Loch Lubnaig
Loch Sloy
BEN VORLICH
Stirling
Strath Gartney
Stronachlachar
Glen Finglas Res.
Anie
Pass of Leny
Inveruglas
ROB ROY'S CAVE
LOCH KATRINE
BEN LEDI
Leny Ho.
ROB ROY & VISITOR CENTRE
NATIONAL
The Trossachs
FALLS OF LENY
Kilmahog
Bochastle
Callander
BEINN IME
Inversnaid Hotel
Loch Arklet
Loch Ard Forest
TROSSACHS PIER COMPLEX
SS SIR WALTER SCOTT
Trossachs Hotel
Brig o'Turk
Coilantogle
A82
WEST HIGHLAND WAY
Frenich
BEN VENUE
Duncraggan
Lendrick Lodge
A821
Teith
Succoth
B829
Loch Achray
THE TROSSACHS
Glen Croe
Tarbet
LOCH
PARK
Loch Chon
Craig Rostan
Loch Venachar
Forest
A83
Arrochar
Achray Forest
Loch Drunkie
Torrie
Ardgartan
LOMOND
Menteith Hills
Loch Rusky
Ardgartan
Stuckgowan
Kinlochard
Altskeith
A821
D. MARSHALL LODGE VISITOR CENTRE
Port of Menteith
A81
Ardmay
BEN LOMOND
Milton
SCOTTISH WOOL CENTRE
TROSSACHS DISCOVERY CENTRE
DUNAVERIG FARMLIFE CENTRE
Ptarmigan Lodge
Loch Ard
B829
Aberfoyle
Kirkton
INCHMAHOME PRIORY
Ruskie
QUEEN ELIZABETH
A81
Malling
Lake of Menteith
Goodie Water
Glen Douglas
Duchray Water
Cobleland
FLANDERS MOSS
Flanders Moss
Rowardennan
ROWARDENNAN LODGE
BEINN UIRD
Loch Ard Forest
DOUNE HILL
Inverbeg
INVERBEG GALLERY
FOREST PARK
Gartmore
Dykehead
Glenmallan
A82
Rowardennan Forest
BEINN BHREAC
Forth
B8034
A814
Kelty Water
Flanders Moss
Dalmary
BEINN EICH
E
NS
B835
Arnprior
Edentaggart
Cauldhame
Glen Luss
Inchlonaig
145
NAT. PARK CENTRE
Milarrochy
Buchlyvie
Whistlefield
Luss
LOCH
Moor Park
A811
THISTLE BAGPIPE WORKS
BEINN CHAORACH
Inchfad
NAT. PARK CENTRE
Buchlyvie Muir
Kippen
Muir
B822
Garelochhead
Aldochlay
Balmaha
Milton of Buchanan
Garadhban Forest
BEINN RUISG
STRONE HOUSE GARDENS
Inchcailloch
B837
ROWAN GALLERY
Balfron Station
Harvieston
Glen Fruin
LOMOND
LOCH LOMOND
Drymen
Balfron
Inchmurrin
A81
A875
Endrick Water
Fintry Hills
CULCREUCH CASTLE
GARE LOCH
A817
Duchlage
Gartness
Boquhan
B818
Ballikinrain
Shandon
Blairglas
Spittal
Killearn
Fintry
LOCH LOMOND & THE TROSSACHS
A814
Gartocharn
Croftamie
GLENARN GARDEN
THE HILL HOUSE
B834
A809
EARL'S SEAT
F
Arden
A811
Rhu
A818
Bannachra Muir
BALLOCH CASTLE
Craighat
Dumgoyne
B822
Rosneath
Helensburgh
LOCH LOMOND
A82
GLENGOYNE DISTILLERY
CAMPSIE FELLS
Craigendoran
Stockiemuir
Blairquhosh
Rosneath Pt.
NAT PK GATEWAY CENTRE
Balloch
Jamestown
Auchencarroch
Blane Water
Strathblane Hills
Kilcreggan
Portkil
ALEXANDRIA
LOCH LOMOND
West
A81
B821
Netherton
Clachan of Campsie
119
Bonhill
118
Dumbarton Muir
Resrs.
Blanefield
Strathblane
A891
Gourock
Renton
Dunbartonshire
East
Balgrochan
Greenock West
G
A813
Lennoxtown
Greenock
DUNCOLM
MUGDOCK
Midton
MCLEAN MUS & ART GALL
HM CUSTOMS & EXCISE MUSEUM & EXHIBITION
Cardross
KILPATRICK HILLS
A809
Mugdock
Dunbartonshire
Castlehill
A812
Townend
DUMBARTON
Blairskaith
Birdston
0 1 2 3 4 5 6 miles
0 1 2 3 4 5 6 7 8 9 10 km

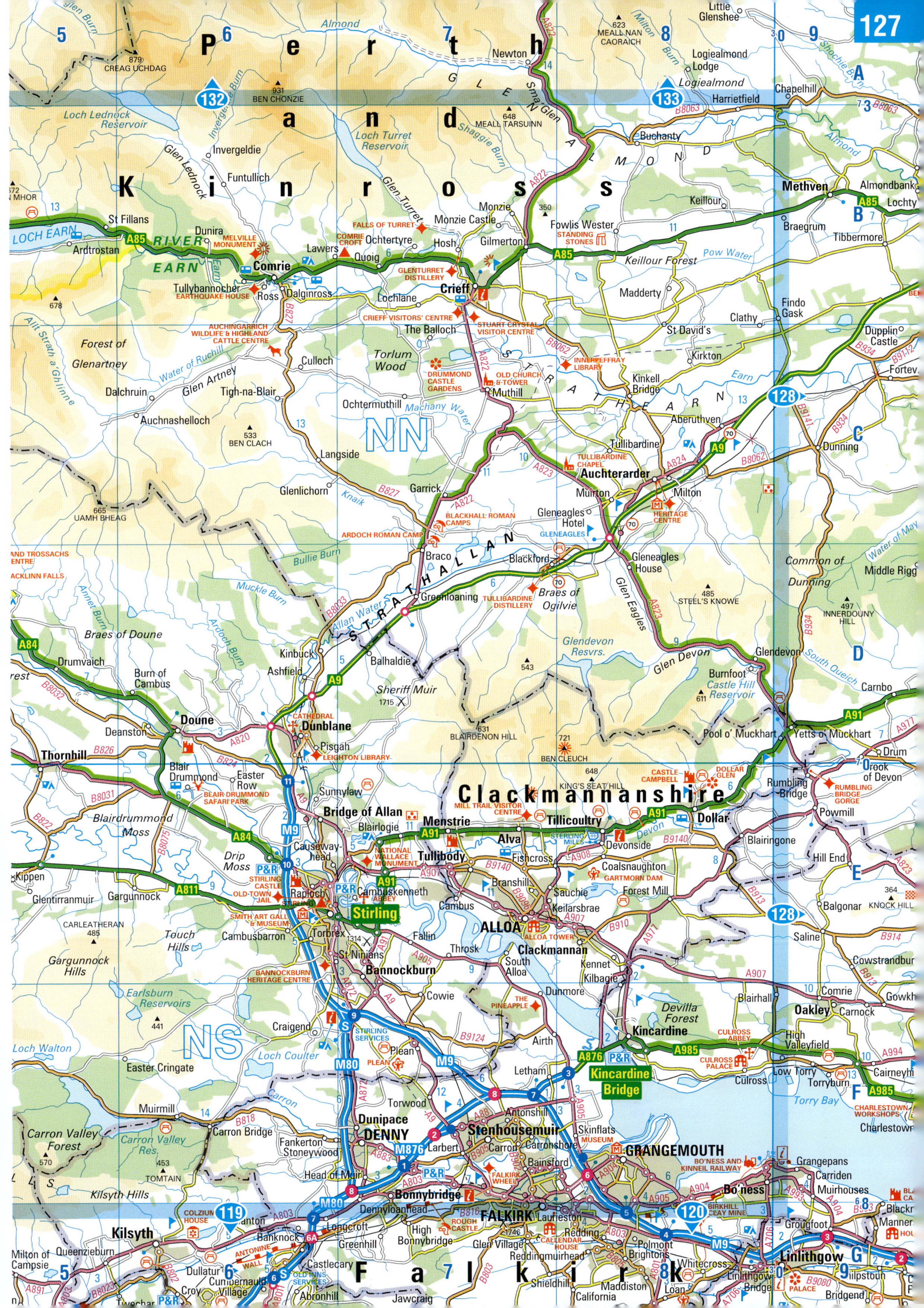
Perth and Kinross
Clackmannanshire
Falkirk
NN
NS
Almond
Glen Almond
879 CREAG UCHDAG
931 BEN CHONZIE
623 MEALL NAN CAORAICH
648 MEALL TARSUINN
Loch Lednock Reservoir
Loch Turret Reservoir
Newton
Little Glenshee
Logiealmond Lodge
Logiealmond
Harrietfield
Chapelhill
Buchanty
Invergeldie
Funtullich
Glen Lednock
Glen Turret
Shaggie Burn
Methven
Almondbank
Lochty
Keillour
Braegrum
Tibbermore
St Fillans
Loch Earn
Ardtrostan
River Earn
Dunira
Melville Monument
Comrie
Lawers
Comrie Croft
Quoig
Ochtertyre
Falls of Turret
Monzie
Monzie Castle
Hosh
Gilmerton
Fowlis Wester
Standing Stones
Keillour Forest
Pow Water
Glenturret Distillery
Crieff
Tullybannocher
Earthquake House
Ross
Dalginross
Lochlane
Madderty
Findo Gask
Clathy
St David's
Crieff Visitors' Centre
Stuart Crystal Visitor Centre
Auchingarrich Wildlife & Highland Cattle Centre
The Balloch
Forest of Glenartney
Water of Ruchill
Culloch
Torlum Wood
Drummond Castle Gardens
Old Church & Tower
Innerpeffray Library
Kirkton
Dupplin Castle
Forteviot
Glen Artney
Dalchruin
Tigh-na-Blair
Muthill
Kinkell Bridge
Strathearn
Ochtermuthill
Machany Water
Auchnashelloch
533 BEN CLACH
Aberuthven
Tullibardine
Dunning
Tullibardine Chapel
Auchterarder
Langside
Garrick
Glenlichorn
Knaik
Muirton
Milton
Heritage Centre
665 UAMH BHEAG
Blackhall Roman Camps
Ardoch Roman Camp
Gleneagles Hotel
Gleneagles
Braco
Blackford
Gleneagles House
Strathallan
Bullie Burn
Muckle Burn
Greenloaning
Tullibardine Distillery
Braes of Ogilvie
Glen Eagles
Common of Dunning
Middle Rigg
485 STEEL'S KNOWE
497 INNERDOUNY HILL
Braes of Doune
Allan Water
Ardoch Burn
Glendevon Resvrs.
Glendevon
Kinbuck
Balhaldie
Glen Devon
Drumvaich
Burn of Cambus
Ashfield
Sheriff Muir
1715
Burnfoot
Castle Hill Reservoir
Carnbo
Deanston
Doune
Cathedral
Dunblane
631 BLAIRDENON HILL
721 BEN CLEUCH
Pool o' Muckhart
Yetts o' Muckhart
Drum
Thornhill
Pisgah
Leighton Library
Crook of Devon
Blair Drummond
Easter Row
Blair Drummond Safari Park
Sunnylaw
648 KING'S SEAT HILL
Castle Campbell
Dollar Glen
Rumbling Bridge
Rumbling Bridge Gorge
Bridge of Allan
Mill Trail Visitor Centre
Menstrie
Tillicoultry
Dollar
Powmill
Blairdrummond Moss
Blairlogie
Alva
Devonside
Blairingone
Drip Moss
Causewayhead
National Wallace Monument
Tullibody
Fishcross
Coalsnaughton
Hill End
Kippen
Stirling Castle
Old Town Jail
Raploch
Cambuskenneth Abbey
Gartmorn Dam
Forest Mill
Glentirranmuir
Gargunnock
Stirling
Cambus
Sauchie
Keilarsbrae
364 KNOCK HILL
Balgonar
Carleatheran 485
Smith Art Gall & Museum
Touch Hills
Cambusbarron
Torbrex
Fallin
ALLOA
Alloa Tower
Saline
Gargunnock Hills
St Ninians
Throsk
Clackmannan
Cowstrandburn
Bannockburn Heritage Centre
Bannockburn
South Alloa
Kennet
Kilbagie
Earlsburn Reservoirs
Cowie
Dunmore
Blairhall
Oakley
Comrie
Carnock
Gowkhall
441
The Pineapple
Devilla Forest
Craigend
Kincardine
Culross Abbey
High Valleyfield
Loch Walton
Stirling Services
Plean
Airth
Culross Palace
Culross
Low Torry
Torryburn
Cairneyhill
Easter Cringate
Loch Coulter
Letham
Kincardine Bridge
Torry Bay
Charlestown Workshops
Charlestown
Muirmill
Carron
Torwood
Antonshill
Dunipace
Denny
Stenhousemuir
Skinflats Museum
Carron Valley Forest
Carron Bridge
Fankerton
Stoneywood
Larbert
Carron
Carronshore
Grangemouth
Grangepans
Carron Valley Res.
453 TOMTAIN
570
Bo'ness and Kinneil Railway
Carriden
Head of Muir
Bainsford
Falkirk Wheel
Kilsyth Hills
Bonnybridge
Bo'ness
Muirhouses
Colzium House
Dennyloanhead
Falkirk
Laurieston
Birkhill Clay Mine
Blackness
Kilsyth
Banton
Banknock
Longcroft
High Bonnybridge
Rough Castle
Redding
Polmont
Grangemouth
Manner
Milton of Campsie
Queenzieburn
Antonine Wall
Greenhill
Glen Village
Callendar House
Brightons
Linlithgow
Castlecary
Reddingmuirhead
Whitecross
Linlithgow Bridge
Linlithgow Palace
Philpstoun
Dullatur
Cumbernauld Village
Croy
Old Inns Services
Abronhill
Jawcraig
Shieldhill
California
Maddiston
Loan
Bridgend
Twechar
Westerton
Gartmore
Allt Strath a' Ghlinne
Loch Lednock Reservoir
Invergeldie Burn
Anner Burn
Water of May
Shochie Burn
South Queich
Glen Burn
Earn
Devon
A85
A822
A823
A824
A9
A84
A91
A811
A820
A907
A908
A905
A977
A876
A985
A994
A904
A803
A883
A872
A88
A801
A706
M9
M80
M876
B8063
B8062
B827
B8033
B826
B824
B8031
B822
B8075
B9140
B908
B910
B913
B914
B934
B9141
B9112
B9124
B818
B816
B905
B902
B8032
B8023
B9080
132
133
128
119
120

Perth and Kinross
NO
NT
FIRTH OF TAY
FIRTH OF FORTH
CARSE OF GOWRIE
BRAES OF THE CARSE
FIFE REGIONAL PARK
LOMOND HILLS
LOCH LEVEN
Perth
Kirkcaldy
EDINBURGH
Forth Road Bridge
DUNFERMLINE
GLENROTHES
GRANGEMOUTH
Stanley
Scone
Methven
Bridge of Earn
Auchterarder
Auchtermuchty
Newburgh
Kinross
Milnathort
Falkland
Ladybank
Leslie
Markinch
Cowdenbeath
Lochgelly
Kelty
Ballingry
Lochore
Cardenden
Burntisland
Kinghorn
Aberdour
Inverkeithing
North Queensferry
Queensferry
Rosyth
Dollar
Oakley
Invergowrie
Bo'ness
Leith
Inchkeith
Inchcolm
Cramond I.
Mugdrum I.
M90
A9
A90
A91
A92
A85
A977
A985
133
134
127
120
121
0 1 2 3 4 5 6 miles
0 1 2 3 4 5 6 7 8 9 10 km

Birkhill
Fintry
Downfield
Baldovie
Mains of Ardestie
Carnoustie
Dundee
Douglas & Angus
Craigie
West Ferry
Monifieth
Barry Links
Lochee
VERDANT WORKS
MUS AND ART GALL
MILLS OBSERVATORY
Stannergate
Broughty Ferry
Barnhill
BROUGHTY CASTLE MUSEUM
FRIGATE UNICORN
Buddon Ness
Dundee
Tay Bridge
DUNDEE
DISCOVERY POINT
UNIVERSITY BOTANIC GARDENS
Tayport
Scotscraig
TENTSMUIR
Newport-on-Tay
Woodhaven
Tay Rail Bridge
Wormit
Tentsmuir Forest
Kirkton
Bottomcraig
Balmerino
Pickletillem
Gauldry
Rhynd
Carrick
Kilmany
Lucklawhill
Leuchars
LEUCHARS NORMAN CHURCH
Rathillet
Logie
Balmullo
Eden Mouth
Guardbridge
EDEN ESTUARY CENTRE
ST ANDREWS BAY
Dairsie or Osnaburgh
Kincaple
ST ANDREWS
ST ANDREWS AQUARIUM
BRITISH GOLF MUS
St Andrews
Kilmaron Castle
Newpark
CATH & ST RULE'S TOWER
Strathkinness
Cupar
Kemback
Blebocraigs
Balone
Brownhills
Buddo Ness
ST ANDREWS BOTANIC GARDEN
CRAIGTOUN
Boarhills
Babbet Ness
Cupar Muir
Denhead
Prior Muir
Pitscottie
HILL OF TARVIT MANSIONHOUSE
Kingsbarns
Cameron Res.
Cameron Burn
Cambo Ness
CAMBO GARDENS
Carr Brigs
Bridgend
Ceres
Baldinnie
Stravithie
Tullybothy Craigs
Dunino
SCOTSTARVIT TOWER
Craigrothie
FIFE FOLK MUSEUM
Balcomie
Craighead
Peat Inn
Fife Ness
Radernie
Kingsmuir
CRAIL TOLBOOTH
Lochty
SCOTLAND'S SECRET BUNKER
Woodside
Lathones
Crail
New Gilston
CRAIL MUSEUM AND HERITAGE CENTRE
Montrave
Largoward
Pitcorthie
Carnbee
West Ness
Pitkierie
Wester Newburn
KELLIE CASTLE AND GARDEN
FIFE COASTAL PATH
PRAYTIS FARM PARK
SCOTLAND'S LARDER
Kilrenny
Arncroach
Kirkton of Largo
NO
Anstruther Easter
Drumeldrie
Colinsburgh
SCOTTISH FISHERIES MUSEUM
Bonnybank
Lundin Links
Abercrombie
Pittenweem
Anstruther Wester
Kennoway
ROBINSON CRUSOE STATUE
Balchrystie
Kilconquhar
Scoonie
Lower Largo
ST FILLAN'S CAVE
ST MONAN'S WINDMILL
SILVERBURN ESTATE
St Monans
Ardross
LETHAM GLEN
Leven
Largo Bay
ST MONAN'S CHURCH
Ruddons Pt.
Innerleven
Elie
Earlsferry
Sauchar Pt.
Methil
ISLE OF MAY
MUSEUM
Chapel Ness
Isle of May
Buckhaven
FIFE COASTAL PATH
FORTH
Fidra
Craigleith
Bass Rock
SCOTTISH SEABIRD CENTRE
Eyebroughy
North Berwick
MUSEUM
TANTALLON CASTLE
DIRLETON CASTLE & GARDENS
MUIRFIELD
Auldhame
NT
Gullane Bay
Dirleton
Scoughall
Gullane
West Fenton
Kingston
Whitekirk
St. Baldred's Cradle
Fenton Barns
Aberlady Bay
Tyne Mouth
Aberlady
JOHN MUIR BIRTHPLACE
MYRETON MOTOR MUSEUM
Drem
JOHN MUIR
Dunbar
Craigielaw
Tyninghame
THE CHESTERS FORT
MUSEUM OF FLIGHT
East Fortune
Belhaven
West Barns
GOSFORD HOUSE
Ballencrieff
Preston
Gosford Bay
Athelstaneford
Peffer Burn
Broxburn
Barns Ness
Spittal
East Linton
Cockenzie and Port Seton
SETON COLLEGIATE CHURCH
HOPETOUN MON
PRESTON MILL & PHANTASSIE DOOCOT
JANE WELSH CARLYLE MUSEUM
Longniddry
Biel Water
East Barns
HAILES CASTLE
Traprain
Pitcox
Spott
Meikle
Skateraw
A
B
C
D
E
F
G

Loch Beoraid
Polnish
Lochailort
A830
Ranochan
796 SGURR AN UTHA
Glen Finnan
Glen Dubh Lighe
Wauchan
Gleann Suileag
Druim Fada
A Ardnish
Laggan
Loch Ailort
Inverailort
A861
Loch Eilt
147
STATION MUSEUM
GLENFINNAN MONUMENT
Glenfinnan
136
Alisary
869 DRUIM FIACLACH
Callop
Drumsallie
Kinlocheil
Fassfern
A830
TREASURES OF THE EARTH
Roshven
882 ROIS-BHEINN
882 BEINN ODHAR BHEAG
LOCH EIL
South Garvan
Duisky
Blaich
Corpach
Achaphubuil
Camusnagaul
Trislaig
B
666 BEINN GAIRE
755 MEALL NAN CREAG LEAC
Glen Garvan
Kinlochmoidart
MOIDART
Gaskan
LOCH SHIEL
Scamodale
Ach'an Todhair
770 STOB COIRE A'CHEARCAILL
Stronchreggan
Ardmolich
Loch Moidart
Brunery
SGOR AN TARMACHAIN 756
Gorstanvorran
Cona Glen
Druimarbin
A82
LOCH SHIEL
Glen Hurich
Dalnabreck
Dalelia
Polloch
786 BEINN MHEADHOIN
Conaglen House
Blarmachfoldach
CLAISH MOSS
Glenhurich
Loch Doilet
888 SGURR DHOMHNUILL
Aryhoulan
Coruanan Lodge
Ardshealach
Kinlochan
Glen Scaddle
Inverscaddle Bay
SUNART
Ardgour
SGURR NA H-EANCHAINNE 730
616 BEINN NA GUCAIG
C
Resipole
845 BEINN RESIPOL
ARIUNDLE CENTRE
ARIUNDLE OAKWOOD
Glen Gour
Glenrigh Forest
Ariundle
Scotstown
Strontian
701
Ardgour
Clovullin
Corran
Inchree
LOCH SUNART
Anaheilt
Sallachan
Corran Narrows
Keppanach
Onich
GLENCRIPESDALE
Ardnastang
Strontian
885 GARBH BHEINN
615
A861
Glen Tarbert
Sallachan Pt.
A82
North Ballachulish
Camuschoirk
Tarbert
Inversanda Bay
Inversanda
LOCH LINNHE
Liddesdale
516 MEALL AN DAMHAIN
NM
583 CREACH BHEINN
B8043
South Ballachulish
Ballachulish
Glencoe
Kentallen
A828
582 BEINN NAM BEATHRACH
765 FUAR BHEINN
Kilmalieu
Glenduror Forest
947
Duror
Rubha Mor
571
D
Lochuisge
A884
Loch Uisge
B8043
Cuil Bay
Beinn a'Bheithir
Glen an Fhiodh
Gleann Dubh
Eilean Balnagowan
Keil
Glen Duror
Beach
Kingairloch
Camasnacroise
Salachan Glen
Loch Arienas
Loch a' Choire
KINGAIRLOCH
879 FRAOCHAIDH
Acharn
739 BEINN MHEADHOIN
Gleann Geal
Shuna I.
Appin House
Glen Stockdale
Elleric
Glen Creran
959
Claggan
147
A828
Fasnacloich
Glen Ure
ARDTORNISH GARDENS
Achranich
Loch Tearnait
437 BEINN A' CHAISIL
Portnacroish
KINLOCHLAICH HOUSE GARDENS
Invercreran
BEINN CHURALAIN 546
GLASDRUM WOOD
Glasdrum
937 BEINN SGULAIRD
Loch Aline
Rannoch
Loch nan Clach
Glensanda
Appin
Strath of Appin
Creagan
E
GLAIS BHEINN 479
Port Ramsay
Port Appin
Druimavuic
LYNN OF LORN
AN SLEAGHACH 513
Clachan
North Shian
839 BEINN TRILLEACHAN
Eignaig
Eriska
South Creagan
ARDTORNISH CASTLE
South Shian
Loch Creran
Lismore
B8045
Barcaldine
Inninmore Bay
Garbh Shlios
Camas Gorm
Achnacroish
SCOTTISH SEA LIFE SANCTUARY
810 CREACH BHEINN
Barcaldine Forest
LYNN OF LORN
Abhainn Dalach
Allt Easach
Scallastle Bay
Rubha an Ridire
Bernera I.
124
Achinduin
Baravullin
Ferlochan
125
Kilcheran
Kiel Crofts
BENDERLOCH
Benderloch
Java
Craignure Bay
Eilean Dubh
Gleann Salach
B845
Craignure
Ledaig
Achnaba
715 BEINN MHEADHONACH
LOCH ETIVE
0:50
Ardmucknish Bay
ARDCHATTAN PRIORY GARDENS
ARDCHATTAN PRIORY
F
Duart Bay
Duart Pt.
DUART CASTLE
Eilean Musdile
Eilean Mor
DUNSTAFFNAGE CASTLE
North Connel
Connel
A828
Black Crofts
FALLS OF LORA
Glen Liver
0:45
Dunbeg
Achnacloich
ACHNACLOICH GARDEN
Bonawe
Lochdon
CASTLEBAY 4:50
COLL 2:40
TIREE 3:35
Ganavan
Black Lochs
A85
Glen Noe
Fearnoch Forest
Brochroy
BONAWE IRON FURNACE
INVERAWE FISHERIES AND SMOKERIES EXHIBITION
A849
Loch Don
Dunollie
OBAN/OBAN LODGE
MCCAIG'S TOWER
OBAN DISTILLERY
Taynuilt
BEN CRUACHAN 1126
Grass Pt.
Altnacraig
BARGUILLEAN GARDENS
Ichrachan
Bridge of Awe
Pass of Brander
Cruachan Res.
Kerrera
Oban
GLEN NANT
Glen Nant
Awe
COLONSAY 2:20
Glenamachrie
383
Glen Lonan
897
Falls of Cruachan
Loch Spelve
0 1 2 3 4 5 6 miles
0 1 2 3 4 5 6 7 8 9 10 km
Gallanach
Loch Nell
Barran
515
CRUACHAN DAM VISITOR CENTRE
Loch-Nant
Loch Tromlee

Gairlochy
Stronaba
Kilmonivaig
COMMANDO MEMORIAL
Spean Bridge
Bohuntine
Bohenie
Inverroy
Roybridge
Achluachrach
Murlaggan
Roughburn
Moy Forest
Moy
Loy Lodge
Glen Loy Forest
Strone
Muirshearlich
Brackletter
Highbridge
Killiechonate
Spean
MONESSIE FALLS
Braes o'Lochaber
GLEN SPEAN
A86
A82
TOR CASTLE
Leanachan Forest
Banavie
NEPTUNE'S STAIRCASE LOCKS
Torlundy
NEVIS RANGE SKI CENTRE
Caol
Lochyside
BEN NEVIS DISTILLERY VISITOR CENTRE
Inverlochy
Claggan
Fort William
Achintee
WEST HIGHLAND MUSEUM
GLEN NEVIS VISITOR CENTRE
GLEN NEVIS
Glen Nevis House
Water of Nevis
1344 BEN NEVIS
1234 AONACH BEAG
1094
1106
1177 STOB CHOIRE CLAURIGH
724 BEINN CHLIANAIG
Allt Laire
Fersit
Lairig Leacach
1115 STOB COIRE EASAIN
LOCH TREIG
1046 CHNO DEARG
Loch Ghuilbinn
Ossian
1114 AONACH BEAG
1087 BEINN A'CHLACHAIR
1049 BEINN A' CHAORUINN
1049 GEAL CHARN
Allt Cam
Uisge Labhair
1148 BEN ALDER
Prince Charlie's Cave
Creaguaineach Lodge
937 BEINN NA LAP
Corrour Shooting Lodge
Loch Ossian
LOCH OSSIAN
Corrour Forest
952 SGOR GAIBHRE
583
Rannoch Forest
Achriabhach
Glen Nevis
Amhainn Rath
Blar a'Chaorainn
1099 SGURR A' MHAIM
1130 BINNEIN MOR
MAMORE FOREST
Loch Eilde Beag
630
789
Loch Eilde Mor
Ciaran Water
906 LEUM UILLEIM
Allt na Caim
WEST HIGHLAND WAY
796 MAM NA GUALAINN
Kinlochmore
Kinlochleven
THE ALUMINIUM STORY
B863
Leven
BLACKWATER RESERVOIR
Black Water
GLENCOE AND NORTH LORN FOLK MUSEUM
867
967 AONACH
953
GLENCOE
NN
Rannoch Station
B846
Loch Eigheach
Gaur
Bridge of Gaur
739 STOB NA CRUAICHE
Altnafeadh
857 BEINN A' CHRULAISTE
Black Corries Lodge
Glen Coe
BEN NEVIS AND GLEN COE
925
1150 BIDEAN NAM BIAN
Coupall
Kingshouse Hotel
Loch Gaineamhach
Loch Laidon
Royal Forest
Etive
GLENCOE SKI CENTRE
MUSEUM OF SCOTTISH SKIING AND MOUNTAINEERING
RANNOCH MOOR
Allt Camghouran
994 SGOR NA H-ULAIDH
Dalness
Glen Etive
Alltchaorunn
1188
547
Loch Bà
931 MEALL BUIDHE
883 STOB DUBH
1099 CLACH LEATHAD
Allt Coire a'Chaolain
Bà
Loch na h-Achlaise
Water of Tulla
Inverchanan
Glenceitlein
879
BLACK MOUNT
Loch an Daimh
Eas Daimh
Gualachulain
Allt Dochard
1090 STOB GHABHAR
WEST HIGHLAND WAY
Loch Tulla
Achallader
907 MEALL BUIDHE
960 STUCHD AN LOCHAIN
1044 STOB COIR'AN ALBANNAICH
Black Mount
1081 BEINN A' CHREACHAIN
Fubil
Cashlie
1078 BEN STARAV
Forest Lodge
Loch Dochard
Inveroran Hotel
Loch Lyon
Stronuich Reservoir
957 BEINN NAN AIGHENAN
Allt Hallater
1004 BIENN AN DOTHAIDH
953 BEINN MHANACH
Bridge of Orchy
BEINN HEASGARNICH 1076
639
1076 BEINN DÒRAIN
Allt Chonoghlais
Kenknock
Glen Lochay
701
Glen Kinglass
Orchy
Glen Orchy
A82
1047 CREAG MHOR
Breadalbane
796 BEINN MHIC-MHONAIDH
Arichastlich
901 BEINN ODHAR
989 BEINN EUNAICH
Glen Strae
840 BEINN UDLAIDH
937 BEINN CHEATHAICH
1025 BEN CHALLUM
Auchlyne West Burn
Allt Mhoille
B8074
Glen Lochy
A85
Arrivain
Lochy
Clifton
Tyndrum
Allt Riobain
B8077
Strath Fillan
KILCHURN CASTLE
Lochawe
Stronmilchan
Strath of Orchy
Achnafalnich
880
Cononish
Inverlochy
GLEN DOCHART
Lochdochart House
Loch Iubhair
Dalmally
MCINTYRE MONUMENT
BEN LUI
1130 BEN LUI
Inverherive
Crianlarich
Loch Dochart
Benmore
Innis Chonain
A85
136
137
132
132
125
126

Moy
Moy Lodge
674 BEINN EILDE
911
Lochan na h-Earba
Ardverikie Forest
1049 GEAL CHARN
Pattack
Loch Ericht Forest
A9
Gaick Forest
Loch Bhrodainn
Allt Gharbh Ghaig
137
774 CREAGAN MOR
941 CARN NA CAIM
138
Loch an Duin
Allt Loraich
Loch Pattack
Ben Alder Lodge
917
Cama Choire
Sronphadruig Lodge
Dail-na-Mine Forest
816 SRON A'CHLEIRICH
1087 BEINN A'CHLACHAIR
Allt Cam
Allt a'Chaoil-reidhe
Ben Alder Forest
936 A'BHUIDHEANACH BHEAG
Allt Glas Choire
FOREST
ATHOLL
Loch Ghuilbinn
LOCH ERICHT
934 BEINN UDLAMAIN
803 THE SOW OF ATHOLL
Dalnacardoch Forest
1114 AONACH BEAG
Loch a' Bhealaich Bheithe
Dalnaspidal Lodge
Edendon Water
Allt a' Chireachain
Ossian
Uisge Labhair
1148 BEN ALDER
Corrievarkie Lodge
Allt na Glaise
Dalnaspidal Forest
Loch Garry
775 MEALL NA LEITREACH
Dalnacardoch Lodge
Corrour Shooting Lodge
Loch Ossian
Prince Charlie's Cave
855
Talla Bheith Forest
GLEN GARRY
Corrour Forest
952 SGOR GAIBHRE
131
Loch Con
Loch Errochty
Allt Ghlas
841 BEINN MHOLACH
612
Rannoch Forest
GRAMPIAN
NN
Trinafour
Dalchalloch
B847
Errochty Water
GLEN ERROCHTY
515 SRON BHEAG
Aulich Burn
891 BEINN A'CHUALLAICH
Tummel Forest
477
Water
Killichonan Burn
Ericht
Craiganor Lodge
Kinloch Rannoch
B846
Tummel Bridge
B8019
Rannoch Station
Bridge of Ericht
Killichonan
LOCH RANNOCH
Dunalastair
Dunalastair Water
Tummel
Foss
Loch Eigheach
Gaur
Bridge of Gaur
Finnart
Carie
Inverhadden
Camghouran
Black Wood of Rannoch
Rannoch Forest
Dall Burn
Allt na Bogair
Innerhadden Burn
Loch Kinardochy
TAY FOREST
1083 SCHIEHALLION
Allt Mor
Allt Camghouran
LOCH RANNOCH AND GLEN LYON
GLENGOULANDIE DEER PARK
Keltney Burn
745 MEALL A'MHUIC
1042 CARN MAIRG
1029 CARN GORM
931 MEALL BUIDHE
Keltneyburn
Appin of Dull
Invervar
Camusvrachan
ST FILLAN'S CHURCH & FORTINGALL YEW
Loch an Daimh
GLEN LYON GALLERY
Innerwick
Lyon
Fortingall
Taymouth Castle
Eas Daimh
Bridge of Balgie
Allt Conait
Gallin
Glen Lyon
Kenmore
A827
907 MEALL BUIDHE
960 STUCHD AN LOCHAIN
Allt Bail a'Mhuilinn
Allt Gleann Da-Eig
Fearnan
SCOTTISH CRANNOG
Remony
780
1118
Acharn
Falls of Acharn
Pubil
Cashlie
Lawers Burn
Loch Lyon
Stronuich Reservoir
LOCH TAY
1214 BEN LAWERS
Loch na Lairige
BEN LAWERS
716 BEINN BHREAC
MEALL NAN TARMACHAN 1043
Lawers
Quaich
Ardtalnaig
BEINN HEASGARNICH 1076
BEN LAWERS VISITOR CENTRE
Carie
Gleann a'Chilleine
Kenknock
Glen Lochay
888
Milton Morenish
Morenish
Ardeonaig
Finglen Burn
Lochay
FALLS OF LOCHAY AND FISH LIFT
Boreland
MOIRLANICH LONGHOUSE
Finlarig
Killin
Achmore
637
Breadalbane
937 BEINN CHEATHAICH
Auchlyne West Burn
Dochart
A827
FALLS OF DOCHART
879 CREAG UCHDAG
Loch Lednock Reservoir
Invergeldie Burn
931 BEN CHONZIE
Allt Ribhainn
126
Auchlyne
A85
Ardchyle
127
Beich Burn
Glen Ogle
Glen Lednock
Invergeldie
Funtullich
Loch Iubhair
Dochart
Benmore
672 SRON MHOR
0 1 2 3 4 5 6 miles
0 1 2 3 4 5 6 7 8 9 10 km

MOUNTAINS
FOREST OF ATHOLL
LOCH TUMMEL
TUMMEL FOREST PARK
NN
NO
Perth and Kinross
GLEN ALMOND
STRATHARDLE
STRATH TAY
RIVER TAY
Bishopric
Glen Shee
994 CARN EALAR
1006 AN SGARSOCH
Bynack Burn
920 CARN BHAC
Baddoch
834
788 UCHD A'CHLARSAIR
138
139
1019 CARN AN TUIRC
958 TOLMO
Tarf Water
1048 BEINN IUTHARN MHOR
Clunie Water
Loch Vrotachan
GLENSHEE SKI CENTRE
933 THE CAIRNWELL
Devil's Elbow
1068 GLAS MAOL
Caenlochan Forest
Glen Bruar
1008 BEINN DEARG
879 BRAIGH SRON GHORM
Loch nan Eun
Tilt
Bruar Lodge
899
Forest Lodge
Loch Loch
1051 GLAS TULAICHEAN
905 FINALTY HILL
Isla
Glen Diridh
Glen Tilt
1120 BEINN A'GHLO
BEN GULABIN 806
Glenlochsie
808 MONAMEANACH
975 CARN LIATH
903 BEN VUIRICH
Gleann Fearnach
801 BEN EARB
Spittal of Glenshee
Auchavan
Loch Beanie
DUCHRAY HILL 702
740 BADENDU HILL
Bruar Water
Falls of the Bruar
CLAN DONNACHAIDH MUSEUM
BLAIR CASTLE
B8079
Pitagowan
Calvine
Struan
Blair Atholl
Old Bridge of Tilt
Lude House
BLAIR ATHOLL MILL
Ballentoul
BLAIR ATHOLL DISTILLERY
TULACH HILL 470
Glen Girnaig
794 MEALL UAINE
134
Dalnaglar Castle
Meikle Forter
Folda
Cray
B951
744 MOUNT BLAIR
Brewlands Bridge
ATHOLL COUNTRY COLLECTION
Aldclune
1689
Killiecrankie
KILLIECRANKIE VISITOR CENTRE
Bonskeid House
B8019
Loch Bhac
841 BEN VRACKIE
Dalnavaid
Tarvie
Straloch
Glen Brerachan
Enochdhu
A924
Ashintully Castle
641 CREAG DHUBH
Tressait
Queen's View
QUEEN'S VIEW CENTRE
Falls of Tummel
LINN OF TUMMEL
A9
Moulin
PITLOCHRY
Pitlochry
Kirkmichael
Blacklunans
B950
520 CAIRN GIBBS
Loch Faskally
EDRADOUR DISTILLERY
Milton of Edradour
Balmore
HYDRO-ELECTRIC VISITOR CENTRE
SCOTTISH PLANT COLLECTORS GARDEN
BLAIR ATHOLL DISTILLERY VISITOR CENTRE
Loch Broom
534 MEALL REAMHAR
KNOCK OF BALMYLE 444
Black Water
Forest of Alyth
780 FARRAGON HILL
Loch Derculich
Tummel
Milton of Dalcapon
Ballintuim
Ardle
561 CREAG NAM MIAL
Strathtay
Ballechin
A827
Tulliemet
Ballinluig
Logierait
Tay
Grandtully
Little Ballinluig
Balnaguard
Edradynate
CLUNY HOUSE GARDENS
ST MARY'S CHURCH
CASTLE MENZIES
Weem
Camserney
Dull
ABERFELDY DISTILLERY & DEWAR'S WORLD OF WHISKY
WADE'S BRIDGE
Aberfeldy
Falls of Moness
BOLFRACKS GARDEN
Balmacneil
Kindallachan
Guay
Dowally
Kincraigie
Loch Skiach
B898
Loch Ordie
Forest of Clunie
Blackcraig Forest
Loch Benachally
Bridge of Cally
Netherton
Tullymurdoch
Cochrage Muir
Riemore
Lornty Burn
Middleton
Tullyfergus
509 DEUCHARY HILL
Riechip
308
Westfields of Rattray
Lornty
A926
Dalguise
Craigvinean Forest
Butterstone
Forneth
Achalader
A923
Blairgowrie
Kinloch
Rattray
Rosemount
532
Loch Kennard
Ballinloan Burn
Urlar Burn
566
Loch Hoil
Glen Cochill
Tombane Burn
SCOTTISH HORSE REGIMENTAL MUSEUM
Loch of the Lowes
LOCH OF LOWES NATURE RESERVE
Concraigie
Loch of Clunie
Clunie
Craigie
Loch of Drumellie
Muirton
Dunkeld
CATHEDRAL
Little Dunkeld
Snaigow House
Kirkton of Lethendy
B947
Lunan Burn
Scotston
THE HERMITAGE
Inver
Birnam
WATERFALL
Ballinlick
Trochry
A822
A984
Spittalfield
Delvine
690 MEALL DEARG
Garrow
404
Caputh
Meikleour
BEECH HEDGE
Kinclaven
Cablea
Strathbraan
Braan
Loch Freuchie
Glen Quaich
Obney Hills
Upper Obney
Gellyburn
Murthly
Muir of Thorn
Ardoch
B867
B9099
Woodside
Burrelton
Cargill
Isla
Amulree
Balquharn
Waterloo
805 MEALL NAM FUARAN
Corrymuckloch
Ordie Burn
Bankfoot
Airntully
Whitefield
Little Glenshee
LIQUEUR CENTRE
Tullybelton
Stanley
West Tofts
Wolfhill
Saucher
623 MEALL NAN CAORAICH
Milton Burn
Shochie Burn
Newton
Logiealmond Lodge
Logiealmond
Guildtown
Kinrossie
Kirkton of Collace
Sma' Glen
Chapelhill
Downhill
Newmiln
St Martins
Harrietfield
B8063
Moneydie
Luncarty
648 MEALL TARSUINN
127
128
B953
Balbeggie
Loch Turret Reservoir
Shaggie Burn
Buchanty
Almond
Redgorton
Pitcairngreen
A93
A94
PERTH AIRPORT
Glen Turret
Methven
Almondbank
CAITHNESS GLASS
PERTH
PERTH MART VISITOR CENTRE
SCONE PALACE
Scone
288 POLE HILL
A85
Lochty
Huntingtower
Muirton
Keillour
Monzie
A822

Baddoch
Glen Callater
Loch Callater
Dubh Loch
Glas-allt Shiel
Spittal of Glenmuick
Loch Muick
Glen Mark
Water of Mark
Burn of Branny
Water of Tarf
Glen Lee
1012 CAIRN BANNOCH
998 BROAD CAIRN
939 AN SOCACH
1019 CARN AN TUIRC
958 TOLMOUNT
696 AWEE
Invermark Lodge
Auchronie
Loch Lee
Inchgrundle
Tarfside
Cairncross
Clunie Water
Loch Vrotachan
GLENSHEE SKI CENTRE
THE CAIRNWELL
Devil's Elbow
1068 GLAS MAOL
Caenlochan Forest
Glen Doll
Glendoll Lodge
Glendoll Forest
CORRIE FEE
Braedownie
832 LAIR OF ALDARARIE
Water of Unich
MUCKLE CAIRN 826
Loch Brandy
Water of Saughs
CRUYS 741
Glen Effock
691 WEST KNOCK
BEN GULABIN 806
905 FINALTY HILL
Isla
947 DRIESH
758
Clova
778 WHITE HILL
Hunthill Lodge
808 MONAMEANACH
Wheen
Angus
756 FINBRACKS
Spittal of Glenshee
Auchavan
Loch Beanie
Glenprosen Lodge
Kilburn
Rottal
794 MEALL UAINE
702 DUCHRAY HILL
740 BADENDUN HILL
NO
Balnaboth
PROSEN
Glenprosen Village
512
Clachnabrain
545 AULD DARKNEY
Glen Shee
Glen Prosen
Glen Clova
Dalnaglar Castle
Meikle Forter
Folda
Glenisla Forest
611
Glenmoy
Auchnacree
Cray
744 MOUNT BLAIR
Brewlands Bridge
Backwater Res.
Glenhead Farm
Easter Lednathie
Glenogil
South Esk
Ashintully Castle
Freuchies
Glenquiech
Ogil
Fern
Kirkmichael
Blacklunans
Kirkton of Glenisla
668 CAT LAW
CAPTAIN SCOTT & DR WILSON CAIRN
Horniehaugh
Dykehead
Newmill of Inshewan
Noran
520 CAIRN GIBBS
Bellaty
497 CREIGH HILL
Balintore
Pearsie
Cortachy
Memus
Tannadice
KNOCK OF BALMYLE 444
Black Water
Forest of Alyth
Dykends
Balloch
Inverquharity
Murthill
Shielhill
Finavon
409 MILE HILL
Oathlaw
Loch of Lintrathen
PEEL FARM TRAIL
Kirkton of Kingoldrum
Northmuir
Ballintuim
Ardle
BALDUFF HILL 425
Bridgend of Lintrathen
LOCH OF KINNORDY NATURE RESERVE
Kinnordy
Kirriemuir
BARRIE'S BIRTHPLACE
Carse Gray
REEKIE LINN WATERFALL
Bridge of Craigisla
Auchrannie
Netherton
Tullymurdoch
Westmuir
GATEWAY TO THE GLENS MUS
Mosside
Lunanhead
RESTENNETH PRIORY
Blackcraig Forest
Bamff
Kirkton of Airlie
Mains of Ballindarg
Padanaram
FORFAR LOCH
Forfar
Bridge of Cally
Craigton
Drumgley
THE MEFFAN GALLERY & MUS
Cochrage Muir
Shanzie
Leys of Cossans
ST ORLAND'S STONE
Dean Water
Kingsmuir
Tullyfergus
Ruthven
Ruthven House
EASSIE SCULPTURED STONE
Lornty Burn
Middleton
Alyth
New Alyth
308
GLAMIS CASTLE
Caldhame
Lownie Moor
Lornty
Westfields of Rattray
Balhary
Castleton
Glamis
Douglastown
Thornton
Kirkton
Charleston
ANGUS FOLK MUSEUM
Foffarty
Achalader
Blairgowrie
Kinloch
Rattray
Leitfie
MEIGLE MUSEUM
Balkeerie
Eassie
Inverarity
Loch of Clunie
Loch of Drumellie
Rosemount
River Ericht
Kirkinch
Meigle
Kinloch
Milton
Gateside
Whigstreet
Clunie
Craigie
Muirton
Ardblair
ARK HILL 340
Wester Denoon
Kirkton of Lethendy
Arthurstone
Gallowfauld
Lunan Burn
Ardler
New-bigging
Newtyle
Nether Handwick
SIDLAW HILLS
Spittalfield
Delvine
Coupar Angus
Keillor
259
Caputh
Tay
Meikleour
BEECH HEDGE
Kinclaven
Isla
Kettins
Markethill
Hallyburton House
Long Loch
Coldstream
Bonnyton
Balkemback
Tealing
Murthly
Ardoch
Campmuir
Leys
Kirkton of Auchterhouse
Newbigging
Monikie
Woodside
Burrelton
Lundie
Auchterhouse
Leoch
Kirkton
Inveraldie
East March
Wellbank
Cargill
Pitcur
Muir of Pert
Burnside of Duntrune
Bucklerheads
Newbigging
Whitefield
Littleton
Dronley
Bridgefoot
Kellas
Drumsturdy
West Tofts
Muirhead
Birkhill
CLATTO
SOUTERRAIN ARDESTIE
Stanley
Saucher
Collace
KING'S SEAT 377
Fowlis
CAMPERDOWN AND TEMPLETON WOODS
Liff
Downfield
Fintry
Douglas & Angus
Baldovie
Wolfhill
Guildtown
Kinrossie
Kirkton of Collace
Abernyte
Denhead of Gray
Knapp
Dundee
VERDANT WORKS
Craigie
West Ferry
Monifieth
St Martins
Newmiln
Lochee
MILLS OBSERVATORY
MUS AND ART GALL
Benvie
Rossie Priory
BRAES OF THE CARSE
Bandirran
Stannergate
Broughty Ferry
BROUGHTY CASTLE MUSEUM
Barnhill
FRIGATE UNICORN
Invergowrie
Longforgan
Dundee
Tay Bridge
Luncarty
Balbeggie
Ballindean
Kingoodie
UNIVERSITY BOTANIC GARDENS
DISCOVERY POINT
Tayport
Inchture
Castle Huntly
Newport-on-Tay
Scotscraig
TENTSMUIR
Kinnaird
Woodhaven
Tay Rail Bridge
Wormit
Tentsmuir Forest
PERTH MART VISITOR CENTRE
Scone
288 POLF HILL
Kilspindie
Grange
0 1 2 3 4 5 6 miles
0 1 2 3 4 5 6 7 8 9 10 km
A93 A923 A984 A94 A926 A928 A90 A92 A85 A9 A932
B955 B951 B954 B950 B947 B953 B957 B9127 B9128 B978 B961 B946 B945
133 139 140 128 129

A
B
C
D
E
F
G
5
6
7
8
140
141
129
NO
Burn of Tennet
778 MOUNT BATTOCK
Glen Dye
525 MELUNCART
464
Drumtochty Forest
Tannachie
Carmont
Nevay Mill
Mains of Dellavaird
BURNS FAMILY MEMORIALS
Glenbervie
Drumlithie
Glenfarquhar Lodge
Drumtochty Castle
Cairn o' Mount
Fiddes
Barras
Mill of Uras
Thornyhive Bay
Crawton
FOWLSHEUGH NATURE RESERVE
Crawton Bay
Pitforthie
Roadside of Catterline
Catterline
Braidon Bay
Todhead Point
Mondynes
Monboddo House
THE RETREAT GLEN ESK FOLK MUS
Millden Lodge
Clatterin Bridge
Glensaugh
Strath Finella
Auchenblae
Brownmuir
East Cairnbeg
Fordoun
Parkneuk
Arbuthnott
Roadside of Kinneff
Kinneff
GRASSIC GIBBON CENTRE
ARBUTHNOTT CHURCH
ARBUTHNOTT HOUSE GARDENS
Mains of Allardice
Little John's Haven
Inverbervie
Bervie Bay
North Esk
Auchmull
Mains of Balnakettle
FASQUE HOUSE
Thainston
FETTERCAIRN DISTILLERY VISITOR CENTRE
Fettercairn
Howe of the Mearns
Scotston
678 HILL OF WIRREN
Dalbog
Bent
Mains of Thornton
Laurencekirk
Tulloch
Inch of Arnhall
Meikle Strath
Gannochy
Witton
EDZELL CASTLE AND GARDENS
Edzell
Sauchieburn
Luthermuir
Luther Water
Garvock
Garvock Hill
Redford
DAMSIDE GARDEN HERBS & ARBORETUM
Benholm
MILL OF BENHOLM
Gourdon
Johnshaven
Dykelands
Bridgend
Balfield
West Water
Dunlappie
440
Tillyarblet
BROWN CATERTHUN
WHITE CATERTHUN
North Water Bridge
Pert
Marykirk
Craigo
Ecclesgreig
Lochside
St Cyrus
ST CYRUS
Milton Ness
Morphie
Logie
Pathhead
Kirkton of Menmuir
Tigerton
Inchbare
Newtonmill
Mains of Balhall
Lochty
Belliehill
Little Brechin
West Muir
Keithock
Trinity
Logie Pert
Muirton of Ballochy
Hillside
Kirkhill
BRECHIN CASTLE CENTRE
Brechin
PICTAVIA
CATHEDRAL & ROUND TOWER
CALEDONIAN RAILWAY
HOUSE OF DUN
Dun
Careston Castle
South Esk
Water
Montrose Basin
Montrose
MUSEUM AND ART GALLERY
Scurdie Ness
WILLIAM LAMB MEMORIAL STUDIO
Bridge of Dun
Barnhead
Aldbar Castle
Netherton
Mains of Melgund
Middle Drums
Kinnaird Castle
Inchbraoch
MONTROSE BASIN VISITOR CENTRE
Ferryden
ABERLEMNO SCULPTURED STONES
Aberlemno
Montreathmont Forest
Farnell
Bonnyton
Maryton
Kirkton of Craig
Carcary
Long Craig
Fishtown of Usan
Pitkennedy
Montreathmont Moor
Rossie Moor
Westerton
Dunninald
Boddin Pt.
252
Turin
Rescobie
Dubton
Braehead of Lunan
Reswallie
Balgavies
Glasterlaw
Bolshan
Lunan
LUNAN BAY
Burnside
Milldens
Guthrie
Kinnell
Redcastle
Pitmuies
HOUSE OF PITMUIES GARDEN
Friockheim
Boysack
Inverkeilor
Dunnichen
Letham
Lunan Water
Lang Craig
Chapelton
Ethie Mains
Idvies
Craichie
Leysmill
Cauldcots
Red Head
Ethie Castle
Tulloes
Drunkendub
Letham Grange
Mosston
Colliston
Auchmithie
Greystone
Redford
Marywell
Meg's Craig
Kirkbuddo
St Vigeans
ST VIGEANS MUSEUM
Hayshead
Hayhillock
Carmyllie
Denhead of Arbilot
Cliffburn
The Deil's Heid
ARBROATH ABBEY
Arbroath
CROMBIE
Arbirlot
SIGNAL TOWER MUSEUM
Res.
Kirkton of Monikie
Balmirmer
Elliot
Monikie Burn
Salmond's Muir
Craigton
CARLUNGIE SOUTERRAIN
Muirdrum
East Haven
BARRY MILL
Panbride
Barry
Mains of Ardestie
Carnoustie
CARNOUSTIE
Barry Links
Buddon Ness
A90
A92
A935
A933
A934
A932
A930
A937
B974
B966
B967
B9120
B960
B9134
B9113
B965
B961
B978
B9128
B9127

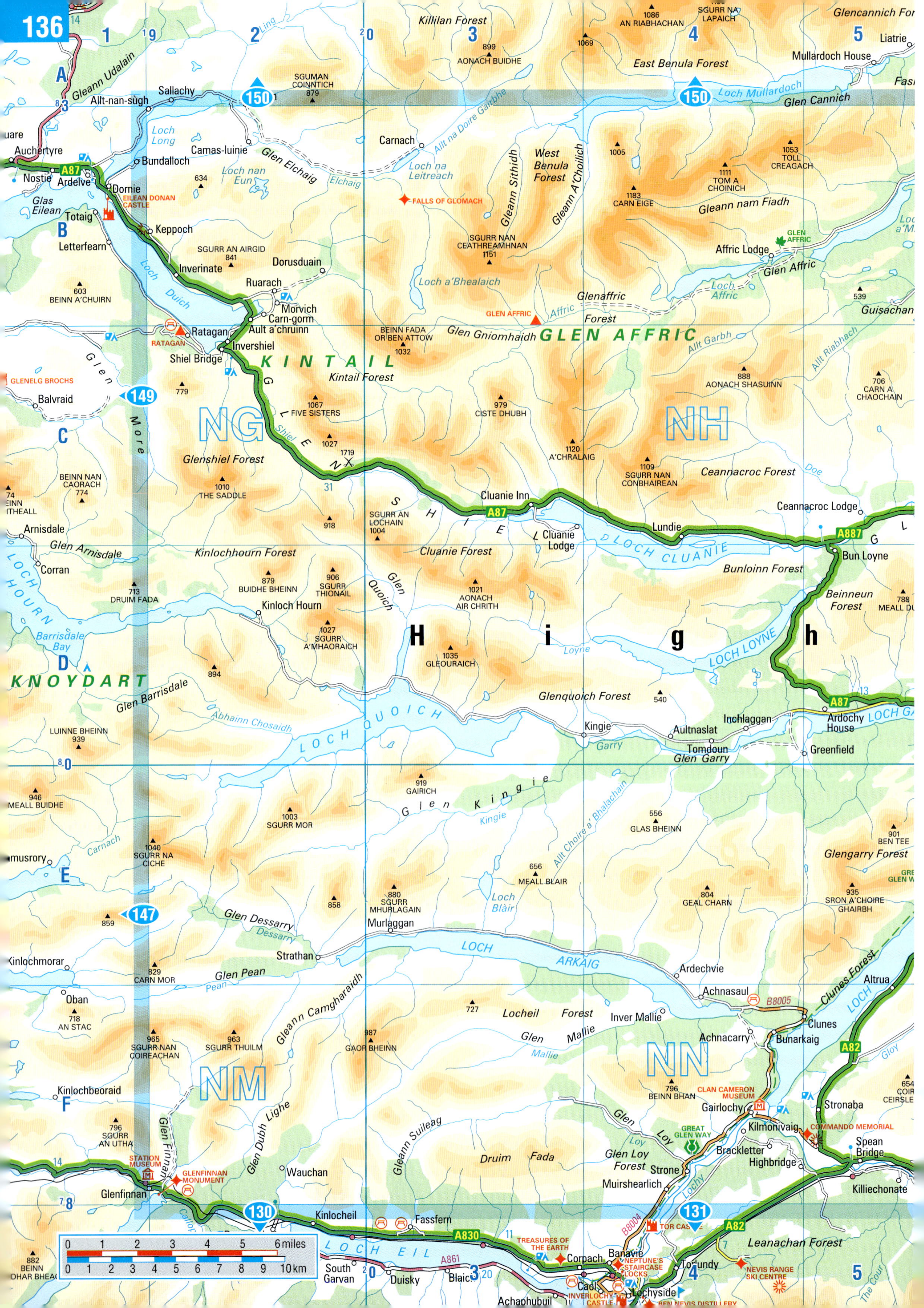
Killilan Forest
899
AONACH BUIDHE
1069
1086
AN RIABHACHAN
SGURR NA LAPAICH
Glencannich Forest
Liatrie
Mullardoch House
East Benula Forest
Loch Mullardoch
Glen Cannich
150
Glenn Udalain
Allt-nan-sugh
Sallachy
SGUMAN COINNTICH
879
Auchertyre
Loch Long
Camas-luinie
Glen Elchaig
Elchaig
Carnach
Allt na Doire Gairbhe
Loch na Leitreach
FALLS OF GLOMACH
Gleann Sithidh
West Benula Forest
Gleann A'Chòilich
1005
1053
TOLL CREAGACH
1111
TOM A CHOINICH
1183
CARN EIGE
Gleann nam Fiadh
Nostie
Ardelve
A87
Bundalloch
Dornie
Loch nan Eun
634
EILEAN DONAN CASTLE
Glas Eilean
Totaig
Keppoch
Letterfearn
SGURR AN AIRGID
841
Inverinate
Dorusduain
SGURR NAN CEATHREAMHNAN
1151
Loch a'Bhealaich
GLEN AFFRIC
Affric Lodge
Glen Affric
Loch Affric
603
BEINN A'CHUIRN
Loch Duich
Ruarach
Morvich
Carn-gorm
Ault a'chruinn
Ratagan
RATAGAN
Inversheil
Shiel Bridge
GLEN AFFRIC
Glenaffric Forest
Affric
539
Guisachan
BEINN FADA OR BEN ATTOW
1032
Glen Gniomhaidh
Allt Garbh
Allt Riabhach
KINTAIL
Kintail Forest
GLENELG BROCHS
Balvraid
Glen More
149
779
1067
FIVE SISTERS
979
CISTE DHUBH
888
AONACH SHASUINN
706
CARN A CHAOCHAIN
NG
NH
C
Shiel
1027
1719
GLEN SHIEL
Glenshiel Forest
1010
THE SADDLE
1120
A'CHRALAIG
1109
SGURR NAN CONBHAIREAN
Ceannacroc Forest
Doe
BEINN NAN CAORACH
774
31
Cluanie Inn
Ceannacroc Lodge
Arnisdale
918
SGURR AN LOCHAIN
1004
Cluanie Lodge
Lundie
A887
Glen Arnisdale
LOCH CLUANIE
Bun Loyne
Corran
Kinlochhourn Forest
Cluanie Forest
Bunloinn Forest
LOCH HOURN
713
DRUIM FADA
879
BUIDHE BHEINN
906
SGURR THIONAIL
Glen Quoich
1021
AONACH AIR CHRITH
Beinneun Forest
788
Kinloch Hourn
1027
SGURR A'MHAORAICH
Barrisdale Bay
Highland
Loyne
LOCH LOYNE
D
KNOYDART
894
1035
GLEOURAICH
Glen Barrisdale
Glenquoich Forest
540
A87
Abhainn Chosaidh
LOCH QUOICH
Inchlaggan
Ardochy House
LUINNE BHEINN
939
Kingie
Aultnaslat
Garry
Tomdoun
Glen Garry
Greenfield
946
MEALL BUIDHE
919
GAIRICH
Glen Kingie
Kingie
Allt Choire a' Bhalachain
1003
SGURR MOR
556
GLAS BHEINN
901
BEN TEE
Glengarry Forest
Carnach
1040
SGURR NA CICHE
E
656
MEALL BLAIR
858
880
SGURR MHURLAGAIN
Loch Blàir
804
GEAL CHARN
935
SRON A'CHOIRE GHAIRBH
859
147
Glen Dessarry
Dessarry
Murlaggan
Strathan
LOCH ARKAIG
Kinlochmorar
829
CARN MOR
Glen Pean
Pean
Ardechvie
Oban
718
AN STAC
727
Achnasaul
B8005
Clunes Forest
Altrua
LOCH
Locheil Forest
Inver Mallie
Clunes
965
SGURR NAN COIREACHAN
963
SGURR THUILM
Gleann Camgharaidh
987
GAOR BHEINN
Glen Mallie
Mallie
Achnacarry
Bunarkaig
A82
NM
NN
Kinlochbeoraid
F
Glen Dubh Lighe
796
BEINN BHAN
CLAN CAMERON MUSEUM
Gairlochy
654
Stronaba
796
SGURR AN UTHA
Glen Finnan
Glen Loy
Loy
GREAT GLEN WAY
Kilmonivaig
COMMANDO MEMORIAL
Spean Bridge
Gleann Suileag
STATION MUSEUM
GLENFINNAN MONUMENT
Wauchan
Druim Fada
Glen Loy Forest
Strone
Brackletter
Highbridge
Killiechonate
Muirshearlich
Lochy
Glenfinnan
130
Kinlocheil
Fassfern
131
TOR CASTLE
A82
B8004
A830
TREASURES OF THE EARTH
Corpach
Banavie
NEPTUNE'S STAIRCASE LOCKS
LOCH EIL
A861
Leanachan Forest
882
South Garvan
Duisky
Blaich
Caol
INVERLOCHY CASTLE
Torlundy
NEVIS RANGE SKI CENTRE
Lochyside
BEN NEVIS DISTILLERY
Achaphubuil
The Cour
0 1 2 3 4 5 6 miles
0 1 2 3 4 5 6 7 8 9 10 km
1
2
3
4
5
A
B

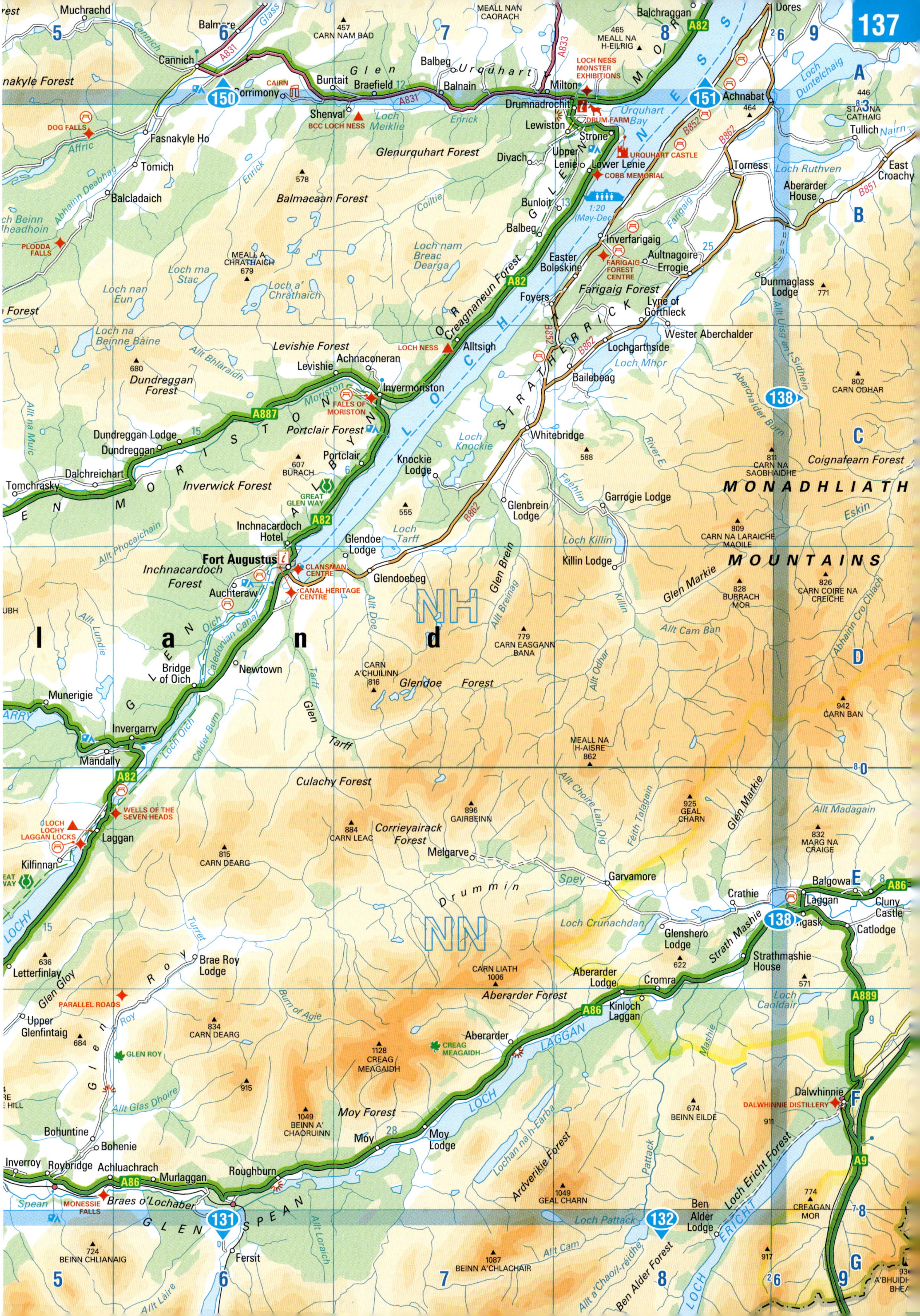
Muchrachd
Balmore
Glass
Cannich
Cannich
Affric
Fasnakyle Ho
Tomich
Balcladaich
DOG FALLS
PLODDA FALLS
150
Corrimony
CAIRN
A831
Buntait
Braefield
Glen Urquhart
Balbeg
Balnain
Shenval
BCC LOCH NESS
Loch Meiklie
Enrick
Glenurquhart Forest
457 CARN NAM BAD
MEALL NAN CAOIRACH
A833
Milton
Drumnadrochit
LOCH NESS MONSTER EXHIBITIONS
DRUM FARM
Urquhart Bay
Lewiston
Strone
Upper Lenie
Lower Lenie
URQUHART CASTLE
COBB MEMORIAL
Divach
Bunloit
Balbeg
1:20 (May-Dec)
Balchraggan
465 MEALL NA H-EILRIG
A82
Dores
151
Achnabat
464
B852
B862
Loch Duntelchaig
446 STAC NA CATHAIG
Tullich
Nairn
Torness
Loch Ruthven
East Croachy
Aberarder House
B851
578
Balmacaan Forest
Coiltie
Loch nam Breac Dearga
MEALL A CHRATHAICH 679
Loch ma Stac
Loch nan Eun
Loch a' Chrathaich
Loch na Beinne Bàine
Allt Bhlàraidh
Levishie Forest
Levishie
Achnaconeran
LOCH NESS
Alltsigh
Creagnaneun Forest
Inverfarigaig
Easter Boleskine
FARIGAIG FOREST CENTRE
Aultnagoire
Errogie
Farigaig Forest
Foyers
Lyne of Gorthleck
Wester Aberchalder
Lochgarthside
Loch Mhor
Bailebeag
Dunmaglass Lodge
771
Allt Uisg an t-Sidhein
Aberchalder Burn
138
802 CARN ODHAR
680
Dundreggan Forest
Invermoriston
FALLS OF MORISTON
Portclair Forest
A887
Dundreggan Lodge
Dundreggan
Dalchreichart
Tomchrasky
Inverwick Forest
607 BURACH
Portclair
Knockie Lodge
Loch Knockie
Whitebridge
588
River E
811 CARN NA SAOBHAIDHE
Coignafearn Forest
MONADHLIATH
MOUNTAINS
GREAT GLEN WAY
555
Glenbrein Lodge
Feehlin
Garrogie Lodge
Eskin
Inchnacardoch Hotel
Allt Phocaichain
Glendoe Lodge
Loch Tarff
B862
Loch Killin
Killin Lodge
809 CARN NA LARAICHE MAOILE
Fort Augustus
CLANSMAN CENTRE
CANAL HERITAGE CENTRE
Inchnacardoch Forest
Auchteraw
Glendoebeg
Glen Brein
Allt Breinag
Glen Markie
828 BURRACH MOR
826 CARN COIRE NA CREICHE
Abhainn Cro Chlach
Allt Cam Ban
NH
Highland
Oich
Caledonian Canal
Allt Lundie
Bridge of Oich
Newtown
Tarff
779 CARN EASGANN BANA
Killin
Allt Odhar
CARN A'CHUILINN 816
Glendoe Forest
Munerigie
Invergarry
Mandally
942 CARN BAN
MEALL NA H-AISRE 862
Glen Tarff
Calder Burn
Loch Oich
Culachy Forest
Allt Choire Lain Oig
Feith Talagain
925 GEAL CHARN
Glen Markie
Allt Madagain
LOCH LOCHY LAGGAN LOCKS
WELLS OF THE SEVEN HEADS
Laggan
Kilfinnan
896 GAIRBEINN
884 CARN LEAC
Corrieyairack Forest
815 CARN DEARG
Melgarve
832 MARG NA CRAIGE
Drummin
Spey
Garvamore
Crathie
Balgowan
Laggan
A86
Cluny Castle
Catlodge
Loch Crunachdan
Glenshero Lodge
Strath Mashie
Strathmashie House
NN
636
Letterfinlay
Turret
Brae Roy Lodge
Glen Roy
Glen Gloy
PARALLEL ROADS
CARN LIATH 1006
Aberarder Lodge
Cromra
622
571
Aberarder Forest
Kinloch Laggan
Loch Caoldair
A889
Upper Glenfintaig
684
Burn of Agie
834 CARN DEARG
GLEN ROY
Roy
1128 CREAG MEAGAIDH
CREAG MEAGAIDH
Aberarder
LOCH LAGGAN
Mashie
Dalwhinnie
DALWHINNIE DISTILLERY
915
Allt Glas Dhoire
1049 BEINN A' CHAORUINN
Moy Forest
Moy
Moy Lodge
674 BEINN EILDE
911
Bohuntine
Bohenie
Lochan na h-Earba
Ardverikie Forest
Pattack
Loch Ericht Forest
A9
Inverroy
Roybridge
Achluachrach
Murlaggan
Roughburn
1049 GEAL CHARN
774 CREAGAN MOR
A86
Spean
MONESSIE FALLS
Braes o'Lochaber
GLEN SPEAN
131
Allt Luraich
Loch Pattack
132
Ben Alder Lodge
ERICHT
Fersit
724 BEINN CHLIANAIG
1087 BEINN A'CHLACHAIR
Allt Cam
Allt a' Chaoil-reidhe
Ben Alder Forest
LOCH ERICHT
917
Allt Làire

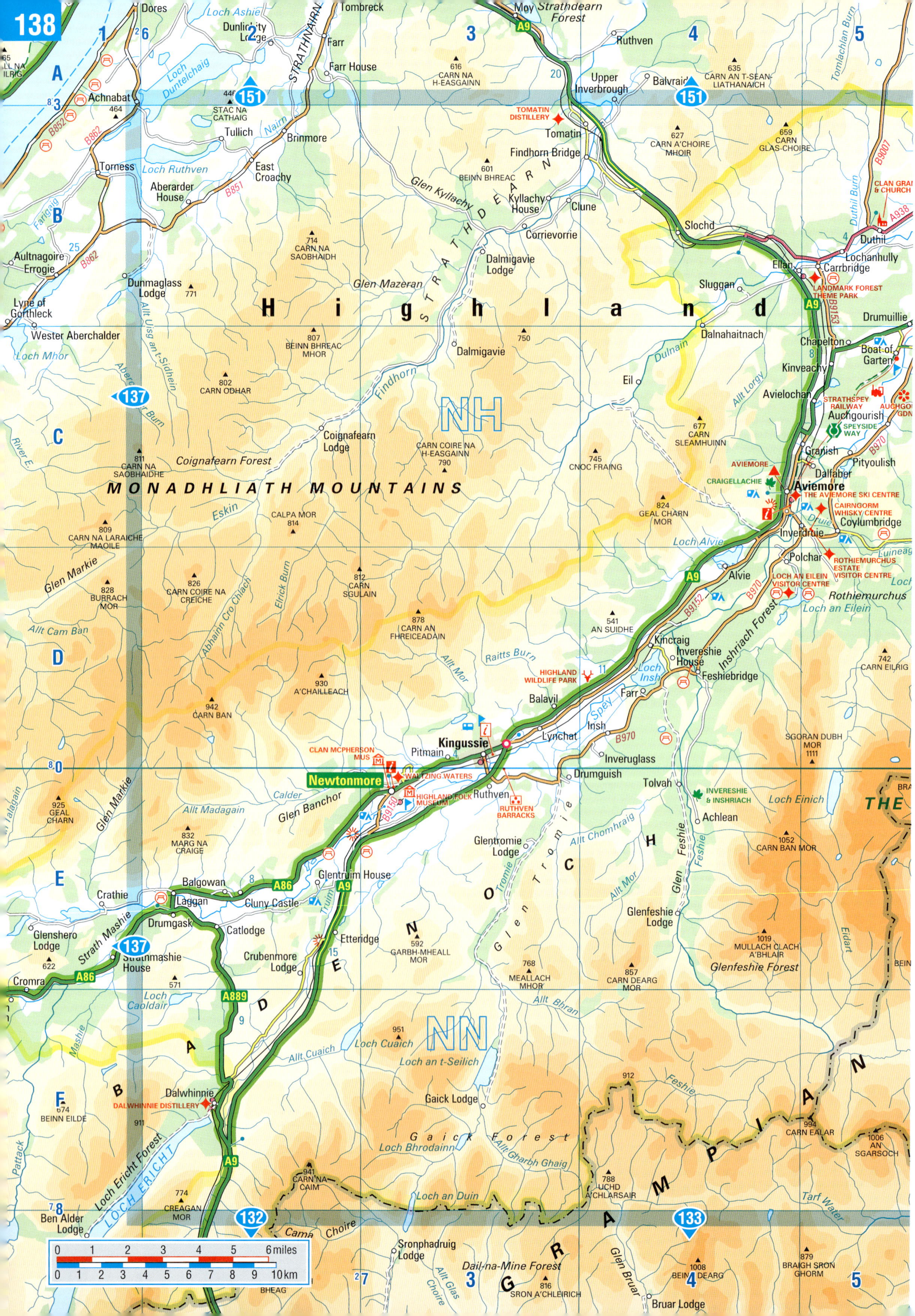
Highland
NH
NN
MONADHLIATH MOUNTAINS
GRAMPIAN
Dores
Loch Ashie
Dunlichity Lodge
STRATHNAIRN
Tombreck
Farr
Farr House
Moy
Strathdearn Forest
Ruthven
Loch Duntelchaig
Achnabat
STAC NA CATHAIG
Tullich
Brinmore
616 CARN NA H-EASGAINN
Upper Inverbrough
Balvraid
635 CARN AN T-SEAN-LIATHANAICH
Tomlachan Burn
TOMATIN DISTILLERY
Tomatin
Findhorn Bridge
627 CARN A'CHOIRE MHOIR
659 CARN GLAS-CHOIRE
Torness
Loch Ruthven
East Croachy
Aberarder House
B851
B862
B852
Farigaig
601 BEINN BHREAC
Glen Kyllachy
Kyllachy House
Clune
Corrievorrie
Slochd
Dulnain Burn
CLAN GRANT & CHURCH
A938
Duthil
Lochanhully
Carrbridge
Ellan
LANDMARK FOREST THEME PARK
Aultnagoire
Errogie
714 CARN NA SAOBHAIDH
Dalmigavie Lodge
Sluggan
Dunmaglass Lodge
771
Glen Mazeran
STRATHDEARN
Lyne of Gorthleck
Wester Aberchalder
807 BEINN BHREAC MHOR
750
Dalnahaitnach
Drumuillie
Chapelton
Boat of Garten
Loch Mhor
Allt Uisg an t-Sidhein
Dalmigavie
Kinveachy
802 CARN ODHAR
Findhorn
Dulnain
Eil
Allt Lorgy
Avielochan
STRATHSPEY RAILWAY
Auchgourish
SPEYSIDE WAY
River E
Coignafearn Lodge
CARN COIRE NA H-EASGAINN 790
677 CARN SLEAMHUINN
Granish
Pityoulish
B970
811 CARN NA SAOBHAIDHE
Coignafearn Forest
745 CNOC FRAING
AVIEMORE
Dalfaber
CRAIGELLACHIE
Aviemore
THE AVIEMORE SKI CENTRE
Eskin
CALPA MOR 814
824 GEAL CHARN MOR
CAIRNGORM WHISKY CENTRE
Coylumbridge
809 CARN NA LARAICHE MAOILE
Inverdruie
Druie
Loch Alvie
Polchar
ROTHIEMURCHUS ESTATE VISITOR CENTRE
Glen Markie
826 CARN COIRE NA CREICHE
Elrick Burn
812 CARN SGULAIN
Alvie
LOCH AN EILEIN VISITOR CENTRE
828 BURRACH MOR
Abhainn Cro Chlach
Rothiemurchus
Loch an Eilein
878 CARN AN FHREICEADAIN
541 AN SUIDHE
Inshriach Forest
Allt Cam Ban
Kincraig
Invereshie House
742 CARN EILRIG
Raitts Burn
Allt Mor
HIGHLAND WILDLIFE PARK
Loch Insh
Feshiebridge
930 A'CHAILLEACH
Farr
942 CARN BAN
Balavil
Spey
Insh
Lynchat
B970
SGORAN DUBH MOR 1111
CLAN MCPHERSON MUS
Pitmain
Kingussie
Inveruglass
Drumguish
Newtonmore
WALTZING WATERS
HIGHLAND FOLK MUSEUM
Ruthven
RUTHVEN BARRACKS
Tolvah
INVERESHIE & INSHRIACH
Loch Einich
925 GEAL CHARN
Calder
Allt Madagain
Glen Banchor
B9150
Achlean
832 MARG NA CRAIGE
Glentromie Lodge
Allt Chomhraig
Glen Feshie
1052 CARN BAN MOR
Glen Tromie
Balgowan
A86
Glentruim House
Crathie
Laggan
Cluny Castle
Truim
A9
Allt Mor
Glenfeshie Lodge
Eidart
Glenshero Lodge
Drumgask
Catlodge
Strath Mashie
592 GARBH-MHEALL MOR
1019 MULLACH CLACH A'BHLAIR
Strathmashie House
Etteridge
Crubenmore Lodge
768 MEALLACH MHOR
857 CARN DEARG MOR
Glenfeshie Forest
622
Cromra
571
A889
Loch Caoldair
Allt Bhran
951
Loch Cuaich
Allt Cuaich
Loch an t-Seilich
Mashie
912
Feshie
Dalwhinnie
DALWHINNIE DISTILLERY
974 BEINN EILDE
911
Gaick Lodge
Gaick Forest
Loch Bhrodainn
Allt Gharbh Ghaig
994 CARN EALAR
1006 AN SGARSOCH
Loch Ericht Forest
LOCH ERICHT
Pattack
941 CARN NA CAIM
788 UCHD A'CHLARSAIR
Loch an Duin
Tarf Water
774 CREAGAN MOR
Ben Alder Lodge
Cama Choire
Sronphadruig Lodge
Dail-na-Mine Forest
Glen Bruar
1008 BEINN DEARG
879 BRAIGH SRON GHORM
Allt Glas Choire
816 SRON A'CHLEIRICH
BHEAG
Bruar Lodge
0 1 2 3 4 5 6 miles
0 1 2 3 4 5 6 7 8 9 10 km
151
137
132
133
THE

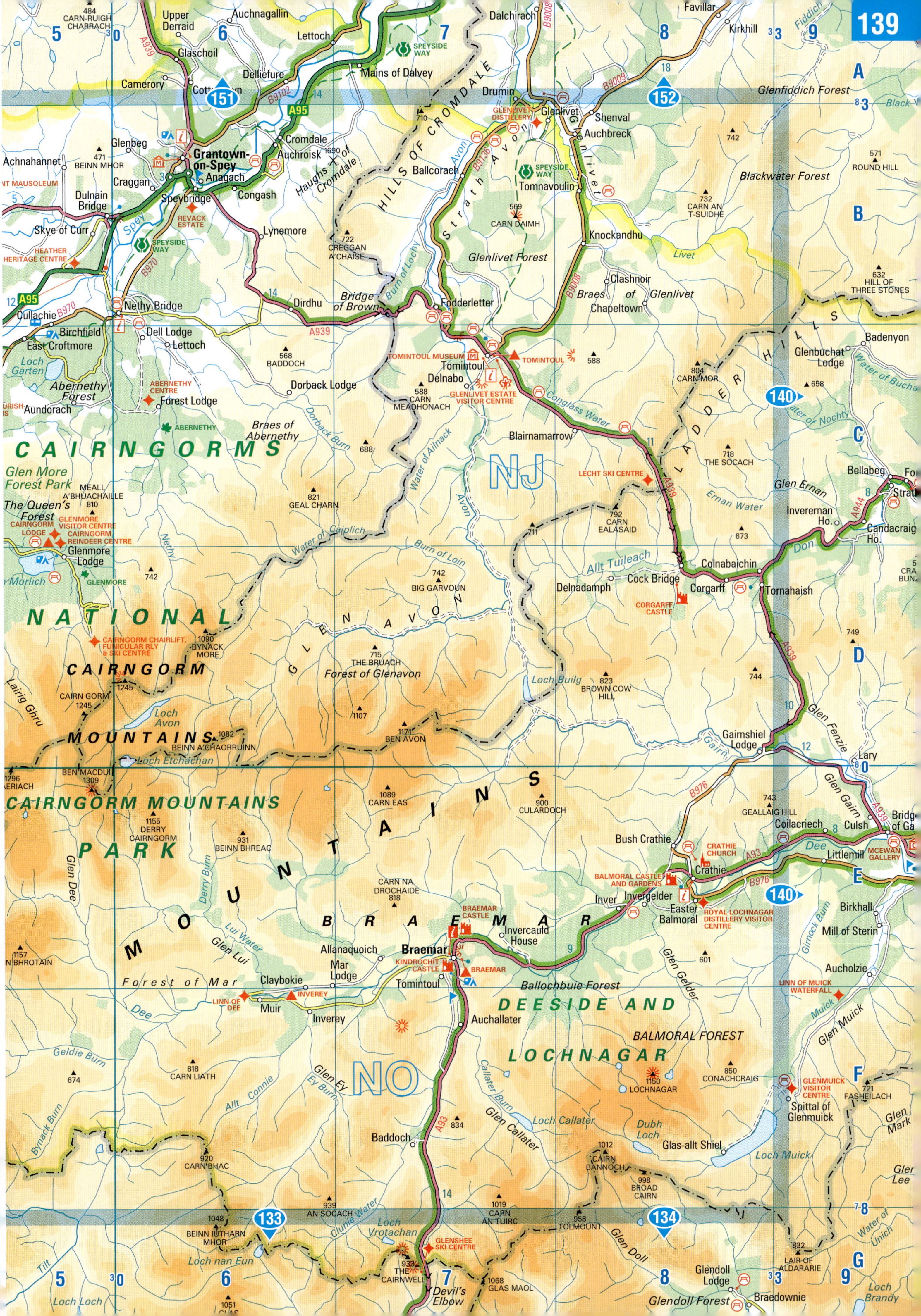
Upper Derraid
Auchnagallin
Lettoch
Glaschoil
Dellefure
Mains of Dalvey
SPEYSIDE WAY
Camerory
Dalchirach
Favillar
Kirkhill
Fiddich
Drumin
Glenlivet
Shenval
Auchbreck
GLENLIVET DISTILLERY
Glenfiddich Forest
Black Water
HILLS OF CROMDALE
Haughs of Cromdale
Cromdale
Auchroisk
Glenbeg
Achnahannet
BEINN MHOR
Grantown-on-Spey
Anagach
Craggan
Congash
Dulnain Bridge
Speybridge
Ballcorach
Strath Avon
Tomnavoulin
Glenlivet
Blackwater Forest
ROUND HILL
CARN AN T-SUIDHE
Skye of Curr
REVACK ESTATE
Lynemore
CREGGAN A'CHAISE
CARN DAIMH
Glenlivet Forest
Knockandhu
Livet
HEATHER HERITAGE CENTRE
Spey
Clashnoir
Braes of Glenlivet
Chapeltown
HILL OF THREE STONES
Cullachie
Nethy Bridge
Dirdhu
Bridge of Brown
Burn of Lochy
Fodderletter
Birchfield
Dell Lodge
Lettoch
East Croftmore
BADDOCH
TOMINTOUL MUSEUM
Tomintoul
TOMINTOUL
Delnabo
GLENLIVET ESTATE VISITOR CENTRE
CARN MEADHONACH
Loch Garten
Abernethy Forest
ABERNETHY CENTRE
Forest Lodge
Dorback Lodge
Dorback Burn
Aundorach
ABERNETHY
Braes of Abernethy
Conglass Water
LADDER HILLS
CARN MOR
Glenbuchat Lodge
Badenyon
Water of Nochty
Blairnamarrow
THE SOCACH
CAIRNGORMS NATIONAL PARK
Glen More Forest Park
MEALL A'BHUACHAILLE
The Queen's Forest
CAIRNGORM LODGE
GLENMORE VISITOR CENTRE
CAIRNGORM REINDEER CENTRE
Glenmore Lodge
GLENMORE
Loch Morlich
GEAL CHARN
Water of Ailnack
NJ
LECHT SKI CENTRE
Glen Ernan
Ernan Water
Bellabeg
Inverernan Ho.
Candacraig Ho.
Water of Caiplich
Burn of Loin
BIG GARVOUN
CARN ELASAID
Allt Tuileach
Delnadamph
Cock Bridge
Colnabaichin
Corgarff
Tornahaish
CORGARFF CASTLE
Don
Nethy
GLEN AVON
CAIRNGORM CHAIRLIFT, FUNICULAR RLY & SKI CENTRE
BYNACK MORE
CAIRNGORM
THE BRUACH
Forest of Glenavon
Loch Builg
BROWN COW HILL
CAIRN GORM
Loch Avon
Lairig Ghru
MOUNTAINS
BEINN A'CHAORRUINN
BEN AVON
Gairnshiel Lodge
Gairn
Glen Fenzie
Lary
Loch Etchachan
BEN MACDUI
CAIRNGORM MOUNTAINS
CARN EAS
CULARDOCH
GEALLAIG HILL
Glen Gairn
Bridge of Gairn
Culsh
Coilacriech
DERRY CAIRNGORM
BEINN BHREAC
Bush Crathie
CRATHIE CHURCH
Crathie
Dee
Littlemill
MCEWAN GALLERY
Derry Burn
Glen Dee
BALMORAL CASTLE AND GARDENS
CARN NA DROCHAIDE
BRAEMAR CASTLE
Inver
Invergelder
Easter Balmoral
ROYAL LOCHNAGAR DISTILLERY VISITOR CENTRE
Birkhall
Mill of Sterin
Girnock Burn
MOUNTAINS
BRAEMAR
Invercauld House
Lui Water
Glen Lui
Allanaquoich
Braemar
Mar Lodge
KINDROCHIT CASTLE
Glen Gelder
Aucholzie
BEN BHROTAIN
Forest of Mar
Claybokie
Tomintoul
Ballochbuie Forest
LINN OF MUICK WATERFALL
LINN OF DEE
INVEREY
Muir
Inverey
DEESIDE AND LOCHNAGAR
Auchallater
Muick
Glen Muick
BALMORAL FOREST
Geldie Burn
CARN LIATH
Glen Ey
Ey Burn
Allt Connie
NO
Callater Burn
LOCHNAGAR
CONACHCRAIG
GLENMUICK VISITOR CENTRE
Spittal of Glenmuick
FASHIELACH
Glen Mark
Bynack Burn
Baddoch
Glen Callater
Loch Callater
Dubh Loch
Glas-allt Shiel
Loch Muick
CARN BHAC
CAIRN BANNOCH
BROAD CAIRN
AN SOCACH
CARN AN TUIRC
TOLMOUNT
Glen Doll
LAIR OF ALDARARIE
Water of Unich
BEINN IUTHARN MHOR
Loch Vrotachan
Clunie Water
GLENSHEE SKI CENTRE
Loch nan Eun
THE CAIRNWELL
Devil's Elbow
GLAS MAOL
Glendoll Lodge
Glendoll Forest
Braedownie
Loch Brandy
Loch Loch
Tilt
A939
A95
A93
A944
B9102
B970
B9008
B9009
B9136
B976
151
152
140
133
134

Ballochford
Tomnaven
Coynachie
Culdrain
Blackburn
Glens of Foudland
A96
HILL OF FOUDLAND
Colpy
Glen Fiddich
Fiddich
Clashindarroch Forest
Clashindarroch
Kirkney
Gartly
Largie
Wrangham
Bridgend
Inverharroch
Glenfiddich Forest
152
Kirkney Water
Cults
Milton of Lesmore
Milton of Noth
Kennethmont
Oldtown
Ardlair
The Shevock
Aulton
Insch
B9002
B992
742
Auchmair
Cabrach
Belhinnie
Rhynie
Cottown
571 ROUND HILL
Blackwater Forest
Aldunie
Wheedlemont
Craig Castle
Clatt
Duncanstone
Kirkton
732 CARN AN SUIDHE
B9002
ST MARY'S CHURCH
Leslie
Knockespock Ho.
Auchleven
Livet
721 THE BUCK
Coldwells Croft
Whitehaugh Forest
632 HILL OF THREE STONES
Clova
SCOTTISH SCULPTURE WORKSHOP
Lumsden
CORREEN HILLS
Muckletown
Chapeltown
A b e r d
Glenton
Tullynessle
Badenyon
LADDER HILLS
Glenbuchat Lodge
Water of Buchat
NJ
Mossat
518 LORD ARTHUR'S CAIRN
Keig
Castle Forbes
804 CARN MOR
Kildrummy
Don
Bridge of Alford
Montgarrie
139
658
Rinmore
Milltown of Kildrummy
A944
ALFORD VALLEY RAILWAY
HAUGHTON
Water of Nochty
Belnacraig
KILDRUMMY CASTLE & GARDEN
Auchintoul
GRAMPIAN TRANSPORT MUS
Gateside
532
Alford
Kirkton of Glenbuchat
HERITAGE CENTRE
Whitehouse
718 THE SOCACH
Asloun
Bellabeg
Forbestown
Glenkindie
Sinnahard
Hillockhead
Kirkton of Tough
Little Lynturk
Glen Ernan
Strathdon
Towie
Milltown of Towie
Ley
Tillyfourie
Ernan Water
Inverernan Ho.
Candacraig Ho.
Heugh-head
Muir of Fowlis
Bridgend
Corrennie Forest
Boultenstone
Milton of Cushnie
Tillyfour
Corrennie Moor
673
Tornashean Forest
Leochel Cushnie
Cock Bridge
Colnabaichin
531 CRAIG OF BUNZEACH
Hillockhead
CRAIGIEVAR CASTLE
Kintocher
Corgarff
Tornahaish
619
494 BENAQUHALLIE
CORGARFF CASTLE
Deskry Water
Easter Davoch
B9119
Migvie
Douneside
Tornaveen
Coynach
Craskins
476
Findrack Ho.
749
CULSH SOUTERRAIN
Drumlasie
744
Logie Coldstone
Tarland
Lumphanan
871 MORVEN
C R O M A R
PEEL RING OF LUMPHANAN
TOMNAVERIE STONE CIRCLE
Milton of Auchinhove
Glen Fenzie
Milton of Logie
Coull
Glendavan Ho.
Auchlossan
Torphins
Gairnshiel Lodge
Ordie
299 SCAR HILL
MUIR OF DINNET
SLUG OF DESS FALLS
Mid Beltie
Lary
604
Loch Davan
Milton of Campfield
Loch Kinord
Kincardine O'Neil
Aboyne
BURN O VAT
Dinnet
Tillydrine
743 GEALLAIG HILL
Glen Gairn
Milton of Tullich
Backhill of Trustach
Muir of Dinnet
Bush
Coilacriech
Culsh
Bridge of Gairn
Birsemore
Birse
Crathie
CRATHIE CHURCH
Glascorrie
Dee
Littlemill
MCEWAN GALLERY
Ballater
Glen Tanar House
BRAELOINE INTERPRETIVE CENTRE
Marywell
Burn of Cattie
Crathie
House of Glenmuick
310 TOM'S CAIRN
Easter Balmoral
ROYAL LOCHNAGAR DISTILLERY CENTRE
Birkhall
529
Tillygarmond
Glen Tanar
Water of Tanar
GLEN TANAR
525 CARNFERG
Finzean
Mill of Sterin
Forest of Birse
Percie
Glen Gelder
601
CLACHAN YELL 526
Ballochan
Aucholzie
Water of Feugh
LINN OF MUICK WATERFALL
Forest of Glen Tanar
617
Water of Aven
Muick
Glen Muick
727 COCK CAIRN
742 HILL OF CAT
MOUNT SHADE 507
BALMORAL FOREST
Glendye Lodge
850 CONACHCRAIG
939 MOUNT KEEN
1150 LOCHNAGAR
GLENMUICK VISITOR CENTRE
721 FASHEILACH
NO
Burn of Branny
Water of Tarf
778 MOUNT BATTOCK
Spittal of Glenmuick
Glen Mark
Water of Mark
Burn of Tennet
Glen Dye
Dubh Loch
Glas-allt Shiel
Loch Muick
Glen Lee
525 MELUNCART
998 BROAD CAIRN
696 MONAWEE
Invermark Lodge
Auchronie
Cairn o' Mount
134
Tarfside
Cairncross
THE RETREAT GLEN ESK FOLK MUS
135
Loch Lee
Inchgrundle
North Esk
0 1 2 3 4 5 6 miles
0 1 2 3 4 5 6 7 8 9 10 km
Glen Doll
Glen Effock
G L E N E S K
Glendoll Forest
Braedownie
Loch Brandy
CRUYS
FASQUE HOUSE

Kirkton of Culsalmond
Rothmaise
Newseat
Folla Rule
St Katherine's
Cross of Jackston
Jackstown
Chapel
Earlsford
Balgove
Tulloch
HADDO HOUSE AND GARDENS
Wedderlairs
Ythanbank
Hilton
Inverebrie
Mains of Birness
Broomfield
Neth Leask
Artrochie
Auchmacoy
Cairnhill
Tocher
Meikle Wartle
Bonnyton
Kirkton of Rayne
Newton Ho.
Old Rayne
Pitmachie
Ardoyne
LOANHEAD STONE CIRCLE
Mounie Castle
Daviot
Durno
Meldrum Ho.
Craigdam
Tarves
Auquhorthies
Raxton
MEDIEVAL TOMB
Ythsie
West Kinharrachie
Esslemont
Ellon
FORMARTINE
TOLQUHON CASTLE
PITMEDDEN GARDENS
Pitmedden
Kirkton of Logie Buchan
VISITOR CENTRE
Kirktown of Slains
Collieston
Waterside
FORVIE
St Catherine's Dub
Hackley Hd. or Forvie Ness
Sands of Forvie
Westhall
Whiteford
Pitcaple
Fingask
Barra Castle
Oldmeldrum
Cairnbrogie
Udny Green
Tipperty
Meikle Tarty
Tarty Burn
Newburgh
Oyne
Kirkton of Oyne
Chapel of Garioch
Pittodrie
Harlaw Ho.
Mill of Kingoodie
Hattoncrook
Kirkton of Bourtie
Pettymuick
Culterculien
Foveran
Foveran Burn
Udny Station
Minnes
Rashiereive
Drums
Newburgh Bar
BENNACHIE
BATTLE OF HARLAW MEMORIAL
Balhalgardy
BRANDSBUTT STONE
Burgh Muir
Hillbrae
Whiterashes
Affleck
Tillygreig
Tillycorthie
INVERURIE MUSEUM
Nether Crimond
Tillykerrie
Straloch
Ardo Ho.
GARIOCH
Inverurie
Aberdeenshire
Manar Ho.
Middlemuir
Delfrigs
Upper Woodend
Bograxie
Burnhervie
Port Elphinstone
Kinmuck
Middleton
Balbithan Ho.
Newmachar
Craigie
Causeyend
Aquhythie
KINKELL CHURCH
Whitecairns
Belhelvie
Don
Rorandle
Pitfichie
Blairdaff
Dalmadilly
Balbithan
Wester Fintray
Cairnpark
Kinmundy
BALMEDIE
Balmedie
Grantlodge
Clovenstone
Cothall
Drumligair
Pitfichie Forest
Pitmunie
MONYMUSK ARTS CENTRE
Kemnay
Cottown
Kintore
Hatton of Fintray
OLD CHURCH
Potterton
Corby Loch
Blackdog
Monymusk
Craigearn
Todlachie
Leylodge
Overton
Parkhill Ho.
Mundurno
Lauchintilly
CASTLE FRASER
Blackburn
Dyce
ABERDEEN
KIRKWALL 6:00
LERWICK 14:30
Haughs of Clinterty
Aberdeen City
Stoneywood
Denmore
Ordhead
Sauchen
Achath
Lyne of Skene
Bankhead
East Auchronie
Bucksburn
Hayton
Bridge of Don
CRUICKSHANK BOTANIC GARDEN
BRIG O' BALGOWNIE
ST MACHAR'S CATHEDRAL
Milton of Corsindae
Old Kinnernie
Corsindae
Dunecht
Skene Ho.
Kirkton of Skene
Woodside
Kittybrewster
Old Aberdeen
Bankhead
Northfield
Mastrick
KING'S COLLEGE VISITOR CENTRE
Midmar
STONE CIRCLE
Loch of Skene
Westhill
Aberdeen
Comers
Tillybirloch
Marionburgh
Echt
Garlogie
Cairnie
Elrick
Kingswells
SATROSPHERE
MARISCHAL MUSEUM
GORDON HIGHLANDERS MUSEUM
Ferryhill
Torry
Girdle Ness
Midmar Forest
South Kirkton
Mannofield
Blacktop
Easter Ord
DAVID WELCH WINTER GARDENS
Nigg Bay
Greg Ness
Landerberry
Redhill
Leuchar Burn
Ruthrieston
Kincorth
HILL OF FARE
Burn of Corrichie
West Cullery
Benthoul
Contlaw
Cults
Bieldside
Garthdee
Hardgate
Craigton
Milton of Murtle
Milltimber
Nigg
Banchory-Devenick
Cove Bay
Charlestown
DRUM CASTLE
Hirn
Peterculter
Kirkton of Maryculter
Auchlunies
Hare Ness
Brathens
Myrebird
Drumoak
Mains of Drum
Maryculter
Marywell
Findon Ness
Bridge of Canny
East Mains
Upper Lochton
The Neuk
CRATHES CASTLE AND GARDENS
Woodside of Arbeadie
Hillside
Findon
BANCHORY MUSEUM
Crathes
Dee
ROYAL DEESIDE RLY
Arbeadie
Banchory
Kirkton of Durris
Woodlands
Denside
Muirskie
Auchlee
Portlethen
Downies
Cammachmore Bay
Deebank
Auchattie
Bridge of Feugh
Upper Burnhaugh
Cammachmore
Belts of Collonach
Crossroads
Durris Forest
Borrowfield
Newtonhill
Strachan
Netherley
Cookney
Muchalls
CAIRN-MON-EARN
Lochton
RAEDYKES ROMAN CAMP
Bridge of Muchalls
Union Cottage
Garrol Hill
MONGOUR
Mergie
Rickarton
Burn of Sheeoch
Water of Dye
Cowie Water
KERLOCH
Garron Pt.
Cowie
Bridge of Dye
Kirktown of Fetteresso
Tewel
Fetteresso Forest
Stonehaven
TOLBOOTH MUSEUM
Carmont
Tannachie
New Mill
Castle Haven
DUNNOTTAR CASTLE
Thornyhive Bay
Drumtochty Forest
Mains of Dellavaird
BURNS FAMILY MEMORIALS
Glenfarquhar Lodge
Drumlithie
Glenbervie
Fiddes
Mill of Uras
Drumtochty Castle
Barras
Crawton
Strath Finella
Auchenblae
Mondynes
Pitforthie
Roadside of Catterline
Crawton Bay
Catterline
Clatterin Bridge
Glensaugh
Brownmuir
Braidon Bay
Todhead Point
East Cairnbeg
Fordoun
Parkneuk
Roadside of Kinneff
Arbuthnott
NJ
NO

1
2
3
4
5
6
A
B
C
D
E
F
G
H
Rubha Bholsa
Rubha a'Mhail
COLONSAY 1:10
(Summer only)
Loch an Aircill
439
J U R
364
SGARBH
BREAC
785
755
PAPS OF JURA
Loch a Chnuic Bhric
JURA FOREST
Corran
Leargybreck
Gleann Astaile
Loch
Nave Island
Ardnave Pt.
Gortantaoid
316
Bunnahabhain
BUNNAHABHAIN DISTILLERY
SOUND OF ISLAY
Carraig Bhan
Ardnave
Killinallan
144
An Clachan
Sanaigmore
Loch Gruinart
Caol Ila
CAOL ILA DISTILLERY
Port Askaig
561
Feolin Ferry
Keils
Braigo
Leckgruinart
B8018
FINLAGGAN CENTRE
Keills
Craighouse
ISLE OF JURA DISTILLERY
Sm
Ballinaby
Carnduncan
LOCH GRUINART NATURE RESERVE VISITORS CENTRE
Loch Finlaggan
Loch Cam
Loch Ballygrant
Gleann Ullibh
Aoradh
Craigens
Ballygrant
A846
Saligo Bay
Loch Gorm
B8017
342
BRAT BHEINN
Coul Pt.
Coull
I S L A Y
Kilmeny
Cabrach
Sunderland
B8018
A847
Blackrock
Redhouses
Sorn
Daill
267
BEINN DUBH
Machir Bay
Kilchoman
Bridgend
Am Fraoch Eilean
Rubha na Tràil
Brosdale I.
Conisby
Bruichladdich
Kilchiaran
Kilchiaran Bay
Bowmore
BOWMORE ROUND CHURCH
A846
ISLAY LIFE MUSEUM
Tormisdale
RHINNS
ISLAY
Port Charlotte
Mulindry
McArthur's Hd.
A r g y l l
Kilennan
15
LOCH INDAAL
Laggan
Lossit
232
OF
471
BEINN BHAN
491
BEINN BHEIGEIR
Carraig Mhór
Lossit Pt.
Nerabus
Laggan Pt.
Laggan
Duich
Ardtalla
ISLAY
Loch Beinn Uraraidh
Claggain Bay
Rubha na Faing
A847
13
B8016
Portnahaven
LAGGAN BAY
Kintour
Port Wemyss
Glenegedale
ISLAY
Ardmore Pt.
Orsay
Rinns Pt.
347
BEINN SHOLUM
KILDALTON CHURCH AND CROSSES
Eilean Craobhach
Port Alsaig
Rubha Mòr
Kintra
Leorin
Eilean a'Chuirn
ARDBEG DISTILLERY
Eilean Bhride
A846
Cornabus
Imeraval
Lagavulin
Lower Cragabus
Port Ellen
Ardbeg
Eilean Imersay
LAGAVULIN DISTILLERY
Dùn Mór Ghil
152
LAPHROAIG DISTILLERY
Laphroaig
THE OA
Texa
Lower Killeyan
Risabus
AMERICAN MONUMENT
Mull of Oa
Inerval
202
NR
Rubha nan Leacan
NORTH CHANNEL
Rathlin Island
Scale : 1:265 000
(approx 4 miles to 1 inch)
0 1 2 3 4 5 6 miles
0 1 2 3 4 5 6 7 8 9 10km

Argyll and Bute
KNAPDALE
KINTYRE
ISLE OF ARRAN
NORTH ARRAN
ISLE OF BUTE
KYLES OF BUTE
Tarbert
West Tarbert
Campbeltown
Brodick
Rothesay
Lochranza
Lamlash
Whiting Bay
Blackwaterfoot
Kilmory
Lagg
Corrie
Sannox
Catacol
Pirnmill
Imachar
Dougarie
Machrie Bay
Shiskine
Kilpatrick
Sliddery
Lochead
Achahoish
Ellary
Clachbreck
Erines
Baile Boidheach
Ormsary
Druimdrishaig
Cretshengan
Coulaghailtro
Kilberry
Carse Ho.
Dunmore
Ardpatrick
Kilchamaig
Whitehouse
Kennacraig
Redhouse
Corranbuie
Glenreasdell Mains
Skipness
Claonaig
Portachoillan
Clachan
Tayinloan
Killean
Beacharr
Muasdale
Bellochantuy
Killocraw
Westport
Kilchenzie
Kilmichael
Machrihanish
Drumlemble
Stewarton
Kilkerran
Knocknaha
Woodbank
Southend
Carskiey
Feochaig
Kildalloig
Saddell
Ugadale
Peninver
Carradale
Grogport
Brackley
Crossaig
Cour
Gigha Island
Ardminish
Tarbert
Sanda Island
Inchmarnock
Portavadie
Millhouse
Kames
Tighnabruaich
Port Driseach
Auchenlochan
Melldalloch
Kilfinan
Ardlamont Ho.
Ardlamont Pt.
Port Bannatyne
Straad
Scalpsie
St Colmac
Ardentraive
Colintraive
Port Lamont
Loch Striven
Sound of Bute
Kilbrannan Sound
Sound of Gigha
Loch Tarbert
Campbeltown Loch
Mull of Kintyre
A83
A841
B842
B8024
B8001
B880
B843
Goat Fell
Beinn Tarsuinn
Cir Mhòr
Glen Rosa
Glen Iorsa
Glen Sannox
Holy Island
Pladda
Kildonan
Ardrossan 0:55
Lochranza Castle
Brodick Castle
Skipness Castle
Kilpatrick Dun
Machrie Moor Standing Stones
King's Cave
Torrylinn Cairn
Carn Ban
Glenashdale Falls
Saddell Abbey
Davaar Island Cave Painting
Campbeltown Heritage Centre
Clan MacAlister Centre
Achamore Gardens
Isle of Arran Distillery
Isle of Arran Heritage Museum
NS
144
145

6 7 8 9 10 11

ARDMEANACH
Killiemore House
Aird of Kinloch
Kilfinichen Bay
THE BURG
LOCH SCRIDAIN
Pennycross
Torrans
BROLASS
Loch Fuaron
BEN BUIE 717
CREACH BEINN 698
Loch Airdeglais
Loch Spelve
Croggan
Rubha nan Sailthean
Bach I.
Ardmore
Rubha Seanach
Kinlochspelve
Lochbuie
Barachandroman
Loch Uisg
503 BEINN NA CROISE
Leidle
Carsaig
Carsaig Bay
Loch Buie
Rubha Dubh
Laggan Deer Forest
405 DRUIM FADA
LORD LOVAT'S CAVE
CARSAIG ARCHES
Malcolm's Pt.
Eilean Annraidh
MACLEAN'S CROSS
IONA ABBEY AND CATHEDRAL
IONA HERITAGE CENTRE
Kintra
Rubha nan Cearc
Loch na Lathaich
ST COLUMBA EXHIBITION & WELCOME CENTRE
Baile Mor
Iona
Sound of Iona
Fionnphort
Aridhglas
Eorabus
Fidden
Tiraghoil
Bunessan
Lee
376 CRUACHAN MIN
Loch Assapol
ROSS OF MULL
Erraid
Ardalanish
Uisken
Scoor
Ardchiavaig
Rubha nam Braithrean
Eilean a'Chalmain
Rubh Ardalanish
146
Torran Rocks
NM
FIRTH OF LORN
Frank Lockwood's Island
Insh I.
Sound of Insh
Seil
Clachan-Seil
Clachan
CLACHAN BRIDGE
Easdale
AN CALA GARDENS
EASDALE ISLAND FOLK MUSEUM
Balvicar
Dubh-fheith
Cuan
Cullipool
Torsa
Seil Sound
Kilchoan
Garbh Eileach
Garvellachs
SCARBA, LUNGA AND THE GARVELLACHS
Eilean Dubh Mor
Eileach an Naoimh
Luing
Achafolla
Sound of Luing
ARDUAINE GARDEN
Arduaine
Toberonochy
Shuna Sound
Shuna
Craobh Haven
Lunga
Shuna Pt.
OBAN 2:20
124
CRUACH SCARBA 449
Scarba
Rubha Aird Luing
Gulf of Corryvreckan
Aird
Rèisa an t-Sruith
Craignish Pt.
Island Macaskin
Loch Craignish
Kinuachdrachd
Kinuachdrachd Harbour
296 CRUACH NA SEILCHEIG
Glengarrisdale Bay
Glendebadel Bay
Loch Crinan
Crinan
Kilmahumaig
Bellanoch
Rubh'a'Geadha
Balnahard
Kiloran Bay
KILORAN GARDENS
Kiloran
Kilchattan
COLONSAY
Scalasaig
Loch Staosnaig
Garvard
Rubha Dubh
PRIORY
Dubh Eilean
Oronsay
Eilean nan Ron
365 BEN GARRISDALE
Corpach Bay
Lussa
Lealt Burn
Lealt
467 BEINN BHREAC
453 RAINBERG MOR
Shian Bay
Shian
Loch Righ Mòr
Ardlussa
Ardlussa Bay
Inverlussa
Lussagiven
Gleann Aoistail
SOUND OF JURA
Gallachoille
KNAPD
Carsaig
Tayvallich
Achanamara
Kilmichael of Inverlussa
Barrahormid
TAYNISH
Taynish
Loch Sween
466 CRUACH LUSACH
Rubh'an t-Sàilein
1:10 (Summer Only)
Tarbert
Loch Tarbert
Rubha Lang-aoinidh
KEILLS CHAPEL
Keillmore
New Ulva
Dunrostan
Island of Danna
CASTLE SWEEN
241
ST COLUMBA'S CAVE
Lochead
Achahoish
Rubha Bholsa
Rubha a'Mhail
Lagg
Loch an Aircill
Loch Lesgamaill
439
364 SGARBH BREAC
Nave Island
Ardnave Pt.
JURA
785 755 PAPS OF JURA
Eilean Mòr
ST CORMAC'S CHAPEL
CHAPEL
Kilmory
Kilmory Bay
Ellary
Clachbreck
Ardnave
Gortantaoid
316
Bunnahabhain
BUNNAHABHAIN DISTILLERY
Loch a Chnuic Bhric
JURA FOREST
Corran
An Dùnan
Knockrome
Lowlandman's Bay
Baile Boidheach
Ormsary
Loch Caolisport
Pt. of Knap
Killinallan
Loch Gruinart
Gleann Astaile
Leargybreck
Loch na Mile
Druimdrishaig
Leckgruinart
Caol Ila
CAOL ILA DISTILLERY
Port Askaig
Feolin Ferry
561
Keils
Small Isles
305
Loch nan Torran
FINLAGGAN CENTRE
Loch Finlaggan
Keills
LOCH GRUINART NATURE RESERVE VISITORS CENTRE
Aoradh
Craigens
Loch Cam
Loch Ballygrant
Gleann Ullibh
Craighouse
ISLE OF JURA DISTILLERY
Miller's Bay
Cretshengan
CRUACH LAGAIN 264
Coulaghailtro
342 BRAT BHEINN
NR
ISLAY
Ballygrant
Kilmeny
142
Cabrach
Kilberry Hd.
SCULPTURED STONES
Kilberry
Blackrock
Redhouses
Daill
267 BEINN DUBH
Bridgend
Rubha na Tràille
Am Fraoch Eilean
Brosdale I.
Carse Ho.
Dunmore
Loch Stornoway
Ardpatrick
Gartnagrenach
WEST LOCH
Bowmore
BOWMORE ROUND CHURCH
Mulindry
McArthur's Hd.
Ardpatrick Ho.
2:05
Portachoillan
ISLAY
Port Charlotte
LOCH INDAAL
Kilennan
Laggan
Ardpatrick Pt.
Eilean Traighe
471 BEINN BHAN
491 BEINN BHEIGEIR
Carraig Mhór
Laggan Pt.
Ronachan Pt.
A83
Clachan
Scale 1:265 000
(approx 4 miles to 1 inch)
Ardtalla
143
Eilean Garbh
West Tarbert Bay
Loch Ciaran
Loch Beinn Uraraidh
Claggain Bay
PORT ELLEN 2:20
East Tarbert Bay
Gigha Island
Tarbert
Balochroy
Ardmore Pt.
KILDALTON CHURCH
0 1 2 3 4 5 6 miles
0 1 2 3 4 5 6 7 8 9 10 km

Argyll and Bute
NN
NS
Loch Lomond and The Trossachs National Park
Argyll Forest Park
Clyde-Muirshiel Regional Park
Inverclyde
Kerrera
Oban
Kilninver
Glen Lonan
Glen Feochan
Barrochreal
Braes of Lorn
Kilmelford
Melfort
Ardanstur
Glenmore
Kames
Lagalochan
Garraron
Kintraw
Arichamish
Torran
Ford
Ederline
Kilmartin
Slockavullin
Poltalloch
Bridgend
Cairnbaan
Lochgilphead
Ardrishaig
Achahoish
Inverneill
Tarbert
West Tarbert
Kennacraig
Whitehouse
Skipness
Claonaig
Crossaig
Dalmally
Lochawe
Pass of Brander
Inverlochy
Strath of Orchy
Tyndrum
Ben Lui
Inishail
Ardanaiseig
Kilchrenan
Annat
North Port
Portsonachan
South Port
Cladich
Inverinan
Ballimeanoch
Tullich
Glen Aray
Dalavich
Portinnisherrich
Eredine
Durran
Eredine Forest
Auchindrain
Dalchenna
Inveraray
Inveraray Castle
Newtown
Furnace
Strachur
Creggans
Strachur Bay
Glen Shira
Clachan
Drishaig
Cairndow
Ardno
Glen Kinglas
St Catherine's
Hell's Glen
Rest and Be Thankful
Monevechadan
Lochgoilhead
Drimsynie
Corrow
Ardgartan
Arrochar
Tarbet
Succoth
Stuckgowan
Ardmay
Inveruglas
Ardlui
Inverarnan
Glen Fyne
Glenfyne Lodge
Ben Vorlich
Loch Sloy
Glen Croe
Ardgoil Forest
Glen Douglas
Inverbeg
Glenmallan
Portincaple
Whistlefield
Garelochhead
Faslane Port
Coulport
Rahane
Shandon
Ardpeaton
Clynder
Rosneath
Rhu
Helensburgh
Cove
Kilcreggan
Craigendoran
Loch Long
Gare Loch
Loch Goil
Loch Eck
Glen Branter
Glenbranter
Invernoaden
Newton
Lachlan Castle
Garbhallt
Strathlachlan Forest
Minard
Crarae
Tullochgorm
Lephinmore
Lephinchapel
Asknish
Lochgair
Castleton
Largiemore
Otter Ferry
Ballimore
Auchnaha
Glendaruel Forest
Clachan of Glendaruel
Glendaruel
Dunans
Conchra
Caol Ghleann
Glenmassan
Benmore
Kilmun
Ardbeg
Blairmore
Sandbank
Holy Loch
Strone
Hunter's Quay
Dunoon
Kirn
Glen Lean
Clachaig
Glenstriven
Inverchaolain
Corlarach Forest
Bullwood
Innellan
Toward
Toward Pt.
Kilfinan
Drum
Melldalloch
Kames
Tighnabruaich
Port Driseach
Millhouse
Portavadie
Kyles of Bute
Loch Fyne
Loch Riddon
Loch Striven
Isle of Bute
Glen More
Port Bannatyne
Rothesay
Rothesay Bay
Craigmore
Montford
Ascog
Kerrycroy
Ardbeg
Straad
Scalpsie
Kingarth
Kilchattan Bay
St Colmac
Ettrick Bay
Inchmarnock
Ardscalpsie Pt.
Sound of Bute
Ardlamont Pt.
Rubha Leathan
Great Cumbrae Island
Millport
Little Cumbrae Island
Largs
Fairlie
Skelmorlie
Wemyss Bay
Inverkip
Gourock
Greenock
Port Glasgow
Kilbirnie
Lochwinnoch
Cock of Arran
Lochranza
Loch Ranza
Garroch Hd.
A83
A85
A815
A886
A82
A78
A8
124
125
126
118
143

NF
NL
Canna
A'Chill
Garrisdale Pt.
Canna Harbour
Sanday
Sound of Canna
Guirdil Bay
Kilmory
Kilmory Glen
Kinloch Glen
Rubha Shamhnan Insir
MALLAIG 2:30 (Sat only)
Rubha na Roinne
Loch Scresort
Kinloch
KINLOCH CASTLE
Rubha Port na Caranean
A'Bhrideanach
571 ORVAL
R Ù M
RÙM
Schooner Pt.
Oigh-sgeir
Harris
Glen Harris
812 ASKIVAL
781 AINSHVAL
Rubha Sgorr an t-Snidhe
Rubha nam Meirleach
THE SMALL ISLES
SOUND OF RÙM
Bay of Laig
Cleadale
Rubha an Fhasaidh
Eigg
393 AN SGURR
Kildonnan
Galmisdale
Eilean nan Each
SOUND OF EIGG
Muck
137
Port Mor
Bhatarsaigh (Vatersay)
Uidh
Bagh Bhatarsaigh
Bhatarsaigh
Caolas Shanndraigh
Flodaigh (Flodday)
Sanndraigh (Sandray)
207
Lingeigh (Lingay)
Greanamul
Caolas Phabaigh
Theisgeir (Heiskers)
Pabaidh (Pabbay)
171
Caolas Mhiui Laigh
Miùgh Laigh (Mingulay)
273
Bearnaraigh (Berneray)
Caolas Bhearnaraigh
Barra Hd.
Sanna Point
Sanna
Sanna Bay
Portuairk
Achnaha
Point of Ardnamurchan
ARDNAMURCHAN LIGHTHOUSE
Achosnich
B8007
Ormsaigmore
Ormsaigbeg
Kilchoan
An Acairseid
Kilchoan Bay
Cairns of Coll
Eilean Mor
Rubha Mor
Sorisdale
Bousd
B8072
Cliad Bay
Arnabost
Gallanach
Grishipoll
B8071
Ballyhaugh
Hogh Bay
104
Loch Cliad
73
COLL
OBAN 2:40
Arinagour
Totronald
Feall Bay
Arileod
Acha
B8070
Breachacha Castle
Friesland
Loch Eatharna
Eilean Ornsay
CASTLEBAY 6:45 (Summer only)
Calgary Pt.
Gunna
Crossapol Bay
Loch Breachacha
Soa
TIREE
Vaul Bay
Salum
Caolas
Vaul
B8069
Rubha Dubh
Hough Skerries
Balephetrish Bay
B8068
Ruaig
Balevullin
Gott Bay
Soa
R. Chraiginis
Kenovay
Kilkenneth
Moss
B8068
TIREE
Scarinish
B8065
Middleton
Heylipol
Port Mor
Crossapol
Heanish
Barrapol
B8065
Rubha Traigh an Duin
Loch a'Phuill
B8067
Hynish Bay
Rinn Thorbhais
Balephuil
141
Balemartine
Mannal
Balephuil Bay
Port Snoig
Hynish
Quinish Pt.
Glengorm Castle
MULL MUSEUM
Ardmore Bay
Ardmore Pt.
Caliach Pt.
Rubha an Aird
Sunipol
Mornish
Penmore Mill
Quinish
Mishnish
S. AIRDE-BEINN
292
MULL THEATRE
Dervaig
Achnadrish
THE OLD BYRE HERITAGE CENTRE
Calgary Bay
Calgary
Treshnish Pt.
Ensay
342 CARN MOR
Haunn
Bellart
Lettermore
Achnacraig
Rubh a'Chaoil
B8073
Burg
Kilninian
Achleck
Fanmore
390
Treshnish Isles
Fladda
LOCH TUATH
Ballygown
EAS FORS WATERFALL
424 BEINN NA DRISE
Eilean Dioghlum
Lagganulva
Lunga
Gometra
Beamus
313
Laggan Bay
Oskamull
Ulva
Ulva House
Sound of Ulva
Killiechronan
LOCH NA KEAL
Bac Mor
Little Colonsay
Eorsa
Staffa
STAFFA
FINGAL'S CAVE
INCH KENNETH CHAPEL
Inch Kenneth
ISLE OF MULL
Derryguaig
Balnahard
MACKINNON'S CAVE
Erisgeir
561
519
BEINN NA SREINE
Glen Seilisdeir
ARDMEANACH
Killiemore House
THE BURG
Kilfinichen Bay
LOCH SCRIDAIN
MACLEAN'S CROSS
Eilean Annraidh
IONA ABBEY AND CATHEDRAL
Rubha nan Cearc
100
IONA HERITAGE CENTRE
Kintra
ST COLUMBA EXHIBITION & WELCOME CENTRE
Iona
Baile Mor
Ardhglas
Loch na Lathaich
Torrans
Stac an Aoineidh
Sound of Iona
Fionnphort
A849
Eorabus
Fidden
Tiraghoil
Lee
Bunessan
Loch Assapol
376 CRUACHAN MIN
Erraid
ROSS OF MULL
Soa I.
Ardalanish
Uisken
Scoor
Ardchiavaig
125
Malcolm's Pt.
Rubha nam Braithrean
Eilean a'Chalmain
Rubh Ardalanish
Torran Rocks
0:55
1:00
1:10
0:35
Scale : 1:332 000
(approx 5 miles to 1 inch)
0 1 2 3 4 5 6 miles
0 1 2 3 4 5 6 7 8 9 10 km

NG
NH
NM
NN
KNOYDART
Highland
Argyll and Bute
MORAR, MOIDART AND ARDNAMURCHAN
SOUND OF SLEAT
SOUND OF ARISAIG
SOUND OF MULL
ISLAND OF MULL
FIRTH OF LORN
LYNN OF LORN
LOCH LINNHE
LOCH SHIEL
LOCH SUNART
LOCH NEVIS
LOCH MORAR
LOCH ARKAIG
LOCH QUOICH
LOCH EIL
LOCH ETIVE
LOCH AWE
MOIDART
SUNART
ARDNAMURCHAN
MORVERN
KINGAIRLOCH
BENDERLOCH
Mallaig
Fort William
Oban
Tobermory
Glenfinnan
Corpach
Ballachulish
Glencoe
Kilchoan
Acharacle
Strontian
Lochaline
Craignure
Lismore
Kerrera
Seil
Luing
Inveraray
Dalmally
Taynuilt
Connel
Arisaig
Lochailort
Salen
Sandaig
Inverie
Point of Sleat
Ard Thurinish
Armadale
Kinlochleven
Appin
Duror
Kentallen
Onich
Inchree
Clovullin
Ardgour
Glen Coe
Glen Etive
Glen Orchy
Glen Lonan
Glen More
Glen Dessarry
Glen Pean
Glen Kingie
Glen Loy
Glen Garry
Ben Nevis
149
136
130
124
8
9
10
11
12
13
14
A
B
C
D
E
F
G
H
J
K

Western Isles
UIBHIST A TUATH (NORTH UIST)
BEINN NA FAOGHLA (BENBECULA)
UIBHIST A DEAS (SOUTH UIST)
EILEAN BHARRAIGH (BARRA)
SOUTH UIST MACHAIR
AN CAOLAS MHONACH
CAOLAS NA HEARADH
LOCH DUNVEGAN
NF
Haskeir I.
Haskeir Eagach
Sound of Spuir
Spuir
Eilean Bhearnaraigh (Berneray)
Ruisigearraidh
Borgh
Baile
Boreray
Ensay
Killegray
Carminish Is.
Cairminis
Srannda
Roghadal
Boirseam
Lingreabhagh
Lingarabay I.
Vallay
Renish Pt.
Langay
ST CLEMENT'S CHURCH
Aird a'Mhòrain
Veilish Pt.
Vallay
Lingay
Oronsay
Port nan Long
Baile Mhic Phail
Torogay
Groay
Gilsay
Lingay
Scaravay
Griminish Pt.
Scolpaig
SCOLPAIG TOWER
Vallay Strand
Solas
Greinetobht
Trumaisgearraidh
Sursay
Tahay
Opsay
Hermetray
Manish Pt.
Baile Mhartainn
Malacleit
Loch nan Geireann
Groatay
Taigh a Ghearraidh
Hosta
Glen Drolla
Causamul
Aird an Rùnair
Hogha Gearraidh
Baile Raghaill
Lochportain
Loch Fada
230 MARRIVAL
Loch nam Madadh (Lochmaddy)
TAIGH CHEARSABHAGH
UIST ANIMAL VISITOR CENTRE
Rubha Port Scolpaig
Ceann a Bhaigh
Claddach-knockline
Paibeil
Baile Mor
Loch Scadabhagh
Weaver's Pt.
UIG 1:45
Rubha nam Pleac
Madadh Gruamach
Cladach Chireboist
BARPA LANGASS CAIRN
250
281 SOUTH LEE
Na h-eileanan Monach (Heisker or Monach Islands)
Stockay
Kirkibost Island
Vorogay
An t-Aigeach
MONACH ISLES
Ceann Iar
Ceann Ear
Clachan na Luib
Loch Euphoirt
Saighdinis
Rubha Mhic Gille-mhicheil
Teanna Mhachair
Samhla
Corunna
Baile Sear (Baleshare)
Bail Uachdraich
TRINITY TEMPLE
Cairinis
Loch Obasaraigh
347 EAVAL
Bail Iochdrach
Oitir Mhòr
Baile Glas
Floddaybeg
Beul an Toim
BENBECULA
Griomasaigh (Grimsay)
Floddaymore
Uachdar
Scotbheinn
Bagh Mor
Ronay
Baile a Mhanaich
Gramsdal
Flodaigh
Flodday
Baile nan Cailleach
124
99
Rubha na Rodagrich
Griminis
Maragay Mor
Torlum
COMMUNITY MUSEUM
Lionacleit
Loch Uisgeabhagh
Loch Chiurabhagh
Maaey Riabhach
Gualan
Creag Ghoraidh
Hornish Pt.
Rubha Carn nan Gall
Ardivachar Pt.
Aird a Mhachair
Iochdar
Clachan
102
Bagh nam Faoileann
Fuidhaigh (Wiay)
Loch Bì
Loch a Charnain
Steisay
Gasay
Sanndabhaig
Loch Càrnan
Geirinis
OUR LADY OF THE ISLES STATUE
Luirsay Dubh
168
Stadhlaigearraidh
Loch Sgioport
Ornish I.
Dreumasdal
HOWMORE
Loch Druidibeg
Mol a'Tuath
Verran I.
Tobha Mor
Snìseabhal
606 HECLA
176
Rubha Rossel
Rubha'Aird-mhicheil
Staoinebrig
527
Rubha Bhilidh
Ormiclate Castle
Loch Olaigh
BEINN MHOR 620
Rubha Hellisdale
Rubha Ardvule
Loch Cill Donnain
Bornais
Taobh a Tuath Loch Aineort
Rubha Bolum
Calvay
KILDONAN MUSEUM
Cill Donnain
Unasary
Gearraidh Bhailteas
Minngearraidh
FLORA MACDONALD'S BIRTHPLACE
Loch Aineort
Loch Sniogaiscleit
Aisgernis
374 STULAVAL
Stuley
Loch Stulabhal
Dalabrog
Taobh a Tuath Loch Baghasdail
357
Rubha na Creige Mòire
Crois Dughaill
Loch Baghasdail (Lochboisdale)
Cille Pheadair
Loch Baghasdail
Calvay
Baghasdal
Ceann a Deas Loch Baghasdail
Rubha Meall na Hoe
Trosaraidh
Gearraidh na Monadh
Smercleit
Cille Bhrighde
South Glendale
Rubha na h-Ordaig
Pol a Charra
Taobh a Chaolais
Ludag
201
Caolas Eiriosgaigh
Sgeir a'Mhill
Lingeigh (Lingay)
Calvay
Haunn
Bun a'Mhuillin
Hartamul
Am Baile
Coilleag
185
Eiriosgaigh (Eriskay)
Fiaraigh (Fiaray)
Caolas Fhiaraigh
Caolas Bhearraigh
Scurrival Pt.
89
Fuideigh (Fuday)
CASTLEBAY 1:30
Eolaigearraidh
CILLE BHARRA
Caolas Fhuideigh
Stack Is.
Orosay
Traigh Mhor
Oitir Mhòr
Greian Head
Cliaid
207 BEN CLIAD
Cuidhir
Hellisay
Gighay
Aird Mhor
Aird Mhidhinis
Bagh Shiarabhagh
Caolas Sheileasaigh
Allathasdal
Bruairnis
Borve Pt.
Baile na Creige
Buaile nam Bodach
CRAIGSTON MUSEUM
Borgh
94
Fuiay
Bagh a Tuath
Bruernish Pt.
Dòirlinn Hd.
Tangasdal
Earsairidh
332
HEAVAL 383
BARRA HERITAGE CENTRE
Breibhig
Bagh a Chaisteil (Castlebay)
KIESSIMUL (KISIMUL) CASTLE
Rubha Mor
LOCHBOISDALE 1:30
190
Uidh
Bhatarsaigh (Vatersay)
Bagh Bhatarsaigh
Bhatarsaigh
Muldoanich
OBAN 4:50
Flodaigh (Flodday)
Caolas Shanndraigh
207
Sanndraigh (Sandray)
SCARINISH (TIREE) 6:45 (Summer only)
Lingeigh (Lingay)
Greanamul
Caolas Phabaigh
Pabaidh
TARBERT 1:40
LOCHMADDY 1:45
Waterish Point
Ard Beag
TRUMPAN CHURCH
BEN GEARY 284
Geary
Trumpan
Knockbreck
Lower Halistra
Upper Halistra
Gillen
Ardmore Pt.
Hallin
Dunvegan Head
Isay
Mingay
Stein
Loch Bay
Galtrigill
Claigan
Borreraig
BORRERAIG PARK MUSEUM
Uig
327 BEINN BHREAC
Husabost
An Ceannaich
Loch Pooltiel
Feriniquarrie
Lower Milovaig
Totaig
Glasphein
Oisgill Bay
Upper Milovaig
Lephin
COLBOST FOLK MUSEUM
Colbost
DUNVEGAN CASTLE
Holmisdale
LIGHTHOUSE
Neist Point
Glen Dale
Skinidin
Dunvegan
Kilmuir
Lonmore
Moonen Bay
HEALABHAL MHOR 468
Ramasaig
Hoe Rape
Macleod's Tables
Orbost
488 HEALABHAL BHEAG
Hoe Point
Geodha Mor
MACLEOD'S MAIDENS
Idrigill P
Canna
A'Chill
Garrisdale Pt.
Oigh-sgeir
154
146
Scale : 1:332 000
(approx 5 miles to 1 inch)
0 1 2 3 4 5 6 miles
0 1 2 3 4 5 6 7 8 9 10 km

Fladda-chùain
Eilean Trodday
Rubha Hunish
Rubha na h-Aiseig
Duntulm
Balmacqueen
Kilmaluag
Hungladder
Bornesketaig
Kilmuir
Kilvaxter
Balgown
Linicro
Totscore
Kilbride Point
Ascrib Islands
Idrigill
Uig
Uig Bay
Ru Chorachan
Balnaknock
Earlish
LOCH SNIZORT
Peinlich
Kingsburgh
Lyndale Pt.
Greshornish Pt.
Greshornish
Lyndale Ho.
Flashader
Treaslane
Suladale
Edinbane
Blackhill
Eyre
The Aird
Kensaleyre
Bernisdale
Tote
Skeabost
Carbost
Borve
Glen Bernisdale
Uigshader
Drumuie
Achachork
Glengrasco
Portree
Torvaig
Shulishadermor
Heatherfield
Penifiler
Glenmore
Mugeary
Camastianavaig
Conordan
Lower Ollach
Upper Ollach
Gedintailor
The Braes
Peinchorran
Sconser
Sligachan Hotel
Glen Varragill
Crossal
Drynoch
Carbost
Merkadale
Fernilea
Fiskavaig
Portnalong
Oronsay
Gleann Oraid
Talisker
Talisker Bay
Eynort
Grula
Glen Brittle Forest
Glenbrittle House
CUILLIN HILLS
THE CUILLIN HILLS
Bualintur
Rubh an Dunain
Soay
Soay Sound
Mol-chlach
Camasunary
Kirkibost
Kilmarie
Elgol
Glasnakille
Rubha Suisnish
Eilean na h-Airde
Rubha na h-Easgainne
Torrin
Kilbride
Strathaird
Loch Slapin
Luib
Dunan
Moll
Scalpay
Scalpay Ho.
Guillamon I.
Pabay
RED HILLS
Corry
Broadford
Harrapool
Waterloo
Lower Breakish
Upper Breakish
Skulamus
Heast
Kinloch
Drumfearn
Duisdalemore
Isleornsay
Ornsay
Camuscross
Teangue
Tokavaig
Ord
Tarskavaig
Tarskavaig Pt.
Achnacloich
Ferindonald
Kilbeg
Kilmore
Armadale Castle
Armadale Bay
Glen Meadhonach
Calligarry
Ardvasar
Aird of Sleat
Ard Thurinish
Point of Sleat
Rubha Charn nan Cearc
Stenscholl
Staffin
Staffin Bay
Staffin I.
Digg
Glashvin
Brogaig
Flodigarry
Eilean Flodigarry
Kilt Rock
Elishader
Maligar
Valtos
Marishader
Garros
Rubha nam Brathairean
Breckrey
Culnaknock
Lealt
Lower Tote
Upper Tote
TROTTERNISH
Ollach
Bearreraig Bay
Holm I.
Manish Pt.
Rubha na h Airde Glaise
Glame
Balmeanach
Balachuirn
Oskaig
Clachan
Raasay Ho.
Inverarish
North Fearns
East Suisnish
Eyre
Eyre Point
ISLAND OF RAASAY
Brochel
Arnish
Torran
Eilean Fladday
Eilean Tigh
Eilean Garbh
Garbh Eilean
An Caol
Island of Rona
SOUND OF RAASAY
INNER SOUND
Crowlin Islands
Eilean Mór
Longay
Rubha na'Leac
Eilean na Bà
ISLE OF SKYE
Bracadale
Struan
Coillore
Ullinish
Tarner I.
Loch Bracadale
Wiay
Roskhill
Roag
Vatten
Harlosh
Balmore
Ose
Orbost
Lusta
Rubha nan Clach
Arnaval
Seana Chamas
Aultgrishan
Midtown
Brae
Peterburn
Naast
Rubha 'Ard na Bà
Tournaig
Inverewe Garden
Londubh
Poolewe
Aird Dubh
Loch Ewe
Fionn Loch
Port Erradale
North Erradale
Big Sand
Rubha Bàn
Longa Island
Strath
Smithstown
Gairloch
Charlestown
Loch Gairloch
Kerrysdale
Port Henderson
Opinan
Aird
Badachro
Shieldaig
South Erradale
Redpoint
Loch Maree
Eilean Subhainn
Talladale
WESTER ROSS
Flowerdale Forest
Shieldaig Forest
Rubha na Fearn
Fearnmore
Fearnbeg
Arinacrinachd
Lower Diabaig
Kenmore
Ardheslaig
Alligin Shuas
Inveralligin
Rechullin
Torridon Ho.
Fasaig
Torridon
Annat
Torridon Forest
Glen Torridon
Ben-damph Forest
Shieldaig
Balgy
Loch Torridon
Upper Loch Torridon
Cuaig
Callakille
Lonbain
Applecross
Applecross Forest
Applecross Bay
Camusteel
Camusterrach
Culduie
Ard-dhubh
Toscaig
Glenshieldaig Forest
Sanachan
Kirkton
Lochcarron
Slumbay
Achintraid
Ardarroch
Kishorn I.
Ardaneaskan
Stromemore
Stromeferry
Ardnarff
Attadale
Plockton
Achmore
An Dubh-aird
Port Cam
Duirinish
Drumbuie
Erbusaig
Badicaul
Black Is.
Balmacara Square
Reraig
Auchertyre
Kyle of Lochalsh
Kyleakin
Balmacara
Kirkton
Nostie
Ardelve
Dornie
Glas Eilean
Totaig
Ardintoul Pt.
Letterfearn
Loch Alsh
Keppoch
Bundalloch
Camas-luinie
Allt-nan-sùgh
Sallachy
Glen Arroch
Kylerhea
Bernera
Galltair
Glenelg
Glenelg Bay
Eilanreach
Balvraid
Ratagan
Shiel Bridge
Invershiel
Glen More
Glenshiel Forest
Upper Sandaig
Sandaig Is.
Corran
Arnisdale
Glen Arnisdale
Loch Hourn
Kinlochhourn Forest
Inverguseran
Rubha Ard Slisneach
Airor
KNOYDART
Glen Barrisdale
Sandaig
Scottas
Inverie
Inverie Bay
Loch Nevis
Mallaig
Glasnacardoch
Beoraidbeg
Morar
Bracara
Bracorina
Brinacory
Tarbet
Kylesmorar
Kylesknoydart
Camusrory
Swordland
Kinlochmorar
Loch Morar
North Morar
South Morar
Bunacaimb
Portnaluchaig
Back of Keppoch
Oban
Eilean Ighe
Rùm
Kinloch
Kinloch Glen
Kilmory
Harris
Glen Harris
Schooner Pt.
Rubha Sgorr an t-Snidhe
Rubha nam Meirleach
Rubha Port na Caranean
Rubha na Roinne
Rubha Shamhnan Insir
Canna Harbour
Sound of Canna
Loch Scresort
SMALL ISLES
SOUND OF RÙM
SOUND OF SLEAT
Bay of Laig
Cleadale

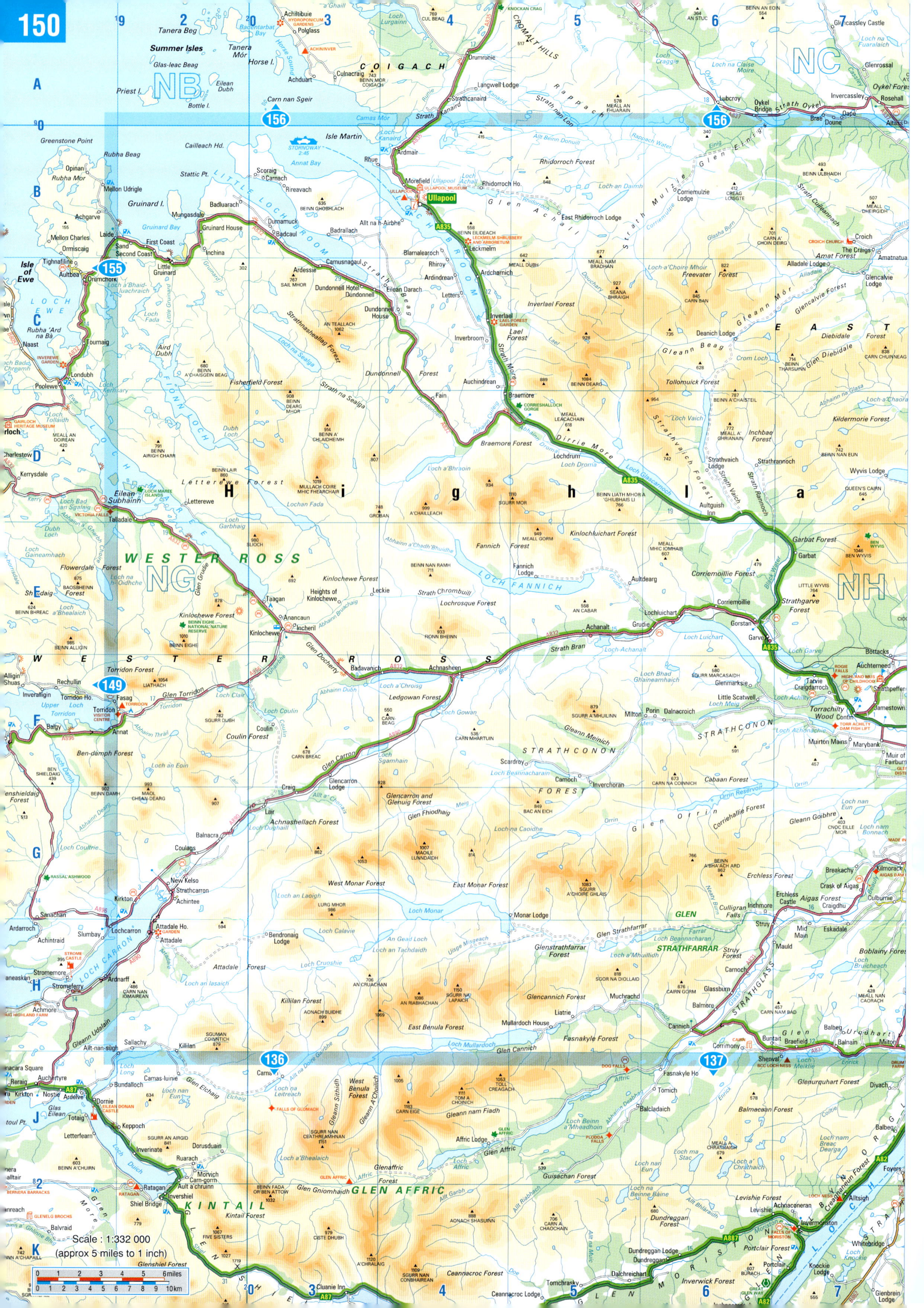
Tanera Beg
Summer Isles
Tanera Mòr
Glas-leac Beag
Horse I.
Achiltibuie
Polglass
Priest I.
Eilean Dubh
Bottle I.
NB
Carn nan Sgeir
COIGACH
Culnacraig
Achduart
Drumrunie
CROMALT HILLS
Langwell Lodge
Strathcanaird
Strath Kanaird
Rappach
Strath nan Lon
NC
Loch Craggie
Glencassley Castle
Glenrossal
Oykel Forest
Rosehall
Invercassley
Lubcroy
Oykel Bridge
Strath Oykel
Brae
Doune
Altass
156
Greenstone Point
Rubha Beag
Cailleach Hd.
Isle Martin
Ardmair
Rhue
Annat Bay
Stattic Pt.
Scoraig
Carnach
Rireavach
Opinan
Rubha Mor
Mellon Udrigle
Gruinard I.
Badluarach
Mungasdale
Gruinard House
Gruinard Bay
LITTLE LOCH BROOM
Morefield
Ullapool
Rhidorroch Forest
Rhidorroch Ho.
Glen Achall
East Rhidorroch Lodge
Strath Mulzie
Corriemulzie Lodge
Glen Einig
Strath Cuileannach
Croick
The Craigs
Amatnatua
Amat Forest
Alladale Lodge
Glencalvie Lodge
Glencalvie Forest
Achgarve
Mellon Charles
Ormiscaig
Laide
Sand
First Coast
Second Coast
Little Gruinard
Inchina
Badcaul
Dundonnell Hotel
Dundonnell
Camusnagaul
Allt na h-Airbhe
Leckmelm
Ardcharnich
Inverlael
Lael Forest
Inverlael Forest
Freevater
Forest
Gleann Mòr
Isle of Ewe
Aultbea
Drumchork
Tighnafiline
155
LOCH EWE
Rubha 'Ard na Bà
Naast
Tournaig
Poolewe
Londubh
Inverewe Garden
Ardessie
Strathnasheallag Forest
Dundonnell House
Inverbroom
Strath More
Auchindrean
Braemore
Fain
Dundonnell Forest
Deanich Lodge
Gleann Beag
Diebidale
Glen Diebidale
Tollomuick Forest
Fisherfield Forest
Strath na Sealga
FIONN LOCH
Gairloch Heritage Museum
Kerrysdale
Charlestown
Letterewe Forest
Letterewe
Eilean Subhainn
Talladale
Braemore Forest
Dirrie More
Lochdrum
Loch Droma
Strathvaich Forest
Strathvaich Lodge
Strath Rannoch
Strathrannoch
Inchbae Forest
Kildermorie Forest
Wyvis Lodge
Highland
Aultguish Inn
Loch Glascarnoch
A835
Kinlochluichart Forest
Fannich
Forest
Fannich Lodge
LOCH FANNICH
Garbat Forest
Garbat
Ben Wyvis
Corriemoillie Forest
Corriemoillie
Strathgarve Forest
Auldearg
Lochluichart
Gorstan
Garve
NH
Flowerdale
Forest
Shieldaig
WESTER ROSS
NG
Kinlochewe Forest
Heights of Kinlochewe
Leckie
Strath Chrombuill
Lochrosque Forest
Taagan
Anancaun
Incheril
Kinlochewe
Glen Docherty
Achnasheen
Achanalt
Strath Bran
Grudie
Loch Luichart
Bottacks
Auchterneed
Strathpeffer
Tarvie
Craigdarroch
Torrachilty Wood
Contin
Jamestown
WESTER ROSS
Torridon Forest
Rechullin
Inveralligin
Torridon Ho.
Fasag
Torridon
Glen Torridon
Badavanich
Ledgowan Forest
Achnasheen
Loch Gowan
Scardroy
STRATHCONON
STRATHCONON FOREST
Milton
Porin
Dalnacroich
Little Scatwell
Murrton Mains
Marybank
Annat
Balgy
Ben-damph Forest
Coulin Forest
Coulin
Glen Carron
Glencarron Lodge
Craig
Glencarron and Glenuig Forest
Glen Fhiodhaig
Carnoch
Inverchoran
Cabaan Forest
Orrin Reservoir
Corriehallie Forest
Glen Orrin
Gleann Goibhre
Achnashellach Forest
Lair
Balnacra
Coulags
Erchless Forest
Breakachy
Crask of Aigas
Aigas Forest
Erchless Castle
Culburnie
Kilmorack
West Monar Forest
East Monar Forest
Monar Lodge
Loch Monar
GLEN
Culligran Falls
Inchmore
Struy
New Kelso
Strathcarron
Achintee
Kirkton
Lochcarron
Slumbay
Attadale Ho.
Attadale
Bendronaig Lodge
Glen Strathfarrar
STRATHFARRAR
Glenstrathfarrar Forest
Struy Forest
Mid Main
Eskadale
Mauld
Carnoch
Boblainy Forest
Sanachan
Ardarroch
Achintraid
Strome Castle
Stromemore
Stromeferry
LOCH CARRON
Ardnarff
Attadale Forest
Killilan Forest
Glencannich Forest
Muchrachd
Glassburn
STRATHGLASS
Balmore
Cannich
Mullardoch House
Liatrie
Fasnakyle Forest
East Benula Forest
Achmore
Gleann Udalain
Sallachy
Killilan
Alt-nan-sùgh
Loch Mullardoch
Glen Cannich
136
137
Corrimony
Shenval
Buntait
Glen Urquhart
Braefield
Balnain
Milton
Balbeg
Auchertyre
Reraig
Kirkton
Nostie
Ardelve
Dornie
Eilean Donan Castle
Bundalloch
Camas-luinie
Carnach
Glen Elchaig
Falls of Glomach
West Benula Forest
Gleann Sithidh
Carn Eige
Gleann nam Fiadh
Fasnakyle Ho
Tomich
Dog Falls
Glenurquhart Forest
Divach
Balmacaan Forest
Glas Eilean
Totaig
Keppoch
Letterfearn
Invernate
Dorusduain
Ruarach
Morvich
Carn-gorm
Affric Lodge
Glen Affric
Balcladaich
Guisachan Forest
Plodda Falls
Glenaffric Forest
GLEN AFFRIC
Glen Gniomhaidh
Ratagan
Shiel Bridge
Invershiel
Ault a chruinn
KINTAIL
Kintail Forest
Dundreggan Forest
Levishie Forest
Achnaconeran
Invermoriston
Alltsigh
Creag nan Eun Forest
Foyers
Balvraid
Glenelg Brochs
Glenshiel Forest
Cluanie Inn
Ceannacroc Forest
Ceannacroc Lodge
Tomchrasky
Dalchreichart
Dundreggan Lodge
Dundreggan
GLEN MORISTON
Portclair Forest
Portclair
Inverwick Forest
Knockie Lodge
Whitebridge
Glenbrein Lodge
LOCH NESS
Scale : 1:332 000
(approx 5 miles to 1 inch)
0 1 2 3 4 5 6 miles
0 1 2 3 4 5 6 7 8 9 10 km

ND
NJ
157
152
138
139
Brora
Golspie
Dornoch
Dornoch Firth
Tain
Tarbat Ness
Balintore
Invergordon
Alness
Cromarty
Cromarty Firth
Black Isle
Moray Firth
Burghead
Burghead Bay
Forres
Nairn
Fortrose
Avoch
Dingwall
Conon Bridge
Muir of Ord
Beauly
Beauly Firth
Inverness
Culloden
Bonar Bridge
Ross
Moray
Grantown-on-Spey
Strathspey
Cairngorms National Park
Aviemore
Carrbridge
Boat of Garten
Nethy Bridge
Tomatin
Drumnadrochit
Loch Ness
Monadhliath Mountains
Hills of Cromdale
Strathdearn
The Aird
Rosemarkie
Ardersier
Dalcross
Cawdor
Dulnain Bridge
Tomintoul

Halliman Skerries
Covesea Skerries
LOSSIEMOUTH FISHERIES & COMMUNITY MUSEUM
Branderburgh
Lossiemouth
Stotfield
Covesea
Burghead
BURGHEAD MUSEUM
Hopeman
Duffus
Gordonstoun
Cummingston
Roseisle
Roseisle Forest
DUFFUS CASTLE
Loch Spynie
PALACE OF SPYNIE
Lossie Forest
SPEY BAY
Spynie
Quarrywood
Lower Hempriggs
Newton
Bishopmill
Elgin
ELGIN MUSEUM
CATHEDRAL
CASHMERE VISITOR CENTRE
OLD MILLS
MORAY MOTOR MUSEUM
Coltfield
Alves
Miltonhill
Pittendreich
New Elgin
Leuchars Ho.
Lochhill
Urquhart
Llanbryde
Lochs Crofts
Kingston
Garmouth
DOLPHIN CENTRE
TUGNET ICE HOUSE
Spey Bay
Portannachy
Nether Dallachy
Upper Dallachy
Bogmoor
SPEYSIDE WAY
Auchenhalrig
Newlands of Tynet
BAXTERS HIGHLAND VILLAGE
FOCHABERS FOLK MUSEUM
Fochabers
Mosstodloch
COXTON TOWER
Moss of Barmuckity
Miltonduff
Mains of Burgie
Monaughty Forest
PLUSCARDEN ABBEY
Barnhill
Auchtertyre
Foresterseat
Paddockhaugh
BIRNIE CHURCH
Thomshill
Longmorn
Blackhills
Dipple
Orbliston
Speymouth Forest
Braes of Enzie
Ordiequish
Teindland Forest
MILLBUIES
Inchberry
Wood of Ordiequish
Califer
Kellas
Dallas Forest
Glenlatterach
Briach
Branchill
Dallas
Craigroy
Moray
Glen of Rothes
Auchinroath
Newlands
365 CAIRN UISH
371 MILL BUIE
Rothes
GLEN GRANT DISTILLERY
Burn of Rothes
SPEYSIDE WAY
471 BEN AIGAN
Mulben
Rosarie Forest
Elchies Forest
404 CARN NA CAILLICHE
Whiteacen
LADYCROFT AGRICULTURAL MUSEUM
MACALLAN DISTILLERY
Dandaleith
Maggieknockater
Archiestown
CARDHU DISTILLERY
Cardow
Ringorm
Craigellachie
SPEYSIDE COOPERAGE VISITOR CENTRE
Kininvie Ho.
Midtown of Buchromb
Upper Knockando
Knockando
Knockando Ho.
SPEYSIDE WAY VISITOR CENTRE
Speyview
Charlestown of Aberlour
Carron
Daugh of Kinermony
Milltown of Edinvillie
BALVENIE CASTLE
GLENFIDDICH DISTILLERY
Dufftown
Kirktown of Mortlach
CARN KITTY 521
545 LARIG HILL
516
Marypark
GLENFARCLAS DISTILLERY
Bellehiglash
MEIKLE CONVAL 569
Glen Rinnes
Dullan Water
CRAGGANMORE DISTILLERY
Advie
Bridge of Avon
Dalchirach
840 BEN RINNES
Favillar
Kirkhill
Glen Fiddich
Lettoch
Mains of Dalvey
STRATH SPEY
Drumin
GLENLIVET DISTILLERY
Glenlivet
Shenval
Auchbreck
Glenfiddich Forest
Black Water
Cromdale
Achroisk
Haughs of Cromdale
HILLS OF CROMDALE
Ballcorach
Tomnavoulin
Strath Avon
509 CARN DAIMH
Blackwater Forest
732 CARN AN T-SUIDHE
742
571 ROUND HILL
722 CREAGAN A' CHAISE
Knockandhu
Livet
Glenlivet Forest
Clashnoir
Braes of Glenlivet
Chapeltown
632 HILL OF THREE STONES
Bridge of Brown
Fodderletter
Dirdhu
TOMINTOUL MUSEUM
Tomintoul
TOMINTOUL
Delnabo
GLENLIVET ESTATE VISITOR CENTRE
568 BADDOCH
Dorback Lodge
588 CARN MEADHONACH
804 CARN MOR
LADDER HILLS
Badenyon
Glenbuchat Lodge
658
Water of Buchat
Water of Nochty
Belnacraig
Kirkton of Glenbuchat
Conglass Water
Blairnamarrow
718 THE SOCACH
LECHT SKI CENTRE
Glen Ernan
Ernan Water
Bellabeg
Forbestown
Strathdon
Inverernan Ho.
Candacraig Ho.
Heugh-head
Tornashean Forest
531 CRAIG OF BUNZEACH
Hillockhead
Deskry Water
821 GEAL CHARN
CAIRNGORMS NATIONAL PARK
792 CARN EALASAID
673
Allt Tuileach
Colnabaichin
Cock Bridge
Corgarff
CORGARFF CASTLE
Delnadamph
Tornahaish
742 BIG GARVOUN
GLEN AVON
749
744
871 MORVEN
823 BROWN COW HILL
Loch Builg
Gairnshiel Lodge
Glen Fenzie
BEN AVON
Scale : 1:265 000
(approx 4 miles to 1 inch)
0 1 2 3 4 5 6 miles
0 1 2 3 4 5 6 7 8 9 10 km
Portknockie
Findochty
THE BUCKIE DRIFTER
Gordonsburgh
Buckie
Portessie
Buckpool
Rathven
Cullen Bay
Logie Hd.
Cullen
FINDLATER CASTLE
Sandend Bay
Sandend
Redhythe Pt.
Portsoy
Seatown
Easter Whyntie
Lintmill
Portgordon
Cairnfield Ho.
Drybridge
Slackhead
320
JOINER'S WORKSHOP
Fordyce
199
Milton
Kirktown of Deskford
DESKFORD CHURCH
Ardiecow
Broadley
ST. GREGORY'S CHAPEL
Clochan
Shiel Muir
Berryhillock
Little Toux
Newmills of Boyne
Oldtown of Ord
Craibstone
301 MILLSTONE HILL
Cornhill
Mains of Edingight
Gordonstown
Deerhill
Grange Crossroads
Edingight Ho.
KNOCK HILL 430
Finnygaud
Broadrashes
Forgie
Aultmore
Crannoch
Sillyearn
Knock
Knowes of Elrick
Glen Barry
Bracobrae
Davoch of Grange
Drumnagorrach
Newmill
Farmtown
Old Crombie
Aberchirder
Keith
STRATHISLA DISTILLERY
Knauchland
Marnoch
311
KEITH AND DUFFTOWN RLY
STRATH ISLA
Balloch Wood
265
Milltown of Rothiemay
Deveron
Mains of Mayen
Hillbrae
339
Towiemore
Edintore
Glen of Coachford
Ruthven
Yonder Bognie
Bognie brae
344 FOURMAN HILL
Little Pitlurg
Coachford
Cairnie
313 THE BIN
The Bin Forest
Drummuir Castle
Drummuir
NJ
Daugh of Cairnborrow
Corse of Kinnoir
GLENDRONACH DISTILLERY
NORDIC SKI CENTRE
HUNTLY CASTLE
Huntly
BRANDER MUSEUM
Lessendrum
Drumblade
Corse
417 Milltown of Auchindoun
Cairnborrow
Torry
Brideswell
Slioch
Haugh of Glass
AUCHINDOUN CASTLE
STRATHBOGIE
487 THE SCALP
Bailiesward
Bridgend
Thomastown
Denend
Hillhead
Bainshole
Ballochford
Succoth
Tillathrowie
Kirkstile
Shanquhar
525
Coynachie
Culdrain
Blackburn
Tomnaven
Glens of Foudland
467 HILL OF FOUDLAND
Clashindarroch Forest
Clashindarroch
Kirkney
Gartly
Cults
434 KNOCKANDY HILL
LEITH HALL
Largie
Kirkney Water
Bridgend
Inverharroch
Milton of Lesmore
Kennethmont
Oldtown
Ardlair
The Shevock
Aulton
Auchmair
505
Cabrach
Aldunie
Belhinnie
Rhynie
Milton of Noth
Cottown
Clatt
Duncanstone
Wheedlemont
Craig Castle
ST MARY'S CHURCH
Leslie
721 THE BUCK
Knockespock Ho.
Coldwells Croft
Whitehaugh Forest
Clova
SCOTTISH SCULPTURE WORKSHOP
Lumsden
CORREEN HILLS
Muckletown
Aberdeen
Mossat
518 LORD ARTHUR'S CAIRN
Tullynessle
Keig
Castle Forbes
Montgarrie
Bridge of Alford
Kildrummy
Rinmore
KILDRUMMY CASTLE & GARDEN
Milltown of Kildrummy
Don
ALFORD VALLEY RAILWAY
HAUGHTON
GRAMPIAN TRANSPORT MUS
Auchintoul
532
Alford
HERITAGE CENTRE
Gateside
Asloun
Whitehouse
Glenkindie
Towie
Milltown of Towie
Sinnahard
Hillockhead
Ley
Little Lynturk
Kirkton of Tough
Muir of Fowlis
Bridgend
Tillyfour
Boultenstone
Milton of Cushnie
Leochel-Cushnie
CRAIGIEVAR CASTLE
Kintocher
Corrennie Moor
494 BENAQUHALLIE
Easter Davoch
619
Migvie
Coynach
Douneside
Craskins
476
Tornaveen
CULSH SOUTERRAIN
Findrack Ho.
Logie Coldstone
Tarland
Lumphanan
PEEL RING OF LUMPHANAN
CROMAR
TOMNAVERIE STONE CIRCLE
Milton of Auchinhove
Milton of Logie
Glendavan Ho.
Ordie
299
Coull
Auchlossan
Torphins
A96
A95
A941
A920
A97
A944
A939
A98
B9002
B9119
151
139
140

Fraserburgh
Peterhead
Aberdeen
Macduff
Banff
Turriff
Rosehearty
Inverallochy
Kinnaird Head
Cairnbulg Pt.
Rattray Head
Scotstown Hd.
Kirkton Hd.
Buchan Ness
Boddam
Cruden Bay
Bay of Cruden
North Haven
Hackley Hd. or Forvie Ness
Newburgh Bar
Girdle Ness
Greg Ness
Nigg Bay
Troup Hd.
Pennan Hd.
Quarry Hd.
Head of Garness
Knock Hd.
Gamrie Bay
New Pitsligo
Strichen
Mintlaw
Maud
Crimond
Longside
Old Deer
Ellon
Oldmeldrum
Inverurie
Kintore
Kemnay
Insch
Newmachar
Dyce
Bridge of Don
Westhill
Cults
Cove Bay
Newburgh
Balmedie
Fyvie
Methlick
Tarves
Pitmedden
Collieston
Whinnyfold
Hatton
Port Erroll
NK
B U C H A N
F O R M A R T I N E
G A R I O C H
e e n s h i r e
A b e r d e e n
C i t y
KIRKWALL 6:00
LERWICK 14:30
A90
A96
A947
A950
A952
A975
A920
A948
A981
A98
141

NA
NF
Western Isles
Na h-Eileanan Flannach
St. Kilda
Boreray
ST KILDA
Soay
CNOC GLAS
Loch a' Ghlinne
CONACHAIR
MULLACH BI
St Kilda or Hirta (Hiort)
Bagh a Bhaile
Dun
Siabost bho Thuath
Siabost bho Dheas
SHAWBOST NORSE MILL
Bagh Dhail Beag
GEARRANNAN BLACKHOUSE VILLAGE
GARENIN
Dail Beag
Dail Mor
Pairc Shiaboist
Na Gearrannan
Borghastan
Carlabhagh
Campay
Loch Chàrlabhaigh
DUN CARLOWAY BROCH
Little Bernera
Dun Charlabhaigh
Floday
Harsgeir
IRON AGE HOUSE
Crothair
Tolastadh a Chaolais
AN CAOLAS
An Galan Uigeach
Pabay Mor
Tobson
Aird Uig
Bhaltos
Vacsay
BERNERA
Breacleit
Great Bernera
Loch Lacsabhat Ard
Bàgh Fhiabhaig
Cliobh
Miabhig
Circebost
Breascleit
Timsgearraidh
Riof
Vuia Mor
Tacleit
Barraglom
Keava
Cradhlastadh
Uigen
Loch Rog
Tobhtarol
Eilean Kearstay
CALANAIS VISITOR CENTRE
Càrnais
Vuia Beag
Crulabhig
Calanais
CALANAIS STANDING STONES
Gearraidh na h-Aibhne
Ard More Mangersta
Cairisiadar
Floday
Linsiadar
Mangurstadh
Eadar Dha Fhadhail
SUAINAVAL
Geisiadar
Loch Smuasabhat
Loch Suaineabhal
Aird Fenish
Loch Tungabhat
Einacleite
Aird Brenish
Islibhig
MEALISVAL
Loch Rog
Brenais
Loch Grunabhat
Giosla
Loch Chaolartan
Loch Fuaroil
Loch Airigh na h-Airde
BEINN MHEADHONACH
Mealasta Island
Caolas an Eilein
Loch Morsgail
Loch Cro Criosdaig
Loch Coirigerod
Loch Beiniseabhal
Loch Strandabhat
Loch Tamanabhaigh
Loch Bòdabhat
Morsgail Forest
Ceann Tarabhaigh
Loch Tealasabhaigh
Loch Reasort
LOCH LANGABHAT
Kearstay
Airidh a Bhruaich
Bràighe Mòr
Aird an Troim
Scarp
Loch Crabhadail
Uladail
Abhainn Bhearnaraig
Loch a' Ghlinne
Gaisgeir
Caolas an Scarp
STULAVAL
Aline Lodge
Huisinis
SOUTH LEWIS,
Seaforth I.
Hushinish Pt.
TIRGA MOR
ULLAVAL
Aird a' Mhulaidh
BEINN MHOR
Bagh Huisinis
Scaladal
Gobhaig
UISGNAVAL MORE
Forest of Harris
Horsanish
Abhainn Suidhe
CLISHAM
Arda Mòra
HARRIS AND
CEANN A TUATH NA HEARADH
Loch Shiphoirt
Taransay Glorigs
Soay Beag
Cliasmol
Maraig
LOCH A SIAR
Miabhag
Soay Mòr
Bun Abhainn Eadarra
Camus an t-suithean
OLD WHALING STATION
NORTH UIST
Aird Asaig
Isay
Loch Lacasdail
RHENIGIDALE
Reinigeadal
Tarasaigh (Taransay)
BEN LUSKENTYRE
Loch Trollamarig
Paible
Losgaintir
Tairbeart (Tarbert)
Urgha
Carragraich
Caolas Tharasaigh
LUSKENTYRE BEACH
South Harris Forest
Caolas Scalpaigh
Carnach
Rubha Sgeirigin
Loch Ceann Dibig
Sgeotasaigh
Rudha Crago
Seilebost
Miabhag
Scalpay
Loch an Tairbeart
Eilean Scalpa (Scalp
Borve Lodge
Toe Head
NA HEARADH (HARRIS)
Drinisiadar
Buirgh
Kennavley
Plocropol Pt.
Coppay
CHAIPAVAL
Sgarasta Mhor
Aird Mhighe
Plocrapol
Greosabhagh
Leac a Li
Lideasto
Scadabhagh
Rubha Bhocaig
Rubha'an Teampuill
BLEAVAL
Geocrab
Cluthar
Little Shillay
Shillay
Loch Langabhat
Beacrabhaic
Caolas Stocinis
Loch Greosabhagh
Sound of Shillay
Brenish Pt.
Taobh Tuath
Stockinish I.
SEALLAM!
Fleoideabhagh
Manais
Pabaidh (Pabbay)
Loch Steiseabhat
Aird Mhighe
An t-Ob (Leverburgh)
Cuidhtinis
UIG 1:40
Quinish
Fionnsbhagh
Loch Fleoideabhagh
Ensay
Carminish Is.
ROINEABHAL
Boirseam
Loch Fionnsbhagh
Sound of Spuir
Caolas Phabaidh
Lingreabhagh
Spuir
Cairminis
Lingarabay I.
Killegray
Srannda
Eilean Bhearnaraigh (Berneray)
Ruisigearraidh
ST CLEMENT'S CHURCH
Roghadal
Haskeir I.
BERNERAY
Valley
Borgh
Langay
Renish Pt.
Haskeir Eagach
Boreray
Baile
CAOLAS NA HEARADH
Caolas a'Mhòrain
Aird a'Mhòrain
Caolas Bhearnaraigh
Groay
Gilsay
148
Lingay
Torogay
Scaravay
Veilish Pt.
Lingay
Port nan Long
Valley
Baile Mhic Phàil
Griminish Pt.
Oronsay
Sursay
Opsay
Scolpaig
Grenetobht
Tahay
Trumaisgearraidh
Valley Strand
Solas
Loch Amhlsaraigh
Baile Mhàrtainn
Malacleit
Hermetray
A859
A865
B8011
B887
Scale : 1:332 000
(approx 5 miles to 1 inch)
0 1 2 3 4 5 6 miles
0 1 2 3 4 5 6 7 8 9 10 km

8
9
10
11
12
13
A
B
C
D
E
F
G
H
J
156
149
150
NB
NG
RUBHA ROBHANAIS
(BUTT OF LEWIS)
Cunndal
CHURCH OF ST MOULAG
Eòropaidh
Coig Peighinnean
HARBOUR VIEW GALLERY
Lional
Port Nis
Cross Sands
Suainebost
Tabost
Cros
Aird Dhail
Dail bho Dheas
Dail bho Thuath
Sgiogarstaigh
Glen Cross
Gabhsann bho Thuath
Gabhsann bho Dheas
Mealabost Bhuirgh
Bail Àrd Bhuirgh
Coig Peighinnean Bhuirgh
Cuiashader
Cellar Head
Siadar
Siadar Iarach
Siadar Uarach
Baile an Truiseil
Rubha Leathann
Aird Barvas
TRUSHAL STONE
Loch Langabhat
Loch Mòr Shanndabhat
Barabhas Iarach
Barabhas Uarach
Barabhas
BLACK HOUSE MUSEUM
Labost
Brù
Arnol
Bragar
Abhainn Ghearadha
Bail' Ur Tholastaidh
Tolastadh bho Thuath
Tolsta Head
248 MUIRNEAG
Loch Urghag
Loch Breibhat
Loch Sgeireach Mòr
Gleann Tholàstaidh
Port Bun a'Ghlinne
Gleann Bhruthadail
Glen Bragar
Gleann Mòr Barvas
Griais
Creag Fhraoch
Bac
Col
Vatisker Pt.
Col Uarach
Breibhig
Coll Sands
Loch Scarabhat Mhòr
Loch Mòr an Stàirr
292 BEINN MHOLACH
Loch nan Stearnag
Aird Thunga
Tunga
Sròn Ruadh
BROAD BAY OR LOCH A TUATH
Port Nan Giùran
Cnoc Amhlaigh
Rubha an t-Siumpain
Port Mholair
Aird
Grianan
An Gleann Ur
Newmarket
Lacasdal
Sulaisiadar
Seisiadar
Loch Urabhal
LEWIS LOOM CENTRE
MUSEUM NAN EILEAN
STORNOWAY
Stornoway
Garrabost
EYE PENINSULA
Mealabost
Aiginis
ST COLUMBA'S
Pabail Uarach
Pabail Iarach
Sanndabhaig
AN LANNTAIR GALLERY
An Cnoc
Suardail
Bàgh Phabail
Tolm
Holm I.
A'Chearc
223
Loch a' Ghainmhich
Arnish Moor
Acha Mòr
Loch Orasaigh
Loch Tobhta Bridein
Loch nam Falcag
Grimsidar
Ben Casgro
Liurbost
Ranais
Raerinish Pt.
ULLAPOOL 2:45
Soval Lodge
Crosbost
Loch Trealabhal
Barkin Is.
Tabhaidh Mhor
Eilean Chaluim Chille
Ceos
Eilean Orasaidh
Baile Ailein
Lacasaidh
Eireasort
Cròmor
Eilean Thoraidh
Sildinis
Cearsiadair
Gearraidh Bhaird
Cabharstadh
Tabost
KERSHADER
Marbhig
Ceann Shiphoirt
Loch Sgibacleit
Loch nan Eilean
Calbost
Taobh a' Ghlinne
Grabhair
Loch Odhairn
Kebock Head
Loch Shanndabhat
PARK OR PAIRC
Orasaigh
Leumrabhagh
Eisgean
Loch Shell or Loch Sealg
Srianach
Eilean Iubhard
470 CRÒNAIG
Mol Truisg
Gob Rubh'Uisenis
Rubha Bhrollum
Rubha a'Bhaird
CAOLAS NAN EILEAN
Garbh Eilean
Eilean Mhuire
Na h-Eileanan Mòra (Shiant Islands)
Eilean an Tighe
Glas-leac Beag
Priest I.
Greenstone Point
Rubha Beag
Opinan
Rubha Mòr
Mellon Udrigle
Gruinard I.
Achgarve
Gruinard Bay
Sròn a' Gheodha Dhuibh
Eilean Furadh Mòr
Rubha Reidh
Camas Mòr
155
Mellon Charles
Laide
Sand
First Coast
Second Coast
Ormiscaig
Loch an Draing
Cove
Isle of Ewe
Tighnafiline
Aultbea
Little Gruinard
296 AN CUAIDH
Drumchork
Loch a' Bhaid-luachraich
Loch Sguod
Melvaig
Inverasdale
Aultgrishan
Midtown
LOCH EWE
Loch Fada
Little Gruinard
Seana Chamas
Brae
Rubha 'Ard na Bà
Peterburn
Naast
Tournaig
Aird Dubh
INVEREWE GARDEN
Loch Bad a' Chreamh
Port Erradale
North Erradale
Londubh
FIONN LOCH
Poolewe
Loch Kernsary
Fladda-chùain
Eilean Trodday
Rubha Bàn
Big Sand
CARN DEARG
Longa Island
Caolas Beag
Loch Tollaidh
Strath
GAIRLOCH HERITAGE MUSEUM
Smithstown
Gairloch
MEALL AN DOIREAN 420
Rubha Hunish
Rubha na h-Aiseig
LOCH GAIRLOCH
Charlestown
791 BEINN AIRIGH CHARR
DUNTULM CASTLE
Duntulm
Kilmaluag
Port Henderson
Aird
Badachro
Kerrysdale

NB
NG
155
150
CAPE WRATH
Kearvaig
Geodha Ruadh na Fola
Bay of Keisgaig
Geodha Ruadh
Am Balg
Rubh'an Fhir Léithe
Faraid Head
Balnakeil Bay
BALNAKEIL CHURCH
BALNAKEIL CRAFT VILLAGE
DURNESS VISITOR CENTRE
SMOO CAVE
Durness
Sangomore
Keoldale
Kyle of Durness
Achiemore
Inshore
Leirinmore
Sangobeg
Eilean Hoan
Geodh'a' Bhrideoin
Eilean Cluimhrig
Whiten
Rispond
Sarsgrum
Loch Keisgaig
Sandwood Loch
Strath Shinary
Loch na Gainimh
Loch Airigh na Beinne
371 SGRIBHIS-BHEINN
457 FASHVEN
423 BEINN DEARG
485 CREAG RIABHACH
332 GHLAS BHEINN
422 MEALL MEADHONACH
521 FARRMHEALL
772 BEINN SPIONNAIDH
800 CRANSTACKIE
Sheigra
Balchrick
Droman
Oldshore Beg
Oldshoremore
Eilean Roin Mor
Loch Clash
Kinlochbervie
Badcall
Achriesgill
Gualin Ho.
Strath Dionard
Strath Beag
Portnancon
Heilam
Hope
Lochside
Eilean Choraidh
Eriboll
Polla
LOCH ERIBOLL
Loch Hope
Bagh Loch an Roin
Loch Dughaill
Rubha Ruadh
Ardmore Pt.
Ardmore
Achlyness
Ceathramh Garbh
Rhiconich
Loch Inchard
L. na Claise Carnaich
GANU MOR 908
Foinaven
521 AN LEAN-CHARN
927 BEN HOPE
Fanagmore
Tarbet
Foindle
Loch Laxford
NORTH-WEST SUTHERLAND
Loch a' Garbh-bhaid Mór
Loch Dionard
Loch Crocach
Handa Island
Sound of Handa
Loch nam Brac
Laxford Bridge
Loch an Easain Uaine
787 ARKLE
777
FEINNE-BHEINN MOR 465
Altnacaillich
DUN DORNAIGIL BROCH
Scourie Bay
Scourie More
Scourie
Rubh'Aird an t-Sionnaich
Gorm Loch
Lochstack Lodge
Glen Golly
Strath More
Upper Badcall
Lower Badcall
719 BEN STACK
Strath Stack
Loch Stack
Gobernuisgach Lodge
Badcall Bay
BEINN AUSKAIRD 386
Eil. a'Bhreitheimh
LOCH A'MHUILINN
Achfary
332
Loch Crocach
REAY FOREST
Lochmore Lodge
759
Rubha a'Mhucard
A894
Meall Mór
Calbha Mór
Calbha Beag
Eddrachillis Bay
Duartmore Forest
Loch More
Aultanrynie
Loch na Creige Duibhe
Loch an Leathaid Bhuain
Loch Coire na Saidhe Duibhe
Point of Stoer
Cirean Geardail
161
R. nan Cósan
Eilean Chrona
Oldany Island
Culkein Drumbeg
Culkein
Loch Nedd
Kylestrome
Kylesku
Unapool
Loch a' Chàirn Bhàin
547
Glendhu Forest
Kinloch
A838
873 BEN HEE
Loch a'Ghorm-choire
Cluas Deas
Clashnessie Bay
Oldany
Drumbeg
Nedd
B869
Loch Glendhu
Gleann Dubh
566
Achnacarnin
Clashmore
Clashnessie
Balchladich
Rienachait
Gleann Leireag
Newton
Loch Glencoul
530 BEINN AIRD DA LOCH
Glen Coul
Loch Merkland
Loch Poll
Rubh'a' Mhill Dheirg
Bay of Stoer
Stoer
Clachtoll
Loch Crocach
Loch Beannach
Loch an Leothaid
808 QUINAG
792 BEINN LEOID
Loch an Eircill
Loch Dubh a'Chuail
Merkland Lodge
Loch Fiag
404
312 CNOC A' ALASKI
H
i
g
R. Leumair
Achmelvich Bay
Rhicarn
Lochassynt Lodge
EAS COUL AULIN WATERFALL
776
BEINN UIDHE 740
Loch a'Ghriama
Corrykinloch
Glen Fiag
Fiag Plantation
Achmelvich
ACHMELVICH BEACH
ASSYNT VISITOR CENTRE
Rubha Rodha
Baddidarach
Lochinver
A837
Brackloch
Inver
Little Assynt
LOCH ASSYNT
Skiag Bridge
ARDVRECK CASTLE
Gorm Loch Mor
Fionn Loch Mor
Overscaig Hotel
Soyea I.
Loch Inver
Glencanisp Lodge
Loch Fèith an Leothaid
540
Inchnadamph
Inchnadamph Forest
A'Chleit
Kirkaig Pt.
Badnaban
Strathan
ASSYNT-
512 MAOVALLY
Flag Bridge
Loch Kirkaig
Inverkirkaig
Glencanisp Forest
INCHNADAMPH
998 BEN MORE ASSYNT
391
Rubha Coigeach
Rubha na Breige
Eilean Mór
SUILVEN 731
846 CANISP
Stronchrubie
Loch na Gainimh
Fionn Loch
718 BREABAG
MEALL AN AONAICH 715
Strath an Lòin
LOCH SHIN
ENARD BAY
Falls
COIGACH
Duchally
Camas Eilean Ghlais
Rubha Mór
Reiff
Rubh'a' Choin
Inverpolly Lodge
Loch Awe
Cam Loch
Benmore Forest
Brae of Achnahaird
Loch Sionascaig
Loch Veyatie
Ledmore
BEINN SGEIREACH 476
Altandhu
SUMMER ISLES SMOKEHOUSE
Loch Vatachan
Aird of Coigach
Inverpolly Forest
849 CUL MOR
HIGHLAND & RARE BREEDS FARM
Elphin
Altnacealgach Hotel
Loch Ailsh
Benmore Lodge
Eilean Mullagrach
Loch Osgaig
613 STAC POLLAIDH
Drumrunie Forest
Loch an Doire Dhuibh
Knockan
Isle Ristol
Polbain
Glas-leac Mór
Loch Bad a'Ghaill
Loch Urigill
KNOCKAN CRAG
A835
364 AN STUC
BEINN AN EOIN 554
Glen Oykel
Glen Cassley
Glencassley Castle
Tanera Beg
Badentarbat Bay
Achiltibuie
HYDROPONICUM GARDENS
Polglass
Loch Lurgainn
769 CUL BEAG
CROMALT HILLS
517
Loch na Fuaralaich
Summer Isles
Tanera Mór
Horse Sound
ACHININVER
Drumrunie
Oykel
Loch Craggie
Loch na Claise Moire
Glenrossal
Glas-leac Beag
Horse I.
Achduart
Culnacraig
743 BEINN MOR COIGACH
COIGACH
Langwell Lodge
Rappach
578 MEALL AN FHUARAIN
Lubcroy
Oykel Bridge
Strath Oykel
Invercassley
Oykel Forest
Rosehall
Priest I.
Eilean Dubh
Carn nan Sgeir
Bottle I.
Strathcanaird
Kanaird
Strath nan Lon
Strath Kanaird
A837
Oape
Brae
Doune
Altass
Camas Mór
Isle Martin
415
Ailt Beinn Donuill
Rappach Water
Greenstone Point
Rubha Beag
Cailleach Hd.
STORNOWAY 2:45
Annat Bay
Ardmair
Glen Einig
Opinan
Stattic Pt.
Scoraig
Carnach
Rhue
Rhidorroch Forest
493 BEINN ULBHAIDH
Rireavach
Morefield
Ullapool
ULLAPOOL MUSEUM
Loch Achall
Rhidorroch Ho.
548
Loch an Daimh
Strath Mulzie
Corriemulzie Lodge
412 CREAG LOISGTE
Strath Cuileannach
LITTLE LOCH BROOM
LOCH BROOM
Badluarach
635 BEINN GHOBHLACH
Glen Achall
East Rhidorroch Lodge
507 MEALL DHEIRGIDH
Gruinard House
Dundonnell
Durnamuck
Badcaul
Badrallach
Allt na h-Airbhe
558 BEINN EILIDEACH
LECKMELM SHRUBBERY AND ARBORETUM
701 CARN A' CHOIN DEIRG
CROICH CHURCH
Croich
Mellon Charles
First Coast
Scale 1:332 000
(approx 5 miles to 1 inch)
0 1 2 3 4 5 6 miles
0 1 2 3 4 5 6 7 8 9 10 km

Strathy Point
Totegan
Brims Ness
Spear Hd.
Holborn Hd.
Thurso Bay
Clardon Hd.
STROMNESS 1:30
Crosskirk
Scrabster
Thurso
Bridge of Forss
Dounreay
Buldoo
Achreamie
Newlands of Geise
Thurso East
Clardon
Murkle
Haimer
Castletown
Olrig Ho.
Weydale
Achingills
Westfield
Shebster
Achvarasdal
Isauld
Reay
Sandside Ho.
Fresgoe
Red Pt.
Sandside Bay
Melvich
Melvich Bay
Portskerra
Bighouse
Baligill
Strathy
Strathy Bay
Aultiphurst
Brawl
Armadale
Armadale Bay
Lednagullin
Kirtomy
Kirtomy Pt.
Ardmore Pt.
Farr Pt.
Farr
Swordly
Bettyhill
Achina
Invernaver
Torrisdale Bay
Torrisdale
Achtoty
Airdtorrisdale
Skerray
Neave I. or Coombe I.
Eilean nan Ron
Rabbit Is.
Caol Raineach
Port Vasgo
Tongue Bay
Strathan
Midfield
West Strathan
Talmine
Skinnet
Midtown
Head
Rubha Thormaid
A' Mhoine
Skullomie
Coldbackie
Borgie
Borgie Forest
Achuvoldrach
Tongue
Kirkiboll
Castle Varrich
Kyle of Tongue
Ribigill
Kinloch Lodge
Loch Craggie
Loch Loyal
Ben Loyal
Loch Loyal Lodge
Cnoc nan Cullean
Loch Coulside
Inchkinloch
Leckfurin
Skelpick
Achanlochy Clearance Village
Strathnaver Museum
Achagary
Carnachy
Rhifail
Skail
Langdale
Syre
Dalvina Lo.
Rosal Clearance Trail
Strathnaver
Strathy Forest
Bowside Lodge
Golval
Achiemore
Upper Bighouse
Craigtown
Dalhalvaig
Trantlemore
Trantlebeg
Strath Halladale
Forsinain
Forsinard
Forsinard Station
The Flows
Sletill Hill
Loch Sletill
Altnabreac Station
Lochdhu
Dalnawillan Lodge
Loch More
Lochmore Cottage
Strathmore Lodge
Westerdale
Halkirk
Spittal
Mybster
Scotscalder Station
Olgrinmore
Harpsdale
Banniskirk Ho.
Georgemas
Roadside
Clayock
Knockdee
Buckies
Sordale
Calder Mains
Loch Calder
Braal Castle
Geise
Lieurary
Broubster
Shurrery
Shurrery Lodge
Brawlbin
Dorrery
Beinn nam Bad Mor
Cnoc Freiceadain Chambered Cairn
Dounreay Exhibition Centre
St Mary's Chapel
Thurso Castle
Thurso Folk Museum
NC
ND
NH
NJ
158
151
Mudale
Altnaharra
Loch Naver
Clebrig
Naver Forest
Loch Rimsdale
Garvault Hotel
Ben Griam More
Ben Griam Beg
Achentoul Forest
Badanloch Forest
Badanloch Lodge
Loch Badanloch
Lochside
Achentoul
Strath Beg
Kinbrace
Knockfin Heights
Glutt Lodge
Ben Alisky
Cnoc Loch Mhadadh
Braehungie
Smerral
Latheronwheel Ho.
Braemore
Dunbeath
Dunbeath Castle
Balnabruich
Knockally
Ramscraigs
Borgue
Newport
Ceann Leathad nam Bò
Berriedale
Langwell Ho.
Badbea Clearance Village
Ousdale
Langwell Forest
Morven
Scaraben
Wag
Aultibea
Cnoc Coire na Fearna
Cnoc an Eireannaich
Creag Scalabsdale
Borrobol Forest
Borrobol Lodge
Altanduin
Creag nam Fiadh
Kildonan Lodge
Baile an Or Goldrush Site
Beinn Dubhain
Strath of Kildonan
Torrish
Kilphedir
Eldrable Hill
Marrel
West Helmsdale
Navidale
Helmsdale
Timespan Heritage Centre
Ord Point
Gartymore
Portgower
Beinn Dhorain
Glen Loth
Glen Sletdale
Lothmore
Lothbeg
Lothbeg Pt.
Craggie
Ben Kilbreck
Meall nan Con
Loch Choire Lodge
Loch Choire Forest
Ben Armine
Meall a' Bhata
Creag Mhòr
Ben Armine Forest
Ben Armine Lodge
Strath na Seilge
Strath Skinsdale
Meallan Liath Mor
Crask Inn
Strath Vagastie
Strath Tirry
Rhian
Shinness
Achnairn
Dalnessie
Dalchork
Dalchork Wood
Colaboll
Sallachy
Saval
Lairg Lodge
Lairg Muir
Lairg
Ferrycroft Countryside Centre
Achnaluachrach
West Langwell
Strath Brora
Dalreavoch
Rhilochan
East Langwell
Farlary
Balnacoil
Gordonbush
Loch Brora
Ben Horn
Loch Horn
Cagar Feosaig
Achrimsdale
East Clyne
West Clyne
Clynelish Distillery
Dalchalm
Brora
Doll
Backies
Beinn Lunndaidh
Dunrobin Castle Museum & Gardens
Golspie
Culmaily
Kirkton
Strath Fleet
Muie
Ardachu
Rogart
Pittentrail
Rogart Station
Hector Macdonald Monument
Morvich
Torroble
Claonel
Gruids
Achany
Shin Forest
Achinduich
Falls of Shin Visitor Centre
Linsidemore
Achnahanat
Inveran
Invershin
Carbisdale Castle
Culrain
Balblair
Craigton
Airdens
Clashcoig
Migdale
Bonar Bridge
Braelangwell Lodge
Wester Gruinards
Soyal
Lower Gledfield
Beinn Domhnaill
Torboll Farm
Little Torboll
Cambusmore Lodge
Loch Fleet
Cambusavie Farm
Skelbo
Skelbo Castle
Littleferry
Fourpenny
Embo
Embo Street
Achvaich
Badninish
Rearquhar
Proncy
Poles
Pitgrudy
Gablon
Evelix
Sutherland

HOY
Flotta
Switha
SOUTH WALLS
SOUTH RONALDSAY
Burray
Swona
PENTLAND FIRTH
Island of Stroma
DUNNET HEAD
DUNCANSBY HEAD
Stacks of Duncansby
DUNNET BAY
SINCLAIR'S BAY
Thurso
Wick
Halkirk
Castletown
Dunnet
John o' Groats
Canisbay
Mey
Keiss
Watten
Lybster
Dunbeath
Berriedale
Helmsdale
Latheron
Scrabster
Reay
Dounreay
Altnabreac Station
Loch Watten
Loch Heilen
Rumster Forest
Langwell Forest
Highland
NC
ND
A9
A99
A836
A882
B874
B876
B870
159
157
Scale : 1:332 000
(approx 5 miles to 1 inch)
0 1 2 3 4 5 6miles
0 1 2 3 4 5 6 7 8 9 10km

Orkney
HY
ND
Papa Westray
Holm of Papa
North Ronaldsay
Hollandstoun
BROCH OF BURRIAN
NORTH RONALDSAY FIRTH
NOUP HEAD
WESTRAY
Aikerness
Holland
Backaskaill
Rackwick
Gayfield
Pierowall
Broughton
Braehead
PIEROWALL CHURCH
NOLTLAND CASTLE
FITTY HILL
Midbea
Skelwick
Langskaill
WESTSIDE CHURCH
Rapness
Sulland
THE NORTH SOUND
KIRKWALL 1:50
Scar
Burness
Lettan
Sellibister
START PT.
Newark
Lady
SANDAY
Broughtown
Overbister
Kettletoft
Laminess
QUOYNESS CHAMBERED CAIRN
SANDAY SOUND
Calf of Eday
Carrick Ho.
CARRICK HOUSE
Calfsound
Braeswick
Guith
Millbounds
Stove
Loth
EDAY
Backaland
Faray
WESTRAY FIRTH
Wasbister
ROUSAY
Sourin
Westness
MIDHOWE BROCH
Eynhallow
EYNHALLOW CHURCH
KNOWE OF YARSO CAIRN
Skaill
ST MAGNUS CHURCH
Egilsay
Veness
Odie
Papa Stronsay
Whitehall Village
Linga Holm
STRONSAY
Wardhill
Everbay
Grobister
Kirbister
Rothiesholm
Dishes
Holland
Muckle Green Holm
BROUGH HEAD
BROUGH OF BIRSAY
Abune-the-Hill
Costa
Burgar
The Barony
EARL'S PALACE
MARWICK HEAD NATURE RESERVE
Marwick
Stara
Kirbuster
Twatt
Evie
Stenso
Redland
BROCH OF GURNESS
Frotoft
Brinian
CUBBIE ROO'S CASTLE AND ST MARY'S CHAPEL
Wyre
Gairsay
Isbister
Beaquoy
Click Mill
CLICK MILL
Tingwall
Scarwell
Northdyke
Quoyloo
Skeabrae
Dounby
Mirbister
Hackland
Kierfiold Ho.
CORRIGALL FARM MUSEUM
Gorseness
Skaill
SKAILL HOUSE
Brough
Settiscarth
Isbister
Breck of Cruan
Aith
Hestwall
Tenston
Netherbrough
Bimbister
Yesnaby
Voy
Arion
Finstown
Shapinsay
Balfour
BALFOUR CASTLE
Edmonstone
Newlot
Auskerry
FIRTH
STRONSAY
Quholm
RING OF BRODGAR
STANDING STONES
TORMISTON MILL
MAES HOWE
Bridge of Waith
Grimbister
WIRELESS MUSEUM
ORKNEY MUSEUM
Work
Craigiefield
Kirkwall
ST MAGNUS CATHEDRAL
BISHOP'S & EARL'S PALACE
HIGHLAND PARK DISTILLERY
Berstane
Scapa
Heddle
Nisthouse
Clouston
Outertown
PIER ARTS CENTRE
Stromness
STROMNESS MUSEUM
Ireland
Kirbister
Hobbister
Greenigoe
Tradespark
Whiteclett
Hall of Tankerness
North Halley
Deerness
Skaill
Grindigar
Gritley
HOY AND WEST MAINLAND
Breckan
Graemsay
Clestrain
Cairnton
Smoogro
Waulkmill Lodge
Swanbister
Toab
Foubister
Orphir
Petertown
Gyre
Houton
ST NICHOLAS CHURCH
Murra
NORTH HOY NATURE RESERVE
Linksness
Hoy
Quoyness
WARD HILL
SCRABSTER 1:30
OLD MAN OF HOY
DWARFIE STANE
Rackwick
RORA HEAD
KNAP OF TROWIEGLEN
SCAPA FLOW
North Dawn
NORWOOD MUSEUM
Upper Sanday
St Mary's
ITALIAN CHAPEL
Braehead
Cornquoy
Copinsay
ABERDEEN 6:00
LERWICK 5:30
Cava
Rysa Little
Fara
FOSSIL AND VINTAGE CENTRE
Hunda
Hillside
Northtown
Burray
Southtown
Burray Village
HOY
SCAPA FLOW VISITOR CENTRE
Lyness
Rinnigill
Bow
Pan
Flotta
Uppertown
St. Margaret's Hope
Grimness
Crockness
Little Ayre
Herston
Quindry
Papley
Widewall
Aikers
Wyng
Hackness
MARTELLO TOWERS
Switha
Longhope
Melsetter
Hurliness
Brims
SOUTH WALLS
Sandwick
Suckquoy
Lythes
SOUTH RONALDSAY
Linklater
Dundas Ho.
Burwick
Cleat
Swona
TOMB OF THE EAGLES AND BRONZE AGE HOUSE
Liddel
PENTLAND FIRTH
158
Island of Stroma
Nethertown
Uppertown
0:40 (May-Sept)
DUNNET HEAD
Scarfskerry
East Mey
Brough
Hunspow
Ham
Rattar
CASTLE OF MEY
Mey
Gills
Kirkstyle
Huna
John o' Groats
DUNCANSBY HEAD
MARY-ANN'S COTTAGE
Dunnet
DUNNET BAY
Corsback
Barrock
Canisbay
STROMNESS 1:30
Scrabster
THURSO CASTLE
FOLK MUSEUM
INTERPRETATIVE TRAIL
Castlehill
Inkstack
Brabster
Skirza
Thurso
Clardon
Castletown
Murkle
Greenland
Lochend
Tofts
Millbank
East Haimer
Olrig Ho.
CASTLETOWN
Tain
Freswick
Slickly
Reaster
Geise
Hillclay
Weydale
Durran
Achingills
Bowermadden
Alterwall
BUCHOLLY CASTLE
CAITHNESS BROCH CENTRE
Auckengill
LYTH ARTS CENTRE
Lyth
Sortat
Nybster
Lieurary
Buckies
Sordale
Bowertower
Barrock Ho.
Knockdee
Stemster Ho.
Halcro
Hastigrow
Howe
Keiss
KEISS CASTLE
Calder Mains
Brael Castle
Roadside
Gillock
Mireland
Halkirk
Clayock
North Watten
Kirk
Myrelandhorn
SINCLAIR'S BAY
Bannskirk Ho.
Mains of Watten
Killimster
Scotscalder Station
Harpsdale
Olgrinmore
Wick
Reiss
CASTLE SINCLAIR
CASTLE GIRNIGOE
Scale : 1:400 000
(approx 6¼ miles to 1 inch)
0 1 2 3 4 5 6miles
0 1 2 3 4 5 6 7 8 9 10km

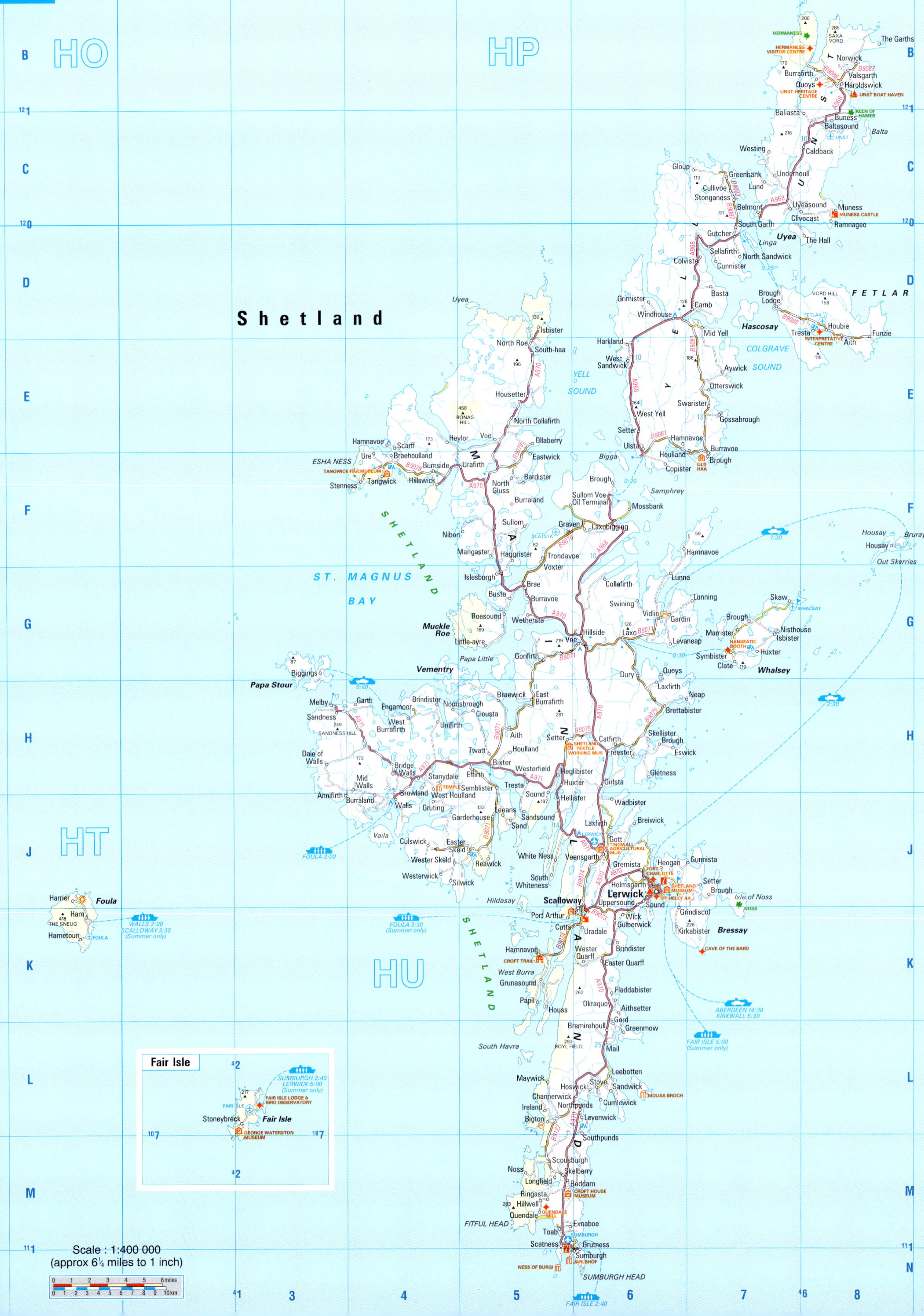

HO
HP
HT
HU
Shetland
Unst
Yell
Mainland
Fetlar
Hermaness
Hermaness Visitor Centre
Saxa Vord
The Garths
Norwick
Burrafirth
Valsgarth
Quoys
Haroldswick
Unst Heritage Centre
Unst Boat Haven
Baliasta
Keen of Hamar
Buness
Baltasound
Unst
Balta
Westing
Caldback
Gloup
Greenbank
Underhoull
Cullivoe
Lund
Stonganess
Belmont
Uyeasound
Muness
Muness Castle
Clivocast
South Garth
Ramnageo
Uyea
Gutcher
Linga
The Hall
Sellafirth
North Sandwick
Colvister
Cunnister
Grimister
Basta
Brough Lodge
Vord Hill
Windhouse
Camb
Hascosay
Tresta
Fetlar
Houbie
Fetlar Interpretative Centre
Funzie
Aith
Harkland
Mid Yell
Colgrave
West Sandwick
Aywick
Sound
Yell Sound
Otterswick
Swarister
West Yell
Gossabrough
Setter
Hamnavoe
Burravoe
Ulsta
Houland
Old Haa
Brough
Copister
Bigga
Samphrey
Uyea
Isbister
North Roe
South-haa
Housetter
Ronas Hill
North Collafirth
Heylor
Voe
Ollaberry
Hamnavoe
Scarff
Braehoulland
Ure
Esha Ness
Tangwick Haa Museum
Burnside
Urafirth
Eastwick
Stenness
Tangwick
Hillswick
Bardister
North Gluss
Burraland
Sullom Voe Oil Terminal
Mossbank
Sullom
Graven
Laxobigging
Scatsta
Nibon
Mangaster
Haggrister
Trondavoe
Hamnavoe
Voxter
Shetland
St. Magnus Bay
Islesburgh
Collafirth
Lunna
Brae
Busta
Burravoe
Lunning
Swining
Skaw
Roesound
Wethersta
Vidlin
Gardin
Brough
Whalsay
Muckle Roe
Laxo
Hillside
Marrister
Nisthouse
Isbister
Little-ayre
Voe
Levaneap
Hanseatic Booth
Huxter
Papa Little
Gonfirth
Symbister
Clate
Whalsey
Biggings
Vementry
Dury
Quoys
Papa Stour
Laxfirth
Neap
Melby
Garth
Brindister
Braewick
East Burrafirth
Brettabister
Sandness
Engamoor
Noonsbrough
Clousta
West Burrafirth
Sandness Hill
Unifirth
Skellister
Brough
Aith
Setter
Catfirth
Shetland Textile Working Mus
Eswick
Dale of Walls
Twatt
Houlland
Frester
Bridge of Walls
Bixter
Westerfield
Heglibister
Gletness
Mid Walls
Stanydale
Effirth
Huxter
Girlsta
Annifirth
Burraland
Temple
Brownland
Sembister
Tresta
West Houlland
Sound
Hellister
Wadbister
Walls
Gruting
Garderhouse
Leeans
Sandsound
Sand
Breiwick
Vaila
Laxfirth
Foula 2:00
Culswick
Easter Skeld
Skeld
Lerwick
Gott
Tingwall Agricultural Mus
Reawick
Wester Skeld
White Ness
Veensgarth
Gremista
Heogan
Gunnista
Fort Charlotte
Westerwick
Silwick
South Whiteness
Holmsgarth
Setter
Shetland Museum
Up Helly Aa
Brough
Harrier
Foula
Hildasay
Scalloway
Uppersound
Sound
Isle of Noss
Ham
The Sneug
Hametoun
Foula
Walls 2:00
Scalloway 3:30
(Summer only)
Foula 3:30
(Summer only)
Port Arthur
Wick
Grindiscol
Noss
Gulberwick
Cutts
Uradale
Kirkabister
Bressay
Hamnavoe
Wester Quarff
Brindister
Cave of the Bard
Croft Trail
Easter Quarff
West Burra
Grunasound
Fladdabister
Papil
Okraquoy
Houss
Aithsetter
Aberdeen 14:30
Kirkwall 5:30
Bremirehoull
Gord
Greenmow
South Havra
Royl Field
Mail
Fair Isle 5:00
(Summer only)
Fair Isle
Sumburgh 2:40
Lerwick 5:00
(Summer only)
Fair Isle Lodge & Bird Observatory
Stoneybreck
Fair Isle
George Waterston Museum
Leebotten
Maywick
Hoswick
Stove
Sandwick
Mousa Broch
Channerwick
Ireland
Northpunds
Cumlewick
Bigton
Levenwick
Southpunds
Scousburgh
Noss
Skelberry
Longfield
Boddam
Croft House Museum
Ringasta
Hillwell
Quendale
Quendale Mill
Fitful Head
Exnaboe
Toab
Sumburgh
Scatness
Grutness
Sumburgh
Jarlshof
Ness of Burgi
Sumburgh Head
Fair Isle 2:40
Out Skerries
Housay
Bruray
Scale : 1:400 000
(approx 6¼ miles to 1 inch)
6 miles
10 km

BRISTOL
Kingswood
Filton
Avonmouth
Bristol approaches
Mangotsfield
Downend
Frenchay
Fishponds
Stapleton
Eastville
Horfield
Henleaze
Westbury on Trym
Southmead
Clifton
Cotham
Redland
Hotwells
Bedminster
Brislington
Knowle
Hengrove
Oldland
Hanham
Warmley
St. George
Speedwell
Shirehampton
Lawrence Weston
Sea Mills
Stoke Bishop
Sneyd Park
Henbury
Brentry
Patchway
Bradley Stoke
Stoke Gifford
Winterbourne
Frampton End
Coalpit Heath
Emersons Green
Pill
Easton-in-Gordano
Portbury
Abbots Leigh
Leigh Woods
Long Ashton
Failand
Flax Bourton
Keynsham
Bitton
River Avon
Avon Gorge
Clifton Suspension Bridge
Bristol Zoo Gardens
Blaise Castle
Avonmouth Docks
The Royal Portbury Dock
Ashton Court Estate
Tyntesfield
Long Ashton
Stockwood
Whitchurch
Hartcliffe
Bishopsworth
M4
M5
M32
M49
A4
A38
A4174
A432
A420
A431
A37
A369
A370
A403
A4018
A4032
2 miles
3 km

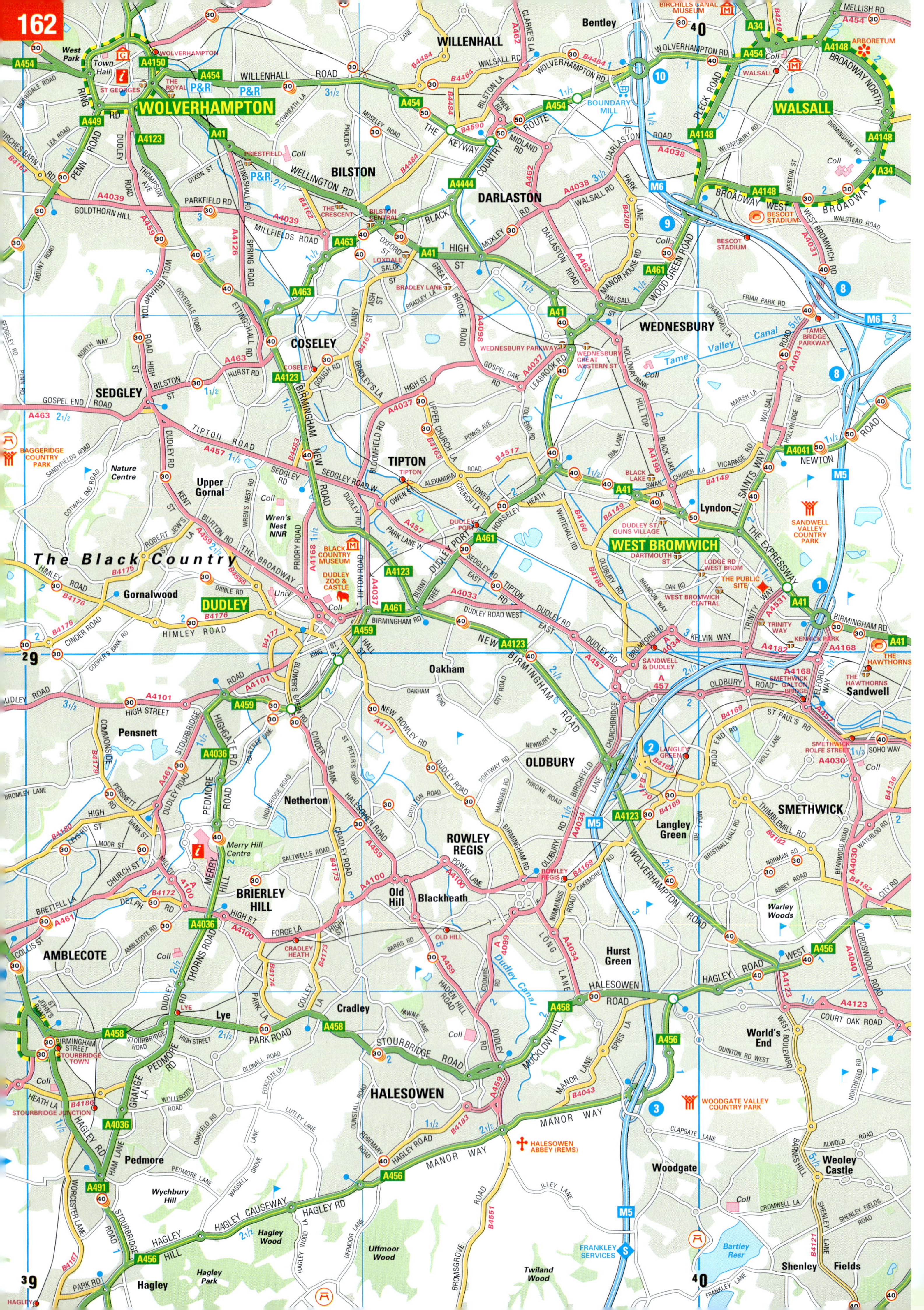

WOLVERHAMPTON
West Park
Town Hall
ST GEORGES
THE ROYAL
P&R
WILLENHALL
WILLENHALL ROAD
Bentley
BIRCHILLS CANAL MUSEUM
WALSALL
ARBORETUM
BROADWAY NORTH
MELLISH RD
BOUNDARY MILL
DARLASTON
BILSTON
BILSTON CENTRAL
THE CRESCENT
PRIESTFIELD
WELLINGTON RD
GOLDTHORN HILL
PARKFIELD RD
MILLFIELDS ROAD
THE KEYWAY
BLACK COUNTRY ROUTE
WOLVERHAMPTON RD
BESCOT STADIUM
BROADWAY WEST
WALSTEAD ROAD
PLECK ROAD
LOXDALE
BRADLEY LANE
WEDNESBURY
WEDNESBURY PARKWAY
WEDNESBURY GREAT WESTERN ST
TAME BRIDGE PARKWAY
Tame Valley Canal
COSELEY
SEDGLEY
GOSPEL END
BAGGERIDGE COUNTRY PARK
Nature Centre
TIPTON
TIPTON ROAD
SEDGLEY ROAD W
Upper Gornal
Wren's Nest NNR
BLACK COUNTRY MUSEUM
DUDLEY ZOO & CASTLE
DUDLEY PORT
The Black Country
Gornalwood
DUDLEY
HIMLEY ROAD
DUDLEY ROAD WEST
WEST BROMWICH
DUDLEY ST GUNS VILLAGE
DARTMOUTH ST
LODGE RD WEST BROM
THE PUBLIC SITE
WEST BROMWICH CENTRAL
TRINITY WAY
KENRICK PARK
THE HAWTHORNS
BLACK LAKE
SWAN
Lyndon
NEWTON
SANDWELL VALLEY COUNTRY PARK
THE EXPRESSWAY
ALL SAINTS WAY
BIRMINGHAM RD
KELVIN WAY
SANDWELL & DUDLEY
Sandwell
Oakham
OLDBURY
Pensnett
HIGH STREET
Netherton
Merry Hill Centre
BRIERLEY HILL
ROWLEY REGIS
Old Hill
Blackheath
LANGLEY GREEN
Langley Green
SMETHWICK
SMETHWICK ROLFE STREET
Warley Woods
AMBLECOTE
CRADLEY HEATH
Cradley
Lye
Hurst Green
HALESOWEN
HALESOWEN ROAD
HAGLEY ROAD
World's End
COURT OAK ROAD
STOURBRIDGE TOWN
STOURBRIDGE JUNCTION
PARK ROAD
STOURBRIDGE ROAD
Dudley Canal
MANOR WAY
HALESOWEN ABBEY (REMS)
WOODGATE VALLEY COUNTRY PARK
Woodgate
Weoley Castle
Pedmore
Wychbury Hill
HAGLEY CAUSEWAY
Hagley Wood
Uffmoor Wood
Hagley Park
Hagley
Twiland Wood
FRANKLEY SERVICES
Bartley Resr
Shenley Fields
M5
M6
A454
A4150
A449
A4123
A41
A4039
A463
A461
A459
A4037
A4033
A457
A458
A4036
A4100
A456
A491
A4148
A34
A4038
A4044
A4098
A462
A4041
A4031
A4168
A4182
A4030
A4034
A4040

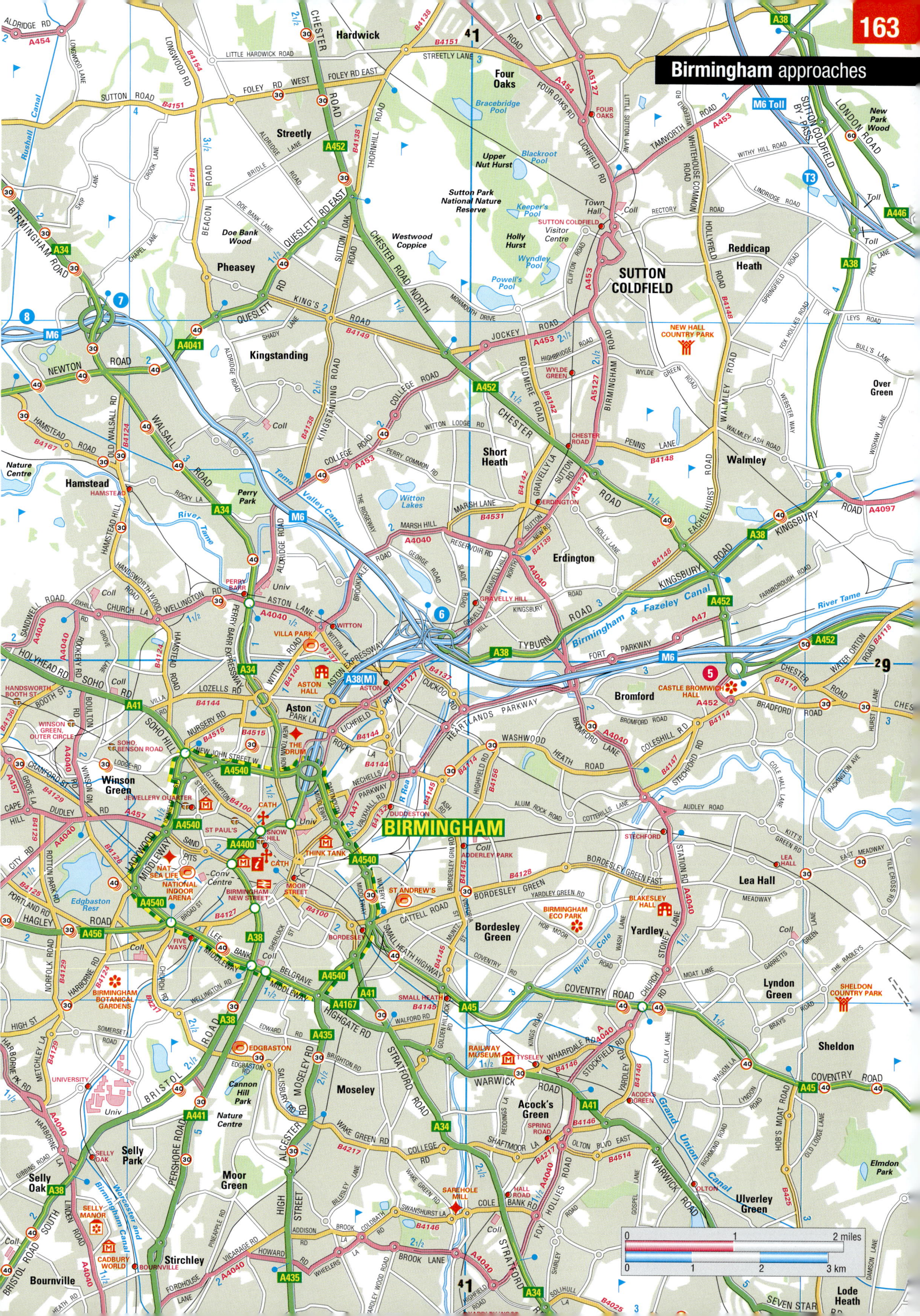
Hardwick
Four Oaks
Bracebridge Pool
Blackroot Pool
Upper Nut Hurst
Sutton Park National Nature Reserve
Keeper's Pool
Holly Hurst
Wyndley Pool
Powell's Pool
Westwood Coppice
Town Hall
SUTTON COLDFIELD
Visitor Centre
Streetly
Doe Bank Wood
Pheasey
Kingstanding
Reddicap Heath
NEW HALL COUNTRY PARK
New Park Wood
Over Green
Walmley
Short Heath
Hamstead
Perry Park
Witton Lakes
Erdington
Tame Valley Canal
River Tame
Birmingham & Fazeley Canal
Bromford
CASTLE BROMWICH HALL
Aston
ASTON HALL
THE DRUM
VILLA PARK
HANDSWORTH BOOTH ST
WINSON GREEN, OUTER CIRCLE
SOHO BENSON ROAD
Winson Green
JEWELLERY QUARTER
BIRMINGHAM
THINK TANK
CATH
ST PAUL'S
SNOW HILL
NAT SEA LIFE
NATIONAL INDOOR ARENA
Conv Centre
BIRMINGHAM NEW STREET
MOOR STREET
Edgbaston Resr
ST ANDREW'S
ADDERLEY PARK
DUDDESTON
BIRMINGHAM ECO PARK
Bordesley Green
BLAKESLEY HALL
Yardley
Lea Hall
Stechford
Lyndon Green
SHELDON COUNTRY PARK
Sheldon
FIVE WAYS
BORDESLEY
SMALL HEATH
BIRMINGHAM BOTANICAL GARDENS
EDGBASTON
Cannon Hill Park
Nature Centre
Moseley
RAILWAY MUSEUM
TYSELEY
Acock's Green
SPRING ROAD
ACOCKS GREEN
Grand Union Canal
River Cole
UNIVERSITY
Univ
Selly Oak
Selly Park
SELLY MANOR
Worcester and Birmingham Canal
CADBURY WORLD
BOURNVILLE
Bournville
Stirchley
Moor Green
SAREHOLE MILL
HALL GREEN
Elmdon Park
OLTON
Ulverley Green
Lode Heath
M6
M6 Toll
A38(M)
0 1 2 miles
0 1 2 3 km

Cardiff approaches

CARDIFF
(CAERDYDD)
St. Mellons
(Llaneirwg)
Trowbridge
Rumney
(Rhymni)
Llanrumney
Llanedeyrn
Pentwyn
Pwll-Mawr
Newton
Marshfield
Castleton
Blacktown
Michaelston-y-Fedw
Began
Tremorfa
Splott
Roath
Roath Park
Cyncoed
Lisvane
(Llys Faen)
Llanishen
Thornhill
Heath
Cathays
Maindy
Gabalfa
Birchgrove
Rhiwbina
Whitchurch
Llandaff North
Llandaff
(Llandaf)
Pontcanna
Canton
Riverside
Grangetown
Butetown
Saltmead
Leckwith
Llandough
Michaelston-le-Pit
Fairwater
Ely
(Tre-lai)
Caerau
Michaelston-super-Ely
St Fagans
(Sain Ffagan)
Radyr
Morganstown
Tongwynlais
Taff's Well
(Ffynnon-Taf)
Nantgarw
Glan-y-llyn
Pentyrch
Gwaelod-y-garth
Church Village
Soar
St Brides-super-Ely
(Llansanffraid-ar-Elai)
St George's
St Nicholas
(San Nicolas)
Culverhouse Cross
Wenvoe
(Gwenfô)
Wallston
Twyn-yr-odyn
Downs
Drope
Peterstone Wentlooge
(Llanbedr Gwynllŵg)
Watford
Cefn Mably Woods
Llwyncelyn
The Warren
Caerphilly Common
Coed-y-Wenallt
Garth Wood
Coed y Gedrys
Grath Hill
Taff vale
Park Wood
Llanishen Reservoir
The Lake
Roath Dock
Bute E Dock
Cardiff Bay
Cardiff Bay Barrage
River Taff
River Ely
Rhymney River
CARDIFF GATE SERVICES
CARDIFF WEST SERVICES
WALES MILLENNIUM CENTRE
NATIONAL ASSEMBLY
CARDIFF BAY VISITOR CENTRE
TECHNIQUEST
MILLENNIUM STADIUM
CARDIFF ARMS PARK
CARDIFF CASTLE
NATIONAL MUSEUM CARDIFF
SOPHIA GDNS
LLANDAFF CATHEDRAL
CASTELL COCH
FOREST FARM
PARC CEFN ONN
ST FAGANS NATIONAL HISTORY MUSEUM
TINKINSWOOD BURIAL CHAMBER
CARDIFF CENTRAL
CARDIFF CITY
M4
A48(M)
A48
A470
A469
A4232
A4119
A4054
A4161
A4160
A4050
A4055
B4562
B4487
B4239
B4267
B4488
B4262
B4263
0
1
2 miles
3 km
31
32
18

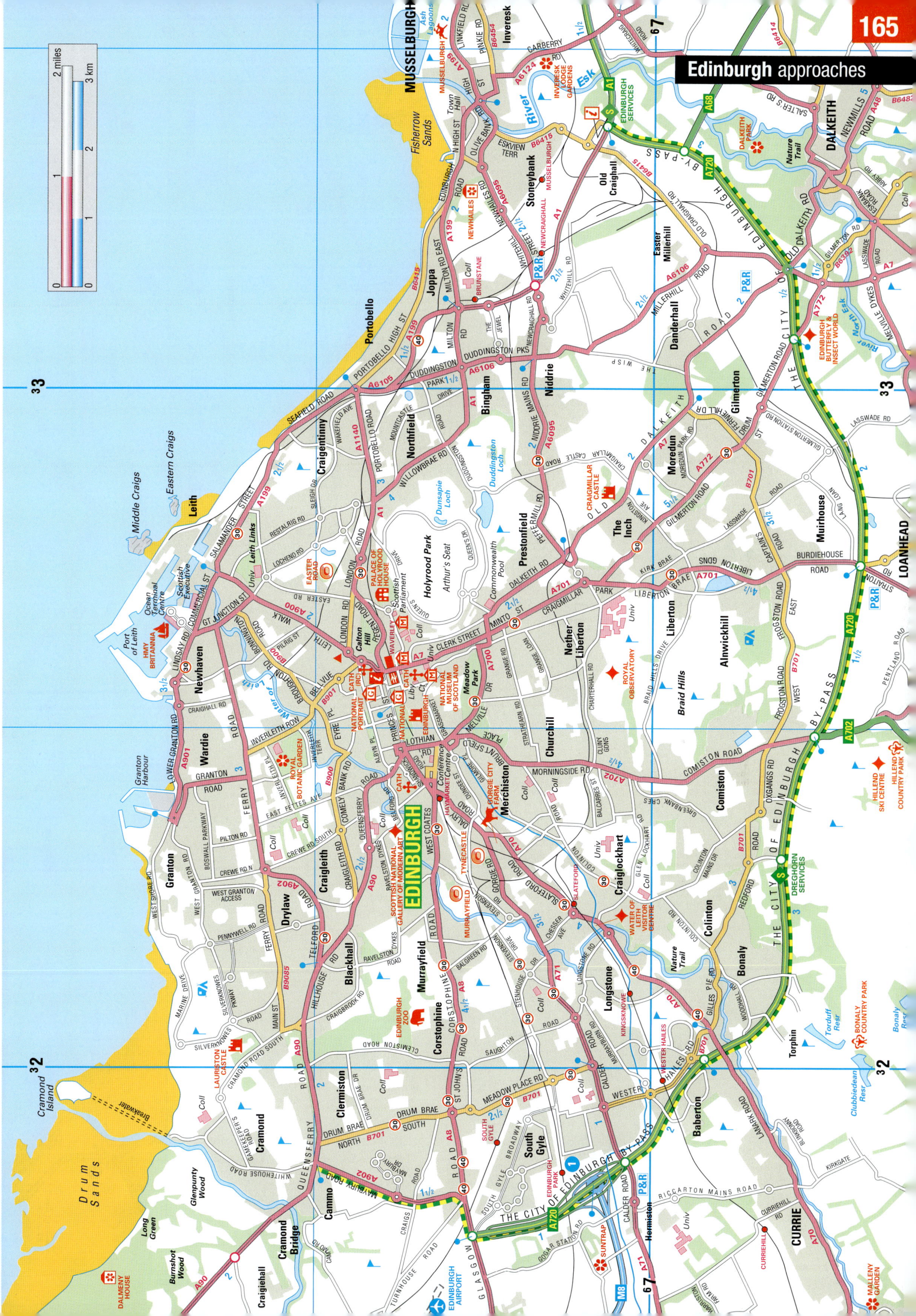
EDINBURGH
MUSSELBURGH
DALKEITH
LOANHEAD
Leith
Portobello
Joppa
Newhaven
Granton
Wardie
Craigleith
Drylaw
Blackhall
Murrayfield
Corstorphine
Clermiston
Cramond
Cammo
Cramond Bridge
Craigiehall
South Gyle
Hermiston
CURRIE
Baberton
Torphin
Bonaly
Colinton
Longstone
Craiglockhart
Merchiston
Churchill
Meadow Park
Nether Liberton
Liberton
Alnwickhill
Braid Hills
Comiston
Muirhouse
Gilmerton
Moredun
The Inch
Prestonfield
Niddrie
Bingham
Northfield
Craigentinny
Danderhall
Easter Millerhill
Old Craighall
Stoneybank
Inveresk
Fisherrow Sands
Drum Sands
Cramond Island
Middle Craigs
Eastern Craigs
Granton Harbour
Port of Leith
Holyrood Park
Arthur's Seat
Dunsapie Loch
Duddingston Loch
Calton Hill
EDINBURGH AIRPORT
DALMENY HOUSE
LAURISTON CASTLE
EDINBURGH ZOO
ROYAL BOTANIC GARDEN
ROYAL OBSERVATORY
CRAIGMILLAR CASTLE
PALACE OF HOLYROODHOUSE
Scottish Parliament
NATIONAL GALLERY OF SCOTLAND
NATIONAL PORTRAIT
NATIONAL MUSEUM OF SCOTLAND
SCOTTISH NATIONAL GALLERY OF MODERN ART
HMY BRITANNIA
GORGIE CITY FARM
TYNECASTLE
MURRAYFIELD
WATER OF LEITH VISITOR CENTRE
HILLEND SKI CENTRE
HILLEND COUNTRY PARK
BONALY COUNTRY PARK
MALLENY GARDEN
SUNTRAP
EDINBURGH BUTTERFLY & INSECT WORLD
NEWHAILES
INVERESK LODGE GARDENS
DALKEITH PARK
DREGHORN SERVICES
EDINBURGH SERVICES
CITY OF EDINBURGH BY-PASS
A1
A7
A8
A70
A71
A90
A199
A702
A720
M8
2 miles
3 km

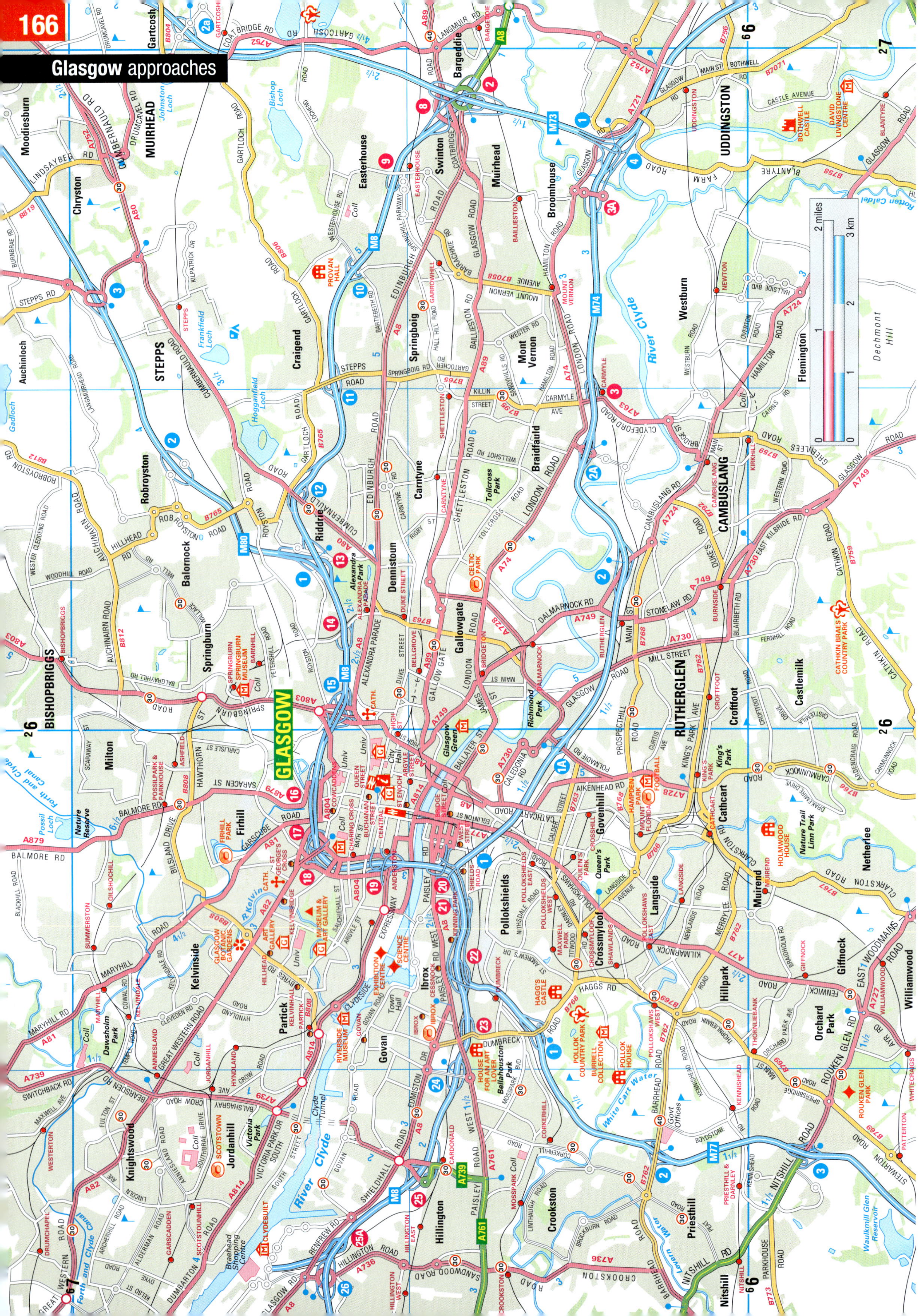
GLASGOW
Moodiesburn
Chryston
MUIRHEAD
Gartcosh
Stepps
Auchinloch
Robroyston
Balornock
Springburn
BISHOPBRIGGS
Milton
Craigend
Ruchazie
Riddrie
Easterhouse
Swinton
Bargeddie
Muirhead
Broomhouse
UDDINGSTON
Springboig
Mont Vernon
Carmyle
Westburn
Flemington
Carntyne
Braidfauld
Tollcross Park
Dennistoun
Gallowgate
Glasgow Green
Richmond Park
RUTHERGLEN
CAMBUSLANG
Castlemilk
Croftfoot
King's Park
Cathcart
Netherlee
Muirend
Giffnock
Williamwood
Orchard Park
Hillpark
Langside
Queen's Park
Govanhill
Crossmyloof
Pollokshields
Ibrox
Govan
Partick
Kelvinside
Firhill
Dawsholm Park
Knightswood
Jordanhill
Victoria Park
Hillington
Crookston
Priesthill
Nitshill
Pollok Country Park
Burrell Collection
Pollok House
Linn Park
Holmwood House
Rouken Glen Park
Provan Hall
Bothwell Castle
David Livingstone Centre
Cathkin Braes Country Park
Springburn Museum
Glasgow Botanic Gardens
Science Centre
Riverside Museum
River Clyde
White Cart Water
Forth and Clyde Canal
Hogganfield Loch
Frankfield Loch
Bishop Loch
Johnston Loch
Possil Loch
Dechmont Hill
Waulkmill Glen Reservoir
Clyde Tunnel
Braehead Shopping Centre
Nature Reserve
2 miles
3 km

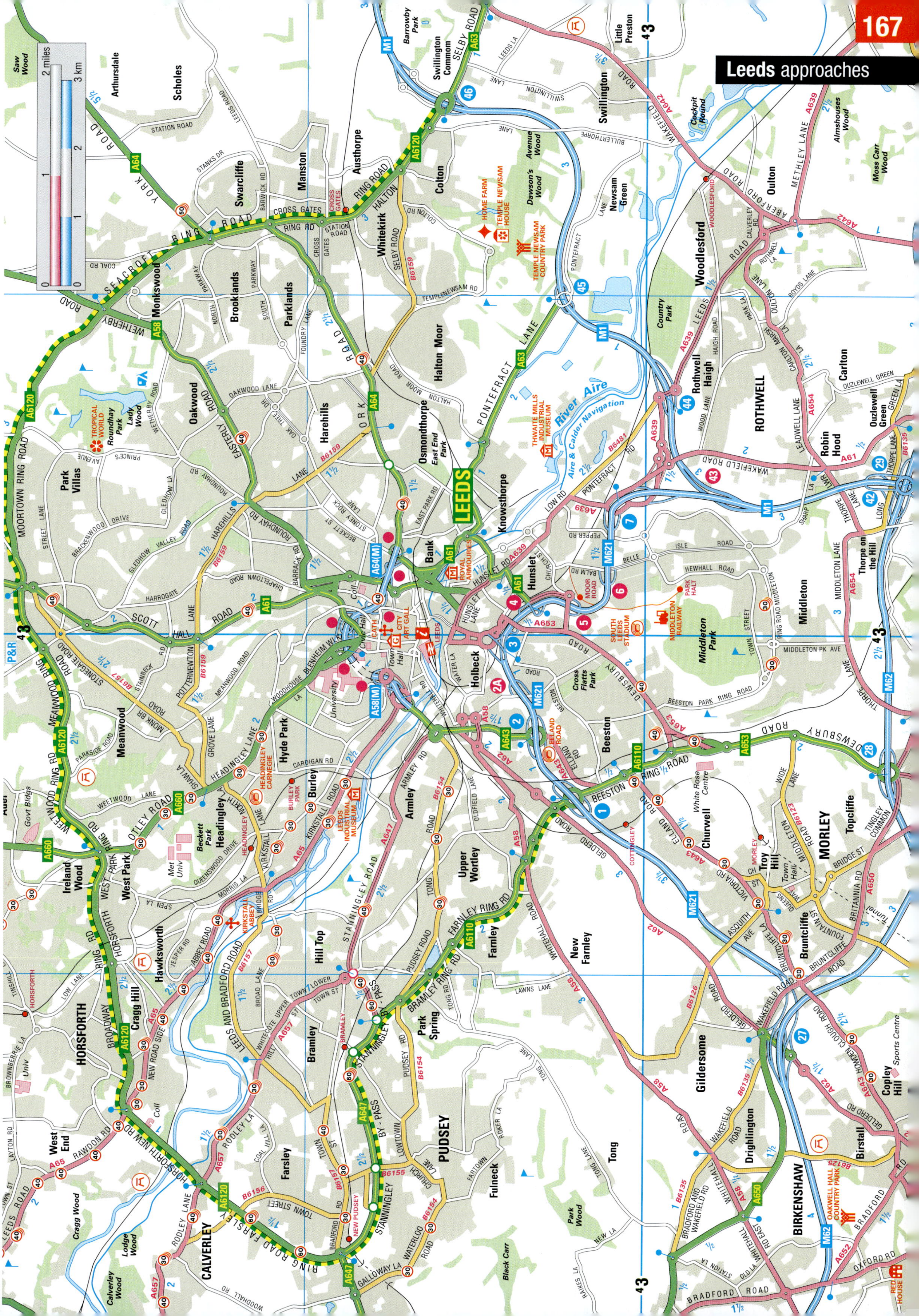
LEEDS
Horsforth
Calverley
Pudsey
Morley
Rothwell
Birkenshaw
Woodlesford
Oulton
Swillington
Colton
Austhorpe
Manston
Swarcliffe
Scholes
Arthursdale
Halton Moor
Osmondthorpe
Harehills
Oakwood
Monkswood
Brooklands
Parklands
Whitekirk
Park Villas
Meanwood
Headingley
Hyde Park
Burley
Armley
Holbeck
Hunslet
Knowsthorpe
Beeston
Churwell
Middleton
Carlton
Robin Hood
Oulton
Topcliffe
Bruntcliffe
Gildersome
Drighlington
Birstall
Tong
Fulneck
Farnley
New Farnley
Upper Wortley
Bramley
Farsley
Hill Top
Park Spring
Stanningley
West End
West Park
Ireland Wood
Hawksworth
Cragg Hill
Newsam Green
Thorpe on the Hill
Oulton
Copley Hill
Ouzlewell Green
Rothwell Haigh
Little Preston
Leeds Bradford Airport
M1
M62
M621
A64(M)
A58(M)
A6120
A64
A58
A61
A63
A639
A642
A653
A643
A62
A647
A65
A660
A657
A6110
A650
A654
River Aire
Aire & Calder Navigation
Temple Newsam House
Temple Newsam Country Park
Home Farm
Tropical World
Roundhay Park
Royal Armouries
Thwaite Mills Industrial Museum
Middleton Railway
Middleton Park
Kirkstall Abbey
Leeds Industrial Museum
Oakwell Hall Country Park
South Leeds Stadium
Headingley Carnegie
Civic Hall
Town Hall
City Art Gall
University
Cath
Country Park
RING ROAD
YORK ROAD
SEACROFT
SELBY ROAD
PONTEFRACT LANE
WAKEFIELD ROAD
DEWSBURY ROAD
BRADFORD ROAD
OTLEY ROAD
SCOTT HALL ROAD
STANNINGLEY BY-PASS
FARNLEY RING RD
BEESTON RING ROAD
MOORTOWN RING ROAD
MEANWOOD RING RD
WEETWOOD RING RD
WEST PARK RING RD
HORSFORTH RING RD
HORSFORTH NEW RD
LEEDS AND BRADFORD ROAD
GELDERD ROAD
ABERFORD ROAD
ELLAND ROAD
HALTON MOOR ROAD
EASTERLY ROAD
ROUNDHAY RD
CHAPELTOWN ROAD
HAREHILLS LANE
OAKWOOD LANE
STATION ROAD
CROSS GATES
COAL RD
WETHERBY ROAD
TOWN STREET
GALLOWAY LA
WATERLOO ROAD
RODLEY LANE
KIRKSTALL ROAD
WOODHOUSE LA
HEADINGLEY LANE
BRAMLEY RING RD
LOWER TOWN ST
TONG ROAD
LEEDS ROAD
METHLEY LANE
BRITANNIA RD
BRIDGE ST
FOUNTAIN ST
MIDDLETON PK AVE
BEESTON PARK RING ROAD
ISLE ROAD
HEWHALL ROAD
LOW RD
PEPPER RD
TEMPLENEWSAM RD
OUZLEWELL GREEN
43

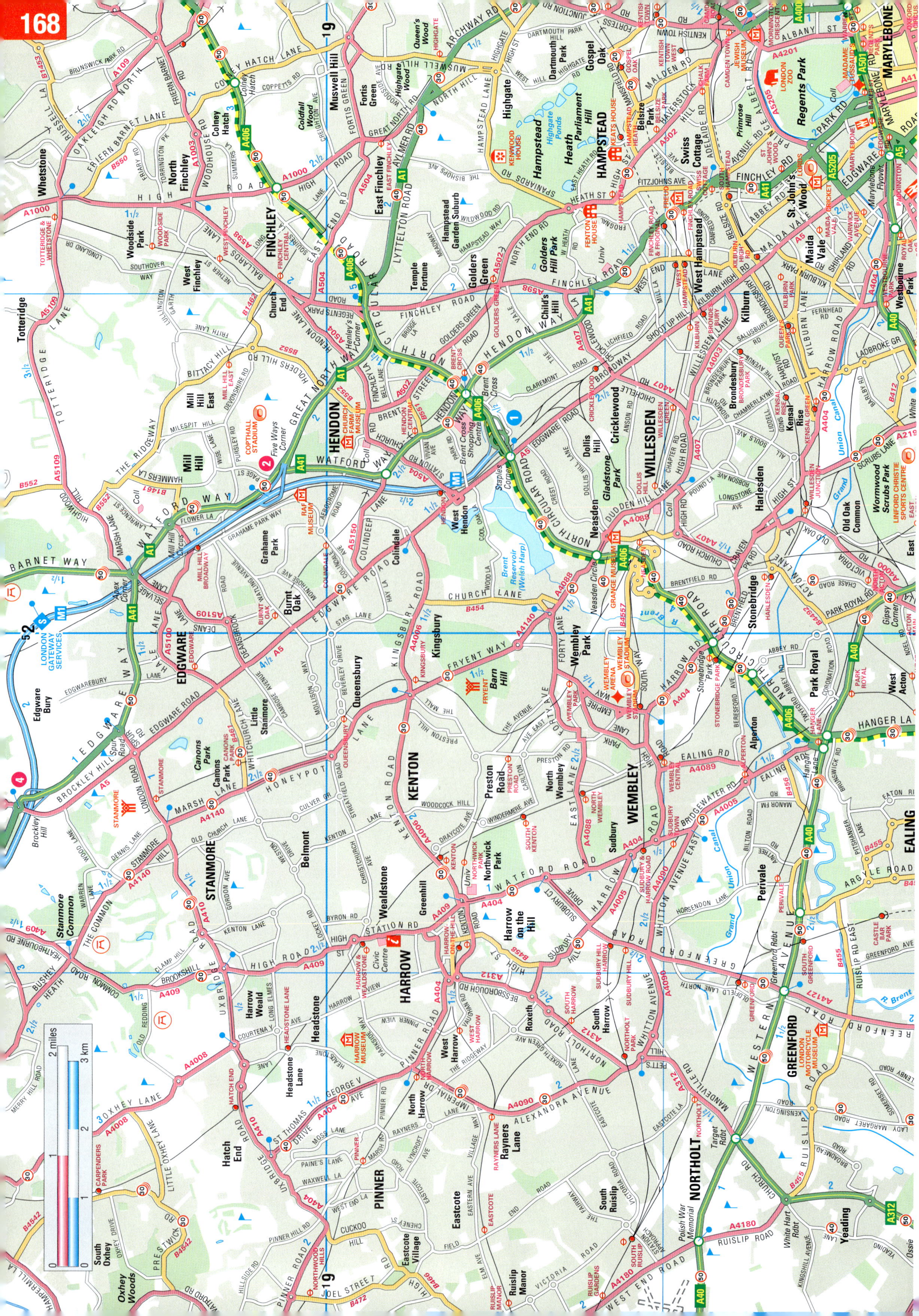

Whetstone
Totteridge
North Finchley
Woodside Park
West Finchley
FINCHLEY
Church End
Muswell Hill
Fortis Green
East Finchley
Hampstead Garden Suburb
Temple Fortune
Golders Green
Highgate
Hampstead Heath
Parliament Hill
Gospel Oak
HAMPSTEAD
Belsize Park
Swiss Cottage
Primrose Hill
Regents Park
MARYLEBONE
St John's Wood
Maida Vale
West Hampstead
Kilburn
Child's Hill
Golders Hill Park
Mill Hill
Mill Hill East
HENDON
West Hendon
Colindale
Brent Cross
Brent Reservoir (Welsh Harp)
Cricklewood
Dollis Hill
Gladstone Park
WILLESDEN
Brondesbury
Kensal Rise
Harlesden
Neasden
Stonebridge
Old Oak Common
Wormwood Scrubs Park
Park Royal
West Acton
EALING
Edgware
Edgware Bury
Burnt Oak
Grahame Park
Queensbury
Kingsbury
Wembley Park
Barn Hill
Little Stanmore
Canons Park
STANMORE
Stanmore Common
Belmont
KENTON
Preston Road
North Wembley
WEMBLEY
Sudbury
Alperton
Perivale
Wealdstone
Harrow Weald
Headstone
HARROW
Harrow on the Hill
Greenhill
Northwick Park
South Harrow
West Harrow
Roxeth
North Harrow
Headstone Lane
Hatch End
PINNER
Rayners Lane
Eastcote
Eastcote Village
South Ruislip
NORTHOLT
GREENFORD
Yeading
Ruislip Manor
South Oxhey
Oxhey Woods
Brockley Hill
London Gateway Services

PADDINGTON
Bayswater
Mayfair
Hyde Park
Kensington Gardens
Knightsbridge
CHELSEA
Pimlico
BATTERSEA
Battersea Park
Clapham Common
Balham
Wandsworth Common
Upper Tooting
Tooting
Colliers Wood
Earlsfield
WANDSWORTH
Parsons Green
FULHAM
Hurlingham Park
West Hill
Southfields
Wimbledon Park
WIMBLEDON
MERTON
MORDEN
Morden Hall Park
Holland Park
Notting Hill
HAMMERSMITH
Shepherd's Bush
River Thames
BARNES
PUTNEY
Putney Heath
Putney Vale
Wimbledon Common
Raynes Park
Crooked Billet
Bedford Park
ACTON
CHISWICK
Mortlake
East Sheen
Roehampton
Richmond Park
Kingston Vale
Coombe
NEW MALDEN
Norbiton
South Acton
North Sheen
Kew
RICHMOND
Richmond Hill
Petersham
KINGSTON UPON THAMES
Gunnersbury Park
Royal Botanic Gardens (Kew)
West Ealing
HANWELL
Northfields
BRENTFORD
Syon Park
Old Deer Park
Ham
TEDDINGTON
Hampton Wick
Hampton Court Park
St Margarets
TWICKENHAM
Strawberry Hill
Bushy Park
Isleworth
ISLEWORTH
HOUNSLOW
Osterley Park
Osterley
Norwood Green
HESTON
Southall
SOUTHALL
Dormer's Wells
Drayton Green
Whitton
Hampton
Hampton Hill
Hounslow Heath
Hounslow West
HANWORTH
Hanworth Park
FELTHAM
North Hyde
Cranford
Hayes Town
SUNBURY
Molesey Reservoirs
Bessborough Res
Richmond Park
Roads in Richmond Park open in daylight hours only

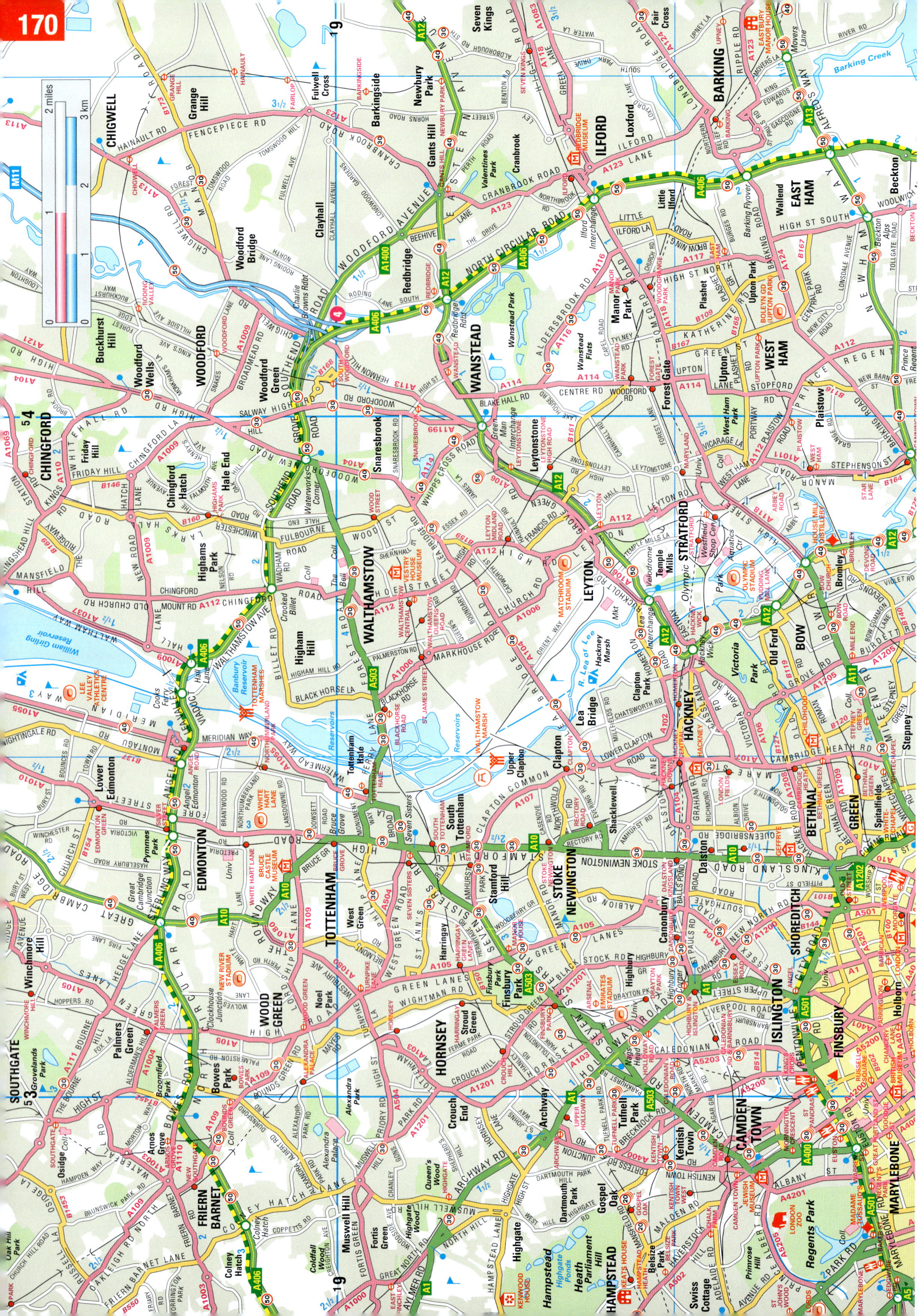
CHIGWELL
Grange Hill
Fulwell Cross
Barkingside
Newbury Park
Seven Kings
Fair Cross
BARKING
Gants Hill
Cranbrook
ILFORD
Loxford
Clayhall
Woodford Bridge
Redbridge
Valentines Park
Little Ilford
Buckhurst Hill
Woodford Wells
WOODFORD
Woodford Green
WANSTEAD
Wanstead Park
Wanstead Flats
Manor Park
Forest Gate
Upton Park
Plashet
EAST HAM
Wallend
Beckton
WEST HAM
Upton
Plaistow
CHINGFORD
Friday Hill
Chingford Hatch
Hale End
Highams Park
Snaresbrook
Leytonstone
WALTHAMSTOW
LEYTON
Temple Mills
STRATFORD
BOW
Old Ford
Bromley
Victoria Park
Hackney Wick
Hackney Marsh
Crooked Billet
Higham Hill
William Girling Reservoir
Banbury Reservoir
Lower Edmonton
Edmonton
EDMONTON
Pymmes Park
TOTTENHAM
West Green
Tottenham Hale
South Tottenham
Upper Clapton
Clapton
Lea Bridge
Clapton Park
Shacklewell
HACKNEY
Dalston
BETHNAL GREEN
Stepney
Spitalfields
SHOREDITCH
STOKE NEWINGTON
Stamford Hill
Canonbury
Highbury
ISLINGTON
FINSBURY
Holborn
Harringay
Finsbury Park
HORNSEY
Stroud Green
Crouch End
WOOD GREEN
Noel Park
Alexandra Park
Alexandra Palace
Muswell Hill
Fortis Green
Highgate
Archway
Tufnell Park
Kentish Town
CAMDEN TOWN
Dartmouth Park
Gospel Oak
HAMPSTEAD
Hampstead Heath
Parliament Hill
Belsize Park
Primrose Hill
Regents Park
MARYLEBONE
Swiss Cottage
Winchmore Hill
Palmers Green
Bowes Park
SOUTHGATE
Arnos Grove
Osidge
FRIERN BARNET
Colney Hatch
Coldfall Wood
Highgate Wood
Queen's Wood
Walthamstow Marsh
Reservoirs
NORTH CIRCULAR ROAD
Barking Creek
Olympic Park
Queen Elizabeth Olympic Park

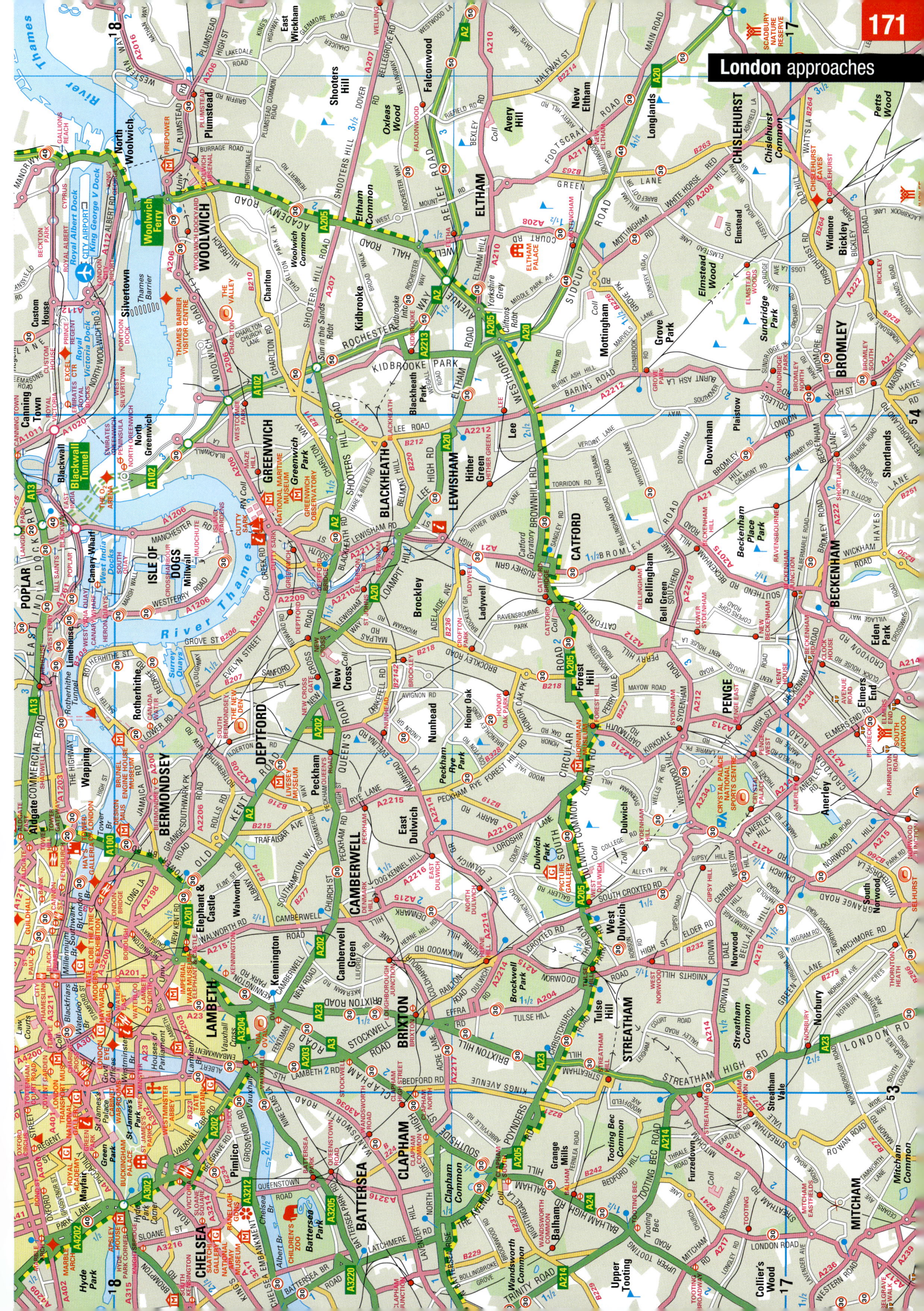
Woolwich
Greenwich
Deptford
Bermondsey
Isle of Dogs
Poplar
Canning Town
Silvertown
Blackheath
Lewisham
Catford
Eltham
Chislehurst
Bromley
Beckenham
Penge
Camberwell
Brixton
Lambeth
Kennington
Clapham
Battersea
Chelsea
Streatham
Mitcham
Dulwich
Peckham
Sydenham
River Thames
Kidbrooke
Charlton
Plumstead
Shooters Hill
Mottingham
Grove Park
Downham
Forest Hill
Norbury
Balham
Tooting
Wandsworth Common
Clapham Common
Herne Hill
Tulse Hill
West Dulwich
East Dulwich
Nunhead
Brockley
Rotherhithe
Wapping
Limehouse
Millwall
Lee
Hither Green
Elmstead Wood
Sundridge Park
Plaistow
Shortlands
Elmers End
Anerley
South Norwood
Norwood
Crystal Palace
Streatham Common
Streatham Vale
Mitcham Common
Collier's Wood
Upper Tooting
Furzedown
Pimlico
Vauxhall
Walworth
Elephant & Castle
Waterloo
Blackfriars
Aldgate
Mayfair
Hyde Park
Bellingham
Bell Green
Beckenham Place Park
Avery Hill
New Eltham
Longlands
Falconwood
Oxleas Wood
Eltham Common
Woolwich Common
Canary Wharf
Blackwall
North Greenwich
North Woolwich
Custom House
Woolwich Ferry
Blackwall Tunnel
Rotherhithe Tunnel
Thames Barrier

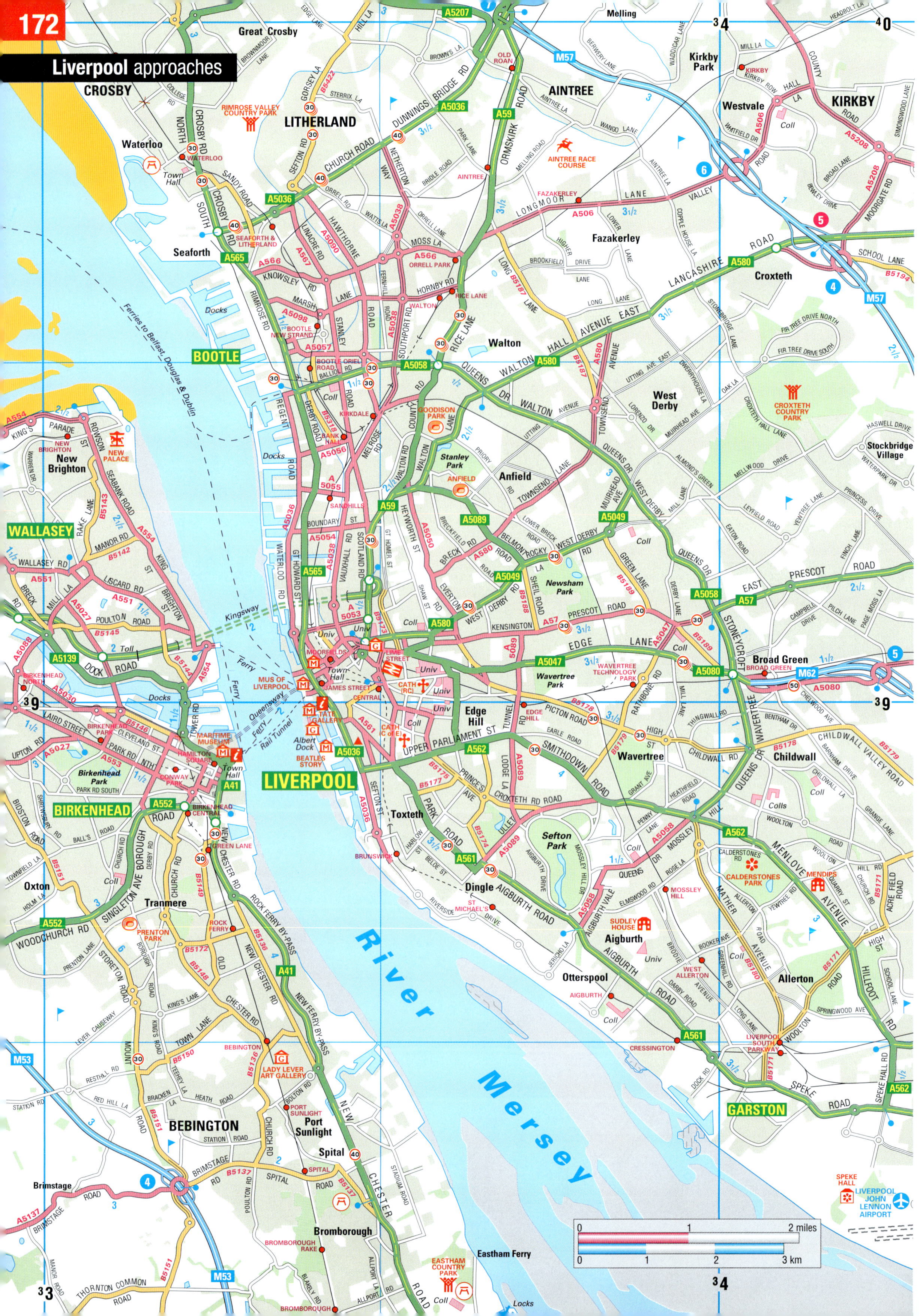
CROSBY
Great Crosby
Waterloo
Seaforth
LITHERLAND
AINTREE
Melling
Kirkby Park
Westvale
KIRKBY
Fazakerley
Croxteth
Walton
BOOTLE
West Derby
New Brighton
WALLASEY
Stanley Park
Anfield
Stockbridge Village
Newsham Park
Kingsway
Broad Green
Wavertree Park
Edge Hill
LIVERPOOL
Wavertree
Childwall
Birkenhead Park
BIRKENHEAD
Toxteth
Sefton Park
Oxton
Tranmere
Dingle
Aigburth
Otterspool
Allerton
GARSTON
BEBINGTON
Port Sunlight
Spital
Brimstage
Bromborough
Eastham Ferry
River Mersey
RIMROSE VALLEY COUNTRY PARK
AINTREE RACE COURSE
CROXTETH COUNTRY PARK
GOODISON PARK
ANFIELD
NEW PALACE
MARITIME MUSEUM
TATE GALLERY
BEATLES STORY
MUS OF LIVERPOOL
PRENTON PARK
CALDERSTONES PARK
SUDLEY HOUSE
MENDIPS
LADY LEVER ART GALLERY
SPEKE HALL
LIVERPOOL JOHN LENNON AIRPORT
EASTHAM COUNTRY PARK
Ferries to Belfast, Douglas & Dublin
Queensway
Rail Tunnel
M57
M62
M53
A5036
A59
A580
A5058
A57
A562
A561
A41
A552
A554
A5080
A5047
A5049
A5089
A565
0 1 2 miles
0 1 2 3 km

MANCHESTER
SALFORD
TRAFFORD PARK
WHITEFIELD
PRESTWICH
PENDLEBURY
SWINTON
ECCLES
STRETFORD
SALE
ALTRINCHAM
WYTHENSHAWE
REDDISH
CHEADLE HULME
GATLEY
Outwood
Ringley
Park Lane
Besses o' th' Barn
Simister
Rhodes
Alkrington Garden Village
Higher Blackley
Heaton Park
Charlestown
Clifton Green
Newtown
Kersal
Broughton Park
Crumpsall
Moston
New Moston
Harpurhey
Ellesmere Park
Little Bolton
Seedley
Patricroft
Strangeways
Miles Platting
Newton Heath
Clayton
Openshaw
Ardwick
Hulme
Gorton
Old Trafford
Moss Side
Rusholme
Ryder Brow
Levenshulme
Firswood
Whalley Range
Longford Park
North Reddish
South Reddish
Chorlton-cum-Hardy
Withington
Burnage
Barlow Moor
West Didsbury
Ashton upon Mersey
Woodhouses
Brooklands
Heaton Mersey
Heaton Norris
Northern Moor
Timperley
Roundthorn
Newall Green
River Irwell
River Mersey
Manchester Ship Canal
Bridgewater Canal
M60
M602
M56
M66
M62
A57(M)
1 mile
2 miles
1 km
2 km
3 km

Brunswick Village
WIDE OPEN
Hazlerigg
NEWCASTLE INTERNATIONAL AIRPORT
P&R
Camperdown
Killingworth
Killingworth Centre
Backworth
SHIREMOOR
NORTHUMBERLAND PARK
BOUNDARY MILL NEWCASTLE
NEWCASTLE
Gosforth Wood
Gosforth Lake
Woolsington
KINGSTON PARK
Fawdon
Gosforth
LONGBENTON
PALMERSVILLE
RISING SUN COUNTRY PARK
STEPHENSON RAILWAY MUSEUM
SOUTH GOSFORTH
Govt Blds
Willington
NEWCASTLE UPON TYNE
Blakelaw
Jesmond
WEST JESMOND
Heaton
WALLSEND
Fenham
MILITARY VEHICLE MUSEUM
SEGEDUNUM ROMAN FORT
Tyne Tunnel
River Tyne
DENTON HALL TURRET
SPORTS DIRECT ARENA
Civic Centre
HAYMARKET
Benwell
Scotswood
Byker
Walker
HEBBURN
DISCOVERY
MONUMENT
MANORS
CENTRAL
BALTIC CENTRE
THE SAGE
Elswick
GATESHEAD
GATESHEAD INTERNATIONAL STADIUM
METRO RADIO ARENA
METROCENTRE
METROLAND
Metro Centre
Dunston
GATESHEAD STADIUM
FELLING
HEWORTH
PELAW
Wardley
WHICKHAM THORNS CENTRE
SHIPLEY ART GALL
Bensham
Felling
Lobley Hill
Sunniside
Hill Head Wood
Wrekenton
Lyndhurst
Chowdene
Springwell
High Park Wood
Usworth
BOWES RAILWAY
ANGEL OF THE NORTH
ANDREWS HOUSE
TANFIELD RAILWAY
Kibblesworth
BIRTLEY
WASHINGTON
WASHINGTON OLD HALL
CAUSEY ARCH
Biddock
Lampton
WASHINGTON BIRTLEY SERVICES
Govt Offices
BEAMISH OPEN AIR MUSEUM
URPETH
OUSTON
Fatfield
Harraton
0 1 2 miles
0 1 2 3 km

Town plan symbols

- Motorway
- **Primary route** – dual, single carriageway
- **A road** – dual, single carriageway
- **B road** – dual, single carriageway
- Minor through road
- One-way street
- Pedestrian roads
- Shopping streets
- Railway with station
- Tramway with station
- Underground or Metro station
- Hospital
- Parking
- Police, Post Office
- Shopmobility
- Youth hostel
- Bus or railway station building
- Shopping precinct or retail park
- Park
- Congestion charge zone
- Abbey or cathedral
- Ancient monument
- Aquarium
- Art gallery
- Bird collection or aviary
- Building of interest
- Castle
- Church of interest
- Cinema
- Garden
- Historic ship
- House
- House and garden
- Museum
- Preserved railway
- Roman antiquity
- Safari park
- Theatre
- Tourist information centre
- Zoo
- Other place of interest

Aberdeen

0 Miles ¼

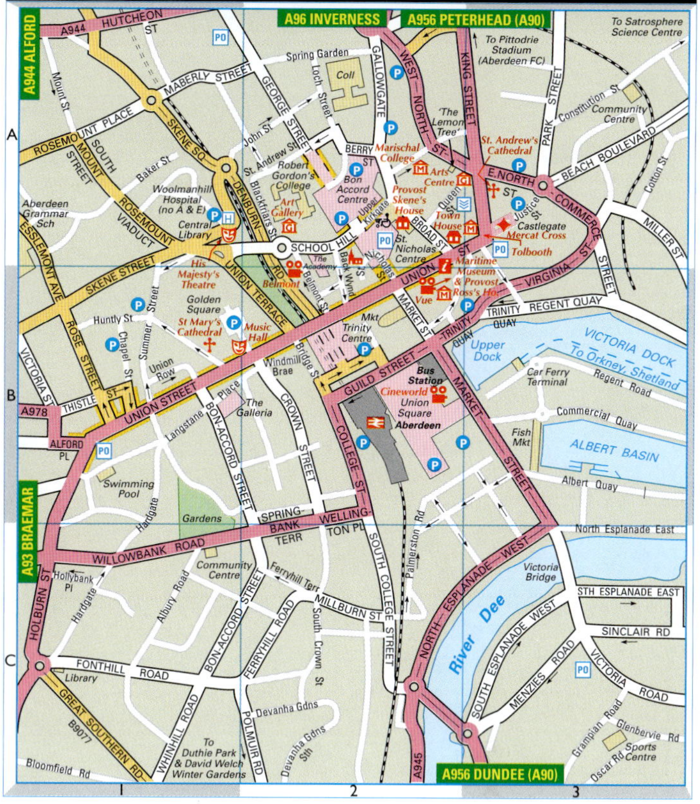

Bath

0 Miles ¼

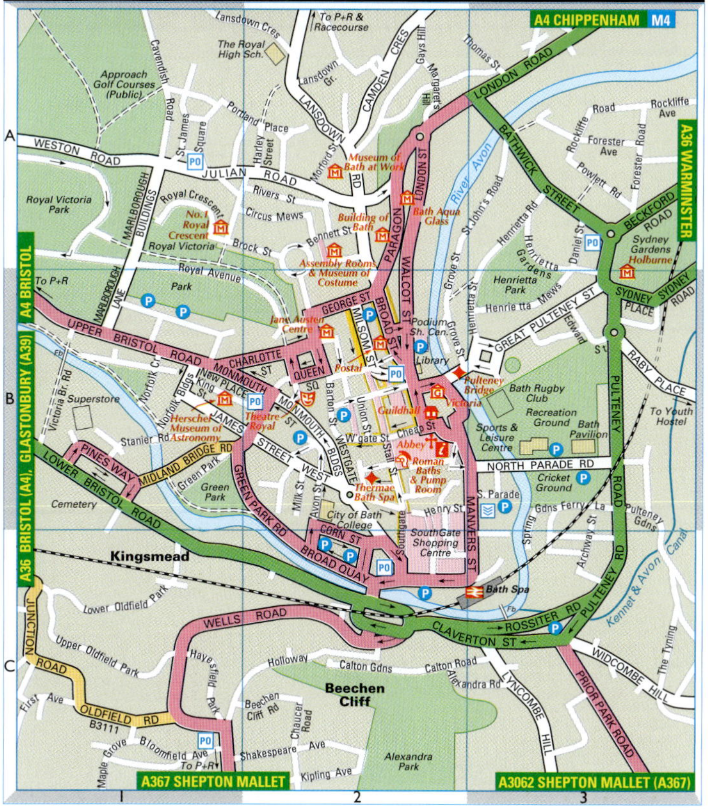

Blackpool

0 Miles ¼

Birmingham

0 Miles ¼

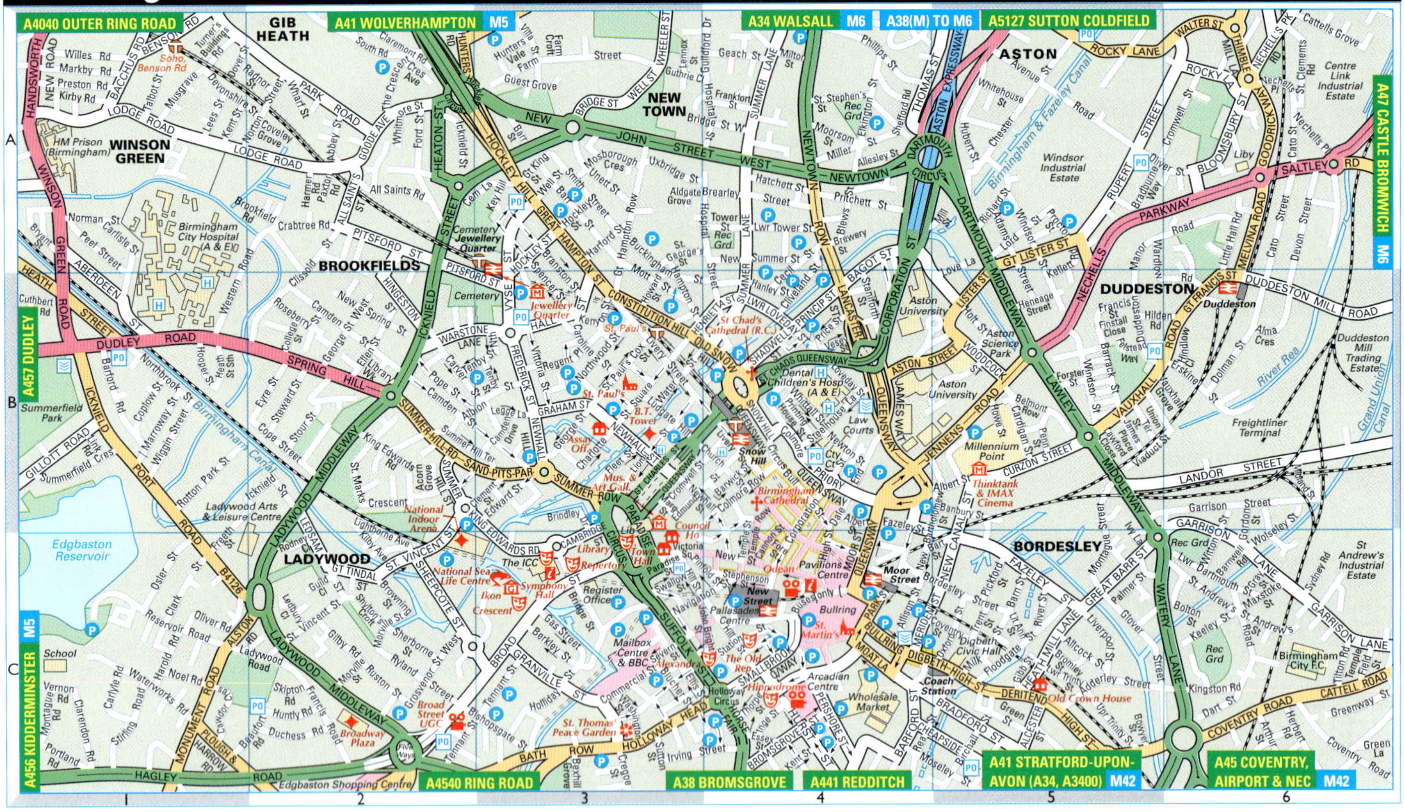

Bournemouth

0 Miles ¼

Bradford

0 Miles ¼

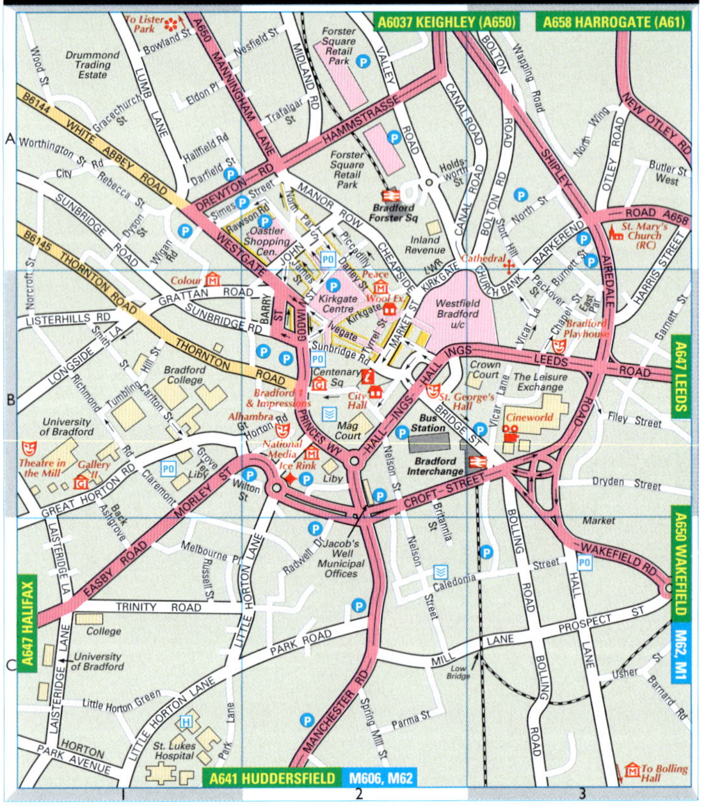

Bristol

0 Miles ¼
A4018 TO M5
A38 TO M5
A4032 TO M32 & M4
A432 MANGOTSFIELD
A420 CHIPPENHAM
A4 AVONMOUTH & M5
A370 WESTON-SUPER-MARE
A38 TAUNTON
A37 SHEPTON MALLET
A4 BATH
CLIFTON
To Clifton Suspension Bridge
To Camp Bristol Zoo Gardens
Goldney Hall
Cabot Tower
Brandon Hill
Queen Elizabeth Hospital School
City of Bristol College
Bristol Cathedral
Council House
Bristol Central Library
Millennium Square
Amphitheatre
The Lloyds' Building
Floating Harbour
Bristol Marina
Cumberland Basin
Merchants Dock
Baltic Wharf Leisure Centre & Caravan Park
SS Great Britain & The Matthew
Maritime Heritage Centre
Spike Island Artspace
M Shed
Bristol Harbour Railway
River Avon (New Cut)
Bathurst Basin
General Hospital
Redcliffe Bridge
St. Mary Redcliffe
Bristol Temple Meads
Temple Church (ruin)
Temple Gardens
Castle Park
The Mall
Broadmead
Quakers Friars
Christchurch
St. Peter's (ruin)
The Exchange & St. Nicholas' Markets
Bristol Bridge
Bristol Royal Infirmary
Bristol Royal Children's Hospital
Bristol Eye Hosp (A & E)
Bus Sta
The Watershed
Arnolfini Arts Centre
Theatre Royal
Landoger Trow
The Create Centre
Greville Smyth Park
The Tobacco Factory
CUMBERLAND ROAD
CORONATION ROAD
HOTWELL ROAD
ANCHOR ROAD
PARK ROW
BALDWIN STREET
VICTORIA STREET
TEMPLE WAY
NEWFOUNDLAND ST
CLIFT HOUSE ROAD
BEDMINSTER PARADE
YORK RD
CLARENCE RD
COMMERCIAL ROAD

Brighton

0 Miles ¼
A23 CRAWLEY M23
A270 LEWES (A27)
A270 WORTHING (A27)
A259 WORTHING
A259 NEWHAVEN
To Booth Museum
To British Engineerium
To Withdean Stadium Park & Ride
Brighton
St. Bartholomew's
Toy & Model
St. Peter's
Phoenix
St. Nicholas'
Churchill Square Shopping Centre
Clock Tower
Theatre Royal
The Dome
Art Gallery & Museum
Royal Pavilion
The Lanes
Town Hall
Brighton Centre
Odeon Film Centre
Brighton Fishing Museum
West Pier (Closed to the public)
Palace Pier
Sea Life Centre
Volk's Electric Railway
To Brighton Marina
To Royal Sussex County Hospital (A & E)
University of Brighton
Law Courts
OLD SHOREHAM ROAD
DYKE ROAD
NEW ENGLAND RD
VIADUCT ROAD
UPPER LEWES RD
LEWES RD
DITCHLING ROAD
WESTERN ROAD
NORTH STREET
KINGS ROAD
GRAND JUNCTION RD
MARINE PARADE
EDWARD STREET
ST. JAMES'S STREET
QUEEN'S ROAD
GRAND PARADE

Cambridge

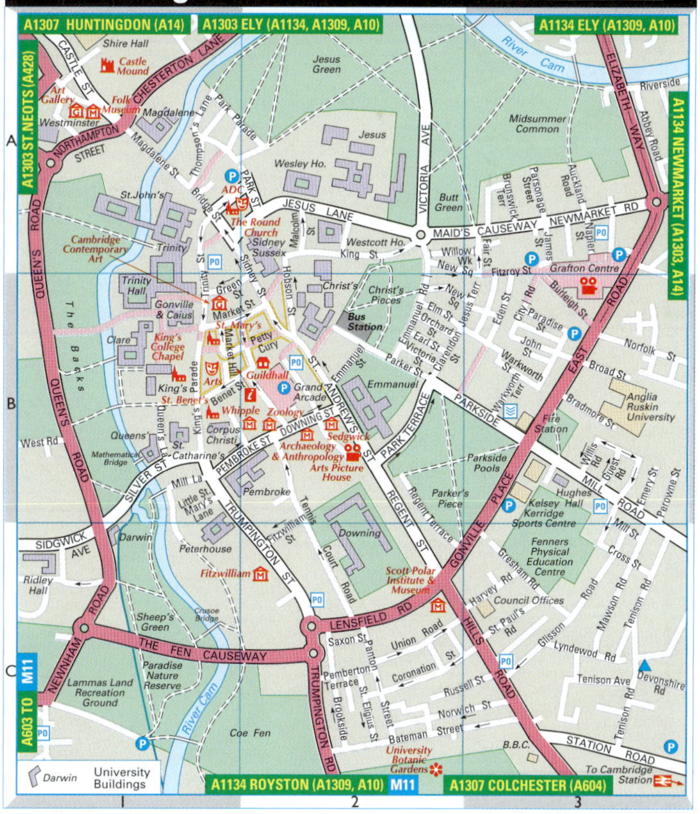
0 Miles ¼
A1307 HUNTINGDON (A14)
A1303 ELY (A1134, A1309, A10)
A1134 ELY (A1309, A10)
A1303 ST. NEOTS (A428)
A1134 NEWMARKET (A1303, A14)
A603 TO M11
A1134 ROYSTON (A1309, A10) M11
A1307 COLCHESTER (A604)
River Cam
Jesus Green
Midsummer Common
Castle Mound
Shire Hall
Art Gallery
Folk Museum
Magdalene
Westminster
Jesus
Wesley Ho.
St. John's
Trinity
Trinity Hall
Gonville & Caius
King's College Chapel
Clare
Queens'
Corpus Christi
St. Catharine's
Pembroke
Peterhouse
Fitzwilliam
Downing
The Round Church
Sidney Sussex
Christ's
Christ's Pieces
Bus Station
Emmanuel
Grand Arcade
Guildhall
Arts
Whipple
Zoology
Sedgwick
Archaeology & Anthropology
Arts Picture House
Scott Polar Institute & Museum
Parker's Piece
Parkside Pools
Kelsey Kerridge Sports Centre
Fenners Physical Education Centre
Anglia Ruskin University
Grafton Centre
Council Offices
University Botanic Gardens
Coe Fen
Sheep's Green
Paradise Nature Reserve
Lammas Land Recreation Ground
Darwin
Ridley Hall
To Cambridge Station
Darwin University Buildings
QUEEN'S ROAD
THE FEN CAUSEWAY
TRUMPINGTON RD
HILLS RD
LENSFIELD ROAD
REGENT ST
EAST ROAD
NEWMARKET RD
MAID'S CAUSEWAY
JESUS LANE
CHESTERTON LANE
ELIZABETH WAY
GONVILLE PLACE
STATION ROAD

Canterbury

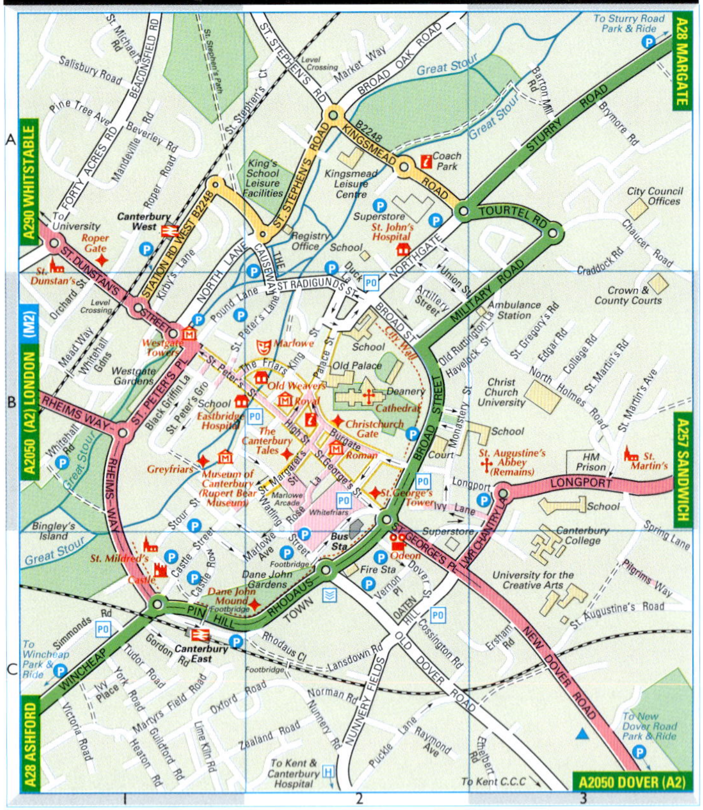

Cardiff / Caerdydd

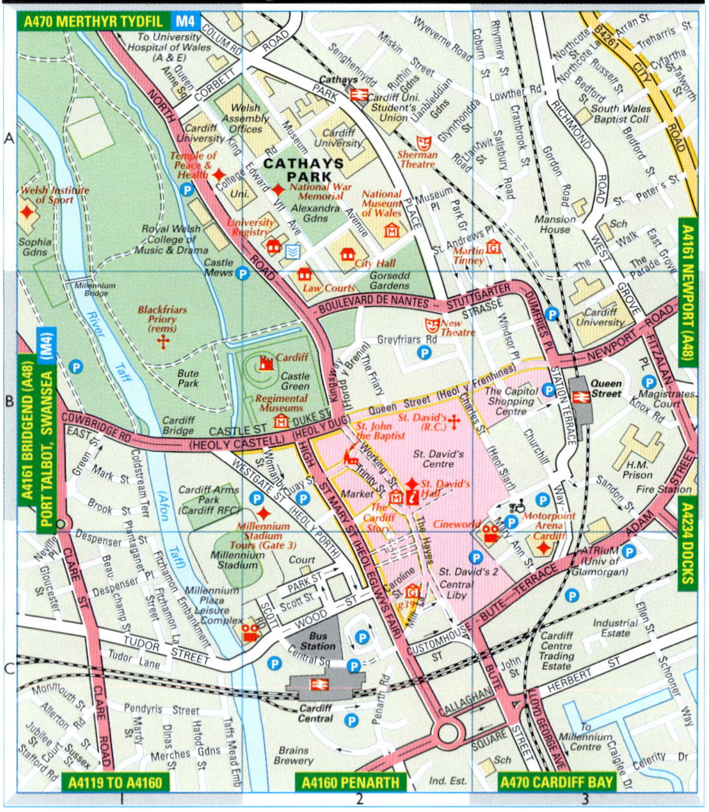

Cheltenham

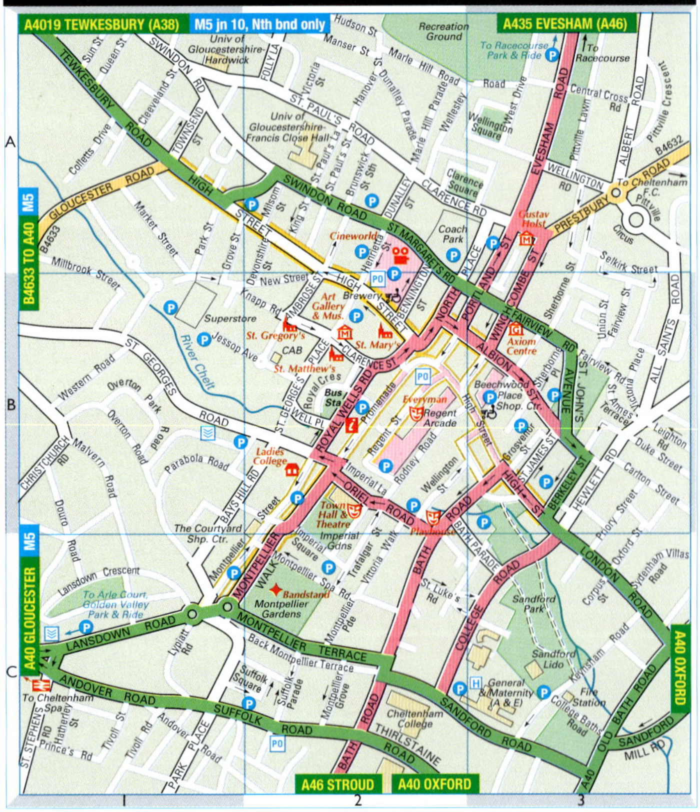

Chester

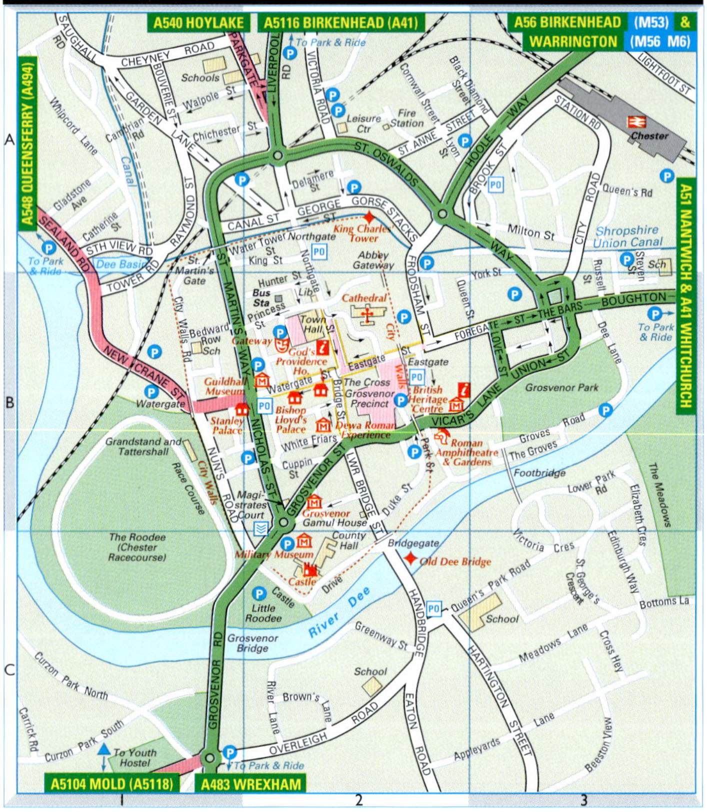

Colchester

0 Miles ¼

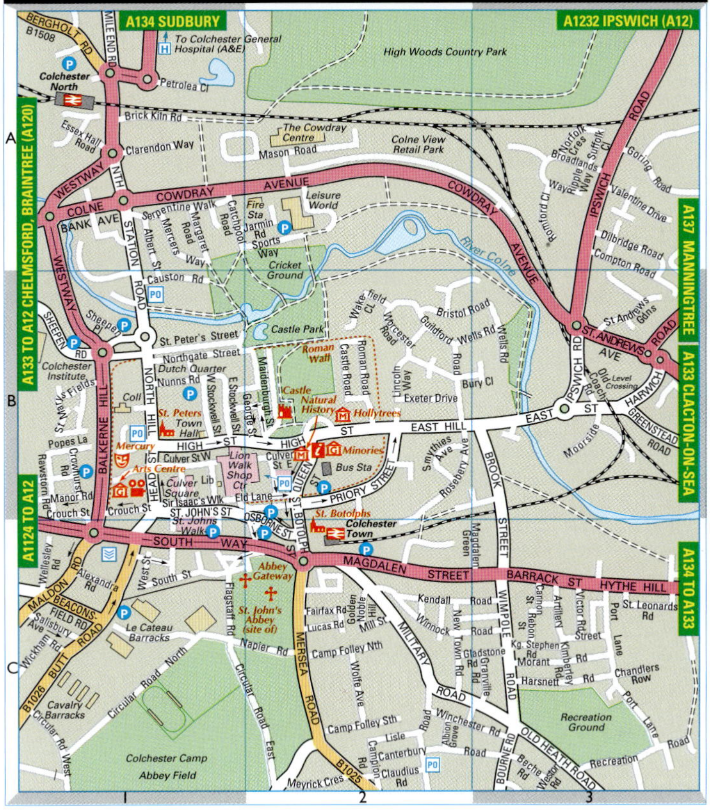

Coventry

0 Miles ¼

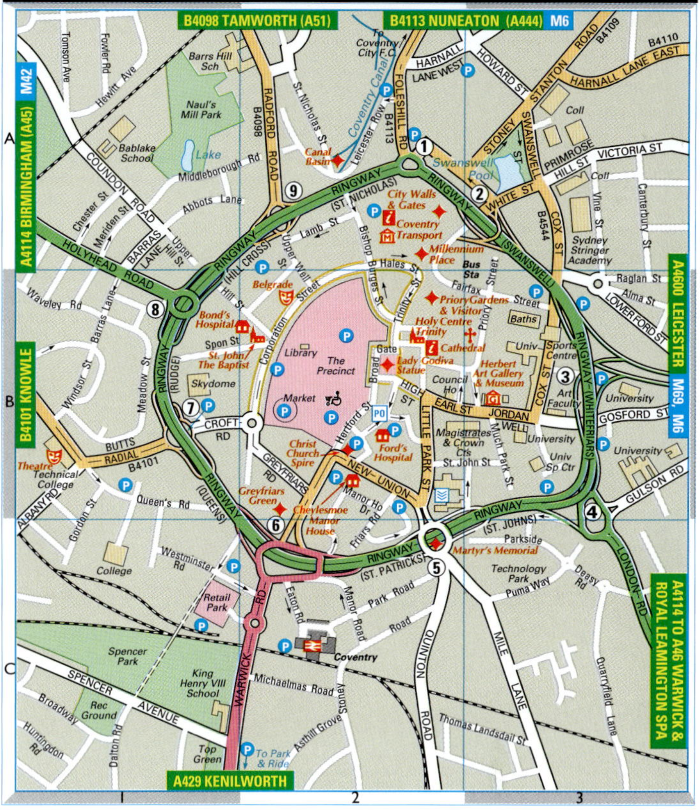

Derby

0 Miles ¼

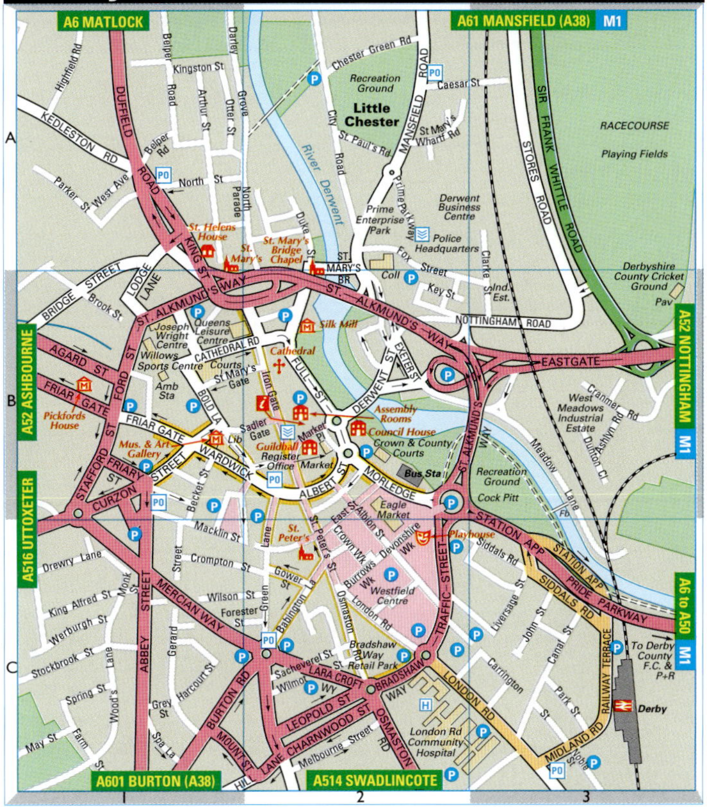

Dundee

0 Miles ¼

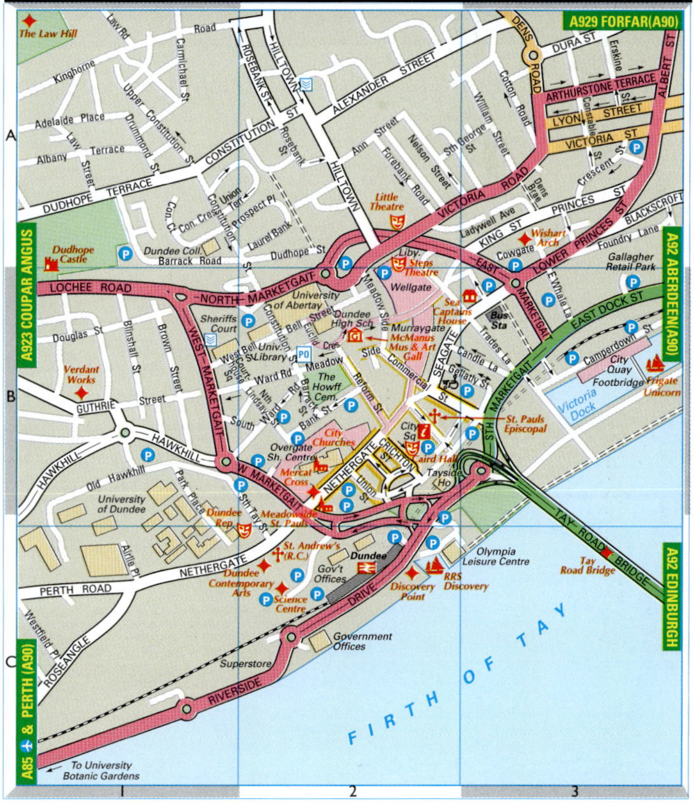

Edinburgh

0 Miles ¼

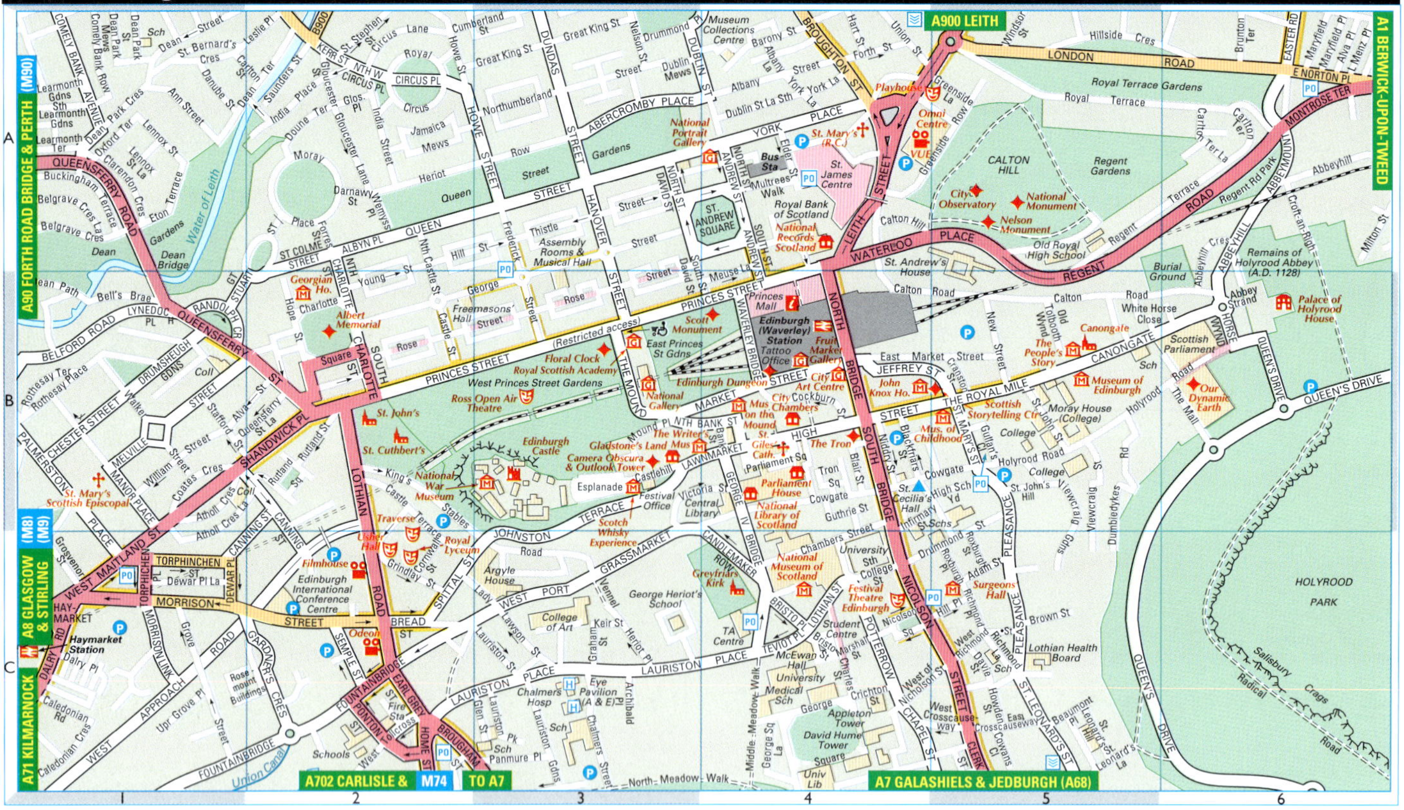

Durham

0 Miles ¼

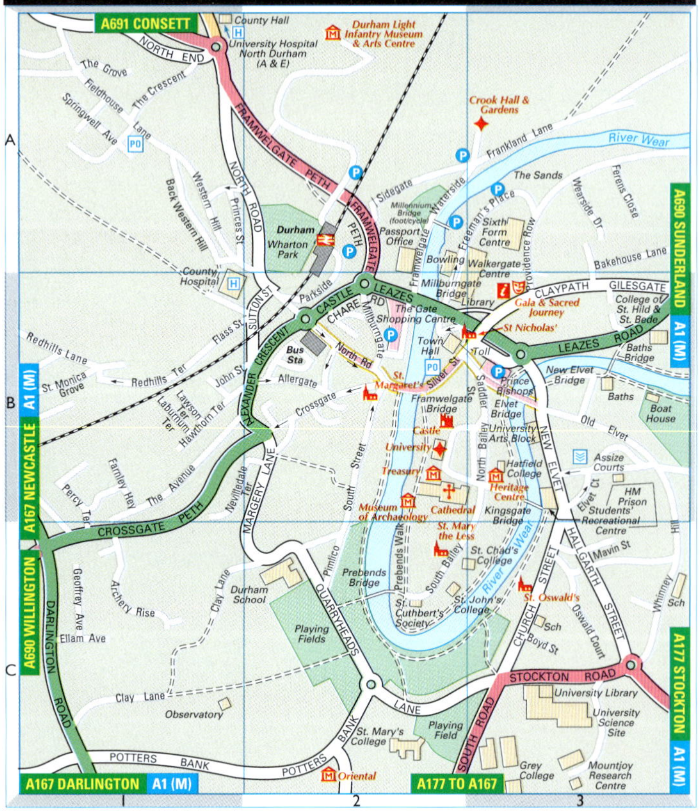

Exeter

0 Miles ¼

Glasgow

0 Miles ¼

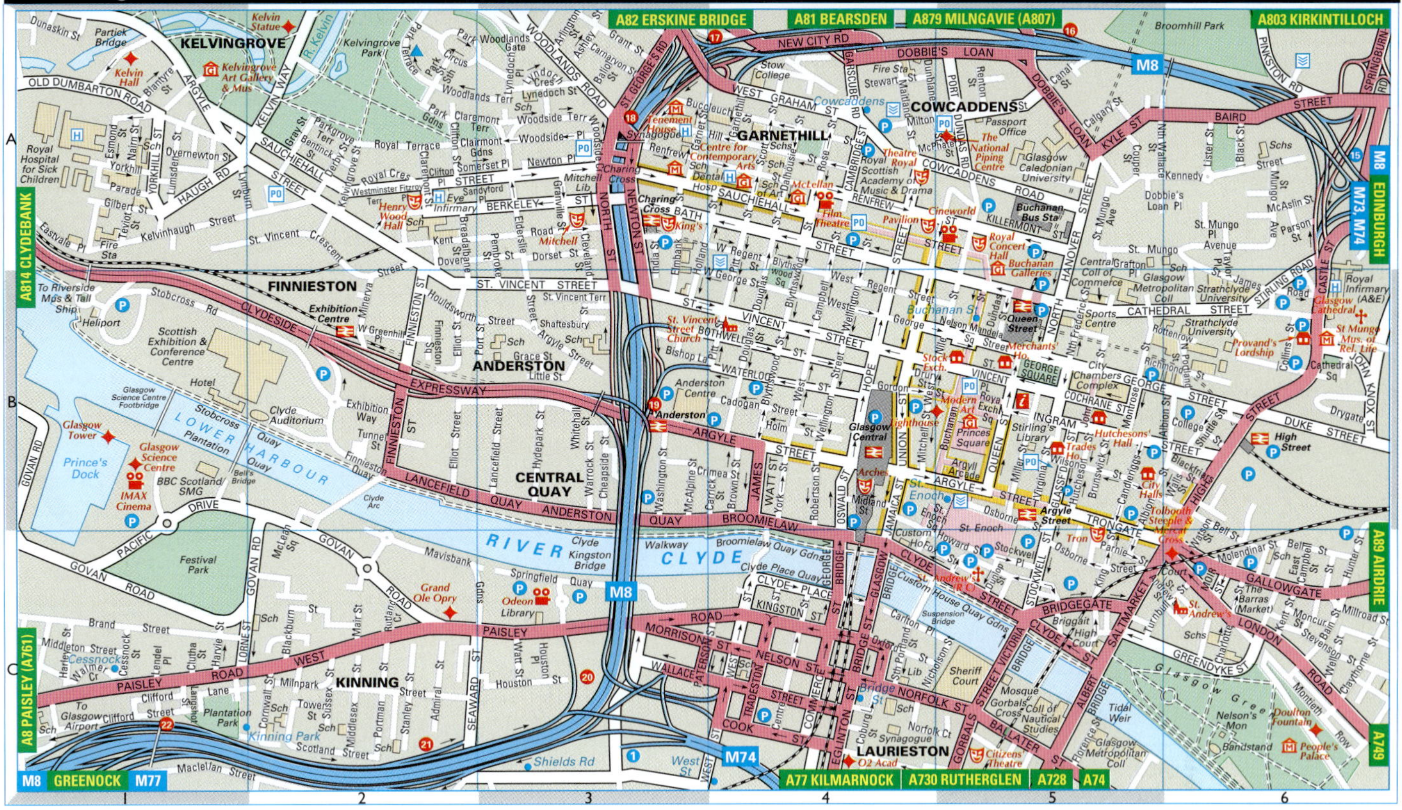

Gloucester

0 Miles ¼

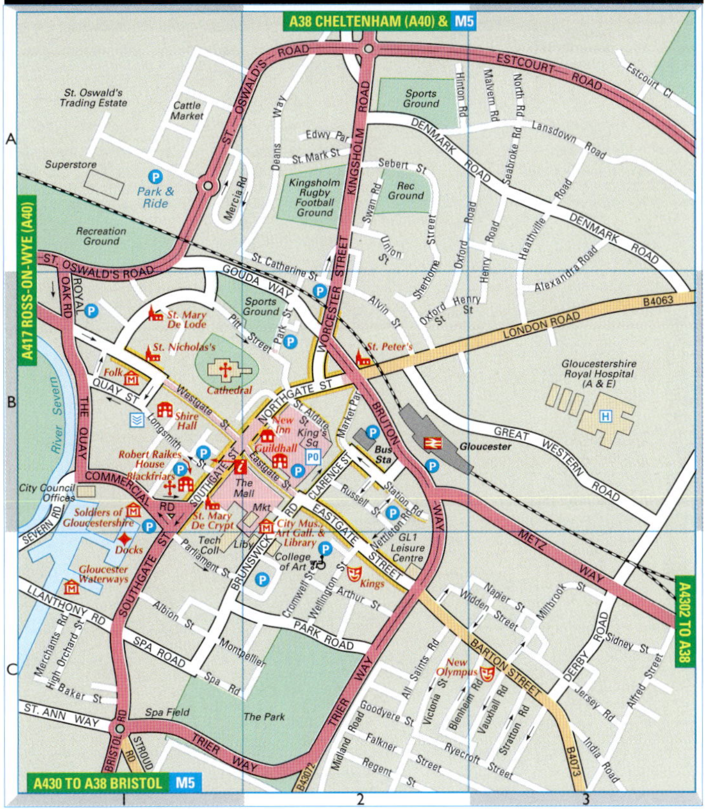

Hanley (Stoke-on-Trent)

0 Miles ¼

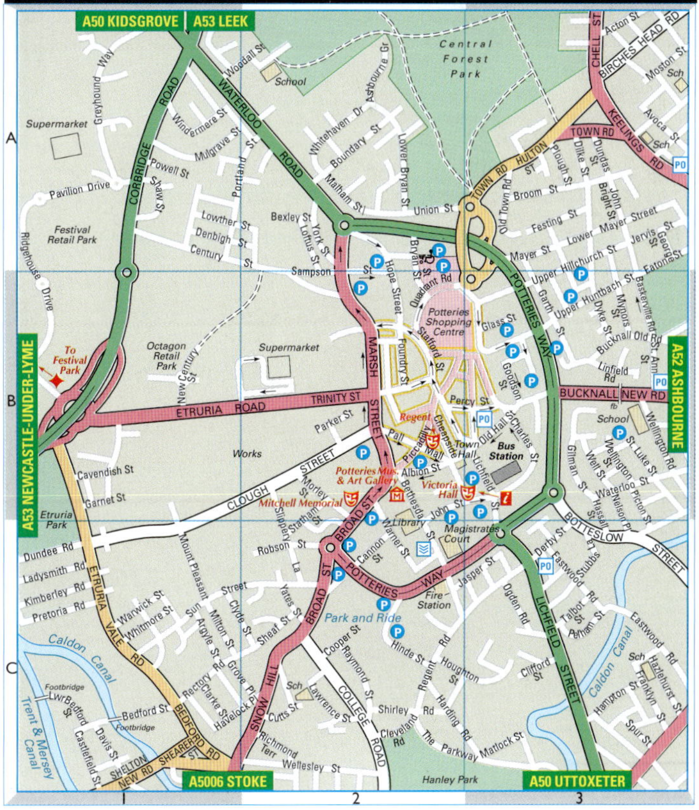

Harrogate

0 Miles ¼

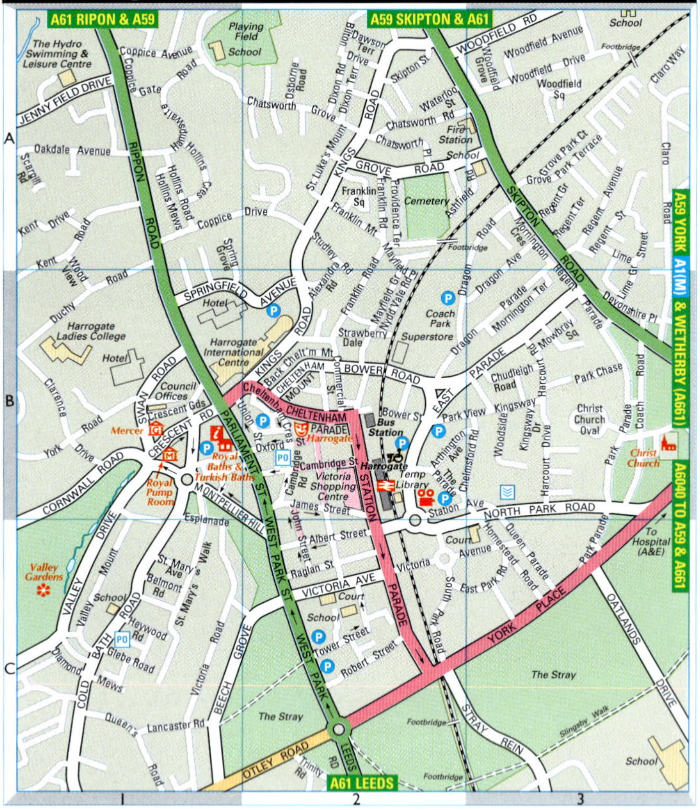

Hull

0 Miles ¼

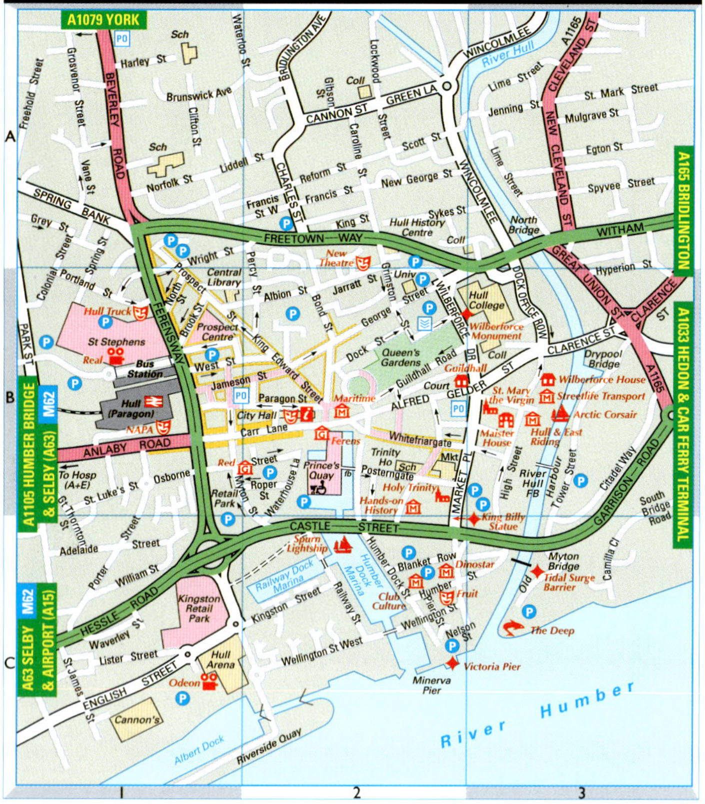

Ipswich

0 Miles ¼

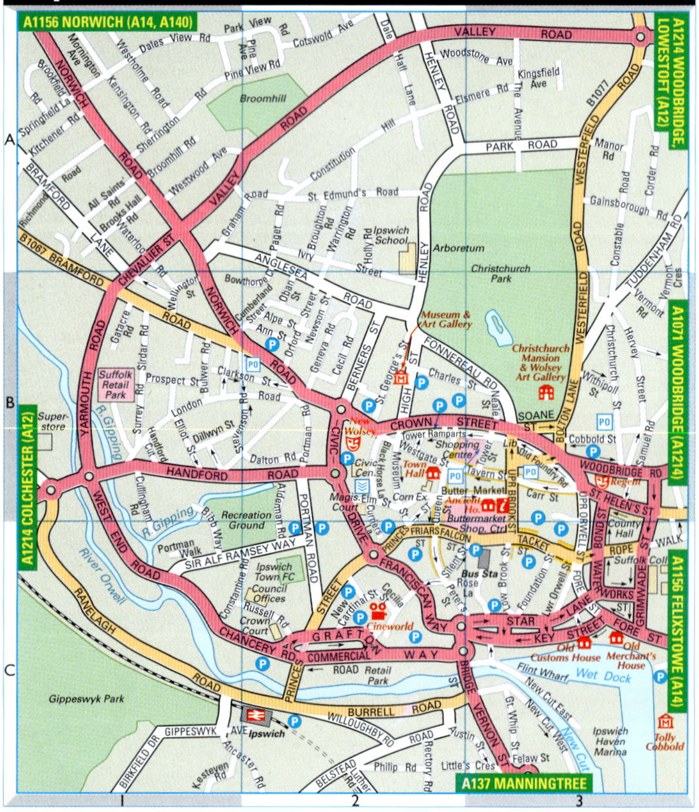

Leicester

0 Miles ¼

Leeds

0 Miles ¼

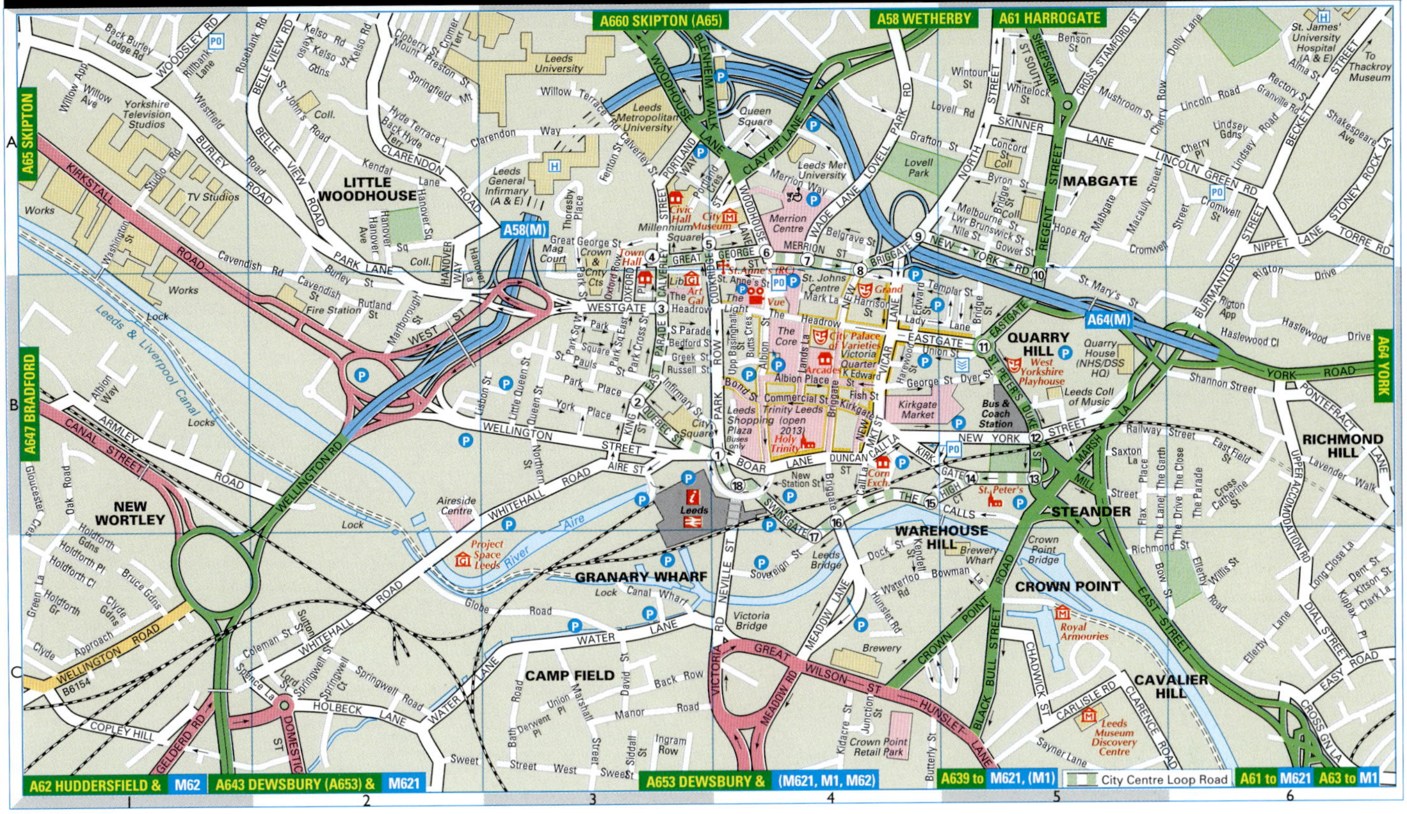
A660 SKIPTON (A65)
A58 WETHERBY
A61 HARROGATE
A65 SKIPTON
A647 BRADFORD
A64 YORK
A62 HUDDERSFIELD & M62
A643 DEWSBURY (A653) & M621
A653 DEWSBURY & (M621, M1, M62)
A639 to M621, (M1)
City Centre Loop Road
A61 to M621
A63 to M1
LITTLE WOODHOUSE
MABGATE
QUARRY HILL
RICHMOND HILL
NEW WORTLEY
STEANDER
WAREHOUSE HILL
GRANARY WHARF
CROWN POINT
CAMP FIELD
CAVALIER HILL
Leeds University
Leeds Metropolitan University
Leeds General Infirmary (A & E)
Yorkshire Television Studios
TV Studios
A58(M)
A64(M)
Leeds & Liverpool Canal
River Aire
Royal Armouries
Leeds Museum Discovery Centre
West Yorkshire Playhouse
Kirkgate Market
Bus & Coach Station
Leeds Shopping Plaza
Trinity Leeds
City Palace of Varieties
Victoria Quarter
Millennium Square
Town Hall
Crown Point Retail Park
Project Space Leeds
Corn Exch
Grand

Liverpool

0 Miles ¼

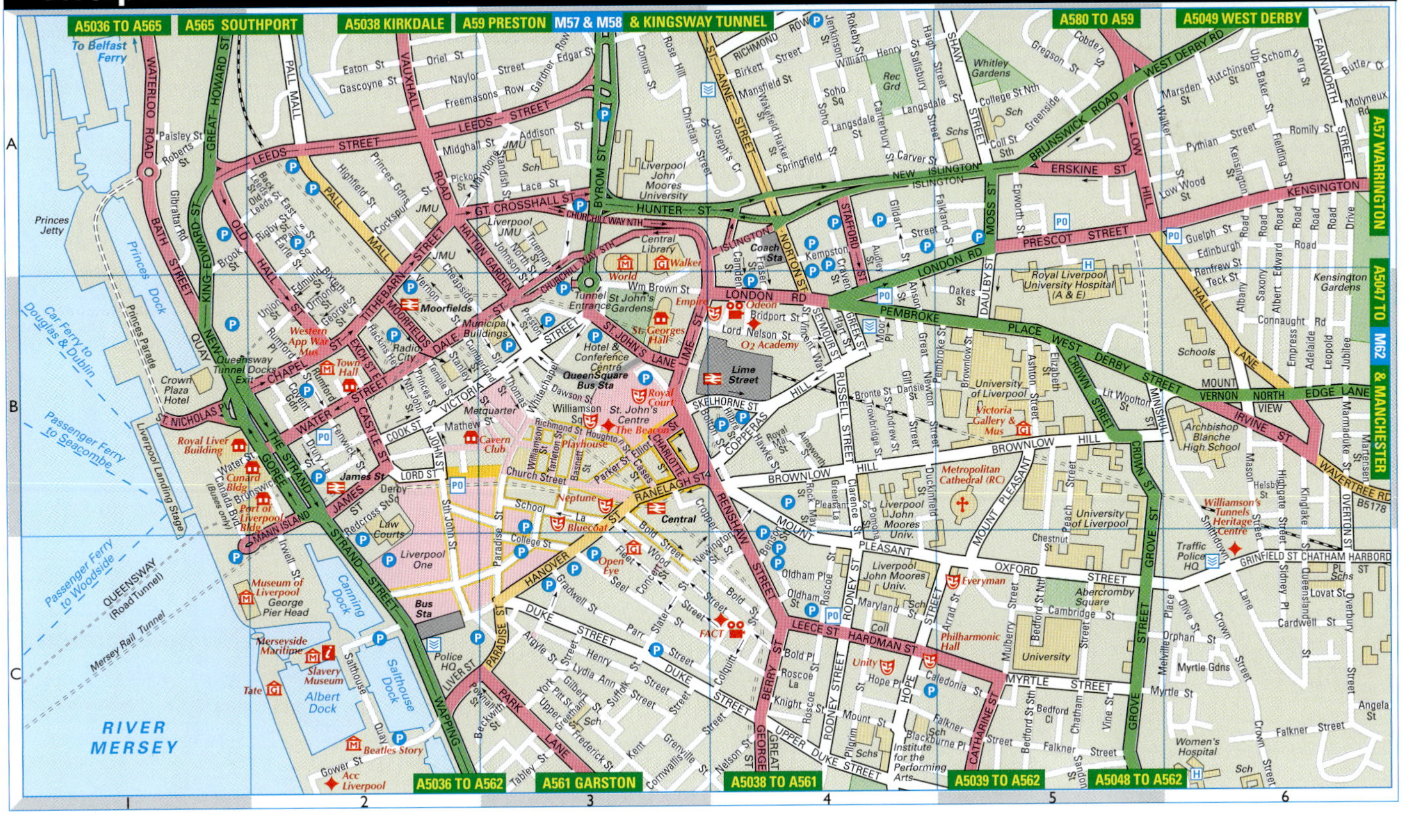
A5036 TO A565
A565 SOUTHPORT
A5038 KIRKDALE
A59 PRESTON
M57 & M58
& KINGSWAY TUNNEL
A580 TO A59
A5049 WEST DERBY
A57 WARRINGTON
A5047 TO M62 & MANCHESTER
A5036 TO A562
A561 GARSTON
A5038 TO A561
A5039 TO A562
A5048 TO A562
To Belfast Ferry
Princes Jetty
Princes Dock
Car Ferry to Douglas & Dublin
Passenger Ferry to Seacombe
Passenger Ferry to Woodside
QUEENSWAY (Road Tunnel)
Mersey Rail Tunnel
RIVER MERSEY
Royal Liver Building
Cunard Bldg
Port of Liverpool Bldg
Museum of Liverpool
Merseyside Maritime Museum
Slavery Museum
Albert Dock
Tate
Beatles Story
Liverpool One
Lime Street
Queen Square Bus Sta
St. John's Centre
Walker
World Museum
Central Library
St. George's Hall
Metropolitan Cathedral (RC)
Liverpool John Moores University
University of Liverpool
Royal Liverpool University Hospital (A & E)
Victoria Gallery & Mus
Philharmonic Hall
Everyman
Unity
Williamson's Tunnels Heritage Centre
Women's Hospital
Cavern Club
Moorfields
Central
Playhouse
Empire
O2 Academy
FACT

REGENT'S PARK
REGENT'S PARK
SOMERS TOWN
St. Pancras International
King's Cross
Euston
FITZROVIA
BLOOMSBURY
MARYLEBONE
British Museum
SOHO
MAYFAIR
ST. JAMES'S
HYDE PARK
GREEN PARK
ST. JAMES'S PARK
Buckingham Palace Gardens
Buckingham Palace
WESTMINSTER
Westminster Abbey
Houses of Parliament
London Eye Pier
BELGRAVIA
Victoria
Charing Cross
Piccadilly Circus
Oxford Circus
Marble Arch
Wellington Arch
OXFORD STREET
PICCADILLY
REGENT STREET
STRAND
PARK LANE
VICTORIA EMBANKMENT
WESTMINSTER BRIDGE
LAMBETH BRIDGE
Miles

HOXTON
SHOREDITCH
FINSBURY
CLERKENWELL
HOLBORN
THE CITY
SOUTHWARK
LAMBETH
BETHNAL GREEN ROAD
RIVER THAMES
Liverpool Street
Fenchurch Street
Cannon Street
Blackfriars
Waterloo
London Bridge
The Barbican
St Paul's Cathedral
Tower of London
Tate Modern
Shakespeare's Globe Theatre
Imperial War Museum
Congestion Charging Zone
London Docklands
STEPNEY
POPLAR
CANNING TOWN
WAPPING
ROTHERHITHE
BERMONDSEY
MILLWALL
ISLE OF DOGS
DEPTFORD
GREENWICH
Miles

Lincoln

0 Miles ¼

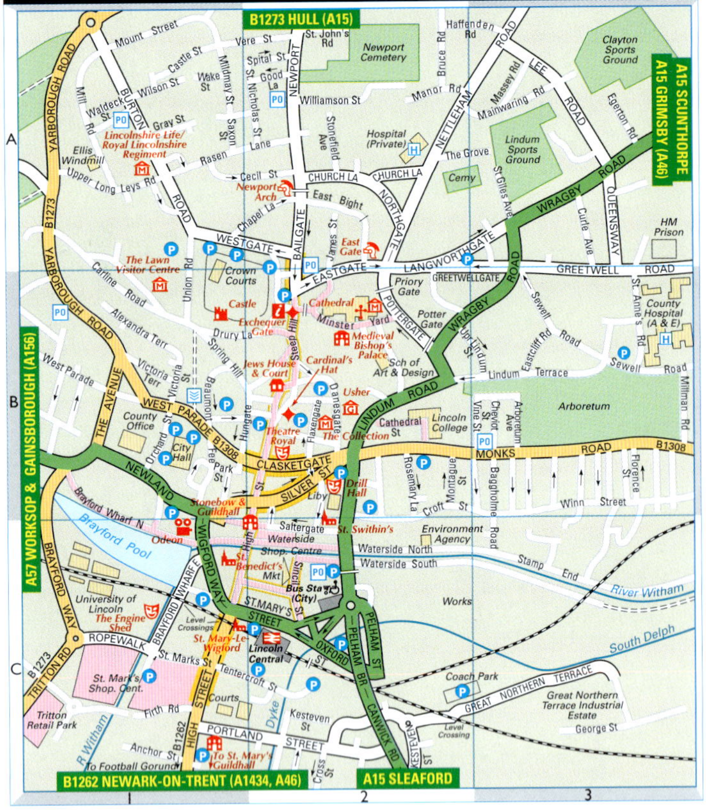

Luton

0 Miles ¼

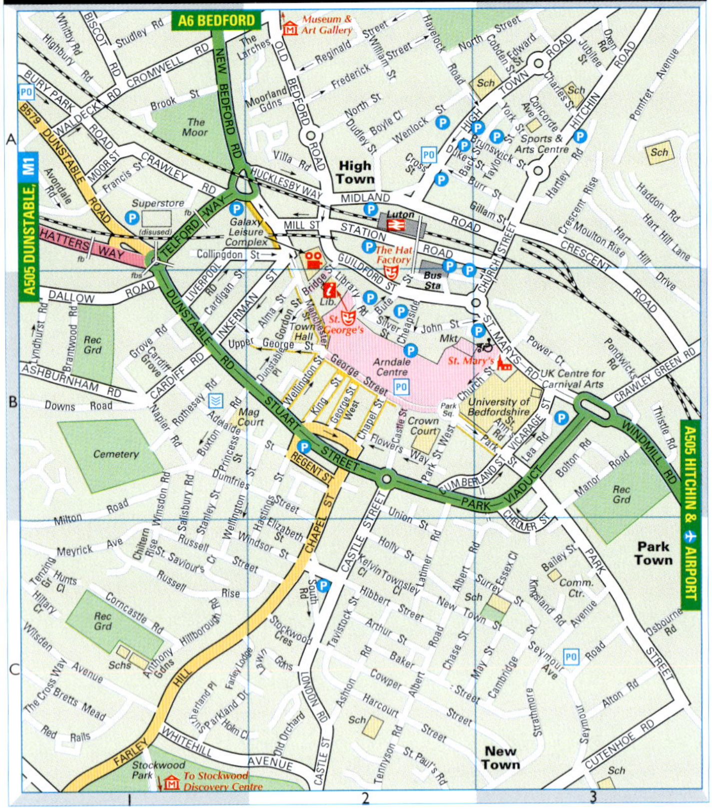

Manchester

0 Miles ¼

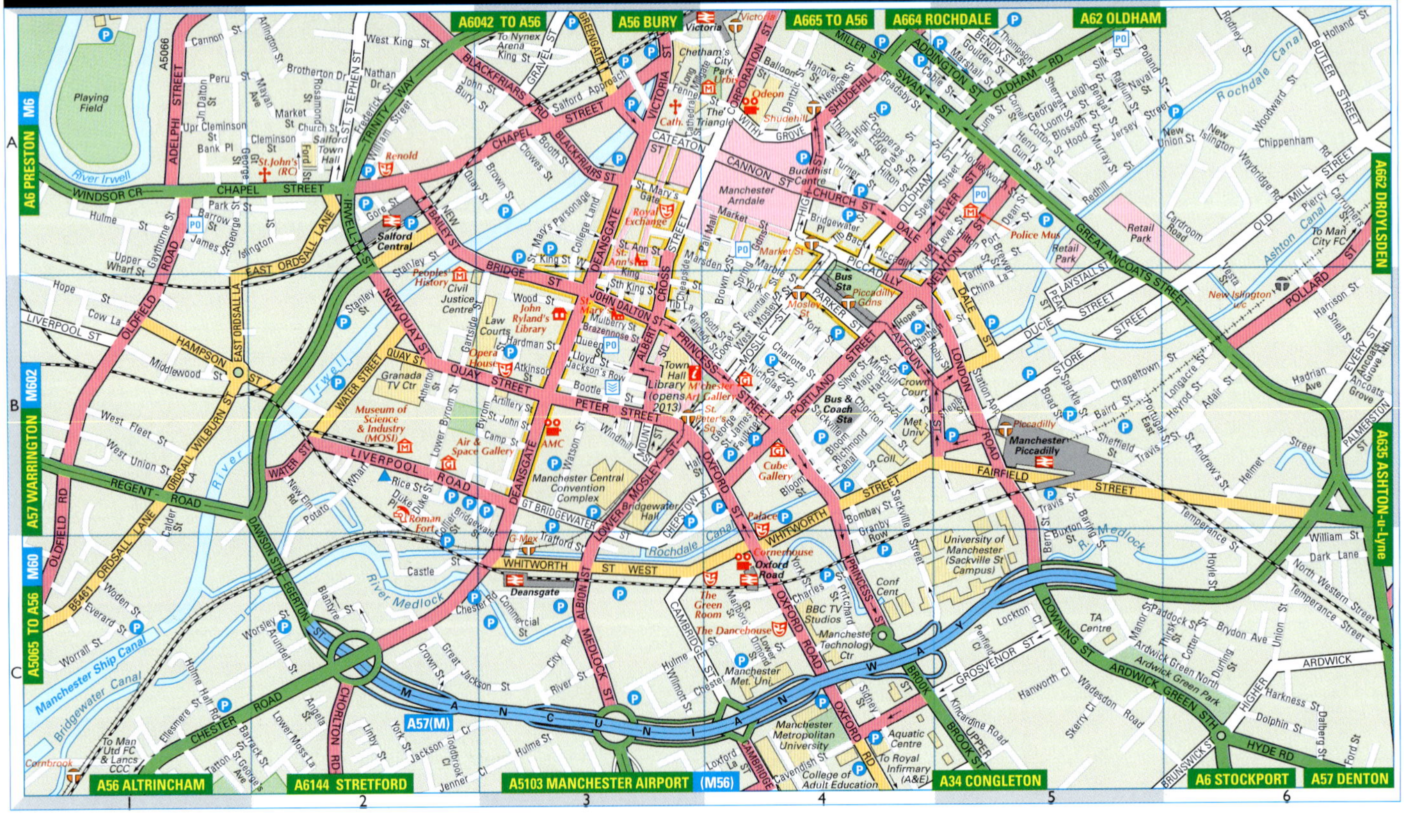

Maidstone

0 Miles ¼

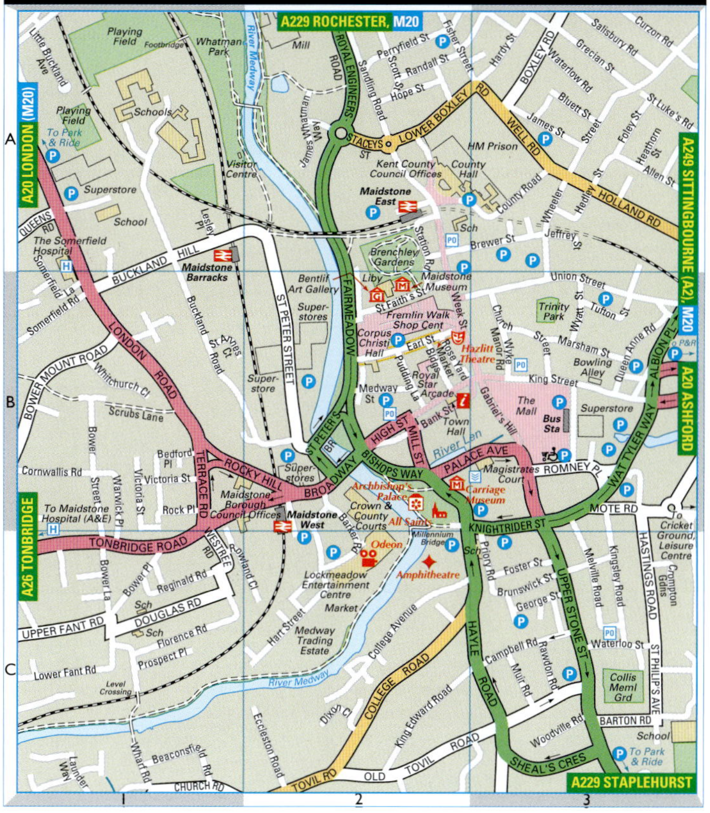

Middlesbrough

0 Miles ¼

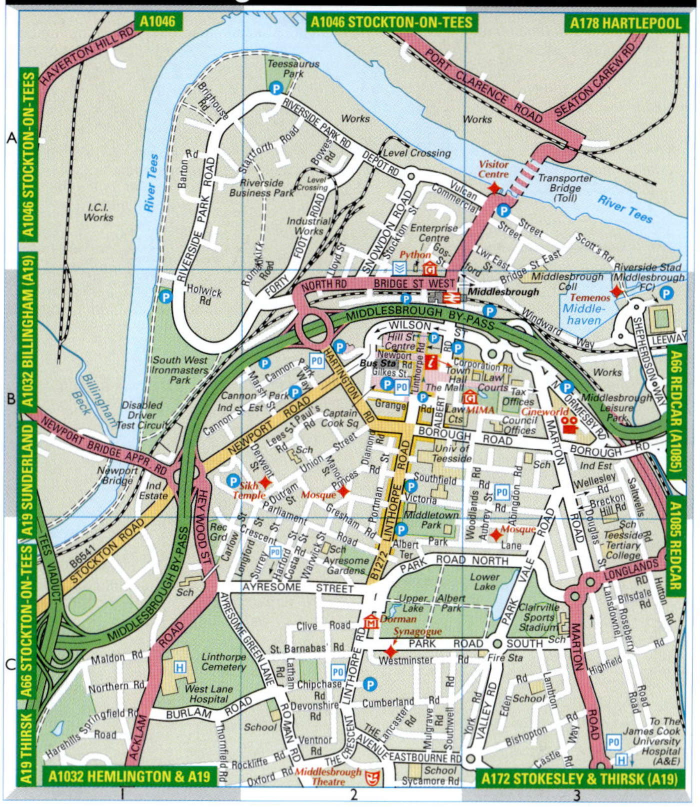

Milton Keynes

0 Miles ¼

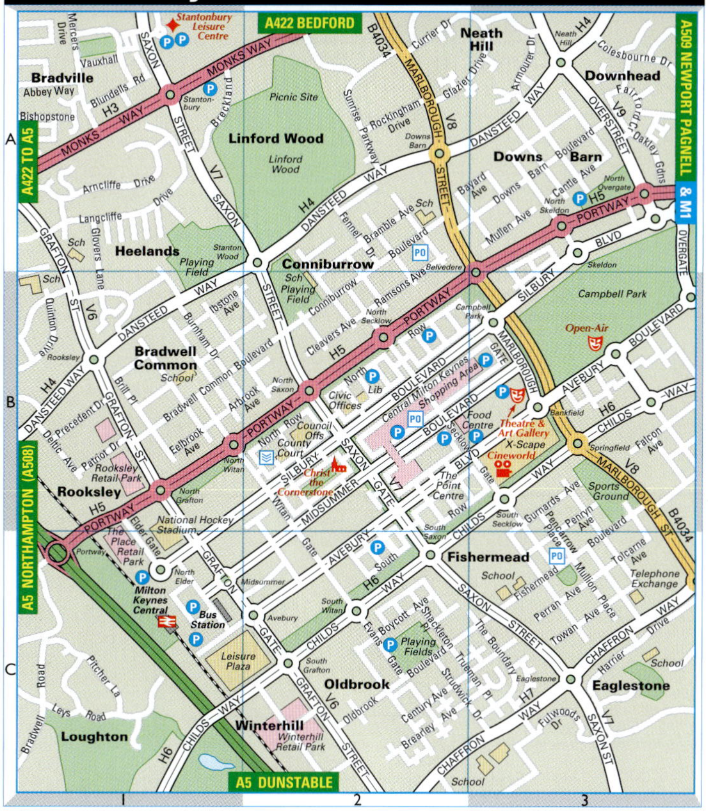

Newcastle upon Tyne

0 Miles ¼

Newport / Casnewydd

0 Miles ¼

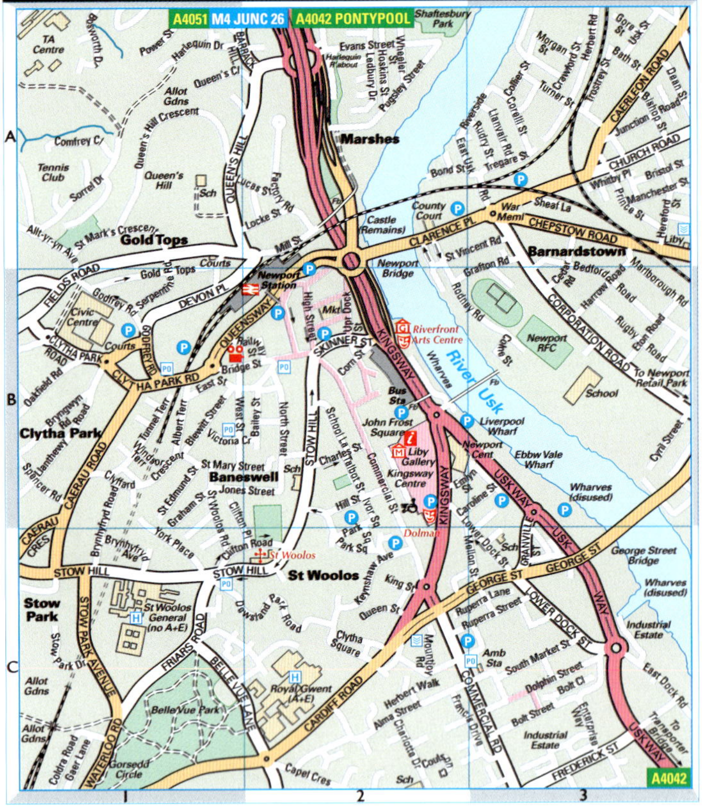

Northampton

0 Miles ¼

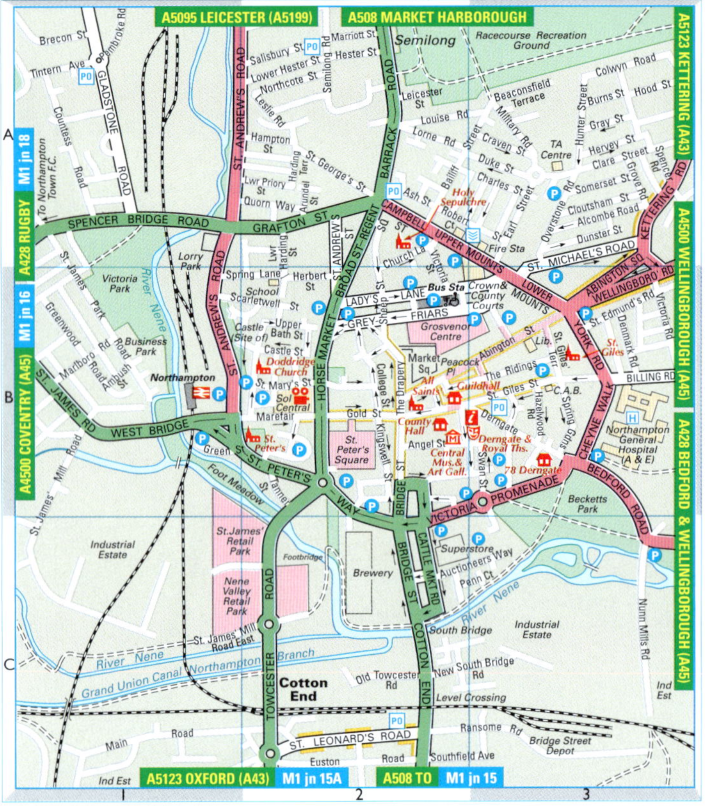

Norwich

0 Miles ¼

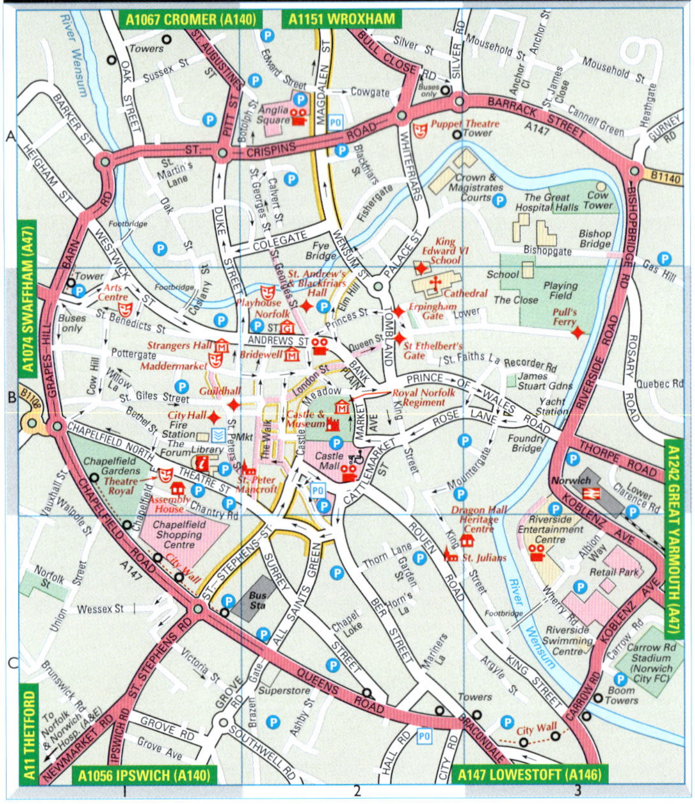

Nottingham

0 Miles ¼

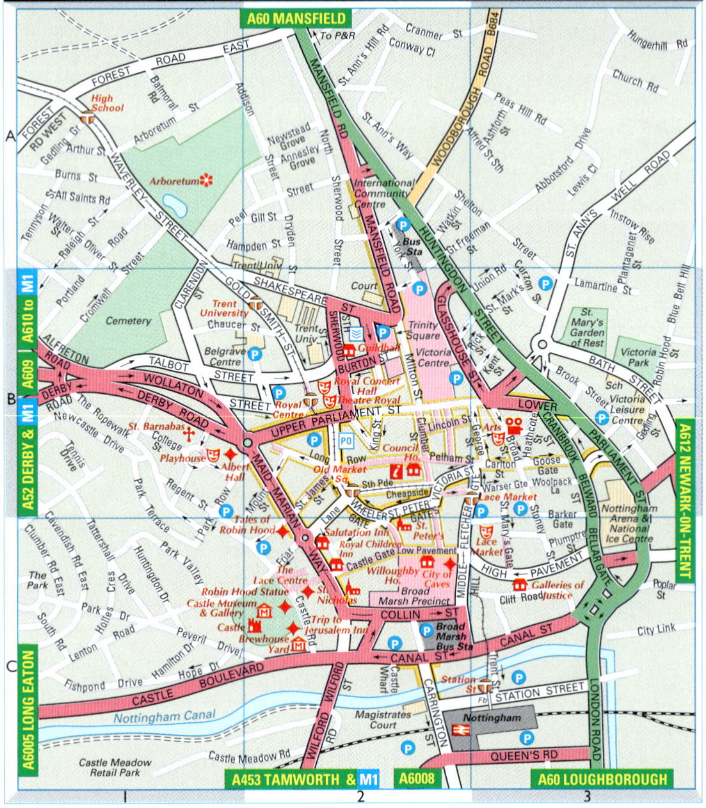

Oxford

0 Miles ¼

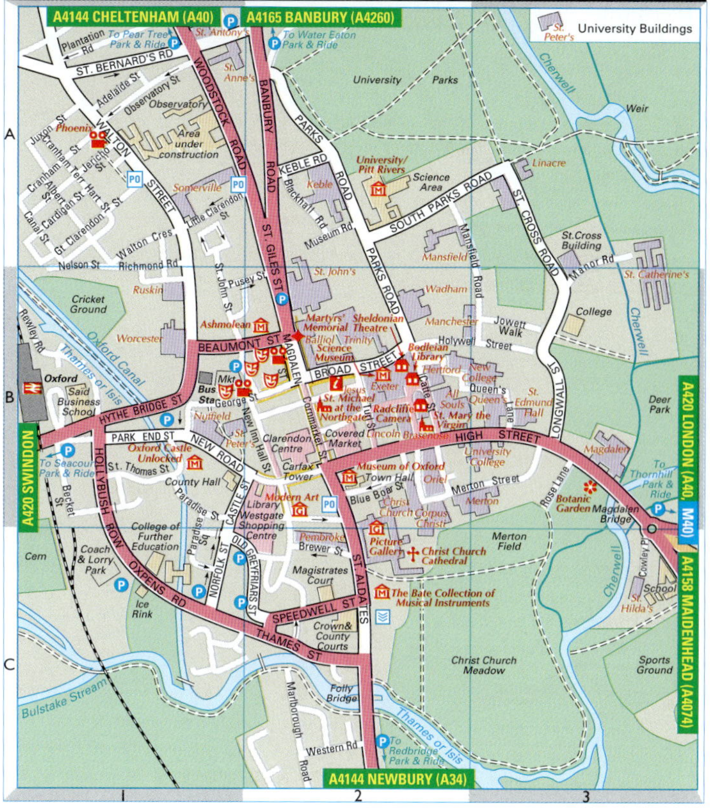

Peterborough

0 Miles ¼

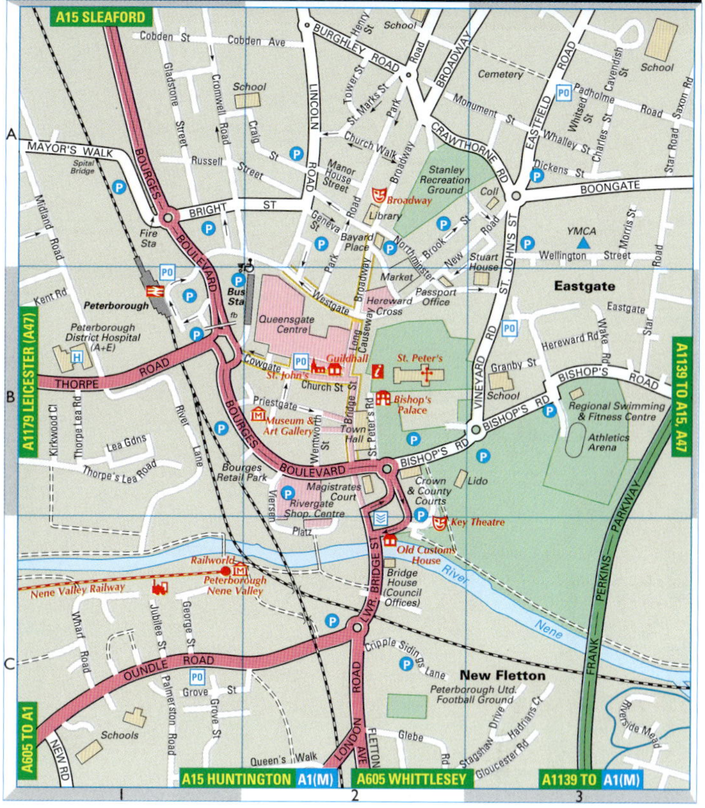

Plymouth

0 Miles ¼

Portsmouth

0 Miles ¼

Reading

0 Miles ¼

Salisbury

0 Miles ¼

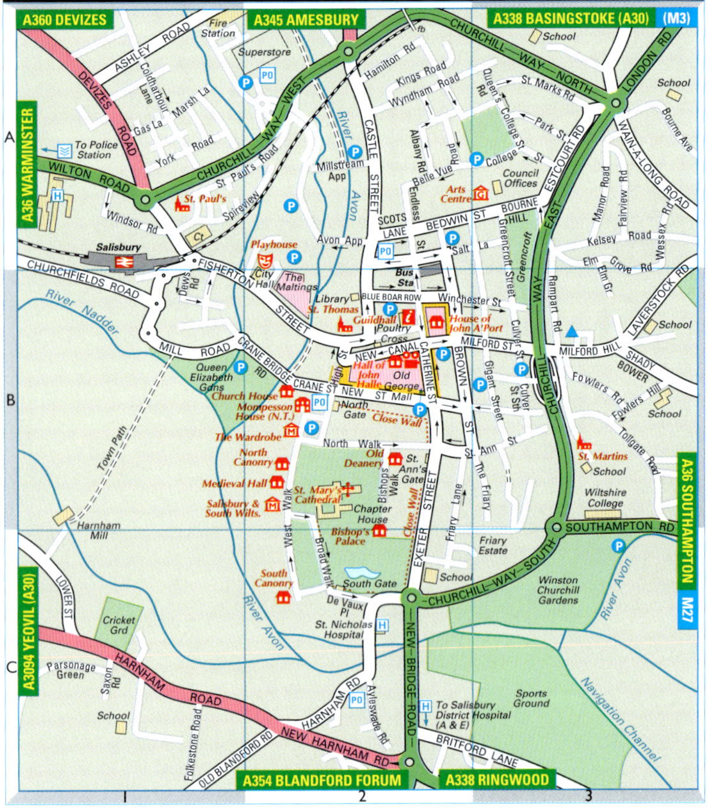

Scarborough

0 Miles ¼

Southampton

0 Miles ¼

Sheffield

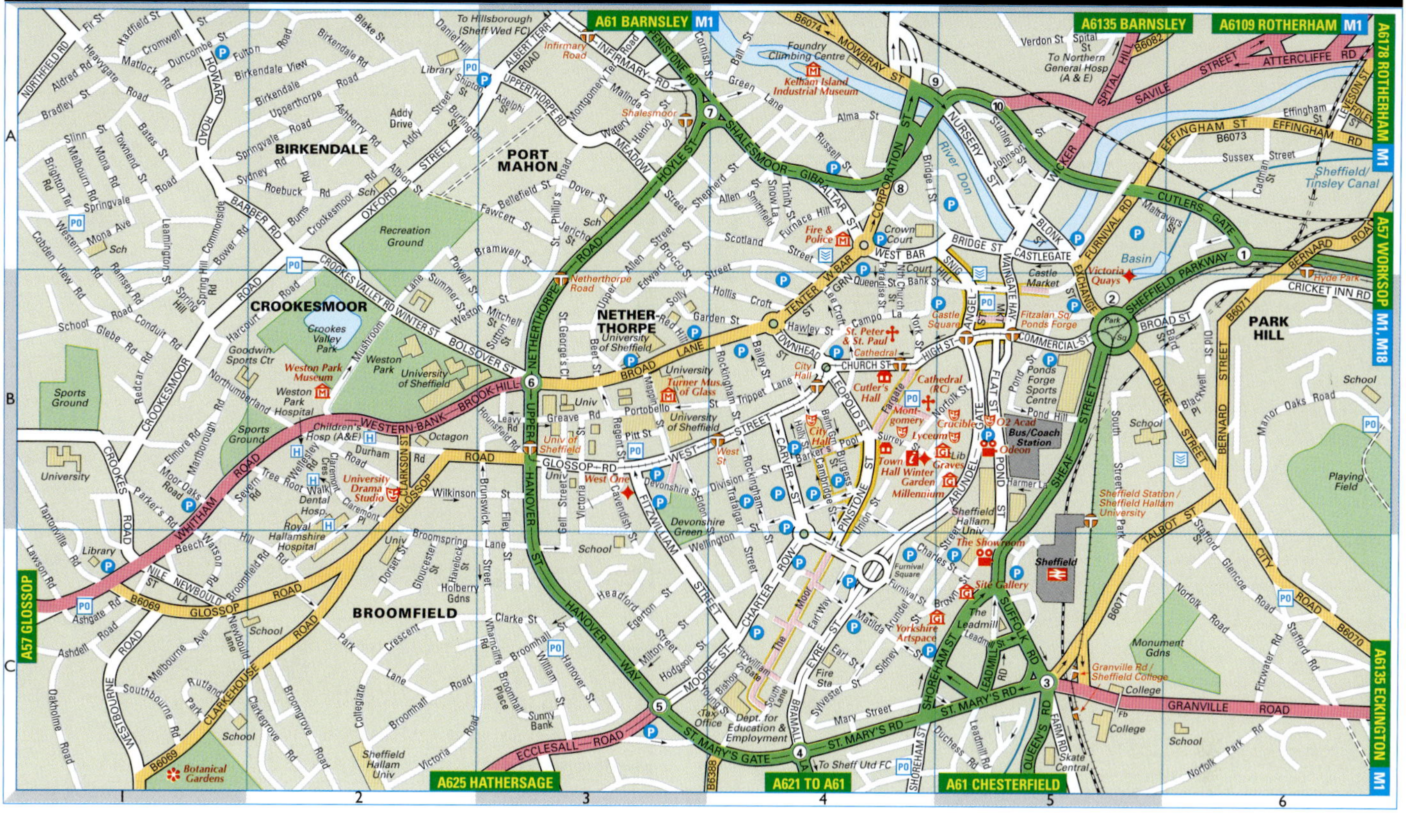
0 Miles ¼
A61 BARNSLEY M1
A6135 BARNSLEY
A6109 ROTHERHAM M1
A6178 ROTHERHAM M1
A57 WORKSOP M1, M18
A6135 ECKINGTON M1
A61 CHESTERFIELD
A621 TO A61
A625 HATHERSAGE
A57 GLOSSOP
BIRKENDALE
PORT MAHON
CROOKESMOOR
NETHER-THORPE
PARK HILL
BROOMFIELD
University of Sheffield
Weston Park Museum
Sheffield Hallam Univ
Sheffield
Bus/Coach Station
Castle Market
Victoria Quays
Crucible
Lyceum
Town Hall
Winter Garden
Millennium
City Hall
Cathedral
Botanical Gardens
To Sheff Utd FC
To Hillsborough (Sheff Wed FC)
Thames
1
2
3
4
5
6
A
B
C

Southend-on-Sea

0 Miles ¼
A127 BASILDON & SOUTHEND AIRPORT
A13 TILBURY
A13 SHOEBURYNESS
Southend United F.C.
Civic Centre
Southend Victoria
The Victoria
Southend Central
Univ of Essex
South Essex College
Beecroft Art Gallery
Cliffs Pavilion
The Royals
Alexandra Yacht Club
Adventure Island
Southend Pier
Southend Pier Railway
Thames Estuary
1
2
3
A
B
C

Stoke

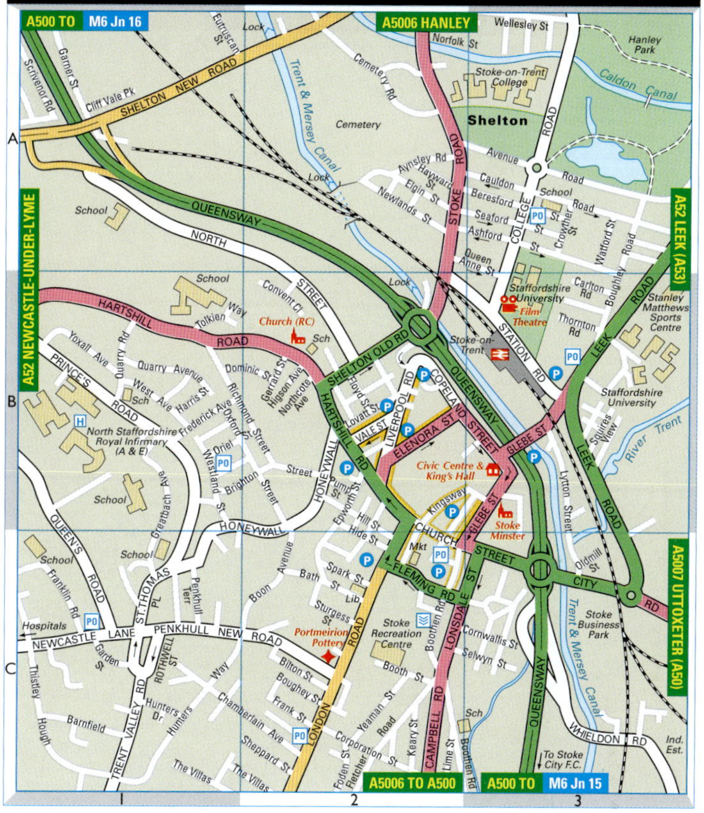
0 Miles ¼
A500 TO M6 Jn 16
A5006 HANLEY
A52 NEWCASTLE-UNDER-LYME
A52 LEEK (A53)
A5007 UTTOXETER (A50)
A5006 TO A500
A500 TO M6 Jn 15
Shelton
Stoke-on-Trent College
Staffordshire University
Stoke-on-Trent
North Staffordshire Royal Infirmary (A & E)
Civic Centre & King's Hall
Stoke Minster
Stoke Recreation Centre
Portmeirion Pottery
Stoke Business Park
To Stoke City F.C.
Trent & Mersey Canal
Caldon Canal
River Trent
Cemetery
1
2
3
A
B
C

Stratford-upon-Avon

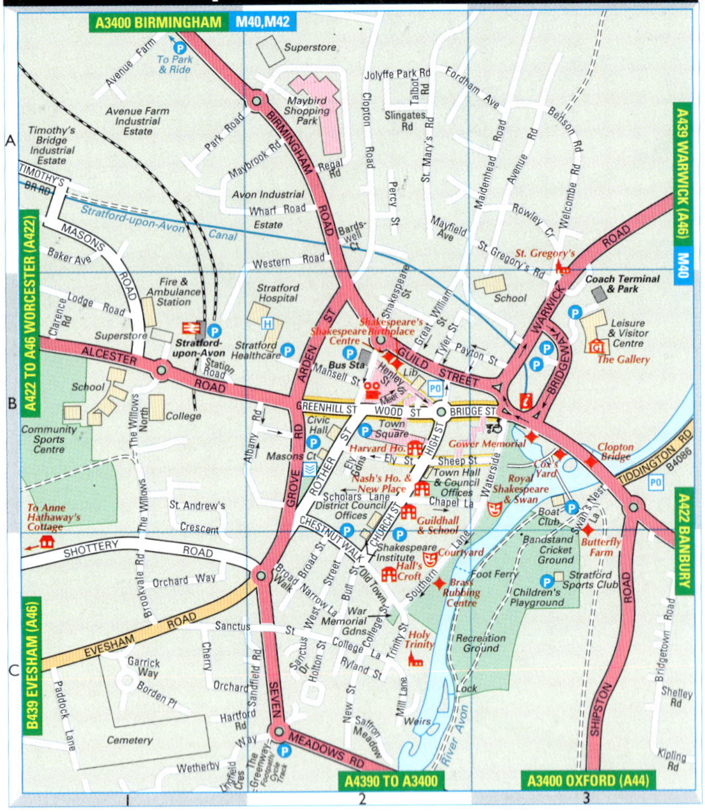

Sunderland

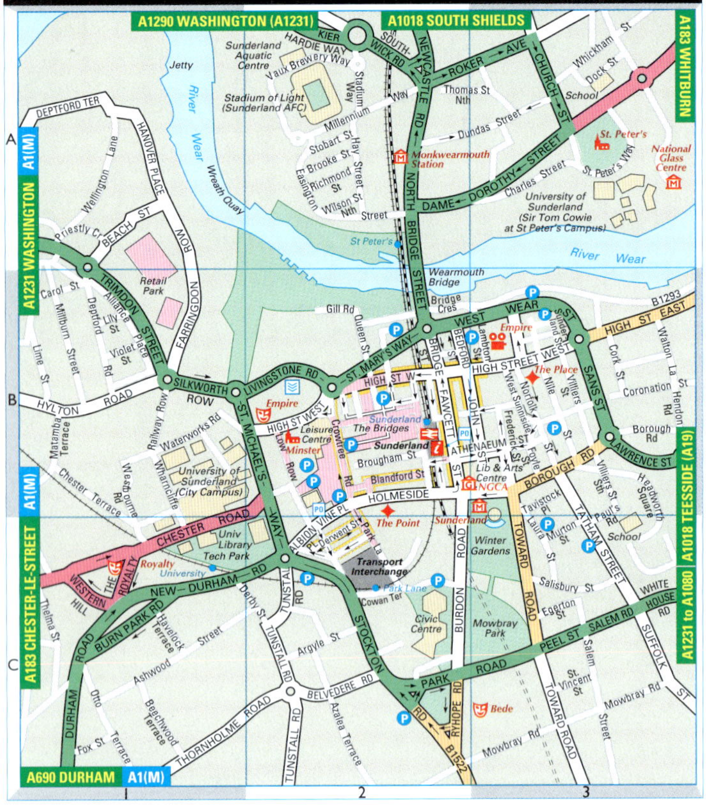

Swansea / Abertawe

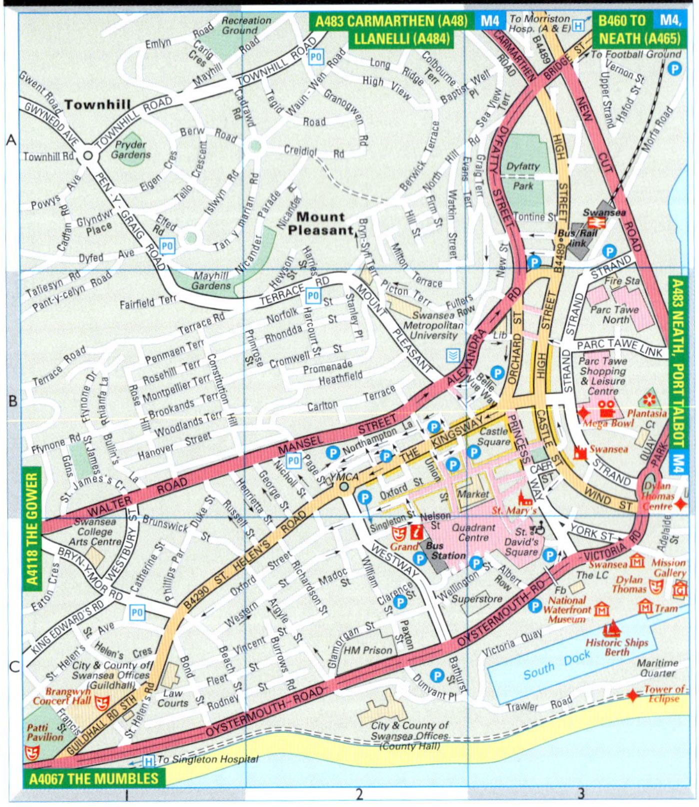

Swindon

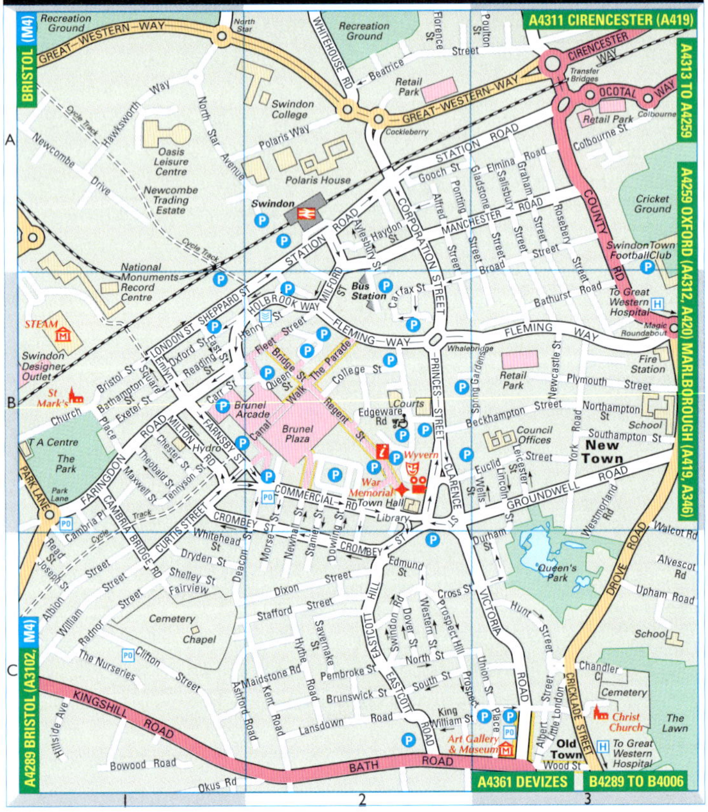

Taunton

0 Miles ¼

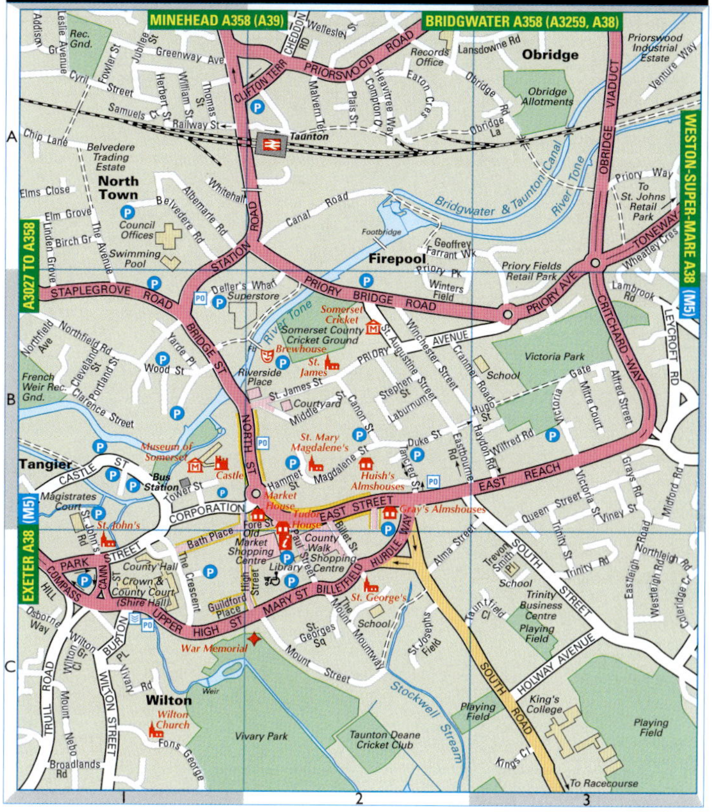

Telford

0 Miles ¼

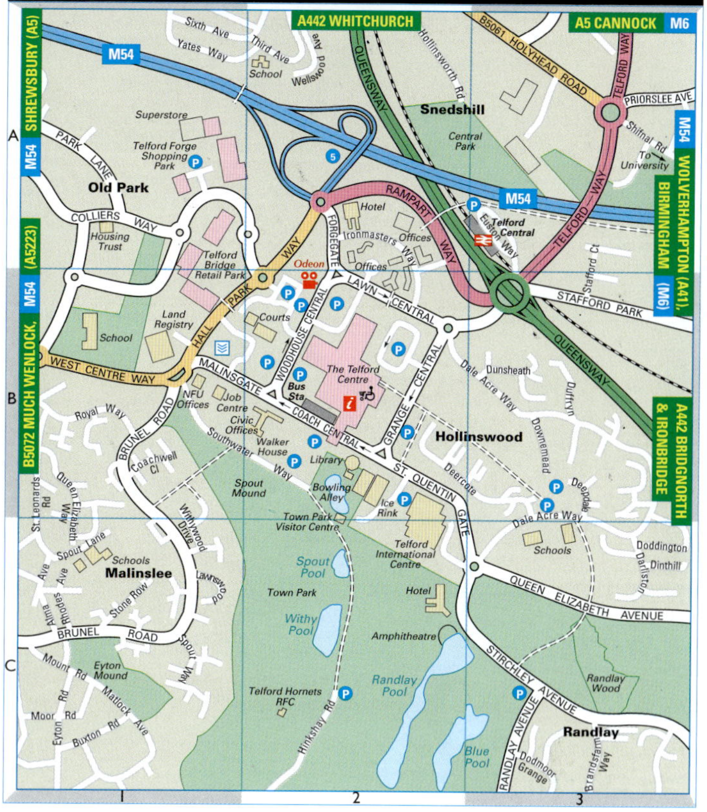

Winchester

0 Miles ¼

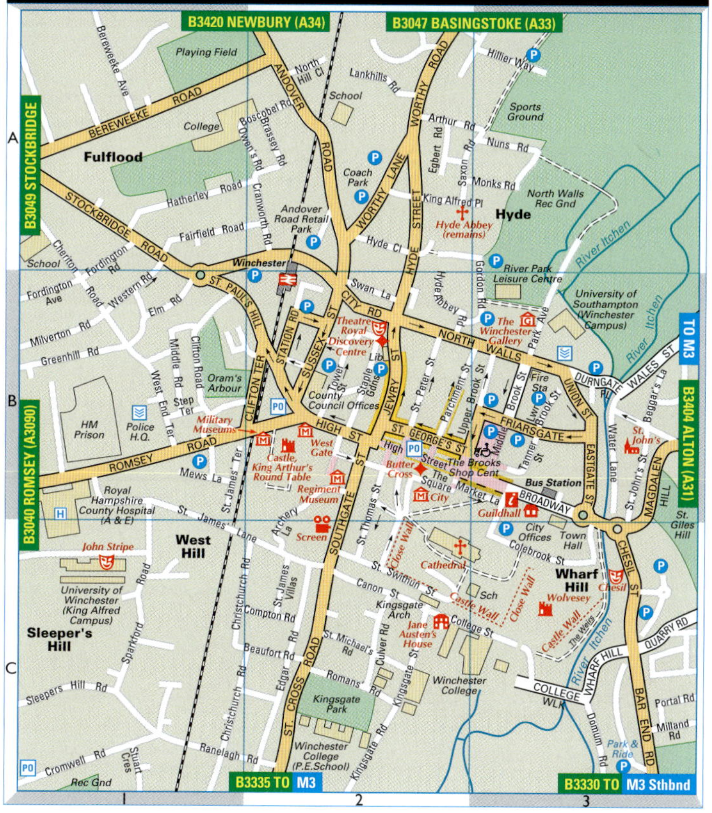

Windsor

0 Miles ¼

Wolverhampton

0 Miles ¼

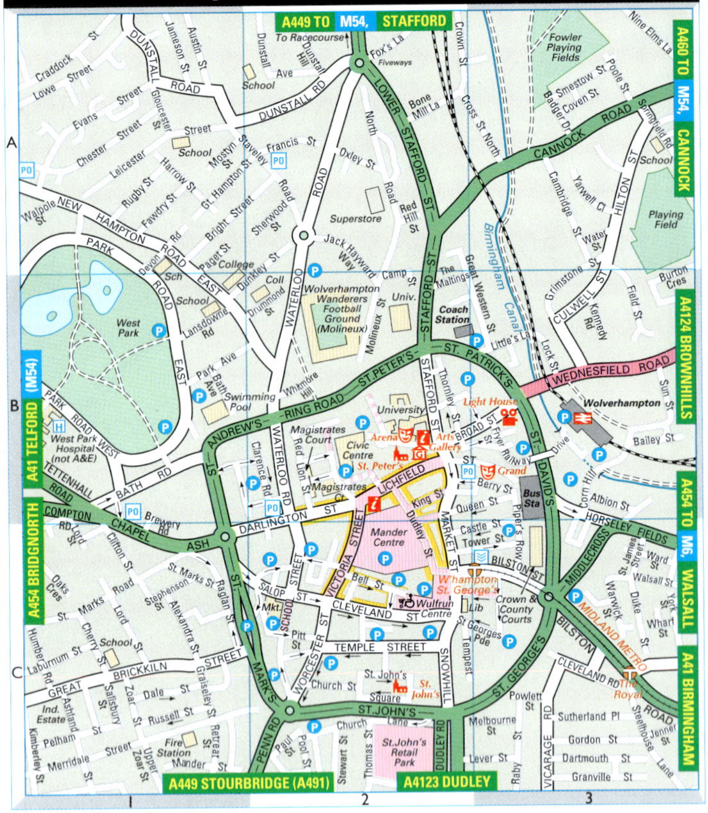

Worcester

0 Miles ¼

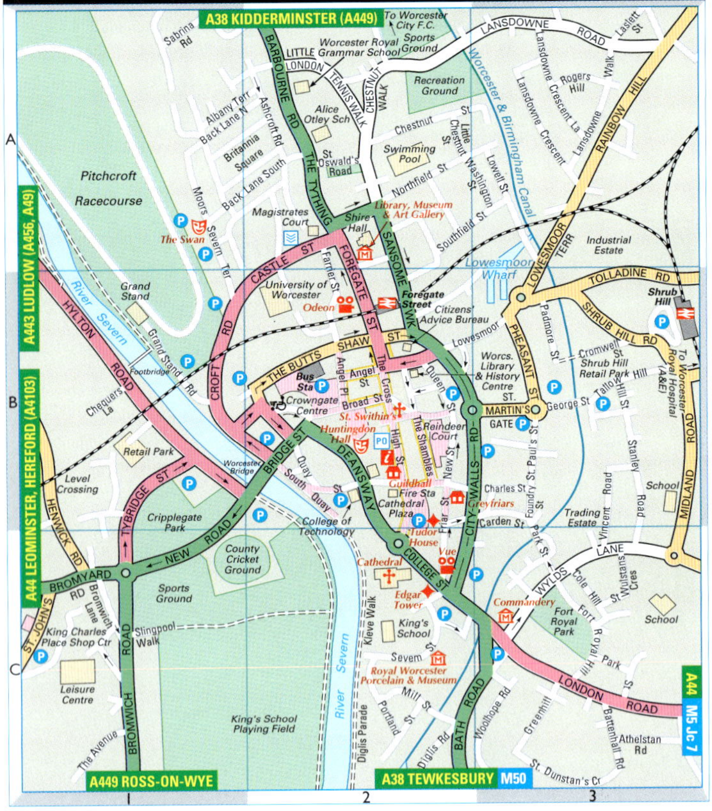

Wrexham / Wrecsam

0 Miles ¼

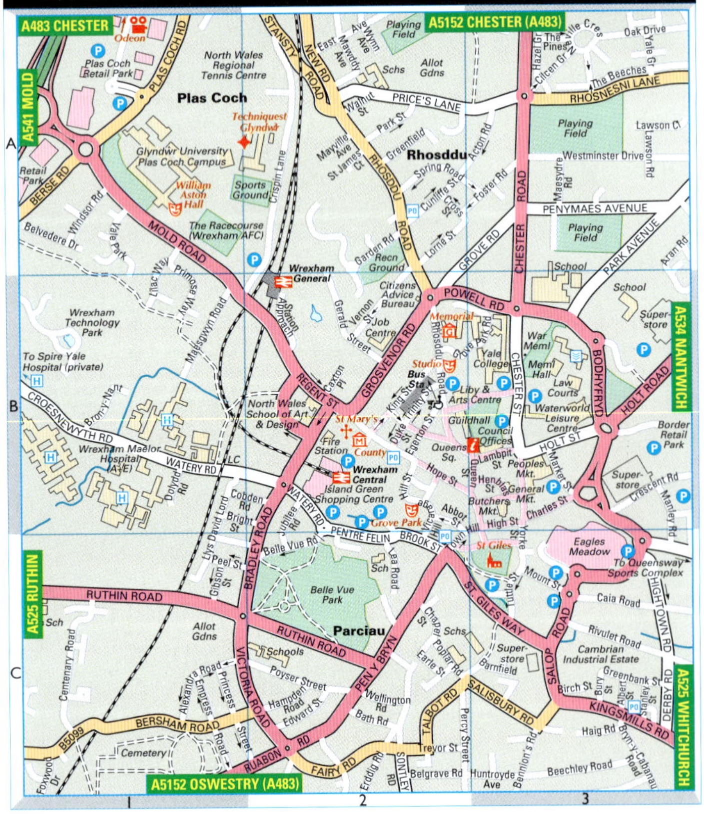

York

0 Miles ¼

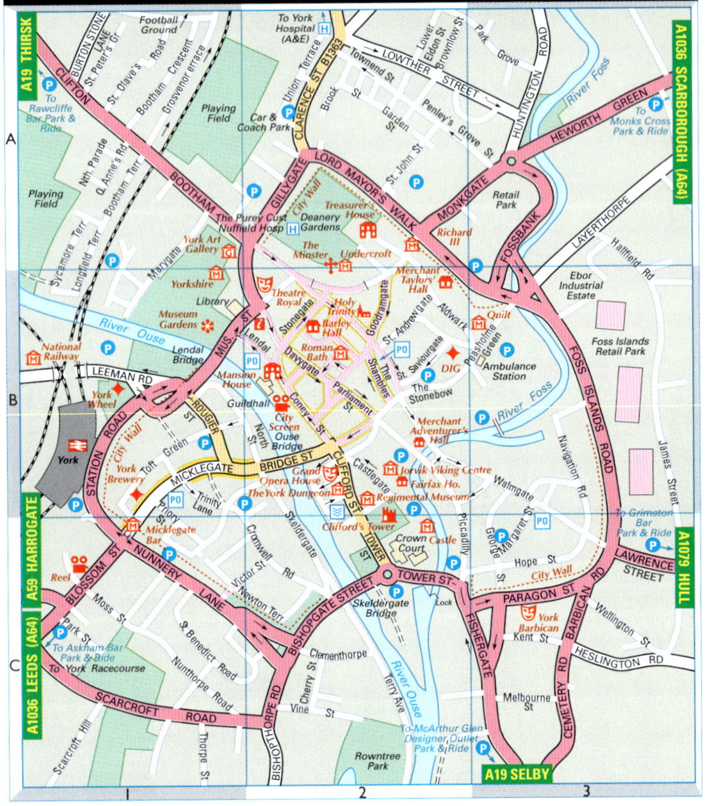

Town plan indexes

Aberdeen 175

Aberdeen B2
Aberdeen Grammar School A1
Academy, The B2
Albert Basin B3
Albert Quay B3
Albury Rd C1
Alford Pl B1
Art Gallery A2
Arts Ctr A2
Back Wynd A2
Baker St A1
Beach Blvd A3
Belmont B2
Belmont St B2
Berry St A2
Blackfriars St A2
Bloomfield Rd C1
Bon Accord Ctr A2
Bon-Accord St B1/C1
Bridge St B2
Broad St A2
Bus Station B2
Car Ferry Terminal B3
Castlegate A3
Central Library A1
Chapel St B1
Cineworld B2
College A2
College St B2
Commerce St A3
Commercial Quay B3
Community Ctr A3/C1
Constitution St A3
Cotton St A3
Crown St B2
Denburn Rd A2
Devanha Gdns C2
Devanha Gdns South C2
East North St A3
Esslemont Ave A1
Ferryhill Rd C2
Ferryhill Terr C2
Fish Market B3
Fonthill Rd C1
Galleria, The B1
Gallowgate A2
George St A2
Glenbervie Rd C3
Golden Sq B1
Grampian Rd C3
Great Southern Rd C1
Guild St B2
Hardgate B1/C1
His Majesty's Theatre A1
Holburn St C1
Hollybank Pl C1
Huntly St B1
Hutcheon St A1
Information Ctr B2
John St A2
Justice St A3
King St A2
Langstane Pl B1
Lemon Tree, The A2
Library C1
Loch St A2
Maberly St A1
Marischal College A2
Maritime Mus & Provost Ross's Ho B2
Market St B2/B3
Menzies Rd C3
Mercat Cross A3
Millburn St C2
Miller St A3
Market B2
Mount St A1
Music Hall B1
North Esp East C3
North Esp West C2
Oscar Rd C3
Palmerston Rd C2
Park St A3
Police Station A2
Polmuir Rd C2
Post Office A1/A2/A3/B1/C3
Provost Skene's House A2
Queen St A2
Regent Quay B3
Regent Road B3
Robert Gordon's Coll A2
Rose St B1
Rosemount Pl A1
Rosemount Viaduct A1
St Andrew St A2
St Andrew's Cath A3
St Mary's Cath B1
St Nicholas Ctr A2
St Nicholas St A2
School Hill A2
Sinclair Rd C3
Skene Sq A1
Skene St B1
South College St C2
South Crown St C2
South Esp East C3
South Esp West C3
South Mount St A1
Sports Ctr C3
Spring Garden A2
Springbank Terr C2
Summer St B1
Swimming Pool B1
Thistle St B1
Tolbooth A3
Town House A2
Trinity Ctr B2
Trinity Quay B3
Union Row B1
Union Square B2
Union St B1/B2
Upper Dock B3
Upper Kirkgate A2
Victoria Bridge C3
Victoria Dock B3
Victoria Rd C3
Victoria St B2
Virginia St A3
Vue B2
Wellington Pl B2
West North St A2
Whinhill Rd C1
Willowbank Rd C1
Windmill Brae B2
Woolmanhill Hospl A1

Bath 175

Alexandra Park C2
Alexandra Rd C2
Approach Golf Courses (Public) A1
Bath Aqua Glass A2
Archway St C3
Assembly Rooms & Mus of Costume A2
Avon St B2
Barton St B2
Bath Abbey B2
Bath City College B2
Bath Pavilion B3
Bath Rugby Club B3
Bath Spa Station C3
Bathwick St A3
Beckford Road A3
Beechen Cliff Rd C2
Bennett St A2
Bloomfield Ave C1
Broad Quay C2
Broad St B2
Brock St A1
Building of Bath Museum A2
Bus Station C2
Calton Gdns C2
Calton Rd C2
Camden Cr A2
Cavendish Rd A1
Cemetery B1
Charlotte St B2
Chaucer Rd C2
Cheap St B2
Circus Mews A2
Claverton St C2
Corn St C2
Cricket Ground B3
Daniel St A3
Edward St B3
Ferry La B3
First Ave C1
Forester Ave A3
Forester Rd A3
Gays Hill A2
George St B2
Great Pulteney St B3
Green Park B1
Green Park Rd B2
Grove St B2
Guildhall B2
Harley St A2
Hayesfield Park C1
Henrietta Gdns A3
Henrietta Mews B3
Henrietta Park B3
Henrietta Rd A3
Henrietta St B3
Henry St B2
Herschel Museum of Astronomy B1
Holburne Museum B3
Holloway C2
Information Ctr B2
James St West B1/B2
Jane Austen Ctr B2
Julian Rd A1
Junction Rd C1
Kipling Ave C2
Lansdown Cr A1
Lansdown Gr A2
Lansdown Rd A2
Library B2
London Rd A3
London St A2
Lower Bristol Rd B1
Lower Oldfield Park C1
Lyncombe Hill C3
Manvers St B3
Maple Gr C1
Margaret's Hill A2
Marlborough Bldgs A1
Marlborough La B1
Midland Bridge Rd B1
Milk St B2
Milsom St B2
Monmouth St B2
Morford St A2
Museum of Bath at Work A2
New King St B1
No 1 Royal Cres A1
Norfolk Bldgs B1
Norfolk Cr B1
North Parade Rd B3
Oldfield Rd C1
Paragon A2
Pines Way B1
Podium Shopping Ctr B2
Police Station B3
Portland Pl A2
Post Office A1/A3/B2/C1/C2
Postal Museum B2
Powlett Rd A3
Prior Park Rd C3
Pulteney Bridge B2
Pulteney Gdns B3
Pulteney Rd B3/C3
Queen Sq B2
Raby Pl B3
Recreation Ground B3
Rivers St A2
Rockliffe Ave A3
Rockliffe Rd A3
Roman Baths & Pump Room B2
Rossiter Rd C3
Royal Ave A1
Royal Cr A1
Royal High School, The A2
Royal Victoria Park A1
St James Sq A1
St John's Rd A3
Shakespeare Ave C2
Southgate C2
South Pde B3
Sports & Leisure Ctr B3
Spring Gdns C3
Stall St B2
Stanier Rd B1
Superstore B1
Sydney Gdns A3
Sydney Pl B3
Sydney Rd B3
Theatre Royal B2
Thermae Bath Spa B2
The Tyning C3
Thomas St A3
Union St B2
Upper Bristol Rd B1
Upper Oldfield Park C1
Victoria Art Gallery B2
Victoria Bridge Rd B1
Walcot St B2
Wells Rd C1
Westgate Buildings B2
Westgate St B2
Weston Rd A1
Widcombe Hill C3

Birmingham 176

Abbey St A2
Aberdeen St A1
Acorn Gr B2
Adams St A5
Adderley St C5
Albert St B4/B5
Albion St B2
Alcester St C5
Aldgate Gr A3
Alexandra Theatre C3
All Saint's St A2
All Saints Rd A2
Allcock St C5
Allesley St A4
Allison St C4
Alma Cr B6
Alston Rd C1
Arcadian Ctr C4
Arthur St C6
Assay Office B3
Aston Expressway A5
Aston Science Park B5
Aston St B4
Aston University B4/B5
Avenue Rd A5
BT Tower B3
Bacchus Rd A1
Bagot St B4
Banbury St B5
Barford Rd B1
Barford St C4
Barn St C5
Barnwell Rd C6
Barr St A3
Barrack St B5
Bartholomew St C4
Barwick St B4
Bath Row C3
Beaufort Rd C1
Belmont Row B5
Benson Rd A1
Berkley St C3
Bexhill Gr C3
Birchall St C5
Birmingham City FC C6
Birmingham City Hospital (A&E) A1
Bishopsgate St C3
Blews St A4
Bloomsbury St A6
Blucher St C3
Bordesley St C4
Bowyer St C5
Bradburne Way A5
Bradford St C5
Branston St A3
Brearley St A4
Brewery St A4
Bridge St A3
Bridge St C3
Bridge St West A4
Brindley Dr B3
Broad St C3
Broad St UGC C2
Broadway Plaza C2
Bromley St C5
Bromsgrove St C4
Brookfield Rd A2
Browning St C2
Bryant St A1
Buckingham St A3
Bullring C4
Bull St B4
Cambridge St C3
Camden Dr B3
Camden St B2
Cannon St C4
Cardigan St B5
Carlisle St A1
Carlyle Rd C1
Caroline St B3
Carver St B2
Cato St A6
Cattell Rd C6
Cattells Gr A6
Cawdor Cr C1
Cecil St B4
Cemetery A2/B2
Cemetery La A2
Ctr Link Ind Est A6
Charlotte St B3
Cheapside C4
Chester St A5
Children's Hospital (A&E) B4
Church St B4
Claremont Rd A2
Clarendon Rd C1
Clark St C1
Clement St B3
Clissold St B2
Cliveland St B4
Coach Station C5
College St B2
Colmore Circus B4
Colmore Row B4
Commercial St C3
Constitution Hill B3
Convention Ctr, The C3
Cope St B2
Coplow St B1
Corporation St B4
Council House B3
County Court B4
Coveley Gr A2
Coventry Rd C6
Coventry St C5
Cox St B3
Crabtree Rd A2
Cregoe St C3
Crescent Ave A2
Crescent Theatre C3
Cromwell St A6
Cromwell St B3
Curzon St B5
Cuthbert Rd B1
Dale End B4
Dart St C6
Dartmouth Circus A4
Dartmouth Middleway A5
Dental Hospital B4
Deritend C5
Devon St A6
Devonshire St A1
Digbeth Civic Hall C5
Digbeth High St C4
Dolman St B6
Dover St A1
Duchess Rd C2
Duddeston B6
Duddeston Manor Rd B5
Duddeston Mill Rd B6
Duddeston Mill Trading Estate B6
Dudley Rd B1
Edgbaston Sh Ctr C2
Edmund St B3
Edward St B3
Elkington St A4
Ellen St B2
Ellis St C3
Erskine St B6
Essex St C4
Eyre St B2
Farm Croft A3
Farm St A3
Fazeley St B4/C5
Felstead Way B5
Finstall Cl B5
Five Ways C2
Fleet St B3
Floodgate St C5
Ford St A2
Fore St C4
Forster St B5
Francis Rd C2
Francis St B5
Frankfort St A4
Frederick St B3
Freeth St C1
Freightliner Terminal B6
Garrison La C6
Garrison St B6
Gas St C3
Geach St A4
George St B3
George St West B2
Gibb St C5
Gillott Rd B1
Gilby Rd C2
Glover St C5
Goode Ave A2
Goodrick Way A6
Gordon St B6
Graham St B3
Granville St C3
Gray St C6
Great Barr St C5
Great Charles St B3
Great Francis St B6
Great Hampton Row A3
Great Hampton St A3
Great King St A3
Great Lister St A5
Great Tindal St C2
Green La C6
Green St C5
Greenway St C6
Grosvenor St West C2
Guest Gr A3
Guild Cl C2
Guildford Dr A4
Guthrie Cl A3
Hagley Rd C1
Hall St B3
Hampton St A3
Handsworth New Rd A1
Hanley St B4
Harford St A3
Harmer Rd A2
Harold Rd C1
Hatchett St A4
Heath Mill La C5
Heath St B1
Heath St South B1
Heaton St A2
Heneage St B5
Henrietta St B4
Herbert Rd C6
High St C4
High St C5
Hilden Rd B5
Hill St C3/C4
Hindlow Cl B6
Hingeston St B2
Hippodrome Theatre C4
HM Prison A1
Hockley Circus A2
Hockley Hill A3
Hockley St A3
Holliday St C3
Holloway Circus C4
Holloway Head C3
Holt St B5
Hooper St B1
Horse Fair C4
Hospital St A4
Howard St B3
Howe St B5
Hubert St A5
Hunters Rd A2
Hunters Vale A3
Huntly Rd C2
Hurst St C4
Icknield Port Rd B1
Icknield Sq B2
Icknield St A2/B2
Ikon Gallery C3
Information Ctr C4
Inge St C4
Irving St C3
Ivy La C5
James Watt Queensway B4
Jennens Rd B5
Jewellery Quarter A3
Jewellery Quarter Museum B3
John Bright St C4
Keeley St C6
Kellett Rd B5
Kent St C4
Kenyon St B3
Key Hill A3
Kilby Ave C2
King Edwards Rd B2
King Edwards Rd C3
Kingston Rd C6
Kirby Rd A1
Ladywood Arts & Leisure Ctr B1
Ladywood Middleway C2/C3
Ladywood Rd C1
Lancaster St B4
Landor St B6
Law Courts B4
Lawford Cl B5
Lawley Middleway B5
Ledbury Cl C2
Ledsam St B2
Lees St A1
Legge La B3
Lennox St A3
Library A6/C3
Library Walk B2
Lighthorne Ave B2
Link Rd B1
Lionel St B3
Lister St B5
Little Ann St C5
Little Hall Rd A6
Liverpool St C5
Livery St B3/B4
Lodge Rd A1
Lord St A5
Love La A5
Loveday St B4
Lower Dartmouth St C6
Lower Loveday St B4
Lower Tower St A4
Lower Trinty St C5
Ludgate Hill B3
Mailbox Ctr & BBC C3
Margaret St B3
Markby Rd A1
Marroway St B1
Maxstoke St C6
Melvina Rd A6
Meriden St C4
Metropolitan (RC) B4
Midland St B6
Milk St C5
Mill St A5
Millennium Point B5
Miller St A4
Milton St A4
Moat La C4
Montague Rd C1
Montague St C5
Monument Rd C1
Moor Street C4
Moor St Queensway C4
Moorsom St A4
Morville St C2
Mosborough Cr A3
Moseley St C4
Mott St B3
Mus & Art Gallery B3
Musgrave Rd A1
National Indoor Arena C2
National Sea Life Ctr C3
Navigation St C3
Nechell's Park Rd A6
Nechells Parkway B5
Nechells Pl A6
New Bartholomew St C4
New Canal St C5
New John St West A3
New Spring St B2
New St C4
New Street C4
New Summer St A4
New Town Row A4
Newhall Hill B3
Newhall St B3
Newton St B4
Newtown A4
Noel Rd C1
Norman St A1
Northbrook St B1
Northwood St B3
Norton St A2
Old Crown House C5
Old Rep Theatre, The C4
Old Snow Hill B4
Oliver Rd C1
Oliver St A5
Osler St C1
Oxford St C5
Pallasades Ctr C4
Palmer St C5
Paradise Circus C3
Paradise St C3
Park Rd A2
Park St C4
Pavilions Ctr C4
Paxton Rd A2
Peel St A1
Penn St B5
Pershore St C4
Phillips St A4
Pickford St C5
Pinfold St C4
Pitsford St A2
Plough & Harrow Rd C1
Police Station A4/B1/B4/C2/C4
Pope St B2
Portland Rd C1
Post Office A3/A5/B1/B3/B4/B5/C2/C3/C5
Preston Rd A1
Price St B4
Princip St B4
Printing House St B4
Priory Queensway B4
Pritchett St A4
Proctor St A5
Queensway B3
Radnor St A2
Rea St C4
Regent Pl B3
Register Office C3
Repertory Theatre C3
Reservoir Rd C1
Richard St A5
River St C5
Rocky La A5/A6
Rodney Cl C2
Roseberry St B2
Rotton Park St B1
Rupert St A5
Ruston St C2
Ryland St C2
St Andrew's Ind Est C6
St Andrew's Rd C6
St Andrew's St C6
St Bolton St C6
St Chads Queensway B4
St Clements Rd A6
St George's St A3
St James Pl B5
St Marks Cr B2
St Martin's C4
St Paul's B3
St Paul's B3
St Paul's Sq B3
St Philip's B4
St Stephen's St A4
St Thomas' Peace Garden C3
St Vincent St C2
Saltley Rd A6
Sand Pits Pde B3
Severn St C3
Shadwell St B4
Sheepcote St C2
Shefford Rd A4
Sherborne St C2
Shylton's Croft C2
Skipton Rd C2
Smallbrook Queensway C4
Smith St A3
Snow Hill B4
Snow Hill Queensway B4
Soho, Benson Rd A1
South Rd A2
Spencer St B3
Spring Hill B2
Staniforth St B4
Station St C4
Steelhouse La B4
Stephenson St C4
Steward St B2
Stirling Rd C1
Stour St B2
Suffolk St C3
Summer Hill Rd B2
Summer Hill St B2
Summer Hill Terr B2
Summer La A4
Summer Row B3
Summerfield Cr B1
Summerfield Park B1
Sutton St C3
Swallow St C3
Sydney Rd C6
Symphony Hall C3
Talbot St A1
Temple Row C4
Temple St C4
Templefield St C6
Tenby St B3
Tenby St North B2
Tennant St C2/C3
The Crescent A2
Thimble Mill La A6
Thinktank (Science & Discovery) B5
Thomas St A4
Thorpe St C4
Tilton Rd C6
Tower St A4
Town Hall C3
Trent St C5
Turner's Buildings A1
Unett St A3
Union Terr B5
Upper Trinity St C5
Uxbridge St A3
Vauxhall Gr B5
Vauxhall Rd B5
Vernon Rd C1
Vesey St B4
Viaduct St B5
Victoria Sq C3
Villa St A3
Vittoria St B3
Vyse St B3
Walter St A6
Wardlow Rd A5
Warstone La B2
Washington St C3
Water St B3
Waterworks Rd C1
Watery La C5
Well St A3
Western Rd B1
Wharf St A2
Wheeler St A3
Whitehouse St A5
Whitmore St A2
Whittall St B4
Wholesale Market C4
Wiggin St B1
Willes Rd A1
Windsor Ind Est A5
Windsor St A5
Windsor St B5
Winson Green Rd A1
Witton St C6
Wolseley St C6
Woodcock St B5

Blackpool 175

Abingdon St A1
Addison Cr A3
Adelaide St B1
Albert Rd B2
Alfred St B2
Ascot Rd A3
Ashton Rd C2
Auburn Gr C3
Bank Hey St B1
Banks St A1
Beech Ave A3
Bela Gr C2
Belmont Ave B2
Birley St A1
Blackpool & Fleetwood Tram B1
Blackpool & The Fylde College B2
Blackpool FC C2
Blackpool North A2
Blackpool Tower B1
Blundell St C1
Bonny St B1
Breck Rd B3
Bryan Rd A3
Buchanan St A2
Cambridge Rd A3
Caunce St A2/A3
Central Dr B1/C2
Central Pier C1
Central Pier C1
Central Pier Theatre C1
Chapel St C1
Charles St A2
Charnley Rd B2
Church St A1/A2
Clinton Ave B2
Coach Station A2/C1
Cocker St A1
Cocker St A1
Coleridge Rd A3
Collingwood Ave A3
Condor Gr C3
Cookson St A2
Coronation St B1
Corporation St A1
Courts B1
Cumberland Ave B3
Cunliffe Rd C3
Dale St C1
Devonshire Rd A3
Devonshire Sq A3
Dickson Rd A1
Elizabeth St A2
Ferguson Rd C3
Forest Gate B3
Foxhall Rd C1
Foxhall Sq C1
Freckleton St C2
George St A2
Gloucester Ave B3
Golden Mile, The C1
Gorse Rd B3
Gorton St A2
Grand Theatre, The B1
Granville Rd A2
Grasmere Rd C2
Grosvenor St A2
Grundy Art Gallery A1
Harvey Rd B3
Hornby Rd B2
Hounds Hill Sh Ctr B1
Hull Rd B1
Ibbison Ct C2
Information Ctr A1
Kent Rd C2
Keswick Rd C2
King St A2
Knox Gr C3
Laycock Gate A3
Layton Rd A3
Leamington Rd B2
Leeds Rd B3
Leicester Rd B2
Levens Gr C2
Library A1
Lifeboat Station B1
Lincoln Rd B2
Liverpool Rd B3
Livingstone Rd B2
London Rd A3
Louis Tussaud's Waxworks B1
Lune Gr C2
Lytham Rd C1
Manchester Sq C1
Manor Rd B3
Maple Ave B3
Market St A1
Marlboro Rd B3
Mere Rd B3
Milbourne St A2
Newcastle Ave B3
Newton Dr A3
North Pier A1
North Pier A1
North Pier Theatre A1
Odeon C2
Olive Gr B3
Palatine Rd B2
Park Rd B2/C3
Peter St A2
Police Station B1
Post Office A1/A3/B1/B2/B3
Princess Pde A1
Princess St C1/C2
Promenade A1/C1
Queen St A1
Queen Victoria Rd C2
Raikes Pde B2
Reads Ave B2
Regent Rd B2
Register Office B2
Ribble Rd B2
Rigby Rd C1/C2
Ripon Rd B3
St Albans Rd B3
St Ives Ave C3
St Vincent Ave C3
Salisbury Rd B3
Salthouse Ave C2
Salvation Army Ctr A2
Sands Way C2
Sealife Ctr B1
Seasiders Way C1
Selbourne Rd A2
Sharrow Gr C3
Somerset Ave C3
Springfield Rd A1
South King St B2
Sutton Pl B2
Talbot Rd A1/A2
Thornber Gr C2
Topping St A1
Tower B1
Town Hall A1
Tram Depot C1
Tyldesley Rd C1
Vance Rd B1
Victoria St B1
Victory Rd A2
Wayman Rd A3
Westmorland Ave C2/C3
Whitegate Dr B3
Winter Gardens Theatre B1
Woodland Gr B3
Woolman Rd B2

Bournemouth 176

Ascham Rd A3
Avenue Rd B1
Bath Rd C2
Beacon Rd C1
Beach Office C2
Beechey Rd A3
Bodorgan Rd B1
Bourne Ave B1
Bournemouth A3
Bournemouth & Poole College B3
Bournemouth Eye C2
Bournemouth Int Ctr C1
Bournemouth Pier C2
Bournemouth Sta B3
Braidley Rd A1
Cavendish Place A2
Cavendish Rd A2
Central Drive A1
Christchurch Rd B3
Cliff Lift C1/C3
Coach House Pl A3
Coach Station A3
Commercial Rd B1
Cotlands Rd B3
Courts B3
Cranborne Rd C1
Cricket Ground A2
Cumnor Rd B2
Dean Park A2
Dean Park Cr B2
Dean Park Rd A2
Durrant Rd B1
East Overcliff Dr C3
Exeter Cr C1
Exeter La C2
Exeter Rd C1
Gervis Place B1
Gervis Rd B3
Glen Fern Rd B2
Golf Club B1
Grove Rd B3
Hinton Rd C2
Holdenhurst Rd B3
Horseshoe Common B2
Nuffield Health Bournemouth Hospl (private) A2
Information Ctr B2
Lansdowne B3
Lansdowne Rd A2
Lorne Park Rd B2
Lower Central Gdns B1/C2
Madeira Rd B2
Methuen Rd A3
Meyrick Park A1
Meyrick Rd B3
Milton Rd A2
Oceanarium C2
Odeon Cinema C2
Old Christchurch Rd B2
Ophir Rd A3
Oxford Rd B3
Park Rd A3
Parsonage Rd B2
Pavilion C2
Pier Approach C2
Pier Theatre C2
Police Station A3/B3
Portchester Rd A3
Post Office B1/B3
Priory Rd C1
Quadrant, The B2
Recreation Ground A1
Richmond Hill Rd B1
Russell Cotes Art Gallery & Mus C2
Russell Cotes Rd C2
St Anthony's Rd A1
St Michael's Rd C1
St Paul's A3
St Paul's La B3
St Paul's Rd A3
St Peter's B2
St Peter's B2
St Peter's Rd B2
St Stephen's Rd B1/B2
St Swithun's B3
St Swithun's Rd B3
St Swithun's Rd South B3
St Valerie Rd A2
St Winifred's Rd A2
Stafford Rd B3
Terrace Rd B1
The Square B1
The Triangle B1
Town Hall B1
Tregonwell Rd C1
Trinity Rd B2
Undercliff Drive C3
Upper Central Gdns B1
Upper Hinton Rd B2
Upper Terr Rd C1
Waterfront, The C2
Wellington Rd A2/A3
Wessex Way A3/B1/B2
West Cliff Prom C1
West Hill Rd C1
West Undercliff Promenade C1
Westover Rd B2
Wimborne Rd A2
Wootton Mount B2
Wychwood Dr A1
Yelverton Rd B2
York Rd B3
Zig-Zag Walks C1/C3

Bradford 176

Alhambra B2
Back Ashgrove B1
Barkerend Rd A3
Barnard Rd C3
Barry St B2
Bolling Rd C3
Bolton Rd A3
Bowland St A1
Bradford 1 B2
Bradford College B1
Bradford Forster Sq A2
Bradford Interchange B3
Bradford Playhouse B3
Bridge St B2
Britannia St B2
Burnett St B3
Bus Station B2
Butler St West A3
Caledonia St C2
Canal Rd A2
Carlton St B1
Cathedral A3
Centenary Sq B2
Chapel St B3
Cheapside A2
Church Bank B3
Cineworld B3
City Hall B2
City Rd A1
Claremont B1
Colour Museum B1
Croft St B2
Crown Court B3
Darfield St A1
Darley St A2
Drewton Rd A1
Drummond Trading Estate A1
Dryden St B3
Dyson St A1
Easby Rd C1
East Parade B3
Eldon Pl A1
Filey St B3
Forster Sq Ret Pk A2
Gallery II B1
Garnett St B3
Godwin St B2
Gracechurch St A1
Grattan Rd B1
Great Horton Rd B1/B2
Grove Terr B1
Hall Ings B2
Hall La C3
Hallfield Rd A1
Hammstrasse A2
Harris St B3
Holdsworth St A2
Ice Rink B2
Impressions B2
Information Ctr B2
Ivegate B2
Inland Revenue A2
Jacob's Well Municipal Offices B2
James St A2
John St A2
Kirkgate B2
Kirkgate Ctr B2
Laisteridge La C1
Leeds Rd B3
Library B1/B2
Listerhills Rd B1
Little Horton La C1
Little Horton Gn C1
Longside La B1
Lower Kirkgate B2
Lumb La A1
Magistrates Court B2
Manchester Rd C2
Manningham La A1
Manor Row A2
Market C3
Market St B2
Melbourne Place C1
Midland Rd A2
Mill La C2
Morley St B1
National Media B2
Nelson St B2/C2
Nesfield St A2
New Otley Rd A3
Norcroft St B1
North Parade A2
North St A3
North Wing A3
Oastler Shopping Ctr A2
Otley Rd A3
Park Ave C1
Park La C1
Park Rd C2
Parma St C2
Peace Museum B2
Peckover St B3
Piccadilly A2
Police Station B2/C2
Post Office A2/B1/B2/C3
Princes Way B2
Prospect St C3
Radwell Drive C2
Rawson Rd A1
Rebecca St A1
Richmond Rd B1
Russell St C1
St George's Hall B2
St Lukes Hospital C1
St Mary's A3
Shipley Airedale Rd A3/B3
Simes St A1
Smith St B1
Spring Mill St C2
Stott Hill A3
Sunbridge Rd A1/B1/B2
The L Exchange B3
Theatre in the Mill B1
Thornton Rd A1/B1
Trafalgar St A2
Trinity Rd C1
Tumbling Hill St B1
Tyrrel St B2
Univ of Bradford B1/C1
Usher St C3
Valley Rd A2
Vicar La B3
Wakefield Rd C3
Wapping Rd A3
Westgate A1
White Abbey Rd A1
Wigan Rd A1
Wilton St B1
Wood St A1
Wool Exchange B2
Worthington St A1

Brighton 177

Addison Rd A1
Albert Rd B2
Albion Hill B3
Albion St B3
Ann St A3
Art Gallery & Mus B3
Baker St A3
Black Lion St C2
Brighton A2
Brighton Ctr C2
Brighton Fishing Museum C2
Broad St C3
Buckingham Pl A2
Buckingham Rd B2
Cannon Pl C1
Carlton Hill B3
Chatham Pl A1
Cheapside A3
Church St B2
Churchill Sq Sh Ctr B2
Clifton Hill B1
Clifton Pl B1
Clifton Rd B1
Clifton St A2
Clifton Terr B1
Clock Tower B2
Clyde Rd A3
Coach Park C3
Compton Ave A2
Davigdor Rd A1
Denmark Terr B1
Ditchling Rd A3
Dome, The B2
Duke St B2
Duke's La C2
Dyke Rd A1/B2
East St C2
Edward St B3
Elmore Rd B3
Frederick St B2
Gardner St B2
Gloucester Pl B3
Gloucester Rd B2
Goldsmid Rd A1
Grand Junction Rd C2
Grand Pde B3
Grove Hill B3

Guildford St A2
Hampton Pl B1
Hanover Terr A3
High St C3
Highdown Rd A1
Information Ctr C2
John St B3
Kemp St B2
Kensington Pl B2
Kings Rd C1
Law Courts B3
Lewes Rd A3
Library B2
London Rd A3
Madeira Dr C3
Marine Pde C3
Middle St C2
Montpelier Pl B1
Montpelier Rd B1
Montpelier St B1
New England Rd A2
New England St A2
New Rd B2
Nizells Ave A1
Norfolk Rd B1
Norfolk Terr B1
North Rd B2
North St B2
Odeon Cinema C2
Old Shoreham Rd A1
Old Steine C3
Osmond Rd A1
Over St B2
Oxford St A3
Palace Pier C3
Park Crescent Terr A3
Phoenix Art Gallery B3
Phoenix Rise A3
Police Station B3
Post Office A1/A2/A3/B1/B2/B3/C3
Preston Rd A2
Preston St B1
Prestonville Rd A1
Queen's Rd B2
Regency Sq C1
Regent St B2
Richmomd Pl B3
Richmond St B3
Richmond Terr A3
Rose Hill Terr A3
Royal Alexandra Hospital B1
Royal Pavilion B2
St Bartholomew's A3
St James's St C3
St Nicholas Rd B2
St Nicholas' B2
St Peter's A3
Sea Life Ctr C3
Shaftesbury Rd A3
Ship St C2
Sillwood Rd B1
Sillwood St B1
Southover St A3
Spring Gdns B2
Stanford Rd A1
Stanley Rd A3
Surrey St B2
Sussex St B3
Sussex Terr B3
Swimming Pool B3
Sydney St B3
Temple Gdns B1
Terminus Rd A2
The Lanes C2
Theatre Royal B2
Tidy St B2
Town Hall C2
Toy & Model Mus A2
Trafalgar St B2
Union Rd A3
Univ of Brighton B3
Upper Lewes Rd A3
Upper North St B1
Viaduct Rd A3
Victoria Gdns B3
Victoria Rd B1
Volk's Electric Railway C3
West Pier (Closed to the Public) C1
West St C2
Western Rd B1
Whitecross St B2
York Ave B1
York Pl B3

Bristol 177

Acramans Rd C4
Albert Rd C6
Alfred Hill A4
All Saint's St A4
All Saints' B4
Allington Rd C3
Alpha Rd C4
Ambra Vale B1
Ambra Vale East B2
Ambrose Rd B2
Amphitheatre C3
Anchor Rd B3
Anvil St B6
Architecture Ctr B4
Argyle Pl B2
Arlington Villas A2
Arnolfini Arts Ctr, The B4
Art Gallery A3
Ashton Gate Rd C2
Ashton Rd C1
at-Bristol B3
Avon Bridge C1
Avon Cr C1
Avon St B6
Baldwin St B4
Baltic Wharf C2
Baltic Wharf Leisure Ctr & Caravan Park C2
Barossa Pl C4
Barton Manor B6
Barton Rd B6
Barton Vale B6
Bath Rd C6
Bathurst Basin C4
Bathurst Parade C4
Beauley Rd C3
Bedminster Bridge C5
Bedminster Parade C4
Bellevue B2
Bellevue Cr B2
Bellevue Rd C6
Berkeley Pl A2
Berkeley Sq A3
Birch Rd C2
Blackfriars A4
Bond St A5
Braggs La A6
Brandon Hill B3
Brandon Steep B3
Bristol Bridge B5
Bristol Cath (CE) B3
Bristol Central Liby B3
Bristol Eye Hospital (A&E) A4
Bristol Grammar School A3
Bristol Harbour Railway C3
Bristol Marina C2
Bristol Royal Children's Hospital A4
Bristol Royal Infirmary (A&E) A4
Bristol Temple Meads Station B6
Broad Plain B6
Broad Quay B4
Broad St A4
Broad Weir A5
Broadcasting House A3
Broadmead A5
Brunel Way C1
Brunswick Sq A5
Burton Cl C5
Bus Station A4
Butts Rd B3
Cabot Tower B3
Caledonia Pl B1
Callowhill Ct A5
Cambridge St C6
Camden Rd C3
Camp Rd A1
Canada Way C2
Cannon St A4
Canon's Rd B3/B4
Canon's Way B3
Cantock's Cl A3
Canynge Rd A1
Canynge Sq A1
Castle Park A5
Castle St A5
Catherine Meade St C4
Cattle Market Rd C6
Charles Pl B1
Charlotte St B3
Charlotte St South B3
Chatterton House B5
Chatterton Sq C5
Chatterton St C5
Cheese La B5
Christchurch A4
Christchurch Rd A1
Christmas Steps A4
Church La B2/B5
Church St B5
City Museum A3
City of Bristol College B3
Clare St B4
Clarence Rd C5
Cliff Rd C1
Clift House Rd C1
Clifton Cath (RC) A2
Clifton Down A1
Clifton Down Rd A1
Clifton Hill B2
Clifton Park A1/A2
Clifton Park Rd A1
Clifton Rd A2
Cliftonwood Cr B2
Cliftonwood Rd B2
Cliftonwood Terr B2
Clifton Vale B1
Cobblestone Mews A1
College Green B3
College Rd A1
College St B3
Colston Almshouses A4
Colston Ave B4
Colston Hall B4
Colston Parade C5
Colston St A4
Commercial Rd C4
Commonwealth Museum B5
Constitution Hill B2
Cooperage La C2
Corn St B4
Cornwallis Ave B1
Cornwallis Cr B1
Coronation Rd C2/C4
Council House B3
Counterslip B5
Courts A4
Create Ctr, The C1
Crosby Row B2
Culver St B3
Cumberland Basin C1
Cumberland Cl C2
Cumberland Rd C2/C3
Dale St A6
David St A6
Dean La C4
Deanery Rd B3
Denmark St B4
Dowry Sq B1
East St A5
Eaton Cr A2
Elmdale Rd A3
Elton Rd A3
Eugene St A4/A6
Exchange, The and St Nicholas' Mkts B4
Fairfax St A4
Fire Station B5
Floating Harbour C3
Foster Almshouses A4
Frayne Rd C1
Frederick Pl A2
Freeland Pl B1
Frogmore St B3
Fry's Hill B2
Gas La B6
Gasferry Rd C3
General Hospital C4
Georgian House B3
Glendale B1
Glentworth Rd B2
Gloucester St A1
Goldney Hall B2
Goldney Rd B1
Gordon Rd A2
Granby Hill B1
Grange Rd A1
Great Ann St A6
Great George St A6/B3
Great George Rd B3
Great Western Way B6
Green St North B1
Green St South B1
Greenay Bush La C2
Greenbank Rd C2
Greville Smyth Park C1
Guildhall A4
Guinea St C4
Hamilton Rd C3
Hanbury Rd A2
Hanover Pl C2
Harbour Way B3
Harley Pl A1
Haymarket A5
Hensman's Hill B1
High St B4
Highbury Villas A3
Hill St B3
Hill St C6
Hippodrome B4
Hopechapel Hill B1
Horfield Rd A4
Horton St B6
Host St A4
Hotwell Rd B1/B2
Houlton St A6
Howard Rd C3
Ice Rink B3
IMAX Cinema B4
Information Ctr B4
Islington Rd C3
Jacob St A5/A6
Jacob's Wells Rd B2
John Carr's Terr B2
John Wesley's Chapel A5
Joy Hill B1
Jubilee St B6
Kensington Pl A2
Kilkenny St B6
King St B4
Kingsland Rd B6
Kingston Rd C3
Lamb St A6
Lansdown Rd A2
Lawford St A6
Lawfords Gate A6
Leighton Rd C3
Lewins Mead A4
Lime Rd C2
Little Ann St A6
Little Caroline Pl B1
Little George St A6
Little King St B4
Litfield Rd A1
Llandoger Trow B4
Lloyds' Building, The C3
Lodge St A4
Lord Mayor's Chapel, The B4
Lower Castle St A5
Lower Church La A4
Lower Clifton Hill B2
Lower Guinea St C4
Lower Lamb St B3
Lower Maudlin St A4
Lower Park Rd A4
Lower Sidney St C2
Lucky La C4
Lydstep Terr C3
Mall (Galleries Shopping Ctr), The A5
Manilla Rd A1
Mardyke Ferry Rd C2
Maritime Heritage Ctr B3
Marlborough Hill A4
Marlborough St A4
Marsh St B4
Mead St C5
Meadow St A5
Merchant Dock B2
Merchant Seamen's Almshouses B4
Merchant St A5
Merchants Rd A1
Merchants Rd C1
Meridian Pl A2
Meridian Vale A2
Merrywood Rd C3
Midland Rd A6
Milford St C3
Millennium Sq B3
Mitchell La B5
Mortimer Rd A1
M Shed C4
Murray Rd C4
Myrtle Rd A3
Narrow Plain B5
Narrow Quay B4
Nelson St A4
New Charlotte St C4
New Kingsley Rd B6
New Queen St C5
New St A6
Newfoundland St A5
Newgate A5
Newton St A6
Norland Rd A1
North St C2
Oakfield Gr A2
Oakfield Pl A2
Oakfield Rd A2
Old Bread St B6
Old Market St A6
Old Park Hill A4
Oldfield Rd B1
Orchard Ave B4
Orchard La B4
Orchard St B4
Osbourne Rd C3
Oxford St B6
Park Pl A2
Park Rd C3
Park Row A3
Park St A3
Passage St B5
Pembroke Gr A2
Pembroke Rd A2
Pembroke Rd C3
Pembroke St A5
Penn St A5
Pennywell Rd A6
Percival Rd A1
Pero's Bridge B4
Perry Rd A4
Pip & Jay A5
Plimsoll Bridge B1
Police Sta A4/A6
Polygon Rd B1
Portland St A1
Portwall La B5
Post Office A1/A3/A4/A5/A6/B1/B4/C4/C5
Prewett St C5
Prince St B4
Prince St Bridge C4
Princess St C5
Princess Victoria St B1
Priory Rd A3
Pump La C5
QEH Theatre A2
Queen Charlotte St B4
Quakers Friars A5
Quay St A4
Queen Elizabeth Hospital School B2
Queen Sq B4
Queen St A5
Queen's Ave A3
Queen's Parade B3
Queen's Rd A2/A3
Raleigh Rd C2
Randall Rd B2
Redcliffe Backs B5
Redcliffe Bridge B4
Redcliffe Hill C5
Redcliffe Parade C4
Redcliffe St B5
Redcliffe Way B5
Redcross La A6
Redcross St A6
Redgrave Theatre A1
Red Lodge A4
Regent St B1
Richmond Hill A2
Richmond Hill Ave A2
Richmond La A2
Richmond Park Rd A2
Richmond St C6
Richmond Terr A2
River St A6
Rownham Mead B2
Royal Fort Rd A3
Royal Park A2
Royal West of England Academy A3
Royal York Cr B1
Royal York Villas B1
Rupert St A4
Russ St B6
St Andrew's Walk B2
St George's B3
St George's Rd B3
St James A4
St John's A4
St John's Rd C4
St Luke's Rd C5
St Mary Redcliffe C5
St Mary's Hospital A3
St Matthias Park A6
St Michael's Hill A3
St Michael's Hospl A4
St Michael's Park A3
St Nicholas St B4
St Paul St A5
St Paul's Rd A2
St Peter's (ruin) A5
St Philip's Bridge B5
St Philips Rd A6
St Stephen's B4
St Stephen's St B4
St Thomas St B5
St Thomas the Martyr B5
Sandford Rd B1
Sargent St C5
Saville Pl B1
Ship La C5
Silver St A4
Sion Hill A1
Small St A4
Smeaton Rd C1
Somerset Sq C5
Somerset St C5
Southernhay Ave B2
Southville Rd C4
Spike Island Artspace C2
Spring St C5
SS Great Britain and The Matthew B2
Stackpool Rd C3
Staight St B6
Stillhouse La C4
Stracey Rd C2
Stratton St A5
Sydney Row C2
Tankard's Cl A3
Temple Back B5
Temple Boulevard B5
Temple Bridge B5
Temple Church B5
Temple Circus B5
Temple Gate C5
Temple St B5
Temple Way B5
Terrell St A4
The Arcade A5
The Fosseway A2
The Grove B4
The Horsefair A5
The Mall A1
Theatre Royal B4
Thomas La B5
Three Kings of Cologne A4
Three Queens La B5
Tobacco Factory, The C2
Tower Hill B5
Tower La A4
Trenchard St A4
Triangle South A3
Triangle West A3
Trinity Rd A6
Trinity St A6
Tucker St A5
Tyndall Ave A3
Union St A5
Union St B6
Unity St A6
Unity St B3
University of Bristol A3
University Rd A3
Upper Maudlin St A4
Upper Perry Hill C3
Upper Byron Pl A3
Upton Rd C2
Valentine Bridge B6
Victoria Gr C5
Victoria Rd C6
Victoria Rooms A2
Victoria Sq A2
Victoria St B5
Vyvyan Rd A1
Vyvyan Terr A1
Wade St A6
Walter St C2
Wapping Rd C4
Water La B5
Waterloo Rd A6
Waterloo St A1
Waterloo St A6
Watershed, The B4
Welling Terr B1
Wellington Rd A6
Welsh Back B4
West Mall A1
West St A6
Westfield Pl A1
Wetherell Pl A2
Whitehouse Pl C5
Whitehouse St C5
Whiteladies Rd A2
Whitson St A4
William St C5
Willway St C5
Windsor Pl B1
Windsor Terr B1
Wine St A4
Woodland Rise A3
Woodland Rd A3
Worcester Rd A1
Worcester Terr A1
YHA B4
York Gdns B1
York Pl A2
York Rd C5

Cambridge 177

Abbey Rd A3
ADC A2
Anglia Ruskin Univ B3
Archaeology & Anthropology B2
Art Gallery A1
Arts Picture House B2
Arts Theatre B1
Auckland Rd A3
Bateman St C2
BBC C3
Benet St B1
Bradmore St B3
Bridge St A1
Broad St B3
Brookside C2
Brunswick Terr A3
Burleigh St B3
Bus Station B2
Butt Green A2
Cambridge Contemporary Art Gallery B1
Castle Mound A1
Castle St A1
Chesterton La A1
Christ's (Coll) B2
Christ's Pieces B2
City Rd B3
Clare (Coll) B1
Clarendon St B2
Coe Fen C2
Coronation St C2
Corpus Christi (Coll) B1
Council Offices C3
Cross St C3
Crusoe Bridge C1
Darwin (Coll) C1
Devonshire Rd C3
Downing (Coll) C3
Downing St B2
Earl St B2
East Rd B3
Eden St B3
Elizabeth Way A3
Elm St B2
Emery St B3
Emmanuel (Coll) B2
Emmanuel Rd B2
Emmanuel St B2
Fair St A3
Fenners Physical Education Ctr C3
Fire Station B3
Fitzroy St A3
Fitzwilliam Mus C2
Fitzwilliam St C2
Folk Museum A1
Glisson Rd C3
Gonville & Caius (Coll) B1
Gonville Place C2
Grafton Ctr A3
Grand Arcade B2
Gresham Rd C3
Green St B1
Guest Rd B3
Guildhall B2
Harvey Rd C3
Hills Rd C3
Hobson St B2
Hughes Hall (Coll) B3
Information Ctr B2
James St A3
Jesus (Coll) A2
Jesus Green A2
Jesus La A2
Jesus Terr B3
John St B3
Kelsey Kerridge Sports Ctr B3
King St A2
King's (Coll) B1
King's Coll Chapel B1
King's Parade B1
Lammas Land Rec Gd C1
Lensfield Rd C2
Little St Mary's La B1
Lyndewod Rd C3
Magdalene (Coll) A1
Magdalene St A1
Maid's Causeway A3
Malcolm St A2
Market Hill B1
Market St B1
Mathematical Bridge B1
Mawson Rd C3
Midsummer Common A3
Mill La B1
Mill Rd B3
Mill St C3
Napier St A3
New Square A2
Newmarket Rd A3
Newnham Rd C1
Norfolk St B3
Northampton St A1
Norwich St C2
Orchard St B2
Panton St C2
Paradise Nature Reserve C1
Paradise St B3
Park Parade A1
Park St A2
Park Terr B2
Parker St B2
Parker's Piece B2
Parkside B3
Parkside Pools B3
Parsonage St A3
Pemberton Terr C2
Pembroke (Coll) B2
Pembroke St B1
Perowne St B3
Peterhouse (Coll) C1
Petty Cury B2
Police Station B3
Post Office A1/A3/B2/B3/C1/C2/C3
Queens' (Coll) B1
Queen's La B1
Queen's Rd B1
Regent St B2
Regent Terr B2
Ridley Hall (Coll) C1
Riverside A3
Round Church, The A1
Russell St C2
St Andrew's St B2
St Benet's B1
St Catharine's (Coll) B1
St Eligius St C2
St John's (Coll) A1
St Mary's B1
St Paul's Rd C3
Saxon St C2
Scott Polar Institute & Museum C2
Sedgwick Museum B2
Sheep's Green C1
Shire Hall A1
Sidgwick Ave C1
Sidney St A2
Sidney Sussex (Coll) A2
Silver St B1
Station Rd C3
Tenison Ave C3
Tenison Rd C3
Tennis Court Rd B2
The Backs B1
The Fen Causeway C1
Thompson's La A1
Trinity (Coll) A1
Trinity Hall (Coll) B1
Trinity St B1
Trumpington Rd C2
Trumpington St B1
Union Rd C2
University Botanic Gardens C2
Victoria Ave A2
Victoria St B2
Warkworth St B3
Warkworth Terr B3
Wesley House (Coll) A2
West Rd B1
Westcott Ho (Coll) A2
Westminster (Coll) A1
Whipple B2
Willis Rd B3
Willow Walk A2
Zoology B2

Canterbury 178

Artillery St B2
Barton Mill Rd A3
Beaconsfield Rd A1
Beverley Rd A1
Bingley's Island B1
Black Griffin La B1
Broad Oak Rd A2
Broad St B2
Brymore Rd A3
Burgate B2
Bus Station C2
Canterbury College C3
Canterbury East C1
Canterbury Tales, The B2
Canterbury West A1
Castle C1
Castle Row C1
Castle St C1
Cathedral B2
Chaucer Rd A3
Christ Church Univ B3
Christchurch Gate B2
City Council Offices A3
City Wall B2
Coach Park A2
College Rd B3
Cossington Rd C2
Court B2
Craddock Rd A3
Crown & County Courts B3
Dane John Gdns C2
Dane John Mound C1
Deanery B2
Dover St C2
Duck La B2
Eastbridge Hospl B1
Edgar Rd B3
Ersham Rd C3
Ethelbert Rd C3
Fire Station C2
Forty Acres Rd A1
Gordon Rd C1
Greyfriars B1
Guildford Rd C1
Havelock St B2
Heaton Rd C1
High St B2
HM Prison B3
Information Ctr A2/B2
Ivy La B2
Ivy Pl C1
King St B2
King's School B2/B3
King's School Leisure Facilities A2
Kingsmead L Ctr A2
Kingsmead Rd A2
Kirby's La B1
Lansdown Rd C2
Lime Kiln Rd C1
Longport B3
Lower Chantry La C3
Mandeville Rd A1
Market Way A2
Marlowe Arcade B2
Marlowe Ave C2
Marlowe Theatre B2
Martyrs Field Rd C1
Mead Way B1
Military Rd B2
Monastery St B2
Museum of Canterbury (Rupert Bear Museum) B1
New Dover Rd C3
Norman Rd C2
North Holmes Rd B3
North La B1
Northgate A2
Nunnery Fields C2
Nunnery Rd C2
Oaten Hill C2
Odeon Cinema C2
Old Dover Rd C2
Old Palace B2
Old Ruttington La B2
Old Weavers B2
Orchard St B1
Oxford Rd C1
Palace St B2
Pilgrims Way C3
Pin Hill C1
Pine Tree Ave A1
Police Station C2
Post Office B2/C1/C2
Pound La B1
Puckle La C2
Raymond Ave C2
Registry Office A2
Rheims Way B1
Rhodaus Cl C2
Rhodaus Town C2
Roman Museum B2
Roper Gateway A1
Roper Rd A1
Rose La B2
Royal Museum B2
St Augustine's Abbey (remains) B3
St Augustine's Rd C3
St Dunstan's A1
St Dunstan's St A1
St George's Pl C2
St George's St B2
St George's Tower B2
St Gregory's Rd B3
St John's Hospital A2
St Margaret's St B2
St Martin's B3
St Martin's Ave B3
St Martin's Rd B3
St Michael's Rd A1
St Mildred's C1
St Peter's Gr B1
St Peter's La B2
St Peter's Pl B1
St Peter's St B1
St Radigunds St B2
St Stephen's Ct A1
St Stephen's Path A1
St Stephen's Rd A2
Salisbury Rd A1
Simmonds Rd C1
Spring La C3
Station Rd West B1
Stour St B1
Sturry Rd A3
The Causeway A2
The Friars B2
Tourtel Rd A3
Tudor Rd C1
Union St B2
University for the Creative Arts C3
Vernon Pl C2
Victoria Rd C1
Watling St B2
Westgate Gdns B1
Westgate Towers B1
Whitefriars B2
Whitehall Gdns B1
Whitehall Rd B1
Wincheap C1
York Rd C1
Zealand Rd C2

Cardiff/*Caerdydd* 178

Adam St B3
Alexandra Gdns A2
Allerton St C1
Arran St A3
ATRiuM (Univ of Glamorgan) C3
Beauchamp St C1
Bedford St A3
Blackfriars Priory (rems) B1
Boulevard De Nantes B2
Brains Brewery C2
Brook St B1
Bus Station C2
Bute Park B1
Bute St C2
Bute Terr C3
Callaghan Sq C2/C3
Capitol Sh Ctr, The B3
Cardiff Arms Park (Cardiff RFC) B1
Cardiff Bridge B1
Cardiff Castle B2
Cardiff Central Sta C2
Cardiff Ctr Trading Estate C3
Cardiff Univ A1/A2/B3
Cardiff University Student's Union A2
Caroline St C2
Castle Green B2
Castle Mews A1
Castle St (Heol y Castell) B1
Cathays Station A2
Celerity Drive C3
Central Library C2
Central Sq C2
Charles St (Heol Siarl) B3
Churchill Way B3
City Hall A2
City Rd A3
Clare Rd C1
Clare St C1
Coburn St A3
Coldstream Terr B1
College Rd A1
Colum Rd A1
Court C2
Court Rd C1
Craiglee Drive C3
Cranbrook St A3
Customhouse St C2
Cyfartha St A3
Despenser Place C1
Despenser St C1
Dinas St C1
Duke St (Heol y Dug) B2
Dumfries Place B3
East Grove A3
Ellen St C3
Fire Station B3
Fitzalan Place B3
Fitzhamon Emb C1
Fitzhamon La C1
g39 B2
Gloucester St C1
Glynrhondda St A2
Gordon Rd A3
Gorsedd Gdns B2
Green St B1
Greyfriars Rd B2
HM Prison B3
Hafod St C1
Herbert St C3
High St B2
Industrial Estate C3
John St C3
Jubilee St C1
King Edward VII Ave A1
Kingsway (Ffordd y Brenin) B2
Knox Rd B3
Law Courts B2
Llanbleddian Gdns A2
Llantwit St A2
Lloyd George Ave C3
Lower Cathedral Rd B1
Lowther Rd A3
Magistrates Court B3
Mansion House A3
Mardy St C1
Mark St B1
Market B2
Mary Ann St C3
Merches Gdns C1
Mill La C2
Millennium Bridge B1
Millennium Plaza Leisure Complex C1
Millennium Stadium C1
Millennium Stadium Tours (Gate 3) B2
Miskin St A2
Monmouth St C1
Motorpoint Arena Cardiff C3
Museum Ave A2
Museum Place A2
National Museum of Wales A2
National War Memorial A2
Neville Place C1
New Theatre B2
Newport Rd B3
Northcote La A3
Northcote St A3
Park Grove A4
Park Place A2
Park St C2
Penarth Rd C2
Pendyris St C1
Plantaganet St C1
Quay St B2
Queen Anne Sq A1
Queen St (Heol y Frenhines) B2
Queen St Station B3
Regimental Museums B2
Rhymney St A3
Richmond Rd A3
Royal Welsh College of Music and Drama A1
Russell St A3
Ruthin Gdns A2
St Andrews Place A2
St David's B2
St David's 2 C2
St David's Ctr B2
St David's Hall B2
St John The Baptist B2
St Mary St (Heol Eglwys Fair) B2
St Peter's St A3
Salisbury Rd A3
Sandon St B3
Schooner Way C3
Scott Rd C2
Scott St C2
Senghennydd Rd A2
Sherman Theatre A2
Sophia Gardens A1
South Wales Baptist College A3
Stafford Rd C1
Station Terr B3
Stuttgarter Strasse B2
Sussex St C1
Taffs Mead Emb C1
Talworth St A3
Temple of Peace & Health A1
The Cardiff Story B2
The Friary B2
The Hayes B2
The Parade A3
The Walk A3
Treharris St A3
Trinity St B2
Tudor La C1
Tudor St C1
Welsh Assembly Offices A1
Welsh Inst of Sport A1
West Grove A3
Westgate St (Heol y Porth) B2
Windsor Place B3
Womanby St B2
Wood St C2
Working St B2
Wyeverne Rd A2

Cheltenham 178

Albert Rd A3
Albion St B3
All Saints Rd B3
Ambrose St B2
Andover Rd C1
Art Gallery & Mus B2
Axiom Ctr B3
Back Montpellier Terr C2
Bandstand C2
Bath Pde B2
Bath Rd C2
Bays Hill Rd C1
Beechwood Pl Sh Ctr B3
Bennington St B2
Berkeley St B3
Brewery A2
Brunswick St South A2
Bus Station B2
CAB B2
Carlton St B3
Central Cross Road A3
Cheltenham College C2
Cheltenham FC A3
Cheltenham General (A&E) C3
Christchurch Rd B1
Cineworld A2
Clarence Rd A2
Clarence Sq A2
Clarence St B2
Cleeveland St A1
Coach Park A2
College Baths Road C3
College Rd C2
Colletts Dr A1
Corpus St C3
Devonshire St A2
Douro Rd B1
Duke St B3
Dunalley Pde A2
Dunalley St A2
Everyman B2
Evesham Rd A3
Fairview Rd B3
Fairview St B3
Fire Station C3
Folly La A2
Gloucester Rd A1
Grosvenor St B3
Grove St A1
Gustav Holst A3
Hanover St A2
Hatherley St C1
Henrietta St A2
Hewlett Rd B3
High St B2/B3
Hudson St A2
Imperial Gdns C2
Imperial La B2
Imperial Sq C2
Information Ctr B2
Keynsham Rd C3
King St A2
Knapp Rd B2
Ladies College B2
Lansdown Cr C1
Lansdown Rd C1
Leighton Rd B3
London Rd C3
Lypiatt Rd C1
Malvern Rd B1
Manser St A2
Market St A1
Marle Hill Pde A2
Marle Hill Rd A2
Millbrook St A1
Milsom St A2
Montpellier Gdns C2
Montpellier Gr C2
Montpellier Pde C2
Montpellier Spa Rd C2
Montpellier St C1
Montpellier Terr C2
Montpellier Walk C2
New St B2
North Pl B2
Old Bath Rd C3
Oriel Rd B2
Overton Park Rd B1
Overton Rd B1
Oxford St C3
Parabola Rd B1
Park Pl C1
Park St A1
Pittville Circus A3
Pittville Cr A3
Pittville Lawn A3
Playhouse B2
Police Station B1/C1
Portland St B3
Post Office B2/C2
Prestbury Rd A3
Prince's Rd C1
Priory St B3
Promenade B2
Queen St A1
Recreation Ground A2
Regent Arcade B2
Regent St B2
Rodney Rd B2
Royal Cr B2
Royal Wells Rd B2
St George's Pl B2
St Georges Rd B1
St Gregory's B2
St James St B3
St John's Ave B3
St Luke's Rd C2
St Margarets Rd A2
St Mary's B2
St Matthew's B2
St Paul's La A2
St Paul's Rd A2
St Paul's St A2
St Stephen's Rd C1
Sandford Lido C3
Sandford Mill Road C3
Sandford Park C3
Sandford Rd C2
Selkirk St A3
Sherborne Pl B3
Sherborne St B3
Suffolk Pde C2
Suffolk Rd C1
Suffolk Sq C1
Sun St A1
Swindon Rd B2
Sydenham Villas Rd C3
Tewkesbury Rd A1
The Courtyard B1
Thirlstaine Rd C2
Tivoli Rd C1
Tivoli St C1
Town Hall & Theatre B2
Townsend St A1
Trafalgar St C2
Union St B3
Univ of Gloucestershire (Francis Cl Hall) A2
Univ of Gloucestershire (Hardwick) A1
Victoria Pl B3
Victoria St A2
Vittoria Walk C2
Wel Pl B2
Wellesley Rd A2
Wellington Rd A3
Wellington Sq A3
Wellington St B2
West Drive A3
Western Rd B1
Winchcombe St B3

Chester 178

Abbey Gateway A2
Appleyards La C3
Bedward Row B1
Beeston View C3
Bishop Lloyd's Pal B2
Black Diamond St A2
Bottoms La C3

Boughton . . . B3
Bouverie St . . . A1
Bridge St . . . B2
Bridgegate . . . C2
British Heritage Ctr . . . B2
Brook St . . . A3
Brown's La . . . C2
Bus Station . . . B2
Cambrian Rd . . . A1
Canal St . . . A2
Carrick Rd . . . C1
Castle . . . C2
Castle Dr . . . C2
Cathedral . . . B2
Catherine St . . . A1
Chester . . . A3
Cheyney Rd . . . A1
Chichester St . . . A1
City Rd . . . A3
City Walls . . . B1/B2
City Walls Rd . . . B1
Cornwall St . . . A2
County Hall . . . C2
Cross Hey . . . C3
Cuppin St . . . B2
Curzon Park North . . . C1
Curzon Park South . . . C1
Dee Basin . . . A1
Dee La . . . B3
Delamere St . . . A2
Dewa Roman Experience . . . B2
Duke St . . . B2
Eastgate . . . B2
Eastgate St . . . B2
Eaton Rd . . . C2
Edinburgh Way . . . C3
Elizabeth Cr . . . B3
Fire Station . . . A2
Foregate St . . . B2
Frodsham St . . . B2
Gamul House . . . B2
Garden La . . . A1
Gateway Theatre . . . B2
George St . . . A2
Gladstone Ave . . . A1
God's Providence House . . . B2
Gorse Stacks . . . A2
Greenway St . . . C2
Grosvenor Bridge . . . C1
Grosvenor Mus . . . B2
Grosvenor Park . . . B3
Grosvenor Precinct . . . B2
Grosvenor Rd . . . C1
Grosvenor St . . . B2
Groves Rd . . . B3
Guildhall Museum . . . B1
Handbridge . . . C2
Hartington St . . . C3
Hoole Way . . . A2
Hunter St . . . B2
Information Ctr . . . B2
King Charles' Tower . . . A2
King St . . . A2
Leisure Ctr . . . A2
Library . . . B2
Lightfoot St . . . A3
Little Roodee . . . C2
Liverpool Rd . . . A2
Love St . . . B3
Lower Bridge St . . . B2
Lower Park Rd . . . B3
Lyon St . . . A2
Magistrates Court . . . B2
Meadows La . . . C3
Military Museum . . . C2
Milton St . . . A3
New Crane St . . . B1
Nicholas St . . . B2
Northgate . . . A2
Northgate St . . . A2
Nun's Rd . . . B1
Old Dee Bridge . . . C2
Overleigh Rd . . . C2
Park St . . . B2
Police Station . . . B2
Post Office . . . A2/A3/B2/C2
Princess St . . . B2
Queen St . . . B2
Queen's Park Rd . . . C3
Queen's Rd . . . A3
Race Course . . . B1
Raymond St . . . A1
River La . . . C2
Roman Amphitheatre & Gardens . . . B2
Roodee, The (Chester Racecourse) . . . B1
Russell St . . . A3
St Anne St . . . A2
St George's Cr . . . C3
St Martin's Gate . . . A1
St Martin's Way . . . B1
St Oswalds Way . . . A2
Saughall Rd . . . A1
Sealand Rd . . . A1
South View Rd . . . A1
Stanley Palace . . . B1
Station Rd . . . A3
Steven St . . . A3
The Bars . . . B3
The Cross . . . B2
The Groves . . . B3
The Meadows . . . B3
Tower Rd . . . B1
Town Hall . . . B2
Union St . . . B3
Vicar's La . . . B2
Victoria Cr . . . C3
Victoria Rd . . . A2
Walpole St . . . A1
Water Tower St . . . A1
Watergate . . . B1
Watergate St . . . B2
Whipcord La . . . A1
White Friars . . . B2
York St . . . B3

Colchester 179

Abbey Gateway . . . C2
Albert St . . . A1
Albion Grove . . . C2
Alexandra Rd . . . C1
Artillery St . . . C3
Arts Ctr . . . B1
Balkerne Hill . . . B1
Barrack St . . . C3
Beaconsfield Rd . . . C1
Beche Rd . . . C3
Bergholt Rd . . . A1
Bourne Rd . . . C3
Brick Kiln Rd . . . A1
Bristol Rd . . . B2
Broadlands Way . . . A3
Brook St . . . B3
Bury Cl . . . B2
Bus Sta . . . B2
Butt Rd . . . C1
Camp Folley North . . . C2
Camp Folley South . . . C2
Campion Rd . . . C2
Cannon St . . . C3
Canterbury Rd . . . C2
Castle . . . B2
Castle Park . . . B2
Castle Rd . . . B2
Catchpool Rd . . . A1
Causton Rd . . . B1
Cavalry Barracks . . . C1
Chandlers Row . . . C3
Circular Rd East . . . C2
Circular Rd North . . . C1
Circular Rd West . . . C1
Clarendon Way . . . A1
Claudius Rd . . . C2
Colchester Camp Abbey Field . . . C1
Colchester Institute . . . B1
Colchester . . . A1
Colchester Town . . . C2
Colne Bank Ave . . . A1
Colne View Retail Pk . . . A2
Compton Rd . . . A3
Cowdray Ave . . . A1/A2
Cowdray Ctr, The . . . A2
Crouch St . . . B1
Crowhurst Rd . . . B1
Culver Square Sh Ctr . . . B1
Culver St East . . . B2
Culver St West . . . B1
Dilbridge Rd . . . A3
East Hill . . . B2
East St . . . B3
East Stockwell St . . . B1
Eld La . . . B1
Essex Hall Rd . . . A1
Exeter Dr . . . B2
Fairfax Rd . . . C2
Fire Station . . . A2
Flagstaff Rd . . . C1
George St . . . B2
Gladstone Rd . . . C2
Golden Noble Hill . . . C2
Goring Rd . . . A3
Granville Rd . . . C3
Greenstead Rd . . . B3
Guildford Rd . . . B2
Harsnett Rd . . . C3
Harwich Rd . . . B3
Head St . . . B1
High St . . . B1/B2
High Woods Ctry Pk . . . A2
Hollytrees . . . B2
Hythe Hill . . . C3
Information Ctr . . . B2
Ipswich Rd . . . A3
Jarmin Rd . . . A2
Kendall Rd . . . C2
Kimberley Rd . . . C3
King Stephen Rd . . . C3
Le Cateau Barracks . . . C1
Leisure World . . . A2
Library . . . B1
Lincoln Way . . . B2
Lion Walk Sh Ctr . . . B1
Lisle Rd . . . C2
Lucas Rd . . . C2
Magdalen Green . . . C3
Magdalen St . . . C2
Maidenburgh St . . . B2
Maldon Rd . . . C1
Manor Rd . . . B1
Margaret Rd . . . A1
Mason Rd . . . A2
Mercers Way . . . A1
Mercury . . . B1
Mersea Rd . . . C2
Meyrick Cr . . . C2
Mile End Rd . . . A1
Military Rd . . . C2
Mill St . . . C2
Minories . . . B2
Moorside . . . B3
Morant Rd . . . C3
Napier Rd . . . C2
Natural History . . . B2
New Town Rd . . . C2
Norfolk Cr . . . A3
North Hill . . . B1
North Station Rd . . . A1
Northgate St . . . B1
Nunns Rd . . . B1
Odeon . . . B1
Old Coach Rd . . . B3
Old Heath Rd . . . C3
Osborne St . . . B2
Petrolea Cl . . . A1
Police Station . . . C1
Popes La . . . B1
Port La . . . C3
Post Office . . . B1/B2/C2
Priory St . . . B2
Queen St . . . B2
Rawstorn Rd . . . B1
Rebon St . . . C3
Recreation Rd . . . C3
Ripple Way . . . A3
Roman Rd . . . B2
Roman Wall . . . B2
Romford Cl . . . A3
Rosebery Ave . . . B2
St Andrews Ave . . . B3
St Andrews Gdns . . . B3
St Botolph St . . . B2
St Botolphs . . . B2
St John's Abbey (site of) . . . C2
St John's St . . . B1
St Johns Walk Sh Ctr . . . B1
St Leonards Rd . . . C3
St Marys Fields . . . B1
St Peters . . . B1
St Peter's St . . . B1
Salisbury Ave . . . C1
Serpentine Walk . . . A1
Sheepen Pl . . . B1
Sheepen Rd . . . B1
Sir Isaac's Walk . . . B1
Smythies Ave . . . B2
South St . . . C1
South Way . . . C1
Sports Way . . . A2
Suffolk Cl . . . A3
Town Hall . . . B1
Valentine Dr . . . A3
Victor Rd . . . C3
Wakefield Cl . . . B2
Wellesley Rd . . . C1
Wells Rd . . . B2/B3
West St . . . C1
West Stockwell St . . . B1
Weston Rd . . . C3
Westway . . . A1
Wickham Rd . . . C1
Wimpole Rd . . . C3
Winchester Rd . . . C2
Winnock Rd . . . C2
Wolfe Ave . . . C2
Worcester Rd . . . B2

Coventry 179

Abbots La . . . A1
Albany Rd . . . B1
Alma St . . . B3
Art Faculty . . . B3
Asthill Grove . . . C2
Bablake School . . . A1
Barras La . . . A1/B1
Barrs Hill School . . . A1
Belgrade . . . B2
Bishop Burges St . . . A2
Bond's Hospital . . . B1
Broad Gate . . . B2
Broadway . . . C1
Bus Station . . . A3
Butts Radial . . . B1
Canal Basin . . . A2
Canterbury St . . . A3
Cathedral . . . B3
Chester St . . . A1
Cheylesmore Manor House . . . B2
Christ Church Spire . . . B2
City Walls & Gates . . . A2
Corporation St . . . B2
Council House . . . B2
Coundon Rd . . . A1
Coventry Station . . . C2
Coventry Transport Museum . . . A2
Cox St . . . A3
Croft Rd . . . B1
Dalton Rd . . . C1
Deasy Rd . . . C3
Earl St . . . B2
Eaton Rd . . . C2
Fairfax St . . . B2
Foleshill Rd . . . A2
Ford's Hospital . . . B2
Fowler Rd . . . A1
Friars Rd . . . C2
Gordon St . . . C1
Gosford St . . . B3
Greyfriars Green . . . B2
Greyfriars Rd . . . B2
Gulson Rd . . . B3
Hales St . . . A2
Harnall Lane East . . . A3
Harnall Lane West . . . A2
Herbert Art Gallery & Museum . . . B3
Hertford St . . . B2
Hewitt Ave . . . A1
High St . . . B2
Hill St . . . B1
Holy Trinity . . . B2
Holyhead Rd . . . A1
Howard St . . . A3
Huntingdon Rd . . . C1
Information Ctr . . . B2
Jordan Well . . . B3
King Henry VIII School . . . C1
Lady Godiva Statue . . . B2
Lamb St . . . A2
Leicester Row . . . A2
Library . . . B2
Little Park St . . . B2
London Rd . . . C3
Lower Ford St . . . B3
Magistrates & Crown Courts . . . B2
Manor House Drive . . . B2
Manor Rd . . . C2
Market . . . B2
Martyr's Memorial . . . C2
Meadow St . . . B1
Meriden St . . . A1
Michaelmas Rd . . . C2
Middleborough Rd . . . A1
Mile La . . . C3
Millennium Place . . . A2
Much Park St . . . B3
Naul's Mill Park . . . A1
New Union . . . B2
Park Rd . . . C2
Parkside . . . C3
Post Office . . . B2
Primrose Hill St . . . A3
Priory Gardens & Visitor Ctr . . . B2
Priory St . . . B3
Puma Way . . . C3
Quarryfield La . . . C3
Queen's Rd . . . B1
Quinton Rd . . . C2
Radford Rd . . . A2
Raglan St . . . B3
Retail Park . . . C1
Ringway (Hill Cross) . . . A1
Ringway (Queens) . . . B1
Ringway (Rudge) . . . B1
Ringway (St Johns) . . . B3
Ringway (St Nicholas) . . . A2
Ringway (St Patricks) . . . C2
Ringway (Swanswell) . . . A2
Ringway (Whitefriars) . . . B3
St John St . . . B2
St John The Baptist . . . B2
St Nicholas St . . . A2
Skydome . . . B1
Spencer Ave . . . C1
Spencer Park . . . C1
Spon St . . . B1
Sports Ctr . . . B3
Stoney Rd . . . C2
Stoney Stanton Rd . . . A3
Swanswell Pool . . . A3
Sydney Stringer Acad . . . A3
Technical College . . . B1
Technology Park . . . C3
The Precinct . . . B2
Theatre . . . B1
Thomas Landsdail St . . . C2
Tomson Ave . . . A1
Top Green . . . C2
Trinity St . . . B2
University . . . B3
University Sports Ctr . . . B3
Upper Hill St . . . A1
Upper Well St . . . A2
Victoria St . . . A3
Vine St . . . A3
Warwick Rd . . . C2
Waveley Rd . . . B1
Westminster Rd . . . C1
White St . . . A3
Windsor St . . . B1

Derby 179

Abbey St . . . C1
Agard St . . . B1
Albert St . . . B2
Albion St . . . B2
Ambulance Station . . . B1
Arthur St . . . A1
Ashlyn Rd . . . B3
Assembly Rooms . . . B2
Babington La . . . C2
Becket St . . . B1
Belper Rd . . . A1
Bold La . . . B1
Bradshaw Way . . . C2
Bradshaw Way Ret Pk . . . C2
Bridge St . . . B1
Brook St . . . B1
Burrows Walk . . . C2
Burton Rd . . . C1
Bus Station . . . B2
Business Park . . . A3
Caesar St . . . A2
Canal St . . . C3
Carrington St . . . C3
Cathedral . . . B2
Cathedral Rd . . . B1
Charnwood St . . . C2
Chester Green Rd . . . A2
City Rd . . . A2
Clarke St . . . A3
Cock Pitt . . . B3
Council House . . . B2
Courts . . . B1
Cranmer Rd . . . B3
Crompton St . . . C1
Crown & County Courts . . . B2
Crown Walk . . . C2
Curzon St . . . B1
Darley Grove . . . A1
Derby . . . C3
Derbyshire County Cricket Ground . . . B3
Derwent Bsns Ctr . . . A2
Derwent St . . . B2
Devonshire Walk . . . C2
Drewry La . . . C1
Duffield Rd . . . A1
Duke St . . . A2
Dunton Cl . . . B3
Eagle Market . . . C2
Eastgate . . . B3
East St . . . B2
Exeter St . . . B2
Farm St . . . C1
Ford St . . . B1
Forester St . . . C1
Fox St . . . A2
Friar Gate . . . B1
Friary St . . . B1
Full St . . . B2
Gerard St . . . C1
Gower St . . . C2
Green La . . . C2
Grey St . . . C1
Guildhall . . . B2
Harcourt St . . . C1
Highfield Rd . . . A1
Hill La . . . C2
Information Ctr . . . B2
Iron Gate . . . B2
John St . . . C3
Joseph Wright Ctr . . . B1
Kedleston Rd . . . A1
Key St . . . B2
King Alfred St . . . C1
King St . . . A1
Kingston St . . . A1
Lara Croft Way . . . C2
Leopold St . . . C2
Library . . . B1
Liversage St . . . C3
Lodge La . . . B1
London Rd . . . C2
London Rd Community Hospital . . . C2
Macklin St . . . C1
Mansfield Rd . . . A2
Market . . . B2
Market Pl . . . B2
May St . . . C1
Meadow La . . . B3
Melbourne St . . . C2
Mercian Way . . . C1
Midland Rd . . . C3
Monk St . . . C1
Morledge . . . B2
Mount St . . . C1
Mus & Art Gallery . . . B1
Noble St . . . C3
North Parade . . . A1
North St . . . A1
Nottingham Rd . . . B3
Osmaston Rd . . . C2
Otter St . . . A1
Park St . . . C3
Parker St . . . A1
Pickfords House . . . B1
Playhouse . . . C2
Police HQ . . . A2
Police Station . . . B2
Post Office . . . A1/A2/B1/B2/C2/C3
Prime Enterprise Pk . . . A3
Pride Parkway . . . C3
Prime Parkway . . . A3
Queens Leisure Ctr . . . B1
Racecourse . . . A3
Railway Terr . . . C3
Register Office . . . B2
Sacheverel St . . . C2
Sadler Gate . . . B1
St Alkmund's Way . . . B1/B2
St Helens House . . . A1
St Mary's . . . A1
St Mary's Bridge . . . A2
St Mary's Bridge Chapel . . . A2
St Mary's Gate . . . B1
St Paul's Rd . . . A2
St Peter's . . . C2
St Peter's St . . . C2
Siddals Rd . . . C3
Silk Mill . . . B2
Sir Frank Whittle Rd . . . A3
Spa La . . . C1
Spring St . . . C1
Stafford St . . . B1
Station Approach . . . C3
Stockbrook St . . . C1
Stores Rd . . . A3
Traffic St . . . C2
Wardwick . . . B1
Werburgh St . . . C1
West Ave . . . A1
Westfield Ctr . . . C2
West Meadows Industrial Estate . . . B3
Wharf Rd . . . A2
Wilmot St . . . C2
Wilson St . . . C1
Wood's La . . . C1

Dundee 179

Adelaide Pl . . . A1
Airlie Pl . . . C1
Albany Terr . . . A1
Albert St . . . A3
Alexander St . . . A2
Ann St . . . A2
Arthurstone Terr . . . A3
Bank St . . . B2
Barrack Rd . . . A1
Barrack St . . . B2
Bell St . . . B2
Blackscroft . . . A3
Blinshall St . . . B1
Brown St . . . B1
Bus Station . . . B3
Caird Hall . . . B2
Camperdown St . . . B3
Candle La . . . B3
Carmichael St . . . A1
City Churches . . . B2
City Quay . . . B3
City Sq . . . B2
Commercial St . . . B2
Constable St . . . A3
Constitution Ct . . . A1
Constitution Cres . . . A1
Constitution St . . . A1/B2
Cotton Rd . . . A3
Courthouse Sq . . . B1
Cowgate . . . A3
Crescent St . . . A3
Crichton St . . . B2
Dens Brae . . . A3
Dens Rd . . . A3
Discovery Point . . . C2
Douglas St . . . B1
Drummond St . . . A1
Dudhope Castle . . . A1
Dudhope St . . . A2
Dudhope Terr . . . A1
Dundee . . . C2
Dundee College . . . A1
Dundee Contemporary Arts . . . C2
Dundee High School . . . B2
Dundee Repertory . . . C2
Dura St . . . A3
East Dock St . . . B3
East Whale La . . . B3
East Marketgait . . . B3
Erskine St . . . A3
Euclid Cr . . . B2
Forebank Rd . . . A2
Foundry La . . . A3
Frigate Unicorn . . . B3
Gallagher Retail Park . . . B3
Gellatly St . . . B3
Government Offices . . . C2
Guthrie St . . . B1
Hawkhill . . . B1
Hilltown . . . A2
Howff Cemetery, The . . . B2
Information Ctr . . . B2
King St . . . A3
Kinghorne Rd . . . A1
Ladywell Ave . . . A3
Laurel Bank . . . A2
Law Hill, The . . . A1
Law Rd . . . A1
Law St . . . A1
Library . . . A2
Little Theatre . . . A2
Lochee Rd . . . B1
Lower Princes St . . . A3
Lyon St . . . A3
McManus Museum & Art Gallery . . . B2
Meadow Side . . . B2
Meadowside St Pauls . . . B2
Mercat Cross . . . B2
Murraygate . . . B2
Nelson St . . . A2
Nethergate . . . B2/C1
North Marketgait . . . B2
North Lindsay St . . . B2
Old Hawkhill . . . B1
Olympia Leisure Ctr . . . C3
Overgate Sh Ctr . . . B2
Park Pl . . . B1
Perth Rd . . . C1
Police Station . . . A2/B1
Post Office . . . B2
Princes St . . . A3
Prospect Pl . . . A2
Reform St . . . B2
Riverside Dr . . . C2
Roseangle . . . C1
Rosebank St . . . A2
RRS Discovery . . . C2
St Andrew's . . . C2
St Pauls Episcopal . . . B3
Science Ctr . . . C2
Seagate . . . B2
Sheriffs Court . . . B1
South George St . . . A2
South Marketgait . . . B3
South Tay St . . . B2
South Ward Rd . . . B2
Steps . . . A2
Tay Road Bridge . . . C3
Tayside House . . . B2
Trades La . . . B3
Union St . . . B2
Union Terr . . . A1
University Library . . . B2
University of Abertay . . . B2
University of Dundee . . . B1
Upper Constitution St . . . A1
Verdant Works . . . B1
Victoria Dock . . . B3
Victoria Rd . . . A2
Victoria St . . . A3
West Marketgait . . . B1/B2
Ward Rd . . . B1
Wellgate . . . B2
West Bell St . . . B1
Westfield Pl . . . C1
William St . . . A3
Wishart Arch . . . A3

Durham 180

Alexander Cr . . . B2
Allergate . . . B2
Archery Rise . . . C1
Assize Courts . . . B3
Back Western Hill . . . A1
Bakehouse La . . . A3
Baths . . . B3
Baths Bridge . . . B3
Boat House . . . B3
Bowling . . . A2
Boyd St . . . C3
Bus Station . . . B2
Castle . . . B2
Castle Chare . . . B2
Cathedral . . . B2
Church St . . . C3
Clay La . . . C1
Claypath . . . B3
College of St Hild & St Bede . . . B3
County Hall . . . A1
County Hospital . . . B1
Crook Hall & Gardens . . . A3
Crossgate . . . B2
Crossgate Peth . . . C1
Darlington Rd . . . C1
Durham . . . A2
Durham Light Infantry Mus & Arts Ctr . . . A2
Durham School . . . C2
Ellam Ave . . . C1
Elvet Bridge . . . B3
Elvet Court . . . B3
Farnley Hey . . . B1
Ferens Cl . . . A3
Fieldhouse La . . . A1
Flass St . . . B1
Framwelgate . . . A2
Framwelgate Bridge . . . B2
Framwelgate Peth . . . A2
Framwelgate Waterside . . . A2
Frankland La . . . A3
Freeman's Pl . . . A3
Gala & Sacred Journey . . . B3
Gate Sh Ctr, The . . . B2
Geoffrey Ave . . . C1
Gilesgate . . . B3
Grey College . . . C3
Hallgarth St . . . C3
Hatfield College . . . B3
Hawthorn Terr . . . B1
Heritage Ctr . . . B3
HM Prison . . . B3
Information Ctr . . . B3
John St . . . B1
Kingsgate Bridge . . . B3
Laburnum Terr . . . B1
Lawson Terr . . . B1
Leazes Rd . . . B2/B3
Library . . . B2
Margery La . . . B2
Mavin St . . . C3
Millburngate . . . B2
Millburngate Bridge . . . B2
Millennium Bridge (foot/cycle) . . . A2
Mountjoy Research Ctr . . . C3
Museum of Archaeology . . . B2
Nevilledale Terr . . . B1
New Elvet . . . B3
New Elvet Bridge . . . B3
North Bailey . . . B3
North End . . . A1
North Rd . . . A1/B2
Observatory . . . C1
Old Elvet . . . B3
Oriental Museum . . . C2
Oswald Court . . . C3
Parkside . . . B2
Passport Office . . . A2
Percy Terr . . . B1
Pimlico . . . C2
Police Station . . . B3
Post Office . . . A1/B2
Potters Bank . . . C1/C2
Prebends Bridge . . . C2
Prebends Walk . . . C2
Prince Bishops Sh Ctr . . . B3
Princes St . . . A1
Providence Row . . . A3
Quarryheads La . . . C2
Redhills La . . . B1
Redhills Terr . . . B1
Saddler St . . . B3
St Chad's College . . . C3
St Cuthbert's Society . . . C2
St John's College . . . C2
St Margaret's . . . B2
St Mary The Less . . . C2
St Mary's College . . . C2
St Monica Grove . . . B1
St Nicholas' . . . B3
St Oswald's . . . C3
Sidegate . . . A2
Silver St . . . B2
Sixth Form Ctr (Durham Gilesgate) . . . A3
South Bailey . . . C2
South Rd . . . C3
South St . . . B2
Springwell Ave . . . A1
Stockton Rd . . . C3
Students' Rec Ctr . . . B3
Sutton St . . . B2
The Avenue . . . B1
The Crescent . . . A1
The Grove . . . A1
The Sands . . . A3
Town Hall . . . B2
Treasury Museum . . . B2
University . . . B2
University Arts Block . . . B3
University Library . . . C3
Univ Science Site . . . C3
Walkergate Ctr . . . A3
Wearside Dr . . . A3
Western Hill . . . A1
Wharton Park . . . A2
Whinney Hill . . . C3

Edinburgh 180

Abbey Strand . . . B6
Abbeyhill . . . B6
Abbeyhill Cr . . . B6
Abbeymount . . . A6
Abercromby Pl . . . A3
Adam St . . . C5
Albany La . . . A4
Albany St . . . A4
Albert Memorial . . . B2
Albyn Pl . . . A2
Alva Pl . . . A6
Alva St . . . B1
Ann St . . . A1
Appleton Tower . . . C4
Archibald Pl . . . C3
Argyle House . . . C3
Assembly Rooms & Musical Hall . . . A3
Atholl Cr . . . B1
Atholl Crescent La . . . C1
Bank St . . . B4
Barony St . . . A4
Beaumont Pl . . . C5
Belford Rd . . . B1
Belgrave Cr . . . A1
Belgrave Crescent La . . . A1
Bell's Brae . . . B1
Blackfriars St . . . B4
Blair St . . . B4
Bread St . . . C2
Bristo Pl . . . C4
Bristo St . . . C4
Brougham St . . . C2
Broughton St . . . A4
Brown St . . . C5
Brunton Terr . . . A6
Buckingham Terr . . . A1
Burial Ground . . . A6
Bus Station . . . A4
Caledonian Cr . . . C1
Caledonian Rd . . . C1
Calton Hill . . . A4
Calton Hill . . . A5
Calton Rd . . . B4
Camera Obscura & Outlook Tower . . . B3
Candlemaker Row . . . C4
Canning St . . . B2
Canongate . . . B5
Canongate . . . B5
Carlton St . . . A1
Carlton Terr . . . A6
Carlton Terrace La . . . A6
Castle St . . . B2
Castle Terr . . . B2
Castlehill . . . B3
Central Library . . . B4
Chalmers Hospital . . . C3
Chalmers St . . . C3
Chambers St . . . C4
Chapel St . . . C4
Charles St . . . C4
Charlotte Sq . . . B2
Chester St . . . B1
Circus La . . . A2
Circus Pl . . . A2
City Art Ctr . . . B4
City Chambers . . . B4
City Observatory . . . A5
Clarendon Cr . . . A1
Clerk St . . . C5
Coates Cr . . . B1
Cockburn St . . . B4
College of Art . . . C3
Comely Bank Ave . . . A1
Comely Bank Row . . . A1
Cornwall St . . . C2
Cowans Cl . . . C5
Cowgate . . . B4
Cranston St . . . B5
Crichton St . . . C4
Croft-An-Righ . . . A6
Cumberland St . . . A2
Dalry Pl . . . C1
Dalry Rd . . . C1
Danube St . . . A1
Darnawy St . . . A2
David Hume Tower . . . C4
Davie St . . . C5
Dean Bridge . . . A1
Dean Gdns . . . A1
Dean Park Cr . . . A1
Dean Park Mews . . . A1
Dean Park St . . . A1
Dean Path . . . B1
Dean St . . . A1
Dean Terr . . . A1
Dewar Pl . . . C1
Dewar Place La . . . C1
Doune Terr . . . A2
Drummond Pl . . . A3
Drummond St . . . C5
Drumsheugh Gdns . . . B1
Dublin Mews . . . A3
Dublin St . . . A4
Dublin St La South . . . A4
Dumbiedykes Rd . . . B5
Dundas St . . . A3
Earl Grey St . . . C2
East Crosscauseway . . . C5
East Market St . . . B4
East Norton Pl . . . A6
East Princes St Gdns . . . B3
Easter Rd . . . A6
Edinburgh (Waverley) . . . B4
Edinburgh Castle . . . B3
Edinburgh Dungeon . . . B4
Edinburgh Int Conference Ctr . . . C2
Elder St . . . A4
Esplanade . . . B3
Eton Terr . . . A1
Eye Pavilion . . . C3
Festival Office . . . B3
Festival Theatre Edinburgh . . . C4
Filmhouse . . . C2
Fire Station . . . C2
Floral Clock . . . B3
Forres St . . . A2
Forth St . . . A4
Fountainbridge . . . C2
Frederick St . . . A3
Freemasons' Hall . . . B3
Fruit Market . . . B4
Gardner's Cr . . . C2
George Heriot's School . . . C3
George IV Bridge . . . B4
George Sq . . . C4
George Sq La . . . C4
George St . . . B3
Georgian House . . . B2
Gladstone's Land . . . B3
Glen St . . . C3
Gloucester La . . . A2
Gloucester Pl . . . A2
Gloucester St . . . A2
Graham St . . . C3
Grassmarket . . . C3
Great King St . . . A3
Great Stuart . . . B1
Greenside La . . . A5
Greenside Row . . . A5
Greyfriars Kirk . . . C4
Grindlay St . . . C2
Grosvenor St . . . C1
Grove St . . . C1
Gullan's Cl . . . B5
Guthrie St . . . B4
Hanover St . . . A3
Hart St . . . A4
Haymarket . . . C1
Haymarket Station . . . C1
Heriot Pl . . . C3
Heriot Row . . . A2
High School Yard . . . B5
High St . . . B4
Hill Pl . . . C5
Hill St . . . A2
Hillside Cr . . . A5
Holyrood Park . . . C6
Holyrood Rd . . . B5
Home St . . . C2
Hope St . . . B2
Horse Wynd . . . B6
Howden St . . . C5
Howe St . . . A2
India Pl . . . A2
India St . . . A2
Infirmary St . . . B4
Information Ctr . . . B4
Jamaica Mews . . . A2
Jeffrey St . . . B4
John Knox House . . . B4
Johnston Terr . . . C3
Keir St . . . C3
Kerr St . . . A2
King's Stables Rd . . . B2
Lady Lawson St . . . C3
Lauriston Gdns . . . C3
Lauriston Park . . . C3
Lauriston Pl . . . C3
Lauriston St . . . C3
Lawnmarket . . . B3
Learmonth Gdns . . . A1
Learmonth Terr . . . A1
Leith St . . . A4
Lennox St . . . A1
Lennox St La . . . A1
Leslie Pl . . . A2
London Rd . . . A5
Lothian Health Board . . . C5
Lothian Rd . . . B2
Lothian St . . . C4
Lower Menz Pl . . . A6
Lynedoch Pl . . . B1
Manor Pl . . . B1
Market St . . . B4
Marshall St . . . C4
Maryfield . . . A6
Maryfield Pl . . . A6
McEwan Hall . . . C4
Medical School . . . C4
Melville St . . . B1
Meuse La . . . B4
Middle Meadow Walk . . . C4
Milton St . . . A6
Montrose Terr . . . A6
Moray House (Coll) . . . B5
Moray Place . . . A2
Morrison Link . . . C1
Morrison St . . . C1
Mound Pl . . . B3
Multrees Walk . . . A4
Mus Collections Ctr . . . A4
Mus of Childhood . . . B5
Mus of Edinburgh . . . B5
Mus on the Mound . . . B4
National Gallery . . . B3
National Library of Scotland . . . B4
National Monument . . . A5
National Museum of Scotland . . . C4
National Portrait Gallery . . . B4
National Records Scotland . . . A4
Nelson Monument . . . A5
Nelson St . . . A3
New St . . . B5
Nicolson Sq . . . C4
Nicolson St . . . C4
Niddry St . . . B4
North Bridge . . . B4
North Meadow Walk . . . C3
North Bank St . . . B3
North Castle St . . . A2
North Charlotte St . . . A2
North St Andrew St . . . A4
North St David St . . . A3
North West Circus Pl . . . A2
Northumberland St . . . A3
Odeon . . . C2
Old Royal High School . . . A5
Old Tolbooth Wynd . . . B5
Omni Ctr . . . A4
Our Dynamic Earth . . . B6
Oxford Terr . . . A1
Pal of Holyrood Ho . . . B6
Palmerston Pl . . . B1
Panmure Pl . . . C3
Parliament House . . . B4
Parliament Sq . . . B4
People's Story, The . . . B5
Playhouse Theatre . . . A4
Pleasance . . . C5
Police Station . . . A4
Ponton St . . . C2
Post Office . . . A3/A4/B5/C1/C2/C4/C5
Potterrow . . . C4
Princes Mall . . . B4
Princes St . . . B3
Queen St . . . A2
Queen Street Gdns . . . A3
Queen's Dr . . . B6/C6
Queensferry Rd . . . A1
Queensferry St . . . B1
Queensferry St La . . . B2
Radical Rd . . . C6
Randolph Cr . . . B1
Regent Gdns . . . A5
Regent Rd . . . B5
Regent Rd Park . . . A6
Regent Terr . . . A5
Remains of Holyrood Abbey (AD 1128) . . . A6
Richmond La . . . C5
Richmond Pl . . . C5
Rose St . . . B2
Rosemount Bldgs . . . C1
Ross Open Air Theatre . . . B3
Rothesay Pl . . . B1
Rothesay Terr . . . B1
Roxburgh Pl . . . C5
Roxburgh St . . . C5
Royal Bank of Scotland . . . A4
Royal Circus . . . A2
Royal Lyceum . . . C2
Royal Scottish Academy . . . B3
Royal Terr . . . A5
Royal Terrace Gdns . . . A5
Rutland Sq . . . B2
Rutland St . . . B2
St Andrew Sq . . . A3
St Andrew's House . . . A4
St Bernard's Cr . . . A1
St Cecilia's Hall . . . B4
St Colme St . . . A2
St Cuthbert's . . . B2
St Giles' . . . B4
St James Ctr . . . A4
St John St . . . B5
St John's . . . B2
St John's Hill . . . B5
St Leonard's Hill . . . C5
St Leonard's La . . . C5
St Leonard's St . . . C5
St Mary's . . . A4
St Mary's (RC) . . . A4
St Mary's Scottish Episcopal . . . B1
St Mary's St . . . B5
St Stephen St . . . A2
Salisbury Crags . . . C6
Saunders St . . . A2
Scotch Whisky Experience . . . B3
Scott Monument . . . B4
Scottish Parliament . . . B6
Scottish Storytelling Ctr . . . B5
Semple St . . . C2
Shandwick Pl . . . B2
South Bridge . . . B4
South Charlotte St . . . B2
South College St . . . C4
South Learmonth Gdns . . . A1
South St Andrew St . . . A4
South St David St . . . A3
Spittal St . . . C2
Stafford St . . . B1
Student Ctr . . . C4
Surgeons' Hall . . . C5
TA Ctr . . . C4
Tattoo Office . . . B4
Teviot Pl . . . C4
The Mall . . . B6
The Mound . . . B3
The Royal Mile . . . B5
The Writer's Mus . . . B4
Thistle St . . . A3
Torphichen Pl . . . C1
Torphichen St . . . C1
Traverse Theatre . . . B2
Tron Sq . . . B4
Tron, The . . . B4
Union St . . . A4
University . . . C4
University Library . . . C4
Upper Grove Pl . . . C1
Usher Hall . . . C2
Vennel . . . C3
Victoria St . . . B3
Viewcraig Gdns . . . B5
Viewcraig St . . . B5
VUE . . . A4
Walker St . . . B1
Waterloo Pl . . . A4
Waverley Bridge . . . B4
Wemyss Pl . . . A2
West Approach Rd . . . C1
West Crosscauseway . . . C5
West Maitland St . . . C1
West of Nicholson St . . . C4
West Port . . . C3
West Princes St Gdns . . . B3
West Richmond St . . . C5
West Tollcross . . . C2
White Horse Cl . . . B5
William St . . . B1
Windsor St . . . A5
York La . . . A4
York Pl . . . A4
Young St . . . B2

Exeter 180

Alphington St . . . C1
Athelstan Rd . . . B3
Bampfylde St . . . B2
Barnardo Rd . . . C3
Barnfield Hill . . . B3
Barnfield Rd . . . B2/B3
Barnfield Theatre . . . B2
Bartholomew St East . . . B1
Bartholomew St West . . . B1
Bear St . . . B2
Beaufort Rd . . . C1
Bedford St . . . B2
Belgrave Rd . . . A3
Belmont Rd . . . A3
Blackall Rd . . . A2
Blackboy Rd . . . A3
Bonhay Rd . . . B1
Bull Meadow Rd . . . C2
Bus & Coach Sta . . . B3
Castle St . . . B2
Cecil Rd . . . C1
Cheeke St . . . A3
Church Rd . . . C1
Chute St . . . A3
City Industrial Estate . . . C2
City Wall . . . B1/B2
Civic Ctr . . . B2
Clifton Rd . . . B3
Clifton St . . . B3
Clock Tower . . . A1
College Rd . . . B3
Colleton Cr . . . C2
Commercial Rd . . . C1
Coombe St . . . B2
Cowick St . . . C1
Crown Courts . . . B2
Custom House . . . C2
Danes' Rd . . . A2
Denmark Rd . . . B3
Devon County Hall . . . C3
Devonshire Pl . . . A3
Dinham Rd . . . B1
East Grove Rd . . . C3
Edmund St . . . C1
Elmgrove Rd . . . A1
Exe St . . . B1
Exeter Cathedral . . . B2

Exeter Central Sta A1
Exeter City Football Ground A3
Exeter College A1
Exeter Picture Ho B1
Fire Station A1
Fore St B1
Friars Walk C2
Guildhall B2
Guildhall Sh Ctr B2
Harlequins Sh Ctr B1
Haven Rd C2
Heavitree Rd B3
Hele Rd A1
High St B2
HM Prison A2
Holloway St C2
Hoopern St A2
Horseguards A2
Howell Rd A1
Information Ctr B3
Iron Bridge B1
Isca Rd C1
Jesmond Rd A3
King William St A2
King St B1
Larkbeare Rd C2
Leisure Ctr C1
Library B2
Longbrook St A2
Longbrook Terr A2
Lower North St B1
Lucky La C2
Lyndhurst Rd C3
Magdalen Rd B3
Magdalen St B2
Magistrates & Crown Courts A2
Market B2
Market St B2
Marlborough Rd C3
Mary Arches St B1
Matford Ave C3
Matford La C3
Matford Rd C3
May St A3
Mol's Coffee Ho B2
New Theatre C2
New Bridge St B1
New North Rd A1/A2
North St B1
Northernhay St B1
Norwood Ave C3
Odeon A3
Okehampton St C1
Old Mill Cl C2
Old Tiverton Rd A3
Oxford Rd A3
Paris St B2
Parr St A3
Paul St B1
Pennsylvania Rd A2
Police HQ B3
Portland Street A3
Post Office A3/B1/B3/C1
Powderham Cr A3
Preston St B1
Princesshay Sh Ctr B2
Queen St A1
Queens Rd C1
Queen's Terr A1
Radford Rd C2
Richmond Rd A1
Roberts Rd C2
Rougemont Castle A2
Rougemont House B2
Royal Albert Memorial Museum B2
St David's Hill A1
St James' Pk Sta A3
St James' Rd A3
St Leonard's Rd C3
St Lukes University B3
St Mary Steps C1
St Nicholas Priory B1
St Thomas Station C1
Sandford Walk B3
School for the Deaf C2
School Rd C1
Sidwell St A2
Smythen St B1
South St B2
Southernhay East B2
Southernhay West B2
Spacex Gallery B1
Spicer Rd B3
Sports Ctr A3
Summerland St A3
Swimming Pool & Leisure Ctr B3
Sydney Rd C1
Tan La C2
The Quay C2
Thornton Hill A2
Topsham Rd C3
Tucker's Hall B1
Tudor St B1
Velwell Rd A1
Verney St A3
Water La C1/C2
Weirfield Rd C2
Well St A3
West Ave A2
West Grove Rd C3
Western Way A3/B1/B2
Wonford Rd B3/C3
York Rd A2

Glasgow 181

Admiral St C2
Albert Bridge C5
Albion St B5
Anderston B3
Anderston Ctr B3
Anderston Quay B3
Arches B4
Argyle St A1/A2/B3/B4/B5
Argyle Street B5
Argyll Arcade B5
Arlington St A3
Arts Ctr B3
Ashley St A3
Bain St C6
Baird St A6
Baliol St A3
Ballater St C5
Barras, The (Market) C6
Bath St A3
BBC Scotland/SMG B1
Bell St C6
Bell's Bridge B1
Bentinck St A2
Berkeley St A3
Bishop La B3
Black St A6
Blackburn St C2
Blackfriars St B6
Blantyre St A1
Blythswood Sq A4
Blythswood St B4
Bothwell St B4
Brand St C1
Breadalbane St A2
Bridge St C4
Bridge St C4
Bridgegate C5
Briggait C5
Broomhill Park A6
Broomielaw B4
Broomielaw Quay Gdns B3
Brown St B4
Brunswick St B5
Buccleuch St A3
Buchanan Bus Sta A5
Buchanan Galleries A5
Buchanan St B5
Buchanan St B5
Cadogan St B4
Caledonian Univ A5
Calgary St A5
Cambridge St A4
Canal St A5
Candleriggs B5
Carlton Pl C4
Carnarvon St A3
Carrick St B4
Castle St B6
Cathedral Sq B6
Cathedral St B5
Central College of Commerce B5
Ctr for Contemporary Arts A4
Centre St C4
Cessnock C1
Cessnock St C1
Charing Cross A3
Charlotte St C6
Cheapside St B3
Cineworld A5
Citizens' Theatre C5
City Chambers Complex B5
City Halls B5
Clairmont Gdns A2
Claremont St A2
Claremont Terr A2
Claythorne St C6
Cleveland St A3
Clifford La C1
Clifford St C1
Clifton Pl A2
Clifton St A2
Clutha St C1
Clyde Arc B2
Clyde Auditorium B2
Clyde Pl C4
Clyde Place Quay C4
Clyde St C5
Clyde Walkway C3
Clydeside Expressway B2
Coburg St C4
Cochrane St B5
College of Nautical Studies C5
College St B6
Collins St B6
Commerce St C4
Cook St C4
Cornwall St C2
Couper St A5
Cowcaddens A4
Cowcaddens Rd A4
Crimea St B3
Custom House C4
Custom House Quay Gdns C4
Dalhousie St A4
Dental Hospital A4
Derby St A2
Dobbie's Loan A4/A5
Dobbie's Loan Pl A5
Dorset St A3
Douglas St B4
Doulton Fountain C6
Dover St A2
Drury St B4
Drygate B6
Duke St B6
Dunaskin St A1
Dunblane St A4
Dundas St B5
Dunlop St C5
East Campbell St C6
Eastvale Pl A1
Eglinton St C4
Elderslie St A3
Elliot St B2
Elmbank St A3
Esmond St A1
Exhibition Ctr B2
Exhibition Way B2
Eye Infirmary A2
Festival Park C1
Film Theatre A4
Finnieston Quay B2
Finnieston Sq B2
Finnieston St B2
Fitzroy Pl A2
Florence St C5
Fox St C5
Gallowgate C6
Garnet St A3
Garnethill St A4
Garscube Rd A4
George Sq B5
George St B5
George V Bridge C4
Gilbert St A1
Glasgow Bridge C4
Glasgow Cathedral B6
Glasgow Central B4
Glasgow Green C6
Glasgow Metropolitan College B5/C5
Glasgow Tower B1
Glasgow Science Ctr B1
Glasgow Science Ctr Footbridge B1
Glassford St B5
Glebe St A6
Gorbals Cross C5
Gorbals St C5
Gordon St B4
Govan Rd B1/C1/C2
Grace St B3
Grand Ole Opry C2
Grafton Pl A5
Grant St A3
Granville St A3
Gray St A2
Greendyke St C6
Harley St C1
Harvie St C1
Haugh Rd A1
Heliport B1
Henry Wood Hall A2
High Court C5
High St B6
High Street B6
Hill St A3
Holland St A3
Holm St B4
Hope St A5
Houldsworth St B2
Houston Pl C3
Houston St C3
Howard St C5
Hunter St C6
Hutcheson St B5
Hutchesons Hall B5
Hydepark St B3
Imax Cinema B1
India St A3
Information Ctr B5
Ingram St B5
Jamaica St B4
James Watt St B4
John Knox St B6
John St B5
Kelvin Hall A1
Kelvin Statue A2
Kelvin Way A2
Kelvingrove Art Gallery & Museum A1
Kelvingrove Park A2
Kelvingrove St A2
Kelvinhaugh St A1
Kennedy St A6
Kent Rd A2
Killermont St A5
King St B5
King's A3
Kingston Bridge C3
Kingston St C4
Kinning Park C2
Kyle St A5
Lancefield Quay B2
Lancefield St B3
Langshot St C1
Lendel Pl C1
Lighthouse B4
Lister St A6
Little St B3
London Rd C6
Lorne St C1
Lower Harbour B1
Lumsden St A1
Lymburn St A1
Lyndoch Cr A3
Lynedoch Pl A3
Lynedoch St A3
Maclellan St C1
Mair St C2
Maitland St A4
Mavisbank Gdns C2
Mcalpine St B3
Mcaslin St A6
McLean Sq C2
McLellan Gallery A4
McPhater St A4
Merchants' House B5
Middlesex St C2
Middleton St C1
Midland St B4
Miller St B5
Millroad St C6
Milnpark St C2
Milton St A4
Minerva St B2
Mitchell Library A3
Mitchell St West B4
Mitchell Theatre A3
Modern Art Gallery B5
Moir St C6
Molendinar St C6
Moncur St C6
Montieth Row C6
Montrose St B5
Morrison St C3
Mosque C5
Nairn St A1
Nelson Mandela Sq B5
Nelson St C4
Nelson's Monument C6
New City Rd A4
Newton St A3
Newton Pl A3
Nicholson St C4
Nile St B5
Norfolk Court C4
Norfolk St C4
North Frederick St B5
North Hanover St B5
North Portland St B6
North St A3
North Wallace St A5
O2 Academy C4
Odeon C3
Old Dumbarton Rd A1
Osborne St B5/C5
Oswald St B4
Overnewton St A1
Oxford St C4
Pacific Dr B1
Paisley Rd C3
Paisley Rd West C1
Park Circus A2
Park Gdns A2
Park St South A2
Park Terr A2
Parkgrove Terr A2
Parnie St C5
Parson St A6
Partick Bridge A1
Passport Office A5
Pavilion Theatre A4
Pembroke St A3
People's Palace C6
Pinkston Rd A6
Piping Ctr, The National A5
Pitt St A4/B4
Plantation Park C1
Plantation Quay B1
Police Sta A4/A6/B5
Port Dundas Rd A5
Port St B2
Portman St C2
Prince's Dock B1
Princes Sq B5
Provand's Lordship B6
Queen St B5
Queen Street B5
Renfrew St A3/A4
Renton St A5
Richmond St B5
Robertson St B4
Rose St A4
Rottenrow B5
Royal Concert Hall A5
Royal Cr A2
Royal Exchange Sq B5
Royal Highland Fusiliers Mus A3
Royal Hospital For Sick Children A1
Royal Infirmary B6
Royal Scottish Academy of Music & Drama A4
Royal Terr A2
Rutland Cr C2
St Kent St C6
St Andrew's (RC) C5
St Andrew's C6
St Andrew's St C5
St Enoch B5
St Enoch Sh Ctr B5
St Enoch Sq B4
St George's Rd A3
St James Rd B6
St Mungo Ave A5/A6
St Mungo Museum of Religious Life B6
St Mungo Pl A6
St Vincent Cr A2
St Vincent Pl B5
St Vincent St B3/B4
St Vincent Street Church B4
St Vincent Terr B3
Saltmarket C5
Sandyford Pl A3
Sauchiehall St A2/A4
School of Art A4
Scotland St C2
Scott St A4
Scottish Exhibition & Conference Ctr B1
Seaward St C2
Shaftesbury St B3
Sheriff Court C5
Shields Rd C3
Shuttle St B6
Somerset Pl A2
South Portland St C4
Springburn Rd A6
Springfield Quay C3
Stanley St C2
Stevenson St C6
Stewart St A4
Stirling Rd B6
Stirling's Library B5
Stobcross Quay B1
Stobcross Rd B1
Stock Exchange B5
Stockwell Pl C5
Stockwell St B5
Stow College A4
Strathclyde Univ B6
Sussex St C2
Synagogues A3/C4
Taylor Pl A6
Tenement House A3
Teviot St A1
Theatre Royal A4
Tolbooth Steeple & Mercat Cross C6
Tower St C2
Trades House B5
Tradeston St C4
Transport Mus A1
Tron C5
Trongate B5
Tunnel St B2
Turnbull St C5
Union St B4
Victoria Bridge C5
Virginia St B5
West Greenhill Pl B2
West Regent St A4
Wallace St C3
Walls St B6
Walmer Cr C1
Warrock St B3
Washington St B3
Waterloo St B4
Watson St B6
Watt St C3
Wellington St B4
West Campbell St B4
West George St B4
West Graham St A4
West Regent St B4
West St C4
West St C4
Westminster Terr A2
Whitehall St B3
Wilson St B5
Woodlands Gate A3
Woodlands Rd A3
Woodlands Terr A2
Woodside Cr A3
Woodside Pl A3
Woodside Terr A3
York St B4
Yorkhill Pde A1
Yorkhill St A1

Gloucester 181

Albion St C1
Alexandra Rd B3
Alfred St C3
All Saints Rd C2
Alvin St B2
Arthur St C2
Baker St C1
Barton St C2
Blackfriars B1
Blenheim Rd C2
Bristol Rd C1
Brunswick Rd C2
Bruton Way B2
Bus Station B2
Cattle Market A1
City Council Offices B1
City Mus, Art Gall & Library B2
Clarence St B2
College of Art C2
Commercial Rd B1
Cromwell St C2
Deans Way A2
Denmark Rd A3
Derby Rd C3
Docks C1
Eastgate St B2
Edwy Parade A2
Estcourt Cl A3
Estcourt Rd A3
Falkner St C2
Folk Museum B1
GL1 Leisure Ctr C2
Gloucester Cath B1
Gloucester Station B2
Gloucestershire Royal Hospital (A&E) B3
Gloucester Waterways C1
Goodyere St C2
Gouda Way A1
Great Western Rd B3
Guildhall B2
Heathville Rd A3
Henry Rd B3
Henry St B2
High Orchard St C1
Hinton Rd A2
India Rd C3
Information Ctr B1
Jersey Rd C3
King's C2
King's Sq B2
Kingsholm Rd A2
Kingsholm Rugby Football Ground A2
Lansdown Rd A3
Library C2
Llanthony Rd C1
London Rd B3
Longsmith St B1
Malvern Rd A3
Market Pde B2
Merchants Rd C1
Mercia Rd A1
Metz Way C3
Midland Rd C2
Millbrook St C3
Market B2
Montpellier C1
Napier St C3
Nettleton Rd C2
New Inn B2
New Olympus C3
North Rd A3
Northgate St B2
Oxford Rd A2
Oxford St B2
Pk & Ride Gloucester A1
Park Rd C2
Park St B2
Parliament St C1
Pitt St B1
Police Station B1
Post Office B2
Quay St B1
Recreation Gd A1/A2
Regent St C2
Robert Raikes Ho B1
Royal Oak Rd B1
Russell St B2
Ryecroft St C2
St Aldate St B2
St Ann Way C1
St Catherine St A2
St Mark St A2
St Mary De Crypt B1
St Mary De Lode B1
St Nicholas's B1
St Oswald's Rd A1
St Oswald's Trading Estate A1
St Peter's B2
Seabroke Rd A3
Sebert St A2
Severn Rd C1
Sherborne St B2
Shire Hall B1
Sidney St C3
Soldiers of Gloucestershire B1
Southgate St B1/C1
Spa Field C1
Spa Rd C1
Sports Ground A2/B2
Station Rd B2
Stratton Rd C3
Stroud Rd C1
Superstore A1
Swan Rd A2
Technical College C1
The Mall B2
The Park C2
The Quay B1
Trier Way C1/C2
Union St A2
Vauxhall Rd C3
Victoria St C2
Wellington St C2
Westgate St B1
Widden St C2
Worcester St B2

Hanley (Stoke-on-Trent) 181

Acton St A3
Albion St B2
Argyle St C1
Ashbourne Gr A2
Avoca St A3
Baskerville Rd B3
Bedford Rd C1
Bedford St C1
Bethesda St B2
Bexley St A2
Birches Head Rd A3
Botteslow St C3
Boundary St A2
Broad St C2
Broom St A3
Bryan St A2
Bucknall New Rd B3
Bucknall Old Rd B3
Bus Station B3
Cannon St C2
Castlefield St C1
Cavendish St B1
Central Forest Pk A2
Charles St B3
Cheapside B2
Chell St A3
Clarke St C1
Cleveland Rd C2
Clifford St C3
Clough St B2
Clyde St C1
College Rd C2
Cooper St C2
Corbridge Rd A1
Cutts St C2
Davis St C1
Denbigh St A1
Derby St C3
Dilke St A3
Dundas St A3
Dundee Rd C1
Dyke St B3
Eastwood Rd C3
Eaton St A3
Etruria Park B1
Etruria Rd B1
Etruria Vale Rd C1
Festing St A3
Festival Retail Park A1
Fire Station C2
Foundry St B2
Franklyn St C3
Garnet St B1
Garth St B3
George St A3
Gilman St B3
Glass St B3
Goodson St B3
Greyhound Way A1
Grove Pl C1
Hampton St C3
Hanley Park C2
Harding Rd C2
Hassall St B3
Havelock Pl C1
Hazlehurst St C3
Hinde St C2
Hope St B2
Houghton St C2
Hulton St A3
Information Ctr B3
Jasper St C2
Jervis St A3
John Bright St A3
John St B2
Keelings Rd A3
Kimberley Rd C1
Ladysmith Rd C1
Lawrence St C2
Leek Rd C3
Library C2
Lichfield St C3
Linfield Rd B3
Loftus St A2
Lower Bedford St C1
Lower Bryan St A2
Lower Mayer St A3
Lowther St A1
Magistrates Court C2
Malham St A2
Marsh St B2
Matlock St C3
Mayer St A3
Milton St C1
Mitchell Memorial Theatre B2
Morley St B2
Moston St A3
Mount Pleasant C1
Mulgrave St A1
Mynors St B3
Nelson Pl B3
New Century St B1
Octagon Retail Park B1
Ogden Rd C3
Old Hall St B3
Old Town Rd A3
Pall Mall B2
Palmerston St C3
Park and Ride C2
Parker St B2
Pavilion Dr A1
Pelham St C3
Percy St B2
Piccadilly B2
Picton St B3
Plough St A3
Police Station C2
Portland St A1
Post Office A3/B3/C3
Potteries Museum & Art Gallery B2
Potteries Sh Ctr B2
Potteries Way C2
Powell St A1
Pretoria Rd C1
Quadrant Rd B2
Ranelagh St C2
Raymond St C2
Rectory Rd C1
Regent Rd C2
Regent Theatre B2
Richmond Terr C2
Ridgehouse Dr A1
Robson St C2
St Ann St B3
St Luke St B3
Sampson St B2
Shaw St A1
Sheaf St C2
Shearer St C1
Shelton New Rd C1
Shirley Rd C2
Slippery La B2
Snow Hill C2
Spur St C3
Stafford St B2
Statham St B2
Stubbs La C3
Sun St C1
Supermarket A1/B2
Talbot St C3
The Parkway C2
Town Hall B2
Town Rd A3
Trinity St B2
Union St A2
Upper Hillchurch St A3
Upper Huntbach St B3
Victoria Hall Theatre B3
Warner St C2
Warwick St C1
Waterloo Rd A1
Waterloo St B3
Well St B3
Wellesley St C2
Wellington Rd B3
Wellington St B3
Whitehaven Dr A2
Whitmore St C1
Windermere St A1
Woodall St A1
Yates St C2
York St A2

Harrogate 182

Albert St C2
Alexandra Rd B2
Arthington Ave B2
Ashfield Rd A2
Back Cheltenham Mount B2
Beech Grove C1
Belmont Rd C1
Bilton Dr A2
Bower Rd B2
Bower St B2
Bus Station B2
Cambridge Rd B2
Cambridge St B2
Cemetery A2
Chatsworth Pl A2
Chatsworth Grove A2
Chatsworth Rd A2
Chelmsford Rd B3
Cheltenham Cr B2
Cheltenham Mt B2
Cheltenham Pde B2
Christ Church B3
Christ Church Oval B3
Chudleigh Rd B3
Clarence Dr B1
Claro Rd A3
Claro Way A3
Coach Park B2
Coach Rd B3
Cold Bath Rd C1
Commercial St B2
Coppice Ave A1
Coppice Dr A1
Coppice Gate A1
Cornwall Rd B1
Council Offices B1
Court C3
Crescent Gdns B1
Crescent Rd B1
Dawson Terr A2
Devonshire Pl B3
Diamond Mews C1
Dixon Rd A2
Dixon Terr A2
Dragon Ave B3
Dragon Parade B2
Dragon Rd B2
Duchy Rd B1
East Parade B2
East Park Rd C3
Esplanade B1
Fire Station A2
Franklin Mount A2
Franklin Rd B2
Franklin Square A2
Glebe Rd C1
Grove Park Ct A3
Grove Park Terr A3
Grove Rd A2
Hampswaite Rd A1
Harcourt Dr B3
Harcourt Rd B3
Harrogate B2
Harrogate Int Ctr B2
Harrogate Ladies Coll B1
Harrogate Theatre B2
Heywood Rd C1
Hollins Cr A1
Hollins Mews A1
Hollins Rd A1
Homestead Rd C3
Hydro L Ctr, The A1
Information Ctr B1
James St B2
Jenny Field Dr A1
John St B2
Kent Dr A1
Kent Rd A1
Kings Rd A2
Kingsway B3
Kingsway Dr B3
Lancaster Rd C1
Leeds Rd C2
Lime Grove B3
Lime St A3
Mayfield Grove B2
Mayfield Pl A2
Mercer B1
Montpellier Hill B1
Mornington Cr A3
Mornington Terr B3
Mowbray Sq B3
North Park Rd B3
Nydd Vale Rd B2
Oakdale Ave A1
Oatlands Dr C3
Odeon B2
Osborne Rd A2
Otley Rd C2
Oxford St B2
Park Chase B3
Park Parade B3
Park View B2
Parliament St B1
Police Station B3
Post Office B2/C1
Providence Terr A2
Queen Parade C3
Queen's Rd C1
Raglan St C2
Regent Ave A3
Regent Grove A3
Regent Parade A3
Regent St A3
Regent Terr A3
Rippon Rd A1
Robert St C2
Royal Baths & Turkish Baths B1
Royal Pump Room B1
St Luke's Mount A2
St Mary's Ave C1
St Mary's Walk C1
St Pancras International A4
Scargill Rd A1
Skipton Rd A3
Skipton St A2
Slingsby Walk C3
South Park Rd C2
Spring Grove A1
Springfield Ave B1
Station Ave B2
Station Parade B2
Strawberry Dale B2
Stray Rein C3
Studley Rd A2
Superstore B2
Swan Rd B1
The Parade B2
The Stray C2/C3
Tower St C2
Trinity Rd C2
Union St B2
Valley Dr C1
Valley Gardens C1
Valley Mount C1
Victoria Ave C2
Victoria Rd C1
Victoria Shopping Ctr B2
Waterloo St A2
West Park C2
West Park St C2
Wood View A1
Woodfield Ave A3
Woodfield Dr A3
Woodfield Grove A3
Woodfield Rd A3
Woodfield Square A3
Woodside B3
York Pl C3
York Rd B1

Hull 182

Adelaide St C1
Albert Dock C1
Albion St B2
Alfred Gelder St B2
Anlaby Rd B1
Arctic Corsair B3
Beverley Rd A1
Blanket Row C2
Bond St B2
Bridlington Ave A2
Brook St B1
Brunswick Ave A1
Bus Station B1
Camilla Cl C3
Cannon St A2
Cannon's C1
Caroline St A2
Carr La B2
Castle St C2
Central Library B1
Charles St A2
Citadel Way B3
City Hall B2
City Hall Theatre B2
Clarence St B3
Cleveland St A3
Clifton St A1
Club Culture C2
Colonial St B1
Court B2
Deep, The C3
Dock Office Row B3
Dock St B2
Dinostar C2
Drypool Bridge B3
Egton St A3
English St C1
Ferens Gallery B2
Ferensway B1
Francis St A2
Francis St West A2
Freehold St A1
Freetown Way A2
Fruit Theatre C2
Garrison Rd B3
George St B2
Gibson St A2
Great Thornton St B1
Great Union St A3
Green La A2
Grey St A1
Grimston St B2
Grosvenor St A1
Guildhall B2
Guildhall Rd B2
Hands-on History B2
Harley St A1
Hessle Rd C1
High St B3
Holy Trinity B2
Hull & East Riding Museum B3
Hull Arena C1
Hull College B3
Hull History Ctr A2
Hull (Paragon) Sta B1
Hull Truck Theatre B1
Humber Dock Marina C2
Humber Dock St C2
Humber St C2
Hyperion St A3
Information Ctr B2
Jameson St B1
Jarratt St B2
Jenning St A3
King Billy Statue C2
King Edward St B2
King St A2
Kingston Retail Park C1
Kingston St C2
Liddell St A1
Lime St A3
Lister St C1
Lockwood St A2
Maister House B3
Maritime Museum B2
Market B2
Market Place B2
Minerva Pier C2
Mulgrave St A3
Myton Bridge C3
Myton St B1
NAPA (Northern Academy of Performing Arts) B1
Nelson St C2
New Cleveland St A3
New George St A2
New Theatre A2
Norfolk St A1
North Bridge A3
North St B1
Odeon C1
Old Harbour C3
Osborne St B1
Paragon St B2
Park St B1
Percy St A2
Pier St C2
Police Station B1
Post Office A1/B1/B2
Porter St C1
Portland St B1
Posterngate B2
Prince's Quay B2
Prospect Ctr B1
Prospect St B1
Queen's Gdns B2
Railway Dock Marina C2
Railway St C2
Real B1
Red Gallery B1
Reform St A2
Retail Park B1
River Hull Footbridge B3
Riverside Quay C2
Roper St B2
St James St C1
St Luke's St B1
St Mark St A3
St Mary the Virgin B3
St Stephens Sh Ctr B1
Scott St A2
South Bridge Rd B3
Spring Bank A1
Spring St B1
Spurn Lightship C2
Spyvee St A3
Streetlife Transport Museum B3
Sykes St A2
Tidal Surge Barrier C3
Tower St B3
Trinity House B2
University B2
Vane St A1
Victoria Pier C2
Waterhouse La C2
Waterloo St A1
Waverley St C1
Wellington St C2
Wellington St West C2
West St B1
Whitefriargate B2
Wilberforce Dr B2
Wilberforce Ho B3
Wilberforce Monument B3
William St C1
Wincolmlee A3
Witham A3
Wright St A1

Ipswich 182

Alderman Rd B2
All Saints' Rd A1
Alpe St B2
Ancaster Rd C1
Ancient House B3
Anglesea Rd B2
Ann St B2
Arboretum A2
Austin St C2
Belstead Rd C2
Berners St B2
Bibb Way B1
Birkfield Dr C1
Black Horse La B2
Bolton La B3
Bond St C3
Bowthorpe Cl B2
Bramford La A1
Bramford Rd A1
Bridge St C2
Brookfield Rd A1
Brooks Hall Rd A1
Broomhill A2
Broomhill Rd A1
Broughton Rd A2
Bulwer Rd B1
Burrell Rd C2
Butter Market B2
Butter Market Ctr B3
Carr St B3
Cecil Rd B2
Cecilia St C2
Chancery Rd C2
Charles St B2
Chevallier St A1
Christchurch Mansion & Wolsey Art Gallery B3
Christchurch Park A3
Christchurch St B3
Cineworld C2
Civic Ctr B2
Civic Dr B2
Clarkson St B1
Cobbold St B3
Commercial Rd C2
Constable Rd A3
Constantine Rd C1
Constitution Hill A2
Corder Rd A3
Corn Exchange B2
Cotswold Ave A2
Council Offices C2
County Hall B3
Crown Court C2
Crown St B2
Cullingham Rd B1
Cumberland St B2
Curriers La B2
Dale Hall La A2
Dales View Rd A1
Dalton Rd B2
Dillwyn St B1
Elliot St B1
Elm St B2
Elsmere Rd A3
Falcon St C2
Felaw St C3
Flint Wharf C3
Fonnereau Rd B2
Fore St C3
Foundation St C3
Franciscan Way C2
Friars St C2
Gainsborough Rd A3
Gatacre Rd B1
Geneva Rd B2
Gippeswyk Ave C1
Gippeswyk Park C1
Grafton Way C2
Graham Rd A1
Grimwade St C3
Great Whip St C3
Handford Cut B1
Handford Rd B1
Henley Rd A2
Hervey St B3
High St B2
Holly Rd A2
Information Ctr B3
Ipswich Haven Marina C3
Ipswich School A2
Ipswich Station C2
Ipswich Town FC (Portman Road) C2
Ivry St A2
Kensington Rd A1
Kesteven Rd C1
Key St C3
Kingsfield Ave A3
Kitchener Rd A1
Magistrates Court B2
Little's Cr C2
London Rd B1
Low Brook St C3
Lower Orwell St C3
Luther Rd C2
Manor Rd A3
Mornington Ave A1
Mus & Art Gallery B2
Museum St B2
Neale St B3
New Cardinal St C2
New Cut East C3
New Cut West C3
New Wolsey B2

Newson St B2
Norwich Rd A1/B1
Oban St B2
Old Customs Ho C3
Old Foundry Rd B3
Old Merchant's House C3
Orford St B2
Paget Rd A2
Park Rd A3
Park View Rd A2
Peter's St C2
Philip Rd C2
Pine Ave A2
Pine View Rd A2
Police Station B2
Portman Rd B2
Portman Walk C1
Post Office B2/B3
Princes St C2
Prospect St B1
Queen St B2
Ranelagh Rd C1
Recreation Ground B1
Rectory Rd C2
Regent Theatre B3
Retail Park C2
Richmond Rd A1
Rope Walk C3
Rose La C2
Russell Rd C2
St Edmund's Rd A2
St George's St B2
St Helen's St B3
Samuel Rd B3
Sherrington Rd A1
Silent St C2
Sir Alf Ramsey Way C1
Sirdar Rd B1
Soane St B3
Springfield La A1
Star La C3
Stevenson Rd B1
Suffolk College C3
Suffolk Retail Park B1
Superstore B1
Surrey Rd B1
Tacket St C3
Tavern St B3
The Avenue A3
Tolly Cobbold Mus C3
Tower Ramparts B2
Tower Ramparts Shopping Ctr B2
Tower St B3
Town Hall B2
Tuddenham Rd A3
Upper Brook St B3
Upper Orwell St B3
Valley Rd A2
Vermont Cr B3
Vermont Rd B3
Vernon St C3
Warrington Rd A2
Waterloo Rd A1
Waterworks St C3
Wellington St B1
West End Rd B1
Westerfield Rd A3
Westgate St B2
Westholme Rd A1
Westwood Ave A1
Willoughby Rd C2
Withipoll St B3
Woodbridge Rd B3
Woodstone Ave A3
Yarmouth Rd B1

Leeds 183

Aire St B3
Aireside Ctr B2
Albion Pl B4
Albion St B4
Albion Way B1
Alma St A6
Arcades B4
Armley Rd B1
Back Burley Lodge Rd A1
Back Hyde Terr A2
Back Row C3
Bath Rd C3
Beckett St A6
Bedford St B3
Belgrave St A4
Belle View Rd A2
Benson St A5
Black Bull St C5
Blenheim Walk A3
Boar La B4
Bond St B4
Bow St C5
Bowman La C4
Brewery C4
Bridge St A5/B5
Briggate B4
Bruce Gdns C1
Burley Rd A1
Burley St B1
Burmantofs St B6
Bus & Coach Station B5
Butterly St C4
Butts Cr B4
Brewery Wharf C5
Byron St A5
Call La B4
Calverley St A3/B3
Canal St B1
Canal Wharf C3
Carlisle Rd C5
Cavendish Rd A1
Cavendish St A2
Chadwick St C5
Cherry Pl A6
Cherry Row A5
City Museum A4
City Palace of Varieties B4
City Sq B3
Civic Hall A3
Clarence Road C5
Clarendon Rd A2
Clarendon Way A3
Clark La C6
Clay Pit La A4
Cloberry St A2
Clyde Approach C1
Clyde Gdns C1
Coleman St C2
Commercial St B4
Concord St A5
Cookridge St A4
Copley Hill C1
Corn Exchange B4
Cromer Terr A2
Cromwell St A5
Cross Catherine St B6
Cross Green La C6
Cross Stamford St A5
Crown & County Courts A3
Crown Point Bridge C5
Crown Point Ret Pk C4
Crown Point Rd C4
David St C3
Dent St C6
Derwent Pl C3
Dial St C6
Dock St C4
Dolly La A6
Domestic St C2
Duke St B5
Duncan St B4
Dyer St B5
East Field St B6
East Pde B3
East St C5
Eastgate B5
Easy Rd C6
Edward St B4
Ellerby La C6
Ellerby Rd C6
Fenton St A3
Fire Station B2
Fish St B4
Flax Pl B5
Gelderd Rd C1
George St B4
Globe Rd C2
Gloucester Cr B1
Gower St A5
Grafton St A4
Grand Theatre B4
Granville Rd A6
Great George St A3
Great Wilson St C4
Greek St B3
Green La C1
Hanover Ave A2
Hanover La A2
Hanover Sq A2
Hanover Way A2
Harewood St B4
Harrison St B4
Haslewood Cl B6
Haslewood Drive B6
High Court B5
Holbeck La C2
Holdforth Cl C1
Holdforth Gdns B1
Holdforth Gr C1
Holdforth Pl C1
Holy Trinity B4
Hope Rd A5
Hunslet La C4
Hunslet Rd C4
Hyde Terr A2
Infirmary St B3
Information Ctr B3
Ingram Row C3
Junction St C4
Kelso Gdns A2
Kelso Rd A2
Kelso St A2
Kendal La A2
Kendell St C4
Kidacre St C4
King Edward St B4
King St B3
Kippax Pl C6
Kirkgate B4
Kirkgate Market B4
Kirkstall Rd A1
Kitson St C6
Lady La B4
Lands La B4
Lavender Walk B6
Leeds Art Gallery B3
Leeds Bridge C4
Leeds Coll of Music B5
Leeds General Infirmary (A&E) A3
Leeds Metropolitan University A3/A4
Leeds Museum Discovery Ctr C5
Leeds Sh Plaza B4
Leeds Station B3
Leeds University A3
Library B3
Lincoln Green Rd A6
Lincoln Rd A6
Lindsey Gdns A6
Lindsey Rd A6
Lisbon St B3
Little Queen St B3
Long Close La C6
Lord St C2
Lovell Park A4
Lovell Park Rd A4
Lovell Rd A5
Lower Brunswick St A5
Mabgate A5
Macauly St A5
Magistrates Court A3
Manor Rd C3
Mark La B4
Marlborough St B2
Marsh La B5
Marshall St C3
Meadow La C4
Meadow Rd C4
Melbourne St A5
Merrion Ctr A4
Merrion St A4
Merrion Way A4
Mill St B5
Millennium Sq A3
Mount Preston St A2
Mushroom St A5
Neville St C4
New Briggate A4/B4
New Market St B4
New Station St B4
New York Rd A5
New York St B5
Nile St A5
Nippet La A6
North St A4
Northern St B3
Oak Rd B1
Oxford Pl B3
Oxford Row A3
Park Cross St B3
Park La A2
Park Pl B3
Park Row B4
Park Sq B3
Park Sq East B3
Park Sq West B3
Park St B3
Police Station B5
Pontefract La B6
Portland Cr A3
Portland Way A3
Post Office B4/B5
Project Space Leeds C2
Quarry House (NHS/DSS Headquarters) B5
Quebec St B3
Queen St B3
Railway St B5
Rectory St A6
Regent St A5
Richmond St C5
Rigton Approach B6
Rigton Dr B6
Rillbank La A1
Rosebank Rd A1
Royal Armouries C5
Russell St B3
Rutland St B2
St Anne's Cath (RC) A4
St Anne's St B4
St James' Hospital A6
St Johns Ctr B4
St John's Rd A2
St Mary's St B5
St Pauls St B3
St Peter's B5
Saxton La B5
Sayner La C5
Shakespeare Ave A6
Shannon St B6
Sheepscar St South A5
Siddall St C3
Skinner La A5
South Pde B3
Sovereign St C4
Spence La C2
Springfield Mount A2
Springwell Ct C2
Springwell Rd C2
Springwell St C2
Stoney Rock La A6
Studio Rd A1
Sutton St C2
Sweet St C3
Sweet St West C3
Swinegate B4
Templar St B5
The Calls B5
The Close B6
The Core B4
The Drive B6
The Garth B5
The Headrow B3/B4
The Lane B5
The Light B4
The Parade B6
Thoresby Pl A3
Torre Rd A6
Town Hall A3
Union Pl C3
Union St B5
Upper Accomodation Rd B6
Upper Basinghall St B4
Vicar La B4
Victoria Bridge C4
Victoria Quarter B4
Victoria Rd C4
Vue B4
Wade La A4
Washington St A1
Water La C3
Waterloo Rd C4
Wellington Rd B2/C1
Wellington St B3
West St B2
West Yorkshire Playhouse B5
Westfield Rd A1
Westgate B3
Whitehall Rd B3/C2
Whitelock St A5
Willis St C6
Willow Approach A1
Willow Ave A1
Willow Terrace Rd A3
Wintoun St A5
Woodhouse La A3/A4
Woodsley Rd A1
York Pl B3
York Rd B6
Yorkshire Television Studios A1

Leicester 182

Abbey St A2
All Saints' A1
Aylestone Rd C2
Bath La A1
Bede Park C1
Bedford St A3
Bedford St South A3
Belgrave Gate A2
Belle Vue A2
Belvoir St B2
Braunstone Gate B1
Burleys Way A2
Burnmoor St C2
Bus Station A2
Canning St A2
Carlton St C2
Castle B1
Castle Gardens B1
Cathedral B2
Causeway La A2
Charles St B3
Chatham St B2
Christow St A3
Church Gate A2
City Gallery B3
Civic Ctr B2
Clank St B2
Clock Tower B2
Clyde St A3
Colton St B3
Conduit St B3
Crafton St A3
Craven St A1
Crown Courts B3
Curve B3
De Lux A2
De Montfort Hall C3
De Montfort St C3
De Montfort Univ C1
Deacon St C2
Dover St B3
Duns La B1
Dunton St A1
East St B3
Eastern Boulevard C1
Edmonton Rd A3
Erskine St A3
Filbert St C1
Filbert St East C2
Fire Station C3
Fleet St A3
Friar La B2
Friday St A2
Gateway St C2
Glebe St B3
Granby St B3
Grange La C2
Grasmere St C1
Great Central St A1
Guildhall B2
Guru Nanak Sikh Museum B1
Halford St B2
Havelock St C2
Haymarket Sh Ctr A2
High St A2
Highcross St A1
Highcross Sh Ctr A2
HM Prison C2
Horsefair St B2
Humberstone Gate B2
Humberstone Rd A3
Infirmary St C2
Information Ctr B2
Jarrom St C2
Jewry Wall B1
Kamloops Cr A3
King Richards Rd B1
King St B2
Lancaster Rd C3
LCB Depot B3
Lee St A3
Leicester RFC C2
Leicester Royal Infirmary (A&E) C2
Leicester Station B3
Library B2
Little Theatre, The B3
London Rd C3
Lower Brown St B2
Magistrates Court B2
Manitoba Rd A3
Mansfield St A2
Market B2
Market St B2
Mill La C2
Montreal Rd A3
Narborough Rd North B1
Nelson Mandela Park C2
New Park St B1
New St B2
New Walk C3
New Walk Museum & Art Gallery C3
Newarke Houses B2
Newarke St B2
Northgate St A1
Orchard St A2
Ottawa Rd A3
Oxford St C2
Upper Brown St B2
Phoenix Square B3
Police Station A3
Post Office A1/B2/C2/C3
Prebend St C3
Princess Rd East C3
Princess Rd West C3
Queen St B3
Regent College C3
Regent Rd C2/C3
Repton St A1
Rutland St B3
St George St B3
St Georges Way B3
St John St A2
St Margaret's A2
St Margaret's Way A2
St Martins B2
St Mary de Castro B1
St Matthew's Way A3
St Nicholas B1
St Nicholas Circle B1
Sanvey Gate A2
Silver St B2
Slater St A1
Soar La A1
South Albion St B3
Southampton St B3
Swain St B3
Swan St A1
The Gateway C2
The Newarke B1
The Rally Com Park A2
Tigers Way C3
Tower St C3
Town Hall B2
Tudor Rd B1
Univ of Leicester C3
University Rd C3
Upperton Rd C1
Vaughan Way A2
Walnut St C2
Watling St A2
Welford Rd B2
Wellington St B2
West Bridge B1
West St C3
West Walk C3
Western Boulevard C1
Western Rd C1
Wharf St North A3
Wharf St South A3
Y' Theatre, The B3
Yeoman St B3
York Rd B2

Lincoln 186

Alexandra Terr B1
Anchor St C1
Arboretum B3
Arboretum Ave B3
Baggholme Rd B3
Bailgate A2
Beaumont Fee B1
Brayford Way C1
Brayford Wharf East C1
Brayford Wharf North B1
Bruce Rd A2
Burton Rd A1
Bus Station (City) C2
Canwick Rd C2
Cardinal's Hat B2
Carline Rd B1
Castle B1
Castle St A1
Cathedral B2
Cathedral St B2
Cecil St A2
Chapel La A2
Cheviot St B3
Church La A2
City Hall B1
Clasketgate B2
Clayton Sports Gd A3
Coach Park C2
Collection, The B2
County Hospital (A&E) B3
County Office B1
Courts C1
Croft St B2
Cross St C2
Crown Courts B1
Curle Ave A3
Danesgate B2
Drill Hall B2
Drury La B1
East Bight A2
East Gate A2
Eastcliff Rd B3
Eastgate B2
Egerton Rd A3
Ellis Windmill A1
Engine Shed, The C1
Environment Agency C2
Exchequer Gate B2
Firth Rd C1
Flaxengate B2
Florence St B3
George St C3
Good La A2
Gray St A1
Great Northern Terr C3
Great Northern Terrace Industrial Estate C3
Greetwell Rd B3
Greetwellgate B3
Haffenden Rd A2
High St B2/C1
HM Prison A3
Hospital (Private) A2
Hungate B2
James St A2
Jews House & Ct B2
Kesteven St C2
Langworthgate A2
Lawn Visitor Ctr, The B1
Lee Rd A3
Library B2
Lincoln College B2
Lincoln Central Station C2
Lincolnshire Life/Royal Lincolnshire Regiment Museum A1
Lindum Rd B2
Lindum Sports Gd A3
Lindum Terr B3
Mainwaring Rd A3
Manor Rd A2
Market C2
Massey Rd A3
Medieval Bishop's Palace B2
Mildmay St A1
Mill Rd A1
Millman Rd B3
Minster Yard B2
Monks Rd B3
Montague St B2
Mount St A1
Nettleham Rd A2
Newland B1
Newport A2
Newport Arch A2
Newport Cemetery A2
Northgate A2
Odeon C1
Orchard St B1
Oxford St C2
Park St B1
Pelham Bridge C2
Pelham St C2
Police Station B1
Portland St C2
Post Office A1/A2/B1/B3/C2
Potter Gate B2
Priory Gate B2
Queensway A3
Rasen La A1
Ropewalk C1
Rosemary La B2
St Anne's Rd B3
St Benedict's C1
St Giles Ave A3
St John's Rd A2
St Marks St C1
St Mark's Sh Ctr C1
St Mary-Le-Wigford C1
St Mary's St C2
St Nicholas St A2
St Swithin's B2
Saltergate C1
Saxon St A1
Sch of Art & Design B2
Sewell Rd B3
Silver St B2
Sincil St C2
Spital St A2
Spring Hill B1
Stamp End C3
Steep Hill B2
Stonebow & Guildhall C2
Stonefield Ave A2
Tentercroft St C1
The Avenue B1
The Grove A3
Theatre Royal B2
Tritton Retail Park C1
Tritton Rd C1
Union Rd B1
University of Lincoln C1
Upper Lindum St B3
Upper Long Leys Rd A1
Usher B2
Vere St A2
Victoria St B1
Victoria Terr B1
Vine St B3
Wake St A1
Waldeck St A1
Waterside Sh Ctr C2
Waterside North C2
Waterside South C2
West Pde B1
Westgate A2
Wigford Way C1
Williamson St A2
Wilson St A1
Winn St B3
Wragby Rd A3
Yarborough Rd A1

Liverpool 183

Abercromby Sq C5
Acc Liverpool C2
Addison St A3
Adelaide Rd B6
Ainsworth St B4
Albany Rd B6
Albert Dock C2
Albert Edward Rd B6
Angela St C6
Anson St B4
Archbishop Blanche High School B6
Argyle St C3
Arrad St C4
Ashton St B5
Audley St A4
Back Leeds St A2
Basnett St B3
Bath St A1
Beatles Story C2
Beckwith St C3
Bedford Close C5
Bedford St North C5
Bedford St South C5
Benson St C4
Berry St C4
Birkett St A4
Bixteth St B2
Blackburne Place C4
Bluecoat B3
Bold Place C4
Bold St C4
Bolton St B3
Bridport St B4
Bronte St B4
Brook St A1
Brownlow Hill B4/B5
Brownlow St B5
Brunswick Rd A5
Brunswick St B1
Bus Station C2
Butler Cr A6
Byrom St A3
Caledonia St C4
Cambridge St C5
Camden St A4
Canada Blvd B1
Canning Dock C2
Canterbury St A4
Cardwell St C6
Carver St A4
Cases St B3
Castle St B2
Catherine St C5
Cavern Club B3
Central Library A3
Central Station B3
Chapel St B2
Charlotte St B3
Chatham Place C6
Chatham St C5
Cheapside B2
Chestnut St C5
Christian St A3
Church St B3
Churchill Way North A3
Churchill Way South B3
Clarence St B4
Coach Station A4
Cobden St A5
Cockspur St A2
College St C3
College St North A5
College St South A5
Colquitt St C4
Comus St A3
Concert St C3
Connaught Rd B6
Cook St B2
Copperas Hill B4
Cornwallis St C3
Covent Garden B2
Craven St A4
Cropper St B3
Crown St B5/C6
Cumberland St B2
Cunard Building B1
Dale St B2
Dansie St B4
Daulby St B5
Dawson St B3
Derby Sq B2
Drury La B2
Duckinfield St B4
Duke St C3
Earle St A2
East St A2
Eaton St A2
Edgar St A3
Edge La B6
Edinburgh Rd A6
Edmund St B2
Elizabeth St B5
Elliot St B3
Empire Theatre B4
Empress Rd B6
Epworth St A5
Erskine St A5
Everyman Theatre C5
Exchange St East B2
Fact Ctr, The C4
Falkland St A5
Falkner St C5/C6
Farnworth St A6
Fenwick St B2
Fielding St A6
Fleet St C3
Fraser St A4
Freemasons Row A2
Gardner Row A3
Gascoyne St A2
George Pier Head C1
George St B2
Gibraltar Road A1
Gilbert St C3
Gildart St A4
Gill St B4
Goree B2
Gower St C2
Gradwell St C3
Great Crosshall St A3
Great George St C4
Great Howard St A1
Great Newton St B4
Greek St B4
Green La B4
Greenside A5
Greetham St C3
Gregson St A5
Grenville St C3
Grinfield St C6
Grove St C5
Guelph St A6
Hackins Hey B2
Haigh St A4
Hall La B6
Hanover St B3
Harbord St C6
Hardman St C4
Harker St A4
Hart St B4
Hatton Garden A2
Hawke St B4
Helsby St B6
Henry St C3
HM Customs & Excise National Mus C2
Highfield St A2
Highgate St B6
Hilbre St B4
Hope Place C4
Hope St C4
Houghton St B3
Hunter St A3
Hutchinson St A6
Information Ctr C2
Institute For The Performing Arts C4
Irvine St B6
Irwell St B2
Islington A4
James St B2
James St Station B2
Jenkinson St A4
Johnson St A3
Jubilee Drive B6
Kempston St A4
Kensington A6
Kensington Gdns B6
Kensington St A6
Kent St C3
King Edward St A1
Kinglake St B6
Knight St C4
Lace St A3
Langsdale St A4
Law Courts C2
Leece St C4
Leeds St A2
Leopold Rd B6
Lime St B3
Lime St Station B4
Little Woolton St B5
Liver St C2
Liverpool John Moores University A3/B4/C4
Liverpool Landing Stage B1
Liverpool One C2
London Rd A4/B4
Lord Nelson St B4
Lord St B2
Lovat St C6
Low Hill A5
Low Wood St A6
Lydia Ann St C3
Mansfield St A4
Marmaduke St B6
Marsden St A6
Martensen St B6
Marybone A3
Maryland St C4
Mason St B6
Mathew St B2
May St B4
Melville Place C6
Merseyside Maritime Museum C2
Metquarter B3
Metropolitan Cathedral (RC) B5
Midghall St A2
Molyneux Rd A6
Moor Place B4
Moorfields B2
Moorfields Station B2
Moss St A5
Mount Pleasant B4/B5
Mount St C4
Mount Vernon B6
Mulberry St C5
Municipal Buildings B2
Mus of Liverpool C2
Myrtle Gdns C6
Myrtle St C5
Naylor St A2
Nelson St C4
Neptune Theatre B3
New Islington A4
New Quay B1
Newington St C3
North John St B2
North St A3
North View B6
Norton St A4
Oakes St B5
O2 Academy
Odeon B4
Old Hall St A1
Old Leeds St A2
Oldham Place C4
Oldham St C4
Olive St C6
Open Eye Gallery C3
Oriel St A2
Ormond St B2
Orphan St C6
Overbury St C6
Overton St B6
Oxford St C5
Paisley St A1
Pall Mall A2
Paradise St C3
Park La C3
Parker St B3
Parr St C3
Peach St B5
Pembroke Place B4
Pembroke St B5
Philharmonic Hall C5
Pickop St A2
Pilgrim St C4
Pitt St C3
Playhouse Theatre B3
Pleasant St B4
Police HQ C2
Police Station A4/B4
Pomona St B4
Port of Liverpool Building B2
Post Office A2/A4/A5/A6/B2/B3/B4/C4
Pownall St C2
Prescot St A5
Preston St B3
Princes Dock A1
Princes Gdns A2
Princes Jetty A1
Princes Pde B1
Princes St B2
Pythian St A6
Queen Sq Bus Station B3
Queensland St C6
Queensway Tunnel (Docks exit) B1
Queensway Tunnel (Entrance) B3
Radio City B2
Ranelagh St B3
Redcross St B2
Renfrew St B6
Renshaw St B4
Richmond Row A4
Richmond St B3
Rigby St A2
Roberts St A1
Rock St B4
Rodney St C4
Rokeby St A4
Romily St A6
Roscoe La C4
Roscoe St C4
Rose Hill A3
Royal Ct Theatre B3
Royal Liver Building B1
Royal Liverpool Hospital (A&E) B5
Royal Mail St B4
Rumford Place B2
Rumford St B2
Russell St B4
St Andrew St B4
St Anne St A4
St Georges Hall B3
St John's Ctr B3
St John's Gdns B3
St John's La B3
St Joseph's Cr A4
St Minishull St B5
St Nicholas Place B1
St Paul's Sq A2
St Vincent Way B4
Salisbury St A4
Salthouse Dock C2
Salthouse Quay C2
Sandon St C5
Saxony Rd B6
Schomberg St A6
School La B2
Seel St C3
Seymour St B4
Shaw St A5
Sidney Place C6
Sir Thomas St B3
Skelhorne St B4
Slater St C3
Slavery Museum C2
Smithdown La B6
Soho Sq A4
Soho St A4
South John St B2
Springfield A4
Stafford St A4
Standish St A3
Stanley St B2
Strand St C2
Suffolk St C3
Tabley St C3
Tarleton St B3
Tate Gallery C2
Teck St B6
Temple St B2
The Beacon B3
The Strand B2
Tithebarn St B2
Town Hall B2
Traffic Police HQ C6
Trowbridge St B4
Trueman St A3
Union St B2
Unity Theatre C4
University C5
Univ of Liverpool B5
Upper Duke St C4
Upper Frederick St C3
Upper Baker St A6
Vauxhall Rd A2
Vernon St B2
Victoria Gallery & Museum B5
Victoria St B2
Vine St C5
Wakefield St A4
Walker Art Gallery A3
Walker St A6
Wapping C2
Water St B1/B2
Waterloo Rd A1
Wavertree Rd B6
West Derby Rd A6
West Derby St B5
Whitechapel B3
Western Approaches War Museum B2
Whitley Gdns A5
William Brown St B3
William Henry St A4
Williamson Sq B3
Williamson St B3
Williamson's Tunnels Heritage Ctr C6
Women's Hospital C6
Wood St B3
World Museum, Liverpool A3
York St C3

London 184

Abbey Orchard St E3
Abchurch La D6
Abingdon St E4
Achilles Way D2
Acton St B4
Addington St E4
Air St D3
Albany St B2
Albemarle St D3
Albert Embankment F4
Aldenham St A3
Aldersgate St C6
Aldford St D2
Aldgate C7
Aldgate High St C7
Aldwych C4
Allsop Pl B1
Amwell St B5
Andrew Borde St C3
Angel A5
Appold St C7
Argyle Sq B4
Argyle St B4
Argyll St C3
Arnold Circus B7
Artillery La C7
Artillery Row E3
Association of Photographers Gallery B6
Baker St B1
Baker St B1
Baldwin's Gdns C5
Baltic St B6
Bank C6
Bank Museum C6
Bank of England C6
Bankside D6
Bankside Gallery D5
Banner St B6
Barbican C6
Barbican Ctr for Arts, The C6
Barbican Gallery C6
Basil St E1
Bastwick St B6
Bateman's Row B7
Bath St B6
Bayley St C3
Baylis Rd E5
Beak St D3
Bedford Row C4
Bedford Sq C3
Bedford St D4
Bedford Way B3
Beech St C6
Belgrave Pl E2
Belgrave Sq E2
Bell La C7
Belvedere Rd E4
Berkeley Sq D2
Berkeley St D2
Bernard St B4
Berners Pl C3
Berners St C3
Berwick St C3
Bethnal Green Rd B7
Bevenden St B6
Bevis Marks C7
BFI London IMAX Cinema D5
Bidborough St B4
Binney St C2
Birdcage Walk E3
Bishopsgate C7
Blackfriars D5
Blackfriars Bridge D5
Blackfriars Rd E5
Blandford St C1
Blomfield St C6
Bloomsbury St C3
Bloomsbury Way C4
Bolton St D2
Bond St C2
Borough High St E6
Boswell St C4
Bow St C4
Bowling Green La B5
Brad St D5
Bressenden Pl E3
Brewer St D3
Brick St D2
Bridge St E4
Britain at War D7
Britannia Walk B6
British Library B3
British Museum C4
Britton St B5
Broad Sanctuary E3
Broadway E3
Brook Dr F5
Brook St D2
Brunswick Pl B6
Brunswick Sq B4
Brushfield St C7
Bruton St D2
Bryanston St C1
Buckingham Gate E3
Buckingham Pal E3
Buckingham Pal Rd F2
Bunhill Row B6
Byward St D7
Cabinet War Rooms & Churchill Mus E3
Cadogan La E2
Cadogan Pl E1
Cadogan Sq F1
Caledonian Rd A4
Calshot St A4
Calthorpe St B4
Calvert Ave B7
Cambridge Circus C3
Camomile St C7
Cannon St D6
Cannon St D6
Carey St C4
Carlisle La E4
Carlisle Pl E3
Carlton House Terr D3
Carmelite St D5
Carnaby St C3
Carter La C5
Carthusian St C6
Cartwright Gdns B4
Castle Baynard St D5
Cavendish Pl C2
Cavendish Sq C2
Caxton Hall E3
Caxton St E3
Central St B6
Chalton St B3
Chancery Lane C5
Chapel St E2
Charing Cross D4
Charing Cross Rd C3
Charles II St D3
Charles Sq B6
Charles St D2
Charlotte Rd B7
Charlotte St C3
Chart St B6
Charterhouse Sq C5
Charterhouse St C5
Cheapside C6
Chenies St C3
Chesham St E2
Chester Sq F2
Chesterfield Hill D2
Chiltern St C2
Chiswell St C6
City Garden Row A5
City Rd B6
City Thameslink C5
City University, The B5
Claremont Sq A5
Clarges St D2
Clerkenwell Cl B5
Clerkenwell Green B5
Clerkenwell Rd B5
Cleveland St C3
Clifford St D3
Clink Prison Mus D6
Clock Museum C6
Club Row B7
Cockspur St D3
Coleman St C6
Columbia Rd B7
Commercial St C7
Compton St B5

Conduit St D2
Constitution Hill E2
Copperfield St E5
Coptic St C4
Cornhill C6
Cornwall Rd D5
Coronet St B7
Courtauld Gallery D4
Covent Garden D4
Covent Garden D4
Cowcross St C5
Cowper St B6
Cranbourn St D3
Craven St D4
Crawford St C1
Creechurch La C7
Cremer St A7
Cromer St B4
Cumberland Gate D1
Cumberland Terr A2
Curtain Rd B7
Curzon St D2
D'arblay St C3
Davies St C2
Dean St C3
Deluxe Gallery B7
Denmark St C3
Dering St C2
Devonshire St C2
Diana, Princess of Wales Meml Wlk E3
Dingley Rd B6
Dorset St C1
Doughty St B4
Dover St D2
Downing St E4
Druid St E7
Drummond St B3
Drury La C4
Drysdale St B7
Duchess St C2
Dufferin St B6
Duke of Wellington Pl E2
Duke St C2
Duke St D3
Duke St Hill D6
Duke's Pl C7
Duncannon St D4
East Rd B6
Eastcastle St C3
Eastcheap D7
Eastman Dental Hospital B4
Eaton Pl E2
Eaton Sq E2
Eccleston St E2
Edgware Rd C1
Eldon St C6
Embankment D4
Endell St C4
Endsleigh Pl B3
Euston B3
Euston Rd B3
Euston Square B3
Evelina Children's Hospital E4
Eversholt St A3
Exmouth Market B5
Fann St B6
Farringdon C5
Farringdon Rd C5
Farringdon St C5
Featherstone St B6
Fenchurch St D7
Fenchurch St D7
Fetter La C5
Finsbury Circus C6
Finsbury Pavement C6
Finsbury Sq B6
Fitzalan St F5
Fitzmaurice Pl D2
Fleet St C5
Floral St D4
Florence Nightingale Museum E4
Folgate St C7
Foot Hospital B3
Fore St C6
Foster La C6
Francis St F3
Frazier St E5
Freemason's Hall C4
Friday St C6
Gainsford St E7
Garden Row E5
Gee St B6
George St C1
Gerrard St D3
Giltspur St C5
Glasshouse St D3
Gloucester Pl C1
Golden Hinde D6
Golden La B6
Golden Sq D3
Goodge St C3
Goodge St C3
Gordon Sq B3
Goswell Rd B5
Gough St B4
Goulston St C7
Gower St B3
Gracechurch St D6
Grafton Way B3
Gray's Inn Rd B4
Great College St E4
Great Cumberland Pl C1
Great Eastern St B7
Great Guildford St D6
Great Marlborough St C3
Great Ormond St B4
Great Ormond St Children's Hospl B4
Great Percy St B4
Great Peter St E3
Great Portland St B2
Great Portland St C2
Great Queen St C4
Great Russell St C3
Great Scotland Yd D4
Great Smith St E3
Great Suffolk St D5
Great Titchfield St C3
Great Tower St D7
Great Windmill St D3
Greek St C3
Green Park D3
Green St D2
Greencoat Pl F3
Gresham St C6
Greville St B4/C5
Greycoat Hosp Sch E3
Greycoat Pl E3
Grosvenor Cres E2
Grosvenor Gdns E2
Grosvenor Pl E2
Grosvenor Sq D2
Grosvenor St D2
Guards Museum and Chapel E3
Guildhall Art Gallery C6
Guilford St B4
Guy's Hospital D6
Haberdasher St B6
Hackney Rd B7
Half Moon St D2
Halkin St E2
Hall St B5
Hallam St C2
Hampstead Rd B3
Hanover Sq C2
Hans Cres E1
Hanway St C3
Hardwick St B5
Harley St C2
Harrison St B4
Hastings St B4
Hatfields D5
Hayles St F5
Haymarket D3
Hayne St C5
Hay's Galleria D7
Hay's Mews D2
Hayward Gallery D4
Helmet Row B6
Herbrand St B4
Hercules Rd E4
Hertford St D2
High Holborn C4
Hill St D2
HMS Belfast D7
Hobart Pl E2
Holborn C4
Holborn C5
Holborn Viaduct C5
Holland St D5
Holmes Mus B1
Holywell La B7
Horse Guards' Rd D3
Houndsditch C7
Houses of Parliament E4
Howland St C3
Hoxton Sq B7
Hoxton St B7
Hunter St B4
Hunterian Mus C4
Hyde Park D1
Hyde Park Cnr E2
Imperial War Mus E5
Inner Circle B2
Inst of Archaeology (London Univ) B2
Ironmonger Row B6
James St C2
James St D4
Jermyn St D3
Jockey's Fields C4
John Carpenter St D5
John St B4
Judd St B4
Kennington Road E5
King Charles St E4
King St D3
King St D4
King William St C6
Kingley St C3
King's Cross A4
King's Cross Rd B4
King's Cross St Pancras A4
King's Rd E2
Kingsland Rd B7
Kingsway C4
Kinnerton St E2
Knightsbridge E1
Lamb St C7
Lambeth Bridge F4
Lambeth High St F4
Lambeth North E5
Lambeth Palace E4
Lambeth Palace Rd E4
Lambeth Rd E5
Lambeth Walk F4
Lamb's Conduit St C4
Lancaster Pl D4
Langham Pl C2
Leadenhall St C7
Leake St E4
Leather La C5
Leicester Sq D3
Leicester St D3
Leonard St B6
Lever St B6
Lexington St D3
Lidlington Pl A3
Lime St D7
Lincoln's Inn Fields C4
Lindsey St C5
Lisle St D3
Liverpool St C7
Liverpool St C7
Lloyd Baker St B5
Lloyd Sq B5
Lombard St C6
London Aquarium E4
London Bridge D6
London Bridge Hospital D6
London City Hall D7
London Dungeon D6
London Film Mus E4
London Guildhall University C6
London Rd E5
London Transport Museum D4
London Wall C6
London-Eye E4
Long Acre D4
Long La C5
Longford St B2
Lower Belgrave St E2
Lower Grosvenor Pl E2
Lower Marsh E5
Lower Thames St D6
Lowndes St E2
Ludgate Circus C5
Ludgate Hill C5
Luxborough St C2
Lyall St E2
Macclesfield Rd B6
Madame Tussaud's B2
Maddox St D2
Malet St C3
Manchester Sq C2
Manchester St C2
Mandeville Pl C2
Mansell St D7
Mansion House C6
Mansion House D6
Maple St C3
Marble Arch C1
Marble Arch D1
Marchmont St B4
Margaret St C3
Margery St B5
Mark La D7
Marlborough Rd D3
Marshall St C3
Marsham St E3
Marylebone High St C2
Marylebone La C2
Marylebone Rd B2
Marylebone St C2
Mecklenburgh Sq B4
Middle Temple La C5
Middlesex St (Petticoat La) C7
Midland Rd A3
Minories C7
Monck St E3
Monmouth St C4
Montagu Pl C1
Montagu Sq C1
Montagu St C4
Montague Pl C3
Monument D6
Monument St D6
Monument, The D6
Moor La C6
Moorfields C6
Moorfields Eye Hospital B6
Moorgate C6
Moorgate C6
Moreland St B5
Morley St E5
Mortimer St C3
Mount Pleasant B5
Mount St D2
Murray Gr A6
Mus of Gdn History E4
Mus of London C6
Museum St C4
Myddelton Sq B5
Myddelton St B5
National Film Theatre D4
National Gallery D3
National Hospital B4
National Portrait Gallery D3
Neal St C4
Nelson's Column D4
New Bond St C2/D2
New Bridge St C5
New Cavendish St C2
New Change C6
New Fetter La C5
New Inn Yard B7
New North Rd A6
New Oxford St C3
New Scotland Yard E3
New Sq C4
Newgate St C5
Newton St C4
Nile St B6
Noble St C6
Noel St C3
North Audley St D2
North Cres C3
North Row D2
Northampton Sq B5
Northington St B4
Northumberland Ave D4
Norton Folgate C7
Nottingham Pl C2
Obstetric Hosp B3
Old Bailey C5
Old Broad St C6
Old Compton St C3
Old County Hall E4
Old Gloucester St C4
Old King Edward St C6
Old Nichol St B7
Old Paradise St F4
Old Spitalfields Mkt C7
Old St B6
Old St B6
Old Vic E5
Open Air Theatre B2
Operating Theatre Museum D6
Orange St D3
Orchard St C2
Ossulston St A3
Outer Circle B1
Oxford Circus C3
Oxford St C2/C3
Paddington St C2
Palace St E3
Pall Mall D3
Pall Mall East D3
Pancras Rd A4
Panton St D3
Paris Gdn D5
Park Cres B2
Park La D2
Park Rd B1
Park St D2
Park St D6
Parker St C4
Parliament Sq E4
Parliament St E4
Paternoster Sq C5
Paul St B6
Pear Tree St B5
Penton Rise B4
Penton St A5
Pentonville Rd A4/A5
Percival St B5
Petticoat La (Middlesex St) C7
Petty France E3
Phoenix Pl B4
Phoenix Rd A3
Photo Gallery D3
Piccadilly D2
Piccadilly Circus D3
Pitfield St B7
Pollock's Toy Mus C3
Polygon Rd A3
Pont St E1
Portland Pl C2
Portman Mews C2
Portman Sq C2
Portman St C1
Portugal St C4
Poultry C6
Primrose St C7
Princes St C6
Procter St C4
Provost St B6
Quaker St B7
Queen Anne St C2
Queen Elizabeth Hall D4
Queen Sq B4
Queen St D6
Queen Street Pl D6
Queen Victoria St D5
Queens Gallery E3
Radnor St B6
Rathbone Pl C3
Rawstorne St B5
Red Lion Sq C4
Red Lion St C4
Redchurch St B7
Redcross Way D6
Regency St F3
Regent Sq B4
Regent St C3
Regent's Park B2
Richmond Terr E4
Ridgmount St C3
Rivington St B7
Robert St B2
Rochester Row F3
Ropemaker St C6
Rosebery Ave B5
Roupell St D5
Royal Acad of Arts D3
Royal Academy of Dramatic Art B3
Royal Acad of Music B2
Royal Coll of Nursing C2
Royal College of Surgeons C4
Royal Festival Hall D4
Royal London Hospital for Integrated Medicine C4
Royal National Theatre D5
Royal National Throat, Nose and Ear Hospital B4
Royal Opera House D4
Russell Sq B3
Russell Square B4
Sackville St D3
Sadlers Wells B5
Saffron Hill C5
Savile Row D3
Savoy Pl D4
Savoy St D4
School of Hygiene & Tropical Medicine C3
Scrutton St B7
Sekforde St B5
Serpentine Rd D1
Seven Dials C4
Seward St B5
Seymour St C1
Shad Thames D7
Shaftesbury Ave D3
Shakespeare's Globe Theatre D6
Shepherd Market D2
Sherwood St D3
Shoe La C5
Shoreditch High St B7
Shoreditch High St B7
Shorts Gdns C4
Sidmouth St B4
Silk St C6
Sir John Soane's Museum C4
Skinner St B5
Sloane St E1
Snow Hill C5
Soho Sq C3
Somerset House D4
South Audley St D2
South Carriage Dr E1
South Molton St C2
South Pl C6
South St D2
Southampton Row C4
Southampton St D4
Southwark D5
Southwark Bridge D6
Southwark Bridge Rd D6
Southwark Cath D6
Southwark St D6
Speakers' Corner D1
Spencer St B5
Spital Sq C7
St Alban's St D3
St Andrew St C5
St Bartholomew's Hospital C5
St Botolph St C7
St Bride St C5
St George's Rd E5
St Giles High St C3
St James's Palace D3
St James's Park E3
St James's St D3
St John St B5
St Margaret St E4
St Mark's Hosp B5
St Martin's La D4
St Martin's Le Grand C6
St Mary Axe C7
St Pancras Int B4
St Paul's C6
St Paul's Cath C6
St Paul's Churchyard C5
St Peter's Hosp D4
St Thomas' Hosp E4
St Thomas St D6
Stamford St D5
Stanhope St B3
Stephenson Way B3
Stock Exchange C5
Stoney St D6
Strand C5
Stratton St D2
Sumner St D5
Sutton's Way B6
Swanfield St B7
Swinton St B4
Tabernacle St B6
Tate Modern D6
Tavistock Pl B4
Tavistock Sq B3
Tea & Coffee Mus D6
Temple D5
Temple Ave D5
Temple Pl D4
Terminus Pl E2
Thayer St C2
The Cut E5
The Mall E3
Theobald's Rd C4
Thorney St F4
Threadneedle St C6
Throgmorton St C6
Tonbridge St B4
Tooley St D7
Torrington Pl B3
Tothill St E3
Tottenham Court Rd B3
Tottenham Ct Rd C3
Tottenham St C3
Tower Bridge D7
Tower Bridge App D7
Tower Bridge Rd E7
Tower Hill D7
Tower Hill D7
Tower of London, The D7
Toynbee St C7
Trafalgar Square D3
Trinity Sq D7
Trocadero Ctr D3
Tudor St D5
Turnmill St C5
Ufford St E5
Union St D5
Univ Coll Hospl B3
University of London C3
Univ of Westminster C2
University St B3
Upper Belgrave St E2
Upper Berkeley St C1
Upper Brook St D2
Upper Grosvenor St D2
Upper Ground D5
Upper Montague St C1
Upper St Martin's La D4
Upper Thames St D6
Upper Wimpole St C2
Upper Woburn Pl B3
Vere St C2
Vernon Pl C4
Vestry St B6
Victoria E2
Victoria Emb D4
Victoria Pl Sh Ctr F2
Victoria St E3
Villiers St D4
Vincent Sq F3
Vinopolis City of Wine D6
Virginia Rd B7
Wakley St B5
Walbrook C6
Wallace Collection C2
Wardour St C3/D3
Warner St B5
Warren St B3
Warren St B3
Waterloo E5
Waterloo Bridge D4
Waterloo East D5
Waterloo Rd E5
Watling St C6
Webber St E5
Welbeck St C2
Wellington Arch E2
Wellington Mus E2
Wells St C3
Wenlock St A6
Wentworth St C7
West Smithfield C5
West Sq E5
Westminster E4
Westminster Abbey E4
Westminster Bridge E4
Westminster Bridge Rd E5
Westminster Cathedral (RC) E3
Westminster City Hall E3
Westminster Hall E4
Weymouth St C2
Wharf Rd A6
Wharton St B4
Whitcomb St D3
White Cube B7
White Lion Hill D5
White Lion St A5
Whitecross St B6
Whitefriars St C5
Whitehall D4
Whitehall Pl D4
Wigmore Hall C2
Wigmore St C2
William IV St D4
Wilmington Sq B5
Wilson St C6
Wilton Cres E2
Wimpole St C2
Windmill Walk D5
Woburn Pl B4
Woburn Sq B3
Women's Hosp C3
Wood St C6
Woodbridge St B5
Wootton St D5
Wormwood St C7
Worship St B6
Wren St B4
Wynyatt St B5
York Rd E4
York St C1
York Terrace East B2
York Terrace West B2

Luton 186

Adelaide St B1
Albert Rd C2
Alma St B2
Alton Rd C3
Anthony Gdns C1
Arndale Ctr B2
Arthur St C2
Ashburnham Rd B1
Ashton Rd C2
Avondale Rd A1
Back St A2
Bailey St C3
Baker St C2
Biscot Rd A1
Bolton Rd B3
Boyle Cl A2
Brantwood Rd B1
Bretts Mead C1
Bridge St B2
Brook St A1
Brunswick St A3
Burr St A3
Bury Park Rd A1
Bus Station B2
Bute St B2
Buxton Rd B2
Cambridge St C3
Cardiff Grove B1
Cardiff Rd B1
Cardigan St A2
Castle St B2/C2
Chapel St C2
Charles St A3
Chase St C2
Cheapside B2
Chequer St C3
Chiltern Rise C1
Church St B2/B3
Cinema A2
Cobden St A3
Collingdon St A1
Community Ctr C3
Concorde Ave A3
Corncastle Rd C1
Cowper St C2
Crawley Green Rd B3
Crawley Rd A1
Crescent Rise A3
Crescent Rd A3
Cromwell Rd A1
Cross St A2
Crown Court B2
Cumberland St B2
Cutenhoe Rd C3
Dallow Rd B1
Downs Rd B1
Dudley St A2
Duke St A2
Dumfries St B1
Dunstable Place B2
Dunstable Rd A1/B1
Edward St A3
Elizabeth St C2
Essex Cl C3
Farley Hill C1
Farley Lodge C1
Flowers Way B2
Francis St A1
Frederick St A2
Galaxy L Complex A2
George St B2
George St West B2
Gillam St A3
Gordon St B2
Grove Rd B1
Guildford St A2
Haddon Rd A3
Harcourt St C2
Hart Hill Drive A3
Hart Hill Lane A3
Hartley Rd A3
Hastings St B2
Hat Factory, The B2
Hatters Way A1
Havelock Rd A2
Hibbert St C2
High Town Rd A3
Highbury Rd A1
Hightown Community Sports & Arts Ctr A3
Hillary Cres C1
Hillborough Rd C1
Hitchin Rd A3
Holly St C2
Holm C1
Hucklesby Way A2
Hunts Cl C1
Information Ctr B2
Inkerman St A2
John St B2
Jubilee St A3
Kelvin Cl C2
King St B2
Kingsland Rd C3
Latimer Rd C2
Lawn Gdns C2
Lea Rd B3
Library B2
Library Rd B2
Liverpool Rd B1
London Rd C2
Luton Station A2
Lyndhurst Rd B1
Magistrates Court B2
Manchester St B2
Manor Rd B3
May St C3
Meyrick Ave C1
Midland Rd A2
Mill St A2
Milton Rd B1
Moor St A1
Moor, The A1
Moorland Gdns A2
Moulton Rise A3
Mus & Art Gallery A2
Napier Rd B1
New Bedford Rd A1
New Town St C2
North St A3
Old Bedford Rd A2
Old Orchard C2
Osbourne Rd C3
Oxen Rd A3
Park Sq B2
Park St B3/C3
Park St West B2
Park Viaduct B3
Parkland Drive C1
Police Station B1
Pomfret Ave A3
Pondwicks Rd B3
Post Office A1/A2/B2/C3
Power Court B3
Princess St B1
Red Rails C1
Regent St B2
Reginald St A2
Rothesay Rd B1
Russell Rise C1
Russell St C1
St Ann's Rd B3
St George's B2
St Mary's B3
St Marys Rd B3
St Paul's Rd C2
St Saviour's Cres C1
Salisbury Rd B1
Seymour Ave C3
Seymour Rd C3
Silver St B2
South Rd C2
Stanley St B1
Station Rd A2
Stockwood Cres C2
Stockwood Park C1
Strathmore Ave C2
Stuart St B2
Studley Rd A1
Surrey St C3
Sutherland Place C1
Tavistock St C2
Taylor St A3
Telford Way A1
Tennyson Rd C2
Tenzing Grove C1
The Cross Way C1
The Larches A2
Thistle Rd B3
Town Hall B2
Townsley Cl C2
UK Ctr for Carnival Arts B3
Union St B2
Univ of Bedfordshire B3
Upper George St B2
Vicarage St B3
Villa Rd A2
Waldeck Rd A1
Wellington St B1/B2
Wenlock St A2
Whitby Rd A1
Whitehill Ave C1
William St A2
Wilsden Ave C1
Windmill Rd B3
Windsor St C2
Winsdon Rd B1
York St A3

Maidstone 187

Albion Pl B3
All Saints B2
Allen St A3
Amphitheatre C2
Archbishop's Pal B2
Bank St B2
Barker Rd C2
Barton Rd C3
Beaconsfield Rd C1
Bedford Pl B1
Bentlif Art Gallery B2
Bishops Way B2
Bluett St A3
Bower La C1
Bower Mount Rd B1
Bower Pl C1
Bower St B1
Bowling Alley B3
Boxley Rd A3
Brenchley Gardens A2
Brewer St A3
Broadway B2
Brunswick St C3
Buckland Hill A1
Buckland Rd B1
Bus Station B3
Campbell Rd C3
Carriage Museum B2
Church Rd C1
Church St B3
Cinema C2
College Ave C2
College Rd C2
Collis Memorial Gdn C3
Cornwallis Rd B1
Corpus Christi Hall B2
County Hall A2
County Rd A3
Crompton Gdns C3
Crown & County Courts B2
Curzon Rd A3
Dixon Cl C2
Douglas Rd C1
Earl St B2
Eccleston Rd C2
Fairmeadow B2
Fisher St A2
Florence Rd C1
Foley St A3
Foster St C3
Fremlin Walk Sh Ctr B2
Gabriel's Hill B3
George St C3
Grecian St A3
Hardy St A3
Hart St C2
Hastings Rd C3
Hayle Rd C3
Hazlitt Theatre B2
Heathorn St A3
Hedley St A3
High St B2
HM Prison A3
Holland Rd A3
Hope St A2
Information Ctr B2
James St A3
James Whatman Way A2
Jeffrey St A3
Kent County Council Offices A2
King Edward Rd C2
King St B3
Kingsley Rd C3
Knightrider St B3
Launder Way C1
Lesley Pl A1
Library B2
Little Buckland Ave A1
Lockmeadow Leisure Complex C2
London Rd B1
Lower Boxley Rd A2
Lower Fant Rd C1
Magistrates Court B3
Maidstone Barracks Station A1
Maidstone Borough Council Offices B1
Maidstone East Station A2
Maidstone Mus B2
Maidstone West Station B2
Market C2
Market Buildings B2
Marsham St B3
Medway St B2
Medway Trading Est C2
Melville Rd C3
Mill St B2
Millennium Bridge C2
Mote Rd B3
Muir Rd C3
Old Tovil Rd C2
Palace Ave B3
Perryfield St A2
Police Station B3
Post Office A2/B2/B3/C3
Priory Rd C3
Prospect Pl C1
Pudding La B2
Queen Anne Rd B3
Queens Rd A1
Randall St A2
Rawdon Rd C3
Reginald Rd C1
Rock Pl B1
Rocky Hill B1
Romney Pl B3
Rose Yard B2
Rowland Cl C1
Royal Engineers' Rd A2
Royal Star Arcade B2
St Annes Ct B1
St Faith's St B2
St Luke's Rd A3
St Peter's Br B2
St Peter St B2
St Philip's Ave C3
Salisbury Rd A3
Sandling Rd A2
Scott St A2
Scrubs La B1
Sheal's Cres C3
Somerfield La B1
Somerfield Rd B1
Staceys St A2
Station Rd A2
Superstore A1/B2/B3
Terrace Rd B1
The Mall B3
The Somerfield Hospital A1
Tonbridge Rd C1
Tovil Rd C2
Town Hall B2
Trinity Park B3
Tufton St B3
Union St B3
Upper Fant Rd C1
Upper Stone St C3
Victoria St B1
Visitor Ctr A1
Warwick Pl B1
Wat Tyler Way B3
Waterloo St C3
Waterlow Rd A3
Week St B2
Well Rd A3
Westree Rd C1
Wharf Rd C1
Whatman Park A1
Wheeler St A3
Whitchurch Cl B1
Woodville Rd C3
Wyatt St B3
Wyke Manor Rd B3

Manchester 186

Adair St B6
Addington St A5
Adelphi St A1
Air & Space Gallery B2
Albert Sq B3
Albion St C3
AMC Great Northern B3
Ancoats Gr B6
Ancoats Gr North B6
Angela St C2
Aquatic Ctr C4
Ardwick Green Park C5
Ardwick Green North C5
Ardwick Green South C5
Arlington St A2
Artillery St B3
Arundel St C2
Atherton St B2
Atkinson St B3
Aytoun St B4
Back Piccadilly A4
Baird St B5
Balloon St A4
Bank Pl A1
Baring St B5
Barrack St C1
Barrow St A1
BBC TV Studios C4
Bendix St A5
Bengal St A5
Berry St C5
Blackfriars Rd A3
Blackfriars St A3
Blantyre St C2
Bloom St B4
Blossom St A5
Boad St B5
Bombay St B4
Booth St A3
Booth St B4
Bootle St B3
Brazennose St B3
Brewer St A5
Bridge St A3
Bridgewater Hall B3
Bridgewater Pl A4
Bridgewater St B2
Brook St C4
Brotherton Dr A2
Brown St A3
Brown St B4
Brunswick St C6
Brydon Ave C6
Buddhist Ctr A4
Bury St A2
Bus & Coach Station B4
Bus Station B4
Butler St A6
Buxton St C5
Byrom St B3
Cable St A5
Calder St B1
Cambridge St C3/C4
Camp St B3
Canal St B4
Cannon St A1
Cannon St A4
Cardroom Rd A6
Carruthers St A6
Castle St C2
Cateaton St A3
Cathedral A3
Cathedral St A3
Cavendish St C4
Chapel St A1/A3
Chapeltown St B5
Charles St C4
Charlotte St B4
Chatham St B4
Cheapside A3
Chepstow St B3
Chester Rd C1/C2
Chester St C4
Chetham's (Dept Store) A3
China La B5
Chippenham Rd A6
Chorlton Rd C2
Chorlton St B4
Church St A2
Church St A4
City Park A4
City Rd C3
Civil Justice Ctr B2
Cleminson St A2
Clowes St A3
College Land A3
Coll of Adult Ed C4
Collier St B2
Commercial St C3
Conference Ctr C4
Cooper St B4
Copperas St A4
Cornbrook C1
Cornell St A5
Cornerhouse C4
Corporation St A4
Cotter St C6
Cotton St A5
Cow La B1
Cross St B3
Crown Court B4
Crown St C2
Cube Gallery B4
Dalberg St C6
Dale St A4/B5
Dancehouse, The C4
Dantzic St A4
Dark La C6
Dawson St C2
Dean St A5
Deansgate A3/B3
Deansgate Station C3
Dolphin St C6
Downing St C5
Ducie St B5
Duke Pl B2
Duke St B2
Durling St C6
East Ordsall La A2/B1
Edge St A4
Egerton St C2
Ellesmere St C1
Everard St C1
Every St B6
Fairfield St B5
Faulkner St B4
Fennel St A3
Ford St A2
Ford St C6
Fountain St B4
Frederick St A2
Gartside St B2
Gaythorne St A1
George Leigh St A5
George St A1
George St B4
G-Mex C3
Goadsby St A4
Gore St A2
Goulden St A5
Granada TV Ctr B2
Granby Row B4
Gravel St A3
Great Ancoats St A5
Great Bridgewater St B3
Great George St A1
Great Jackson St C2
Great Marlborough St C4
Greengate A3
Green Room, The C4
Grosvenor St C5
Gun St A5
Hadrian Ave B6
Hall St B3
Hampson St B1
Hanover St A4
Hanworth Cl C5
Hardman St B3
Harkness St C6
Harrison St B6
Hart St B4
Helmet St B6
Henry St A5
Heyrod St B6
High St A4
Higher Ardwick C6
Hilton St A4/A5
Holland St A6
Hood St A5
Hope St B1
Hope St B4
Houldsworth St A5
Hoyle St C6
Hulme Hall Rd C1
Hulme St A1
Hulme St C3
Hyde Rd C6
Information Ctr B3
Irwell St A2
Islington St A2
Jackson Cr C2
Jackson's Row B3
James St A1
Jenner Cl C2
Jersey St A5
John Dalton St A1
John Dalton St B3
John Ryland's Liby B3
John St A2
Kennedy St B3
Kincardine Rd C5
King St A3
King St West A3
Law Courts B3
Laystall St B5
Lever St A5
Library B3
Linby St C2
Little Lever St A4
Liverpool Rd B2
Liverpool St B1
Lloyd St B3
Lockton Cl C5
London Rd B5
Long Millgate A3
Longacre St B6
Loom St A5
Lower Byrom St B2
Lower Mosley St B3
Lower Moss La C2
Lower Ormond St C4
Loxford La C4
Luna St A5
Major St B4
Manchester Arndale A4
Manchester Art Gallery B4
Manchester Central Convension Complex B3
Manchester Metropolitan University B4/C4
Manchester Piccadilly Station B5
Manchester Technology Ctr C4
Mancunian Way C3
Manor St C5
Marble St A4
Market St A2
Market St A4
Market St A4
Marsden St A3
Marshall St A5
Mayan Ave A2

Medlock St . . . C3
Middlewood St . . . B1
Miller St . . . A4
Minshull St . . . B4
Mosley St . . . A4
Mosley St . . . B4
Mount St . . . B3
Mulberry St . . . B3
Murray St . . . A5
Museum of Science & Industry (MOSI) . . . B2
Nathan Dr . . . A2
Naval St . . . A5
New Bailey St . . . A2
New Elm Rd . . . B2
New Islington . . . A6
New Quay St . . . B2
New Union St . . . A6
Newgate St . . . A4
Newton St . . . A5
Nicholas St . . . B4
North Western St . . . C6
Oak St . . . A4
Odeon . . . A4
Old Mill St . . . A6
Oldfield Rd . . . A1/C1
Oldham Rd . . . A5
Oldham St . . . A4
Opera House . . . B3
Ordsall La . . . C1
Oxford Rd . . . C4
Oxford Rd . . . C4
Oxford St . . . B4
Paddock St . . . C6
Palace Theatre . . . B4
Pall Mall . . . A3
Palmerston St . . . B6
Park St . . . A1
Parker St . . . B4
Peak St . . . B5
Penfield Cl . . . C5
Peoples' History Museum . . . B2
Peru St . . . A1
Peter St . . . B3
Piccadilly . . . A4
Piccadilly . . . B5
Piccadilly Gdns . . . B4
Piercy St . . . A6
Poland St . . . A5
Police Museum . . . A5
Police Station . . . B3/B5
Pollard St . . . B6
Port St . . . A5
Portland St . . . B4
Portugal St East . . . B5
Post Office . . . A1/A4/A5/B3
Potato Wharf . . . B2
Princess St . . . B3/C4
Pritchard St . . . C4
Quay St . . . A2
Quay St . . . B2
Queen St . . . B3
Radium St . . . A5
Redhill St . . . A5
Regent Rd . . . B1
Renold Theatre . . . A2
Retail Park . . . A5
Rice St . . . B2
Richmond St . . . B4
River St . . . C3
Roby St . . . B5
Rodney St . . . A6
Roman Fort . . . B2
Rosamond St . . . A2
Royal Exchange . . . A3
Sackville St . . . B4
St Andrew's St . . . B6
St Ann St . . . A3
St Ann's . . . A3
St George's Ave . . . C1
St James St . . . B4
St John St . . . B3
St John's Cath (RC) . . . A2
St Mary's . . . B3
St Mary's Gate . . . A3
St Mary's Parsonage . . . A3
St Peter's Sq . . . B3
St Stephen St . . . A2
Salford Approach . . . A3
Salford Central . . . A2
Sheffield St . . . B5
Shepley St . . . B5
Sherratt St . . . A5
Shudehill . . . A4
Shudehill . . . A4
Sidney St . . . C4
Silk St . . . A5
Silver St . . . B4
Skerry Cl . . . C5
Snell St . . . B6
South King St . . . B3
Sparkle St . . . B5
Spear St . . . A4
Spring Gdns . . . A4
Stanley St . . . A2/B2
Station Approach . . . B5
Store St . . . B5
Swan St . . . A4
Tariff St . . . B5
Tatton St . . . C1
Temperance St . . . B6/C6
The Triangle . . . A4
Thirsk St . . . C6
Thomas St . . . A4
Thompson St . . . A5
Tib La . . . B3
Tib St . . . A4
Town Hall (Manchester) . . . B3
Town Hall (Salford) . . . A2
Trafford St . . . C3
Travis St . . . B5
Trinity Way . . . A2
Turner St . . . A4
Union St . . . C6
University of Manchester (Sackville Street Campus) . . . C5
Upper Brook St . . . C5
Upper Cleminson St . . . A1
Upper Wharf St . . . A1
Urbis Museum . . . A4
Vesta St . . . B6
Victoria . . . A4
Victoria Station . . . A4
Victoria St . . . A3
Wadesdon Rd . . . C5
Water St . . . B2
Watson St . . . B3
West Fleet St . . . B1
West King St . . . A2
West Mosley St . . . B4
West Union St . . . B1
Weybridge Rd . . . A6
Whitworth St . . . B4
Whitworth St West . . . C3
Wilburn St . . . B1
William St . . . A2
William St . . . C6
Wilmott St . . . C3
Windmill St . . . B3
Windsor Cr . . . A1
Withy Gr . . . A4
Woden St . . . C1
Wood St . . . B3
Woodward St . . . A6
Worrall St . . . C1
Worsley St . . . C2
York St . . . B4
York St . . . C2
York St . . . C4

Middlesbrough 187

Abingdon Rd . . . C3
Acklam Rd . . . C1
Albert Park . . . C2
Albert Rd . . . B2
Albert Terr . . . C2
Aubrey St . . . C3
Ayresome Gdns . . . C2
Ayresome Green La . . . C1
Ayresome St . . . C2
Barton Rd . . . A1
Bilsdale Rd . . . C3
Bishopton Rd . . . C3
Borough Rd . . . B2/B3
Bowes Rd . . . A2
Breckon Hill Rd . . . B3
Bridge St East . . . B3
Bridge St West . . . B2
Brighouse Rd . . . A1
Burlam Rd . . . C1
Bus Station . . . B2
Cannon Park . . . B1
Cannon Park Way . . . B2
Cannon St . . . B1
Captain Cook Sq . . . B2
Carlow St . . . C1
Castle Way . . . C3
Chipchase Rd . . . C2
Cineworld . . . B3
Clairville Sports Stadium . . . C3
Cleveland Ctr . . . B2
Clive Rd . . . C2
Commercial St . . . A2
Corporation Rd . . . B2
Costa St . . . C2
Council Offices . . . B3
Crescent Rd . . . C2
Cumberland Rd . . . C2
Depot Rd . . . A2
Derwent St . . . B2
Devonshire Rd . . . C2
Diamond Rd . . . B2
Disabled Driver Test Circuit . . . B1
Dorman Museum . . . C2
Douglas St . . . B3
Eastbourne Rd . . . C2
Eden Rd . . . C3
Enterprise Ctr . . . A2
Forty Foot Rd . . . A2
Gilkes St . . . B2
Gosford St . . . A2
Grange Rd . . . B2
Gresham Rd . . . B2
Harehills Rd . . . C1
Harford St . . . C2
Hartington Rd . . . B2
Haverton Hill Rd . . . A1
Hey Wood St . . . B1
Highfield Rd . . . C3
Hill St Ctr . . . B2
Holwick Rd . . . B1
Hutton Rd . . . C3
ICI Works . . . A1
Information Ctr . . . B2
Lambton Rd . . . C3
Lancaster Rd . . . C2
Lansdowne Rd . . . C3
Latham Rd . . . C2
Law Courts . . . B2/B3
Lees Rd . . . B2
Leeway . . . B3
Linthorpe Cemetery . . . C1
Linthorpe Rd . . . B2
Lloyd St . . . B2
Longford St . . . C2
Longlands Rd . . . C3
Lower East St . . . A3
Lower Lake . . . C3
Maldon Rd . . . C1
Manor St . . . B2
Marsh St . . . B2
Marton Rd . . . B3
Middlehaven . . . B3
Middlesbrough By-Pass . . . B2/C1
Middlesbrough Coll . . . B3
Middlesbrough L Pk . . . B3
Middlesbrough Station . . . B2
Middlesbrough Theatre . . . C2
Middletown Park . . . C2
MIMA . . . B3
Mosque . . . B2
Mosque . . . C3
Mulgrave Rd . . . C2
North Ormesby Rd . . . B3
Newport Bridge . . . B1
Newport Bridge Approach Rd . . . B1
Newport Rd . . . B2
North Rd . . . B2
Northern Rd . . . C1
Outram St . . . B2
Oxford Rd . . . C2
Park La . . . C2
Park Rd North . . . C2
Park Rd South . . . C2
Park Vale Rd . . . C3
Parliament Rd . . . B1
Police Station . . . A2
Port Clarence Rd . . . A3
Portman St . . . B2
Post Office . . . B2/B3/C1/C2/C3
Princes Rd . . . B2
Python . . . A2
Riverside Bsns Park . . . A2
Riverside Park Rd . . . A1
Riverside Stadium (Middlesbrough FC) . . . B3
Rockliffe Rd . . . C2
Romaldkirk Rd . . . B1
Roman Rd . . . C2
Roseberry Rd . . . C3
St Barnabas' Rd . . . C2
St Paul's Rd . . . B2
Saltwells Rd . . . B3
Scott's Rd . . . A3
Seaton Carew Rd . . . A3
Shepherdson Way . . . B3
Sikh Temple . . . B2
Snowdon Rd . . . A2
South West Ironmasters Park . . . B1
Southfield Rd . . . B2
Southwell Rd . . . C2
Springfield Rd . . . C1
Startforth Rd . . . A2
Stockton Rd . . . C1
Stockton St . . . A2
Surrey St . . . C2
Sycamore Rd . . . C2
Synagogue . . . C2
Tax Offices . . . B3
Tees Viaduct . . . C1
Teessaurus Park . . . A2
Teesside Tertiary College . . . C3
Temenos . . . B3
The Avenue . . . C2
The Crescent . . . C2
Thornfield Rd . . . C1
Town Hall . . . B2
Transporter Bridge (Toll) . . . A3
Union St . . . B2
Univ of Teesside . . . B2
Upper Lake . . . C2
Valley Rd . . . C3
Ventnor Rd . . . C2
Victoria Rd . . . B2
Visitor Ctr . . . A3
Vulcan St . . . A2
Warwick St . . . C2
Wellesley Rd . . . B3
West Lane Hospl . . . C1
Westminster Rd . . . C2
Wilson St . . . B2
Windward Way . . . B3
Woodlands Rd . . . B2
York Rd . . . C3

Milton Keynes 187

Abbey Way . . . A1
Arbrook Ave . . . B1
Armourer Dr . . . A3
Arncliffe Dr . . . A1
Avebury . . . C2
Avebury Blvd . . . C2
Bankfield . . . B3
Bayard Ave . . . A2
Belvedere . . . A2
Bishopstone . . . A1
Blundells Rd . . . A1
Boycott Ave . . . C2
Bradwell Comm Blvd . . . B1
Bradwell Rd . . . C1
Bramble Ave . . . A2
Brearley Ave . . . C2
Breckland . . . A1
Brill Place . . . B1
Burnham Dr . . . B1
Bus Station . . . C1
Campbell Park . . . B3
Cantle Ave . . . A3
Central Milton Keynes Shopping Area . . . B2
Century Ave . . . C2
Chaffron Way . . . C3
Childs Way . . . C1
Christ the Cornerstone . . . B2
Cineworld . . . B2
Civic Offices . . . B2
Cleavers Ave . . . B2
Colesbourne Dr . . . A3
Conniburrow Blvd . . . B2
County Court . . . B2
Currier Dr . . . A2
Dansteed Way . . . A2/A3/B1
Deltic Ave . . . B1
Downs Barn . . . A2
Downs Barn Blvd . . . A3
Eaglestone . . . C3
Eelbrook Ave . . . B1
Elder Gate . . . B1
Evans Gate . . . C2
Fairford Cr . . . A3
Falcon Ave . . . B3
Fennel Dr . . . A2
Fishermead Blvd . . . C3
Food Ctr . . . B3
Fulwoods Dr . . . C3
Glazier Dr . . . A2
Glovers La . . . A1
Grafton Gate . . . C1
Grafton St . . . A1/C2
Gurnards Ave . . . B3
Harrier Dr . . . C3
Ibstone Ave . . . B1
Langcliffe Dr . . . A1
Leisure Plaza . . . C1
Leys Rd . . . C1
Library . . . B2
Linford Wood . . . A2
Marlborough Gate . . . B3
Marlborough St . . . A2/B3
Mercers Dr . . . A1
Midsummer . . . C2
Midsummer Blvd . . . B2
Milton Keynes Central . . . C1
Monks Way . . . A1
Mullen Ave . . . A3
Mullion Pl . . . C3
National Hockey Stadium . . . B1
Neath Hill . . . A3
North Elder . . . C1
North Grafton . . . B1
North Overgate . . . A3
North Row . . . B2
North Saxon . . . B2
North Secklow . . . B2
North Skeldon . . . A3
North Witan . . . B1
Oakley Gdns . . . A3
Oldbrook Blvd . . . C2
Open-Air Theatre . . . B3
Overgate . . . A3
Overstreet . . . A3
Patriot Dr . . . B1
Pencarrow Pl . . . B3
Penryn Ave . . . B3
Perran Ave . . . C3
Pitcher La . . . C1
Place Retail Pk, The . . . C1
Point Ctr, The . . . B2
Police Station . . . B2
Portway . . . B2
Post Office . . . A2/B2/C3
Precedent Dr . . . B1
Quinton Dr . . . B1
Ramsons Ave . . . B2
Rockingham Dr . . . A2
Rooksley . . . B1
Rooksley Retail Park . . . C1
Saxon Gate . . . B2
Saxon St . . . A1/C3
Secklow Gate . . . B2
Shackleton Pl . . . C2
Silbury Blvd . . . B2
Skeldon . . . A3
South Grafton . . . C2
South Row . . . C2
South Saxon . . . C2
South Secklow . . . B3
South Witan . . . C2
Springfield . . . B3
Stanton Wood . . . A1
Stantonbury . . . A1
Stantonbury L Ctr . . . A1
Strudwick Dr . . . C2
Sunrise Parkway . . . A2
Telephone Exchange . . . C3
The Boundary . . . C3
Theatre & Art Gallery . . . B3
Tolcarne Ave . . . C3
Towan Ave . . . C3
Trueman Pl . . . C2
Vauxhall . . . A1
Winterhill Retail Park . . . C2
Witan Gate . . . B2
X-Scape . . . B3

Newcastle upon Tyne 187

Albert St . . . B3
Argyle St . . . B3
Back New Bridge St . . . B3
BALTIC Ctr for Contemporary Art . . . C3
Barker St . . . A3
Barrack Rd . . . B1
Bath La . . . B1
Bell's Court . . . B2
Bessie Surtees Ho . . . C2
Bigg Market . . . C2
Biscuit Factory . . . B3
Black Gate . . . C2
Blackett St . . . B2
Blandford Sq . . . C1
Boating Lake . . . A1
Boyd St . . . B3
Brandling Park . . . A2
Bus Station . . . B2
Buxton St . . . B3
Byron St . . . A3
Camden St . . . B2
Castle Keep . . . C2
Central . . . C1
Central Library . . . B2
Central Motorway . . . B2
Chester St . . . A3
City Hall . . . B2
City Rd . . . B3/C3
City Walls . . . C1
Civic Ctr . . . A2
Claremont Rd . . . A1
Clarence St . . . B3
Clarence Walk . . . B3
Clayton St . . . C1/B1
Clayton St West . . . C1
Coach Station . . . C1
College St . . . B2
Collingwood St . . . C2
Copland Terr . . . B3
Coppice Way . . . B3
Corporation St . . . B1
Courts . . . C3
Crawhall Rd . . . B3
Dean St . . . C2
Discovery . . . C1
Dinsdale Pl . . . A3
Dinsdale Rd . . . A3
Doncaster Rd . . . A3
Durant Rd . . . B2
Eldon Sq . . . B1
Eldon Sq Sh Ctr . . . B3
Ellison Pl . . . B2
Empire . . . B1
Eskdale Terr . . . A2
Eslington Terr . . . A2
Exhibition Park . . . A1
Falconar St . . . B3
Fenkle St . . . C1
Forth Banks . . . C1
Forth St . . . C1
Gallowgate . . . B1
Gateshead Heritage @ St Mary's . . . C3
Gateshead Millennium Bridge . . . C3
Gibson St . . . B3
Goldspink La . . . A3
Grainger Market . . . B2
Grainger St . . . B2
Grantham Rd . . . A3
Granville Rd . . . A3
Great North Mus:Hancock . . . A2
Grey St . . . B2
Groat Market . . . C2
Guildhall . . . C2
Hancock St . . . A2
Hanover St . . . C2
Hatton Gallery . . . A1
Hawks Rd . . . C3
Haymarket . . . B2
Heber St . . . B1
Helmsley Rd . . . A3
High Bridge . . . B2
High Level Bridge . . . C2
Hillgate . . . C3
Howard St . . . B3
Hutton Terr . . . A3
Information Ctr . . . C3
Jesmond . . . A2
Jesmond Rd . . . A2/A3
John Dobson St . . . B2
John George Joicey Museum . . . C2
Jubilee Rd . . . B3
Kelvin Gr . . . A3
Kensington Terr . . . A2
Laing Gallery . . . B2
Lambton Rd . . . A2
Leazes Cr . . . B1
Leazes La . . . B1
Leazes Park . . . B1
Leazes Park Rd . . . B1
Leazes Terr . . . B1
Live . . . C2
Low Friar St . . . C1
Manor Chare . . . C2
Manors . . . B2
Manors Station . . . B2
Market St . . . B2
Melbourne St . . . B2
Mill Rd . . . C3
Mill Volvo Tyne . . . C1
Monument . . . B2
Monument Mall Shopping Ctr . . . B2
Morpeth St . . . A2
Mosley St . . . C2
Napier St . . . A3
Nazareth House . . . A3
New Bridge St . . . B2/B3
Newcastle Central Station . . . C1
Newcastle University . . . A1
Newgate Sh Ctr . . . C1
Newgate St . . . B1
Newington Rd . . . A3
Northern Stage Theatre . . . A2
Northumberland Rd . . . B2
Northumberland St . . . B2
Northumbria Univ . . . A2
Northwest Radial Rd . . . A1
O2 Academy . . . C1
Oakwellgate . . . C3
Orchard St . . . C2
Osborne Rd . . . A2
Osborne Terr . . . A3
Pandon . . . C3
Pandon Bank . . . B3
Park Terr . . . A1
Percy St . . . B1
Pilgrim St . . . B2
Pipewellgate . . . C2
Pitt St . . . B1
Plummer Tower . . . A2
Police Station . . . B2
Portland Rd . . . A3/B3
Portland Terr . . . A3
Post Office . . . A3/B1/B2/B3
Pottery La . . . C1
Prudhoe Pl . . . B1
Prudhoe St . . . B1
Quayside . . . C2
Queen Elizabeth II Bridge . . . C2
Queen Victoria Rd . . . A1
Richardson Rd . . . A1
Ridley Pl . . . B2
Rock Terr . . . B3
Rosedale Terr . . . A3
Royal Victoria Infirmary . . . A1
Sage Gateshead, The . . . C3
St Andrew's St . . . B1
St James . . . B1
St James' Blvd . . . C1
Sports Direct Arena (St James' Park) (Newcastle Utd FC) . . . B1
St Mary's (RC) . . . C1
St Mary's Place . . . B2
St Nicholas . . . C2
St Nicholas St . . . C2
St Thomas' St . . . B1
Sandyford Rd . . . A2/A3
Science Park . . . B2
Shield St . . . B3
Shieldfield . . . B3
Simpson Terr . . . B3
South Shore Rd . . . C3
South St . . . C1
Starbeck Ave . . . A3
Stepney Rd . . . B3
Stoddart St . . . B3
Stowell St . . . B1
Strawberry Pl . . . B1
Swing Bridge . . . C2
Temple St . . . C1
Terrace Pl . . . B1
The Close . . . C2
The Gate . . . B1
The Side . . . C2
Theatre Royal . . . B2
Times Sq . . . C1
Tower St . . . B3
Trinity House . . . C2
Tyne Bridge . . . C2
Tyne Bridges . . . C2
Tyneside . . . B2
Victoria Sq . . . A2
Warwick St . . . A3
Waterloo St . . . C1
Wellington St . . . B1
Westgate Rd . . . C1/C2
Windsor Terr . . . A2
Worswick St . . . B2
Wretham Pl . . . B3

Newport

Casnewydd 188

Albert Terr . . . B1
Allt-yr-Yn Ave . . . A1
Alma St . . . C2
Ambulance Station . . . C3
Bailey St . . . B2
Barrack Hill . . . A2
Bath St . . . A3
Bedford Rd . . . B3
Belle Vue La . . . C1
Belle Vue Park . . . C1
Bishop St . . . A3
Blewitt St . . . B1
Bolt Cl . . . C3
Bolt St . . . C3
Bond St . . . A2
Bosworth Dr . . . A1
Bridge St . . . B1
Bristol St . . . A3
Bryngwyn Rd . . . B1
Brynhyfryd Ave . . . C1
Brynhyfryd Rd . . . C1
Bus Station . . . B2
Caerau Cres . . . C1
Caerau Rd . . . B1
Caerleon Rd . . . A3
Capel Cres . . . C2
Cardiff Rd . . . C2
Caroline St . . . B3
Castle (Remains) . . . A2
Cedar Rd . . . B3
Charles St . . . B2
Charlotte Dr . . . C2
Chepstow Rd . . . A3
Church Rd . . . A3
City Cinema . . . B1
Civic Ctr . . . B1
Clarence Pl . . . A2
Clifton Pl . . . B1
Clifton Rd . . . C1
Clyffard Cres . . . B1
Clytha Park Rd . . . B1
Clytha Sq . . . C2
Coldra Rd . . . C1
Collier St . . . A3
Colne St . . . B3
Comfrey Cl . . . A1
Commercial Rd . . . C3
Commercial St . . . B2
Corelli St . . . A3
Corn St . . . B2
Corporation Rd . . . B3
Coulson Cl . . . C2
County Court . . . A2
Courts . . . A1
Courts . . . B1
Crawford St . . . A3
Cyril St . . . B3
Dean St . . . A3
Devon Pl . . . B1
Dewsland Park Rd . . . C2
Dolman . . . B2
Dolphin St . . . C3
East Dock Rd . . . C3
East St . . . B1
East Usk Rd . . . A3
Ebbw Vale Wharf . . . B3
Emlyn St . . . B2
Enterprise Way . . . C3
Eton Rd . . . B3
Evans St . . . A2
Factory Rd . . . A2
Fields Rd . . . B1
Francis Dr . . . C2
Frederick St . . . C3
Friars Rd . . . C1
Gaer La . . . C1
George St . . . C3
George Street Bridge . . . C3
Godfrey Rd . . . B1
Gold Tops . . . B1
Gore St . . . A3
Gorsedd Circle . . . C1
Grafton Rd . . . A3
Graham St . . . B1
Granville St . . . C3
Harlequin Dr . . . A1
Harrow Rd . . . B3
Herbert Rd . . . A3
Herbert Walk . . . C2
Hereford St . . . A3
High St . . . B2
Hill St . . . B2
Hoskins St . . . A2
Information Ctr . . . B2
Ivor Sq . . . B2
John Frost Sq . . . B2
Jones St . . . B1
Junction Rd . . . A3
Keynshaw Ave . . . C2
King St . . . C2
Kingsway . . . B2
Kingsway Ctr . . . B2
Ledbury Dr . . . A2
Library . . . A3
Library, Museum & Art Gallery . . . B2
Liverpool Wharf . . . B3
Llanthewy Rd . . . B1
Llanvair Rd . . . A3
Locke St . . . A2
Lower Dock St . . . C3
Lucas St . . . A2
Manchester St . . . A3
Market . . . B2
Marlborough Rd . . . B3
Mellon St . . . C3
Mill St . . . A2
Morgan St . . . A3
Mountjoy Rd . . . C2
Newport Bridge . . . A2
Newport Ctr . . . B2
Newport RFC . . . B3
Newport Station . . . B2
North St . . . B2
Oakfield Rd . . . B1
Park Sq . . . C2
Police Station . . . A3/C2
Post Office . . . B1/B2/C1/C3
Power St . . . A1
Prince St . . . A3
Pugsley St . . . A2
Queen St . . . C2
Queen's Cl . . . A1
Queen's Hill . . . A1
Queen's Hill Cres . . . A1
Queensway . . . B2
Railway St . . . B2
Riverfront Arts Ctr . . . B2
Riverside . . . A3
Rodney Rd . . . B2
Royal Gwent (A+E) . . . C2
Rudry St . . . A3
Rugby Rd . . . B3
Ruperra La . . . C3
Ruperra St . . . C3
St Edmund St . . . B1
St Mark's Cres . . . A1
St Mary St . . . B1
St Vincent Rd . . . A3
St Woolos . . . C2
St Woolos General (no A+E) . . . C1
St Woolos Rd . . . B1
School La . . . B2
Serpentine Rd . . . B1
Shaftesbury Park . . . A2
Sheaf La . . . A3
Skinner St . . . B2
Sorrel Dr . . . A1
South Market St . . . C3
Spencer Rd . . . B1
Stow Hill . . . B2/C1/C2
Stow Park Ave . . . C1
Stow Park Dr . . . C1
TA Ctr . . . A1
Talbot St . . . B2
Tennis Club . . . A1
Tregare St . . . A3
Trostrey St . . . A3
Tunnel Terr . . . B1
Turner St . . . A3
Upper Dock St . . . B2
Usk St . . . A3
Usk Way . . . B3/C3
Victoria Cr . . . B1
War Memorial . . . A3
Waterloo Rd . . . C1
West St . . . B1
Wharves . . . B2
Wheeler St . . . A2
Whitby Pl . . . A3
Windsor Terr . . . B1
York Pl . . . C1

Northampton 188

78 Derngate . . . B3
Abington Sq . . . B3
Abington St . . . B3
Alcombe St . . . A3
All Saints' . . . B2
Ambush St . . . B1
Angel St . . . B2
Arundel St . . . A2
Ash St . . . A2
Auctioneers Way . . . C2
Bailiff St . . . A2
Barrack Rd . . . A2
Beaconsfield Terr . . . A3
Becketts Park . . . C3
Bedford Rd . . . B3
Billing Rd . . . B3
Brecon St . . . A1
Brewery . . . C2
Bridge St . . . C2
Bridge St Depot . . . C3
Broad St . . . B2
Burns St . . . A3
Bus Station . . . B2
Campbell St . . . A2
Castle (Site of) . . . B2
Castle St . . . B2
Cattle Market Rd . . . C2
Central Museum & Art Gallery . . . B2
Charles St . . . A3
Cheyne Walk . . . B3
Church La . . . A2
Clare St . . . A3
Cloutsham St . . . A3
College St . . . B2
Colwyn Rd . . . A3
Cotton End . . . C2
Countess Rd . . . A1
County Hall . . . B2
Court . . . A2
Craven St . . . A3
Crown & County Courts . . . B3
Denmark Rd . . . B3
Derngate . . . B3
Derngate & Royal Theatres . . . B3
Doddridge Church . . . B2
Duke St . . . A3
Dunster St . . . A3
Earl St . . . A3
Euston Rd . . . C2
Fire Station . . . A3
Foot Meadow . . . B2
Gladstone Rd . . . A1
Gold St . . . B2
Grafton St . . . A2
Gray St . . . A3
Green St . . . B1
Greenwood Rd . . . B1
Greyfriars . . . B2
Grosvenor Ctr . . . B2
Grove Rd . . . A3
Guildhall . . . B2
Hampton St . . . A2
Harding Terr . . . A2
Hazelwood Rd . . . B3
Herbert St . . . B2
Hervey St . . . A3
Hester St . . . A2
Holy Sepulchre . . . A2
Hood St . . . A3
Horse Market . . . B2
Hunter St . . . A3
Information Ctr . . . B1
Kettering Rd . . . A3
Kingswell St . . . B2
Lady's La . . . B2
Leicester St . . . A2
Leslie Rd . . . A2
Library . . . B3
Lorne Rd . . . A2
Lorry Park . . . A1
Louise Rd . . . A2
Lower Harding St . . . A2
Lower Hester St . . . A2
Lower Mounts . . . B3
Lower Priory St . . . A2
Main Rd . . . C1
Marefair . . . B2
Market Sq . . . B2
Marlboro Rd . . . B1
Marriott St . . . A2
Military Rd . . . A3
Nene Valley Retail Pk . . . C1
New South Bridge Rd . . . C2
Northampton General Hospital (A&E) . . . B3
Northampton Sta . . . B1
Northcote St . . . A2
Nunn Mills Rd . . . C3
Old Towcester Rd . . . C2
Overstone Rd . . . A3
Peacock Pl . . . B2
Pembroke Rd . . . A1
Penn Court . . . C2
Police Station . . . B3
Post Office . . . A1/A2/B3/C2
Quorn Way . . . A2
Ransome Rd . . . C3
Regent Sq . . . A2
Robert St . . . A2
St Andrew's Rd . . . B1
St Andrew's St . . . A2
St Edmund's Rd . . . B3
St George's St . . . A2
St Giles . . . B3
St Giles St . . . B3
St Giles' Terr . . . B3
St James' Mill Rd . . . B1
St James' Mill Rd East . . . C1
St James Park Rd . . . B1
St James Retail Park . . . C1
St James Rd . . . B1
St Leonard's Rd . . . C2
St Mary's St . . . B2
St Michael's Rd . . . A3
St Peter's . . . B2
St Peter's Sq Sh Prec . . . B2
St Peter's Way . . . B2
Salisbury St . . . A2
Scarletwell St . . . B2
Semilong Rd . . . A2
Sheep St . . . B2
Sol Central (L Ctr) . . . B2
Somerset St . . . A3
South Bridge . . . C2
Southfield Ave . . . C2
Spencer Bridge Rd . . . A1
Spencer Rd . . . A3
Spring Gdns . . . B3
Spring La . . . B2
Swan St . . . B3
TA Ctr . . . A3
Tanner St . . . B2
The Drapery . . . B2
The Ridings . . . B3
Tintern Ave . . . A1
Towcester Rd . . . C2
Upper Bath St . . . B2
Upper Mounts . . . A2
Victoria Park . . . A1
Victoria Promenade . . . B2
Victoria Rd . . . B3
Victoria St . . . A2
Wellingborough Rd . . . B3
West Bridge . . . B1
York Rd . . . B3

Norwich 188

Albion Way . . . C3
All Saints Green . . . C2
Anchor Cl . . . A3
Anchor St . . . A3
Anglia Sq . . . A2
Argyle St . . . C3
Arts Ctr . . . B1
Ashby St . . . C2
Assembly House . . . B1
Bank Plain . . . B2
Barker St . . . A1
Barn Rd . . . A1
Barrack St . . . A3
Ber St . . . C2
Bethel St . . . B1
Bishop Bridge . . . A3
Bishopbridge Rd . . . A3
Bishopgate . . . A3
Blackfriars St . . . A2
Botolph St . . . A2
Bracondale . . . C3
Brazen Gate . . . C2
Bridewell . . . B2
Brunswick Rd . . . C1
Bull Close Rd . . . A2
Bus Station . . . C2
Calvert St . . . A2
Cannell Green . . . A3
Carrow Rd . . . C3
Castle Mall . . . B2
Castle Meadow . . . B2
Castle & Mus . . . B2
Cathedral . . . B2
Cattlemarket St . . . B2
Chantry Rd . . . B1
Chapel Loke . . . C2
Chapelfield East . . . B1
Chapelfield Gdns . . . B1
Chapelfield North . . . B1
Chapelfield Rd . . . B1
Chapelfield Sh Ctr . . . C1
City Hall . . . B1
City Rd . . . C2
City Wall . . . C1/C3
Colegate . . . A2
Coslany St . . . B1
Cow Hill . . . B1
Cow Tower . . . A3
Cowgate . . . A2
Crown & Magistrates Courts . . . A2
Dragon Hall Heritage Ctr . . . C3
Duke St . . . A1
Edward St . . . A2
Elm Hill . . . B2
Erpingham Gate . . . B2
Fire Station . . . B1
Fishergate . . . A2
Foundry Bridge . . . B3
Fye Bridge . . . A2
Garden St . . . C2
Gas Hill . . . B3
Grapes Hill . . . B1
Great Hospital Halls, The . . . A3
Grove Ave . . . C1
Grove Rd . . . C1
Guildhall . . . B1
Gurney Rd . . . A3
Hall Rd . . . C2
Heathgate . . . A3
Heigham St . . . A1
Horn's La . . . C2
Information Ctr . . . B1
Ipswich Rd . . . C1
James StUart Gdns . . . B3
King Edward VI School . . . B2
King St . . . B2
King St . . . C3
Koblenz Ave . . . C3
Library . . . B1
London St . . . B2
Lower Clarence Rd . . . B3
Lower Cl . . . B3
Maddermarket . . . B1
Magdalen St . . . A2
Mariners La . . . C2
Market . . . B2
Market Ave . . . B2
Mountergate . . . B3
Mousehold St . . . A3
Newmarket Rd . . . C1
Norfolk Gallery . . . B2
Norfolk St . . . C1
Norwich City FC . . . C3
Norwich Station . . . B3
Oak St . . . A1
Palace St . . . A2
Pitt St . . . A1
Playhouse . . . B2
Post Office . . . A2/B2/C2
Pottergate . . . B1
Prince of Wales Rd . . . B2
Princes St . . . B2
Pull's Ferry . . . B3
Puppet Theatre . . . A2
Quebec Rd . . . B3
Queen St . . . B2
Queens Rd . . . C2
Recorder Rd . . . B3
Retail Park . . . C3
Riverside Entertainment Ctr . . . C3
Riverside Swimming Ctr . . . C3
Riverside Rd . . . B3
Rosary Rd . . . B3
Rose La . . . B2
Rouen Rd . . . C2
Royal Norfolk Regiment Museum . . . B2
St Andrew's & Blackfriars Hall . . . B2
St Andrews St . . . B2
St Augustines St . . . A1
St Benedicts St . . . B1
St Ethelbert's Gate . . . B2
St Faiths La . . . B3
St Georges St . . . A2
St Giles St . . . B1
St James Cl . . . A3
St Julians . . . C2
St Martin's La . . . A1
St Peter Mancroft . . . B2
St Peters St . . . B1
St Stephens Rd . . . C1
St Stephens St . . . C1
Silver Rd . . . A2
Silver St . . . A2
Southwell Rd . . . C2
Strangers Hall . . . B1
Superstore . . . C2
Surrey St . . . C2
Sussex St . . . A1
The Close . . . B3
The Forum . . . B1
The Walk . . . B2
Theatre Royal . . . B1
Theatre St . . . B1
Thorn La . . . C2
Thorpe Rd . . . B3
Tombland . . . B2
Union St . . . C1
Vauxhall St . . . B1
Victoria St . . . C1
Walpole St . . . B1
Wensum St . . . A2
Wessex St . . . C1
Westwick St . . . A1
Wherry Rd . . . C3
Whitefriars . . . A2
Willow La . . . B1
Yacht Station . . . B3

Nottingham 188

Abbotsford Dr . . . A3
Addison St . . . A1
Albert Hall . . . B1
Alfred St South . . . A3
Alfreton Rd . . . B1
All Saints Rd . . . A1
Annesley Gr . . . A2
Arboretum . . . A1
Arboretum St . . . A1
Arthur St . . . A1
Arts Theatre . . . B3
Ashforth St . . . A3
Balmoral Rd . . . A1
Barker Gate . . . B3
Bath St . . . B3
Belgrave Ctr . . . B1
Bellar Gate . . . B3
Belward St . . . B3
Blue Bell Hill Rd . . . B3
Brewhouse Yard . . . C2
Broad Marsh Bus Sta . . . C2
Broad Marsh Prec . . . C2
Broad St . . . B3
Brook St . . . B3
Burns St . . . A1
Burton St . . . B2
Bus Station . . . A2
Canal St . . . C2
Carlton St . . . B3
Carrington St . . . C2
Castle Blvd . . . C1
Castle . . . C2
Castle Gate . . . C2
Castle Mdw Retail Pk . . . C1
Castle Meadow Rd . . . C2
Castle Museum & Gallery . . . C2
Castle Rd . . . C2
Castle Wharf . . . C2
Cavendish Rd East . . . C1
Cemetery . . . B1
Chaucer St . . . B1
Cheapside . . . B2
Church Rd . . . A3
City Link . . . C3
City of Caves . . . C2
Clarendon St . . . B1
Cliff Rd . . . C3
Clumber Rd East . . . C1
Clumber St . . . B2
College St . . . B1
Collin St . . . C2
Conway Cl . . . A2
Council House . . . B2
Court . . . B2
Cranbrook St . . . B3
Cranmer St . . . A2
Cromwell St . . . B1
Curzon St . . . B3
Derby Rd . . . B1
Dryden St . . . A2
Fishpond Dr . . . C1
Fletcher Gate . . . B3
Forest Rd East . . . A1
Forest Rd West . . . A1
Friar La . . . C2
Galleries of Justice . . . C3
Gedling Gr . . . A1
Gedling St . . . B3
George St . . . B3
Gill St . . . A2
Glasshouse St . . . B2
Goldsmith St . . . B2
Goose Gate . . . B3
Great Freeman St . . . A2
Guildhall . . . B2
Hamilton Dr . . . C1
Hampden St . . . A1
Heathcote St . . . B3
High Pavement . . . C3
High School . . . A1
Holles Cr . . . C1
Hope Dr . . . C1
Hungerhill Rd . . . A3
Huntingdon Dr . . . C1
Huntingdon St . . . A2
Information Ctr . . . B2
Instow Rise . . . A3
Int Com Ctr . . . A2
Kent St . . . B3
King St . . . B2
Lace Ctr, The . . . C2
Lace Market . . . B3
Lace Mkt Theatre . . . C3
Lamartine St . . . B3
Lenton Rd . . . C1
Lewis Cl . . . A3
Lincoln St . . . B2
London Rd . . . C3
Long Row . . . B2
Low Pavement . . . C2
Lower Parliament St . . . B3
Magistrates Court . . . C2
Maid Marian Way . . . B2
Mansfield Rd . . . A2/B2
Middle Hill . . . C2
Milton St . . . B2

Mount St B2
National Ice Ctr C3
Newcastle Dr B1
Newstead Gr A2
North Sherwood St A2
Nottingham Arena C3
Nottingham Sta C3
Old Market Square B2
Oliver St A1
Park Dr C1
Park Row C1
Park Terr B1
Park Valley C1
Peas Hill Rd A3
Peel St A1
Pelham St B2
Peveril Dr C1
Plantagenet St A3
Playhouse Theatre B1
Plumptre St C3
Police Station B2
Poplar St C3
Portland Rd B1
Post Office B2
Queen's Rd C3
Raleigh St A1
Regent St B1
Rick St B3
Robin Hood Statue C2
Robin Hood St B3
Royal Ctr B2
Royal Children Inn C2
Royal Concert Hall B2
St Ann's Hill Rd A2
St Ann's Way A2
St Ann's Well Rd A3
St Barnabas B1
St James' St B2
St Mark's St B3
St Mary's Gdn of Rest B3
St Mary's Gate B3
St Nicholas C2
St Peter's C2
St Peter's Gate B2
Salutation Inn C2
Shakespeare St B2
Shelton St A2
South Pde B2
South Rd C1
South Sherwood St B2
Station St C3
Station Street C3
Stoney St B3
Talbot St B1
Tales of Robin Hood C2
Tattershall Dr C1
Tennis Dr B1
Tennyson St A1
The Park C1
The Ropewalk B1
Theatre Royal B2
Trent St C3
Trent University A2/B2
Trent University B2
Trinity Square Sh Ctr B2
Trip To Jerusalem Inn C2
Union Rd B3
Upper Parliament St B2
Victoria Ctr B2
Victoria Leisure Ctr B3
Victoria Park B3
Victoria St B2
Walter St A1
Warser Gate B3
Watkin St A2
Waverley St A1
Wheeler Gate B2
Wilford Rd C2
Wilford St C2
Willoughby House C2
Wollaton St B1
Woodborough Rd A2
Woolpack La B3
York St A2

Oxford 189

Adelaide St A1
Albert St A1
All Souls (Coll) B2
Ashmolean Mus B2
Balliol (Coll) B2
Banbury Rd A2
Bate Collection of Musical Instruments C2
Beaumont St B1
Becket St B1
Blackhall Rd A2
Blue Boar St B2
Bodleian Library B2
Botanic Garden B3
Brasenose (Coll) B2
Brewer St C2
Broad St B2
Burton-Taylor Theatre B2
Bus Station B1
Canal St A1
Cardigan St A1
Carfax Tower B2
Castle B1
Castle St B1
Catte St B2
Cemetery C1
Christ Church (Coll) B2
Christ Church Cath C2
Christ Church Mdw C2
Clarendon Ctr B2
Coach & Lorry Park C1
College B3
Coll of Further Ed C1
Cornmarket St B2
Corpus Christi (Coll) B2
County Hall B1
Covered Market B2
Cowley Pl C3
Cranham St A1
Cranham Terr A1
Cricket Ground B1
Crown & County Courts C2
Deer Park B3
Exeter (Coll) B2
Folly Bridge C2
George St B1
Great Clarendon St A1
Hart St A1
Hertford (Coll) B2
High St B3
Hollybush Row B1
Holywell St B2
Hythe Bridge St B1
Ice Rink C1
Information Ctr B2
Jericho St A1
Jesus (Coll) B2
Jowett Walk B3
Juxon St A1
Keble (Coll) A2
Keble Rd A2
Library B2
Linacre (Coll) A3
Lincoln (Coll) B2
Little Clarendon St A1
Longwall St B3
Magdalen (Coll) B3
Magdalen Bridge B2
Magdalen St B2
Magistrate's Court C2
Manchester (Coll) B2
Manor Rd B3
Mansfield (Coll) A2
Mansfield Rd A3
Market B1
Marlborough Rd C2
Martyrs' Memorial B2
Merton Field B3
Merton (Coll) B3
Merton St B2
Mus of Modern Art B2
Museum of Oxford B2
Museum Rd A2
New College (Coll) B3
New Inn Hall St B2
New Rd B1
New Theatre B2
Norfolk St C1
Nuffield (Coll) B1
Observatory A1
Observatory St A1
Odeon B1/B2
Old Fire Station B1
Old Greyfriars St C2
Oriel (Coll) B2
Oxford Station B1
Oxford Story, The B2
Oxford University Research Ctrs A1
Oxpens Rd C1
Paradise Sq C1
Paradise St B1
Park End St B1
Parks Rd A2/B2
Pembroke (Coll) C2
Phoenix A1
Picture Gallery C2
Plantation Rd A1
Playhouse B2
Police Station C2
Post Office A1/B2
Pusey St B1
Queen's La B3
Queen's (Coll) B3
Radcliffe Camera B2
Rewley Rd B1
Richmond Rd A1
Rose La B3
Ruskin (Coll) B1
Saïd Business School B1
St Aldates C2
St Anne's (Coll) A1
St Antony's (Coll) A1
St Bernard's Rd A1
St Catherine's (Coll) B3
St Cross Building A3
St Cross Rd A3
St Edmund Hall (Coll) B3
St Giles St A2
St Hilda's (Coll) C3
St John St B2
St John's (Coll) B2
St Mary the Virgin B2
St Michael at the Northgate B2
St Peter's (Coll) B1
St Thomas St B1
Science Area A2
Science Museum B2
Sheldonian Theatre B2
Somerville (Coll) A1
South Parks Rd A2
Speedwell St C2
Sports Ground C3
Thames St C2
Town Hall B2
Trinity (Coll) B2
Turl St B2
University Coll (Coll) B3
Univ Mus & Pitt Rivers Mus A2
University Parks A2
Wadham (Coll) B2
Walton Cr A1
Walton St A1
Western Rd C2
Westgate Sh Ctr B2
Woodstock Rd A1
Worcester (Coll) B1

Peterborough 189

Athletics Arena B3
Bishop's Palace B2
Bishop's Rd B2/B3
Boongate A3
Bourges Boulevard A1
Bourges Retail Pk B1/B2
Bridge House (Council Offices) C2
Bridge St B2
Bright St A1
Broadway A2
Broadway A2
Brook St A2
Burghley Rd A2
Bus Station B2
Cavendish St A3
Charles St A3
Church St B2
Church Walk A2
Cobden Ave A1
Cobden St A1
Cowgate B2
Craig St A2
Crawthorne Rd A2
Cripple Sidings La C2
Cromwell Rd A1
Dickens St A3
Eastfield Rd A3
Eastgate B3
Fire Station A1
Fletton Ave C2
Frank Perkins Parkway C3
Geneva St A2
George St C1
Gladstone St A1
Glebe Rd C2
Gloucester Rd C3
Granby St B3
Grove St C1
Guildhall B2
Hadrians Ct C3
Henry St A2
Hereward Cross (Sh) B2
Hereward Rd B3
Information Ctr B2
Jubilee St C1
Key Theatre C2
Kent Rd B1
Kirkwood Cl B1
Lea Gdns B1
Library A2
Lincoln Rd A2
London Rd C2
Long Causeway B2
Lower Bridge St C2
Magistrates Court B2
Manor House St A2
Mayor's Walk A1
Midland Rd A1
Monument St A2
Morris St A3
Mus & Art Gallery B2
Nene Valley Railway C1
New Rd A2
New Rd C1
Northminster A2
Old Customs Ho C2
Oundle Rd C1
Padholme Rd A3
Palmerston Rd C1
Park Rd A2
Passport Office B2
Peterborough District Hospital (A+E) B1
Peterborough Sta B1
Peterborough Nene Valley C1
Peterborough United FC C2
Police Station B2
Post Office A3/B1/B2/B3/C1
Priestgate B2
Queen's Walk C2
Queensgate Ctr B2
Railworld C1
Regional Swimming & Fitness Ctr B3
River La B1
Rivergate Sh Ctr B2
Riverside Mead C3
Russell St A1
St John's B2
St John's St A3
St Marks St A2
St Peter's B2
St Peter's Rd B2
Saxon Rd A3
Spital Bridge A1
Stagshaw Dr C3
Star Rd B3
Thorpe Lea Rd B1
Thorpe Rd B1
Thorpe's Lea Rd B1
Tower St A2
Town Hall B2
Viersen Platz B2
Vineyard Rd B3
Wake Rd B3
Wellington St A3
Wentworth St B2
Westgate B2
Whalley St A3
Wharf Rd C1
Whitsed St A3
YMCA A3

Plymouth 189

Alma Rd A1
Anstis St B1
Armada Ctr B2
Armada St A3
Armada Way B2
Arts Ctr B2
Athenaeum B1
Athenaeum St C1
Barbican C3
Barbican C3
Baring St A3
Bath St B1
Beaumont Park B3
Beaumont Rd B3
Black Friars Gin Distillery C2
Breton Side B3
Bus Station B2
Castle St C3
Cathedral (RC) B1
Cecil St B1
Central Park A1
Central Park Ave A2
Charles Church B3
Charles Cross B3
Charles St B2
City Museum & Art Gallery B2
Citadel Rd C2
Citadel Rd East C2
Civic Ctr B2
Cliff Rd C1
Clifton Pl A3
Cobourg St A2
College of Art B2
Continental Ferry Port B1
Cornwall St B2
Dale Rd A2
Deptford Pl A3
Derry Ave A2
Derry's Cross B1
Drake Circus B2
Drake Cir Sh Ctr B2
Drake's Memorial C2
Drum B2
Eastlake St B2
Ebrington St B3
Elizabethan House C3
Elliot St C1
Endsleigh Pl A2
Exeter St B3
Fire Station A3
Fish Quay C3
Gibbons St A3
Glen Park Ave A2
Grand Pde C1
Great Western Rd C1
Greenbank Rd A3
Greenbank Terr A3
Guildhall B2
Hampton St B3
Harwell St B1
Hill Park Cr A3
Hoe Approach B2
Hoe Rd C2
Hoegate St C2
Houndiscombe Rd A2
Information Ctr C3
James St A2
Kensington Rd A3
King St B1
Lambhay Hill C3
Leigham St C1
Library B2
Lipson Rd A3/B3
Lockyer St C2
Lockyers Quay C3
Madeira Rd C2
Marina B3
Market Ave B1
Martin St B1
Mayflower Stone & Steps C3
Mayflower St B2
Mayflower Visitor Ctr C3
Merchants House B2
Millbay Rd B1
National Marine Aquarium C3
Neswick St B1
New George St B2
New St C3
North Cross A2
North Hill A3
North Quay B2
North Rd East A2
North Rd West A1
North St B3
Notte St B2
Octagon St B1
Pannier Market B1
Pennycomequick A1
Pier St C1
Plymouth Pavilions B1
Plymouth Station A2
Police Station B3
Portland Sq A2
Post Office A1/B1/B2
Princess St B2
Prysten House B2
Queen Anne's Battery Seasports Ctr C3
Radford Rd C1
Regent St B3
Rope Walk C3
Royal Citadel C2
Royal Pde B2
St Andrew's B2
St Andrew's Cross B2
St Andrew's St B2
St Lawrence Rd A2
Saltash Rd A2
Smeaton's Tower C2
Southern Terr A3
Southside St C2
Stuart Rd A1
Sutherland Rd A2
Sutton Rd B3
Sydney St A1
Teats Hill Rd C3
The Crescent B1
The Hoe C2
The Octagon B1
The Promenade C2
Tothill Ave B3
Union St B1
Univ of Plymouth A2
Vauxhall St B2/3
Victoria Park A1
West Hoe Rd C1
Western Approach B1
Whittington St A1
Wyndham St B1
YMCA B2
YWCA C2

Portsmouth 189

Action Stations C1
Admiralty Rd A1
Alfred Rd A2
Anglesea Rd B2
Arundel St B3
Aspex B1
Bishop St A2
Broad St C1
Buckingham Ho C2
Burnaby Rd B2
Bus Station B1
Camber Dock C1
Cambridge Rd B2
Car Ferry to Isle of Wight B1
Cascades Sh Ctr A3
Castle Rd C3
City Museum & Art Gallery B2
Civic Offices B3
Clarence Pier C2
College St B1
Commercial Rd A3
Cottage Gr B3
Cross St A1
Cumberland St A2
Duisburg Way C2
Durham St A3
East St B1
Edinburgh Rd A2
Elm Gr C3
Great Southsea St C3
Green Rd B3
Greetham St B3
Grosvenor St B3
Groundlings A2
Grove Rd North C3
Grove Rd South C3
Guildhall B3
Guildhall Walk B3
Gunwharf Quays Retail Park B1
Gunwharf Rd B1
Hambrook St C2
Hampshire Terr B2
Hanover St A1
High St C2
HM Naval Base A1
HMS Nelson (Royal Naval Barracks) A2
HMS Victory A1
HMS Warrior A1
Hovercraft Terminal C2
Hyde Park Rd B3
Information Ctr A1/B3
Isambard Brunel Rd B3
Isle of Wight Car Ferry Terminal B1
Kent Rd C3
Kent St A2
King St B3
King's Rd C3
King's Terr C2
Lake Rd A3
Law Courts B3
Library B3
Long Curtain Rd C2
Market Way A3
Marmion Rd C3
Mary Rose Mus A1
Middle St B3
Millennium Prom B1/C1
Museum Rd B2
National Museum of the Royal Navy A1
Naval Recreation Gd C2
Nightingale Rd C3
Norfolk St B3
North St A2
Osborne Rd C3
Park Rd B2
Passenger Catamaran to Isle of Wight B1
Passenger Ferry to Gosport B1
Pelham Rd C3
Pembroke Gdns C2
Pier Rd C2
Point Battery C1
Police Station B3
Portsmouth & Southsea A3
Portsmouth Harbour B1
Portsmouth Historic Dockyard A1
Post Office A2/A3/B1/B3/C3
Queen St A1
Queen's Cr C3
Round Tower C1
Royal Garrison Church C1
St Edward's Rd C3
St George's Rd B2
St George's Sq B1
St George's Way B2
St James's Rd B3
St James's St A2
St John's Cath (RC) A3
St Thomas's Cath C1
St Thomas's St B2
Somers Rd B3
Southsea Common C2
Southsea Terr C2
Spinnaker Tower B1
Square Tower C1
Station St A3
Swimming Pool A2
The Hard B1
Town Fortifications C1
Unicorn Rd A2
United Services Recreation Ground B2
University of Portsmouth A2/B2
Univ of Portsmouth – Coll of Art, Design & Media B3
Upper Arundel St A3
Victoria Ave C2
Victoria Park A2
Victory Gate A1
Vue B1
Warblington St B1
Western Pde C2
White Hart Rd C1
Winston Churchill Ave B3

Reading 190

Abbey Ruins B2
Abbey Sq B2
Abbey St B2
Abbot's Walk B2
Acacia Rd C2
Addington Rd C3
Addison Rd A1
Allcroft Rd C3
Alpine St C2
Baker St B1
Berkeley Ave C1
Bridge St B1
Brigham Rd A1
Broad St B1
Broad Street Mall B1
Carey St B1
Castle Hill C1
Castle St B1
Caversham Rd A1
Christchurch Playing Fields A2
Civic Offices & Magistrate's Court B1
Coley Hill C1
Coley Pl C1
Craven Rd C3
Crown St C2
De Montfort Rd A1
Denmark Rd C3
Duke St B2
East St B2
Edgehill St C2
Eldon Rd B3
Eldon Terr B3
Elgar Rd C1
Erleigh Rd C3
Field Rd C1
Fire Station A1
Fobney St B1
Forbury Gdns B2
Forbury Retail Park B2
Forbury Rd B2
Francis St C1
Friar St B1
Garrard St B1
Gas Works Rd B3
George St A2
Great Knollys St B1
Greyfriars B1
Gun St B1
Henry St C1
Hexagon Theatre, The B1
Hill's Meadow A2
HM Prison B2
Howard St B1
Information Ctr B1
Inner Distribution Rd B1
Katesgrove La C1
Kenavon Dr B2
Kendrick Rd C2
King's Mdw Rec Gd A2
King's Rd B2
Library B2
London Rd C3
London St B2
Lynmouth Rd A1
Market Pl B2
Mill La B2
Mill Rd A2
Minster St B1
Morgan Rd C3
Mount Pleasant C2
Museum of English Rural Life C3
Napier Rd A2
Newark St C2
Newport Rd A1
Old Reading Univ C3
Oracle Sh Ctr, The B1
Orts Rd B3
Pell St C1
Queen Victoria St B1
Queen's Rd A2
Queen's Rd B2
Police Station B1
Post Office B2
Randolph Rd A1
Reading Bridge A2
Reading Station A1
Redlands Rd C3
Renaissance Hotel B1
Riverside Museum B3
Rose Kiln La C1
Royal Berks Hospital (A & E) C3
St Giles C2
St Laurence B2
St Mary's B1
St Mary's Butts B1
St Saviour's Rd C1
Send Rd A3
Sherman Rd C2
Sidmouth St B2
Silver St C2
South St B2
Southampton St C2
Station Hill A1
Station Rd B1
Superstore A3
Swansea Rd A1
Technical College B3
The Causeway A3
The Grove B2
Valpy St B2
Vastern Rd A1
Vue B2
Waldeck St C2
Watlington St B3
West St B1
Whitby Dr C3
Wolseley St C1
York Rd A1
Zinzan St B1

Salisbury 190

Albany Rd A2
Arts Ctr A3
Ashley Rd A1
Avon Approach A2
Ayleswade Rd C2
Bedwin St A2
Belle Vue A2
Bishop's Palace C2
Bishops Walk B2
Blue Boar Row B2
Bourne Ave A3
Bourne Hill A3
Britford La C2
Broad Walk C2
Brown St B2
Bus Station B2
Castle St A2
Catherine St B2
Chapter House B2
Church House B2
Churchfields Rd B1
Churchill Way East B3
Churchill Way North A3
Churchill Way South C2
Churchill Way West A1
City Hall B2
Close Wall B2
Coldharbour La A1
College St A3
Council Offices A3
Court A1
Crane Bridge Rd B2
Crane St B2
Cricket Ground C1
Culver St South B3
De Vaux Pl C2
Devizes Rd A1
Dews Rd B1
Elm Grove B3
Elm Grove Rd A3
Endless St A2
Estcourt Rd A3
Exeter St C2
Fairview Rd A3
Fire Station A1
Fisherton St A1
Folkestone Rd C1
Fowlers Hill B3
Fowlers Rd B3
Friary Estate C3
Friary La B2
Gas La A1
Gigant St B3
Greencroft B3
Greencroft St A3
Guildhall B2
Hall of John Halle B2
Hamilton Rd A2
Harnham Mill B1
Harnham Rd C1/C2
High St B2
Hospital A1
House of John A'Port B2
Information Ctr B2
Kelsey Rd A3
King's Rd A2
Laverstock Rd B3
Library B2
London Rd A3
Lower St C1
Maltings, The B2
Manor Rd A3
Marsh La A1
Medieval Hall B2
Milford Hill B3
Milford St B3
Mill Rd B1
Millstream Approach A2
Mompesson House (NT) B2
New Bridge Rd C2
New Canal B2
New Harnham Rd C2
New St B2
North Canonry B2
North Gate B2
North Walk B2
Old George Hall B2
Old Blandford Rd C1
Old Deanery B2
Park St A3
Parsonage Green C1
Playhouse Theatre A2
Post Office A2/B2/C2
Poultry Cross B2
Queen Elizabeth Gdns B1
Queen's Rd A3
Rampart Rd B3
St Ann's Gate B2
St Ann St B2
St Marks Rd A3
St Martins B3
St Mary's Cath B2
St Nicholas Hospl C2
St Paul's A1
St Paul's Rd A1
St Thomas B2
Salisbury & South Wiltshire Mus B2
Salisbury General Hospital (A&E) C2
Salisbury Station A1
Salt La A3
Saxon Rd C1
Scots La A2
Shady Bower B3
South Canonry C2
South Gate C2
Southampton Rd B2
Spire View A1
Sports Ground C3
The Friary B3
Tollgate Rd B3
Town Path B1
Wain-a-Long Rd A3
Wardrobe, The B2
Wessex Rd A3
West Walk C2
Wilton Rd A1
Wiltshire College B3
Winchester St B3
Windsor Rd A1
Winston Churchill Gdns C3
Wyndham Rd A2
YHA B3
York Rd A1

Scarborough 190

Aberdeen Walk B2
Albert Rd A2
Albion Rd C2
Alexandra Bowling Hall A1
Alexandra Gardens A1
Auborough St B2
Belle Vue St C1
Belmont Rd C2
Brunswick Sh Ctr B2
Castle Dykes B3
Castlegate B3
Castle Holms A3
Castle Hill A3
Castle Rd B2
Castle Walls A3
Cemetery B1
Central Lift C2
Clarence Gardens A2
Coach Park B1
Columbus Ravine A1
Court B1
Cricket Ground A1
Cross St B2
Crown Terr C2
Dean Rd B1
Devonshire Dr A1
East Harbour B3
East Pier B3
Eastborough B2
Elmville Ave B1
Esplanade C2
Falconers Rd B2
Falsgrave Rd C1
Fire Station B2
Foreshore Rd B2
Friargate B2
Futurist Theatre B2
Gladstone Rd B1
Gladstone St B1
Hoxton Rd B1
Information Ctr B2/B3
King St B2
Londesborough Rd C1
Longwestgate B3
Marine Dr A3
Miniature Railway A1
Nelson St B1
Newborough B2
Nicolas St B2
North Marine Rd A1
North St B2
Northway B1
Old Harbour B3
Peasholm Park A1
Peasholm Rd A1
Plaza A1
Police Station B1
Post Office B2/C1
Princess St B3
Prospect Rd B1
Queen St B2
Queen's Parade A2
Queen's Tower (Remains) A3
Ramshill Rd C2
Roman Signal Sta A3
Roscoe St C1
Rotunda Museum C2
Royal Albert Dr A2
St Martin-on-the-Hill C2
St Martin's Ave C2
St Mary's B3
St Thomas St B2
Sandside B3
Scarborough Art Gallery and Crescent Art Studio C2
Scarborough Castle A3
Scarborough C1
Somerset Terr C2
South Cliff Lift C2
Spa, The C2
Spa Theatre, The C2
Stephen Joseph Theatre B1
Tennyson Ave B1
The Crescent C2
Tollergate B2
Town Hall B2
Trafalgar Rd B1
Trafalgar Square A1
Trafalgar St West B1
Valley Bridge Parade C2
Valley Rd C1
Vernon Rd C2
Victoria Park Mount A1
Victoria Rd B1
West Pier B3
Westborough C1
Westover Rd C1
Westwood C1
Woodall Ave A1
York Pl B2
Yorkshire Coast College (Westwood Campus) C1

Sheffield 191

Addy Dr A2
Addy St A2
Adelphi St A3
Albert Terrace Rd A3
Albion St A2
Aldred Rd A1
Allen St A4
Alma St A4
Angel St B5
Arundel Gate B5
Arundel St C4
Ashberry Rd A2
Ashdell Rd C1
Ashgate Rd C1
Athletics Ctr B2
Attercliffe Rd A6
Bailey St B4
Ball St A4
Balm Green B4
Bank St B4
Barber Rd A2
Bard St B5
Barker's Pool B4
Bates St A1
Beech Hill Rd C1
Beet St B3
Bellefield St A3
Bernard Rd A6
Bernard St B6
Birkendale A2
Birkendale Rd A2
Birkendale View A1
Bishop St C4
Blackwell Pl B6
Blake St A2
Blonk St A5
Bolsover St B2
Botanical Gdns C1
Bower Rd A1
Bradley St A1
Bramall La C4
Bramwell St A3
Bridge St A4/A5
Brighton Terrace Rd A1
Broad La B3
Broad St B6
Brocco St A3
Brook Hill B3
Broomfield Rd C1
Broomgrove Rd C2
Broomhall Pl C3
Broomhall Rd C2
Broomhall St C3
Broomspring La C2
Brown St C5
Brunswick St B3
Burgess St B4
Burlington St A2
Burns Rd A2
Bus/Coach Station B5
Cadman St A6
Cambridge St B4
Campo La B4
Carver St B4
Castle Market B5
Castle Square B5
Castlegate A5
Cathedral (RC) B4
Cathedral B4
Cavendish St B3
Charles St C4
Charter Row C4
Children's Hospital (A&E) B2
Church St B4
City Hall B4
City Hall B4
City Rd C6
Claremont Cr B2
Claremont Pl B2
Clarke St C3
Clarkegrove Rd C2
Clarkehouse Rd C1
Clarkson St B2
Cobden View Rd A1
Collegiate Cr C2
Commercial St B5
Commonside A1
Conduit Rd B1
Cornish St A3
Corporation St A4
Court B4
Cricket Inn Rd B6
Cromwell St A1
Crookes Rd B1
Crookes Valley Park B2
Crookes Valley Rd B2
Crookesmoor Rd A2
Crown Court A4
Crucible Theatre B5
Cutlers Gate A6
Cutler's Hall B4
Daniel Hill A2
Dental Hospital B2
Dept for Education & Employment C4
Devonshire Green B3
Devonshire St B3
Division St B4
Dorset St C2
Dover St A3
Duchess Rd C5
Duke St B5
Duncombe St A1
Durham Rd B2
Earl St C4
Earl Way C4
Ecclesall Rd C3
Edward St B3
Effingham Rd A6
Effingham St A6
Egerton St C3
Eldon St B3
Elmore Rd B1
Exchange St B5
Eyre St C4
Fargate B4
Farm Rd C5
Fawcett St A3
Filey St B3
Fire & Police Mus A4
Fire Station C4
Fir St A1
Fitzalan Sq/Ponds Forge B5
Fitzwater Rd C6
Fitzwilliam Gate C4
Fitzwilliam St B3
Flat St B5
Foley St A6
Foundry Climbing Ctr A4
Fulton Rd A1
Furnace Hill A4
Furnival Rd A5
Furnival Sq C4
Furnival St C4
Garden St B3
Gell St B3
Gibraltar St A4
Glebe Rd B1
Glencoe Rd C6
Glossop Rd B2/B3/C1
Gloucester St C2
Granville Rd C6
Granville Rd/ Sheffield College C5
Graves Gallery B5
Greave Rd B3
Green La A4
Hadfield St A1
Hanover St C3
Hanover Way C3
Harcourt Rd B1
Harmer La B5
Havelock St C2
Hawley St B4
Haymarket B5
Headford St C3
Heavygate Rd A1
Henry St A3
High St B4
Hodgson St C3
Holberry Gdns C2
Hollis Croft B4
Holly St B4
Hounsfield Rd B3
Howard Rd A1
Hoyle St A3
Hyde Park A6
Infirmary Rd A3
Infirmary Rd A3
Information Ctr B4
Jericho St A3
Johnson St A5
Kelham Island Ind Mus A4
Lawson Rd C1
Leadmill Rd C5
Leadmill St C5
Leadmill, The C5
Leamington St A1
Leavy Rd B3
Lee Croft B4
Leopold St B4
Leveson St A6
Library A2
Library B5
Library C1
Lyceum Theatre B5
Malinda St A3
Maltravers St A5
Manor Oaks Rd B6
Mappin St B3
Marlborough Rd B1
Mary St C4
Matilda St C4
Matlock Rd A1
Meadow St A3
Melbourn Rd A1
Melbourne Ave C1
Millennium Galleries B5
Milton St C3
Mitchell St B3
Mona Ave A1
Mona Rd A1
Montgomery Terr Rd A3
Montgomery Theatre B4
Monument Gdns C6
Moor Oaks Rd B1
Moore St C3
Mowbray St A4
Mushroom La B2
Netherthorpe Rd B3
Netherthorpe Rd B3
Newbould La C1
Nile St C1
Norfolk Park Rd C6
Norfolk Rd C6
Norfolk St B4
North Church St B4
Northfield Rd A1
Northumberland Rd B1
Nursery St A5
O2 Academy B5
Oakholme Rd C1
Octagon B2
Odeon B5
Old St B6
Oxford St A2
Paradise St B4
Park La C2
Park Sq B5
Parker's Rd B1
Pearson Building (Univ) C2
Penistone Rd A3
Pinstone St B4
Pitt St B3
Police Station A4/B5
Pond Hill B5
Pond St B5
Ponds Forge Sports Ctr B5
Portobello St B3
Post Office A1/A2/B3/B4/B5/B6/C1/C3/C4/C6
Powell St A2
Queen St B4
Queen's Rd C5
Ramsey Rd B1
Red Hill B3
Redcar Rd B1
Regent St B3
Rockingham St B4
Roebuck Rd A2
Royal Hallamshire Hospital C2
Russell St A4
Rutland Park C1
St George's Cl B3

St Mary's Gate C3
St Mary's Rd C4/C5
St Peter & St Paul Cathedral † B4
St Philip's Rd A3
Savile St A5
School Rd B1
Scotland St A4
Severn Rd B1
Shalesmoor A4
Shalesmoor A3
Sheaf St B5
Sheffield Hallam Univ B5
Sheffield Ice Sports Ctr - Skate Central C5
Sheffield Parkway A6
Sheffield Station C5
Sheffield Sta/ Sheffield Hallam Univ B5
Sheffield University B2
Shepherd St A3
Shipton St A2
Shoreham St C4
Showroom, The C5
Shrewsbury Rd C5
Sidney St C4
Site Gallery C5
Slinn St A1
Smithfield A4
Snig Hill A5
Snow La A4
Solly St B3
Southbourne Rd C1
South La C4
South Street Park B6
Spital Hill A5
Spital St A5
Spring Hill B1
Spring Hill Rd B1
Springvale Rd A1
Stafford Rd C6
Stafford St B6
Stanley St A5
Suffolk Rd C5
Summer St B2
Sunny Bank C3
Surrey St B4
Sussex St A6
Sutton St B3
Sydney Rd A2
Sylvester St C4
Talbot St B5
Taptonville Rd B1
Tax Office C4
Tenter St B4
The Moor C4
Town Hall B4
Townend St A1
Townhead St B4
Trafalgar St B4
Tree Root Walk B2
Trinity St A4
Trippet La B4
Turner Museum of Glass B3
Union St B4
Univ Drama Studio B2
Univ of Sheffield B3
Upper Allen St A3
Upper Hanover St B3
Upperthorpe Rd A2/A3
Verdon St A5
Victoria Quays B5
Victoria Rd C2
Victoria St B3
Waingate B5
Watery St A3
Watson Rd C1
Wellesley Rd B2
Wellington St C3
West Bar A4
West Bar Green A4
West One B3
West St B3
West St B4
Westbourne Rd C1
Western Bank B2
Western Rd A1
Weston Park B2
Weston Park Hospl B2
Weston Park Mus B2
Weston St A2
Wharncliffe Rd C3
Whitham Rd B1
Wicker A5
Wilkinson St B2
William St C3
Winter Garden B4
Winter St B2
York St B4
Yorkshire Artspace C5
Young St C4

Southampton 190

Above Bar St A2
Albert Rd North B3
Albert Rd South C3
Anderson's Rd B3
Archaeology Mus (God's Ho Tower) C2
Argyle Rd A2
Arundel Tower B1
Bargate, The B2
Bargate Shopping Ctr B2
BBC Regional Ctr A1
Bedford Pl A1
Belvidere Rd A3
Bernard St C2
Blechynden Terr A1
Brazil Rd C3
Brinton's Rd A2
Britannia Rd A3
Briton St C2
Brunswick Pl A2
Bugle St C1
Canute Rd C3
Castle Way C2
Catchcold Tower B1
Central Bridge C3
Central Rd C2
Channel Way C3
Chapel Rd B3
Cineworld C3
City Art Gallery A1
City College B3
Civic Ctr A1
Civic Ctr Rd A1
Coach Station B1
Commercial Rd A1
Cumberland Pl A1
Cunard Rd C2
Derby Rd A3
Devonshire Rd A1
Dock Gate 4 C2
Dock Gate 8 B1
East Park A2
East Park Terr A2
East St B2
East St Shopping Ctr B2
Endle St B3
European Way C2
Fire Station A2
Floating Bridge Rd C3
Golden Gr A3
Graham Rd A2
Guildhall A1
Hanover Bldgs B2
Harbour Lights C3
Harbour Pde B1
Hartington Rd A3
Havelock Rd A1
Henstead Rd A1
Herbert Walker Ave B1
High St B2
Hoglands Park B2
Holy Rood (Rems), Merchant Navy Memorial B2
Houndwell Park B2
Houndwell Pl B2
Hythe Ferry C2
Information Ctr A1
Isle of Wight Ferry Terminal C1
James St B3
Java Rd C2
Kingsway A2
Leisure World B1
Library A1
Lime St B2
London Rd A2
Marine Pde B3
Maritime C1
Marsh La B2
Mayflower Meml C1
Mayflower Park C1
Mayflower Theatre, The A1
Medieval Merchant's House C1
Melbourne St B3
Millais A2
Morris Rd A1
National Oceanography Ctr C3
Neptune Way C3
New Rd A2
Nichols Rd A3
North Front A2
Northam Rd A3
Ocean Dock C2
Ocean Village Marina C3
Ocean Way C3
Odeon B1
Ogle Rd B1
Old Northam Rd A2
Orchard La B2
Oxford Ave A2
Oxford St C2
Palmerston Park A2
Palmerston Rd A2
Parsonage Rd A3
Peel St A3
Platform Rd C2
Police Station A1
Portland Terr B1
Post Office A2/A3/B2
Pound Tree Rd B2
Quays Swimming & Diving Complex, The B1
Queen's Park C2
Queen's Peace Fountain A2
Queen's Terr C2
Queen's Way B2
Radcliffe Rd A3
Rochester St A3
Royal Pier C1
Royal South Hants Hospital A2
St Andrew's Rd A2
St Mary St A2
St Mary's B3
St Mary's Leisure Ctr A2
St Mary's Pl B2
St Mary's Rd A2
St Mary's Stadium (Southampton FC) A3
St Michael's C1
Solent Sky C3
South Front B2
Southampton Central Station A1
Southampton Solent University A2
SS Shieldhall C2
Terminus Terr C2
The Mall, Marlands A1
The Polygon A1
Threefield La B2
Titanic Engineers' Memorial A2
Town Quay C1
Town Walls B2
Tudor House C1
Vincent's Walk B2
West Gate Hall C1
West Marlands Rd A1
West Park A1
West Park Rd A1
West Quay Rd B1
West Quay Retail Pk B1
West Quay Sh Ctr B1
West Rd C2
Western Esplanade B1
Winton St A2

Southend-on-Sea 191

Adventure Island C3
Albany Ave A1
Albert Rd C3
Alexandra Rd C2
Alexandra St C2
Alexandra Yacht Club C2
Ashburnham Rd B2
Ave Rd B1
Avenue Terr B1
Balmoral Rd B1
Baltic Ave B3
Baxter Ave A2/B2
Beecroft Art Gallery C1
Bircham Rd A2
Boscombe Rd B3
Boston Ave A1/B2
Bournemouth Pk Rd A3
Browning Ave A3
Bus Station C3
Byron Ave A3
Cambridge Rd C1/C2
Canewdon Rd B1
Carnarvon Rd A2
Central Ave A3
Chelmsford Ave A1
Chichester Rd B2
Church Rd C3
Civic Ctr A2
Clarence Rd C2
Clarence St C2
Cliff Ave B1
Cliffs Pavilion C1
Clifftown Parade C2
Clifftown Rd C2
Colchester Rd A1
College Way B2
Coleman St B3
County Court B3
Cromer Rd B3
Crowborough Rd A2
Dryden Ave A3
East St A2
Elmer App B2
Elmer Ave B2
Gainsborough Dr A1
Gayton Rd A2
Glenhurst Rd A2
Gordon Pl B2
Gordon Rd B2
Grainger Rd A2
Greyhound Way A3
Guildford Rd B3
Hamlet Ct Rd B1
Hamlet Rd C1
Harcourt Ave A1
Hartington Rd C3
Hastings Rd B3
Herbert Gr C3
Heygate Ave C3
High St B2/C2
Information Ctr C3
Kenway A2
Kilworth Ave B3
Lancaster Gdns B3
Library B2
London Rd B1
Lucy Rd C3
MacDonald Ave A1
Magistrates Court A2
Maldon Rd A2
Maine Ave C1
Marine Rd C1
Marine Parade C3
Milton Rd B1
Milton St B2
Napier Ave B2
North Ave A3
North Rd A1/B1
Odeon B2
Osborne Rd B1
Park Cres B1
Park Rd B1
Park St B1
Park Terr B1
Pier Hill C3
Pleasant Rd C3
Police Station A2
Post Office B2/B3
Princes St B2
Queens Rd B2
Queensway B2/B3/C3
Rayleigh Ave A1
Redstock Rd A2
Rochford Ave A1
Royal Mews C2
Royal Terr C2
Royals Sh Ctr, The C3
Ruskin Ave A3
St Ann's Rd B3
St Helen's Rd B1
St John's Rd B1
St Leonard's Rd C3
St Lukes Rd A3
St Vincent's Rd C1
Salisbury Ave A1/B1
Scratton Rd C2
Shakespeare Dr A1
Short St A2
South Ave A3
Southchurch Rd B3
South Essex College B2
Southend Central B2
Southend Pier Railway C3
Southend Radio C2
Southend United FC A1
Southend Victoria B2
Stadium Rd A2
Stanfield Rd A2
Stanley Rd C3
Sutton Rd A3/B3
Swanage Rd B3
Sweyne Ave A1
Sycamore Gr A3
Tennyson Ave A3
The Grove A3
Tickfield Ave A2
Tudor Rd A1
Tunbridge Rd A2
Tylers Ave B3
Tyrrel Dr B3
Univ of Essex B2/C2
Vale Ave A2
Victoria Ave A2
Victoria Sh Ctr, The B2
Warrior Sq B3
Wesley Rd C3
West Rd A1
West St A1
Westcliff Ave C1
Westcliff Parade C1
Western Esplanade C1
Weston Rd C2
Whitegate Rd B3
Wilson Rd C1
Wimborne Rd B3
York Rd C3

Stoke 191

Ashford St A3
Avenue Rd A3
Aynsley Rd A2
Barnfield C1
Bath St C2
Beresford St A3
Bilton St C2
Boon Ave C2
Booth St C2
Boothen Rd C2/C3
Boughey St C2
Boughley Rd B3
Brighton St B1
Campbell Rd C2
Carlton Rd B2
Cauldon Rd A3
Cemetery A2
Cemetery Rd A2
Chamberlain Ave C1
Church (RC) B2
Church St C2
City Rd C3
Civic Ctr & King's Hall B3
Cliff Vale Pk A1
College Rd A2
Convent Cl B2
Copeland St B2
Cornwallis St C3
Corporation St C2
Crowther St A3
Dominic St B1
Elenora St B2
Elgin St B2
Epworth St A3
Etruscan St A1
Film Theatre B3
Fleming Rd C2
Fletcher Rd C2
Floyd St B2
Foden St C2
Frank St C2
Franklin Rd C1
Frederick Ave B1
Garden St C1
Garner St A1
Gerrard St B2
Glebe St B3
Greatbach Ave B1
Hanley Park A3
Harris St B1
Hartshill Rd B1
Hayward St A2
Hide St B2
Higson Ave B2
Hill St B2
Honeywall B2
Hunters Dr C1
Hunters Way C1
Keary St C2
Kingsway B2
Leek Rd B3
Library C2
Lime St C2
Liverpool Rd B2
London Rd C2
Lonsdale St C2
Lovatt St B2
Lytton St B3
Market C2
Newcastle La C1
Newlands St A2
Norfolk St A2
North St A1/B2
North Staffordshire Royal Infirmary (A&E) B1
Northcote Ave B2
Oldmill St C3
Oriel St B1
Oxford St B1
Penkhull New Rd C1
Penkhull St C1
Police Station C2
Portmeirion Pottery C2
Post Office A3/B1/B3/C1/C2
Prince's Rd B1
Pump St B2
Quarry Ave B2
Quarry Rd B2
Queen Anne St A3
Queen's Rd C1
Queensway A1/B2/C3
Richmond St B1
Rothwell St C1
St Peter's B3
St Thomas Pl C1
Scrivenor Rd A1
Seaford St A3
Selwyn St C3
Shelton New Rd A1
Shelton Old Rd B2
Sheppard St C2
Spark St C2
Spencer Rd B3
Spode St C2
Squires View B3
Staffordshire Univ B3
Stanley Matthews Sports Ctr B3
Station Rd B3
Stoke Business Park C3
Stoke Recreation Ctr C2
Stoke Rd A2
Stoke-on-Trent Coll A3
Stoke-on-Trent Station B3
Sturgess St C2
The Villas C1
Thistley Hough C1
Thornton Rd B3
Tolkien Way B1
Trent Valley Rd C1
Vale St B2
Watford St A3
Wellesley St A3
West Ave B1
Westland St B1
Yeaman St C2
Yoxall Ave B1

Stratford-upon-Avon 192

Albany Rd B1
Alcester Rd B1
Ambulance Station B1
Arden St B1
Avenue Farm A1
Ave Farm Ind Est A1
Avenue Rd A3
Avon Industrial Est A2
Baker Ave A1
Bandstand C3
Benson Rd A3
Birmingham Rd A2
Boat Club B3
Borden Pl C1
Brass Rubbing Ctr C2
Bridge St B2
Bridgetown Rd C3
Bridgeway B3
Broad St C2
Broad Walk C2
Brookvale Rd C1
Bull St C2
Bus Station B2
Butterfly Farm C3
Cemetery C1
Chapel La B2
Cherry Orchard C1
Chestnut Walk B2
Children's Playground C3
Church St C2
Civic Hall B2
Clarence Rd B1
Clopton Bridge B3
Clopton Rd A2
Coach Terminal & Pk B3
College B1
College La C2
College St C2
Com Sports Ctr B1
Council Offices (District) B2
Courtyard C2
Cox's Yard B3
Cricket Ground C3
Ely Gdns B2
Ely St B2
Evesham Rd C1
Fire Station B1
Foot Ferry C3
Fordham Ave A2
Gallery, The B3
Garrick Way C1
Gower Memorial B3
Great William St B2
Greenhill St B2
Grove Rd B2
Guild St B2
Guildhall & School B2
Hall's Croft C2
Hartford Rd C1
Harvard House B2
Henley St B2
High St B2
Holton St C2
Holy Trinity C2
Information Ctr B3
Jolyffe Park Rd A2
Kipling Rd C3
Library B2
Lodge Rd B1
Maidenhead Rd A3
Mansell St B2
Masons Court B2
Masons Rd A1
Maybird Shopping Pk A2
Maybrook Rd A1
Mayfield Ave A2
Meer St B2
Mill La C2
Moat House Hotel B3
Narrow La C2
Nash's House & New Place B2
New St C2
Old Town C2
Orchard Way C1
Paddock La C1
Park Rd A1
Payton St B2
Percy St A2
Police Station B2
Post Office B2/B3
Recreation Ground C2
Regal Road A2
Rother St B2
Rowley Cr A3
Royal Shakespeare & Swan Theatres B3
Ryland St C2
Saffron Meadow C2
St Andrew's Cr B1
St Gregory's A3
St Gregory's Rd A3
St Mary's Rd A2
Sanctus Dr C2
Sanctus St C1
Sandfield Rd C2
Scholars La B2
Seven Meadows Rd C2
Shakespeare Ctr B2
Shakespeare Inst C2
Shakespeare St B2
Shakespeare's Birthplace B2
Shelley Rd C3
Shipston Rd C3
Shottery Rd C1
Slingates Rd A2
Southern La C2
Station Rd B1
Stratford Healthcare B2
Stratford Hospital B2
Stratford Sports Club B1
Stratford-upon-Avon Station B1
Swan's Nest La B3
Talbot Rd A2
The Greenway C2
The Willows B1
The Willows North B1
Tiddington Rd B3
Timothy's Bridge Industrial Estate A1
Timothy's Bridge Rd A1
Town Hall & Council Offices B2
Town Sq B2
Trinity St C2
Tyler St B2
War Memorial Gdns B3
Warwick Rd B3
Waterside B3
Welcombe Rd A3
West St C2
Western Rd A2
Wharf Rd A2
Wood St B2

Sunderland 192

Albion Pl C2
Alliance Pl B1
Argyle St C2
Ashwood St C1
Athenaeum St B2
Azalea Terr C2
Beach St A1
Bede Theatre C3
Bedford St B2
Beechwood Terr C1
Belvedere Rd C2
Blandford St B2
Borough Rd B3
Bridge Cr B2
Bridge St B2
Brooke St A2
Brougham St B2
Burdon Rd C2
Burn Park C1
Burn Park Rd C1
Burn Park Tech Park C1
Carol St B1
Charles St A3
Chester Rd C1
Chester Terr B1
Church St A3
Civic Ctr C2
Cork St B3
Coronation St B3
Cowan Terr C2
Crowtree Rd B2
Dame Dorothy St A2
Deptford Rd B1
Deptford Terr A1
Derby St C2
Derwent St C2
Dock St A3
Dundas St A2
Durham Rd C1
Easington St A2
Egerton St C3
Empire B2
Empire Theatre B2
Farringdon Row B1
Fawcett St B2
Fox St C1
Foyle St B3
Frederick St B3
Gill Rd B2
Hanover Pl A1
Havelock Terr C1
Hay St A2
Headworth Sq B3
Hendon Rd B3
High St East B3
High St West B2/B3
Holmeside B2
Hylton Rd B1
Information Ctr B2
John St B3
Kier Hardie Way A2
Lambton St B3
Laura St C3
Lawrence St B3
Leisure Ctr B2
Library & Arts Ctr B3
Lily St B1
Lime St B1
Livingstone Rd B2
Low Row B2
Matamba Terr B1
Millburn St B1
Millennium Way A2
Minster B2
Monkwearmouth Station Museum A2
Mowbray Park C3
Mowbray Rd C3
Murton St C3
National Glass Ctr A3
New Durham Rd C1
Newcastle Rd A2
Nile St B3
Norfolk St B3
North Bridge St A2
Northern Gallery for Contemporary Art B3
Otto Terr C1
Park La C2
Park Lane C2
Park Rd C2
Paul's Rd B3
Peel St C3
Police Station B2
Post Office B2
Priestly Cr A1
Queen St B2
Railway Row B1
Retail Park B1
Richmond St A2
Roker Ave A2
Royalty Theatre C1
Ryhope Rd C2
St Mary's Way B2
St Michael's Way B2
St Peter's A3
St Peter's A2
St Peter's Way A3
St Vincent St C3
Salem Rd C3
Salem St C3
Salisbury St C3
Sans St B3
Silkworth Row B1
Southwick Rd A2
Stadium of Light (Sunderland AFC) A2
Stadium Way A2
Stobart St A2
Stockton Rd C2
Suffolk St C3
Sunderland Aquatic Ctr A2
Sunderland B2
Sunderland Mus B3
Sunderland Sta B2
Sunderland St B3
Tatham St C3
Tavistock Pl B3
The Bridges B2
The Place B3
The Royalty C1
Thelma St C1
Thomas St North A2
Thornholme Rd C1
Toward Rd C3
Transport Intc C2
Trimdon St Way B1
Tunstall Rd C2
University B1
University Library C1
Univ of Sunderland (City Campus) B1
Univ of Sunderland (Sir Tom Cowie at St Peter's Campus) A3
Vaux Brewery Way A2
Villiers St B3
Villiers St South B3
Vine Pl C2
Violet St B1
Walton La B3
Waterworks Rd B1
Wearmouth Bridge B2
Wellington La A1
West Sunniside B3
West Wear St B3
Westbourne Rd B1
Western Hill C1
Wharncliffe B1
Whickham St A3
White House Rd C3
Wilson St North A2
Winter Gdns C3
Wreath Quay A1

Swansea Abertawe 192

Adelaide St C3
Albert Row C3
Alexandra Rd B3
Argyle St C1
Baptist Well Pl A2
Beach St C1
Belle Vue Way B3
Berw Rd A1
Berwick Terr A2
Bond St C1
Brangwyn Concert Hall C1
Bridge St A3
Brookands Terr B1
Brunswick St C1
Bryn-Syfi Terr A2
Bryn-y-Mor Rd C1
Bullins La B1
Burrows Rd C1
Bus/Rail link A3
Bus Station C2
Cadfan Rd A1
Cadrawd Rd A1
Caer St B3
Carig Cr A1
Carlton Terr B2
Carmarthen Rd A3
Castle Square B3
Castle St B3
Catherine St C1
City & County of Swansea Offices (County Hall) C2
City & County of Swansea Offices (Guildhall) C1
Clarence St C2
Colbourne Terr A2
Constitution Hill B1
Court B3
Creidiol Rd A2
Cromwell St B2
Duke St B1
Dunvant Pl C2
Dyfatty Park A3
Dyfatty St A3
Dyfed Ave A1
Dylan Thomas Ctr B3
Dylan Thomas Theatre C3
Eaton Cr C1
Eigen Cr A1
Elfed Rd A1
Emlyn Rd A1
Evans Terr A3
Fairfield Terr B1
Ffynone Dr B1
Ffynone Rd B1
Fire Station B3
Firm St A2
Fleet St C1
Francis St C1
Fullers Row B2
George St B2
Glamorgan St C2
Glyndŵr Pl A1
Graig Terr A3
Grand Theatre C2
Granogwen Rd A2
Guildhall Rd South C1
Gwent Rd A1
Gwynedd Ave A1
Hafod St A3
Hanover St B1
Harcourt St B2
Harries St A2
Heathfield B2
Henrietta St B1
Hewson St B2
High St A3/B3
High View A2
Hill St A2
Historic Ships Berth C3
HM Prison C2
Information Ctr C2
Islwyn Rd A1
King Edward's Rd C1
Law Courts C1
Library B3
Long Ridge A2
Madoc St C2
Mansel St B2
Maritime Quarter C3
Market B3
Mayhill Gdns B1
Mayhill Rd A1
Mega Bowl B3
Milton Terr A2
Mission Gallery C3
Montpellier Terr B1
Morfa Rd A3
Mount Pleasant B2
National Waterfront Museum C3
Nelson St C2
New Cut Rd A3
New St A3
Nicander Pde A2
Nicander Pl A2
Nicholl St B2
Norfolk St B2
North Hill Rd A2
Northampton La B2
Orchard St B3
Oxford St B2
Oystermouth Rd C1
Page St B2
Pant-y-Celyn Rd B1
Parc Tawe Link B3
Parc Tawe North B3
Parc Tawe Sh & L Ctr B3
Patti Pavilion C1
Paxton St C2
Penmaen Terr B1
Pen-y-Graig Rd A1
Phillips Pde C1
Picton Terr B2
Plantasia B3
Police Station B2
Post Office A1/A2/B2/C1
Powys Ave A1
Primrose St B2
Princess Way B3
Promenade B2
Pryder Gdns A1
Quadrant Ctr C2
Quay Park B3
Rhianfa La B1
Rhondda St B2
Richardson St C2
Rodney St C1
Rose Hill B1
Rosehill Terr B1
Russell St B1
St David's Sq C3
St Helen's Ave C1
St Helen's Cr C1
St Helen's Rd C1
St James Gdns B1
St James's Cr B1
St Mary's B3
Sea View Terr A3
Singleton St C2
South Dock C3
Stanley Pl B2
Strand B3
Swansea Castle B3
Swansea Coll Arts Ctr C1
Swansea Metropolitan University B2
Swansea Museum C3
Swansea Station A3
Taliesyn Rd B1
Tan y Marian Rd A1
Tegid Rd A2
Teilo Cr A1
Terrace Rd B1/B2
The Kingsway B2
The LC C3
Tontine St A3
Tower of Eclipse C3
Townhill Rd A1
Tram Museum C3
Trawler Rd C3
Union St B2
Upper Strand A3
Vernon St A3
Victoria Quay C3
Victoria Rd B3
Vincent St C1
Walter Rd B1
Watkin St A2
Waun-Wen Rd A2
Wellington St C2
Westbury St C1
Western St C1
Westway C2
William St C2
Wind St B3
Woodlands Terr B1
YMCA B2
York St C3

Swindon 192

Albert St C3
Albion St C1
Alfred St A2
Alvescot Rd C3
Art Gallery & Mus C3
Ashford Rd C1
Aylesbury St A2
Bath Rd C2
Bathampton St B1
Bathurst Rd B3
Beatrice St A2
Beckhampton St B3
Bowood Rd C1
Bristol St B1
Broad St A3
Brunel Arcade B2
Brunel Plaza B2
Brunswick St C2
Bus Station B2
Cambria Bridge Rd B1
Cambria Place B1
Canal Walk B2
Carfax St B2
Carr St B1
Cemetery C1/C3
Chandler Cl C3
Chapel C1
Chester St B1
Christ Church C3
Church Place B1
Cirencester Way A3
Clarence St B2
Clifton St C1
Cockleberry A2
Colbourne A3
Colbourne St A3
College St B2
Commercial Rd B2
Corporation St A2
Council Offices B3
County Rd A3
Courts B2
Cricket Ground A3
Cricklade Street C3
Crombey St B1/C2
Cross St C2
Curtis St B1
Deacon St C1
Designer Outlet (Great Western) B1
Dixon St C2
Dover St C2
Dowling St C2
Drove Rd C3
Dryden St C1
Durham St C3
East St B1
Eastcott Hill C2
Eastcott Rd C2
Edgeware Rd B2
Edmund St C2
Elmina Rd A3
Emlyn Square B1
Euclid St B3
Exeter St B1
Fairview C1
Faringdon Rd B1
Farnsby St B1
Fire Station B3
Fleet St B2
Fleming Way B2/B3
Florence St A2
Gladstone St A3
Gooch St A2
Graham St A3
Great Western Way A1/A2
Groundwell Rd B3
Hawksworth Way A1
Haydon St A2
Henry St B2
Hillside Ave C1
Holbrook Way B2
Hunt St C3
Hydro B1
Hythe Rd C2
Information Ctr B2
Joseph St C1
Kent Rd C2
King William St C2
Kingshill Rd C1
Lansdown Rd C2
Leicester St B3
Library B2
Lincoln St B3
Little London C3
London St B1
Magic Roundabout B3
Maidstone Rd C2
Manchester Rd A3
Maxwell St B1
Milford St B2
Milton Rd B1
Morse St C2
National Monuments Record Ctr B1
Newcastle St B3
Newcombe Drive A1
Newcombe Trading Estate A1
Newhall St C2
North St C2
North Star Ave A1
North Star A1
Northampton St B3
Oasis Leisure Ctr A1
Ocotal Way A3
Okus Rd C1
Old Town C3
Oxford St B1
Park Lane B1
Park Lane B1
Pembroke St C2
Plymouth St B3
Polaris House A2
Polaris Way A2
Police Station B2
Ponting St A2
Post Office B1/B2/C1/C3
Poulton St A3
Princes St B2
Prospect Hill C2
Prospect Place C2
Queen St B2
Queen's Park C3
Radnor St C1
Read St C1
Reading St B1
Regent St B2
Retail Park A2/A3/B3
Rosebery St A3
St Mark's B1
Salisbury St A3
Savernake St C2
Shelley St C1
Sheppard St B1
South St C2
Southampton St B3
Spring Gardens B3
Stafford Street C2
Stanier St C2
Station Road A2
STEAM B1
Swindon College A2
Swindon Rd C2
Swindon Station A2
Swindon Town Football Club A3
T A Ctr B1
Tennyson St B1
The Lawn C3
The Nurseries C1
The Parade B2
The Park B1
Theobald St B1
Town Hall B2
Transfer Bridges A3
Union St C2
Upham Rd C3
Victoria Rd C3
Walcot Rd B3
War Memorial B2
Wells St B3
Western St C2
Westmorland Rd B3
Whalebridge B2
Whitehead St C1
Whitehouse Rd A2
William St C1
Wood St C3
Wyvern Theatre & Arts Ctr B2
York Rd B3

Taunton 193

Addison Gr A1
Albemarle Rd A1
Alfred St B3
Alma St C2
Bath Pl C1
Belvedere Rd A1
Billet St B2
Billetfield C2
Birch Gr A1
Brewhouse Theatre B2
Bridge St B1
Bridgwater & Taunton Canal A2
Broadlands Rd C1
Burton Pl C1
Bus Station B1
Canal Rd A2
Cann St C1
Canon St B2
Castle B1
Castle St B1
Cheddon Rd A2
Chip Lane A1
Clarence St B1
Cleveland St B1
Clifton Terr A2
Coleridge Cres C3
Compass Hill C1
Compton Cl A2
Corporation St B1
Council Offices A1
County Walk Sh Ctr C2
Courtyard B2
Cranmer Rd B2
Critchard Way B3
Cyril St A1
Deller's Wharf B1
Duke St B2
East Reach B3
East St B3
Eastbourne Rd B2
Eastleigh Rd C3
Eaton Cres A2
Elm Gr A1
Elms Cl A1
Fons George C1
Fore St B2
Fowler St A1
French Weir Rec Grd B1
Geoffrey Farrant Wk A2
Gray's Almshouses B2

Grays Rd B3
Greenway Ave A1
Guildford Pl C1
Hammet St B2
Haydon Rd B3
Heavitree Way A2
Herbert St A1
High St C2
Holway Ave C3
Hugo St B3
Huish's Almshouses B2
Hurdle Way C2
Information Ctr C2
Jubilee St A1
King's College C3
Kings Cl C3
Laburnum St B2
Lambrook Rd B3
Lansdowne Rd A3
Leslie Ave A1
Leycroft Rd B3
Library C2
Linden Gr A1
Magdalene St B2
Magistrates Court B1
Malvern Terr A2
Market House B2
Mary St C2
Middle St B2
Midford Rd B3
Mitre Court B3
Mount Nebo C1
Mount St C2
Mountway C2
Mus of Somerset B1
North St B2
Northfield Ave B1
Northfield Rd B1
Northleigh Rd C3
Obridge Allotments A3
Obridge Lane A3
Obridge Rd A3
Obridge Viaduct A3
Old Mkt Shopping Ctr C2
Osborne Way C1
Park St C1
Paul St C2
Plais St A2
Playing Field C3
Police Station C1
Portland St B1
Post Office B1/B2/C1
Priorswood Ind Est A3
Priorswood Rd A2
Priory Ave B2
Priory Bridge Rd B2
Priory Fields Ret Pk A3
Priory Park A2
Priory Way A3
Queen St B3
Railway St A1
Records Office A2
Recreation Grd A1
Riverside Place B2
St Augustine St B2
St George's C2
St Georges Sq C2
St James B2
St James St B2
St John's C1
St John's Rd B1
St Josephs Field C2
St Mary Magdalene's B2
Samuels Ct A1
Shire Hall & Law Courts C1
Somerset County Cricket Ground B2
Somerset County Hall C1
Somerset Cricket B2
South Rd C3
South St C3
Staplegrove Rd B1
Station Rd A1
Stephen St B2
Swimming Pool A1
Tancred St B2
Tauntfield Cl C3
Taunton Dean Cricket Club C2
Taunton Station A2
The Avenue A1
The Crescent C1
The Mount C2
Thomas St A1
Toneway A3
Tower St B1
Trevor Smith Pl C3
Trinity Business Ctr C3
Trinity Rd C3
Trinity St B3
Trull Rd C1
Tudor House B2
Upper High St C1
Venture Way A3
Victoria Gate B3
Victoria Park B3
Victoria St B3
Viney St B3
Vivary Park C2
Vivary Rd C1
War Memorial C1
Wellesley St A2
Wheatley Cres A3
Whitehall A1
Wilfred Rd B3
William St A1
Wilton Church C1
Wilton Cl C1
Wilton Gr C1
Wilton St C1
Winchester St B2
Winters Field B2
Wood St B1
Yarde Pl B1

Telford 193
Alma Ave C1
Amphitheatre C2
Bowling Alley B2
Brandsfarm Way C3
Brunel Rd B1
Bus Station B2
Buxton Rd C1
Central Park A2
Civic Offices B2
Coach Central B2
Coachwell Cl B1
Colliers Way A1
Courts B2
Dale Acre Way B3
Darliston C3
Deepdale B3
Deercote B2
Dinthill C3
Doddington C3
Dodmoor Grange C3
Downemead B3
Duffryn B3
Dunsheath B3
Euston Way A3
Eyton Mound C1
Eyton Rd C1
Forgegate A2
Grange Central B2
Hall Park Way B1
Hinkshay Rd C2
Hollinsworth Rd A2
Holyhead Rd A3
Housing Trust A1
Ice Rink B2
Information Ctr B2
Ironmasters Way A2
Job Ctr B1
Land Registry B1
Lawn Central B2
Lawnswood C1
Library B2
Malinsgate B1
Matlock Ave C1
Moor Rd C1
Mount Rd C1
NFU Offices B1
Odeon B2
Park Lane A1
Police Station B2
Priorslee Ave A3
Queen Elizabeth Ave C3
Queen Elizabeth Way B1
Queensway A2/B3
Rampart Way A2
Randlay Ave C3
Randlay Wood C3
Rhodes Ave C1
Royal Way B1
St Leonards Rd A1
St Quentin Gate B2
Shifnal Rd A3
Sixth Ave A1
Southwater Way B1
Spout Lane C1
Spout Mound B1
Spout Way C1
Stafford Court B3
Stafford Park B3
Stirchley Ave C3
Stone Row C1
Telford Bridge Ret Pk A1
Telford Central Station A3
Telford Ctr, The B2
Telford Forge Ret Pk A1
Telford Hornets RFC C2
Telford Int Ctr C2
Telford Way A3
Third Ave A2
Town Park C2
Town Park Visitor Ctr B2
Walker House B2
Wellswood Ave A2
West Ctr Way B1
Withywood Drive C1
Woodhouse Central B2
Yates Way A1

Winchester 193
Andover Rd A2
Andover Rd Retail Pk A2
Archery La C2
Arthur Rd A2
Bar End Rd C3
Beaufort Rd C2
Beggar's La B3
Bereweeke Ave A1
Bereweeke Rd A1
Boscobel Rd A2
Brassey Rd A2
Broadway B3
Brooks Sh Ctr, The B3
Bus Station B3
Butter Cross B2
Canon St C2
Castle Wall C2/C3
Castle, King Arthur's Round Table B2
Cathedral C2
Cheriton Rd A1
Chesil St C3
Chesil Theatre C3
Christchurch Rd C1
City Museum B2
City Offices C3
City Rd B2
Clifton Rd B1
Clifton Terr B2
Close Wall C2/C3
Coach Park A2
Colebrook St C3
College St C2
College Walk C3
Compton Rd C2
County Council Offices B2
Cranworth Rd A2
Cromwell Rd C1
Culver Rd C2
Domum Rd C3
Durngate Pl B3
Eastgate St B3
Edgar Rd C2
Egbert Rd A2
Elm Rd B1
Fairfield Rd A1
Fire Station B3
Fordington Ave B1
Fordington Rd A1
Friarsgate B3
Gordon Rd B3
Greenhill Rd B1
Guildhall B3
HM Prison B1
Hatherley Rd A1
High St B2
Hillier Way A3
Hyde Abbey (Remains) A2
Hyde Abbey Rd B2
Hyde Cl A2
Hyde St A2
Information Ctr B3
Jane Austen's Ho C2
Jewry St B2
John Stripe Theatre C1
King Alfred Pl A2
Kingsgate Arch C2
Kingsgate Park C2
Kingsgate Rd C2
Kingsgate St C2
Lankhills Rd A2
Library B2
Lower Brook St B3
Magdalen Hill B3
Market La B2
Mews La B1
Middle Brook St B3
Middle Rd B1
Military Museums B2
Milland Rd C3
Milverton Rd B1
Monks Rd A3
North Hill Cl A2
North Walls B2
North Walls Rec Gnd A3
Nuns Rd A3
Oram's Arbour B1
Owen's Rd A2
Parchment St B2
Park & Ride C3
Park Ave B3
Playing Field A1
Police HQ B1
Police Station B3
Portal Rd C3
Post Office B2/C1
Quarry Rd C3
Ranelagh Rd C1
Regiment Museum B2
River Park L Ctr B3
Romans' Rd C2
Romsey Rd B1
Royal Hampshire County Hospital (A&E) B1
St Cross Rd C2
St George's St B2
St Giles Hill C3
St James' La B1
St James' Terr B1
St James Villas C2
St John's B3
St John's St B3
St Michael's Rd C2
St Paul's Hill B1
St Peter St B2
St Swithun St C2
St Thomas St C2
Saxon Rd A2
School of Art B3
Screen B2
Sleepers Hill Rd C1
Southgate St B2
Sparkford Rd C1
Staple Gdns B2
Station Rd B2
Step Terr B1
Stockbridge Rd A1
Stuart Cres C1
Sussex St B2
Swan Lane B2
Tanner St B3
The Square B2
The Weirs C3
The Winchester Gallery B3
Theatre Royal B2
Tower St B2
Town Hall C3
Union St B3
University of Winchester (King Alfred Campus) C1
Upper Brook St B2
Wales St B3
Water Lane B3
West End Terr B1
West Gate B2
Western Rd B1
Wharf Hill C3
Winchester College C2
Winchester Sta A2
Wolvesey Castle C3
Worthy Lane A2
Worthy Rd A2

Windsor 193
Adelaide Sq C3
Albany Rd C2
Albert St B1
Alexandra Gdns B2
Alexandra Rd C2
Alma Rd B2
Ambulance Station B1
Arthur Rd B2
Bachelors Acre B3
Barry Ave B2
Beaumont Rd C2
Bexley St B1
Boat House B2
Brocas St B2
Brook St C3
Bulkeley Ave C1
Castle Hill B3
Charles St B2
Claremont Rd C2
Clarence Cr B2
Clarence Rd B1
Clewer Court Rd B1
Coach Park B2
College Cr C1
Courts C2
Cricket Ground C3
Dagmar Rd C2
Datchet Rd B3
Devereux Rd C2
Dorset Rd C2
Duke St B1
Elm Rd C1
Eton College A3
Eton Ct A2
Eton Sq A2
Eton Wick Rd A2
Fire Station C2
Farm Yard B3
Frances Rd C2
Frogmore Dr B3
Gloucester Pl C3
Goslar Way C1
Goswell Hill B2
Goswell Rd B2
Green La C1
Grove Rd C2
Guildhall B3
Helena Rd C2
Helston La B1
High St A2/B3
Holy Trinity C2
Hospital (Private) C2
Household Cavalry C2
Imperial Rd C1
Information Ctr B2/B3
Keats La A2
King Edward Ct B2
King Edward VII Ave A3
King Edward VII Hospital C2
King George V Meml B3
King's Rd C3
King Stable St A2
Library C2
Maidenhead Rd B1
Meadow La A2
Municipal Offices C3
Nell Gwynne's Ho B3
Osborne Rd C2
Oxford Rd B1
Park St B3
Peascod St B2
Police Station C2
Post Office A2
Princess Margaret Hospital C2
Queen Victoria's Wlk B3
Queen's Rd C2
River St B2
Romney Island A3
Romney Lock A3
Romney Lock Rd A3
Russell St C2
St John's B3
St John's Chapel A2
St Leonards Rd C2
St Mark's Rd C2
Sheet St C3
South Meadow A2
South Meadow La A2
Springfield Rd C1
Stovell Rd B1
Sunbury Rd A3
Tangier La A2
Tangier St A3
Temple Rd C2
Thames St B3
The Brocas A2
The Home Park A3/C3
The Long Walk C3
Theatre Royal B3
Trinity Pl C2
Vansittart Rd B1/C1
Vansittart Rd Gdns C1
Victoria Barracks C2
Victoria St C2
Ward Royal B2
Westmead C1
White Lilies Island A1
William St B2
Windsor Arts Ctr C2
Windsor Castle B3
Windsor & Eton Central B2
Windsor & Eton Riverside A3
Windsor Bridge B3
Windsor Great Park C3
Windsor Leisure Ctr B1
Windsor Relief Rd A1
Windsor Royal Sh B2
York Ave C1
York Rd C1

Wolverhampton 194
Albion St B3
Alexandra St C1
Arena B2
Arts Gallery B2
Ashland St C1
Austin St A1
Badger Dr A3
Bailey St B3
Bath Ave B1
Bath Rd B1
Bell St C2
Berry St B3
Bilston Rd C3
Bilston St C3
Birmingham Canal A3
Bone Mill La A2
Brewery Rd B1
Bright St A1
Burton Cres B3
Bus Station B3
Cambridge St A3
Camp St B2
Cannock Rd A3
Castle St C2
Chapel Ash C1
Cherry St C1
Chester St A1
Church La C2
Church St C2
Civic Ctr B2
Clarence Rd B2
Cleveland St C2
Clifton St C1
Coach Station B2
Compton Rd B1
Corn Hill B3
Coven St A3
Craddock St A1
Cross St North A2
Crown & County Courts C3
Crown St A2
Culwell St B3
Dale St C1
Darlington St C1
Dartmouth St C3
Devon Rd A1
Drummond St B2
Dudley Rd C2
Dudley St B2
Duke St C3
Dunkley St B2
Dunstall Ave A2
Dunstall Hill A2
Dunstall Rd A1/A2
Evans St A1
Fawdry St A1
Field St B3
Fire Station C1
Fiveways A2
Fowler Playing Fields A3
Fox's La A2
Francis St A2
Fryer St B3
Gloucester St A1
Gordon St C3
Graiseley St C1
Grand B3
Granville St C3
Great Brickkiln St C1
Great Hampton St A1
Great Western St A2
Grimstone St B3
Harrow St A1
Hilton St A3
Horseley Fields C3
Humber Rd C1
Jack Hayward Way A2
Jameson St A1
Jenner St C3
Kennedy Rd B3
Kimberley St C1
King St B2
Laburnum St C1
Lansdowne Rd B1
Leicester St A1
Lever St C3
Library C3
Lichfield St B2
Light House B3
Little's La B3
Lock St B3
Lord St C1
Lowe St A1
Lower Stafford St A2
Magistrates Court B2
Mander Ctr C2
Mander St C1
Market St B2
Market C3
Melbourne St C3
Merridale St C1
Middlecross C3
Molineux St B2
Mostyn St A1
New Hampton Rd East A1
Nine Elms La A3
North Rd A2
Oaks Cres C1
Oxley St A2
Paget St A1
Park Ave B1
Park Road East A1
Park Road West B1
Paul St C2
Pelham St C1
Penn Rd C2
Piper's Row B3
Pitt St C2
Police Station C3
Pool St C2
Poole St A3
Post Office A1/A2/B2/B2
Powlett St C3
Queen St B2
Raby St C3
Raglan St C1
Railway Dr B3
Red Hill St A2
Red Lion St B2
Retreat St C1
Ring Rd B2
Rugby St A1
Russell St C1
St Andrew's B1
St David's B3
St George's C3
St George's Pde C2
St James St C3
St John's C2
St John's A2
St John's Retail Park C2
St John's Square C2
St Mark's C1
St Marks Rd C1
St Marks St C1
St Patrick's B2
St Peter's B2
St Peter's B2
Salisbury St C1
Salop St C2
School St C2
Sherwood St A2
Smestow St A3
Snowhill C2
Springfield Rd A3
Stafford St B2
Staveley Rd A1
Steelhouse La C3
Stephenson St C1
Stewart St C2
Sun St B3
Sutherland Pl C3
Tempest St C2
Temple St C2
Tettenhall Rd B1
The Maltings B2
The Royal (Metro) C3
Thomas St C2
Thornley St B2
Tower St C2
University B2
Upper Zoar St C1
Vicarage Rd C3
Victoria St C2
Walpole St A1
Walsall St C3
Ward St C3
Warwick St C3
Water St A3
Waterloo Rd B2
Wednesfield Rd B3
West Pk (not A&E) B1
West Park Swimming Pool B1
Wharf St C3
Whitmore Hill B2
Wolverhampton B3
Wolverhampton St George's (Metro) C2
Wolverhampton Wanderers Football Ground (Molineux) B2
Worcester St C2
Wulfrun Ctr C2
Yarwell Cl A3
York St C3
Zoar St C1

Worcester 194
Albany Terr A1
Alice Otley School A2
Angel Pl B2
Angel St B2
Ashcroft Rd A2
Athelstan Rd C3
Back Lane North A1
Back Lane South A1
Barbourne Rd A2
Bath Rd C2
Battenhall Rd C3
Bridge St B2
Britannia Sq A1
Broad St B2
Bromwich La C1
Bromwich Rd C1
Bromyard Rd C1
Bus Station B2
Carden St B3
Castle St A2
Cathedral C2
Cathedral Plaza B2
Charles St B3
Chequers La B1
Chestnut St A2
Chestnut Walk A2
Citizens' Advice Bureau B2
City Walls Rd B2
Cole Hill C3
Coll of Technology B2
College St C2
Commandery C3
County Cricket Gd C1
Cripplegate Park B1
Croft Rd B1
Cromwell St B3
Crowngate Ctr B2
Deansway B2
Diglis Pde C2
Diglis Rd C2
Edgar Tower C2
Farrier St A2
Fire Station B2
Foregate St B2
Foregate Street B2
Fort Royal Hill C3
Fort Royal Park C3
Foundry St B3
Friar St C2
George St B3
Grand Stand Rd B1
Greenhill C3
Greyfriars B2
Guildhall B2
Henwick Rd B1
High St B2
Hill St B3
Huntingdon Hall B2
Hylton Rd B1
Information Ctr B2
King Charles Place Shopping Ctr C1
King's School C2
King's School Playing Field C2
Kleve Walk C2
Lansdowne Cr A3
Lansdowne Rd A3
Lansdowne Walk A3
Laslett St A3
Leisure Ctr A3
Library, Museum & Art Gallery A2
Little Chestnut St A2
Little London A2
London Rd C3
Lowell St A3
Lowesmoor B2
Lowesmoor Terr A3
Lowesmoor Wharf A3
Magistrates Court A2
Midland Rd B3
Mill St C2
Moors Severn Terr A1
New Rd C1
New St B2
Northfield St A2
Odeon B2
Padmore St B3
Park St C3
Pheasant St B3
Pitchcroft Racecourse A1
Police Station A2
Portland St C2
Post Office B2
Quay St B2
Queen St B2
Rainbow Hill A3
Recreation Ground A2
Reindeer Court B2
Rogers Hill A3
Sabrina Rd A1
St Dunstan's Cr C3
St John's C1
St Martin's Gate B3
St Oswald's Rd A2
St Paul's St B3
St Swithin's Church B2
St Wulstans Cr C3
Sansome Walk A2
Severn St C2
Shaw St B2
Shire Hall A2
Shrub Hill B3
Shrub Hill Retail Park B3
Shrub Hill Rd B3
Slingpool Walk C1
South Quay B2
Southfield St A2
Sports Ground A2/C1
Stanley Rd B3
Swan, The A1
Swimming Pool A2
Tallow Hill B3
Tennis Walk A2
The Avenue C1
The Butts B2
The Cross B2
The Shambles B2
The Tything A2
Tolladine Rd B3
Tudor House B2
Tybridge St B1
Univ of Worcester B2
Vincent Rd B3
Vue C2
Washington St A3
Woolhope Rd C3
Worcester Bridge B2
Worcester Library & History Ctr B3
Worcester Porcelain Museum C2
Worcester Royal Grammar School A2
Wylds La C3

Wrexham *Wrecsam* 194
Abbot St B2
Acton Rd A3
Albert St C3
Alexandra Rd C1
Aran Rd A3
Barnfield C3
Bath Rd C2
Beechley Rd C3
Belgrave Rd C2
Belle Vue Park C2
Belle Vue Rd C2
Belvedere Dr A1
Bennion's Rd C3
Berse Rd A1
Bersham Rd C1
Birch St C3
Bodhyfryd B3
Border Retail Park B3
Bradley Rd C2
Bright St B1
Bron-y-Nant B1
Brook St C2
Bryn-y-Cabanau Rd C3
Bury St C3
Bus Station B2
Butchers Market B3
Caia Rd C3
Cambrian Ind Est C3
Caxton Pl B2
Cemetery C1
Centenary Rd C1
Chapel St C2
Charles St B3
Chester Rd A3
Chester St B3
Cilcen Gr A3
Citizens Advice Bureau B2
Cobden Rd B1
Council Offices B3
County B2
Crescent Rd B3
Crispin La A2
Croesnewyth Rd B1
Cross St A2
Cunliffe St A2
Derby Rd C3
Dolydd Rd B1
Duke St B2
Eagles Meadow C3
Earle St C2
East Ave A2
Edward St C2
Egerton St B2
Empress Rd C1
Erddig Rd C2
Fairy Rd C2
Fire Station B2
Foster Rd A3
Foxwood Dr C1
Garden Rd A2
General Market B3
Gerald St B2
Gibson St C1
Glyndŵr University Plas Coch Campus A1
Greenbank St C3
Greenfield A2
Grosvenor Rd B2
Grove Park B2
Grove Park Rd B3
Grove Rd A3
Guildhall B2
Haig Rd C3
Hampden Rd C2
Hazel Gr A3
Henblas St B3
High St B3
Hightown Rd C3
Hill St B2
Holt Rd B3
Holt St B3
Hope St B2
Huntroyde Ave C3
Information Ctr B3
Island Gn Sh Ctr B2
Job Ctr B2
Jubilee Rd B2
King St B2
Kingsmills Rd C3
Lambpit St B3
Law Courts B3
Lawson Cl A3
Lawson Rd A3
Lea Rd C2
Library & Arts Ctr B2
Lilac Way B1
Llys David Lord B1
Lorne St A2
Maesgwyn Rd B1
Maesydre Rd A3
Manley Rd B3
Market St B3
Mawddy Ave A2
Mayville Ave A2
Memorial Gallery B2
Memorial Hall B3
Mold Rd A1
Mount St C3
Neville Cres A3
New Rd A2
North Wales Regional Tennis Ctr A1
North Wales School of Art & Design B2
Oak Dr A3
Park Ave A3
Park St A2
Peel St C1
Pentre Felin C2
Pen y Bryn C2
Penymaes Ave A3
Peoples Market B3
Percy St C2
Plas Coch Retail Park A1
Plas Coch Rd A1
Police Station B3
Poplar Rd C2
Post Office A2/B2/C2/C3
Powell Rd B3
Poyser St C2
Price's La A2
Primose Way B1
Princess St C1
Queen St B3
Queens Sq B2
Regent St B2
Rhosddu Rd A2/B2
Rhosnesni La A3
Rivulet Rd C3
Ruabon Rd C2
Ruthin Rd C1/C2
St Giles C3
St Giles Way C3
St James Ct A2
St Mary's B2
Salisbury Rd C3
Salop Rd C3
Sontley Rd C2
Spring Rd A2
Stanley St C3
Stansty Rd A2
Station Approach B2
Studio B2
Talbot Rd C2
Techniquest Glyndŵr A2
The Beeches A3
The Pines A3
Town Hill C2
Trevor St C2
Trinity St B2
Tuttle St C3
Vale Park A1
Vernon St B2
Vicarage Hill B2
Victoria Rd C2
Walnut St A2
War Memorial B3
Waterworld L Ctr B3
Watery Rd B1/B2
Wellington Rd C2
Westminster Dr A3
William Aston Hall A1
Windsor Rd A1
Wrexham AFC A1
Wrexham Central B2
Wrexham General B2
Wrexham Maelor Hospital (A+E) B1
Wrexham Technology Park B1
Wynn Ave A2
Yale College B3
Yale Gr A3
Yorke St C3

York 194
Aldwark B2
Ambulance Station B3
Barbican Rd C3
Barley Hall B2
Bishopgate St C2
Bishopthorpe Rd C2
Blossom St C1
Bootham A1
Bootham Cr A1
Bootham Terr A1
Bridge St B2
Brook St A2
Brownlow St A2
Burton Stone La A1
Castle Museum C2
Castlegate B2
Cemetery Rd C3
Cherry St C2
City Screen B2
City Wall A2/B1/C3
Clarence St A2
Clementhorpe C2
Clifford St B2
Clifford's Tower B2
Clifton A1
Coach park A2
Coney St B2
Cromwell Rd C2
Crown Court C2
Davygate B2
Deanery Gdns A2
DIG B2
Ebor Industrial Estate B3
Fairfax House B2
Fishergate C3
Foss Islands Retail Pk B3
Foss Islands Rd B3
Fossbank A3
Garden St A2
George St C3
Gillygate A2
Goodramgate B2
Grand Opera Ho B2
Grosvenor Terr A1
Guildhall B2
Hallfield Rd A3
Heslington Rd C3
Heworth Green A3
Holy Trinity B2
Hope St C3
Huntington Rd A3
Information Ctr B2
James St B3
Jorvik Viking Ctr B2
Kent St C3
Lawrence St C3
Layerthorpe A3
Leeman Rd B1
Lendal B2
Lendal Bridge B1
Library B1
Longfield Terr A1
Lord Mayor's Walk A2
Lower Eldon St A2
Lowther St A2
Mansion House B2
Margaret St C3
Marygate A1
Melbourne St C3
Merchant Adventurer's Hall B2
Merchant Taylors' Hall B2
Micklegate B1
Micklegate Bar C1
Minster, The A2
Monkgate A2
Moss St C1
Museum Gdns B1
Museum St B1
National Railway Museum B1
Navigation Rd B3
Newton Terr C2
North Pde A1
North St B2
Nunnery La C1
Nunthorpe Rd C1
Ouse Bridge B2
Paragon St C3
Park Gr A3
Park St C1
Parliament St B2
Peasholme Green B3
Penley's Grove St A2
Piccadilly B2
Police Station B2
Post Office B1/B2/C3
Priory St B1
Purey Cust Nuffield Hospital, The A2
Quilt Museum B3
Reel C1
Regimental Mus B2
Richard III Mus A2
Roman Bath B2
Rowntree Park C2
St Andrewgate B2
St Benedict Rd C1
St John St A2
St Olave's Rd A1
St Peter's Gr A1
St Saviourgate B2
Scarcroft Hill C1
Scarcroft Rd C1
Skeldergate C2
Skeldergate Bridge C2
Station Rd B1
Stonegate B2
Sycamore Terr A1
Terry Ave C2
The Shambles B2
The Stonebow B2
Theatre Royal B2
Thorpe St C1
Toft Green B1
Tower St C2
Townend St A2
Treasurer's House A2
Trinity La B1
Undercroft Mus A2
Union Terr A2
Victor St C2
Vine St C2
Walmgate B3
Wellington St C3
York Art Gallery A1
York Barbican C3
York Brewery B1
York Dungeon, The B2
York Station B1

Index to road maps of Britain

Abbreviations used in the index

Abbreviation	Full name
Aberdeen	Aberdeen City
Aberds	Aberdeenshire
Ald	Alderney
Anglesey	Isle of Anglesey
Angus	Angus
Argyll	Argyll and Bute
Bath	Bath and North East Somerset
Bedford	Bedford
Bl Gwent	Blaenau Gwent
Blackburn	Blackburn with Darwen
Blackpool	Blackpool
Bmouth	Bournemouth
Borders	Scottish Borders
Brack	Bracknell
Bridgend	Bridgend
Brighton	City of Brighton and Hove
Bristol	City and County of Bristol
Bucks	Buckinghamshire
C Beds	Central Bedfordshire
Caerph	Caerphilly
Cambs	Cambridgeshire
Cardiff	Cardiff
Carms	Carmarthenshire
Ceredig	Ceredigion
Ches E	Cheshire East
Ches W	Cheshire West and Chester
Clack	Clackmannanshire
Conwy	Conwy
Corn	Cornwall
Cumb	Cumbria
Darl	Darlington
Denb	Denbighshire
Derby	City of Derby
Derbys	Derbyshire
Devon	Devon
Dorset	Dorset
Dumfries	Dumfries and Galloway
Dundee	Dundee City
Durham	Durham
E Ayrs	East Ayrshire
E Dunb	East Dunbartonshire
E Loth	East Lothian
E Renf	East Renfrewshire
E Sus	East Sussex
E Yorks	East Riding of Yorkshire
Edin	City of Edinburgh
Essex	Essex
Falk	Falkirk
Fife	Fife
Flint	Flintshire
Glasgow	City of Glasgow
Glos	Gloucestershire
Gtr Man	Greater Manchester
Guern	Guernsey
Gwyn	Gwynedd
Halton	Halton
Hants	Hampshire
Hereford	Herefordshire
Herts	Hertfordshire
Highld	Highland
Hrtlpl	Hartlepool
Hull	Hull
IoM	Isle of Man
IoW	Isle of Wight
Invclyd	Inverclyde
Jersey	Jersey
Kent	Kent
Lancs	Lancashire
Leicester	City of Leicester
Leics	Leicestershire
Lincs	Lincolnshire
London	Greater London
Luton	Luton
M Keynes	Milton Keynes
M Tydf	Merthyr Tydfil
Mbro	Middlesbrough
Medway	Medway
Mers	Merseyside
Midloth	Midlothian
Mon	Monmouthshire
Moray	Moray
N Ayrs	North Ayrshire
N Lincs	North Lincolnshire
N Lanark	North Lanarkshire
N Som	North Somerset
N Yorks	North Yorkshire
NE Lincs	North East Lincolnshire
Neath	Neath Port Talbot
Newport	City and County of Newport
Norf	Norfolk
Northants	Northamptonshire
Northumb	Northumberland
Nottingham	City of Nottingham
Notts	Nottinghamshire
Orkney	Orkney
Oxon	Oxfordshire
Pboro	Peterborough
Pembs	Pembrokeshire
Perth	Perth and Kinross
Plym	Plymouth
Poole	Poole
Powys	Powys
Ptsmth	Portsmouth
Reading	Reading
Redcar	Redcar and Cleveland
Renfs	Renfrewshire
Rhondda	Rhondda Cynon Taff
Rutland	Rutland
S Ayrs	South Ayrshire
S Glos	South Gloucestershire
S Lanark	South Lanarkshire
S Yorks	South Yorkshire
Scilly	Scilly
Shetland	Shetland
Shrops	Shropshire
Slough	Slough
Som	Somerset
Soton	Southampton
Staffs	Staffordshire
Southend	Southend-on-Sea
Stirling	Stirling
Stockton	Stockton-on-Tees
Stoke	Stoke-on-Trent
Suff	Suffolk
Sur	Surrey
Swansea	Swansea
Swindon	Swindon
T&W	Tyne and Wear
Telford	Telford and Wrekin
Thurrock	Thurrock
Torbay	Torbay
Torf	Torfaen
V Glam	The Vale of Glamorgan
W Berks	West Berkshire
W Dunb	West Dunbartonshire
W Isles	Western Isles
W Loth	West Lothian
W Mid	West Midlands
W Sus	West Sussex
W Yorks	West Yorkshire
Warks	Warwickshire
Warr	Warrington
Wilts	Wiltshire
Windsor	Windsor and Maidenhead
Wokingham	Wokingham
Worcs	Worcestershire
Wrex	Wrexham
York	City of York

How to use the index

Example

Trudoxhill Som **24** E2

- grid square
- page number
- county or unitary authority

A

Ab Kettleby Leics 64 B4
Ab Lench Worcs 50 D5
Abbas Combe Som 12 B5
Abberley Worcs 50 C2
Abberton Essex 43 C6
Abberton Worcs 50 D4
Abberwick Northumb 117 C7
Abbess Roding Essex 42 C1
Abbey Devon 11 C6
Abbey-cwm-hir Powys 48 B2
Abbey Dore Hereford 49 F5
Abbey Field Essex 43 B5
Abbey Hulton Stoke 75 E6
Abbey St Bathans Borders 122 C3
Abbey Town Cumb 107 D8
Abbey Village Lancs 86 B4
Abbey Wood London 29 B5
Abbeydale S Yorks 88 F4
Abbeystead Lancs 93 D5
Abbots Bickington Devon 9 C5
Abbots Bromley Staffs 62 B4
Abbots Langley Herts 40 D3
Abbots Leigh N Som 23 B7
Abbots Morton Worcs 50 D5
Abbots Ripton Cambs 54 B3
Abbots Salford Warks 51 D5
Abbotsbury Dorset 12 F3
Abbotsham Devon 9 B6
Abbotskerswell Devon 7 C6
Abbotsley Cambs 54 D3
Abbotswood Hants 14 B4
Abbotts Ann Hants 25 E8
Abcott Shrops 49 B5
Abdon Shrops 61 F5
Aber Ceredig 46 E3
Aber-Arad Carms 46 F2
Aber-banc Ceredig 46 E2
Aber Cowarch Gwyn 59 C5
Aber-Giâr Carms 46 E4
Aber-gwynfi Neath 34 E2
Aber-Hirnant Gwyn 72 F3
Aber-nant Rhondda 34 D4
Aber-Rhiwlech Gwyn 59 B6
Aber-Village Powys 35 B5
Aberaeron Ceredig 46 C3
Aberaman Rhondda 34 D4
Aberangell Gwyn 58 C5
Aberarder Highld 137 F7
Aberarder House Highld 138 B2
Aberarder Lodge Highld 137 F8
Aberargie Perth 128 C3
Aberarth Ceredig 46 C3
Aberavon Neath 33 E8
Aberbeeg Bl Gwent 35 D6
Abercanaid M Tydf 34 D4
Abercarn Caerph 35 E6
Abercastle Pembs 44 B3
Abercegir Powys 58 D5
Aberchirder Aberds 152 C6
Abercraf Powys 34 C2
Abercrombie Fife 129 D7
Abercych Pembs 45 E4
Abercynafon Powys 34 C4
Abercynon Rhondda 34 E4
Aberdalgie Perth 128 B2
Aberdâr = Aberdare Rhondda 34 D3
Aberdare = Aberdâr Rhondda 34 D3
Aberdaron Gwyn 70 E2
Aberdaugleddau = Milford Haven Pembs 44 E4
Aberdeen Aberdeen 141 D8
Aberdesach Gwyn 82 F4
Aberdour Fife 128 F3
Aberdovey Gwyn 58 E3
Aberdulais Neath 34 D1
Aberedw Powys 48 E2
Abereiddy Pembs 44 B2
Abererch Gwyn 70 D4
Aberfan M Tydf 34 D4
Aberfeldy Perth 133 E5
Aberffraw Anglesey 82 E3
Aberffrwd Ceredig 47 B5
Aberford W Yorks 95 F7
Aberfoyle Stirling 126 D4
Abergavenny = Y Fenni Mon 35 C6
Abergele Conwy 72 B3
Abergorlech Carms 46 F4
Abergwaun = Fishguard Pembs 44 B4
Abergwesyn Powys 47 D7
Abergwili Carms 33 B5
Abergwynant Gwyn 58 C3
Abergwyngregyn Gwyn 83 D6
Abergynolwyn Gwyn 58 D3
Aberhonddu = Brecon Powys 34 B4
Aberhosan Powys 58 E5
Aberkenfig Bridgend 34 F2
Aberlady E Loth 129 F6
Aberlemno Angus 135 D5
Aberllefenni Gwyn 58 D4
Abermagwr Ceredig 47 B5
Abermaw = Barmouth Gwyn 58 C3
Abermeurig Ceredig 46 D4
Abermule Powys 59 E8
Abernaint Powys 59 B8
Abernant Carms 32 B4
Abernethy Perth 128 C3
Abernyte Perth 134 F2
Aberpennar = Mountain Ash Rhondda 34 E4
Aberporth Ceredig 45 D4
Abersoch Gwyn 70 E4
Abersychan Torf 35 D6
Abertawe = Swansea Swansea 33 E7
Aberteifi = Cardigan Ceredig 45 E3
Aberthin V Glam 22 B2
Abertillery = Abertyleri Bl Gwent 35 D6
Abertridwr Caerph 35 F5
Abertridwr Powys 59 C7
Abertyleri = Abertillery Bl Gwent 35 D6
Abertysswg Caerph 35 D5
Aberuthven Perth 127 C8
Aberyscir Powys 34 B3
Aberystwyth Ceredig 58 F2
Abhainn Suidhe W Isles 154 G5
Abingdon Oxon 38 E4
Abinger Common Sur 28 E2
Abinger Hammer Sur 27 E8
Abington S Lanark 114 B2
Abington Pigotts Cambs 54 E4
Ablington Glos 37 D8
Ablington Wilts 25 E6
Abney Derbys 75 B8
Aboyne Aberds 140 E4
Abram Gtr Man 86 D4
Abriachan Highld 151 H8
Abridge Essex 41 E7
Abronhill N Lanark 119 B7
Abson S Glos 24 B2
Abthorpe Northants 52 E4
Abune-the-Hill Orkney 159 F3
Aby Lincs 79 B7
Acaster Malbis York 95 E8
Acaster Selby N Yorks 95 E8
Accrington Lancs 87 B5
Acha Argyll 146 F4
Acha Mor W Isles 155 E8
Achabraid Argyll 145 E7
Achachork Highld 149 D9
Achafolla Argyll 124 D3
Achagary Highld 157 D10
Achahoish Argyll 144 F6
Achalader Perth 133 E8
Achallader Argyll 131 E7
Ach'an Todhair Highld 130 B4
Achanalt Highld 150 E5
Achanamara Argyll 144 E6
Achandunie Highld 151 D9
Achany Highld 157 J8
Achaphubuil Highld 130 B4
Acharacle Highld 147 E9
Acharn Highld 147 F10
Acharn Perth 132 E4
Acharole Highld 158 E4
Achath Aberds 141 C6
Achavanich Highld 158 F3
Achavraat Highld 151 G12
Achddu Carms 33 D5
Achduart Highld 156 J3
Achentoul Highld 157 F11
Achfary Highld 156 F5
Achgarve Highld 155 H13
Achiemore Highld 156 C6
Achiemore Highld 157 D11
A'Chill Highld 148 H7
Achiltibuie Highld 156 J3
Achina Highld 157 C10
Achinduich Highld 157 J8
Achinduin Argyll 124 B4
Achingills Highld 158 D3
Achintee Highld 131 B5
Achintee Highld 150 G2
Achintraid Highld 149 E13
Achlean Highld 138 E4
Achleck Argyll 146 G7
Achluachrach Highld 137 F5
Achlyness Highld 156 D5
Achmelvich Highld 156 G3
Achmore Highld 149 E13
Achmore Stirling 132 F2
Achnaba Argyll 124 B5
Achnaba Argyll 145 E8
Achnabat Highld 151 H8
Achnacarnin Highld 156 F3
Achnacarry Highld 136 F4
Achnacloich Argyll 125 B5
Achnacloich Highld 149 H10
Achnaconeran Highld 137 C7
Achnacraig Argyll 146 G7
Achnacroish Argyll 130 E2
Achnadrish Argyll 146 F7
Achnafalnich Argyll 125 C8
Achnagarron Highld 151 E9
Achnaha Highld 146 E7
Achnahanat Highld 151 B8
Achnahannet Highld 139 B5
Achnairn Highld 157 H8
Achnaluachrach Highld 157 J9
Achnasaul Highld 136 F4
Achnasheen Highld 150 F4
Achosnich Highld 146 E7
Achranich Highld 147 G10
Achreamie Highld 157 C13
Achriabhach Highld 131 C5
Achriesgill Highld 156 D5
Achrimsdale Highld 157 J12
Achtoty Highld 157 C9
Achurch Northants 65 F7
Achuvoldrach Highld 157 D8
Achvaich Highld 151 B10
Achvarasdal Highld 157 C12
Ackergill Highld 158 E5
Acklam Mbro 102 C2
Acklam N Yorks 96 C3
Ackleton Shrops 61 E7
Acklington Northumb 117 D8
Ackton W Yorks 88 B5
Ackworth Moor Top W Yorks 88 C5
Acle Norf 69 C7
Acock's Green W Mid 62 F5
Acol Kent 31 C7
Acomb Northumb 110 C2
Acomb York 95 D8
Aconbury Hereford 49 F7
Acre Lancs 87 B5
Acre Street W Sus 15 E8
Acrefair Wrex 73 E6
Acton Ches E 74 D3
Acton Dorset 13 G7
Acton London 41 F5
Acton Shrops 60 F3
Acton Suff 56 E2
Acton Wrex 73 D7
Acton Beauchamp Hereford 49 D8
Acton Bridge Ches W 74 B2
Acton Burnell Shrops 60 D5
Acton Green Hereford 49 D8
Acton Pigott Shrops 60 D5
Acton Round Shrops 61 E6
Acton Scott Shrops 60 F4
Acton Trussell Staffs 62 C3
Acton Turville S Glos 37 F5
Adbaston Staffs 61 B7
Adber Dorset 12 B3
Adderley Shrops 74 E3
Adderstone Northumb 123 F7
Addiewell W Loth 120 C2
Addingham W Yorks 94 E3
Addington Bucks 39 B7
Addington Kent 29 D7
Addington London 28 C4
Addinston Borders 121 D8
Addiscombe London 28 C4
Addlestone Sur 27 C8
Addlethorpe Lincs 79 C8
Adel W Yorks 95 F5
Adeney Telford 61 C7
Adfa Powys 59 D7
Adforton Hereford 49 B6
Adisham Kent 31 D6
Adlestrop Glos 38 B2
Adlingfleet E Yorks 90 B2
Adlington Lancs 86 C4
Admaston Staffs 62 B4
Admaston Telford 61 C6
Admington Warks 51 E7
Adstock Bucks 52 F5
Adstone Northants 52 D3
Adversane W Sus 16 B4
Advie Highld 152 E1
Adwalton W Yorks 88 B3
Adwell Oxon 39 E6
Adwick le Street S Yorks 89 D6
Adwick upon Dearne S Yorks 89 D5
Adziel Aberds 153 C9
Ae Village Dumfries 114 F2
Affleck Aberds 141 B7
Affpuddle Dorset 13 E6
Affric Lodge Highld 136 B4
Afon-wen Flint 72 B5
Afton IoW 14 F4
Agglethorpe N Yorks 101 F5
Agneash IoM 84 D4
Aigburth Mers 85 F4
Aiginis W Isles 155 D9
Aike E Yorks 97 E6
Aikerness Orkney 159 C5
Aikers Orkney 159 J5
Aiketgate Cumb 108 E4
Aikton Cumb 108 D2
Ailey Hereford 48 E5
Ailstone Warks 51 D7
Ailsworth Pboro 65 E8
Ainderby Quernhow N Yorks 102 F1
Ainderby Steeple N Yorks 101 E8
Aingers Green Essex 43 B7
Ainsdale Mers 85 C4
Ainsdale-on-Sea Mers 85 C4
Ainstable Cumb 108 E5
Ainsworth Gtr Man 87 C5
Ainthorpe N Yorks 103 D5
Aintree Mers 85 E4
Aird Argyll 124 E3
Aird Dumfries 104 C4
Aird Highld 149 A12
Aird W Isles 155 D10
Aird a Mhachair W Isles 148 D2
Aird a' Mhulaidh W Isles 154 F6
Aird Asaig W Isles 154 G6
Aird Dhail W Isles 155 A9
Aird Mhidhinis W Isles 148 H2
Aird Mhighe W Isles 154 H6
Aird Mhighe W Isles 154 J5
Aird Mhor W Isles 148 H2
Aird of Sleat Highld 149 H10
Aird Thunga W Isles 155 D9
Aird Uig W Isles 154 D5
Airdens Highld 151 B9
Airdrie N Lanark 119 C7
Airdtorrisdale Highld 157 C9
Airidh a Bhruaich W Isles 154 F7
Airieland Dumfries 106 D4
Airmyn E Yorks 89 B8
Airntully Perth 133 F7
Airor Highld 149 H12
Airth Falk 127 F7
Airton N Yorks 94 D2
Airyhassen Dumfries 105 E7
Aisby Lincs 78 F3
Aisby Lincs 90 E2
Aisgernis W Isles 148 F2
Aiskew N Yorks 101 F7
Aislaby N Yorks 103 D6
Aislaby N Yorks 103 F5
Aislaby Stockton 102 C2
Aisthorpe Lincs 78 A2
Aith Orkney 159 G3
Aith Shetland 160 D8
Aith Shetland 160 H5
Aithsetter Shetland 160 K6
Aitkenhead S Ayrs 112 D3
Aitnoch Highld 151 H12
Akeld Northumb 117 B5
Akeley Bucks 52 F5
Akenham Suff 56 E5
Albaston Corn 6 B2
Alberbury Shrops 60 C3
Albourne W Sus 17 C6
Albrighton Shrops 60 C4
Albrighton Shrops 62 D2
Alburgh Norf 69 F5
Albury Herts 41 B7
Albury Sur 27 E8
Albury End Herts 41 B7
Alby Hill Norf 81 D7
Alcaig Highld 151 F8
Alcaston Shrops 60 F4
Alcester Warks 51 D5
Alciston E Sus 18 E2
Alcombe Som 21 E8
Alcombe Wilts 24 C3
Alconbury Cambs 54 B2
Alconbury Weston Cambs 54 B2
Aldbar Castle Angus 135 D5
Aldborough N Yorks 95 C7
Aldborough Norf 81 D7
Aldbourne Wilts 25 B7
Aldbrough E Yorks 97 F8
Aldbrough St John N Yorks 101 C7
Aldbury Herts 40 C2
Aldcliffe Lancs 92 C4
Aldclune Perth 133 C6
Aldeburgh Suff 57 D8
Aldeby Norf 69 E7
Aldenham Herts 40 E4
Alderbury Wilts 14 B2
Aldercar Derbys 76 E4
Alderford Norf 68 C4
Alderholt Dorset 14 C2
Alderley Glos 36 E4
Alderley Edge Ches E 74 B5
Aldermaston W Berks 26 C3
Aldermaston Wharf W Berks 26 C4
Alderminster Warks 51 E7
Alder's End Hereford 49 E8
Aldersey Green Ches W 73 D8
Aldershot Hants 27 D6
Alderton Glos 50 F5
Alderton Northants 52 E5
Alderton Shrops 60 B4
Alderton Suff 57 E7
Alderton Wilts 37 F5
Alderwasley Derbys 76 D3
Aldfield N Yorks 95 C5
Aldford Ches W 73 D8
Aldham Essex 43 B5
Aldham Suff 56 E4
Aldie Highld 151 C10
Aldingbourne W Sus 16 D3
Aldingham Cumb 92 B2
Aldington Kent 19 B7
Aldington Worcs 51 E5
Aldington Frith Kent 19 B7
Aldochlay Argyll 126 E2
Aldreth Cambs 54 B5
Aldridge W Mid 62 D4
Aldringham Suff 57 C8
Aldsworth Glos 38 C1
Aldunie Moray 140 B2
Aldwark Derbys 76 D2
Aldwark N Yorks 95 C7
Aldwick W Sus 16 E3
Aldwincle Northants 65 F7
Aldworth W Berks 26 B3
Alexandria W Dunb 118 B3
Alfardisworthy Devon 8 C4
Alfington Devon 11 E6
Alfold Sur 27 F8
Alfold Bars W Sus 27 F8
Alfold Crossways Sur 27 F8
Alford Aberds 140 C4
Alford Lincs 79 B7
Alford Som 23 F8
Alfreton Derbys 76 D4
Alfrick Worcs 50 D2
Alfrick Pound Worcs 50 D2
Alfriston E Sus 18 E2
Algaltraig Argyll 145 F9
Algarkirk Lincs 79 F5
Alhampton Som 23 F8
Aline Lodge W Isles 154 F6
Alisary Highld 147 D10
Alkborough N Lincs 90 B2
Alkerton Oxon 51 E8
Alkham Kent 31 E6
Alkington Shrops 74 F2
Alkmonton Derbys 75 F8
All Cannings Wilts 25 C5
All Saints South Elmham Suff 69 F6
All Stretton Shrops 60 E4
Alladale Lodge Highld 150 C7
Allaleigh Devon 7 D6
Allanaquoich Aberds 139 E7
Allangrange Mains Highld 151 F9
Allanton Borders 122 D4
Allanton N Lanark 119 D8
Allathasdal W Isles 148 H1
Allendale Town Northumb 109 D8
Allenheads Northumb 109 E8
Allens Green Herts 41 C7
Allensford Durham 110 D3
Allensmore Hereford 49 F6
Allenton Derby 76 F3
Aller Som 12 B2
Allerby Cumb 107 F7
Allerford Som 21 E8
Allerston N Yorks 103 F6
Allerthorpe E Yorks 96 E3
Allerton Mers 86 F2
Allerton W Yorks 94 F4
Allerton Bywater W Yorks 88 B5
Allerton Mauleverer N Yorks 95 D7
Allesley W Mid 63 F7
Allestree Derby 76 F3
Allet Corn 3 B6
Allexton Leics 64 D5
Allgreave Ches E 75 C6
Allhallows Medway 30 B2
Allhallows-on-Sea Medway 30 B2
Alligin Shuas Highld 149 C13
Allimore Green Staffs 62 C2
Allington Lincs 77 E8
Allington Wilts 25 C5
Allington Wilts 25 F7
Allithwaite Cumb 92 B3
Alloa Clack 127 E7
Allonby Cumb 107 E7
Alloway S Ayrs 112 C3
Allt Carms 33 D6
Allt na h-Airbhe Highld 150 B4
Allt-nan-sùgh Highld 136 B2
Alltchaorunn Highld 131 D5
Alltforgan Powys 59 B6
Alltmawr Powys 48 E2
Alltnacaillich Highld 156 E7
Alltsigh Highld 137 C7
Alltwalis Carms 46 F3
Alltwen Neath 33 D8
Alltyblaca Ceredig 46 E4
Allwood Green Suff 56 B4
Almeley Hereford 48 D5
Almer Dorset 13 E7
Almholme S Yorks 89 D6
Almington Staffs 74 F4
Alminstone Cross Devon 8 B5
Almondbank Perth 128 B2
Almondbury W Yorks 88 C2
Almondsbury S Glos 36 F3
Alne N Yorks 95 C7
Alness Highld 151 E9
Alnham Northumb 117 C5
Alnmouth Northumb 117 C8
Alnwick Northumb 117 C7
Alperton London 40 F4
Alphamstone Essex 56 F2
Alpheton Suff 56 D2
Alphington Devon 10 E4
Alport Derbys 76 C2
Alpraham Ches E 74 D2
Alresford Essex 43 B6
Alrewas Staffs 63 C5
Alsager Ches E 74 D4
Alsagers Bank Staffs 74 E5
Alsop en le Dale Derbys 75 D8
Alston Cumb 109 E7
Alston Devon 11 D8
Alstone Glos 50 F4
Alstonefield Staffs 75 D8
Alswear Devon 10 B2
Altandhu Highld 156 H2
Altanduin Highld 157 G11
Altarnun Corn 8 F4
Altass Highld 156 J7
Alterwall Highld 158 D4
Altham Lancs 93 F7
Althorne Essex 43 E5
Althorpe N Lincs 90 D2
Alticry Dumfries 105 D6
Altnabreac Station Highld 157 E13
Altnacealgach Hotel Highld 156 H5
Altnacraig Argyll 124 C4
Altnafeadh Highld 131 D6
Altnaharra Highld 157 F8
Altofts W Yorks 88 B4
Alton Derbys 76 C3
Alton Hants 26 F5
Alton Staffs 75 E7
Alton Pancras Dorset 12 D5
Alton Priors Wilts 25 C6
Altrincham Gtr Man 87 F5
Altrua Highld 136 F5
Altskeith Stirling 126 D3
Altyre Ho. Moray 151 F13
Alva Clack 127 E7
Alvanley Ches W 73 B8
Alvaston Derby 76 F3
Alvechurch Worcs 50 B5
Alvecote Warks 63 D6
Alvediston Wilts 13 B7
Alveley Shrops 61 F7
Alverdiscott Devon 9 B7
Alverstoke Hants 15 E7
Alverstone IoW 15 F6
Alverton Notts 77 E7
Alves Moray 152 B1
Alvescot Oxon 38 D2
Alveston S Glos 36 F3
Alveston Warks 51 D7
Alvie Highld 138 D4
Alvingham Lincs 91 E7
Alvington Glos 36 D3
Alwalton Cambs 65 E8
Alweston Dorset 12 C4
Alwinton Northumb 116 D5
Alwoodley W Yorks 95 E5
Alyth Perth 134 E2
Am Baile W Isles 148 G2
Am Buth Argyll 124 C4
Amatnatua Highld 150 B7
Amber Hill Lincs 78 E5
Ambergate Derbys 76 D3
Amberley Glos 37 D5
Amberley W Sus 16 C4
Amble Northumb 117 D8
Amblecote W Mid 62 F2
Ambler Thorn W Yorks 87 B8
Ambleside Cumb 99 D5
Ambleston Pembs 44 C5
Ambrosden Oxon 39 C6
Amcotts N Lincs 90 C2
Amersham Bucks 40 E2
Amesbury Wilts 25 E6
Amington Staffs 63 D6
Amisfield Dumfries 114 F2
Amlwch Anglesey 82 B4
Amlwch Port Anglesey 82 B4
Ammanford = Rhydaman Carms 33 C7
Amod Argyll 143 E8
Amotherby N Yorks 96 B3
Ampfield Hants 14 B5
Ampleforth N Yorks 95 B8
Ampney Crucis Glos 37 D7
Ampney St Mary Glos 37 D7
Ampney St Peter Glos 37 D7
Amport Hants 25 E7
Ampthill C Beds 53 F8
Ampton Suff 56 B2
Amroth Pembs 32 D2
Amulree Perth 133 F5
An Caol Highld 149 C11
An Cnoc W Isles 155 D9
An Gleann Ur W Isles 155 D9
An t-Ob = Leverburgh W Isles 154 J5
Anagach Highld 139 B6
Anaheilt Highld 130 C2
Anancaun Highld 150 E3
Ancaster Lincs 78 E2
Anchor Shrops 59 F8
Anchorsholme Blackpool 92 E3
Ancroft Northumb 123 E5
Ancrum Borders 116 B2
Anderby Lincs 79 B8
Anderson Dorset 13 E6
Anderton Ches W 74 B3
Andover Hants 25 E8
Andover Down Hants 25 E8
Andoversford Glos 37 C7
Andreas IoM 84 C4
Anfield Mers 85 E4
Angersleigh Som 11 C6
Angle Pembs 44 E3
Angmering W Sus 16 D4
Angram N Yorks 95 E8
Angram N Yorks 100 E3
Anie Stirling 126 C4
Ankerville Highld 151 D11
Anlaby E Yorks 90 B4
Anmer Norf 80 E3
Anna Valley Hants 25 E8
Annan Dumfries 107 C8
Annat Argyll 125 C6
Annat Highld 149 C13
Annbank S Ayrs 112 B4
Annesley Notts 76 D5
Annesley Woodhouse Notts 76 D4
Annfield Plain Durham 110 D4
Annifirth Shetland 160 J3
Annitsford T&W 111 B5
Annscroft Shrops 60 D4
Ansdell Lancs 85 B4
Ansford Som 23 F8
Ansley Warks 63 E6
Anslow Staffs 63 B6
Anslow Gate Staffs 63 B5
Anstey Herts 54 F5
Anstey Leics 64 D2
Anstruther Easter Fife 129 D7
Anstruther Wester Fife 129 D7
Ansty Hants 26 E5
Ansty W Sus 17 B6
Ansty Warks 63 F7

Place	County/Region	Page	Grid
Baulking	Oxon	38	E3
Baumber	Lincs	78	B5
Baunton	Glos	37	D7
Baverstock	Wilts	24	F5
Bawburgh	Norf	68	D4
Bawdeswell	Norf	81	E6
Bawdrip	Som	22	F5
Bawdsey	Suff	57	E7
Bawtry	S Yorks	89	E7
Baxenden	Lancs	87	B5
Baxterley	Warks	63	E6
Baybridge	Hants	15	B6
Baycliff	Cumb	92	B2
Baydon	Wilts	25	B7
Bayford	Herts	41	D6
Bayford	Som	12	B5
Bayles	Cumb	109	E7
Baylham	Suff	56	D5
Baynard's Green	Oxon	39	B5
Bayston Hill	Shrops	60	D4
Baythorn End	Essex	55	E8
Bayton	Worcs	49	B8
Beach	Highld	130	D1
Beachampton	Bucks	53	F5
Beachamwell	Norf	67	D7
Beachans	Moray	151	G13
Beacharr	Argyll	143	D7
Beachborough	Kent	19	B8
Beachley	Glos	36	E2
Beacon	Devon	11	D6
Beacon End	Essex	43	B5
Beacon Hill	Sur	27	F6
Beacon's Bottom	Bucks	39	E7
Beaconsfield	Bucks	40	F2
Beacrabhaic	W Isles	154	H6
Beadlam	N Yorks	102	F4
Beadlow	C Beds	54	F2
Beadnell	Northumb	117	B8
Beaford	Devon	9	C7
Beal	N Yorks	89	B6
Beal	Northumb	123	E6
Beamhurst	Staffs	75	F7
Beaminster	Dorset	12	D2
Beamish	Durham	110	D5
Beamsley	N Yorks	94	D3
Bean	Kent	29	B6
Beanacre	Wilts	24	C4
Beanley	Northumb	117	C6
Beaquoy	Orkney	159	F4
Bear Cross	Bmouth	13	E8
Beardwood	Blackburn	86	B4
Beare Green	Sur	28	E2
Bearley	Warks	51	C6
Bearnus	Argyll	146	G6
Bearpark	Durham	110	E5
Bearsbridge	Northumb	109	D7
Bearsden	E Dunb	119	C5
Bearsted	Kent	29	D8
Bearstone	Shrops	74	F4
Bearwood	Hereford	49	D6
Bearwood	Poole	13	E8
Bearwood	W Mid	62	F4
Beattock	Dumfries	114	D3
Beauchamp Roding	Essex	42	C1
Beauchief	S Yorks	88	F4
Beaufort	Bl Gwent	35	C5
Beaufort Castle	Highld	151	G8
Beaulieu	Hants	14	D4
Beauly	Highld	151	G8
Beaumaris	Anglesey	83	D6
Beaumont	Cumb	108	D3
Beaumont	Essex	43	B7
Beaumont Hill	Darl	101	C7
Beausale	Warks	51	B7
Beauworth	Hants	15	B6
Beazley End	Essex	42	B3
Bebington	Mers	85	F4
Bebside	Northumb	117	F8
Beccles	Suff	69	E7
Becconsall	Lancs	86	B2
Beck Foot	Cumb	99	E8
Beck Hole	N Yorks	103	D6
Beck Row	Suff	55	B7
Beck Side	Cumb	98	F4
Beckbury	Shrops	61	D7
Beckenham	London	28	C4
Beckermet	Cumb	98	D2
Beckfoot	Cumb	98	D3
Beckfoot	Cumb	107	E7
Beckford	Worcs	50	F4
Beckhampton	Wilts	25	C5
Beckingham	Lincs	77	D8
Beckingham	Notts	89	F8
Beckington	Som	24	D3
Beckley	E Sus	19	C5
Beckley	Hants	14	E3
Beckley	Oxon	39	C5
Beckton	London	41	F7
Beckwithshaw	N Yorks	95	D5
Becontree	London	41	F7
Bed-y-coedwr	Gwyn	71	E8
Bedale	N Yorks	101	F7
Bedburn	Durham	110	F4
Bedchester	Dorset	13	C6
Beddau	Rhondda	34	F4
Beddgelert	Gwyn	71	C6
Beddingham	E Sus	17	D8
Beddington	London	28	C4
Bedfield	Suff	57	C6
Bedford	Bedford	53	D8
Bedham	W Sus	16	B4
Bedhampton	Hants	15	D8
Bedingfield	Suff	57	C5
Bedlam	N Yorks	95	C5
Bedlington	Northumb	117	F8
Bedlington Station	Northumb	117	F8
Bedlinog	M Tydf	34	D4
Bedminster	Bristol	23	B7
Bedmond	Herts	40	D3
Bednall	Staffs	62	C3
Bedrule	Borders	116	C2
Bedstone	Shrops	49	B5
Bedwas	Caerph	35	F5
Bedworth	Warks	63	F7
Bedworth Heath Warks		63	F7
Beeby	Leics	64	D3
Beech	Hants	26	F4
Beech	Staffs	75	F5
Beech Hill	Gtr Man	86	D3
Beech Hill	W Berks	26	C4
Beechingstoke	Wilts	25	D5
Beedon	W Berks	26	B2
Beeford	E Yorks	97	D7
Beeley	Derbys	76	C2
Beelsby	NE Lincs	91	D6
Beenham	W Berks	26	C3
Beeny	Corn	8	E3
Beer	Devon	11	F7
Beer Hackett	Dorset	12	C4
Beercrocombe	Som	11	B8
Beesands	Devon	7	E6
Beesby	Lincs	91	F8
Beeson	Devon	7	E6
Beeston	C Beds	54	E2
Beeston	Ches W	74	D2
Beeston	Norf	68	C2
Beeston	Notts	76	F5
Beeston	W Yorks	95	F5
Beeston Regis	Norf	81	C7
Beeswing	Dumfries	107	C5
Beetham	Cumb	92	B4
Beetley	Norf	68	C2
Begbroke	Oxon	38	C4
Begelly	Pembs	32	D2
Beggar's Bush	Powys	48	D4
Beguildy	Powys	48	B3
Beighton	Norf	69	D6
Beighton	S Yorks	88	F5
Beighton Hill	Derbys	76	D2
Beith	N Ayrs	118	D3
Bekesbourne	Kent	31	D5
Belaugh	Norf	69	C5
Belbroughton	Worcs	50	B4
Belchamp Otten	Essex	56	E2
Belchamp St Paul Essex		55	E8
Belchamp Walter	Essex	56	E2
Belchford	Lincs	79	B5
Belford	Northumb	123	F7
Belhaven	E Loth	122	B2
Belhelvie	Aberds	141	C8
Belhinnie	Aberds	140	B3
Bell Bar	Herts	41	D5
Bell Busk	N Yorks	94	D2
Bell End	Worcs	50	B4
Bell o'th'Hill	Ches W	74	E2
Bellabeg	Aberds	140	C2
Bellamore	S Ayrs	112	F2
Bellanoch	Argyll	144	D6
Bellaty	Angus	134	D2
Belleau	Lincs	79	B7
Bellehiglash	Moray	152	E1
Bellerby	N Yorks	101	E6
Bellever	Devon	6	B4
Belliehill	Angus	135	C5
Bellingdon	Bucks	40	D2
Bellingham	Northumb	116	F4
Belloch	Argyll	143	E7
Bellochantuy	Argyll	143	E7
Bells Yew Green E Sus		18	B3
Bellsbank	E Ayrs	112	D4
Bellshill	N Lanark	119	C7
Bellshill	Northumb	123	F7
Bellspool	Borders	120	F4
Bellsquarry	W Loth	120	C3
Belmaduthy	Highld	151	F9
Belmesthorpe	Rutland	65	C7
Belmont	Blackburn	86	C4
Belmont	London	28	C3
Belmont	S Ayrs	112	B3
Belmont	Shetland	160	C7
Belnacraig	Aberds	140	C2
Belowda	Corn	4	C4
Belper	Derbys	76	E3
Belper Lane End Derbys		76	E3
Belsay	Northumb	110	B4
Belses	Borders	115	B8
Belsford	Devon	7	D5
Belstead	Suff	56	E5
Belston	S Ayrs	112	B3
Belstone	Devon	9	E8
Belthorn	Blackburn	86	B5
Beltinge	Kent	31	C5
Beltoft	N Lincs	90	D2
Belton	Leics	63	B8
Belton	Lincs	78	F2
Belton	N Lincs	89	D8
Belton	Norf	69	D7
Belton in Rutland Rutland		64	D5
Beltring	Kent	29	E7
Belts of Collonach Aberds		141	E5
Belvedere	London	29	B5
Belvoir	Leics	77	F8
Bembridge	IoW	15	F7
Bemersyde	Borders	121	F8
Bemerton	Wilts	25	F6
Bempton	E Yorks	97	B7
Ben Alder Lodge Highld		132	B2
Ben Armine Lodge Highld		157	H10
Ben Casgro	W Isles	155	E9
Benacre	Suff	69	F8
Benbuie	Dumfries	113	E7
Benderloch	Argyll	124	B5
Bendronaig Lodge Highld		150	H3
Benenden	Kent	18	B5
Benfield	Dumfries	105	C7
Bengate	Norf	69	B6
Bengeworth	Worcs	50	E5
Benhall Green	Suff	57	C7
Benhall Street	Suff	57	C7
Benholm	Aberds	135	C8
Beningbrough	N Yorks	95	D8
Benington	Herts	41	B5
Benington	Lincs	79	E6
Benllech	Anglesey	82	C5
Benmore	Argyll	145	E10
Benmore Lodge Highld		156	H6
Bennacott	Corn	8	E4
Bennan	N Ayrs	143	F10
Benniworth	Lincs	91	F6
Benover	Kent	29	E8
Bensham	T&W	110	C5
Benslie	N Ayrs	118	E3
Benson	Oxon	39	E6
Bent	Aberds	135	B6
Bent Gate	Lancs	87	B5
Benthall	Northumb	117	B8
Benthall	Shrops	61	D6
Bentham	Glos	37	C6
Benthoul	Aberdeen	141	D7
Bentlawnt	Shrops	60	D3
Bentley	E Yorks	97	F6
Bentley	Hants	27	E5
Bentley	S Yorks	89	D6
Bentley	Suff	56	F5
Bentley	Warks	63	E6
Bentley	Worcs	50	C4
Bentley Heath	W Mid	51	B6
Benton	Devon	21	F5
Bentpath	Dumfries	115	E6
Bents	W Loth	120	C2
Bentworth	Hants	26	E4
Benvie	Dundee	134	F3
Benwick	Cambs	66	E3
Beoley	Worcs	51	C5
Beoraidbeg	Highld	147	B9
Bepton	W Sus	16	C2
Berden	Essex	41	B7
Bere Alston	Devon	6	C2
Bere Ferrers	Devon	6	C2
Bere Regis	Dorset	13	E6
Berepper	Corn	3	D5
Bergh Apton	Norf	69	D6
Berinsfield	Oxon	39	E5
Berkeley	Glos	36	E3
Berkhamsted	Herts	40	D2
Berkley	Som	24	E3
Berkswell	W Mid	51	B7
Bermondsey	London	28	B4
Bernera	Highld	149	F13
Bernice	Argyll	145	D10
Bernisdale	Highld	149	C9
Berrick Salome	Oxon	39	E6
Berriedale	Highld	158	H3
Berrier	Cumb	99	B5
Berriew	Powys	59	D8
Berrington	Northumb	123	E6
Berrington	Shrops	60	D5
Berrow	Som	22	D5
Berrow Green	Worcs	50	D2
Berry Down Cross Devon		20	E4
Berry Hill	Glos	36	C2
Berry Hill	Pembs	45	E2
Berry Pomeroy	Devon	7	C6
Berryhillock	Moray	152	B5
Berrynarbor	Devon	20	E4
Bersham	Wrex	73	E7
Berstane	Orkney	159	G5
Berwick	E Sus	18	E2
Berwick Bassett Wilts			
Berwick Hill	Northumb	110	B4
Berwick St James Wilts		25	F5
Berwick St John Wilts		13	B7
Berwick St Leonard Wilts		24	F4
Berwick-upon-Tweed Northumb		123	D5
Bescar	Lancs	85	C4
Besford	Worcs	50	E4
Bessacarr	S Yorks	89	D7
Bessels Leigh	Oxon	38	D4
Bessingby	E Yorks	97	C7
Bessingham	Norf	81	D7
Bestbeech Hill	E Sus	18	B3
Besthorpe	Norf	68	E3
Besthorpe	Notts	77	C8
Bestwood	Nottingham	77	E5
Bestwood Village Notts		77	E5
Beswick	E Yorks	97	E6
Betchworth	Sur	28	E3
Bethania	Ceredig	46	C4
Bethania	Gwyn	71	C8
Bethania	Gwyn	83	F6
Bethel	Anglesey	82	D3
Bethel	Gwyn	72	E3
Bethel	Gwyn	82	E4
Bethersden	Kent	30	E3
Bethesda	Gwyn	83	E6
Bethesda	Pembs	32	C1
Bethlehem	Carms	33	B7
Bethnal Green	London	41	F6
Betley	Staffs	74	E4
Betsham	Kent	29	B7
Betteshanger	Kent	31	D7
Bettiscombe	Dorset	11	E8
Bettisfield	Wrex	73	F8
Betton	Shrops	60	D3
Betton	Shrops	74	F3
Bettws	Bridgend	34	F3
Bettws	Mon	35	C6
Bettws	Newport	35	E6
Bettws Cedewain Powys		59	E8
Bettws Gwerfil Goch Denb		72	E4
Bettws Ifan	Ceredig	46	E2
Bettws Newydd	Mon	35	D7
Bettws-y-crwyn Shrops		60	F2
Bettyhill	Highld	157	C10
Betws	Carms	33	C7
Betws Bledrws	Ceredig	46	D4
Betws-Garmon	Gwyn	82	F5
Betws-y-Coed	Conwy	83	F7
Betws-yn-Rhos	Conwy	72	B3
Beulah	Ceredig	45	E4
Beulah	Powys	47	D8
Bevendean	Brighton	17	D7
Bevercotes	Notts	77	B6
Beverley	E Yorks	97	F6
Beverston	Glos	37	E5
Bevington	Glos	36	E3
Bewaldeth	Cumb	108	F2
Bewcastle	Cumb	109	B5
Bewdley	Worcs	50	B2
Bewerley	N Yorks	94	C4
Bewholme	E Yorks	97	D7
Bexhill	E Sus	18	E4
Bexley	London	29	B5
Bexleyheath	London	29	B5
Bexwell	Norf	67	D6
Beyton	Suff	56	C3
Bhaltos	W Isles	154	D5
Bhatarsaigh	W Isles	148	J1
Bibury	Glos	37	D8
Bicester	Oxon	39	B5
Bickenhall	Som	11	C7
Bickenhill	W Mid	63	F5
Bicker	Lincs	78	F5
Bickershaw	Gtr Man	86	D4
Bickerstaffe	Lancs	86	D2
Bickerton	Ches E	74	D2
Bickerton	N Yorks	95	D7
Bickington	Devon	7	B5
Bickington	Devon	20	F4
Bickleigh	Devon	6	C3
Bickleigh	Devon	10	D4
Bickleton	Devon	20	F4
Bickley	London	28	C5
Bickley Moss	Ches W	74	E2
Bicknacre	Essex	42	D3
Bicknoller	Som	22	F3
Bicknor	Kent	30	D2
Bickton	Hants	14	C2
Bicton	Shrops	60	C4
Bicton	Shrops	60	F2
Bidborough	Kent	29	E6
Biddenden	Kent	19	B5
Biddenham	Bedford	53	E8
Biddestone	Wilts	24	B3
Biddisham	Som	23	D5
Biddlesden	Bucks	52	E4
Biddlestone	Northumb	117	D5
Biddulph	Staffs	75	D5
Biddulph Moor	Staffs	75	D6
Bideford	Devon	9	B6
Bidford-on-Avon Warks		51	D6
Bidston	Mers	85	E3
Bielby	E Yorks	96	E3
Bieldside	Aberdeen	141	D7
Bierley	IoW	15	G6
Bierley	W Yorks	94	F4
Bierton	Bucks	39	C8
Big Sand	Highld	149	A12
Bigbury	Devon	6	E4
Bigbury on Sea	Devon	6	E4
Bigby	Lincs	90	D4
Biggar	Cumb	92	C1
Biggar	S Lanark	120	F3
Biggin	Derbys	75	D8
Biggin	Derbys	76	E2
Biggin	N Yorks	95	F8
Biggin Hill	London	28	D5
Biggings	Shetland	160	G3
Biggleswade	C Beds	54	E2
Bighouse	Highld	157	C11
Bighton	Hants	26	F4
Bignor	W Sus	16	C3
Bigton	Shetland	160	L5
Bilberry	Corn	4	C5
Bilborough	Nottingham	76	E5
Bilbrook	Som	22	E2
Bilbrough	N Yorks	95	E8
Bilbster	Highld	158	E4
Bildershaw	Durham	101	B7
Bildeston	Suff	56	E3
Billericay	Essex	42	E2
Billesdon	Leics	64	D4
Billesley	Warks	51	D6
Billingborough	Lincs	78	F4
Billinge	Mers	86	D3
Billingford	Norf	81	E6
Billingham	Stockton	102	B2
Billinghay	Lincs	78	D4
Billingley	S Yorks	88	D5
Billingshurst	W Sus	16	B4
Billingsley	Shrops	61	F7
Billington	C Beds	40	B2
Billington	Lancs	93	F7
Billockby	Norf	69	C7
Billy Row	Durham	110	F4
Bilsborrow	Lancs	92	F5
Bilsby	Lincs	79	B7
Bilsham	W Sus	16	D3
Bilsington	Kent	19	B7
Bilson Green	Glos	36	C3
Bilsthorpe	Notts	77	C6
Bilsthorpe Moor Notts		77	D6
Bilston	Midloth	121	C5
Bilston	W Mid	62	E3
Bilstone	Leics	63	D7
Bilting	Kent	30	E4
Bilton	E Yorks	97	F7
Bilton	N Yorks	95	D6
Bilton	Warks	52	B2
Bilton in Ainsty N Yorks		95	E7
Bimbister	Orkney	159	G4
Binbrook	Lincs	91	E6
Binchester Blocks Durham		110	F5
Bincombe	Dorset	12	F4
Bindal	Highld	151	C12
Binegar	Som	23	E8
Binfield	Brack	27	B6
Binfield Heath	Oxon	26	B5
Bingfield	Northumb	110	B2
Bingham	Notts	77	F7
Bingley	W Yorks	94	F4
Bings Heath	Shrops	60	C5
Binham	Norf	81	D5
Binley	Hants	26	D2
Binley	W Mid	51	B8
Binley Woods	Warks	51	B8
Binniehill	Falk	119	B8
Binsoe	N Yorks	94	B5
Binstead	IoW	15	E6
Binsted	Hants	27	E5
Bintree	Norf	81	E6
Binweston	Shrops	60	D3
Birch	Essex	43	C5
Birch	Gtr Man	87	D6
Birch Green	Essex	43	C5
Birch Heath	Ches W	74	C2
Birch Hill	Ches W	74	B2
Birch Vale	Derbys	87	F8
Bircham Newton Norf		80	D3
Bircham Tofts	Norf	80	D3
Birchanger	Essex	41	B8
Bircher	Hereford	49	C6
Birchgrove	Cardiff	22	B3
Birchgrove	Swansea	33	E8
Birchington	Kent	31	C6
Birchmoor	Warr	86	E4
Birchover	Derbys	76	C2
Birchwood	Lincs	78	C2
Birchwood	Warr	86	E4
Bircotes	Notts	89	E7
Birdbrook	Essex	55	E8
Birdforth	N Yorks	95	B7
Birdham	W Sus	16	E2
Birdholme	Derbys	76	C4
Birdingbury	Warks	52	C2
Birdlip	Glos	37	C6
Birds Edge	W Yorks	88	D3
Birdsall	N Yorks	96	C4
Birdsgreen	Shrops	61	F7
Birdsmoor Gate Dorset		11	D8
Birdston	E Dunb	119	B6
Birdwell	S Yorks	88	D4
Birdwood	Glos	36	C4
Birgham	Borders	122	F3
Birkby	N Yorks	101	D8
Birkdale	Mers	85	C4
Birkenhead	Mers	85	F4
Birkenhills	Aberds	153	D7
Birkenshaw	N Lanark	119	C6
Birkenshaw	W Yorks	88	B3
Birkhall	Aberds	140	E2
Birkhill	Angus	134	F3
Birkhill	Borders	114	C5
Birkholme	Lincs	65	B6
Birkin	N Yorks	89	B6
Birley	Hereford	49	D6
Birling	Kent	29	C7
Birling	Northumb	117	D8
Birling Gap	E Sus	18	F2
Birlingham	Worcs	50	E4
Birmingham	W Mid	62	F4
Birnam	Perth	133	E7
Birse	Aberds	140	E4
Birsemore	Aberds	140	E4
Birstall	Leics	64	D2
Birstall	W Yorks	88	B3
Birstwith	N Yorks	94	D5
Birthorpe	Lincs	78	F4
Birtley	Hereford	49	C5
Birtley	Northumb	109	B8
Birtley	T&W	111	D5
Birts Street	Worcs	50	F2
Birtsmorton	Worcs	50	F3
Bisbrooke	Rutland	65	E5
Biscathorpe	Lincs	91	F6
Biscot	Luton	40	B3
Bish Mill	Devon	10	B2
Bisham	Windsor	39	F8
Bishampton	Worcs	50	D4
Bishop Auckland Durham		101	B7
Bishop Burton	E Yorks	97	F5
Bishop Middleham Durham		111	F6
Bishop Monkton N Yorks		95	C6
Bishop Norton	Lincs	90	E3
Bishop Sutton	Bath	23	D7
Bishop Thornton N Yorks		95	C5
Bishop Wilton	E Yorks	96	D3
Bishopbridge	Lincs	90	E4
Bishopbriggs	E Dunb	119	C6
Bishopmill	Moray	152	B2
Bishops Cannings Wilts		24	C5
Bishop's Castle Shrops		60	F3
Bishop's Caundle Dorset		12	C4
Bishop's Cleeve Glos		37	B6
Bishops Frome Hereford		49	E8
Bishop's Green	Essex	42	C2
Bishop's Hull	Som	11	B7
Bishop's Itchington Warks		51	D8
Bishops Lydeard Som		11	B6
Bishops Nympton Devon		10	B2
Bishop's Offley Staffs		61	B7
Bishop's Stortford Herts		41	B7
Bishop's Sutton Hants		26	F4
Bishop's Tachbrook Warks		51	C8
Bishops Tawton Devon		20	F4
Bishop's Waltham Hants		15	C6
Bishop's Wood	Staffs	62	D2
Bishopsbourne	Kent	31	D5
Bishopsteignton Devon		7	B7
Bishopstoke	Hants	15	C5
Bishopston	Swansea	33	F6
Bishopstone	Bucks	39	C8
Bishopstone	E Sus	17	D8
Bishopstone	Hereford	49	E6
Bishopstone	Swindon	38	F2
Bishopstone	Wilts	13	B8
Bishopstrow	Wilts	24	E3
Bishopswood	Som	11	C7
Bishopsworth	Bristol	23	C7
Bishopthorpe	York	95	E8
Bishopton	Darl	102	B1
Bishopton	Dumfries	105	E8
Bishopton	N Yorks	95	B6
Bishopton	Renfs	118	B4
Bishopton	Warks	51	D6
Bishton	Newport	35	F7
Bisley	Glos	37	D6
Bisley	Sur	27	D7
Bispham	Blackpool	92	E3
Bispham Green	Lancs	86	C2
Bissoe	Corn	3	B6
Bisterne Close	Hants	14	D3
Bitchfield	Lincs	65	B6
Bittadon	Devon	20	E4
Bittaford	Devon	6	D4
Bittering	Norf	68	C2
Bitterley	Shrops	49	B7
Bitterne	Soton	15	C5
Bitteswell	Leics	64	F2
Bitton	S Glos	23	C8
Bix	Oxon	39	F7
Bixter	Shetland	160	H5
Blaby	Leics	64	E2
Black Bourton	Oxon	38	D2
Black Callerton	T&W	110	C4
Black Clauchrie S Ayrs		112	F2
Black Corries Lodge Highld		131	D6
Black Crofts	Argyll	124	B5
Black Dog	Devon	10	D3
Black Heddon Northumb		110	B3
Black Lane	Gtr Man	87	D5
Black Marsh	Shrops	60	E3
Black Mount	Argyll	131	E5
Black Notley	Essex	42	B3
Black Pill	Swansea	33	E7
Black Tar	Pembs	44	E4
Black Torrington Devon		9	D6
Blackacre	Dumfries	114	E3
Blackawton	Devon	7	D6
Blackborough	Devon	11	D5
Blackborough End Norf		67	C6
Blackboys	E Sus	18	C2
Blackbrook	Derbys	76	E3
Blackbrook	Mers	86	E3
Blackbrook	Staffs	74	F4
Blackburn	Aberds	141	C7
Blackburn	Aberds	152	E5
Blackburn	Blackburn	86	B4
Blackburn	W Loth	120	C2
Blackcraig	Dumfries	113	F7
Blackden Heath	Ches E	74	B4
Blackdog	Aberds	141	C8
Blackfell	T&W	111	D5
Blackfield	Hants	14	D5
Blackford	Cumb	108	C3
Blackford	Perth	127	D7
Blackford	Som	23	E6
Blackford	Som	12	B4
Blackfordby	Leics	63	C7
Blackgang	IoW	15	G5
Blackhall Colliery Durham		111	F7
Blackhall Mill	T&W	110	D4
Blackhall Rocks Durham		111	F7
Blackham	E Sus	29	F5
Blackhaugh	Borders	121	F7
Blackheath	Essex	43	B6
Blackheath	Suff	57	B8
Blackheath	Sur	27	E8
Blackheath	W Mid	62	F3
Blackhill	Aberds	153	C10
Blackhill	Aberds	153	D10
Blackhill	Highld	149	C8
Blackhills	Highld	151	F12
Blackhills	Moray	152	C2
Blackhorse	S Glos	23	B8
Blackland	Wilts	24	C5
Blacklaw	Aberds	153	C6
Blackley	Gtr Man	87	D6
Blacklunans	Perth	134	C1
Blackmill	Bridgend	34	F3
Blackmoor	Hants	27	F5
Blackmoor Gate Devon		21	E5
Blackmore	Essex	42	D2
Blackmore End	Essex	55	F8
Blackmore End	Herts	40	C4
Blackness	Falk	120	B3
Blacknest	Hants	27	E5
Blacko	Lancs	93	E8
Blackpool	Blackpool	92	F3
Blackpool	Devon	7	E6
Blackpool	Pembs	32	C1
Blackpool Gate	Cumb	108	B5
Blackridge	W Loth	119	C8
Blackrock	Argyll	142	B4
Blackrock	Mon	35	C6
Blackrod	Gtr Man	86	C4
Blackshaw	Dumfries	107	C7
Blackshaw Head W Yorks		87	B7
Blacksmith's Green Suff		56	C5
Blackstone	W Sus	17	C6
Blackthorn	Oxon	39	C6
Blackthorpe	Suff	56	C3
Blacktoft	E Yorks	90	B2
Blacktop	Aberdeen	141	D7
Blackwall Tunnel London		41	F6
Blackwater	Corn	3	B6
Blackwater	Hants	27	D6
Blackwater	IoW	15	F6
Blackwaterfoot N Ayrs		143	F9
Blackwell	Darl	101	C7
Blackwell	Derbys	75	B8
Blackwell	Derbys	76	D4
Blackwell	W Sus	28	F4
Blackwell	Warks	51	E7
Blackwell	Worcs	50	B4
Blackwood = Coed Duon Caerph		35	E5
Blackwood	S Lanark	119	E7
Blackwood Hill	Staffs	75	D6
Blacon	Ches W	73	C7
Bladnoch	Dumfries	105	D8
Bladon	Oxon	38	C4
Blaen-gwynfi	Neath	34	E2
Blaen-waun	Carms	32	B3
Blaen-y-coed	Carms	32	B4
Blaen-y-cwm	Denb	72	F4
Blaen-y-cwm	Powys	59	B7
Blaenannerch	Ceredig	45	E4
Blaenau Ffestiniog Gwyn		71	C8
Blaenavon	Torf	35	D6
Blaencelyn	Ceredig	46	D2
Blaendyryn	Powys	47	F8
Blaenffos	Pembs	45	F3
Blaengarw	Bridgend	34	E3
Blaengwrach	Neath	34	D2
Blaenpennal	Ceredig	46	C5
Blaenplwyf	Ceredig	46	B4
Blaenporth	Ceredig	45	E4
Blaenrhondda	Rhondda	34	D3
Blaenycwm	Ceredig	47	B7
Blagdon	N Som	23	D7
Blagdon	Torbay	7	C6
Blagdon Hill	Som	11	C7
Blagill	Cumb	109	E7
Blaguegate	Lancs	86	D2
Blaich	Highld	130	B4
Blain	Highld	147	E9
Blaina	Bl Gwent	35	D6
Blair Atholl	Perth	133	C5
Blair Drummond Stirling		127	E6
Blairbeg	N Ayrs	143	E11
Blairdaff	Aberds	141	C5
Blairglas	Argyll	126	F2
Blairgowrie	Perth	134	E1
Blairhall	Fife	128	F2
Blairingone	Perth	127	E8
Blairland	N Ayrs	118	E3
Blairlogie	Stirling	127	E7
Blairlomond	Argyll	125	F7
Blairmore	Argyll	145	E10
Blairnamarrow	Moray	139	C8
Blairquhosh	Stirling	126	F4
Blair's Ferry	Argyll	145	G8
Blairskaith	E Dunb	119	B5
Blaisdon	Glos	36	C4
Blakebrook	Worcs	50	B3
Blakedown	Worcs	50	B3
Blakelaw	Borders	122	F3
Blakeley	Staffs	62	E2
Blakeley Lane	Staffs	75	E6
Blakemere	Hereford	49	E5
Blakeney	Glos	36	D3
Blakeney	Norf	81	C6
Blakenhall	Ches E	74	E4
Blakenhall	W Mid	62	E3
Blakeshall	Worcs	62	F2
Blakesley	Northants	52	D4
Blanchland	Northumb	110	D2
Bland Hill	N Yorks	94	D5
Blandford Forum Dorset		13	D6
Blandford St Mary Dorset		13	D6
Blanefield	Stirling	119	B5
Blankney	Lincs	78	C3
Blantyre	S Lanark	119	D6
Blar a'Chaorainn Highld		131	C5
Blaran	Argyll	124	D4
Blarghour	Argyll	125	D5
Blarmachfoldach Highld		130	C4
Blarnalearoch	Highld	150	B4
Blashford	Hants	14	D2
Blaston	Leics	64	E5
Blatherwycke	Northants	65	E6
Blawith	Cumb	98	F4
Blaxhall	Suff	57	D7
Blaxton	S Yorks	89	D7
Blaydon	T&W	110	C4
Bleadon	N Som	22	D5
Bleak Hey Nook	Gtr Man	87	D8
Blean	Kent	30	C5
Bleasby	Lincs	90	F5
Bleasby	Notts	77	E7
Bleasdale	Lancs	93	E5
Bleatarn	Cumb	100	C2
Blebocraigs	Fife	129	C6
Bleddfa	Powys	48	C4
Bledington	Glos	38	B2
Bledlow	Bucks	39	D7
Bledlow Ridge	Bucks	39	E7
Blegbie	E Loth	121	C7
Blencarn	Cumb	109	F6
Blencogo	Cumb	107	E8
Blendworth	Hants	15	C8
Blenheim Park	Norf	80	D4
Blennerhasset Cumb		107	E8
Blervie Castle	Moray	151	F13
Bletchingdon	Oxon	39	C5
Bletchingley	Sur	28	D4
Bletchley	M Keynes	53	F6
Bletchley	Shrops	74	F3
Bletherston	Pembs	32	B1
Bletsoe	Bedford	53	D8
Blewbury	Oxon	39	F5
Blickling	Norf	81	E7
Blidworth	Notts	77	D5
Blindburn	Northumb	116	C4
Blindcrake	Cumb	107	F8
Blindley Heath	Sur	28	E4
Blisland	Corn	5	B6
Bliss Gate	Worcs	50	B2
Blissford	Hants	14	C2
Blisworth	Northants	52	D5
Blithbury	Staffs	62	B4
Blitterlees	Cumb	107	D8
Blockley	Glos	51	F6
Blofield	Norf	69	D6
Blofield Heath	Norf	69	C6
Blo' Norton	Norf	56	B4
Bloomfield	Borders	115	B8
Blore	Staffs	75	E8
Blount's Green	Staffs	75	F7
Blowick	Mers	85	C4
Bloxham	Oxon	52	F2
Bloxholm	Lincs	78	D3
Bloxwich	W Mid	62	D3
Bloxworth	Dorset	13	E6
Blubberhouses N Yorks		94	D4
Blue Anchor	Som	22	E2
Blue Anchor	Swansea	33	E6
Blue Row	Essex	43	C6
Blundeston	Suff	69	E8
Blunham	C Beds	54	D2
Blunsdon St Andrew Swindon		37	F8
Bluntington	Worcs	50	B3
Bluntisham	Cambs	54	B4
Blunts	Corn	5	C8
Blyborough	Lincs	90	E3
Blyford	Suff	57	B8
Blymhill	Staffs	62	C2
Blyth	Northumb	117	F9
Blyth	Notts	89	F7
Blyth Bridge	Borders	120	E4
Blythburgh	Suff	57	B8
Blythe	Borders	121	E8
Blythe Bridge	Staffs	75	E6
Blyton	Lincs	90	E2
Boarhills	Fife	129	C7
Boarhunt	Hants	15	D7
Boars Head	Gtr Man	86	D3
Boars Hill	Oxon	38	D4
Boarshead	E Sus	18	B2
Boarstall	Bucks	39	C6
Boasley Cross	Devon	9	E6
Boat of Garten	Highld	138	C5
Boath	Highld	151	D8
Bobbing	Kent	30	C2
Bobbington	Staffs	62	E2
Bobbingworth	Essex	41	D8
Bocaddon	Corn	5	D6
Bochastle	Stirling	126	D5
Bocking	Essex	42	B3
Bocking Churchstreet Essex		42	B3
Boddam	Aberds	153	D11
Boddam	Shetland	160	M5
Boddington	Glos	37	B5
Bodedern	Anglesey	82	C3
Bodelwyddan	Denb	72	B4
Bodenham	Hereford	49	D7
Bodenham	Wilts	14	B2
Bodenham Moor Hereford		49	D7
Bodermid	Gwyn	70	E2
Bodewryd	Anglesey	82	B3
Bodfari	Denb	72	B4
Bodffordd	Anglesey	82	D4
Bodham	Norf	81	C7
Bodiam	E Sus	18	C4
Bodicote	Oxon	52	F2
Bodieve	Corn	4	B4
Bodinnick	Corn	5	D6
Bodle Street Green E Sus		18	D3
Bodmin	Corn	5	C5
Bodney	Norf	67	E8
Bodorgan	Anglesey	82	E3
Bodsham	Kent	30	E5
Boduan	Gwyn	70	D4
Bodymoor Heath Warks		63	E5
Bogallan	Highld	151	F9
Bogbrae	Aberds	153	E10
Bogend	S Ayrs	118	F3
Bogend	Borders	122	E3
Boghall	W Loth	120	C2
Boghead	S Lanark	119	E7
Bogmoor	Moray	152	B3
Bogniebrae	Aberds	152	D5
Bognor Regis	W Sus	16	E3
Bograxie	Aberds	141	C6
Bogside	N Lanark	119	E8
Bogton	Aberds	153	C6
Bogue	Dumfries	113	F6
Bohenie	Highld	137	F5
Bohortha	Corn	3	C7
Bohuntine	Highld	137	F5
Boirseam	W Isles	154	J5
Bojewyan	Corn	2	C2
Bolam	Durham	101	B6
Bolam	Northumb	117	F6
Bolberry	Devon	6	F4
Bold Heath	Mers	86	F3
Boldon	T&W	111	C6
Boldon Colliery	T&W	111	C6
Boldre	Hants	14	E4
Boldron	Durham	101	C5
Bole	Notts	89	F8
Bolehill	Derbys	76	D2
Boleside	Borders	121	F7
Bolham	Devon	10	C4
Bolham Water	Devon	11	C6
Bolingey	Corn	4	D2
Bollington	Ches E	75	B6
Bollington Cross Ches E		75	B6
Bolney	W Sus	17	B6
Bolnhurst	Bedford	53	D8
Bolshan	Angus	135	D6
Bolsover	Derbys	76	B4
Bolsterstone	S Yorks	88	E3
Bolstone	Hereford	49	F7
Boltby	N Yorks	102	F2
Bolter End	Bucks	39	E7
Bolton	Cumb	99	B8
Bolton	E Loth	121	B8
Bolton	E Yorks	96	D3
Bolton	Gtr Man	86	D5
Bolton	Northumb	117	C7
Bolton Abbey	N Yorks	94	D3
Bolton Bridge	N Yorks	94	D3
Bolton-by-Bowland Lancs		93	E7
Bolton-le-Sands Lancs		92	C4
Bolton Low Houses Cumb		108	E2
Bolton-on-Swale N Yorks		101	E7
Bolton Percy	N Yorks	95	E8
Bolton Town End Lancs		92	C4
Bolton upon Dearne S Yorks		89	D5
Boltonfellend	Cumb	108	C4
Boltongate	Cumb	108	E2
Bolventor	Corn	5	B6
Bomere Heath	Shrops	60	C4
Bon-y-maen	Swansea	33	E7
Bonar Bridge	Highld	151	B9
Bonawe	Argyll	125	B6
Bonby	N Lincs	90	C4
Boncath	Pembs	45	F4
Bonchester Bridge Borders		115	C8
Bonchurch	IoW	15	G6
Bondleigh	Devon	9	D8
Bonehill	Devon	6	B5
Bonehill	Staffs	63	D5
Bo'ness	Falk	127	F8
Bonhill	W Dunb	118	B3
Boningale	Shrops	62	D2
Bonjedward	Borders	116	B2
Bonkle	N Lanark	119	D8
Bonnavoulin	Highld	147	F8
Bonnington	Edin	120	B4
Bonnington	Kent	19	B7
Bonnybank	Fife	129	D5
Bonnybridge	Falk	127	F7
Bonnykelly	Aberds	153	C8
Bonnyrigg and Lasswade Midloth		121	C6
Bonnyton	Aberds	153	E6
Bonnyton	Angus	134	F3
Bonnyton	Angus	135	D6
Bonsall	Derbys	76	D2
Bonskeid House Perth		133	C5
Bont	Mon	35	C7
Bont-Dolgadfan Powys		59	D5
Bont-goch	Ceredig	58	F3
Bont Newydd	Conwy	83	F8
Bont Newydd	Gwyn	71	E8
Bont-newydd	Conwy	72	B4
Bontddu	Gwyn	58	C3
Bonthorpe	Lincs	79	B7
Bontnewydd	Ceredig	46	C5
Bontnewydd	Gwyn	82	F4
Bontuchel	Denb	72	D4
Bonvilston	V Glam	22	B2
Booker	Bucks	39	E8
Boon	Borders	121	E8
Boosbeck	Redcar	102	C4
Boot	Cumb	98	D3
Boot Street	Suff	57	E6
Booth	W Yorks	87	B8
Booth Wood	W Yorks	87	C8
Boothby Graffoe Lincs		78	D2
Boothby Pagnell	Lincs	78	F2
Boothen	Stoke	75	E5
Boothferry	E Yorks	89	B8
Boothville	Northants	53	C5
Bootle	Cumb	98	F3
Bootle	Mers	85	E4
Booton	Norf	81	E7
Boquhan	Stirling	126	F4
Boraston	Shrops	49	B8
Borden	Kent	30	C2
Borden	W Sus	16	B2
Bordley	N Yorks	94	C2
Bordon	Hants	27	F5
Bordon Camp	Hants	27	F5
Boreham	Essex	42	D3
Boreham	Wilts	24	E3
Boreham Street	E Sus	18	D3
Borehamwood	Herts	40	E4
Boreland	Dumfries	114	E4
Boreland	Stirling	132	F2
Borgh	W Isles	148	H1
Borgh	W Isles	154	J4
Borghastan	W Isles	154	C7
Borgie	Highld	157	D9
Borgue	Dumfries	106	E3
Borgue	Highld	158	H3
Borley	Essex	56	E2
Bornais	W Isles	148	F2
Bornesketaig	Highld	149	A8
Borness	Dumfries	106	E3
Boroughbridge N Yorks		95	C6
Borras Head	Wrex	73	D7
Borreraig	Highld	148	C6
Borrobol Lodge Highld		157	G11
Borrowash	Derbys	76	F4
Borrowby	N Yorks	102	F2
Borrowdale	Cumb	98	C4
Borrowfield	Aberds	141	E7
Borth	Ceredig	58	E3
Borth-y-Gest	Gwyn	71	D6
Borthwickbrae	Borders	115	C7
Borthwickshiels Borders		115	C7
Borve	Highld	149	D9
Borve Lodge	W Isles	154	H5
Borwick	Lancs	92	B5
Bosavern	Corn	2	C2
Bosbury	Hereford	49	E8
Boscastle	Corn	8	E3
Boscombe	Bmouth	14	E2
Boscombe	Wilts	25	F7
Boscoppa	Corn	4	D5
Bosham	W Sus	16	D2
Bosherston	Pembs	44	F4
Boskenna	Corn	2	D3
Bosley	Ches E	75	C6
Bossall	N Yorks	96	C3
Bossiney	Corn	8	F2
Bossingham	Kent	31	E5
Bossington	Som	21	E7
Bostock Green	Ches W	74	C3
Boston	Lincs	79	E6
Boston Long Hedges Lincs		79	E6
Boston Spa	W Yorks	95	E7
Boston West	Lincs	79	E5
Boswinger	Corn	3	B8
Botallack	Corn	2	C2
Botany Bay	London	41	E5
Botcherby	Cumb	108	D4
Botcheston	Leics	63	D8
Botesdale	Suff	56	B4
Bothal	Northumb	117	F8
Bothamsall	Notts	77	B6
Bothel	Cumb	107	F8
Bothenhampton Dorset		12	E2
Bothwell	S Lanark	119	D7
Botley	Bucks	40	D2
Botley	Hants	15	C6
Botley	Oxon	38	D4
Botolph Claydon Bucks		39	B7
Botolphs	W Sus	17	D5
Bottacks	Highld	150	E7
Bottesford	Leics	77	F8
Bottesford	N Lincs	90	D2
Bottisham	Cambs	55	C6
Bottlesford	Wilts	25	D6
Bottom Boat	W Yorks	88	B4
Bottom House	Staffs	75	D7
Bottom o'th'Moor Gtr Man		86	C4
Bottom of Hutton Lancs		86	B2
Bottomcraig	Fife	129	B5
Botusfleming	Corn	6	C2
Botwnnog	Gwyn	70	D3
Bough Beech	Kent	29	E5
Boughrood	Powys	48	F3
Boughspring	Glos	36	E2
Boughton	Norf	67	D6
Boughton	Northants	53	C5
Boughton	Notts	77	C6
Boughton Aluph	Kent	30	E4
Boughton Lees	Kent	30	E4
Boughton Malherbe Kent		30	E2
Boughton Monchelsea Kent		29	D8
Boughton Street Kent		30	D4
Boulby	Redcar	103	C5
Boulden	Shrops	60	F5
Boulmer	Northumb	117	C8
Boulston	Pembs	44	D4
Boultenstone	Aberds	140	C3
Boultham	Lincs	78	C2
Bourn	Cambs	54	D4
Bourne	Lincs	65	B7
Bourne End	Bucks	40	F1
Bourne End	C Beds	53	E7
Bourne End	Herts	40	D3
Bournemouth	Bmouth	13	E8
Bournes Green	Glos	37	D6
Bournes Green Southend		43	F5
Bournheath	Worcs	50	B4
Bournmoor	Durham	111	D6
Bournville	W Mid	62	F4
Bourton	Dorset	24	F2
Bourton	N Som	23	C5
Bourton	Oxon	38	F2
Bourton	Shrops	61	E5
Bourton on Dunsmore Warks		52	B2
Bourton on the Hill Glos		51	F6
Bourton-on-the-Water Glos		38	B1
Bousd	Argyll	146	E5
Boustead Hill	Cumb	108	D2
Bouth	Cumb	99	F5
Bouthwaite	N Yorks	94	B4
Boveney	Bucks	27	B7
Boverton	V Glam	21	C8
Bovey Tracey	Devon	7	B6
Bovingdon	Herts	40	D3
Bovingdon Green Bucks		39	F8
Bovingdon Green Herts		40	D3
Bovinger	Essex	41	D8
Bovington Camp Dorset		13	F6
Bow	Borders	121	E7
Bow	Devon	10	D2
Bow	Orkney	159	J4
Bow Brickhill	M Keynes	53	F7
Bow of Fife	Fife	128	C5
Bow Street	Ceredig	58	F3
Bowbank	Durham	100	B4
Bowburn	Durham	111	F6
Bowcombe	IoW	15	F5
Bowd	Devon	11	E6
Bowden	Borders	121	F8
Bowden	Devon	7	E6
Bowden Hill	Wilts	24	C4
Bowderdale	Cumb	100	D1
Bowdon	Gtr Man	87	F5
Bower	Northumb	116	F3
Bower Hinton	Som	12	C2
Bowerchalke	Wilts	13	B8
Bowerhill	Wilts	24	C4
Bowermadden	Highld	158	D4
Bowers Gifford Essex		42	F3
Bowershall	Fife	128	E2
Bowertower	Highld	158	D4
Bowes	Durham	100	C4
Bowgreave	Lancs	92	E4
Bowhill	Borders	115	B7
Bowhouse	Dumfries	107	C7
Bowland Bridge	Cumb	99	F6
Bowley	Hereford	49	D7
Bowlhead Green Sur		27	F7
Bowling	W Dunb	118	B4
Bowling	W Yorks	94	F4
Bowling Bank	Wrex	73	E7
Bowling Green	Worcs	50	D3
Bowmanstead	Cumb	99	E5
Bowmore	Argyll	142	C4
Bowness-on-Solway Cumb		108	C2
Bowness-on-Windermere Cumb		99	E6
Bowsden	Northumb	123	E5
Bowside Lodge	Highld	157	C11
Bowston	Cumb	99	E6
Bowthorpe	Norf	68	D4
Box	Glos	37	D5
Box	Wilts	24	C3
Box End	Bedford	53	E8
Boxbush	Glos	36	C4
Boxford	Suff	56	E3
Boxford	W Berks	26	B2
Boxgrove	W Sus	16	D3
Boxley	Kent	29	D8
Boxmoor	Herts	40	D3
Boxted	Essex	56	F4
Boxted	Suff	56	D2
Boxted Cross	Essex	56	F4
Boxted Heath	Essex	56	F4
Boxworth	Cambs	54	C4
Boxworth End	Cambs	54	C4
Boyden Gate	Kent	31	C6
Boylestone	Derbys	75	F8
Boyndie	Aberds	153	B6
Boynton	E Yorks	97	C7
Boysack	Angus	135	E6
Boyton	Corn	8	E5
Boyton	Suff	57	E7
Boyton	Wilts	24	F4
Boyton Cross	Essex	42	D2
Boyton End	Suff	55	E8
Bozeat	Northants	53	D7

Bau-Boz 207

Chu–Cro

Column 1:

Churchtown Mers 85 C4
Churnside Lodge Northumb 109 B6
Churston Ferrers Torbay 7 D7
Churt Sur 27 F6
Churton Ches W 73 D8
Churwell W Yorks 88 B3
Chute Standen Wilts 25 D8
Chwilog Gwyn 70 D5
Chyandour Corn 2 C3
Cilan Uchaf Gwyn 70 E3
Cilcain Flint 73 C5
Cilcennin Ceredig 46 C4
Cilfor Gwyn 71 D7
Cilfrew Neath 34 D1
Cilfynydd Rhondda 34 E4
Cilgerran Pembs 45 E3
Cilgwyn Carms 33 B8
Cilgwyn Gwyn 82 F4
Cilgwyn Pembs 45 F2
Ciliau Aeron Ceredig 46 D3
Cill Donnain W Isles 148 F2
Cille Bhrighde W Isles 148 G2
Cille Pheadair W Isles 148 G2
Cilmery Powys 48 D2
Cilsan Carms 33 B6
Ciltalgarth Gwyn 72 E2
Cilwendeg Pembs 45 F4
Cilybebyll Neath 33 D8
Cilycwm Carms 47 F6
Cimla Neath 34 E1
Cinderford Glos 36 C3
Cippyn Pembs 45 E3
Circebost W Isles 154 D6
Cirencester Glos 37 D7
Ciribhig W Isles 154 C6
City London 41 F6
City Powys 60 F2
City Dulas Anglesey 82 C4
Clachaig Argyll 145 E10
Clachan Argyll 124 D3
Clachan Argyll 125 D7
Clachan Argyll 130 E2
Clachan Argyll 144 H6
Clachan Highld 149 E10
Clachan W Isles 148 D2
Clachan na Luib W Isles 148 B3
Clachan of Campsie E Dunb 119 B6
Clachan of Glendaruel Argyll 145 E8
Clachan-Seil Argyll 124 D3
Clachan Strachur Argyll 125 E6
Clachaneasy Dumfries 105 B7
Clachanmore Dumfries 104 E4
Clachbreck Argyll 144 F6
Clachnabrain Angus 134 C3
Clachtoll Highld 156 G3
Clackmannan Clack 127 E8
Clacton-on-Sea Essex 43 C7
Cladach Chireboist W Isles 148 B2
Cladach-knockline W Isles 148 B2
Cladich Argyll 125 C6
Claggan Highld 131 B5
Claggan Highld 147 G9
Claigan Highld 148 C7
Claines Worcs 50 D3
Clandown Bath 23 D8
Clanfield Hants 15 C7
Clanfield Oxon 38 D2
Clanville Hants 25 E8
Claonaig Argyll 145 H7
Claonel Highld 157 J8
Clap Hill Kent 19 B7
Clapgate Dorset 13 D8
Clapgate Herts 41 B7
Clapham Bedford 53 D8
Clapham London 28 B3
Clapham N Yorks 93 C7
Clapham W Sus 16 D4
Clappers Borders 122 D5
Clappersgate Cumb 99 D5
Clapton Som 12 D2
Clapton-in-Gordano N Som 23 B6
Clapton-on-the-Hill Glos 38 C1
Clapworthy Devon 9 B8
Clara Vale T&W 110 C4
Clarach Ceredig 58 F3
Clarbeston Pembs 32 B1
Clarbeston Road Pembs 32 B1
Clarborough Notts 89 F8
Clardon Highld 158 D3
Clare Suff 55 E8
Clarebrand Dumfries 106 C4
Clarencefield Dumfries 107 C7
Clarilaw Borders 115 C8
Clark's Green Sur 28 F2
Clarkston E Renf 119 D5
Clashandorran Highld 151 G8
Clashcoig Highld 151 B9
Clashindarroch Aberds 152 E4
Clashmore Highld 151 C10
Clashmore Highld 156 F3
Clashnessie Highld 156 F3
Clashnoir Moray 139 B8
Clate Shetland 160 G7
Clathy Perth 127 C8
Clatt Aberds 140 B4
Clatter Powys 59 E6
Clatterford IoW 15 F5
Clatterin Bridge Aberds 135 B6
Clatworthy Som 22 F2
Claughton Lancs 92 E5
Claughton Lancs 93 C5
Claughton Mers 85 F4
Claverdon Warks 51 C6
Claverham N Som 23 C6
Clavering Essex 55 F5
Claverley Shrops 61 E7
Claverton Bath 24 C2
Clawdd-newydd Denb 72 D4
Clawthorpe Cumb 92 B5
Clawton Devon 9 E5
Claxby Lincs 90 E5
Claxby Lincs 91 F7
Claxton Norf 69 D6
Claxton N Yorks 96 C2
Clay Common Suff 69 F7
Clay Coton Northants 52 B3
Clay Cross Derbys 76 C3
Clay Hill W Berks 26 B3
Clay Lake Lincs 66 B2
Claybokie Aberds 139 E6
Claybrooke Magna Leics 63 F8

Column 2:

Claybrooke Parva Leics 63 F8
Claydon Oxon 52 D2
Claydon Suff 56 D5
Claygate Dumfries 108 B3
Claygate Kent 29 E8
Claygate Sur 28 C2
Claygate Cross Kent 29 D7
Clayhanger Devon 10 B5
Clayhanger W Mid 62 D4
Clayhidon Devon 11 C6
Clayhill E Sus 18 C5
Clayhill Hants 14 D4
Claylock Highld 158 E3
Claypole Lincs 77 E8
Clayton S Yorks 89 D5
Clayton Staffs 75 E5
Clayton W Sus 17 C6
Clayton W Yorks 94 F4
Clayton Green Lancs 86 B3
Clayton-le-Moors Lancs 93 F7
Clayton-le-Woods Lancs 86 B3
Clayton West W Yorks 88 C3
Clayworth Notts 89 F8
Cleadale Highld 146 C7
Cleadon T&W 111 C6
Clearbrook Devon 6 C3
Clearwell Glos 36 D2
Cleasby N Yorks 101 C7
Cleat Orkney 159 K5
Cleatlam Durham 101 C6
Cleator Cumb 98 C2
Cleator Moor Cumb 98 C2
Clebrig Highld 157 F8
Cleckheaton W Yorks 88 B2
Clee St Margaret Shrops 61 F5
Cleedownton Shrops 61 F5
Cleehill Shrops 49 B7
Cleethorpes NE Lincs 91 D7
Cleeton St Mary Shrops 49 B8
Cleeve N Som 23 C6
Cleeve Hill Glos 37 B6
Cleeve Prior Worcs 51 E5
Clegyrnant Powys 59 D6
Clehonger Hereford 49 F6
Cleish Perth 128 E2
Cleland N Lanark 119 D8
Clench Common Wilts 25 C6
Clenchwarton Norf 67 B5
Clent Worcs 50 B4
Cleobury Mortimer Shrops 49 B8
Cleobury North Shrops 61 F6
Cleongart Argyll 143 F7
Clephanton Highld 151 F11
Clerklands Borders 115 B8
Clestrain Orkney 159 H4
Cleuch Head Borders 115 C8
Cleughbrae Dumfries 107 B7
Clevancy Wilts 25 B5
Clevedon N Som 23 B6
Cleveley Oxon 38 B3
Cleveleys Lancs 92 E3
Cleverton Wilts 37 F6
Clevis Bridgend 21 B7
Clewer Som 23 D6
Cley next the Sea Norf 81 C6
Cliaid W Isles 148 H1
Cliasmol W Isles 154 G5
Cliburn Cumb 99 B7
Click Mill Orkney 159 F4
Cliddesden Hants 26 E4
Cliff End E Sus 19 D5
Cliffburn Angus 135 E6
Cliffe Medway 29 B8
Cliffe N Yorks 96 F2
Cliffe Woods Medway 29 B8
Clifford Hereford 48 E4
Clifford W Yorks 95 E7
Clifford Chambers Warks 51 D6
Clifford's Mesne Glos 36 B4
Cliffsend Kent 31 C7
Clifton Bristol 23 B7
Clifton C Beds 54 F2
Clifton Cumb 99 B7
Clifton Derbys 75 E8
Clifton Devon 20 E4
Clifton N Yorks 94 E4
Clifton Northumb 117 F8
Clifton Nottingham 77 F5
Clifton Oxon 52 F2
Clifton S Yorks 89 E6
Clifton Stirling 131 F7
Clifton Worcs 50 E3
Clifton York 95 D8
Clifton Campville Staffs 63 C6
Clifton Green Gtr Man 87 D5
Clifton Hampden Oxon 39 E5
Clifton Reynes M Keynes 53 D7
Clifton upon Dunsmore Warks 52 B3
Clifton upon Teme Worcs 50 C2
Cliftoncote Borders 116 B4
Cliftonville Kent 31 B7
Climaen gwyn Neath 33 D8
Climping W Sus 16 D4
Climpy S Lanark 120 D2
Clink Som 24 E2
Clint N Yorks 95 D5
Clint Green Norf 68 C3
Clintmains Borders 122 F2
Cliobh W Isles 154 D5
Clippesby Norf 69 C7
Clipsham Rutland 65 C6
Clipston Northants 64 F4
Clipstone Notts 77 C5
Clitheroe Lancs 93 E7
Cliuthar W Isles 154 H6
Clive Shrops 60 B5
Clivocast Shetland 160 C8
Clixby Lincs 90 D5
Clocaenog Denb 72 D4
Clochan Moray 152 B4
Clock Face Mers 86 E3
Clockmill Borders 122 D3
Cloddiau Powys 60 D2
Clodock Hereford 35 B7
Clola Aberds 153 D10
Clophill C Beds 53 F8
Clopton Northants 65 F7
Clopton Suff 57 D6
Clopton Corner Suff 57 D6
Clopton Green Suff 55 D8
Close Clark IoM 84 E2
Closeburn Dumfries 113 E8
Closworth Som 12 C3
Clothall Herts 54 F3
Clotton Ches W 74 C2
Clough Foot W Yorks 87 B7
Cloughton N Yorks 103 E8
Cloughton Newlands N Yorks 103 E8
Clousta Shetland 160 H5
Clouston Orkney 159 G3
Clova Aberds 140 B3
Clova Angus 134 B3
Clove Lodge Durham 100 C4
Clovelly Devon 8 B5
Clovenfords Borders 121 F7
Clovenstone Aberds 141 C6
Clovullin Highld 130 C4
Clow Bridge Lancs 87 B6
Clowne Derbys 76 B4
Clows Top Worcs 50 B2
Cloy Wrex 73 E7
Cluanie Inn Highld 136 C3
Cluanie Lodge Highld 136 C3
Clun Shrops 60 F3
Clunbury Shrops 60 F3
Clunderwen Carms 32 C2
Clune Highld 138 B3
Clunes Highld 136 F5
Clungunford Shrops 49 B5
Clunie Aberds 153 C6
Clunie Perth 133 E8
Clunton Shrops 60 F3
Cluny Fife 128 E4
Cluny Castle Highld 138 E2
Clutton Bath 23 D8
Clutton Ches W 73 D8
Clwt-grugoer Conwy 72 C3
Clwt-y-bont Gwyn 83 E5
Clydach Mon 35 C6

Column 3:

Clydach Swansea 33 D7
Clydach Vale Rhondda 34 E3
Clydebank W Dunb 118 B4
Clydey Pembs 45 F4
Clyffe Pypard Wilts 25 B5
Clynder Argyll 145 E11
Clyne Neath 34 D2
Clynelish Highld 157 J11
Clynnog-fawr Gwyn 82 F4
Clyro Powys 48 E4
Clyst Honiton Devon 10 E4
Clyst Hydon Devon 10 D5
Clyst St George Devon 10 F4
Clyst St Lawrence Devon 10 D5
Clyst St Mary Devon 10 E4
Cnoc Amhlaigh W Isles 155 D10
Cnwch-coch Ceredig 47 B5
Coachford Aberds 152 D4
Coad's Green Corn 5 B7
Coal Aston Derbys 76 B3
Coalbrookdale Telford 61 D6
Coalbrookvale Bl Gwent 35 D5
Coalburn S Lanark 119 F8
Coalburns T&W 110 C4
Coalcleugh Northumb 109 E8
Coaley Glos 36 D4
Coalhall E Ayrs 112 C4
Coalhill Essex 42 E3
Coalpit Heath S Glos 36 F3
Coalport Telford 61 D6
Coalsnaughton Clack 127 E8
Coaltown of Balgonie Fife 128 E4
Coaltown of Wemyss Fife 128 E5
Coalville Leics 63 C8
Coalway Glos 36 C2
Coat Som 12 B2
Coatbridge N Lanark 119 C7
Coatdyke N Lanark 119 C7
Coate Swindon 38 F1
Coate Wilts 24 C5
Coates Cambs 66 E3
Coates Glos 37 D6
Coates Lancs 93 E8
Coates Notts 90 F2
Coates W Sus 16 C3
Coatham Redcar 102 B3
Coatham Mundeville Darl 101 B7
Coatsgate Dumfries 114 D3
Cobbaton Devon 9 B8
Cobbler's Green Norf 69 E5
Coberley Glos 37 C6
Cobham Kent 29 C7
Cobham Sur 28 C2
Cobholm Island Norf 69 D8
Cobleland Stirling 126 E4
Cobnash Hereford 49 C6
Coburty Aberds 153 B9
Cock Bank Wrex 73 E7
Cock Bridge Aberds 139 D8
Cock Clarks Essex 42 D4
Cockayne N Yorks 102 E4
Cockayne Hatley Cambs 54 E3
Cockburnspath Borders 122 B3
Cockenzie and Port Seton E Loth 121 B7
Cockerham Lancs 92 D4
Cockermouth Cumb 107 F8
Cockernhoe Green Herts 40 B4
Cockfield Durham 101 B6
Cockfield Suff 56 D3
Cockfosters London 41 E5
Cocking W Sus 16 C2
Cockington Torbay 7 C6
Cocklake Som 23 E6
Cockley Beck Cumb 98 D4
Cockley Cley Norf 67 D7
Cockshutt Shrops 60 B4
Cockthorpe Norf 81 C5
Cockwood Devon 10 F4
Cockyard Hereford 49 F6
Codda Corn 5 B6
Coddenham Suff 56 D5
Coddington Ches W 73 D8
Coddington Hereford 50 E2
Coddington Notts 77 D8
Codford St Mary Wilts 24 F4
Codford St Peter Wilts 24 F4
Codicote Herts 41 C5
Codmore Hill W Sus 16 B4
Codnor Derbys 76 E4
Codrington S Glos 24 B2
Codsall Staffs 62 D2
Codsall Wood Staffs 62 D2
Coed Duon = Blackwood Caerph 35 E5
Coed Mawr Gwyn 83 D5
Coed Morgan Mon 35 C7
Coed-Talon Flint 73 D6
Coed-y-bryn Ceredig 46 E2
Coed-y-paen Mon 35 E7
Coed-yr-ynys Powys 35 B5
Coed Ystumgwern Gwyn 71 E6
Coedely Rhondda 34 F4
Coedkernew Newport 35 F6
Coedpoeth Wrex 73 D6
Coedway Powys 60 C3
Coelbren Powys 34 C2
Coffinswell Devon 7 C6
Cofton Hackett Worcs 50 B5
Cogan V Glam 22 B3
Cogenhoe Northants 53 C6
Cogges Oxon 38 D3
Coggeshall Essex 42 B4
Coggeshall Hamlet Essex 42 B4
Coggins Mill E Sus 18 C2
Coig Peighinnean W Isles 155 A10
Coig Peighinnean Bhuirgh W Isles 155 B9
Coignafearn Lodge Highld 138 C2
Coilacriech Aberds 140 E2
Coilantogle Stirling 126 D4
Coilleag W Isles 148 G2
Coillore Highld 149 E8
Coity Bridgend 34 F3
Col W Isles 155 C9
Col Uarach W Isles 155 D9
Colaboll Highld 157 H8
Colan Corn 4 C3
Colaton Raleigh Devon 11 F5
Colbost Highld 148 D7
Colburn N Yorks 101 E6
Colby Cumb 100 B1
Colby IoM 84 E2
Colby Norf 81 D8
Colchester Essex 43 B6
Colcot V Glam 22 C3
Cold Ash W Berks 26 C3
Cold Ashby Northants 52 B4
Cold Ashton S Glos 24 B2
Cold Aston Glos 37 C8
Cold Blow Pembs 32 C2
Cold Brayfield M Keynes 53 D7
Cold Hanworth Lincs 90 F4
Cold Harbour Lincs 78 F2
Cold Hatton Telford 61 B6
Cold Hesleden Durham 111 E7
Cold Higham Northants 52 D4
Cold Kirby N Yorks 102 F3
Cold Newton Leics 64 D4
Cold Northcott Corn 8 F4
Cold Norton Essex 42 D4

Column 4:

Cold Overton Leics 64 C5
Coldbackie Highld 157 D9
Coldbeck Cumb 100 D2
Coldblow London 29 B6
Coldean Brighton 17 D7
Coldeast Devon 7 B6
Colden W Yorks 87 B7
Colden Common Hants 15 B5
Coldfair Green Suff 57 C8
Coldham Cambs 66 D4
Coldharbour Glos 36 D2
Coldharbour Kent 29 D6
Coldharbour Sur 28 E2
Coldingham Borders 122 C5
Coldrain Perth 128 D2
Coldred Kent 31 E6
Coldridge Devon 9 D8
Coldstream Angus 134 F3
Coldstream Borders 122 F4
Coldwaltham W Sus 16 C4
Coldwells Aberds 153 D11
Coldwells Croft Aberds 140 B4
Coldyeld Shrops 60 E3
Cole Som 23 F8
Cole Green Herts 41 C5
Cole Henley Hants 26 D2
Colebatch Shrops 60 F3
Colebrook Devon 10 D5
Colebrooke Devon 10 E2
Coleby Lincs 78 C2
Coleby N Lincs 90 C2
Coleford Devon 10 D2
Coleford Glos 36 C2
Coleford Som 23 E8
Colehill Dorset 13 D8
Coleman's Hatch E Sus 29 F5
Colemere Shrops 73 F8
Colemore Hants 26 F5
Coleorton Leics 63 C8
Colerne Wilts 24 B3
Cole's Cross Devon 7 E5
Cole's Green Suff 57 C6
Coles Green Suff 56 E4
Colesbourne Glos 37 C6
Colesden Bedford 54 D2
Coleshill Bucks 40 E2
Coleshill Oxon 38 E2
Coleshill Warks 63 F6
Colestocks Devon 11 D5
Colgate W Sus 28 F3
Colgrain Argyll 126 F2
Colinsburgh Fife 129 D6
Colinton Edin 120 C5
Colintraive Argyll 145 F9
Colkirk Norf 80 E5
Collace Perth 134 F2
Collafirth Shetland 160 G6
College Milton S Lanark 119 D6
Collessie Fife 128 C4
Collier Row London 41 E8
Collier Street Kent 29 E8
Collier's End Herts 41 B6
Collier's Wood London 28 B3
Colliery Row T&W 111 E6
Collieston Aberds 141 B9
Collin Dumfries 107 B7
Collingbourne Ducis Wilts 25 D7
Collingbourne Kingston Wilts 25 D7
Collingham Notts 77 C8
Collingham W Yorks 95 E6
Collington Hereford 49 C8
Collingtree Northants 53 D5
Collins Green Warr 86 E3
Colliston Angus 135 E6
Collycroft Warks 63 F7
Collynie Aberds 153 E8
Collyweston Northants 65 D6
Colmonell S Ayrs 104 A5
Colmworth Bedford 54 D2
Coln Rogers Glos 37 D7
Coln St Aldwyn's Glos 37 D8
Coln St Dennis Glos 37 C7
Colnabaichin Aberds 139 D8
Colnbrook Slough 27 B8
Colne Cambs 54 B4
Colne Lancs 93 E8
Colne Edge Lancs 93 E8
Colne Engaine Essex 56 F2
Colney Norf 68 D4
Colney Heath Herts 41 D5
Colney Street Herts 40 D4
Colpy Aberds 153 E6
Colquhar Borders 121 E6
Colsterworth Lincs 65 B6
Colston Bassett Notts 77 F6
Coltfield Moray 151 E14
Colthouse Cumb 99 E5
Coltishall Norf 69 C5
Coltness N Lanark 119 D8
Colton Cumb 99 F5
Colton Norf 68 D4
Colton N Yorks 95 E8
Colton Staffs 62 B4
Colton W Yorks 95 F6
Colva Powys 48 D4
Colvend Dumfries 107 D5
Colvister Shetland 160 D7
Colwall Green Hereford 50 E2
Colwall Stone Hereford 50 E2
Colwell Northumb 110 B2
Colwich Staffs 62 B4
Colwick Notts 77 E6
Colwinston V Glam 21 B8
Colworth W Sus 16 D3
Colwyn Bay = Bae Colwyn Conwy 83 D8
Colyford Devon 11 E7
Colyton Devon 11 E7
Combe Hereford 48 C5
Combe Oxon 38 C4
Combe W Berks 25 C8
Combe Common Sur 27 F7
Combe Down Bath 24 C2
Combe Florey Som 22 F3
Combe Hay Bath 24 D2
Combe Martin Devon 20 E4
Combe Moor Hereford 49 C5
Combe Raleigh Devon 11 D6
Combe St Nicholas Som 11 C8
Combeinteignhead Devon 7 B7
Comberbach Ches W 74 B3
Comberton Cambs 54 D4
Comberton Hereford 49 C6
Combpyne Devon 11 E7
Combridge Staffs 75 F7
Combrook Warks 51 D8
Combs Derbys 75 B7
Combs Suff 56 D4
Combs Ford Suff 56 D4
Combwich Som 22 E4
Comers Aberds 141 D5
Comins Coch Ceredig 58 F3
Commercial End Cambs 55 C6
Commins Capel Betws Ceredig 46 D5
Commins Coch Powys 58 D5
Common Edge Blackpool 92 F3
Common Side Derbys 76 B3
Commondale N Yorks 102 C4
Commonmoor Corn 5 C7
Commonside Ches W 74 B2
Compstall Gtr Man 87 E7
Compton Devon 7 C6
Compton Hants 15 B5
Compton Sur 27 E6

Column 5:

Compton Sur 27 E7
Compton W Berks 26 B3
Compton W Sus 15 C8
Compton Wilts 25 D6
Compton Abbas Dorset 13 C6
Compton Abdale Glos 37 C7
Compton Bassett Wilts 24 B5
Compton Beauchamp Oxon 38 F2
Compton Bishop Som 23 D5
Compton Chamberlayne Wilts 13 B8
Compton Dando Bath 23 C8
Compton Dundon Som 23 F6
Compton Martin Bath 23 D7
Compton Pauncefoot Som 12 B4
Compton Valence Dorset 12 E3
Comrie Fife 128 F2
Comrie Perth 127 B6
Conaglen House Highld 130 C4
Conchra Argyll 145 E9
Concraigie Perth 133 E8
Conder Green Lancs 92 D4
Conderton Worcs 50 F4
Condicote Glos 38 B1
Condorrat N Lanark 119 B7
Condover Shrops 60 D4
Coney Weston Suff 56 B3
Coneyhurst W Sus 16 B5
Coneysthorpe N Yorks 96 B3
Coneythorpe N Yorks 95 D6
Conford Hants 27 F6
Congash Highld 139 B6
Congdon's Shop Corn 5 B7
Congerstone Leics 63 D7
Congham Norf 80 E3
Congl-y-wal Gwynn 71 C8
Congleton Ches E 75 C5
Congresbury N Som 23 C6
Congreve Staffs 62 C3
Conicavel Moray 151 F12
Coningsby Lincs 78 D5
Conington Cambs 54 C4
Conington Cambs 65 F8
Conisbrough S Yorks 89 E6
Conisby Argyll 142 B3
Conisholme Lincs 91 E8
Coniston Cumb 99 E5
Coniston E Yorks 97 F7
Coniston Cold N Yorks 94 D2
Conistone N Yorks 94 C2
Connah's Quay Flint 73 C6
Connel Argyll 124 B5
Connel Park E Ayrs 113 C6
Connor Downs Corn 2 C4
Conon Bridge Highld 151 F8
Conon House Highld 151 F8
Cononley N Yorks 94 E2
Conordan Highld 149 E10
Consall Staffs 75 E6
Consett Durham 110 D4
Constable Burton N Yorks 101 E6
Constantine Corn 3 D6
Constantine Bay Corn 4 B3
Contin Highld 150 F7
Contlaw Aberdeen 141 D7
Conwy Conwy 83 D7
Conyer Kent 30 C3
Conyers Green Suff 56 C2
Cooden E Sus 18 E4
Cooil IoM 84 E3
Cookbury Devon 9 D6
Cookham Windsor 40 F1
Cookham Dean Windsor 40 F1
Cookham Rise Windsor 40 F1
Cookhill Worcs 51 D5
Cookley Suff 57 B7
Cookley Worcs 62 F2
Cookley Green Oxon 39 E6
Cookney Aberds 141 E7
Cookridge W Yorks 95 E5
Cooksbridge E Sus 17 C8
Cooksmill Green Essex 42 D2
Coolham W Sus 16 B5
Cooling Medway 29 B8
Coombe Corn 8 C4
Coombe Corn 4 D4
Coombe Hants 15 B7
Coombe Wilts 25 D6
Coombe Bissett Wilts 14 B2
Coombe Hill Glos 37 B5
Coombe Keynes Dorset 13 F6
Coombes W Sus 17 D5
Coopersale Common Essex 41 D7
Cootham W Sus 16 C4
Copdock Suff 56 E5
Copford Green Essex 43 B5
Copgrove N Yorks 95 C6
Copister Shetland 160 F6
Cople Bedford 54 E2
Copley Durham 101 B5
Coplow Dale Derbys 75 B8
Copmanthorpe York 95 E8
Coppathorne Corn 8 D4
Coppenhall Staffs 62 C3
Coppenhall Moss Ches E 74 D4
Copperhouse Corn 2 C4
Coppingford Cambs 65 F8
Copplestone Devon 10 D2
Coppull Lancs 86 C3
Coppull Moor Lancs 86 C3
Copsale W Sus 17 B5
Copster Green Lancs 93 F6
Copston Magna Warks 63 F8
Copt Heath W Mid 51 B6
Copt Hewick N Yorks 95 B6
Copt Oak Leics 63 C8
Copthorne Shrops 60 C4
Copthorne Sur 28 F4
Copy's Green Norf 80 D5
Copythorne Hants 14 C4
Corbets Tey London 42 F1
Corbridge Northumb 110 C2
Corby Northants 65 F5
Corby Glen Lincs 65 B6
Cordon N Ayrs 143 E11
Coreley Shrops 49 B8
Cores End Bucks 40 F2
Corfe Som 11 C7
Corfe Castle Dorset 13 F7
Corfe Mullen Dorset 13 E7
Corfton Shrops 60 F4
Corgarff Aberds 139 D8
Corhampton Hants 15 B7
Corlae Dumfries 113 E6
Corley Warks 63 F7
Corley Ash Warks 63 F6
Corley Moor Warks 63 F6
Cornaa IoM 84 D4
Cornabus Argyll 142 D4
Cornel Conwy 83 E7
Corner Row Lancs 92 F4
Corney Cumb 98 E3
Cornforth Durham 111 F6
Cornhill Aberds 152 C5
Cornhill-on-Tweed Northumb 122 F4
Cornholme W Yorks 87 B7
Cornish Hall End Essex 55 F7
Cornquoy Orkney 159 H6
Cornsay Durham 110 E4
Cornsay Colliery Durham 110 E4
Corntown Highld 151 F8
Corntown V Glam 21 B8
Cornwell Oxon 38 B2
Cornwood Devon 6 D4
Cornworthy Devon 7 D6

Column 6:

Corpach Highld 130 B4
Corpusty Norf 81 D7
Corran Highld 130 C4
Corran Highld 149 H13
Corranbuie Argyll 145 G7
Corrany IoM 84 D4
Corrie N Ayrs 143 D11
Corrie Common Dumfries 114 F5
Corriecravie N Ayrs 143 F10
Corriemoillie Highld 150 E6
Corriemulzie Lodge Highld 150 B6
Corrievarkie Lodge Perth 132 B2
Corrievorrie Highld 138 B3
Corrimony Highld 150 H6
Corringham Lincs 90 E2
Corringham Thurrock 42 F3
Corris Gwyn 58 D4
Corris Uchaf Gwyn 58 D4
Corrour Shooting Lodge Highld 131 C6
Corrow Argyll 125 E7
Corry Highld 149 F11
Corry of Ardnagrask Highld 151 G8
Corrykinloch Highld 156 G6
Corrymuckloch Perth 133 F5
Corrynachenchy Argyll 147 G9
Cors-y-Gedol Gwyn 71 E6
Corsback Highld 158 C4
Corscombe Dorset 12 D3
Corse Aberds 152 D6
Corse Glos 36 B4
Corse Lawn Worcs 50 F3
Corse of Kinnoir Aberds 152 D5
Corsewall Dumfries 104 C4
Corsham Wilts 24 B3
Corsindae Aberds 141 D5
Corsley Wilts 24 E3
Corsley Heath Wilts 24 E3
Corsock Dumfries 106 B4
Corston Bath 23 C8
Corston Wilts 37 F6
Corstorphine Edin 120 B4
Cortachy Angus 134 D3
Corton Suff 69 E8
Corton Wilts 24 E4
Corton Denham Som 12 B4
Coruanan Lodge Highld 130 C4
Corunna W Isles 148 B3
Corwen Denb 72 E4
Coryton Devon 9 F6
Coryton Thurrock 42 F3
Cosby Leics 64 E2
Coseley W Mid 62 E3
Cosgrove Northants 53 E5
Cosham Ptsmth 15 D7
Cosheston Pembs 32 D1
Cossall Notts 76 E4
Cossington Leics 64 C3
Cossington Som 23 E5
Costa Orkney 159 F4
Costessey Norf 68 C4
Costock Notts 64 B2
Coston Leics 64 B5
Cote Oxon 38 D3
Cotebrook Ches W 74 C2
Cotehill Cumb 108 D4
Cotes Cumb 99 F6
Cotes Leics 64 B2
Cotes Staffs 74 F5
Cotesbach Leics 64 F2
Cotgrave Notts 77 F6
Cothall Aberds 141 C7
Cotham Notts 77 E7
Cothelstone Som 22 F3
Cotherstone Durham 101 C5
Cothill Oxon 38 E4
Cotleigh Devon 11 D7
Cotmanhay Derbys 76 E4
Cotmaton Devon 11 F6
Coton Cambs 54 D5
Coton Northants 52 B4
Coton Staffs 62 B2
Coton Staffs 75 F6
Coton Clanford Staffs 62 B2
Coton Hill Shrops 60 C4
Coton Hill Staffs 75 F6
Coton in the Elms Derbys 63 C6
Cott Devon 7 C5
Cottam E Yorks 96 C5
Cottam Lancs 92 F4
Cottam Notts 77 B8
Cottartown Highld 151 H13
Cottenham Cambs 54 C5
Cotterdale N Yorks 100 E3
Cottered Herts 41 B6
Cotteridge W Mid 50 B5
Cotterstock Northants 65 E7
Cottesbrooke Northants 52 B5
Cottesmore Rutland 65 C6
Cotteylands Devon 10 C4
Cottingham E Yorks 97 F6
Cottingham Northants 64 E5
Cottingley W Yorks 94 F4
Cottisford Oxon 52 F3
Cotton Staffs 75 E7
Cotton Suff 56 C4
Cotton End Bedford 53 E8
Cottown Aberds 140 B4
Cottown Aberds 141 C6
Cottown Aberds 153 D8
Cotwalton Staffs 75 F6
Couch's Mill Corn 5 D6
Coughton Hereford 36 B2
Coughton Warks 51 C5
Coulaghailtro Argyll 144 G6
Coulags Highld 150 G2
Coulby Newham Mbro 102 C3
Coulderton Cumb 98 D1
Coulin Highld 150 F3
Coull Aberds 140 D4
Coull Argyll 142 B3
Coulport Argyll 145 E11
Coulsdon London 28 D3
Coulston Wilts 24 D4
Coulter S Lanark 120 F3
Coulton N Yorks 96 B2
Cound Shrops 61 D5
Coundon Durham 101 B7
Coundon W Mid 63 F7
Coundon Grange Durham 101 B7
Countersett N Yorks 100 F4
Countess Wilts 25 E6
Countess Wear Devon 10 F4
Countesthorpe Leics 64 E2
Countisbury Devon 21 E6
Coupar Angus Perth 134 E2
Coupland Northumb 122 F5
Cour Argyll 143 D9
Courance Dumfries 114 E3
Court-at-Street Kent 19 B7
Court Henry Carms 33 B6
Courteenhall Northants 53 D5
Courtsend Essex 43 E6
Courtway Som 22 F4
Cousland Midloth 121 C6
Cousley Wood E Sus 18 B3
Cove Argyll 145 E11
Cove Borders 122 B3
Cove Devon 10 C4
Cove Hants 27 D6
Cove Highld 155 H13
Cove Bay Aberdeen 141 D8
Cove Bottom Suff 57 B8

Column 7:

Covehithe Suff 69 F8
Coven Staffs 62 D3
Coveney Cambs 66 F4
Covenham St Bartholomew Lincs 91 E7
Covenham St Mary Lincs 91 E7
Coventry W Mid 51 B8
Coverack Corn 3 E6
Coverham N Yorks 101 F6
Covesea Moray 152 A1
Covington Cambs 53 B8
Covington S Lanark 120 F2
Cow Ark Lancs 93 E6
Cowan Bridge Lancs 93 B6
Cowbeech E Sus 18 D3
Cowbit Lincs 66 C2
Cowbridge Lincs 79 E6
Cowbridge Som 21 E8
Cowbridge = Y Bont-Faen V Glam 21 B8
Cowdale Derbys 75 B7
Cowden Kent 29 E5
Cowdenbeath Fife 128 E3
Cowdenburn Borders 120 D5
Cowers Lane Derbys 76 E3
Cowes IoW 15 E5
Cowesby N Yorks 102 F2
Cowfold W Sus 17 B6
Cowgill Cumb 100 F2
Cowie Aberds 141 F7
Cowie Stirling 127 F7
Cowley Devon 10 E4
Cowley Glos 37 C6
Cowley London 40 F3
Cowley Oxon 39 D5
Cowleymoor Devon 10 C4
Cowling N Yorks 94 E2
Cowling N Yorks 101 F7
Cowlinge Suff 55 D8
Cowpe Lancs 87 B6
Cowpen Northumb 117 F8
Cowpen Bewley Stockton 102 B2
Cowplain Hants 15 C7
Cowshill Durham 109 E8
Cowslip Green N Som 23 C6
Cowstrandburn Fife 128 E2
Cowthorpe N Yorks 95 D7
Cox Common Suff 69 F6
Cox Green Windsor 27 B6
Cox Moor Notts 76 D5
Coxbank Ches E 74 E3
Coxbench Derbys 76 E3
Coxford Norf 80 E4
Coxford Soton 14 C4
Coxheath Kent 29 D8
Coxhill Kent 31 E6
Coxhoe Durham 111 F6
Coxley Som 23 E7
Coxwold N Yorks 95 B8
Coychurch Bridgend 21 B8
Coylton S Ayrs 112 B4
Coylumbridge Highld 138 C5
Coynach Aberds 140 D3
Coynachie Aberds 152 E4
Coytrahen Bridgend 34 F2
Crabadon Devon 7 D5
Crabbs Cross Worcs 50 C5
Crabtree W Sus 17 B6
Crackenthorpe Cumb 100 B1
Crackington Haven Corn 8 E3
Crackley Warks 51 B7
Crackleybank Shrops 61 C7
Crackpot N Yorks 100 E4
Cracoe N Yorks 94 C2
Craddock Devon 11 C5
Cradhlastadh W Isles 154 D5
Cradley Hereford 50 E2
Cradley Heath W Mid 62 F3
Crafthole Corn 5 D8
Cragg Vale W Yorks 87 B8
Craggan Highld 139 B6
Craggie Highld 151 H10
Craggie Highld 157 H11
Craghead Durham 110 D5
Crai Powys 34 B2
Craibstone Moray 152 C4
Craichie Angus 135 E5
Craig Dumfries 106 B3
Craig Dumfries 106 C3
Craig Highld 150 G3
Craig Castle Aberds 140 B3
Craig-cefn-parc Swansea 33 D7
Craig Penllyn V Glam 21 B8
Craig-y-don Conwy 83 C7
Craig-y-nos Powys 34 C2
Craiganor Lodge Perth 132 D3
Craigdam Aberds 153 E8
Craigdarroch Dumfries 113 E7
Craigdarroch Highld 150 F7
Craigdhu Highld 150 G7
Craigearn Aberds 141 C6
Craigellachie Moray 152 D2
Craigencross Dumfries 104 C4
Craigend Perth 128 B3
Craigend Stirling 127 F6
Craigendive Argyll 145 E9
Craigendoran Argyll 126 F2
Craigends Renfs 118 C4
Craigens Argyll 142 B3
Craigens E Ayrs 113 C5
Craighall Edin 120 B4
Craighat Stirling 126 F4
Craighead Fife 129 D8
Craighlaw Mains Dumfries 105 C7
Craighouse Argyll 144 G4
Craigie Aberds 141 C8
Craigie Dundee 134 F4
Craigie Perth 128 B3
Craigie Perth 133 E8
Craigie S Ayrs 118 F4
Craigiefield Orkney 159 G5
Craigielaw E Loth 121 B7
Craiglockhart Edin 120 B5
Craigmalloch E Ayrs 112 E4
Craigmaud Aberds 153 C8
Craigmillar Edin 121 B5
Craigmore Argyll 145 G10
Craignant Shrops 73 F6
Craigneuk N Lanark 119 C7
Craigneuk N Lanark 119 D7
Craignure Argyll 124 B3
Craigo Angus 135 C6
Craigow Perth 128 D2
Craigrothie Fife 129 C5
Craigroy Moray 151 F14
Craigruie Stirling 126 B3
Craigston Castle Aberds 153 C7
Craigton Aberdeen 141 D7
Craigton Angus 134 D3
Craigton Angus 135 F5
Craigton Highld 151 B9
Craigton Highld 151 F9
Craigtown Highld 157 D11
Craik Borders 115 D6
Crail Fife 129 D8
Crailing Borders 116 B2
Crailinghall Borders 116 B2
Craiselound N Lincs 89 E8
Crakehill N Yorks 95 B7
Crakemarsh Staffs 75 F7
Crambe N Yorks 96 C3
Crambeck N Yorks 96 C3
Cramlington Northumb 111 B5
Cramond Edin 120 B4
Cramond Bridge Edin 120 B4
Cranage Ches E 74 C4
Cranberry Staffs 74 F5
Cranborne Dorset 13 C8
Cranbourne Brack 27 B7
Cranbrook Kent 18 B4

Column 8:

Cranbrook Common Kent 18 B4
Crane Moor S Yorks 88 D4
Crane's Corner Norf 68 C2
Cranfield C Beds 53 E7
Cranford London 28 B2
Cranford St Andrew Northants 53 B7
Cranford St John Northants 53 B7
Cranham Glos 37 C5
Cranham London 42 F1
Crank Mers 86 E3
Crank Wood Gtr Man 86 D4
Cranleigh Sur 27 F8
Cranley Suff 57 B5
Cranmer Green Suff 56 B4
Cranmore IoW 14 F4
Cranna Aberds 153 C6
Crannich Argyll 147 G8
Crannoch Moray 152 C4
Cranoe Leics 64 E4
Cransford Suff 57 C7
Cranshaws Borders 122 C2
Cranstal IoM 84 B4
Crantock Corn 4 C2
Cranwell Lincs 78 E3
Cranwich Norf 67 E7
Cranworth Norf 68 D2
Craobh Haven Argyll 124 E3
Crapstone Devon 6 C3
Crarae Argyll 125 F5
Crask Inn Highld 157 G8
Crask of Aigas Highld 150 G7
Craskins Aberds 140 D4
Craster Northumb 117 C8
Craswall Hereford 48 F4
Cratfield Suff 57 B7
Crathes Aberds 141 E6
Crathie Aberds 139 E8
Crathie Highld 137 E8
Crathorne N Yorks 102 D2
Craven Arms Shrops 60 F4
Crawcrook T&W 110 C4
Crawford Lancs 86 D2
Crawford S Lanark 114 B2
Crawfordjohn S Lanark 113 B8
Crawick Dumfries 113 C7
Crawley Hants 26 F2
Crawley Oxon 38 C3
Crawley W Sus 28 F3
Crawley Down W Sus 28 F4
Crawleyside Durham 110 E2
Crawshawbooth Lancs 87 B6
Crawton Aberds 135 B8
Cray N Yorks 94 B2
Cray Perth 133 C8
Crayford London 29 B6
Crayke N Yorks 95 B8
Crays Hill Essex 42 E3
Cray's Pond Oxon 39 F6
Creacombe Devon 10 C3
Creag Ghoraidh W Isles 148 D2
Creaguaineach Lodge Highld 131 C7
Creaksea Essex 43 E5
Creaton Northants 52 B5
Creca Dumfries 108 B2
Credenhill Hereford 49 E6
Crediton Devon 10 D3
Creebridge Dumfries 105 C8
Creech Heathfield Som 11 B7
Creech St Michael Som 11 B7
Creed Corn 3 B8
Creekmouth London 41 F7
Creeting Bottoms Suff 56 D5
Creeting St Mary Suff 56 D4
Creeton Lincs 65 B7
Creetown Dumfries 105 D8
Creg-ny-Baa IoM 84 D3
Creggans Argyll 125 E6
Cregneash IoM 84 F1
Cregrina Powys 48 D3
Creich Fife 128 B5
Creigiau Cardiff 34 F4
Cremyll Corn 6 D2
Creslow Bucks 39 B8
Cressage Shrops 61 D5
Cressbrook Derbys 75 B8
Cresselly Pembs 32 D1
Cressing Essex 42 B3
Cresswell Northumb 117 E8
Cresswell Staffs 75 F6
Cresswell Quay Pembs 32 D1
Creswell Derbys 76 B5
Cretingham Suff 57 C6
Cretshengan Argyll 144 G6
Crewe Ches E 74 D4
Crewe Ches W 73 D8
Crewgreen Powys 60 C3
Crewkerne Som 12 D2
Crianlarich Stirling 126 B2
Cribyn Ceredig 46 D4
Criccieth Gwyn 71 D5
Crich Derbys 76 D3
Crichie Aberds 153 D9
Crichton Midloth 121 C6
Crick Mon 36 E1
Crick Northants 52 B3
Crickadarn Powys 48 E2
Cricket Malherbie Som 11 C8
Cricket St Thomas Som 11 D8
Crickheath Shrops 60 B2
Crickhowell Powys 35 C6
Cricklade Wilts 37 E8
Cricklewood London 41 F5
Cridling Stubbs N Yorks 89 B6
Crieff Perth 127 B7
Criggion Powys 60 C2
Crigglestone W Yorks 88 C4
Crimond Aberds 153 C10
Crimonmogate Aberds 153 C10
Crimplesham Norf 67 D6
Crinan Argyll 144 D6
Cringleford Norf 68 D4
Cringles W Yorks 94 E3
Crinow Pembs 32 C2
Cripplesease Corn 2 C4
Cripplestyle Dorset 13 C8
Cripp's Corner E Sus 18 C4
Croasdale Cumb 98 C2
Crock Street Som 11 C8
Crockenhill Kent 29 C6
Crockernwell Devon 10 E2
Crockerton Wilts 24 E3
Crocketford or Ninemile Bar Dumfries 106 B5
Crockey Hill York 96 E2
Crockham Hill Kent 28 D5
Crockleford Heath Essex 43 B6
Crockness Orkney 159 J4
Croes-goch Pembs 44 B3
Croes-lan Ceredig 46 E2
Croes-y-mwyalch Torf 35 E7
Croeserw Neath 34 E2
Croesor Gwyn 71 C7
Croesyceiliog Carms 33 C5
Croesyceiliog Torf 35 E7
Croeswaun Gwyn 82 E4
Croft Leics 64 E2
Croft Lincs 79 C8
Croft Pembs 45 E3
Croft Warr 86 E4
Croft-on-Tees N Yorks 101 D7
Croftamie Stirling 126 F4
Croftmalloch W Loth 120 C2
Crofton W Yorks 88 C4

D

E

F

Felingwm uchaf Carms 33 B6
Felinwynt Ceredig 45 D4
Felixkirk N Yorks 102 F2
Felixstowe Suff 57 F6
Felixstowe Ferry Suff 57 F7
Felkington Northumb 122 E5
Felkirk W Yorks 88 C4
Fell Side Cumb 108 F3
Felling T&W 111 C5
Felmersham Bedford 53 D7
Felmingham Norf 81 E8
Felpham W Sus 16 E3
Felsham Suff 56 D3
Felsted Essex 42 B2
Feltham London 28 B2
Felthorpe Norf 68 C4
Felton Hereford 49 E7
Felton N Som 23 C7
Felton Northumb 117 D7
Felton Butler Shrops 60 C3
Feltwell Norf 67 E7
Fen Ditton Cambs 55 C5
Fen Drayton Cambs 54 C4
Fen End W Mid 51 B7
Fen Side Lincs 79 D6
Fenay Bridge W Yorks 88 C2
Fence Lancs 93 F8
Fence Houses T&W 111 D6
Fengate Norf 81 E7
Fengate Pboro 66 E2
Fenham Northumb 123 E6
Fenhouses Lincs 79 E5
Feniscliffe Blackburn 86 B4
Feniscowles Blackburn 86 B4
Feniton Devon 11 E6
Fenlake Bedford 53 E8
Fenny Bentley Derbys 75 D8
Fenny Bridges Devon 11 E6
Fenny Compton Warks 52 D2
Fenny Drayton Leics 63 E7
Fenny Stratford M Keynes 53 F6
Fenrother Northumb 117 E7
Fenstanton Cambs 54 C4
Fenton Cambs 54 B4
Fenton Lincs 77 B8
Fenton Lincs 77 D8
Fenton Stoke 75 E5
Fenton Barns E Loth 129 F7
Fenton Town Northumb 123 F5
Fenwick E Ayrs 118 E4
Fenwick Northumb 110 B3
Fenwick Northumb 123 E6
Fenwick S Yorks 89 C6
Feochaig Argyll 143 G8
Feock Corn 3 C7
Feolin Ferry Argyll 144 G3
Ferindonald Highld 149 H11
Feriniquarrie Highld 148 C6
Ferlochan Argyll 130 E3
Fern Angus 134 C4
Ferndale Rhondda 34 E4
Ferndown Dorset 13 D8
Ferness Highld 151 G12
Ferney Green Cumb 99 E6
Fernham Oxon 38 E2
Fernhill Heath Worcs 50 D3
Fernhurst W Sus 16 B2
Fernie Fife 128 C5
Ferniegair S Lanark 119 D7
Fernilea Highld 149 E8
Fernilee Derbys 75 B7
Ferrensby N Yorks 95 C6
Ferring W Sus 16 D4
Ferry Hill Cambs 66 F3
Ferry Point Highld 151 C10
Ferrybridge W Yorks 89 B5
Ferryden Angus 135 D7
Ferryhill Aberdeen 141 D8
Ferryhill Durham 111 F5
Ferryhill Station Durham 111 F6
Ferryside Carms 32 C4
Fersfield Norf 68 F3
Fersit Highld 131 B7
Ferwig Ceredig 45 E3
Feshiebridge Highld 138 D4
Fetcham Sur 28 D2
Fetterangus Aberds 153 C9
Fettercairn Aberds 135 B6
Fettes Highld 151 F8
Fewcott Oxon 39 B5
Fewston N Yorks 94 D4
Ffair-Rhos Ceredig 47 C6
Ffairfach Carms 33 B7
Ffaldybrenin Carms 46 E5
Ffarmers Carms 47 E5
Ffawyddog Powys 35 C6
Fforest Carms 33 D6
Fforest-fâch Swansea 33 E7
Ffos-y-ffin Ceredig 46 C3
Ffostrasol Ceredig 46 E2
Ffridd-Uchaf Gwyn 83 F5
Ffrith Wrex 73 D6
Ffrwd Gwyn 82 F4
Ffynnon ddrain Carms 33 B5
Ffynnon-oer Ceredig 46 D4
Ffynnongroyw Flint 85 F2
Fidden Argyll 146 J6
Fiddes Aberds 141 F7
Fiddington Glos 50 F4
Fiddington Som 22 E4
Fiddleford Dorset 13 C6
Fiddlers Hamlet Essex 41 D7
Field Staffs 75 F7
Field Broughton Cumb 99 F5
Field Dalling Norf 81 D6
Field Head Leics 63 D8
Fifehead Magdalen Dorset 13 B5
Fifehead Neville Dorset 13 C5
Fifield Oxon 38 C2
Fifield Wilts 25 D6
Fifield Windsor 27 B7
Fifield Bavant Wilts 13 B8
Figheldean Wilts 25 E6
Filands Wilts 37 F6
Filby Norf 69 C7
Filey N Yorks 97 A7
Filgrave M Keynes 53 E6
Filkins Oxon 38 D2
Filleigh Devon 9 B8
Filleigh Devon 10 C2
Fillingham Lincs 90 F3
Fillongley Warks 63 F6
Filton S Glos 23 B8
Fimber E Yorks 96 C4
Finavon Angus 134 D4
Finchairn Argyll 124 E5
Fincham Norf 67 D6
Finchampstead Wokingham 27 C5
Finchdean Hants 15 C8
Finchingfield Essex 55 F7
Finchley London 41 E5
Findern Derbys 76 F3
Findhorn Moray 151 E13
Findhorn Bridge Highld 138 B4
Findo Gask Perth 128 B2
Findochty Moray 152 B4
Findon Aberds 141 E8
Findon W Sus 16 D5
Findon Mains Highld 151 E9
Findrack Ho. Aberds 140 D5
Finedon Northants 53 B7
Fingal Street Suff 57 C6
Fingask Aberds 141 B6
Fingerpost Worcs 50 B2
Fingest Bucks 39 E7
Finghall N Yorks 101 F6
Fingland Cumb 108 D2
Fingland Dumfries 113 C7
Finglesham Kent 31 D7
Fingringhoe Essex 43 B6
Finlarig Stirling 132 F2
Finmere Oxon 52 F4
Finnart Perth 132 D2
Finningham Suff 56 C4
Finningley S Yorks 89 E7
Finnygaud Aberds 152 C5
Finsbury London 41 F6
Finstall Worcs 50 C4
Finsthwaite Cumb 99 F5
Finstock Oxon 38 C3
Finstown Orkney 159 G4
Fintry Aberds 153 C7
Fintry Dundee 134 F4
Fintry Stirling 126 F5
Finzean Aberds 140 E5
Fionnphort Argyll 146 J6
Fionnsbhagh W Isles 154 J5
Fir Tree Durham 110 F4
Firbeck S Yorks 89 F6
Firby N Yorks 96 C3
Firby N Yorks 101 F7
Firgrove Gtr Man 87 C7
Firsby Lincs 79 C7
Firsdown Wilts 25 F7
First Coast Highld 150 B2
Fishbourne IoW 15 E6
Fishbourne W Sus 16 D2
Fishburn Durham 111 F6
Fishcross Clack 127 E7
Fisher Place Cumb 99 C5
Fisherford Aberds 153 E6
Fisher's Pond Hants 15 B5
Fisherstreet W Sus 27 F7
Fisherton Highld 151 F10
Fisherton S Ayrs 112 C2
Fishguard = Abergwaun Pembs 44 B4
Fishlake S Yorks 89 C7
Fishleigh Barton Devon 9 B7
Fishponds Bristol 23 B8
Fishpool Glos 36 B3
Fishtoft Lincs 79 E6
Fishtoft Drove Lincs 79 E6
Fishtown of Usan Angus 135 D7
Fishwick Borders 122 D5
Fiskavaig Highld 149 E8
Fiskerton Lincs 78 B3
Fiskerton Notts 77 D7
Fitling E Yorks 97 F8
Fittleton Wilts 25 E6
Fittleworth W Sus 16 C4
Fitton End Cambs 66 C4
Fitz Shrops 60 C4
Fitzhead Som 11 B6
Fitzwilliam W Yorks 88 C5
Fiunary Highld 147 G9
Five Acres Glos 36 C2
Five Ashes E Sus 18 C2
Five Oak Green Kent 29 E7
Five Oaks Jersey 17
Five Oaks W Sus 16 B4
Five Roads Carms 33 D5
Fivecrosses Ches W 74 B2
Fivehead Som 11 B8
Flack's Green Essex 42 C3
Flackwell Heath Bucks 40 F1
Fladbury Worcs 50 E4
Fladdabister Shetland 160 K6
Flagg Derbys 75 C8
Flamborough E Yorks 97 B8
Flamstead Herts 40 C3
Flamstead End Herts 41 D6
Flansham W Sus 16 D3
Flanshaw W Yorks 88 B4
Flasby N Yorks 94 D2
Flash Staffs 75 C7
Flashader Highld 149 C8
Flask Inn N Yorks 103 D7
Flaunden Herts 40 D3
Flawborough Notts 77 E7
Flawith N Yorks 95 C7
Flax Bourton N Som 23 C7
Flaxby N Yorks 95 D6
Flaxholme Derbys 76 E3
Flaxley Glos 36 C3
Flaxpool Som 22 F3
Flaxton N Yorks 96 C2
Fleckney Leics 64 E3
Flecknoe Warks 52 C3
Fledborough Notts 77 B8
Fleet Hants 15 D8
Fleet Hants 27 D6
Fleet Lincs 66 B3
Fleet Hargate Lincs 66 B3
Fleetham Northumb 117 B7
Fleetlands Hants 15 D6
Fleetville Herts 40 D4
Fleetwood Lancs 92 E3
Flemingston V Glam 22 B2
Flemington S Lanark 119 D6
Flempton Suff 56 C2
Fleoideabhagh W Isles 154 J5
Fletchertown Cumb 108 E2
Fletching E Sus 17 B8
Flexbury Corn 8 D4
Flexford Sur 27 E7
Flimby Cumb 107 F7
Flimwell E Sus 18 B4
Flint = Y Fflint Flint 73 B6
Flint Mountain Flint 73 B6
Flintham Notts 77 E7
Flinton E Yorks 97 F8
Flintsham Hereford 48 D5
Flitcham Norf 80 E3
Flitton C Beds 53 F8
Flitwick C Beds 53 F8
Flixborough N Lincs 90 C2
Flixborough Stather N Lincs 90 C2
Flixton Gtr Man 86 E5
Flixton N Yorks 97 B6
Flixton Suff 69 F6
Flockton W Yorks 88 C3
Flodaigh W Isles 148 C3
Flodden Northumb 122 F5
Flodigarry Highld 149 A9
Flood's Ferry Cambs 66 E3
Flookburgh Cumb 92 B3
Florden Norf 68 E4
Flore Northants 52 C4
Flotterton Northumb 117 D5
Flowton Suff 56 E4
Flush House W Yorks 88 D2
Flushing Aberds 153 D10
Flushing Corn 3 C7
Flyford Flavell Worcs 50 D4
Foals Green Suff 57 B6
Fobbing Thurrock 42 F3
Fochabers Moray 152 C3
Fochriw Caerph 35 D5
Fockerby N Lincs 90 C2
Fodderletter Moray 139 B7
Fodderty Highld 151 F8
Foel Powys 59 C6
Foel-gastell Carms 33 C6
Foffarty Angus 134 E4
Foggathorpe E Yorks 96 F3
Fogo Borders 122 E3
Fogorig Borders 122 E3
Foindle Highld 156 E4
Folda Angus 134 C1
Fole Staffs 75 F7
Foleshill W Mid 63 F7
Folke Dorset 12 C4
Folkestone Kent 31 F6
Folkingham Lincs 78 F3
Folkington E Sus 18 E2
Folksworth Cambs 65 F8
Folkton N Yorks 97 B6
Folla Rule Aberds 153 E7
Follifoot N Yorks 95 D6
Folly Gate Devon 9 E7
Fonthill Bishop Wilts 24 F4
Fonthill Gifford Wilts 24 F4
Fontmell Magna Dorset 13 C6
Fontwell W Sus 16 D3
Foolow Derbys 75 B8
Foots Cray London 29 B5
Forbestown Aberds 140 C2
Force Mills Cumb 99 E5
Forcett N Yorks 101 C6
Ford Argyll 124 E4
Ford Bucks 39 D7
Ford Devon 9 B6
Ford Glos 37 B7
Ford Northumb 122 F5
Ford Shrops 60 C4
Ford Staffs 75 D7
Ford W Sus 16 D3
Ford Wilts 24 B3
Ford End Essex 42 C2
Ford Street Som 11 C6
Fordcombe Kent 29 E6
Fordell Fife 128 F3
Forden Powys 60 D2
Forder Green Devon 7 C5
Fordham Cambs 55 B7
Fordham Essex 43 B5
Fordham Norf 67 E6
Fordhouses W Mid 62 D3
Fordingbridge Hants 14 C2
Fordon E Yorks 97 B6
Fordoun Aberds 135 B7
Ford's Green Suff 56 C4
Fordstreet Essex 43 B5
Fordwells Oxon 38 C3
Fordwich Kent 31 D5
Fordyce Aberds 152 B5
Forebridge Staffs 62 B3
Forest Durham 109 F8
Forest Becks Lancs 93 D7
Forest Gate London 41 F7
Forest Green Sur 28 E2
Forest Hall Cumb 99 D7
Forest Head Cumb 109 D5
Forest Hill Oxon 39 D5
Forest Lane Head N Yorks 95 D6
Forest Lodge Argyll 131 E6
Forest Lodge Highld 139 C6
Forest Lodge Perth 133 B6
Forest Mill Clack 127 E8
Forest Row E Sus 28 F5
Forest Town Notts 77 C5
Forestburn Gate Northumb 117 E6
Foresterseat Moray 152 C1
Forestside W Sus 15 C8
Forfar Angus 134 D4
Forgandenny Perth 128 C2
Forge Powys 58 E4
Forge Side Torf 35 D6
Forgewood N Lanark 119 D7
Forgie Moray 152 C3
Forglen Ho. Aberds 153 C6
Formby Mers 85 D4
Forncett End Norf 68 E4
Forncett St Mary Norf 68 E4
Forncett St Peter Norf 68 E4
Forneth Perth 133 E7
Fornham All Saints Suff 56 C2
Fornham St Martin Suff 56 C2
Forres Moray 151 F13
Forrest Lodge Dumfries 113 F5
Forrestfield N Lanark 119 C8
Forsbrook Staffs 75 E6
Forse Highld 158 G4
Forse Ho. Highld 158 G4
Forsinain Highld 157 E12
Forsinard Highld 157 E11
Forsinard Station Highld 157 E11
Forston Dorset 12 E4
Fort Augustus Highld 137 D6
Fort George Guern 16
Fort George Highld 151 F10
Fort William Highld 131 B5
Forteviot Perth 128 C2
Forth S Lanark 120 D2
Forth Road Bridge Edin 120 B4
Forthampton Glos 50 F3
Fortingall Perth 132 E4
Forton Hants 26 E2
Forton Lancs 92 D4
Forton Shrops 60 C4
Forton Som 11 D8
Forton Staffs 61 B7
Forton Heath Shrops 60 C4
Fortrie Aberds 153 D6
Fortrose Highld 151 F10
Fortuneswell Dorset 12 G4
Forty Green Bucks 40 E2
Forty Hill London 41 E6
Forward Green Suff 56 D4
Fosbury Wilts 25 D8
Fosdyke Lincs 79 F6
Foss Perth 132 D4
Foss Cross Glos 37 D7
Fossebridge Glos 37 C7
Foster Street Essex 41 D7
Fosterhouses S Yorks 89 C7
Foston Derbys 75 F8
Foston Lincs 77 E8
Foston N Yorks 96 C2
Foston on the Wolds E Yorks 97 D7
Fotherby Lincs 91 E7
Fotheringhay Northants 65 E7
Foubister Orkney 159 H6
Foul Mile E Sus 18 D3
Foulby W Yorks 88 C4
Foulden Borders 122 D5
Foulden Norf 67 E7
Foulis Castle Highld 151 E8
Foulridge Lancs 93 E8
Foulsham Norf 81 E6
Fountainhall Borders 121 E7
Four Ashes Staffs 62 F2
Four Ashes Suff 56 B4
Four Crosses Powys 59 D7
Four Crosses Powys 60 C2
Four Crosses Wrex 73 D6
Four Elms Kent 29 E5
Four Forks Som 22 F4
Four Gotes Cambs 66 C4
Four Lane Ends Ches W 74 C2
Four Lanes Corn 3 C5
Four Marks Hants 26 F4
Four Mile Bridge Anglesey 82 D2
Four Oaks E Sus 19 C5
Four Oaks W Mid 62 E5
Four Oaks W Mid 63 F6
Four Roads Carms 33 D5
Four Roads IoM 84 F2
Four Throws Kent 18 C4
Fourlane Ends Derbys 76 D3
Fourlanes End Ches E 74 D5
Fourpenny Highld 151 B11
Fourstones Northumb 109 C8
Fovant Wilts 13 B8
Foveran Aberds 141 B8
Fowey Corn 5 D6
Fowley Common Warr 86 E4
Fowlis Angus 134 F3
Fowlis Wester Perth 127 B8
Fowlmere Cambs 54 E5
Fownhope Hereford 49 F7
Fox Corner Sur 27 D7
Fox Lane Hants 27 D6
Fox Street Essex 43 B6
Foxbar Renfs 118 C4
Foxcombe Hill Oxon 38 D4
Foxdale IoM 84 E2
Foxearth Essex 56 E2
Foxfield Cumb 98 F4
Foxham Wilts 24 B4
Foxhole Corn 4 D4
Foxhole Swansea 33 E7
Foxholes N Yorks 97 B6
Foxhunt Green E Sus 18 D2
Foxley Norf 81 E6
Foxley Wilts 37 F5
Foxt Staffs 75 E7
Foxton Cambs 54 E5
Foxton Durham 102 B1
Foxton Leics 64 E4
Foxup N Yorks 93 B8
Foxwist Green Ches W 74 C3
Foxwood Shrops 49 B8
Foy Hereford 36 B2
Foyers Highld 137 B7
Fraddam Corn 2 C4
Fraddon Corn 4 D4
Fradley Staffs 63 C5
Fradswell Staffs 75 F6
Fraisthorpe E Yorks 97 C7
Framfield E Sus 17 B8
Framingham Earl Norf 69 D5
Framingham Pigot Norf 69 D5
Framlingham Suff 57 C6
Frampton Dorset 12 E4
Frampton Lincs 79 F6
Frampton Cotterell S Glos 36 F3
Frampton Mansell Glos 37 D6
Frampton on Severn Glos 36 D4
Frampton West End Lincs 79 E5
Framsden Suff 57 D5
Framwellgate Moor Durham 111 E5
Franche Worcs 50 B3
Frankby Mers 85 F3
Frankley Worcs 62 F3
Frank's Bridge Powys 48 D3
Frankton Warks 52 B2
Frant E Sus 18 B2
Fraserburgh Aberds 153 B9
Frating Green Essex 43 B6
Fratton Ptsmth 15 E7
Freathy Corn 5 D8
Freckenham Suff 55 B7
Freckleton Lancs 86 B2
Freeby Leics 64 B5
Freehay Staffs 75 E7
Freeland Oxon 38 C4
Freester Shetland 160 H6
Freethorpe Norf 69 D7
Freiston Lincs 79 E6
Fremington Devon 20 F4
Fremington N Yorks 101 E5
Frenchay S Glos 23 B8
Frenchbeer Devon 9 F8
Frenich Stirling 126 D3
Frensham Sur 27 E6
Fresgoe Highld 157 C12
Freshfield Mers 85 D3
Freshford Bath 24 C2
Freshwater IoW 14 F4
Freshwater Bay IoW 14 F4
Freshwater East Pembs 32 E1
Fressingfield Suff 57 B6
Freston Suff 57 F5
Freswick Highld 158 D5
Fretherne Glos 36 D4
Frettenham Norf 68 C5
Freuchie Fife 128 D4
Freuchies Angus 134 C2
Freystrop Pembs 44 D4
Friar's Gate E Sus 29 F5
Friarton Perth 128 B3
Friday Bridge Cambs 66 D4
Friday Street E Sus 18 E3
Fridaythorpe E Yorks 96 D4
Friern Barnet London 41 E5
Friesland Argyll 146 F4
Friesthorpe Lincs 90 F4
Frieston Lincs 78 E2
Frieth Bucks 39 E7
Frilford Oxon 38 E4
Frilsham W Berks 26 B3
Frimley Sur 27 D6
Frimley Green Sur 27 D6
Frindsbury Medway 29 B8
Fring Norf 80 D3
Fringford Oxon 39 B6
Frinsted Kent 30 D2
Frinton-on-Sea Essex 43 B8
Friockheim Angus 135 E5
Friog Gwyn 58 C3
Frisby on the Wreake Leics 64 C3
Friskney Lincs 79 D7
Friskney Eaudike Lincs 79 D7
Friskney Tofts Lincs 79 D7
Friston E Sus 18 F2
Friston Suff 57 C8
Fritchley Derbys 76 D3
Frith Bank Lincs 79 E6
Frith Common Worcs 49 C8
Fritham Hants 14 C3
Frithelstock Devon 9 C6
Frithelstock Stone Devon 9 C6
Frithville Lincs 79 D6
Frittenden Kent 30 E2
Frittiscombe Devon 7 E6
Fritton Norf 68 E5
Fritton Norf 69 D7
Fritwell Oxon 39 B5
Frizinghall W Yorks 94 F4
Frizington Cumb 98 C2
Frocester Glos 36 D4
Frodesley Shrops 60 D5
Frodingham N Lincs 90 C2
Frodsham Ches W 74 B2
Frogden Borders 116 B3
Froggatt Derbys 76 B2
Froghall Staffs 75 E7
Frogmore Devon 7 E5
Frogmore Hants 27 D6
Frognall Lincs 65 C8
Frogshail Norf 81 D8
Frolesworth Leics 64 E2
Frome Som 24 E2
Frome St Quintin Dorset 12 D3
Fromes Hill Hereford 49 E8
Fron Denb 72 C4
Fron Gwyn 70 D4
Fron Gwyn 82 F5
Fron Powys 48 C2
Fron Powys 59 E8
Fron Powys 60 D2
Froncysyllte Wrex 73 E6
Frongoch Gwyn 72 F3
Frostenden Suff 69 F7
Frosterley Durham 110 F3
Frotoft Orkney 159 F5
Froxfield Wilts 25 C7
Froxfield Green Hants 15 B8
Froyle Hants 27 E5
Fryerning Essex 42 D2
Fryton N Yorks 96 B2
Fulbeck Lincs 78 D2
Fulbourn Cambs 55 D6
Fulbrook Oxon 38 C2
Fulford Som 11 B7
Fulford Staffs 75 F6
Fulford York 96 E2
Fulham London 28 B3
Fulking W Sus 17 C6
Full Sutton E Yorks 96 D3
Fullarton Glasgow 119 C6
Fullarton N Ayrs 118 F3
Fuller Street Essex 42 C3
Fuller's Moor Ches W 73 D8
Fullerton Hants 25 F8
Fulletby Lincs 79 B5
Fullwood E Ayrs 118 D4
Fulmer Bucks 40 F2
Fulmodestone Norf 81 D5
Fulnetby Lincs 78 B3
Fulstow Lincs 91 E7
Fulwell T&W 111 D6
Fulwood Lancs 92 F5
Fulwood S Yorks 88 F4
Fundenhall Norf 68 E4
Fundenhall Street Norf 68 E4
Funtington W Sus 15 D8
Funtley Hants 15 D6
Funtullich Perth 127 B6
Funzie Shetland 160 D8
Furley Devon 11 D7
Furnace Argyll 125 E6
Furnace Carms 33 D6
Furnace End Warks 63 E6
Furneaux Pelham Herts 41 B7
Furness Vale Derbys 87 F8
Furze Platt Windsor 40 F1
Furzehill Devon 21 E6
Fyfett Som 11 C7
Fyfield Essex 42 D1
Fyfield Glos 38 D2
Fyfield Hants 25 E7
Fyfield Oxon 38 E4
Fyfield Wilts 25 C6
Fylingthorpe N Yorks 103 D7
Fyvie Aberds 153 E7

G

Gabhsann bho Dheas W Isles 155 B9
Gabhsann bho Thuath W Isles 155 B9
Gablon Highld 151 B10
Gabroc Hill E Ayrs 118 D4
Gaddesby Leics 64 C3
Gadebridge Herts 40 D3
Gaer Powys 35 B5
Gaerllwyd Mon 35 E8
Gaerwen Anglesey 82 D4
Gagingwell Oxon 38 B4
Gaick Lodge Highld 138 F3
Gailey Staffs 62 C3
Gainford Durham 101 C6
Gainsborough Lincs 90 E2
Gainsborough Suff 57 E5
Gainsford End Essex 55 F8
Gairloch Highld 149 A13
Gairlochy Highld 136 F4
Gairney Bank Perth 128 E3
Gairnshiel Lodge Aberds 139 D8
Gaisgill Cumb 99 D8
Gaitsgill Cumb 108 E3
Galashiels Borders 121 F7
Galgate Lancs 92 D4
Galhampton Som 12 B4
Gallaberry Dumfries 114 F2
Gallachoille Argyll 144 E6
Gallanach Argyll 124 C4
Gallanach Argyll 146 E5
Gallantry Bank Ches E 74 D2
Gallatown Fife 128 E4
Galley Common Warks 63 E7
Galley Hill Cambs 54 C4
Galleyend Essex 42 D3
Galleywood Essex 42 D3
Gallin Perth 132 E2
Gallowfauld Angus 134 E4
Gallows Green Staffs 75 E7
Galltair Highld 149 F13
Galmisdale Highld 146 C7
Galmpton Devon 6 E4
Galmpton Torbay 7 D6
Galphay N Yorks 95 B5
Galston E Ayrs 118 F5
Galtrigill Highld 148 C6
Gamblesby Cumb 109 F6
Gamesley Derbys 87 E8
Gamlingay Cambs 54 D3
Gammersgill N Yorks 101 F5
Gamston Notts 77 B7
Ganarew Hereford 36 C2
Ganavan Argyll 124 B4
Gang Corn 5 C8
Ganllwyd Gwyn 71 E8
Gannochy Angus 135 B5
Gannochy Perth 128 B3
Gansclet Highld 158 F5
Ganstead E Yorks 97 F7
Ganthorpe N Yorks 96 B2
Ganton N Yorks 97 B5
Garbat Highld 150 E7
Garbhallt Argyll 125 F6
Garboldisham Norf 68 F3
Garden City Flint 73 C7
Garden Village W Yorks 95 F7
Garden Village Wrex 73 D7
Gardenstown Aberds 153 B7
Garderhouse Shetland 160 J5
Gardham E Yorks 97 E5
Gardin Shetland 160 G6
Gare Hill Som 24 E2
Garelochhead Argyll 145 D11
Garford Oxon 38 E4
Garforth W Yorks 95 F7
Gargrave N Yorks 94 D2
Gargunnock Stirling 127 E6
Garlic Street Norf 68 F5
Garlieston Dumfries 105 E8
Garlinge Green Kent 30 D5
Garlogie Aberds 141 D6
Garmond Aberds 153 C8
Garmony Argyll 147 G9
Garmouth Moray 152 B3
Garn-yr-erw Torf 35 C6
Garnant Carms 33 C7
Garndiffaith Torf 35 D6
Garndolbenmaen Gwyn 71 C5
Garnedd Conwy 83 F7
Garnett Bridge Cumb 99 E7
Garnfadryn Gwyn 70 D3
Garnkirk N Lanark 119 C6
Garnlydan Bl Gwent 35 C5
Garnswllt Swansea 33 D7
Garrabost W Isles 155 D10
Garraron Argyll 124 E4
Garras Corn 3 D6
Garreg Gwyn 71 C7
Garrick Perth 127 C7
Garrigill Cumb 109 E7
Garriston N Yorks 101 E6
Garroch Dumfries 113 F5
Garrogie Lodge Highld 137 C8
Garros Highld 149 B9
Garrow Perth 133 E5
Garryhorn Dumfries 113 E5
Garsdale Cumb 100 F2
Garsdale Head Cumb 100 E2
Garsdon Wilts 37 F6
Garshall Green Staffs 75 F6
Garsington Oxon 39 D5
Garstang Lancs 92 E4
Garston Mers 86 F2
Garswood Mers 86 E3
Gartcosh N Lanark 119 C6
Garth Bridgend 34 E2
Garth Gwyn 83 D5
Garth Powys 47 E8
Garth Shetland 160 H4
Garth Wrex 73 E6
Garth Row Cumb 99 E7
Garthamlock Glasgow 119 C6
Garthbrengy Powys 48 F2
Garthdee Aberdeen 141 D8
Gartheli Ceredig 46 D4
Garthmyl Powys 59 E8
Garthorpe Leics 64 B5
Garthorpe N Lincs 90 C2
Gartly Aberds 152 E5
Gartmore Stirling 126 E4
Gartnagrenach Argyll 144 H6
Gartness N Lanark 119 C7
Gartness Stirling 126 F4
Gartocharn W Dunb 126 F3
Garton E Yorks 97 F8
Garton-on-the-Wolds E Yorks 97 D5
Gartsherrie N Lanark 119 C7
Gartymore Highld 157 H13
Garvald E Loth 121 B8
Garvamore Highld 137 E8
Garvard Argyll 144 D2
Garvault Hotel Highld 157 F10
Garve Highld 150 E6
Garvestone Norf 68 D3
Garvock Aberds 135 B7
Garvock Invclyd 118 B2
Garway Hereford 36 B1
Garway Hill Hereford 35 B8
Gaskan Highld 130 B1
Gastard Wilts 24 C3
Gasthorpe Norf 68 F2
Gatcombe IoW 15 F5
Gate Burton Lincs 90 F2
Gate Helmsley N Yorks 96 D2
Gateacre Mers 86 F2
Gatebeck Cumb 99 F7
Gateford Notts 89 F6
Gateforth N Yorks 89 B6
Gatehead E Ayrs 118 F3
Gatehouse Northumb 116 F3
Gatehouse of Fleet Dumfries 106 D3
Gatelawbridge Dumfries 114 E2
Gateley Norf 81 E5
Gatenby N Yorks 101 F8
Gateshead T&W 111 C5
Gatesheath Ches W 73 C8
Gateside Aberds 140 C5
Gateside Angus 134 E4
Gateside E Renf 118 D4
Gateside Fife 128 D3
Gateside N Ayrs 118 D3
Gathurst Gtr Man 86 D3
Gatley Gtr Man 87 F6
Gattonside Borders 121 F8
Gatwick Airport W Sus 28 E3
Gaufron Powys 47 C8
Gaulby Leics 64 D3
Gauldry Fife 129 B5
Gaunt's Common Dorset 13 D8
Gautby Lincs 78 B4
Gavinton Borders 122 D3
Gawber S Yorks 88 D4
Gawcott Bucks 52 F4
Gawsworth Ches E 75 C5
Gawthorpe W Yorks 88 B3
Gawthrop Cumb 100 F1
Gawthwaite Cumb 98 F4
Gay Street W Sus 16 B4
Gaydon Warks 51 D8
Gayfield Orkney 159 C5
Gayhurst M Keynes 53 E6
Gayle N Yorks 100 F3
Gayles N Yorks 101 D6
Gayton Mers 85 F3
Gayton Norf 67 C7
Gayton Northants 52 D5
Gayton Staffs 62 B3
Gayton le Marsh Lincs 91 F8
Gayton le Wold Lincs 91 F6
Gayton Thorpe Norf 67 C7
Gaywood Norf 67 B6
Gazeley Suff 55 C8
Geanies House Highld 151 D11
Gearraidh Bhailteas W Isles 148 F2
Gearraidh Bhaird W Isles 155 E8
Gearraidh na h-Aibhne W Isles 154 D7
Gearraidh na Monadh W Isles 148 G2
Geary Highld 148 B7
Geddes House Highld 151 F11
Gedding Suff 56 D3
Geddington Northants 65 F5
Gedintailor Highld 149 E10
Gedling Notts 77 E6
Gedney Lincs 66 B4
Gedney Broadgate Lincs 66 B4
Gedney Drove End Lincs 66 B4
Gedney Dyke Lincs 66 B4
Gedney Hill Lincs 66 C3
Gee Cross Gtr Man 87 E7
Geilston Argyll 118 B3
Geirinis W Isles 148 D2
Geise Highld 158 D3
Geisiadar W Isles 154 D6
Geldeston Norf 69 E6
Gell Conwy 83 E8
Gelli Pembs 32 C1
Gelli Rhondda 34 E3
Gellideg M Tydf 34 D4
Gellifor Denb 72 C5
Gelligaer Caerph 35 E5
Gellilydan Gwyn 71 D7
Gellinudd Neath 33 D8
Gellyburn Perth 133 F7
Gellywen Carms 32 B3
Gelston Dumfries 106 D4
Gelston Lincs 78 E2
Gembling E Yorks 97 D7
Gentleshaw Staffs 62 C4
Geocrab W Isles 154 H6
George Green Bucks 40 F3
George Nympton Devon 10 B2
Georgefield Dumfries 115 E5
Georgeham Devon 20 F3
Georgetown Bl Gwent 35 D5
Gerlan Gwyn 83 E6
Germansweek Devon 9 E6
Germoe Corn 2 D4
Gerrans Corn 3 C7
Gerrards Cross Bucks 40 F3
Gestingthorpe Essex 56 F2
Geuffordd Powys 60 C2
Gib Hill Ches W 74 B3
Gibbet Hill Warks 64 F2
Gibbshill Dumfries 106 B4
Gidea Park London 41 F8
Gidleigh Devon 9 F8
Giffnock E Renf 119 D5
Gifford E Loth 121 C8
Giffordland N Ayrs 118 E2
Giffordtown Fife 128 C4
Giggleswick N Yorks 93 C8
Gilberdyke E Yorks 90 B2
Gilchriston E Loth 121 C7
Gilcrux Cumb 107 F8
Gildersome W Yorks 88 B3
Gildingwells S Yorks 89 F6
Gileston V Glam 22 C2
Gilfach Caerph 35 E5
Gilfach Goch Rhondda 34 F3
Gilfachrheda Ceredig 46 D3
Gillamoor N Yorks 102 F4
Gillar's Green Mers 86 E2
Gillen Highld 148 C7
Gilling East N Yorks 96 B2
Gilling West N Yorks 101 D6
Gillingham Dorset 13 B6
Gillingham Medway 29 C8
Gillingham Norf 69 E7
Gillock Highld 158 E4
Gillow Heath Staffs 75 D5
Gills Highld 158 C5
Gill's Green Kent 18 B4
Gilmanscleuch Borders 115 B6
Gilmerton Edin 121 C5
Gilmerton Perth 127 B7
Gilmonby Durham 100 C4
Gilmorton Leics 64 F2
Gilmourton S Lanark 119 E6
Gilsland Northumb 109 C6
Gilsland Spa Cumb 109 C6
Gilston Borders 121 D7
Gilston Herts 41 C7
Gilwern Mon 35 C6
Gimingham Norf 81 D8
Giosla W Isles 154 E6
Gipping Suff 56 C4
Gipsey Bridge Lincs 79 E5
Girdle Toll N Ayrs 118 E3
Girlsta Shetland 160 H6
Girsby N Yorks 102 D1
Girtford C Beds 54 D2
Girthon Dumfries 106 D3
Girton Cambs 54 C5
Girton Notts 77 C8
Girvan S Ayrs 112 E1
Gisburn Lancs 93 E8
Gisleham Suff 69 F8
Gislingham Suff 56 B4
Gissing Norf 68 F4
Gittisham Devon 11 E6
Gladestry Powys 48 D4
Gladsmuir E Loth 121 B7
Glais Swansea 33 D8
Glaisdale N Yorks 103 D5
Glame Highld 149 D10
Glamis Angus 134 E3
Glan Adda Gwyn 83 D5
Glan Conwy Conwy 83 D8
Glan-Conwy Conwy 83 F8
Glan-Duar Carms 46 E4
Glan-Dwyfach Gwyn 71 C5
Glan Gors Anglesey 82 D4
Glan-rhyd Gwyn 82 F4
Glan-traeth Anglesey 82 D2
Glan-y-don Flint 73 B5
Glan-y-nant Powys 59 F6
Glan-y-wern Gwyn 71 D7
Glan-yr-afon Anglesey 83 C6
Glan-yr-afon Gwyn 72 E3
Glan-yr-afon Gwyn 72 E4
Glanaman Carms 33 C7
Glandford Norf 81 C6
Glandwr Pembs 32 B2
Glandy Cross Carms 32 B2
Glandyfi Ceredig 58 E3
Glangrwyney Powys 35 C6
Glanmule Powys 59 E8
Glanrafon Ceredig 58 F3
Glanrhyd Gwyn 70 D3
Glanrhyd Pembs 45 E3
Glanton Northumb 117 C6
Glanton Pike Northumb 117 C6
Glanvilles Wootton Dorset 12 D4
Glapthorn Northants 65 E7
Glapwell Derbys 76 C4
Glas-allt Shiel Aberds 139 F8
Glasbury Powys 48 F3
Glaschoil Highld 151 H13
Glascoed Denb 72 B3
Glascoed Mon 35 D7
Glascoed Powys 59 C8
Glascorrie Aberds 140 E2
Glascote Staffs 63 D6
Glascwm Powys 48 D3
Glasdrum Argyll 130 E4
Glasfryn Conwy 72 D3
Glasgow Glasgow 119 C5
Glashvin Highld 149 B9
Glasinfryn Gwyn 83 E5
Glasnacardoch Highld 147 B9
Glasnakille Highld 149 G10
Glasphein Highld 148 D6
Glaspwll Powys 58 E4
Glassburn Highld 150 H6
Glasserton Dumfries 105 F8
Glassford S Lanark 119 E7
Glasshouse Hill Glos 36 B4
Glasshouses N Yorks 94 C4
Glasslie Fife 128 D4
Glasson Cumb 108 C2
Glasson Lancs 92 D4
Glassonby Cumb 109 F5
Glasterlaw Angus 135 D5
Glaston Rutland 65 D5
Glastonbury Som 23 F7
Glatton Cambs 65 F8
Glazebrook Warr 86 E4
Glazebury Warr 86 E4
Glazeley Shrops 61 F7
Gleadless S Yorks 88 F4
Gleadsmoss Ches E 74 C5
Gleann Tholàstaidh W Isles 155 C10
Gleaston Cumb 92 B2
Gleiniant Powys 59 E6
Glemsford Suff 56 E2
Glen Dumfries 106 B5
Glen Dumfries 106 D2
Glen Auldyn IoM 84 C4
Glen Bernisdale Highld 149 D9
Glen Ho Borders 121 F5
Glen Mona IoM 84 D4
Glen Nevis House Highld 131 B5
Glen Parva Leics 64 E2
Glen Sluain Argyll 125 F6
Glen Tanar House Aberds 140 E3
Glen Trool Lodge Dumfries 112 F4
Glen Village Falk 119 B8
Glen Vine IoM 84 E3
Glenamachrie Argyll 124 C5
Glenbarr Argyll 143 E7
Glenbeg Highld 139 B6
Glenbeg Highld 147 E8
Glenbervie Aberds 141 F6
Glenboig N Lanark 119 C7
Glenborrodale Highld 147 E9
Glenbranter Argyll 125 F7
Glenbreck Borders 114 B3
Glenbrein Lodge Highld 137 C7
Glenbrittle House Highld 149 F9
Glenbuchat Lodge Aberds 140 C2
Glenbuck E Ayrs 113 B7
Glenburn Renfs 118 C4
Glencalvie Lodge Highld 150 C7
Glencanisp Lodge Highld 156 G4
Glencaple Dumfries 107 C6
Glencarron Lodge Highld 150 F3
Glencarse Perth 128 B3
Glencassley Castle Highld 156 J7
Glenceitlein Highld 131 E5
Glencoe Highld 130 D4
Glencraig Fife 128 E3
Glencripesdale Highld 147 F9
Glencrosh Dumfries 113 F7
Glendavan Ho. Aberds 140 D3
Glendevon Perth 127 D8
Glendoe Lodge Highld 137 D7
Glendoebeg Highld 137 D7
Glendoick Perth 128 B4
Glendoll Lodge Angus 134 B2
Glendoune S Ayrs 112 E1
Glenduckie Fife 128 C4
Glendye Lodge Aberds 140 F5
Gleneagles Hotel Perth 127 C8
Gleneagles House Perth 127 D8
Glenegedale Argyll 142 C4
Glenelg Highld 149 G13
Glenernie Moray 151 G13
Glenfarg Perth 128 C3
Glenfarquhar Lodge Aberds 141 F6
Glenferness House Highld 151 G12
Glenfeshie Lodge Highld 138 E4
Glenfield Leics 64 D2
Glenfinnan Highld 147 C11
Glenfoot Perth 128 C3
Glenfyne Lodge Argyll 125 D8
Glengap Dumfries 106 D3
Glengarnock N Ayrs 118 D3
Glengorm Castle Argyll 146 F7
Glengrasco Highld 149 D9
Glenhead Farm Angus 134 C2
Glenhoul Dumfries 113 F6
Glenhurich Highld 130 C2
Glenkerry Borders 115 C5
Glenkiln Dumfries 106 B5
Glenkindie Aberds 140 C3
Glenlatterach Moray 152 C1
Glenlee Dumfries 113 F6
Glenlichorn Perth 127 C6
Glenlivet Moray 139 B7
Glenlochsie Perth 133 B7
Glenloig N Ayrs 143 E10
Glenluce Dumfries 105 D6
Glenmallan Argyll 125 F8
Glenmarksie Highld 150 F6
Glenmassan Argyll 145 E10
Glenmavis N Lanark 119 C7
Glenmaye IoM 84 E2
Glenmidge Dumfries 113 F8
Glenmore Argyll 124 D4
Glenmore Highld 149 D9
Glenmore Lodge Highld 139 D5
Glenmoy Angus 134 C4
Glenogil Angus 134 C4
Glenprosen Lodge Angus 134 C2
Glenprosen Village Angus 134 C3
Glenquiech Angus 134 C4
Glenreasdell Mains Argyll 145 H7
Glenree N Ayrs 143 F10
Glenridding Cumb 99 C5
Glenrossal Highld 156 J7
Glenrothes Fife 128 D4
Glensanda Highld 130 E2
Glensaugh Aberds 135 B6
Glenshero Lodge Highld 137 E8
Glenstockadale Dumfries 104 C4
Glenstriven Argyll 145 F9
Glentaggart S Lanark 113 B8
Glentham Lincs 90 E4
Glentirranmuir Stirling 127 E5
Glenton Aberds 140 B5
Glentress Borders 121 F5
Glentromie Lodge Highld 138 E3
Glentrool Village Dumfries 105 B7
Glentruan IoM 84 B4
Glentruim House Highld 138 E2
Glentworth Lincs 90 F3
Glenuig Highld 147 D9
Glenurquhart Highld 151 E10
Glespin S Lanark 113 B8
Gletness Shetland 160 H6
Glewstone Hereford 36 B2
Glinton Pboro 65 D8
Glooston Leics 64 E4
Glororum Northumb 123 F7
Glossop Derbys 87 E8
Gloster Hill Northumb 117 D8
Gloucester Glos 37 C5
Gloup Shetland 160 C7
Glusburn N Yorks 94 E3
Glutt Lodge Highld 157 F12
Glutton Bridge Staffs 75 C7
Glympton Oxon 38 B4
Glyn-Ceiriog Wrex 73 F6
Glyn-cywarch Gwyn 71 D7
Glyn Ebwy = Ebbw Vale Bl Gwent 35 D5
Glyn-neath = Glynedd Neath 34 D2
Glynarthen Ceredig 46 E2
Glynbrochan Powys 59 F6
Glyncoch Rhondda 34 E4
Glyncorrwg Neath 34 E2
Glynde E Sus 17 D8
Glyndebourne E Sus 17 C8
Glyndyfrdwy Denb 72 E5
Glynedd = Glyn-neath Neath 34 D2
Glynogwr Bridgend 34 F3
Glyntaff Rhondda 34 F4
Glyntawe Powys 34 C2
Gnosall Staffs 62 B2
Gnosall Heath Staffs 62 B2
Goadby Leics 64 E4
Goadby Marwood Leics 64 B4
Goat Lees Kent 30 E4
Goatacre Wilts 24 B5
Goathill Dorset 12 C4
Goathland N Yorks 103 D6
Goathurst Som 22 F4
Gobernuisgach Lodge Highld 156 E7
Gobhaig W Isles 154 G5
Gobowen Shrops 73 F7
Godalming Sur 27 E7
Godley Gtr Man 87 E7
Godmanchester Cambs 54 B3
Godmanstone Dorset 12 E4
Godmersham Kent 30 D4
Godney Som 23 E6
Godolphin Cross Corn 2 C5
Godre'r-graig Neath 34 D1
Godshill Hants 14 C2
Godshill IoW 15 F6
Godstone Sur 28 D4
Godwinscroft Hants 14 E2
Goetre Mon 35 D7
Goferydd Anglesey 82 C2
Goff's Oak Herts 41 D6
Gogar Edin 120 B4
Goginan Ceredig 58 F3
Golan Gwyn 71 C6
Golant Corn 5 D6
Golberdon Corn 5 B8
Golborne Gtr Man 86 E4
Golcar W Yorks 88 C2
Gold Hill Norf 66 E5
Goldcliff Newport 35 F7
Golden Cross E Sus 18 D2
Golden Green Kent 29 E7
Golden Grove Carms 33 C6

H

Hat–Hul 215

Gazetteer index entries, columns left to right:

Column 1:
Hatherton Ches E 74 E3; Hatherton Staffs 62 C3; Hatley St George Cambs 54 D3; Hatt Corn 5 C8; Hattingley Hants 26 F4; Hatton Aberds 153 E10; Hatton Derbys 63 B6; Hatton Lincs 78 B4; Hatton Shrops 60 E4; Hatton Warks 51 C7; Hatton Warr 86 F3; Hatton Castle Aberds 153 D7; Hatton Heath Ches W 73 C8; Hatton of Fintray Aberds 141 C7; Hattoncrook Aberds 141 B7; Haugh E Ayrs 112 B4; Haugh Gtr Man 87 C7; Haugh Lincs 79 B7; Haugh Head Northumb 117 B6; Haugh of Glass Moray 152 E4; Haugh of Urr Dumfries 106 C5; Haugham Lincs 91 F7; Haughley Suff 56 C4; Haughley Green Suff 56 C4; Haughs of Clinterty Aberdeen 141 C7; Haughton Notts 77 B6; Haughton Shrops 60 B3; Haughton Shrops 60 C3; Haughton Shrops 61 C6; Haughton Staffs 62 B2; Haughton Castle Northumb 110 B2; Haughton Green Gtr Man 87 E7; Haughton Moss Ches E 74 D2; Haultwick Herts 41 B6; Haunn Argyll 146 G6; Haunn W Isles 148 G2; Haunton Staffs 63 C6; Hauxley Northumb 117 D8; Hauxton Cambs 54 D5; Havant Hants 15 D8; Haven Hereford 49 D6; Haven Bank Lincs 78 D5; Haven Side E Yorks 91 B5; Havenstreet IoW 15 E6; Havercroft W Yorks 88 C4; Haverfordwest = Hwlffordd Pembs 44 D4; Haverhill Suff 55 E7; Haverigg Cumb 92 B1; Havering-atte-Bower London 41 E8; Haveringland Norf 81 E7; Haversham M Keynes 53 E6; Haverthwaite Cumb 99 F5; Haverton Hill Stockton 102 B2; Hawarden = Penarlâg Flint 73 C7; Hawcoat Cumb 92 B2; Hawen Ceredig 46 E2; Hawes N Yorks 100 F3; Hawes' Green Norf 68 E5; Hawes Side Blackpool 92 F3; Hawford Worcs 50 C3; Hawick Borders 115 C8; Hawk Green Gtr Man 87 F7; Hawkchurch Devon 11 D8; Hawkedon Suff 55 D8; Hawkenbury Kent 31 F6; Hawkenbury Kent 30 E2; Hawkeridge Wilts 24 D3; Hawkerland Devon 11 F5; Hawkes End W Mid 63 F7; Hawkesbury S Glos 36 F4; Hawkesbury Warks 63 F7; Hawkesbury Upton S Glos 36 F4; Hawkhill Northumb 117 C8; Hawkhurst Kent 18 B4; Hawkinge Kent 31 F6; Hawkley Hants 15 B8; Hawkridge Som 21 F7; Hawkshead Cumb 99 E5; Hawkshead Hill Cumb 99 E5; Hawksland S Lanark 119 F8; Hawkswick N Yorks 94 B2; Hawksworth Notts 77 E7; Hawksworth W Yorks 94 F4; Hawksworth W Yorks 95 F5; Hawkwell Essex 42 E4; Hawley Hants 27 D6; Hawley Kent 29 B6; Hawling Glos 37 B7; Hawnby N Yorks 102 F3; Haworth W Yorks 94 F3; Hawstead Suff 56 D2; Hawthorn Durham 111 E7; Hawthorn Rhondda 35 F5; Hawthorn Wilts 24 C3; Hawthorn Hill Brack 27 B6; Hawthorn Hill Lincs 78 D5; Hawthorpe Lincs 65 B7; Hawton Notts 77 D7; Haxby York 96 D2; Haxey N Lincs 89 E8; Hay Green Norf 66 C5; Hay-on-Wye = Y Gelli Gandryll Powys 48 E4; Hay Street Herts 41 B6; Haydock Mers 86 E3; Haydon Dorset 12 C4; Haydon Bridge Northumb 109 C8; Haydon Wick Swindon 37 F8; Haye Corn 5 C8; Hayes London 28 C5; Hayes London 40 F4; Hayfield Derbys 87 F8; Hayfield Fife 128 E4; Hayhill E Ayrs 112 C4; Hayhillock Angus 135 E5; Hayle Corn 2 C4; Haynes C Beds 53 E8; Haynes Church End C Beds 53 E8; Hayscastle Pembs 44 C3; Hayscastle Cross Pembs 44 C4; Hayshead Angus 135 E6; Hayton Aberdeen 141 D8; Hayton Cumb 107 E8; Hayton Cumb 108 D5; Hayton E Yorks 96 E4; Hayton Notts 89 F8; Hayton's Bent Shrops 60 F5; Haytor Vale Devon 7 B5; Haywards Heath W Sus 17 B7; Haywood S Yorks 89 C6; Haywood Oaks Notts 77 D6; Hazel Grove Gtr Man 87 F7; Hazel Street Kent 18 B3; Hazelbank S Lanark 119 E8; Hazelbury Bryan Dorset 12 D5; Hazeley Hants 26 D5; Hazelhurst Gtr Man 87 D7; Hazelslade Staffs 62 C4; Hazelton Glos 37 C7; Hazelton Walls Fife 128 B5; Hazelwood Derbys 76 E3; Hazlemere Bucks 40 E1; Hazlerigg T&W 110 B5; Hazlewood N Yorks 94 D3; Hazon Northumb 117 D7; Heacham Norf 80 D2; Head of Muir Falk 127 F7; Headbourne Worthy Hants 26 F2; Headbrook Hereford 48 D5; Headcorn Kent 30 E2; Headingley W Yorks 95 F5; Headington Oxon 39 D5; Headlam Durham 101 C6; Headless Cross Worcs 50 C5; Headley Hants 26 F5; Headley Hants 27 F6;

Column 2:
Headley Sur 28 D3; Headon Notts 77 B7; Heads S Lanark 119 E7; Heads Nook Cumb 108 D4; Heage Derbys 76 D3; Healaugh N Yorks 95 F7; Healaugh N Yorks 101 E5; Heald Green Gtr Man 87 F6; Heale Devon 20 E5; Heale Som 23 E8; Healey Gtr Man 87 C6; Healey N Yorks 101 F6; Healey Northumb 110 D3; Healing NE Lincs 91 C6; Heamoor Corn 2 C3; Heanish Argyll 146 G3; Heanor Derbys 76 E4; Heanton Punchardon Devon 20 F4; Heapham Lincs 90 F2; Hearthstane Borders 114 B4; Heasley Mill Devon 21 F6; Heast Highld 149 G11; Heath Cardiff 22 B3; Heath Derbys 76 C4; Heath and Reach C Beds 40 B2; Heath End Hants 26 C3; Heath End Sur 27 E6; Heath End Warks 51 C7; Heath Hayes Staffs 62 C4; Heath Hill Shrops 61 C7; Heath House Som 23 E6; Heathcote Derbys 75 C8; Heather Leics 63 C7; Heatherfield Highld 149 D9; Heathfield Devon 7 B6; Heathfield E Sus 18 C2; Heathfield Som 11 B6; Heathhall Dumfries 107 B6; Heathrow Airport London 27 B8; Heathstock Devon 11 D7; Heathton Shrops 62 E2; Heatley Warr 86 F5; Heaton Lancs 92 C4; Heaton Staffs 75 C6; Heaton T&W 111 C5; Heaton W Yorks 94 F4; Heaton Moor Gtr Man 87 E6; Heaverham Kent 29 D6; Heaviley Gtr Man 87 F7; Heavitree Devon 10 E4; Hebburn T&W 111 C6; Hebden N Yorks 94 C3; Hebden Bridge W Yorks 87 B7; Hebron Anglesey 82 C4; Hebron Carms 32 B2; Hebron Northumb 117 F7; Heck Dumfries 114 F3; Heckfield Hants 26 C5; Heckfield Green Suff 57 B5; Heckfordbridge Essex 43 B5; Heckington Lincs 78 E4; Heckmondwike W Yorks 88 B3; Heddington Wilts 24 C4; Heddle Orkney 159 G4; Heddon-on-the-Wall Northumb 110 C4; Hedenham Norf 69 E6; Hedge End Hants 15 C5; Hedgerley Bucks 40 F2; Hedging Som 11 B8; Hedley on the Hill Northumb 110 D3; Hednesford Staffs 62 C4; Hedon E Yorks 91 B5; Hedsor Bucks 40 F2; Hedworth T&W 111 C6; Hegdon Hill Hereford 49 D7; Heggerscales Cumb 100 C3; Heglibister Shetland 160 H5; Heighington Darl 101 B7; Heighington Lincs 78 C3; Heights of Brae Highld 151 E8; Heights of Kinlochewe Highld 150 E3; Heilam Highld 156 C7; Heiton Borders 122 F3; Hele Devon 10 D4; Hele Devon 20 E4; Helensburgh Argyll 145 E11; Helford Corn 3 D6; Helford Passage Corn 3 D6; Helhoughton Norf 80 E4; Helions Bumpstead Essex 55 E7; Hellaby S Yorks 89 E6; Helland Corn 5 B5; Hellesdon Norf 68 C5; Hellidon Northants 52 D3; Hellifield N Yorks 93 D8; Hellingly E Sus 18 D2; Hellington Norf 69 D6; Hellister Shetland 160 J5; Helm Northumb 117 E7; Helmdon Northants 52 E3; Helmingham Suff 57 D5; Helmington Row Durham 110 F4; Helmsdale Highld 157 H13; Helmshore Lancs 87 B5; Helmsley N Yorks 102 F4; Helperby N Yorks 95 C7; Helperthorpe N Yorks 97 B5; Helpringham Lincs 78 E4; Helpston Pboro 65 D8; Helsby Ches W 73 B8; Helsey Lincs 79 B8; Helston Corn 3 D5; Helstone Corn 8 F2; Helton Cumb 99 B7; Helwith Bridge N Yorks 93 C8; Hemblington Norf 69 C6; Hemel Hempstead Herts 40 D3; Hemingbrough N Yorks 96 F2; Hemingby Lincs 78 B5; Hemingford Abbots Cambs 54 B3; Hemingford Grey Cambs 54 B3; Hemingstone Suff 57 D5; Hemington Leics 63 B8; Hemington Northants 65 F7; Hemington Som 24 D2; Hemley Suff 57 E6; Hemlington Mbro 102 C3; Hemp Green Suff 57 C7; Hempholme E Yorks 97 D6; Hempnall Norf 68 E5; Hempnall Green Norf 68 E5; Hempriggs House Highld 158 F5; Hempstead Essex 55 F7; Hempstead Medway 29 C8; Hempstead Norf 81 D7; Hempstead Norf 69 C7; Hempsted Glos 37 C5; Hempton Norf 80 E5; Hempton Oxon 52 F2; Hemsby Norf 69 C7; Hemswell Lincs 90 E3; Hemswell Cliff Lincs 90 F3; Hemsworth W Yorks 88 C5; Hemyock Devon 11 C6; Hen-feddau fawr Pembs 45 F4; Henbury Bristol 23 B7; Henbury Ches E 75 B5; Hendon London 41 F5; Hendon T&W 111 D7;

Column 3:
Hendre Flint 73 C5; Hendre-ddu Conwy 83 E8; Hendreforgan Rhondda 34 F3; Hendy Carms 33 D6; Heneglwys Anglesey 82 D4; Henfield W Sus 17 C6; Henford Devon 9 E5; Hengherst Kent 19 B6; Hengoed Caerph 35 E5; Hengoed Powys 48 D4; Hengoed Shrops 73 F6; Hengrave Suff 56 C2; Henham Essex 41 B8; Heniarth Powys 59 D8; Henlade Som 11 B7; Henley Shrops 49 B7; Henley Som 23 F6; Henley Suff 57 D5; Henley W Sus 16 B2; Henley-in-Arden Warks 51 C6; Henley-on-Thames Oxon 39 F7; Henley's Down E Sus 18 D4; Henllan Ceredig 46 E2; Henllan Denb 72 C4; Henllan Amgoed Carms 32 B2; Henllys Torf 35 E6; Henlow C Beds 54 F2; Hennock Devon 10 F3; Henny Street Essex 56 F2; Henryd Conwy 83 D7; Henry's Moat Pembs 32 B1; Hensall N Yorks 89 B6; Henshaw Northumb 109 C7; Hensingham Cumb 98 C1; Henstead Suff 69 F7; Henstridge Som 12 C5; Henstridge Ash Som 12 B5; Henstridge Marsh Som 12 B5; Henton Oxon 39 D7; Henton Som 23 E6; Henwood Corn 5 B7; Heogan Shetland 160 J6; Heol-las Swansea 33 E7; Heol Senni Powys 34 B3; Heol-y-Cyw Bridgend 34 F3; Hepburn Northumb 117 B6; Hepple Northumb 117 D5; Hepscott Northumb 117 F8; Heptonstall W Yorks 87 B7; Hepworth Suff 56 B3; Hepworth W Yorks 88 D2; Herbrandston Pembs 44 E3; Hereford Hereford 49 E7; Heriot Borders 121 D6; Hermiston Edin 120 B4; Hermitage Borders 115 E8; Hermitage Dorset 12 D4; Hermitage W Berks 26 B3; Hermitage W Sus 15 D8; Hermon Anglesey 82 E3; Hermon Carms 33 B7; Hermon Carms 46 F2; Hermon Pembs 45 F4; Herne Kent 31 C5; Herne Bay Kent 31 C5; Herner Devon 9 B7; Hernhill Kent 30 C4; Herodsfoot Corn 5 C7; Herongate Essex 42 E2; Heronsford S Ayrs 104 A5; Herriard Hants 26 E4; Herringfleet Suff 69 E7; Herringswell Suff 55 B8; Hersden Kent 31 C6; Hersham Corn 8 D4; Hersham Sur 28 C2; Herstmonceux E Sus 18 D3; Herston Orkney 159 J5; Hertford Herts 41 C6; Hertford Heath Herts 41 C6; Hertingfordbury Herts 41 C6; Hesket Newmarket Cumb 108 F3; Hesketh Bank Lancs 86 B2; Hesketh Lane Lancs 93 E6; Heskin Green Lancs 86 C3; Hesleden Durham 111 F7; Hesleyside Northumb 116 F4; Heslington York 96 D2; Hessay York 95 D8; Hessenford Corn 5 D8; Hessett Suff 56 C3; Hessle E Yorks 90 B4; Hest Bank Lancs 92 C4; Heston London 28 B2; Hestwall Orkney 159 G3; Heswall Mers 85 F3; Hethe Oxon 39 B5; Hethel Norf 68 D4; Hethersett Norf 68 D4; Hethersgill Cumb 108 C4; Hethpool Northumb 116 B4; Hett Durham 111 F5; Hetton N Yorks 94 D2; Hetton-le-Hole T&W 111 E6; Hetton Steads Northumb 123 F6; Heugh Northumb 110 B3; Heugh-head Aberds 140 C2; Heveningham Suff 57 B7; Hever Kent 29 E5; Heversham Cumb 99 F6; Hevingham Norf 81 E7; Hewas Water Corn 3 B8; Hewelsfield Glos 36 D2; Hewish N Som 23 C6; Hewish Som 12 D2; Heworth York 96 D2; Hexham Northumb 110 C2; Hextable Kent 29 B6; Hexton Herts 54 F2; Hexworthy Devon 6 B4; Hey Lancs 93 E8; Heybridge Essex 42 D4; Heybridge Essex 42 E2; Heybridge Basin Essex 42 D4; Heybrook Bay Devon 6 E3; Heydon Cambs 54 E5; Heydon Norf 81 E7; Heydour Lincs 78 F3; Heylipoll Argyll 146 G2; Heylor Shetland 160 E4; Heysham Lancs 92 C4; Heyshott W Sus 16 C2; Heytesbury Wilts 24 E4; Heythrop Oxon 38 B3; Heywood Gtr Man 87 C6; Heywood Wilts 24 D3; Hibaldstow N Lincs 90 D3; Hickleton S Yorks 89 D5; Hickling Norf 69 B7; Hickling Notts 64 B3; Hickling Green Norf 69 B7; Hickling Heath Norf 69 B7; Hickstead W Sus 17 B6; Hidcote Boyce Glos 51 E6; High Ackworth W Yorks 88 C5; High Bankhill Cumb 109 E5; High Barnes T&W 111 D6; High Beach Essex 41 E7; High Bentham N Yorks 93 C6; High Bickington Devon 9 B7; High Birkwith N Yorks 93 B7; High Blantyre S Lanark 119 D6; High Bonnybridge Falk 119 B8; High Bradfield S Yorks 88 E3; High Bray Devon 21 F5; High Brooms Kent 29 E6;

Column 4:
High Bullen Devon 9 B7; High Buston Northumb 117 D8; High Callerton Northumb 110 B4; High Catton E Yorks 96 D3; High Cogges Oxon 38 D3; High Conisclifffe Darl 101 C7; High Cross Hants 15 B8; High Cross Herts 41 C6; High Easter Essex 42 C2; High Eggborough N Yorks 89 B6; High Ellington N Yorks 101 F6; High Ercall Telford 61 C5; High Etherley Durham 101 B6; High Garrett Essex 42 B3; High Grange Durham 110 F4; High Green Norf 68 D4; High Green S Yorks 88 E4; High Green Worcs 50 E3; High Halden Kent 19 B5; High Halstow Medway 29 B8; High Ham Som 23 F6; High Harrington Cumb 98 B2; High Hatton Shrops 61 B6; High Hawsker N Yorks 103 D7; High Hesket Cumb 108 E4; High Hesleden Durham 111 F7; High Hoyland S Yorks 88 C3; High Hunsley E Yorks 97 F5; High Hurstwood E Sus 17 B8; High Hutton N Yorks 96 C3; High Ireby Cumb 108 F2; High Kelling Norf 81 C7; High Kilburn N Yorks 95 B8; High Lands Durham 101 B6; High Lane Gtr Man 87 F7; High Lane Worcs 49 C8; High Laver Essex 41 D8; High Legh Ches E 86 F5; High Leven Stockton 102 C2; High Littleton Bath 23 D8; High Lorton Cumb 98 B3; High Marishes N Yorks 96 B4; High Marnham Notts 77 B8; High Melton S Yorks 89 D6; High Mickley Northumb 110 C3; High Mindork Dumfries 105 D7; High Moorsley T&W 111 E6; High Newton Cumb 99 F6; High Newton-by-the-Sea Northumb 117 B8; High Nibthwaite Cumb 98 F4; High Offley Staffs 61 B7; High Ongar Essex 42 D1; High Onn Staffs 62 C2; High Roding Essex 42 C2; High Row Cumb 108 F3; High Salvington W Sus 16 D5; High Sellafield Cumb 98 D2; High Shaw N Yorks 100 F3; High Spen T&W 110 D4; High Stoop Durham 110 E4; High Street Corn 4 D4; High Street Kent 18 B4; High Street Suff 56 F2; High Street Suff 57 B8; High Street Suff 57 D8; High Street Green Suff 56 D4; High Throston Hrtlpl 111 F7; High Toynton Lincs 79 C5; High Trewhitt Northumb 117 D6; High Valleyfield Fife 128 F2; High Westwood Durham 110 D4; High Wray Cumb 99 E5; High Wych Herts 41 C7; High Wycombe Bucks 40 E1; Higham Derbys 76 D3; Higham Kent 29 B8; Higham Lancs 93 F8; Higham Suff 55 B8; Higham Suff 56 F4; Higham Dykes Northumb 110 B4; Higham Ferrers Northants 53 C7; Higham Gobion C Beds 54 F2; Higham on the Hill Leics 63 E7; Higham Wood Kent 29 E6; Highampton Devon 9 D6; Highbridge Highld 136 F4; Highbridge Som 22 E5; Highbrook W Sus 28 F4; Highburton W Yorks 88 C2; Highbury Som 23 E8; Highclere Hants 26 C2; Highcliffe Dorset 14 E3; Higher Ansty Dorset 13 D5; Higher Ashton Devon 10 F3; Higher Ballam Lancs 92 F3; Higher Bartle Lancs 92 F5; Higher Boscaswell Corn 2 C2; Higher Burwardsley Ches W 74 D2; Higher Clovelly Devon 8 B5; Higher End Gtr Man 86 D3; Higher Kinnerton Flint 73 C7; Higher Penwortham Lancs 86 B3; Higher Town Scilly 2 E4; Higher Walreddon Devon 6 B2; Higher Walton Lancs 86 B3; Higher Walton Warr 86 F4; Higher Wheelton Lancs 86 B4; Higher Whitley Ches W 86 F4; Higher Wincham Ches W 74 B3; Higher Wych Ches W 73 E8; Highfield E Yorks 96 F3; Highfield Gtr Man 86 D5; Highfield N Ayrs 118 D3; Highfield Oxon 39 B5; Highfield S Yorks 88 F4; Highfield T&W 110 D4; Highfields Cambs 54 D4; Highfields Northumb 123 D5; Highgate London 41 F5; Highlane Ches E 75 C5; Highlane Derbys 88 F5; Highlaws Cumb 107 E7; Highleadon Glos 36 B4; Highleigh W Sus 16 E2; Highley Shrops 61 F7; Highmoor Cross Oxon 39 F7; Highmoor Hill Mon 35 F8; Highnam Glos 36 C4; Highnam Green Glos 36 B4; Highsted Kent 30 C3; Highstreet Green Essex 55 F8; Hightae Dumfries 107 B7; Hightown Ches E 75 C5; Hightown Mers 85 D4; Hightown Green Suff 56 D3; Highway Wilts 24 B5; Highweek Devon 7 B6; Highworth Swindon 38 E2; Hilborough Norf 67 D8; Hilcote Derbys 76 D4; Hilcott Wilts 25 D6; Hilden Park Kent 29 E6; Hildenborough Kent 29 E6; Hildersham Cambs 55 E6; Hilderstone Staffs 75 F6; Hilderthorpe E Yorks 97 C7; Hilfield Dorset 12 D4; Hilgay Norf 67 E6; Hill Pembs 32 D2; Hill S Glos 36 E3; Hill W Mid 62 E5;

Column 5:
Hill Brow W Sus 15 B8; Hill Dale Lancs 86 C2; Hill Dyke Lincs 79 E6; Hill End Durham 110 F3; Hill End Fife 128 E2; Hill End N Yorks 94 D3; Hill Head Hants 15 D6; Hill Head Northumb 110 C2; Hill Mountain Pembs 44 E4; Hill of Beath Fife 128 E3; Hill of Fearn Highld 151 D11; Hill of Mountblairy Aberds 153 C6; Hill Ridware Staffs 62 C4; Hill Top Durham 100 B4; Hill Top Hants 14 D5; Hill Top W Mid 62 E3; Hill Top W Yorks 88 C4; Hill View Dorset 13 E7; Hillam N Yorks 89 B6; Hillbeck Cumb 100 C2; Hillborough Kent 31 C6; Hillbrae Aberds 141 B6; Hillbrae Aberds 152 D6; Hillbutts Dorset 13 D7; Hillclifflane Derbys 76 E2; Hillcommon Som 11 B6; Hillend Fife 128 F3; Hillerton Devon 10 E2; Hillesden Bucks 39 B6; Hillesley Glos 36 F4; Hillfarrance Som 11 B6; Hillhead Aberds 152 E5; Hillhead Devon 7 D7; Hillhead S Ayrs 112 C4; Hillhead of Auchentumb Aberds 153 C9; Hillhead of Cocklaw Aberds 153 D10; Hillhouse Borders 121 D8; Hilliclay Highld 158 D3; Hillingdon London 40 F3; Hillington Glasgow 118 C5; Hillington Norf 80 E3; Hillmorton Warks 52 B3; Hillockhead Aberds 140 C3; Hillockhead Aberds 140 D2; Hillside Aberds 141 E8; Hillside Angus 135 C7; Hillside Mers 85 C4; Hillside Orkney 159 J5; Hillside Shetland 160 G6; Hillswick Shetland 160 F4; Hillway IoW 15 F7; Hillwell Shetland 160 M5; Hilmarton Wilts 24 B5; Hilperton Wilts 24 D3; Hilsea Ptsmth 15 D7; Hilston E Yorks 97 F8; Hilton Aberds 153 E9; Hilton Cambs 54 C3; Hilton Cumb 100 B2; Hilton Derbys 76 F2; Hilton Dorset 13 D5; Hilton Durham 101 B6; Hilton Highld 151 C10; Hilton Shrops 61 E7; Hilton Stockton 102 C2; Hilton of Cadboll Highld 151 D11; Himbleton Worcs 50 D4; Himley Staffs 62 E3; Hincaster Cumb 99 F7; Hinckley Leics 63 E8; Hinderclay Suff 56 B4; Hinderton Ches W 73 B7; Hinderwell N Yorks 103 C5; Hindford Shrops 73 F7; Hindhead Sur 27 F6; Hindley Gtr Man 86 D4; Hindley Green Gtr Man 86 D4; Hindlip Worcs 50 D3; Hindolveston Norf 81 E6; Hindon Wilts 24 F4; Hindringham Norf 81 D5; Hingham Norf 68 D3; Hinstock Shrops 61 B6; Hintlesham Suff 56 E4; Hinton Hants 14 E3; Hinton Hereford 48 F5; Hinton Northants 52 D3; Hinton S Glos 24 B2; Hinton Shrops 60 D4; Hinton Ampner Hants 15 B6; Hinton Blewett Bath 23 D7; Hinton Charterhouse Bath 24 D2; Hinton-in-the-Hedges Northants 52 F3; Hinton Martell Dorset 13 D8; Hinton on the Green Worcs 50 E5; Hinton Parva Swindon 38 F2; Hinton St George Som 12 C2; Hinton St Mary Dorset 13 C5; Hinton Waldrist Oxon 38 E3; Hints Shrops 49 B8; Hints Staffs 63 D5; Hinwick Bedford 53 C7; Hinxhill Kent 30 E4; Hinxton Cambs 55 E5; Hinxworth Herts 54 E3; Hipperholme W Yorks 88 B2; Hipswell N Yorks 101 E6; Hirael Gwyn 83 D5; Hiraeth Carms 32 B2; Hirn Aberds 141 D6; Hirnant Powys 59 B7; Hirst N Lanark 119 C8; Hirst Northumb 117 F8; Hirst Courtney N Yorks 89 B7; Hirwaen Denb 72 C5; Hirwaun Rhondda 34 D3; Hiscott Devon 9 B7; Histon Cambs 55 C5; Hitcham Suff 56 D3; Hitchin Herts 40 B4; Hither Green London 28 B4; Hittisleigh Devon 10 E2; Hive E Yorks 96 F4; Hixon Staffs 62 B4; Hoaden Kent 31 D6; Hoaldalbert Mon 35 B7; Hoar Cross Staffs 62 B5; Hoarwithy Hereford 36 B2; Hoath Kent 31 C6; Hobarris Shrops 48 B5; Hobbister Orkney 159 H4; Hobkirk Borders 115 C8; Hobson Durham 110 D4; Hoby Leics 64 C3; Hockering Norf 68 C3; Hockerton Notts 77 D7; Hockley Essex 42 E4; Hockley Heath W Mid 51 B6; Hockliffe C Beds 40 B2; Hockwold cum Wilton Norf 67 F7; Hockworthy Devon 10 C5; Hoddesdon Herts 41 D6; Hoddlesden Blackburn 86 B5; Hoddom Mains Dumfries 107 B8; Hoddomcross Dumfries 107 B8; Hodgeston Pembs 32 E1; Hodley Powys 59 E8; Hodnet Shrops 61 B6; Hodthorpe Derbys 76 B5; Hoe Hants 15 C6; Hoe Norf 68 C2; Hoe Gate Hants 15 C7; Hoff Cumb 100 C1; Hog Patch Sur 27 E6;

Column 6:
Hoggard's Green Suff 56 D2; Hoggeston Bucks 39 B8; Hogha Gearraidh W Isles 148 A2; Hoghton Lancs 86 B4; Hognaston Derbys 76 D2; Hogsthorpe Lincs 79 B8; Holbeach Lincs 66 B3; Holbeach Bank Lincs 66 B3; Holbeach Clough Lincs 66 B3; Holbeach Drove Lincs 66 C3; Holbeach Hurn Lincs 66 B3; Holbeach St Johns Lincs 66 C3; Holbeach St Marks Lincs 79 F6; Holbeach St Matthew Lincs 79 F7; Holbeck Notts 76 B5; Holbeck W Yorks 95 F5; Holbeck Woodhouse Notts 76 B5; Holberrow Green Worcs 50 D5; Holbeton Devon 6 D4; Holborn London 41 F6; Holbrook Derbys 76 E3; Holbrook S Yorks 88 F5; Holbrook Suff 57 F5; Holburn Northumb 123 F6; Holbury Hants 14 D5; Holcombe Devon 7 B7; Holcombe Som 23 E8; Holcombe Rogus Devon 11 C5; Holcot Northants 53 C5; Holden Lancs 93 E7; Holdenby Northants 52 C4; Holdenhurst Bmouth 14 E2; Holdgate Shrops 61 F5; Holdingham Lincs 78 E3; Holditch Dorset 11 D8; Hole-in-the-Wall Hereford 36 B3; Holefield Borders 122 F4; Holehouses Ches E 74 B4; Holemoor Devon 9 D6; Holestane Dumfries 113 E8; Holford Som 22 E3; Holgate York 95 D8; Holker Cumb 92 B3; Holkham Norf 80 C4; Hollacombe Devon 9 D5; Holland Orkney 159 C5; Holland Orkney 159 F7; Holland Fen Lincs 79 E5; Holland-on-Sea Essex 43 C8; Hollandstoun Orkney 159 C8; Hollee Dumfries 108 C2; Hollesley Suff 57 E7; Hollicombe Torbay 7 C6; Hollingbourne Kent 30 D2; Hollington Derbys 76 F2; Hollington E Sus 18 D4; Hollington Staffs 75 F7; Hollington Grove Derbys 76 F2; Hollingworth Gtr Man 87 E8; Hollins Gtr Man 87 D6; Hollins Green Warr 86 E4; Hollins Lane Lancs 92 D4; Hollinsclough Staffs 75 C7; Hollinwood Gtr Man 87 D7; Hollinwood Shrops 74 F2; Hollocombe Devon 9 C8; Holloway Derbys 76 D3; Hollowell Northants 52 B4; Holly End Norf 66 D4; Holly Green Worcs 50 E3; Hollybush Caerph 35 D5; Hollybush E Ayrs 112 C3; Hollybush Worcs 50 F2; Hollym E Yorks 91 B7; Hollywood Worcs 51 B5; Holmbridge W Yorks 88 D2; Holmbury St Mary Sur 28 E2; Holmbush Corn 4 D5; Holmcroft Staffs 62 B3; Holme Cambs 65 F8; Holme Cumb 92 B5; Holme N Yorks 102 F1; Holme Notts 77 D8; Holme W Yorks 88 D2; Holme Chapel Lancs 87 B6; Holme Green N Yorks 95 E8; Holme Hale Norf 67 D8; Holme Lacy Hereford 49 F7; Holme Marsh Hereford 48 D5; Holme next the Sea Norf 80 C3; Holme-on-Spalding-Moor E Yorks 96 F4; Holme on the Wolds E Yorks 97 E5; Holme Pierrepont Notts 77 F6; Holme St Cuthbert Cumb 107 E7; Holme Wood W Yorks 94 F4; Holmer Hereford 49 E7; Holmer Green Bucks 40 E2; Holmes Chapel Ches E 74 C4; Holmesfield Derbys 76 B3; Holmeswood Lancs 86 C2; Holmewood Derbys 76 C4; Holmfirth W Yorks 88 D2; Holmhead Dumfries 113 F7; Holmhead E Ayrs 113 B5; Holmisdale Highld 148 D6; Holmpton E Yorks 91 B7; Holmrook Cumb 98 E2; Holmsgarth Shetland 160 J6; Holmwrangle Cumb 108 E5; Holne Devon 6 C5; Holnest Dorset 12 D4; Holsworthy Devon 8 D5; Holsworthy Beacon Devon 9 D5; Holt Dorset 13 D8; Holt Norf 81 D6; Holt Wilts 24 C3; Holt Worcs 50 C3; Holt Wrex 73 D8; Holt End Hants 26 F4; Holt End Worcs 51 C5; Holt Fleet Worcs 50 C3; Holt Heath Worcs 50 C3; Holt Park W Yorks 95 E5; Holtby York 96 D2; Holton Oxon 39 D6; Holton Som 12 B4; Holton Suff 57 B7; Holton cum Beckering Lincs 90 F5; Holton Heath Dorset 13 E7; Holton le Clay Lincs 91 D6; Holton le Moor Lincs 90 E4; Holton St Mary Suff 56 F4; Holwell Dorset 12 C5; Holwell Herts 54 F2; Holwell Leics 64 B4; Holwell Oxon 38 D2; Holwick Durham 100 B4; Holworth Dorset 13 F5; Holy Cross Worcs 50 B4; Holy Island Northumb 123 E7; Holybourne Hants 27 E5; Holyhead = Caergybi Anglesey 82 C2; Holymoorside Derbys 76 C3; Holyport Windsor 27 B6; Holystone Northumb 117 D5; Holytown N Lanark 119 C7;

Column 7:
Holywell Cambs 54 B4; Holywell Corn 4 D2; Holywell Dorset 12 D3; Holywell E Sus 18 F2; Holywell = Treffynnon Flint 73 B5; Holywell Northumb 111 B6; Holywell Green W Yorks 87 C8; Holywell Lake Som 11 B6; Holywell Row Suff 55 B8; Holywood Dumfries 114 F2; Hom Green Hereford 36 B2; Homer Shrops 61 D6; Homersfield Suff 69 F5; Homington Wilts 14 B2; Honey Hill Kent 30 C5; Honey Street Wilts 25 C6; Honey Tye Suff 56 F3; Honeyborough Pembs 44 E4; Honeybourne Worcs 51 E6; Honeychurch Devon 9 D8; Honiley Warks 51 B7; Honing Norf 69 B6; Honingham Norf 68 C4; Honington Lincs 78 E2; Honington Suff 56 B3; Honington Warks 51 E7; Honiton Devon 11 D6; Honley W Yorks 88 C2; Hoo St Werburgh Medway 29 B8; Hood Green S Yorks 88 D4; Hooe E Sus 18 E3; Hooe Plym 6 D3; Hooe Common E Sus 18 D3; Hook E Yorks 89 B8; Hook Hants 26 D5; Hook Hants 15 D7; Hook London 28 C2; Hook Pembs 44 D4; Hook Wilts 37 F7; Hook Green Kent 18 B3; Hook Green Kent 29 E7; Hook Norton Oxon 51 F8; Hook's Cross Herts 41 B5; Hookgate Staffs 74 F4; Hookway Devon 10 E3; Hookwood Sur 28 E3; Hoole Ches W 73 C8; Hooley Sur 28 D3; Hoop Mon 36 D2; Hooton Ches W 73 B7; Hooton Levitt S Yorks 89 E6; Hooton Pagnell S Yorks 89 D5; Hooton Roberts S Yorks 89 E5; Hop Pole Lincs 65 C8; Hope Derbys 88 F2; Hope Devon 6 F4; Hope Highld 156 D7; Hope Powys 60 D2; Hope Shrops 60 D3; Hope Staffs 75 D8; Hope = Yr Hôb Flint 73 D7; Hope Bagot Shrops 49 B7; Hope Bowdler Shrops 60 E4; Hope End Green Essex 42 B1; Hope Green Ches E 87 F7; Hope Mansell Hereford 36 C3; Hope under Dinmore Hereford 49 D7; Hopeman Moray 152 B1; Hopesay Shrops 60 F3; Hopley's Green Hereford 48 D5; Hopperton N Yorks 95 D7; Hopstone Shrops 61 E7; Hopton Derbys 76 D2; Hopton Shrops 60 B3; Hopton Shrops 60 B4; Hopton Staffs 62 B3; Hopton Suff 56 B3; Hopton Cangeford Shrops 60 F5; Hopton Castle Shrops 49 B5; Hopton on Sea Norf 69 D8; Hopton Wafers Shrops 49 B8; Hoptonheath Shrops 49 B5; Hopwas Staffs 63 D5; Hopwood Gtr Man 87 D6; Hopwood Worcs 50 B5; Horam E Sus 18 D2; Horbling Lincs 78 F4; Horbury W Yorks 88 C3; Horcott Glos 38 D1; Horden Durham 111 E7; Horderley Shrops 60 F4; Hordle Hants 14 E3; Hordley Shrops 73 F7; Horeb Carms 33 B6; Horeb Carms 46 F3; Horeb Ceredig 46 E2; Horfield Bristol 23 B8; Horham Suff 57 B6; Horkesley Heath Essex 43 B5; Horkstow N Lincs 90 C3; Horley Oxon 52 E2; Horley Sur 28 E3; Hornblotton Green Som 23 F7; Hornby Lancs 93 C5; Hornby N Yorks 101 E7; Hornby N Yorks 102 D1; Horncastle Lincs 78 C5; Hornchurch London 41 F8; Horncliffe Northumb 122 E5; Horndean Borders 122 E4; Horndean Hants 15 C8; Horndon Devon 6 B3; Horndon on the Hill Thurrock 42 F2; Horne Sur 28 E4; Horniehaugh Angus 134 C4; Horning Norf 69 C6; Horninghold Leics 64 E5; Horninglow Staffs 63 B6; Horningsea Cambs 55 C5; Horningsham Wilts 24 E3; Horningtoft Norf 80 E5; Horns Corner Kent 18 B4; Horns Cross Devon 9 B5; Horns Cross E Sus 18 C5; Hornsby Cumb 108 D5; Hornsea E Yorks 97 E8; Hornsea Bridge E Yorks 97 E8; Hornsey London 41 F6; Hornton Oxon 51 E8; Horrabridge Devon 6 C3; Horringer Suff 56 C2; Horringford IoW 15 F6; Horse Bridge Staffs 75 D6; Horsebridge Devon 6 B2; Horsebridge Hants 25 F8; Horsebrook Staffs 62 D2; Horsehay Telford 61 D6; Horseheath Cambs 55 E7; Horsehouse N Yorks 101 F5; Horsell Sur 27 D7; Horseman's Green Wrex 73 E8; Horseway Cambs 66 F4; Horsey Norf 69 B7; Horsford Norf 68 C4; Horsforth W Yorks 94 F5; Horsham W Sus 28 F2; Horsham Worcs 50 D2; Horsham St Faith Norf 68 C5; Horsington Lincs 78 C4; Horsington Som 12 B5; Horsley Derbys 76 E3; Horsley Glos 37 E5; Horsley Northumb 110 C3; Horsley Northumb 116 E4; Horsley Cross Essex 43 B7;

Column 8 (rightmost):
Horsleycross Street Essex 43 B7; Horsleyhill Borders 115 C8; Horsleyhope Durham 110 E3; Horsmonden Kent 29 E7; Horspath Oxon 39 D5; Horstead Norf 69 C5; Horsted Keynes W Sus 17 B7; Horton Bucks 40 C2; Horton Dorset 13 D8; Horton Lancs 93 D8; Horton Northumb 123 F7; Horton S Glos 36 F4; Horton Shrops 60 B4; Horton Som 11 C8; Horton Staffs 75 D6; Horton Swansea 33 F5; Horton Wilts 25 C5; Horton Windsor 27 B8; Horton-cum-Studley Oxon 39 C5; Horton Green Ches W 73 E8; Horton Heath Hants 15 C5; Horton in Ribblesdale N Yorks 93 B8; Horton Kirby Kent 29 C6; Hortonlane Shrops 60 C4; Horwich Gtr Man 86 C4; Horwich End Derbys 87 F8; Horwood Devon 9 B7; Hose Leics 64 B4; Hoselaw Borders 122 F4; Hoses Cumb 98 E4; Hosh Perth 127 B7; Hosta W Isles 148 A2; Hoswick Shetland 160 L6; Hotham E Yorks 96 F4; Hothfield Kent 30 E3; Hoton Leics 64 B2; Houbie Shetland 160 D8; Houdston S Ayrs 112 E1; Hough Ches E 74 D4; Hough Ches E 74 B5; Hough Green Halton 86 F2; Hough-on-the-Hill Lincs 78 E2; Houghams Lincs 78 E2; Houghton Cambs 54 B3; Houghton Cumb 108 D4; Houghton Hants 25 F8; Houghton Pembs 44 E4; Houghton W Sus 16 C4; Houghton Conquest C Beds 53 E8; Houghton Green E Sus 19 C6; Houghton Green Warr 86 E4; Houghton-le-Side Darl 101 B7; Houghton-Le-Spring T&W 111 E6; Houghton on the Hill Leics 64 D3; Houghton Regis C Beds 40 B3; Houghton St Giles Norf 80 D5; Houlland Shetland 160 H5; Houlland Shetland 160 F7; Houlsyke N Yorks 103 D5; Hound Hants 15 D5; Hound Green Hants 26 D5; Houndslow Borders 122 E2; Houndwood Borders 122 C4; Hounslow London 28 B2; Hounslow Green Essex 42 C2; Housay Shetland 160 F8; House of Daviot Highld 151 G10; House of Glenmuick Aberds 140 E2; Housetter Shetland 160 E5; Houss Shetland 160 K5; Houston Renfs 118 C4; Houstry Highld 158 G3; Houton Orkney 159 H4; Hove Brighton 17 D6; Hoveringham Notts 77 E6; Hoveton Norf 69 C6; Hovingham N Yorks 96 B2; How Cumb 108 D5; How Caple Hereford 49 F8; How End C Beds 53 E8; How Green Kent 29 E5; Howbrook S Yorks 88 E4; Howden Borders 116 B2; Howden E Yorks 89 B8; Howden-le-Wear Durham 110 F4; Howe Highld 158 D5; Howe N Yorks 101 F8; Howe Norf 69 D5; Howe Bridge Gtr Man 86 D4; Howe Green Essex 42 D3; Howe of Teuchar Aberds 153 D7; Howe Street Essex 42 C2; Howe Street Essex 55 F7; Howell Lincs 78 E4; Howey Powys 48 D2; Howgate Midloth 120 D5; Howick Northumb 117 C8; Howle Durham 101 B5; Howle Telford 61 B6; Howlett End Essex 55 F6; Howley Som 11 C7; Hownam Borders 116 C3; Hownam Mains Borders 116 B3; Howpasley Borders 115 D6; Howsham N Lincs 90 D4; Howsham N Yorks 96 C3; Howslack Dumfries 114 D3; Howtel Northumb 122 F4; Howton Hereford 35 B8; Howtown Cumb 99 C6; Howwood Renfs 118 D3; Hoxne Suff 57 B5; Hoy Orkney 159 H3; Hoylake Mers 85 F3; Hoyland S Yorks 88 D4; Hoylandswaine S Yorks 88 D3; Hubberholme N Yorks 94 B2; Hubbert's Bridge Lincs 79 E5; Huby N Yorks 95 E5; Huby N Yorks 95 C8; Hucclecote Glos 37 C5; Hucking Kent 30 D2; Hucknall Notts 76 E5; Huddersfield W Yorks 88 C2; Huddington Worcs 50 D4; Hudswell N Yorks 101 D6; Huggate E Yorks 96 D4; Hugglescote Leics 63 C8; Hugh Town Scilly 2 E4; Hughenden Valley Bucks 40 E1; Hughley Shrops 61 E5; Huish Devon 9 C7; Huish Wilts 25 C6; Huish Champflower Som 11 B5; Huish Episcopi Som 12 B2; Huisinis W Isles 154 F4; Hulcott Bucks 40 C1; Hulland Derbys 76 E2; Hulland Ward Derbys 76 E2; Hullavington Wilts 37 F5; Hullbridge Essex 42 E4; Hulme Gtr Man 87 E6

Hat–Hul 215

Hulme End Staffs 75 D8
Hulme Walfield Ches E 74 C5
Hulver Street Suff 69 F7
Hulverstone IoW 14 F4
Humber Hereford 49 D7
Humber Bridge N Lincs 90 B4
Humberston NE Lincs 91 D7
Humbie E Loth 121 C7
Humbleton E Yorks 97 F8
Humbleton Northumb 117 B5
Humby Lincs 78 F3
Hume Borders 122 E3
Humshaugh Northumb 110 B2
Huna Highld 158 C5
Huncoat Lancs 93 F7
Huncote Leics 64 E2
Hundalee Borders 116 C2
Hunderthwaite Durham 100 B4
Hundle Houses Lincs 79 D5
Hundleby Lincs 79 C6
Hundleton Pembs 44 E4
Hundon Suff 55 E8
Hundred Acres Hants 15 C6
Hundred End Lancs 86 B2
Hundred House Powys 48 D3
Hungarton Leics 64 D3
Hungerford Hants 14 C2
Hungerford W Berks 25 C8
Hungerford Newtown W Berks 25 B8
Hungerton Lincs 65 B5
Hungladder Highld 149 A8
Hunmanby N Yorks 97 B6
Hunmanby Moor N Yorks 97 B7
Hunningham Warks 51 C8
Hunny Hill IoW 15 F5
Hunsdon Herts 41 C7
Hunsingore N Yorks 95 D7
Hunslet W Yorks 95 F6
Hunsonby Cumb 109 F5
Hunspow Highld 158 C4
Hunstanton Norf 80 C2
Hunstanworth Durham 110 E2
Hunsterson Ches E 74 E3
Hunston Suff 56 C3
Hunston W Sus 16 D2
Hunstrete Bath 23 C8
Hunt End Worcs 50 C5
Hunter's Quay Argyll 145 F10
Hunthill Lodge Angus 134 B4
Hunting-tower Perth 128 B2
Huntingdon Cambs 54 B3
Huntingfield Suff 57 B7
Huntingford Dorset 24 F3
Huntington E Loth 121 B7
Huntington Hereford 48 D4
Huntington Staffs 62 C3
Huntington York 96 D2
Huntley Glos 36 C4
Huntly Aberds 152 E5
Huntlywood Borders 122 E2
Hunton Kent 29 E8
Hunton N Yorks 101 E6
Hunt's Corner Norf 68 F3
Hunt's Cross Mers 86 F2
Huntsham Devon 10 B5
Huntspill Som 22 E5
Huntworth Som 22 F5
Hunwick Durham 110 F4
Hunworth Norf 81 D6
Hurdsfield Ches E 75 B6
Hurley Warks 63 E6
Hurley Windsor 39 F8
Hurlford E Ayrs 118 F4
Hurliness Orkney 159 K3
Hurn Dorset 14 E2
Hurn's End Lincs 79 E7
Hursley Hants 14 B5
Hurst N Yorks 101 D5
Hurst Som 12 C2
Hurst Wokingham 27 B5
Hurst Green E Sus 18 C4
Hurst Green Lancs 93 F6
Hurst Wickham W Sus 17 C6
Hurstbourne Priors Hants 26 E2
Hurstbourne Tarrant Hants 25 D8
Hurstpierpoint W Sus 17 C6
Hurstwood Lancs 93 F8
Hurtmore Sur 27 E7
Hurworth Place Darl 101 D7
Hury Durham 100 C4
Husabost Highld 148 C7
Husbands Bosworth Leics 64 F3
Husborne Crawley C Beds 53 F7
Husthwaite N Yorks 95 B8
Hutchwns Bridgend 21 B7
Huthwaite Notts 76 D4
Huttoft Lincs 79 B8
Hutton Borders 122 D5
Hutton Cumb 99 B6
Hutton E Yorks 97 D6
Hutton Essex 42 E2
Hutton Lancs 86 B2
Hutton N Som 22 D5
Hutton Buscel N Yorks 103 F7
Hutton Conyers N Yorks 95 B6
Hutton Cranswick E Yorks 97 D6
Hutton End Cumb 108 F4
Hutton Gate Redcar 102 C3
Hutton Henry Durham 111 F7
Hutton-le-Hole N Yorks 103 E5
Hutton Magna Durham 101 C6
Hutton Roof Cumb 93 B5
Hutton Roof Cumb 108 F3
Hutton Rudby N Yorks 102 D2
Hutton Sessay N Yorks 95 B7
Hutton Village Redcar 102 C3
Hutton Wandesley N Yorks 95 D8
Huxley Ches W 74 C2
Huxter Shetland 160 G7
Huxter Shetland 160 H5
Huxton Borders 122 C4
Huyton Mers 86 E2
Hwlffordd = Haverfordwest Pembs 44 D4
Hycemoor Cumb 98 F2
Hyde Glos 37 D5
Hyde Gtr Man 87 E7
Hyde Hants 14 C2
Hyde Heath Bucks 40 D2
Hyde Park S Yorks 89 D6
Hydestile Sur 27 E7
Hylton Castle T&W 111 D6
Hyndford Bridge S Lanark 120 E2
Hynish Argyll 146 H2
Hyssington Powys 60 E3
Hythe Hants 14 D5
Hythe Kent 19 B8
Hythe End Windsor 27 B8
Hythie Aberds 153 C10

I

Ibberton Dorset 13 D5
Ible Derbys 76 D2
Ibsley Hants 14 D2
Ibstock Leics 63 C8
Ibstone Bucks 39 E7
Ibthorpe Hants 25 D8
Ibworth Hants 26 D3
Ichrachan Argyll 125 B6
Ickburgh Norf 67 E8
Ickenham London 40 F3
Ickford Bucks 39 D6
Ickham Kent 31 D6
Ickleford Herts 54 F2
Icklesham E Sus 19 D5
Ickleton Cambs 55 E5
Icklingham Suff 55 B8
Ickwell Green C Beds 54 E2
Icomb Glos 38 B2
Idbury Oxon 38 C2
Iddesleigh Devon 9 D7
Ide Devon 10 E3
Ide Hill Kent 29 D5
Ideford Devon 7 B6
Iden E Sus 19 C6
Iden Green Kent 18 B4
Iden Green Kent 18 B5
Idle W Yorks 94 F4
Idlicote Warks 51 E7
Idmiston Wilts 25 F6
Idole Carms 33 C5
Idridgehay Derbys 76 E2
Idrigill Highld 149 B8
Idstone Oxon 38 F2
Idvies Angus 135 E5
Iffley Oxon 39 D5
Ifield W Sus 28 F3
Ifold W Sus 27 F8
Iford E Sus 17 D8
Ifton Heath Shrops 73 F7
Ightfield Shrops 74 F2
Ightham Kent 29 D6
Iken Suff 57 D8
Ilam Staffs 75 D8
Ilchester Som 12 B3
Ilderton Northumb 117 B6
Ilford London 41 F7
Ilfracombe Devon 20 E4
Ilkeston Derbys 76 E4
Ilketshall St Andrew Suff 69 F6
Ilketshall St Lawrence Suff 69 F6
Ilketshall St Margaret Suff 69 F6
Ilkley W Yorks 94 E4
Illey W Mid 62 F3
Illingworth W Yorks 87 B8
Illogan Corn 3 B5
Illston on the Hill Leics 64 E4
Ilmer Bucks 39 D7
Ilmington Warks 51 E7
Ilminster Som 11 C8
Ilsington Devon 7 B5
Ilston Swansea 33 E6
Ilton N Yorks 94 B4
Ilton Som 11 C8
Imachar N Ayrs 143 D9
Imeraval Argyll 142 D4
Immingham NE Lincs 91 C5
Impington Cambs 54 C5
Ince Ches W 73 B8
Ince Blundell Mers 85 D4
Ince in Makerfield Gtr Man 86 D3
Inch of Arnhall Aberds 135 B6
Inchbare Angus 135 C6
Inchberry Moray 152 C3
Inchbraoch Angus 135 D7
Incheril Highld 150 E3
Inchgrundle Angus 134 B4
Inchina Highld 150 B2
Inchinnan Renfs 118 C4
Inchkinloch Highld 157 E8
Inchlaggan Highld 136 D4
Inchlumpie Highld 151 D8
Inchmore Highld 150 G6
Inchnacardoch Hotel Highld 137 C6
Inchnadamph Highld 156 G5
Inchree Highld 130 C4
Inchture Perth 128 B4
Inchyra Perth 128 B3
Indian Queens Corn 4 D4
Inerval Argyll 142 D4
Ingatestone Essex 42 E2
Ingbirchworth S Yorks 88 D3
Ingestre Staffs 62 B3
Ingham Lincs 90 F3
Ingham Norf 69 B6
Ingham Suff 56 B2
Ingham Corner Norf 69 B6
Ingleborough Norf 66 C4
Ingleby Derbys 63 B7
Ingleby Lincs 77 B8
Ingleby Arncliffe N Yorks 102 D2
Ingleby Barwick Stockton 102 C2
Ingleby Greenhow N Yorks 102 D3
Inglemire Hull 97 F6
Inglesbatch Bath 24 C2
Inglesham Swindon 38 E2
Ingleton Durham 101 B6
Ingleton N Yorks 93 B6
Inglewhite Lancs 92 E5
Ingliston Edin 120 B4
Ingoe Northumb 110 B3
Ingol Lancs 92 F5
Ingoldisthorpe Norf 80 D2
Ingoldmells Lincs 79 C8
Ingoldsby Lincs 78 F3
Ingon Warks 51 D7
Ingram Northumb 117 C6
Ingrow W Yorks 94 F3
Ings Cumb 99 E6
Ingst S Glos 36 F2
Ingworth Norf 81 E7
Inham's End Cambs 66 E2
Inkberrow Worcs 50 D5
Inkpen W Berks 25 C8
Inkstack Highld 158 C4
Inn Cumb 99 D6
Innellan Argyll 145 F10
Innerleithen Borders 121 F6
Innerleven Fife 129 D5
Innermessan Dumfries 104 C4
Innerwick E Loth 122 B3
Innerwick Perth 132 E2
Innis Chonain Argyll 125 C7
Insch Aberds 140 B5
Insh Highld 138 D4
Inshore Highld 156 C6
Inskip Lancs 92 F4
Instoneville S Yorks 89 C6
Instow Devon 20 F3
Intake S Yorks 89 D6
Inver Aberds 139 E8
Inver Highld 151 C11
Inver Perth 133 E7
Inver Mallie Highld 136 F4
Inverailort Highld 147 C10
Inveraldie Angus 134 F4
Inverallign Highld 149 C13
Inverallochy Aberds 153 B10
Inveran Highld 151 B8
Inveraray Argyll 125 E6
Inverarish Highld 149 E10
Inverarity Angus 134 E4
Inverarnan Stirling 126 C2
Inverasdale Highld 155 J13
Inverbeg Argyll 126 E2
Inverbervie Aberds 135 B8
Inverboyndie Aberds 153 B6
Inverbroom Highld 150 C4
Invercassley Highld 156 J7
Invercauld House Aberds 139 E7
Inverchaolain Argyll 145 F9
Invercharnan Highld 131 E5
Inverchoran Highld 150 F5
Invercreran Argyll 130 E4
Inverdruie Highld 138 C5
Inverebrie Aberds 153 E9
Invereck Argyll 145 E10
Inverernan Ho. Aberds 140 C2
Invereshie House Highld 138 D4
Inveresk E Loth 121 B6
Inverey Aberds 139 F6
Inverfarigaig Highld 137 B8
Invergarry Highld 137 D6
Invergelder Aberds 139 E8
Invergeldie Perth 127 B6
Invergordon Highld 151 E10
Invergowrie Perth 134 F3
Inverguseran Highld 149 H12
Inverhadden Perth 132 D3
Inverharroch Moray 152 E3
Inverherive Stirling 126 B2
Inverie Highld 147 B10
Inverinan Argyll 125 D5
Inverinate Highld 136 B2
Inverkeilor Angus 135 E6
Inverkeithing Fife 128 F3
Inverkeithny Aberds 153 D6
Inverkip Invclyd 118 B2
Inverkirkaig Highld 156 H3
Inverlael Highld 150 C4
Inverlochlarig Stirling 126 C3
Inverlochy Argyll 125 C7
Inverlochy Highld 131 B5
Inverlussa Argyll 144 E5
Invermark Lodge Angus 140 F3
Invermoidart Highld 147 D9
Invermoriston Highld 137 C7
Invernaver Highld 157 C10
Inverneill Argyll 145 E7
Inverness Highld 151 G9
Invernettie Aberds 153 D11
Invernoaden Argyll 125 F7
Inveroran Hotel Argyll 131 E6
Inverpolly Lodge Highld 156 H3
Inverquharity Angus 134 D4
Inverquhomery Aberds 153 D10
Inverroy Highld 137 F5
Inversanda Highld 130 D3
Invershiel Highld 136 C2
Invershin Highld 151 B8
Inversnaid Hotel Stirling 126 D2
Inverugie Aberds 153 D11
Inveruglas Argyll 126 D2
Inveruglass Highld 138 D4
Inverurie Aberds 141 B6
Invervar Perth 132 E3
Inverythan Aberds 153 D7
Inwardleigh Devon 9 E7
Inworth Essex 42 C4
Iochdar W Isles 148 D2
Iping W Sus 16 B2
Ipplepen Devon 7 C6
Ipsden Oxon 39 F6
Ipsley Worcs 51 C5
Ipstones Staffs 75 D7
Ipswich Suff 57 E5
Irby Mers 85 F3
Irby in the Marsh Lincs 79 C7
Irby upon Humber NE Lincs 91 D5
Irchester Northants 53 C7
Ireby Cumb 108 F2
Ireby Lancs 93 B6
Ireland Orkney 159 H4
Ireland Shetland 160 L5
Ireland's Cross Shrops 74 E4
Ireleth Cumb 92 B2
Ireshopeburn Durham 109 F8
Irlam Gtr Man 86 E5
Irnham Lincs 65 B7
Iron Acton S Glos 36 F3
Iron Cross Warks 51 D5
Ironbridge Telford 61 D6
Irongray Dumfries 107 B6
Ironmacannie Dumfries 106 B3
Ironside Aberds 153 C8
Ironville Derbys 76 D4
Irstead Norf 69 B6
Irthington Cumb 108 C4
Irthlingborough Northants 53 B7
Irton N Yorks 103 F8
Irvine N Ayrs 118 F3
Isauld Highld 157 C12
Isbister Orkney 159 F3
Isbister Orkney 159 G4
Isbister Shetland 160 D5
Isbister Shetland 160 G7
Isfield E Sus 17 C8
Isham Northants 53 B6
Isle Abbotts Som 11 B8
Isle Brewers Som 11 B8
Isle of Whithorn Dumfries 105 F8
Isleham Cambs 55 B7
Isleornsay Highld 149 G12
Islesburgh Shetland 160 G5
Islesteps Dumfries 107 B6
Isleworth London 28 B2
Isley Walton Leics 63 B8
Islibhig W Isles 154 E4
Islington London 41 F6
Islip Northants 53 B7
Islip Oxon 39 C5
Istead Rise Kent 29 C7
Isycoed Wrex 73 D8
Itchen Soton 14 C5
Itchen Abbas Hants 26 F3
Itchen Stoke Hants 26 F3
Itchingfield W Sus 16 B5
Itchington S Glos 36 F3
Itteringham Norf 81 D7
Itton Devon 9 E8
Itton Common Mon 36 E1
Ivegill Cumb 108 E4
Iver Bucks 40 F3
Iver Heath Bucks 40 F3
Iveston Durham 110 D4
Ivinghoe Bucks 40 C2
Ivinghoe Aston Bucks 40 C2
Ivington Hereford 49 D6
Ivington Green Hereford 49 D6
Ivy Chimneys Essex 41 D7
Ivy Cross Dorset 13 B6
Ivy Hatch Kent 29 D6
Ivybridge Devon 6 D4
Ivychurch Kent 19 C7
Iwade Kent 30 C3
Iwerne Courtney or Shroton Dorset 13 C6
Iwerne Minster Dorset 13 C6
Ixworth Suff 56 B3
Ixworth Thorpe Suff 56 B3

J

Jack Hill N Yorks 94 D5
Jack in the Green Devon 10 E5
Jacksdale Notts 76 D4
Jackstown Aberds 153 E7
Jacobstow Corn 8 E3
Jacobstowe Devon 9 D7
Jameston Pembs 32 E1
Jamestown Dumfries 115 E6
Jamestown Highld 150 F7
Jamestown W Dunb 126 F2
Jarrow T&W 111 C6
Jarvis Brook E Sus 18 C2
Jasper's Green Essex 42 B3
Java Argyll 124 B3
Jawcraig Falk 119 B8
Jaywick Essex 43 C7
Jealott's Hill Brack 27 B6
Jedburgh Borders 116 B2
Jeffreyston Pembs 32 D1
Jellyhill E Dunb 119 B6
Jemimaville Highld 151 E10
Jersey Farm Herts 40 D4
Jesmond T&W 111 C5
Jevington E Sus 18 E2
Jockey End Herts 40 C3
John o'Groats Highld 158 C5
Johnby Cumb 108 F4
John's Cross E Sus 18 C4
Johnshaven Aberds 135 C7
Johnston Pembs 44 D4
Johnstone Renfs 118 C4
Johnstonebridge Dumfries 114 E3
Johnstown Carms 33 C5
Johnstown Wrex 73 E7
Joppa Edin 121 B6
Joppa S Ayrs 112 C4
Jordans Bucks 40 E2
Jordanthorpe S Yorks 88 F4
Jump S Yorks 88 D4
Jumpers Green Dorset 14 E2
Juniper Green Edin 120 C4
Jurby East IoM 84 C3
Jurby West IoM 84 C3

K

Kaber Cumb 100 C2
Kaimend S Lanark 120 E2
Kaimes Edin 121 C5
Kalemouth Borders 116 B3
Kames Argyll 124 D4
Kames Argyll 145 F8
Kames E Ayrs 113 B6
Kea Corn 3 B7
Keadby N Lincs 90 C2
Keal Cotes Lincs 79 C6
Kearsley Gtr Man 87 D5
Kearstwick Cumb 99 F8
Kearton N Yorks 100 E4
Kearvaig Highld 156 B5
Keasden N Yorks 93 C7
Keckwick Halton 86 F3
Keddington Lincs 91 F7
Kedington Suff 55 E8
Kedleston Derbys 76 E3
Keelby Lincs 91 C5
Keele Staffs 74 E5
Keeley Green Bedford 53 E8
Keeston Pembs 44 D4
Keevil Wilts 24 D4
Kegworth Leics 63 B8
Kehelland Corn 2 B5
Keig Aberds 140 C5
Keighley W Yorks 94 E3
Keil Highld 130 D3
Keilarsbrae Clack 127 E7
Keilhill Aberds 153 C7
Keillmore Argyll 144 E5
Keillor Perth 134 E2
Keillour Perth 127 B8
Keills Argyll 142 B5
Keils Argyll 144 G4
Keinton Mandeville Som 23 F7
Keir Mill Dumfries 113 E8
Keisby Lincs 65 B7
Keiss Highld 158 D5
Keith Moray 152 C4
Keith Inch Aberds 153 D11
Keithock Angus 135 C6
Kelbrook Lancs 94 E2
Kelby Lincs 78 E3
Keld Cumb 99 C7
Keld N Yorks 100 D3
Keldholme N Yorks 103 F5
Kelfield N Lincs 90 D2
Kelfield N Yorks 95 F8
Kelham Notts 77 D7
Kellan Argyll 147 G8
Kellas Angus 134 F4
Kellas Moray 152 C1
Kellaton Devon 7 F6
Kelleth Cumb 100 D1
Kelleythorpe E Yorks 97 D5
Kelling Norf 81 C6
Kellingley N Yorks 89 B6
Kellington N Yorks 89 B6
Kelloe Durham 111 F6
Kelloholm Dumfries 113 C7
Kelly Devon 9 F5
Kelly Bray Corn 5 B8
Kelmarsh Northants 52 B5
Kelmscot Oxon 38 E2
Kelsale Suff 57 C7
Kelsall Ches W 74 C2
Kelsall Hill Ches W 74 C2
Kelshall Herts 54 F4
Kelsick Cumb 107 D8
Kelso Borders 122 F3
Kelstedge Derbys 76 C3
Kelstern Lincs 91 E6
Kelston Bath 24 C2
Keltneyburn Perth 132 E4
Kelton Dumfries 107 B6
Kelty Fife 128 E3
Kelvedon Essex 42 C4
Kelvedon Hatch Essex 42 E1
Kelvin S Lanark 119 D6
Kelvinside Glasgow 119 C5
Kelynack Corn 2 C2
Kemback Fife 129 C6
Kemberton Shrops 61 D7
Kemble Glos 37 E6
Kemerton Worcs 50 F4
Kemeys Commander Mon 35 D7
Kemnay Aberds 141 C6
Kemp Town Brighton 17 D7
Kempley Glos 36 B3
Kemps Green Warks 51 B6
Kempsey Worcs 50 E3
Kempsford Glos 38 E1
Kempshott Hants 26 D4
Kempston Bedford 53 E8
Kempston Hardwick Bedford 53 E8
Kempton Shrops 60 F3
Kemsing Kent 29 D6
Kemsley Kent 30 C3
Kenardington Kent 19 B6
Kenchester Hereford 49 E6
Kencot Oxon 38 D2
Kendal Cumb 99 E7
Kendoon Dumfries 113 F6
Kendray S Yorks 88 D4
Kenfig Bridgend 34 F2
Kenfig Hill Bridgend 34 F2
Kenilworth Warks 51 B7
Kenknock Stirling 132 F1
Kenley London 28 D4
Kenley Shrops 61 D5
Kenmore Highld 149 C12
Kenmore Perth 132 E4
Kenn Devon 10 F4
Kenn N Som 23 C6
Kennacley W Isles 154 H6
Kennacraig Argyll 145 G7
Kennerleigh Devon 10 D3
Kennet Clack 127 E8
Kennethmont Aberds 140 B4
Kennett Cambs 55 C7
Kennford Devon 10 F4
Kenninghall Norf 68 F3
Kenninghall Heath Norf 68 F3
Kennington Kent 30 E4
Kennington Oxon 39 D5
Kennoway Fife 129 D5
Kenny Hill Suff 55 B7
Kennythorpe N Yorks 96 C3
Kenovay Argyll 146 G2
Kensaleyre Highld 149 C9
Kensington London 28 B3
Kensworth C Beds 40 C3
Kensworth Common C Beds 40 C3
Kent's Oak Hants 14 B4
Kent Street E Sus 18 D4
Kent Street Kent 29 D7
Kent Street W Sus 17 B6
Kentallen Highld 130 D4
Kentchurch Hereford 35 B8
Kentford Suff 55 C8
Kentisbeare Devon 11 D5
Kentisbury Devon 20 E5
Kentisbury Ford Devon 20 E5
Kentmere Cumb 99 D6
Kenton Devon 10 F4
Kenton Suff 57 C5
Kenton T&W 110 C5
Kenton Bankfoot T&W 110 C5
Kentra Highld 147 E9
Kents Bank Cumb 92 B3
Kent's Green Glos 36 B4
Kenwick Shrops 73 F8
Kenwyn Corn 3 B7
Keoldale Highld 156 C6
Keppanach Highld 130 C4
Keppoch Highld 136 B2
Keprigan Argyll 143 G7
Kepwick N Yorks 102 E2
Kerchesters Borders 122 F3
Keresley W Mid 63 F7
Kernborough Devon 7 E5
Kerne Bridge Hereford 36 C2
Kerris Corn 2 D3
Kerry Powys 59 F8
Kerrycroy Argyll 145 G10
Kerry's Gate Hereford 49 F5
Kerrysdale Highld 149 A13
Kersall Notts 77 C7
Kersey Suff 56 E4
Kershopefoot Cumb 115 F7
Kersoe Worcs 50 F4
Kerswell Devon 11 D5
Kerswell Green Worcs 50 E3
Kesgrave Suff 57 E6
Kessingland Suff 69 F8
Kessingland Beach Suff 69 F8
Kessington E Dunb 119 B5
Kestle Corn 3 B8
Kestle Mill Corn 4 D3
Keston London 28 C5
Keswick Cumb 98 B4
Keswick Norf 68 D5
Keswick Norf 81 D9
Ketley Telford 61 C6
Ketley Bank Telford 61 C6
Ketsby Lincs 79 B6
Kettering Northants 53 B6
Ketteringham Norf 68 D4
Kettins Perth 134 F2
Kettle Green Herts 41 C7
Kettlebaston Suff 56 D3
Kettlebridge Fife 128 D5
Kettleburgh Suff 57 C6
Kettlehill Fife 128 D5
Kettleholm Dumfries 107 B8
Kettleness N Yorks 103 C6
Kettleshume Ches E 75 B6
Kettlesing Bottom N Yorks 94 D5
Kettlesing Head N Yorks 94 D5
Kettlestone Norf 81 D5
Kettlethorpe Lincs 77 B8
Kettletoft Orkney 159 E7
Kettlewell N Yorks 94 B2
Ketton Rutland 65 D6
Kew London 28 B2
Kew Br. London 28 B2
Kewstoke N Som 22 C5
Kexbrough S Yorks 88 D4
Kexby Lincs 90 F2
Kexby York 96 D3
Key Green Ches E 75 C5
Keyham Leics 64 D3
Keyhaven Hants 14 E4
Keyingham E Yorks 91 B6
Keymer W Sus 17 C7
Keynsham Bath 23 C8
Keysoe Bedford 53 C8
Keysoe Row Bedford 53 C8
Keyston Cambs 53 B8
Keyworth Notts 77 F6
Kibblesworth T&W 110 D5
Kibworth Beauchamp Leics 64 E3
Kibworth Harcourt Leics 64 E3
Kidbrooke London 28 B5
Kiddemore Green Staffs 62 D2
Kidderminster Worcs 50 B3
Kiddington Oxon 38 B4
Kidlington Oxon 38 C4
Kidmore End Oxon 26 B4
Kidsgrove Staffs 74 D5
Kidstones N Yorks 100 F4
Kidwelly = Cydweli Carms 33 D5
Kiel Crofts Argyll 124 B5
Kielder Northumb 116 E2
Kierfiold Ho Orkney 159 G3
Kilbagie Fife 127 F8
Kilbarchan Renfs 118 C4
Kilbeg Highld 149 H11
Kilberry Argyll 144 G6
Kilbirnie N Ayrs 118 D3
Kilbride Argyll 124 C4
Kilbride Argyll 124 C5
Kilbride Highld 149 F10
Kilburn Angus 134 C3
Kilburn Derbys 76 E3
Kilburn London 41 F5
Kilburn N Yorks 95 B8
Kilby Leics 64 E3
Kilchamaig Argyll 145 G7
Kilchattan Argyll 144 D2
Kilchattan Bay Argyll 145 H10
Kilchenzie Argyll 143 F7
Kilcheran Argyll 124 B4
Kilchiaran Argyll 142 B3
Kilchoan Argyll 124 D3
Kilchoan Highld 146 E7
Kilchoman Argyll 142 B3
Kilchrenan Argyll 125 C6
Kilconquhar Fife 129 D6
Kilcot Glos 36 B3
Kilcoy Highld 151 F8
Kilcreggan Argyll 145 E11
Kildale N Yorks 102 D4
Kildalloig Argyll 143 G8
Kildary Highld 151 D10
Kildermorie Lodge Highld 151 D8
Kildonan N Ayrs 143 F11
Kildonan Lodge Highld 157 G12
Kildonnan Highld 146 C7
Kildrummy Aberds 140 C3
Kildwick N Yorks 94 E3
Kilfinan Argyll 145 F8
Kilfinnan Highld 137 E5
Kilgetty Pembs 32 D2
Kilgwrrwg Common Mon 36 E1
Kilham E Yorks 97 C6
Kilham Northumb 122 F4
Kilkenneth Argyll 146 G2
Kilkerran Argyll 143 G8
Kilkhampton Corn 9 E6
Killamarsh Derbys 89 F5
Killay Swansea 33 E7
Killbeg Argyll 147 G9
Killean Argyll 143 D7
Killearn Stirling 126 F4
Killen Highld 151 F9
Killerby Darl 101 C6
Killichonan Perth 132 D2
Killiechonate Highld 136 F5
Killiechronan Argyll 147 G8
Killiecrankie Perth 133 C6
Killiemor Argyll 146 H7
Killiemore House Argyll 146 J7
Killilan Highld 150 H2
Killimster Highld 158 E5
Killin Stirling 132 F2
Killin Lodge Highld 137 D8
Killinallan Argyll 142 A4
Killinghall N Yorks 95 D5
Killington Cumb 99 F8
Killingworth T&W 111 B5
Killmahumaig Argyll 144 D6
Killochyett Borders 121 E7
Killocraw Argyll 143 E7
Killundine Highld 147 G8
Kilmacolm Invclyd 118 C3
Kilmaha Argyll 124 E5
Kilmahog Stirling 126 D5
Kilmalieu Highld 130 D2
Kilmaluag Highld 149 A9
Kilmany Fife 129 B5
Kilmarie Highld 149 G10
Kilmarnock E Ayrs 118 F4
Kilmaron Castle Fife 129 C5
Kilmartin Argyll 124 F4
Kilmaurs E Ayrs 118 E4
Kilmelford Argyll 124 D4
Kilmeny Argyll 142 B4
Kilmersdon Som 23 D8
Kilmeston Hants 15 B6
Kilmichael Argyll 143 F7
Kilmichael Glassary Argyll 145 D7
Kilmichael of Inverlussa Argyll 144 E6
Kilmington Devon 11 E7
Kilmington Wilts 24 F2
Kilmonivaig Highld 136 F4
Kilmorack Highld 150 G7
Kilmore Argyll 124 C4
Kilmore Highld 149 H11
Kilmory Argyll 144 F6
Kilmory Highld 147 D8
Kilmory Highld 149 H8
Kilmory N Ayrs 143 F10
Kilmuir Highld 148 D7
Kilmuir Highld 149 A8
Kilmuir Highld 151 D10
Kilmuir Highld 151 G9
Kilmun Argyll 124 D5
Kilmun Argyll 145 E10
Kiln Pit Hill Northumb 110 D3
Kilncadzow S Lanark 119 E8
Kilndown Kent 18 B4
Kilnhurst S Yorks 89 E5
Kilninian Argyll 146 G6
Kilninver Argyll 124 C4
Kilnsea E Yorks 91 C8
Kilnsey N Yorks 94 C2
Kilnwick E Yorks 97 E5
Kilnwick Percy E Yorks 96 D4
Kiloran Argyll 144 D2
Kilpatrick N Ayrs 143 F10
Kilpeck Hereford 49 F6
Kilphedir Highld 157 H12
Kilpin E Yorks 89 B8
Kilpin Pike E Yorks 89 B8
Kilrenny Fife 129 D7
Kilsby Northants 52 B3
Kilspindie Perth 128 B4
Kilsyth N Lanark 119 B7
Kiltarlity Highld 151 G8
Kilton Notts 77 B5
Kilton Som 22 E3
Kilton Thorpe Redcar 102 C4
Kilvaxter Highld 149 B8
Kilve Som 22 E3
Kilvington Notts 77 E7
Kilwinning N Ayrs 118 E3
Kimber worth S Yorks 88 E5
Kimberley Norf 68 D3
Kimberley Notts 76 E5
Kimble Wick Bucks 39 D8
Kimblesworth Durham 111 E5
Kimbolton Cambs 53 C8
Kimbolton Hereford 49 C7
Kimcote Leics 64 F2
Kimmeridge Dorset 13 G7
Kimmerston Northumb 123 F5
Kimpton Hants 25 E7
Kimpton Herts 40 C4
Kinbrace Highld 157 F11
Kinbuck Stirling 127 D6
Kincaple Fife 129 C6
Kincardine Fife 127 F8
Kincardine Highld 151 C9
Kincardine Bridge Falk 127 F8
Kincardine O'Neil Aberds 140 E4
Kinclaven Perth 134 F1
Kincorth Aberdeen 141 D8
Kincorth Ho. Moray 151 E13
Kincraig Highld 138 D4
Kincraigie Perth 133 E6
Kindallachan Perth 133 E6
Kineton Glos 37 B7
Kineton Warks 51 D8
Kinfauns Perth 128 B3
King Edward Aberds 153 C7
King Sterndale Derbys 75 B7
Kingairloch Highld 130 D2
Kingarth Argyll 145 H9
Kingcoed Mon 35 D8
Kingerby Lincs 90 E4
Kingham Oxon 38 B2
Kingholm Quay Dumfries 107 B6
Kinghorn Fife 128 F4
Kingie Highld 136 D4
Kinglassie Fife 128 E4
Kingoodie Perth 128 B5
King's Acre Hereford 49 E6
King's Bromley Staffs 62 C5
King's Caple Hereford 36 B2
King's Cliffe Northants 65 E7
King's Coughton Warks 51 D5
King's Heath W Mid 62 F4
Kings Hedges Cambs 55 C5
Kings Langley Herts 40 D3
King's Hill Kent 29 D7
King's Lynn Norf 67 B6
King's Meaburn Cumb 99 B8
King's Mills Wrex 73 E7
Kings Muir Borders 121 F5
King's Newnham Warks 52 B2
King's Newton Derbys 63 B7
King's Norton Leics 64 D3
King's Norton W Mid 51 B5
King's Nympton Devon 9 C8
King's Pyon Hereford 49 D6
King's Ripton Cambs 54 B3
King's Somborne Hants 25 F8
King's Stag Dorset 12 C5
King's Stanley Glos 37 D5
King's Sutton Northants 52 F2
King's Thorn Hereford 49 F7
King's Walden Herts 40 B4
Kings Worthy Hants 26 F2
Kingsand Corn 6 D2
Kingsbarns Fife 129 C7
Kingsbridge Devon 6 E5
Kingsbridge Som 21 F8
Kingsburgh Highld 149 C8
Kingsbury London 41 F5
Kingsbury Warks 63 E6
Kingsbury Episcopi Som 12 B2
Kingsclere Hants 26 D3
Kingscote Glos 37 E5
Kingscott Devon 9 C7
Kingscross N Ayrs 143 F11
Kingsdon Som 12 B3
Kingsdown Kent 31 E7
Kingseat Fife 128 E3
Kingsey Bucks 39 D7
Kingsfold W Sus 28 F2
Kingsford E Ayrs 118 E4
Kingsford Worcs 62 F2
Kingsforth N Lincs 90 C4
Kingsgate Kent 31 B7
Kingsheanton Devon 20 F4
Kingshouse Hotel Highld 131 D6
Kingside Hill Cumb 107 D8
Kingskerswell Devon 7 C6
Kingskettle Fife 128 D5
Kingsland Anglesey 82 C2
Kingsland Hereford 49 C6
Kingsley Ches W 74 B2
Kingsley Hants 27 F5
Kingsley Staffs 75 E7
Kingsley Green W Sus 27 F6
Kingsley Holt Staffs 75 E7
Kingsley Park Northants 53 C5
Kingsmuir Angus 134 E4
Kingsmuir Fife 129 D7
Kingsnorth Kent 19 B7
Kingstanding W Mid 62 E4
Kingsteignton Devon 7 B6
Kingsthorpe Northants 53 C5
Kingston Cambs 54 D4
Kingston Devon 6 E4
Kingston Dorset 13 D5
Kingston Dorset 13 G7
Kingston E Loth 129 F7
Kingston Hants 14 D2
Kingston IoW 15 F5
Kingston Kent 31 D5
Kingston Moray 152 B3
Kingston Bagpuize Oxon 38 E4
Kingston Blount Oxon 39 E7
Kingston by Sea W Sus 17 D6
Kingston Deverill Wilts 24 F3
Kingston Gorse W Sus 16 D4
Kingston Lisle Oxon 38 F3
Kingston Maurward Dorset 12 E5
Kingston near Lewes E Sus 17 D7
Kingston on Soar Notts 64 B2
Kingston Russell Dorset 12 E3
Kingston Seymour N Som 23 C6
Kingston St Mary Som 11 B7
Kingston Upon Hull Hull 90 B4
Kingston upon Thames London 28 C2
Kingston Vale London 28 B3
Kingstone Hereford 49 F6
Kingstone Som 11 C8
Kingstone Staffs 62 B4
Kingstown Cumb 108 D3
Kingswear Devon 7 D6
Kingswells Aberdeen 141 D7
Kingswinford W Mid 62 F2
Kingswood Bucks 39 C6
Kingswood Glos 36 E4
Kingswood Hereford 48 D4
Kingswood Kent 30 D2
Kingswood Powys 60 D2
Kingswood S Glos 23 B8
Kingswood Sur 28 D3
Kingswood Warks 51 B6
Kingthorpe Lincs 78 B4
Kington Hereford 48 D4
Kington Worcs 50 D4
Kington Langley Wilts 24 B4
Kington Magna Dorset 13 B5
Kington St Michael Wilts 24 B4
Kingussie Highld 138 D3
Kingweston Som 23 F7
Kininvie Ho. Moray 152 D3
Kinkell Bridge Perth 127 C8
Kinknockie Aberds 153 D10
Kinlet Shrops 61 F7
Kinloch Fife 128 C4
Kinloch Highld 146 B6
Kinloch Highld 149 G11
Kinloch Highld 156 F6
Kinloch Perth 133 E8
Kinloch Perth 134 E2
Kinloch Hourn Highld 136 D2
Kinloch Laggan Highld 137 F8
Kinloch Lodge Highld 157 D8
Kinloch Rannoch Perth 132 D3
Kinlochan Highld 130 C2
Kinlochard Stirling 126 D3
Kinlochbeoraid Highld 147 C11
Kinlochbervie Highld 156 D5
Kinlocheil Highld 130 B3
Kinlochewe Highld 150 E3
Kinlochleven Highld 131 C5
Kinlochmoidart Highld 147 D10
Kinlochmorar Highld 147 B11
Kinlochmore Highld 131 C5
Kinlochspelve Argyll 124 C2
Kinloid Highld 147 C9
Kinloss Moray 151 E13
Kinmel Bay Conwy 72 A3
Kinmuck Aberds 141 C7
Kinmundy Aberds 141 C7
Kinnadie Aberds 153 D9
Kinnaird Perth 128 B4
Kinnaird Castle Angus 135 D6
Kinneff Aberds 135 B8
Kinnelhead Dumfries 114 D3
Kinnell Angus 135 D6
Kinnerley Shrops 60 B3
Kinnersley Hereford 48 E5
Kinnersley Worcs 50 E3
Kinnerton Powys 48 C4
Kinnesswood Perth 128 D3
Kinninvie Durham 101 B5
Kinnordy Angus 134 D3
Kinoulton Notts 77 F6
Kinross Perth 128 D3
Kinrossie Perth 134 F1
Kinsbourne Green Herts 40 C4
Kinsey Heath Ches E 74 E3
Kinsham Hereford 49 C5
Kinsham Worcs 50 F4
Kinsley W Yorks 88 C5
Kinson Bmouth 13 E8
Kintbury W Berks 25 C8
Kintessack Moray 151 E12
Kintillo Perth 128 C3
Kintocher Aberds 140 D4
Kinton Hereford 49 B6
Kinton Shrops 60 C3
Kintore Aberds 141 C6
Kintour Argyll 142 C5
Kintra Argyll 142 D4
Kintra Argyll 146 J6
Kintraw Argyll 124 E4
Kinuachdrachd Argyll 124 F3
Kinveachy Highld 138 C5
Kinver Staffs 62 F2
Kippax W Yorks 95 F7
Kippen Stirling 127 E5
Kippford or Scaur Dumfries 106 D5
Kirbister Orkney 159 F7
Kirbister Orkney 159 H4
Kirbuster Orkney 159 F3
Kirby Bedon Norf 69 D5
Kirby Bellars Leics 64 C4
Kirby Cane Norf 69 E6
Kirby Cross Essex 43 B8
Kirby Grindalythe N Yorks 96 C5
Kirby Hill N Yorks 95 C6
Kirby Hill N Yorks 101 D6
Kirby Knowle N Yorks 102 F2
Kirby-le-Soken Essex 43 B8
Kirby Misperton N Yorks 96 B3
Kirby Muxloe Leics 64 D2
Kirby Row Norf 69 E6
Kirby Sigston N Yorks 102 E2
Kirby Underdale E Yorks 96 D4
Kirby Wiske N Yorks 102 F1
Kirdford W Sus 16 B4
Kirk Highld 158 E4
Kirk Bramwith S Yorks 89 C7
Kirk Deighton N Yorks 95 D6
Kirk Ella E Yorks 90 B4
Kirk Hallam Derbys 76 E4
Kirk Hammerton N Yorks 95 D7
Kirk Ireton Derbys 76 D2
Kirk Langley Derbys 76 F2
Kirk Merrington Durham 111 F5
Kirk Michael IoM 84 C3
Kirk of Shotts N Lanark 119 C8
Kirk Sandall S Yorks 89 D7
Kirk Smeaton N Yorks 89 C6
Kirk Yetholm Borders 116 B4
Kirkabister Shetland 160 K6
Kirkandrews Dumfries 106 E3
Kirkandrews upon Eden Cumb 108 D3
Kirkbampton Cumb 108 D3
Kirkbean Dumfries 107 D6
Kirkbride Cumb 108 D2
Kirkbuddo Angus 135 E5
Kirkburn Borders 121 F5
Kirkburn E Yorks 97 D5
Kirkburton W Yorks 88 C2
Kirkby Lincs 90 E4
Kirkby Mers 86 E2
Kirkby N Yorks 102 D3
Kirkby Fleetham N Yorks 101 E7
Kirkby Green Lincs 78 D3
Kirkby In Ashfield Notts 76 D5
Kirkby-in-Furness Cumb 98 F4
Kirkby la Thorpe Lincs 78 E3
Kirkby Lonsdale Cumb 93 B6
Kirkby Malham N Yorks 93 C8
Kirkby Mallory Leics 63 D8
Kirkby Malzeard N Yorks 94 B5
Kirkby Mills N Yorks 103 F5
Kirkby on Bain Lincs 78 C5
Kirkby Overflow N Yorks 95 E6
Kirkby Stephen Cumb 100 D2
Kirkby Thore Cumb 99 B8
Kirkby Underwood Lincs 65 B7
Kirkby Wharfe N Yorks 95 E8
Kirkbymoorside N Yorks 102 F4
Kirkcaldy Fife 128 E4
Kirkcambeck Cumb 108 C5
Kirkcarswell Dumfries 106 E4
Kirkcolm Dumfries 104 C4
Kirkconnel Dumfries 113 C7
Kirkconnell Dumfries 107 C6
Kirkcowan Dumfries 105 C7
Kirkcudbright Dumfries 106 D3
Kirkdale Mers 85 E4
Kirkfieldbank S Lanark 119 E8
Kirkgunzeon Dumfries 107 C5
Kirkham Lancs 92 F4
Kirkham N Yorks 96 C3
Kirkhamgate W Yorks 88 B3
Kirkharle Northumb 117 F6
Kirkheaton Northumb 110 B3
Kirkheaton W Yorks 88 C2
Kirkhill Angus 135 C6
Kirkhill Highld 151 G8
Kirkhill Midloth 120 C5
Kirkhill Moray 152 E2
Kirkhope Borders 115 B6
Kirkhouse Borders 121 F6
Kirkiboll Highld 157 D8
Kirkibost Highld 149 G10
Kirkinch Angus 134 E3
Kirkinner Dumfries 105 D8
Kirkintilloch E Dunb 119 B6
Kirkland Cumb 98 C2
Kirkland Cumb 109 F6
Kirkland Dumfries 113 C7
Kirkland Dumfries 113 E8
Kirkland Dumfries 114 E2
Kirkleatham Redcar 102 B3
Kirklevington Stockton 102 D2
Kirkley Suff 69 E8
Kirklington N Yorks 101 F8
Kirklington Notts 77 D6
Kirklinton Cumb 108 C4
Kirkliston Edin 120 B4
Kirkmaiden Dumfries 104 F5
Kirkmichael Perth 133 D7
Kirkmichael S Ayrs 112 D3
Kirkmuirhill S Lanark 119 E7
Kirknewton Northumb 122 F5
Kirknewton W Loth 120 C4
Kirkney Aberds 152 E5
Kirkoswald Cumb 109 E5
Kirkoswald S Ayrs 112 D2
Kirkpatrick Durham Dumfries 106 B4
Kirkpatrick-Fleming Dumfries 108 B2
Kirksanton Cumb 98 F3
Kirkstall W Yorks 95 F5
Kirkstead Lincs 78 C4
Kirkstile Aberds 152 E5
Kirkstyle Highld 158 C5
Kirkton Aberds 140 B5
Kirkton Aberds 153 D6
Kirkton Angus 134 E4
Kirkton Angus 134 F4
Kirkton Borders 115 C8
Kirkton Dumfries 114 F2
Kirkton Fife 129 B5
Kirkton Highld 149 F13
Kirkton Highld 150 G2
Kirkton Highld 151 B10
Kirkton Highld 151 F10
Kirkton Perth 127 C8
Kirkton S Lanark 114 B2
Kirkton Stirling 126 D4
Kirkton Manor Borders 120 F5
Kirkton of Airlie Angus 134 D3

L

Man–Mou 219

(Index entries, arranged in columns)

Column 1:
- Manar Ho. Aberds 141 B6
- Manaton Devon 10 F2
- Manby Lincs 91 F7
- Mancetter Warks 63 E7
- Manchester Gtr Man 87 E6
- Manchester Airport Gtr Man 87 F6
- Mancot Flint 73 C7
- Mandally Highld 137 D5
- Manea Cambs 66 F4
- Manfield N Yorks 101 C7
- Mangaster Shetland 160 F5
- Mangotsfield S Glos 23 B8
- Mangurstadh W Isles 154 D5
- Mankinholes W Yorks 87 B7
- Manley Ches W 74 B2
- Mannal Argyll 146 G2
- Mannerston W Loth 120 B3
- Manningford Bohune Wilts 25 D6
- Manningford Bruce Wilts 25 D6
- Manningham W Yorks 94 F4
- Mannings Heath W Sus 17 B6
- Mannington Dorset 13 D8
- Manningtree Essex 56 F4
- Mannofield Aberdeen 141 D8
- Manor London 41 F7
- Manor Estate S Yorks 88 F4
- Manorbier Pembs 32 E1
- Manordeilo Carms 33 B7
- Manorhill Borders 122 F2
- Manorowen Pembs 44 B4
- Mansel Lacy Hereford 49 E6
- Manselfield Swansea 33 F6
- Mansell Gamage Hereford 49 E5
- Mansergh Cumb 99 F8
- Mansfield E Ayrs 113 C6
- Mansfield Notts 76 C5
- Mansfield Woodhouse Notts 76 C5
- Mansriggs Cumb 98 F4
- Manston Dorset 13 C6
- Manston Kent 31 C7
- Manston W Yorks 95 F6
- Manswood Dorset 13 D7
- Manthorpe Lincs 65 C7
- Manthorpe Lincs 78 F2
- Manton N Lincs 90 D3
- Manton Notts 77 B5
- Manton Rutland 65 D5
- Manton Wilts 25 C6
- Manuden Essex 41 B7
- Maperton Som 12 B4
- Maple Cross Herts 40 E3
- Maplebeck Notts 77 C7
- Mapledurham Oxon 26 B4
- Mapledurwell Hants 26 D4
- Maplehurst W Sus 17 B5
- Maplescombe Kent 29 C6
- Mapleton Derbys 75 E8
- Mapperley Derbys 76 E4
- Mapperley Park Nottingham 77 E5
- Mapperton Dorset 12 E3
- Mappleborough Green Warks 51 C5
- Mappleton E Yorks 97 E8
- Mappowder Dorset 12 D5
- Mar Lodge Aberds 139 E6
- Maraig W Isles 154 G6
- Marazanvose Corn 4 D3
- Marazion Corn 2 C4
- Marbhig W Isles 155 F9
- Marbury Ches E 74 E2
- March Cambs 66 E4
- March S Lanark 114 C2
- Marcham Oxon 38 E4
- Marchamley Shrops 61 B5
- Marchington Staffs 75 F8
- Marchington Woodlands Staffs 62 B5
- Marchroes Gwyn 70 E4
- Marchwiel Wrex 73 E7
- Marchwood Hants 14 C4
- Marcross V Glam 21 C8
- Marden Hereford 49 E7
- Marden Kent 29 E8
- Marden T&W 111 B6
- Marden Wilts 25 D5
- Marden Beech Kent 29 E8
- Marden Thorn Kent 29 E8
- Mardy Mon 35 C7
- Marefield Leics 64 D4
- Mareham le Fen Lincs 79 C5
- Mareham on the Hill Lincs 79 C5
- Marehay Derbys 76 E3
- Marehill W Sus 16 C4
- Maresfield E Sus 17 B8
- Marfleet Hull 90 B5
- Marford Wrex 73 D7
- Margam Neath 34 F1
- Margaret Marsh Dorset 13 C6
- Margaret Roding Essex 42 C1
- Margaretting Essex 42 D2
- Margate Kent 31 B7
- Margnaheglish N Ayrs 143 E11
- Margrove Park Redcar 102 C4
- Marham Norf 67 C7
- Marhamchurch Corn 8 D4
- Marholm Pboro 65 D8
- Mariandyrys Anglesey 83 C6
- Marianglas Anglesey 82 C5
- Mariansleigh Devon 10 B2
- Marionburgh Aberds 141 D6
- Marishader Highld 149 B9
- Marjoriebanks Dumfries 114 F3
- Mark Dumfries 105 D6
- Mark S Ayrs 104 B4
- Mark Som 23 E5
- Mark Causeway Som 23 E5
- Mark Cross E Sus 17 C7
- Mark Cross E Sus 18 B2
- Markbeech Kent 29 E5
- Markby Lincs 79 B7
- Market Bosworth Leics 63 D8
- Market Deeping Lincs 65 D8
- Market Drayton Shrops 74 F3
- Market Harborough Leics 64 F4
- Market Lavington Wilts 24 D5
- Market Overton Rutland 65 C5
- Market Rasen Lincs 90 F5
- Market Stainton Lincs 78 B5
- Market Warsop Notts 77 C5
- Market Weighton E Yorks 96 E4
- Market Weston Suff 56 B3
- Markethill Perth 134 F2
- Markfield Leics 63 C8
- Markham Caerph 35 D6
- Markham Moor Notts 77 B7
- Markinch Fife 128 D4
- Markington N Yorks 95 C5
- Marks Tey Essex 43 B5
- Marksbury Bath 23 C8
- Markyate Herts 40 C3
- Marland Gtr Man 87 C6
- Marlborough Wilts 25 C6
- Marlbrook Hereford 49 D7
- Marlbrook Worcs 50 B4
- Marlcliff Warks 51 D5
- Marldon Devon 7 C6
- Marlesford Suff 57 D7
- Marley Green Ches E 74 E2
- Marley Hill T&W 110 D5
- Marley Mount Hants 14 E3

Column 2:
- Marlingford Norf 68 D4
- Marloes Pembs 44 E2
- Marlow Bucks 39 F8
- Marlow Hereford 49 B6
- Marlow Bottom Bucks 40 F1
- Marlpit Hill Kent 28 E5
- Marlpool Derbys 76 E4
- Marnhull Dorset 13 C5
- Marnoch Aberds 152 C5
- Marnock N Lanark 119 C7
- Marple Gtr Man 87 F7
- Marple Bridge Gtr Man 87 F7
- Marr S Yorks 89 D6
- Marrel Highld 157 H13
- Marrick N Yorks 101 E5
- Marrister Shetland 160 G7
- Marros Carms 32 D3
- Marsden T&W 111 C6
- Marsden W Yorks 87 C8
- Marsett N Yorks 100 F4
- Marsh Bucks 39 D8
- Marsh W Yorks 94 F3
- Marsh Baldon Oxon 39 E5
- Marsh Bottom Oxon 39 F7
- Marsh Gibbon Bucks 39 B6
- Marsh Green Devon 10 E5
- Marsh Green Kent 28 E5
- Marsh Green Staffs 75 D5
- Marsh Lane Derbys 76 B4
- Marsh Street Som 21 E8
- Marshall's Heath Herts 40 C4
- Marshalsea Dorset 11 D8
- Marshalswick Herts 40 D4
- Marsham Norf 81 E7
- Marshaw Lancs 93 D5
- Marshborough Kent 31 D7
- Marshbrook Shrops 60 F4
- Marshchapel Lincs 91 E7
- Marshfield Newport 35 F6
- Marshfield S Glos 24 B2
- Marshgate Corn 8 E3
- Marshland St James Norf 66 D5
- Marshside Mers 85 C4
- Marshwood Dorset 11 E8
- Marske N Yorks 101 D6
- Marske-by-the-Sea Redcar 102 B4
- Marston Ches W 74 B3
- Marston Hereford 49 D5
- Marston Lincs 77 E8
- Marston Oxon 39 D5
- Marston Staffs 62 B3
- Marston Staffs 62 C2
- Marston Warks 63 E6
- Marston Wilts 24 D4
- Marston Doles Warks 52 D2
- Marston Green W Mid 63 F5
- Marston Magna Som 12 B3
- Marston Meysey Wilts 37 E8
- Marston Montgomery Derbys 75 F8
- Marston Moretaine C Beds 53 E7
- Marston on Dove Derbys 63 B6
- Marston St Lawrence Northants 52 E3
- Marston Stannett Hereford 49 D7
- Marston Trussell Northants 64 F3
- Marstow Hereford 36 C2
- Marsworth Bucks 40 C2
- Marten Wilts 25 D7
- Marthall Ches E 74 B5
- Martham Norf 69 C7
- Martin Hants 13 C8
- Martin Kent 31 E7
- Martin Lincs 78 C5
- Martin Lincs 78 C4
- Martin Dales Lincs 78 C4
- Martin Drove End Hants 13 B8
- Martin Hussingtree Worcs 50 C3
- Martin Mill Kent 31 E7
- Martinhoe Devon 21 E5
- Martinhoe Cross Devon 21 E5
- Martinscroft Warr 86 F4
- Martinstown Dorset 12 F4
- Martlesham Suff 57 E6
- Martlesham Heath Suff 57 E6
- Martletwy Pembs 32 C1
- Martley Worcs 50 D2
- Martock Som 12 C2
- Marton Ches E 75 C5
- Marton E Yorks 97 F7
- Marton Lincs 90 F2
- Marton Mbro 102 C3
- Marton N Yorks 95 C7
- Marton N Yorks 103 F5
- Marton Shrops 60 B4
- Marton Shrops 60 D2
- Marton Warks 52 C2
- Marton-le-Moor N Yorks 95 B6
- Martyr Worthy Hants 26 F3
- Martyr's Green Sur 27 D8
- Marwick Orkney 159 F3
- Marwood Devon 20 F4
- Mary Tavy Devon 6 B3
- Marybank Highld 150 F7
- Maryburgh Highld 151 F8
- Maryhill Glasgow 119 C5
- Marykirk Aberds 135 C6
- Marylebone Gtr Man 86 D3
- Marypark Moray 152 E1
- Maryport Cumb 107 F7
- Maryport Dumfries 104 F5
- Maryton Angus 135 D6
- Marywell Aberds 140 E4
- Marywell Aberds 141 E8
- Marywell Angus 135 E6
- Masham N Yorks 101 F7
- Mashbury Essex 42 C2
- Masongill N Yorks 93 B6
- Masonleys Aberds 140 C5
- Mastin Moor Derbys 76 B4
- Mastrick Aberdeen 141 D7
- Matching Essex 41 C8
- Matching Green Essex 41 C8
- Matching Tye Essex 41 C8
- Matfen Northumb 110 B3
- Matfield Kent 29 E7
- Mathern Mon 36 E2
- Mathon Hereford 50 E2
- Mathry Pembs 44 B3
- Matlaske Norf 81 D7
- Matlock Derbys 76 C2
- Matlock Bath Derbys 76 D2
- Matson Glos 37 C5
- Matterdale End Cumb 99 B5
- Mattersey Notts 89 F7
- Mattersey Thorpe Notts 89 F7
- Mattingley Hants 26 D5
- Mattishall Norf 68 C3
- Mattishall Burgh Norf 68 C3
- Mauchline E Ayrs 112 B4
- Maud Aberds 153 D9
- Maugersbury Glos 38 B2
- Maughold IoM 84 C4
- Mauld Highld 150 H7
- Maulden C Beds 53 F8
- Maulds Meaburn Cumb 99 C8
- Maunby N Yorks 102 F1
- Maund Bryan Hereford 49 D7
- Maundown Som 11 B5
- Mautby Norf 69 C7
- Mavis Enderby Lincs 79 C6
- Maw Green Ches E 74 D4
- Mawbray Cumb 107 E7
- Mawdesley Lancs 86 C2
- Mawdlam Bridgend 34 F2
- Mawgan Corn 3 D6
- Mawla Corn 3 B6
- Mawnan Corn 3 D6
- Mawnan Smith Corn 3 D6
- Mawsley Northants 53 B6

Column 3:
- Maxey Pboro 65 D8
- Maxstoke Warks 63 F6
- Maxton Borders 122 F2
- Maxton Kent 31 E7
- Maxwellheugh Borders 122 F3
- Maxwelltown Dumfries 107 B6
- Maxworthy Corn 8 E4
- May Bank Staffs 75 E5
- Mayals Swansea 33 E7
- Maybole S Ayrs 112 D3
- Mayfield E Sus 18 C2
- Mayfield Midloth 121 C6
- Mayfield Staffs 75 E8
- Mayfield W Loth 120 C2
- Mayford Sur 27 D7
- Mayland Essex 43 D5
- Maynard's Green E Sus 18 D2
- Maypole Mon 36 C1
- Maypole Scilly 2 E4
- Maypole Green Essex 43 B5
- Maypole Green Norf 69 E7
- Maypole Green Suff 57 C6
- Maywick Shetland 160 L5
- Meadle Bucks 39 D8
- Meadowtown Shrops 60 D3
- Meaford Staffs 75 F5
- Meal Bank Cumb 99 E7
- Mealabost W Isles 155 D9
- Mealabost Bhuirgh W Isles 155 B9
- Mealsgate Cumb 108 E2
- Meanwood W Yorks 95 F5
- Mearbeck N Yorks 93 C8
- Meare Som 23 E6
- Meare Green Som 11 B8
- Mears Ashby Northants 53 C6
- Measham Leics 63 C7
- Meath Green Sur 28 E3
- Meathop Cumb 99 F6
- Meaux E Yorks 97 F6
- Meavy Devon 6 C3
- Medbourne Leics 64 E4
- Medburn Northumb 110 B4
- Meden Vale Notts 77 C5
- Medlam Lincs 79 D6
- Medmenham Bucks 39 F8
- Medomsley Durham 110 D4
- Medstead Hants 26 F4
- Meer End W Mid 51 B7
- Meerbrook Staffs 75 C6
- Meers Bridge Lincs 91 F8
- Meesden Herts 54 F5
- Meeth Devon 9 D7
- Meggethead Borders 114 B4
- Meidrim Carms 32 B3
- Meifod Denb 72 D4
- Meifod Powys 59 C8
- Meigle N Ayrs 118 C1
- Meigle Perth 134 E2
- Meikle Earnock S Lanark 119 D7
- Meikle Ferry Highld 151 C10
- Meikle Forter Angus 134 C1
- Meikle Gluich Highld 151 C9
- Meikle Pinkerton E Loth 122 B3
- Meikle Strath Aberds 135 B6
- Meikle Tarty Aberds 141 B8
- Meikle Wartle Aberds 153 E7
- Meikleour Perth 134 F1
- Meinciau Carms 33 C5
- Meir Stoke 75 E6
- Meir Heath Staffs 75 E6
- Melbourn Cambs 54 E4
- Melbourne Derbys 63 B7
- Melbourne E Yorks 96 E3
- Melbourne S Lanark 120 E3
- Melbury Abbas Dorset 13 B6
- Melbury Bubb Dorset 12 D3
- Melbury Osmond Dorset 12 D3
- Melbury Sampford Dorset 12 D3
- Melby Shetland 160 H3
- Melchbourne Bedford 53 C8
- Melcombe Bingham Dorset 13 D5
- Melcombe Regis Dorset 12 F4
- Meldon Devon 9 E7
- Meldon Northumb 117 F7
- Meldreth Cambs 54 E4
- Meldrum Ho. Aberds 141 B7
- Melfort Argyll 124 D4
- Melgarve Highld 137 E7
- Meliden Denb 72 A4
- Melin-y-coed Conwy 83 E8
- Melin-y-ddôl Powys 59 D7
- Melin-y-grug Powys 59 D7
- Melin-y-Wig Denb 72 E4
- Melinbyrhedyn Powys 58 E5
- Melincourt Neath 34 D2
- Melin-Y-Wig Denb 72 E4
- Melkinthorpe Cumb 99 B7
- Melkridge Northumb 109 C7
- Melksham Wilts 24 C4
- Melldalloch Argyll 145 F8
- Melling Lancs 93 B5
- Melling Mers 85 D4
- Melling Mount Mers 86 D2
- Mellis Suff 56 B5
- Mellon Charles Highld 155 H13
- Mellon Udrigle Highld 155 H13
- Mellor Gtr Man 87 F7
- Mellor Lancs 93 F6
- Mellor Brook Lancs 93 F6
- Mells Som 24 E2
- Melmerby Cumb 109 F6
- Melmerby N Yorks 95 B6
- Melmerby N Yorks 101 F5
- Melplash Dorset 12 E2
- Melrose Borders 121 F8
- Melsetter Orkney 159 K3
- Melsonby N Yorks 101 D6
- Meltham W Yorks 88 C2
- Melton Suff 57 D6
- Melton Constable Norf 81 D6
- Melton Mowbray Leics 64 C4
- Melton Ross N Lincs 90 C4
- Meltonby E Yorks 96 D3
- Melvaig Highld 155 J12
- Melverley Shrops 60 C3
- Melverley Green Shrops 60 C3
- Melvich Highld 157 C11
- Membury Devon 11 D7
- Memsie Aberds 153 B9
- Memus Angus 134 D4
- Menabilly Corn 5 D5
- Menai Bridge = Porthaethwy Anglesey 83 D5
- Mendham Suff 69 F5
- Mendlesham Suff 56 C5
- Mendlesham Green Suff 56 C4
- Menheniot Corn 5 C7
- Mennock Dumfries 113 D8
- Menston W Yorks 94 E4
- Menstrie Clack 127 E7
- Menthorpe N Yorks 96 F2
- Mentmore Bucks 40 C2
- Meoble Highld 147 C10
- Meole Brace Shrops 60 C4
- Meols Mers 85 E3
- Meonstoke Hants 15 C7
- Meopham Kent 29 C7
- Meopham Station Kent 29 C7
- Mepal Cambs 66 F4
- Meppershall C Beds 54 F2
- Merbach Hereford 48 E5
- Mere Ches E 86 F5

Column 4:
- Mere Wilts 24 F3
- Mere Brow Lancs 86 C2
- Mere Green W Mid 62 E5
- Mereclough Lancs 93 F8
- Mereside Blackpool 92 F3
- Mereworth Kent 29 D7
- Mergie Aberds 141 F6
- Meriden W Mid 63 F6
- Merkadale Highld 149 E8
- Merkland Dumfries 106 B4
- Merkland S Ayrs 112 E2
- Merkland Lodge Highld 156 G7
- Merley Poole 13 E8
- Merlin's Bridge Pembs 44 D4
- Merrington Shrops 60 B4
- Merrion Pembs 44 F4
- Merriott Som 12 C2
- Merrivale Devon 6 B3
- Merrow Sur 27 D8
- Merrymeet Corn 5 C7
- Mersham Kent 19 B7
- Merstham Sur 28 D3
- Merston W Sus 16 D2
- Merstone IoW 15 F6
- Merther Corn 3 B7
- Merthyr Carms 32 B4
- Merthyr Cynog Powys 47 F8
- Merthyr-Dyfan V Glam 22 C3
- Merthyr Mawr Bridgend 21 B7
- Merthyr Tudful = Merthyr Tydfil M Tydf 34 D4
- Merthyr Tydfil M Tydf 34 D4
- Merthyr Vale M Tydf 34 E4
- Merton Devon 9 C7
- Merton London 28 B3
- Merton Norf 68 E2
- Merton Oxon 39 C5
- Mervinslaw Borders 116 C2
- Meshaw Devon 10 C2
- Messing Essex 42 C4
- Messingham N Lincs 90 D2
- Metfield Suff 69 F5
- Metheringham Lincs 78 C3
- Methil Fife 129 E5
- Methlem Gwyn 70 D2
- Methley W Yorks 88 B4
- Methlick Aberds 153 E8
- Methven Perth 128 B2
- Methwold Norf 67 E7
- Methwold Hythe Norf 67 E7
- Mettingham Suff 69 F6
- Mevagissey Corn 3 B9
- Mewith Head N Yorks 93 C7
- Mexborough S Yorks 89 D5
- Mey Highld 158 C4
- Meysey Hampton Glos 37 E8
- Miabhag W Isles 154 G5
- Miabhag W Isles 154 H6
- Miabhig W Isles 154 D5
- Michaelchurch Hereford 36 B2
- Michaelchurch Escley Hereford 48 F5
- Michaelchurch on Arrow Powys 48 D4
- Michaelston-le-Pit V Glam 22 B3
- Michaelston-y-Fedw Newport 35 F6
- Michaelstow Corn 5 B5
- Michaelston-super-Ely Cardiff 22 B3
- Micheldever Hants 26 F3
- Michelmersh Hants 14 B4
- Mickfield Suff 56 C5
- Mickle Trafford Ches W 73 C8
- Micklebring S Yorks 89 E6
- Mickleby N Yorks 103 C6
- Mickleham Sur 28 D2
- Micklehurst Gtr Man 87 D7
- Mickleover Derby 76 F3
- Micklethwaite W Yorks 94 E4
- Mickleton Durham 100 B4
- Mickleton Glos 51 E6
- Mickletown W Yorks 88 B4
- Mickley N Yorks 95 B5
- Mickley Square Northumb 110 C3
- Mid Ardlaw Aberds 153 B9
- Mid Auchinlech Involyd 118 B3
- Mid Beltie Aberds 140 D5
- Mid Calder W Loth 120 C3
- Mid Cloch Forbie Aberds 153 C7
- Mid Clyth Highld 158 G4
- Mid Lavant W Sus 16 D2
- Mid Main Highld 150 H7
- Mid Urchany Highld 151 G11
- Mid Walls Shetland 160 H4
- Mid Yell Shetland 160 D7
- Mid Bea Orkney 159 D5
- Middle Assendon Oxon 39 F7
- Middle Aston Oxon 38 B4
- Middle Barton Oxon 38 B4
- Middle Cairncake Aberds 153 D8
- Middle Claydon Bucks 39 B7
- Middle Drums Angus 135 D5
- Middle Handley Derbys 76 B4
- Middle Littleton Worcs 51 E5
- Middle Maes-coed Hereford 48 F5
- Middle Mill Pembs 44 C3
- Middle Rasen Lincs 90 F4
- Middle Rigg Perth 128 D2
- Middle Tysoe Warks 51 E8
- Middle Wallop Hants 25 F7
- Middle Winterslow Wilts 25 F7
- Middle Woodford Wilts 25 F6
- Middlebie Dumfries 108 B2
- Middleforth Green Lancs 86 B3
- Middleham N Yorks 101 F6
- Middlehope Shrops 60 F4
- Middlemarsh Dorset 12 D4
- Middlemuir Aberds 141 B8
- Middlesbrough Mbro 102 B2
- Middleshaw Cumb 99 F7
- Middleshaw Dumfries 107 B8
- Middlesmoor N Yorks 94 B3
- Middlestone Durham 111 F5
- Middlestone Moor Durham 110 F5
- Middlestown W Yorks 88 C3
- Middlethird Borders 122 E2
- Middleton Aberds 141 C7
- Middleton Argyll 146 G2
- Middleton Cumb 99 F8
- Middleton Derbys 75 D8
- Middleton Derbys 76 C2
- Middleton Essex 56 F2
- Middleton Gtr Man 87 D6
- Middleton Hants 26 E2
- Middleton Hereford 49 C7
- Middleton Lancs 92 D4
- Middleton Midloth 121 D6
- Middleton Norf 67 C6
- Middleton Northants 64 F5
- Middleton Northumb 110 B2
- Middleton Northumb 117 F6
- Middleton N Yorks 94 E4
- Middleton N Yorks 103 F5
- Middleton Perth 128 D3
- Middleton Shrops 49 B7

Column 5:
- Middleton Shrops 60 B3
- Middleton Shrops 60 F2
- Middleton Suff 57 C8
- Middleton Swansea 33 F5
- Middleton Warks 63 E5
- Middleton W Yorks 88 B3
- Middleton Cheney Northants 52 E2
- Middleton Green Staffs 75 F6
- Middleton Hall Northumb 117 B5
- Middleton-in-Teesdale Durham 100 B4
- Middleton Moor Suff 57 C8
- Middleton-on-Leven N Yorks 102 D2
- Middleton-on-Sea W Sus 16 D3
- Middleton on the Hill Hereford 49 C7
- Middleton-on-the-Wolds E Yorks 96 E5
- Middleton One Row Darl 102 C1
- Middleton Priors Shrops 61 E6
- Middleton Quernham N Yorks 95 B6
- Middleton Scriven Shrops 61 F6
- Middleton St George Darl 101 C8
- Middleton Stoney Oxon 39 B5
- Middleton Tyas N Yorks 101 D7
- Middletown Cumb 98 D1
- Middletown Powys 60 C3
- Middlewich Ches E 74 C3
- Middlewood Green Suff 56 C4
- Middlezoy Som 23 F5
- Middridge Durham 101 B7
- Midfield Highld 157 C8
- Midge Hall Lancs 86 B3
- Midgeholme Cumb 109 D6
- Midgham W Berks 26 C3
- Midgley W Yorks 87 B8
- Midgley W Yorks 88 C3
- Midhopestones S Yorks 88 E3
- Midhurst W Sus 16 B2
- Midlem Borders 115 B8
- Midmar Aberds 141 D6
- Midsomer Norton Bath 23 D8
- Midton Inclyd 118 B2
- Midtown Highld 155 J13
- Midtown Highld 157 C8
- Midtown of Buchromb Moray 152 D3
- Midville Lincs 79 D6
- Midway Ches E 87 F7
- Migdale Highld 151 B9
- Migvie Aberds 140 D3
- Milarrochy Stirling 126 E3
- Milborne Port Som 12 C4
- Milborne St Andrew Dorset 13 E6
- Milborne Wick Som 12 B4
- Milbourne Northumb 110 B4
- Milburn Cumb 100 B1
- Milbury Heath S Glos 36 E3
- Milcombe Oxon 52 F2
- Milden Suff 56 E3
- Mildenhall Suff 55 B8
- Mildenhall Wilts 25 C7
- Mile Cross Norf 68 C5
- Mile Elm Wilts 24 C4
- Mile End Essex 43 B5
- Mile End Glos 36 C2
- Mileham Norf 68 C2
- Milesmark Fife 128 F2
- Milfield Northumb 122 F5
- Milford Derbys 76 E3
- Milford Devon 8 B4
- Milford Powys 59 E7
- Milford Staffs 62 B3
- Milford Sur 27 E7
- Milford Wilts 14 B2
- Milford Haven = Aberdaugleddau Pembs 44 E4
- Milford on Sea Hants 14 E3
- Milkwall Glos 36 D2
- Milkwell Wilts 13 B7
- Mill Bank W Yorks 87 B8
- Mill Common Suff 69 F7
- Mill End Bucks 39 F7
- Mill End Herts 54 F4
- Mill Green Essex 42 D2
- Mill Green Norf 68 F4
- Mill Green Suff 56 E3
- Mill Hill London 41 E5
- Mill Lane Hants 27 D5
- Mill of Kingoodie Aberds 141 B7
- Mill of Muiresk Aberds 153 D6
- Mill of Sterin Aberds 140 E2
- Mill of Uras Aberds 141 F7
- Mill Place N Lincs 90 D3
- Mill Side Cumb 99 F6
- Mill Street Norf 68 C3
- Milland W Sus 16 B2
- Millarston Renfs 118 C4
- Millbank Aberds 153 D11
- Millbank Highld 158 D3
- Millbeck Cumb 98 B4
- Millbounds Orkney 159 E6
- Millbreck Aberds 153 D10
- Millbridge Sur 27 E6
- Millbrook C Beds 53 F8
- Millbrook Corn 6 D2
- Millbrook Soton 14 C4
- Millburn S Ayrs 112 B4
- Millcombe Devon 7 E6
- Millcorner E Sus 18 C5
- Milldale Staffs 75 D8
- Millden Lodge Angus 135 B5
- Milldens Angus 135 D5
- Millerhill Midloth 121 C6
- Miller's Dale Derbys 75 B8
- Miller's Green Derbys 76 D2
- Millgreen Shrops 61 B6
- Millhalf Hereford 48 E4
- Millhayes Devon 11 D7
- Millhead Lancs 92 B4
- Millheugh S Lanark 119 D7
- Millholme Cumb 99 E7
- Millhouse Argyll 145 F8
- Millhouse Cumb 108 F3
- Millhouse Green S Yorks 88 D3
- Millhousebridge Dumfries 114 F4
- Millhouses S Yorks 88 F4
- Millikenpark Renfs 118 C4
- Millin Cross Pembs 44 D4
- Millington E Yorks 96 D4
- Millmeece Staffs 74 F5
- Millom Cumb 98 F3
- Millook Corn 8 E3
- Millpool Corn 5 B6
- Millport N Ayrs 145 H10
- Millquarter Dumfries 113 F6
- Millthorpe Lincs 78 F4
- Millthrop Cumb 100 E1
- Milltimber Aberdeen 141 D7
- Milltown Corn 5 D6
- Milltown Derbys 76 C3
- Milltown Devon 20 F4
- Milltown Dumfries 108 B3

Column 6:
- Milltown of Aberdalgie Perth 128 B2
- Milltown of Auchindoun Moray 152 D3
- Milltown of Craigston Aberds 153 C7
- Milltown of Edinvillie Moray 152 D2
- Milltown of Kildrummy Aberds 140 C3
- Milltown of Rothiemay Moray 152 D5
- Milltown of Towie Aberds 140 C3
- Milnathort Perth 128 D3
- Milner's Heath Ches W 73 C8
- Milngavie E Dunb 119 B5
- Milnrow Gtr Man 87 C7
- Milnshaw Lancs 87 B5
- Milnthorpe Cumb 99 F6
- Milo Carms 33 C6
- Milson Shrops 49 B8
- Milstead Kent 30 D2
- Milston Wilts 25 E6
- Milton Angus 134 E3
- Milton Cambs 55 C5
- Milton Cumb 109 C5
- Milton Derbys 63 C7
- Milton Dumfries 105 D6
- Milton Dumfries 106 B5
- Milton Dumfries 113 F8
- Milton Highld 150 F7
- Milton Highld 150 H6
- Milton Highld 150 H7
- Milton Highld 151 G8
- Milton Highld 151 G11
- Milton Moray 152 B5
- Milton Notts 77 B7
- Milton N Som 22 C5
- Milton Oxon 38 E4
- Milton Oxon 52 F2
- Milton Pembs 32 D1
- Milton Perth 127 B8
- Milton Ptsmth 15 E7
- Milton Stirling 126 D4
- Milton Stoke 75 D6
- Milton W Dunb 118 B4
- Milton Abbas Dorset 13 D6
- Milton Abbot Devon 6 B2
- Milton Bridge Midloth 120 C5
- Milton Bryan C Beds 53 F7
- Milton Clevedon Som 23 F8
- Milton Coldwells Aberds 153 E9
- Milton Combe Devon 6 C2
- Milton Damerel Devon 9 C5
- Milton End Glos 37 D8
- Milton Ernest Bedford 53 D8
- Milton Green Ches W 73 D8
- Milton Hill Oxon 38 E4
- Milton Keynes M Keynes 53 F6
- Milton Keynes Village M Keynes 53 F6
- Milton Lilbourne Wilts 25 C6
- Milton Malsor Northants 52 D5
- Milton Morenish Perth 132 F2
- Milton of Auchinhove Aberds 140 D4
- Milton of Balgonie Fife 128 E5
- Milton of Buchanan Stirling 126 E3
- Milton of Campfield Aberds 140 D5
- Milton of Campsie E Dunb 119 B6
- Milton of Corsindae Aberds 141 D6
- Milton of Cushnie Aberds 140 C4
- Milton of Dalcapon Perth 133 D6
- Milton of Edradour Perth 133 D6
- Milton of Gollanfield Highld 151 F10
- Milton of Lesmore Aberds 140 B3
- Milton of Logie Aberds 140 D3
- Milton of Murtle Aberdeen 141 D7
- Milton of Noth Aberds 140 B4
- Milton of Tullich Aberds 140 E2
- Milton on Stour Dorset 13 B5
- Milton Regis Kent 30 C2
- Milton under Wychwood Oxon 38 C2
- Miltonduff Moray 152 B1
- Miltonise Dumfries 105 B5
- Miltonhill Moray 151 E13
- Milverton Som 11 B6
- Milverton Warks 51 C8
- Milwich Staffs 75 F6
- Minard Argyll 125 F5
- Minchington Dorset 13 C7
- Minchinhampton Glos 37 D5
- Mindrum Northumb 122 F4
- Minehead Som 21 E8
- Minera Wrex 73 D6
- Minety Wilts 37 E7
- Minffordd Gwyn 58 A4
- Minffordd Gwyn 71 D6
- Minffordd Gwyn 83 D5
- Miningsby Lincs 79 C6
- Minions Corn 5 B7
- Minishant S Ayrs 112 C3
- Minllyn Gwyn 59 C5
- Minnes Aberds 141 B8
- Minngearraidh W Isles 148 F2
- Minnigaff Dumfries 105 C8
- Minnonie Aberds 153 B7
- Minskip N Yorks 95 C6
- Minstead Hants 14 C3
- Minsted W Sus 16 B2
- Minster Kent 30 B3
- Minster Kent 31 C7
- Minster Lovell Oxon 38 C3
- Minsterley Shrops 60 D3
- Minsterworth Glos 36 C4
- Minterne Magna Dorset 12 D4
- Minting Lincs 78 B4
- Mintlaw Aberds 153 D10
- Minto Borders 115 B8
- Minton Shrops 60 E4
- Minwear Pembs 32 C1
- Minworth W Mid 63 E5
- Mirbister Orkney 159 F4
- Mirehouse Cumb 98 C1
- Mireland Highld 158 D5
- Mirfield W Yorks 88 C3
- Miserden Glos 37 D6
- Miskin Rhondda 34 F4
- Misson Notts 89 E7
- Misterton Leics 64 F2
- Misterton Notts 89 E8
- Misterton Som 12 D2
- Mistley Essex 56 F5
- Mitcham London 28 C3
- Mitchel Troy Mon 36 C1
- Mitcheldean Glos 36 C3
- Mitchell Corn 4 D3
- Mitchellslacks Dumfries 114 E2
- Mitford Northumb 117 F7
- Mithian Corn 4 D2
- Mitton Staffs 62 C2
- Mixbury Oxon 52 F4
- Mixenden W Yorks 87 B8
- Moat Cumb 108 B4
- Moats Tye Suff 56 D4
- Mobberley Ches E 74 B4
- Mobberley Staffs 75 E7

Column 7:
- Moccas Hereford 49 E5
- Mochdre Conwy 83 D8
- Mochdre Powys 59 F7
- Mochrum Dumfries 105 E7
- Mockbeggar Hants 14 D2
- Mockerkin Cumb 98 B2
- Modbury Devon 6 D4
- Moddershall Staffs 75 F6
- Moelfre Anglesey 82 C5
- Moelfre Powys 59 B8
- Moffat Dumfries 114 D3
- Moggerhanger C Beds 54 E2
- Moira Leics 63 C7
- Mol-chlach Highld 149 G9
- Molash Kent 30 D4
- Mold = Yr Wyddgrug Flint 73 C6
- Moldgreen W Yorks 88 C2
- Molehill Green Essex 42 B1
- Molescroft E Yorks 97 E6
- Molesden Northumb 117 F7
- Molesworth Cambs 53 B8
- Moll Highld 149 E10
- Molland Devon 10 B3
- Mollington Ches W 73 B7
- Mollington Oxon 52 E2
- Mollinsburn N Lanark 119 B7
- Monachty Ceredig 46 C4
- Monachylemore Stirling 126 C3
- Monar Lodge Highld 150 G5
- Monaughty Powys 48 C4
- Monboddo House Aberds 135 B7
- Mondynes Aberds 135 B7
- Monevechadan Argyll 125 E7
- Monewden Suff 57 D6
- Moneydie Perth 128 B2
- Moniaive Dumfries 113 E7
- Monifieth Angus 134 F4
- Monikie Angus 135 F4
- Monimail Fife 128 C4
- Monington Pembs 45 E3
- Monk Bretton S Yorks 88 D4
- Monk Fryston N Yorks 89 B6
- Monk Sherborne Hants 26 D4
- Monk Soham Suff 57 C6
- Monk Street Essex 42 B2
- Monken Hadley London 41 E5
- Monkhopton Shrops 61 E6
- Monkland Hereford 49 D6
- Monkleigh Devon 9 B6
- Monknash V Glam 21 B8
- Monkokehampton Devon 9 D7
- Monks Eleigh Suff 56 E3
- Monk's Gate W Sus 17 B6
- Monks Heath Ches E 74 B5
- Monks Kirby Warks 63 F8
- Monks Risborough Bucks 39 D8
- Monkseaton T&W 111 B6
- Monkshill Aberds 153 D7
- Monksilver Som 22 F2
- Monkspath W Mid 51 B6
- Monkswood Mon 35 D7
- Monkton Devon 11 D6
- Monkton Kent 31 C6
- Monkton Pembs 44 E4
- Monkton S Ayrs 112 B3
- Monkton Combe Bath 24 C2
- Monkton Deverill Wilts 24 F3
- Monkton Farleigh Wilts 24 C3
- Monkton Heathfield Som 11 B7
- Monkton Up Wimborne Dorset 13 C8
- Monkwearmouth T&W 111 D6
- Monkwood Hants 26 F4
- Monmouth = Trefynwy Mon 36 C2
- Monmouth Cap Mon 35 B7
- Monnington on Wye Hereford 49 E5
- Monreith Dumfries 105 E7
- Monreith Mains Dumfries 105 E7
- Mont Saint Guern 16
- Montacute Som 12 C2
- Montcoffer Ho. Aberds 153 B6
- Montford Argyll 145 G10
- Montford Shrops 60 C4
- Montford Bridge Shrops 60 C4
- Montgarrie Aberds 140 C4
- Montgomery = Trefaldwyn Powys 60 E2
- Montrave Fife 129 D5
- Montrose Angus 135 D7
- Montsale Essex 43 E6
- Monxton Hants 25 E8
- Monyash Derbys 75 C8
- Monymusk Aberds 141 C5
- Monzie Perth 127 B7
- Monzie Castle Perth 127 B7
- Moodiesburn N Lanark 119 B6
- Moonzie Fife 128 C5
- Moor Allerton W Yorks 95 F5
- Moor Crichel Dorset 13 D7
- Moor End E Yorks 96 F4
- Moor End York 96 D2
- Moor Monkton N Yorks 95 D8
- Moor of Granary Moray 151 F13
- Moor of Ravenstone Dumfries 105 E7
- Moor Row Cumb 98 C2
- Moor Street Kent 30 C2
- Moorby Lincs 79 C5
- Moordown Bmouth 13 E8
- Moore Halton 86 F3
- Moorend Glos 36 D4
- Moorends S Yorks 89 C7
- Moorgate S Yorks 89 E5
- Moorgreen Notts 76 E4
- Moorhall Derbys 76 B3
- Moorhampton Hereford 49 E5
- Moorhead W Yorks 94 F4
- Moorhouse Cumb 108 D3
- Moorhouse Notts 77 C7
- Moorlinch Som 23 F5
- Moorsholm Redcar 102 C4
- Moorside Gtr Man 87 D7
- Moorthorpe W Yorks 89 C5
- Moortown Hants 14 D2
- Moortown IoW 14 F5
- Moortown Lincs 90 E4
- Morangie Highld 151 C10
- Morar Highld 147 B9
- Morborne Cambs 65 E8
- Morchard Bishop Devon 10 D2
- Morcombelake Dorset 12 E2
- Morcott Rutland 65 D6
- Morda Shrops 60 B2
- Morden Dorset 13 E7
- Morden London 28 C3
- Mordiford Hereford 49 F7
- Mordon Durham 101 B8
- More Shrops 60 E3
- Morebath Devon 10 B4
- Morebattle Borders 116 B3
- Morecambe Lancs 92 C4
- Morefield Highld 150 B4
- Moreleigh Devon 7 D5
- Morenish Perth 132 F2
- Moresby Cumb 98 B1
- Moresby Parks Cumb 98 C1
- Morestead Hants 15 B6
- Moreton Dorset 13 F6

Column 8:
- Moreton Essex 41 D8
- Moreton Mers 85 E3
- Moreton Oxon 39 D6
- Moreton Staffs 61 C7
- Moreton Corbet Shrops 61 B5
- Moreton-in-Marsh Glos 51 F7
- Moreton Jeffries Hereford 49 E8
- Moreton Morrell Warks 51 D8
- Moreton on Lugg Hereford 49 E7
- Moreton Pinkney Northants 52 E3
- Moreton Say Shrops 74 F3
- Moreton Valence Glos 36 D4
- Moretonhampstead Devon 10 F2
- Morfa Carms 33 C6
- Morfa Carms 33 E6
- Morfa Bach Carms 32 C4
- Morfa Bychan Gwyn 71 D6
- Morfa Dinlle Gwyn 82 F4
- Morfa Glas Neath 34 D2
- Morfa Nefyn Gwyn 70 C3
- Morfydd Denb 72 E5
- Morgan's Vale Wilts 14 B2
- Moriah Ceredig 46 B5
- Morland Cumb 99 B7
- Morley Derbys 76 E3
- Morley Durham 101 B6
- Morley W Yorks 88 B3
- Morley Green Ches E 87 F6
- Morley St Botolph Norf 68 E3
- Morningside Edin 120 B5
- Morningside N Lanark 119 D8
- Morningthorpe Norf 68 E5
- Morpeth Northumb 117 F8
- Morphie Aberds 135 C7
- Morrey Staffs 62 C5
- Morris Green Essex 55 F8
- Morriston Swansea 33 E7
- Morston Norf 81 C6
- Mortehoe Devon 20 E3
- Mortimer W Berks 26 C4
- Mortimer's Cross Hereford 49 C6
- Mortlake London 28 B3
- Morton Cumb 108 D3
- Morton Derbys 76 C4
- Morton Lincs 65 B7
- Morton Lincs 77 C8
- Morton Lincs 90 E2
- Morton Norf 68 C4
- Morton Notts 77 D7
- Morton S Glos 36 E3
- Morton Shrops 60 B2
- Morton Bagot Warks 51 C6
- Morton-on-Swale N Yorks 101 E8
- Morvah Corn 2 C3
- Morval Corn 5 D7
- Morvich Highld 136 B2
- Morvich Highld 157 J10
- Morville Shrops 61 E6
- Morville Heath Shrops 61 E6
- Morwenstow Corn 8 C4
- Mosborough S Yorks 88 F5
- Moscow E Ayrs 118 E4
- Mosedale Cumb 108 F3
- Moseley W Mid 62 F4
- Moseley W Mid 62 F3
- Moseley Worcs 50 D3
- Moss Argyll 146 G2
- Moss Highld 147 E9
- Moss S Yorks 89 C6
- Moss Wrex 73 D7
- Moss Bank Mers 86 E3
- Moss Edge Lancs 92 E4
- Moss End Brack 27 B6
- Moss of Barmuckity Moray 152 B2
- Moss Pit Staffs 62 B3
- Moss-side Highld 151 F11
- Moss Side Lancs 92 F3
- Mossat Aberds 140 C3
- Mossbank Shetland 160 F6
- Mossbay Cumb 98 B1
- Mossblown S Ayrs 112 B4
- Mossbrow Gtr Man 86 F5
- Mossburnford Borders 116 C2
- Mossdale Dumfries 106 B3
- Mossend N Lanark 119 C7
- Mosser Cumb 98 B3
- Mossfield Highld 151 D9
- Mossgiel E Ayrs 112 B4
- Mosside Angus 134 D4
- Mossley Ches E 75 C5
- Mossley Gtr Man 87 D7
- Mossley Hill Mers 85 F4
- Mosstodloch Moray 152 B3
- Mosston Angus 135 E5
- Mossy Lea Lancs 86 C3
- Mosterton Dorset 12 D2
- Moston Gtr Man 87 D6
- Moston Shrops 61 B5
- Moston Green Ches E 74 C4
- Mostyn Flint 85 F2
- Mostyn Quay Flint 85 F2
- Motcombe Dorset 13 B6
- Mothecombe Devon 6 E4
- Motherby Cumb 99 B6
- Motherwell N Lanark 119 D7
- Mottingham London 28 B5
- Mottisfont Hants 14 B4
- Mottistone IoW 14 F5
- Mottram in Longdendale Gtr Man 87 E7
- Mottram St Andrew Ches E 75 B5
- Mouilpied Guern 16
- Mouldsworth Ches W 74 B2
- Moulin Perth 133 D6
- Moulsecoomb Brighton 17 D7
- Moulsford Oxon 39 F5
- Moulsoe M Keynes 53 E7
- Moulton Ches W 74 C3
- Moulton Lincs 66 B3
- Moulton Northants 53 C5
- Moulton N Yorks 101 D7
- Moulton Suff 55 C8
- Moulton V Glam 22 B2
- Moulton Chapel Lincs 66 C2
- Moulton Eaugate Lincs 66 C3
- Moulton Seas End Lincs 66 B3
- Moulton St Mary Norf 69 D6
- Mounie Castle Aberds 141 B6
- Mount Corn 4 D2
- Mount Corn 5 C6
- Mount Highld 151 G12
- Mount Bures Essex 56 F3
- Mount Canisp Highld 151 D10
- Mount Hawke Corn 3 B6
- Mount Pleasant Ches E 74 D5
- Mount Pleasant Derbys 63 C6
- Mount Pleasant Derbys 76 E3
- Mount Pleasant Flint 73 B6
- Mount Pleasant Hants 14 E3
- Mount Pleasant W Yorks 88 B3
- Mount Sorrel Wilts 13 B8
- Mount Tabor W Yorks 87 B8
- Mountain W Yorks 94 F3
- Mountain Ash = Aberpennar Rhondda 34 E4
- Mountain Cross Borders 120 E4

N

S

Sto–Thw 225

Column 1

- Stoke sub Hamdon Som 12 C2
- Stoke Talmage Oxon 39 E6
- Stoke Trister Som 12 B5
- Stoke Wake Dorset 13 D5
- Stokeford Dorset 13 F6
- Stokeham Notts 77 B7
- Stokeinteignhead Devon 7 B7
- Stokenchurch Bucks 39 E7
- Stokenham Devon 7 E6
- Stokesay Shrops 60 F4
- Stokesby Norf 69 C7
- Stokesley N Yorks 102 D3
- Stolford Som 22 E4
- Ston Easton Som 23 D8
- Stondon Massey Essex 42 D1
- Stone Bucks 39 C7
- Stone Glos 36 E3
- Stone Kent 29 B6
- Stone S Yorks 89 F6
- Stone Staffs 75 F6
- Stone Worcs 50 B3
- Stone Allerton Som 23 D6
- Stone Bridge Corner Pboro 66 D2
- Stone Chair W Yorks 88 B2
- Stone Cross E Sus 18 E3
- Stone Cross Kent 31 D7
- Stone-edge Batch N Som 23 B6
- Stone House Cumb 100 F2
- Stone Street Kent 29 D6
- Stone Street Suff 56 F3
- Stone Street Suff 69 F6
- Stonebroom Derbys 76 D4
- Stonefield S Lanark 119 D6
- Stonegate E Sus 18 C3
- Stonegate N Yorks 103 D5
- Stonegrave N Yorks 96 B2
- Stonehaugh Northumb 109 B7
- Stonehaven Aberds 141 F7
- Stonehouse Glos 37 D5
- Stonehouse Northumb 109 D6
- Stonehouse S Lanark 119 E7
- Stoneleigh Warks 51 B8
- Stonely Cambs 54 C2
- Stoner Hill Hants 15 B8
- Stone's Green Essex 43 B7
- Stonesby Leics 64 B5
- Stonesfield Oxon 38 C3
- Stonethwaite Cumb 98 C4
- Stoney Cross Hants 14 C3
- Stoney Middleton Derbys 76 B2
- Stoney Stanton Leics 63 E8
- Stoney Stoke Som 24 F2
- Stoney Stratton Som 23 F8
- Stoney Stretton Shrops 60 D3
- Stoneybreck Shetland 160 N8
- Stoneyburn W Loth 120 C2
- Stoneygate Aberds 153 E10
- Stoneygate Leicester 64 D3
- Stoneyhills Essex 43 E5
- Stoneykirk Dumfries 104 D4
- Stoneywood Aberdeen 141 C7
- Stoneywood Falk 127 F6
- Stonganess Shetland 160 C7
- Stonham Aspal Suff 56 D5
- Stonnall Staffs 62 D4
- Stonor Oxon 39 F7
- Stonton Wyville Leics 64 E4
- Stony Cross Hereford 50 E2
- Stony Stratford M Keynes 53 E5
- Stonyfield Highld 151 D10
- Stoodleigh Devon 10 C4
- Stopes S Yorks 88 F3
- Stopham W Sus 16 C4
- Stopsley Luton 40 B4
- Stores Corner Suff 57 E7
- Storeton Mers 85 F4
- Stornoway W Isles 155 D9
- Storridge Hereford 50 E2
- Storrington W Sus 16 C4
- Storrs Cumb 99 E5
- Storth Cumb 99 F6
- Storwood E Yorks 96 E3
- Stotfield Moray 152 A2
- Stotfold C Beds 54 F3
- Stottesdon Shrops 61 F6
- Stoughton Leics 64 D3
- Stoughton Sur 27 D7
- Stoughton W Sus 16 C2
- Stoul Highld 147 B10
- Stoulton Worcs 50 E4
- Stour Provost Dorset 13 B5
- Stour Row Dorset 13 B6
- Stourbridge W Mid 62 F3
- Stourpaine Dorset 13 D6
- Stourport on Severn Worcs 50 B3
- Stourton Staffs 62 F2
- Stourton Warks 51 F7
- Stourton Wilts 24 F2
- Stourton Caundle Dorset 12 C5
- Stove Orkney 159 E7
- Stove Shetland 160 L6
- Stoven Suff 69 F7
- Stow Borders 121 E7
- Stow Lincs 78 B3
- Stow Lincs 90 F2
- Stow Bardolph Norf 67 D6
- Stow Bedon Norf 68 E2
- Stow cum Quy Cambs 55 C5
- Stow Longa Cambs 54 B2
- Stow Maries Essex 42 E4
- Stow-on-the-Wold Glos 38 B1
- Stowbridge Norf 67 D6
- Stowe Shrops 48 B5
- Stowe-by-Chartley Staffs 62 B4
- Stowe Green Glos 36 D2
- Stowell Som 12 B4
- Stowford Devon 9 F6
- Stowlangtoft Suff 56 C3
- Stowmarket Suff 56 D4
- Stowting Kent 30 E5
- Stowupland Suff 56 D4
- Straad Argyll 145 G9
- Strachan Aberds 141 E5
- Stradbroke Suff 57 B6
- Stradishall Suff 55 D8
- Stradsett Norf 67 D6
- Stragglethorpe Lincs 78 D2
- Straid S Ayrs 112 E1
- Straith Dumfries 113 E8
- Straiton Edin 121 C5
- Straiton S Ayrs 112 D3
- Straloch Aberds 141 B7
- Straloch Perth 133 C7
- Stramshall Staffs 75 F7
- Strang IoM 84 E3
- Stranraer Dumfries 104 C4
- Stratfield Mortimer W Berks 26 C4
- Stratfield Saye Hants 26 C4
- Stratfield Turgis Hants 26 D4
- Stratford London 41 F7
- Stratford St Andrew Suff 57 C7
- Stratford St Mary Suff 56 F4
- Stratford Sub Castle Wilts 25 F6
- Stratford Tony Wilts 13 B8
- Stratford-upon-Avon Warks 51 D6
- Strath Highld 149 A12
- Strath Highld 158 E4
- Strathan Highld 136 D2
- Strathan Highld 156 G3

Column 2

- Strathan Highld 157 C8
- Strathaven S Lanark 119 E7
- Strathblane Stirling 119 B5
- Strathcanaird Highld 156 J4
- Strathcarron Highld 150 G2
- Strathcoil Argyll 124 B2
- Strathdon Aberds 140 C2
- Strathellie Aberds 153 B10
- Strathkinness Fife 129 C6
- Strathmashie House Highld 137 E8
- Strathmiglo Fife 128 C4
- Strathmore Lodge Highld 158 F3
- Strathpeffer Highld 150 F7
- Strathrannoch Highld 150 D6
- Strathtay Perth 133 D6
- Strathvaich Lodge Highld 150 D6
- Strathwhillan N Ayrs 143 E11
- Strathy Highld 157 C11
- Stratton Corn 8 D4
- Stratton Dorset 12 E4
- Stratton Glos 37 D7
- Stratton Audley Oxon 39 B6
- Stratton on the Fosse Som 23 D8
- Stratton St Margaret Swindon 38 F1
- Stratton St Michael Norf 68 E5
- Stratton Strawless Norf 81 E8
- Stravithie Fife 129 C7
- Streat E Sus 17 C7
- Streatham London 28 B4
- Streatley C Beds 40 B3
- Streatley W Berks 39 F5
- Street Lancs 92 D5
- Street N Yorks 103 D5
- Street Som 23 F6
- Street Dinas Shrops 73 F7
- Street End Kent 30 D5
- Street End W Sus 16 E2
- Street Gate T&W 110 D5
- Street Lydan Wrex 73 F8
- Streethay Staffs 62 C5
- Streetlam N Yorks 101 E8
- Streetly W Mid 62 E4
- Streetly End Cambs 55 E7
- Strefford Shrops 60 F4
- Strelley Notts 76 E5
- Strensall York 96 C2
- Stretcholt Som 22 E4
- Strete Devon 7 E6
- Stretford Gtr Man 87 E6
- Strethall Essex 55 F5
- Stretham Cambs 55 B6
- Strettington W Sus 16 D2
- Stretton Ches W 73 D8
- Stretton Derbys 76 C3
- Stretton Rutland 65 C6
- Stretton Staffs 62 C2
- Stretton Staffs 63 B6
- Stretton Warr 86 F4
- Stretton Grandison Hereford 49 E8
- Stretton-on-Dunsmore Warks 52 B2
- Stretton-on-Fosse Warks 51 F7
- Stretton Sugwas Hereford 49 E6
- Stretton under Fosse Warks 63 F8
- Stretton Westwood Shrops 61 E5
- Strichen Aberds 153 C9
- Strines Gtr Man 87 F7
- Stringston Som 22 E3
- Strixton Northants 53 C7
- Stroat Glos 36 E2
- Stromeferry Highld 149 E13
- Stromemore Highld 149 E13
- Stromness Orkney 159 H3
- Stronaba Highld 136 F5
- Stronachlachar Stirling 126 C3
- Stronchreggan Highld 130 B4
- Stronchrubie Highld 156 H5
- Strone Argyll 145 E10
- Strone Highld 136 F4
- Strone Highld 137 B8
- Strone Inverclyd 118 B2
- Stronmilchan Argyll 125 C7
- Strontian Highld 130 C2
- Strood Medway 29 C8
- Strood Green Sur 28 E3
- Strood Green W Sus 16 B4
- Strood Green W Sus 28 F2
- Stroud Glos 37 D5
- Stroud Hants 15 B8
- Stroud Green Essex 42 E4
- Stroxton Lincs 78 F2
- Struan Highld 149 E8
- Struan Perth 133 C5
- Strubby Lincs 91 F8
- Strumpshaw Norf 69 D6
- Strutherhill S Lanark 119 E7
- Struy Highld 150 H6
- Stryt-issa Wrex 73 E6
- Stuartfield Aberds 153 D9
- Stub Place Cumb 98 E2
- Stubbington Hants 15 D6
- Stubbins Lancs 87 C5
- Stubbs Cross Kent 19 B6
- Stubb's Green Norf 69 E5
- Stubhampton Dorset 13 C7
- Stubton Lincs 77 E8
- Stuckgowan Argyll 126 D2
- Stuckton Hants 14 C2
- Stud Green Windsor 27 B6
- Studham C Beds 40 C3
- Studland Dorset 13 F8
- Studley Warks 51 C5
- Studley Wilts 24 B4
- Studley Roger N Yorks 95 B5
- Stump Cross Essex 55 E6
- Stuntney Cambs 55 B6
- Sturbridge Staffs 74 F5
- Sturmer Essex 55 E7
- Sturminster Marshall Dorset 13 D7
- Sturminster Newton Dorset 13 C5
- Sturry Kent 31 C5
- Sturton N Lincs 90 D3
- Sturton by Stow Lincs 90 F2
- Sturton le Steeple Notts 89 F8
- Stuston Suff 56 B5
- Stutton N Yorks 95 E7
- Stutton Suff 57 F5
- Styal Ches E 87 F6
- Styrrup Notts 89 E7

Column 3

- Suffield Norf 81 D8
- Sugnall Staffs 74 F4
- Suladale Highld 149 C8
- Sulaisiadar W Isles 155 D10
- Sulby IoM 84 C3
- Sulgrave Northants 52 E3
- Sulham W Berks 26 B4
- Sulhamstead W Berks 26 C4
- Sulland Orkney 159 D6
- Sullington W Sus 16 C4
- Sullom Shetland 160 F5
- Sullom Voe Oil Terminal Shetland 160 F5
- Sully V Glam 22 C3
- Sumburgh Shetland 160 N6
- Summer Bridge N Yorks 94 C5
- Summer-house Darl 101 C7
- Summercourt Corn 4 D3
- Summerfield Norf 80 D3
- Summergangs Hull 97 F7
- Summerleaze Mon 35 F8
- Summersdale W Sus 16 D2
- Summerseat Gtr Man 87 C5
- Summertown Oxon 39 D5
- Summit Gtr Man 87 D7
- Sunbury-on-Thames Sur 28 C2
- Sundaywell Dumfries 113 F8
- Sunderland Argyll 142 B3
- Sunderland Cumb 107 F8
- Sunderland T&W 111 D6
- Sunderland Bridge Durham 111 F5
- Sundhope Borders 115 B6
- Sundon Park Luton 40 B3
- Sundridge Kent 29 D5
- Sunipol Argyll 146 F6
- Sunk Island E Yorks 91 C6
- Sunningdale Windsor 27 C7
- Sunninghill Windsor 27 C7
- Sunningwell Oxon 38 D4
- Sunniside Durham 110 F4
- Sunniside T&W 110 D5
- Sunnyhurst Blackburn 86 B4
- Sunnylaw Stirling 127 E6
- Sunnyside W Sus 28 F4
- Sunton Wilts 25 D7
- Surbiton London 28 C2
- Surby IoM 84 E2
- Surfleet Lincs 66 B2
- Surfleet Seas End Lincs 66 B2
- Surlingham Norf 69 D6
- Sustead Norf 81 D7
- Susworth Lincs 90 D2
- Sutcombe Devon 8 C5
- Suton Norf 68 E3
- Sutors of Cromarty Highld 151 E11
- Sutterby Lincs 79 B6
- Sutterton Lincs 79 F5
- Sutton C Beds 54 E3
- Sutton Cambs 54 B5
- Sutton Kent 31 E7
- Sutton London 28 C3
- Sutton Mers 86 E3
- Sutton N Yorks 89 B5
- Sutton Norf 69 B6
- Sutton Notts 77 F7
- Sutton Notts 89 F7
- Sutton Oxon 38 D4
- Sutton Pboro 65 E7
- Sutton S Yorks 89 C6
- Sutton Shrops 61 F7
- Sutton Shrops 74 F3
- Sutton Som 23 F8
- Sutton Staffs 61 B7
- Sutton Suff 57 E7
- Sutton Sur 27 E8
- Sutton W Sus 16 C3
- Sutton at Hone Kent 29 B6
- Sutton Bassett Northants 64 E4
- Sutton Benger Wilts 24 B4
- Sutton Bonington Notts 64 B2
- Sutton Bridge Lincs 66 B4
- Sutton Cheney Leics 63 D8
- Sutton Coldfield W Mid 62 E5
- Sutton Courtenay Oxon 39 E5
- Sutton Crosses Lincs 66 B4
- Sutton Grange N Yorks 95 B5
- Sutton Green Sur 27 D8
- Sutton Howgrave N Yorks 95 B6
- Sutton In Ashfield Notts 76 D4
- Sutton-in-Craven N Yorks 94 E3
- Sutton in the Elms Leics 64 E2
- Sutton Ings Hull 97 F7
- Sutton Lane Ends Ches E 75 B6
- Sutton Leach Mers 86 E3
- Sutton Maddock Shrops 61 D7
- Sutton Mallet Som 23 F5
- Sutton Mandeville Wilts 13 B7
- Sutton Manor Mers 86 E3
- Sutton Montis Som 12 B4
- Sutton on Hull Hull 97 F7
- Sutton on Sea Lincs 91 F9
- Sutton-on-the-Forest N Yorks 95 C8
- Sutton on the Hill Derbys 76 F2
- Sutton on Trent Notts 77 C7
- Sutton Scarsdale Derbys 76 C4
- Sutton Scotney Hants 26 F2
- Sutton St Edmund Lincs 66 C3
- Sutton St James Lincs 66 C3
- Sutton St Nicholas Hereford 49 E7
- Sutton under Brailes Warks 51 F8
- Sutton-under-Whitestonecliffe N Yorks 102 F2
- Sutton upon Derwent E Yorks 96 E3
- Sutton Valence Kent 30 E2
- Sutton Veny Wilts 24 E3
- Sutton Waldron Dorset 13 C6
- Sutton Weaver Ches W 74 B2
- Sutton Wick Bath 23 D7
- Swaby Lincs 79 B6
- Swadlincote Derbys 63 C7
- Swaffham Norf 67 D8
- Swaffham Bulbeck Cambs 55 C6
- Swaffham Prior Cambs 55 C6
- Swafield Norf 81 D8
- Swainby N Yorks 102 D2
- Swainshill Hereford 49 E6
- Swainsthorpe Norf 68 D5
- Swainswick Bath 24 C2
- Swalcliffe Oxon 51 F8
- Swalecliffe Kent 30 C5
- Swallow Lincs 91 D5
- Swallowcliffe Wilts 13 B7
- Swallowfield Wokingham 26 C5
- Swallownest S Yorks 89 F5
- Swallows Cross Essex 42 E2
- Swan Green Ches W 74 B4
- Swan Green Suff 57 B6
- Swanage Dorset 13 G8

Column 4

- Swanbister Orkney 159 H4
- Swanbourne Bucks 39 B8
- Swanland E Yorks 90 B3
- Swanley Kent 29 C6
- Swanley Village Kent 29 C6
- Swanmore Hants 15 C6
- Swannington Leics 63 C8
- Swannington Norf 68 C4
- Swanscombe Kent 29 B7
- Swansea = Abertawe Swansea 33 E7
- Swanton Abbott Norf 81 E8
- Swanton Morley Norf 68 C3
- Swanton Novers Norf 81 D6
- Swanton Street Kent 30 D2
- Swanwick Derbys 76 D4
- Swanwick Hants 15 D6
- Swarby Lincs 78 E3
- Swardeston Norf 68 D5
- Swarister Shetland 160 E7
- Swarkestone Derbys 63 B7
- Swarland Northumb 117 D7
- Swarthmoor Cumb 92 B2
- Swathwick Derbys 76 C3
- Swaton Lincs 78 F4
- Swavesey Cambs 54 C4
- Sway Hants 14 E3
- Swayfield Lincs 65 B6
- Swaythling Soton 14 C5
- Sweet Green Worcs 49 C8
- Sweetham Devon 10 E3
- Sweethouse Corn 5 C5
- Sweffling Suff 57 C7
- Swepstone Leics 63 C7
- Swerford Oxon 51 F8
- Swettenham Ches E 74 C5
- Swetton N Yorks 94 B4
- Swffryd Caerph 35 E6
- Swiftsden E Sus 18 C4
- Swilland Suff 57 D5
- Swillington W Yorks 95 F6
- Swimbridge Devon 9 B8
- Swimbridge Newland Devon 20 F5
- Swinbrook Oxon 38 C2
- Swinderby Lincs 77 C8
- Swindon Glos 37 B6
- Swindon Staffs 62 E2
- Swindon Swindon 38 F1
- Swine E Yorks 97 F7
- Swinefleet E Yorks 89 B8
- Swineshead Bedford 53 C8
- Swineshead Lincs 78 E5
- Swineshead Bridge Lincs 78 E5
- Swiney Highld 158 G4
- Swinford Leics 52 B3
- Swinford Oxon 38 D4
- Swingate Notts 76 E5
- Swingfield Minnis Kent 31 E6
- Swingfield Street Kent 31 E6
- Swinhoe Northumb 117 B8
- Swinhope Lincs 91 E6
- Swining Shetland 160 G6
- Swinithwaite N Yorks 101 F5
- Swinnow Moor W Yorks 94 F5
- Swinscoe Staffs 75 E8
- Swinside Hall Borders 116 C3
- Swinstead Lincs 65 B7
- Swinton Borders 122 E4
- Swinton Gtr Man 87 D5
- Swinton N Yorks 94 B5
- Swinton N Yorks 96 B3
- Swinton S Yorks 88 E5
- Swintonmill Borders 122 E4
- Swithland Leics 64 C2
- Swordale Highld 151 E8
- Swordland Highld 147 B10
- Swordly Highld 157 C10
- Sworton Heath Ches E 86 F4
- Swydd-ffynnon Ceredig 47 C5
- Swynnerton Staffs 75 F5
- Swyre Dorset 12 F3
- Sychtyn Powys 59 D6
- Syde Glos 37 C6
- Sydenham London 28 B4
- Sydenham Oxon 39 D7
- Sydenham Damerel Devon 6 B2
- Syderstone Norf 80 D4
- Sydling St Nicholas Dorset 12 E4
- Sydmonton Hants 26 D2
- Syerston Notts 77 E7
- Syke Gtr Man 87 C6
- Sykehouse S Yorks 89 C7
- Sykes Lancs 93 D6
- Syleham Suff 57 B6
- Sylen Carms 33 D6
- Symbister Shetland 160 G7
- Symington S Ayrs 118 F3
- Symington S Lanark 120 F2
- Symonds Yat Hereford 36 C2
- Symondsbury Dorset 12 E2
- Synod Inn Ceredig 46 D3
- Syre Highld 157 E9
- Syreford Glos 37 B7
- Syresham Northants 52 E4
- Syston Leics 64 C3
- Syston Lincs 78 E2
- Sytchampton Worcs 50 C3
- Sywell Northants 53 C6

Column 5

T

- Taagan Highld 150 E3
- Tàbost W Isles 155 A10
- Tabost W Isles 155 F8
- Tackley Oxon 38 B4
- Tacleit W Isles 154 D6
- Tacolneston Norf 68 E4
- Tadcaster N Yorks 95 E7
- Taddington Derbys 75 B8
- Taddiport Devon 9 C6
- Tadley Hants 26 C4
- Tadlow C Beds 54 E3
- Tadmarton Oxon 51 F8
- Tadworth Sur 28 D3
- Tafarn-y-gelyn Denb 73 C5
- Tafarnau-bach Bl Gwent 35 C5
- Taff's Well Rhondda 35 F5
- Tafolwern Powys 59 D5
- Tai Conwy 83 E7
- Tai-bach Powys 59 B8
- Tai-mawr Conwy 72 E3
- Tai-Ucha Denb 72 D4
- Taibach Neath 34 F1
- Taigh a Ghearraidh W Isles 148 A2
- Tain Highld 151 C10
- Tain Highld 158 D4
- Tainant Wrex 73 E6
- Tainlon Gwyn 82 F4
- Tai'r-Bull Powys 34 B3
- Tairgwaith Neath 33 C8
- Takeley Essex 42 B1
- Takeley Street Essex 41 B8
- Tal-sarn Ceredig 46 D4
- Tal-y-bont Ceredig 58 F3
- Tal-y-Bont Conwy 83 E7
- Tal-y-bont Gwyn 71 E6
- Tal-y-bont Gwyn 83 D6
- Tal-y-cafn Conwy 83 D7
- Tal-y-llyn Gwyn 58 D4

Column 6

- Tal-y-wern Powys 58 D5
- Talachddu Powys 48 F2
- Talacre Flint 85 F2
- Tadley Hants 59 B5
- Talaton Devon 11 E5
- Talbenny Pembs 44 D3
- Talbot Green Rhondda 34 F4
- Talbot Village Poole 13 E8
- Tale Devon 11 D5
- Talerddig Powys 59 D6
- Talgarreg Ceredig 46 D3
- Talgarth Powys 48 F3
- Talisker Highld 149 E8
- Talke Staffs 74 D5
- Talkin Cumb 109 D5
- Talla Linnfoots Borders 114 B4
- Talladale Highld 150 D2
- Tallarn Green Wrex 73 E8
- Tallentire Cumb 107 F8
- Talley Carms 46 F5
- Tallington Lincs 65 D7
- Talmine Highld 157 C8
- Talog Carms 32 B4
- Talsarn Carms 34 B1
- Talsarnau Gwyn 71 D7
- Talskiddy Corn 4 C4
- Talwrn Anglesey 82 D4
- Talwrn Wrex 73 E6
- Talybont-on-Usk Powys 35 B5
- Talyllyn Powys 35 B5
- Talysarn Gwyn 82 F4
- Talywain Torf 35 D6
- Tame Bridge N Yorks 102 D3
- Tamerton Foliot Plym 6 C2
- Tamworth Staffs 63 D6
- Tan Hinon Powys 59 F5
- Tan-lan Conwy 83 F7
- Tan-lan Gwyn 71 C7
- Tan-y-bwlch Gwyn 71 C7
- Tan-y-fron Conwy 72 C3
- Tan-y-graig Anglesey 82 D5
- Tan-y-graig Gwyn 70 D4
- Tan-y-groes Ceredig 45 E4
- Tan-y-pistyll Powys 59 B7
- Tan-yr-allt Gwyn 82 F4
- Tandem W Yorks 88 C2
- Tanden Kent 19 B6
- Tandridge Sur 28 D4
- Tanerdy Carms 33 B5
- Tanfield Durham 110 D4
- Tanfield Lea Durham 110 D4
- Tangasdal W Isles 148 J1
- Tangiers Pembs 44 D4
- Tangley Hants 25 D8
- Tanglwst Carms 46 F2
- Tangmere W Sus 16 D3
- Tangwick Shetland 160 F4
- Tankerness Orkney 159 H6
- Tankersley S Yorks 88 D4
- Tankerton Kent 30 C5
- Tannach Highld 158 F5
- Tannachie Aberds 141 F6
- Tannadice Angus 134 D4
- Tannington Suff 57 C6
- Tansley Derbys 76 D3
- Tansley Knoll Derbys 76 C3
- Tansor Northants 65 E7
- Tantobie Durham 110 D4
- Tanton N Yorks 102 C3
- Tanworth-in-Arden Warks 51 B6
- Tanygrisiau Gwyn 71 C7
- Tanyrhydiau Ceredig 47 C6
- Taobh a Chaolais W Isles 148 G2
- Taobh a Thuath Loch Aineort W Isles 148 F2
- Taobh a Tuath Loch Baghasdail W Isles 148 F2
- Taobh a'Ghlinne W Isles 155 F8
- Taobh Tuath W Isles 154 J4
- Taplow Bucks 40 F2
- Tapton Derbys 76 B3
- Tarbat Ho. Highld 151 D10
- Tarbert Argyll 143 C7
- Tarbert Argyll 144 E5
- Tarbert Argyll 145 G7
- Tairbeart = Tarbert W Isles 154 G6
- Tarbet Argyll 126 D2
- Tarbet Highld 147 B10
- Tarbet Highld 156 E4
- Tarbock Green Mers 86 F2
- Tarbolton S Ayrs 112 B4
- Tarbrax S Lanark 120 D3
- Tardebigge Worcs 50 C5
- Tarfside Angus 134 B4
- Tarland Aberds 140 D3
- Tarleton Lancs 86 B2
- Tarlogie Highld 151 C10
- Tarlscough Lancs 86 C2
- Tarlton Glos 37 E6
- Tarnbrook Lancs 93 D5
- Tarporley Ches W 74 C2
- Tarr Som 22 F3
- Tarrant Crawford Dorset 13 D7
- Tarrant Gunville Dorset 13 C7
- Tarrant Hinton Dorset 13 C7
- Tarrant Keyneston Dorset 13 D7
- Tarrant Launceston Dorset 13 D7
- Tarrant Monkton Dorset 13 D7
- Tarrant Rawston Dorset 13 D7
- Tarrant Rushton Dorset 13 D7
- Tarrel Highld 151 C11
- Tarring Neville E Sus 17 D8
- Tarrington Hereford 49 E8
- Tarsappie Perth 128 B3
- Tarskavaig Highld 149 H10
- Tarves Aberds 153 E8
- Tarvie Highld 150 F7
- Tarvie Perth 133 C7
- Tarvin Ches W 73 C8
- Tasburgh Norf 68 E5
- Tasley Shrops 61 E6
- Taston Oxon 38 B3
- Tatenhill Staffs 63 B6
- Tathall End M Keynes 53 E6
- Tatham Lancs 93 C6
- Tathwell Lincs 91 F7
- Tatling End Bucks 40 F3
- Tatsfield Sur 28 D5
- Tattenhall Ches W 73 D8
- Tattenhoe M Keynes 53 F6
- Tatterford Norf 80 E4
- Tattersett Norf 80 D4
- Tattershall Lincs 78 D5
- Tattershall Bridge Lincs 78 D5
- Tattershall Thorpe Lincs 78 D5
- Tattingstone Suff 56 F5
- Tatworth Som 11 D8
- Taverham Norf 68 C4
- Tavernspite Pembs 32 C2
- Tavistock Devon 6 B2
- Taw Green Devon 9 E8
- Tawstock Devon 9 B7
- Taxal Derbys 75 B7
- Tay Bridge Dundee 129 B6
- Tayinloan Argyll 143 D7
- Taymouth Castle Perth 132 E4
- Taynish Argyll 144 E6
- Taynton Glos 36 B4

Column 7

- Taynton Oxon 38 C2
- Taynuilt Argyll 125 B6
- Tayport Fife 129 B6
- Tayvallich Argyll 144 E6
- Tealby Lincs 91 E5
- Tealing Angus 134 F4
- Teangue Highld 149 H11
- Teanna Mhachair W Isles 148 B2
- Tebay Cumb 99 D8
- Tebworth C Beds 40 B2
- Tedburn St Mary Devon 10 E3
- Teddington Glos 50 F4
- Teddington London 28 B2
- Tedstone Delamere Hereford 49 D8
- Tedstone Wafre Hereford 49 D8
- Teeton Northants 52 B4
- Teffont Evias Wilts 24 F4
- Teffont Magna Wilts 24 F4
- Tegryn Pembs 45 F4
- Teigh Rutland 65 C5
- Teigncombe Devon 9 F8
- Teigngrace Devon 7 B6
- Teignmouth Devon 7 B7
- Telford Telford 61 D6
- Telham E Sus 18 D4
- Tellisford Som 24 D3
- Telscombe E Sus 17 D8
- Telscombe Cliffs E Sus 17 D7
- Templand Dumfries 114 F3
- Temple Corn 5 B6
- Temple Glasgow 118 C5
- Temple Midloth 121 D6
- Temple Balsall W Mid 51 B7
- Temple Bar Carms 33 C6
- Temple Bar Ceredig 46 D4
- Temple Cloud Bath 23 D8
- Temple Combe Som 12 B5
- Temple Ewell Kent 31 E6
- Temple Grafton Warks 51 D6
- Temple Guiting Glos 37 B7
- Temple Herdewyke Warks 51 D8
- Temple Hirst N Yorks 89 B7
- Temple Normanton Derbys 76 C4
- Temple Sowerby Cumb 99 B8
- Templehall Fife 128 E4
- Templeton Devon 10 C3
- Templeton Pembs 32 C2
- Templeton Bridge Devon 10 C3
- Templetown Durham 110 D4
- Tempsford C Beds 54 D2
- Ten Mile Bank Norf 67 E6
- Tenbury Wells Worcs 49 C7
- Tenby = Dinbych-Y-Pysgod Pembs 32 D2
- Tendring Essex 43 B7
- Tendring Green Essex 43 B7
- Tenston Orkney 159 G3
- Tenterden Kent 19 B5
- Terling Essex 42 C3
- Ternhill Shrops 74 F3
- Terregles Banks Dumfries 107 B6
- Terrick Bucks 39 D8
- Terrington N Yorks 96 B2
- Terrington St Clement Norf 66 C5
- Terrington St John Norf 66 C5
- Teston Kent 29 D8
- Testwood Hants 14 C4
- Tetbury Glos 37 E5
- Tetbury Upton Glos 37 E5
- Tetchill Shrops 73 F7
- Tetcott Devon 8 E5
- Tetford Lincs 79 B6
- Tetney Lincs 91 D7
- Tetney Lock Lincs 91 D7
- Tetsworth Oxon 39 D6
- Tettenhall W Mid 62 E2
- Teuchan Aberds 153 E10
- Teversal Notts 76 C4
- Teversham Cambs 55 D5
- Teviothead Borders 115 D7
- Tewel Aberds 141 F7
- Tewin Herts 41 C5
- Tewkesbury Glos 50 F3
- Teynham Kent 30 C3
- Thackthwaite Cumb 98 B3
- Thainston Aberds 135 B6
- Thakeham W Sus 16 C5
- Thame Oxon 39 D7
- Thames Ditton Sur 28 C2
- Thames Haven Thurrock 42 F3
- Thamesmead London 41 F7
- Thanington Kent 30 D5
- Thankerton S Lanark 120 F2
- Tharston Norf 68 E4
- Thatcham W Berks 26 C3
- Thatto Heath Mers 86 E3
- Thaxted Essex 55 F7
- The Aird Highld 149 C9
- The Arms Norf 67 E8
- The Bage Hereford 48 E4
- The Balloch Perth 127 C7
- The Barony Orkney 159 F3
- The Bog Shrops 60 E3
- The Bourne Sur 27 E6
- The Braes Highld 149 E10
- The Broad Hereford 49 C6
- The Butts Som 24 E2
- The Camp Glos 37 D6
- The Camp Herts 40 D4
- The Chequer Wrex 73 E8
- The City Bucks 39 E7
- The Common Wilts 25 F7
- The Craigs Highld 150 B7
- The Cronk IoM 84 C3
- The Dell Suff 69 E7
- The Den N Ayrs 118 D3
- The Eals Northumb 116 F3
- The Eaves Glos 36 D3
- The Flatt Cumb 109 B5
- The Four Alls Shrops 74 F3
- The Garths Shetland 160 B8
- The Green Cumb 98 F3
- The Green Wilts 24 F3
- The Grove Dumfries 107 B6
- The Hall Shetland 160 D8
- The Haven W Sus 27 F8
- The Heath Norf 81 E7
- The Heath Suff 56 F5
- The Hill Cumb 98 F3
- The Howe Cumb 99 F6
- The Howe IoM 84 F1
- The Hundred Hereford 49 C7
- The Lee Bucks 40 D2
- The Lhen IoM 84 B3
- The Marsh Powys 60 E3
- The Marsh Wilts 37 F7
- The Middles Durham 110 D5
- The Moor Kent 18 C4
- The Mumbles = Y Mwmbwls Swansea 33 F7
- The Murray S Lanark 119 D6
- The Neuk Aberds 141 E6
- The Oval Bath 24 C2
- The Pole of Itlaw Aberds 153 C6
- The Quarry Glos 36 E4
- The Rhos Pembs 32 C1
- The Rock Telford 61 D6
- The Ryde Herts 41 D5
- The Sands Sur 27 E6
- The Stocks Kent 19 C6
- The Throat Wokingham 27 C6
- The Vauld Hereford 49 E7
- The Wyke Shrops 61 D7

Column 8

- Theakston N Yorks 101 F8
- Thealby N Lincs 90 C2
- Theale Som 23 E6
- Theale W Berks 26 B4
- Thearne E Yorks 97 F6
- Theberton Suff 57 C8
- Theddingworth Leics 64 F3
- Theddlethorpe All Saints Lincs 91 F8
- Theddlethorpe St Helen Lincs 91 F8
- Thelbridge Barton Devon 10 C2
- Thenetham Suff 56 B4
- Thelveton Norf 68 F4
- Thelwall Warr 86 F4
- Themelthorpe Norf 81 E6
- Thenford Northants 52 E3
- Therfield Herts 54 F4
- Thetford Lincs 65 C8
- Thetford Norf 67 F8
- Theydon Bois Essex 41 E7
- Thickwood Wilts 24 B3
- Thimbleby Lincs 78 C5
- Thimbleby N Yorks 102 E2
- Thingwall Mers 85 F3
- Thirdpart N Ayrs 118 E1
- Thirlby N Yorks 102 F2
- Thirlestane Borders 121 E8
- Thirn N Yorks 101 F7
- Thirsk N Yorks 102 F2
- Thirtleby E Yorks 97 F7
- Thistleton Lancs 92 F4
- Thistleton Rutland 65 C6
- Thistley Green Suff 55 B7
- Thixendale N Yorks 96 C4
- Thockrington Northumb 110 B2
- Tholomas Drove Cambs 66 D3
- Tholthorpe N Yorks 95 C7
- Thomas Chapel Pembs 32 D2
- Thomas Close Cumb 108 E4
- Thomastown Aberds 152 E5
- Thompson Norf 68 E2
- Thomshill Moray 152 C2
- Thong Kent 29 B7
- Thongsbridge W Yorks 88 D2
- Thoralby N Yorks 101 F5
- Thoresway Lincs 91 E5
- Thorganby Lincs 91 E6
- Thorganby N Yorks 96 E2
- Thorgill N Yorks 103 E5
- Thorington Suff 57 B8
- Thorington Street Suff 56 F4
- Thorlby N Yorks 94 D2
- Thorley Herts 41 C7
- Thorley Street IoW 14 F4
- Thormanby N Yorks 95 B7
- Thornaby-on-Tees Stockton 102 C2
- Thornage Norf 81 D6
- Thornborough Bucks 52 F5
- Thornborough N Yorks 95 B5
- Thornbury Devon 9 D6
- Thornbury Hereford 49 D8
- Thornbury S Glos 36 E3
- Thornbury W Yorks 94 F4
- Thornby Northants 52 B4
- Thorncliffe Staffs 75 D7
- Thorncombe Dorset 11 D8
- Thorncombe Dorset 13 C7
- Thorncombe Street Sur 27 E8
- Thorncote Green C Beds 54 E2
- Thorncross IoW 14 F5
- Thorndon Suff 56 C5
- Thorndon Cross Devon 9 E7
- Thorne S Yorks 89 C7
- Thorne St Margaret Som 11 B5
- Thorner W Yorks 95 E6
- Thorney Notts 77 B8
- Thorney Pboro 66 D2
- Thorney Crofts E Yorks 91 B6
- Thorney Green Suff 56 C4
- Thorney Hill Hants 14 E2
- Thorney Toll Pboro 66 D3
- Thornfalcon Som 11 B7
- Thornford Dorset 12 C4
- Thorngumbald E Yorks 91 B6
- Thornham Norf 80 C3
- Thornham Magna Suff 56 B5
- Thornham Parva Suff 56 B5
- Thornhaugh Pboro 65 D7
- Thornhill Cardiff 35 F5
- Thornhill Cumb 98 D2
- Thornhill Derbys 88 F2
- Thornhill Dumfries 113 E8
- Thornhill Soton 15 C5
- Thornhill Stirling 126 E4
- Thornhill W Yorks 88 C3
- Thornhill Edge W Yorks 88 C3
- Thornhill Lees W Yorks 88 C3
- Thornholme E Yorks 97 C7
- Thornley Durham 110 F4
- Thornley Durham 111 F6
- Thornliebank E Renf 118 D5
- Thorns Suff 55 D8
- Thorns Green Ches E 87 F5
- Thornsett Derbys 87 F8
- Thornthwaite Cumb 98 B4
- Thornthwaite N Yorks 94 D4
- Thornton Angus 134 E3
- Thornton Bucks 53 F5
- Thornton E Yorks 96 E3
- Thornton Fife 128 E4
- Thornton Lancs 92 E3
- Thornton Leics 63 D8
- Thornton Lincs 78 C5
- Thornton Mbro 102 C2
- Thornton Mers 85 D4
- Thornton Northumb 123 E5
- Thornton Pembs 44 E4
- Thornton W Yorks 94 F4
- Thornton Curtis N Lincs 90 C4
- Thornton Heath London 28 C4
- Thornton Hough Mers 85 F4
- Thornton in Craven N Yorks 94 E2
- Thornton-le-Beans N Yorks 102 E2
- Thornton-le-Clay N Yorks 96 C2
- Thornton-le-Dale N Yorks 96 B4
- Thornton le Moor Lincs 90 E4
- Thornton-le-Moor N Yorks 102 F1
- Thornton-le-Moors Ches W 73 B8
- Thornton-le-Street N Yorks 102 F2
- Thornton Rust N Yorks 100 F4
- Thornton Steward N Yorks 101 F6
- Thornton Watlass N Yorks 101 F7
- Thorntonhall S Lanark 119 D5
- Thorntonloch E Loth 122 B3
- Thorntonpark Northumb 122 E5
- Thornwood Common Essex 41 D7
- Thornydykes Borders 122 E2
- Thoroton Notts 77 E7

Column 9

- Thorp Arch W Yorks 95 E7
- Thorpe Derbys 75 D8
- Thorpe E Yorks 97 E5
- Thorpe Lincs 91 F8
- Thorpe N Yorks 94 C3
- Thorpe Norf 69 E7
- Thorpe Notts 77 E7
- Thorpe Sur 27 C8
- Thorpe Abbotts Norf 57 B5
- Thorpe Acre Leics 64 B2
- Thorpe Arnold Leics 64 B4
- Thorpe Audlin W Yorks 89 C5
- Thorpe Bassett N Yorks 96 B4
- Thorpe Bay Southend 43 F5
- Thorpe by Water Rutland 65 E5
- Thorpe Common Suff 57 F6
- Thorpe Constantine Staffs 63 D6
- Thorpe Culvert Lincs 79 C7
- Thorpe End Norf 69 C5
- Thorpe Fendykes Lincs 79 C7
- Thorpe Green Essex 43 B7
- Thorpe Green Suff 56 D3
- Thorpe Hesley S Yorks 88 E4
- Thorpe in Balne S Yorks 89 C6
- Thorpe in the Fallows Lincs 90 F3
- Thorpe Langton Leics 64 E4
- Thorpe Larches Durham 102 B1
- Thorpe-le-Soken Essex 43 B7
- Thorpe le Street E Yorks 96 E4
- Thorpe Malsor Northants 53 B6
- Thorpe Mandeville Northants 52 E3
- Thorpe Market Norf 81 D8
- Thorpe Marriott Norf 68 C4
- Thorpe Morieux Suff 56 D3
- Thorpe on the Hill Lincs 78 C2
- Thorpe Salvin S Yorks 89 F6
- Thorpe Satchville Leics 64 C4
- Thorpe St Andrew Norf 69 D5
- Thorpe St Peter Lincs 79 C7
- Thorpe Thewles Stockton 102 B2
- Thorpe Tilney Lincs 78 D4
- Thorpe Underwood N Yorks 95 D7
- Thorpe Waterville Northants 65 F7
- Thorpe Willoughby N Yorks 95 F8
- Thorpeness Suff 57 D8
- Thorrington Essex 43 C6
- Thorverton Devon 10 D4
- Thrandeston Suff 56 B5
- Thrapston Northants 53 B7
- Thrashbush N Lanark 119 C7
- Threapland Cumb 107 F8
- Threapland N Yorks 94 C2
- Threapwood Ches W 73 E8
- Threapwood Staffs 75 E7
- Three Ashes Hereford 36 B2
- Three Bridges W Sus 28 F3
- Three Burrows Corn 3 B6
- Three Chimneys Kent 19 B5
- Three Cocks Powys 48 F3
- Three Crosses Swansea 33 E6
- Three Cups Corner E Sus 18 C3
- Three Holes Norf 66 D5
- Three Leg Cross E Sus 18 B3
- Three Legged Cross Dorset 13 D7
- Three Oaks E Sus 18 D5
- Threehammer Common Norf 69 C6
- Threekingham Lincs 78 F3
- Threemile Cross Wokingham 26 C5
- Threemilestone Corn 3 B6
- Threemiletown W Loth 120 B3
- Threlkeld Cumb 99 B5
- Threshfield N Yorks 94 C2
- Thrigby Norf 69 C7
- Thringarth Durham 100 B4
- Thringstone Leics 63 C8
- Thrintoft N Yorks 101 E8
- Thriplow Cambs 54 E5
- Throckenholt Lincs 66 D3
- Throcking Herts 54 F4
- Throckley T&W 110 C4
- Throckmorton Worcs 50 E4
- Throphill Northumb 117 F7
- Thropton Northumb 117 D6
- Throsk Stirling 127 E7
- Throwleigh Devon 9 E8
- Throwley Kent 30 D3
- Thrumster Highld 158 F5
- Thrunton Northumb 117 C6
- Thrupp Glos 37 D5
- Thrupp Oxon 38 C4
- Thrushelton Devon 9 F6
- Thrussington Leics 64 C3
- Thruxton Hants 25 E7
- Thruxton Hereford 49 F6
- Thrybergh S Yorks 89 E5
- Thulston Derbys 76 F4
- Thundergay N Ayrs 143 D9
- Thundersley Essex 42 F3
- Thundridge Herts 41 C6
- Thurcaston Leics 64 C2
- Thurcroft S Yorks 89 F5
- Thurgarton Norf 81 D7
- Thurgarton Notts 77 E6
- Thurgoland S Yorks 88 D3
- Thurlaston Leics 64 E2
- Thurlaston Warks 52 B2
- Thurlbear Som 11 B7
- Thurlby Lincs 65 C8
- Thurlby Lincs 78 C2
- Thurleigh Bedford 53 D8
- Thurlestone Devon 6 E4
- Thurloxton Som 22 F4
- Thurlstone S Yorks 88 D3
- Thurlton Norf 69 E7
- Thurlwood Ches E 74 D5
- Thurmaston Leics 64 D3
- Thurnby Leics 64 D3
- Thurne Norf 69 C7
- Thurnham Kent 30 D2
- Thurnham Lancs 92 D4
- Thurning Norf 81 E6
- Thurning Northants 65 F7
- Thurnscoe S Yorks 89 D5
- Thurnscoe East S Yorks 89 D5
- Thursby Cumb 108 D3
- Thursford Norf 81 D5
- Thursley Sur 27 F7
- Thurso Highld 158 D3
- Thurso East Highld 158 D3
- Thurstaston Mers 85 F3
- Thurston Suff 56 C3
- Thurstonfield Cumb 108 D3
- Thurstonland W Yorks 88 C2
- Thurton Norf 69 D6
- Thurvaston Derbys 76 F2
- Thuxton Norf 68 D3
- Thwaite N Yorks 100 E3

Thwaite Suff 56 C5
Thwaite St Mary Norf 69 E6
Thwaites W Yorks 94 E3
Thwaites Brow W Yorks 94 E3
Thwing E Yorks 97 B6
Tibbermore Perth 128 B2
Tibberton Glos 36 B4
Tibberton Telford 61 B6
Tibberton Worcs 50 D4
Tibenham Norf 68 F4
Tibshelf Derbys 76 C4
Tibthorpe E Yorks 97 D5
Ticehurst E Sus 18 B3
Tichborne Hants 26 F3
Tickencote Rutland 65 D6
Tickenham N Som 23 B6
Tickhill S Yorks 89 E6
Ticklerton Shrops 60 E4
Ticknall Derbys 63 B7
Tickton E Yorks 97 E6
Tidcombe Wilts 25 D7
Tiddington Oxon 39 D6
Tiddington Warks 51 D7
Tidebrook E Sus 18 C3
Tideford Corn 5 D8
Tideford Cross Corn 5 C8
Tidenham Glos 36 E2
Tideswell Derbys 75 B8
Tidmarsh W Berks 26 B4
Tidmington Warks 51 F7
Tidpit Hants 13 C8
Tidworth Wilts 25 E7
Tiers Cross Pembs 44 D4
Tiffield Northants 52 D4
Tifty Aberds 153 D7
Tigerton Angus 135 C5
Tigh-na-Blair Perth 127 C6
Tighnabruaich Argyll 145 F8
Tighnafiline Highld 155 J13
Tigley Devon 7 C5
Tilbrook Cambs 53 C8
Tilbury Thurrock 29 B7
Tilbury Juxta Clare Essex 55 E8
Tile Cross W Mid 63 F5
Tile Hill W Mid 51 B7
Tilehurst Reading 26 B4
Tilford Sur 27 E6
Tilgate W Sus 28 F3
Tilgate Forest Row W Sus 28 F3
Tillathrowie Aberds 152 E4
Tilley Shrops 60 B5
Tillicoultry Clack 127 E8
Tillingham Essex 43 D5
Tillington Hereford 49 E6
Tillington W Sus 16 B3
Tillington Common Hereford 49 E6
Tillyarblet Angus 135 C5
Tillybirloch Aberds 141 D5
Tillycorthie Aberds 141 B8
Tillydrine Aberds 140 E5
Tillyfour Aberds 140 C4
Tillyfourie Aberds 140 C5
Tillygarmond Aberds 140 E5
Tillygreig Aberds 141 B7
Tillykerrie Aberds 141 B7
Tilmanstone Kent 31 D7
Tilney All Saints Norf 67 C5
Tilney High End Norf 67 C5
Tilney St Lawrence Norf 66 C5
Tilshead Wilts 24 E5
Tilstock Shrops 74 F2
Tilston Ches W 73 D8
Tilstone Fearnall Ches W 74 C2
Tilsworth C Beds 40 B2
Tilton on the Hill Leics 64 D4
Timberland Lincs 78 D4
Timbersbrook Ches E 75 C5
Timberscombe Som 21 E8
Timble N Yorks 94 D4
Timperley Gtr Man 87 F5
Timsbury Bath 23 D8
Timsbury Hants 14 B4
Timsgearraidh W Isles 154 D5
Timworth Green Suff 56 C2
Tincleton Dorset 13 E5
Tindale Cumb 109 D6
Tingewick Bucks 52 F4
Tingley W Yorks 88 B3
Tingrith C Beds 53 F8
Tingwall Orkney 159 F4
Tinhay Devon 9 F5
Tinshill W Yorks 95 F5
Tinsley S Yorks 88 E5
Tintagel Corn 8 F2
Tintern Parva Mon 36 D2
Tintinhull Som 12 C3
Tintwistle Derbys 87 E8
Tinwald Dumfries 114 F3
Tinwell Rutland 65 D7
Tipperty Aberds 141 B8
Tipsend Norf 66 E5
Tipton W Mid 62 E3
Tipton St John Devon 11 E5
Tiptree Essex 42 C4
Tir-y-dail Carms 33 C7
Tirabad Powys 47 E7
Tiraghoil Argyll 146 J6
Tirley Glos 37 B5
Tirphil Caerph 35 D5
Tirril Cumb 99 B7
Tisbury Wilts 13 B7
Tisman's Common W Sus 27 F8
Tissington Derbys 75 D8
Titchberry Devon 8 B4
Titchfield Hants 15 D6
Titchmarsh Northants 53 B8
Titchwell Norf 80 C3
Tithby Notts 77 F6
Titley Hereford 48 C5
Titlington Northumb 117 C7
Titsey Sur 28 D5
Tittensor Staffs 75 F5
Tittleshall Norf 80 E4
Tiverton Ches W 74 C2
Tiverton Devon 10 C4
Tivetshall St Margaret Norf 68 F4
Tivetshall St Mary Norf 68 F4
Tividale W Mid 62 E3
Tivy Dale S Yorks 88 D3
Tixall Staffs 62 B3
Tixover Rutland 65 D6
Toab Orkney 159 H6
Toab Shetland 160 M5
Toadmoor Derbys 76 D3
Tobermory Argyll 147 F8
Toberonochy Argyll 124 E3
Tobha Mor W Isles 148 E2
Tobhtarol W Isles 154 D6
Tobson W Isles 154 D6
Tocher Aberds 153 E6
Tockenham Wilts 24 B5
Tockenham Wick Wilts 37 F7
Tockholes Blackburn 86 B4
Tockington S Glos 36 F3
Tockwith N Yorks 95 D7
Todber Dorset 13 B6
Todding Hereford 49 B6
Toddington C Beds 40 B3
Toddington Glos 50 F5
Todenham Glos 51 F7
Todhills Cumb 108 C3
Todlachie Aberds 141 C5
Todmorden W Yorks 87 B7
Todrig Borders 115 C7
Todwick S Yorks 89 F5
Toft Cambs 54 D4
Toft Lincs 65 C7
Toft Hill Durham 101 B6
Toft Hill Lincs 78 C5
Toft Monks Norf 69 E7
Toft next Newton Lincs 90 F4
Toftrees Norf 80 E4
Tofts Highld 158 D5
Toftwood Norf 68 C2
Togston Northumb 117 D8
Tokavaig Highld 149 G11
Tokers Green Oxon 26 B5
Tolastadh a Chaolais W Isles 154 D6
Tolastadh bho Thuath W Isles 155 C10
Toll Bar S Yorks 89 D6
Toll End W Mid 62 E3
Toll of Birness Aberds 153 E10
Tolland Som 22 F3
Tollard Royal Wilts 13 C7
Tollbar End W Mid 51 B8
Toller Fratrum Dorset 12 E3
Toller Porcorum Dorset 12 E3
Tollerton N Yorks 95 C8
Tollerton Notts 77 F6
Tollesbury Essex 43 C5
Tolleshunt D'Arcy Essex 43 C5
Tolleshunt Major Essex 43 C5
Tolm W Isles 155 D9
Tolpuddle Dorset 13 E5
Tolvah Highld 138 E4
Tolworth London 28 C2
Tomatin Highld 138 B4
Tombreck Highld 151 H9
Tomchrasky Highld 137 C5
Tomdoun Highld 136 D4
Tomich Highld 137 B6
Tomich Highld 151 D9
Tomich House Highld 151 G8
Tomintoul Aberds 139 E7
Tomintoul Moray 139 C7
Tomnaven Moray 152 E4
Tomnavoulin Moray 139 B8
Ton-Pentre Rhondda 34 E3
Tonbridge Kent 29 E6
Tondu Bridgend 34 F2
Tonfanau Gwyn 58 D2
Tong Shrops 61 D7
Tong W Yorks 94 F5
Tong Norton Shrops 61 D7
Tonge Leics 63 B8
Tongham Sur 27 E6
Tongland Dumfries 106 D3
Tongue Highld 157 D8
Tongue End Lincs 65 C8
Tongwynlais Cardiff 35 F5
Tonna Neath 34 E1
Tonwell Herts 41 C6
Tonypandy Rhondda 34 E3
Tonyrefail Rhondda 34 F4
Toot Baldon Oxon 39 D5
Toot Hill Essex 41 D8
Toothill Hants 14 C4
Top of Hebers Gtr Man 87 D6
Topcliffe N Yorks 95 B7
Topcroft Norf 69 E5
Topcroft Street Norf 69 E5
Toppesfield Essex 55 F8
Toppings Gtr Man 86 C5
Topsham Devon 10 F4
Torbay Torbay 7 D7
Torbeg N Ayrs 143 F10
Torboll Farm Highld 151 B10
Torbrex Stirling 127 E6
Torbryan Devon 7 C6
Torcross Devon 7 E6
Tore Highld 151 F9
Torinturk Argyll 145 G7
Torksey Lincs 77 B8
Torlum W Isles 148 C2
Torlundy Highld 131 B5
Tormarton S Glos 24 B2
Tormisdale Argyll 142 C2
Tormitchell S Ayrs 112 E2
Tormore N Ayrs 143 E9
Tornagrain Highld 151 G10
Tornahaish Aberds 139 D8
Tornaveen Aberds 140 D5
Torness Highld 137 B8
Toronto Durham 110 F4
Torpenhow Cumb 108 F2
Torphichen W Loth 120 B2
Torphins Aberds 140 D5
Torpoint Corn 6 D2
Torquay Torbay 7 C7
Torquhan Borders 121 E7
Torran Argyll 124 E4
Torran Highld 149 D10
Torran Highld 151 D10
Torrance E Dunb 119 B6
Torrans Argyll 146 J7
Torranyard N Ayrs 118 E3
Torre Torbay 7 C7
Torridon Highld 150 F2
Torridon Ho. Highld 149 C13
Torrin Highld 149 F10
Torrisdale Highld 157 C9
Torrisdale-Square Argyll 143 E8
Torrish Highld 157 H12
Torrisholme Lancs 92 C4
Torroble Highld 157 J8
Torry Aberdeen 141 D8
Torry Aberds 152 E4
Torryburn Fife 128 F2
Torterston Aberds 153 D10
Torthorwald Dumfries 107 B7
Tortington W Sus 16 D4
Tortworth S Glos 36 E4
Torvaig Highld 149 D9
Torver Cumb 98 E4
Torwood Falk 127 F7
Torworth Notts 89 F7
Tosberry Devon 8 B4
Toscaig Highld 149 E12
Toseland Cambs 54 C3
Tosside N Yorks 93 D7
Tostock Suff 56 C3
Totaig Highld 148 C7
Totaig Highld 149 F13
Tote Highld 149 D9
Totegan Highld 157 C11
Tothill Lincs 91 F8
Totland IoW 14 F4
Totnes Devon 7 C6
Toton Notts 76 F5
Totronald Argyll 146 F4
Totscore Highld 149 B8
Tottenham London 41 E6
Tottenhill Norf 67 C6
Tottenhill Row Norf 67 C6
Totteridge London 41 E5
Totternhoe C Beds 40 B2
Tottington Gtr Man 87 C5
Totton Hants 14 C4
Touchen End Windsor 27 B6
Tournaig Highld 155 J13
Toux Aberds 153 C9
Tovil Kent 29 D8
Tow Law Durham 110 F4
Toward Argyll 145 G10
Towcester Northants 52 E4
Towednack Corn 2 C3
Tower End Norf 67 C6
Towersey Oxon 39 D7
Towie Aberds 140 C3
Towie Aberds 153 B8
Towiemore Moray 152 D3
Town End Cambs 66 E4
Town End Cumb 99 F6
Town Row E Sus 18 B2
Town Yetholm Borders 116 B4
Townend W Dunb 118 B4
Towngate Lincs 65 C8
Townhead Cumb 108 F5
Townhead Dumfries 106 E3
Townhead S Ayrs 112 D2
Townhead S Yorks 88 D2
Townhead of Greenlaw Dumfries 106 C4
Townhill Fife 128 F3
Townsend Bucks 39 D7
Townsend Herts 40 D4
Townshend Corn 2 C4
Towthorpe York 96 D2
Towton N Yorks 95 F7
Towyn Conwy 72 B3
Toxteth Mers 85 F4
Toynton All Saints Lincs 79 C6
Toynton Fen Side Lincs 79 C6
Toynton St Peter Lincs 79 C7
Toy's Hill Kent 29 D5
Trabboch E Ayrs 112 B4
Traboe Corn 3 D6
Tradespark Highld 151 F11
Tradespark Orkney 159 H5
Trafford Park Gtr Man 87 E5
Trallong Powys 34 B3
Tranent E Loth 121 B7
Tranmere Mers 85 F4
Trantlebeg Highld 157 D11
Trantlemore Highld 157 D11
Tranwell Northumb 117 F7
Trapp Carms 33 C7
Traprain E Loth 121 B8
Traquair Borders 121 F6
Trawden Lancs 94 F2
Trawsfynydd Gwyn 71 D8
Tre-Gibbon Rhondda 34 D3
Tre-Taliesin Ceredig 58 E3
Tre-vaughan Carms 32 B4
Tre-wyn Mon 35 B7
Trealaw Rhondda 34 E4
Treales Lancs 92 F4
Trearddur Anglesey 82 D2
Treaslane Highld 149 C8
Trebanog Rhondda 34 E4
Trebanos Neath 33 D8
Trebartha Corn 5 B7
Trebarwith Corn 8 F2
Trebetherick Corn 4 B4
Treborough Som 22 F2
Trebudannon Corn 4 C3
Trebullett Corn 5 B8
Treburley Corn 5 B8
Trebyan Corn 5 C5
Trecastle Powys 34 B2
Trecenydd Caerph 35 F5
Trecwn Pembs 44 B4
Trecynon Rhondda 34 D3
Tredavoe Corn 2 D3
Treddiog Pembs 44 C3
Tredegar Bl Gwent 35 D5
Tredegar = Newydd New Tredegar Caerph 35 D5
Tredington Glos 37 B6
Tredington Warks 51 E7
Tredinnick Corn 4 B4
Tredomen Powys 48 F3
Tredunnock Mon 35 E7
Tredustan Powys 48 F3
Treen Corn 2 D2
Treeton S Yorks 88 F5
Tref-Y-Clawdd = Knighton Powys 48 B4
Trefaldwyn = Montgomery Powys 60 E2
Trefasser Pembs 44 B3
Trefdraeth Anglesey 82 D4
Trefdraeth = Newport Pembs 45 F2
Trefecca Powys 48 F3
Trefechan Ceredig 58 F2
Trefeglwys Powys 59 E6
Trefenter Ceredig 46 C5
Treffgarne Pembs 44 C4
Treffynnon = Holywell Flint 73 B5
Treffynnon Pembs 44 C3
Trefgarn Owen Pembs 44 C3
Trefil Bl Gwent 35 C5
Trefilan Ceredig 46 D4
Trefin Pembs 44 B3
Treflach Shrops 60 B2
Trefnanney Powys 60 C2
Trefnant Denb 72 B4
Trefonen Shrops 60 B2
Trefor Anglesey 82 C3
Trefor Gwyn 70 C4
Treforest Rhondda 34 F4
Trefriw Conwy 83 E7
Trefynwy = Monmouth Mon 36 C2
Tregadillett Corn 8 F4
Tregaian Anglesey 82 D4
Tregare Mon 35 C8
Tregaron Ceredig 47 D5
Tregarth Gwyn 83 E6
Tregeare Corn 8 F4
Tregeiriog Wrex 73 F5
Tregele Anglesey 82 B3
Tregidden Corn 3 D6
Treglemais Pembs 44 C3
Tregole Corn 8 E3
Tregonetha Corn 4 C4
Tregony Corn 3 B8
Tregoss Corn 4 C4
Tregoyd Powys 48 F4
Tregroes Ceredig 46 E3
Tregurrian Corn 4 C3
Tregynon Powys 59 E7
Trehafod Rhondda 34 E4
Treharris M Tydf 34 E4
Treherbert Rhondda 34 E3
Trekenner Corn 5 B8
Treknow Corn 8 F2
Trelan Corn 3 E6
Trelash Corn 8 E3
Trelassick Corn 4 D3
Trelawnyd Flint 72 B4
Trelech Carms 45 F4
Treleddyd-fawr Pembs 44 C2
Trelewis M Tydf 35 E5
Treligga Corn 8 F2
Trelights Corn 4 B4
Trelill Corn 4 B5
Trelissick Corn 3 C7
Trellech Mon 36 D2
Trelleck Grange Mon 36 D1
Trelogan Flint 85 F2
Trelystan Powys 60 D2
Tremadog Gwyn 71 C6
Tremail Corn 8 F3
Tremain Ceredig 45 E4
Tremaine Corn 8 F4
Tremar Corn 5 C7
Trematon Corn 5 D8
Tremeirchion Denb 72 B4
Trenance Corn 4 C3
Trenarren Corn 3 B9
Trench Telford 61 C6
Treneglos Corn 8 F4
Trenewan Corn 5 D6
Trent Dorset 12 C3
Trent Vale Stoke 75 E5
Trentham Stoke 75 E5
Trentishoe Devon 20 E5
Treoes V Glam 21 B8
Treorchy = Treorci Rhondda 34 E3
Treorci = Treorchy Rhondda 34 E3
Tre'r-ddôl Ceredig 58 E3
Trerule Foot Corn 5 D8
Tresaith Ceredig 45 D4
Tresawle Corn 3 B7
Trescott Staffs 62 E2
Trescowe Corn 2 C4
Tresham Glos 36 E4
Tresillian Corn 3 B7
Tresinwen Pembs 44 A4
Treskinnick Cross Corn 8 E4
Tresmeer Corn 8 F4
Tresparrett Corn 8 E3
Tresparrett Posts Corn 8 E3
Tressait Perth 133 C5
Tresta Shetland 160 D8
Tresta Shetland 160 H5
Treswell Notts 77 B7
Trethosa Corn 4 D4
Trethurgy Corn 4 D5
Tretio Pembs 44 C2
Tretire Hereford 36 B2
Tretower Powys 35 B5
Treuddyn Flint 73 D6
Trevalga Corn 8 F2
Trevalyn Wrex 73 D7
Trevanson Corn 4 B4
Trevarren Corn 4 C4
Trevarrian Corn 4 C3
Trevarrick Corn 3 B8
Trevaughan Carms 32 C2
Treveighan Corn 5 B5
Trevellas Corn 4 D2
Treverva Corn 3 C6
Trevethin Torf 35 D6
Trevigro Corn 5 C8
Treviscoe Corn 4 D4
Trevone Corn 4 B3
Trewarmett Corn 8 F2
Trewassa Corn 8 F3
Trewellard Corn 2 C2
Trewen Corn 8 F4
Trewennack Corn 3 D5
Trewern Powys 60 C2
Trewethern Corn 4 B5
Trewidland Corn 5 D7
Trewint Corn 8 E3
Trewint Corn 8 F4
Trewithian Corn 3 C7
Trewoofe Corn 2 D3
Trewoon Corn 4 D4
Treworga Corn 3 B7
Treworlas Corn 3 C7
Treyarnon Corn 4 B3
Treyford W Sus 16 C2
Trezaise Corn 4 D4
Triangle W Yorks 87 B8
Trickett's Cross Dorset 13 D8
Triffleton Pembs 44 C4
Trimdon Durham 111 F6
Trimdon Colliery Durham 111 F6
Trimdon Grange Durham 111 F6
Trimingham Norf 81 D8
Trimley Lower Street Suff 57 F6
Trimley St Martin Suff 57 F6
Trimley St Mary Suff 57 F6
Trimpley Worcs 50 B2
Trimsaran Carms 33 D5
Trimstone Devon 20 E3
Trinafour Perth 132 C4
Trinant Caerph 35 D6
Tring Herts 40 C2
Tring Wharf Herts 40 C2
Trinity Angus 135 C6
Trinity Jersey 17
Trisant Ceredig 47 B6
Trislaig Highld 130 B4
Trispen Corn 4 D3
Tritlington Northumb 117 E8
Trochry Perth 133 E6
Trodigal Argyll 143 F7
Troed-rhiwdalar Powys 47 D8
Troedyraur Ceredig 46 E2
Troedyrhiw M Tydf 34 D4
Tromode IoM 84 E3
Trondavoe Shetland 160 F5
Troon Corn 3 C5
Troon S Ayrs 118 F3
Trosaraidh W Isles 148 G2
Trossachs Hotel Stirling 126 D4
Troston Suff 56 B2
Trottiscliffe Kent 29 C7
Trotton W Sus 16 B2
Troutbeck Cumb 99 B5
Troutbeck Cumb 99 D6
Troutbeck Bridge Cumb 99 D6
Trow Green Glos 36 D2
Trowbridge Wilts 24 D3
Trowell Notts 76 F4
Trowle Common Wilts 24 D3
Trowley Bottom Herts 40 C3
Trows Borders 122 F2
Trowse Newton Norf 68 D5
Trudoxhill Som 24 E2
Trull Som 11 B7
Trumaisgearraidh W Isles 148 A3
Trumpan Highld 148 B7
Trumpet Hereford 49 F8
Trumpington Cambs 54 D5
Trunch Norf 81 D8
Trunnah Lancs 92 E3
Truro Corn 3 B7
Trusham Devon 10 F3
Trusley Derbys 76 F2
Trusthorpe Lincs 91 F9
Trysull Staffs 62 E2
Tubney Oxon 38 E4
Tuckenhay Devon 7 D6
Tuckhill Shrops 61 F7
Tuckingmill Corn 3 B5
Tuddenham Suff 55 B8
Tuddenham St Martin Suff 57 E5
Tudeley Kent 29 E7
Tudhoe Durham 111 F5
Tudorville Hereford 36 B2
Tudweiliog Gwyn 70 D3
Tuesley Sur 27 E7
Tuffley Glos 37 C5
Tufton Hants 26 E2
Tufton Pembs 32 B1
Tugby Leics 64 D4
Tugford Shrops 61 F5
Tullibardine Perth 127 C8
Tullibody Clack 127 E7
Tullich Argyll 125 D6
Tullich Highld 138 B2
Tullich Muir Highld 151 D10
Tulliemet Perth 133 D6
Tulloch Aberds 135 B7
Tulloch Aberds 153 E8
Tulloch Perth 128 B2
Tulloch Castle Highld 151 E8
Tullochgorm Argyll 125 F5
Tulloes Angus 135 E5
Tullybannocher Perth 127 B6
Tullybelton Perth 133 F7
Tullyfergus Perth 134 E2
Tullymurdoch Perth 134 D1
Tullynessle Aberds 140 C4
Tumble Carms 33 C6
Tumby Woodside Lincs 79 D5
Tummel Bridge Perth 132 D4
Tunga W Isles 155 D9
Tunstall E Yorks 97 F9
Tunstall Kent 30 C2
Tunstall Lancs 93 B6
Tunstall N Yorks 101 E7
Tunstall Norf 69 D7
Tunstall Stoke 75 D5
Tunstall Suff 57 D7
Tunstall T&W 111 D6
Tunstead Derbys 75 B8
Tunstead Gtr Man 87 D8
Tunstead Norf 81 E8
Tunworth Hants 26 E4
Tupsley Hereford 49 E7
Tupton Derbys 76 C3
Tur Langton Leics 64 E4
Turgis Green Hants 26 D4
Turin Angus 135 D5
Turkdean Glos 37 C8
Turleigh Wilts 24 C3
Turn Lancs 87 C6
Turnastone Hereford 49 F5
Turnberry S Ayrs 112 D2
Turnditch Derbys 76 E2
Turners Hill W Sus 28 F4
Turners Puddle Dorset 13 E6
Turnford Herts 41 D6
Turnhouse Edin 120 B4
Turnworth Dorset 13 D6
Turriff Aberds 153 C7
Turton Bottoms Blackburn 86 C5
Turves Cambs 66 E3
Turvey Bedford 53 D7
Turville Bucks 39 E7
Turville Heath Bucks 39 E7
Turweston Bucks 52 F4
Tushielaw Borders 115 C6
Tutbury Staffs 63 B6
Tutnall Worcs 50 B4
Tutshill Glos 36 E2
Tuttington Norf 81 E8
Tutts Clump W Berks 26 B3
Tuxford Notts 77 B7
Twatt Orkney 159 F3
Twatt Shetland 160 H5
Twechar E Dunb 119 B7
Tweedmouth Northumb 123 D5
Tweedsmuir Borders 114 B3
Twelve Heads Corn 3 B6
Twemlow Green Ches E 74 C4
Twenty Lincs 65 B8
Twerton Bath 24 C2
Twickenham London 28 B2
Twigworth Glos 37 B5
Twineham W Sus 17 C6
Twinhoe Bath 24 D2
Twinstead Essex 56 F2
Twinstead Green Essex 56 F2
Twiss Green Warr 86 E4
Twiston Lancs 93 E8
Twitchen Devon 21 F6
Twitchen Shrops 49 B5
Two Bridges Devon 6 B4
Two Dales Derbys 76 C2
Two Mills Ches W 73 B7
Twycross Leics 63 D7
Twyford Bucks 39 B6
Twyford Derbys 63 B7
Twyford Hants 15 B5
Twyford Leics 64 C4
Twyford Lincs 65 B6
Twyford Norf 81 E6
Twyford Wokingham 27 B5
Twyford Common Hereford 49 F7
Twyn-y-Sheriff Mon 35 D8
Twynholm Dumfries 106 D3
Twyning Glos 50 F3
Twyning Green Glos 50 F4
Twynllanan Carms 34 B1
Twynmynydd Carms 33 C7
Twywell Northants 53 B7
Ty-draw Conwy 83 F8
Ty-hen Carms 32 B4
Ty-hen Gwyn 70 D2
Ty-mawr Anglesey 82 C4
Ty Mawr Carms 46 E4
Ty Mawr Cwm Conwy 72 E3
Ty-nant Conwy 72 E3
Ty-nant Gwyn 59 B6
Ty-uchaf Powys 59 B7
Tyberton Hereford 49 F5
Tyburn W Mid 62 E5
Tycroes Carms 33 C7
Tycrwyn Powys 59 C8
Tydd Gote Lincs 66 C4
Tydd St Giles Cambs 66 C4
Tydd St Mary Lincs 66 C4
Tyddewi = St David's Pembs 44 C2
Tyddyn-mawr Gwyn 71 C6
Tye Green Essex 41 D7
Tye Green Essex 42 B3
Tye Green Essex 55 F6
Tyldesley Gtr Man 86 D4
Tyler Hill Kent 30 C5
Tylers Green Bucks 40 E2
Tylorstown Rhondda 34 E4
Tylwch Powys 59 F6
Tyn-y-celyn Wrex 73 F5
Tyn-y-coed Shrops 60 B2
Tyn-y-fedwen Powys 72 F5
Tyn-y-ffridd Powys 72 F5
Tyn-y-graig Powys 48 D2
Ty'n-y-groes Conwy 83 D7
Ty'n-y-maes Gwyn 83 E6
Tyn-y-pwll Anglesey 82 C4
Ty'n-yr-eithin Ceredig 47 C5
Tyncelyn Ceredig 46 C5
Tyndrum Stirling 131 F7
Tyne Tunnel T&W 111 C6
Tyneham Dorset 13 F6
Tynehead Midloth 121 D6
Tynemouth T&W 111 C6
Tynewydd Rhondda 34 E3
Tyninghame E Loth 122 B2
Tynron Dumfries 113 E8
Tynygongl Anglesey 82 C5
Tynygraig Ceredig 47 C5
Tŷ'r-felin-isaf Conwy 83 E8
Tyrie Aberds 153 B9
Tyringham M Keynes 53 E6
Tythecott Devon 9 C6
Tythegston Bridgend 21 B7
Tytherington Ches E 75 B6
Tytherington S Glos 36 F3
Tytherington Som 24 E2
Tytherington Wilts 24 E4
Tytherleigh Devon 11 D8
Tywardreath Corn 5 D5
Tywyn Conwy 83 D7
Tywyn Gwyn 58 D2

U

Uachdar W Isles 148 C2
Uags Highld 149 E12
Ubbeston Green Suff 57 B7
Ubley Bath 23 D7
Uckerby N Yorks 101 D7
Uckfield E Sus 17 B8
Uckington Glos 37 B6
Uddingston S Lanark 119 C6
Uddington S Lanark 119 F8
Udimore E Sus 19 D5
Udny Green Aberds 141 B7
Udny Station Aberds 141 B8
Udston S Lanark 119 D6
Udstonhead S Lanark 119 E7
Uffcott Wilts 25 B6
Uffculme Devon 11 C5
Uffington Lincs 65 D7
Uffington Oxon 38 F3
Uffington Shrops 60 C5
Ufford Pboro 65 D7
Ufford Suff 57 D6
Ufton Warks 51 C8
Ufton Nervet W Berks 26 C4
Ugadale Argyll 143 F8
Ugborough Devon 6 D4
Uggeshall Suff 69 F7
Ugglebarnby N Yorks 103 D6
Ughill S Yorks 88 E3
Ugley Essex 41 B8
Ugley Green Essex 41 B8
Ugthorpe N Yorks 103 C5
Uidh W Isles 148 J1
Uig Argyll 145 E10
Uig Highld 148 C6
Uig Highld 149 B8
Uigen W Isles 154 D5
Uigshader Highld 149 D9
Uisken Argyll 146 K6
Ulbster Highld 158 F5
Ulceby Lincs 79 B7
Ulceby N Lincs 90 C5
Ulceby Skitter N Lincs 90 C5
Ulcombe Kent 30 E2
Uldale Cumb 108 F2
Uley Glos 36 E4
Ulgham Northumb 117 E8
Ullapool Highld 150 B4
Ullenhall Warks 51 C6
Ullenwood Glos 37 C6
Ulleskelf N Yorks 95 E8
Ullesthorpe Leics 64 F2
Ulley S Yorks 89 F5
Ullingswick Hereford 49 E7
Ullinish Highld 149 E8
Ullock Cumb 98 B2
Ulnes Walton Lancs 86 C3
Ulpha Cumb 98 E3
Ulrome E Yorks 97 D7
Ulsta Shetland 160 E6
Ulva House Argyll 146 H7
Ulverston Cumb 92 B2
Ulwell Dorset 13 F8
Umberleigh Devon 9 B8
Unapool Highld 156 F5
Unasary W Isles 148 F2
Underbarrow Cumb 99 E6
Undercliffe W Yorks 94 F4
Underhoull Shetland 160 C7
Underriver Kent 29 D6
Underwood Notts 76 D4
Undy Mon 35 F8
Unifirth Shetland 160 H4
Union Cottage Aberds 141 E7
Union Mills IoM 84 E3
Union Street E Sus 18 B4
Unstone Derbys 76 B3
Unstone Green Derbys 76 B3
Unthank Cumb 108 F4
Unthank Cumb 109 E6
Unthank End Cumb 108 F4
Up Cerne Dorset 12 D4
Up Exe Devon 10 D4
Up Hatherley Glos 37 B6
Up Holland Lancs 86 D3
Up Marden W Sus 15 C8
Up Nately Hants 26 D4
Up Somborne Hants 25 F8
Up Sydling Dorset 12 D4
Upavon Wilts 25 D6
Upchurch Kent 30 C2
Upcott Hereford 48 D5
Upend Cambs 55 D7
Upgate Norf 68 C4
Uphall W Loth 120 B3
Uphall Station W Loth 120 B3
Upham Devon 10 D3
Upham Hants 15 B6
Uphampton Worcs 50 C3
Uphill N Som 22 D5
Uplawmoor E Renf 118 D4
Upleadon Glos 36 B4
Upleatham Redcar 102 C4
Uplees Kent 30 C3
Uploders Dorset 12 E3
Uplowman Devon 10 C5
Uplyme Devon 11 E8
Upminster London 42 F1
Upnor Medway 29 B8
Upottery Devon 11 D7
Upper Affcot Shrops 60 F4
Upper Ardchronie Highld 151 C9
Upper Arley Worcs 61 F7
Upper Arncott Oxon 39 C6
Upper Astrop Northants 52 F3
Upper Badcall Highld 156 E4
Upper Basildon W Berks 26 B3
Upper Beeding W Sus 17 C5
Upper Benefield Northants 65 F6
Upper Bighouse Highld 157 D11
Upper Boddington Northants 52 D2
Upper Borth Ceredig 58 F3
Upper Boyndlie Aberds 153 B9
Upper Brailes Warks 51 F8
Upper Breakish Highld 149 F11
Upper Breinton Hereford 49 E6
Upper Broadheath Worcs 50 D3
Upper Broughton Notts 64 B3
Upper Bucklebury W Berks 26 C3
Upper Burnhaugh Aberds 141 E7
Upper Caldecote C Beds 54 E2
Upper Catesby Northants 52 D3
Upper Chapel Powys 48 E2
Upper Church Village Rhondda 34 F4
Upper Chute Wilts 25 D7
Upper Clatford Hants 25 E8
Upper Clynnog Gwyn 71 C5
Upper Cumberworth W Yorks 88 D3
Upper Cwm-twrch Powys 34 C1
Upper Cwmbran Torf 35 E6
Upper Dallachy Moray 152 B3
Upper Dean Bedford 53 C8
Upper Denby W Yorks 88 D3
Upper Denton Cumb 109 C6
Upper Derraid Highld 151 H13
Upper Dicker E Sus 18 E2
Upper Dovercourt Essex 57 F6
Upper Druimfin Argyll 147 F8
Upper Dunsforth N Yorks 95 C7
Upper Eathie Highld 151 E10
Upper Elkstone Staffs 75 D7
Upper End Derbys 75 B7
Upper Farringdon Hants 26 F5
Upper Framilode Glos 36 C4
Upper Glenfintaig Highld 137 F5
Upper Gornal W Mid 62 E3
Upper Gravenhurst C Beds 54 F2
Upper Green Mon 35 C7
Upper Green W Berks 25 C8
Upper Grove Common Hereford 36 B2
Upper Hackney Derbys 76 C2
Upper Hale Sur 27 E6
Upper Halistra Highld 148 C7
Upper Halling Medway 29 C7
Upper Hambleton Rutland 65 D6
Upper Hardres Court Kent 31 D5
Upper Hartfield E Sus 29 F5
Upper Haugh S Yorks 88 E5
Upper Heath Shrops 61 F5
Upper Hellesdon Norf 68 C5
Upper Helmsley N Yorks 96 D2
Upper Hergest Hereford 48 D4
Upper Heyford Northants 52 D4
Upper Heyford Oxon 38 B4
Upper Hill Hereford 49 D6
Upper Hopton W Yorks 88 C2
Upper Horsebridge E Sus 18 D2
Upper Hulme Staffs 75 C7
Upper Inglesham Swindon 38 E2
Upper Inverbrough Highld 151 H11
Upper Killay Swansea 33 E6
Upper Knockando Moray 152 D1
Upper Lambourn W Berks 38 F3
Upper Leigh Staffs 75 F7
Upper Lenie Highld 137 B8
Upper Lochton Aberds 141 E5
Upper Longdon Staffs 62 C4
Upper Lybster Highld 158 G4
Upper Lydbrook Glos 36 C3
Upper Maes-coed Hereford 48 F5
Upper Midway Derbys 63 B6
Upper Milovaig Highld 148 D6
Upper Minety Wilts 37 E7
Upper Mitton Worcs 50 B3
Upper North Dean Bucks 39 E8
Upper Obney Perth 133 F7
Upper Ollach Highld 149 E10
Upper Padley Derbys 76 B2
Upper Pollicott Bucks 39 C7
Upper Poppleton York 95 D8
Upper Quinton Warks 51 E6
Upper Ratley Hants 14 B4
Upper Rissington Glos 38 C2
Upper Rochford Worcs 49 C8
Upper Sandaig Highld 149 G12
Upper Sanday Orkney 159 H6
Upper Sapey Hereford 49 C8
Upper Saxondale Notts 77 F6
Upper Seagry Wilts 37 F6
Upper Shelton C Beds 53 E7
Upper Sheringham Norf 81 C7
Upper Skelmorlie N Ayrs 118 C2
Upper Slaughter Glos 38 B1
Upper Soudley Glos 36 C3
Upper Stondon C Beds 54 F2
Upper Stowe Northants 52 D4
Upper Stratton Swindon 38 F1
Upper Street Hants 14 C2
Upper Street Norf 69 C6
Upper Street Norf 69 C6
Upper Street Suff 56 F5
Upper Strensham Worcs 50 F4
Upper Sundon C Beds 40 B3
Upper Swell Glos 38 B1
Upper Tean Staffs 75 F7
Upper Tillyrie Perth 128 D3
Upper Tooting London 28 B3
Upper Tote Highld 149 C10
Upper Town N Som 23 C7
Upper Treverward Shrops 48 B4
Upper Tysoe Warks 51 E8
Upper Upham Wilts 25 B7
Upper Wardington Oxon 52 E2
Upper Weald M Keynes 53 F5
Upper Weedon Northants 52 D4
Upper Wield Hants 26 F4
Upper Winchendon Bucks 39 C7
Upper Witton W Mid 62 E4
Upper Woodend Aberds 141 C5
Upper Woodford Wilts 25 F6
Upper Wootton Hants 26 D3
Upper Wyche Hereford 50 E2
Upperby Cumb 108 D4
Uppermill Gtr Man 87 D7
Uppersound Shetland 160 J6
Upperthong W Yorks 88 D2
Upperthorpe N Lincs 89 D8
Upperton W Sus 16 B3
Uppertown Derbys 76 C3
Uppertown Highld 158 C5
Uppertown Orkney 159 J5
Uppingham Rutland 65 E5
Uppington Shrops 61 D6
Upsall N Yorks 102 F2
Upshire Essex 41 D7
Upstreet Kent 31 C6
Upthorpe Suff 56 B3
Upton Cambs 54 B2
Upton Ches W 73 C8
Upton Corn 8 D4
Upton Dorset 12 F5
Upton Dorset 13 E7
Upton Hants 14 C4
Upton Hants 25 D8
Upton Leics 63 E7
Upton Lincs 90 F2
Upton Mers 85 F3
Upton Norf 69 C6
Upton Northants 52 C5
Upton Notts 77 B7
Upton Notts 77 D7
Upton Oxon 39 F5
Upton Pboro 65 D8
Upton Slough 27 B7
Upton Som 10 B4
Upton W Yorks 89 C5
Upton Bishop Hereford 36 B3
Upton Cheyney S Glos 23 C8
Upton Cressett Shrops 61 E6
Upton Cross Corn 5 B7
Upton Grey Hants 26 E4
Upton Hellions Devon 10 D3
Upton Lovell Wilts 24 E4
Upton Magna Shrops 61 C5
Upton Noble Som 24 F2
Upton Pyne Devon 10 E4
Upton Scudamore Wilts 24 E3
Upton St Leonard's Glos 37 C5
Upton Snodsbury Worcs 50 D4
Upton upon Severn Worcs 50 E3
Upton Warren Worcs 50 C4
Upwaltham W Sus 16 C3
Upware Cambs 55 B6
Upwell Norf 66 D4
Upwey Dorset 12 F4
Upwood Cambs 66 F2
Uradale Shetland 160 K6
Urafirth Shetland 160 F5
Urchfont Wilts 24 D5
Urdimarsh Hereford 49 E7
Ure Shetland 160 F4
Ure Bank N Yorks 95 B6
Urgha W Isles 154 H6
Urishay Common Hereford 48 F5
Urlay Nook Stockton 102 C1
Urmston Gtr Man 87 E5
Urpeth Durham 110 D5
Urquhart Highld 151 F8
Urquhart Moray 152 B2
Urra N Yorks 102 D3
Urray Highld 151 F8
Ushaw Moor Durham 110 E5
Usk = Brynbuga Mon 35 D7
Usselby Lincs 90 E4
Usworth T&W 111 D6
Utkinton Ches W 74 C2
Utley W Yorks 94 E3
Uton Devon 10 E3
Utterby Lincs 91 E7
Uttoxeter Staffs 75 F7
Uwchmynydd Gwyn 70 E2
Uxbridge London 40 F3
Uyeasound Shetland 160 C7
Uzmaston Pembs 44 D4

V

Valley Anglesey 82 D2
Valley Truckle Corn 8 F2
Valleyfield Dumfries 106 D3
Valsgarth Shetland 160 B8
Valtos Highld 149 B10
Van Powys 59 F6
Vange Essex 42 F3
Varteg Torf 35 D6
Vatten Highld 149 D7
Vaul Argyll 146 G3
Vaynor M Tydf 34 C4
Veensgarth Shetland 160 J6
Velindre Powys 48 F3
Vellow Som 22 F2
Veness Orkney 159 F6
Venn Green Devon 9 C5
Venn Ottery Devon 11 E5
Vennington Shrops 60 D3
Venny Tedburn Devon 10 E3
Ventnor IoW 15 G6
Vernham Dean Hants 25 D8
Vernham Street Hants 25 D8
Vernolds Common Shrops 60 F4
Verwood Dorset 13 D8
Veryan Corn 3 C8
Vicarage Devon 11 F7
Vickerstown Cumb 92 C1
Victoria Corn 4 C4
Victoria S Yorks 88 D2
Vidlin Shetland 160 G6
Viewpark N Lanark 119 C7
Vigo Village Kent 29 C7
Vinehall Street E Sus 18 C4
Vine's Cross E Sus 18 D2
Viney Hill Glos 36 D3
Virginia Water Sur 27 C8
Virginstow Devon 9 E5
Vobster Som 24 E2
Voe Shetland 160 E5
Voe Shetland 160 G6
Vowchurch Hereford 49 F5
Voxter Shetland 160 F5
Voy Orkney 159 G3

W

Wackerfield Durham 101 B6
Wacton Norf 68 E4
Wadbister Shetland 160 J6
Wadborough Worcs 50 E4
Waddesdon Bucks 39 C7
Waddingham Lincs 90 E3
Waddington Lancs 93 E7
Waddington Lincs 78 C2
Wadebridge Corn 4 B4
Wadeford Som 11 C8
Wadenhoe Northants 65 F7
Wadesmill Herts 41 C6
Wadhurst E Sus 18 B3
Wadshelf Derbys 76 B3
Wadsley S Yorks 88 E4
Wadsley Bridge S Yorks 88 E4
Wadworth S Yorks 89 E6
Waen Denb 72 C3
Waen Denb 72 C5
Waen Fach Powys 60 C2
Waen Goleugoed Denb 72 B4
Wag Highld 157 G13
Wainfleet All Saints Lincs 79 D7
Wainfleet Bank Lincs 79 D7
Wainfleet St Mary Lincs 79 D8
Wainfleet Tofts Lincs 79 D7
Wainhouse Corner Corn 8 E3
Wainscott Medway 29 B8
Wainstalls W Yorks 87 B8
Waitby Cumb 100 D2
Waithe Lincs 91 D6
Wake Lady Green N Yorks 102 E4
Wakefield W Yorks 88 B4
Wakerley Northants 65 E6
Wakes Colne Essex 42 B4
Walberswick Suff 57 B8
Walberton W Sus 16 D3
Walbottle T&W 110 C4
Walcot Lincs 78 F3
Walcot N Lincs 90 B2
Walcot Shrops 60 F3
Walcot Swindon 38 F1
Walcot Telford 61 C5
Walcot Green Norf 68 F4
Walcote Leics 64 F2
Walcote Warks 51 D6
Walcott Lincs 78 D4
Walcott Norf 69 A6
Walden N Yorks 101 F5
Walden Head N Yorks 100 F4
Walden Stubbs N Yorks 89 C6
Waldersey Cambs 66 D4
Walderslade Medway 29 C8
Walderton W Sus 15 C8
Walditch Dorset 12 E2
Waldley Derbys 75 F8
Waldridge Durham 111 D5
Waldringfield Suff 57 E6
Waldringfield Heath Suff 57 E6
Waldron E Sus 18 D2
Wales S Yorks 89 F5
Walesby Lincs 90 E5
Walesby Notts 77 B6
Walford Hereford 36 B2
Walford Hereford 49 B5
Walford Shrops 60 B4

Walford Heath Shrops 60 C4
Walgherton Ches E 74 E3
Walgrave Northants 53 B6
Walhampton Hants 14 E4
Walk Mill Lancs 93 F8
Walkden Gtr Man 86 D5
Walker T&W 111 C5
Walker Barn Ches E 75 B6
Walker Fold Lancs 93 E6
Walkerburn Borders 121 F6
Walkeringham Notts 89 E8
Walkerith Lincs 89 E8
Walkern Herts 41 B5
Walker's Green Hereford 49 E7
Walkerville N Yorks 101 E7
Walkford Dorset 14 E3
Walkhampton Devon 6 C3
Walkington E Yorks 97 F5
Walkley S Yorks 88 F4
Wall Northumb 110 C2
Wall Staffs 62 D5
Wall Bank Shrops 60 E5
Wall Heath W Mid 62 F2
Wall under Heywood Shrops 60 E5
Wallaceton Dumfries 113 F8
Wallacetown S Ayrs 112 B3
Wallacetown S Ayrs 112 D2
Wallands Park E Sus 17 C8
Wallasey Mers 85 E4
Wallcrouch E Sus 18 B3
Wallingford Oxon 39 F6
Wallington Hants 15 D6
Wallington Herts 54 F3
Wallington London 28 C3
Wallis Pembs 32 B1
Walliswood Sur 28 F2
Walls Shetland 160 J4
Wallsend T&W 111 C5
Wallston V Glam 22 B3
Wallyford E Loth 121 B6
Walmer Kent 31 D7
Walmer Bridge Lancs 86 B2
Walmersley Gtr Man 87 C6
Walmley W Mid 62 E5
Walpole Suff 57 B7
Walpole Cross Keys Norf 66 C5
Walpole Highway Norf 66 C5
Walpole Marsh Norf 66 C4
Walpole St Andrew Norf 66 C5
Walpole St Peter Norf 66 C5
Walsall W Mid 62 E4
Walsall Wood W Mid 62 D4
Walsden W Yorks 87 B7
Walsgrave on Sowe W Mid 63 F7
Walsham le Willows Suff 56 B3
Walshaw Gtr Man 87 C5
Walshford N Yorks 95 D7
Walsoken Cambs 66 C4
Walston S Lanark 120 E3
Walsworth Herts 54 F3
Walters Ash Bucks 39 E8
Walterston V Glam 22 B2
Walterstone Hereford 35 B7
Waltham Kent 30 E5
Waltham NE Lincs 91 D6
Waltham Abbey Essex 41 D6
Waltham Chase Hants 15 C6
Waltham Cross Herts 41 D6
Waltham on the Wolds Leics 64 B5
Waltham St Lawrence Windsor 27 B6
Walthamstow London 41 F6
Walton Cumb 108 C5
Walton Derbys 76 C3
Walton Leics 64 F2
Walton M Keynes 53 F6
Walton Mers 85 E4
Walton Pboro 65 D8
Walton Powys 48 D4
Walton Som 23 F6
Walton Staffs 75 F5
Walton Suff 57 F6
Walton Telford 61 C5
Walton W Yorks 88 C4
Walton W Yorks 95 E7
Walton Warks 51 D7
Walton Cardiff Glos 50 F4
Walton East Pembs 32 B1
Walton-in-Gordano N Som 23 B6
Walton-le-Dale Lancs 86 B3
Walton-on-Thames Sur 28 C2
Walton on the Hill Staffs 62 B3
Walton on the Hill Sur 28 D3
Walton-on-the-Naze Essex 43 B8
Walton on the Wolds Leics 64 C2
Walton-on-Trent Derbys 63 C6
Walton West Pembs 44 D3
Walwen Flint 73 B6
Walwick Northumb 110 B2
Walworth Darl 101 C7
Walworth Gate Darl 101 B7
Walwyn's Castle Pembs 44 D3
Wambrook Som 11 D7
Wanborough Sur 27 E7
Wanborough Swindon 38 F2
Wandsworth London 28 B3
Wangford Suff 57 B8
Wanlockhead Dumfries 113 C8
Wansford E Yorks 97 D6
Wansford Pboro 65 E7
Wanstead London 41 F7
Wanstrow Som 24 E2
Wanswell Glos 36 D3
Wantage Oxon 38 F3
Wapley S Glos 24 B2
Wappenbury Warks 51 C8
Wappenham Northants 52 E4
Warbleton E Sus 18 D3
Warblington Hants 15 D8
Warborough Oxon 39 E5
Warboys Cambs 66 F3
Warbreck Blackpool 92 F3
Warbstow Corn 8 E4
Warburton Gtr Man 86 F5
Warcop Cumb 100 C2
Ward End W Mid 62 F5
Ward Green Suff 56 C4
Warden Kent 30 B4
Warden Northumb 110 C2
Wardhill Orkney 159 F7
Wardington Oxon 52 E2
Wardlaw Borders 115 C5
Wardle Ches E 74 D3
Wardle Gtr Man 87 C7
Wardley Rutland 64 D5
Wardlow Derbys 75 B8
Wardy Hill Cambs 66 F4
Ware Herts 41 C6
Ware Kent 31 C6
Wareham Dorset 13 F7
Warehorne Kent 19 B6
Waren Mill Northumb 123 F7
Warenford Northumb 117 B7
Warenton Northumb 123 F7
Wareside Herts 41 C6
Waresley Cambs 54 D3
Waresley Worcs 50 B3
Warfield Brack 27 B6
Warfleet Devon 7 D6
Wargrave Wokingham 27 B5
Warham Norf 80 C5
Warhill Gtr Man 87 E7
Wark Northumb 109 B8
Wark Northumb 122 F4
Warkleigh Devon 9 B8
Warkton Northants 53 B6
Warkworth Northants 52 E2
Warkworth Northumb 117 D8
Warlaby N Yorks 101 E8
Warland W Yorks 87 B7
Warleggan Corn 5 C6
Warlingham Sur 28 D4
Warmfield W Yorks 88 B4
Warmingham Ches E 74 C4
Warmington Northants 65 E7
Warmington Warks 52 E2
Warminster Wilts 24 E3
Warmlake Kent 30 D2
Warmley S Glos 23 B8
Warmley Tower S Glos 23 B8
Warmonds Hill Northants 53 C7
Warmsworth S Yorks 89 D6
Warmwell Dorset 13 F5
Warndon Worcs 50 D3
Warnford Hants 15 B7
Warnham W Sus 28 F2
Warninglid W Sus 17 B6
Warren Ches E 75 B5
Warren Pembs 44 F4
Warren Heath Suff 57 E6
Warren Row Windsor 39 F8
Warren Street Kent 30 D3
Warrington M Keynes 53 D6
Warrington Warr 86 F4
Warsash Hants 15 D5
Warslow Staffs 75 D7
Warter E Yorks 96 D4
Warthermarske N Yorks 94 B5
Warthill N Yorks 96 D2
Wartling E Sus 18 E3
Wartnaby Leics 64 B4
Warton Lancs 86 B2
Warton Lancs 92 B4
Warton Northumb 117 D6
Warton Warks 63 D6
Warwick Warks 51 C7
Warwick Bridge Cumb 108 D4
Warwick on Eden Cumb 108 D4
Wasbister Orkney 159 E4
Wasdale Head Cumb 98 D3
Wash Common W Berks 26 C2
Washaway Corn 4 C5
Washbourne Devon 7 D5
Washfield Devon 10 C4
Washfold N Yorks 101 D5
Washford Som 22 E2
Washford Pyne Devon 10 C3
Washingborough Lincs 78 B3
Washington T&W 111 D6
Washington W Sus 16 C5
Wasing W Berks 26 C3
Waskerley Durham 110 E3
Wasperton Warks 51 D7
Wasps Nest Lincs 78 C3
Wass N Yorks 95 B8
Watchet Som 22 E2
Watchfield Oxon 38 E2
Watchfield Som 22 E5
Watchgate Cumb 99 E7
Watchhill Cumb 107 E8
Watcombe Torbay 7 C7
Watendlath Cumb 98 C4
Water Devon 10 F2
Water Lancs 87 B6
Water End E Yorks 96 F3
Water End Herts 40 C3
Water End Herts 41 D5
Water Newton Cambs 65 E8
Water Orton Warks 63 E5
Water Stratford Bucks 52 F4
Water Yeat Cumb 98 F4
Waterbeach Cambs 55 C5
Waterbeck Dumfries 108 B2
Waterden Norf 80 D4
Waterfall Staffs 75 D7
Waterfoot E Renf 119 D5
Waterfoot Lancs 87 B6
Waterford Hants 14 E4
Waterford Herts 41 C6
Waterhead Cumb 99 D5
Waterhead Dumfries 114 E4
Waterheads Borders 120 D5
Waterhouses Durham 110 E4
Waterhouses Staffs 75 D7
Wateringbury Kent 29 D7
Waterloo Gtr Man 87 D7
Waterloo Highld 149 F11
Waterloo Mers 85 E4
Waterloo N Lanark 119 D8
Waterloo Norf 68 C5
Waterloo Perth 133 F7
Waterloo Poole 13 E8
Waterloo Shrops 74 F2
Waterloo Port Gwyn 82 E4
Waterlooville Hants 15 D7
Watermeetings S Lanark 114 C2
Watermillock Cumb 99 B6
Waterperry Oxon 39 D6
Waterrow Som 11 B5
Water's Nook Gtr Man 86 D4
Waters Upton Telford 61 C6
Watersfield W Sus 16 C4
Waterside Aberds 141 B9
Waterside Blackburn 86 B5
Waterside Cumb 108 E2
Waterside E Ayrs 112 D4
Waterside E Ayrs 118 E4
Waterside E Dunb 119 B6
Waterside E Renf 118 D5
Waterstock Oxon 39 D6
Waterston Pembs 44 E4
Watford Herts 40 E4
Watford Northants 52 C4
Watford Gap Staffs 62 D5
Wath N Yorks 94 C4
Wath N Yorks 95 B6
Wath N Yorks 96 B2
Wath Brow Cumb 98 C2
Wath upon Dearne S Yorks 88 D5
Watlington Norf 67 C6
Watlington Oxon 39 E6
Watnall Notts 76 E5
Watten Highld 158 E4
Wattisfield Suff 56 B4
Wattisham Suff 56 D4
Wattlesborough Heath Shrops 60 C3
Watton E Yorks 97 D6
Watton Norf 68 D2
Watton at Stone Herts 41 C6
Wattston N Lanark 119 B7
Wattstown Rhondda 34 E4
Wauchan Highld 136 F2
Waulkmill Lodge Orkney 159 H4
Waun Powys 59 D5
Waun-y-clyn Carms 33 D5
Waunarlwydd Swansea 33 E7
Waunclunda Carms 47 F5
Waunfawr Gwyn 82 F5
Waungron Swansea 33 D6
Waunlwyd Bl Gwent 35 D5
Wavendon M Keynes 53 F7
Waverbridge Cumb 108 E2
Waverton Ches W 73 C8
Waverton Cumb 108 E2
Wavertree Mers 85 F4
Wawne E Yorks 97 F6
Waxham Norf 69 B7
Waxholme E Yorks 91 B7
Way Kent 31 C7
Way Village Devon 10 C3
Wayfield Medway 29 C8
Wayford Som 12 D2
Waymills Shrops 74 E2
Wayne Green Mon 35 C8
Wdig = Goodwick Pembs 44 B4
Weachyburn Aberds 153 C6
Weald Oxon 38 D3
Wealdstone London 40 F4
Weardley W Yorks 95 E5
Weare Som 23 D6
Weare Giffard Devon 9 B6
Wearhead Durham 109 F8
Weasdale Cumb 100 D1
Weasenham All Saints Norf 80 E4
Weasenham St Peter Norf 80 E4
Weatherhill Sur 28 E4
Weaverham Ches W 74 B3
Weaverthorpe N Yorks 97 B5
Webheath Worcs 50 C5
Wedderlairs Aberds 153 E8
Wedderlie Borders 122 D2
Weddington Warks 63 E7
Wedhampton Wilts 25 D5
Wedmore Som 23 E6
Wednesbury W Mid 62 E3
Wednesfield W Mid 62 D3
Weedon Bucks 39 C8
Weedon Bec Northants 52 D4
Weedon Lois Northants 52 E4
Weeford Staffs 62 D5
Week Devon 10 C2
Week St Mary Corn 8 E4
Weeke Hants 26 F2
Weekley Northants 65 F5
Weel E Yorks 97 F6
Weeley Essex 43 B7
Weeley Heath Essex 43 B7
Weem Perth 133 E5
Weeping Cross Staffs 62 B3
Weethley Gate Warks 51 D5
Weeting Norf 67 F7
Weeton E Yorks 91 B7
Weeton Lancs 92 F3
Weeton N Yorks 95 E5
Weetwood Hall Northumb 117 B6
Weir Lancs 87 B6
Weir Quay Devon 6 C2
Welborne Norf 68 D3
Welbourn Lincs 78 D2
Welburn N Yorks 96 C3
Welburn N Yorks 102 F4
Welbury N Yorks 102 D1
Welby Lincs 78 F2
Welches Dam Cambs 66 F4
Welcombe Devon 8 C4
Weld Bank Lancs 86 C3
Weldon Northumb 117 E7
Welford Northants 64 F3
Welford W Berks 26 B2
Welford-on-Avon Warks 51 D6
Welham Leics 64 E4
Welham Notts 89 F8
Welham Green Herts 41 D5
Well Hants 27 E5
Well Lincs 79 B7
Well N Yorks 101 F7
Well End Bucks 40 F1
Well Heads W Yorks 94 F3
Well Hill Kent 29 C5
Well Town Devon 10 D4
Welland Worcs 50 E2
Wellbank Angus 134 F4
Welldale Dumfries 107 C8
Wellesbourne Warks 51 D7
Welling London 29 B5
Wellingborough Northants 53 C6
Wellingham Norf 80 E4
Wellingore Lincs 78 D2
Wellington Cumb 98 D2
Wellington Hereford 49 E6
Wellington Som 11 B6
Wellington Telford 61 C6
Wellington Heath Hereford 50 E2
Wellington Hill W Yorks 95 F6
Wellow Bath 24 D2
Wellow IoW 14 F4
Wellow Notts 77 C6
Wellpond Green Herts 41 B7
Wells Som 23 E7
Wells Green Ches E 74 D3
Wells-Next-The-Sea Norf 80 C5
Wellsborough Leics 63 D7
Wellswood Torbay 7 C7
Wellwood Fife 128 F2
Welney Norf 66 E5
Welsh Bicknor Hereford 36 C2
Welsh End Shrops 74 F2
Welsh Frankton Shrops 73 F7
Welsh Hook Pembs 44 C4
Welsh Newton Hereford 36 C1
Welsh St Donats V Glam 22 B2
Welshampton Shrops 73 F8
Welshpool = Y Trallwng Powys 60 D2
Welton Cumb 108 E3
Welton E Yorks 90 B3
Welton Lincs 78 B3
Welton Northants 52 C3
Welton Hill Lincs 90 F4
Welton le Marsh Lincs 79 C7
Welton le Wold Lincs 91 F6
Welwick E Yorks 91 B7
Welwyn Herts 41 C5
Welwyn Garden City Herts 41 C5
Wem Shrops 60 B5
Wembdon Som 22 F4
Wembley London 40 F4
Wembury Devon 6 E3
Wembworthy Devon 9 D8
Wemyss Bay Invclyd 118 C1
Wenallt Ceredig 47 B5
Wenallt Gwyn 72 E3
Wendens Ambo Essex 55 F6
Wendlebury Oxon 39 C5
Wendling Norf 68 C2
Wendover Bucks 40 D1
Wendron Corn 3 C5
Wendy Cambs 54 E4
Wenfordbridge Corn 5 B5
Wenhaston Suff 57 B8
Wennington Cambs 54 B3
Wennington Lancs 93 B6
Wennington London 41 F8
Wensley Derbys 76 C2
Wensley N Yorks 101 F5
Wentbridge W Yorks 89 C5
Wentnor Shrops 60 E3
Wentworth Cambs 55 B5
Wentworth S Yorks 88 E4
Wenvoe V Glam 22 B3
Weobley Hereford 49 D6
Weobley Marsh Hereford 49 D6
Wereham Norf 67 D6
Wergs W Mid 62 D2
Wern Powys 59 C6
Wern Powys 60 C2
Wernffrwd Swansea 33 E6
Wernyrheolydd Mon 35 C7
Werrington Corn 8 F5
Werrington Pboro 65 D8
Werrington Staffs 75 E6
Wervin Ches W 73 B8
Wesham Lancs 92 F4
Wessington Derbys 76 D3
West Acre Norf 67 C7
West Adderbury Oxon 52 F2
West Allerdean Northumb 123 E5
West Alvington Devon 6 E5
West Amesbury Wilts 25 E6
West Anstey Devon 10 B3
West Ashby Lincs 79 B5
West Ashling W Sus 16 D2
West Ashton Wilts 24 D3
West Auckland Durham 101 B6
West Ayton N Yorks 103 F7
West Bagborough Som 22 F3
West Barkwith Lincs 91 F5
West Barnby N Yorks 103 C6
West Barns E Loth 122 B2
West Barsham Norf 80 D5
West Bay Dorset 12 E2
West Beckham Norf 81 D7
West Bedfont Sur 27 B8
West Benhar N Lanark 119 C8
West Bergholt Essex 43 B5
West Bexington Dorset 12 F3
West Bilney Norf 67 C7
West Blatchington Brighton 17 D6
West Bowling W Yorks 94 F4
West Bradford Lancs 93 E7
West Bradley Som 23 F7
West Bretton W Yorks 88 C3
West Bridgford Notts 77 F5
West Bromwich W Mid 62 E4
West Buckland Devon 21 F5
West Buckland Som 11 B6
West Burrafirth Shetland 160 H4
West Burton N Yorks 101 F5
West Burton W Sus 16 C3
West Butterwick N Lincs 90 D2
West Byfleet Sur 27 C8
West Caister Norf 69 C8
West Calder W Loth 120 C3
West Camel Som 12 B3
West Challow Oxon 38 F3
West Chelborough Dorset 12 D3
West Chevington Northumb 117 E8
West Chiltington W Sus 16 C4
West Chiltington Common W Sus 16 C4
West Chinnock Som 12 C2
West Chisenbury Wilts 25 D6
West Clandon Sur 27 D8
West Cliffe Kent 31 E7
West Clyne Highld 157 J11
West Clyth Highld 158 G4
West Coker Som 12 C3
West Compton Dorset 12 E3
West Compton Som 23 E7
West Cowick E Yorks 89 B7
West Cranmore Som 23 E8
West Cross Swansea 33 F7
West Cullery Aberds 141 D6
West Curry Corn 8 E4
West Curthwaite Cumb 108 E3
West Darlochan Argyll 143 F7
West Dean W Sus 16 C2
West Dean Wilts 14 B3
West Deeping Lincs 65 D8
West Derby Mers 85 E4
West Dereham Norf 67 D6
West Didsbury Gtr Man 87 E6
West Ditchburn Northumb 117 B7
West Down Devon 20 E4
West Drayton London 27 B8
West Drayton Notts 77 B7
West Ella E Yorks 90 B4
West End Bedford 53 D7
West End E Yorks 96 F5
West End E Yorks 97 F7
West End Hants 15 C5
West End Lancs 86 B5
West End N Som 23 C6
West End N Yorks 94 D4
West End Norf 68 D2
West End Norf 69 C8
West End Oxon 38 D4
West End S Lanark 120 E2
West End S Yorks 89 D7
West End Suff 69 F7
West End Sur 27 C7
West End W Sus 17 C6
West End Wilts 13 B7
West End Wilts 24 B4
West End Green Hants 26 C4
West Farleigh Kent 29 D8
West Felton Shrops 60 B3
West Fenton E Loth 129 F6
West Ferry Dundee 134 F4
West Firle E Sus 17 D8
West Ginge Oxon 38 F4
West Grafton Wilts 25 C7
West Green Hants 26 D5
West Greenskares Aberds 153 B7
West Grimstead Wilts 14 B3
West Grinstead W Sus 17 B5
West Haddlesey N Yorks 89 B6
West Haddon Northants 52 B4
West Hagbourne Oxon 39 F5
West Hagley Worcs 62 F3
West Hall Cumb 109 C5
West Hallam Derbys 76 E4
West Halton N Lincs 90 B3
West Ham London 41 F7
West Handley Derbys 76 B3
West Hanney Oxon 38 E4
West Hanningfield Essex 42 E3
West Hardwick W Yorks 88 C5
West Harnham Wilts 14 B2
West Harptree Bath 23 D7
West Hatch Som 11 B7
West Head Norf 67 D5
West Heath Ches E 74 C5
West Heath Hants 26 D3
West Heath Hants 27 D6
West Helmsdale Highld 157 H13
West Hendred Oxon 38 F4
West Heslerton N Yorks 96 B5
West Hill Devon 11 E5
West Hill E Yorks 97 C7
West Hill N Som 23 B6
West Hoathly W Sus 28 F4
West Holme Dorset 13 F6
West Horndon Essex 42 F2
West Horrington Som 23 E7
West Horsley Sur 27 D8
West Horton Northumb 123 F6
West Hougham Kent 31 E6
West Houlland Shetland 160 H4
West-houses Derbys 76 D4
West Huntington York 96 D2
West Hythe Kent 19 B8
West Ilsley W Berks 38 F4
West Itchenor W Sus 15 D8
West Keal Lincs 79 C6
West Kennett Wilts 25 C6
West Kilbride N Ayrs 118 E2
West Kingsdown Kent 29 C6
West Kington Wilts 24 B3
West Kinharrachie Aberds 153 E9
West Kirby Mers 85 F3
West Knapton N Yorks 96 B4
West Knighton Dorset 12 F5
West Knoyle Wilts 24 F3
West Kyloe Northumb 123 E6
West Lambrook Som 12 C2
West Langdon Kent 31 E7
West Langwell Highld 157 J9
West Lavington W Sus 16 B2
West Lavington Wilts 24 D5
West Layton N Yorks 101 D6
West Lea Durham 111 E7
West Leake Notts 64 B2
West Learmouth Northumb 122 F4
West Leigh Devon 9 D8
West Lexham Norf 67 C8
West Lilling N Yorks 96 C2
West Linton Borders 120 D4
West Liss Hants 15 B8
West Littleton S Glos 24 B2
West Looe Corn 5 D7
West Luccombe Som 21 E7
West Lulworth Dorset 13 F6
West Lutton N Yorks 96 C5
West Lydford Som 23 F7
West Lyng Som 11 B8
West Lynn Norf 67 B6
West Malling Kent 29 D7
West Malvern Worcs 50 E2
West Marden W Sus 15 C8
West Marina E Sus 18 E4
West Markham Notts 77 B7
West Marsh NE Lincs 91 C6
West Marton N Yorks 93 D8
West Meon Hants 15 B7
West Mersea Essex 43 C6
West Milton Dorset 12 E3
West Minster Kent 30 B3
West Molesey Sur 28 C2
West Monkton Som 11 B7
West Moors Dorset 13 D8
West Morriston Borders 122 E2
West Muir Angus 135 C5
West Ness N Yorks 96 B2
West Newham Northumb 110 B3
West Newton E Yorks 97 F7
West Newton Norf 67 B6
West Norwood London 28 B4
West Ogwell Devon 7 B6
West Orchard Dorset 13 C6
West Overton Wilts 25 C6
West Park Hrtlpl 111 F7
West Parley Dorset 13 E8
West Peckham Kent 29 D7
West Pelton Durham 110 D5
West Pennard Som 23 F7
West Pentire Corn 4 C2
West Perry Cambs 54 C2
West Putford Devon 9 C5
West Quantoxhead Som 22 E3
West Rainton Durham 111 E6
West Rasen Lincs 90 F4
West Raynham Norf 80 E4
West Retford Notts 89 F7
West Rounton N Yorks 102 D2
West Row Suff 55 B7
West Rudham Norf 80 E4
West Runton Norf 81 C7
West Saltoun E Loth 121 C7
West Sandwick Shetland 160 E6
West Scrafton N Yorks 101 F5
West Sleekburn Northumb 117 F8
West Somerton Norf 69 C7
West Stafford Dorset 12 F5
West Stockwith Notts 89 E8
West Stoke W Sus 16 D2
West Stonesdale N Yorks 100 D3
West Stoughton Som 23 E6
West Stour Dorset 13 B5
West Stourmouth Kent 31 C6
West Stow Suff 56 B2
West Stowell Wilts 25 C6
West Strathan Highld 157 C8
West Stratton Hants 26 E3
West Street Kent 30 D3
West Tanfield N Yorks 95 B5
West Taphouse Corn 5 C6
West Tarbert Argyll 145 G7
West Thirston Northumb 117 E7
West Thorney W Sus 15 D8
West Thurrock Thurrock 29 B6
West Tilbury Thurrock 29 B7
West Tisted Hants 15 B7
West Tofts Norf 67 E8
West Tofts Perth 133 F8
West Torrington Lincs 90 F5
West Town Hants 15 E8
West Town N Som 23 C6
West Tytherley Hants 14 B3
West Tytherton Wilts 24 B4
West Walton Norf 66 C4
West Walton Highway Norf 66 C4
West Wellow Hants 14 C3
West Wemyss Fife 128 E5
West Wick N Som 23 C5
West Wickham Cambs 55 E7
West Wickham London 28 C4
West Williamston Pembs 32 D1
West Willoughby Lincs 78 E2
West Winch Norf 67 C6
West Winterslow Wilts 25 F7
West Wittering W Sus 15 E8
West Witton N Yorks 101 F5
West Woodburn Northumb 116 F4
West Woodhay W Berks 25 C8
West Woodlands Som 24 E2
West Worldham Hants 26 F5
West Worlington Devon 10 C2
West Worthing W Sus 16 D5
West Wratting Cambs 55 D7
West Wycombe Bucks 39 E8
West Wylam Northumb 110 C4
West Yell Shetland 160 E6
Westacott Devon 20 F4
Westbere Kent 31 C5
Westborough Lincs 77 E8
Westbourne Bmouth 13 E8
Westbourne Suff 56 E5
Westbourne W Sus 15 D8
Westbrook W Berks 26 B2
Westbury Bucks 52 F4
Westbury Shrops 60 D3
Westbury Wilts 24 D3
Westbury Leigh Wilts 24 D3
Westbury-on-Severn Glos 36 C4
Westbury on Trym Bristol 23 B7
Westbury-sub-Mendip Som 23 E7
Westby Lancs 92 F3
Westcliff-on-Sea Southend 42 F4
Westcombe Som 23 F8
Westcote Glos 38 B2
Westcott Bucks 39 C7
Westcott Devon 10 D5
Westcott Sur 28 E2
Westcott Barton Oxon 38 B4
Westdean E Sus 18 F2
Westdene Brighton 17 D6
Wester Aberchalder Highld 137 B8
Wester Balgedie Perth 128 D3
Wester Culbeuchly Aberds 153 B6
Wester Dechmont W Loth 120 C3
Wester Denoon Angus 134 E3
Wester Fintray Aberds 141 C7
Wester Gruinards Highld 151 B8
Wester Lealty Highld 151 D9
Wester Milton Highld 151 F12
Wester Newburn Fife 129 D6
Wester Quarff Shetland 160 K6
Wester Skeld Shetland 160 J4
Westerdale Highld 158 E3
Westerdale N Yorks 102 D4
Westerfield Shetland 160 H5
Westerfield Suff 57 E5
Westergate W Sus 16 D3
Westerham Kent 28 D5
Westerhope T&W 110 C4
Westerleigh S Glos 23 B9
Westerton Angus 135 D6
Westerton Durham 110 F5
Westerton W Sus 16 D2
Westerwick Shetland 160 J4
Westfield Cumb 98 B1
Westfield E Sus 18 D5
Westfield Hereford 50 E2
Westfield Highld 158 D2
Westfield N Lanark 119 B7
Westfield Norf 68 D2
Westfield W Loth 120 B2
Westfields Dorset 12 D5
Westfields of Rattray Perth 134 E1
Westgate Durham 110 F2
Westgate N Lincs 89 D8
Westgate Norf 80 C4
Westgate Norf 81 C5
Westgate on Sea Kent 31 B7
Westhall Aberds 141 B5
Westhall Suff 69 F7
Westham Dorset 12 G4
Westham E Sus 18 E3
Westham Som 23 E6
Westhampnett W Sus 16 D2
Westhay Som 23 E6
Westhead Lancs 86 D2
Westhide Hereford 49 E7
Westhill Aberds 141 D7
Westhill Highld 151 G10
Westhope Hereford 49 D6
Westhope Shrops 60 F4
Westhorpe Lincs 78 F5
Westhorpe Suff 56 C4
Westhoughton Gtr Man 86 D4
Westhouse N Yorks 93 B6
Westhumble Sur 28 D2
Westing Shetland 160 C7
Westlake Devon 6 D4
Westleigh Devon 9 B6
Westleigh Devon 11 C5
Westleigh Gtr Man 86 D4
Westleton Suff 57 C8
Westley Shrops 60 D3
Westley Suff 56 C2
Westley Waterless Cambs 55 D7
Westlington Bucks 39 C7
Westlinton Cumb 108 C3
Westmarsh Kent 31 C6
Westmeston E Sus 17 C7
Westmill Herts 41 B6
Westminster London 28 B4
Westmuir Angus 134 D3
Westness Orkney 159 F4
Westnewton Cumb 107 E8
Westnewton Northumb 122 F5
Westoe T&W 111 C6
Weston Bath 24 C2
Weston Ches E 74 D4
Weston Devon 11 F6
Weston Dorset 12 G4
Weston Halton 86 F3
Weston Hants 15 B8
Weston Herts 54 F3
Weston Lincs 66 B2
Weston N Yorks 94 E4
Weston Northants 52 E3
Weston Notts 77 C7
Weston Shrops 61 B5
Weston Shrops 61 E5
Weston Staffs 62 B3
Weston W Berks 25 B8
Weston Beggard Hereford 49 E7
Weston by Welland Northants 64 E4
Weston Colville Cambs 55 D7
Weston Coyney Stoke 75 E6
Weston Favell Northants 53 C5
Weston Green Cambs 55 D7
Weston Green Norf 68 C4
Weston Heath Shrops 61 C7
Weston Hills Lincs 66 B2
Weston-in-Gordano N Som 23 B6
Weston Jones Staffs 61 B7
Weston Longville Norf 68 C4
Weston Lullingfields Shrops 60 B4
Weston-on-the-Green Oxon 39 C5
Weston-on-Trent Derbys 63 B8
Weston Patrick Hants 26 E4
Weston Rhyn Shrops 73 F6
Weston-Sub-Edge Glos 51 E6
Weston-super-Mare N Som 22 C5
Weston Turville Bucks 40 C1
Weston under Lizard Staffs 62 C2
Weston under Penyard Hereford 36 B3
Weston under Wetherley Warks 51 C8
Weston Underwood Derbys 76 E2
Weston Underwood M Keynes 53 D6
Westonbirt Glos 37 F5
Westoncommon Shrops 60 B4
Westoning C Beds 53 F8
Westonzoyland Som 23 F5
Westow N Yorks 96 C3
Westport Argyll 143 F7
Westport Som 11 C8
Westrigg W Loth 120 C2
Westruther Borders 122 E2
Westry Cambs 66 E3
Westville Notts 76 E5
Westward Cumb 108 E2
Westward Ho! Devon 9 B6
Westwell Kent 30 E3
Westwell Oxon 38 D2
Westwell Leacon Kent 30 E3
Westwick Cambs 54 C5
Westwick Durham 101 C5
Westwick Norf 81 E8
Westwood Devon 10 E5
Westwood Wilts 24 D3
Westwoodside N Lincs 89 E8
Wetheral Cumb 108 D4
Wetherby W Yorks 95 E7
Wetherden Suff 56 C4
Wetheringsett Suff 56 C5
Wethersfield Essex 55 F8
Wethersta Shetland 160 G5
Wetherup Street Suff 56 C5
Wetley Rocks Staffs 75 E6
Wettenhall Ches E 74 C3
Wetton Staffs 75 D8
Wetwang E Yorks 96 D5
Wetwood Staffs 74 F4
Wexcombe Wilts 25 D7
Wexham Street Bucks 40 F2
Weybourne Norf 81 C7
Weybread Suff 68 F5
Weybridge Sur 27 C8
Weycroft Devon 11 E8
Weydale Highld 158 D3
Weyhill Hants 25 E8
Weymouth Dorset 12 G4
Whaddon Bucks 53 F6
Whaddon Cambs 54 E4
Whaddon Glos 37 C5
Whaddon Wilts 14 B2
Whale Cumb 99 B7
Whaley Derbys 76 B5
Whaley Bridge Derbys 87 F8
Whaley Thorns Derbys 76 B5
Whaligoe Highld 158 F5
Whalley Lancs 93 F7
Whalton Northumb 117 F7
Wham N Yorks 93 C7
Whaplode Lincs 66 B3
Whaplode Drove Lincs 66 C3
Whaplode St Catherine Lincs 66 B3
Wharfe N Yorks 93 C7
Wharles Lancs 92 F4
Wharncliffe Side S Yorks 88 E3
Wharram le Street N Yorks 96 C4
Wharton Ches W 74 C3
Wharton Green Ches W 74 C3
Whashton N Yorks 101 D6
Whatcombe Dorset 13 D6
Whatcote Warks 51 E8
Whatfield Suff 56 E4
Whatley Som 11 D8
Whatley Som 24 E2
Whatlington E Sus 18 D4
Whatstandwell Derbys 76 D3
Whatton Notts 77 F7
Whauphill Dumfries 105 E8
Whaw N Yorks 100 D4
Wheatacre Norf 69 E7
Wheatcroft Derbys 76 D3
Wheathampstead Herts 40 C4
Wheathill Shrops 61 F6
Wheatley Devon 10 E4
Wheatley Hants 27 E5
Wheatley Oxon 39 D5
Wheatley S Yorks 89 D6
Wheatley W Yorks 87 B8
Wheatley Hill Durham 111 F6
Wheaton Aston Staffs 62 C2
Wheddon Cross Som 21 F8
Wheedlemont Aberds 140 B3
Wheelerstreet Sur 27 E7
Wheelock Ches E 74 D4
Wheelock Heath Ches E 74 D4
Wheelton Lancs 86 B4
Wheen Angus 134 B3
Wheldrake York 96 E2
Whelford Glos 38 E1
Whelpley Hill Herts 40 D2
Whempstead Herts 41 B6
Whenby N Yorks 96 C2
Whepstead Suff 56 D2
Wherstead Suff 57 E5
Wherwell Hants 25 E8
Wheston Derbys 75 B8
Whetsted Kent 29 E7
Whetstone Leics 64 E2
Whicham Cumb 98 F3
Whichford Warks 51 F8
Whickham T&W 110 C5
Whiddon Down Devon 9 E8
Whigstreet Angus 134 E4
Whilton Northants 52 C4
Whim Farm Borders 120 D5
Whimble Devon 9 D5
Whimple Devon 10 E5
Whimpwell Green Norf 69 B6
Whinburgh Norf 68 D3
Whinnieliggate Dumfries 106 D4
Whinnyfold Aberds 153 E10
Whippingham IoW 15 E6
Whipsnade C Beds 40 C3
Whipton Devon 10 E4
Whirlow S Yorks 88 F4
Whisby Lincs 78 C2
Whissendine Rutland 64 C5
Whissonsett Norf 80 E5
Whistlefield Argyll 145 D10
Whistlefield Argyll 145 D11
Whistley Green Wokingham 27 B5
Whiston Mers 86 E2
Whiston Northants 53 C6
Whiston S Yorks 88 F5
Whiston Staffs 62 C2
Whiston Staffs 75 E7
Whitbeck Cumb 98 F3
Whitbourne Hereford 50 D2
Whitburn T&W 111 C7
Whitburn W Loth 120 C2
Whitburn Colliery T&W 111 C7
Whitby Ches W 73 B7
Whitby N Yorks 103 C6
Whitbyheath Ches W 73 B7
Whitchurch Bath 23 C8
Whitchurch Bucks 39 B7
Whitchurch Cardiff 35 F5
Whitchurch Devon 6 B2
Whitchurch Hants 26 E2
Whitchurch Hereford 36 C2
Whitchurch Oxon 26 B4
Whitchurch Pembs 44 C2
Whitchurch Shrops 74 E2
Whitchurch Canonicorum Dorset 11 E8
Whitchurch Hill Oxon 26 B4
Whitcombe Dorset 12 F5
Whitcott Keysett Shrops 60 F2
White Coppice Lancs 86 C4
White Lackington Dorset 12 E5
White Ladies Aston Worcs 50 D4
White Lund Lancs 92 C4
White Mill Carms 33 B5
White Ness Shetland 160 J5
White Notley Essex 42 C3
White Pit Lincs 79 B6
White Post Notts 77 D6
White Rocks Hereford 35 B8
White Roding Essex 42 C1
White Waltham Windsor 27 B6
Whiteacen Moray 152 D2
Whiteacre Heath Warks 63 E6
Whitebridge Highld 137 C7
Whitebrook Mon 36 D2
Whiteburn Borders 121 E8
Whitecairn Dumfries 105 D6
Whitecairns Aberds 141 C8
Whitecastle S Lanark 120 E3
Whitechapel Lancs 93 E5
Whitecleat Orkney 159 H6
Whitecraig E Loth 121 B6
Whitecroft Glos 36 D3
Whitecross Corn 4 B4
Whitecross Falk 120 B2
Whitecross Staffs 62 B2
Whiteface Highld 151 C10
Whitefarland N Ayrs 143 D9
Whitefaulds S Ayrs 112 D2
Whitefield Gtr Man 87 D6
Whitefield Perth 134 F1
Whiteford Aberds 141 B6
Whitegate Ches W 74 C3
Whitehall Blackburn 86 B4
Whitehall W Sus 16 B5
Whitehall Village Orkney 159 F7
Whitehaven Cumb 98 C1
Whitehill Hants 27 F5
Whitehills Aberds 153 B6
Whitehills S Lanark 119 D6
Whitehough Derbys 87 F8
Whitehouse Aberds 140 C5
Whitehouse Argyll 145 G7
Whiteinch Glasgow 118 C5
Whitekirk E Loth 129 F7
Whitelaw S Lanark 119 E6
Whiteleas T&W 111 C6
Whiteley Bank IoW 15 F6
Whiteley Green Ches E 75 B6
Whiteley Village Sur 27 C8
Whitemans Green W Sus 17 B7
Whitemire Moray 151 F12
Whitemoor Corn 4 D4
Whitemore Staffs 75 C5
Whitenap Hants 14 B4
Whiteoak Green Oxon 38 C3
Whiteparish Wilts 14 B3
Whiterashes Aberds 141 B7
Whiterow Highld 158 F5
Whiteshill Glos 37 D5
Whiteside Northumb 109 C7
Whiteside W Loth 120 C2
Whitesmith E Sus 18 D2
Whitestaunton Som 11 C7
Whitestone Devon 10 E3
Whitestone Devon 20 E3
Whitestone Warks 63 F7
Whitestones Aberds 153 C8
Whitestreet Green Suff 56 F3
Whitewall Corner N Yorks 96 B3
Whiteway Glos 37 C6
Whiteway Glos 37 E5
Whitewell Aberds 153 B9
Whitewell Lancs 93 E6
Whitewell Bottom Lancs 87 B6
Whiteworks Devon 6 B4
Whitfield Kent 31 E7
Whitfield Northants 52 F4
Whitfield Northumb 109 D7
Whitfield S Glos 36 E3
Whitford Devon 11 E7
Whitford Flint 72 B5
Whitgift E Yorks 90 B2
Whitgreave Staffs 62 B2
Whithorn Dumfries 105 E8
Whiting Bay N Ayrs 143 F11
Whitkirk W Yorks 95 F6
Whitland Carms 32 C2
Whitletts S Ayrs 112 B3
Whitley N Yorks 89 B6
Whitley Reading 26 B5
Whitley Wilts 24 C3
Whitley Bay T&W 111 B6
Whitley Chapel Northumb 110 D2
Whitley Lower W Yorks 88 C3
Whitley Row Kent 29 D5
Whitlock's End W Mid 51 B6
Whitminster Glos 36 D4
Whitmore Staffs 74 E5
Whitnage Devon 10 C5
Whitnash Warks 51 C8
Whitney-on-Wye Hereford 48 E4
Whitrigg Cumb 108 D2
Whitrigg Cumb 108 F2
Whitsbury Hants 14 C2
Whitsome Borders 122 D4
Whitson Newport 35 F7
Whitstable Kent 30 C5
Whitstone Corn 8 E4
Whittingham Northumb 117 C6
Whittingslow Shrops 60 F4
Whittington Glos 37 B7
Whittington Lancs 93 B6
Whittington Norf 67 E7
Whittington Shrops 73 F7
Whittington Staffs 62 F2
Whittington Staffs 63 D5
Whittington Worcs 50 D3
Whittle-le-Woods Lancs 86 B3
Whittlebury Northants 52 E4
Whittlesey Cambs 66 E2
Whittlesford Cambs 55 E5
Whittlestone Head Blackburn 86 C5
Whitton Borders 116 B3
Whitton N Lincs 90 B3
Whitton Northumb 117 D6
Whitton Powys 48 C4
Whitton Shrops 49 B7
Whitton Stockton 102 B1
Whitton Suff 56 E5
Whittonditch Wilts 25 B7
Whittonstall Northumb 110 D3
Whitway Hants 26 D2
Whitwell Derbys 76 B5
Whitwell Herts 40 B4
Whitwell IoW 15 G6
Whitwell N Yorks 101 E7

Whitwell Rutland 65 D6
Whitwell-on-the-Hill N Yorks 96 C3
Whitwell Street Norf 81 E7
Whitwick Leics 63 C8
Whitwood W Yorks 88 B5
Whitworth Lancs 87 C6
Whixall Shrops 74 F2
Whixley N Yorks 95 D7
Whoberley W Mid 51 B8
Whorlton Durham 101 C6
Whorlton N Yorks 102 D2
Whygate Northumb 109 B7
Whyle Hereford 49 C7
Whyteleafe Sur 28 D4
Wibdon Glos 36 E2
Wibsey W Yorks 88 A2
Wibtoft Leics 63 F8
Wichenford Worcs 50 C2
Wichling Kent 30 D3
Wick Bmouth 14 E2
Wick Devon 11 D6
Wick Highld 158 E5
Wick S Glos 24 B2
Wick Shetland 160 K6
Wick V Glam 21 B8
Wick W Sus 16 D4
Wick Wilts 14 B2
Wick Worcs 50 E4
Wick Hill Wokingham 27 C5
Wick St Lawrence N Som 23 C5
Wicken Cambs 55 B6
Wicken Northants 52 F5
Wicken Bonhunt Essex 55 F5
Wicken Green Village Norf 80 D4
Wickenby Lincs 90 F4
Wickersley S Yorks 89 E5
Wickford Essex 42 E3
Wickham Hants 15 C6
Wickham W Berks 25 B8
Wickham Bishops Essex 42 C4
Wickham Market Suff 57 D7
Wickham Skeith Suff 56 C4
Wickham St Paul Essex 56 F2
Wickham Street Suff 55 D8
Wickham Street Suff 56 C4
Wickhambreux Kent 31 D6
Wickhambrook Suff 55 D8
Wickhamford Worcs 51 E5
Wickhampton Norf 69 D7
Wicklewood Norf 68 D3
Wickmere Norf 81 D7
Wickwar S Glos 36 F4
Widdington Essex 55 F6
Widdrington Northumb 117 E8
Widdrington Station Northumb 117 E8
Wide Open T&W 110 B5
Widecombe in the Moor Devon 6 B5
Widegates Corn 5 D7
Widemouth Bay Corn 8 D4
Widewall Orkney 159 J5
Widford Essex 42 D2
Widford Herts 41 C7
Widham Wilts 37 F7
Widmer End Bucks 40 E1
Widmerpool Notts 64 B3
Widnes Halton 86 F3
Wigan Gtr Man 86 D3
Wiggaton Devon 11 E6
Wiggenhall St Germans Norf 67 C5
Wiggenhall St Mary Magdalen Norf 67 C5
Wiggenhall St Mary the Virgin Norf 67 C5
Wigginton Herts 40 C2
Wigginton Oxon 51 F8
Wigginton Staffs 63 D6
Wigginton York 95 D8
Wigglesworth N Yorks 93 D8
Wiggonby Cumb 108 D2
Wiggonholt W Sus 16 C4
Wighill N Yorks 95 E7
Wighton Norf 80 D5
Wigley Hants 14 C4
Wigmore Hereford 49 C6
Wigmore Medway 30 C2
Wigsley Notts 77 B8
Wigsthorpe Northants 65 F7
Wigston Leics 64 E3
Wigthorpe Notts 89 F6
Wigtoft Lincs 79 F5
Wigton Cumb 108 E2
Wigtown Dumfries 105 D8
Wigtwizzle S Yorks 88 E3
Wike W Yorks 95 E6
Wike Well End S Yorks 89 C7
Wilbarston Northants 64 F5
Wilberfoss E Yorks 96 D3
Wilberlee W Yorks 87 C8
Wilburton Cambs 55 B5
Wilby Norf 68 F3
Wilby Northants 53 C6
Wilby Suff 57 B6
Wilcot Wilts 25 C6
Wilcott Shrops 60 C3
Wilcrick Newport 35 F8
Wilday Green Derbys 76 B3
Wildboarclough Ches E 75 C6
Wilden Bedford 53 D8
Wilden Worcs 50 B3
Wildhern Hants 25 D8
Wildhill Herts 41 D5
Wildmoor Worcs 50 B4
Wildsworth Lincs 90 E2
Wilford Nottingham 77 F5
Wilkesley Ches E 74 E3
Wilkhaven Highld 151 C12
Wilkieston W Loth 120 C4
Willand Devon 10 C5
Willaston Ches E 74 D3
Willaston Ches W 73 B7
Willen M Keynes 53 E6
Willenhall W Mid 51 B8
Willenhall W Mid 62 E3
Willerby E Yorks 97 F6
Willerby N Yorks 97 B6
Willersey Glos 51 F6
Willersley Hereford 48 E5
Willesborough Kent 30 E4
Willesborough Lees Kent 30 E4
Willesden London 41 F5
Willett Som 22 F3
Willey Shrops 61 E6
Willey Warks 63 F8
Willey Green Sur 27 D7
Williamscott Oxon 52 E2
Willian Herts 54 F3
Willingale Essex 42 D1
Willingdon E Sus 18 E2
Willingham Cambs 54 B5
Willingham by Stow Lincs 90 F2
Willington Bedford 54 E2
Willington Derbys 63 B6
Willington Durham 110 F4
Willington T&W 111 C6
Willington Warks 51 F7
Willington Corner Ches W 74 C2
Willisham Tye Suff 56 D4
Willitoft E Yorks 96 F3
Williton Som 22 E2
Willoughbridge Staffs 74 E4
Willoughby Lincs 79 B7
Willoughby Warks 52 C3
Willoughby-on-the-Wolds Notts 64 B3
Willoughby Waterleys Leics 64 E2
Willoughton Lincs 90 E3
Willows Green Essex 42 C3
Willsbridge S Glos 23 B8
Willsworthy Devon 9 F7
Wilmcote Warks 51 D6
Wilmington Devon 11 E7
Wilmington E Sus 18 E2
Wilmington Kent 29 B6
Wilminstone Devon 6 B2
Wilmslow Ches E 87 F6
Wilnecote Staffs 63 D6
Wilpshire Lancs 93 F6
Wilsden W Yorks 94 F3
Wilsford Lincs 78 E3
Wilsford Wilts 25 D6
Wilsford Wilts 25 F6
Wilsill N Yorks 94 C4
Wilsley Pound Kent 18 B4
Wilsom Hants 26 F5
Wilson Leics 63 B8
Wilsontown S Lanark 120 D2
Wilstead Bedford 53 E8
Wilsthorpe Lincs 65 C7
Wilstone Herts 40 C2
Wilton Borders 115 C7
Wilton Cumb 98 C2
Wilton N Yorks 103 F6
Wilton Redcar 102 C3
Wilton Wilts 25 C7
Wilton Wilts 25 F5
Wimbish Essex 55 F6
Wimbish Green Essex 55 F7
Wimblebury Staffs 62 C4
Wimbledon London 28 B3
Wimblington Cambs 66 E4
Wimborne Minster Dorset 13 E8
Wimborne St Giles Dorset 13 C8
Wimbotsham Norf 67 D6
Wimpson Soton 14 C4
Wimpstone Warks 51 E7
Wincanton Som 12 B5
Wincham Ches W 74 B3
Winchburgh W Loth 120 B3
Winchcombe Glos 37 B7
Winchelsea E Sus 19 D6
Winchelsea Beach E Sus 19 D6
Winchester Hants 15 B5
Winchet Hill Kent 29 E8
Winchfield Hants 27 D5
Winchmore Hill Bucks 40 E2
Winchmore Hill London 41 E6
Wincle Ches E 75 C6
Wincobank S Yorks 88 E4
Windermere Cumb 99 E6
Winderton Warks 51 E8
Windhill Highld 151 G8
Windhouse Shetland 160 D6
Windlehurst Gtr Man 87 F7
Windlesham Sur 27 C7
Windley Derbys 76 E3
Windmill Hill E Sus 18 D3
Windmill Hill Som 11 C8
Windrush Glos 38 C1
Windsor N Lincs 89 C8
Windsor Windsor 27 B7
Windsoredge Glos 37 D5
Windygates Fife 128 D5
Windyknowe W Loth 120 C2
Windywalls Borders 122 F3
Wineham W Sus 17 B6
Winestead E Yorks 91 B6
Winewall Lancs 94 E2
Winfarthing Norf 68 F4
Winford IoW 15 F6
Winford N Som 23 C7
Winforton Hereford 48 E4
Winfrith Newburgh Dorset 13 F6
Wing Bucks 40 B1
Wing Rutland 65 D5
Wingate Durham 111 F7
Wingates Gtr Man 86 D4
Wingates Northumb 117 E7
Wingerworth Derbys 76 C3
Wingfield C Beds 40 B2
Wingfield Suff 57 B6
Wingfield Wilts 24 D3
Wingham Kent 31 D6
Wingmore Kent 31 E5
Wingrave Bucks 40 C1
Winkburn Notts 77 D7
Winkfield Brack 27 B7
Winkfield Row Brack 27 B6
Winkhill Staffs 75 D7
Winklebury Hants 26 D4
Winkleigh Devon 9 D8
Winksley N Yorks 95 B5
Winkton Dorset 14 E2
Winlaton T&W 110 C4
Winless Highld 158 E5
Winmarleigh Lancs 92 E4
Winnal Hereford 49 F6
Winnall Hants 15 B5
Winnersh Wokingham 27 B5
Winscales Cumb 98 B2
Winscombe N Som 23 D6
Winsford Ches W 74 C3
Winsford Som 21 F8
Winsham Som 11 D8
Winshill Staffs 63 B6
Winskill Cumb 109 F5
Winslade Hants 26 E4
Winsley Wilts 24 C3
Winslow Bucks 39 B7
Winson Glos 37 D7
Winson Green W Mid 62 F4
Winsor Hants 14 C4
Winster Cumb 99 E6
Winster Derbys 76 C2
Winston Durham 101 C6
Winston Suff 57 C5
Winston Green Suff 57 C5
Winstone Glos 37 D6
Winswell Devon 9 C6
Winter Gardens Essex 42 F3
Winterborne Clenston Dorset 13 D6
Winterborne Herringston Dorset 12 F4
Winterborne Houghton Dorset 13 D6
Winterborne Kingston Dorset 13 E6
Winterborne Monkton Dorset 12 F4
Winterborne Stickland Dorset 13 D6
Winterborne Whitechurch Dorset 13 D6
Winterborne Zelston Dorset 13 E6
Winterbourne S Glos 36 F3
Winterbourne W Berks 26 B2
Winterbourne Abbas Dorset 12 E4
Winterbourne Bassett Wilts 25 B6
Winterbourne Dauntsey Wilts 25 F6
Winterbourne Down S Glos 23 B8
Winterbourne Earls Wilts 25 F6
Winterbourne Gunner Wilts 25 F6
Winterbourne Monkton Wilts 25 B6
Winterbourne Steepleton Dorset 12 F4
Winterbourne Stoke Wilts 25 E5
Winterburn N Yorks 94 D2
Winteringham N Lincs 90 B3
Winterley Ches E 74 D4
Wintersett W Yorks 88 C4
Wintershill Hants 15 C6
Winterton N Lincs 90 C3
Winterton-on-Sea Norf 69 C7
Winthorpe Lincs 79 C8
Winthorpe Notts 77 D8
Winton Bmouth 13 E8
Winton Cumb 100 C2
Winton N Yorks 102 E2
Wintringham N Yorks 96 B4
Winwick Cambs 65 F8
Winwick Northants 52 B4
Winwick Warr 86 E4
Wirksworth Derbys 76 D2
Wirksworth Moor Derbys 76 D3
Wirswall Ches E 74 E2
Wisbech Cambs 66 D4
Wisbech St Mary Cambs 66 D4
Wisborough Green W Sus 16 B4
Wiseton Notts 89 F8
Wishaw N Lanark 119 D7
Wishaw Warks 63 E5
Wisley Sur 27 D8
Wispington Lincs 78 B5
Wissenden Kent 30 E3
Wissett Suff 57 B7
Wistanstow Shrops 60 F4
Wistanswick Shrops 61 B6
Wistaston Ches E 74 D3
Wistaston Green Ches E 74 D3
Wiston Pembs 32 C1
Wiston S Lanark 120 F2
Wiston W Sus 16 C5
Wistow Cambs 66 F2
Wistow N Yorks 95 F8
Wiswell Lancs 93 F7
Witcham Cambs 66 F4
Witchampton Dorset 13 D7
Witchford Cambs 55 B6
Witham Essex 42 C4
Witham Friary Som 24 E2
Witham on the Hill Lincs 65 C7
Withcall Lincs 91 F6
Withdean Brighton 17 D7
Witherenden Hill E Sus 18 C3
Witheridge Devon 10 C3
Witherley Leics 63 E7
Withern Lincs 91 F8
Withernsea E Yorks 91 B7
Withernwick E Yorks 97 E7
Withersdale Street Suff 69 F5
Withersfield Suff 55 E7
Witherslack Cumb 99 F6
Withiel Corn 4 C4
Withiel Florey Som 21 F8
Withington Glos 37 C7
Withington Gtr Man 87 E6
Withington Hereford 49 E7
Withington Shrops 61 C5
Withington Staffs 75 F7
Withington Green Ches E 74 B5
Withleigh Devon 10 C4
Withnell Lancs 86 B4
Withybrook Warks 63 F8
Withycombe Som 22 E2
Withycombe Raleigh Devon 10 F5
Withyham E Sus 29 F5
Withypool Som 21 F7
Witley Sur 27 F7
Witnesham Suff 57 D5
Witney Oxon 38 C3
Wittering Pboro 65 D7
Wittersham Kent 19 C5
Witton Angus 135 B5
Witton Worcs 50 C3
Witton Bridge Norf 69 A6
Witton Gilbert Durham 110 E5
Witton-le-Wear Durham 110 F4
Witton Park Durham 110 F4
Wiveliscombe Som 11 B5
Wivelrod Hants 26 F4
Wivelsfield E Sus 17 B7
Wivelsfield Green E Sus 17 B7
Wivenhoe Essex 43 B6
Wivenhoe Cross Essex 43 B6
Wiveton Norf 81 C6
Wix Essex 43 B7
Wixford Warks 51 D5
Wixhill Shrops 61 B5
Wixoe Suff 55 E8
Woburn C Beds 53 F7
Woburn Sands M Keynes 53 F7
Wokefield Park W Berks 26 C4
Woking Sur 27 D8
Wokingham Wokingham 27 C6
Wolborough Devon 7 B6
Wold Newton E Yorks 97 B6
Wold Newton NE Lincs 91 E6
Woldingham Sur 28 D4
Wolfclyde S Lanark 120 F3
Wolferton Norf 67 B6
Wolfhill Perth 134 F1
Wolf's Castle Pembs 44 C4
Wolfsdale Pembs 44 C4
Woll Borders 115 B7
Wollaston Northants 53 C7
Wollaston Shrops 60 C3
Wollaton Nottingham 76 F5
Wollerton Shrops 74 F3
Wollescote W Mid 62 F3
Wolsingham Durham 110 F3
Wolstanton Staffs 75 E5
Wolston Warks 52 B2
Wolvercote Oxon 38 D4
Wolverhampton W Mid 62 E3
Wolverley Shrops 73 F8
Wolverley Worcs 50 B3
Wolverton Hants 26 D3
Wolverton M Keynes 53 E6
Wolverton Warks 51 C7
Wolverton Common Hants 26 D3
Wolvesnewton Mon 36 E1
Wolvey Warks 63 F8
Wolviston Stockton 102 B2
Wombleton N Yorks 102 F4
Wombourne Staffs 62 E2
Wombwell S Yorks 88 D4
Womenswold Kent 31 D6
Womersley N Yorks 89 C6
Wonastow Mon 36 C1
Wonersh Sur 27 E8
Wonson Devon 9 F8
Wonston Hants 26 F2
Wooburn Bucks 40 F2
Wooburn Green Bucks 40 F2
Wood Dalling Norf 81 E6
Wood End Herts 41 B6
Wood End Warks 51 B6
Wood End Warks 63 E6
Wood Enderby Lincs 79 C5
Wood Field Sur 28 D2
Wood Green London 41 E6
Wood Hayes W Mid 62 D3
Wood Lanes Ches E 87 F7
Wood Norton Norf 81 E6
Wood Street Norf 69 B6
Wood Street Sur 27 D7
Wood Walton Cambs 66 F2
Woodacott Devon 9 D5
Woodale N Yorks 94 B3
Woodbank Argyll 143 G7
Woodbastwick Norf 69 C6
Woodbeck Notts 77 B7
Woodborough Notts 77 E6
Woodborough Wilts 25 D6
Woodbridge Dorset 12 C5
Woodbridge Suff 57 E6
Woodbury Devon 10 F5
Woodbury Salterton Devon 10 F5
Woodchester Glos 37 D5
Woodchurch Kent 19 B6
Woodchurch Mers 85 F3
Woodcombe Som 21 E8
Woodcote Oxon 39 F6
Woodcott Hants 26 D2
Woodcroft Glos 36 E2
Woodcutts Dorset 13 C7
Woodditton Cambs 55 D7
Woodeaton Oxon 39 C5
Woodend Cumb 98 E3
Woodend Northants 52 E4
Woodend W Sus 16 D2
Woodend Green Northants 52 E4
Woodfalls Wilts 14 B2
Woodfield Oxon 39 B5
Woodfield S Ayrs 112 B3
Woodford Corn 8 C4
Woodford Devon 7 D5
Woodford Glos 36 E3
Woodford Gtr Man 87 F6
Woodford London 41 E7
Woodford Northants 53 B7
Woodford Bridge London 41 E7
Woodford Halse Northants 52 D3
Woodgate Norf 68 C3
Woodgate W Mid 62 F3
Woodgate W Sus 16 D3
Woodgate Worcs 50 C4
Woodgreen Hants 14 C2
Woodhall Herts 41 C5
Woodhall Invclyd 118 B3
Woodhall N Yorks 100 E4
Woodhall Spa Lincs 78 C4
Woodham Sur 27 C8
Woodham Ferrers Essex 42 E3
Woodham Mortimer Essex 42 D4
Woodham Walter Essex 42 D4
Woodhaven Fife 129 B6
Woodhead Aberds 153 E7
Woodhey Gtr Man 87 C5
Woodhill Shrops 61 F7
Woodhorn Northumb 117 F8
Woodhouse Leics 64 C2
Woodhouse N Lincs 89 D8
Woodhouse S Yorks 88 F5
Woodhouse W Yorks 88 B4
Woodhouse W Yorks 95 F5
Woodhouse Eaves Leics 64 C2
Woodhouse Park Gtr Man 87 F6
Woodhouselee Midloth 120 C5
Woodhouselees Dumfries 108 B3
Woodhouses Staffs 63 C5
Woodhurst Cambs 54 B4
Woodingdean Brighton 17 D7
Woodkirk W Yorks 88 B3
Woodland Devon 7 C5
Woodland Durham 101 B5
Woodlands Aberds 141 E6
Woodlands Dorset 13 D8
Woodlands Hants 14 C4
Woodlands Highld 151 E8
Woodlands N Yorks 95 D6
Woodlands S Yorks 89 D6
Woodlands Park Windsor 27 B6
Woodlands St Mary W Berks 25 B8
Woodlane Staffs 62 B5
Woodleigh Devon 6 E5
Woodlesford W Yorks 88 B4
Woodley Gtr Man 87 E7
Woodley Wokingham 27 B5
Woodmancote Glos 36 E4
Woodmancote Glos 37 B6
Woodmancote Glos 37 D7
Woodmancote W Sus 15 D8
Woodmancote W Sus 17 C6
Woodmancott Hants 26 E3
Woodmansey E Yorks 97 F6
Woodmansterne Sur 28 D3
Woodminton Wilts 13 B8
Woodnesborough Kent 31 D7
Woodnewton Northants 65 E7
Woodplumpton Lancs 92 F5
Woodrising Norf 68 D2
Wood's Green E Sus 18 B3
Woodseaves Shrops 74 F3
Woodseaves Staffs 61 B7
Woodsend Wilts 25 B7
Woodsetts S Yorks 89 F6
Woodsford Dorset 13 E5
Woodside Aberdeen 141 D8
Woodside Aberds 153 D10
Woodside Brack 27 B7
Woodside Fife 129 D6
Woodside Hants 14 E4
Woodside Herts 41 D5
Woodside Perth 134 F2
Woodside of Arbeadie Aberds 141 E6
Woodstock Oxon 38 C4
Woodstock Pembs 32 B1
Woodthorpe Derbys 76 B4
Woodthorpe Leics 64 C2
Woodthorpe Lincs 91 F8
Woodthorpe York 95 E8
Woodton Norf 69 E5
Woodtown Devon 9 B6
Woodtown Devon 9 B6
Woodvale Mers 85 C4
Woodville Derbys 63 C7
Woodyates Dorset 13 C8
Woofferton Shrops 49 C7
Wookey Som 23 E7
Wookey Hole Som 23 E7
Wool Dorset 13 F6
Woolacombe Devon 20 E3
Woolage Green Kent 31 E6
Woolaston Glos 36 E2
Woolavington Som 22 E5
Woolbeding W Sus 16 B2
Wooldale W Yorks 88 D2
Wooler Northumb 117 B5
Woolfardisworthy Devon 8 B5
Woolfardisworthy Devon 10 D3
Woolfords Cottages S Lanark 120 D3
Woolhampton W Berks 26 C3
Woolhope Hereford 49 F8
Woolhope Cockshoot Hereford 49 F8
Woolland Dorset 13 D5
Woollaton Devon 9 C6
Woolley Bath 24 C2
Woolley Cambs 54 B2
Woolley Corn 8 C4
Woolley Derbys 76 C3
Woolley W Yorks 88 C4
Woolmer Green Herts 41 C5
Woolmere Green Worcs 50 C4
Woolpit Suff 56 C3
Woolscott Warks 52 C2
Woolsington T&W 110 C4
Woolstanwood Ches E 74 D3
Woolstaston Shrops 60 E4
Woolsthorpe Lincs 65 B6
Woolsthorpe Lincs 77 F8
Woolston Devon 6 E5
Woolston Shrops 60 B3
Woolston Shrops 60 F4
Woolston Soton 14 C5
Woolston Warr 86 F4
Woolstone M Keynes 53 F6
Woolstone Oxon 38 F2
Woolton Mers 86 F2
Woolton Hill Hants 26 C2
Woolverstone Suff 57 F5
Woolverton Som 24 D2
Woolwich London 28 B5
Woolwich Ferry London 28 B5
Woonton Hereford 49 D5
Wooperton Northumb 117 B6
Woore Shrops 74 E4
Wootten Green Suff 57 B6
Wootton Bedford 53 E8
Wootton Hants 14 E3
Wootton Hereford 48 D5
Wootton Kent 31 E6
Wootton N Lincs 90 C4
Wootton Northants 53 D5
Wootton Oxon 38 C4
Wootton Oxon 38 D4
Wootton Shrops 49 B6
Wootton Shrops 60 B3
Wootton Staffs 62 B2
Wootton Staffs 75 E8
Wootton Bridge IoW 15 E6
Wootton Common IoW 15 E6
Wootton Courtenay Som 21 E8
Wootton Fitzpaine Dorset 11 E8
Wootton Rivers Wilts 25 C6
Wootton St Lawrence Hants 26 D3
Wootton Wawen Warks 51 C6
Worcester Worcs 50 D3
Worcester Park London 28 C3
Wordsley W Mid 62 F2
Worfield Shrops 61 E7
Work Orkney 159 G5
Workington Cumb 98 B1
Worksop Notts 77 B5
Worlaby N Lincs 90 C4
World's End W Berks 26 B2
Worle N Som 23 C5
Worleston Ches E 74 D3
Worlingham Suff 69 F7
Worlington Suff 55 B7
Worlingworth Suff 57 C6
Wormald Green N Yorks 95 C6
Wormbridge Hereford 49 F6
Wormegay Norf 67 C6
Wormelow Tump Hereford 49 F6
Wormhill Derbys 75 B8
Wormingford Essex 56 F3
Worminghall Bucks 39 D6
Wormington Glos 50 F5
Worminster Som 23 E7
Wormit Fife 129 B5
Wormleighton Warks 52 D2
Wormley Herts 41 D6
Wormley Sur 27 F7
Wormley West End Herts 41 D6
Wormshill Kent 30 D2
Wormsley Hereford 49 E6
Worplesdon Sur 27 D7
Worrall S Yorks 88 E4
Worsbrough S Yorks 88 D4
Worsbrough Common S Yorks 88 D4
Worsley Gtr Man 86 D5
Worstead Norf 69 B6
Worsthorne Lancs 93 F8
Worston Lancs 93 E7
Worswell Devon 6 E3
Worth Kent 31 D7
Worth W Sus 28 F4
Worth Matravers Dorset 13 G7
Wortham Suff 56 B4
Worthen Shrops 60 D3
Worthenbury Wrex 73 E8
Worthing Norf 68 C2
Worthing W Sus 16 D5
Worthington Leics 63 B8
Worting Hants 26 D4
Wortley S Yorks 88 E4
Wortley W Yorks 95 F5
Worton N Yorks 100 E4
Worton Wilts 24 D4
Wortwell Norf 69 F5
Wotherton Shrops 60 D2
Wotter Devon 6 C3
Wotton Sur 28 E2
Wotton-under-Edge Glos 36 E4
Wotton Underwood Bucks 39 C6
Woughton on the Green M Keynes 53 F6
Wouldham Kent 29 C8
Wrabness Essex 57 F5
Wrafton Devon 20 F3
Wragby Lincs 78 B4
Wragby W Yorks 88 C5
Wragholme Lincs 91 E7
Wramplingham Norf 68 D4
Wrangbrook W Yorks 89 C5
Wrangham Aberds 153 E6
Wrangle Lincs 79 D7
Wrangle Bank Lincs 79 D7
Wrangle Lowgate Lincs 79 D7
Wrangway Som 11 C6
Wrantage Som 11 B8
Wrawby N Lincs 90 D4
Wraxall Dorset 12 D3
Wraxall N Som 23 B6
Wraxall Som 23 F8
Wray Lancs 93 C6
Wraysbury Windsor 27 B8
Wrayton Lancs 93 B6
Wrea Green Lancs 92 F3
Wreay Cumb 99 B6
Wreay Cumb 108 E4
Wrecclesham Sur 27 E6
Wrecsam = Wrexham Wrex 73 D7
Wrekenton T&W 111 D5
Wrelton N Yorks 103 F5
Wrenbury Ches E 74 E2
Wrench Green N Yorks 103 F7
Wreningham Norf 68 E4
Wrentham Suff 69 F7
Wrenthorpe W Yorks 88 B4
Wrentnall Shrops 60 D4
Wressle E Yorks 96 F3
Wressle N Lincs 90 D3
Wrestlingworth C Beds 54 E3
Wretham Norf 68 F2
Wretton Norf 67 E6
Wrexham = Wrecsam Wrex 73 D7
Wrexham Industrial Estate Wrex 73 E7
Wribbenhall Worcs 50 B2
Wrightington Bar Lancs 86 C3
Wrinehill Staffs 74 E4
Wrington N Som 23 C6
Writhlington Bath 24 D2
Writtle Essex 42 D2
Wrockwardine Telford 61 C6
Wroot N Lincs 89 D8
Wrotham Kent 29 D7
Wrotham Heath Kent 29 D7
Wroughton Swindon 37 F8
Wroxall IoW 15 G6
Wroxall Warks 51 B7
Wroxeter Shrops 61 D5
Wroxham Norf 69 C6
Wroxton Oxon 52 E2
Wyaston Derbys 75 E8
Wyberton Lincs 79 E6
Wyboston Bedford 54 D2
Wybunbury Ches E 74 E4
Wych Cross E Sus 28 F5
Wychbold Worcs 50 C4
Wyck Hants 27 F5
Wyck Rissington Glos 38 B1
Wycoller Lancs 94 F2
Wycomb Leics 64 B4
Wycombe Marsh Bucks 40 E1
Wyddial Herts 54 F4
Wye Kent 30 E4
Wyesham Mon 36 C2
Wyfordby Leics 64 C4
Wyke Dorset 13 B5
Wyke Shrops 61 D6
Wyke Sur 27 D7
Wyke W Yorks 88 B2
Wyke Regis Dorset 12 G4
Wykeham N Yorks 96 B4
Wykeham N Yorks 103 F7
Wyken W Mid 63 F7
Wykey Shrops 60 B3
Wylam Northumb 110 C4
Wylde Green W Mid 62 E5
Wyllie Caerph 35 E5
Wylye Wilts 24 F5
Wymering Ptsmth 15 D7
Wymeswold Leics 64 B3
Wymington Bedford 53 C7
Wymondham Leics 65 C5
Wymondham Norf 68 D4
Wyndham Bridgend 34 E3
Wynford Eagle Dorset 12 E3
Wyng Orkney 159 J4
Wynyard Village Stockton 102 B2
Wyre Piddle Worcs 50 E4
Wysall Notts 64 B3
Wythall Worcs 51 B5
Wytham Oxon 38 D4
Wythburn Cumb 99 C5
Wythenshawe Gtr Man 87 F6
Wythop Mill Cumb 98 B3
Wyton Cambs 54 B3
Wyverstone Suff 56 C4
Wyverstone Street Suff 56 C4
Wyville Lincs 65 B5
Wyvis Lodge Highld 150 D7

Y

Y Bala = Bala Gwyn 72 F3
Y Barri = Barry V Glam 22 C3
Y Bont-Faen = Cowbridge V Glam 21 B8
Y Drenewydd = Newtown Powys 59 E8
Y Felinheli Gwyn 82 E5
Y Fenni = Abergavenny Mon 35 C6
Y Fflint = Flint Flint 73 B6
Y Ffôr Gwyn 70 D4
Y-Ffrith Denb 72 A4
Y Gelli Gandryll = Hay-on-Wye Powys 48 E4
Y Mwmbwls = The Mumbles Swansea 33 F7
Y Pîl = Pyle Bridgend 34 F2
Y Rhws = Rhoose V Glam 22 C2
Y Rhyl = Rhyl Denb 72 A4
Y Trallwng = Welshpool Powys 60 D2
Y Waun = Chirk Wrex 73 F6
Yaddlethorpe N Lincs 90 D2
Yafford IoW 14 F5
Yafforth N Yorks 101 E8
Yalding Kent 29 D7
Yanworth Glos 37 C7
Yapham E Yorks 96 D3
Yapton W Sus 16 D3
Yarburgh Lincs 91 E7
Yarcombe Devon 11 D7
Yard Som 22 F2
Yardley W Mid 62 F5
Yardley Gobion Northants 53 E5
Yardley Hastings Northants 53 D6
Yardro Powys 48 D4
Yarkhill Hereford 49 E8
Yarlet Staffs 62 B3
Yarlington Som 12 B4
Yarlside Cumb 92 C2
Yarm Stockton 102 C2
Yarmouth IoW 14 F4
Yarnbrook Wilts 24 D3
Yarnfield Staffs 75 F5
Yarnscombe Devon 9 B7
Yarnton Oxon 38 C4
Yarpole Hereford 49 C6
Yarrow Borders 115 B6
Yarrow Feus Borders 115 B6
Yarsop Hereford 49 E6
Yarwell Northants 65 E7
Yate S Glos 36 F4
Yateley Hants 27 C6
Yatesbury Wilts 25 B5
Yattendon W Berks 26 B3
Yatton Hereford 49 C6
Yatton N Som 23 C6
Yatton Keynell Wilts 24 B3
Yaverland IoW 15 F7
Yaxham Norf 68 C3
Yaxley Cambs 65 E8
Yaxley Suff 56 B5
Yazor Hereford 49 E6
Yeading London 40 F4
Yeadon W Yorks 94 E5
Yealand Conyers Lancs 92 B5
Yealand Redmayne Lancs 92 B5
Yealmpton Devon 6 D3
Yearby Redcar 102 B4
Yearsley N Yorks 95 B8
Yeaton Shrops 60 C4
Yeaveley Derbys 75 E8
Yedingham N Yorks 96 B4
Yeldon Bedford 53 C8
Yelford Oxon 38 D3
Yelland Devon 20 F3
Yelling Cambs 54 C3
Yelvertoft Northants 52 B3
Yelverton Devon 6 C3
Yelverton Norf 69 D5
Yenston Som 12 B5
Yeo Mill Devon 10 B3
Yeoford Devon 10 E2
YeoImbridge Corn 8 F5
Yeovil Som 12 C3
Yeovil Marsh Som 12 C3
Yeovilton Som 12 B3
Yerbeston Pembs 32 D1
Yesnaby Orkney 159 G3
Yetlington Northumb 117 D6
Yetminster Dorset 12 C3
Yettington Devon 11 F5
Yetts o'Muckhart Clack 128 D2
Yieldshields S Lanark 119 D8
Yiewsley London 40 F3
Ynys-meudwy Neath 33 D8
Ynysboeth Rhondda 34 E4
Ynysddu Caerph 35 E5
Ynysgyfflog Gwyn 58 C3
Ynyshir Rhondda 34 E4
Ynyslas Ceredig 58 E3
Ynystawe Swansea 33 D7
Ynysybwl Rhondda 34 E4
Yockenthwaite N Yorks 94 B2
Yockleton Shrops 60 C3
Yokefleet E Yorks 90 B2
Yoker W Dunb 118 C5
Yonder Bognie Aberds 152 D5
York York 95 D8
York Town Sur 27 C6
Yorkletts Kent 30 C4
Yorkley Glos 36 D3
Yorton Shrops 60 B5
Youlgreave Derbys 76 C2
Youlstone Devon 8 C4
Youlthorpe E Yorks 96 D3
Youlton N Yorks 95 C7
Young Wood Lincs 78 B4
Young's End Essex 42 C3
Yoxall Staffs 62 C5
Yoxford Suff 57 C7
Yr Hôb = Hope Flint 73 D7
Yr Wyddgrug = Mold Flint 73 C6
Ysbyty-Cynfyn Ceredig 47 B6
Ysbyty Ifan Conwy 72 E2
Ysbyty Ystwyth Ceredig 47 B6
Ysceifiog Flint 73 B5
Yspitty Carms 33 E6
Ystalyfera Neath 34 D1
Ystrad Rhondda 34 E3
Ystrad Aeron Ceredig 46 D4
Ystrad-mynach Caerph 35 E5
Ystradfellte Powys 34 C3
Ystradffin Carms 47 E6
Ystradgynlais Powys 34 C1
Ystradmeurig Ceredig 47 C6
Ystradowen Carms 33 C8
Ystradowen V Glam 22 B2
Ystumtuen Ceredig 47 B6
Ythanbank Aberds 153 E9
Ythanwells Aberds 153 E6
Ythsie Aberds 153 E8

Z

Zeal Monachorum Devon 10 D2
Zeals Wilts 24 F2
Zelah Corn 4 D3
Zennor Corn 2 C3